'... when it comes to helping wine drinkers make sense of the
now thousands of wines being produced in this country,
(Halliday) is in a class of his own.'
— *Sunday Herald Sun*

'An annual "must have" for those racing to keep up with the hurly-
burly of the Australian wine industry, and it's easy to see why.'
— *The Age*

'Halliday has refined the art of tucking diverse information ... into a
readable and compact package.'
— *Melbourne Times*

'Halliday brings a vast knowledge to the subject, so even a few words
carry a weight unmatched by lesser mortals.'
— *Gold Coast Bulletin*

'(Wine) buyers will find his assessments expert and informative,
and those with cellars, however modest, will be helped by his assessment
of past vintages.'
— *Herald Sun*

james halliday

australia & new zealand

wine

companion

2001 EDITION

james halliday

australia & new zealand

wine

companion

2001 EDITION

GRUB STREET • LONDON

This edition published in 2000 by
Grub Street
The Basement
10 Chivalry Road
London SW11 1HT
email: food@grubstreet.co.uk
Web: www.grubstreet.co.uk

A CIP record for this book is available from the British Library

ISBN 1 902304 67 5

Cover inset photograph by Kevin Judd

Set in Bembo 8/9.5
Printed in Australia by Griffin Press Pty Ltd on 65gsm Bulky Paperback

about the author

James Halliday is Australia's most respected wine writer. Over the past thirty years he has worn many hats: lawyer, winemaker and grape grower, wine judge, wine consultant, journalist and author. He has now discarded his legal hat, but actively continues in his other roles, incessantly travelling, researching and tasting wines in all the major wine-producing countries. He judges regularly at wine shows in Australia, the UK, the US, South Africa and New Zealand.

James Halliday has written or contributed to over 40 books on wine since he began writing in 1979 (notable contributions include the *Oxford Companion* and *Larousse Encylopedia of Wine*). Various of his books have been translated into Japanese, French and German, and have been published in the UK and the US as well as Australia.

His most recent works include *Classic Wines of Australia, An Introduction to Australian Wine, Wine Atlas of Australia and New Zealand* and *Collecting Wine: You and Your Cellar.*

Co-founder of the new wine website, www.winepros.com.au, Halliday is proving to be as popular on the World Wide Web as he is in other mediums.

contents

how to use this book

he *Wine Companion* is arranged with wineries in alphabetical order, and the entries should be self-explanatory, but here I will briefly take you through the information for each entry.

winery entries

cape mentelle ★★★★★
Off Wallcliffe Road, Margaret River, WA 6285   **region** Margaret River
phone (08) 9757 3266 **fax** (08) 9757 3233 **open** 7 days 10–4.30
winemaker John Durham **production** 50 000 **est.** 1970
prod. range ($20–44 R) Chardonnay, Semillon Sauvignon Blanc, Cabernet Sauvignon, Cabernet Merlot, Shiraz, Zinfandel, Trinders Cabernet Merlot.
summary Notwithstanding majority ownership by Veuve Clicquot, David Hohnen remains very much in command of one of Australia's foremost medium-sized wineries. Exceptional marketing skills and wine of the highest quality, with the back-up of New Zealand's Cloudy Bay, are a potent combination. The Chardonnay and Semillon Sauvignon Blanc are among Australia's best, the potent Shiraz usually superb, and the berry/spicy Zinfandel makes one wonder why this grape is not as widespread in Australia as it is in California.

winery name   Cape Mentelle

Although it might seem that stating the winery name is straightforward, this is not necessarily so. To avoid confusion, wherever possible I use the name that appears most prominently on the wine label and do not refer to any associated trading name.

ratings ★★★★★

The winery star system may be interpreted as follows:

★★★★★ Outstanding winery regularly producing exemplary wines.
★★★★☆ Extremely good; virtually on a par with a five-star winery.
 ★★★★ Consistently produces high-quality wines.
 ★★★☆ A solid, reliable producer of good wine.
  ★★★ Typically good, but may have a few lesser wines.
  ★★☆ Adequate.
   ★★ Hard to recommend.

If the ratings seem generous, so be it. The fact is that Australia is blessed with a marvellous climate for growing grapes, a high degree of technological skill, and a remarkable degree of enthusiasm and dedication on the part of its winemakers. Across the price spectrum, Australian wines stand tall in the markets of the world. I see no reason, therefore, to shrink from recognising excellence. NR = not rated, either because the winery is new or because I have not tasted enough of its wines.

address Off Wallcliffe Road, Margaret River, WA 6285
phone (08) 9757 3266 **fax** (08) 9757 3233

The details are usually those of the winery and cellar door but in a few instances may simply be of the winery; this occurs when the wine is made at another winery under contract and is sold only through retail.

region Margaret River

The mapping of Australia into Zones and Regions with legally defined boundaries is now well underway. This edition sees radical changes (and additions) to the regional names and boundaries. Wherever possible the official 'Geographic Indication' name has been adopted, and where the registration process is incomplete, I have used the most likely name.

cellar door sales hours open 7 days 10–4.30

Although a winery might be listed as not open or only open on weekends, some may in fact be prepared to open by appointment. Many will, some won't; a telephone call will establish whether it is possible or not. Also, virtually every winery that is shown as being open only for weekends is in fact open for public holidays as well. Once again, a telephone call will confirm this.

winemaker John Durham

In the large companies the winemaker is simply the head of a team; there may be many executive winemakers actually responsible for specific wines.

production 50 000

This figure given (representing the number of cases produced each year) is merely an indication of the size of the operation. Some wineries (principally but not exclusively the large companies) regard this information as confidential; in that event, NFP (not for publication) will appear. NA = information was not available.

year of establishment est. 1970

A more or less self-explanatory item, but keep in mind that some makers consider the year in which they purchased the land to be the year of establishment, others the year in which they first planted grapes, others the year they first made wine, others the year they first offered wine for sale, and so on. There may also be minor complications where there has been a change of ownership or a break in production.

price range and prod. range ($20–44 R) Chardonnay, Semillon Sauvignon Blanc, Cabernet Sauvignon, Cabernet Merlot, Shiraz, Zinfandel, Trinders Cabernet Merlot.

The **price range** given covers the least expensive through to the most expensive wines usually made by the winery in question (where the information was available). Hence there may be a significant spread. That spread, however, may not fully cover fluctuations that occur in retail pricing, particularly with the larger companies. Erratic and often savage discounting remains a feature of the wine industry, and prices must therefore be seen as approximate.

For Australia, this spread has been compounded by the introduction on July 1 2000 of the Goods and Services Tax (GST) of 10 per cent and the special and uniquely discriminatory Wine Equalisation Tax (WET) of 29 per cent imposed on top of one another in a tax-on-tax pyramid.

Notwithstanding Federal Government assurances that the price of wine would not increase by more than 1.5 per cent, and notwithstanding the fierce scrutiny of Professor Allan Fels and the ACCC, most prices will have risen by 3–5 per cent since this book went to print. The Australian winery prices are for purchase in Australia, in Australian dollars; those for New Zealand are for purchase in New Zealand, in New Zealand dollars.

I have indicated whether the price is cellar door (CD), mailing list (ML) or retail (R). By and large, the choice has been determined by which of the three methods of sale is most important to the winery. The price of Australian and New Zealand wines in other countries is affected by a number of factors, including excise and customs duty, distribution mark-up and currency fluctuations. Contact the winery for details.

product range   Particularly with the larger companies, it is not possible to give a complete list of the wines. The saving grace is that these days most of the wines are simply identified on their label by their varietal composition.

summary   Notwithstanding majority ownership by Veuve Clicquot, David Hohnen remains very much in command of one of Australia's foremost medium-sized wineries. Exceptional marketing skills and wine of the highest quality, with the back-up of New Zealand's Cloudy Bay, are a potent combination. The Chardonnay and Semillon Sauvignon Blanc are among Australia's best, the potent Shiraz usually superb, and the berry/spicy Zinfandel makes one wonder why this grape is not as widespread in Australia as it is in California.

My summary of the winery. Little needs to be said, except that I have tried to vary the subjects I discuss in this part of the winery entry.

🍂   The vine leaf symbol indicates wineries that are new entries in this year's listing.

wine entries
and tasting notes

Cape Mentelle Cabernet Sauvignon
The wine which started the Cape Mentelle juggernaut, with the '82 and '83 vintages winning the Jimmy Watson Trophy in successive years. Both style and quality wandered somewhat in the second half of the 1980s, but has steadied (and improved greatly) in the 1990s as David Hohnen has come to terms with the now fully mature vineyard (and it with him).
▼▼▼▼♈ **1995** Medium to full red-purple; a bouquet with uncommon depth and complexity, and a range of secondary earthy/cedary/berry characters already starting to appear. A wine with similarly good structure and depth to the palate although the flavours are tending more towards the savoury end of the spectrum than the opulently fruity. **rating:** 90
best drinking 2000–2010 **best vintages** '76, '78, '82, '83, '86, '90, '91, '93, '94, '95 **drink with** Loin of lamb   • $43.20

wine name   Cape Mentelle Cabernet Sauvignon

In most instances, the wine's name will be prefaced by the name of the winery.

ratings ▼▼▼▼♈

Two ratings are given for each wine; the ratings apply to the vintage reviewed, and may vary from one year to the next.

Points scale	Glass symbol	
98–100	–	Perfection which exists only as an idea.
94–97	▼▼▼▼▼	As close to perfection as the real world will allow.
90–93	▼▼▼▼♈	Excellent wine full of character; of gold medal standard.
85–89	▼▼▼▼	Very good wine; clear varietal definition/style; silver verging on gold medal standard.
80–84	▼▼▼♈	Good fault-free, flavoursome; high bronze to silver medal standard.

You will see that nearly all of the wines reviewed in this book rate 84 points (3½ glasses) or better. This is not wanton generosity on my part. It simply reflects the fact that the 1000 or so wines selected for specific review are the tip of more than 5000 tasting notes accumulated over the past year. In other words, the wines described are among Australia's top 20 per cent. NR = not rated.

background   The wine which started the Cape Mentelle juggernaut, with the '82 and '83 vintages winning the Jimmy Watson Trophy in successive years. Both style and quality wandered somewhat in the second half of the 1980s, but has steadied (and improved greatly) in the 1990s as David Hohnen has come to terms with the now fully mature vineyard (and it with him).

Like the summary information given in the winery entries, I have tried to vary the approach of my discussions.

♥♥♥♥♀ **1995** Medium to full red-purple; a bouquet with uncommon depth and complexity, and a range of secondary earthy/cedary/berry characters already starting to appear. A wine with similarly good structure and depth to the palate although the flavours are tending more towards the savoury end of the spectrum than the opulently fruity.   **rating:** 90

The tasting note opens with the vintage of the wine tasted. With the exception of a very occasional classic wine, this tasting note will have been made within the 12 months prior to publication. Even that is a long time, and during the life of this book the wine will almost certainly change. More than this, remember that tasting is a highly subjective and imperfect art. NV = non-vintage.

best drinking   2000–2010

I will usually give a range of years or a more specific comment (such as 'quick-developing style'), but whatever my best drinking recommendation, always consider it with extreme caution and as an approximate guide at best. When to drink a given wine is an intensely personal decision, which only you can make.

best vintages   '76, '78, '82, '83, '86, '90, '91, '93, '94, '95

Self-explanatory information, but a note of caution: wines do change in the bottle, and it may be that were I to taste all of the best vintages listed, I would demote some and elevate some not mentioned.

drink with   Loin of lamb

Again, merely a suggestion – a subliminal guide to the style of wine.

price   • $43.20

This is a (GST exclusive) guide only.

$NA = information not available.

Abbreviation: mlf = malolactic fermentation.

key to regions

wine regions of australia

1 Lower Hunter Valley
2 Upper Hunter Valley
3 Hastings River
4 Mudgee
5 Orange
6 Cowra
7 Swan Hill
8 Murray Darling
9 Riverina
10 Pericoota
11 Hilltops
12 Canberra District
13 Tumbarumba
14 Shoalhaven
15 Far South West Victoria
16 Grampians
17 Pyrenees
18 Ballarat
19 Bendigo
20 Goulburn Valley
21 Central Victorian Mountain Country
22 Rutherglen and Glenrowan
23 King Valley
24 Alpine Valleys and Beechworth
25 Gippsland
26 Mornington Peninsula
27 Yarra Valley
28 Geelong
29 Sunbury
30 Macedon Ranges
31 Northern Tasmania
32 Southern Tasmania
33 Mount Gambier
34 Robe
35 Coonawarra
36 Wrattonbully
37 Mount Benson
38 Padthaway
39 Langhorne Creek
40 McLaren Vale
41 Adelaide Hills
42 Eden Valley
43 Adelaide Plains
44 Barossa Valley
45 Riverland
46 Clare Valley
47 Port Lincoln
48 Great Southern
49 Pemberton, Warren Valley and Manjimup
50 Blackwood Valley
51 Margaret River
52 Geographe
53 South-west Coast
54 Perth Hills
55 Swan District
56 South Burnett
57 Granite Belt

Western
Australia

perth

55
54
53
52
50
51 49 48

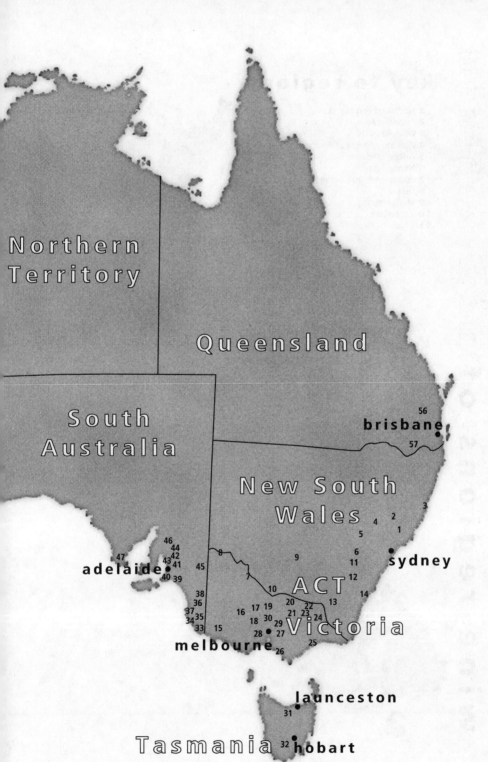

Northern
Territory

Queensland

South
Australia

56
brisbane
57

New South
Wales
3
4 2
5 1
6
11 sydney
12
14
8
9
ACT
10
20 22 13
16 17 19 21 23 24 Victoria
18 30 29
28 27
melbourne 26 25

adelaide
46
44
47 42
43 41 45
40 39
38
36
37 35
34 33
15

launceston

31

Tasmania 32 hobart

wine regions of new zealand

key to regions

1 Northland and Matakana
2 Auckland Area
3 Waiheke Island
4 Waikato and Bay of Plenty
5 Gisborne/Poverty Bay
6 Hawke's Bay
7 Wairarapa/Martinborough
8 Nelson
9 Marlborough
10 Canterbury
11 Otago

1

2 3

auckland

4

North
Island

5

6

8
9

7
wellington

10
christchurch

South
Island

11

the best
of the best
by variety

the following lists are the arithmetic results of numerous tastings of over 5000 wines during a seven-month period from October 1999 to the end of April 2000. They vividly expose the inherent frailties and shortcomings of assigning precise numbers (or points) to wines. The process may have validity in the context of a particular tasting on a particular day but it inevitably becomes compromised once multiple tastings are brought together at a later date.

Some of the points (and omissions) seem as strange to me as they may to you. However, having elected to live by the sword, I must die by it and so I have refrained from any massaging of the rank each wine has been given.

Inclusion in the list of the top 20 wines in each category has one qualification: a minimum score of 90 points. On the other side of the coin, where more than 20 wines have scored 94 points or above, all have been included. Wines with the same point score have been listed alphabetically.

Finally, for obvious reasons, I have listed Australian and New Zealand wines separately.

australia

riesling

The strong showing of Tasmanian Rieslings in this list will surprise some — especially those tasters who are sensitive to higher levels of acidity. This apart, there is an interesting mix of styles from cool to warmer (e.g. Clare Valley) regions. 21 wines have been included and another 18 scored 90 points or more.

1999 Crawford River Wines Reserve Riesling	97 points
1999 Grosset Polish Hill Riesling	96
1999 East Arm Vineyard Riesling	95
1999 Tamar Ridge Riesling	95
1998 Ashton Hills Riesling	94
1999 Grosset Watervale Riesling	94
1999 Howard Park Riesling	94
1996 Kelly's Creek Riesling	94
1999 Mt Lofty Ranges Five Vines Riesling	94
1999 Petaluma Riesling	94
1999 Pipers Brook Riesling	94
1998 Seppelt Drumborg Riesling	94
1998 Katnook Estate Riesling	93
1999 The Clare Essentials Carlsfield Vineyard Riesling	93
1999 Treehouse Vineyard Riesling	93
1999 Coombend Estate Riesling	92
1999 Crawford River Wines Riesling	92
1995 Leo Buring Leonay Riesling	92
1999 Annie's Lane Riesling	92
1999 Richmond Grove Watervale Riesling	92
1999 St Matthias Riesling	92

semillon

There are only 14 wines in this list and all but three are from the Hunter Valley. The small number of wines reflects the very reserved nature of young Semillon; many wines with lesser ratings will coast past 90 as they start to reach maturity five years (or more) after their vintage date.

1995 Tyrrell's Vat 1 Semillon	96 points
1998 Alkoomi Wandoo	94
1995 McWilliam's Mount Pleasant Elizabeth	94
1995 McWilliam's Mount Pleasant Lovedale Semillon	94
1996 Tyrrell's Stevens Semillon	94
1998 Clarendon Hills Hickinbotham Semillon	93

1999 Tyrrell's Old Winery Semillon	93
1999 Glenguin The Old Broke Block Semillon	92
1996 McWilliam's Mount Pleasant Elizabeth	92
1999 Brokenwood Semillon	91
1999 Molly Morgan Old Vines Semillon	91
1998 Penfolds Adelaide Hills Semillon	91
1998 Rosemount Estate Show Reserve Semillon	90
1998 Terrace Vale Bin 1 Semillon	90

sauvignon blanc and sauvignon blanc semillon blends

This group takes in both Sauvignon-dominant and Semillon-dominant blends. It is the basis for white Bordeaux wines (plus a little Muscadelle) and works every bit as well in Australia as it does there. In particular, it comes to the aid of the painfully shy Semillon, and the subtle use of barrel fermentation (often of a portion of the blend) also helps.

1999 Cape Mentelle Semillon Sauvignon Blanc	94 points
1999 Chain of Ponds Semillon Sauvignon Blanc	94
1997 Yarra Yarra Semillon Sauvignon Blanc	94
1998 Brown Brothers Gewurztraminer	93
1999 Cullen Wines Sauvignon Blanc Semillon	93
1999 Shaw & Smith Sauvignon Blanc	93
1997 Suckfizzle Augusta Semillon Sauvignon Blanc	93
1999 Brookland Valley Verse 1 Semillon Sauvignon Blanc	92
1999 Grosset Semillon Sauvignon Blanc	92
1999 Moss Brothers Sauvignon Blanc	92
1999 Primo Estate La Biondina Colombard	92
1996 Voyager Estate Tom Price Sauvignon Blanc Semillon	91
1999 Brookland Valley Sauvignon Blanc	90
1999 Hillstowe Buxton Sauvignon Blanc	90
1999 Ravenswood Lane Vineyard The Gathering Sauvignon Blanc	90

chardonnay

Having made some rules for inclusion, I have slightly bent them for this group because of the break point between 94 and 93 points. Although 27 wines are included, another 36 scored between 90 and 92 points inclusive. If nothing else, it suggests Chardonnay is alive and well — and flourishing indeed.

1997 Leeuwin Estate Art Series Chardonnay	97 points
1995 Penfolds Reserve Bin Chardonnay	97
1997 Bannockburn Chardonnay	96
1998 Pipers Brook Summit Vineyard Chardonnay	96

1997 Voyager Estate Chardonnay	96
1998 Cape Mentelle Chardonnay	95
1998 Cullen Chardonnay	95
1996 Penfolds Yattarna Chardonnay	95
1999 Tyrrell's Vat 47 Pinot Chardonnay	95
1998 Alkoomi Frankland River Chardonnay	94
1998 Bannockburn Chardonnay	94
1998 Geoff Weaver Lenswood Chardonnay	94
1998 Giaconda Chardonnay	94
1996 Leeuwin Estate Art Series Chardonnay	94
1997 Métier Tarraford Vineyard Chardonnay	94
1998 Pipers Brook Vineyard Reserve Chardonnay	94
1997 Rosemount Estate Roxburgh Chardonnay	94
1998 Shaw & Smith Reserve Chardonnay	94
1997 Wellington Chardonnay	94
1998 Ashbrook Estate Chardonnay	93
1997 Brookland Valley Chardonnay	93
1998 Chain of Ponds Chardonnay	93
1997 Craiglee Chardonnay	93
1998 Penfolds Adelaide Hills Chardonnay	93
1999 Rothvale Vineyard Reserve Chardonnay F	93
1998 Tyrrell's Vat 47 Pinot Chardonnay	93
1999 Wynns Coonawarra Estate Chardonnay	93

sweet white wines

A gross under-representation; there are far more botrytised wines which deserve 90 points or above. Next year I shall make sure more are reviewed.

1998 De Bortoli Noble One Botrytis Semillon	96 points
1997 Miranda Golden Botrytis	95
1999 Winstead Ensnared Riesling	94
1999 Bloodwood Ice Riesling	92

sparkling wines

Here, too, there should be more entries. Part of the problem comes with the major companies, where space can limit the inclusion of tasting notes for wines that would otherwise qualify.

1995 Yarrabank Brut Cuvée	95 points
1995 Hardys Arras	94
NV Rockford Black Shiraz	94
1995 Domaine Chandon Blanc de Noirs	93
1997 Petaluma Croser	93
1996 Clover Hill	91

pinot noir

As well as the 20 wines listed, another 19 scored 90 or 91 points. One of the more controversial aspects is what seems to be the under-representation of the Yarra Valley. Part of the answer lies in the fact that while 1997 was a great vintage for Pinot in that neck of the woods (and elsewhere), 1998 was good rather than very good or great. Conversely, it was a fantastic year in Tasmania, which has seven wines in the top 20.

1997 Ashton Hills Reserve Pinot Noir	97	points
1997 Bannockburn Pinot Noir	97	
1997 Bass Phillip Premium Pinot Noir	95	
1998 Elsewhere Pinot Noir	95	
1998 Freycinet Pinot Noir	95	
1998 Meadowbank Henry James Pinot Noir	95	
1998 Oyster Cove Vineyard Pinot Noir	95	
1998 Ashton Hills Piccadilly Pinot Noir	94	
1998 Ashton Hills Pinot Noir	94	
1998 Diamond Valley Estate Pinot Noir	94	
1998 Hillstowe Udy's Mill Pinot Noir	94	
1998 Port Phillip Estate Reserve Pinot Noir	94	
1999 Barratt Piccadilly Valley Pinot Noir	93	
1999 Freycinet Pinot Noir	93	
1998 Phillip Island Vineyard The Nobbies	93	
1998 Wellington Pinot Noir	93	
1999 Kings Creek Reserve Pinot Noir	92	
1998 Stefano Lubiana Pinot Noir	92	
1998 Tuck's Ridge Reserve Pinot Noir	92	
1998 Yarra Yering Pinot Noir	92	

shiraz

Not surprisingly, this is the strongest varietal group, with 28 wines scoring 94 points or more, and another 72 wines receiving 90 to 93 points. This very strength gives rise to omissions such as Penfolds Grange (93 points). Yet every style of Shiraz is represented, ranging from the blood and thunder of McLaren Vale through to elegant, cool climate wines such as Craiglee.

1997 Abercorn Shiraz	97	points
1998 Bannockburn Vineyards Shiraz	97	
1997 Best's Wines Thomson Family Shiraz	97	
1996 Henschke Hill of Grace	97	
1997 Craiglee Shiraz	96	
1996 Brand's of Coonawarra Stentilford's Reserve Shiraz	95	
1998 Burge Family Draycott Reserve Shiraz	95	
1997 Haselgrove 'H' Reserve Shiraz	95	

1998 Turkey Flat Shiraz	95
1998 Barwang Vineyard Shiraz	94
1998 Berrys Bridge Shiraz	94
1997 Bowen Estate Shiraz	94
1998 Brindabella Hills Shiraz	94
1998 Clarendon Hills Hickinbotham Shiraz	94
1998 d'Arenberg Dead Arm Shiraz	94
1998 Fergusson Jeremy Shiraz	94
1996 Hardys Eileen Hardy Shiraz	94
1998 Heritage Wines Rossco's Shiraz	94
1998 Hewitson Barossa Shiraz	94
1998 Kilikanoon Oracle Shiraz	94
1997 Maglieri Shark Block Shiraz	94
1996 Mitchelton Print Label Shiraz	94
1998 Pertaringa Shiraz	94
1998 Ravenswood Lane Starvedog Lane Shiraz	94
1996 Reynell Basket Pressed Shiraz	94
1997 Tatachilla Foundation Shiraz	94
1998 Tim Gramp McLaren Vale Shiraz	94
1998 Zema Estate Shiraz	94

shiraz blends

A reasonably select group, with Shiraz Cabernet blends dominating. (Interestingly, the Cabernet-dominant blends had very few Cabernet Shirazes). It is unlikely this dominance will last: every day the number of Rhône Valley blends — Shiraz, Grenache and Mourvedre — increases and the trend will continue.

1997 Rosemount Estate Mountain Blue Shiraz Cabernet	95 points
1994 Grant Burge MS Shiraz Cabernet	94
1997 Lindemans Limestone Ridge	94
1998 Majella The Malleea Shiraz Cabernet	94
1998 Yarra Yering Dry Red No 2	94
1998 d'Arenberg d'Arry's Original Shiraz Grenache	93
1998 Henschke Johann's Garden Grenache Shiraz Mourvedre	93
1997 Majella The Malleea Shiraz Cabernet	93
1998 Passing Clouds Graeme's Blend Shiraz Cabernet	93
1997 Tyrrell's Vat 8 Shiraz Cabernet	92
1998 Charles Melton Nine Popes	91
1996 Andrew Harris The Vision	90

merlot

Hmm. Obviously, there is much more talk than action here. There are two problems: Australia's most common clone of merlot is very bad, forever finding ways of refusing to set (that is, failing to produce grapes on the numerous bunches which promise so much at flowering stage) and then by aborting. Second, it is the least temperamental in terms of setting in warmer climates when it actually needs a cool climate to produce good varietal character.

1998 Leconfield Merlot	93 points
1997 Haan Wines Merlot Prestige	92
1997 Capel Vale Howecroft Merlot	91
1998 Shaw & Smith Incognito Merlot	91
1996 James Irvine Grand Merlot	90
1997 Mountadam Merlot	90
1998 Oakridge Estate Merlot	90
1998 Tatachilla Clarendon Vineyard Merlot	90

cabernet sauvignon

With 19 wines at 93 points or more and another 26 scoring 90 to 92 points, this is a distinguished group. However, in many instances the best is still to come as some hitherto unreleased '98 vintage Cabernets come onto the market. As with Shiraz, there is a full spectrum of style from (surprisingly, perhaps) three Tasmanian Cabernets which are akin to fugitives from Bordeaux to the opulence of wines such as John Riddoch and Red Edge.

1996 Penfolds Block 42 Kalimna Cabernet Sauvignon	96 points
1998 Clarendon Hills Sandown Cabernet Sauvignon	95
1997 Crawford River Cabernet Sauvignon	95
1997 Katnook Estate Cabernet Sauvignon	95
1998 Moorilla Estate Cabernet Sauvignon	95
1998 Balnaves of Coonawarra Cabernet Sauvignon	94
1997 Coombend Estate Cabernet Sauvignon	94
1997 Edwards & Chaffey Section 353 Cabernet Sauvignon	94
1996 Henschke Cyril Henschke Cabernet	94
1998 Heritage Wines Cabernet Sauvignon	94
1998 Legana Vineyard Cabernet Sauvignon	94
1998 Pertaringa Cabernet Sauvignon	94
1998 Red Edge Cabernet Sauvignon	94
1997 Wirra Wirra The Angelus Cabernet Sauvignon	94
1997 Wynns Coonawarra Estate John Riddoch Cabernet Sauvignon	94
1997 Yarra Yarra Reserve Cabernet Sauvignon	94
1998 Zema Estate Family Selection Cabernet Sauvignon	94
1996 Glenara Adelaide Hills Cabernet Sauvignon	93
1998 Tim Adams Cabernet	93

cabernet blends

The points break has led to the inclusion of 23 (rather than 20) wines, which are majestically headed by the Cullen Cabernet Merlot. The net has once again been cast wide, although the representation of Australia's best wine-growing regions seems eminently appropriate.

1998 Cullen Cabernet Sauvignon Merlot	97 points
1996 Houghton Jack Mann	95
1998 Laurel Bank Cabernet Sauvignon Merlot	95
1998 Petaluma Coonawarra	95
1997 Yarra Yarra Cabernets	95
1997 Ashton Hills Obliqua Cabernet Merlot	94
1997 Brookland Valley Cabernet Merlot	94
1998 Lake's Folly Cabernets	94
1997 Petaluma Coonawarra	94
1998 Primo Estate Joseph Moda Amarone Cabernet Merlot	94
1992 Voyager Estate Tom Price Cabernet Merlot	94
1995 De Bortoli Melba Barrel Select	93
1997 Jim Barry McCrae Wood Cabernet Malbec	93
1998 Yeringberg Dry Red	93
1996 Evans & Tate Redbrook	92
1997 Leasingham Bin 56 Cabernet Malbec	92
1998 Matilda's Meadow Cabernet Sauvignon Cabernet Franc	92
1997 Rosemount Estate Traditional	92
1997 Henschke Abbott's Prayer Cabernet Merlot	91
1997 Mount Langi Ghiran Langi Cabernet Merlot	91
1996 Passing Clouds Cabernet Shiraz	91
1996 Salitage Pemberton	91
1998 Yarra Yering Dry Red No 1	91

fortified wines

Familiarity has long since bred contempt for these magical wines; they are among Australia's greatest, with the Iberian Peninsula alone offering wines of comparable quality. The absence of vintage ports is, with one exception (Stanton and Killeen), no surprise: Australia has missed the boat here. The other omissions are Chambers Rosewood (it doesn't provide samples of its sublime fortified wines, which sell themselves) and Morris, the latter a glitch in the system.

NV Seppelt Show Tawny Port DP90	97 points
NV All Saints Show Reserve Tokay	96
NV Seppelt Show Reserve Muscat DP63	96
NV Seppelt Show Fino Sherry DP117	96
NV Bullers Calliope Rare Liqueur Tokay	95

NV Penfolds Great Grandfather Port	95
NV Seppelt Show Oloroso Sherry DP38	95
NV All Saints Classic Release Tokay	94
NV Bullers Calliope Rare Liqueur Muscat	94
NV Campbells Rutherglen Tokay	94
NV Campbells Merchant Prince Muscat	94
NV Seppelt Rutherglen Show Tokay DP57	94
NV Seppelt Amontillado Sherry DP116	94
1998 Yarra Yering Portsorts	94
NV Campbells Isabella Tokay	93
NV Campbells Liquid Gold Tokay	91
1969 Talijancich Liqueur Tokay 375 ml	91

australian vintage charts

Each number represents a mark out of ten for the quality
of vintages in each region.

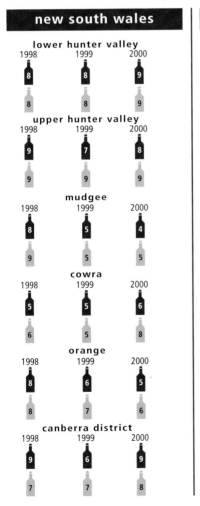

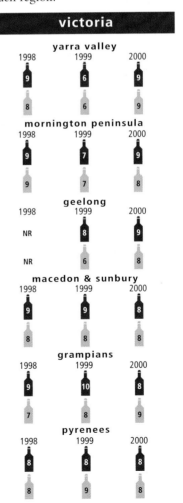

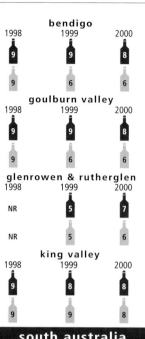

bendigo

	1998	1999	2000
	9	9	8
	9	6	6

goulburn valley

	1998	1999	2000
	9	9	8
	9	6	6

glenrowen & rutherglen

	1998	1999	2000
	NR	5	7
	NR	5	6

king valley

	1998	1999	2000
	9	8	8
	9	9	8

south australia

barossa valley

	1998	1999	2000
	10	5	4
	7	6	6

eden valley

	1998	1999	2000
	8	7	6
	7	6	6

clare valley

	1998	1999	2000
	10	9	6
	8	8	7

adelaide hills

	1998	1999	2000
	7	7	5
	7	8	6

coonawarra

	1998	1999	2000
	10	9	6
	8	7	7

padthaway

	1998	1999	2000
	10	9	7
	8	8	9

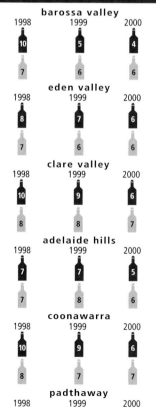

mclaren vale

	1998	1999	2000
	10	6	5
	8	7	5

langhorne creek

	1998	1999	2000
	8	6	7
	8	8	8

western australia

margaret river

	1998	1999	2000
	7	10	9
	7	8	8

great southern

	1998	1999	2000
	6	7	7
	7	6	6

swan district

	1998	1999	2000
	9	8	7
	9	6	6

queensland

granite belt

	1998	1999	2000
	8	10	8
	6	9	7

tasmania

northern tasmania

	1998	1999	2000
	10	9	9
	9	9	9

southern tasmania

	1998	1999	2000
	9	8	10
	8	7	9

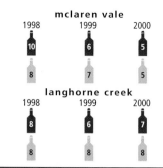
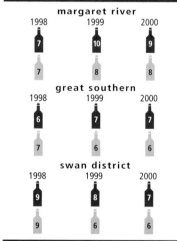

new zealand

sauvignon blanc

Both by the force of numbers (or hectares) and by the force of its flavour, Sauvignon Blanc is New Zealand's premier wine. It is as ubiquitous as Chardonnay is in Australia, even if 60 per cent of its production comes from Marlborough. Here it achieves a razor-sharp clarity of varietal character, bitingly aromatic and flavoured, the descriptors ranging through asparagus, herb, grass, mineral, citrus, gooseberry, passionfruit and redcurrant. Some makers — notably Cloudy Bay — use a little bit of this and that, including touches of barrel fermentation, Semillon and malolactic fermentation to add texture and ever-so-slightly soften the razor's edge of the fruit. Others, such as Hunter's, produce a fully barrel-fermented style as a clear alternative. But Marlborough does not have a mortgage either on the variety or on the choice of wine making options, so you see these approaches (including, of course, simple stainless steel fermentation and early bottling) repeated up and down the length of both the North and South Islands.

1999 Lawson's Dry Hills Sauvignon Blanc	97 points
1999 Gladstone Vineyard Sauvignon Blanc	95
1999 Cloudy Bay Sauvignon Blanc	94
1999 Goldwater Estate Dog Point Marlborough Sauvignon Blanc	94
1999 Hawkesbridge Willowbank Vineyard Sauvignon Blanc	94
1999 Hunter's Winemakers Reserve Sauvignon Blanc	94
1999 Seresin Estate Sauvignon Blanc	94
1999 Sherwood Estate Sauvignon Blanc	94
1999 Whitehaven Sauvignon Blanc	94
1999 Charles Wiffen Sauvignon Blanc	93
1999 Fairhall Downs Estate Sauvignon Blanc	93
1999 Forrest Estate Sauvignon Blanc	93
1999 Isabel Estate Marlborough Sauvignon Blanc	93
1999 Villa Maria Reserve Clifford Bay Sauvignon Blanc	93
1999 Chancellor Wines of Waipara Mount Cass Waipara Sauvignon Blanc	92
1999 Giesen Estate Marlborough Sauvignon Blanc	92
1999 Hunter's Sauvignon Blanc	92
1999 Kaikoura Sauvignon Blanc	92
1999 Alan McCorkindale Sauvignon Blanc	91
1999 De Redcliffe Estates Marlborough Estates Sauvignon Blanc	91

1999 Jackson Estate Sauvignon Blanc	91
1999 Morworth Estate Sauvignon Blanc	91
1999 Le Grys Sauvignon Blanc	91
1999 Waimea Estates Waimea Plains Nelson Sauvignon Blanc	91

riesling

Surprisingly, a latecomer on the scene, and largely restricted to Wairarapa (at the southern end of the North Island) and to the South Island, with all the regions there producing excellent and very distinctive wines. The naturally high acidity makes the retention of residual sugar almost mandatory if a balanced wine is to be made. What at first blush seems to be a dry wine may well have more than 10 grams per litre of residual sugar and for good measure carry the word 'dry' on its label. Overall, the wines have an intensity of flavour akin to that of the Mosel-Suar Ruwer of Germany, with mineral and lime juice the counterpoints of aroma and flavour. I should add that there are some marvellous botrytised styles also made.

1999 Dry River Craighall Riesling	94 points
1999 Drylands Estate Dry Riesling	94
1999 Giesen Estate Canterbury Riesling	94
1999 Dry River Marlborough Gewurztraminer	94
1999 Felton Road Riesling	93
1999 Forrest Estate Gewurztraminer	93
1999 Kaikoura Riesling	93
1999 Grove Mill Winemakers Reserve Riesling	92
1999 Saint Clair Estate Marlborough Riesling	92
1998 Villa Maria Reserve Gewurztraminer	92
1999 Chard Farm Riesling	91
1999 Felton Road Dry Riesling	91
1998 Giesen Estate Canterbury Riesling Reserve Selection	91
1999 Clifford Bay Estate Riesling	90
1999 De Redcliffe Estates Marlborough Estates Riesling	90
1999 Framingham Gewurztraminer	90
1999 Hunter's Riesling	90
1998 Lawson's Dry Hills Riesling	90
1999 Trinity Hill Wairarapa Riesling	90

chardonnay

New Zealand has had less than 20 years experience with Chardonnay, and seems to be still in the throes of an insatiable adolescent love affair. If much is good, more must be better still. Over and above the winemaking excesses this implies, there seems to be an 'x' factor that very quickly turns the wines into a glowing buttercup yellow, often accompanied by phenolic break-up of the flavour. By and large, then, they are at their best within a year of being bottled. All of these comments describe Australian Chardonnays 15 years ago, so it is fair to assume the best New Zealand Chardonnays of today point the way for the future — and the best are very good indeed. Also, as with Australia, Chardonnay is grown and made in every wine region, providing a panoply of flavours and styles.

1998 Giesen Estate Reserve Marlborough Chardonnay	96 points
1998 Grove Mill Winemakers Reserve Chardonnay	95
1998 Villa Maria Reserve Hawke's Bay Chardonnay	95
1998 Ata Rangi Petrie Chardonnay	94
1998 C J Pask Winery Reserve Chardonnay	94
1998 Clearview Estate Reserve Chardonnay	94
1998 Foxes Island Chardonnay	94
1998 Giesen Estate Canterbury/Marlborough School Road Chardonnay	94
1997 Hunter's Chardonnay	94
1998 Hunter's Reserve Chardonnay	94
1998 Sileni Estates Chardonnay	94
1998 Vidal Estate Reserve Hawke's Bay Chardonnay	94
1999 Neudorf Nelson Chardonnay	93
1998 Palliser Estate Chardonnay	93
1998 Seresin Estate Chardonnay Reserve	93
1998 Ata Rangi Craighall Chardonnay	92
1998 Chard Farm Judge and Jury Chardonnay	92
1998 Cloudy Bay Chardonnay	92
1998 Coopers Creek Swamp Reserve Chardonnay	92
1998 Neudorf Moutere Chardonnay	92
1998 Te Mania Estate Nelson Chardonnay	92

pinot gris

Every New World winemaking country must have a mini-arsenal of trendy new varieties, and one of New Zealand's most important is Pinot Gris. The volumes aren't yet great, of course, and the further south you go, the better the variety performs. Thus, Central Otago and Canterbury are presently the leaders. As with Riesling, there is a tendency to balance acidity with residual sugar, and an apparent acceptance by winemakers and judges of distinctly off-dry styles. It works with Riesling, but I am less convinced it can or should be so with Pinot Gris. Thus the wines I give the highest points to are basically dry.

1999 Quartz Reef Pinot Gris	92 points
1999 Gibbston Valley Central Otago Pinot Gris	90
1999 Kumeu River Pinot Gris	90
1999 Seresin Estate Pinot Gris	90

pinot noir

In terms of total production, Pinot Noir will never challenge Sauvignon Blanc in New Zealand but has every likelihood of displacing it as the national wine flag-bearer. As most Pinot Noir devotees know, there are all too few places outside Burgundy where the grape flourishes and the wine shows the hauntingly beautiful aroma and flavour of great Pinot. Nor can mere climatic statistics or soil analyses tell in advance where Pinot will flourish (though climate may tell where it won't). New Zealand is uniquely blessed with a considerable number of regions in which the variety performs admirably. Although initially the suitability of the terrain and climatic combinations of some of these regions was disguised by some poor clones (notably bachtabel), that time is now long gone. Martinborough/Wairarapa is the one outstanding region in the North Island, although careful site selection in Hawke's Bay may be rewarding. In the South Island it's an embarrassment of riches: Marlborough, Nelson, Waipara, Canterbury and Otago are all capable of producing outstanding Pinots in vintages such as 1998; wines with astonishing colour, flavour and power.

1998 Felton Road Pinot Noir Block 3	97 points
1998 Wither Hills Pinot Noir	97
1998 Daniel Schuster Omihi Hills Selection Pinot Noir	96
1998 Gibbston Valley Reserve Pinot Noir	96
1998 Felton Road Pinot Noir	95
1998 McCashin's Marlborough Pinot Noir	95
1998 Highfield Estate Elstree Reserve Pinot Noir	94
1998 Kaituna Valley Pinot Noir	94
1998 Mud House Marlborough Pinot Noir	94
1998 Palliser Estate Pinot Noir	94

1998 Ata Rangi Pinot Noir	93
1998 Alana Estate Pinot Noir	92
1998 Giesen Estate Canterbury Pinot Noir Reserve Barrel Selection	92
1998 Quartz Reef Pinot Noir	92
1998 Chard Farm Bragato Pinot Noir	91
1998 Gibbston Valley Pinot Noir	91
1998 Isabel Estate Marlborough Pinot Noir	91
1998 Pegasus Bay Canterbury Pinot Noir	91
1999 Mt Difficulty Pinot Noir	90
1998 Te Kairanga Reserve Pinot Noir	90
1998 Two Paddocks Neill Pinot Noir	90

cabernet sauvignon and merlot

Hawke's Bay and Waiheke Island are locked in a battle to establish supremacy in the minds of New Zealand's wine connoisseurs. John Buck of Te Mata will dismiss Waiheke Island with a snort of derision; Stephen White of Waiheke's Stonyridge will repay the compliment with equal vigour, aided by the Goldwaters of Goldwater Estate. Hawke's Bay has dozens of top producers, Waiheke Island a handful. Then add in the spice that the 1998 vintage should surely change New Zealand's own perspectives on what is and what is not ripe flavour for these two varieties. Banished were the tamarillo flavours, a biting green core within a superficially ripe coating; ripe, sweet tannins, not green ones. Ten years ago Dr Richard Smart suggested New Zealand's wine industry had a vested interest in the continuation of global warming. Perhaps he was right.

1998 Esk Valley Estate The Terraces	96 points
1998 Hyperion Wines Gaia Merlot	96
1998 Te Kairanga Wines Cabernet Sauvignon	96
1998 Esk Valley Estate Reserve Merlot Malbec Cabernet Sauvignon	95
1998 Matariki Wines Anthology	95
1998 Mills Reef Winery Elspeth Cabernet Sauvignon	95
1998 C J Pask Winery Gimblett Road Merlot	94
1998 C J Pask Winery Reserve Merlot	94
1998 C J Pask Winery Gimblett Road Cabernet Sauvignon	94
1998 Forrest Estate Merlot	94
1998 Mills Reef Winery Elspeth Merlot Cabernet Syrah	94
1997 Te Mata Estate Coleraine Cabernet Franc Merlot	94
1998 Thornbury Wines Hawke's Bay Merlot	94
1998 Unison Vineyard Selection	94
1998 Clearview Estate Reserve Merlot	93
1998 Dry River Arapoff Amaranth Syrah	93

australian

wineries and wines

abbey vale ★★★★

Wildwood Road, Yallingup, WA 6282 **region** Margaret River
phone (08) 9755 2121 **fax** (08) 9755 2286 **open** 7 days 10–5
winemaker Dorham Mann **production** 35 000 **est.** 1986
product range ($15–45 CD) Festival White, Semillon, Verdelho, Sauvignon Blanc, Sunburst Verdelho, Contessa, Chardonnay, Monseigneur, Yallingup Mist, Merlot Shiraz, Cabernet Merlot, Cabernet Sauvignon, Reserve Cabernet Sauvignon; Moonshine Ale brewed on the premises.
summary Abbey Vale has gone from strength to strength in recent years, vinifying an ever-increasing proportion of the production from its large 30-hectare vineyard (plus another 60 under contract), and winning a significant number of show awards. The wines are exported to Japan, the US, Canada, the UK, Bangkok, France and Germany.

abercorn ★★★☆

Cassilis Road, Mudgee, NSW 2850 **region** Mudgee
phone (02) 6373 3106 **fax** (02) 6373 3108 **open** 7 days 10–4
winemaker Tim Stevens, Simon Gilbert (Contract) **production** 3000 **est.** 1996
product range ($9.95–30 CD) Sauvignon Blanc, Chardonnay, Reserve Chardonnay, Shiraz; Barons Court is second label, comprising Chardonnay and Shiraz.
summary Tim and Connie Stevens acquired the 25-year-old Abercorn Vineyard in 1996 which, while admirably located next door to Huntington Estate, had become somewhat run down. Rejuvenation of the vineyard is well under way, and contract-winemaking has moved to Simon Gilbert (with considerable involvement by Tim Stevens), with excellent results. The wine is starting to find retail distribution throughout Sydney in addition to its cellar-door and mail-order business.

Abercorn Chardonnay

Fifty per cent of the wine is barrel-fermented in new French oak, and roughly one-third taken through malolactic fermentation. The fruit comes from 30-year-old vines. Low yields and high alcohol levels were an unavoidable fact of life in the 1998 vintage.
▼▼▼♀ **1998** Medium yellow-green; fairly obvious barrel-ferment oak, but of good quality (the oak, that is). The palate is clean and well made, moderately rich, although the finish is a touch hot/alcoholic. **rating:** 83
best drinking 1999–2001 **best vintages** NA **drink with** Pasta • $17.50

Abercorn Shiraz

Produced from 3 hectares of 30-year-old estate vines. After a warm ferment the wine is matured in French hogsheads from the Allier, Vosges and Nevers regions, 80 per cent new. Has an impressive show record.
▼▼▼▼ **1998** Dense red-purple; rich, ripe blackberry and mulberry fruit is more than a match for the French oak on the bouquet. The palate, too, is fruit-driven, with rich, ripe concentrated sweet fruit set against a background of stylish oak. **rating:** 89
▼▼▼▼▼ **1997** Medium to full red-purple; a clean bouquet with an attractive balance of sweet cherry fruit and vanilla oak. The palate is similarly attractive and balanced, with sweet fruit and oak and soft tannins all making for a very approachable wine. **rating:** 97
best drinking 2003–2013 **best vintages** '97, '98 **drink with** Rare roast beef • $22

ada river ★★★

Main Road, Neerim South, Vic 3831 **region** Gippsland
phone (03) 5628 1221 **fax** (03) 5466 2333 **open** 10–6 weekends and public holidays
winemaker Peter Kelliher, Chris Kelliher **production** 1000 **est.** 1983
product range ($13–18 CD) From Gippsland-grown grapes Chardonnay, Pinot Noir, and Cabernet Sauvignon; from Yarra Valley grapes Traminer, Chardonnay and Pinot Noir; Baw Baw Port.
summary The Kelliher family first planted vines on their dairy farm at Neerim South in 1983, extending the original Millstream Vineyard in 1989 and increasing plantings yet further by establishing the nearby Manilla Vineyard in 1994. The family also has the Goondalahg Vineyard at Steels Creek in the Yarra Valley under long-term lease, thus providing two distinct wine ranges. Wine production began in 1991, the first wines going on sale in 1995.

Ada River Yarra Valley Pinot Noir

In some prior vintages Ada River has opted to blend its Yarra Valley and Gippsland Pinot Noirs, but in 1998 chose to keep them separate.
▼▼▼♀ **1998** Medium red-purple; the aromas run through the savoury, spicy and forest spectrum, although there is a touch of plum there, too. A soft, fairly light palate, but well-balanced and well-priced. **rating:** 80
best drinking 2000–2003 **best vintages** '94, '95 **drink with** Grilled salmon • $16

affleck NR

154 Millynn Road off Bungendore Road, Bungendore, NSW 2621 **region** Canberra District
phone (02) 6236 9276 **fax** (02) 6236 9090 **open** 7 days 9–5
winemaker Ian Hendry **production** 400 **est.** 1976
product range ($8–18 CD) Chardonnay, Pinot Noir, Semillon, Late Picked Sauvignon Blanc, Cabernet Shiraz, Muscat, Ruby Port.
summary The cellar-door and mail-order price list says that the wines are 'grown, produced and bottled on the estate by Ian and Susie Hendry with much dedicated help from family and friends'. The original 2.5-hectare vineyard has been expanded to 7 hectares, and a new tasting room (offering light lunches) opened in1999.

aldinga bay winery NR

Main South Road, Aldinga, SA 5173 **region** McLaren Vale
phone (08) 8556 3179 **fax** (08) 8556 3350 **open** 7 days 10–5
winemaker Nick Girolamo **production** 6000 **est.** 1979
product range ($7.80–15 CD) Chardonnay, Sauvignon Blanc, Riesling, Cabernet Sauvignon, Shiraz, Merlot, Port.
summary The former Donolga Winery has had a name and image change since Nick Girolamo, the son of founders Don and Olga Girolamo, returned from Roseworthy College with a degree in oenology. Nick Girolamo has taken over both the winemaking and marketing; prices remain modest, though not as low as they once were, reflecting an increase in the quality and an upgrade in packaging. Aldinga Bay also has some very interesting varietal plantings,16 in all, including petit verdot, nebbiolo, barbera and sangiovese.

🐌 alexandra bridge estate NR

Brockman Highway, Karridale, WA 6288 **region** Margaret River
phone (08) 9758 5000 **fax** (08) 9384 4811 **open** 7 days 10–4.30
winemaker Philip Tubb **production** 20 000 **est.** 1994
product range ($15–30 R) Semillon, Sauvignon Blanc, Chardonnay, Margaret River Classic, Shiraz, Cabernet Sauvignon.
summary Alexandra Bridge Estate is one of the fast-developing Margaret River ventures; 30 hectares of vines have been established since 1994, and production is planned to rise from 3000 cases in 1999 to 24 000 cases in 2001 via an estate winery which opened in late 1999.

alkoomi ★★★★★

Wingebellup Road, Frankland, WA 6396 **region** Great Southern
phone (08) 9855 2229 **fax** (08) 9855 2284 **open** 7 days 10.30–5
winemaker Michael Staniford, Merv Lange **production** 60 000 **est.** 1971
product range ($11.50–47 CD) Classic White, Riesling, Chardonnay, Sauvignon Blanc, Late Harvest Riesling, Classic Red, Malbec, Shiraz, Cabernet Sauvignon, Sparkling Alkoomi, Tawny Port.
summary For those who see the wineries of Western Australia as suffering from the tyranny of distance, this most remote of all wineries shows there is no tyranny after all. It is a story of unqualified success due to sheer hard work, and no doubt to Merv and Judy Lange's aversion to borrowing a single dollar from the bank. The substantial production is entirely drawn from the ever-expanding estate vineyards, which by 1999 amounted to 50 hectares. Wine quality across the range is impeccable, always with precisely defined varietal character. National retail distribution; exports to Hong Kong, Japan, Malaysia, the UK, Denmark and France.

Alkoomi Frankland River Riesling

As with all of the Alkoomi wines, produced from estate-grown fruit. Yet another example of the symbiotic relationship between Mount Barker and Riesling, for it is usually an excellent wine.
▼▼▼▼ 1999 Very pale green-yellow; a delicate, restrained crisp bouquet leads into a long, clean palate, with gentle citrus/lime fruit neatly balanced by crisp acidity on the finish. Guaranteed to develop beautifully. **rating:** 89
best drinking 2003–2009 **best vintages** '94, '95, '96, '98, '99 **drink with** Salad • $15

Alkoomi Wandoo

The current flagship from Alkoomi in the Frankland River region of Western Australia underlines both the quality of the region and in particular that of the 25-year-old vineyards of Alkoomi (not to mention first class winemaking). The '97 was Semillon Sauvignon Blanc, the '98 is made from 100 per cent Semillon.
▼▼▼▼▼ 1998 Light green-yellow; a clean bouquet with gentle fruit and very subtle oak is followed by a palate which is quite delicate yet well structured and long. Stylish and sophisticated. **rating:** 94
best drinking 2000–2004 **best vintages** '97, '98 **drink with** Mussels • $28

Alkoomi Sauvignon Blanc

Alkoomi has 2.5 hectares of sauvignon blanc and was one of the first vineyards in the region to experiment with the variety. Some of the early vintages lacked varietal character, but every year since 1995 has displayed great depth of flavour and strong varietal character.

TTTT 1999 Very light green-yellow; the aromas are fresh and fragrant, with passionfruit and a touch of gooseberry; the palate has similarly attractive flavour and feel, but is a fraction on the light side.   **rating: 89**

best drinking Drink now **best vintages** '95, '96, '97, '98 **drink with** Ginger prawns • $17

Alkoomi Mount Frankland White

An abbreviated name from what was previously called Classic White; the varietal composition varies from year to year.

TTTT 1999 1999 Alkoomi Mount Frankland White is one of those 'classic' blends favoured by the Margaret River and Great Southern regions. Sauvignon Blanc and Semillon must play a part in what is a deliciously aromatic passionfruit and gooseberry-accent bouquet, with a lively, fresh, aromatic palate with a hint of fruit sweetness before a dry, crisp finish. Far better than most in its price class.   **rating: 86**

best drinking 2000–2003 **best vintages** NA **drink with** Smoked chicken salad • $13

Alkoomi Frankland River Chardonnay

Produced from 5 hectares of estate plantings, and barrel-fermented and matured in a mixture of oak, predominantly French Nevers and Vosges from Seguin Moreau.

TTTTT 1998 A complex array of citrus, nectarine and melon fruit with a posy of spicy oak on the bouquet announces a very attractive, elegant and lingering palate sustained by balanced but positive French oak. **rating: 94**

best drinking 2000–2005 **best vintages** '85, '88, '90, '92, '94, '97, '98 **drink with** Stir-fried chicken with cashew nuts • $22

Alkoomi Frankland River Shiraz

Yet another wine to underline the quality of Great Southern Shiraz. As with all the Alkoomi wines, made exclusively from estate-grown grapes, of which there are 6 hectares. Not a powerhouse style by any means, but with clear varietal definition.

TTTT 1998 Medium red-purple; the bouquet is clean, but not particularly concentrated or rich; there is nice cherry fruit and well-balanced fine tannins on the elegant palate; on the lighter side of the spectrum, but hangs together well.   **rating: 88**

best drinking 2001–2006 **best vintages** '90, '93, '94, '97, '98 **drink with** Lamb fillet • $21

Alkoomi Classic Red

Predominantly made from estate-grown shiraz, with a significant percentage of cabernet sauvignon, and small amounts of merlot, malbec and cabernet franc. It is the shiraz which drives the wine; it is not surprising that each release of this wine sells out long before the next becomes available.

TTTY 1998 Medium purple-red; the bouquet is firm, with slight gamey canopy characters. The palate is fresh and firm, with young vine/green fruit notes. Has been much better in other vintages.   **rating: 80**

best drinking 2000–2002 **best vintages** '83, '84, '86, '90, '93, '94, '97 **drink with** Steak Diane • $14

Alkoomi Blackbutt

A new super-premium release from Alkoomi, first made in 1994 from a blend of Cabernet Sauvignon, Malbec and Merlot, with the first blend made after the components had already been in barrel for 20 months, thereafter being transferred to 100 per cent new French oak for a further eight months before bottling. Only very small quantities are made.

TTTY 1996 Medium red-purple; the bouquet is fragrant, but relatively light, with cassis and cedar; the palate is elegant, but has more weight than the bouquet suggests; once again, cassis and cedar flavours are neatly held together with fine tannins.   **rating: 90**

best drinking 2001–2011 **best vintages** '94, '95, '96 **drink with** Rare beef • $47

Alkoomi Frankland River Cabernet Sauvignon

Typically a blend of 85 per cent Cabernet Sauvignon, 10 per cent Malbec and 5 per cent Merlot; matured for almost two years in a mix of new (30 per cent) and used French oak.

TTTT 1997 Medium red-purple; the bouquet is clean and elegant with berry and leaf aromas running into sweet redcurrant/cassis on the palate, replete with very fine-grained tannins. However, there is just a shadow of green fruit on the background.   **rating: 87**

best drinking 2002–2006 **best vintages** '83, '84, '86, '90, '93, '94, '95 **drink with** Rare rump steak • $23

allandale ★★★★

Lovedale Road, Lovedale, NSW 2320 **region** Lower Hunter Valley
phone (02) 4990 4526 **fax** (02) 4990 1714 **open** Mon–Sat 9–5, Sun 10–5
winemaker Bill Sneddon, Steve Langham **production** 17 000 **est.** 1978
product range ($16–25.50 R) Hilltops Riesling, Late Picked Hilltops Riesling, Hilltops Semillon, Semillon, Sauvignon Blanc, Chardonnay, Chardonnay Semillon, Verdelho, Lombardo (Pinot Noir Shiraz blend), Matthew Shiraz, McLaren Vale Shiraz, Mudgee Cabernet Sauvignon, William Méthode Champenoise.
summary Without ostentation, this medium-sized winery has been under the control of winemaker Bill Sneddon for well over a decade. Allandale has developed something of a reputation as a Chardonnay specialist, but does offer a broad range of wines of good quality, with an increasing number of wines produced from grapes grown in the Hilltops region. The wines are exported to the UK, the US and Switzerland.

Allandale Verdelho

Yet another wine from this variety, which is fast becoming par for the course in the Hunter Valley.
ΨΨΨΨ **1999** Light green-yellow; the bouquet has light, tropical fruit salad varietal character; clean and well made with some quite attractive mid-palate weight, and a clean, non-phenolic finish. Good example of the breed.

rating: 83

best drinking 1999–2000 **best vintages** NA **drink with** Smoked salmon pasta • $17

Allandale Hunter River Chardonnay

Draws upon 3 hectares of estate plantings. At its best, the wine shows excellent use of a mix of French and American oak. The wine is given extended lees contact and taken through partial malolactic fermentation.
ΨΨΨΨ **1999** Medium yellow-green; the bouquet shows gentle, tangy barrel-ferment influences which give an attractively bready note to the aromas. The palate is quite complex, with a neatly blended mix of tangy fruit, oak and those slightly bready characters of the bouquet. Has good length.

rating: 88

best drinking 2000–2001 **best vintages** '91, '94, '96, '98, '99 **drink with** Smoked salmon • $18.50

Allandale McLaren Vale Shiraz

Allandale has been making forays into the Hilltops region for some time now to supplement its fruit sources; for this wine it has followed the example set by Brokenwood and gone to McLaren Vale, with excellent results.
ΨΨΨΨ **1998** Medium to full purple-red; good, cherry varietal character and a nice touch of gout de terroir on the bouquet. There is excellent fruit weight and richness on the palate with sweet black cherry fruit and a touch of regional chocolate. Subtle oak; great potential for bottle development.

rating: 92

best drinking 2005–2015 **best vintages** '98 **drink with** Marinated lamb • $25

allanmere NR

Allandale Road, Allandale via Pokolbin, NSW 2321 **region** Lower Hunter Valley
phone (02) 4930 7387 **fax** (02) 4930 7900 **open** 7 days 9.30–5
winemaker Greg Silkman **production** 7000 **est.** 1984
product range ($15–20 CD) Gold Label Chardonnay, Semillon, Trinity White (Chardonnay, Semillon, Sauvignon Blanc), Cabernet Sauvignon, Trinity Red (Cabernet blend), Cabernet Shiraz. Durham Chardonnay is top-of-the-range Chardonnay.
summary Now owned by Monarch Winemaking Services. While it has a relatively low profile in conventional retail markets, cellar-door sales are flourishing in response to the ever-increasing tourist traffic in the Hunter Valley. No recent tastings. Exports to Japan, Switzerland, the US, Taiwan and the UK.

allinda NR

119 Lorimers Lane, Dixons Creek, Vic 3775 **region** Yarra Valley
phone (03) 5965 2450 **fax** (03) 5965 2467 **open** Weekends and public holidays 11–5
winemaker Al Fencaros **production** 2500 **est.** 1991
product range ($16.50–24.50 CD) Riesling, Sauvignon Blanc, Chardonnay, Late Harvest Riesling, Shiraz, Cabernets.
summary Winemaker Al Fencaros is a graduate of Bachelor of Wine Science from Charles Sturt University and was formerly employed by De Bortoli in the Yarra Valley. All of the Allinda wines are produced on site; all except the Shiraz (from Heathcote) are estate-grown from a little over 3 hectares of vineyards. Limited retail distribution in Melbourne and Sydney.

Allinda Cabernets

Primary fermentation at around 24°C is followed by two weeks post-fermentation maceration. The wine is then matured in a mix of French and American oak barriques. The concentrated 1997 vintage was a blend of 76 per cent Cabernet Sauvignon, 12 per cent Cabernet Franc and 12 per cent Merlot.

▼▼▼♀ **1997** Medium red-purple; the moderately intense bouquet offers a range of savoury/spicy nuances over sweet berry fruit. The palate has quite warm cassis berry fruit with commensurately sweet tannins, and just a touch of vanilla oak. **rating:** 84

best drinking 2000–2007 **best vintages** '95, '97 **drink with** Lasagne • $24.50

all saints ★★★★☆

All Saints Road, Wahgunyah, Vic 3687 **region** Rutherglen and Glenrowan
phone (02) 6033 1922 **fax** (02) 6033 3515 **open** Mon–Sat 9–5.30, Sun 10–5.30
winemaker Peter Brown **production** NFP **est.** 1864
product range ($9.80–90 CD) Riesling, Chenin Blanc, Muscadelle, Chardonnay, Marsanne, Orange Muscat (a winery specialty), Aleatico, Merlot, Shiraz, Cabernet Sauvignon, Late Harvest Semillon, Late Picked Muscadelle, Sparkling. The real focus is on Classic Release Muscat and Tokay and on Show Reserve Muscat and Tokay.
summary The winery rating principally reflects the Show Reserve fortified wines, but the table wines are more than adequate. An excellent winery restaurant makes this a compulsory and most enjoyable stop for any visitor to the northeast. All Saints and St Leonards are now wholly owned by Peter Brown; the vast majority of the wines are sold through cellar door and by mailing list.

All Saints Orange Muscat

Orange muscat was first planted by Brown Brothers, and seems to have stayed close to home, notwithstanding its ability to produce a drop-dead cellar-door style.

▼▼▼♀ **1999** Light to medium yellow-green; light honeysuckle and orange blossom aromas, clean and pure, are followed by a light but tangy orange zest-accented, fruity palate. **rating:** 82

best drinking Drink now **best vintages** NA **drink with** Dappled sunlight • $13

All Saints Classic Release Tokay

An exceptionally good wine at the price, with an average blend age of eight years. The varietal definition is excellent, the blend a delightful amalgam of old and young material.

▼▼▼▼▼ **NV** Light golden-brown; rich and sweet malt and tea-leaf aromas with barely perceptible fortifying spirit. The palate is of medium to full weight, with malty/toffee/caramel/tea-leaf flavours, finishing with well-balanced acidity. **rating:** 94

best drinking 2000–2010 **best vintages** NA **drink with** Try it as an aperitif • $36

All Saints Show Reserve Tokay

While some of the best stocks of All Saints were sold to other purchasers before Brown Brothers completed the acquisition of the entire property, certain of the very best material remained. This has in turn formed the base of this show blend, which has an average age of 20 years, and which has already accumulated a large number of trophies and gold medals.

▼▼▼▼▼ **NV** Deep golden-brown; wonderfully concentrated and rich caramel, toffee and molasses aromas lead on to a sensuously luscious and complex toffee, tea-leaf and butterscotch-flavoured palate. **rating:** 96

best drinking 2000–2010 **best vintages** NA **drink with** A meal in itself • $90

All Saints Classic Release Muscat

The blend has an average age of ten years, and, even if not showing the same outstanding varietal character as its sister wine, the Liqueur Tokay, is an impressive wine, attesting to the depth of the fortified stocks still held at All Saints. Won two trophies at the 1998 Sydney International Wine Competition, including the Millers Trophy for runner-up to Best Wine of Show.

▼▼▼▼♀ **NV** Medium tawny with just a hint of brown on the rim; soft, raisiny varietal muscat with fractionally earthy spirit. The palate is quite luscious, with good raisined fruit, starting sweet and finishing with cleansing acidity. **rating:** 90

best drinking 2000–2010 **best vintages** NA **drink with** Coffee and chocolates • $36

amberley estate ★★★★

Thornton Road, Yallingup, WA 6282 **region** Margaret River
phone (08) 9755 2288 **fax** (08) 9755 2171 **open** 7 days 10–4.30
winemaker Eddie Price, Greg Tilbrook **production** 80 000 **est.** 1986

product range ($17–60 CD) Semillon Sauvignon Blanc, Semillon, Chardonnay, Chenin, Cabernet Merlot, Shiraz, Cabernet Reserve.

summary Based its initial growth on the basis of its ultra-commercial, fairly sweet Chenin Blanc, which continues to provide the volume for the brand, selling out well prior to the following release. However, the quality of all of the other wines has risen markedly over recent years as the 31 hectares of estate plantings have become fully mature. Production has virtually doubled over the past few years, and exports to the UK and Japan have been established.

Amberley Estate Semillon

Typically spends some months in French oak, and some wild yeast fermentations are incorporated.

▼▼▼▼ **1999** Light to medium yellow-green; obvious barrel-ferment complexes the tangy bouquet with its rich fruit. The palate opens with attractive tangy fruit, and it is not until the aftertaste that the strong vanillin oak flexes its considerable muscle. **rating:** 87

best drinking 2000–2005 **best vintages** '95, '98 **drink with** Roast chicken • $21.50

Amberley Estate Chardonnay

Made in the usual opulent style of Amberley, building on the natural propensity of the region to produce strongly built Chardonnay.

▼▼▼▼ **1999** Medium yellow-green; complex, spicy, smoky barrel-ferment oak mingles with tangy, peachy fruit on the bouquet, characters which flow continuously into a highly flavoured palate that looks as if it will develop fairly quickly. **rating:** 87

best drinking 2000–2002 **best vintages** NA **drink with** Veal ravioli • $21.50

Amberley Estate Shiraz

Strongly flavoured and positively styled wine; first made in 1994 and has since established itself as one of Amberley's showcase wines.

▼▼▼▼ **1998** Medium to full red-purple; a gently complex range of spicy, savoury berry fruit aromas invest the bouquet with some elegance. The theme is continued on the well-balanced and composed palate, showing the intelligent use of oak, and finishing with fine tannins. A definite change in style, and a change for the better. **rating:** 89

best drinking 2002–2008 **best vintages** '94, '95, '96, '98 **drink with** Moroccan lamb • $32

Amberley Estate Cabernet Merlot

A blend of Cabernet Sauvignon, Merlot and Cabernet Franc.

▼▼▼▼ **1997** Medium red-purple; the bouquet is in traditional savoury style, with sweet fruit aromas hard to define. The palate has very long, tangy, savoury — almost lemony — flavours. An interesting wine from a varietal viewpoint. **rating:** 87

best drinking 2000–2007 **best vintages** '91, '92, '94, '97 **drink with** Rack of lamb • $22

Amberley Estate Cabernet Reserve

In 1992, and again in 1993, a Reserve Cabernet Sauvignon was held back five or so years for release as a mature wine.

▼▼▼▼ **1993** Medium red; the bouquet is clean, with attractive chocolate and cedar aromas; the palate has plenty of blackberry/blackcurrant fruit overlain with chocolate and cedar; the tannins are still powerful and have little hope of fully softening before the fruit dies. **rating:** 85

best drinking 2000–2008 **best vintages** NA **drink with** Rib of beef • $60

anderson   NR

Lot 12 Chiltern Road, Rutherglen, Vic 3685 **region** Rutherglen and Glenrowan
phone (02) 6032 8111 **open** 7 days 10–5
winemaker Howard Anderson **production** 1500 **est.** 1993
product range ($11–25 CD) Semillon, Chenin Blanc, Doux Blanc, Chardonnay, Soft Cabernet, Shiraz, Cabernet Merlot, Cabernet Sauvignon, Late Harvest Tokay, Pinot Chardonnay, Fortifieds.
summary Having notched up a winemaking career spanning 30 years, including a stint at Seppelt Great Western, Howard Anderson and family have started their own winery, ultimately intending to specialise in sparkling wine made entirely on site.

andrew garrett ★★★★

Kangarilla Road, McLaren Vale, SA 5171 **region** McLaren Vale
phone (08) 8323 8853 **fax** (08) 8323 8271 **open** 7 days 10–4
winemaker Charles Hargrave **production** 80 000 **est.** 1983
product range ($24.50 R) Semillon, Sauvignon Blanc, Chardonnay, Cabernet Merlot, Bold Shiraz, Vintage
Pinot Chardonnay.
summary Effectively another brand in the Mildara Blass Wine Group, with many of the wines now not having a
sole McLaren Vale source but instead being drawn from regions across southeastern Australia. Over the past few
years, the winemaker has produced some excellent wines which provide great value for money, particularly for the
smooth, peachy Chardonnay. Exports and distribution via Mildara Blass.

Garrett Sauvignon Blanc

No-frills winemaking, cold-fermented in tank; the the logical choice for the style.
▼▼▼▽ 1999 Light yellow-green; a light, clean, crisp bouquet is followed by a clean, nicely balanced palate helped
by good acidity; modest varietal fruit flavour in a herbaceous spectrum. **rating:** 83
best drinking 2000–2001 **best vintages** NA **drink with** Fish and chips • $10

andrew garrett vineyard estates ★★★☆

McLarens on the Lake, Kangarilla Road, McLaren Vale, SA 5171 **region** McLaren Vale
phone (08) 8323 8911 **fax** (08) 8323 9010 **open** 7 days 10–5
winemaker Andrew Garrett **production** NA **est.** 1986
product range ($9.70–37.20 CD) There are three premium wine ranges: from the Yarra Valley in Victoria
comes the Yarra Glen label, from the Adelaide Hills in South Australia the Springwood Park label, and
Marandoo Run Cabernet Sauvignon from Langhorne Creek. In much lower price and quality category come
the McLarens on the Lake blended wines of Colombard Semillon Chardonnay, Chardonnay, Cabernet Shiraz,
Grenache Shiraz and Brut Cuvée; now also Martindale Hall from Clare Valley, Macedon Ridge from Macedon
Ranges.
summary The irrepressible Andrew Garrett has risen once again after 20 years in the wine industry as
'winemaker, innovator, entrepreneur, marketer and personality' (to use his own words). Andrew Garrett Vineyard
Estates is now the umbrella for the Yarra Valley-based Yarra Glen label, the Adelaide Hills-based Springwood Park
label, and for the far longer established and more humble McLarens on the Lake range. Martindale Hall (Clare
Valley) and Macedon Range are the most recent additions.

Andrew Garrett Vineyard Estates Martindale Hall Riesling

A rich, concentrated Clare Valley style.
▼▼▼▼ 1998 Light green-yellow; a very forward bouquet with powerful toasty lime fruit and hints of kerosene.
The palate, likewise, has lots of flavour, but looks like a five-year-old wine. **rating:** 87
best drinking 2000–2003 **best vintages** NA **drink with** Sugar-cured tuna • $18.60

Andrew Garrett Vineyard Estates Springwood Park Sauvignon Blanc

A wine with greater fruit concentration (and quality) than the standard release.
▼▼▼▼ 1999 Light green-yellow; the moderately intense bouquet has touches of herb and asparagus, followed by
fuller flavour and texture, quite round in the mouth. **rating:** 87
best drinking 2000–2001 **best vintages** NA **drink with** Grilled scallops • $19

Andrew Garrett Vineyard Estates Macedon Ridge Sauvignon Blanc Chardonnay

An unusual blend of convenience which seldom rises above its station.
▼▼▼▽ 1998 Medium yellow-green; the bouquet is powerful, quite rich, but does reflect the uneasy blend of
varieties; the palate is surprisingly low in acidity, leaving one even less convinced about the merits of the blend.
rating: 81
best drinking Drink now **best vintages** NA **drink with** Takeaway • $19

Andrew Garrett Vineyard Estates Yarra Glen Chardonnay

Produced from the 100-hectare Yarra Valley vineyard established by the Andrew Garrett Group in the mid-1990s. The wine is not given any oak treatment.

♥♥♥♀ 1998 Light green-yellow; a light, clean bouquet ranging through lemon, peach and nectarine. The palate is very delicate, but lacks depth and intensity, perhaps due to high cropping levels or young vines. At least it is not swamped by oak. **rating:** 83

best drinking 2000–2003 **best vintages** NA **drink with** Baby calamari • $35

Andrew Garrett Vineyard Estates Macedon Ridge Chardonnay

Sourced from the Macedon Ranges in Victoria, and is a well-made wine.

♥♥♥♀ 1998 Light green-yellow; strong spicy nutmeg oak comes to the fore on both bouquet and palate; this is good oak, coming from genuine barrel-ferment, but it really needed more fruit. **rating:** 84

best drinking 2000–2003 **best vintages** NA **drink with** Chicken pasta • $25

Andrew Garrett Vineyard Estates McLarens on the Lake Chardonnay

This label is used for the wines at the base of the Garrett wine empire, intended for everyday drinking.

♥♥♥♀ 1999 Medium yellow-green; quite strong, spicy, chippy oak comes through on the bouquet and likewise on the palate. There is, however, some fruit there to partially balance that oak. **rating:** 80

best drinking 2000–2002 **best vintages** NA **drink with** KFC • $12.40

Andrew Garrett Vineyard Estates Macedon Ridge Pinot Noir

The reborn Garrett empire takes in many regions in the cooler parts of Victoria and South Australia.

♥♥♥♀ 1998 Light to medium red; there is some varietal character with those slightly sweet and sour, boiled fruit aromas; the palate is predominantly sappy/stemmy, again showing varietal character, but lacking richness. **rating:** 84

best drinking 2000–2001 **best vintages** NA **drink with** Asian • $25.44

Andrew Garrett Vineyard Estates Yarra Glen Grand Cabernet Sauvignon

The principal vineyard plantings of Andrew Garrett's Victorian holdings are on the outskirts of Yarra Glen, hence the name.

♥♥♥♥ 1997 Medium purple-red; abundant new oak, not fully integrated, swamps the bouquet, but sweet cabernet fruit, with fine tannins, comes through on the palate, where the oak is less assertive. **rating:** 88

best drinking 2004–2012 **best vintages** NA **drink with** Roast beef • $37.20

andrew harris vineyards ★★★★

Sydney Road, Mudgee, NSW 2850 **region** Mudgee
phone (02) 6373 1213 **fax** (02) 6373 1296 **open** Not
winemaker Frank Newman **production** 12 000 **est.** 1991
product range ($16–45 R) Premium Chardonnay, Shiraz, Premium Cabernet Sauvignon; at the top come Reserve Chardonnay, Reserve Shiraz and Reserve Cabernet Sauvignon; super premium is Shiraz Cabernet Sauvignon The Vision.
summary Andrew and Debbie Harris have lost no time since purchasing a 300-hectare sheep station southeast of Mudgee in 1991. The first 6 hectares of vineyard were planted in that year and have since been expanded to 90 hectares. A substantial portion of the production is sold to others, but right from the first vintage limited quantities of high-quality wines have been made under the Andrew Harris label (by Simon Gilbert as contract-winemaker), which deservedly enjoyed considerable show success.

Andrew Harris Premium Chardonnay

Drawn from a little over 20 hectares of estate plantings; the oak handling is less flamboyant and opulent than in the Reserve range, with brief French and American oak maturation.

♥♥♥♀ 1998 Light to medium green-yellow; the bouquet is clean, quite light, with some nectarine fruit and a hint of charry oak. The palate is pleasant, but does not have a lot of life. **rating:** 82

best drinking Drink now **best vintages** NA **drink with** Fillet of pork • $14.95

Andrew Harris The Vision

A super-premium Shiraz Cabernet release which won two trophies at the 1997 Royal Sydney Wine Show, and has matured well since doing so.

TTTT 1996 Medium red, starting to show some development. The bouquet is quite complex, already showing some secondary leafy/earthy/savoury aromas together with some oak lift. The palate is attractive, with sweet earthy/berry fruit, soft, sweet, fine tannins and subtle American oak. **rating: 90**

best drinking 2000–2006 **best vintages** NA **drink with** Steak and kidney pie • $45

Andrew Harris Premium Cabernet Sauvignon

Produced from 20 hectares of estate plantings; as with the Chardonnay, the oak handling is less pronounced than in the Reserve range, but here the choice is less clear-cut. Both styles will have their proponents. The Premium wine is matured in a mix of used French and American oak.

TTT 1997 Medium red-purple; the bouquet is literally swamped with American oak, as is the palate. If you like drinking American oak, you will love drinking this wine. **rating: 80**

best drinking 2000–2003 **best vintages** '94, '95 **drink with** Illabo lamb • $14.95

andrew peace wines NR

Wood Wood, Swan Hill, Vic 3585 **region** Swan Hill
phone (03) 5030 5291 **fax** (03) 5030 5605 **open** By appointment
winemaker Andrew Peace **production** 50 000 **est.** 1995
product range ($9.95–15.95 R) Sauvignon Blanc, Chardonnay, Colombard Chardonnay, Mourvedre Shiraz, Grenache Shiraz, Shiraz, Cabernet, Merlot.
summary The Peace family has been a major Swan Hill grape grower since 1980 and moved into winemaking with the opening of a $3 million winery in 1997. The modestly priced wines are aimed at supermarket-type outlets in Australia and, in particular, at the export market in the major destinations for Australian wine.

angove's ★★★☆

Bookmark Avenue, Renmark, SA 5341 **region** Riverland
phone (08) 8595 1311 **fax** (08) 8595 1583 **open** Mon–Fri 9–5
winemaker Garry Wall **production** 1 million **est.** 1886
product range ($3.15–45 CD) A range of new label designs and packaging for the five varietal ranges. At the top comes Sarnia Farm Chardonnay and Cabernet Sauvignon; then Mondiale White and Red (blends); then Classic Reserve, covering virtually all varieties; and then Stonegate blended whites and reds; Butterfly Ridge wines; and, bringing up the rear, Misty Vineyards.
summary Exemplifies the economies of scale achievable in the Australian Riverland without compromising potential quality. Very good technology provides wines which are never poor and which can sometimes exceed their theoretical station in life. The white varietals are best. Angove's expansion into Padthaway has resulted in estate-grown premium wines at the top of the range. As well as national distribution, Angove's is exported to virtually all the major markets in Europe, North America and Asia. For good measure, it also acts as a distributor of Perrier Jouet Champagne and several small Australian wineries.

Angove's Sarnia Farm Chardonnay

The twin of Sarnia Farm Cabernet Sauvignon, and if only by virtue of the superior grape resource (Angove's Padthaway vineyard), the best of the always competently crafted and made Angove's white wines.

TTTT 1999 Medium to full yellow-green; a clean, smooth bouquet with ripe nectarine fruit and subtle oak is followed by a clean, gentle and well-balanced palate, without any particular complexity or claim to greatness. **rating: 83**

best drinking 2000–2003 **best vintages** NA **drink with** Creamy pasta • $NA

Angove's Classic Reserve Cabernet Sauvignon

Part of the smartly newly packaged Classic Reserve range. The great strength of these well-priced wines is that the winemakers have resisted the temptation to load up the wines with chippy oak.

TTT 1998 Light to medium red; the bouquet, while relatively light, is quite fragrant, with redcurrant/raspberry fruit. The palate provides more of the same in a light-bodied but pleasant mode, finishing with soft tannins. **rating: 82**

best drinking 2000–2003 **best vintages** NA **drink with** Alfresco • $NA

Angove's Sarnia Farm Cabernet Sauvignon

A new venture for Angove's, which has hitherto produced almost all of its wines from its Nanya Vineyard in the Riverland, making occasional Limited Release/Winemaker Selection with grapes purchased from various premium areas. 1993 was the inaugural vintage. As with the Chardonnay, gained the name 'Sarnia Farm' with the second release, and which really impresses with its most recent release. It may well be that a maturing vineyard and/or better viticulture is playing a role.

▼▼▼▼ 1998 Medium red-purple; the bouquet is firm and fresh with earthy cabernet varietal character and echoes of mint and cedar. The palate is similarly quite firm and fresh, with blackcurrant/cassis fruit and fine tannins to close.   **rating:** 85

best drinking 2001–2006 **best vintages** '93, '98 **drink with** Beef Provençale • $NA

annie's lane ★★★★

Main North Road, Watervale, SA 5452 **region** Clare Valley
phone (08) 8843 0003 **fax** (08) 8843 0096 **open** Mon–Fri 8.30–5, weekends 11–4
winemaker David O'Leary **production** 150 000 **est.** 1856
product range ($12–34 CD) Annie's Lane Riesling, Annie's Lane Semillon, Annie's Lane Chardonnay, Annie's Lane Shiraz and Annie's Lane Cabernet Merlot, Annie's Lane Contour Vineyard Shiraz, The Clare Essentials Prospect Vineyard Riesling, The Clare Essentials Carlsfield Vineyard Riesling, The Clare Essentials Polish Hill River Vineyard Riesling, Red Essentials Schultz's Wrattonbully Vineyard Shiraz, The Essentials O'Deas Vineyard Coonawarra Cabernet.
summary The wheel has turned full circle and, after some regrettable decisions to progressively change the name of Quelltaler to Eaglehawk Estate and Black Opal, this great legacy of the nineteenth century once again proudly bears the Quelltaler name. The Eaglehawk brand continues but is made at Wolf Blass in the Barossa Valley and has a southeastern Australia origin; Black Opal is made, but only for export; Quelltaler as a brand name is, at least for the time being, in suspense; and the Clare Valley portfolio made at Quelltaler is sold under the Annie's Lane label. The name comes from Annie Weyman, a turn-of-the-century local identity. The winery, incidentally, has been leased to some Clare Valley vignerons determined to keep it in going-concern condition.

Annie's Lane Riesling

Produced from a blend of Watervale and Polish Hill-grown grapes. Notwithstanding the emergence of three Quelltaler single vineyard Rieslings, this wine suffers nothing in comparison.

▼▼▼▼♀ 1999 Winner of the Trophy for Best Value Wine in the under $15 consumer classes at the Royal Adelaide Wine Show in September 1999. Abundant floral/lime aromas introduce a snappy palate, crisp, clean and long, with lime/mineral flavours and perfect acidity to leave the mouth as fresh as a spring day.   **rating:** 92

best drinking 1999–2009 **best vintages** '96, '97, '98 **drink with** Asparagus • $14

The Clare Essentials Carlsfield Vineyard Riesling

Carlsfield Vineyard was planted in 1935 on a sweeping hillside of red loam over limestone. The vineyard is situated just to the southeast of the Quelltaler winery at an elevation of 470 metres. The riesling is the celebrated Geisenheim clone.

▼▼▼▼♀ 1999 Very pure, tight lime juice aromas lead into an excellent, tight lime/minerally palate, with a long, clean finish. Wholly deceptive simplicity.   **rating:** 93

best drinking 2000–2014 **best vintages** '98, '99 **drink with** Eggplant terrine • $16

Annie's Lane Semillon

The semillon vines at Quelltaler are clonal selections from the Hunter Valley, and have an average age of 45 years. Grown on red loam over limestone, hand-pruned and hand-picked, they have always produced a white wine of exceptional concentration and character. The wine is cool-fermented, and 50 per cent matured in two-year-old French oak on its lees for a period of six weeks, giving a barely subliminal hint of oak.

▼▼▼♀ 1999 Medium yellow-green; a smooth, clean and soft bouquet offers a hint of honey; the palate is already showing some weight but will develop further in the short term.   **rating:** 83

best drinking 2000–2003 **best vintages** '94, '96 **drink with** Poached salmon • $14

Annie's Lane Chardonnay

Sourced from two quite distinct pockets of the Clare Valley, 60 per cent coming from the Annie's Lane Vineyard in Polish Hill, the coolest part of the valley which ripens three weeks later than the Quelltaler Estate vineyard at Watervale, from which the remaining 40 per cent comes. Twenty per cent of the wine is barrel-fermented in new French oak, the remainder being fermented in steel before being oak-matured and bottled in August of the year of vintage.

▼▼▼♀ **1999** Good green-yellow; the bouquet is solid, but not particularly aromatic. The palate lacks any real distinguishing features, but is fault-free. **rating:** 80

best drinking Drink now **best vintages** '94, '96 **drink with** Grilled chicken • $14

Annie's Lane Shiraz

Comes from predominantly old vines on both the Annie's Lane Vineyard in Polish Hill as well as from contract growers throughout the Clare Valley. Fermented in small 4-tonne open fermenters, and matured in a mix of French and American oak hogsheads for 20 months. As with all the Annie's Lane wines, a consistent show winner.

▼▼▼▼♀ **1998** Medium purple-red; fresh, sweet cherry/berry fruit on the bouquet is followed by lush cherry fruit on the palate. The oak is just a fraction raw, but an outstanding wine at its price. **rating:** 91

best drinking 2002–2008 **best vintages** '94, '96, '98 **drink with** Pepper steak • $16

Red Essentials Schultz's Wrattonbully Vineyard Shiraz

This is the second red wine to be released under the slightly quixotic 'The Essentials' banner, nominally anchored to the Quelltaler winery in the Clare Valley, but produced from grapes grown in Wrattonbully aka Koppamurra.

▼▼▼▼ **1997** Medium red-purple; the bouquet is clean, with hints of pepper and spice throughout the light red cherry fruit. The palate is fresh and lively, with moderately weighted Shiraz, and just a touch of the spice and pepper of the bouquet coming through on the finish. **rating:** 86

best drinking 1999–2003 **best vintages** NA **drink with** Pasta • $19

Annie's Lane Cabernet Merlot

A blend of 85 per cent Cabernet Sauvignon and 15 per cent Merlot, the Cabernet Sauvignon coming in part from Annie's Lane Vineyard in Polish Hill and from other Clare Valley growers, the Merlot component from the Quelltaler Estate vineyard. Fermented in small 4-tonne open fermenters, then matured in French oak (20 per cent new) for a period of 15 months.

▼▼▼▼ **1998** Medium red-purple; the bouquet is full of ripe, dark berry fruit aromas, without a hint of green. The palate is bolstered by American oak to provide a rich, easily enjoyed mainstream Australian red. **rating:** 89

best drinking 2002–2007 **best vintages** '94, '95, '97 **drink with** Illabo spring lamb • $16

antcliff's chase NR

RMB 4510, Caveat via Seymour, Vic 3660 **region** Central Victorian Mountain Country
phone (03) 5790 4333 **fax** (03) 5790 4333 **open** Weekends 10–5
winemaker Chris Bennett, Ian Leamon **production** 800 **est.** 1982
product range ($14–30 CD) Riesling, Chardonnay, Pinot Noir, Cabernet Franc.
summary A small family enterprise which commenced planting the vineyards at an elevation of 600 metres in the Strathbogie Ranges in 1982 but which has only recently commenced wine production from the 4-hectare vineyard. As the scarecrow label indicates, birds are a major problem for remote vineyards such as this.

apsley gorge vineyard ★★★★☆

Rosedale Road, Bicheno, Tas 7215 **region** Southern Tasmania
phone (03) 6375 1221 **fax** (03) 6375 1589 **open** By appointment
winemaker Brian Franklin **production** 2000 **est.** 1988
product range ($20–25 CD) Chardonnay, Pinot Noir.
summary While nominally situated at Bicheno on the east coast, Apsley Gorge is in fact some distance inland, taking its name from a mountain pass. Clearly, it shares with the other east coast wineries the capacity to produce Chardonnay and Pinot Noir of excellent quality, with skilled winemaking by Andrew Hood doing the rest. Retail distribution in most States; exports to the UK, Switzerland, the Netherlands, Austria, California and Canada.

Apsley Gorge Chardonnay

Contract-made by Andrew Hood in tiny quantities since 1994. It is a wine that has grown in stature year by year, and at the top of the Tasmanian quality tree. Interestingly, was the first Chardonnay to be made by Andrew Hood which undergoes malolactic fermentation, this being the express wish of Apsley Gorge owners Brian Frankland and Greg Walch.

▼▼▼▼ **1998** Excellent green-yellow colour; clean, smooth peachy fruit on both the bouquet and palate is the driving force of the wine, which is nicely balanced and has good, ripe flavours. If there is a criticism, the oak is slightly pedestrian. **rating:** 89

best drinking 2000–2004 **best vintages** '96, '97, '98 **drink with** Sugar-cured tuna • $25

aquila estate ★★★

85 Carabooda Road, Carabooda, WA 6033 **region** Swan District
phone (08) 9561 5415 **fax** (08) 9561 5415 **open** Not
winemaker Andrew Spencer Wright **production** 19 500 **est.** 1993
product range ($9.99–18.99 R) Semillon, Sauvignon Blanc, Boyup Brook Chardonnay, Reflections (white blend), Cabernet Sauvignon, Flame (red blend).
summary As Aquila Estate has matured, so have its grape sources centred on the Margaret River (principally) and Boyup Brook. The white wines are quite attractive, particularly the Margaret River Sauvignon Blanc and Boyup Brook Chardonnay.

arlewood estate NR

Harmans Road South, Willyabrup, WA 6284 **region** Margaret River
phone (08) 9755 6267 **fax** (08) 9755 6267 **open** Weekends 11–5
winemaker Voyager Estate (Contract) **production** 2000 **est.** 1988
product range ($19–29 CD) Semillon, Sauvignon Blanc, Liaison (sweet), Cabernet Sauvignon Reserve, Port.
summary Liz and John Wojturski have expanded their initial plantings of 2.5 hectares to over 9 hectares and now have limited distribution through agents in Sydney, New South Wales and Perth and exports to New York.

armstrong vineyards ★★★★

Lot 1 Military Road, Armstrong, Vic 3381 **region** Grampians
phone (08) 8277 6073 **fax** (08) 8277 6035 **open** Not
winemaker Tony Royal **production** 1000 **est.** 1989
product range ($47.95 R) Shiraz.
summary Armstrong Vineyards is the brain- or love-child of Tony Royal, former Seppelt Great Western winemaker who now runs the Australian business of Seguin Moreau, the largest of the French coopers. Armstrong Vineyards has 6.5 hectares of shiraz, the first 2 hectares planted in 1989, the remainder in 1995–96. Low yields (4.5 to 5.5 tonnes per hectare) mean the wine will always be produced in limited quantities.

Armstrong Vineyards Shiraz

The wine was made with a four-day pre-fermentation cold-soak, and is then fermented in small open fermenters which are hand-plunged. Fermentation is completed in French oak (70 per cent new, 30 per cent one-year-old, Seguin Moreau, of course) where it spends a little under two years.
TTTTY 1998 Dense red-purple; rich, ripe complex dark plum fruit and touches of spice flood the rich bouquet; the same flavours are repeated on the palate, supported by well-balanced and integrated oak, and good tannins. None of the mint of lesser vintages. **rating:** 90
best drinking 2003–2013 **best vintages** '96, '98 **drink with** Yearling steak • $47.95

arranmore vineyard NR

Rangeview Road, Carey Gully, SA 5144 **region** Adelaide Hills
phone (08) 8390 3034 **fax** (08) 8390 3034 **open** By appointment
winemaker John Venus **production** 250 **est.** 1998
product range ($20–23 CD) Sauvignon Blanc, Chardonnay, Black Pinot Noir, Cleggett's Block Shiraz Cabernet.
summary One of the tiny operations which are appearing all over the beautiful Adelaide Hills. The 2-hectare vineyard is planted to pinot noir, chardonnay and sauvignon blanc, and the wines are basically sold through word of mouth and mail order.

Arranmore Vineyard Black Pinot Noir

Made by owner/winemaker John Venus on the estate. Partial destemming (70 per cent) and whole bunches (30 per cent) in open stainless steel vats with frequent hand-plunging. The wine spends 12 months in refurbished French (predominant) and American oak barrels.
TTTT 1998 Medium to full red-purple; the bouquet has plenty of rich cherry/plum pinot fruit, as does the palate, where the flavours are of plum rather than cherry. A very promising start. **rating:** 85
best drinking 2001–2004 **best vintages** '98 **drink with** Coq au vin • $23

arrowfield ★★★

Denman Road, Jerry's Plains, NSW 2330 **region** Upper Hunter Valley
phone (02) 6576 4041 **fax** (02) 6576 4144 **open** 7 days 10–5
winemaker Blair Duncan **production** 100 000 **est.** 1968
product range ($8.95–19.95 R) Top-of-the-range Show Reserve range of Chardonnay, Semillon, Shiraz, Cabernet Sauvignon; Cowra Chardonnay, Merlot, Late Harvest Gewurztraminer; Arrowfield varietals Chardonnay, Semillon Chardonnay, Sauvignon Blanc, Traminer Riesling, Late Harvest Riesling, Shiraz, Cabernet Merlot; Sparkling and Fortifieds.
summary After largely dropping the Arrowfield name in favour of Mountarrow and a plethora of other brands, this Japanese-owned company has come full circle, once again marketing the wines solely under the Arrowfield label. Its principal grape sources are Cowra and the Upper Hunter, but it does venture further afield from time to time. Tragically, during the 1999 vintage, the Arrowfield winery (and some of its wine stocks) were severely damaged in a $10 million fire.

Arrowfield Sauvignon Blanc

A blend of grapes from the Hunter Valley and Cowra, cool-fermented in stainless steel and early-bottled.
▼▼▼▽ 1999 Light green-yellow; the bouquet is clean and crisp, but very delicate and light. The palate is clean, but lacks fruit intensity; cleverly fleshed out with a touch of residual sugar on the finish.   **rating: 82**
best drinking 2000–2001 **best vintages** NA **drink with** Light seafood • $12

Arrowfield Cowra Chardonnay

Cold-fermented in stainless steel except for the pressings fraction which finished its ferment in American oak. Clever commercial winemaking.
▼▼▼▽ 1999 Medium yellow-green; the bouquet is clean, with predominant melon and a little peach; a pleasant commercial Chardonnay on the palate until a faint touch of slightly coarse oak comes on the finish.   **rating: 81**
best drinking 2000–2001 **best vintages** NA **drink with** Takeaway • $14

arthurs creek estate ★★★★★

Strathewen Road, Arthurs Creek, Vic 3099 **region** Yarra Valley
phone (03) 9827 6629 **fax** (03) 9824 0252 **open** Not
winemaker Mitchelton (Contract), Gary Baldwin (Consultant) **production** 1600 **est.** 1976
product range ($27.25–44.30 R) Chardonnay, Cabernet Sauvignon.
summary A latter-day folly of leading Melbourne QC, S E K Hulme, who planted 1.5 hectares each of semillon, chardonnay, and cabernet sauvignon at Arthurs Creek in the mid-1970s, and commenced to have wine made by various people for 15 years before deciding to sell any of it. A ruthless weeding-out process followed, with only the best of the older vintages offered. The Cabernets from the 1990s are absolutely outstanding, deeply fruited and marvellously structured. Exports to UK and Japan.

Arthurs Creek Chardonnay

Produced from 1.5 hectares of estate plantings. The two initial releases were 1988 and 1990, which came on to the market in late 1993. As with the Cabernet Sauvignon, winemaking has been done at Mitchelton since 1992 and the quality and consistency of the vintages since that time have been wholly admirable.
▼▼▼▼ 1998 Light green-yellow; the bouquet is light and crisp, with subtle oak. The palate, too, seems light, and certainly needs time to develop. This is produced from an old vineyard with a distinguished series of wines preceding it, so the prospects simply have to be good.   **rating: 85**
best drinking 2002–2008 **best vintages** '88, '90, '92, '93, '94, '95, '97 **drink with** Veal fricassee • $27.25

ashbrook estate ★★★★★

Harmans Road South, Willyabrup, WA 6284 **region** Margaret River
phone (08) 9755 6262 **fax** (08) 9755 6290 **open** 7 days 11–5
winemaker Tony Devitt, Brian Devitt **production** 8000 **est.** 1975
product range ($15–24 CD) Gold Label Riesling, Black Label Riesling, Semillon, Sauvignon Blanc, Chardonnay, Verdelho, Cabernet Merlot, Cabernet Sauvignon.
summary A fastidious maker of consistently outstanding estate-grown table wines but which shuns publicity and the wine show system alike and is less well-known than it deserves to be, selling much of its wine through the cellar door and by an understandably very loyal mailing list clientele. All of the white wines are of the highest quality, year in, year out. Small quantities of the wines now find their way to Japan, Singapore, Hong Kong, the US and Taiwan.

Ashbrook Estate Gold Label Riesling

The Margaret River region, unlike the neighbouring Great Southern, isn't known for its Rieslings, but the Devitt brothers haven't been told that.

TTTTY 1999 Light green-yellow; a fresh, crisp, fine lemony bouquet with no toasty characters. The palate is immaculate, with lemon/lime/herb flavours, and a fine, non-phenolic finish; much tighter and crisper than most Margaret River Rieslings. **rating: 91**

best drinking 2000–2005 **best vintages** '99 **drink with** Asparagus and salmon terrine • $15

Ashbrook Estate Semillon

All of the Ashbrook Estate wines are estate-grown, the Semillon from 2.6 hectares of vines. Fermented in stainless steel, and not given any time in oak, the wine shows the herbaceous style of Margaret River Semillon to best advantage.

TTTT 1999 Medium yellow-green; the bouquet is quite aromatic, with ripe fruit running through a mix of tropical and more zesty characters. A soft, easy style, fresh and clean on the palate although not quite the intensity of prior vintages. **rating: 89**

best drinking 2000–2005 **best vintages** '87, '92, '93, '94, '95, '97, '99 **drink with** Blanquette of veal • $15

Ashbrook Estate Verdelho

A wine which proves even the gods are mortal or, at the very least, susceptible to the economic blandishments of the cellar door.

TTTY 1999 Medium yellow-green; the bouquet is highly aromatic but has slightly reductive/armpit aromas. The palate is full, but very sweet, in uncompromising cellar-door style. **rating: 84**

best drinking Drink now **best vintages** NA **drink with** Chicken takeaway • $16

Ashbrook Estate Chardonnay

Produced from a little over 3 hectares of estate plantings. The wine is 50 per cent fermented in new French oak barriques, and spends approximately six months maturing in wood before being bottled. Immaculate winemaking produces an immaculate wine.

TTTTY 1998 Medium yellow-green; the bouquet offers a sophisticated and seamless marriage between fruit and oak; the very elegant palate is exceptionally smooth, with melon and citrus fruit the driver, subtle oak the backdrop. **rating: 93**

best drinking 2000–2008 **best vintages** '87, '92, '93, '94, '95, '98 **drink with** Grilled spatchcock • $23

asher   NR

360 Goldsworthy Road, Lovely Banks, Geelong, Vic 3231 **region** Geelong
phone (03) 5276 1365 **open** Sat, public holidays 10–5, Sun 12–5
winemaker Brian Moten **production** Minuscule **est.** 1975
product range ($10 CD) Sauvignon Blanc, Cabernet Sauvignon, Malbec.
summary A tiny, semi-home-winemaking operation situated at the picturesquely named town of Lovely Banks on the outskirts of Geelong.

ashton hills   ★★★★☆

Tregarthen Road, Ashton, SA 5137 **region** Adelaide Hills
phone (08) 8390 1243 **fax** (08) 8390 1243 **open** Weekends 11–5.30
winemaker Stephen George **production** 1500 **est.** 1982
product range ($16–40 CD) Chardonnay, Riesling, Salmon Brut, Blanc de Blanc, Pinot Noir, Obliqua (Cabernet Merlot).
summary Stephen George wears three winemaker hats: one for Ashton Hills, drawing upon a 3.5-hectare estate vineyard high in the Adelaide Hills; one for Galah Wines; and one for Wendouree. It would be hard to imagine three wineries producing more diverse styles, with the elegance and finesse of Ashton Hills at one end of the spectrum, the awesome power of Wendouree at the other. The Riesling and Pinot Noir have moved into the highest echelon. Export markets have been developed in the UK and the US.

Ashton Hills Riesling

A wine of unusually consistent style, and which invariably ages slowly. The natural acidity is high, and the fruit sometimes tight and inexpressive when the wine is young, slowly opening up as it evolves in bottle. These elegant wines are ideal to complement food.

TTTTT 1998 Light green-yellow; a very pure manifestation of Riesling, with lovely, crisp lime and mineral aromas. The palate, likewise, has crystal clear varietal fruit, lime-accented, with great length. Will develop beautifully. **rating: 94**

best drinking 2001–2011 **best vintages** '89, '90, '91, '93, '94, '96, '97, '98 **drink with** Fresh asparagus • $16

Ashton Hills Pinot Noir
As with all the Ashton Hills wines, these are Pinots relying on finesse and elegance, rather than extract. Winemaker Stephen George employs the full gamut of winemaking techniques, and has an extraordinary 19 different clones of pinot planted in 1 hectare of vines, necessarily providing yet further complexity. Now the third Pinot Noir release from Ashton Hills, and yet another gold medal-pointed wine on my score sheet at the 1999 Adelaide Hills Wine Show. Indeed, the only three gold medals I awarded all went to the Ashton Hills wines sprinkled throughout the class, which I decribed (before knowing the identity of any of the wines) as a great class of Pinot Noirs in the full-bodied style of Adelaide Hills at its very best.

▼▼▼▼▼ **1998** Medium red, with some purple. Intense, fragrant sappy Burgundian aromas are followed by a palate literally loaded with style. The only problem, if such it be, is that the wine is very advanced. This was yet another gold medal-pointed wine on my score sheet at the 1999 Adelaide Hills Wine Show. **rating:** 94

best drinking 2000–2003 **best vintages** '88, '91, '92, '93, '94, '97, '98 **drink with** Peking duck • $25

Ashton Hills Piccadilly Pinot Noir
Another beautifully crafted Adelaide Hills Pinot Noir from the hands of Stephen George.

▼▼▼▼▼ **1998** Medium red with a tinge of purple. Although tasted when only 18 months old, the wine had already developed complex, secondary bottle-developed aromas, suggesting more rapid developments than the '97 Reserve. The wine comes into its own on the palate, with tremendous length and grip to the foresty/earthy flavours. **rating:** 94

best drinking 2000–2004 **best vintages** NA **drink with** Braised duck • $20

Ashton Hills Reserve Pinot Noir
The vines at the Ashton Hills vineyard are now over 15 years old, producing better grapes year by year. In 1997 Ashton Hills produced a freakish Pinot Noir, a wine of immense intensity and complexity, and a benchmark achievement for Australia at the start of the new millennium. Swept all before it every time I tasted it in the second half of 1999, fulfilling all the promise the wine showed when first bottled.

▼▼▼▼▼ **1997** Medium red-purple; an exceptionally complex bouquet of plum, game and spice aromas; masses of plum and spice flood the mouth in a multi-dimensional, multi-textural way. The oak handling is impeccable. **rating:** 97

best drinking 2000–2005 **best vintages** '97 **drink with** Smoked duck • $40

Ashton Hills Obliqua Cabernet Merlot
The Ashton Hills vineyard is in a distinctly cool part of the Adelaide Hills, and the Bordeaux varieties — particularly cabernet sauvignon — struggle to achieve the flavour ripeness Australians are used to. The '97 Obliqua topped its class at the 1999 Adelaide Hills Wine Show, and was the only gold medal winner.

▼▼▼▼▼ **1997** Medium red-purple; a high-toned bouquet with some faintly leafy/stemmy aromas does not prepare one for the palate, which is complex, soft and stylish in a way which is not often achieved in the Adelaide Hills. **rating:** 94

best drinking 2001–2007 **best vintages** '97 **drink with** Rack of lamb • $26

ashworths hill NR
Ashworths Road, Lancefield, Vic 3435 **region** Macedon Ranges
phone (03) 5429 1689 **fax** (03) 5429 1689 **open** 7 days 10–6
winemaker Anne Manning, John Ellis **production** 100 **est.** 1982
product range ($12–20 CD) Macedon Ranges Cabernet Sauvignon is the flagship; Victorian Riesling and Chardonnay also available.
summary Peg and Ken Reaburn offer light refreshments throughout the day, the property offering scenic views of the Macedon Ranges.

audrey wilkinson NR
Oakdale, DeBeyers Road, Pokolbin, NSW 2320 **region** Lower Hunter Valley
phone (02) 4998 7411 **fax** (02) 4998 7303 **open** By appointment
winemaker Chris Cameron **production** 6000 **est.** 1999
product range ($19–20 CD) Semillon, Traminer, Chardonnay, Shiraz.
summary One of the most historic properties in the Hunter Valley, with a particularly beautiful location. The four wines come from the old plantings on the property.

auldstone ★★★☆

Booths Road, Taminick via Glenrowan, Vic 3675 **region** Rutherglen and Glenrowan
phone (03) 5766 2237 **fax** (03) 5766 2131 **open** Thur–Sat and school holidays 9–5, Sun 10–5
winemaker Michael Reid **production** 2000 **est.** 1987
product range ($10–24 CD) Riesling, Traminer Riesling, Chardonnay, Late Picked Riesling, Shiraz, Cabernet, Herceynia Tawny Port, Boweya Muscat, Sparkling Shiraz.
summary Michael and Nancy Reid have restored a century-old stone winery and have replanted the largely abandoned 24-hectare vineyard around it. Gourmet lunches are available on weekends.

austin's barrabool ★★★★

50 Lemins Road, Waurn Ponds, Vic 3221 **region** Geelong
phone (03) 5241 8114 **fax** (03) 5241 8122 **open** By appointment
winemaker John Ellis (Contract), Pamela Austin **production** 1800 **est.** 1982
product range ($18–40 CD) Riesling, Chardonnay, Reserve Shiraz, Cabernet Sauvignon.
summary Pamela and Richard Austin have quietly built their business from a tiny base, but one which is now poised for much bigger things. The vineyard has been extended to 16.4 hectares, and instead of selling part of the production to others, they intend to significantly increase wine production under their own label — it doubled between 1998 and 1999. Wine quality, too, has risen sharply, with high-quality wines being skilfully made by John Ellis at Hanging Rock.

avalon vineyard ★★☆

RMB 9556 Whitfield Road, Wangaratta, Vic 3678 **region** King Valley
phone (03) 5729 3629 **fax** (03) 5729 3635 **open** 7 days 10–5
winemaker Doug Groom **production** 900 **est.** 1981
product range ($12–16 CD) Riesling, Chardonnay, Sauvignon Blanc Semillon, Late Harvest Semillon, Shiraz, Cabernet Sauvignon, Pinot Noir, Pinot Noir Méthode Champenoise.
summary Avalon Vineyard is situated in the King Valley, 4 kilometres north of Whitfield. Much of the production from the 10-hectare vineyard is sold to other makers, with limited quantities made by Doug Groom, a graduate of Roseworthy, and one of the owners of the property.

avalon wines NR

1605 Bailey Road, Glen Forrest, WA 6071 **region** Perth Hills
phone (08) 9298 8049 **fax** (08) 9298 8049 **open** By appointment
winemaker Caspar van der Meer (1999) Rob Marshall (2000) **production** 650 **est.** 1986
product range ($10–14.95 CD) Chardonnay, Semillon, Cabernet Merlot.
summary One of the newer wineries in the Perth Hills, drawing upon three-quarters of a hectare each of chardonnay, semillon and cabernet sauvignon.

Avalon Wines Cabernet Merlot

Estate-grown, drawing on 0.7 hectares of cabernet sauvignon and 0.6 hectares of merlot. The wine itself is a blend of 67 per cent Cabernet and 33 per cent Merlot.
 1999 Medium red, with just a touch of purple; the light to moderately intense bouquet is clean, with savoury/foresty fruit and subtle oak. The palate is clean, well made and balanced, with gentle berry fruit; the tannin and oak extract does not threaten the wine. **rating:** 80
best drinking 2000–2004 **best vintages** NA **drink with** Smoked beef •$14.95

bacchus estate NR

381 Milbrodale Road, Broke, NSW 2330 **region** Lower Hunter Valley
phone (02) 6579 1153 **fax** (02) 6579 1069 **open** By appointment
winemaker Andrew Margan (Contract) **production** 1000 **est.** 1993
product range ($14–20 CD) Chardonnay, Unwooded Chardonnay, Shiraz.
summary Another of the wineries springing up like mushrooms after spring rain in the Hunter Valley, in this instance at Broke. A little over 10 hectares of vineyard have been established, with a further 12 hectares to be planted in the near future. As the new plantings mature, production will increase significantly.

badger's brook   NR

874 Maroondah Highway, Coldstream, Vic 3770 **region** Yarra Valley
phone (03) 5962 4130 **fax** (03) 5962 4238 **open** Weekends and public holidays 10–5
winemaker Contract **production** 5300 **est.** 1993
product range Badger's Brook and Storm Ridge.
summary Situated prominently on the Maroondah Highway next door to the well-known Eyton-on-Yarra. Location is all, although not for the wines which come from various sources.

bago vineyards   NR

Milligans Road, off Bago Road, Wauchope, NSW 2446 **region** Hastings River
phone (02) 6585 7099 **fax** (02) 6585 7099 **open** 7 days 11–5
winemaker John Cassegrain (Contract) **production** 4000 **est.** 1985
product range ($12–17.50 CD) Chardonnay, Jazz Classic White, Verdelho, Chambourcin, Sparkling, Tawny Port.
summary Jim and Kay Mobs commenced planting the Broken Bago Vineyards in 1985 with 1 hectare of chardonnay and have now increased the total plantings to 12 hectares. Regional specialist John Cassegrain (no longer with Cassegrain Vineyards) is contract-winemaker.

Bago Vineyards Chambourcin

Very sensibly, chambourcin is the dominant variety in the vineyards, with 4 hectares under vine. It stands up far better to the often wet and humid conditions of the north coast than any other variety.
 1998 Dense purple-red; the bouquet is quite rich, with that intriguing gamey varietal character which can easily be mistaken as a sign of bacterial activity. The palate is clean, fruity and quite well balanced, but with that slight structural dip or hollow towards the end which is another hallmark of the variety.   **rating: 80**
best drinking 2000–2002 **best vintages** NA **drink with** Beef pie • $14.50

baileys of glenrowan   ★★★★★

Corner Taminick Gap and Upper Taminick Roads, Glenrowan, Vic 3675 **region** Rutherglen and Glenrowan
phone (03) 5766 2392 **fax** (03) 5766 2596 **open** Mon–Fri 9–5, weekends 10–5
winemaker Nick Walker **production** 30 0000 **est.** 1870
product range ($15–50 CD) Classic Chardonnay, Riesling, Touriga, Shiraz, 1920's Block Shiraz are the principal wines; Warby Range, Founders and Winemaker's Selection Tokay and Muscat; Phantom's Lake Chardonnay and Shiraz were introduced in 1997 in fancy bottles.
summary Now part of the sprawling Mildara Blass empire, inherited via the Rothbury takeover. Has made some excellent Shiraz in recent years, but its greatest strength lies in its fortified wines. It is for these wines that the winery rating is given. Exports and distribution via Mildara Blass.

baldivis estate   ★★☆

291 River Road, Serpentine, WA 6205 **region** South West Coast
phone (08) 9525 2066 **fax** (08) 9525 2411 **open** Mon–Fri 10–4, weekends, holidays 11–5
winemaker Mark Kailis, Sarah Siddons **production** 20 000 **est.** 1982
product range ($17–45 CD) Wooded and Unwooded Chardonnay, Sauvignon Blanc, Semillon Sauvignon Blanc, Pinot Noir Cabernet, Cabernet Merlot, Cabernet Sauvignon Reserve.
summary Part of a very large mixed horticultural enterprise on the Tuart Sands of the coastal plain. There is ample viticultural and winemaking expertise; although the wines are pleasant, soft and light-bodied, they lack concentration.

Baldivis Estate Cabernet Sauvignon Reserve

A rose amidst a sea of thorns, something which it would appear Baldivis itself recognises, because the price is roughly twice that of the rest of the wines in the portfolio.
 1997 Dark red; the bouquet has ripe, dark savoury blackberry/blackcurrant fruit married with nicely handled oak. A big wine on the palate, the flavours running through dark berry, plum and prune, complexed by more savoury notes and supported by good tannins.   **rating: 88**
best drinking 2003–2008 **best vintages** '97 **drink with** Prime rib of beef • $45

bald mountain   ★★★☆

Hickling Lane, Wallangarra, Qld 4383 **region** Granite Belt
phone (07) 4684 3186 **fax** (07) 4684 3433 **open** 7 days 10–5
winemaker Simon Gilbert (Contract) **production** 5000 **est.** 1985
product range ($11–19 CD) Classic Queenslander (in fact 100 per cent Sauvignon Blanc), Chardonnay, Late Harvest Sauvignon Blanc, Shiraz, Shiraz Cabernet.

summary Denis Parsons is a self-taught but exceptionally competent vigneron who has turned Bald Mountain into the viticultural showpiece of the Granite Belt. In various regional and national shows since 1988, Bald Mountain has won almost 70 show awards, placing it at the forefront of the Granite Belt wineries. The two Sauvignon Blanc-based wines, Classic Queenslander and the occasional non-vintage Late Harvest Sauvignon Blanc, are interesting alternatives to the mainstream wines. Future production will also see grapes coming from new vineyards near Tenterfield just across the border in New South Wales. No recent tastings.

balgownie estate ★★★★

Hermitage Road, Maiden Gully, Vic 3551 **region** Bendigo
phone (03) 5449 6222 **fax** (03) 5449 6506 **open** Mon–Sat 10.30–5, Sun 12–4
winemaker Lindsay Ross **production** 8000 **est.** 1969
product range ($24–28 CD) Estate-produced Chardonnay, Pinot Noir, Shiraz, Cabernet Sauvignon; Premier Cuvée (second, non-estate label), Chardonnay and Cabernet Shiraz.
summary The sale of Balgownie foreshadowed in the previous edition of the *Wine Companion* has now eventuated, but Lindsay Ross remains as winemaker, and there is every reason for Balgownie to continue its renaissance, with the '98 red wines building on the 1997 vintage.

Balgownie Estate Shiraz

Produced from fully-mature estate vineyards established in the early 1970s, and with a proud history dating back to that time. After an uncertain period in the second half of the 1980s and early '90s, has returned to form in no uncertain fashion.
▼▼▼▼ 1998 Very dense purple-red; the bouquet is clean, with concentrated blackberry fruit; a massive wine on the palate, with similarly concentrated fruit and oak, and the tannins needing time to soften. I am confident this will happen with sufficient time in bottle. **rating: 91**
best drinking 2003–2013 **best vintages** '91, '93, '96, '97, '98 **drink with** Beef in red wine •$27

Balgownie Estate Cabernet Sauvignon

The best known of the Balgownie wines in the height of its glory days of the mid-1970s, partly because there were so few small-winemaker Cabernet Sauvignons around at the time. After a period in the wilderness, has bounced back to top form.
▼▼▼▼ 1998 Medium to full red-purple; the bouquet has quite concentrated blackcurrant and more earthy cabernet varietal character, supported by subtle oak. There is an abundance of rich cassis fruit on the palate, with ample tannins and well-handled oak. **rating: 90**
best drinking 2002–2012 **best vintages** '75, '76, '80, '94, '96, '97, '98 **drink with** Beef casserole •$27

ballandean estate ★★★

Sundown Road, Ballandean, Qld 4382 **region** Granite Belt
phone (07) 4684 1226 **fax** (07) 4684 1288 **open** 7 days 9–5
winemaker Mark Ravenscroft **production** 10 000 **est.** 1970
product range ($10.50–22 CD) Riesling, Semillon, Semillon Sauvignon Blanc, Black Label Sauvignon Blanc, Viognier, Chardonnay, Sylvaner Late Harvest, White Pearl (semi-sweet white), Lambrusco, Summer Shiraz, Estate Shiraz, Black Label Shiraz, Black Label Merlot, Fortifieds, Sparkling.
summary The senior winery of the Granite Belt and by far the largest. The white wines are of diverse but interesting styles, the red wines smooth and usually well made. The estate specialty Sylvaner Late Harvest is a particularly interesting wine of good flavour. No recent tastings.

balnaves of coonawarra ★★★★

Main Road, Coonawarra, SA 5263 **region** Coonawarra
phone (08) 8737 2946 **fax** (08) 8737 2945 **open** Mon–Fri 9–5, weekends 10–5
winemaker Peter Bissell **production** 10 000 **est.** 1975
product range ($19–30 R) Chardonnay, The Blend (Merlot Cabernet Franc), Shiraz, Cabernet Merlot, Cabernet Sauvignon.
summary Former Hungerford Hill vineyard manager and now viticultural consultant-cum-grape grower Doug Balnaves established his vineyard in 1975 but did not launch into winemaking until 1990, with colleague Ralph Fowler as contract-maker in the early years. A striking new 300-tonne winery was built and was in operation for the 1996 vintage, with former Wynns Coonawarra Estate assistant winemaker Peter Bissell in charge. The expected leap in quality has indeed materialised with the 1996 and subsequent vintages. The wines are sold through Majestic Wines in the UK, and are also exported to Japan, Switzerland and Germany.

Balnaves Chardonnay

Produced from a careful selection from part of the estate vineyards. The clarified juice is barrel-fermented in new Seguin Moreau French oak hogsheads followed by lees stirring for two months, followed by a further two months oak maturation before relatively early bottling.

TTTT 1998 Light green-yellow; light nectarine/citrus/melon aromas are supported by subtle oak on the bouquet; subtle, spicy oak is woven through quite delicate nectarine and melon fruit on the palate. An elegant style which should age well. **rating: 88**

best drinking 2001–2005 **best vintages** '92, '93, '94, '96, '98 **drink with** Robe crayfish • $24

Balnaves Shiraz

Only produced when seasonal conditions permit; not made, for example, in either 1994 or 1995. Selected from estate-grown grapes from the highest and stoniest part of the Balnaves shiraz plantings. The fermentation in a vinimatic is completed in new and second-use American oak barrels.

TTTTY 1998 Very deep, almost impenetrable, purple; the bouquet offers a concentrated array of dark berry, earth, spice and liquorice fruit aromas; an opulently ripe, rich and concentrated palate also features good oak handling. **rating: 92**

best drinking 2003–2013 **best vintages** '93, '96, '97, '98 **drink with** Cotechino sausages • $23

Balnaves The Blend

The blend varies according to vintage; in 1998 it was one-third each of Merlot, Cabernet Sauvignon and Cabernet Franc. Fermented in open-topped fermenters for 6-11 days, it is then matured for 15 months in a mix of new (20 per cent) and used French oak barriques.

TTTT 1998 Medium to full red-purple; a fruit-driven bouquet with ripe blackberry/mulberry/plum fruit is followed by a nicely constructed and quite elegant palate, which does lighten off slightly on the finish. **rating: 89**

best drinking 2001–2006 **best vintages** NA **drink with** Lamb loin • $19

Balnaves Cabernet Merlot

A blend of 75 per cent Cabernet Sauvignon and 25 per cent Merlot, matured in used French and American hogsheads for 12 months.

TTTT 1998 Medium to full red-purple; the bouquet opens with concentrated dark berry fruit then shows distinct earthy notes. The medium- to full-bodied palate does much the same, with sweet, dark berry fruit on the mid-palate followed by persistent, slightly dry, tannins on the finish. **rating: 86**

best drinking 2003–2008 **best vintages** '90, '91, '92, '96 **drink with** Calf's liver Italian style • $24

Balnaves Cabernet Sauvignon

Drawn from a little over 16 hectares of estate plantings, the majority of the grapes are sold to other leading Coonawarra winemakers. The '96 won the trophy for Best Varietal Cabernet in Show at the 1998 Royal Sydney Wine Show, and the '98 is every bit as good.

TTTTY 1998 Medium to full red-purple; strong, dark blackberry, mulberry cassis fruit on the bouquet is followed by a richly textured and structured wine, with tannins running right through the length of the palate; subtle, sweet oak. **rating: 94**

best drinking 2003–2013 **best vintages** '90, '91, '96, '98 **drink with** Veal chops • $30

bannockburn vineyards ★★★★★

Midland Highway, Bannockburn, Vic 3331 **region** Geelong
phone (03) 5281 1363 **fax** (03) 5281 1349 **open** Not
winemaker Gary Farr **production** 8000 **est.** 1974
product range ($18–105 R) Riesling, Sauvignon Blanc, Chardonnay, Pinot Noir, Saignee (Rosé), Serré, Shiraz, Cabernet Merlot, Cabernet Sauvignon.
summary With the qualified exception of the Cabernet Merlot, which can be a little leafy and gamey, produces outstanding wines across the range, all with individuality, style, great complexity and depth of flavour. The low-yielding estate vineyards play their role, but so does the French-influenced winemaking of Gary Farr. In the wake of a devastating hail storm on 10 November 1997 the '98 vintage wines were all made from grapes grown around southeast Australia provided by other winemakers and fermented (and bottled) at Bannockburn. Export markets have been established in the UK, the US, Hong Kong, New Zealand and Switzerland.

Bannockburn Chardonnay

As with all the Bannockburn wines, 100 per cent estate-grown from plantings made in 1974, 1981 and 1987 which are typically low-yielding and produce fully ripe grapes with very concentrated flavour. Made with what I describe as traditional French techniques, with roughly settled juice, barrel-fermented, natural yeast and natural malolactic fermentation, resulting in wines of great complexity.

▼▼▼▼▼ 1998 Inevitably, less dense than the normal Bannockburn style, but it makes up for that by its finesse. Every detail of the wine is exactly calibrated, the lemony citrus fruit vibrant (despite 100 per cent malolactic fermentation), the French oak subtle. **rating:** 94

▼▼▼▼▼ 1997 The grizzly bear face and booming laugh of Gary Farr are appropriate for a wine so rich and full of character. Opulent, complex barrel-ferment oak input is balanced by powerful fruit on the bouquet; the palate has concentrated, ripe fig fruit and oak. Overall, harmonious and balanced. **rating:** 96

best drinking 2001–2008 **best vintages** '88, '90, '91, '92, '94, '96, '98 **drink with** Rich white meat dishes • $45

Bannockburn Pinot Noir

Widely acknowledged as one of Australia's best Pinot Noirs, made in a very distinctive style with strong French influences from low-yielding vineyards at Geelong, near Melbourne. Winemaker Gary Farr begins making the Pinot Noir in the vineyard but does not finish his work until the wine is bottled. Even then, a certain degree of patience is required to allow the wine to show its best.

▼▼▼▼▼ 1997 Medium red-purple; the aromas are exceptionally complex, savoury/foresty/plummy/oaky, but it is the palate that lifts the wine into the highest class — intense and with the ultimate peacock's tail finish. **rating:** 97

best drinking 2000–2005 **best vintages** '84, '86, '88, '89, '90, '91, '92, '94, '97 **drink with** Rare roast squab • $42.85

Bannockburn Shiraz

Gary Farr has made wine in France every year since 1983. While based at Domaine Dujac in Burgundy he has closely watched the methods of Rhône winemakers, including Alain Graillot of Crozes Hermitage (who himself worked at Dujac), and this wine is strongly, and very deliberately, Rhône-influenced in style.

▼▼▼▼▼ 1998 For whatever reason, the winemaking techniques employed by Gary Farr in making Shiraz succeeded even more brilliantly than usual with this wine. Wonderfully aromatic, its flavours flow together so seamlessly it is impossible to decide whether dark cherry, plum or prune is dominant. The French oak certainly isn't dominant, nor are the supple, fine tannins. A seductively brilliant wine. **rating:** 97

best drinking 2002–2012 **best vintages** '88, '91, '92, '94, '95, '98 **drink with** Rich game, strong cheese • $41.25

banrock station ★★★☆

Holmes Road, off Sturt Highway, Kingston-on-Murray, SA 5331 **region** Riverland
phone (08) 8583 0299 **fax** (08) 8583 0288 **open** 9–5 Mon–Sat, 10–4 Sunday
winemaker Glenn James **production** NFP **est.** 1994
product range ($6.30–14.95 R) Semillon Chardonnay, Wigley Reach Unwooded Chardonnay, Nappers Verdelho, Shiraz Cabernet, Ball Island Shiraz, Cave Cliff Merlot. The Semillon Chardonnay and Shiraz Cabernet are packaged both in 750 ml bottles and 2-litre casks; Oak matured Port (available only at visitors centre), also Sparkling Chardonnay.
summary The $1 million visitors centre at Banrock Station was opened in February 1999. Owned by BRL Hardy, the Banrock Station property covers over 1700 hectares, with 230 hectares of vineyard and the remainder being a major wildlife and wetland preservation area. The wines have consistently offered excellent value for money.

Banrock Station Wigley Reach Unwooded Chardonnay

Right from day one, the Banrock Chardonnay has exhibited above-average flavour (and quality) for a Riverland wine. What is more, it is an unwooded Chardonnay which succeeds where so many fail. The new Wigley Reach name is part of the branding upgrade, but the wine remains the same.

▼▼▼▽ 1999 Light to medium yellow-green; the bouquet has distinct melon and fig varietal character; the palate offers plenty of flavour and varietal fruit, without pretensions to finesse. As always, towards the top end of this price point/varietal market. **rating:** 83

best drinking 2000–2001 **best vintages** '98, '99 **drink with** Takeaway • $10.95

Banrock Station Ball Island Shiraz

As one should expect with a wine at this price, the oak influence seems to be provided by the use of oak chips, but it avoids the evil of over-use.

▼▼▼▼ 1998 Excellent red-purple; strong black cherry and vanilla oak flood the bouquet; American oak is a little overplayed on the palate, but there is plenty of flavour and horsepower at the price. **rating:** 86

best drinking 2000–2003 **best vintages** '98 **drink with** Steak sandwich • $10.95

Banrock Station Shiraz Cabernet

Typical of the Banrock Station range, offering excellent value for money.

▼▼▼▽ NV Youthful light to medium red-purple; fresh, with distinct spicy aromas. Similar spicy fruit characters come through red fruit flavours on the palate; very good at the price, but the non-vintage label is a worry; there is no way of knowing which bottling you are tasting. **rating: 83**

best drinking 2000–2001 **best vintages** NA **drink with** Any red meat dish • $6.95

Banrock Station Cave Cliff Merlot

Another in the new series, made in a straightforward, no-frills fashion.

▼▼▼▽ 1998 Dense red-purple; there is plenty of solid, sweet fruit on the bouquet, although it is not particularly varietal. Luscious berry fruit flavour to a full-bodied wine; needed more work in the winery to maximise its potential. **rating: 84**

best drinking 2000–2003 **best vintages** '98 **drink with** Kransky sausages • $10.95

barak estate   NR

Barak Road, Moorooduc, Vic 3933 **region** Mornington Peninsula
phone (03) 5978 8439 **fax** (03) 5978 8439 **open** Weekends and public holidays 11–5
winemaker James Williamson **production** 500 **est.** 1996
product range ($15–17 CD) Chardonnay, Shiraz, Merlot, Cabernet Sauvignon, Cherry Port.
summary When James Williamson decided to plant vines on his 4-hectare Moorooduc property and establish a micro-winery, he already knew it was far cheaper to buy wine by the bottle than to make it. Undeterred, he ventured into grape growing and winemaking, picking the first grapes in 1993 and opening Barak Estate in 1996. Old telegraph poles, railway sleepers, old palings and timber shingles have all been used in the construction of the picturesque winery.

barambah ridge   NR

79 Goschnicks Road, Redgate via Murgon, Qld 4605 **region** South Burnett and Other Wineries of Qld
phone (07) 4168 4766 **fax** (07) 4168 4770 **open** 7 days 10–5
winemaker Bruce Humphery-Smith **production** 10 000 **est.** 1997
product range ($10.50–16.50 CD) Semillon, Ridge Semillon, Ridge White, Chardonnay, French Oaked Chardonnay, Ridge Red, Reserve Shiraz, Cabernet Sauvignon.
summary Barambah Ridge is owned by South Burnett Wines, an unlisted public company, and is a major new entrant on the Queensland wine scene. The winery constructed for the 1998 vintage has a crush of 150 tonnes. The 1997 wines were made by the omnipresent Bruce Humphery-Smith, winning an array of medals at the annual Sheraton/*Courier-Mail* Brisbane Queensland Wine Awards, including the trophy and gold medal for Best White Wine (with the 1997 unwooded Chardonnay). No recent tastings.

baratto's   NR

Farm 678, Hanwood, NSW 2680 **region** Riverina
phone (02) 6963 0171 **fax** (02) 6963 0171 **open** 7 days 10–5
winemaker Peter Baratto **production** NA **est.** 1975
product range Semillon, Chardonnay, Dry White, Barbera, Shiraz, Cabernet Sauvignon.
summary Baratto's is in many ways a throwback to the old days. Peter Baratto has 15 hectares of vineyards and sells the wine in bulk or in 10- and 20-litre casks from the cellar door at old-time prices, from as little as $3 per litre.

barletta bros   NR

95a Walkerville Terrace, Walkerville, SA 5081 **region** Clare Valley
phone (08) 8342 3395 **fax** (08) 8344 2180 **open** By appointment
winemaker Neil Pike (Polish Hill River Winery) **production** 1000 **est.** 1993
product range ($15–20 CD) Bros Hand Picked Riesling, Shiraz, Dry Grown Grenache Shiraz.
summary There have been many twists since 1993 when Mario, Ben and Julio Barletta started an 'own brand' for their then-retail business, Walkerville Cellars. They no longer own Walkerville Cellars, and the winemaking business is now the sole business of Mario, who has an active involvement with contract-winemaker Neil Pike. The Barletta tanks and barrels reside at Pikes, but Mario Barletta intends to ultimately establish his own independent vineyard and winery and operation. Retail distribution in South Australia and Melbourne; exports to the US and Germany.

🐦 barnadown run   NR

390 Cornella Road, Toolleen, Vic 3551 **region** Bendigo
phone (03) 5433 6376 **fax** (03) 5433 6386 **open** 7 days 10–5
winemaker Andrew Millis **production** 500 **est.** 1995
product range ($12–25 CD) Chardonnay, Heathcote Chardonnay, Shiraz, Cabernet, Botrytis Semillon; also
Millis + Millis Chardonnay Semillon and Shiraz Cabernet.
summary Named after the original pastoral lease of which the vineyard forms part, established on rich terra rossa
soil for which the best Heathcote vineyards are famous. Owner Andrew Millis carries out both the viticulture and
winemaking at the 5-hectare vineyard.

Barnadown Run Cabernet

Produced from the 1 hectare of estate cabernet sauvignon, basket-pressed, and matured in a mix of French and
American oak.
▼▼▼▽ **1998** Medium purple-red; the bouquet is of light to moderate intensity, with minty/berry fruit; the mint
characters are powerful on the palate, typical of the region, but offset by a touch of chocolate and quite sweet oak.
Good tannins help the structure.   **rating:** 83
best drinking 2002–2008 **drink with** Rare beef • $25

barossa ridge wine estate   ★★★☆

Light Pass Road, Tanunda, SA 5352 **region** Barossa Valley
phone (08) 8563 2811 **fax** (08) 8563 2811 **open** By appointment
winemaker Marco Litterini **production** 1500 **est.** 1987
product range ($19–22 CD) Valley of Vines Merlot Cabernet Franc Cabernet Sauvignon Petit Verdot, Old
Creek Shiraz, Mardia's Vineyard Cabernet Franc, Bamboo Creek Merlot, Rocky Valley Cabernet Sauvignon.
summary A grape grower turned winemaker with a small list of interesting red varietals, including the Valley of
Vines blend of Merlot, Cabernet Franc, Cabernet Sauvignon and Petit Verdot (what a mouthful), the only such
wine produced in the Barossa Valley. Production has doubled, and the National Wine Merchant been appointed as
distributor through all States. All of its wines are built in an impressively heroic style.

Barossa Ridge Old Creek Shiraz

The precise origin of the name is not explained, but the wine comes from half a hectare of estate plantings.
▼▼▼▼ **1998** Dense red-purple; the bouquet has massive dark fruit and chocolate, with oak just discernible in the
background. The palate is equally rich and concentrated, with dark plum and chocolate fruit flavours; once again,
the oak is subtle.   **rating:** 89
best drinking 2003–2013 **best vintages** '98 **drink with** Thick rump steak • $22

Barossa Ridge Mardia's Vineyard Cabernet Franc

Once again, no explanation of the name. Barossa Ridge has 0.3 of a hectare planted, but also produces a varietal
blend incorporating cabernet franc, so the limited release tag given to the wine is undoubtedly justified. This apart,
it is a pretty impressive example of this variety.
▼▼▼▼ **1998** Medium to full red-purple; a quite sweet and concentrated bouquet, with well-integrated and
balanced oak, leads into a palate with solid blackcurrant fruit, the oak once again in the background. **rating:** 85
best drinking 2002–2007 **best vintages** '98 **drink with** Braised lamb • $19

Barossa Ridge Bamboo Creek Merlot

Barossa Ridge has 1 hectare of merlot planted, or one-third of its small vineyard plantings. Quite obviously, Marco
Litterini believes in fully ripe grapes.
▼▼▼▽ **1998** Incredibly dense colour; a powerful, rich, dry red, nothing to do with Merlot in its traditional guise,
is the story of the bouquet. The palate is huge, with rich, dark berry fruit, and lots of tannin and extract. The
points are a compromise, reflecting the power of the wine and in no way indicative of varietal typicity. **rating:** 84
best drinking 2005–2010 **best vintages** NA **drink with** Leave it in the cellar • $19

Barossa Ridge Rocky Valley Cabernet Sauvignon

Yet another evocative name; drawn from 0.8 hectares of estate plantings, and made in the typical winery style.
▼▼▼▽ **1998** Medium to full red-purple; there are distinctly earthy/leathery varietal aromas showing some
development, followed by a very ripe sweet and slightly jammy berry palate. The tannin and extract are at a
slightly lesser level than some of the other wines.   **rating:** 84
best drinking 2003–2008 **best vintages** NA **drink with** Pot roast • $21

barossa settlers ★★★

Trial Hill Road, Lyndoch, SA 5351 **region** Barossa Valley
phone (08) 8524 4017 **fax** (08) 8524 4519 **open** Mon–Sat 10–4, Sun 11–4
winemaker Howard Haese **production** 1500 **est.** 1983
product range ($10–26 CD) Gully Winds Riesling, Semillon, Woolshed Flat Chardonnay, Megan's White (Semillon Chardonnay), Festive Champagne, Millstowe Royale (Sparkling Red), Late Harvest Riesling, Old Home Block (Light Red), Hoffnungsthal Settlement Shiraz, Rostock Red (Shiraz), Cabernet Sauvignon, Port, Sherry.
summary A superbly located cellar door is the only outlet (other than mail order) for the wines from this excellent vineyard owned by the Haese family. Production has slowed in recent years, with the grapes from the 31-hectare vineyard being sold to others, picking up pace again in 1997.

barossa valley estate ★★★★

Heaslip Road, Angle Vale, SA 5117 **region** Adelaide Plains
phone (08) 8284 7000 **fax** (08) 8284 7219 **open** Mon–Fri 9–5, Sat 10–5
winemaker Natasha Mooney **production** 60 000 **est.** 1984
product range ($10–50 R) Spires Chardonnay Semillon, Shiraz Cabernet Sauvignon; Moculta Semillon, Chardonnay, Shiraz, Cabernet Merlot; Ebenezer Chardonnay, Sparkling Pinot Noir, Shiraz, Cabernet Sauvignon Merlot; and the premium E & E Sparkling Shiraz and Black Pepper Shiraz.
summary Barossa Valley Estate is now part-owned by BRL Hardy, marking the end of a period during which it was one of the last significant co-operative-owned wineries in Australia. Across the board, the wines are full flavoured and honest. E & E Black Pepper Shiraz is an upmarket label with a strong reputation and following, the Ebenezer range likewise. Over-enthusiastic use of American oak (particularly with the red wines) has been the Achilles heel in the past. The wines are distributed in Australia and the UK by BRL Hardy, and by independent distributors in North America.

Barossa Valley Estate E & E Black Pepper Shiraz

The flagship of Barossa Valley Estate, made from grapes grown on a number of low-yielding vineyards from the northeastern corner of the unirrigated vineyards, planted on ironstone-laced soil over a limestone base, yields as little as 1 tonne per acre, and the grapes are hand-picked when very ripe. Notwithstanding the implication of the name, pepper and spice are not aromas or flavours to be found in this luscious, traditional Barossa style.
♆♆♆♆ 1996 Medium to full red-purple; rich, ripe, sweet and concentrated chocolate and vanilla aromas of the bouquet are followed by a concentrated, almost essencey choc-mint, cherry and vanilla-flavoured palate. Very good in its style context but, as ever, not a hint of pepper. **rating:** 89
best drinking 2000–2010 **best vintages** '90, '91, '94, '96 **drink with** Rich red meat dishes • $50

Barossa Valley Estate Ebenezer Shiraz

Ebenezer takes its name from the small Ebenezer settlement in the northeastern corner of the Barossa Valley, first settled and named in 1851. This premium Barossa Shiraz finishes its primary fermentation in new American oak barriques, where it spends the following 24 months prior to bottling.
♆♆♆♆♆ 1996 Medium to full red-purple; the bouquet is rich and concentrated, with masses of sweet vanilla oak floating on top of the fruit. The roles are more or less reversed on the palate, with richly opulent and concentrated dark cherry fruit with a smooth coating of oak and a base of soft tannins. **rating:** 91
best drinking 2001–2011 **best vintages** '90, '91, '94, '96 **drink with** Lamb, rabbit or hare • $26.50

Barossa Valley Estate Moculta Shiraz

A well-priced, reliable, traditional Barossa style.
♆♆♆♆ 1997 Medium red-purple; there is a mix of clean, earthy shiraz varietal character plus vanilla American oak on the bouquet. Sweet, earthy shiraz in traditional style is nicely complemented by vanilla oak on the generously flavoured palate. Good value. **rating:** 87
best drinking 1999–2004 **best vintages** NA **drink with** Shepherd's pie • $14

barratt ★★★★★

PO Box 204, Summertown, SA 5141 **region** Adelaide Hills
phone (08) 8390 1788 **fax** (08) 8390 1788 **open** By appointment
winemaker Jeffrey Grosset (Contract) **production** 1000 **est.** 1993
product range ($25–35 ML) Chardonnay, Pinot Noir.

summary Lindsay and Carolyn Barratt purchased the Uley Vineyard, situated at the northern end of the Piccadilly Valley at a height of 500 metres, from the late Ian Wilson in August 1990. Part of the production from the 5.2-hectare vineyard is sold to other makers, with a small proportion being contract-made by Jeffrey Grosset. Both wines are complex and of high quality. Limited quantities are sold in the UK, the US and Singapore.

Barratt Chardonnay
Made from hand-harvested grapes selected from particular blocks within the Uley Vineyard, and matured in a mix of new and one-year-old French oak barriques for approximately ten months. Forty per cent of the wine undergoes malolactic fermentation.

ŸŸŸŸŸ 1999 Glowing yellow-green; the intense bouquet features a seamless marriage of melon, nectarine and barrel-ferment oak. The palate opens with pristine nectarine fruit then showing hints of cashew and melon; the oak is judged to perfection, being very subtle, as is the malolactic influence. An elegant, light-bodied wine.   **rating:** 90

best drinking 2001–2008 **best vintages** '97, '99 **drink with** Trout mousse • $25

Barratt Piccadilly Valley Pinot Noir
Fermented in tiny, open half-tonne fermenters with foot-stamping and plunging of whole bunches, and matured in a mix of new and one-year-old French oak barriques for 11 months prior to bottling. The wine is neither fined nor filtered. Various vintages have had great show success.

ŸŸŸŸŸ 1999 Light to medium red; fragrant and very sappy/Burgundian, typical of the estate (and of Jeffrey Grosset's winemaking). The palate is intense and long, with a cascade of spicy, sappy, savoury and cherry flavours which dance on the tongue.   **rating:** 93

best drinking 2000–2004 **best vintages** '96, '97, '99 **drink with** Jugged hare • $35

barretts wines   NR
Portland–Nelson Highway, Portland, Vic 3305 **region** Far South West Victoria
phone (03) 5526 5251 **open** 7 days 11–5
winemaker Rod Barrett **production** 1000 **est.** 1983
product range ($12–15 CD) Riesling, Traminer, Late Harvest Riesling, Pinot Noir, Cabernet Sauvignon, Port.
summary The second (and newer) winery in the Portland region. The initial releases were made at Best's, but since 1992 all wines have been made on the property by Rod Barrett.

barrington estate   ★★★☆
Yarraman Road, Wybong, NSW 2333 **region** Upper Hunter Valley
phone (02) 6547 8118 **fax** (02) 6547 8039 **open** By appointment
winemaker Daniel Crane **production** 75 000 **est.** 1967
product range ($10.99–24 R) Yarraman Road is the top label with Black Clay Chardonnay and Sandy Slopes Cabernet Shiraz; Barrington Estate is cheaper label; also Narrambla Verdelho and Chardonnay, and The Banjo Shiraz.
summary Yarraman Road/Barrington Estate is the reincarnation of Penfolds Wybong Estate, into which Penfolds poured millions of dollars between 1960 and 1978, then selling the winery and surrounding vineyards to Rosemount Estate. Rosemount removed most of the unproductive vineyards and used the winery for red wine production until 1992, then converting it to pure storage area. In 1994 Gary and Karen Blom purchased the property from Rosemount after they returned from the US, where Australian-born entrepreneur Gary Blom had a highly successful career; their main investment is the IMAX Theatre in Darling Harbour, but they intend to spend $3 to 4 million in redeveloping Barrington Estate.

Barrington Estate Semillon
Produced from contract-grown grapes and machine-harvested at night. Conventional making techniques, with cold fermentation in stainless steel and early bottling. No frills needed or offered.

ŸŸŸŸ 1998 Light to medium yellow-green; the bouquet is lean, moderately intense, with correct, faintly grassy/mineral aromas. The palate is tightly structured and crisp, again with minerally notes; seems to have the structure and flavour for good development in the medium term.   **rating:** 87

best drinking 2000–2015 **best vintages** NA **drink with** Crustacea • $15

Barrington Estate Narrambla Verdelho
Night-harvested, stainless steel-fermented and early-bottled to retain freshness.

ŸŸŸ 1999 Light green-yellow; the bouquet is clean and crisp, as much like Sauvignon Blanc as Verdelho with some mineral components. The palate is a replay of the bouquet; a pleasant although unremarkable commercial wine.   **rating:** 79

best drinking 2000–2001 **best vintages** NA **drink with** Takeaway • $10.99

Barrington Estate Narrambla Chardonnay

Principally fermented in stainless steel, but with a small portion in a mix of French oak; three months on yeast lees.

▼▼▼▼ **1998** Medium to full yellow-green; there is quite strong peachy/buttery fruit on the bouquet, characters which come through on the solid, peachy palate; fast-developing but flavoursome and good value. **rating: 85**

best drinking 2000–2001 **best vintages** NA **drink with** Chicken pasta • $10.90

Barrington Estate Yarraman Road Black Clay Chardonnay

Produced from estate-grown grapes coming from individual blocks on Barrington Estate's Upper Hunter vineyard. Various fermentation techniques are used, including warmer, higher solids ferments for the more full-flavoured fruit. Part of the wine is barrel-fermented and aged for nine months in new French oak hogsheads.

▼▼▼▼ **1998** Medium to full yellow-green; there is depth to the bouquet with ripe peach fruit and relatively subtle oak. The palate is muscular, although quite well balanced and structured in a distinctly regional fashion; best consumed sooner rather than later. **rating: 86**

best drinking 1999–2001 **best vintages** NA **drink with** Roast chicken • $24

Barrington Estate Chambourcin

Chambourcin is a French hybrid which is highly disease-resistant, and well suited to wetter, warmer climates. This wine comes from estate-grown grapes, with the vines heavily pruned to reduce yields. In recognition of the fact that Chambourcin normally lacks structure, the wine spends seven days on skins, with fermentation temperature in the mid-twenties.

▼▼▼▼ **1998** Dark red; the bouquet is sweet and ripe, with faintly spicy, warm cinnamon-bread aromas. The palate is quite rich, with sweet flavour and more structure on the finish than usual, although there is little or no perceptible tannin. **rating: 87**

best drinking 1999–2001 **best vintages** NA **drink with** Coq au Vin • $17

barwang vineyard ★★★★☆

Postal c/o McWilliam's Wines, Doug McWilliam Road, Yenda, NSW 2681 **region** Hilltops
phone (02) 9722 1200 **fax** (02) 9707 4408 **open** Not
winemaker Jim Brayne **production** NA **est.** 1975
product range ($15.95–19.95 R) Chardonnay, Semillon, Shiraz, Cabernet Sauvignon.
summary Peter Robertson pioneered viticulture in the Young region when he planted his first vines in 1975 as part of a diversification programme for his 400-hectare grazing property. When McWilliam's acquired Barwang in 1989, the vineyard amounted to 13 hectares; today the plantings exceed 100 hectares. Wine quality has been exemplary from the word go, always elegant, restrained and deliberately understated, repaying extended cellaring. Interestingly, the name has been adopted for a large-volume, relatively low-priced range of wines for distribution in the US.

Barwang Semillon

Produced from 20-year-old estate semillon vines. The wine is barrel-fermented in new French oak, and matured in a mix of new and used oak, and given lees contact. Notwithstanding this oak treatment, the wine is driven by its fruit.

▼▼▼♀ **1999** Very pale straw-green; very crisp, light and incredibly youthful; the palate has the length to promise much given sufficient time in bottle; faintly lemony fruit and minerally acid round off the finish. I cannot see any oak in this wine, and it may have been handled differently. The points are for the wine as it is today, not as it may be in the future. **rating: 84**

best drinking 2004–2009 **best vintages** NA **drink with** Crab cakes • $16.95

Barwang Chardonnay

Made in a restrained style, with subtle oak, and which evolves steadily but slowly given time in bottle.

▼▼▼▼ **1998** Glowing yellow-green; the moderately intense bouquet is clean, with discreet melon/peach fruit and subtle oak. The gentle, rounded palate has good mouthfeel and flavour, with touches of cashew and spicy oak; it all comes together nicely. **rating: 86**

best drinking 2001–2004 **best vintages** '94, '98 **drink with** Calamari • $16.95

Barwang Shiraz

Overall, the Shiraz has been the best performer in a classy stable. Each vintage has been extremely good, with very clear varietal character, the only problem being a slight hardness in the mouth in the lesser years.

▼▼▼▼▼ **1998** Deep red-purple; the bouquet is rich, with concentrated, dark small berry fruit and touches of chocolate. Lovely rich plum, dark berry, chocolate and blackberry fruit floods the bouquet, the oak as subtle as ever. The best Barwang for years, if not ever. **rating:** 94

▼▼▼▼♀ **1997** A wine which has improved wonderfully in bottle over the past nine months. Strong, deep red-purple; the bouquet is smooth with nicely balanced fruit and oak, and a mix of dark berry and chocolate aromas. The palate is full and well balanced, with dark berry and more savoury/earthy flavours finishing with tannins that have now softened and integrated. **rating:** 90

best drinking 2003–2012 **best vintages** '90, '91, '92, '93, '94, '97, '98 **drink with** Kraft Australian Parmesan • $19.95

Barwang Cabernet Sauvignon

The continental climate of the Barwang Vineyard, marked by cold nights and warm summer days, but with the growing season finishing much later than it does in either the Hunter Valley or Mudgee, produces red wines of considerable flavour, power and extract, exemplified by this wine.

▼▼▼▼♀ **1998** Medium to full red-purple; the bouquet is quite ripe, with earthy/chocolatey cabernet varietal aromas; the powerful and concentrated palate has more of those blackberry/blackcurrant and chocolate fruit characters promised by the bouquet; substantial tannins add to the texture and structure. **rating:** 90

▼▼▼▼♀ **1997** Like the Barwang Shiraz of the same vintage, has benefited enormously from an additional 12 months in bottle; while the bouquet is quite oaky, with cedar and cigar box aromas, the palate has developed quite excellent texture and weight. Quite sweet overall, with touches of vanilla and chocolate, finishing with fine tannins. **rating:** 90

best drinking 2003–2013 **best vintages** '89, '91, '92, '93, '96, '97, '98 **drink with** Beef Wellington • $19.95

basedow ★★★☆

161–165 Murray Street, Tanunda, SA 5352 **region** Barossa Valley
phone (08) 8563 3666 **fax** (08) 8563 3597 **open** Mon–Fri 10–5, weekends and public holidays 11–5
winemaker Craig Stansborough **production** 100 000 **est.** 1896
product range ($9.95–65 CD) Eden Valley Riesling, Barossa Valley Semillon (White Burgundy), Sauvignon Blanc Semillon, Barossa Chardonnay, Unwooded Chardonnay, Late Harvest, Oscar's Heritage, Grenache, Johannes Shiraz, Barossa Shiraz, Mistella, Old Tawny Port; Museum Release Watervale Riesling, Barossa Cabernet Sauvignon.
summary An old and proud label, particularly well known for its oak-matured Semillon (called White Burgundy on the Australian market), which underwent a number of changes of ownership during the 1990s. Overall, a reliable producer of solidly flavoured wines. Exports to the UK, the US, Canada, Hong Kong, The Netherlands, New Zealand, Singapore, Switzerland and Thailand.

Basedow Riesling

A fast-developing full-flavoured wine, presumably from Barossa Valley floor vineyards.
▼▼▼▼ **1998** Medium to full yellow-green; the bouquet is extraordinarily developed, with powerful lime/toast aromas; the powerful palate is in an uncompromising old-fashioned style, with petrolly overtones and masses of character. **rating:** 85
best drinking 2000–2003 **best vintages** NA **drink with** Rich fish dishes • $14

Basedow Johannes Shiraz

The first super-premium release from Basedow; two years in American oak and 18 months bottle age. Five gold medals.
▼▼▼▼ **1996** Medium red-purple; the bouquet is clean, with sweet, rich fruit and voluminous vanilla oak. An interesting wine which in some ways is the epitome of Barossa Valley style, but the oak is formidable. **rating:** 89
best drinking 2001–2011 **best vintages** '89 **drink with** Strong meat stews • $65

basket range wines NR

c/o PO, Basket Range, SA 5138 **region** Adelaide Hills
phone (08) 9390 1515 **open** Not
winemaker Phillip Broderick **production** 500 **est.** 1980
product range ($18 ML) A single Bordeaux-blend of Cabernet Sauvignon, Cabernet Franc, Merlot, Malbec drawn from 3 hectares of estate plantings.
summary A tiny operation known to very few, run by civil and Aboriginal rights lawyer Phillip Broderick, a most engaging man with a disarmingly laid-back manner.

bass fine wines   NR

686 Richmond Road, Cambridge, Tas 7170 **region** Southern Tasmania
phone 0417 596 234 **fax** (03) 6231 6222 **open** Not
winemaker Various Contract **production** 1000 **est.** 1999
product range ($18–25 R) Chardonnay, Pinot Noir, Strait Pinot Noir.
summary Bass Fine Wines runs entirely counter to the usual Tasmanian pattern of tiny, estate-based businesses. Guy Wagner has set up Bass as a classic negociant operation, working backwards from the marketplace. He is halfway through a wine marketing degree at the University of Adelaide, and intends to continue studies in oenology and viticulture while being involved in the making of the wines by contract makers Jim Chatto and Andrew Hood. The wines have been purchased from various vineyards in bottle and in barrel, but from the 2000 vintage also purchased as grapes. It has been set up as a Pinot Noir specialist with three levels of Pinot in the business plan, commencing with Strait Pinot in the fighting sector of the market, then Bass as a premium brand, and ultimately there will be a super-premium Pinot, possibly to come from 30-year-old plantings which have been contracted.

bass phillip   ★★★★★

Tosch's Road, Leongatha South, Vic 3953 **region** Gippsland
phone (03) 5664 3341 **fax** (03) 5664 3209 **open** By appointment
winemaker Phillip Jones **production** 1500 **est.** 1979
product range ($35–145 ML) Tiny quantities of Pinot Noir in three categories: standard, Premium and an occasional barrel of Reserve. A hatful of Chardonnay also made; plus Pinot Rosé and Gamay.
summary Phillip Jones has retired from the Melbourne rat-race to handcraft tiny quantities of superlative Pinot Noir which, at its best, has no equal in Australia. Painstaking site selection, ultra-close vine spacing and the very, very cool climate of South Gippsland are the keys to the magic of Bass Phillip and its eerily Burgundian Pinots. The quality, and longevity, of the '96 and '97 wines have added to the reputation of the brand.

Bass Phillip Premium Pinot Noir

Produced from the oldest vines which are ultra-close planted. The wine receives substantially more new oak than does the standard release.
♥♥♥♥♥ 1997 An exceptionally deep, almost opaque purple-red; the bouquet is extremely complex, with savoury/bacony oak woven through the lusciously ripe fruit. The same velvety richness runs through the depths of the palate, where plum intersects with spice, bacony oak and tannins. An exceptional example of the impact vintage can make on terroir, for this is way outside the mainstream style of Bass Phillip, however good the wine undoubtedly is.   **rating:** 95
best drinking 2000–2010 **best vintages** '84, '85, '89, '91, '92, '93, '94, '95, '96, '97 **drink with** Venison • $75

batista   ★★★★

Franklin Road, Middlesex, WA 6258 **region** Pemberton, Warren Valley and Manjimup
phone (08) 9772 3530 **fax** (08) 9772 3530 **open** By appointment
winemaker Bob Peruch **production** 1200 **est.** 1993
product range ($19–28 CD) Pinot Noir, Pinot Chardonnay Reserve Brut.
summary Batista is in fact the baptismal name of owner Bob Peruch, a Pinot Noir devotee whose father planted 1 hectare of vines back in the 1950s, although these have since gone. Between 1993 and 1996 Bob Peruch has planted 1.5 hectares of pinot noir, a hectare each of shiraz and the cabernet family, and half a hectare of chardonnay destined for sparkling wine. The estate has two vineyards, one selected for pinot noir and chardonnay, and the other, 2 kilometres away, for shiraz, cabernet sauvignon, cabernet franc and merlot. The well-drained soils are of quartz and ironstone gravel; yields are restricted to around 7 tonnes per hectare.

Batista Pinot Noir

With 1.5 hectares (out of a total of 3.55 hectares of a total of six varieties) pinot noir has the lion's share at Batista. It is a mix of four clones described by Bob Peruch as being D5V12, 115, Droopy and Meunier.
♥♥♥♥▽ 1998 Strong red-purple; a complex, powerful and fragrant bouquet has aromas of leather and spice over a foundation of plum. The elegant palate has good flavour and structure, the flavours running through plum, spice and sweet leather, all strongly varietal.   **rating:** 90
best drinking 2001–2006 **best vintages** NA **drink with** Braised oxtail • $27

baxter stokes wines   NR

65 Memorial Avenue, Baskerville, WA 6065   **region** Swan District
phone (08) 9296 4831   **fax** (08) 9296 4831   **open** 9.30–5 weekends and public holidays
winemaker Greg Stokes   **production** 750   **est.** 1988
product range ($10–14 CD) Chardonnay, Verdelho, Shiraz Pinot Noir, Shiraz Cabernet Sauvignon.
summary A weekend and holiday operation for Greg and Lucy Stokes, with the production sold by mail order and through cellar door.

beckett's flat   ★★★☆

Beckett Road, Metricup, WA 6280   **region** Margaret River
phone (08) 9755 7402   **fax** (08) 9755 7344   **open** 7 days 10–6
winemaker Belizar Ilic, Mark Lane (Consultant)   **production** 5000   **est.** 1992
product range ($18–29.90 CD) Sauvignon Blanc Semillon, Oak Matured Semillon Sauvignon Blanc, Autumn Harvest Semillon, Verdelho, Chardonnay, Shiraz, Reserve Merlot, Cabernet Sauvignon.
summary Bill and Noni Ilic opened Beckett's Flat in September 1997. Situated just off the Bussell Highway, at Metricup, midway between Busselton and the Margaret River, it draws upon 8 hectares of estate vineyards, first planted in 1992. As from 1998 the wines have been made at the on-site winery. Accommodation is available.

Beckett's Flat Chardonnay

The wine is stainless steel-fermented, and then matured in new American oak barriques for a period of four months, with 50 per cent undergoing malolactic fermentation. As from the 2000 vintage, French oak has replaced American.
▼▼▼▽ **1999** Medium yellow-green; strong, spicy clove barrel-ferment oak dominates both the bouquet and palate. A pity, because there is nice fruit underneath that oak.   **rating:** 80
best drinking 2000–2004   **best vintages** NA   **drink with** Roast turkey   • $24.80

Beckett's Flat Shiraz

The warmer end of the Margaret River should prove to be a reliable producer of shiraz; certainly Beckett's Flat believes so, for shiraz has a major share (3 hectares) of the total estate vineyards. The grapes are open-fermented and hand-plunged, with 12 months maturation in new and older American and French oak barriques. Light filtration deliberately leaves a light sediment in the wine.
▼▼▼▽ **1998** Medium red-purple; some slightly gamey overtones to the bouquet, which may or may not be varietal, are followed by a bright, fresh cherry palate, not particularly complex but not over-oaked either.   **rating:** 82
best drinking 2001–2005   **best vintages** NA   **drink with** Pizza   • $23.80

Beckett's Flat Cabernet Sauvignon

Produced from 3 hectares of cabernet sauvignon and 1 hectare of merlot. Has consistently been the best of the Beckett's Flat wines.
▼▼▼▼ **1998** Medium red-purple; Attractive chocolately fruit merges with subtle oak on the bouquet; similarly appealing chocolate and soft cassis fruit is supported by fine tannins and subtle oak on the palate.   **rating:** 85
best drinking 2002–2007   **best vintages** '97   **drink with** Ox kidney   • $23.80

belbourie   ★★☆

Branxton Road, Rothbury, NSW 2330   **region** Lower Hunter Valley
phone (02) 4938 1556   **open** Weekends, holidays 10–sunset
winemaker Bob Davies   **production** 2000   **est.** 1963
product range ($15–16 CD) Barramundi Chardonnay, Belah Semillon Chardonnay, Hermitage.
summary A winery with a rich, and at times highly controversial history of wine and winemaking, but these days tending more to the conventional. It has always sought to encourage cellar-door and mailing list sales, focusing on monthly wine and food events, and has a loyal clientele.

bellingham vineyard   ★★★

Pipers Brook, Tas 7254   **region** Northern Tasmania
phone (03) 6382 7149   **open** By appointment
winemaker Greg O'Keefe (Contract)   **production** 500   **est.** 1984
product range ($5.50–8 ML) Riesling, Chardonnay, Pinot Noir, Cabernet Sauvignon.
summary Long-term owner of Bellingham Vineyard, Dallas Targett, was in the course of selling both the vineyard and the vineyard name (though not the label design) as this book was going to press. No details available of the purchaser, but Dallas Targett has plans to start another vineyard close to Launceston.

belubula valley vineyards   NR

Golden Gully, Mandurama, NSW 2798 **region** Orange
phone (02) 6367 5236 **fax** (02) 6362 4726 **open** Not
winemaker David Somervaille **production** 1000 **est.** 1986
product range Cabernet Sauvignon.
summary Belubula Valley is a foundation member of the Central Highlands Grapegrowers Association, centred on Orange; the vineyard is located on the Belubula River, near Carcoar, and the small amounts of wine made to date have not yet been commercially released. David Somervaille, incidentally, was the chairman of partners of the national law firm Blake Dawson Waldron.

beresford wines   ★★★

49 Fraser Avenue, Happy Valley, SA 5159 **region** McLaren Vale
phone (08) 8322 3611 **fax** (08) 8322 3610 **open** Mon–Fri 9–5, weekends 11–5
winemaker Robert Dundon, John Davey **production** 158 000 **est.** 1985
product range ($8–18 CD) Beacon Hill Semillon Chardonnay, Shiraz Cabernet, Tawny Port; Highwood Sauvignon Blanc, Chardonnay, Shiraz; the Saints range of St Yvette Chardonnay, St Helene Cabernet Shiraz, St Martine Sparkling Brut; followed by the Belleville range of Riesling, Chardonnay, Semillon Sauvignon Blanc, Shiraz and Cabernet Merlot.
summary The Beresford brand sits at the top of a range of labels primarily and successfully aimed at export markets in the UK, the US, Hong Kong and China. The accent is on price, and the wines do not aspire to great complexity. Quality, however, has improved in the latter part of the1990s. No tastings in 2000.

berlingieri wines   NR

Lot 69 Tiers Road, Lenswood, SA 5240 **region** Adelaide Hills
phone (08) 8371 1962 **fax** (08) 8371 4117 **open** Not
winemaker Vincenzo Berlingieri **production** 15 000 **est.** 1992
product range ($9–13 ML) The Piccolo label of wines sourced from Langhorne Creek include Verdelho, Shiraz, Cabernet Sauvignon Malbec Merlot Cabernet Franc.
summary Vincenzo Berlingieri is one of the great characters of the wine industry who arrived in Sydney with beard flowing and arms waving in the 1970s as he successfully gained considerable publicity for his then McLaren Vale winery. Fortune did not follow marketing success for this research scientist who had arrived to work in plant genetics at Melbourne University's Botany Department in 1964 armed with a doctorate in agricultural science from Perugia University, Italy. However, after various moves he is in business again with his children Jason John and Annika, for the time being sourcing most of the grapes from Langhorne Creek and McLaren Vale, but with Adelaide Hills wines in the planning pipeline. Most of the business is in unlabelled cleanskin form at yesterday's prices sold only through a mailing list/direct order system.

berri estates   ★★

Sturt Highway, Glossop, SA 5344 **region** Riverland
phone (08) 8582 0300 **fax** (08) 8583 2224 **open** Mon–Sat 9–5
winemaker Paul Kasselbaum, Peter Hensel, Graham Buller **production** NFP **est.** 1916
product range Light Fruity Lexia, Fruity Gordo Moselle, Chablis, Claret, Rosé, White Lambrusco, all in cask form.
summary Strictly a producer of cask and bulk wine with no pretensions to grandeur and with a substantial part of the production exported in bulk. Part of the BRL Hardy Group.

berrys bridge   ★★★★☆

Forsters Road, Carapooee, St Arnaud, Vic 3478 **region** Pyrenees
phone (03) 5496 3220 **fax** (03) 5496 3322 **open** Weekends 10–5, or by appointment
winemaker Jane Holt **production** 500 **est.** 1990
product range ($30 CD) Shiraz, Cabernet Sauvignon.
summary While the date of establishment is 1990, Roger Milner purchased the property in 1975, intending to plant a vineyard having worked for three years at Reynell winery in South Australia. Four hectares of vines were planted (chiefly by his friends) but his then career in mineral exploration meant that the vines were neglected and ultimately ploughed in. In the mid-1980s he returned with Jane Holt, and together they began the construction of the stone house-cum-winery. Planting of existing 7 hectares of vineyard commenced in 1990, around the time that Jane commenced her viticultural studies at Charles Sturt University (she completed the course in 1993, and will have completed a subsequent wine science degree course in 2000). Until 1997 the grapes were sold to others, the first vintage (from 1997) being released in November 1998. The wines are distributed in Victoria through Winestock to a number of well-known retailers. Not surprisingly, the limited quantity sells out with great speed.

best's wines ★★★★☆

1 kilometre off Western Highway, Great Western, Vic 3377 **region** Grampians
phone (03) 5356 2250 **fax** (03) 5356 2430 **open** Mon–Sat and public holidays 10–5, Sun of Vic school holidays 12–4
winemaker Viv Thomson, Michael Unwin **production** 30 000 **est.** 1866
product range ($8–52 R) Great Western Chardonnay, Great Western Gewurztraminer, Victoria Riesling, Victoria Chenin Blanc, Great Western Pinot Noir, Great Western Dolcetto, Great Western Merlot, Great Western Shiraz, Bin O Shiraz, Thomson Family Shiraz, Great Western Cabernet Sauvignon, together with a large range of fortified wines sourced from St Andrews at Lake Boga. Some of these wines are available only at cellar door.
summary An historic winery, owning some priceless vineyards planted as long ago as 1867 (other plantings are, of course, much more recent), which has consistently produced elegant, supple wines which deserve far greater recognition than they in fact receive. The Shiraz is a classic; the Thomson Family Shiraz magnificent. Exports to the UK, Canada, The Netherlands, Belgium and Switzerland.

Best's Shiraz

One of the more understated classic wines, produced entirely from estate-grown grapes, made with a minimum of artifice and with high-quality fruit, rather than oak, doing the work.
▼▼▼▼♈ **1997** Medium red-purple; the bouquet is quite fragrant, with a mix of cherry, berry and mint, the palate with fresh, lively fruit, fine acid and tannin balance, and subtle oak. **rating:** 92
best drinking 2002–2012 **best vintages** '62, '70, '77, '78, '85, '88, '90, '91, '92, '94, '97 **drink with** Roast veal, mature cheddar • $34

Best's Thomson Family Shiraz

An outstanding wine first released in late 1994 to commemorate the Centenary of Best's Great Western Vineyards. What might have been a one-off event is now an annual one (vintage permitting) under the Thomson Family label. The '95 was a superb successor to the Centenary vintage, made entirely from vines planted adjacent to the winery in 1867 by Henry Best, and matured in small French oak.
▼▼▼▼▼ **1997** Deep, bright purple-red, it has seductive sweet cherry fruit, a hint of spice and finely balanced oak on the bouquet; the concentrated yet smooth and velvety palate has perfectly balanced tannins and oak. **rating:** 97
best drinking 2000–2002 **best vintages** '95, '96, '97 **drink with** Stir-fried beef • $52

Best's Cabernet Sauvignon

Has been overshadowed by the Shiraz but is a more than useful wine, produced entirely from estate-grown grapes. In recent vintages, a small percentage of Merlot has usually been included in the blend.
▼▼▼▼♈ **1997** Medium purple-red; pronounced sweet and sour aromas and flavours run throughout the wine, ranging from leaf and mint at the one end to raisin at the other. **rating:** 82
best drinking 2000–2003 **best vintages** '88, '91, '92, '93, '96 **drink with** Sirloin of beef • $30

bethany wines ★★★★

Bethany Road, Bethany via Tanunda, SA 5352 **region** Barossa Valley
phone (08) 8563 2086 **fax** (08) 8563 0046 **open** Mon–Sat 10–5, Sun 1–5
winemaker Geoff Schrapel, Robert Schrapel **production** 25 000 **est.** 1977
product range ($14–65 CD) Riesling (Reserve Dry, Special Select Late Harvest), Chardonnay, Wood Aged Semillon, The Manse (Semillon Riesling Chardonnay), Cabernet Merlot, Shiraz, Reserve Shiraz, Grenache, Shiraz Cabernet, Old Quarry Barossa Tawny Port, Old Quarry Barossa Fronti (White Port), Vintage Brut Chardonnay Blanc de Blanc.
summary The Schrapel family has been growing grapes in the Barossa Valley for over 140 years, but the winery has only been in operation since 1977. Nestling high on a hillside in the site of an old quarry, it is run by Geoff and Rob Schrapel, who produce a range of consistently well-made and attractively packaged wines. They have 36 hectares of vineyards in the Barossa Valley, 8 in the Eden Valley and (recently and interestingly) 2 hectares of chardonnay and 2 hectares of cabernet sauvignon on Kangaroo Island. The wines enjoy national distribution in Australia, and are exported to the UK, New Zealand, Europe, Taiwan and the US.

Bethany Barossa Riesling

A typical Barossa floor style from mature vines, generous in flavour if not finesse.
▼▼▼▼♈ **1999** Medium to full yellow-green; a big, rich, full Barossa style, with lime and a touch of mineral on the bouquet. There is abundant ripe, tropical lime fruit flavour in an early-developing style. **rating:** 84
best drinking 2000–2003 **best vintages** NA **drink with** Seafood risotto • $13.85

Bethany Wines Reserve Shiraz

A new deluxe, Reserve bottling for Bethany, which has always made good Shiraz. Replete with ultra-heavy imported bottle. The Bin number advances with each vintage, hence GR3 for 1995 and GR4 for 1996.

▼▼▼▼ **1996** GR4. Medium red-purple; soft cherry/berry fruit on the bouquet is supported by obvious, slightly dusty vanilla oak. The palate has round cherry and mint fruit in typical, ripe Barossa style. No shortage of flavour here. **rating:** 90

best drinking 2001–2006 **best vintages** '95, '96 **drink with** Rack of lamb • $65

Bethany Shiraz Cabernet

With estate plantings of shiraz in the Barossa Valley and the Eden Valley, and cabernet sauvignon in the Barossa Valley and Kangaroo Island, there is ample scope for subtle blending, not only of variety but vineyard sources. The result is a nice, early-release style.

▼▼▼ **1999** Medium red-purple; the bouquet is clean and soft, with predominantly dark berry fruit and hints of chocolate. There is plenty of ripe, juicy flavour on the palate and, not surprisingly, an ever-so-slightly callow finish. Should settle down with a little bottle age. **rating:** 84

best drinking 2001–2004 **best vintages** NA **drink with** Spaghetti Milanese • $15.75

Bethany Grenache

Sourced from 2 hectares of grenache in the Barossa Valley and 1.5 hectares in the Eden Valley.

▼▼▼ **1999** Medium red, with just a touch of purple. The bouquet has jammy, juicy varietal fruit and just a touch of charry oak, the palate following logically on in a light to medium weight, user-friendly style. **rating:** 81

best drinking 2000–2001 **best vintages** NA **drink with** Anything except oysters • $15.75

Bethany Barossa Cabernet Merlot

A blend of around 60 per cent Cabernet Sauvignon grown on the Mulberry Vineyard, 15 per cent Cabernet Franc grown on the Homestead Block and 25 per cent Merlot from the Munzberg Vineyard, aged for 12 to 15 months in a mix of new and used French and American oak.

▼▼▼ **1998** Medium red-purple; a moderately intense bouquet shows that ever-so-typical touch of slightly gamey fruit from the Merlot component. The palate, however, is much more attractive with pleasantly sweet fruit, soft tannins and a well-balanced finish. **rating:** 84

best drinking 2001–2008 **best vintages** '88, '90, '91, '92, '94, '98 **drink with** Fillet of lamb • $23.50

beyond broke vineyard NR

Cobcroft Road, Broke, NSW 2330 **region** Lower Hunter Valley
phone (02) 6026 2043 **fax** (02) 6026 2043 **open** Tastings available at Broke Village Store 10–4
winemaker Pete Howland (Contract) **production** 4000 **est.** 1996
product range ($12.50–18.30 R) Semillon, Verdelho, Chardonnay, Unwooded Chardonnay, Sparkling Semillon, Shiraz.
summary Beyond Broke Vineyard is the reincarnation of a former Lindemans vineyard purchased by Bob and Terry Kennedy in 1996. In a more than slightly ironical twist, the 1997 Beyond Broke Semillon won two trophies at the Hunter Valley Wine Show of that year, the first for the Best Current Vintage Semillon and the second, the Henry John Lindeman Memorial Trophy for the Best Current Vintage Dry White Wine. Subsequent shows have been less spectacularly kind, but there is nothing surprising in that, and its turn will come again when vintage conditions permit.

bianchet ★★★☆

Lot 3 Victoria Road, Lilydale, Vic 3140 **region** Yarra Valley
phone (03) 9739 1779 **fax** (03) 9739 1277 **open** Thurs–Mon 11–5
winemaker Keith Salter, Martin Williams (Consultant) **production** 2000 **est.** 1976
product range ($16–25 CD) Traminer, Copestone Semillon Sauvignon Blanc, Chardonnay Cuvée, Marsanne, Verduzzo, Verduzzo Gold, Pinot Noir, Shiraz, Merlot.
summary Recently sold by the founding Bianchet family to a small Melbourne-based syndicate, with Keith Salter (one of the syndicate members) and consultant Martin Williams taking on winemaking responsibilities. One of the most unusual wines from the winery is Verduzzo Gold, a late-harvest, sweet white wine made from the Italian grape variety. The wines are still basically sold through cellar door, although there is limited export to Japan.

Bianchet Traminer

Estate-grown, the vines being fully mature.

TTTY 1999 Light to medium yellow-green; the bouquet is light, but has distinct lychee and spice varietal character; it follows through pleasantly on to a light palate; a good outcome for a difficult vintage. **rating:** 80

best drinking 2000–2003 **best vintages** NA **drink with** Light Asian dishes • $19

Bianchet Pinot Noir

Produced from mature estate plantings in a very warm vintage.

TTTY 1998 Medium to full red; very ripe, slightly raisiny plum and prune fruit on the bouquet and palate suggests the grapes may have been picked a little too late; does have considerable flavour and may develop well. **rating:** 80

best drinking 2001–2004 **best vintages** NA **drink with** Jugged hare • $25

bimbadgen estate ★★★☆

Lot 21 McDonalds Road, Pokolbin, NSW 2321 **region** Lower Hunter Valley
phone (02) 4998 7585 **fax** (02) 4998 7732 **open** 7 days 9.30–5
winemaker Kees Van De Scheur, Thomas Jung **production** up to 100 000 **est.** 1968
product range ($12.50–28 R) Semillon, Chardonnay, Verdelho, Pinot Noir, Shiraz, Cabernet Sauvignon; Signature range is the super-premium range of Semillon, Chardonnay and Shiraz; Grand Ridge Estate is the lower-priced label.
summary Established as McPherson Wines, then successively Tamalee, then Sobels, then Parker Wines and now Bimbadgen, this substantial winery has had what might politely be termed a turbulent history. It has the great advantage of having 45 hectares of estate plantings, mostly with now relatively old vines. The restaurant is open seven days for lunch and from Wednesday to Saturday inclusive for dinner. Exports to Hong Kong and the US.

Bimbadgen Estate Semillon

Stainless steel-fermented but seemingly made in a fast-developing style, possibly with skin contact.

TTTY 1998 Medium yellow-green, quite advanced; the bouquet is solid and full, with citrus fruit, the palate big and rich in an early-developing style. **rating:** 81

best drinking 2000–2002 **best vintages** NA **drink with** Pasta • $17.50

Bimbadgen Estate Shiraz

As with the Chardonnay, three vintages are available from cellar door, made in a traditional style, American oak-matured, and offering plenty of flavour.

TTTT 1998 Medium red-purple; attractive sweet leather, spice and vanilla aromas of the bouquet are followed by a palate essentially driven by warm vanillin oak that is, however, neatly integrated, and gently fine tannins provide overall balance. **rating:** 85

best drinking 2000–2005 **best vintages** NA **drink with** Lamb cutlets • $18.50

Bimbadgen Estate Signature Shiraz

Produced from the best blocks of the 30-year-old vineyard and matured in new American oak.

TTTTY 1998 Full red-purple; concentrated, dark berry fruit is matched with lashings of oak on the bouquet; on the palate the fruit flavours move towards sweet cherry, and again there is heaps of vanilla oak. Overall, the fruit handles the oak, and the wine should mature well. **rating:** 90

best drinking 2003–2008 **best vintages** '90 **drink with** Game pie • $28

bindi wine growers ★★★★★

343 Melton Road, Gisborne, Vic 3437 **region** Macedon Ranges
phone (03) 5428 2564 **fax** (03) 5428 2564 **open** Not
winemaker Michael Dhillon, Stuart Anderson **production** 1000 **est.** 1988
product range ($30–50 ML) Macedon Chardonnay, Chardonnay, Chardonnay Quartz, Original Vineyard Pinot Noir, Block 5 Pinot Noir.
summary A relatively new arrival in the Macedon region which has gone from strength to strength. The Chardonnay is top-shelf, the Pinot Noir as remarkable (albeit in a very different idiom) as Bass Phillip, Giaconda or any of the other tiny-production, icon wines. Notwithstanding the tiny production, the wines are exported (in small quantities, of course) to the UK, Italy, Singapore and the US.

Bindi Chardonnay

Bindi produces complex rich and notably long-lived Chardonnay. A four-vintage mini vertical tasting in January 1998 produced top points for the still-youthful, complex and powerful '91 vintage (92 points), followed by the citrussy '94, with an exceptionally long, fine palate (87 points), then a curiously garlicky '95, which I did not like at all (73 points), finally the very different '96, most deeply coloured of all of the wines, and showing what appears to be some botrytis influence. Both that tasting and subsequent tastings demonstrate the slow-devloping style of the wine.

▼▼▼▼ 1998 Quartz ($40). Medium to full yellow-green; complex barrel-ferment aromas are joined with melon, biscuit and cashew on the bouquet. The palate is smooth and powerful but seems locked up at the moment. Rated as it is today, not how it will be in the future. **rating: 86**

best drinking 2002–2007 **best vintages** '91, '94, '95, '96, '97 **drink with** Corn-fed chicken • $30

Bindi Block 5 Pinot Noir

A new departure for Bindi, which in 1997 yielded only 1 tonne per acre, less even than the Original Vineyard which produced 1.3 tonnes per acre — this on close-planted vines. As I did with the '97 vintage, I have given marginally higher points to the '98 Original Vineyard than to Block 5.

▼▼▼▼ 1998 Medium red-purple; a solid bouquet with plenty of ripe plum fruit, but seems to lack the spark of the '97. The palate follows down much the same track, with flavours of plum and forest, and quite good length, but doesn't sing. Time may change matters. **rating: 88**

best drinking 2001–2006 **best vintages** '97 **drink with** Rich game • $50

Bindi Original Vineyard Pinot Noir

I cannot help but wonder what Rick Kinzbrunner (of Giaconda) would achieve if given the Bindi pinot noir grapes to vinify. In saying this I am not suggesting any shortcoming on the part of Michael Dhillon or Stuart Anderson; on the contrary. It is simply that I think the quality of the Bindi grapes, in all except the wettest, coldest years, is utterly exceptional, and in years like 1997, to die for if you are a passionate Pinot Noir maker. Since 1997 there have been two Bindi Pinot Noirs: Original Vineyard and Block 5.

▼▼▼▼▽ 1998 Medium to full red-purple, slightly brighter than Block 5. The bouquet is clean, with firm plum fruit, a touch of spice, and also a little more oak evident. While the palate is still locked up, it is more powerful and seems to have more structure than Block 5. Time may prove that I have under-pointed both wines. **rating: 91**

best drinking 2001–2008 **best vintages** '93, '94, '96, '97, '98 **drink with** Squab • $37.50

birdwood estate ★★★☆

Mannum Road, Birdwood, SA 5234 **region** Adelaide Hills
phone (08) 8263 0986 **fax** (08) 8263 0986 **open** Not
winemaker Oli Cucchiarelli **production** 700 **est.** 1990
product range ($14–23 ML) Chardonnay, Riesling, Merlot, Cabernet Sauvignon.
summary Birdwood Estate draws upon 5 hectares of estate vineyards progressively established since 1990. The quality of the white wines, and in particular the Chardonnay, has generally been good. The tiny production is principally sold through retail in Adelaide, with limited distribution in Sydney and Melbourne.

birnam wood wines NR

Turanville Road, Scone, NSW 2337 **region** Upper Hunter Valley
phone (02) 6545 3286 **fax** (02) 6545 3431 **open** 7 days 10–4
winemaker Simon Gilbert (Contract) **production** 4000 **est.** 1994
product range ($14.95–18.95 CD) Semillon, Semillon Sauvignon Blanc, Chardonnay, Premium Reserve Chardonnay.
summary Former Sydney car dealer Mike Eagan and wife Min moved to Scone to establish a horse stud; the vineyard came later (in 1994) but is now a major part of the business, with over 30 hectares of vines. Most of the grapes are sold; part only is vinified for Birnam Wood.

black george NR

Black Georges Road, Manjimup, WA 6258 **region** Pemberton, Warren Valley and Manjimup
phone (08) 9772 3569 **fax** (08) 9772 3102 **open** 7 days 10.30–4.45
winemaker Dr Shelley E Wilson **production** 4000 **est.** 1991
product range ($17.50–32 CD) Unwooded Chardonnay, The Captains Reserve Chardonnay, Late Picked Verdelho, Classic White, Pinot Noir, Cabernet Franc Merlot.
summary A relatively recent arrival on the scene, with particular aspirations to make high-quality Pinot Noir. As with so much of the Pemberton region, it remains to be seen whether the combination of soil and climate will permit this. Distributors have been appointed in New South Wales, Victoria and Queensland, with direct exports to the UK.

blackjack vineyards ★★★☆

Corner Blackjack Road and Calder Highway, Harcourt, Vic 3453 **region** Bendigo
phone (03) 5474 2355 **fax** (03) 5474 2355 **open** Weekends and public holidays 11–5
winemaker Ian McKenzie, Ken Pollock **production** 2400 **est.** 1987
product range ($22 CD) Shiraz, Cabernet Merlot.
summary Established by the McKenzie and Pollock families on the site of an old apple and pear orchard in the Harcourt Valley. Best known for some very good Shirazes. Ian McKenzie, incidentally, is not to be confused with Ian McKenzie of Seppelt Great Western.

BlackJack Shiraz

Produced from the hillside vineyards of BlackJack and aged in American and French oak barriques for 18 months prior to bottling. The name 'BlackJack' derives from an American sailor who jumped ship during the gold-rush days of the 1850s and 1860s and earned himself this nickname.
▼▼▼▼ 1998 Deep, bright purple-red; there is excellent rich and ripe dark cherry/sweet leather varietal fruit on the bouquet. That black cherry follows through on the palate, with a positive contribution from oak; soft tannins to close. By far the best BlackJack Shiraz to date. **rating:** 90
best drinking 2003–2012 **best vintages** '93, '96, '97, '98 **drink with** Barbecued T-bone • $22

BlackJack Cabernet Merlot

Usually the lesser of the two wines from BlackJack, but it is still a nice wine.
▼▼▼▽ 1998 Medium to full purple-red; the moderately intense bouquet has a mix of spicy/savoury/earthy fruit and just a hint of oak. The medium-bodied palate has some slightly earthy astringency, moving back into spicy territory; the oak and tannins have been well handled. **rating:** 84
best drinking 2003–2008 **best vintages** '98 **drink with** Lamb casserole • $22

✿ black wattle vineyards NR

RSD 106 Mt Benson, via Kingston, SA 5275 (postal) **region** Mount Benson
phone (08) 8768 6264 **fax** (08) 8778 6114 **open** Not
winemaker Ashley Hooper **production** NA **est.** NA
product range ($13.99–32.99) Mount Benson Chardonnay and Cabernet Sauvignon; Lysander Mount Benson Sauvignon Blanc and Cabernet Merlot; Wrights Bay Chardonnay Verdelho and Cabernet blend.
summary Black Wattle Vineyards is owned by Cellarmaster, but is unusual in that it has an estate base, with almost 42 hectares of vines planted to chardonnay, verdelho, sauvignon blanc, cabernet sauvignon, shiraz, cabernet franc, merlot and a dash of petit verdot.

blackwood crest wines ★★☆

RMB 404A, Boyup Brook, WA 6244 **region** Blackwood Valley
phone (08) 9767 3029 **fax** (08) 9767 3029 **open** 7 days 10–6
winemaker Max Fairbrass **production** 3000 **est.** 1976
product range ($13–21 CD) Riesling, Blackwood Classic (Sauvignon Blanc Chardonnay), White Cascade (Semillon Riesling), Sauvignon Blanc, Chardonnay, Shiraz, Cabernet Sauvignon.
summary A remote and small winery which has produced one or two striking red wines full of flavour and character; worth watching.

blanche barkly wines NR

Rheola Road, Kingower, Vic 3517 **region** Bendigo
phone (03) 5443 3664 **open** Weekends, public holidays 10–5
winemaker David Reimers **production** NFP **est.** 1972
product range ($10–16.50 CD) Shiraz, Cabernet Sauvignon.
summary Sporadic but small production and variable quality seem to be the order of the day; the potential has always been there. No recent tastings.

blaxlands wines NR

Broke Road, Pokolbin, NSW 2320 **region** Lower Hunter Valley
phone (02) 4998 7550 **fax** (02) 4998 7802 **open** 7 days 10.30–4.30
winemaker Trevor Drayton (Contract) **production** 1000 **est.** 1976
product range ($17–18 CD) Chardonnay, Chardonnay Semillon, Shiraz.

summary Chris Barnes is an industry veteran who ran Blaxlands Restaurant and Wine Centre in Pokolbin for almost 20 years before selling it to Len Evans in 1999. He is also the owner of 1.5 hectares each of chardonnay and semillon, the wines from which are included in the comprehensive range of Hunter Valley wines available from the Wine Centre (and the restaurant).

bleasdale vineyards ★★★☆

Wellington Road, Langhorne Creek, SA 5255 **region** Langhorne Creek
phone (08) 8537 3001 **fax** (08) 8537 3224 **open** Mon–Sat 9–5, Sun 11–5
winemaker Michael Potts **production** 100 000 **est.** 1850
product range ($9–29 CD) Langhorne Crossing White and Dry Red; Chardonnay, Sandhill Verdelho, Malbec, Mulberry Tree Cabernet Sauvignon, Bremerview Shiraz, Frank Potts Cabernet Malbec Merlot, Sparkling, Fortified.
summary One of the most historic wineries in Australia, drawing upon vineyards that are flooded every winter by diversion of the Bremer River, which provides moisture throughout the dry, cool, growing season. The wines offer excellent value for money, all showing that particular softness which is the hallmark of the Langhorne Creek region. Production has soared; export markets established in the UK, Canada, New Zealand and Switzerland.

bloodwood ★★★★

4 Griffin Road, Orange, NSW 2800 **region** Orange
phone (02) 6362 5631 **fax** (02) 6361 1173 **open** By appointment
winemaker Stephen Doyle, Jon Reynolds **production** 3000 **est.** 1983
product range ($11–25 ML) Riesling, Rosé of Malbec, Chardonnay, Schubert Chardonnay, Ice Riesling, Maurice (Bordeaux-blend), Cabernet, Merlot Noir, Chirac (Pinot Chardonnay).
summary Rhonda and Stephen Doyle are two of the pioneers of the burgeoning Orange district. The wines are sold mainly through cellar door and an energetically and informatively run mailing list; the principal retail outlet is Ian Cook's Fiveways Cellar, Paddington, Sydney. Bloodwood has done best with elegant but intense Chardonnay and the intermittent releases of super-late-harvest Ice Riesling.

Bloodwood Chardonnay

Made by Jon Reynolds at Reynolds Yarraman and has consistently shown that it needs time in bottle to evolve. A delicate style, usually light-bodied but texturally complex, with malolactic cashew notes.
▼▼▼♀ **1998** Medium to full yellow-green; the moderately intense bouquet has a pleasant array of nutty/melon/nectarine supported by subtle oak. The palate is less rewarding, lacking mid-palate intensity and thinning out on the finish. **rating: 82**
best drinking 2000–2003 **best vintages** NA **drink with** White-fleshed fish • $16.60

Bloodwood Schubert Chardonnay

Named in honour of Max Schubert because Stephen Doyle was in the course of preparing the block from which the wine now comes when he heard the news of Max's death on the radio. Hence Chardonnay rather than Shiraz. The wine is whole-bunch pressed and fermented in 50 per cent new French oak, the remainder being two and three years old. The malolactic fermentation is deliberately suppressed.
▼▼▼▼ **1998** Light to medium yellow-green; the bouquet is clean and subtle, with attractive nutty/melon fruit and oak; the palate is fresh, elegant and understated, with fine citrus/melon fruit and a long, clean finish. **rating: 87**
best drinking 2000–2003 **best vintages** NA **drink with** Creamy pasta • $22.80

Bloodwood Ice Riesling

So far as I am aware, the last grapes to be harvested in Australia in the years in which the wine is made. In 1994 the grapes were harvested in July, those for the '97 vintage were picked on June 20. The quality of the wine justifies the patience and faith of the Doyles.
▼▼▼▼♀ **1999** Light to medium yellow-green; the bouquet is clean, moderately intense, with quite tight herbal and mineral aromas. The palate is crisp and lively, with a mix of lime, herb and passionfruit flavours, and a strong streak of brisk acidity running throughout. A great achievement from a very difficult vintage. **rating: 92**
best drinking 2000–2009 **best vintages** '94, '97, '99 **drink with** Any fruit-based dessert • $13

Bloodwood Rosé Of Malbec

Bloodwood has always used its malbec to produce a Rosé, with consistent and convincing results. Malbec tends to crop heavily, and while it has high colour potential, tends to be hollow on the mid to back palate when made as a varietal red wine. On the other hand, the juicy flavours are very well suited to Rosé.

▼▼▼▽ **1999** Bright pink; the bouquet is fresh and lively, the palate likewise fresh but unexpectedly — and perhaps unnecessarily — sweet, however well balanced the acidity may be. **rating:** 83

best drinking 2000–2001 **best vintages** NA **drink with** Mediterranean eggplant • $11

Bloodwood Merlot Noir

A mysterious name for Merlot, which indeed is (except abberationally) a red grape.

▼▼▼▽ **1997** Light to medium red; the bouquet has some earthy, spicy notes before the oak comes into play; the palate is chewy, extremely oaky and finishing with earthy tannins. Not the right style for Merlot. **rating:** 80

best drinking 2000–2003 **best vintages** NA **drink with** Lasagne • $20.85

☙ bluebush estate   NR

Wilderness Road, Cessnock, NSW 2325 **region** Lower Hunter Valley
phone (02) 4930 7177 **fax** (02) 4930 7666 **open** Not
winemaker Contract **production** 200 **est.** 1991
product range Chardonnay, Shiraz.
summary Two hectares of vineyards have been established by David McGain; the two wines (Chardonnay and Shiraz) are contract-made and sold by mail order.

blue pyrenees estate   ★★★

Vinoca Road, Avoca, Vic 3467 **region** Pyrenees
phone (03) 5465 3202 **fax** (03) 5465 3529 **open** Mon–Fri 10–4.30, weekends and public holidays 10–5
winemaker Kim Hart, Greg Dedman **production** 80 000 **est.** 1963
product range ($9–55 R) Brut, Midnight Cuvée, Chardonnay, Estate Red; Fiddlers Creek Chardonnay, Sauvignon Blanc, Semillon, Pinot Noir, Cabernet Shiraz, Brut. Leydens Vale has recently been introduced as a mid-priced range between the Estate wines and Fiddlers Creek.
summary Notwithstanding its distinguished French ownership, the perseverance of former winemaker Vincent Gere, a very well-equipped winery, and lavish marketing expenditure, the former Chateau Remy has struggled. The 1996 renaming of the winery as Blue Pyrenees is a sign of that struggle, and also of a progressive shift in production towards still table wine, a sensible move. The second label, multi-region-sourced Fiddlers Creek range makes steady progress and offers real value for money at around $12. Not surprisingly, the wines are exported throughout Asia (frequently through Remy subsidiaries), the UK and the US.

Blue Pyrenees Estate Chardonnay

Introduced in the early 1990s as part of the move towards greater reliance on table wine. Produced from estate-grown grapes and barrel-fermented.

▼▼▼▽ **1998** Light green-yellow; the bouquet is very light with faint citrus/mineral fruit aromas and just a trace of oak. The palate follows down the same track, seemingly undermade and underdeveloped. **rating:** 81

best drinking 2000–2002 **best vintages** NA **drink with** Veal scaloppine • $21

Blue Pyrenees Estate Midnight Cuvée

Made from 90 per cent Chardonnay and 10 per cent Pinot Noir, 100 per cent estate-grown and, as the name suggests, hand-picked at night, the pickers being fitted with miner's helmets. Whole-bunch pressed at 8°C.

▼▼▼▼ **NV** Pale straw-green; the bouquet is clean, with some slightly herbaceous/minerally characters. The palate is not succulent, but is stylish, with crisp lemon and mineral flavours running through to a long finish. The best Blue Pyrenees sparkling wine for some considerable time. **rating:** 87

best drinking 1999–2001 **best vintages** NA **drink with** Oysters • $30

Blue Pyrenees Estate Red

A blend of estate-grown Shiraz, Cabernet Sauvignon and Merlot, packaged in the very distinctive Blue Pyrenees label.

▼▼▼▽ **1997** Medium red-purple; the moderately intense bouquet has faintly gamey nuances, probably vineyard-derived. The palate is powerful, but distinctly undermade. **rating:** 81

best drinking 2000–2002 **best vintages** '86, '89, '91, '94 **drink with** Beef Bordelaise • $26

Blue Pyrenees Estate Cabernet Blend

The flag-bearer for the estate; a Bordeaux-inspired blend of Cabernet Sauvignon, Shiraz, Merlot and Cabernet Franc. Only in the best vintages does it live up to its reputation and price. A re-release in 1999.

▼▼▼▽ **1992** Medium red, with just a touch of purple. The bouquet seems tired and to lack character, and although the palate is better, it is hard to see the justification for the price. **rating:** 82

best drinking 2000–2003 **best vintages** NA **drink with** Yearling beef • $55

Blue Pyrenees Leydens Vale Cabernet Sauvignon

A blend of Pyrenees and McLaren Vale Cabernet Sauvignon which may soften and develop nicely in bottle.

▼▼▼▽ 1997 Vivid, strong purple-red; there is generous blackberry fruit, a touch of herb and subtle oak on the bouquet, all of which promise much. In the mouth the wine appears slightly underworked, leading to some hardness, but the fruit flavour is there. Could be worth cellaring.　　　　　　　　　　**rating: 83**

best drinking 2003–2008　**best vintages** NA　**drink with** Char-grilled beef　• $16.95

✿ blue wren　　NR

Lot 8 Stoney Creek Road, Mudgee, NSW 2850　**region** Mudgee
phone (02) 6373 5320　**fax** (02) 6373 5488　**open** Weekends and public holidays10–4, or by appointment
winemaker Pieter Van Gent, Simon Gilbert (Contract)　**production** 2000　**est.** 1985
product range ($13–16 CD) Semillon, Chardonnay, Unwooded Chardonnay, Cabernet Sauvignon Merlot, Chardonnay Port.
summary James and Diana Anderson have two vineyards, the first called Stoney Creek, planted in 1985 and acquired from the Britten family in early 1999. It has 2 hectares each of chardonnay and semillon, 1.5 hectares of cabernet and 0.5 hectare of merlot, situated 20 kilometres north of Mudgee, and the vines are dry-grown. The second vineyard has been planted to 2.4 hectares of shiraz and 1.4 hectares of verdelho, leaving more than 20 hectares as yet unplanted. The Bombira Vineyard, as it is known, is adjacent to the old Augustine vineyards owned by Mildara Blass.

Blue Wren Semillon

Produced from 1.8 hectares of mature estate plantings. Well received at the 1999 Winewise Small Vigneron Awards, but really needs five years to realise its potential, and will almost certainly be thwarted by the agglomerate cork.

▼▼▼ 1999 Very pale straw-green; the bouquet is, of course, youthful, crisp and with relatively little fruit aroma. The palate has excellent minerally, crispy acidity, and won't start to develop flavour for at least five years.　　**rating:** 79

best drinking 2005–2010　**drink with** Oysters　• $14

✿ boireann　　NR

Donnellys Castle Road, The Summit, Qld, 4377　**region** Queensland Zone
phone (07) 4683 2194　**open** Fri–Sun 10–4
winemaker Peter Stark　**production** 300　**est.** 1998
product range ($17.50 CD) Cabernet Sauvignon.
summary Peter and Therese Stark have a 10-hectare property set amongst the great granite boulders and trees which are so much part of the Granite Belt. Luxury accommodation is provided, and supplements the winemaking activities. They have established a little over 1 hectare of vines planted to no less than seven varieties, including the four Bordeaux varieties which will go to make a Bordeaux-blend; grenache and mourvedre will provide a Rhône-blend, and there will also be a straight Merlot. The one wine so far released is a very creditable start.

Boireann Granite Belt Cabernet Sauvignon

An estate-grown, produced and bottled wine.

▼▼▼▽ 1998 Strong purple-red colour; there is dense fruit and lots of chippy oak on the bouquet, characters which come through equally powerfully on the palate. Seems undermade, and with fairly sharp acidity. On the other hand, it certainly has character and is a more than creditable first vintage.　　**rating:** 82

best drinking 2002–2006　**drink with** Rich meat casserole　• $17.50

boneo plains　　NR

RMB 1400, Browns Road, South Rosebud, Vic 3939　**region** Mornington Peninsula
phone (03) 5988 6208　**fax** (03) 5988 6208　**open** By appointment
winemaker R D Tallarida　**production** 2500　**est.** 1988
product range ($10–22 CD) Chardonnay, Cabernet Sauvignon; Roch Unwooded Chardonnay, Roch Rosé.
summary A 9-hectare vineyard and winery established by the Tallarida family, well known as manufacturers and suppliers of winemaking equipment to the industry. The Chardonnay is the best of the wines so far released.

bonneyview   NR

Sturt Highway, Barmera, SA 5345 **region** Riverland
phone (08) 8588 2279 **open** 7 days 9–5.30
winemaker Robert Minns **production** 5000 **est.** 1975
product range ($6–25 CD) Riesling, Chardonnay, Frontignan Blanc, Shiraz Petit Verdot, Cabernet Petit Verdot, Cabernet Blend, Fortifieds.
summary The smallest Riverland winery selling exclusively cellar door, with an ex-Kent cricketer and Oxford University graduate as its owner/winemaker. The Shiraz Petit Verdot (unique to Bonneyview) and Cabernet Petit Verdot add a particular dimension of interest to the wine portfolio.

booth's taminick cellars   NR

Taminick via Glenrowan, Vic 3675 **region** Rutherglen and Glenrowan
phone (03) 5766 2282 **fax** (03) 5766 2151 **open** Mon–Sat 9–5, Sun 10–5
winemaker Peter Booth **production** 4000 **est.** 1904
product range ($6.50–12 CD) Trebbiano, Chardonnay, Late Harvest Trebbiano, Shiraz, Cabernet Merlot, Cabernet Sauvignon, Ports, Muscat.
summary Ultra-conservative producer of massively flavoured and concentrated red wines, usually with more than a few rough edges which time may or may not smooth over.

boston bay wines   ★★★☆

Lincoln Highway, Port Lincoln, SA 5606 **region** Other Wineries of SA
phone (08) 8684 3600 **fax** (08) 8684 3637 **open** Weekends, school/public holidays 11.30–4.30
winemaker David O'Leary (Contract) **production** 2500 **est.** 1984
product range ($11–17.50 CD) Riesling, Spatlese Riesling, Chardonnay, Cabernet Sauvignon, Merlot, Baudin's Blend (Magnum), Mistelle.
summary A strongly tourist-oriented operation which has extended the viticultural map in South Australia. It is situated at the same latitude as Adelaide, overlooking the Spencer Gulf at the southern tip of the Eyre Peninsula. Say proprietors Graham and Mary Ford, 'It is the only vineyard in the world to offer frequent sightings of whales at play in the waters at its foot'. No tastings in 1999/2000.

botobolar   ★★★☆

89 Botobolar Road, Mudgee, NSW 2850 **region** Mudgee
phone (02) 6373 3840 **fax** (02) 6373 3789 **open** Mon–Sat 10–5, Sun 10–3
winemaker Kevin Karstrom **production** 6000 **est.** 1971
product range ($7–18 CD) Sauvignon Blanc, Rain Goddess Dry White, Rain Goddess Sweet White, Chardonnay, Shiraz, Cabernet Sauvignon; Preservative Free White and Preservative Free Shiraz.
summary One of the first organic vineyards in Australia, with present owner Kevin Karstrom continuing the practices established by founder Gil Wahlquist. Preservative Free Dry White and Dry Red extend the organic practice of the vineyard to the winery. Shiraz is consistently the best wine to appear under the Botobolar label. Exports to the UK, Denmark, Germany and Japan.

bowen estate   ★★★★

Riddoch Highway, Coonawarra, SA 5263 **region** Coonawarra
phone (08) 8737 2229 **fax** (08) 8737 2173 **open** 7 days 10–5
winemaker Doug Bowen **production** 11 000 **est.** 1972
product range ($18–25 CD) Chardonnay, Shiraz, The Blend, Cabernet Sauvignon, Sanderson Sparkling.
summary One of the best-known names among the smaller Coonawarra wineries, with a great track record of red winemaking; Chardonnay and Sanderson Sparkling have joined the band, and the Riesling ended with the '93 vintage. Full-bodied reds at the top end of the ripeness spectrum are the winery trademarks, with a chewy richness uncommon in Coonawarra. Exports to the UK, Germany and New Zealand.

Bowen Estate Shiraz

A wine which has given tremendous pleasure over the years, always crammed full of personality and flavour. Doug Bowen certainly prefers to allow the grapes to ripen fully, sometimes to frightening levels. The ripe style does not always turn me on, but the '94, '95 and '97 did so in spades.

▼▼▼▼▼ **1997** Medium to full red-purple; an ultra-classic Australian red bouquet; rich, with complex fruit and sweet oak. The palate delivers all that the bouquet promises, with abundant flavour in the red berry spectrum coupled with almost Italianate tannins, and complementary oak. **rating:** 94

best drinking 2000–2010 **best vintages** '86, '90, '91, '92, '94, '95, '97 **drink with** Kangaroo fillet • $22.95

Bowen Estate The Blend

A relatively new direction for Bowen Estate, usually made in a different different style from the normal Bowen Estate reds, earlier picked and with less opulently ripe flavour. A Cabernet Sauvignon, Merlot and Cabernet Franc.

▼▼▼▼ **1997** Medium red-purple; the bouquet has greater ripeness and substance than any previous release of this wine I can remember, with a pleasant touch of earthy Cabernet Sauvignon providing backbone. A really nice wine on the palate, with no green characters, simply red berry and a hint of mint supported by well-handled oak.

rating: 89

best drinking 2002–2007 **best vintages** '95, '97 **drink with** Lasagne • $21

Bowen Estate Cabernet Sauvignon

Normally made in the ripe Bowen style, which succeeds in most, but not all, warm vintages. The approach seems to be validated by the outcome for less ripe years (such as '97) where the wine tends to austerity.

▼▼▼▽ **1997** Medium red-purple; the aromas are in the olive/herb/earth spectrum, undoubtedly varietal but a fraction austere. The palate is pleasant enough but seems to have that doughnut, hole-in-the-middle structure which Cabernet is often accused of having, but which is far from inevitable, particularly in Coonawarra. **rating: 84**

best drinking 2001–2005 **best vintages** '86, '90, '91, '93, '94 **drink with** Richly sauced beef casserole • $25

boynton's ★★★☆

Great Alpine Road, Porepunkah, Vic 3741 **region** Alpine Valleys and Beechworth
phone (03) 5756 2356 **fax** (03) 5756 2610 **open** 7 days 10–5
winemaker Kel Boynton **production** 12 000 **est.** 1987
product range ($14–60 CD) Riesling, Semillon, Sauvignon Blanc, Chardonnay, Boynton's Gold (Noble Riesling Chardonnay blend), Pinots (Pinot Meunier Pinot Noir), Shiraz, Merlot, Cabernet Sauvignon, Reserve (Cabernet Sauvignon Merlot, Petit Verdot), Port, Vintage Brut, Boynton's Black (Sparkling Burgundy).
summary The original 12.5-hectare vineyard, expanded to almost 16 hectares by 1996 plantings of pinot gris, durif and sauvignon blanc, is situated in the Ovens Valley north of the township of Bright, under the lee of Mount Buffalo. In the early years a substantial part of the crop was sold, but virtually all is now vinified at the winery. Overall, the red wines have always outshone the whites, initially with very strong American oak input, but in more recent years with better fruit/oak balance. Striking, indeed strident new labelling has led to a minor name change by the dropping of the words 'of Bright'. The wines have distribution through the east coast of Australia, Germany and the US.

Boynton's Pinots

An interesting blend of Pinot Meunier (80 per cent) and Pinot Noir (20 per cent), a rarely encountered table wine.

▼▼▼▽ **1998** Medium purple-red; the bouquet is quite ripe, with aromas of caramel, toffee and strawberry conserve. The palate flavours offer strawberry and a touch of mint; there is a lack of mid-palate vinosity, although it is remotely possible this will build with a little more bottle age. **rating: 81**

best drinking 2000–2003 **best vintages** NA **drink with** Risotto • $21

Boynton's Shiraz

Sourced from a little under 2.5 hectares of estate plantings, which are now fully mature. As ever, American oak is omnipresent, though less than in earlier vintages.

▼▼▼▽ **1998** Medium red-purple; an ultra-traditional, earthy American oak-style bouquet is followed by a palate in two compartments: first, quite fresh, juicy cherry fruit; and second, American oak. **rating: 82**

best drinking 2000–2004 **best vintages** '89, '90, '91, '93 **drink with** Pizza • $18

Boynton's Cabernet Sauvignon

Cabernet sauvignon is the most widely planted variety on the estate, with 4 hectares under vine. It provides some of the richest of the Boynton reds.

▼▼▼▼ **1998** Medium purple-red; the bouquet offers attractive cassis/berry fruit, and the oak is under control. Rich, cassis berry floods the mouth and here, too, the oak has been kept under control. **rating: 86**

best drinking 2000–2005 **best vintages** '90, '92, '93, '94 **drink with** Yearling beef • $18

⚘ braewattie NR

Woodend Road, Rochford, Vic 3442 **region** Macedon Ranges
phone (03) 9818 5742 **fax** (03) 9818 8361 **open** By appointment
winemaker John Flynn, John Ellis **production** 250 **est.** 1993
product range ($18–25 R) Chardonnay, Pinot Noir.
summary A tiny operation with the wines sold by mail order to friends and acquaintances.

brand's of coonawarra ★★★★

Main Road, Coonawarra, SA 5263 **region** Coonawarra
phone (08) 8736 3260 **fax** (08) 8736 3208 **open** Mon–Fri 9–4.30, weekends 10–4
winemaker Jim Brand, Jim Brayne **production** NFP **est.** 1965
product range ($13.95–55 R) Riesling, Chardonnay, Cabernet Merlot, Shiraz, Stentiford's Reserve Shiraz, Merlot, Cabernet Sauvignon, Patron's Reserve Cabernet Sauvignon.
summary Part of a very substantial investment in Coonawarra by McWilliam's, which first acquired a 50 per cent interest from the founding Brand family then moved to 100 per cent, and followed this with the purchase of 100 hectares of additional vineyard land. Significantly increased production of the smooth wines for which Brand's is known will follow past the end of the decade.

Brand's of Coonawarra Riesling

Just when one makes up one's mind that growing riesling in Coonawarra is a capital offence, or at the very least a terrible waste of a rare and finite resource (Coonawarra terra rossa), a wine such as the '98 comes along to confound you; the '99 is pleasant.
▼▼▼▼ 1999 Light yellow-green; the aromas are crisp, predominantly minerally, with some herb; a pleasant wine on the palate, with moderate intensity and length. **rating:** 84
best drinking 2000–2003 **best vintages** '98 **drink with** Caesar salad • $10.95

Brand's of Coonawarra Shiraz

As the Coonawarra vineyard resources of McWilliam's (and hence Brand's) have increased, so has the style of the Brand's wines subtly changed, becoming more elegant and (perhaps) understated.
▼▼▼▼▼ 1998 Medium to full red-purple; the fragrant bouquet offers dark cherry together with hints of mint and leaf; the finely balanced and elegant palate has more of those dark cherry fruit flavours supported by crisp acidity and subtle oak. **rating:** 90
best drinking 2003–2012 **best vintages** '90, '91, '96, '98 **drink with** Braised lamb shanks • $22.50

Brand's of Coonawarra Stentiford's Reserve Shiraz

A new addition to the brand range, commemorating Captain Stentilford, the sea captain who established the original vineyard around the turn of the century and whose ship was called *Laira*.
▼▼▼▼▼ 1997 Medium red-purple; the moderately intense bouquet is spotlessly clean, with smooth red berry/cherry and nicely handled vanillin oak. Intense, bright, sweet cherry fruit fills the palate; fine, soft tannins and subtle vanilla oak complete a particularly good wine. **rating:** 91
▼▼▼▼▼ 1996 This debut release is packed with complex, dark red stone-fruit aroma; the palate has much more substance and structure than the standard release, with hints of cedar and fine tannins. **rating:** 95
best drinking 2003–2013 **best vintages** '96, '97 **drink with** Rack of lamb • $55

Brand's of Coonawarra Merlot

A new release reflecting the increasing vineyard production at Brand's. Still feeling the way, but with potential.
▼▼▼▼ 1998 Medium red-purple; the bouquet shows authentic varietal character with a mix of savoury/earthy/leafy aromas; some lively, sweet red berry fruit lifts the palate, as do the fine tannins. **rating:** 87
best drinking 2002–2006 **best vintages** '97 **drink with** Veal chops • $29.95

Brand's of Coonawarra Cabernet Sauvignon

First made in 1971, and over the intervening years has produced some wonderful wines; the earlier vintages, in particular, were pacesetters. Since then the field has caught up and for a period passed Brand's, but the viticultural resources are there, and there is no doubting the honesty of the wine. Has been a consistent gold medal winner at national shows over more recent vintages.
▼▼▼▼▼ 1998 Medium to full red-purple; the bouquet is quite rich, with ample blackberry, cassis and dark chocolate fruit aromas. The palate is full, round, soft and fleshy with ripe tannins and good oak. **rating:** 90
best drinking 2003–2010 **best vintages** '86, '90, '91, '93, '94, '95, '98 **drink with** Yearling steak • $22.50

Brand's of Coonawarra Patron's Reserve Cabernet Sauvignon

Another new addition to the range, sitting alongside the Stentilford's Reserve Shiraz. In both instances the wines come from the '97 vintage; the '98s are an enticing prospect.
▼▼▼▼ 1997 Medium to full red-purple; the bouquet is clean, quite intense and very smooth, flowing logically into the fresh blackberry, mint and leaf flavours of the lively palate. **rating:** 88
best drinking 2002–2007 **best vintages** NA **drink with** Osso bucco • $55

brangayne of orange ★★★★☆

49 Pinnacle Road, Orange, NSW 2880 **region** Orange
phone (02) 6365 3229 **fax** (02) 6365 3170 **open** By appointment
winemaker Simon Gilbert (Contract) **production** 4500 **est.** 1994
product range ($15.50–23.50 CD) Sauvignon Blanc, Premium Chardonnay, Reserve Chardonnay, Orange
Pinot Noir, Reserve Chardonnay, Shiraz, Merlot, The Tristan (Cabernet blend), Cabernet Sauvignon.
summary Orchardists Don and Pamela Hoskins decided to diversify into grape growing in 1994 and have
progressively established 25 hectares of high-quality vineyards. With viticultural consultancy advice from Dr
Richard Smart and skilled contract-winemaking by Simon Gilbert, Brangayne has made an extraordinarily
auspicious debut, emphatically underlining the potential of the Orange region.

Brangayne of Orange Premium Chardonnay

The first vintage (1997) was a silver medal winner at the 1997 Liquorland National Wine Show, and well-
deserving of that award. Skilful winemaking, subtle use of oak and excellent cool-climate fruit are the ingredients.
▼▼▼♈ 1999 Light to medium yellow-green; the bouquet is quite fragrant though delicate; happily, the oak is
subtle. The palate has delicate melon fruit, with pleasant acid balance and the barest suggestion of oak; nicely
restrained, and should cellar well. **rating: 84**
best drinking 2000–2005 **best vintages** '97 **drink with** Calamari • $15.50

Brangayne of Orange Reserve Chardonnay

The best chardonnay, picked riper (13.5 degrees versus 13 degrees than the Premium Chardonnay) is barrel-
fermented in a mix of Allier and Vosges French oak barriques, before spending five months on lees. Sophisticated
winemaking with excellent base material.
▼▼▼▼ 1999 Light to medium green-yellow; gentle, melon/nectarine fruit aromas and imperceptible oak on the
bouquet leads into a pleasant, well-made, well-balanced wine on the palate. It seems to lack the intensity and focus
of the '98. **rating: 85**
best drinking 2000–2005 **best vintages** '97, '98 **drink with** Flathead fillets • $20

Brangayne Orange Pinot Noir

The first release of Pinot Noir from Brangayne, and a particularly interesting wine, which suggests this area may
well be suited to this finicky variety.
▼▼▼▼ 1998 Medium red-purple, bright and clear; the overall impression of the bouquet is sweetness, with some spice
and plum fruit and minimal oak. There is plenty of ripe plum fruit showing some varietal character on the palate,
supported by attractive, dusty tannins and subtle oak. Overall, a better red wine than a Pinot Noir. **rating: 87**
best drinking 2000–2003 **best vintages** '98 **drink with** Jugged hare • $23.50

Brangayne of Orange The Tristan

A blend of Cabernet Sauvignon, Shiraz and Merlot, and which reinforces the suggestion that the Hoskins are not
only skilled viticulturists, but have chosen an exceptionally good vineyard site.
▼▼▼▼ 1998 Medium to full red-purple; the bouquet offers a range of cassis/blackberry fruit aromas with no leafy
characters whatsoever. The palate opens with sweet juicy berry fruit, closing with tannins and slightly jumpy
acidity. **rating: 87**
best drinking 2003–2008 **best vintages** '97, '98 **drink with** Grain-fed beef • $22

🐾 branson wines NR.

Seppeltsfield Road, Greenock, SA 5360 **region** Barossa Valley
phone (08) 8562 8085 **fax** (08) 8562 8085 **open** Wed–Mon 10.30–5
winemaker Vicky Louise Bartier **production** 1000 **est.** 1997
product range ($10–35 CD) Semillon, Chardonnay, Spatlese, JB Brut Champagne, Highway Shiraz, Coach
House Shiraz, Cabernet Sauvignon Merlot, Fine Old Tawny Port.
summary If you drive up the main highway from Adelaide to the Barossa Valley, the first large road sign you
come across at the entrance to the Valley is one pointing the way to Seppeltsfield. Almost immediately after you
leave the highway, and with Seppeltsfield only a couple of kilometres away, you will pass Branson Wines on the
right-hand side. The property was acquired by James Branson in 1848, and vines first planted in 1924, although at
some point along the way, the vineyards were removed. Malcolm Aspden and his family purchased the property in
1987, and three years later began a planting programme centred on shiraz, and now have 5 hectares of shiraz, and
1 each of semillon, cabernet sauvignon and chardonnay. The cellar door was opened in 1997, and all wine
produced is sold through the cellar door with the exception of small exports to New York.

bream creek ★★★★

Marion Bay Road, Bream Creek, Tas 7175 **region** Southern Tasmania
phone (03) 6231 4646 **fax** (03) 6231 4646 **open** At Potters Croft, Dunally, phone (03) 6253 5469
winemaker Steve Lubiana (Contract) **production** 3000 **est.** 1975
product range ($16–19 CD) Riesling, Gewürztraminer, Schonburger, Chardonnay, Pinot Noir, Cabernet
Pinot, Cabernet Sauvignon.
summary Until 1990 the Bream Creek fruit was sold to Moorilla Estate, but since that time the winery has been
independently owned and managed under the control of Fred Peacock, legendary for the care he bestows on the
vines under his direction. Peacock's skills have seen both an increase in production and also a vast lift in wine
quality across the range, headed by the Pinot Noir. The 1996 acquisition of a second vineyard in the Tamar Valley
has significantly strengthened the business base of the venture.

Bream Creek Riesling

Bream Creek is situated on one of the coldest sites in Tasmania, with a constant maritime influence. Conventional
fruit ripeness will always be difficult to achieve, with the evident residual sugar needed to balance higher than
usual acidity.
▼▼▼▽ **1998** Medium yellow-green; the bouquet is solid, not particularly aromatic, but with limey fruit quite evident.
The palate has plenty of flavour, but the support of residual sugar is just a little on the heavy side. **rating:** 84
best drinking 2000–2005 **best vintages** NA **drink with** Spring rolls • $17

Bream Creek Schonburger

Both the 1998 and 1999 vintages won bronze medals at succeeding Tasmanian Wine Shows. Schonburger is a
hybrid bred for ultra-cool climates in Germany and England, and has a distinctive slightly oily character.
▼▼▼▽ **1999** Light green-yellow; the bouquet has intense jujube/pastille fruit leading into a palate with slightly
oily overtones. Distinctive and rare. **rating:** 80
best drinking Drink now **best vintages** NA **drink with** Asian food • $16.40

Bream Creek Pinot Noir

Bream Creek has two vineyards, one established many years ago on the east coast of Tasmania, the other more
recently in the Tamar Valley. This wine comes entirely from the often temperamental east coast vineyard. The 1997
was a monumental wine; the '98 is good, but not in the same Olympian class.
▼▼▼▼ **1998** Youthful purple-red; the bouquet offers dark, juicy plum aromas with hints of hay and straw; one
wonders whether the wine may have spent some time in stainless steel. A very concentrated and powerful palate
picks up the plum and dark cherry fruit, with oak very much in the background. **rating:** 87
best drinking 2001–2004 **best vintages** '97 **drink with** Braised duck • $19

Bream Creek Cabernet Sauvignon

Initially sourced from the Bream Creek east coast vineyard, but now using grapes from the vineyard near Rowella
in the Tamar Valley acquired late in 1996.
▼▼▼▽ **1998** Medium red-purple; the aromas are of light to moderate intensity, tending earthy/leafy. However,
sweeter fruit is to be found on the palate alongside some gamey canopy characters. **rating:** 80
best drinking 2003–2008 **best vintages** NA **drink with** Venison • $16

bremerton wines ★★★★

Strathalbyn Road, Langhorne Creek, SA 5255 **region** Langhorne Creek
phone (08) 8537 3093 **fax** (08) 8537 3109 **open** 7 days 10–5
winemaker Rebecca Willson **production** 17 500 **est.** 1988
product range ($13.50–28 CD) Sauvignon Blanc Semillon, Botrytised Chenin Blanc, Verdelho, Young Vine
Shiraz, Old Adam Shiraz, Bremerton Blend (red), Cabernet Sauvignon, Tamblyn (Cabernet Shiraz Merlot).
summary The Willsons have been grape growers in the Langhorne Creek region for some considerable time but
their dual business as grape growers and winemakers has expanded significantly over the past few years. Their
vineyards have more than doubled to over 100 hectares (predominantly cabernet sauvignon, shiraz and merlot), as
has their production of wine under the Bremerton label, no doubt in recognition of the quality of the wines.
Wholesale distribution in all States of Australia; exports to the UK, the US, Canada, Hong Kong and Switzerland.

Bremerton Young Vine Shiraz

What a remarkable piece of honesty in a world which seems to be only populated with Old Vines. The vines in
question are between six and eight years old, and the wine spends 15 months in American oak.

TTTT 1998 Medium red-purple; the bouquet opens with clean cherry and plum fruit, then moves into a more open phase, but not excessively so. The palate is fresh and well made, the fruit nicely framed, and avoids the trap of over-extraction. **rating: 86**

best drinking 2002–2007 **best vintages** NA **drink with** Lasagne • $16

Bremerton Tamblyn

A newly introduced blend of Cabernet Sauvignon, Shiraz and Merlot. Excellent value.

TTTT 1998 Bright, youthful red-purple. The moderately intense bouquet is clean, with a mix of red berry and more savoury fruit supported by just a touch of oak. The palate has plenty of depth and good structure except for a slight dip on the mid-palate, which will very probably fill out with a few more years in bottle. **rating: 85**

best drinking 2002–2007 **best vintages** NA **drink with** Grilled calf's liver • $15

brewery hill winery   NR

Olivers Road, McLaren Vale, SA 5171 **region** McLaren Vale
phone (08) 8323 7344 **fax** (08) 8323 7355 **open** Mon–Fri 9–5, weekends 10–5
winemaker Warren Randall (Consultant) **production** 12 000 **est.** 1869
product range ($6.20–22 CD) Classic Dry White, Sauvignon Blanc, Riesling, Chardonnay, Botrytis Riesling, Classic Dry Red, Grenache, Shiraz, Shiraz Cabernet, Sparkling and Fortifieds.
summary A change of name and of address for the former St Francis Winery, which has moved into the former Manning Park Winery and is now known as Brewery Hill Winery.

briagolong estate   ★★☆

Valencia–Briagolong Road, Briagolong, Vic 3860 **region** Gippsland
phone (03) 5147 2322 **fax** (03) 5147 2400 **open** By appointment
winemaker Gordon McIntosh **production** 300 **est.** 1979
product range ($35 ML) Chardonnay, Pinot Noir.
summary This is very much a weekend hobby for medical practitioner Gordon McIntosh, who tries hard to invest his wines with Burgundian complexity, although with mixed success. Dr McIntosh must have established an all-time record with the 15.4 degrees alcohol in the '92 Pinot Noir.

brian barry wines   ★★★☆

PO Box 128, Stepney, SA 5069 **region** Clare Valley
phone (08) 8363 6211 **fax** (08) 8362 0498 **open** Not
winemaker Brian Barry **production** 10 000 **est.** 1977
product range ($14.99–30 R) Jud's Hill Handpicked Riesling, Chardonnay, Handpicked Merlot, Handpicked Cabernet Sauvignon; Gleeson's Ridge Shiraz Merlot and Semillon Chardonnay.
summary Brian Barry is an industry veteran with a wealth of winemaking and show-judging experience. His is nonetheless in reality a vineyard-only operation, with a substantial part of the output sold as grapes to other wineries and the wines made under contract at various wineries, albeit under Brian Barry's supervision. As one would expect, the quality is reliably good. Retail distribution through all States, and exports to the US, Canada, Taiwan, Switzerland and New Zealand.

brian mcguigan wines   ★★★

PO Box 300, Cessnock, NSW 2335 **region** Lower Hunter Valley
phone (02) 4998 7700 **fax** (02) 4998 7401 **open** 7 days 10–5
winemaker Brian McGuigan, Peter Hall, Rodney Kemp, Sarah-Kate Wilson **production** 750 000 **est.** 1992
product range ($9–35 R) The wines are sold in several price brackets: at the bottom, Harvest Range First Harvest, Night Harvest and Autumn Harvest; the Black Label range of Verdelho Chardonnay, Chardonnay, Traminer Riesling and Black Label Red; Vineyard Selection Gewurztraminer and Petite Verdot; then the Bin range of 2000 Hermitage, 3000 Merlot, 4000 Cabernet Sauvignon, 5000 Malbec, 6000 Verdelho, 7000 Chardonnay, 8000 Sauvignon Blanc, 9000 Semillon; finally Shareholder Reserve range and Personal Reserve range.
summary A public-listed company which is the ultimate logical expression of Brian McGuigan's marketing drive and vision, on a par with that of Wolf Blass in his heyday. Highly successful in its chosen niche market notwithstanding exceedingly garish labels. Has been particularly active in export markets, notably the US and more recently in China. Wine quality seems less important than marketing magic.

briar ridge ★★★☆

Mount View Road, Mount View, NSW 2325 **region** Lower Hunter Valley
phone (02) 4990 3670 **fax** (02) 4990 7802 **open** Mon–Sat 9.30–5, Sun 10–5
winemaker Karl Stockhausen, Neil McGuigan **production** 20 000 **est.** 1972
product range ($17–24.50 CD) Varietal range of Méthode Champenoise, Early Harvest Semillon, Hand Picked Chardonnay, Verdelho, Late Harvest Gewurztraminer, Botrytis Semillon, Old Vines Shiraz, Cabernet Sauvignon, Tawny Port; Signature Stockhausen Semillon, and Hermitage; and Signature McGuigan Chardonnay and Cabernet Merlot.
summary Semillon and Hermitage, each in various guises, have been the most consistent performers, underlying the suitability of these varieties to the Hunter Valley. The Semillon, in particular, invariably shows intense fruit and cellars well. Briar Ridge has been a model of stability with the winemaking duo of Neil McGuigan and Karl Stockhausen and also has the comfort of over 40 hectares of estate vineyards, from which it is able to select the best grapes. Exports to the US and Switzerland.

bridgeman downs NR

Barambah Road, Moffatdale via Murgon, Qld 4605 **region** Granite Belt
phone (07) 4168 4784 **fax** (07) 4168 4767 **open** By appointment
winemaker Bruce Humphery-Smith **production** NA **est.** NA
product range ($11.50–16.50 CD) Cellar White and Red; Chardonnay, Verdelho, Shiraz, Merlot Cabernet.
summary A substantial, albeit new, vineyard with 4 hectares of vines, the major plantings being of verdelho, chardonnay and shiraz and lesser amounts of merlot and cabernet sauvignon. The perpetual-motion Bruce Humphery-Smith has been retained as consultant winemaker, which should ensure wine quality. The first wines were released from the 1998 vintage but were not tasted.

bridgewater mill ★★★★

Mount Barker Road, Bridgewater, SA 5155 **region** Adelaide Hills
phone (08) 8339 3422 **fax** (08) 8339 5253 **open** Mon–Fri 9.30–5, weekends 10–5
winemaker Brian Croser **production** 20 000 **est.** 1986
product range ($15–33 R) Sauvignon Blanc, Chardonnay, Millstone Shiraz, Cabernet Malbec.
summary The second label of Petaluma, which consistently provides wines most makers would love to have as their top label. The fruit sources are diverse, with the majority of the sauvignon blanc and chardonnay coming from Petaluma-owned or managed vineyards, while the Shiraz is made from purchased grapes.

Bridgewater Mill Sauvignon Blanc

A blend of material coming from the Adelaide Hills, Clare Valley and Coonawarra, cold-fermented in stainless steel and relatively early-bottled.
▼▼▼▽ **1999** Light to medium yellow-green; the bouquet is quite full, but not overly varietal; there is a similar, solidly fruited palate; simply doesn't sparkle. **rating:** 83
best drinking Drink now **best vintages** '92, '94, '95 **drink with** Mousseline of scallops • $19

Bridgewater Mill Chardonnay

Produced from chardonnay grown in the Coonawarra, the Adelaide Hills and the Clare Valley, barrel-fermented in French oak barriques of unspecified age, but fairly evidently, not new. A pleasant, simple and direct style.
▼▼▼▼▽ **1997** Medium yellow-green; there are some bottle-developed aromas of melon and a hint of hay. It is on the palate that the wine really comes alive, with melon and citrus fruit, good length and balance; still remarkably fresh. **rating:** 90
best drinking 2000–2004 **best vintages** '97 **drink with** Whiting • $21

brindabella hills ★★★★

Woodgrove Close, via Hall, ACT 2618 **region** Canberra District
phone (02) 6230 2583 **fax** (02) 6230 2023 **open** Weekends, public holidays 10–5
winemaker Dr Roger Harris **production** 2000 **est.** 1989
product range ($18–25 CD) Riesling, Sauvignon Blanc Semillon, Chardonnay, Reserve Chardonnay, Shiraz, Cabernet.
summary Distinguished research scientist Dr Roger Harris presides over Brindabella Hills, which increasingly relies on estate-produced grapes, with small plantings of cabernet sauvignon, cabernet franc, merlot, shiraz, chardonnay, sauvignon blanc, semillon and riesling. Wine quality has been consistently impressive. All of the wine is sold direct ex winery.

Brindabella Hills Sauvignon Blanc Semillon

One hundred per cent estate-grown, with the components picked over a range of degrees of ripeness, cold-fermented to dryness and early-bottled.

▼▼▼▼ 1999 Light straw-yellow; crisp herb and lemon aromas take time to evolve, but do so progressively; the palate has good length and intensity, with lingering lemon/mineral flavours. **rating:** 85

best drinking 2000–2002 **best vintages** NA **drink with** Gravlax • $16.50

Brindabella Hills Chardonnay

Produced from estate-grown grapes (20 per cent) from vineyards at Orange (70 per cent) and the Yarra Valley (10 per cent). Fully barrel-fermented, lees stirring and 50 per cent malolactic fermentation.

▼▼▼▼ 1999 Medium yellow-green; the bouquet is complex, with quite pronounced charry barrel-ferment characters. Attractive citrus and melon fruit comes to the fore on the palate; the oak is far less strident, and the finish long. **rating:** 87

best drinking 2000–2004 **best vintages** NA **drink with** Pan-fried veal • $20

Brindabella Hills Shiraz

Fermented in small open fermenters and hand-plunged; basket-pressed and then taken to American oak where it spends 18 months. An outstanding wine with an excellent show pedigree. The entire crop was destroyed by the October 1998 frost; the grapes for the '99 vintage were sourced through BRL Hardy.

▼▼▼▼ 1999 Langhorne Creek Shiraz. Medium to full red-purple; a civilised and complex wine with sweet, savoury berry aromas and excellent oak handling. The palate is elegant and restrained, with soft tannins and subtle oak; it is just a little lacking on the mid-palate. Nonetheless, a very interesting example of what can be done with Langhorne Creek fruit. **rating:** 86

▼▼▼▼▼ 1998 Vivid, deep red-purple; the bouquet is spotlessly clean, with attractive dark berry/plum fruit and subtle oak. While quite focused and concentrated, there is a mirror-smooth texture to the palate; raspberry fruit has soaked up the oak, and the wine finishes with good acidity. **rating:** 94

best drinking 2001–2006 **best vintages** '92, '98 **drink with** Lamb casserole • $15

britannia creek wines NR

75 Britannia Creek Road, Wesburn, Vic 3799 **region** Yarra Valley
phone (03) 5780 1426 **fax** (03) 5780 1426 **open** Weekends 10–6
winemaker Charlie Brydon **production** 1200 **est.** 1982
product range ($12–18 CD) Sauvignon Blanc, Semillon, Cabernets.
summary The wines (from Britannia Creek Wines) are made under the Britannia Falls label from 4 hectares of estate-grown grapes. A range of vintages are available from cellar door, with some interesting, full-flavoured Semillon.

broadview estates NR

Rowbottoms Road, Granton, Tas 7030 **region** Southern Tasmania
phone (03) 6263 6882 **open** Tues–Sun 10–5
winemaker Andrew Hood (Contract) **production** 250 **est.** 1996
product range ($15.50–18 CD) Riesling, Chardonnay.
summary David and Kaye O'Neil planted their vineyard in the spring of 1996, picking the first precious 200 kilograms of chardonnay in 1998 and producing a fine minerally wine.

broke estate ★★★☆

Wollombi Road, Broke, NSW 2330 **region** Lower Hunter Valley
phone (02) 6579 1065 **fax** (02) 6579 1065 **open** 7 days 10–5
winemaker Matthew Ryan **production** 22 000 **est.** 1988
product range ($14–48 ML) Broke Estate is the premium label with Chardonnay, Cabernets, Lacrima Angelorum (sweet white) and Moussant Sparkling; the second label, which accounts for 20 000 of the 22 000 case production, is Ryan Free Run Chardonnay and Basket Pressed Shiraz.
summary With a high-profile consultant viticulturist (Dr Richard Smart) achieving some spectacular early results, Broke Estate has seldom been far from the headlines. Contrary to what one might expect, the opulent red wines (rather than the whites) have been the most successful.

Ryan Free Run Chardonnay

An interesting name for what I take to be an unwooded, early-bottled Chardonnay.

▼▼▼▽ **1999** Light to medium yellow-green; there is fair fruit on the bouquet, slightly inhibited by a whisper of burnt match. A pleasant, commercial wine with residual sugar and acidity designed to balance each other. **rating:** 80

best drinking 2000–2001 **best vintages** NA **drink with** Pizza • $13

Broke Estate Cabernets

A blend of Cabernet Sauvignon and Cabernet Franc which, in appropriate years without too much rain, can produce good wine.

▼▼▼▽ **1998** Medium red-purple; the moderately intense bouquet has a mix of sweet berry, chocolate and earth aromas; the palate doesn't quite deliver the promise of the bouquet, with slightly stewy fruit characters counterbalanced by some sweet tannins, possibly oak-derived. **rating:** 81

best drinking 2001–2004 **best vintages** '91, '94 **drink with** Smoked lamb • $23.75

---

brokenwood ★★★★★

McDonalds Road, Pokolbin, NSW 2321 **region** Lower Hunter Valley
phone (02) 4998 7559 **fax** (02) 4998 7893 **open** 7 days 10–5
winemaker Iain Riggs **production** 70 000 **est.** 1970
product range ($10–45 R) Semillon, Cricket Pitch Sauvignon Blanc Semillon, ILR Semillon, Cricket Pitch Unwooded Chardonnay, Graveyard Chardonnay, Harlequin White, Jelka Riesling (dessert), Cricket Pitch Red, Harlequin Red, Cricket Pitch Cabernet Merlot, Shiraz, Pinot Noir, Cabernet Sauvignon, Rayner Vineyard Shiraz, Graveyard Shiraz, Mistress Block Shiraz.
summary Deservedly fashionable winery producing consistently excellent wines. Cricket Pitch Sauvignon Blanc Semillon has an especially strong following, as has Cabernet Sauvignon; the Graveyard Shiraz is one of the best Hunter reds available today, the unwooded Semillon a modern classic. In 1997 acquired a controlling interest in Seville Estate (Yarra Valley) and has also been involved in the establishment of substantial vineyards in Cowra. National distribution in Australia; exports to the US, the UK, Canada, Switzerland and Asia.

Brokenwood Semillon

A wine much appreciated by the Sydney market, which ensures that each release sells out long before the next becomes available. It is made in traditional style: in other words, without the use of oak, and unforced by techniques such as skin contact. Most is drunk young as a crisp, quasi-Chablis style, but as tastings show, can develop into a Hunter classic. (Specially made Reserve releases are in the maturation pipeline.)

▼▼▼▼▽ **1999** Light green-yellow; a fragrant bouquet with lots of lemongrass and citrus aromas is followed by a highly flavoured, lively, zesty palate with very good acidity and length. **rating:** 91

best drinking 2000–2004 **best vintages** '85, '86, '89, '92, '94, '95, '96, '97, '98, '99 **drink with** Balmain bugs • $17.50

Brokenwood Harlequin

Introduced with the 1998 vintage, utilising shiraz (40 per cent), cabernet franc (30 per cent) and cabernet sauvignon (30 per cent) grapes grown in McLaren Vale and designed to be an easy, early-drinking style. It is placed alongside the Harlequin White, first released a year earlier.

▼▼▼▼ **1998** Medium red-purple; the bouquet is clean, quite ripe with nice, smooth berry fruit and oak. The palate is well balanced, quite sweet, with soft tannins and subtle oak, precisely achieving the aim of the winemaking team. **rating:** 85

best drinking 2000–2003 **best vintages** NA **drink with** Asian red meat dishes • $16

---

brook eden vineyard NR

Adams Road, Lebrina, Tas 7254 **region** Northern Tasmania
phone (03) 6395 6244 **open** 7 days 10–5
winemaker Jan Bezemer **production** 800 **est.** 1988
product range ($15–18 CD) Chardonnay, Pinot Noir.
summary Jan and Sheila Bezemer own a 60-hectare Angus beef property which they purchased in 1987 but have diversified with the establishment of 2.5 hectares of vines. Jan Bezemer makes the wine at Delamere, the first vintage being 1993. The vineyard site is beautiful, with viticultural advice from the noted Fred Peacock.

brookland valley ★★★★☆

Caves Road, Willyabrup, WA 6284 **region** Margaret River
phone (08) 9755 6250 **fax** (08) 9755 6214 **open** Tues–Sun 11–4.30
winemaker Larry Cherubino **production** 8000 **est.** 1984
product range ($18–32.95 R) Sauvignon Blanc, Chardonnay, Merlot, Cabernet Merlot; Verse 1 Semillon Sauvignon Blanc, Chardonnay and Cabernet Merlot.
summary Brookland Valley has an idyllic setting, with its much enlarged Flutes Cafe one of the best winery restaurants in the Margaret River region. In 1997 BRL Hardy acquired a 50 per cent interest in the venture and has taken responsibility for viticulture and winemaking. The move towards richer and more complex red wines evident before the takeover has continued; the white wines have an extra degree of finesse and elegance.

Brookland Valley Sauvignon Blanc

Has consistently impressed, gaining in power and concentration as the vines have matured. The wine is produced from 2 hectares of estate plantings and is at the richer end of the Margaret River spectrum — an area noted for producing Sauvignon Blanc with excellent varietal character.
▼▼▼▼▽ 1999 Light green-yellow; quite fragrant and clean with a mix of gooseberry and passionfruit, flavours which are repeated on the crisp and lively palate, finishing with bright acidity. **rating:** 90
best drinking 2000–2001 **best vintages** '92, '93, '94, '95, '97, '99 **drink with** Calamari • $23.95

Brookland Valley Verse 1 Semillon Sauvignon Blanc

The bronze statue of Pan has been resident at Brookland Valley since it opened. Thus the step to Verse 1, labelled with music by Jane Rutter, Australia's leading flautist, is entirely logical.
▼▼▼▼▽ 1999 Light green-yellow; the moderately intense bouquet has a mix of fragrant and potent passionfruit/gooseberry fruit with a more minerally underlay. The palate is bright, lively and zesty, with a lovely combination of fruit and mineral, and a crisp, clean finish. **rating:** 92
best drinking 2000–2003 **best vintages** NA **drink with** Avocado salad • $16.80

Brookland Valley Chardonnay

A wine which shows the benefit of the skilled winemaking inputs from majority owner BRL Hardy.
▼▼▼▼▽ 1997 Medium yellow-green; the moderately intense bouquet has a range of nectarine, peach and fig fruit allied with some more bready/cashew notes. The moderately weighted palate is well balanced, with a nice spicy oak addition to the fruit, and a clean finish. **rating:** 93
best drinking 2000–2007 **best vintages** NA **drink with** Pan-fried veal • $28.95

Brookland Valley Merlot

Does nothing to answer the eternal question asked in Australia: what should Merlot taste like? For all that, a relatively new direction for Brookland Valley, and a variety which does appear suited to the Margaret River region.
▼▼▼▽ 1997 Medium red-purple; strong, spicy/charry oak dominates the bouquet, although fruit fights back to a degree on the palate — but doesn't win. The texture is the strong point of the wine. **rating:** 84
best drinking 2002–2006 **best vintages** NA **drink with** Devilled steak • $32.95

Brookland Valley Cabernet Merlot

Since the arrival of BRL Hardy on the scene, the already good quality of the Brookland Valley wines has improved. So, in some instances, has the style changed for the better, particularly with the Cabernet Merlot, which is now produced in a much sweeter, softer and fruitier style than hitherto.
▼▼▼▼▼ 1997 Medium purple-red; a fragrant bouquet with seductive cedary/savoury overtones to sweet fruit; a stylish medium-bodied wine, with very sweet berry fruit on the palate supported by fine tannins. **rating:** 94
best drinking 2000–2007 **best vintages** '90, '91, '92, '93, '95, '97 **drink with** Char-grilled steak • $32.95

Brookland Valley Verse 1 Cabernet Merlot

This is the sister wine to Verse 1 Semillon Sauvignon Blanc with an identical background to the inspiration for the label.
▼▼▼▼ 1998 Medium red-purple; the bouquet is fresh and fragrant, offering a mix of berry, mint and leaf supported by subtle oak. On the palate, a lighter, minty, leafy, early-drinking style with a beguiling finish. **rating:** 88
best drinking 2000–2004 **best vintages** NA **drink with** Pasta • $17.80

brookside vineyard NR

5 Loaring Road, Bickley Valley, WA 6076 **region** Perth Hills
phone (08) 9291 8705 **fax** (08) 9291 5316 **open** Weekends and public holidays 10–5
winemaker Darlington Estate (Contract) **production** 400 **est.** 1984
product range ($15–17 CD) Chardonnay, Cabernet Sauvignon, Méthode Champenoise.
summary Brookside is one of the many doll's house-scale vineyard operations which dot the Perth Hills. It has a quarter of a hectare each of chardonnay and cabernet sauvignon, basically selling the wine through a mailing list. It does, however, offer bed and breakfast accommodation at the house with its attractive views of the Bickley Valley.

brown brothers ★★★★

Snow Road, Milawa, Vic 3678 **region** King Valley
phone (03) 5720 5500 **fax** (03) 5720 5511 **open** 7 days 9–5
winemaker Terry Barnett, Wendy Cameron, Matt Fawcett **production** 300 000 **est.** 1885
product range ($10.95–45.50 R) A kaleidoscopic array of varietal wines, with a cross-hatch of appellations, the broadest being Victorian (e.g. Victorian Shiraz), more specific being King Valley (e.g. NV Brut and Pinot Chardonnay) and Milawa (e.g. Noble Riesling), then the Limited Release, Family Selection (e.g. Very Old Tokay and King Valley Chardonnay), and the Family Reserve ranges. Dinning's Shiraz is a cellar-door special.
summary Brown Brothers draws upon a considerable number of vineyards spread throughout a range of site climates, ranging from very warm to very cool, with the climate varying according to altitude. It is also known for the diversity of varieties with which it works, and the wines always represent excellent value for money. Deservedly one of the most successful family wineries in Australia. The wines are exported to over 20 countries spread throughout Europe, the UK, Asia and the Far East. Conspicuously, Brown Brothers still remains out of the US market.

Brown Brothers Whitlands Riesling
From the high altitude Whitlands Vineyard with a genuinely cool, if not downright cold, climate.
▼▼▼▼▽ 1998 Light green-yellow; the bouquet is fresh, moderately intense, with quite Germanic lime/mineral aromas. The palate is still crisp, minerally and light, developing slowly. Give it time. **rating:** 90
best drinking 2003–2008 **best vintages** '98 **drink with** Fresh asparagus • $16.50

Brown Brothers Gewurztraminer
A wine which does not always fire the imagination, but which did so emphatically in 1998.
▼▼▼▼▽ 1998 Light to medium green-yellow; a power-packed bouquet with masses of spice and lychee, almost Alsatian. The palate is not quite as powerful as the bouquet, but still truly remarkable. **rating:** 93
best drinking 2000–2003 **best vintages** '98 **drink with** Asian • $17.60

Brown Brothers Sauvignon Blanc
Sourced from a number of vineyards in the King Valley.
▼▼▼▽ 1999 Light to medium yellow-green; some tropical fruit aromas but not particularly varietal, with the same slightly offbeat flavour edges, probably reflecting the 14 degrees alcohol. **rating:** 83
best drinking Drink now **best vintages** NA **drink with** Light seafood. • $17.60

Brown Brothers Moscato
With an alcohol content of only 6.5 degrees, this is in fact an alcohol-reduced wine. Prior vintages have been very attractive.
▼▼▼▽ 1999 Light yellow-green; the bouquet has lively grapey/spicy fruit; the spritz on the palate picks up the intensity of the fruit, but I really find the wine altogether too sweet. **rating:** 80
best drinking Drink now **best vintages** NA **drink with** Fresh fruit • $12.90

Brown Brothers Verdelho
Having broken the ground with so many varietals, it seems strange that Brown Brothers should be a relative latecomer into the Verdelho game, but it has done so with success.
▼▼▼▼ 1998 Medium yellow-green; the wine has acquired some pleasant bottle-developed aromas in a raisin toast spectrum, the palate likewise having built good flavour in a relatively short time. Drink soon. **rating:** 89
best drinking Drink now **best vintages** NA **drink with** Pasta • $16.80

Brown Brothers Victorian Chardonnay

The King Valley provides the grapes, Brown Brothers the well-oiled winemaking.

❦❦❦❦ **1998** Medium yellow-green; a well-crafted commercial Chardonnay offering nicely balanced fruit and oak; smooth and easy. **rating: 85**

best drinking 2000–2002 **best vintages** NA **drink with** Wiener Schnitzel • $17.60

Brown Brothers Whitlands Chardonnay

A limited release wine produced from Brown Brothers' high altitude vineyard at Whitlands, on the very roof of the King Valley. This is a serious cool-climate area.

❦❦❦❦❦ **1998** Medium yellow-green; a complex wine with obvious high toast, spicy barrel-ferment aromas, which in no way threaten the palate, where ripe melon fruit is the key, running through to a long finish, the oak playing a perfectly judged support role. **rating: 90**

best drinking 2000–2004 **best vintages** NA **drink with** Yabbies • $20.50

Brown Brothers Dinning's Shiraz

A cellar-door release which, over the years, has enjoyed major show successes. I must confess I have wondered whether it was the wine or the oak which attracted the judges' attention.

❦❦❦❦ **1997** Medium red-purple; as ever, a very, very oaky bouquet; the attractive sweet fruit lurking on the palate is similarly swamped by oak. **rating: 84**

best drinking 2001–2004 **best vintages** NA **drink with** Moroccan lamb • $35.80

Brown Brothers Victorian Shiraz

Sourced from Brown Brothers' estate in Milawa and Mystic Park Vineyards, the balance coming from contract growers in the King Valley. Typically harvested over a long period running from mid-March to late April, which invests the wine with an extra degree of complexity. American oak is used at a level which is in the mainstream of Australian commercial red winemaking.

❦❦❦❦ **1997** Medium red-purple; the moderately intense bouquet offers nicely balanced fruit and vanillin American oak. The palate opens up in the same fashion, although charry American oak is a little too emphatic on the finish for my liking. **rating: 84**

best drinking 2001–2007 **best vintages** '91, '92, '93, '94 **drink with** Braised beef Chinese-style • $17.30

Brown Brothers Milawa Shiraz
Mondeuse Cabernet

Brown Brothers have used the rare mondeuse red grape variety for many decades. This wine is in fact a blend of Shiraz, Mondeuse, Cabernet Sauvignon and Ruby Cabernet sourced from the King Valley.

❦❦❦❦ **1995** Medium red-purple; the bouquet is quite aromatic with ripe prune/mulberry/blackberry fruit; the sweet fruit flavours of the palate track the bouquet, finishing with soft tannins. **rating: 87**

best drinking 2000–2010 **best vintages** NA **drink with** Shepherd's pie • $NA

Brown Brothers Barbera

Brown Brothers has long been in the vanguard of the promotion of Italian varieties such as this.

❦❦❦❦ **1998** The colour is slightly dull, not unusual for this variety. The bouquet creeps up on you, with some tobacco and cinnamon spice characters which flow through into the pleasantly savoury palate, finishing with soft tannins. Sotto voce from start to finish. **rating: 83**

❦❦❦❦ **1997** Medium red-purple; the bouquet offers a mix of savoury/cedary/leafy/minty fruit, characters which flow through to the pleasantly balanced palate with soft tannins on the finish. **rating: 85**

best drinking 2000–2003 **best vintages** NA **drink with** Spiced Italian sausages • $15

Brown Brothers King Valley Merlot

There are relatively large plantings of merlot in the King Valley. At higher elevations the climate should be ideal; the problems will come in restraining yield — merlot is very nearly as sensitive to over-cropping as is pinot noir.

❦❦❦❦ **1997** Light to medium red-purple; leafy, cedary earthy aromas lead into a plain wine with a relatively short finish, but reasonable overall balance. **rating: 80**

best drinking 2000–2003 **best vintages** NA **drink with** Loin of lamb • $18.50

Brown Brothers Classic Release Cabernet Sauvignon Malbec Shiraz Merlot

A Bordeaux-blend with a couple of Australian flourishes: the inclusion of Shiraz and (lots of) American oak.

TTTT 1994 Medium to full red-purple; quite complex fruit does battle with heaps of American oak on the bouquet; the oak attack diminishes on the palate, where solid, ripe mulberry and plum fruit flavours and well-balanced tannins come together with the oak. A traditional style.　　　　　　　　**rating:** 88

best drinking 2000–2009 **best vintages** NA **drink with** Beef ragout with olives • $45.50

Brown Brothers Family Reserve Cabernet Sauvignon

Matured in barrel and then in bottle in Brown Brothers' cellars for eight years prior to release; their flag-bearing red wine.

TTTTT 1992 Medium red-purple; the bouquet is clean and smooth with gentle, ripe berry and cedar aromas. The palate is pleasantly smooth, with ripe berry fruit and subtle oak. Ageing surely and slowly.　　**rating:** 90

best drinking 2000–2010 **best vintages** NA **drink with** Roast rib of beef • $45.50

browns of padthaway　　★★☆

Keith Road, Padthaway, SA 5271 **region** Padthaway
phone (08) 8765 6063 **fax** (08) 8765 6083 **open** At Padthaway Estate
winemaker Contract **production** 35 000 **est.** 1993
product range ($10–20 R) Classic Diamond, Riesling, Sauvignon Blanc, Non Wooded Chardonnay, Verdelho, T-Trellis Shiraz, Redwood Cabernet Malbec, Myra Family Reserve Cabernet Sauvignon, Sparkling Shiraz.
summary The Brown family has for many years been the largest independent grape grower in Padthaway, a district in which most of the vineyards were established and owned by Wynns, Seppelts, Lindemans and Hardys, respectively. A rapidly expanding range of wines is now appearing under the Browns of Padthaway label, the majority being pleasant but very light in body and flavour.

brush box vineyard　　NR

40 Rodd Street, Broke, NSW 2101 **region** Lower Hunter Valley
phone (02) 9913 1419 **fax** (02) 9913 1419 **open** Not
winemaker Peter Howland (Contract) **production** 600 **est.** 1997
product range ($13.50–14.50 ML) Verdelho, Chardonnay, Cabernet Merlot.
summary Paul and Suzanne Mackay have established their 6.5-hectare Brushbox Vineyard at Broke; it is planted to chardonnay, verdelho, cabernet sauvignon and merlot, and so far sold by mail order only.

bullers beverford　　★★★

Murray Valley Highway, Beverford, Vic 3590 **region** Swan Hill
phone (03) 5037 6305 **fax** (03) 5037 6803 **open** Mon–Sat 9–5
winemaker Richard Buller (Jnr) **production** 50 000 **est.** 1952
product range ($9.50–39 CD) Victoria Chenin Blanc Colombard and Shiraz Grenache Malbec; The Magee Semillon Chardonnay and Cabernet Sauvignon Shiraz; White Label range of Semillon Chenin Blanc, Spätlese Lexia, Rosé, Shiraz, Cabernet Sauvignon; Victoria range of fortifieds, including Port, Tokay and Muscat; also Sails Unwooded Chardonnay and Cabernet Shiraz Merlot.
summary Traditional wines which in the final analysis reflect both their Riverland origin and a fairly low-key approach to style in the winery. It is, however, one of the few remaining sources of reasonable quality bulk fortified wine available to the public, provided in 22-litre Valorex barrels at $6.50 per litre. Some recent table wines have impressed.

Bullers Beverford Chardonnay

Made from 100 per cent chardonnay grown in the Swan Hill region; stainless steel-fermented, with 40 per cent matured in oak.

TTTY 1998 Light to medium yellow-green; very ripe peach/canned fruit aromas are classic sunshine in a bottle; the ripe, peachy fruit is lusciously sweet, probably due to the 14.5 degrees alcohol. Oak barely intrudes into the picture.　　　　　　　　**rating:** 82

best drinking 2000–2001 **best vintages** NA **drink with** Prosciutto and melon • $13.50

Bullers Beverford Cabernet Sauvignon

An attractive wine from the irrigated Beverford Vineyard on the Murray River. No-frills winemaking; after fermentation the wine spends 12 months in oak, the majority old.

▼▼▼♀ **1998** Medium red, with just a touch of purple; the bouquet offers ripe, slightly jammy fruit with undertones of spice and cedar. A pleasant, light-bodied wine on the palate, again slightly jammy, but not offensively so. Easy early-drinking style.   **rating:** 82

best drinking 2000–2003 **best vintages** NA **drink with** Simple food   • $18

Bullers Beverford Vintage Port

A classic old-style Vintage Port which added to its already formidable show record of 2 trophies, 5 gold, 9 silver and 6 bronze medals at the 1999 Australian Inland Wine Show, held in Swan Hill and chaired by Bill Chambers with Chris Killeen and David Morris among the judges. At this show it won the trophy for Best Vintage Port.

▼▼▼▼ **1978** Medium red-tawny; the bouquet is very sweet with raisin and spice aromas backed by gentle spirit. The palate is rich and round with flavours of chocolate, raisin and spice, finishing with fine tannins. Ultra-traditional style.   **rating:** 87

best drinking Drink now **best vintages** NA **drink with** Coffee and chocolate   • $39

bullers calliope   ★★★★☆

Three Chain Road, Rutherglen, Vic 3685 **region** Rutherglen and Glenrowan
phone (02) 6032 9660 **fax** (02) 6032 8005 **open** Mon–Sat 9–5, Sun 10–5
winemaker Andrew Buller **production** 5000 **est.** 1921
product range ($16–55 CD) Limited Release Shiraz, Mondeuse Shiraz, Grenache Cinsaut; Premium Black Label range and Museum Release range of old and rare material.
summary The winery rating is very much influenced by the recent superb releases of Museum fortified wines. Limited releases of Calliope Shiraz and Shiraz Mondeuse can also be exceptionally good.

Bullers Calliope Limited Release

The flagship table wine for Bullers, first released under this label in 1991. One hundred per cent Shiraz, made in open fermenters, hand-plunged and basket-pressed before maturation in American oak.

▼▼▼▼ **1996** Medium to full red-purple; quite complex savoury/dark berry/blackberry fruit aromas on the bouquet are followed by a full-bodied palate with a mix of dark berry, chocolate and more savoury flavours, and chewy but ripe tannins on the finish.   **rating:** 88

best drinking 2000–2010 **best vintages** NA **drink with** Rich meat dishes   • $42

Bullers Calliope Rare Liqueur Tokay

Both the Rare Liqueur Muscat and Tokay are of extreme quality and of great age, with the older material in the blend dating back to the 1940s, and picked from Bullers' 1920 Rutherglen dryland vineyard. The base wine is over 20 years old, and only 150 dozen 375-ml bottles are released each year to protect the integrity of the base material. Like the Liquid Gold Tokay, very smartly packaged in a 375-ml bottle.

▼▼▼▼▼ **NV** Deep golden brown; a classic mix of sweet tea-leaf and crème brûlée aromas is followed by an outstanding palate showing the complexity which only age (and first class base material) can bring; some nutty characters join the tea-leaf and crème brûlée of the bouquet.   **rating:** 95

best drinking 2000–2010 **best vintages** NA **drink with** Strictly unnecessary, a meal in itself   • $55

Bullers Calliope Rare Liqueur Muscat

Emerged from the shadows in spectacular fashion at the 1994 Sydney International Wine Competition, where it won the trophy for Best Wine of Show. A magnificent wine of great age and complexity. Originally released as Very Old Rutherglen Muscat, but now under the Rare Liqueur label, and in the new package.

▼▼▼▼▼ **NV** Deep brown with a touch of olive on the rim; full and deep, almost into chocolate, with intense raisined fruit; richly textured, with great structure to the raisined/plum pudding fruit flavours, and obvious rancio age.   **rating:** 94

best drinking 2000–2010 **best vintages** NA **drink with** Strictly unnecessary, a meal in itself   • $55

bungawarra   NR

Bents Road, Ballandean, Qld 4382 **region** Granite Belt
phone (07) 4684 1128 **fax** (07) 4684 1128 **open** 7 days 10.30–4.30
winemaker Bruce Humphery-Smith, Jeff Harden **production** 1300 **est.** 1975
product range ($10–20 CD) Traminer, Thomas Semillon, Block Six Chardonnay, Foundation Chardonnay, Bliss, Festival Red, Shiraz, Cabernet Sauvignon, Liquid Amber, Paragon Liqueur, Liqueur Muscat.
summary Now owned by Jeff Harden. It draws upon 5 hectares of mature vineyards which over the years have shown themselves capable of producing red wines of considerable character.

burge family winemakers ★★★★

Barossa Way, Lyndoch, SA 5351 **region** Barossa Valley
phone (08) 8524 4644 **fax** (08) 8524 4444 **open** 7 days 10–5
winemaker Rick Burge **production** 3500 **est.** 1928
product range ($14.80–48 CD) Olive Hill Riesling, Olive Hill Semillon, Chardonnay, Muscat Blanc Late Harvest, Clochmerle (Grenache), Olive Hill Grenache Shiraz, Draycott Shiraz Grenache, Draycott Shiraz, Draycott Reserve Shiraz, Draycott Cabernet Merlot, Draycott Sparkling Red, Fortifieds.
summary Rick Burge came back to the family winery after a number of years successfully running St Leonards; there was much work to be done, but he has achieved much, using the base of very good fortified wines and markedly improving table wine quality, with Draycott Shiraz (both standard and Reserve) leading the way. The wines are exported to the US, Singapore, Germany, The Netherlands, the UK and Canada.

Burge Family Olive Hill Semillon

Barossa Semillon is not an easy wine to make well, often tending to heaviness and prone to rapid development, particularly when exposed to phenolic, German oak. This wine has been very well handled, 20 per cent being barrel-fermented in new French (Allier) oak. It should, nonetheless, be drunk sooner rather than later.

▼▼▼▽ **1999** Deep, glowing green-yellow; the bouquet shows quite strong herbal varietal character, the palate right in the groove for this style in a 'drink today rather than drink tomorrow' mode. **rating:** 83

best drinking 2000–2001 **best vintages** NA **drink with** Chicken pasta • $19.80

Burge Family Draycott Reserve Shiraz

A similar fruit base to the standard Draycott Shiraz, but given Rolls Royce treatment in new oak. The '96 was runner-up in the Shiraz Class at the 1998 *Winewise* Small Makers Competition, and perhaps a tad unlucky not to win its class. The '98 is even better, the only problem is that only 174 cases of the wine were made.

▼▼▼▼▼ **1998** Medium to full red-purple; the bouquet offers everything imaginable in a rich, ripe and concentrated mode, ranging through dark berry, plum and prune. The opulently rich palate shows excellent handling of oak with fermentation finished in new French and American oak barrels. This contributes to the outstanding texture and structure of an irresistible wine. **rating:** 95

best drinking 2003–2023 **best vintages** '96, '98 **drink with** Char-grilled rump • $48

Burge Family Draycott Shiraz Grenache

A varying blend of between 70 and 77 per cent Shiraz and 23 and 30 per cent old vine Grenache.

▼▼▼▼ **1998** Medium to full red-purple; the bouquet is solid, with dark berry and blackberry fruit. The palate is very powerful, with lots of extract in a big frame; here a touch of the jammy grenache fruit is to be found, as are plentiful tannins. **rating:** 89

best drinking 2001–2005 **best vintages** '98 **drink with** Rich casserole • $19.80

burnbrae NR

Hill End Road, Erudgere via Mudgee, NSW 2850 **region** Mudgee
phone (02) 6373 3504 **fax** (02) 6373 3601 **open** Wed–Mon 9–5
winemaker Alan Cox **production** NFP **est.** 1976
product range ($10–18 CD) Sauvignon Blanc, Chardonnay, Pinot Noir, Shiraz, Malbec, Cabernet Sauvignon, Vintage Port, Liqueur Muscat.
summary The founding Mace family sold Burnbrae to Alan Cox in 1996. It continues as an estate-based operation with 23 hectares of vineyards. No recent tastings.

burramurra NR

Barwood Park, Nagambie, Vic 3608 **region** Goulburn Valley
phone (03) 5794 2181 **fax** (03) 5794 2755 **open** Not
winemaker Mitchelton (Contract) **production** 800 **est.** 1988
product range ($18 R) Cabernet Merlot.
summary Burramurra is the relatively low-profile vineyard operation of the former Deputy Premier of Victoria, the Hon. Pat McNamara. Most of the grapes are sold to Mitchelton; a small amount is contract-made for the Burramurra label. Glowing reveiws in the United States have led to brisk export business with that country.

🐚 burrundulla   NR

Sydney Road, Mudgee, NSW 2850 **region** Mudgee
phone (02) 6372 1620 **fax** (02) 6372 4058 **open** Not
winemaker Contract **production** NA **est.** 1996
product range NA.
summary A very substantial venture but one which is still in its infancy; the Cox family (Chris, Michael and Ted) are in the course of establishing 54 hectares of vineyards planted to chardonnay, shiraz and cabernet sauvignon.

calais estates   ★★★

Palmers Lane, Pokolbin, NSW 2321 **region** Lower Hunter Valley
phone (02) 4998 7654 **fax** (02) 4998 7813 **open** Mon–Fri 9–5, weekends 10–5
winemaker Adrian Sheridan **production** 11 000 **est.** 1987
product range ($12–30 CD) Chenin Blanc, Semillon, Chardonnay, Reserve Chardonnay, Late Harvest Riesling, Sauterne, Shiraz Pinot, Shiraz, Reserve Shiraz, Cabernet Sauvignon.
summary A quite substantial operation but off the beaten track in Palmers Lane; at the time of writing an auction sale was scheduled, and it is likely it will emerge with new ownership.

cambewarra estate   ★★★☆

520 Illaroo Road, Cambewarra, NSW 2540 **region** Shoalhaven
phone (02) 4446 0170 **fax** (02) 4446 0170 **open** Weekends and public holidays Wed–Sun 10–5, Mon–Fri by appointment
winemaker Tamburlaine (Contract) **production** 3500 **est.** 1991
product range ($15–29 CD) Chardonnay (wooded and unwooded), Verdelho, Petit Rouge, Chambourcin, Cabernet Sauvignon, Vintage Port.
summary Geoffrey and Louise Cole founded Cambewarra Estate near the Shoalhaven River on the central southern coast of New South Wales, with contract-winemaking competently carried out (a considerable distance away) at Tamburlaine Winery in the Hunter Valley. Cambewarra continues to produce attractive wines which have had significant success in wine shows.

Cambewarra Estate Chambourcin

Chambourcin is a French-bred hybrid which is highly resistant to mildew and rot, and particularly suited to warmer, wetter growing regions. Cassegrain on the north coast of New South Wales has the largest plantings, but they are scattered through various parts of the State. At Cambewarra, as elsewhere, it produces a strongly coloured wine which is typically best consumed when young. Cambewarra makes two versions: one a lighter style, without oak, the other a fuller, oak-matured wine.

 1999 Typically dense purple; the bouquet has that gamey varietal character of Chambourcin which can deceive you into thinking it is due to bacterial activity. The palate has rich, sweet juicy fruit flavours, again ever-so-typical.   **rating:** 84
best drinking 2000–2001 **best vintages** '94, '97, '98 **drink with** Italian cuisine   • $20

Cambewarra Estate Chambourcin Vintage Port 375 ml

It might seem inherently unlikely that chambourcin should produce good fortified wine, but Cambewarra Estate has done it consistently, and there are one or two other examples around the country. A gold medal winner at Cowra Show 1999, believed to be the first gold medal for a Chambourcin Port.

1998 Full purple-red; spice and chocolate aromas come through on the bouquet, which, like the palate, has pleasantly neutral fortifying spirit. The palate is well balanced, fruity yet not overly sweet, the base wine working very well.   **rating:** 86
best drinking 2000–2003 **best vintages** '98 **drink with** After dinner   • $14

campbells   ★★★★

Murray Valley Highway, Rutherglen, Vic 3685 **region** Rutherglen and Glenrowan
phone (02) 6032 9458 **fax** (02) 6032 9870 **open** Mon–Sat 9–5, Sun 10–5
winemaker Colin Campbell **production** 35 000 **est.** 1870
product range ($7.50–79.50 R) Semillon, Riesling, Pedro Ximenez, Trebbiano, Bobbie Burns Chardonnay, Silverburn Dry White and Red, Bobbie Burns Shiraz, The Barkly Durif, Malbec, Shiraz Durif Cabernet, Cabernets, Liquid Gold Tokay, Isabella Tokay, Rutherglen Muscat, Merchant Prince Muscat.

summary A wide range of table and fortified wines of ascending quality and price, which are always honest; as so often happens in this part of the world, the fortified wines are the best, with the extremely elegant Isabella Tokay and Merchant Prince Muscat at the top of the tree. For all that, the table wines are impressive in a full-bodied style; the winery rating is something of a compromise between that for the fortified wines and for the table wines. A feature of the cellar door is an extensive range of back vintage releases of small parcels of wine not available through any other outlet. National distribution through FD&C Wines; exports to the UK, the US and Singapore.

Campbells Bobbie Burns Shiraz

An always interesting wine made from very ripe grapes, typically with alcohol levels of around 14 degrees, and with a relatively high pH, which gives the wine softness and roundness in the mouth. One hundred per cent estate-grown. Ranged alongside the Chardonnay as the premium table wine release from Campbells.

▼▼▼▼ 1998 Medium to full red-purple; very rich, high-toned plum and prune aromas are followed by a big, juicy, ripe, fleshy palate in archetypal Bobbie Burns style; tannins are controlled, as is the oak. A mere 14.6 degrees alcohol. **rating:** 88

best drinking 2002–2007 **best vintages** '86, '88, '90, '91, '92, '94, '96, '98 **drink with** Rich game dishes • $17.50

Campbells Isabella Tokay

One of a pair of super-premium fortified wines produced by Campbells, the other being Campbells Merchant Prince Muscat. The Campbells wine is, and always has been, lighter and fresher than that of the other major producers, with more emphasis thrown on the underlying varietal fruit of the wines. It is a question of style rather than quality; these deluxe wines deserve their price.

▼▼▼▼▼ NV Light tawny-gold; fragrant grapey, sweet tea-leaf aromas with clean spirit; the palate is luscious with sweet juicy berry and tea-leaf flavours, finishing with good acidity and a very clean aftertaste. **rating:** 93

best drinking 2000–2001 **best vintages** NA **drink with** As fine an aperitif as it is a digestif • $79.50

Campbells Liquid Gold Tokay

Repackaged into the slender, clear glass 'olive oil' type of 375-ml bottle much favoured these days, but done extremely well, with an attractive label and capsule design. Externalities to one side, a beautiful expression of young Rutherglen Tokay, the sort of wine one should drink, rather than sip — especially on a cold winter's night.

▼▼▼▼▼ NV Glowing golden brown; totally delicious, sweet tea-leaf and caramel varietal aromas leap from the glass, with the flavour precisely tracking the bouquet. Clean spirit, sweet but not the least bit cloying. **rating:** 91

best drinking 2000–2001 **best vintages** NA **drink with** Cake and coffee • $18

Campbells Rutherglen Tokay

Campbells are one of the best makers of young Tokay (average age five years or so) in Rutherglen. The wine has perfectly defined varietal character, and is to be drunk, rather than just sipped.

▼▼▼▼▼ NV Bright golden brown; lovely young cold tea, tea-leaf varietal aromas flowing without a break into the palate, where the spirit is harmonious and does not threaten the wonderful tokay flavour. **rating:** 94

best drinking 2000–2001 **best vintages** NA **drink with** As fine an aperitif as it is a digestif • $15.50

Campbells Liquid Gold Muscat

The sister wine to the Tokay, again featuring relatively fresh material, and again in the style one can drink in generous quantities. Shares the same attractive packaging.

▼▼▼▼▼ NV Orange-brown; classic raisiny/grapey aromas lead into a young Muscat at its very best, with intense raisiny fruit, just a hint of nuttiness, and finishing with clean spirit. **rating:** 90

best drinking 2000–2001 **best vintages** NA **drink with** Walnuts and almonds • $18

Campbells Merchant Prince Muscat

A superbly balanced and constructed Muscat in a distinctly lighter mould than Baileys, Chambers or Morris, the big names of the district. For all that, it has an average age of 25 years, with the oldest component dating back over 60 years. One of those rare Muscats which actually invites a second glass.

▼▼▼▼▼ NV Light to medium brown; intense but fragrant spice and raisin aromas with clean spirit. The palate is remarkably fresh and light given the age of the wine, with raisin, spice, malt and toffee flavours all intermingling, followed by cleansing acidity. **rating:** 94

best drinking 2000–2001 **best vintages** NA **drink with** Coffee, high-quality biscuits • $79.50

Campbells Rutherglen Muscat

Again the second tier of Campbells fortifieds, like the Tokay showing largely unmodified varietal character.

ŢŢŢŢŢ NV Light tawny red; very youthful raisiny fruit aromas, with the spirit fractionally jumpy — quite why, I am not sure. High-toned fruit on the palate adds a haunting edge to the flavour, almost floral. Intriguing and delicious. **rating:** 90

best drinking 2000–2001 **best vintages** NA **drink with** Fruit cake • $15.50

candlebark hill ★★★★

Fordes Lane, Kyneton, Vic 3444 **region** Macedon Ranges
phone (03) 9836 2712 **fax** (03) 9836 2712 **open** By appointment
winemaker David Forster, Llew Knight (Consultant) **production** 600 **est.** 1987
product range ($17–30 CD) Chardonnay, Pinot Noir, Cabernet Merlot, Cabernet Shiraz.
summary Candlebark Hill has been established by David Forster on the northern end of the Macedon Ranges, enjoying magnificent views over the central Victorian countryside north of the Great Dividing Range. The 3.5-hectare vineyard is planted to pinot noir (1.5 hectares) together with 1 hectare each of chardonnay and the three Bordeaux varieties, complete with half a hectare of shiraz and malbec. The quality of the 1997 vintage wines was exemplary, promising much for the future, but no tastings of the 1998 wines.

canobolas-smith ★★★★

Boree Lane, off Cargo Road, Lidster via Orange, NSW 2800 **region** Orange
phone (02) 6365 6113 **fax** (02) 6365 6113 **open** Weekends, public holidays 11–5
winemaker Murray Smith **production** 2500 **est.** 1986
product range ($28 CD) Aurora, Chardonnay, Highland Chardonnay, Pinot Noir, Highland Red, Cabernets, Alchemy (Cabernet blend).
summary After a tentative start with early experimental vintages, Canobolas-Smith has established itself as one of the leading Orange district wineries with its distinctive blue wrap-around labels. Much of the wine is sold from the cellar door, which is well worth a visit. Exports through Australian Prestige Wines to Japan and Peter Weygandt to the US.

Canobolas-Smith Chardonnay

Produced from 2.2 hectares of estate plantings at an elevation of 820 metres on Mount Canobolas. The vines are not irrigated and are grown on red volcanic soils. Each vintage has shown distinct improvement, the '95 and '96 being the best to that point of time, but the '97 towering above those two vintages.

ŢŢŢŢ 1997 Medium yellow-green; the bouquet is clean and attractive, with melon fruit and subtle oak. The wine picks up pace on the very fresh palate, which has impressive citrus and melon fruit and great intensity and length. **rating:** 92

best drinking 2000–2005 **best vintages** '94, '95, '96, '97 **drink with** Pasta • $28

Canobolas-Smith Alchemy

The over-size, striking blue labels may not be to everyone's taste, but they certainly are evocative. So is the name of this wine, a blend of Cabernet Sauvignon, Cabernet Franc, Merlot and Shiraz, disparate parts which come together well.

ŢŢŢŢ 1997 Medium red-purple; the bouquet is a tad hard, with a mix of savoury/cedar/leafy/green aromas. However, the palate offers sweet plummy fruit alongside the characters flowing through from the bouquet; the tannins are balanced and the oak subtle. **rating:** 83

best drinking 2001–2007 **best vintages** NA **drink with** Milk-fed veal • $28

canungra valley vineyards NR

Lamington National Park Road, Canungra Valley, Qld 4275 **region** Other Wineries of Qld
phone (07) 5543 4011 **fax** (07) 5543 4162 **open** 7 days 10–5
winemaker Martin Millard, Ashley Smith, Philippa Hambleton **production** NFP **est.** 1997
product range ($15–29 CD) Picnic range of White, Red, Semillon Chardonnay and Bubbles; Platypus Play range of Chardonnay, Cabernet and Port; Preston Peak range of Sauvignon Blanc, Cabernet Sauvignon; Molly O'Reilly Reserve Chardonnay, Golden Gleam, Emily Rosé.
summary Canungra Valley Vineyards has been established in the hinterland of the Gold Coast with a clear focus on broad-based tourism. Two hectares of vines have been established around the nineteenth century homestead (relocated to the site from its original location in Warrick) but these provide only a small part of the wine offered for sale. In deference to the climate, 70 per cent is chambourcin, the rain and mildrew-resistent hybrid, the remainder being semillon. As the product range makes perfectly obvious, all the wine being offered at this early stage has been purchased from other winemakers. On the other hand, Canungra Valley offers a great deal of natural beauty for the general tourist.

cape bouvard   NR

Mount John Road, Mandurah, WA 6210   **region** South West Coast
phone (08) 9739 1360 **fax** (08) 9739 1360 **open** 7 days 10–5
winemaker Gary Grierson **production** 2000 **est.** 1990
product range ($13–20 CD) Chenin Blanc, Dry White, Tuart Shiraz, Cabernet Sauvignon, Port.
summary Doggerel poet-cum-winemaker Gary Grierson draws upon 1 hectare of estate plantings but also purchases grapes from other growers for the new Cape Bouvard label. The few wines tasted have been light but inoffensive.

cape clairault   ★★★★

Henry Road, Willyabrup, WA 6280   **region** Margaret River
phone (08) 9755 6225 **fax** (08) 9755 6229 **open** 7 days 10–5
winemaker Ian Lewis, Peter Stark **production** 8000 **est.** 1976
product range ($13–22 CD) Under the Cape Clairault label: Sauvignon Blanc, Unwooded Chardonnay, Semillon Sauvignon Blanc, Riesling, Claireau (sweet white), Clairault (Cabernet blend); under the second Cape label, Cape White, Cape Rosé, Cape Late Harvest and Cape Red.
summary Ian and Ani Lewis have been joined by two of their sons and, in consequence, have not only decided not to sell the business but to double its size, with winery capacity being almost doubled from 85 tonnes to 150 tonnes. Notwithstanding increasing production, demand for the wines is so great that Cape Clairault has withdrawn from export to concentrate on the local market. A vineyard specialty is guinea fowl, not to be eaten (I think) but to control grasshopper plagues.

cape jaffa wines   NR

Limestone Coast Road, Cape Jaffa, SA 5276   **region** Mount Benson and Robe
phone (08) 8768 5053 **fax** (08) 8768 5040 **open** 7 days 10–5
winemaker Derek Hooper **production** 12 000 **est.** 1993
product range ($14.40–18 CD) Unwooded Chardonnay (McLaren Vale), Semillon Sauvignon Blanc, Barrel Fermented Chardonnay (Mount Benson and Padthaway), Shiraz (McLaren Vale) Cabernet Sauvignon (Mount Benson).
summary Cape Jaffa is the first of the Mount Benson wineries to come into production, albeit with most of the initial releases coming from other regions. Ultimately all of the wines will come from the substantial estate plantings of 20 hectares, which include the four major Bordeaux red varieties, shiraz, chardonnay, sauvignon blanc and semillon. It is a joint venture between the Hooper and Fowler families, and the winery (built of local paddock rock) has been designed to allow eventual expansion to1000 tonnes, or 70 000 cases.

capel vale   ★★★★

Lot 5 Stirling Estate, Mallokup Road, Capel, WA 6271   **region** Geographe
phone (08) 9727 1986 **fax** (08) 9727 1904 **open** 7 days 10–4
winemaker Rob Bowen, Krister Jonsson **production** 90 000 **est.** 1979
product range ($10.50–48 R) CV 'Bistro' range of Chenin, Unwooded Chardonnay, Sauvignon Blanc Chardonnay, Pinot Noir, Shiraz, Cabernets Merlot; Capel Vale 'Fine Dining' Riesling, Verdelho, Sauvignon Blanc Semillon, Chardonnay, Merlot, Shiraz, Cabernet Sauvignon; 'Reserve Connoisseur' range of Whispering Hill Riesling, Seven Day Road Sauvignon Blanc, Frederick Chardonnay, Kinaird Shiraz and Howecroft; Tawny Port.
summary Capel Vale continues to expand its viticultural empire, its contract-grape sources and its marketing, the last through the recent introduction of a series of vineyard or similarly named super-premium wines. Against the run of play, as it were, the most successful of these super-premiums are the red wines, for I have long admired the elegance and finesse of the Capel Vale whites. The strong marketing focus the company has always had is driven by its indefatigable owner, Dr Peter Pratten, who has developed export markets throughout Europe, the US and Asia.

Capel Vale WA Riesling

Over the long term Riesling has been one of the best wines in the Capel Vale portfolio, but, typically for the estate, is far from consistent.
▼▼▼▼ 1999 Light to medium yellow-green; the bouquet is of light to medium intensity, with a mix of floral and lime aromas. The mid-weight palate has lime and passionfruit flavours, good length and equally good balance.

rating: 88

best drinking 2002–2009 **best vintages** '86, '87, '91, '92, '93, '95, '96, '99 **drink with** Caesar salad • $16

Capel Vale Whispering Hill Riesling

First produced under the top Reserve label in 1996, and drawn from Capel Vale's Whispering Hill Vineyard at Mount Barker. Particularly powerful wines were made in 1997 and 1998.

▼▼▼▼♈ **1998** Light green-yellow; powerful, bottle-developed lime/kerosene aromas are followed by a palate with abundant flavour and character; has great depth but is quite idiosyncratic, particularly its precocity. **rating:** 90

best drinking 2000–2003 **best vintages** '97, '98 **drink with** Thai cuisine • $21

Capel Vale Sauvignon Blanc Semillon

Typically a complex blend of both region and variety, the regions taking in Mount Barker, Pemberton and Capel; Sauvignon Blanc normally constitutes two-thirds of the blend.

▼▼▼♈ **1999** Light green-yellow; the moderately intense bouquet is clean, with crisp mineral/herb aromas. The palate is quite tight, with more of those crisp, mineral characters, finishing with good acidity. **rating:** 83

best drinking 2000–2002 **best vintages** NA **drink with** Shellfish • $16

Capel Vale Verdelho

Little to be said: the ubiquitous Verdelho is everywhere, making wines which are as hard to praise as they are to damn.

▼▼▼♈ **1999** Light to medium yellow-green; the bouquet is clean but, as with the palate, rather bland and soft, all adding up to a pleasant but unremarkable commercial wine. **rating:** 82

best drinking Drink now **best vintages** NA **drink with** Takeaway • $16

Capel Vale CV Unwooded Chardonnay

Drawn from the same spread of vineyard sources utilised by Capel Vale in making its conventional (i.e. wooded) Chardonnays, and neatly puts an argument that regional blending adds to complexity. Certainly one of the better unwooded Chardonnays on the market.

▼▼▼▼ **1999** Light green-yellow; a highly fragrant bouquet with a mix of melon, white peach and citrus flows logically into a fresh and lively palate with nice length and balance. **rating:** 85

best drinking 2000–2002 **best vintages** NA **drink with** Terrine of salmon • $15

Capel Vale Howecroft Merlot

In prior vintages the premium Howecroft has been a Cabernet-dominant blend with Merlot; in 1997 it is a varietal Merlot. Like the Kinnaird Shiraz, presented in a dreadnought-class bottle.

▼▼▼▼♈ **1997** Medium to full red-purple; a concentrated, smooth bouquet with a mix of berry, cedar and cigar box aromas flows into a smooth, harmonious palate with excellent overall balance and integration of fruit, oak and tannins. **rating:** 91

best drinking 2002–2012 **best vintages** '95, '97 **drink with** Rare eye fillet • $48

cape mentelle ★★★★★

Off Wallcliffe Road, Margaret River, WA 6285 **region** Margaret River
phone (08) 9757 3266 **fax** (08) 9757 3233 **open** 7 days 10–4.30
winemaker John Durham **production** 50 000 **est.** 1970
product range ($15.35–49.80 R) Chardonnay, Semillon Sauvignon Blanc, Georgiana, Marmaduke, Cabernet Sauvignon, Cabernet Merlot, Shiraz, Zinfandel, Trinders Cabernet Merlot.
summary Notwithstanding majority ownership by Veuve Clicquot, David Hohnen remains very much in command of one of Australia's foremost medium-sized wineries. Exceptional marketing skills and wine of the highest quality, with the back-up of New Zealand's Cloudy Bay, are a potent combination. The Chardonnay and Semillon Sauvignon Blanc are among Australia's best, the potent Shiraz usually superb, and the berry/spicy Zinfandel makes one wonder why this grape is not as widespread in Australia as it is in California.

Cape Mentelle Semillon Sauvignon Blanc

Part of the Cape Mentelle portfolio since 1985, and is consistently one of the outstanding examples of its style.

▼▼▼▼▼ **1999** Light to medium yellow-green; the usual rich, gooseberry, passionfruit and nectarine aromas with perfectly balanced oak. As ever, plenty of flavour and weight, with balanced varietal character and subtle oak. **rating:** 94

best drinking 1999–2001 **best vintages** '85, '88, '91, '93, '95, '96, '97, '98, '99 **drink with** Fish, Asian cuisine • $21.60

Cape Mentelle Chardonnay

First made in 1988 and immediately established itself as another classic. The 1990 vintage was selected for British Airways First Class; each succeeding year has reached new heights. These are wines of exceptional complexity, Chardonnays made by a red winemaker (but in the best possible way). The 1993 won the George Mackey Award for best wine exported from Australia in 1994; subsequent vintages have all been in the same class.

▼▼▼▼▼ 1998 Medium to full straw-green; the bouquet is complex, with a mix of barrel-ferment and malolactic-ferment aromas; creamy, nutty and figgy. As ever, great texture and oak handling. A long finish. **rating:** 95

best drinking 2000–2010 **best vintages** '90, '91, '92, '93, '94, '95, '96, '97, '98 **drink with** Tasmanian salmon • $31.50

Cape Mentelle Shiraz

Made its debut in 1981, and over the intervening years has produced some spectacular wines which — to my palate at least — have not infrequently outclassed the Cabernet Sauvignon. The wines typically show wonderful spice, game and liquorice characters reminiscent of the Rhône Valley. Since 1986 a small percentage of Grenache has been included in some years.

▼▼▼▼▽ 1998 Medium to full red-purple; complex, concentrated plum, liquorice and spice aromas on the bouquet are followed by a similar array of sweet, lush, complex flavours on the palate, finishing with fine tannins. Another in a series of lovely wines. **rating:** 93

best drinking 2003–2013 **best vintages** '86, '88, '90, '91, '93, '94, '96, '97, '98 **drink with** Stir-fried Asian beef • $28.10

Cape Mentelle Zinfandel

Also made its first appearance in 1981, a direct reflection of David Hohnen's early winemaking experiences in California. Of exceptional quality, it remains the only Zinfandel worth mentioning in Australia; it is most surprising that it has not encouraged others to try.

▼▼▼▼ 1998 Medium to full red-purple; fragrant mint and plum fruit with a hint of vanilla lead into a chewy palate with rich fruit appearing early, then lingering tannins. **rating:** 89

best drinking 2000–2005 **best vintages** '86, '87, '91, '92, '93, '94, '95, '97, '98 **drink with** Rare char-grilled rump steak • $32.30

capercaillie ★★★

Londons Road, Lovedale, NSW 2325 **region** Lower Hunter Valley
phone (02) 4990 2904 **fax** (02) 4991 1886 **open** Mon–Sat 9–5, Sun 10–5
winemaker Alasdair Sutherland **production** 6000 **est.** 1995
product range ($17–25 CD) Watervale Riesling, Gewurztraminer, Semillon, Hunter Valley Chardonnay, Chardonnay, Dessert Style Gewurztraminer, Hunter Valley Chambourcin, Orange Highlands Merlot, Clan (Cabernet blend from Orange and Coonawarra), C Sparkling (Red).
summary The former Dawson Estate, now run by Hunter Valley veteran Alasdair Sutherland (no relation to Neil Sutherland of Sutherland Estate). The Capercaillie wines, and the Chardonnays in particular, are always extremely full flavoured and generous.

capogreco estate NR

Riverside Avenue, Mildura, Vic 3500 **region** Murray Darling
phone (03) 5023 3060 **open** Mon–Sat 10–6
winemaker Bruno Capogreco **production** NFP **est.** 1976
product range ($8–12 CD) Riesling, Moselle, Shiraz-Mataro, Cabernet Sauvignon, Claret, Rosé, Fortifieds.
summary Italian-owned and run, the wines are a blend of Italian and Australian Riverland influences; the herb-infused Rosso Dolce is a particularly good example of its kind.

captain's paddock NR

Booie–Crawford Road, Kingaroy, Qld 4610 **region** South Burnett and Other Wineries of Qld
phone (07) 4162 4534 **fax** (07) 4162 4502 **open** Weekends 9–4
winemaker Adam Chapman **production** 400 **est.** 1995
product range ($10–15 CD) Chardonnay, Shiraz, Captain's Red (semi-sweet).
summary Don and Judy McCallum planted the first hectare of vineyard in 1995, followed by a further 3 hectares in 1996, focusing on shiraz and chardonnay. It is a family affair; the mudbrick cellar-door building was made with bricks crafted by Don McCallum and Judy's screen printing adorns the tables and chairs and printed linen for sale to the public. Their two children are both sculptors, with works on display at the winery. Captain's Paddock is fully licensed, offering either light platters or full dishes incorporating local produce. Meals are served either inside or alfresco in the courtyard, with its views over the Booie Ranges.

carabooda estate NR

297 Carabooda Road, Carabooda, WA 6033 **region** Swan District
phone (08) 9407 5283 **fax** (08) 9407 5283 **open** 7 days 10–6
winemaker Terry Ord **production** 2000 **est.** 1989
product range ($12.50–18 CD) Sauvignon Blanc, Chenin Blanc, Shiraz, Cabernet Shiraz, Cabernet Sauvignon.
summary 1989 is the year of establishment given by Terry Ord, but it might as well have been 1979 (when he made his first wine) or 1981 (when he and wife Simonne planted their first vines). But it has been a slowly, slowly exercise, with production from the 3 hectares of estate plantings now supplemented by purchased grapes, the first public release not being made until mid-1994. As at March 1999 red wines from the 1994 and 1995 vintages were available ex cellar door, the whites from 1998. Since that time production has risen significantly.

carbunup estate ★★★

Bussel Highway, Carbunup, WA 6280 **region** Margaret River
phone (08) 9755 1111 **open** 7 days 10–5
winemaker Robert Credaro **production** NFP **est.** 1988
product range ($12–16 CD) Under the premium Vasse River Wines label: Chardonnay, Semillon, Sauvignon Blanc; under Carbunup Estate label: Verdelho, Shiraz.
summary A relative newcomer, selling part of the grapes produced from the 18 hectares of vineyards but keeping part for release under the Carbunup Estate and Vasse River labels — strikingly different in design, and giving no clue that they emanate from the same winery. It has had immediate success with its white wines and in particular its Chardonnay and Semillon.

🐝 cargo road wines NR

Cargo Road, Orange, NSW 2800 **region** Orange
phone (02) 6365 6100 **fax** (02) 6365 6001 **open** Weekends 11–5
winemaker James Sweetapple **production** 1200 **est.** 1983
product range ($14–22.50 CD) Riesling, Gewürztraminer, Sauvignon Blanc, Merlot, Zinfandel, Cabernet Merlot.
summary This is one of the oldest vineyards in Orange, although it has been extended by recent plantings, and now comprises zinfandel (3 hectares), sauvignon blanc (2.5 hectares), merlot (1.4 hectares), cabernet sauvignon (1.3 hectares), riesling (1.5 hectares) and gewurztraminer (0.4 hectare).

carindale wines NR

Palmers Lane, Pokolbin, NSW 2321 **region** Lower Hunter Valley
phone (02) 4998 7665 **fax** (02) 4998 7665 **open** Fri–Mon 10–4.30
winemaker Brian Walsh (Contract) **production** 1500 **est.** 1996
product range ($18–25 CD) Chardonnay, Blackthorn (Cabernet blend).
summary Carindale is still in its infancy, drawing upon 2 hectares of chardonnay, 1.2 hectares of cabernet franc and 0.4 hectares of merlot (together with few muscat vines). At this juncture the wines are available only through cellar door and by mail order.

🐝 carlei estate NR

1 Albert Road, Upper Beaconsfield, Vic 3808 **region** Port Phillip Zone
phone (03) 5944 4599 **fax** (03) 5944 4599 **open** Weekends 11–5
winemaker Sergio Carlei **production** 400 **est.** 1998
product range ($25–55 CD) Chardonnay, Pinot Noir, Shiraz.
summary Sergio Carlei has established 3 hectares of vineyard using biodynamic and organic methods. The tiny production is sold through the cellar door and by mail order only.

carosa NR

310 Houston Street, Mount Helena, WA 6082 **region** Perth Hills
phone (08) 9572 1603 **fax** (08) 9572 1604 **open** Weekends, holidays 11–5 or by appointment
winemaker James Elson **production** 450 **est.** 1984
product range ($13–18 CD) Chardonnay, Summer White, Pinot Noir, Cabernet Merlot, Sparkling Pinot Noir, Pinot Noir, Cabernet Merlot, Old Tawny Port, White Port.
summary Very limited production and small-scale winemaking result in wines which can only be described as rustic, but which sell readily enough into the local market. Winemaker Jim Elson has extensive eastern Australia winemaking experience (with Seppelt) so should succeed. Almost all of the wine is sold through cellar door and by mailing list, but there is limited retail distribution through McLaren Vale Cellars, Canberra.

casa fontana   NR

4 Cook Street, Lutana, Tas 7009 **region** Southern Tasmania
phone (03) 6272 3180 **open** Not
winemaker Mark Fontana, Steve Lubiana (Contract) **production** 200 **est.** 1994
product range ($20–22.50 ML) Riesling, Chardonnay, Pinot Noir.
summary Mark Fontana and his Japanese wife Shige planted their first pinot noir in 1994 and over the following two years expanded the vineyard to its present level of 2.6 hectares, 1 hectare each of pinot noir and chardonnay, and 0.6 hectares of riesling. Mark Fontana is a metallurgist with Pasminco and came into grape growing through his love of fine wine. The '98 Pinot Noir, tasted ex barrel, was very rich and concentrated, with lovely plum and cherry fruit.

Casa Fontana The Dromedary Pinot Noir

A four-barrel selection which might well have been labelled as Reserve; the lesser barrels were sold in bulk.
♥♥♥♥ 1998 Vivid purple-red; vibrant, juicy, almost essencey blackberry and plum fruit floods the bouquet; the palate is rich and sensually smooth; it will develop great complexity with age.   **rating: 87**
best drinking 2002–2006 **best vintages** NA **drink with** Braised quail   •$22.50

cascabel

Rogers Road, Willunga, SA 5172 **region** McLaren Vale
phone (08) 8557 4434 **fax** (08) 8557 4435 **open** By appointment
winemaker Susana Fernandez, Duncan Ferguson **production** 1500 **est.** 1998
product range ($14–28 R) Eden Valley Riesling, Fleurieu Sauvignon Blanc, Adelaide Hills Pinot Noir, Shiraz, McLaren Vale Grenache Shiraz, Sparkling Shiraz.
summary Cascabel's proprietors, Duncan Ferguson and Susana Fernandez, established Cascabel when they purchased a property at Willunga on the Fleurieu Peninsula and planted it to roussanne, tempranillo, graciano, monastrel, grenache, shiraz and viognier. The choice of grapes reflects the winemaking experience of the proprietors in Australia, the Rhône Valley, Bordeaux, Italy, Germany and New Zealand — and also Susana Fernandez's birthplace, Spain. Both are fully qualified and intend to move the production base steadily towards the style of the Rhône Valley, Rioja and other parts of Spain. In the meantime the 4000-case capacity winery which they erected on site prior to the 1998 vintage is being kept busy with grapes sourced from areas throughout South Australia. The initial releases left no doubt that the proprietors know what they are doing, and it will be interesting to watch the development of the wines from the estate plantings. Exports to the US and Japan.

Cascabel Eden Valley Riesling

Made from grapes purchased from a single vineyard with dry-grown, low-yielding 40-year-old vines. Production varies between 200 and 400 cases.
♥♥♥♥♡ 1999 Bright, light green-yellow; the bouquet has a mix of minerally, chalky and lime juice aromas in classic Eden Valley style. The palate is well made and balanced, with mineral and lime flavours running through a long, intense finish.   **rating: 91**
best drinking 2000–2009 **best vintages** '99 **drink with** Stir-fried prawns   •$16

Cascabel Adelaide Hills Pinot Noir

Produced from a single vineyard near Summertown in one of the cooler parts of the Adelaide Hills.
♥♥♥♡ 1998 Light to medium red-purple; there is pleasant, gentle sweet cherry fruit on the bouquet and on the palate; given the sophisticated winemaking methods used, the wine is curiously empty on entry to the mouth. Perhaps it was in one of those sulky periods through which Pinots are prone to pass when tasted.   **rating: 84**
best drinking 2000–2004 **best vintages** NA **drink with** Carpaccio of smoked kangaroo   •$21

Cascabel Fleurieu Peninsula Shiraz

570 cases made from a vineyard near Victor Harbour and matured in a mix of new (30 per cent) and older French oak.
♥♥♥♥♡ 1998 Full red-purple; rich, dark cherry, plum and liquorice fruit aromas are supported by subtle oak. The full, powerful and fleshy palate has a lovely core of fruit surrounded by soft, almost silky, tannins and excellently balanced and integrated oak.   **rating: 93**
best drinking 2003–2013 **best vintages** '98 **drink with** Ox cheek   •$25

casella ★★★☆

Wakely Road, Yenda, NSW 2681 **region** Riverina
phone (02) 6968 1346 **fax** (02) 6968 1196 **open** Not
winemaker Alan Kennett **production** 1.2 million **est.** 1969
product range ($4.95–19.50 R) Chardonnay, Shiraz, Cabernet Sauvignon; under the Carramar Estate label Semillon Sauvignon Blanc, Chardonnay, Unwooded Chardonnay, Botrytis Semillon, Merlot, Shiraz, Shiraz Cabernet, Cabernet Sauvignon; also Cottlers Bridge at significantly lower prices.
summary Casella is typical of the new wave sweeping through the Riverina. It draws upon 285 hectares of estate vineyards, selling much of its wine in bulk or as cleanskin bottled wine to other producers, but also marketing a range of varietals under the Carramar Estate label. Casella is part of the Semillon of the Riverina group (promoting dry Semillon), and overall its wines offer good value for money. Predictably, the Botrytis Semillon is the outstanding release. Retail distribution through the eastern States and South Australia; exports to the US, the UK, Japan and New Zealand.

Casella Carramar Estate Chardonnay

Made in the typical, fast-developing Riverina style, with the generous use of oak. In this instance the wine is said to be barrel-fermented for three months in a mix of French and American oak.
▼▼▼▽ 1999 Deep, glowing green-yellow; the bouquet is complex in a heavy hitting fashion, vaguely reminiscent of some of the more baroque New Zealand Chardonnays. The no-holds-barred palate enthusiastically delivers more of the same. The only option is to relax and enjoy it. **rating: 82**
best drinking Drink now **best vintages** NA **drink with** KFC • $9.95

Casella Carramar Estate Botrytis Semillon

Fully botrytised semillon is picked at 23° baumé and cold-fermented at 12°C in stainless steel. An excellent example of Riverina Botrytis Semillon, the '97 winning the trophy for Best New South Wales Sweet Wine at the 1998 New South Wales Wine Awards.
▼▼▼▼ 1998 Golden yellow; a rich bouquet with peach, cumquat and mandarin aromas; the palate is similarly ripe and luscious, with peach, cumquat and honey, but is just a little simple, and you can see why this vintage has never won a gold medal, instead harvesting a string of silvers. **rating: 85**
best drinking 2000–2003 **best vintages** '97 **drink with** Any rich dessert • $14.95

Casella Shiraz

A richly flavoured and oaked wine.
▼▼▼▼ 1999 Medium to full red-purple; the bouquet is quite rich and clean with berry fruit and some smoky oak. Smoky bacon/resinous oak leads the way on the palate, although there is plenty of fruit and tannin swimming around under the oak. **rating: 86**
best drinking 2001–2004 **best vintages** NA **drink with** Picnic barbecues • $19.50

Casella Cottlers Bridge Shiraz

Notwithstanding its station and low price, this wine won a bronze medal at Brisbane and a gold medal at the Cowra Show, both in 1999. It went on to win the Australian Wine & Brandy Corporation Perpetual Trophy at the Royal Sydney Wine Show, awarded to the best red wine under $15.
▼▼▼▼ 1999 Medium red-purple; a leafy berry bouquet gives way to a pretty wine on the palate, quite rich and with plenty of soft juicy berry fruit and — thankfully — only a touch of oak. **rating: 87**
best drinking Drink now **best vintages** NA **drink with** Pasta • $14.95

cassegrain ★★★☆

Hastings River Winery, Fernbank Creek Road, Port Macquarie, NSW 2444 **region** Hastings River
phone (02) 6583 7777 **fax** (02) 6584 0354 **open** 7 days 9–5
winemaker John Cassegrain **production** 55 000 **est.** 1980
product range ($11.95–28.95 CD) Semillon, Sauvignon Blanc, Unwooded Chardonnay, Oaked Chardonnay, Verdelho, Traminer Riesling, Rosé, White Pinot, Chambourcin, Shiraz, Cabernet Merlot, Merlot, Cabernet Sauvignon; Five Mile Hollow Semillon Chardonnay, White, Classic Red; The Premiere Collection series of Fromenteau Reserve Chardonnay, Reserve Semillon, Reserve Chambourcin, Maximus; also a selection of sparkling, dessert and fortifieds.
summary A very substantial operation based in the Hastings Valley on the north coast of New South Wales. In earlier years it drew fruit from many parts of Australia but is now entirely supplied by the 154 hectares of estate plantings which offer 14 varieties, including the rare chambourcin, a French-bred cross. Exports to the UK, the US, Japan, Switzerland, Germany, The Netherlands, Canada and Asia.

Cassegrain Fromenteau Chardonnay

Compelling proof that the Hastings Valley, on the north coast of New South Wales, can produce Chardonnay of exceptional quality. Initially sourced from a single vineyard bearing the Fromenteau name, but is now used simply to denote the best Chardonnay made each year, always in limited quantities (between 650 and 950 cases).

TTTT 1996 Full yellow-green; the bouquet is very smooth and round, with honeyed fruit, the palate offering similarly luscious flavour, with peach, honeycomb and malt backed by a touch of toasty oak.　　**rating:** 86

best drinking 1999–2001　**best vintages** '89, '91, '93, '95, '96　**drink with** Rich chicken or veal　• $22.95

Cassegrain Maximus XCVII Cabernet Blend

One of a new range of flagship wines from Cassegrain, primarily a blend of Cabernet Franc, Cabernet Sauvignon and Malbec grown on various vineyards in the Hastings River region.

TTTTY 1997 Medium red-purple, slightly opaque. Soft, ripe berry/dark chocolate/blackcurrant aromas introduce a most attractive wine, with soft, dark berry, chocolate and more savoury fruit flavours. The tannins are fine, the oak well-balanced and integrated.　　**rating:** 90

best drinking 2001–2006　**best vintages** NA　**drink with** Sautéed kidneys　• $28.95

🐛 castagna vineyard　　NR

Ressom Lane, Beechworth, Vic 3747　**region** North East Victoria
phone (03) 5728 2888　**fax** (03) 5728 2898　**open** Not
winemaker Julian Castagna　**production** 2000　**est.** 1997
product range ($23–27 ML) Allegro Rosé, Genesis Syrah.
summary The elegantly labelled wines of Castagna will ultimately come from 2.5 hectares of estate shiraz and viognier (the latter making up 15 per cent of the total). Winemaker Julian Castagna is intent on making wines which reflect the terroir as closely as possible, declining to use cultured yeast or filtration. The initial release of 1998 Genesis Syrah was in fact made from grapes purchased from a nextdoor neighbour, but all future wines will be estate-grown.

Castagna Vineyard Genesis Syrah

Initially intended as an experiment to validate the minimalist winemaking approach of Julian Castagna and not for commercial sale. Reaction to the wine was sufficiently positive to lead to its release.

TTTT 1998 Medium to full purple-red; the bouquet is clean, with attractive, warm spicy fruit while the palate has a most interesting, soft texture; very light tannins seem to shorten the finish somewhat, but an attractive wine nonetheless.　　**rating:** 87

best drinking 2000–2005　**drink with** Braised rabbit　• $27

castle rock estate　　★★★★

Porongurup Road, Porongurup, WA 6324　**region** Great Southern
phone (08) 9853 1035　**fax** (08) 9853 1010　**open** Mon–Fri 10–4, weekends and public holidays 10–5
winemaker Michael Staniford　**production** 5000　**est.** 1983
product range ($14.50–22 CD) Riesling, Late Harvest Riesling, Great Southern White, Chardonnay, Pinot Noir, Cabernet Merlot, Merlot Cabernet Franc, Cabernet Sauvignon, Muscat Liqueur.
summary An exceptionally beautifully sited vineyard and cellar-door sales area with sweeping vistas from the Porongurups, operated by the Diletti family. The standard of viticulture is very high, and the site itself ideally situated (quite apart from its beauty). The Rieslings have always been elegant and handsomely repaid time in bottle. In the most recent vintages the other wines of Castle Rock have improved considerably, with far greater weight and flavour than hitherto.

cathcart ridge estate　　NR

Moyston Road, Cathcart via Ararat, Vic 3377　**region** Grampians
phone (03) 5352 1997　**fax** (03) 5352 1558　**open** 7 days 10–5
winemaker David Farnhill, Simon Clayfield　**production** NA　**est.** 1977
product range ($9–60 CD) Estate Reserve Chardonnay, Grampians Riesling, Shiraz, Merlot, Cabernet Sauvignon; Rhymney Reef Colombard Chenin Blanc, Sauvignon Blanc, Shiraz, Shiraz Cabernet, Merlot, Cabernet Merlot, Cabernet Sauvignon, Old Tawny Port; and, at the bottom of the price range, Mount Ararat Dry White, Pinot Noir, Shiraz.
summary In 1999 sought significant funds from the public by a prospectus in order to provide the finance for a significant expansion programme of both vineyards and the winery. I am uncertain of the outcome.

catherine vale vineyard ★★★☆

656 Milbrodale Road, Bulga, NSW 2330 **region** Lower Hunter Valley
phone (02) 6579 1334 **fax** (02) 6579 1334 **open** Weekends and public holidays 10–5 or by appointment
winemaker John Hordern (Contract) **production** 1000 **est.** 1994
product range ($11–14.50 CD) Semillon, Chardonnay, Semillon Chardonnay.
summary Former schoolteachers Bill and Wendy Lawson have established Catherine Vale as a not-so-idle retirement venture. Both were involved in school athletics and sports programmes, handy training for do-it-yourself viticulturists. Most of the grapes from the 3.5-hectare vineyard are sold to contract-winemaker John Hordern; a small proportion is vinified for the Catherine Vale label.

celtic farm NR

Level 1, Rear 351 Whitehorse Road, Balwyn, Vic 3103 **region** Other Wineries of Victoria
phone (03) 9836 2666 **fax** (03) 9836 2888 **open** Not
winemaker Gerry Taggert **production** 4900 **est.** 1997
product range ($18–29 R) South Block Riesling (Clare Valley), The Gridge Pinot Grigio (King Valley), Raisin Hell Rutherglen Muscat, Far Canal Shiraz (Coonawarra).
summary Yet another Warehouse winery, the brainchild of a marketing and sales team of Mark McKenzie and Gerry Taggert. The proprietors say, 'Celtic Farm is produced from classic varieties selected from Australia's premium wine regions and made with a total commitment to quality. While we have a desire to pay homage to our Celtic (drinking) heritage we are also acutely aware that wine should be about enjoyment, fun and not taking yourself too seriously'.

chain of ponds ★★★★☆

Adelaide Road, Gumeracha, SA 5233 **region** Adelaide Hills
phone (08) 8389 1415 **fax** (08) 8389 1877 **open** 7 days 10.30–4.30
winemaker Caj Amadio (Contract) **production** 8000 **est.** 1993
product range ($10–29 CD) Riesling, Semillon, Sauvignon Blanc Semillon, Special Release Sauvignon Blanc, Chardonnay, Novello Rosso, Pinot Noir, Ledge Shiraz, Amadeus Cabernet Sauvignon, Diva Pinot Chardonnay.
summary Caj and Genny Amadio are the largest growers in the Adelaide Hills, with 100 hectares of vineyards established on a Scott-Henry trellis producing 1000 tonnes of grapes a year, almost all sold to Penfolds, but with a small amount made into wine for sale under the Chain of Ponds label. The first vintage was 1993, and the wines first offered for sale in 1995. The full-flavoured white wines have enjoyed consistent show success. The Vineyard Balcony restaurant provides lunches on weekends and public holidays.

Chain of Ponds Semillon Sauvignon Blanc

First produced in 1997, and has headed its class at the Adelaide Hills Wine Show each year since then.
 1999 Light green-yellow; the initially shy bouquet progressively unfolded with gently lemony/grassy fruit. Asserts its class in the mouth with lovely mid-palate fruit and exceptionally good length.   **rating:** 94
best drinking 2000–2004 **best vintages** '97, '98, '99 **drink with** Richer seafood dishes • $17

Chain Of Ponds Chardonnay

Has the winemaker's fingerprints all over it, with the full gamut of winemaking techniques being used. Barrel-ferment, lees contact and malolactic fermentation are all evident, but there is the fruit intensity there to support these inputs. Never less than good, often outstanding. Highly rated in the *Wine Spectator* Top 100 in 1999.
1998 Medium green-yellow; a supremely stylish and smooth bouquet with perfect integration of fruit and oak. Nice citrussy/lemony fruit on the palate, which is long and harmonious; once again, the oak has been judged to perfection. Topped the very strong Chardonnay class at the 1999 Adelaide Wine Show.   **rating:** 93
best drinking 2000–2006 **best vintages** '94, '97, '98 **drink with** Veal saltimbocca • $28

chalk hill ★★★☆

Field Street, McLaren Vale, SA 5171 **region** McLaren Vale
phone (08) 8556 2121 **fax** (08) 8556 2121 **open** Not
winemaker Contract **production** 2500 **est.** 1973
product range ($22–25 CD) Shiraz, Cabernet Sauvignon.
summary Chalk Hill is in full flight again, drawing upon the vineyards of grape-growing owners John and Di Harvey, who acquired Chalk Hill in 1996.

Chalk Hill Shiraz

Produced from high-quality McLaren Vale shiraz which has been allowed to ripen to 14.5° baumé (producing 14.5 degrees alcohol) and matured in American oak. The power and density of the fruit happily accommodates that oak.

TTTT 1998 Medium to full red-purple; powerful earthy, dark, savoury berry shiraz fruit on the bouquet is followed by masses of black cherry and chocolate fruit on the palate; overall, seems to have been slightly over-extracted; the oak is balanced, however. **rating:** 85

best drinking 2003–2013 **best vintages** '97, '98 **drink with** Rich game dishes • $25

Chalk Hill Cabernet Sauvignon

Both the 1997 and 1998 Cabernet Sauvignon seem to run along the same pattern as the Shiraz of those two years, the '98s being less approachable and needing more time than the '97s.

TTTY 1998 Medium red-purple; the bouquet is clean, moderately intense, with attractive blackberry fruit aromatics. However, the palate is massively extracted, with huge tannins surrounding the great volume of fruit hidden in the forest. Needs 20 years. **rating:** 84

best drinking 2008–2018 **best vintages** NA **drink with** Leave it in the cellar • $24

chambers rosewood

Barkley Street, Rutherglen, Vic 3685 **region** Rutherglen and Glenrowan
phone (02) 6032 8641 **fax** (02) 6032 8101 **open** Mon–Sat 9–5, Sun 11–5
winemaker Bill Chambers **production** 10 000 **est.** 1858
product range ($8–75 CD) A wide range of table wines, including such rarities as a Riesling and Gouias blend, Blue Imperial (which is in fact Cinsaut) and a wide range of fortified wines. The supremely great wines are the Rare Tokay and Rare Muscat, and the very good Special Muscat and Special Tokay. These are now offered in 375-ml bottles at prices which are starting to reflect their intrinsic value, and are rather higher than the prices for the same wines when last offered in 750-ml bottles.
summary The winery rating is given for the Muscats and Tokays and is in fact a compromise between the Special Muscat and Tokay (rated 'grand' under the Rutherglen Classification system) and the Rare wines, which are on a level all of their own, somewhere higher than five stars. The chief virtue of the table wines is that they are cheap.

chapel hill

Chapel Hill Road, McLaren Vale, SA 5171 **region** McLaren Vale
phone (08) 8323 8429 **fax** (08) 8323 9245 **open** 7 days 12–5
winemaker Pam Dunsford (Consultant), Angela Meaney **production** 51 000 **est.** 1979
product range ($14.95–33 CD) Eden Valley Riesling, Unwooded Chardonnay, Reserve Chardonnay, Verdelho, McLaren Vale Shiraz, The Vicar (Cabernet Shiraz), Reserve Cabernet Shiraz, McLaren Vale/Coonawarra Cabernet Sauvignon, Tawny Port.
summary A winery which, in the 1990s, leapt from obscurity to national prominence after a change of ownership, a very large capital injection, and the installation of Pam Dunsford as consultant winemaker. In the early phases of the growth the wines were superb and, after a period of uncertainty, is coming back towards its best. Exports to the UK, Germany and Switzerland.

Chapel Hill Unwooded Chardonnay

Taking the oak out of Chardonnay is not a magic solution which, through some process of alchemy, produces a better wine. It simply produces a different, more direct style, and the fruit base has to be there. A blend of McLaren Vale, Padthaway and Barossa Valley fruit.

TTTY 1999 Light green-yellow; the bouquet offers melon fruit of light to medium intensity, the palate pleasant mouthfeel and nice length. A clean, well-made wine of above-average quality for this category. **rating:** 84

best drinking 2000–2003 **best vintages** NA **drink with** Pasta, salads • $14.95

Chapel Hill Reserve Chardonnay

Fully deserves the Reserve label. It is sourced from premium vineyards in McLaren Vale, Padthaway and Coonawarra and barrel-fermented and then matured for 11 months in high-quality French oak to produce a wine of great style which is a consistent medal winner in shows.

TTTTY 1998 Medium yellow-green; quite pronounced charry oak is matched by rich, tangy fruit on the bouquet; the palate, similarly, is well balanced, albeit powerful, with lots of depth and structure. **rating:** 90

best drinking 2000–2004 **best vintages** '91, '92, '93, '94, '97, '98 **drink with** Slow-cooked fresh salmon • $23

Chapel Hill Shiraz

Produced from grapes grown on three different vineyard sites in McLaren Vale: Blewitt Springs, Bakers Gully and Kangarilla. These have widely spread ripening dates, and harvest typically extends from late March to early May. The wine is matured for 18 months in 50 per cent French and 50 per cent American oak hogsheads, half new and the remainder second and third use.

▼▼▼▼ 1997 Medium to full purple-red; the bouquet is rich, complex and concentrated with lush dark berry fruit aromas and well-balanced and integrated oak. The palate shows the same excellent balance and structure, finishing with soft tannins. However, it dries out just a fraction on the mid-palate, in contrast to the lush fruit of the bouquet. **rating:** 89

best drinking 2002–2010 **best vintages** '91, '94, '95, '96 **drink with** Grilled calf's liver • $27.50

Chapel Hill McLaren Vale/Coonawarra Cabernet Sauvignon

The '97 is A blend of 79 per cent McLaren Vale and 21 per cent Coonawarra grapes, although the blend does vary slightly from one vintage to the next, matured in a mix of quality French and American oak. Consistently good over the years, peaking with the '92 vintage, which capped a distinguished show career by winning three trophies at the 1994 National Wine Show in Canberra, including Best Table Wine of Show.

▼▼▼▼ 1997 Medium to full red-purple; the bouquet is strongly regional, with that sweet chocolatey fruit so typical of McLaren Vale. The palate moves decidedly towards mint and cassis flavours, and part reflecting the Coonawarra component. As always, well-handled oak, and soft tannins. **rating:** 88

best drinking 2002–2010 **best vintages** '88, '90, '91, '92, '95 **drink with** Marinated beef • $27.50

chapman's creek vineyard NR

RMS 447 Yelverton Road, Willyabrup, WA 6280 **region** Margaret River
phone (08) 9755 7545 **fax** (08) 9755 7571 **open** 7 days 10.30–4.30
winemaker Various Contract **production** 5000 **est.** 1989
product range ($15–26 R) Chenin Blanc, Unoaked Chardonnay, Chardonnay, Merlot, Cabernet Merlot, Tawny Port.
summary Tony Lord is an extremely experienced wine journalist who for many years was editor and part-owner of *Decanter* magazine of the United Kingdom, one of the leaders in the field. He still writes for Australian magazines and newspapers and knows the industry extremely well. Notwithstanding this, he has been positively reclusive about Chapman's Creek Vineyard, which he owns. I have unofficially tasted a number of the wines over the past two years, and those I have tasted have been excellent, fully reflecting the outstanding quality of the Willyabrup subregion of the Margaret River.

charles cimicky ★★★☆

Gomersal Road, Lyndoch, SA 5351 **region** Barossa Valley
phone (08) 8524 4025 **fax** (08) 8524 4772 **open** Tues–Sat 10.30–4.30
winemaker Charles Cimicky **production** 15 000 **est.** 1972
product range ($15–25 CD) Sauvignon Blanc, Chardonnay, Cabernet Franc, Classic Merlot, Cabernet Sauvignon, Signature Shiraz, Old Fireside Tawny Port.
summary These wines are of very good quality, thanks to the lavish (but sophisticated) use of new French oak in tandem with high-quality grapes. The intense, long-flavoured Sauvignon Blanc has been a particularly consistent performer, as has the rich, voluptuous American-oaked Signature Shiraz. Limited retail distribution in South Australia, Victoria, New South Wales and Western Australia, with exports to the UK, the US, Switzerland, Canada, Malaysia and Hong Kong.

charles melton ★★★★★

Krondorf Road, Tanunda, SA 5352 **region** Barossa Valley
phone (08) 8563 3606 **fax** (08) 8563 3422 **open** 7 days 11–5
winemaker Charlie Melton **production** 10 000 **est.** 1984
product range ($16.90–44.90 R) Rosé of Virginia, Grenache, Shiraz, Nine Popes (Shiraz Grenache Mourvedre), Cabernet Sauvignon, Sparkling Red.
summary Charlie Melton, one of the Barossa Valley's great characters, with wife Virginia by his side, makes some of the most eagerly sought à la mode wines in Australia. Inevitably, the Melton empire grew in response to the insatiable demand, with a doubling of estate vineyards to 13 hectares (and the exclusive management and offtake of a further 10 hectares) and the erection of a new barrel store in 1996. The expanded volume has had no adverse effect on the wonderfully rich, sweet and well-made wines. Exports to the UK, Ireland, Switzerland, France, the US and Southeast Asia.

Charles Melton Rosé Of Virginia

One of the most interesting Rosés currently made in Australia, produced from grenache, and presumably a partial by-product of Nine Popes juice run-off. It has much more fruit flavour than a standard Rosé, at least being more a cross between a standard Rosé and a Beaujolais style. Tremendous summer drinking.

▼▼▼▼ 1999 Vivid fuchsia; the bouquet is bright and fresh with hints of earth along with strawberry fruit. The palate is lively and zingy, with a touch of residual sugar as the commercial market wishes; serve chilled. **rating:** 85

best drinking Drink now **best vintages** '97, '98 **drink with** Light Mediterranean dishes • $14.90

Charles Melton Shiraz

Produced from small patches of old low-yielding shiraz scattered across the Barossa Valley, but also showing the sophisticated use of American oak to produce a very modern style.

▼▼▼▼♀ 1998 Full red-purple; rich, smoky/gamey/leathery shiraz aromas marry with attractive vanilla oak on the bouquet. Rich, ripe dark plum fruit with slightly smoky notes, and round, ripe, soft tannins give the wine lovely mouthfeel. Totally seductive. **rating:** 93

best drinking 2001–2011 **best vintages** '95, '96, '98 **drink with** Spiced lamb • $36.80

Charles Melton Nine Popes

A label which is Australia's answer to California's Bonny Doon, where Randall Grahm is the genius pulling the strings. Charlie Melton is no slouch either, as this blend of low-yielding, dry-grown shiraz, grenache and mourvedre handsomely shows. Melton realised the supreme quality of these vines well before most others, and the market has now caught up with his vision.

▼▼▼▼♀ 1998 Medium red-purple; complex, scented, savoury cedar aromas are followed by a medium-bodied palate, with fine-grained tannins and subtle oak; more elegant than lush. **rating:** 91

best drinking 2000–2004 **best vintages** '90, '91, '92, '93, '94, '95, '96, '98 **drink with** Full-blooded Italian cuisine • $36.80

Charles Melton Cabernet Sauvignon

Charles Melton is best known for his Shiraz and Rhône-style reds, but also makes an exceptionally good Cabernet Sauvignon, which he skilfully moulds into the winery style one expects of the label without compromising varietal character.

▼▼▼▼ 1998 Medium red-purple; the bouquet is at the cedary/leafy end of the spectrum but the palate brings sweet berry, mint and a touch of chocolate into play. The tannins are soft, the oak playing a pure support role. **rating:** 89

best drinking 2002–2008 **best vintages** '96 **drink with** Braised ox cheek with demi glaze • $36.80

charles reuben estate   NR

777 Middle Tea Tree Road, Tea Tree, Tas 7017 **region** Southern Tasmania
phone (03) 6268 1702 **fax** (03) 6231 3571 **open** Wed–Sun 10–5
winemaker Tim Krushka **production** 450 **est.** 1990
product range ($15–22 CD) Semillon Sauvignon Blanc, Chardonnay, Riesling, Pinot Noir, Bordeaux-blend red.
summary Charles Reuben Estate has 1.5 hectares of pinot noir, half a hectare of chardonnay and a few rows of riesling in production. It has also planted 1.2 hectares of the four Bordeaux varieties, headed by cabernet sauvignon with a little cabernet franc, merlot and petit verdot, and 0.6 hectare of sauvignon blanc accompanied by a few rows of semillon. The principal wines will be Pinot Noir, Chardonnay, a Bordeaux-blend red and a Sauvignon Blanc Semillon, although there is an element of trial in the plantings to establish which varieties succeed best on the estate.

charles sturt university winery   ★★★☆

Boorooma Street, North Wagga Wagga, NSW 2650 **region** Other Wineries of NSW
phone (02) 6933 2435 **fax** (02) 6933 4072 **open** Mon–Fri 11–5, weekends 11–4
winemaker Greg Gallagher **production** 15 000 **est.** 1977
product range ($10–22 R) The precise composition varies from one release to the next but is divided into two sections: the top-of-the-range Limited Release Series (e.g. Cabernet Sauvignon Shiraz, Cowra Chardonnay, Méthode Champenoise, Cabernet Sauvignon, Botrytis Semillon, Liqueur Port and Liqueur Muscat) and a basic range of lower-priced varietals, including Chardonnay, Traminer Riesling, Sauvignon Blanc Semillon and Cabernet Sauvignon Shiraz.

summary Between 1990 and 1996 winemaking at Charles Sturt University was carried out under the direction of Rodney Hooper, who managed to resolve the dual roles of producing commercial wines and teaching students with consummate skill. Neither the '97 nor '98 vintages seemed to be in the same class as those made by Hooper, although they do offer quite good value at their price points. The wines are exported to the US.

Charles Sturt Chardonnay

Receives restricted maturation in French oak, and is sourced from the University's own plantings at Wagga Wagga, and from Riverina grapes.

ΨΨΨΨ 1998 Light to medium yellow-green; the bouquet is clean and smooth, quite light, but with attractive citrus, nectarine and melon fruit. The very pleasant, smooth and supple palate likewise offers melon and nectarine fruit running through a long finish. **rating: 88**

best drinking 2000–2004 **best vintages** '98 **drink with** Turkey • $12

Charles Sturt McLaren Vale Shiraz

As with many of the Charles Sturt wines, produced from grapes trucked halfway across Australia.

ΨΨΨΨ 1997 Medium red-purple; the moderately intense bouquet has a mix of red fruits and more savoury/earthy overtones. The palate opens with sweet berry fruit but then rather hard, bitter tannins take over on the finish. A pity; I seriously doubt whether the tannins will soften sufficiently quickly. **rating: 81**

best drinking 2002–2007 **best vintages** NA **drink with** Barbecued steak • $22

charley brothers ★★☆

The Ruins Way, Inneslake, Port Macquarie, NSW 2444 **region** Hastings River
phone (02) 6581 1332 **fax** (02) 6581 0391 **open** Mon–Fri 1–5, weekends 10–5
winemaker Cassegrain (Contract) **production** 1000 **est.** 1988
product range ($10–15 CD) Semillon, Chardonnay, Summer White, Pinot Noir, Shiraz Cabernet Merlot, Cabernet Sauvignon.
summary The property upon which the Charley Brothers vineyard is established has been in the family's ownership since the turn of the century but in fact had been planted to vines by a Major Innes in the 1840s. After carrying on logging and fruit growing at various times, the Charley family planted vines in 1988 with the encouragement of John Cassegrain. A little over 10.5 hectares of vines have been established. The '98 vintage wines are pleasant and certainly appropriate to the cellar door.

charlotte plains NR

RMB 3180, Dooleys Road, Maryborough, Vic 3465 **region** Bendigo
phone (03) 5361 3137 **open** By appointment
winemaker Roland Kaval **production** 80 **est.** 1990
product range ($16 ML) Shiraz.
summary Charlotte Plains is a classic example of miniaturism. Production comes from a close-planted vineyard which is only one-third of a hectare, a quarter being shiraz, the remainder sauvignon blanc. The minuscule production is sold solely through the mailing list and by phone, but the '96 Shiraz (the second vintage from Charlotte Plains) was awarded four stars in *Winestate* magazine in mid-1997 and judged as the Equal Best Shiraz for Central Victoria.

chateau doré NR

Mandurang Road, via Bendigo, Vic 3551 **region** Bendigo
phone (03) 5439 5278 **open** Tues–Sun 10–6
winemaker Ivan Gross **production** 1000 **est.** 1860
product range ($9–14 CD) Riesling, Shiraz, Cabernet Sauvignon, Tawny Port.
summary Has been in the ownership of the Gross family since 1860, with the winery buildings dating back respectively to 1860 and 1893. All wine is sold through cellar door.

chateau dorrien NR

Corner Seppeltsfield Road and Barossa Valley Way, Dorrien, SA 5352 **region** Barossa Valley
phone (08) 8562 2850 **fax** (08) 8562 1416 **open** 7 days 10–5
winemaker Fernando Martin **production** 2000 **est.** 1983
product range ($10–18 CD) Riesling, Semillon Chardonnay, Traminer, Frontignac Traminer, Frontignac Spaetlese, Late Harvest Frontignac, Semillon Chardonnay Sparkling Brut, Prima Vera (light red), Limited Release Grenache, Shiraz, Cabernet Sauvignon, Tawny Port.
summary Unashamedly and successfully directed at the tourist trade.

chateau francois ★★★

Broke Road, Pokolbin, NSW 2321 **region** Lower Hunter Valley
phone (02) 4998 7548 **fax** (02) 4998 7805 **open** Weekends 9–5 or by appointment
winemaker Don Francois **production** 700 **est.** 1969
product range ($11 ML) Pokolbin Mallee Semillon, Chardonnay, Shiraz Pinot Noir.
summary The retirement hobby of former NSW Director of Fisheries, Don Francois. Soft-flavoured and structured wines which frequently show regional characters but which are modestly priced and are all sold through the cellar door and mailing list to a loyal following. The tasting room is available for private dinners for 12–16 people. Don Francois has sailed through a quadruple-bypass followed by a mild stroke with his sense of humour intact, if not enhanced. A recent newsletter says (inter alia) '… my brush with destiny has changed my grizzly personality and I am now sweetness and light … Can you believe? Well, almost!' He even promises comfortable tasting facilities.

chateau hornsby NR

Petrick Road, Alice Springs, NT 0870 **region** Alice Springs
phone (08) 8955 5133 **fax** (08) 8955 5133 **open** 7 days 11–4
winemaker Gordon Cook **production** 1000 **est.** 1976
product range ($12–17 CD) Riesling, Semillon, Chardonnay, Shiraz, Cabernet Sauvignon.
summary Draws in part upon 3 hectares of estate plantings, and in part from grapes and wines purchased from other regions. Very much a tourist-oriented operation, with numerous allied entertainments on offer.

chateau leamon ★★★

5528 Calder Highway, Bendigo, Vic 3550 **region** Bendigo
phone (03) 5447 7995 **fax** (03) 5447 0855 **open** Wed–Mon 10–5
winemaker Ian Leamon **production** 2000 **est.** 1973
product range ($15–30 CD) Riesling, Semillon, Chardonnay, Shiraz, Reserve Shiraz, Cabernet Merlot.
summary After a period of uncertainty, Chateau Leamon is (a little tentatively) returning to some of its former glory. Ian Leamon is using locally grown grapes but is also looking to the Strathbogie Ranges for grapes for other wines, including Pinot Noir. Limited retail distribution in Victoria and Queensland; exports to Asia and the US.

Chateau Leamon Riesling
Made from grapes grown by Christopher Bennett in the Strathbogie Ranges.
1998 Light green-yellow; the bouquet is clean but seems to have closed down at the start of its transition from young to mature Riesling. The same impression is given on the palate, which, while well made and balanced, isn't singing at the moment. **rating: 82**
best drinking 2003–2008 **best vintages** NA **drink with** Leave it in the cellar • $15

Chateau Leamon Reserve Shiraz
First made in 1996, and produced from 26-year-old vines grown at Chateau Leamon's Big Hill Vineyard near Bendigo. It is open fermented, and spends a little over 12 months in 100 per cent new American oak hogsheads.
1998 Medium red-purple; a major disappointment after the '97 vintage, which so brilliantly matched fruit and oak. Here the oak floods both the bouquet and palate, even though you can see the cherry fruit hiding under the vanilla oak. **rating: 84**
best drinking 2003–2008 **best vintages** '97 **drink with** Rich game • $30

Chateau Leamon Cabernet Merlot
Produced from a blend of 78 per cent Cabernet Sauvignon, 12 per cent Merlot and 10 per cent Cabernet Franc estate-grown on the Big Hill Vineyard.
1998 A slightly dull colour is followed by a savoury, leafy bouquet, neither rich nor sweet. The palate is pleasant, in a lighter style, with light, leafy berry fruit flavours and almost no tannins to speak of. **rating: 78**
best drinking 2000–2003 **best vintages** NA **drink with** Rack of lamb • $20

chateau pato ★★★★

Thompson's Road, Pokolbin, NSW 2321 **region** Lower Hunter Valley
phone (02) 4998 7634 **fax** (02) 4998 7860 **open** By appointment
winemaker Nicholas Paterson **production** 300 **est.** 1978
product range ($18–25 CD) Pinot Noir, Shiraz.

summary Nicholas and Roger Paterson have taken over responsibility for this tiny winery following the death of their father David Paterson during the 1993 vintage. Two and a half hectares of shiraz, 1 hectare of chardonnay and half a hectare of pinot noir; most of the grapes are sold, with a tiny quantitiy of shiraz being made into a marvellous wine. On all the evidence, David Paterson's inheritance is being handsomely guarded.

Chateau Pato Shiraz

Produced from the 2 hectares of estate plantings, just across the road from Brokenwood's Graveyard Vineyard.
▼▼▼▼▽ **1998** Dense purple-red; the bouquet is concentrated and complex, giving full expression to Hunter terroir. The palate, too, is classic, earthy Hunter shiraz, which has the intensity and depth to evolve over decades.
rating: 90

best drinking 2005–2015 **best vintages** '86, '87, '90, '91, '94, '98 **drink with** Barbecued beef • $25

chateau tahbilk ★★★★

Goulburn Valley Highway, Tabilk, Vic 3607 **region** Goulburn Valley
phone (03) 5794 2555 **fax** (03) 5794 2360 **open** Mon–Sat 9–5, Sun 11–5
winemaker Alister Purbrick, Neil Larson, Alan George **production** 105 000 **est.** 1860
product range ($9.95–99.95 R) Riesling, Chardonnay, Marsanne, Roussanne, Viognier, Sauvignon Blanc, Semillon, Verdelho, Grenache, Cabernet Franc, Malbec, Cabernet Malbec, Shiraz, Cabernet Sauvignon; 1860 Vines Shiraz is rare flagship, with a Reserve Red released from each vintage.
summary A winery steeped in tradition (with high National Trust classification), which should be visited at least once by every wine-conscious Australian, and which makes wines — particularly red wines — utterly in keeping with that tradition. The essence of that heritage comes in the form of the tiny quantities of Shiraz made entirely from vines planted in 1860. As well as Australian national distribution through Tucker Seabrook, Chateau Tahbilk has agents in every principal wine market, including the UK, Europe, Asia and North America.

Chateau Tahbilk Riesling

Chateau Tahbilk is not particularly well known for its Riesling, yet has accumulated a trophy, 11 gold, 26 silver and 51 bronze medals for this wine since its introduction in 1980. As with all the Tahbilk wines, estate-grown, and again, as with all Tahbilk wines, particularly generous in flavour.
▼▼▼▼ **1999** Light yellow-green; a full, solid, lime-accented bouquet, with some toast in the background. A full-bodied food style, with plenty of richness in the mouth. **rating:** 86
best drinking 2000–2003 **best vintages** '86, '90, '92, '94, '99 **drink with** Seafood salad • $13.95

Chateau Tahbilk Marsanne

The best known of Chateau Tahbilk's wines, with an illustrious history. Made in a very simple and direct fashion, in total contrast to neighbour Mitchelton, and in particular without the use of oak. Like young traditional Semillon, frequently needs time to come into its own. As a matter of interest, the 40 hectares of marsanne planted at Chateau Tahbilk is the largest single vineyard planting of that variety in the world.
▼▼▼▼ **1998** Light green-yellow; the bouquet is light, with a mix of honeysuckle (dominant) and herb. The palate has length, intensity and good acidity. Absolutely guaranteed to flower with age into a 90-plus-point wine. **rating:** 86
best drinking 2003–2013 **best vintages** '53, '74, '79, '81, '84, '85, '87, '88, '91, '92, '93, '95, '96, '98 **drink with** Lighter Italian or Asian dishes • $10.95

Chateau Tahbilk Shiraz

A rock of ages, deliberately made by Alister Purbrick in precisely the same way as the wines of ten, 20, 30 and 40 years ago. Normally there is tremendous colour, flavour and extract, with little or no oak influence. The only question about the better vintages was whether they need five, 10 or 20 years in the cellar. Quite why some of the more recent vintages have been (relatively speaking) weak and somewhat dilute I do not know.
▼▼▼▼ **1997** Excellent, bright red-purple; the bouquet is straightforward but seems hampered by some off aromas from old oak. The palate is better, with moderate length and grip. **rating:** 85
best drinking 2000–2007 **best vintages** '61, '62, '65, '68, '71, '74, '76, '78, '81, '84, '85, '86, '91 **drink with** Barbecued T-bone steak • $18.95

Chateau Tahbilk Cabernet Sauvignon

As with all of the Tahbilk wines, estate-grown, produced from a significant percentage of old vines. This is terroir speaking, the hand of the maker being deliberately withdrawn. As from 1995, 10 per cent Cabernet Franc was incorporated in the wine. A wine which seems to have picked up the pace a bit after a couple of disappointing vintages.

♥♥♥♥ **1997** Medium red-purple; the bouquet is moderately intense, with distinctive earthy cabernet varietal character; the palate has quite sweet berry fruit flavours, likewise moderately intense, but also a hint of sweet new oak. **rating:** 86

best drinking 2002–2007 **best vintages** '65, '71, '72, '75, '76, '78, '79, '86, '90, '92, '97 **drink with** Strong mature cheddar, stilton • $18.95

chatsfield ★★★★

O'Neil Road, Mount Barker, WA 6324 **region** Great Southern
phone (08) 9851 1704 **fax** (08) 9851 1704 **open** Tues–Sun, public holidays 10.30–4.30
winemaker Rob Lee, John Wade (Consultant) **production** 6000 **est.** 1976
product range ($14–17 CD) Mount Barker Riesling, Gewurztraminer, Chardonnay, Cabernet Franc, Shiraz.
summary Irish-born medical practitioner Ken Lynch can be very proud of his achievements at Chatsfield, as can the various contract-winemakers who have taken the high-quality estate-grown material and made such impressive wines, notably the Riesling, vibrant Cabernet Franc (as an unwooded nouveau style) and spicy liquorice Shiraz. Exports to Ireland, the UK, the US, Canada, Japan, Hong Kong and Singapore.

🐌 chepstowe vineyard NR

Fitzpatricks Lane, Carngham, Vic 3351 **region** Ballarat
phone (03) 5344 9412 **fax** (03) 5344 9403 **open** 7 days 10–5
winemaker John Ellis (Contract) **production** 700 **est.** 1994
product range ($20 CD) Chardonnay, Pinot Noir.
summary Way back in 1983 Bill Wallace asked the then Yellowglen winemaker Dominique Landragin what he thought about the suitability of a block of steeply sloping grazing land on the side of the Chepstowe Hill, looking northeast across to the Grampians and its various mountains, including Mount Misery. Landragin replied 'it might be possible to grow grapes there', and Wallace subsequently acquired the property. It was not until November 1994 that 1 hectare each of pinot noir and chardonnay was planted, followed by an additional hectare of pinot noir in 1996. In the warmest of vintages it may be possible to obtain full ripeness for table wines, but in normal years I suspect sparkling wine (of potentially high quality) might be the best option. Certainly the two 1998 wines show unflinching, ultra-cool-climate characteristics.

Chepstowe Vineyard Pinot Noir

A wine which shows how delicately poised the Ballarat climate is for the production of table wine.
♥♥♥♡ **1998** Medium red-purple; the bouquet is very stemmy, with some offsetting spice. There is a range of spicy, stemmy, tomato vine flavours on the palate, which finishes with relatively high acidity. **rating:** 81

best drinking 2000–2003 **drink with** Teriyaki chicken • $20

chestnut grove ★★★☆

Chestnut Grove Road, Manjimup, WA 6258 **region** Pemberton, Warren Valley and Manjimup
phone (08) 9772 4345 **fax** (08) 9772 4543 **open** Weekends by appointment
winemaker Kim Horton, John Griffiths (Consultant) **production** 10 000 **est.** 1988
product range ($16.95–23.95 CD) Chardonnay, Sauvignon Blanc, Verdelho, Pinot Noir, Cabernet Merlot, Merlot.
summary A joint venture between the Lange family of Alkoomi and Vic Kordic and his family, through to grandson Darren Cook. Initial vintages were slightly weak and dilute, but increasing vine age (and one suspects better viticulture) has resulted in a significant lift in wine quality, particularly with the Cabernet Merlot. Production, too, has been more than doubled, with distribution in all States and exports to the UK and Germany.

chestnut hill vineyard NR

1280 Pakenham Road, Mount Burnett, Vic 3781 **region** Gippsland
phone (03) 5942 7314 **fax** (03) 5942 7314 **open** Weekends and public holidays 10.30–5.30, or by appointment
winemaker Charlie Javor **production** 1100 **est.** 1995
product range ($15–18 CD) Chardonnay, Sauvignon Blanc, Shiraz.
summary Charlie and Ivka Javor started Chestnut Hill with small plantings of chardonnay and shiraz in 1985 and have slowly increased the vineyards to their present total of a little over 3 hectares. The first wines were made in 1995, and all distribution is through the cellar door and direct to a few restaurants. Situated less than one hour's drive from Melbourne, the picturesque vineyard is situated among the rolling hills in the southeast of the Dandenongs near Mount Burnett. The wines reflect the cool climate.

🐌 chislett's lachlan valley wines   NR

Wandary Lane, Forbes, NSW 2871 **region** Western Plains Zone
phone (02) 6852 3983 **open** NA
winemaker Frank Chislett **production** NA **est.** 1920
product range Chardonnay, Riesling, Semillon, Shiraz, Pinot Noir, Cabernet Sauvignon.
summary The Chislett family (Frank, Les and Annette) have been quietly making wines in a century-old winery since the 1920s, but the wines are seldom, if ever, seen outside cellar door.

chittering estate   NR

Chittering Valley Road, Lower Chittering, WA 6084 **region** Other Wineries of WA
phone (08) 9273 6255 **fax** (08) 9273 6101 **open** Weekends and public holidays 11–4.30 (Apr–Dec)
winemaker Francois Jacquard **production** 12 000 **est.** 1982
product range ($14.90–21 R) Chardonnay, Hill Top Reserve Chardonnay, Semillon Sauvignon Blanc, Pinot Noir, Cabernet Merlot, Hill Top Reserve Cabernet Sauvignon.
summary Chittering Estate was sold in late1997, and no information has been forthcoming about its new owner's intentions.

ciavarella   ★★★

Evans Lane, Oxley, Vic 3678 **region** King Valley
phone (03) 5727 3384 **fax** (03) 5727 3384 **open** Mon–Sat 9–6, Sun 10–6
winemaker Cyril Ciavarella **production** 2000 **est.** 1978
product range ($14–18 CD) Semillon, Chenin Blanc, Late Harvest Chenin Blanc, Chardonnay, Dolcino (medium-bodied sweet red), Shiraz, Cabernet Sauvignon.
summary The Ciavarellas have been grape growers in the King Valley for almost 20 years, selling their grapes to wineries such as Brown Brothers. Changes in the grape marketplace led to Ciavarella deciding to make limited quantities of wines, which were first offered for sale from the cellar door in early 1994.

Ciavarella Semillon

Estate-grown; the wine spends six months in used French oak barriques, and the approach works well.
▼▼▼♀ 1999 Light to medium yellow-green; slightly hard oak, not yet integrated but not oppressive, is evident on the bouquet, but the palate is far better where oak does add a dimension to the tangy herb and lime fruit.   **rating:** 82
best drinking 2000–2003 **best vintages** NA **drink with** Shellfish • $14

Ciavarella Cabernet Sauvignon

Made without pretensions and in particular without the extravagant use of oak; it spends 12 months in a mix of new and predominantly used French oak barriques.
▼▼▼♀ 1998 Medium red-purple; the bouquet is of light to medium intensity, with savoury, leafy/berry aromas; the medium-bodied palate has attractive berry fruit, soft tannins and just a faint lick of oak on the finish.   **rating:** 84
best drinking 2000–2003 **best vintages** NA **drink with** Roast lamb • $16

clarendon hills   ★★★★☆

Brookmans Road, Blewitt Springs, SA 5171 **region** McLaren Vale
phone (08) 8364 1484 **fax** (08) 8364 1484 **open** By appointment
winemaker Roman Bratasiuk **production** 20 000 **est.** 1989
product range ($60–175 R) Hickinbotham Vineyard Semillon, Chardonnay (from the Norton Summit, Kangarilla and Hickinbotham Vineyards), Hickinbotham Vineyard Pinot Noir, Old Vine Grenache (from the Kangarilla, Blewitt Springs Vineyards), Shiraz (Hickinbotham, Piggott Range Vineyards), Astralis, Merlot (from the Brookman and Hickinbotham Vineyards) and Cabernet Sauvignon (from the Brookman, Sandown and Hickinbotham Vineyards).
summary Clarendon Hills produces some of the most startlingly concentrated, rich and full-bodied red wines to be found in Australia, rivalled in this respect only by Wendouree. Roman Bratasiuk is a larger-than-life figure who makes larger-than-life wines. Technocrats may quibble about this or that aspect, but influential judges such as Robert Parker have neither reservations about nor problems with the immense, brooding red wines which Bratasiuk regularly produces from small patches of old, low-yielding vines which he ferrets out. Exports to New Zealand, the US, Canada, Germany, Switzerland, Belgium, The Netherlands, Sweden, the UK and Japan.

Clarendon Hills Hickinbotham Semillon

From the Alan Hickinbotham vineyard in the Onkaparinga Valley perched near the boundary between the Adelaide Hills and McLaren Vale.

▼▼▼▼▽ 1998 Medium yellow-green; the bouquet is clean, with pleasantly ripe, weighty semillon fruit with reassuring nuances of herb and nettle. The palate is precisely as expected, nicely weighted, fully ripe and with considerable length. **rating:** 93

best drinking 2000–2005 **best vintages** '98 **drink with** Trout mousse • $39.50

Clarendon Hills Kangarilla Chardonnay

One hundred per cent barrel-fermented in new French oak; a wine which will soften with bottle age.

▼▼▼▼▽ 1998 Medium yellow-green; the bouquet is clean, quite firm, with a mix of cashew and mineral aromas; subtle oak. Some oak spice comes through on the mid-palate, then crisp acid picks up and lengthens the palate. **rating:** 91

best drinking 2003–2008 **best vintages** '98 **drink with** Crumbed brains • $45

Clarendon Hills Hickinbotham Pinot Noir

Made from grapes grown on the extensive vineyard holdings of Alan Hickinbotham, a real estate developer who is indeed the brother of oenologist Ian Hickinbotham.

▼▼▼▼▽ 1998 Light to medium red-purple; there is a mix of sappy, spicy, stemmy fruit aromas strongly suggesting whole-bunch maceration. The palate is intense, long, sappy and lingering, finishing with fine tannins; clever winemaking and sophisticated use of oak throughout. **rating:** 90

best drinking 2000–2003 **best vintages** NA **drink with** Chinese deep-fried quail • $69

Clarendon Hills Brookman Shiraz

Made from 75-year-old vines planted on a northwest-facing slope on the Brookman Vineyard; the soil is a mix of sand, gravel, ironstone and clay.

▼▼▼▼▽ 1998 Medium red-purple; the bouquet is clean, showing some slightly stemmy notes, that promptly disappear on the palate, which has good structure, and fine, sweet tannins throughout its length. At 14 degrees alcohol, a conundrum. **rating:** 90

best drinking 2003–2008 **best vintages** '98 **drink with** Kangaroo fillet • $99

Clarendon Hills Hickinbotham Shiraz

The vineyard is situated in the Onkaparinga Valley; the particular vines are 35 years old, and planted on a hard clay and ironstone soil with a northwest aspect.

▼▼▼▼▼ 1998 Medium to full red-purple; the bouquet is rich and clean, with pronounced earthy shiraz varietal character. A substantial wine on the palate, with masses of dark cherry fruit and just a hint of spice; subtle oak and good acidity. **rating:** 94

best drinking 2005–2015 **best vintages** '98 **drink with** Braised lamb shanks • $99

Clarendon Hills Liandra Shiraz

There are two distinct blocks with quite different terroir. The first is on deep sand soil and is west-facing; it produces highly perfumed grapes. The second is a north-facing slope on black clay, which provides far more tannic wine. In each instance the vines are 75 years old.

▼▼▼▼ 1998 Medium red-purple; the bouquet is perfumed and clean, the palate likewise, with earthy cherry fruit and the hallmark fine tannins that distinguish the '98 trio of Shiraz from Clarendon Hills. **rating:** 89

best drinking 2003–2008 **best vintages** '98 **drink with** Oxtail • $99

Clarendon Hills Brookman Merlot

The wine comes from a single east-facing block planted 30 years ago on deep clay soil.

▼▼▼▼ 1998 Medium red-purple; there is clean, fresh bright fruit on the bouquet with spicy, toasty oak; then the wheels fall off somewhat on the palate, where charry oak sits firmly on top of the fruit, followed by dry tannins on the finish. **rating:** 85

best drinking 2003–2006 **best vintages** NA **drink with** Tea-smoked lamb • $85

Clarendon Hills Old Vines Blewitt Springs Grenache

The 75-year-old vineyard is established on a very steep slope, with rocky quartz on top, and ironstone and clay subsoil. It faces due east, and the vines are 75 years old.

▼▼▼▼ 1998 Surprisingly light colour; the bouquet is clean, light and fresh, with flowery redcurrant aromas. Similar fresh fruit flavours open the palate but are followed by utterly unexpected tannins. It is far from certain that the two components will ever unite. **rating: 87**

best drinking 2003–2007 **best vintages** '98 **drink with** Beef in red wine • $60

Clarendon Hills Old Vines Clarendon Grenache

The 80-year-old vines grow in a natural amphitheatre at a height of 240 metres; the steep slope is of heavy clay soil, and the southerly aspect creates a cool site climate.

▼▼▼▼▽ 1998 Light to medium red-purple; the bouquet offers authentic, varietal juicy, jammy berry fruit; the palate is quite rich, complex and spicy, although once again the tannins on the finish seem to be contained in a separate add-on compartment. **rating: 91**

best drinking 2003–2008 **best vintages** '98 **drink with** Grilled calf's liver • $60

Clarendon Hills Sandown Cabernet Sauvignon

One of a series of technically flawless and often elegant wines from the 1998 vintage made by Roman Bratasiuk.

▼▼▼▼▼ 1998 Brilliant colour; lovely sweet, ripe blackcurrant fruit is swathed in fine oak on the bouquet; the palate has powerful, pure, perfectly ripened Cabernet flavours, well-handled oak and plenty of tannins. **rating: 95**

best drinking 2003–2013 **best vintages** '98 **drink with** Rare roast beef • $85

🦘 clemens hill   NR

686 Richmond Road, Cambridge, Tas 7170 **region** Southern Tasmania
phone (03) 6248 5985 **fax** (03) 6231 6222 **open** By appointment
winemaker Andrew Hood (Contract) **production** 180 **est.** 1994
product range ($16 CD) Sauvignon Blanc, Chardonnay, Pinot Noir.
summary Owned by Kevin and Jacqueline Wagner, whose son Ben Wagner is one of Tasmania's foremost viticulturists. 1998 was the first vintage, and both it and 1999 have produced wines of show medal quality.

Clemens Hill Sauvignon Blanc

Produced from half a hectare of estate plantings, and matured for four months in new French oak.

▼▼▼▽ 1999 Light green-yellow; the bouquet is fresh and clean, the oak almost imperceptible on both bouquet and palate. A nicely balanced wine, with gentle gooseberry flavours and well balanced by acidity. **rating: 84**

best drinking 2000–2001 **drink with** Shellfish • $16

Clemens Hill Pinot Noir

The first release for Clemens Hill from this variety which was of silver medal quality on my score sheet at the Tasmanian Wines Show 2000.

▼▼▼▼ 1999 Light to medium red-purple; clean, fresh aromas with some spice and cherry lead into a palate with good intensity, length and attack. Cherry flavours manifest again, driving a stylish wine. **rating: 85**

best drinking 2000–2003 **drink with** Smoked quail • $16

cleveland   ★★★☆

Shannons Road, Lancefield, Vic 3435 **region** Macedon Ranges
phone (03) 5429 1449 **fax** (03) 5429 2017 **open** 7 days 9–6
winemaker Keith Brien **production** 2000 **est.** 1985
product range ($10–28 CD) Macedon Brut, Chardonnay, Pinot Noir, Redcastle Shiraz, Cabernet Merlot; Brien Family Chardonnay Gordo, Muscat Gordo Blanco and Shiraz Mourvedre.
summary The Cleveland homestead was built in 1889 in the style of a Gothic Revival manor house but had been abandoned for 40 years when purchased by the Briens in 1983. It has since been painstakingly restored, and 3.8 hectares of surrounding vineyard established. Cleveland has done best with Pinot Noir and Chardonnay, but the occasional Cabernet Sauvignon attests to an unusually favourable vineyard site in a very cool region. Exports to the UK.

cliff house ★★★☆

57 Camms Road, Kayena, Tas 7270 **region** Northern Tasmania
phone (03) 6394 7454 **fax** (03) 6394 7454 **open** By appointment
winemaker Julian Alcorso (Contract) **production** 2500 **est.** 1983
product range ($18–20 R) Riesling, Chardonnay, Pinot Noir, Devil's Elbow (Pinot Cabernet blend), Cabernet Sauvignon.
summary Cliff House has undergone a metamorphosis. In 1999 Geoff and Cheryl Hewitt sold the 4-hectare vineyard they established in the Tamar Valley area in 1983. They have now turned a two-hole golf course around their house into a second, new vineyard, planted to riesling and pinot noir. Until this comes into production they will sell their remaining stocks of wine contract-made from the old plantings.

Cliff House Riesling

The 1998 vintage was a gold medal winner at the 1999 Tasmanian Wines Show, the following vintage winning a silver medal at the 2000 show.
▼▼▼▼ 1999 Light to medium green-yellow; a big, soft passionfruit/tropical bouquet introduces a generous wine, with abundant tropical and lime juice flavours on a rich palate. Excellent early-drinking style. **rating:** 90
best drinking 2000–2004 **best vintages** '98, '99 **drink with** Fresh shellfish • $18

Cliff House Chardonnay

The last of the line from Cliff House, winning a silver medal at the 1999 Tasmanian Wines Show, and a high bronze in 2000. Made by Alain Rousseau at Moorilla Estate.
▼▼▼▼ 1998 Medium green-yellow; a slightly burnt edge to the bouquet may be due to oak or possibly a yeast fermentation problem. However, the wine comes into its own on the rich palate, which is complexed by good oak handling. **rating:** 84
best drinking 2000–2003 **best vintages** NA **drink with** Chinese pork • $NA

clonakilla ★★★★

Crisps Lane, Murrumbateman, NSW 2582 **region** Canberra District
phone (02) 6227 5877 **fax** (02) 6227 5871 **open** 7 days 11–5
winemaker Tim Kirk **production** 2500 **est.** 1971
product range ($16–36 CD) Riesling, Chardonnay, Semillon Sauvignon Blanc, Viognier, Muscat, Shiraz, Shiraz Viognier, Cabernet Merlot.
summary The indefatigable Tim Kirk, who has many of the same personality characteristics as Frank Tate (of Evans & Tate), has taken over the management of Clonakilla from father and scientist Dr John Kirk. The quality of the wines is good, but none more so than the highly regarded Shiraz, which sells out quickly every year. Exports to the US.

Clonakilla Riesling

Made in a consistent style throughout the 1990s, always showing considerable flavour, and quite often exhibiting a not unpleasant character which I can only describe as slightly cosmetic.
▼▼▼▼ 1999 Medium yellow-green; the bouquet is clean but rather neutral and closed, with no obvious aromatics. The palate is similarly closed and unevolved, although you can see the latent fruit there, and the wine has good acidity. Certainly shows the result of a killer frost which reduced the crop to 20 per cent of its normal level. Guaranteed to flower with age. **rating:** 85
best drinking 2004–2009 **best vintages** '91, '93, '94, '95, '97 **drink with** Spiced Asian dishes • $18

Clonakilla Shiraz Viognier

Now firmly established as Clonakilla's best wine, and indeed one of the best wines to come out of the Canberra District each year. Since 1994 the wine has been a blend of Shiraz and Viognier, with the Shiraz component typically accounting for between 80 per cent and 85 per cent of the blend. Interestingly, too, the grapes are not crushed but are placed as whole bunches in open fermenters, foot-trodden, and the fermentation is completed in new and used French oak barriques. Originally simply labelled Shiraz, with 'Viognier' added to the label since 1997.
▼▼▼▼ 1998 Dark, ever-so-slightly dull, red-purple. The bouquet is quite striking, with wonderfully aromatic and complex spicy/earthy fruit. The palate has plenty of substance, with dark berry/cherry fruit, and savoury touches of liquorice and spice; the oak is well handled, and the tannins quite gentle. **rating:** 92
best drinking 2003–2013 **best vintages** '90, '92, '93, '94, '95, '97, '98 **drink with** Jugged hare • $36

Clonakilla Cabernet Merlot

Since 1991 a Bordeaux-style blend typically composed of 50 per cent Cabernet Franc, 30 per cent Cabernet Sauvignon and 20 per cent Merlot. The wine is given extensive maceration on skins (up to three weeks) before being pressed, and spends 18 months in French oak.

▼▼▼▼ 1997 Medium to full red-purple; the bouquet is distinctly savoury, with leafy, cedary aromas. The palate is concentrated, with savoury chocolate and berry fruit, and slightly less assertive tannins than are present in the upcoming '98 release.   **rating: 87**

best drinking 2002–2010 **best vintages** '97 **drink with** Tea-smoked lamb   • $24

clos clare   NR

Government Road, Watervale, SA 5452 **region** Clare Valley
phone (08) 8843 0161 **fax** (08) 8843 0161 **open** Weekends and public holidays 10–5
winemaker Various Contract **production** 1000 **est.** 1993
product range ($15–19 CD) Riesling, Shiraz.
summary Clos Clare is based on a small (1.5 hectares), unirrigated section of the original Florita Vineyard once owned by Leo Buring and which produces Riesling of extraordinary concentration and power. Exports to the US and Canada.

🐦 clovely estate   NR

Steinhardts Road, Moffatdale via Murgon, Qld 4605 **region** South Burnett
phone (07) 3876 5200 **fax** (07) 3876 5200 **open** 7 days 10–5
winemaker David Lowe, Adam Chapman (Contract) **production** 15 000 **est.** 1998
product range ($12.95–14.95 CD) Left Field Semillon Chardonnay, Chardonnay, Shiraz; Fifth Row Chardonnay, Shiraz Cabernet.
summary Although new-born, Clovely Estate has the largest vineyards in Queensland, having established 174 hectares of vines at two locations just to the east of Murgon in the Burnett Valley. There are 127 hectares of red grapes (including 74 hectares of shiraz) and 47 hectares of white grapes. The attractively packaged wines are sold in four tiers: Clovely Estate at the top end, and which will not be produced every year; Left Field, strongly fruity and designed to age; Fifth Row, for early drinking; and Outback, primarily designed for the export market.

clover hill   ★★★★☆

Clover Hill Road, Lebrina, Tas 7254 **region** Northern Tasmania
phone (03) 6395 6114 **fax** (03) 6395 6257 **open** 7 days 10–5; by appointment in winter
winemaker Shane Clohesy, Chris Markell **production** 5000 **est.** 1986
product range ($33.20 R) Clover Hill (Sparkling).
summary Clover Hill was established by Taltarni in 1986 with the sole purpose of making a premium sparkling wine. Its 20 hectares of vineyards, comprising 12 hectares of chardonnay, 6.5 of pinot noir and 1.5 of pinot meunier, are still coming into bearing, and production is steadily increasing. Wine quality is excellent, combining finesse with power and length.

Clover Hill

A Chardonnay-predominant style, given not less than 24 months on yeast lees and invariably clean, fresh and finishing with pronounced acidity — a testament to the very cool climate in which the grapes are grown.

▼▼▼▼▽ 1996 Light, bright green-yellow; it has complex citrus and bread aromas followed by attractive citrus-accented flavours which run evenly along the palate, with crisp but not excessive acidity.   **rating: 91**

best drinking 2000–2001 **best vintages** '90, '91, '92, '95, '96 **drink with** Caviar, shellfish   • $33.20

coalville vineyard   ★★★

RMB 4750 Moe South Road, Moe South, Vic 3825 **region** Gippsland
phone (03) 5127 4229 **fax** (03) 5127 2148 **open** 7 days 10–5
winemaker Peter Beasley **production** 250 **est.** 1985
product range ($15 ML) A single wine, predominantly Cabernet Sauvignon with a little Cabernet Franc, Malbec and Merlot, labelled Coalville Red.
summary This is the new name for Mair's Coalville, following the sale of the property by Dr Stewart Mair to Peter Beasley. I am unaware of any other changes.

cobanov   NR

Stock Road, Herne Hill, WA 6056 **region** Swan District
phone (08) 9296 4210 **open** Wed–Sun 9–5.30
winemaker Steve Cobanov **production** 10 000 **est.** 1960
product range ($6–10 CD) Chenin Blanc, Chardonnay, Sauvignon Blanc, Verdelho, Shiraz, Grenache, Cabernet Sauvignon.
summary A substantial family-owned operation producing a mix of bulk and bottled wine from 21 hectares of estate grapes. Part of the annual production is sold as grapes to other producers, including Houghton; part is sold in bulk; part sold in 2-litre flagons, and the remainder in modestly priced bottles.

cobaw ridge   ★★★☆

Perc Boyer's Lane, East Pastoria via Kyneton, Vic 3444 **region** Macedon Ranges
phone (03) 5423 5227 **fax** (03) 5423 5227 **open** Most weekends 10–5
winemaker Alan Cooper **production** 1400 **est.** 1985
product range ($28–35 CD) Chardonnay, Lagrein (375 ml), Shiraz, Shiraz Reserve.
summary Nelly and Alan Cooper have established Cobaw Ridge's 4-hectare vineyard at an altitude of 610 metres in the hills above Kyneton complete with self-constructed pole-framed mudbrick house and winery. Wine quality has been somewhat variable, but overall Alan Cooper has done extremely well. The plantings of cabernet sauvignon have been removed and partially replaced by lagrein, a variety which sent me scuttling to Jancis Robinson's seminal book on grape varieties, from which I learned it is a northeast Italian variety typically used to make delicate Rosé. Cooper believes it to be the only commercial planting in Australia, a claim disputed by at least one other winery, but no matter.

Cobaw Ridge Chardonnay

Produced from 2 hectares of estate plantings, and, like all the Cobaw Ridge wines, made and bottled on the estate.
▼▼▼▽ 1998 Medium yellow-green; the moderately intense bouquet of mineral and melon is followed by a palate that is relatively austere, neither fleshy nor lush, but which has the balance and oak integration to develop slowly but surely.   **rating: 83**
best drinking 2002–2007 **best vintages** NA **drink with** Honey chicken • $28

Cobaw Ridge Shiraz

Cobaw Ridge has established a solid reputation for its Shiraz, which flourishes in the warmer vintages.
▼▼▼▼ 1998 Medium red-purple; there is some gamey complexity to the bouquet derived from the character of the vineyard. The palate has welcome fruit sweetness, with cherry and mint flavours, finishing with pleasant tannins.   **rating: 86**
best drinking 2003–2008 **best vintages** '97, '98 **drink with** Rare beef • $31

cobbitty wines   NR

Cobbitty Road, Cobbitty, NSW 2570 **region** Other Wineries of NSW
phone (02) 4651 2281 **fax** (02) 4651 2671 **open** Mon–Sat 10–5, Sun 12–6
winemaker Giovanni Cogno **production** 5000 **est.** 1964
product range ($5–14 CD) A full range of generic table, fortified and sparkling wines under the Cobbitty Wines label; also cocktail wines.
summary Draws upon 10 hectares of estate plantings of muscat, barbera, grenache and trebbiano, relying very much on local and ethnic custom.

cockfighter's ghost vineyard   ★★★

Lot 251 Milbrodale Road, Broke, NSW 2330 **region** Lower Hunter Valley
phone (02) 9667 1622 **fax** (02) 9667 1442 **open** Not
winemaker Various Contract **production** 12 000 **est.** 1994
product range ($16–22 ML) Semillon, Unwooded Chardonnay, Chardonnay, Pinot Noir, Shiraz.
summary Like Poole's Rock Vineyard, owned by eminent Sydney merchant banker David Clarke but run and marketed as a separate venture, with lower wine prices. The wine has retail distribution throughout Australia, and is exported to the UK and New Zealand.

Cockfighter's Ghost Semillon

Made in the traditional Hunter fashion, unoaked and begging to be given time in bottle. It is made from 100 per cent semillon grapes grown on the sandy loam soils of the Broke/Fordwich subdistrict, and is contract-made by Neil McGuigan.

TTTY 1998 Medium yellow-green; a clean bouquet with pleasant, young herbaceous varietal character. The palate shows fairly high levels of dissolved CO_2, which lead to a prickle on the tongue but which will help the ageing and development over the long term.   **rating:** 83

best drinking 2000–2004 **best vintages** '96, '98 **drink with** Fresh asparagus • $15.95

cofield ★★★☆

Distillery Road, Wahgunyah, Vic 3687 **region** Rutherglen and Glenrowan
phone (02) 6033 3798 **fax** (02) 6033 3798 **open** Mon–Sat 9–5, Sun 10–5
winemaker Max Cofield, Damien Cofield **production** 7000 **est.** 1990
product range ($11.50–20 CD) Riesling, Chenin Blanc, Semillon, Semillon Chardonnay, Chardonnay, Late Harvest Tokay, Max's Blend Dry White, Max's Blend Dry Red, Shiraz, Merlot, Cabernet Sauvignon, Cabernet Merlot, Sparkling, Fortified.
summary District veteran Max Cofield, together with wife Karen and sons Damien, Ben and Andrew, is developing a strong cellar-door sales base by staging in-winery functions with guest chefs, and also providing a large barbecue and picnic area. (The Pickled Sisters Cafe is open for lunch Wed–Mon; telephone (02) 6033 2377.) The quality of the red wines, in particular, is good and improving all the time. Limited retail distribution in Melbourne and Tasmania.

Cofield Shiraz

Estate-grown, with the vineyard utilising the Scott-Henry trellis system which simultaneously increases yield and ripeness. Consistently reliable.

TTTY 1998 Medium red-purple; the bouquet is clean and smooth, with gently sweet vanillin oak wrapped around the fruit. A medium-bodied wine, with similarly pleasant, smooth berry fruit and soft tannins on the finish.   **rating:** 84

best drinking 2001–2005 **best vintages** NA **drink with** Marinated beef • $15

Cofield Merlot

Another well-made Cofield wine; on the face of it, Rutherglen is not the most logical home for merlot, but there can be no complaints about this wine.

TTTY 1998 Medium red-purple; a clean, smooth and basically sweet bouquet, with some more spicy/savoury edges appropriate to the variety; a well-crafted wine on the palate, with sweet berry fruit and balanced tannins.
rating: 83

best drinking 2001–2004 **best vintages** NA **drink with** Veal piccata • $16

Cofield Cabernet Sauvignon

Yet another honest, flavoursome and easy-drinking style, albeit with a touch more character than the other wines in the portfolio.

TTTT 1998 Medium red-purple; a solid, clean bouquet with blackberry and chocolate fruit is followed by a sweet, berry-fruited palate with nice structure, extract and tannins.   **rating:** 85

best drinking 2001–2007 **best vintages** NA **drink with** Rolled shoulder of lamb • $15

coldstream hills NR

31 Maddens Lane, Coldstream, Vic 3770 **region** Yarra Valley
phone (03) 5964 9410 **fax** (03) 5964 9389 **open** 7 days 10–5
winemaker James Halliday, Paul Lapsley **production** 50 000 **est.** 1985
product range ($24–45 CD) Pinot Gris, Sauvignon Blanc, Chardonnay, Reserve Chardonnay, Pinot Noir, Reserve Pinot Noir, Merlot, Reserve Merlot, Briarston (Cabernet Merlot), Reserve Cabernet Sauvignon; Limited Release Shiraz, Blanc de Noirs and Botrytis Chardonnay.
summary Founded by the author, who continues to be involved with the winemaking with Paul Lapsley, but acquired by Southcorp in mid-1996. Expansion plans already then underway have been accelerated, with well in excess of 100 hectares of owned or managed estate vineyards as the base. Chardonnay and Pinot Noir continue to be the principal focus; Merlot came on-stream from the 1997 vintage. Vintage conditions permitting, these three wines are made in both varietal and Reserve form, the latter in restricted quantities.

Coldstream Hills Sauvignon Blanc

1997 was the first varietal Sauvignon Blanc produced by Coldstream Hills. In prior years the Sauvignon Blanc was blended with a greater volume of Semillon to produce a wine labelled Fumé Blanc. It is a blend of 90 per cent Sauvignon Blanc cold-fermented in stainless steel, principally sourced from Upper Yarra Valley vineyards, and 10 per cent barrel-fermented Semillon.

1999 Light yellow-green; a highly fragrant bouquet with a strongly varietal mix of gooseberry and passionfruit. The palate is crisp yet intense, with an excellent balance of the ripe fruit flavours promised by the bouquet and minerally acidity on the finish.

best drinking 2000–2001 **best vintages** '97, '98 **drink with** Salad • $20

Coldstream Hills Chardonnay

Made from Yarra Valley grapes, part estate-grown and part purchased from other Yarra Valley growers. Largely barrel-fermented in a mix of new and used French oak under strictly controlled temperatures. Prolonged lees contact but no malolactic fermentation.

1998 Light to medium yellow-green; aromas of sweet fig and white peach on the bouquet, supported as always, by subtle oak. Similar, particularly sweet, fig and nectarine fruit flavours on the palate, no doubt deriving from the warm vintage. The wine has the hallmark length of flavour, a lingering aftertaste and good acidity.

best drinking 1999–2006 **best vintages** '86, '88, '91, '92, '93, '94, '96, '97 **drink with** Oven-roasted blue eye cod • $25.50

Coldstream Hills Reserve Chardonnay

Made primarily from estate-grown grapes which are 100 per cent barrel-fermented in a mix of new (over 50 per cent) and used French oak barriques, principally Vosges but with Troncais and Allier also used. Six months lees contact; 20 per cent malolactic fermentation.

1998 Medium yellow-green; an extremely smooth bouquet with total integration of fruit and barely perceptible oak; the fruit aromas are of melon, fig and a hint of cashew. The same seamless integration of fruit and oak appears on the surprisingly elegant palate, where fig and ripe pear flavours come to the fore.

best drinking 2000–2004 **best vintages** '88, '91, '92, '93, '94, '96, '97 **drink with** Veal, chicken • $41.50

Coldstream Hills Pinot Noir

Part estate-grown and part sourced from other Yarra Valley growers, with a range of site climates. It is made using the full gamut of Burgundian techniques, including substantial use of whole bunches, foot-stamped and macerated. The primary fermentation is completed in a mix of new and used Troncais (French) oak.

1998 Medium red, with a touch of purple; has plum and forest characters on the bouquet, which will continue to grow and evolve over the next few years. There are pleasant plum and cherry flavours on the medium-weight palate. The wine has good structure and fine tannins running through a lingering finish.

best drinking 1999–2003 **best vintages** '87, '88, '91, '92, '94, '96, '97 **drink with** Seared or slow-cooked salmon, Asian cuisine • $26.80

Coldstream Hills Reserve Pinot Noir

Produced entirely from estate-grown grapes, in turn coming mainly from the Amphitheatre Block established in 1985. The same making techniques are used with the Reserve wine as with the standard, the difference being fruit selection and a much higher percentage of new Dargaud & Jaegle Troncais oak barriques.

1998 Medium purple-red; there is excellent balance and integration of the fruit and oak; spice and plum aromas will progressively develop as the wine settles down in bottle. A classically proportioned and structured wine in the mainstream of Coldstream Hills style; a long palate, which expands exponentially on the finish, rounded off with fine tannins. Has come on considerably since being bottled, but will not really open up until around 2001.

best drinking 2001–2004 **best vintages** '87, '88, '91, '92, '94, '96, '97 **drink with** Quail, Asian cuisine • $45

Coldstream Hills Merlot

The '98 is the third release of our varietal merlot. The wine comes from a very warm vintage which allowed the berries to fully develop complex flavours and excellent sugar levels.

1998 Bright and healthy with purple hues predominant; sweet berry fruit with seamless French oak, hints of cedar and spice. Similar fruit, fully ripe savoury berries and plum, fine tannins; by far the best Merlot to date.

best drinking 2000–2004 **best vintages** '90, '97, '98 **drink with** All red meats, cheeses and game • $27.50

Coldstream Hills Briarston

A blend of Cabernet Sauvignon, Cabernet Franc and Merlot. The percentages vary a little from year to year, but the Cabernet Sauvignon component is usually 80 per cent or more. As with the other wines, part estate-grown, part purchased from other Yarra Valley growers. It is matured in a mix of new and used French oak (predominantly Nevers and Allier, with lesser amounts of Troncais) for 18–20 months before bottling.

1998 Medium red-purple; the bouquet is rich and full, showing dark berry/chocolate and fine spicy oak. The richest Briarston to date; round and fleshy, fine lingering tannins, judicious oak.

best drinking 2000–2004 **best vintages** '88, '90, '91, '92, '94, '97, '98 **drink with** Lamb with redcurrant sauce • $25.50

☙ collina wines   NR

Princes Highway, Mogo, NSW 2536 **region** Other Wineries of NSW
phone (02) 4474 0005 **fax** (02) 4474 0007 **open** 7 days 10–5
winemaker Nicola Collins **production** NA **est.** 1999
product range ($15–22 CD) Chardonnay, Classic White, Gewurztraminer, Late Harvest Riesling Traminer, South Coast Cabernets, Rougon (semi-sweet red).
summary In the spring of 1980, Jim Collins planted the first vines on the south coast at Bega's Grevillea Estate. His daughter Nicola was winemaker from the outset, and having completed 16 vintages, encouraged her father to build a second winery at Mogo in the Eurobodalla region. The winery does not have vineyards of its own, sourcing grapes in part from Grevillea Estate and from the growing number of South Coast vineyards. As with Grevillea Estate, the operation is aimed at the general tourist rather than the wine connoisseur.

connor park winery   NR

59 Connors Road, Leichardt, Vic 3516 **region** Bendigo
phone (03) 5437 5234 **fax** (03) 5437 5204 **open** 7 days 10–6
winemaker Ross Lougoon **production** 2000 **est.** 1994
product range ($16–20 CD) Riesling, Semillon, Pinot Noir, Merlot, Shiraz, Cabernet Sauvignon, Port, Muscat.
summary The original planting of 2 hectares of vineyard dates back to the mid-1960s and to the uncle of the present owners, who had plans for designing an automatic grape harvester. The plans came to nothing, and when the present owners purchased the property in 1985 the vineyard had run wild. They resuscitated the vineyard (which formed part of a much larger mixed farming operation) and until 1994 were content to sell the grapes to other winemakers. Since then the vineyard has been expanded to 10 hectares, and while part of the grapes is sold to others, significant quantities are made under the Connor Park label and sold through cellar door and by mail order.

constable & hershon   NR

1 Gillards Road, Pokolbin, NSW 2320 **region** Lower Hunter Valley
phone (02) 4998 7887 **fax** (02) 4998 7887 **open** 7 days 10–5
winemaker Neil McGuigan (Contract) **production** 3000 **est.** 1981
product range ($18.50–24.95 CD) Chardonnay, Unwooded Chardonnay, Pinot Noir, Cabernet Merlot, Reserve Cabernet Merlot.
summary Features four spectacular formal gardens, the Rose, Knot and Herb, Secret and Sculpture; a free garden tour is conducted every Monday to Friday at 10.30 am lasting 30 minutes. The 7-hectare vineyard is itself spectacularly situated under the backdrop of the Brokenback Range. Typically offers a range of several vintages of each variety ex cellar door or by mailing list.

constables   ★★★

Graphite Road, West Manjimup, WA 6258 **region** Pemberton, Warren Valley and Manjimup
phone (08) 9772 1375 **open** 7 days 9–5
winemaker Houghton (Contract) **production** NFP **est.** 1988
product range ($10–15 CD) Riesling, Sauvignon Blanc, Chardonnay, Cabernet Sauvignon.
summary Father John and son Michael, together with other members of the Constable family, have established an 11-hectare vineyard at Manjimup. Most of the grapes are sold to Houghton under a long-term contract, and limited quantities are made for the Constable label by Houghton under contract.

coolangatta estate ★★★☆

1335 Bolong Road, Shoalhaven Heads, NSW 2535 **region** Shoalhaven
phone (02) 4448 7131 **fax** (02) 4448 7997 **open** 7 days 10–5
winemaker Tyrrell's (Contract) **production** 4000 **est.** 1988
product range ($14–20 CD) Sauvignon Blanc, Semillon Sauvignon Blanc, Sauvignon Blanc Chardonnay, Unwooded Chardonnay, Alexander Berry Chardonnay, Verdelho, Chambourcin, Cabernet Shiraz, Merlot, Cabernet Sauvignon, Vintage Port.
summary Coolangatta Estate is part of a 150-hectare resort with accommodation, restaurants, golf course, etc, with some of the oldest buildings convict-built in 1822. It might be thought that the wines are tailored purely for the tourist market, but in fact the standard of viticulture is exceptionally high (immaculate Scott-Henry trellising), and the winemaking is wholly professional (contract by Tyrrell's).

Coolangatta Estate Sauvignon Blanc Chardonnay

The Scott-Henry trellis system used at Shoalhaven is ideal for high-vigour vineyards, particularly where (as in the case of Shoalhaven) the risk of summer rainfall is high. The canopy is split vertically, allowing sunlight and wind penetration, optimising air movement and reducing disease. For all that, the tempering effect of the nearby Shoalhaven River delays maturity, for vintage typically does not get under way until mid-March. Over the years several different blends involving Sauvignon Blanc have been made, initially incorporating Semillon, but since 1998 using Chardonnay in a 70 per cent/30 per cent blend.

♥♥♥♡ **1999** Light green-yellow; the bouquet is light and crisp, with minerally Sauvignon Blanc dominant. The palate is slightly sharp, as if the acidity had either been recently adjusted or perhaps over-zealously so. **rating:** 81
best drinking 1999–2000 **best vintages** '91, '94, '98 **drink with** Whitebait • $14

Coolangatta Estate Verdelho

An early-ripening variety, typically picked at the end of February (chardonnay follows in March) which is a distinct advantage in a climate in which summer rainfall always poses a threat. It is no doubt for the same reason that chambourcin has been planted, and likewise does well.

♥♥♥♡ **1999** Light to medium straw-yellow; the bouquet is clean, of light to medium intensity and essentially neutral. On the palate some pleasant tropical fruit comes through; once again, the acidity is a little sharp, but may well settle down given time; will then deserve a higher rating. **rating:** 82
best drinking 2000–2001 **best vintages** NA **drink with** Pasta • $17

Coolangatta Estate Elizabeth Berry Cabernet Sauvignon

Named after the wife of Alexander Berry, one of the founders of Coolangatta Estate. Competent contract-winemaking at Tyrrell's has produced a light but pleasant wine.

♥♥♥♥ **1998** Very youthful and deep purple-red, the hue suggesting there may be a touch of Chambourcin in the blend. Ripe, sweet cassis berry fruit, together with a touch of varietally derived earth is followed by a spotlessly clean, fresh, berry-flavoured palate, with little or no evident oak influence. Fractionally angular, and needs a year or two in bottle to settle down. **rating:** 86
best drinking 2001–2004 **best vintages** NA **drink with** Italian cuisine • $19

coombend estate ★★★★☆

Coombend via Swansea, Tas 7190 **region** Southern Tasmania
phone (03) 6257 8256 **fax** (03) 6257 8484 **open** 7 days 9–6
winemaker Andrew Hood (Contract) **production** 3000 **est.** 1985
product range ($17.50–26 CD) Riesling, Sauvignon Blanc, Cabernet Sauvignon.
summary John Fenn Smith originally established 1.75 hectares of cabernet sauvignon, 2.2 hectares of sauvignon blanc and 0.5 hectare of riesling (together with a little cabernet franc) on his 2600-hectare sheep station, choosing that part of his property which is immediately adjacent to Freycinet. This slightly quixotic choice of variety has been justified by the success of the wine in limited show entries. In December 1998 Coombend opened a brand new, purpose-built cellar-door sales area and has also significantly expanded its plantings to include riesling and sauvignon blanc.

Coombend Estate Riesling

Being graziers by background, the Fenn Smiths calculate their vineyard holdings not by area but by vine numbers, of which there are 4000 riesling. The wine is contract-made by Andrew Hood.

♥♥♥♥♡ **1999** Light green-yellow; the highly aromatic, high-toned bouquet has voluminous tropical passionfruit aromas; similar tropical/lime fruit swirls through the palate which, against the odds, retains finesse. Gold medal winner Tasmanian Wines Show 2000. **rating:** 92
best drinking 2000–2007 **best vintages** '99 **drink with** Avocado salad • $17.50

Coombend Estate Sauvignon Blanc

Produced from 3000 estate vines, and spends six weeks in French oak.

▼▼▼▼ 1999 Medium yellow-green; the bouquet is potent, rich and powerful, with fruit rather than oak the driving force. The abundantly flavoured palate is no less strongly fruit-driven by ripe sauvignon flavours. **rating: 86**

best drinking 2000–2002 **best vintages** NA **drink with** Sugar-cured tuna • $26

Coombend Cabernet Sauvignon

Situated adjacent to Freycinet, and shares the same remarkable site climate, proving yet again how difficult it is to generalise about the Tasmanian climate. Since 1990 Coombend's Cabernets have been at or near the top of the Tasmanian hierarchy. Rotherhythe, Stoney Vineyard Domaine A and, more recently, Moorilla Estate are the only other serious contenders.

▼▼▼▼▽ 1998 Medium purple-red; fresh, bright cassis berry aromas flow through into a palate which has lovely sweet fruit but slightly cloying tannins on the finish. **rating: 92**

▼▼▼▼▼ 1997 Medium to full purple-red; smooth, sweet ripe berry and chocolate aromas and flavours enrich a wine with excellent structure and sure oak handling. **rating: 94**

best drinking 2003–2010 **best vintages** '90, '91, '92, '94, '95, '97, '98 **drink with** Ragout of lamb • $26

🐾 cooperage estate NR

15 Markovitch Lane, Junortoun, Vic 3551 **region** Bendigo
phone 0418 544 743 **fax** (03) 5449 3681 **open** Not
winemaker Graham Gregurek **production** NA **est.** 1995
product range NA.
summary The Gregurek family has established 2.2 hectares of shiraz and cabernet sauvignon at their vineyard on the southern outskirts of the town of Bendigo. As the name suggests, there is also a cooperage on site.

coorinja ★★☆

Toodyay Road, Toodyay, WA 6566 **region** Other wineries of WA
phone (08) 9626 2280 **open** Mon–Sat 8–5
winemaker Michael Wood **production** 3200 **est.** 1870
product range ($8–10.50 CD) Dry White, Claret, Hermitage, Burgundy, Fortifieds; the latter account for 50 per cent of Coorinja's production.
summary An evocative and historic winery nestling in a small gully which seems to be in a time-warp, begging to be used as a set for a film. A recent revamp of the packaging accompanied a more than respectable Hermitage, with lots of dark chocolate and sweet berry flavour, finishing with soft tannins.

cope-williams ★★★☆

Glenfern Road, Romsey, Vic 3434 **region** Macedon Ranges
phone (03) 5429 5428 **fax** (03) 5429 5655 **open** 7 days 11–5
winemaker Michael Cope-Williams **production** 7000 **est.** 1977
product range ($14–25 R) Chardonnay, Cabernet Merlot; d'Vine is second label, Riesling, Chardonnay and Cabernet Sauvignon; winery specialty sparkling wine Macedon R.O.M.S.E.Y.
summary One of the high country Macedon pioneers, specialising in sparkling wines which are full flavoured but also producing excellent Chardonnay and Pinot Noir table wines in the warmer vintages. A traditional 'English Green'-type cricket ground is available for hire and booked out most days of the week from spring through till autumn.

coriole ★★★★

Chaffeys Road, McLaren Vale, SA 5171 **region** McLaren Vale
phone (08) 8323 8305 **fax** (08) 8323 9136 **open** Mon–Fri 10–5, weekends 11–5
winemaker Grant Harrison **production** 30 000 **est.** 1967
product range ($14–52 R) Lalla Rookh Semillon, Semillon Sauvignon Blanc, Chenin Blanc, Semillon, Chardonnay, Sangiovese, Shiraz, Redstone (Shiraz Cabernet Grenache), Diva (Sangiovese blend), Cabernet Sauvignon; Mary Kathleen (Cabernet blend), Lloyd Reserve Shiraz, Lalla Rookh Grenache Shiraz.
summary Justifiably best known for its Shiraz, which — both in the rare Lloyd Reserve and also like standard form — is extremely impressive. It has spread its wings in recent years, being one of the first wineries to catch onto the Italian fashion with its Sangiovese, but its white varietal wines lose nothing by comparison. It is also a producer of high-quality olive oil distributed commercially through all Australian States. The wines are exported to the UK, the US, Canada, Switzerland, Germany, The Netherlands, Taiwan, Japan and New Zealand.

Coriole Shiraz

Produced from estate plantings on red loam over ironstone and limestone subsoils. While the vines are new in comparison to those used to make Lloyd Reserve, they are in fact old by any normal standards, dating back to the late 1960s. This has usually been a distinguished wine.

TTTT 1997 Medium red-purple; the bouquet is moderately intense, but quite complex, with a range of earthy/savoury/berry/chocolate aromas. The palate is smoother, with attractive cherry and blackberry fruit neatly offset by fine tannins and subtle oak. **rating:** 89

best drinking 2002–2010 **best vintages** '90, '91, '96 **drink with** Steak and kidney pie • $24

Coriole Sangiovese

Together with Montrose, Coriole has been one of the pioneers in the growing and making of Sangiovese in Australia, making its first wine from this variety in 1986. Traditionally made in open fermenters and matured in aged American and French oak.

TTTY 1998 Medium red-purple; the bouquet is fresh, with quite bright mint, leaf and cherry fruit. The palate is very, very minty; I simply cannot see this as a true varietal expression. **rating:** 82

best drinking 2001–2004 **best vintages** '96 **drink with** Osso buco • $18

Coriole Mary Kathleen Cabernet Blend

Second in the Coriole hierarchy after the scarce Lloyd Shiraz, but still very much a super-premium wine. Typically made from roughly equal quantities of Merlot and Cabernet Sauvignon, with a dash of Cabernet Franc (in 1995 45 per cent Merlot, 41 per cent Cabernet Sauvignon and 14 per cent Cabernet Franc) it is a distinguished wine, utterly different from the others in the Coriole stable.

TTTTY 1997 Medium red-purple; the bouquet is quite complex, with woody/briary/canopy notes, which disappear altogether on the palate, where solid berry fruit and some archetypal McLaren Valley chocolate flavours come through, finishing with balanced oak and good tannins. **rating:** 90

best drinking 2002–2007 **best vintages** '90, '91, '92, '94, '95, '97 **drink with** Mature cheddar • $33

cosham NR

101 Union Road, Carmel via Kalamunda, WA 6076 **region** Perth Hills
phone (08) 9293 5424 **fax** (08) 9293 5062 **open** Weekends and public holidays 10–5
winemaker Julie White **production** 1000 **est.** 1989
product range ($16 CD) Chardonnay, Pinot Noir, Cabernet Merlot, Méthode Champenoise Brut.
summary The newest of the Perth Hills ventures, with a microscopic amount of wine available. Both the Chardonnay and Pinot Noir spend two years in French oak barriques before bottling — a long time by any standards. Improbable though it may seem, exports to the US.

Cosham Chardonnay

A well-made wine which has won bronze medals at the Australian Small Winemakers Show and the Swan Valley Show in 1999.

TTTY 1998 Very light green-yellow; the bouquet is light, with some slight creamy/biscuity notes but not over-much fruit. The palate is slightly tart; any shortcomings in the wine stem from the grapes rather than the winemaking. **rating:** 81

best drinking 2000–2001 **best vintages** NA **drink with** Roast chicken • $16

Cosham Cabernet Merlot

Like the Cosham Chardonnay, competently made, winning bronze medals at the Swan Valley Show and the Perth Hills Wine Show in 1999.

TTT 1998 Medium red, with just a touch of purple; light berry fruit has some earthy overtones and a slightly varnishy lift; the palate is light, with sweet, slight confection, fruit. **rating:** 79

best drinking 2000–2002 **best vintages** NA **drink with** Cold meat salad • $16

cowra estate ★★★

Boorowa Road, Cowra, NSW 2794 **region** Cowra
phone (02) 6342 1136 **fax** (02) 6342 4286 **open** 7 days 9–6
winemaker Simon Gilbert (Contract) **production** 20 000 **est.** 1973
product range ($12–15 CD) Chardonnay, Unwooded Chardonnay, Verdelho, Cabernet Rosé, Cabernet Sauvignon Shiraz, Cabernets. The Classic Bat series of Chardonnay, Pinot Noir and Cabernet Merlot is now at the head of the range.

summary Cowra Estate was purchased from the family of founder Tony Gray by South African-born food and beverage entrepreneur John Geber in 1995. A vigorous promotional campaign has gained a higher domestic profile for the once export-oriented brand. John Geber is actively involved in the promotional effort and rightly proud of the excellent value for money which the wines represent. The Quarry Wine Cellars and Restaurant offer visitors a full range of all of the Cowra Estate's wines but also wines from the other producers in the region, including Richmond Grove, Hungerford Hill, Arrowfield, Mulyan and Chiverton.

Cowra Estate Chardonnay

The principal wine produced by Cowra Estate, drawn in part from vineyards which in bygone days were responsible for the first Petaluma Chardonnays, and thereafter the early Rothbury Estate Chardonnays. Always reliable wine. Six family-owned vineyards form the viticultural base from which Cowra Estate draws its grapes.

▼▼▼▽ **1998** Medium yellow-green; the bouquet has some character and weight, with peach and citrus fruit, but the wine doesn't quite deliver the same fruit on the palate, possibly due to the masking effect of indifferent oak.
rating: 80

best drinking 1999–2000 **best vintages** NA **drink with** Red Rooster • $11.90

Cowra Estate Cabernet Rosé

If one wished to be cruel, it would be possible to argue that Rosé is the best use to which Cowra cabernet can be put. Certainly, this is always a pleasant wine, right in the commercial slot. Its only problem is that Rosé is an unwanted child in the general market.

▼▼▼▽ **1999** Bright pink. The bouquet is quite fresh and lively, the palate fresh, clean and just off-dry; a pleasant, inoffensive commercial style, excellent for summer drinking. **rating:** 80

best drinking Drink now **best vintages** NA **drink with** Summer lunch • $12

Cowra Estate Cabernets

As the name suggests, a Bordeaux-blend, which offers a pretty good value at the price. The brand had its moment of glory as the winner of the Riedel Crystal Trophy for Best Lighter Bodied Dry Red Table Wine of Show at the 1998 Sydney International Wine Competition.

▼▼▼▽ **1998** Medium red-purple; there is sweet, slightly stewy, berry fruit on the bouquet; the palate has some concentration and some unresolved tannins. Would have benefited from a bit more work in barrel, but the underlying fruit is quite good. **rating:** 80

best drinking 2000–2002 **best vintages** NA **drink with** Lasagne • $12

crabtree of watervale ★★★☆

North Terrace, Watervale SA 5452 **region** Clare Valley
phone (08) 8843 0069 **fax** (08) 8843 0144 **open** 7 days 11–5
winemaker Robert Crabtree, Stuart Bourne **production** 4000 **est.** 1979
product range ($15–20 CD) Riesling, Late Harvest Riesling, Semillon, Watervale Dry Red, Grenache, Shiraz Cabernet Sauvignon, Cabernet Sauvignon, Muscat, Windmill Tawny.
summary The gently eccentric Robert Crabtree and wife Elizabeth are once again very much part of the business, making full flavoured, classic Clare Valley styles.

Crabtree of Watervale Riesling

Produced from hand-picked estate-grown grapes; the wine is partially whole-bunch pressed and conventionally fermented in stainless steel at low temperatures using two yeasts.

▼▼▼▼ **1999** Light yellow-green; the bouquet is highly scented, with lime and hints of passionfruit; abundant, tropical lime fruit flavours flood the palate; a rich, early-drinking style. **rating:** 87

best drinking 2000–2001 **best vintages** '99 **drink with** Ginger prawns • $15

Crabtree of Watervale Shiraz Cabernet Sauvignon

A blend of 80 per cent Shiraz and 20 per cent Cabernet Sauvignon. Made the old-fashioned way, from hand-pruned and hand-picked vines, then fermented and pressed in a basket press. The wine spends 14 months in French oak hogsheads, principally used, before being egg white-fined and lightly filtered.

▼▼▼▼ **1996** Medium red-purple; the bouquet is clean and firm, with a touch of earthy austerity from the Cabernet component. The palate is lively, helped by good acidity; there are red berry flavours, with a hint of mint and minimal tannin. **rating:** 85

best drinking 1999–2005 **best vintages** NA **drink with** Sirloin steak • $18

craig avon vineyard ★★★☆

Craig Avon Lane, Merricks North, Vic 3926 **region** Mornington Peninsula
phone (03) 5989 7465 **fax** (03) 5989 7615 **open** Weekends and public holidays 12–5
winemaker Ken Lang **production** 1000 **est.** 1986
product range ($29–33 CD) Chardonnay, Pinot Noir, Cabernet, Cabernet Merlot.
summary All of the wines are sold cellar door and by mailing list. The wines are competently made, clean and
with pleasant fruit flavour.

craigie knowe ★★★

Glen Gala Road, Cranbrook, Tas 7190 **region** Southern Tasmania
phone (03) 6223 5620 **fax** (03) 6223 5009 **open** Weekends or by appointment
winemaker Dr John Austwick **production** 500 **est.** 1979
product range ($20–23 ML) Cabernet Sauvignon, Pinot Noir.
summary John Austwick makes a small quantity of full flavoured, robust Cabernet Sauvignon in a tiny winery as
a weekend relief from a busy metropolitan dental practice. The Pinot Noir is made in a style which will appeal to
confirmed Cabernet Sauvignon drinkers, and John Austwick has a couple of barrels of 1998 Cabernet Sauvignon
which, if bottled separately, would appeal to everyone who has ever lifted a wine glass.

craiglee ★★★★★

Sunbury Road, Sunbury, Vic 3429 **region** Sunbury
phone (03) 9744 4489 **fax** (03) 9744 4489 **open** Sun, public holidays 10–5, or by appointment
winemaker Patrick Carmody **production** 2000 **est.** 1976
product range ($17–34 CD) Chardonnay, Pinot Noir, Shiraz, Cabernet Sauvignon.
summary An historic winery with a proud nineteenth-century record which recommenced winemaking in
1976 after a prolonged hiatus. Produces one of the finest cool-climate Shirazes in Australia, redolent of cherry,
liquorice and spice in the better (i.e. warmer) vintages, lighter-bodied in the cooler ones. Maturing vines and
improved viticulture have made the wines more consistent (and even better) over the past ten years or so.

Craiglee Chardonnay

Has stood in the shadow of the Craiglee Shiraz, but a vertical tasting late in 1997 with vintages back to 1982
showed it to be a very fine wine in its own right, and with true cellaring potential. Since 1991 the move to barrel-
fermentation in French oak and the exclusion of malolactic fermentation has both tightened the style, and
increased its longevity.
1997 Light to medium green-yellow; a stylish, complex wine, with tangy, citrus-accented fruit aromas
and perfectly balanced and integrated oak. The palate follows down the same track, with persistent citrus and
melon fruit coming through to a long finish, supported by subtle oak.   **rating:** 93
best drinking 2000–2005 **best vintages** '87, '90, '92, '96, '97 **drink with** Pan-fried veal • $NA

Craiglee Shiraz

Produced from 4 hectares of estate plantings, almost invariably producing wines of the highest imaginable
quality, with wonderful cherry, pepper and spice aromas and flavours. The wines are fruit- rather than oak-
driven; they are immaculately structured, having the fruit weight and vinous sweetness to balance the
peppery/spicy tang.
1997 Medium to full purple-red; a clean and powerful bouquet, with classic black cherry and spice
aromas; a lovely wine on the palate, with black cherry fruit together with hints of spice and liquorice; fine tannins
and subtle oak.   **rating:** 96
best drinking 2001–2007 **best vintages** '84, '86, '88, '91, '92, '93, '94, '96, '97 **drink with** Italian cuisine • $34

craigow NR

528 Richmond Road, Cambridge, Tas 7170 **region** Southern Tasmania
phone (03) 6248 5379 **fax** (03) 6248 5482 **open** Fri–Sun 10–5
winemaker Alain Rousseau (Contract) **production** 500 **est.** 1989
product range ($18–24 CD) Riesling, Gewurztraminer, Chardonnay, Pinot Noir.
summary Craigow has substantial vineyards, with 5 hectares of pinot noir and another 5 hectares divided
between riesling, chardonnay and gewurztraminer. Barry and Cathy have moved from being grape growers with
only one wine made for sale. Their cellar door opened early in December 1999.

Craigow Riesling

A particularly attractive style; the 1998 vintage won a silver medal at the Tasmanian Wines Show 2000.

▼▼▼▼ 1998 Light green-yellow; the bouquet is quite delicate, with passionfruit nuances which come through on the palate, where floral passionfruit and spice flavours run through to a fractionally heavy finish.   **rating: 85**

best drinking 2000–2005 **best vintages** NA **drink with** Fish terrine •$18

Craigow Pinot Noir

A full-bodied Coal River style, providing great flavour without undue effort in the winery.

▼▼▼▼ 1998 Medium to full purple-red; the bouquet is solid and ripe, with dark plum fruit cascading over into the rich, full and sweet palate. The wine has literally eaten the oak.   **rating: 87**

best drinking 2001–2008 **best vintages** NA **drink with** Duck casserole •$24

craneford   ★★★☆

Moorundie Street, Truro, SA 5356 **region** Barossa Valley
phone (08) 8564 0003 **fax** (08) 8564 0008 **open** Wed–Mon 11–5
winemaker John Zilm **production** 3000 **est.** 1978
product range ($9–25 CD) Eden Valley Riesling, Barossa Valley Chardonnay, Barossa Valley Unwooded Chardonnay, Barossa Valley Semillon, Frontignac, Shiraz, Quartet, Grenache, Fortified and Sparkling.
summary The purchase of Craneford by owner/winemaker John Zilm has wrought many changes. It has moved to a new winery (and café) and is supported by 15 hectares of Barossa Valley shiraz. Wine quality, too, has leapt. Retail distribution in Sydney and Melbourne, and exports to Japan through Australian Prestige Wines.

Craneford Premium Barossa Semillon

Made from grapes grown on the Barossa Valley floor and described as lightly oaked, which it is. Other Barossa Valley winemakers of Semillon could well pay attention.

▼▼▼▼ 1999 Glowing yellow-green; a clean and solid bouquet with herb and citrus aromas is followed by a palate where subtle oak adds more to the texture than to the flavour. Admirable.   **rating: 86**

best drinking 2000–2003 **best vintages** NA **drink with** Maggie Beer chicken •$13

Craneford Shiraz

Produced from the substantial estate plantings; it comes as no surprise to find that the wine has received medals at both the Melbourne and Adelaide Wine Shows, and received four and a half stars in *Winestate* magazine.

▼▼▼▼ 1998 Dense red-purple; concentrated, deep blackberry and black pepper fruit on the bouquet is followed by a palate which is, happily, of medium body and not over-extracted. Here sweet blackberry fruit, supple tannins and subtle oak all contribute to a richly stylish wine.   **rating: 87**

best drinking 2002–2012 **best vintages** '98 **drink with** Kangaroo fillet •$25

Craneford Quartet

Produced from a blend of Cabernet Sauvignon, Cabernet Franc, Petit Verdot and Shiraz; like the Shiraz, well made.

▼▼▼▼ 1998 The colour is dark, the hue not entirely convincing. An earthy/savoury bouquet is followed by a far better and more convincing palate, with blackberry and blackcurrant fruit running all the way through to a soft, lingering finish.   **rating: 86**

best drinking 2001–2008 **best vintages** '98 **drink with** Barbecued lamb chops •$20

crane winery   NR

Haydens Road, Kingaroy, Qld 4610 **region** South Burnett and Other Wineries of Queensland
phone (07) 4162 7647 **fax** (07) 4162 7647 **open** 7 days 9–4
winemaker John Crane **production** 4000 **est.** 1996
product range ($10–16 ML) Marsanne Verdelho, Semillon, Chardonnay, Hillside White and Red, Ruby Cabernet, Merlot, Shiraz, Shiraz Cabernet Sauvignon, Cabernet Sauvignon, Sparkling Burgundy, Vintage Liqueur Shiraz, Liqueur Muscat.
summary Established by John and Sue Crane, Crane Winery is one of several in the burgeoning Kingaroy (or South Burnett) region in Queensland, drawing upon 3 hectares of estate plantings but also purchasing grapes from other growers in the region. Interestingly, Sue Crane's great-grandfather established a vineyard planted to shiraz over 100 years ago (in 1898) and which remained in production until 1970. Four hectares of estate vineyards are supplemented by grapes from over 20 contract growers.

Crane Winery Shiraz

The first varietal Shiraz produced by the winery; would appear to be made from locally-grown grapes.

▼▼▼♀ **1999** Medium to full red-purple; a rich and very sweet bouquet; chocolate, leather and vanilla flows into a rich, almost soupy, chocolatey/berry/meaty palate. **rating:** 80

best drinking 2000–2003 **best vintages** NA **drink with** Steak and kidney pie • $15

cranswick estate ★★★

Walla Avenue, Griffith, NSW 2680 **region** Riverina
phone (02) 6962 4133 **fax** (02) 6962 2888 **open** 7 days 10–4
winemaker Andrew Schulz, Tim Pearce **production** 800 000 **est.** 1976
product range ($7–22 R) There are three ranges in two price sectors: at the top come the Premium and Regional Selection ranges (with Autumn Gold Botrytis Semillon off to one side and higher priced again) comprising Barrel Fermented Semillon, Young Vine Chardonnay, Conlon Block Marsanne, McLaren Vale Sauvignon Blanc, Gnarled Vine Barossa Grenache, Cocoparra Vineyard Shiraz, Dry Country Cabernet Sauvignon and NV Sparkling Shiraz; then there is the volume-selling Vignette range of Fruition (White Frontignac), Unoaked Chardonnay, Semillon Sauvignon Blanc, Semillon Cabernet Merlot, Shiraz.
summary Taking full advantage of the buoyant share market and the continuing export success of Australian wines, Cranswick Estate made a highly successful entry to the lists of the Australian Associated Stock Exchanges in 1997. The substantial capital raised will see the further expansion of an already thriving business, firmly aimed at the export market in the UK and Europe, the US and Japan and Southeast Asia.

Cranswick Estate Vignette Range Cabernet Merlot

While most of the Cranswick Estate wines in the Vignette Range are no better than their price ($10–12) would suggest, the Cabernet Merlot sometimes rises above its station. A blend of 52 per cent Cabernet Sauvignon, 42 per cent Merlot and 6 per cent Ruby Cabernet, it is sourced from various vineyards in the Griffith region.

▼▼▼♀ **1997** Light to medium red-purple; the bouquet is light but clean, with aromas of leaf and hay. The palate has the typical savoury leafy/tobacco notes from the Merlot component, and a touch of berry from the Cabernet. The acidity has been neatly adjusted to give freshness. Well priced. **rating:** 81

best drinking 2000–2001 **best vintages** NA **drink with** Cheddar • $10

crawford river wines ★★★★★

Hotspur Upper Road, Condah, Vic 3303 **region** Far South West Victoria
phone (03) 5578 2267 **fax** (03) 5578 2240 **open** 7 days 10–4
winemaker John Thomson **production** 3600 **est.** 1975
product range ($18–30 CD) Riesling, Reserve Riesling, Semillon Sauvignon Blanc, Chardonnay, Cabernet Merlot, Cabernet Sauvignon, Nektar.
summary Exemplary wines right across the range are made by full-time grazier, part-time winemaker John Thomson, who clearly has the winemaker's equivalent of the gardener's green thumb. The Riesling is consistently outstanding, the Cabernet-based wines excellent in warmer vintages. Exports to the UK, Germany, Singapore and Austria.

Crawford River Riesling

A wine of exemplary quality over the years, tight and reserved, and fully reflecting the very cool climate in which it is grown. It is 100 per cent estate-grown (as are all of the Crawford River wines).

▼▼▼▼♀ **1999** Light green-yellow; the bouquet is very fragrant, with lots of passionfruit, partially ex fermentation; just a touch reductive. The palate is potent, with abundant passionfruit/lime flavours running through a long, slightly smoky finish. **rating:** 92

best drinking 2002–2007 **best vintages** '86, '88, '89, '91, '94, '96, '97, '98, '99 **drink with** Antipasto • $22

Crawford River Reserve Riesling

First made in 1999, and then in tiny quantities which were effectively pre-sold. It is not hard to see why.

▼▼▼▼▼ **1999** Medium yellow-green; a spotlessly clean bouquet with intense, sweet lime juice aromas flows into an intense, powerful and long palate, which has an extra dimension on the mid-palate coming from fruit rather then sweetness. Perfect balance. **rating:** 97

best drinking 2001–2020 **best vintages** '99 **drink with** Richer fish dishes • $NA

Crawford River Semillon Sauvignon Blanc

Yet another testament to the winemaking skills, and in particular the white winemaking skills, of John Thomson. In vintages such a 1997, it is hard to imagine a more perfect evocation of a blend such as this, with the two varieties seamlessly merging with each other, and reflecting the cool climate.

TTTT 1999 Light to medium green-yellow; the bouquet is clean and fresh, with a hint of gooseberry; the palate is delicate, fresh and crisp, gaining momentum towards the finish, but without the depth of fruit of the '97. **rating: 85**

best drinking 2000–2003 **best vintages** '96, '97 **drink with** Crab or shellfish • $18

Crawford River Nektar

A clever name for a strongly botrytised wine; the varieties are nowhere specified, and one suspects come from all three white varieties planted at the vineyard (semillon, sauvignon blanc and riesling).

TTTT 1998 Glowing yellow-green; the bouquet is clean and powerful, but without any particular varietal character. The palate would seem to include Semillon as well as Riesling; powerful and well-balanced honey and cumquat flavours. **rating: 85**

best drinking 2000–2005 **best vintages** NA **drink with** Any rich dessert • $24

Crawford River Cabernet Sauvignon

Grown at the extreme edge for Cabernet Sauvignon, and always presents a rather austere, minerally, European cast, but in most years redeems itself with the length of its finish and the way the flavour builds up with the second glass.

TTTTT 1997 The fragrant, cedary, savoury bouquet is classic cool-grown Cabernet, yet is not green or leafy. The elegant palate swells into sweeter blackberry/blackcurrant flavours, with fine-grained tannins and subtle oak. **rating: 95**

best drinking 2002–2012 **best vintages** '86, '88, '90, '91, '93, '97 **drink with** Roast veal • $27

crisford winery   NR

556 Hermitage Road, Pokolbin, NSW 2022 **region** Lower Hunter Valley
phone (02) 9387 1100 **fax** (02) 9387 6688 **open** Not
winemaker David Hook (Contract) **production** NA **est.** 1990
product range A single wine — Synergy (Merlot Cabernet Franc blend).
summary Carol and Neal Crisford have established 2.6 hectares of merlot and cabernet franc which go to produce Synergy (a name which I fancy has been trademarked by Hamilton).

crosswinds vineyard   NR

10 Vineyard Drive, Tea Tree, Tas 7017 **region** Southern Tasmania
phone (03) 6268 1091 **fax** (03) 6268 1091 **open** 7 days 10–5 Oct–May, weekends Sept–June
winemaker Andrew Vasiljuk **production** 20 tonnes **est.** 1990
product range ($15.85–20.60 R) Riesling, Chardonnay, Pinot Noir.
summary Crosswinds has two vineyards, with the 1-hectare Tea Tree Vineyard and the 2-hectare Margate Vineyard. As well as cellar-door sales, has retail distribution in Melbourne and small exports to the UK and Southeast Asia.

Crosswinds Unwooded Chardonnay

A wine which shows Andrew Vasiljuk is highly skilled in making both wooded and unwooded Chardonnay. The 1997 vintage of this was selected by *Decanter* as its Wine of the Month in July 1999, and in my view, the '98 is an even better wine; certainly I gave it gold medal points on my score sheet at the Tasmanian Wines Show 2000.

TTTTY 1998 Medium yellow-green; the moderately intense bouquet is clean, with a mix of apple, citrus and mineral aromas. The palate is delicate and crisp in the manner of a French Chablis from a lighter vintage. **rating: 91**

best drinking 2000–2004 **best vintages** '99 **drink with** Tasmanian salmon • $18

cruickshank callatoota estate   ★★☆

2656 Wybong Road, Wybong, NSW 2333 **region** Upper Hunter Valley
phone (02) 6547 8149 **fax** (02) 6547 8144 **open** 7 days 9–5
winemaker Hartley Smithers **production** 7000 **est.** 1973
product range ($9–13.50 CD) Cabernet Rosé, Cask 12 Cabernet Sauvignon, Two Cabernets, Show Reserve, Cabernet Franc, Old Tawny Port.
summary Owned by Sydney management consultant John Cruickshank and family. Wine quality definitely improved in the 1990s, although the wines still show strong regional, rather earthy, characters; the label itself likewise doggedly remains old-fashioned.

cubbaroo cellars   NR

Cubbaroo Station, Wee Waa, NSW 2388 **region** Western Plains Zone
phone (02) 6796 1741 **fax** (02) 6796 1751 **open** Thurs–Sun 12–10
winemaker Simon Gilbert (Contract) **production** NA **est.** 1972
product range ($10–15 CD) Shiraz, Port.

summary Cubbaroo Cellars has been in existence since the early 1970s in the heart of the Namoi Valley cotton country. For a while it seemed that it had ceased production under the Cubbaroo Cellars label, selling its grapes to wineries in the Hunter Valley. However, the 10.8 hectares of shiraz planted long ago has now been supplemented by 4 hectares of cabernet sauvignon (not yet producing), so its fortunes may be on the rise. The two wines presently available are sold only through the cellar door.

cullen wines   ★★★★★

Caves Road, Cowaramup, WA 6284 **region** Margaret River
phone (08) 9755 5277 **fax** (08) 9755 5550 **open** 7 days 10–4
winemaker Vanya Cullen, Trevor Kent **production** 15 000 **est.** 1971
product range ($16–60 CD) Flagship wines: Chardonnay, Sauvignon Blanc, Pinot Noir, Semillon Sauvignon Blanc, Reserve Cabernet Sauvignon Merlot; premium wines: Classic Dry White, Blanc de Noir, Velvet Red, Autumn Harvest.

summary One of the pioneers of Margaret River which has always produced long-lived wines of highly individual style from the substantial and mature estate vineyards. Winemaking is now in the hands of Vanya Cullen, daughter of the founders; she is possessed of an extraordinarily good palate. The Cabernet Merlot goes from strength to strength; indeed, I would rate it Australia's best. The wines are distributed throughout Australia and also make their way to significant export markets in the UK, the US, Europe and Asia.

Cullen Sauvignon Blanc Semillon

An extremely complex wine, a blend of 70 per cent Sauvignon Blanc, 25 per cent Semillon and 5 per cent Chardonnay, the Chardonnay having been taken through malolactic fermentation in oak. The Sauvignon Blanc component is entirely barrel-fermented in new French oak. This approach deliberately softens primary varietal characters.

▼▼▼▼▽ **1999** Medium yellow-green; the bouquet is quite complex and concentrated, with barrel-ferment oak obvious but not aggressive. A multiflavoured palate with a mix of herb, gooseberry, spice and mineral is as complex as it is long.   **rating:** 93

best drinking 2000–2005 **best vintages** '97, '98, '99 **drink with** Margaret River marron   • $40

Cullen Classic Dry White

A blend of 28 per cent Sauvignon Blanc, 27 per cent Chardonnay, 21 per cent Verdelho, 14 per cent Semillon and 10 per cent Chenin Blanc.

▼▼▼▼ **1999** Light green-yellow; there are soft, generous fruit salad aromas followed by plenty of ripe, rich, rounded fruit in an easy-drinking style.   **rating:** 89

best drinking Drink now **best vintages** NA **drink with** Rich seafood   • $17

Cullen Chardonnay

An exceptionally complex wine which has really hit the heights since 1993; both that vintage and 1994 stand high among the more powerful, structured Chardonnays made in Australia. One hundred per cent barrel-fermentation, 100 per cent malolactic fermentation and prolonged lees contact all make their mark.

▼▼▼▼▼ **1998** Stephen Lake has mastered the intricacies of Hunter Valley Chardonnay, no doubt assisted by the great terroir of the Folly Vineyard. The wine exudes style from start to finish, with nectarine and cashew aromas and perfectly weighted ripe fig and nectarine flavours in a silken web of vanillan oak.   **rating:** 95

best drinking 2000–2003 **best vintages** '93, '94, '96, '98 **drink with** Sweetbreads   • $45

Cullen Cabernet Sauvignon Merlot

An estate-grown wine of the highest quality; since 1990 has been the best Margaret River Cabernet Merlot blend. Up to 1995 both a varietal and a Reserve version were made, but as from that vintage the decision was taken to only release one wine. Consistently outstanding. A blend of 75 per cent Cabernet Sauvignon, 20 per cent Merlot and 5 per cent Cabernet Franc.

▼▼▼▼▼ **1998** Dense red-purple; the spotlessly clean, smooth bouquet is flooded with wonderfully rich cassis fruit; an imperious wine on the palate, with layer upon layer of fruit woven through with ripe tannins and oak.   **rating:** 97

best drinking 2003–2018 **best vintages** '77, '84, '86, '90, '91, '92, '93, '95, '96, '97, '98 **drink with** Lamb, strong cheddar   • $60

currency creek wines ★★★

Winery Road, Currency Creek, SA 5214 **region** Other Wineries of SA
phone (08) 8555 4069 **fax** (08) 8555 4100 **open** 7 days 10–5
winemaker Phillip Tonkin **production** 4500 **est.** 1969
product range ($9.80–30 CD) Dry White, Semillon, Sauvignon Blanc, Chardonnay, Princess Alexandrina
Noble Riesling, Gamay, Pinot Noir, Harmony (Shiraz Merlot), Ostrich Hill Shiraz, Cabernet Sauvignon,
Sparkling, Fortifieds.
summary Constant name changes early in the piece (Santa Rosa, Tonkins have also been tried) did not help the
quest for identity or recognition in the marketplace, but the winery has nonetheless produced some outstanding
wood-matured whites and pleasant, soft reds selling at attractive prices.

Currency Creek Sauvignon Blanc

Made from a small portion of the grapes harvested from over 11 hectares of estate plantings. Over the years, has
been one of the better Currency Creek wines, always showing some varietal character, in some years tropical and
in other years more herbaceous.
▼▼▼▽ **1999** Light straw; a crisp, light and fairly herbaceous bouquet leads into a similar, slightly old-fashioned-
style palate; at least it has character.   **rating:** 81
best drinking 2000–2001 **best vintages** '93, '95 **drink with** Seafood •$13.10

curtis NR

Foggo Road, McLaren Vale, SA 5171 **region** McLaren Vale
phone (08) 8323 8389 **open** Weekends 11–4.30
winemaker P Curtis **production** 1500 **est.** 1988
product range ($4–5.50 CD) Riesling, Moselle, Claret, Shiraz Grenache, Ruby Port, Tawny Port.
summary A small and relatively new producer in McLaren Vale, whose wines I have not tasted.

dalfarras ★★★★

PO Box 123, Nagambie, Vic 3608 **region** Goulburn Valley
phone (03) 5794 2637 **fax** (03) 5794 2360 **open** Not
winemaker Alister Purbrick, Alan George **production** 35 000 **est.** 1991
product range ($13.95–49.95 R) Riesling, Unwooded Chardonnay, Barrel Fermented Chardonnay, Sauvignon
Blanc, Marsanne, Shiraz, Cabernet Sauvignon, Reserve Cabernet Sauvignon.
summary The personal project of Alister Purbrick and artist-wife Rosa (née) Dalfarra, whose paintings adorn
the labels of the wines. Alister, of course, is best known as winemaker at Chateau Tahbilk, the family winery and
home, but this range of wines is intended to (in Alister's words) 'allow me to expand my winemaking horizons and
mould wines in styles different to Chateau Tahbilk'. It now draws upon 37 hectares of its own plantings in the
Goulburn Valley, and the business continues to grow year by year. In the 1998 show season the Dalfarras wines had
outstanding success, with the 1991 Reserve Cabernet Sauvignon winning two trophies, a gold, two silver and
seven bronze medals, backed up by the 1998 Sauvignon Blanc and 1997 Marsanne, both of which won gold
medals and a number of silver and bronze awards. Exports to the UK.

Dalfarras Marsanne

A wood-matured version; the grapes are grown at Chateau Tahbilk.
▼▼▼▼ **1997** Medium yellow-green; the bouquet is bottle-developed and complex, with obvious oak input. The
palate, likewise, is quite complex; made in the Mitchelton style, rather than the Chateau Tahbilk style, which gives
it major points of difference from the latter.   **rating:** 85
best drinking 2000–2005 **best vintages** NA **drink with** Brains in black butter •$14.95

dalrymple ★★★★

1337 Pipers Brook Road, Pipers Brook, Tas 7254 **region** Northern Tasmania
phone (03) 6382 7222 **fax** (03) 6382 7222 **open** 7 days 10–5
winemaker Bertel Sundstrup **production** 3800 **est.** 1987
product range ($16–35 CD) Chardonnay, Unwooded Chardonnay, Sauvignon Blanc, Pinot Noir, Pinot Noir
Special Bin.
summary A partnership between Jill Mitchell and her sister and brother-in-law, Anne and Bertel Sundstrup,
inspired by father Bill Mitchell's establishment of the Tamarway Vineyard in the late 1960s. In 1991 Tamarway
reverted to the Sundstrup and Mitchell families and it, too, will be producing wine in the future, probably under
its own label but sold ex the Dalrymple cellar door. As production has grown (significantly), so has that of wine
quality across the board, often led by its Sauvignon Blanc.

Dalrymple Unwooded Chardonnay

An unusually full-flavoured wine which almost always has utterly distinctive characters.

ŸŸŸŸ 1999 Light green-yellow; a potent, aromatic bouquet with a mix of tropical/citrus/grapefruit aromas leads into a pretty powerful palate, which does, however, tend to cloy just a fraction. Seems to have been boosted by botrytis. **rating:** 80

best drinking 2000–2002 **best vintages** '98 **drink with** Scampi • $16

Dalrymple Pinot Noir

Yet another of a range of very good wines coming from Dalrymple out of the 1998 vintage. Re-entered in the Tasmanian Wines Show 2000, showing good development.

ŸŸŸŸ 1998 Light to medium red-purple; while the bouquet is only of light to medium intensity, the fruit is sweet and complexed by a touch of forest. The same play occurs on the palate which ranges through plum, leaf and forest flavours in a delicate but appealing fashion. When retasted in January 2000 it seemed to have picked up weight and flesh. **rating:** 90

best drinking 2000–2002 **best vintages** '98 **drink with** Chinese barbecued pork • $25

dalwhinnie ★★★★★

Taltarni Road, RMB 4378, Moonambel, Vic 3478 **region** Pyrenees
phone (03) 5467 2388 **fax** (03) 5467 2237 **open** 7 days 10–5
winemaker David Jones, Rick Kinzbrunner (Contract) **production** 4500 **est.** 1976
product range ($27–39 CD) Dalwhinnie Chardonnay and Pinot Noir, Moonambel Shiraz and Cabernet, Eagle Series Shiraz.
summary David and Jenny Jones have now acquired full ownership of Dalwhinnie from Ewan Jones, and have three children of their own to ensure the future succession. In the meantime, Dalwhinnie goes from strength to strength, making outstanding wines right across the board. The wines all show tremendous depth of fruit flavour, reflecting the relatively low-yielding but very well-maintained vineyards. It is hard to say whether the Chardonnay or the Shiraz is the more distinguished, the Pinot Noir (made with assistance from Rick Kinzbrunner) a startling arrival from out of nowhere. A further 8 hectares of shiraz (with a little viognier) were planted in the spring of 1999 on a newly acquired block on Taltarni Road, permitting the further development of export markets already established in the UK, Asia, Germany and the US.

Dalwhinnie Chardonnay

Produced from a little under 4 hectares of low-yielding, unirrigated estate-grown vines, with an ancestry going back to the clone introduced in the nineteenth century and discovered at Mudgee in the late 1960s. Barrel-fermentation adds to the richness to produce an invariably extremely complex wine.

ŸŸŸŸŸ 1998 Medium yellow-green; a very smooth bouquet with creamy/figgy aromas woven through subtle barrel-ferment oak; a fine, understated palate with a mix of cashew, fig and more minerally flavours, again supported by subtle oak. Perfect balance and harmony. **rating:** 91

best drinking 2001–2006 **best vintages** '87, '88, '90, '92, '93, '94, '96, '99 **drink with** Turkey • $27

Dalwhinnie Eagle Series Pyrenees Shiraz

A new wine to celebrate the millennium, made by David and Charlie Jones in the small winery overlooking the vineyard. Made in small 1500-litre open fermenters, foot-crushed and pigeaged, and basket-pressed. It then spends two years in small French oak barrels with lees contact and minimal sulphur. A mix of backyard and Burgundy winemaking techniques.

ŸŸŸŸ 1997 Medium to full red-purple; the bouquet is rich, with the contribution of the French oak quite evident, resulting in a mix of cedar and spice aromas. The palate is complex and savoury, in radically different style the glorious direct fruit of the '98 Moonambel. The oak, too, is just a little assertive, however good it may be. **rating:** 89

best drinking 2002–2009 **best vintages** NA **drink with** Game • $20

Dalwhinnie Moonambel Shiraz

An exceptionally concentrated and powerful wine, fully reflecting the low yields and the influence of the quartz, clay and gravel soils. These are not wines for the faint-hearted, positively demanding long cellaring but having the balance to repay patience.

ŸŸŸŸŸ 1998 Medium to full red-purple; the very rich bouquet has masses of ripe blood plum and pronounced spice, together with hints of vanilla. Sweet fruit carries right through from the start to the very finish of the complex flavour and structure of the palate. **rating:** 93

best drinking 2003–2013 **best vintages** '86, '88, '90, '91, '92, '94, '95, '97, '98 **drink with** Potent cheeses, strong red meats • $39

dalyup river estate   NR

Murrays Road, Esperance, WA 6450 **region** Other Wineries of WA
phone (08) 9076 5027 **fax** (08) 9076 5027 **open** Weekends 10–4
winemaker Tom Murray **production** 700 **est.** 1987
product range ($12–15 CD) Hellfire White, Esperance Sauvignon Blanc, Esperance Shiraz, Esperance Cabernet Sauvignon, Port.
summary Arguably the most remote winery in Australia other than Chateau Hornsby in Alice Springs. The quantities are as small as the cellar-door prices are modest; this apart, the light but fragrant wines show the cool climate of this ocean-side vineyard.

dal zotto wines   NR

Edi Road, Cheshunt, Vic 3678 **region** King Valley
phone (03) 5729 8321 **fax** (03) 5729 8490 **open** Fri–Mon 10–5
winemaker Otto Dal Zotto, Warren Proft **production** 2000 **est.** 1987
product range ($17–18 CD) Chardonnay, Merlot, Cabernet Merlot, Cabernet Sauvignon.
summary Dal Zotto Wines remains primarily a contract grape grower, with almost 26 hectares of vineyards (predominantly chardonnay, cabernet sauvignon and merlot, but with trial plantings of sangiovese, barbera and marzemimo) but does make a small amount of wine for local sale (and by mail order).

danbury estate   NR

Billimari, NSW 2794 (PO Box 605, Cowra, NSW 2794) **region** Cowra
phone (02) 6341 2204 **fax** (02) 6341 4690 **open** By appointment
winemaker Peter Howland (Contract) **production** 4600 **est.** 1996
product range ($12.95–15.30 CD) Middleton Chardonnay, Reserve Chardonnay.
summary A specialist Chardonnay producer established by Jonathon Middleton, with 8 hectares in production, and the wine made under contract.

d'arenberg   ★★★★★

Osborn Road, McLaren Vale, SA 5171 **region** McLaren Vale
phone (08) 8323 8206 **fax** (08) 8323 8423 **open** 7 days 10–5
winemaker Chester Osborn, Phillip Dean **production** 150 000 **est.** 1912
product range ($10–60 R) Dry Dam Riesling, Dryland Sauvignon Blanc, Broken Fishplate Sauvignon Blanc, Last Ditch Viognier, Olive Grove Chardonnay, Other Side Chardonnay, Noble Riesling, Peppermint Paddock Sparkling Chambourcin, Twenty Eight Road Mourvedre, d'Arry's Original Shiraz Grenache, Custodian Grenache, Dead Arm Shiraz, Footbolt Old Vine Shiraz, Red Ochre, Ironstone Pressings, High Trellis Cabernet Sauvignon, The Coppermine Road Cabernet Sauvignon; Fortified.
summary d'Arenberg has adopted a much higher profile in the second half of the 1990s, with a cascade of volubly worded labels and the opening of a spectacularly situated and high-quality restaurant, d'Arry's Verandah. Happily, wine quality has more than kept pace with the label uplifts. An incredible number of export markets spread across Europe, North America and Asia, with all of the major countries represented.

d'Arenberg The Last Ditch Viognier

This is the second vintage of the wine, which has the usual convoluted story about its label, involving Pedlers Creek and Palomino. An interesting wine with a touch more character than many featureless examples of the variety.
▼▼▼▽ 1999 Medium yellow-green; the bouquet is tangy, with plenty of character from both fruit and oak. It has that glycerol mouthfeel of the variety, which, as in this case, seems to involve slight phenolic characters. Whether it is worth the price is an interesting question.   **rating:** 83
best drinking 2000–2002 **best vintages** NA **drink with** Roast turkey •$30

d'Arenberg The Other Side Chardonnay

If my memory serves me right, The Other Side is precisely that: the other side of the estate vineyards. The wine is made using the full bunch of Chardonnay winemaker inputs.
▼▼▼▽ 1998 Medium yellow-green; a big, fleshy bouquet, slightly broad and oily, is followed by a similarly full-framed palate in its own particular style.   **rating:** 82
best drinking 2000–2002 **best vintages** NA **drink with** Roast turkey •$35

d'Arenberg Dead Arm Shiraz

Part of a veritable cascade of new labels which tumbled out from d'Arenberg in the mid-1990s, and a decidedly strange name for the super-premium flagship of the winery. The name comes from a fungal disease (phomopsis viticola) that attacks vines in many parts of the world, and which can cause one half (or one side) of the vine to die, leaving the other side unaffected (at least for the time being). The older the vines, the more likely the incidence of attack. So much for the name, the wine itself can be absolutely outstanding, bringing together concentrated fruit with 12–18 months maturation in new American oak barriques.

♥♥♥♥♥ **1998** Dense red-purple; a typically rich, dense and concentrated bouquet oozing dark plum and berry fruit is followed by a massively rich and ripe palate with powerful tannins to boot. **rating:** 94

best drinking 2005–2015 **best vintages** '94, '95, '96, '97, '98 **drink with** Marinated beef • $60

d'Arenberg The Footbolt Old Vine Shiraz

Produced from vines dating back as far as 1890 but harvested over a long period to achieve differing flavour and sugar levels to add complexity. Made traditionally in open fermenters, basket-pressed, and aged in a mix of French and American barriques and hogsheads for one year, all of which have been previously used, and which are not intended to impart excessive oak flavour. The adddition of the word 'Footbolt' on the front label has given rise to a world record back label, best read with a microscope and a spellcheck, the latter to tell you that the 'absinent' Joe Osborn was really abstinent.

♥♥♥♡ **1998** Medium purple-red; the bouquet is very earthy/stalky, and lacking the richness one expects from d'Arenberg. The palate, too, has some atypical, harsh green fruit characters. Possibly a poor bottle. **rating:** 81

best drinking 2002–2004 **best vintages** '82, '88, '90, '91, '94, '95, '96, '97 **drink with** Smoked lamb with redcurrant sauce • $18.50

d'Arenberg Ironstone Pressings

Since 1994 has become a permanent part of the d'Arenberg portfolio. Typically a blend of 70 per cent Grenache, 20 per cent Shiraz and 10 per cent Mourvedre, it is not — as the name might suggest — made up of the pressings component of the various Grenache and Shiraz blends and wines made by d'Arenberg. In other words, it contains the usual mix of free-run and pressings material; to the extent it has extra weight, it comes from the late harvesting, with the ripest components nearing 16° baumé — terrorising stuff for the uninitiated.

♥♥♥♥ **1998** Medium to full red-purple; the bouquet is very ripe, with slightly jammy grenache setting the tone, together with a hint of mint. The palate has massive body and extract, with the tannins running throughout; a convincing demonstration of raw power. **rating:** 88

best drinking 2003–2013 **best vintages** '91, '94, '95, '97, '98 **drink with** Leave it in the cellar • $60

d'Arenberg Red Ochre

Presumably the repository of the bits and pieces from the innumerable d'Arenberg labels which do not quite make the grade. Sometimes predominantly Shiraz, at other times a blend of Shiraz and Grenache it can represent extraordinary value for money.

♥♥♥♡ **1998** Light to medium red-purple; a clean, fresh bouquet with light cherry/cherry pip fruit; the palate has similar fruit flavour on entry, but finishes with quite good tannins, which add complexity. **rating:** 82

best drinking Drink now **best vintages** '94, '95 **drink with** Barbecue • $10

d'Arenberg d'Arry's Original Shiraz Grenache

A classic wine style with an illustrious show record and, as the classic wine entry indicates, dating back to 1961. Made from roughly equal proportions of low-yielding, old vine Shiraz and Grenache, held in a mix of large and small oak (principally old) for ten months prior to bottling. Quite deliberately made in a slightly old-fashioned style, fruit- rather than oak-driven, but none the worse for that.

♥♥♥♥♡ **1998** First made in 1961, when it was simply called Burgundy, and became famous with the 1967 vintage (seven trophies, 25 gold medals). There are bright, spicy/peppery notes to clean red berry fruit aromas; lovely, juicy red berry fruit with spice and mint runs along the palate, finishing with soft, fine tannins. **rating:** 93

best drinking 2000–2013 **best vintages** '63, '76, '86, '87, '88, '91, '95, '96, '97 **drink with** Jugged hare • $18.50

d'Arenberg The Custodian Grenache

As with all of the d'Arenberg wines, if you get to read the back label, these background notes will be as superfluous as they are brief. Suffice it to say that Grenache has always been a major part of the d'Arenberg red wine production, and the best parcels of old vine grenache are used to produce the wine. It is kept in tank and in large wood for part of the time, before spending six months in new and old American oak barriques, thus putting the major emphasis on the luscious fruit — which is as it should be.

▼▼▼▼ **1997** Medium red-purple; an aromatic bouquet, quite scented, with cedar and spice, and typical slightly jammy varietal character. The palate has much more texture, structure and concentration than one normally finds with Grenache. **rating:** 89

best drinking 2000–2007 **best vintages** '91, '92, '94, '95, '96, '98 **drink with** Ragout of venison • $20

---

d'Arenberg The Coppermine Road Cabernet Sauvignon

The name comes from a road adjoining the vineyard (which in fact has four different names along parts of its not very great length, which is somehow appropriate). It spends 18 months in new and used French and American oak barriques.

▼▼▼▼ **1998** Medium to full red-purple; the bouquet has strong, savoury/earthy cabernet varietal character; curiously, given the very good vintage, the palate does not have as much luscious red fruit as usual, tending austere and tannic. **rating:** 86

best drinking 2003–2008 **best vintages** '97 **drink with** Leave it in the cellar • $60

---

d'Arenberg The High Trellis Cabernet Sauvignon

The original and near-universal method of training vines was in the so-called bush or goblet shape; the vines are pruned severely and are free-standing, without the aid of a wire trellis. The next step was a single-wire low trellis, with high trellis systems of relatively recent origin.

▼▼▼▽ **1998** Dense red-purple; the bouquet is clean, with firm cassis berry fruit and subtle oak. The palate has good weight and ripeness, rounded off with soft tannins and subtle oak. All in all, an excellent expression of ripe cabernet varietal character. **rating:** 91

best drinking 2003–2013 **best vintages** NA **drink with** Leg of lamb • $18.50

---

dargo valley winery NR

Lower Dargo Road, Dargo, Vic 3682 **region** Gippsland
phone (03) 5140 1228 **fax** (03) 5140 1388 **open** Mon–Thur 12–8, weekends, holidays 10–8 (closed Fridays)
winemaker Hermann Bila **production** 200 **est.** 1985
product range ($12–14 CD) Traminer, Rhine Riesling, Sauvignon Blanc, Chardonnay, Pinot Noir, Cabernet Sauvignon, Port.
summary Two and a half hectares are situated in mountain country north of Maffra and looking towards the Bogong National Park. Hermann Bila comes from a family of European winemakers; there is an on-site restaurant, and Devonshire teas and ploughman's lunches are provided — very useful given the remote locality. The white wines tend to be rustic, the sappy/earthy/cherry Pinot Noir the pick of the red wines.

darling estate ★★★

Whitfield Road, Cheshunt, Vic 3678 **region** King Valley
phone (03) 5729 8396 **fax** (03) 5729 8396 **open** By appointment
winemaker Guy Darling, Rick Kinzbrunner (Consultant) **production** 500 **est.** 1990
product range ($6.25–18.75 ML) Koombahla Riesling, Nambucca Chenin Blanc, Koombahla Chardonnay, Koombahla Pinot Noir, Nambucca Gamay Koombahla Shiraz, Koombahla Cabernet Franc, Koombahla Cabernet Sauvignon.
summary Guy Darling was one of the pioneers of the King Valley when he planted his first vines in 1970. For many years the entire production was purchased by Brown Brothers, providing their well-known Koombahla Estate label. Much of the production from the 23 hectares is still sold to Brown Brothers (and others), but since 1991 Guy Darling has had a fully functional winery established on the vineyard, making a small portion of the production into wine — which was, in fact, his original motivation for planting the first vines. All the wines on sale have considerable bottle age.

darling park ★★★★

Red Hill Road, Red Hill, Vic 3937 **region** Mornington Peninsula
phone (03) 5989 2324 **fax** (03) 5989 2254 **open** Weekends and public holidays 11–5 and any time the vineyard gates are open
winemaker John Sargeant, John Brooks (Red), Kevin McCarthy (White) **production** 1000 **est.** 1986
product range ($16–30 CD) Chardonnay, Pinot Gris, Querida (Rosé), Tempranillo, Decadence, Pinot Noir, Pinot Noir Reserve, Shiraz, Merlot, Cabernet Merlot, Halcyon Cabernet.

summary John and Delys Sargeant have now opened their cellar door-cum-restaurant at Darling Park, which is open every day through January of each year. The labels are the most gloriously baroque of any to be found in Australia and would give the American Bureau of Alcohol, Tobacco and Firearms (which governs such matters in the United States) total cardiac arrest. At the ripe young age of 70 John Sargeant took over the winemaking of the red wines as from the 1996 vintage.

Darling Park Pinot Noir Reserve

Distinguished from the varietal Pinot Noir merely by virtue of the clones; it does show the higher yields of the 1998 vintage.

▼▼▼▽ **1998** Medium red; the bouquet offers a mix of cherry, forest and slightly stemmy aromas, the palate being cast in a similar firm, savoury/foresty mode. The varietal character is, within this context, clear, and the wine well priced. **rating:** 83

best drinking 2000–2003 **best vintages** NA **drink with** Smoked quail • $22

Darling Park Shiraz

A debut vintage, made from grapes grown at Merricks Grove, Balnarring, and was bottled immediately prior to tasting, which makes the quality all the more impressive.

▼▼▼▼ **1999** Medium red, with a touch of purple. There is surprisingly ripe and sweet dark cherry fruit supported by subtle oak on the bouquet. The palate does not disappoint, with powerful, rich, spicy dark berry fruit and just a hint of oak in support. **rating:** 89

best drinking 2003–2009 **best vintages** NA **drink with** Game • $NA

darlington estate ★★★☆

Lot 39 Nelson Road, Darlington, WA 6070 **region** Perth Hills
phone (08) 9299 6268 **fax** (08) 9299 7107 **open** Thurs–Sun and holidays 12–5
winemaker Caspar van der Meer (previous) **production** 3000 **est.** 1983
product range ($10–24 CD) Sonata (Sauvignon Blanc), Semillon, Chardonnay, Symphony (Verdelho), Serenade (Chardonnay), Shiraz, Cabernet Sauvignon, Ruby Port; Darling Red (Grenache), Darling White (Unwooded Chardonnay).
summary By far the largest producer in the Perth Hills region, and the best. Winemaking responsibilities passed to Caspar van der Meer, Balt's son, who graduated from Roseworthy in 1995 and, after a vintage at Chateau de Landiras in Bordeaux, joined the family business in 1996, returning to Languedoc in 1997 to make a large quantity of wine for the American market. He has now left to pursue further overseas winemaking opportunities.

david traeger ★★★

139 High Street, Nagambie, Vic 3608 **region** Goulburn Valley
phone (03) 5794 2514 **fax** (03) 5794 1776 **open** 7 days 10–5
winemaker David Traeger **production** 8000 **est.** 1986
product range ($16.50–25.50 R) Classic Verdelho, Shiraz, Cabernet, Reserve Cabernet (premium aged release); Helvetia (available from cellar door only), Riesling, Late Harvest Riesling, Cabernet Dolce.
summary David Traeger learned much during his years as assistant winemaker at Mitchelton, and knows central Victoria well. The red wines are solidly crafted, the Verdelho interesting but more variable in quality. Reasonably active retail distribution through Melbourne, Sydney, Brisbane and Canberra, with exports to Germany, Hong Kong, the UK and Singapore.

deakin estate ★★★★

Kulkyne Way, via Red Cliffs, Vic 3496 **region** Murray Darling
phone (03) 5029 1666 **fax** (03) 5024 3316 **open** Not
winemaker Mark Zeppel **production** 200 000 **est.** 1980
product range ($9.99–12.99 R) Colombard, Sauvignon Blanc, Chardonnay, Shiraz, Cabernet Sauvignon, Brut; Alfred Chardonnay and Alfred Shiraz are flag-bearers.
summary Effectively replaces the Sunnycliff label in the Yunghanns-owned Katnook Estate, Riddoch and (now) Deakin Estate triumvirate, which constitutes the Wingara Wine Group. Sunnycliff is still used for export purposes but does not appear on the domestic market any more. Deakin Estate draws on 346 hectares of its own vineyards, making it largely self-sufficient, and produces competitively priced wines of consistent quality and impressive value, getting better year by year. Exports to the UK, the US, Canada, Switzerland, Hong Kong and the Philippines.

Deakin Estate Sauvignon Blanc

Picking of different sites over a two-week period is intended to provide a range of flavour ripeness; standard cold fermentation in stainless steel follows.

▼▼▼▽ **1999** Very light straw-green; a clean, delicate bouquet is followed by a similarly crisp and delicate palate with a hint of passionfruit and faint grassy undertones. **rating:** 82

best drinking 2000–2001 **best vintages** NA **drink with** Vegetarian • $9.90

Deakin Estate Colombard

Brown Brothers was one of the pioneers in the planting of colombard in Australia, but it is now widely grown through all of the warmer regions and in particular the Riverland areas. Here, as in California (where enormous acreages are planted), its particular virtue is its ability to retain high levels of natural acidity and hence to produce a bright, fresh wine which is often blended with softer, broader varieties but which does well in its own right.

▼▼▼▽ **1999** Light green-yellow; the bouquet is clean, with some of that tinned fruit salad aroma and flavour that is part and parcel of the variety. The palate is delicate and fresh, with crisp acidity. **rating:** 81

best drinking 2000–2001 **best vintages** NA **drink with** Spicy Asian dishes • $9.90

Deakin Estate Alfred Chardonnay

A fast-developing style, with skin contact taking the place of oak chips.

▼▼▼▽ **1998** Medium to full yellow-green; quite complex, tangy bottle-developed aromas are followed by a palate with plenty of weight, though it finishes short. The wine was distinctly better when younger. **rating:** 83

best drinking Drink now **best vintages** NA **drink with** Any fish or white meat • $12.99

Deakin Estate Shiraz

Producing an early-bottled red wine from the Riverland and investing it with both flavour and structure is no easy task. Deakin Estate has seemingly completely mastered the techniques, producing a wine which is far superior to most in its price range. For the record, it has a touch of Merlot and an irrelevant (1 per cent) dash of Cabernet Sauvignon.

▼▼▼▼ **1999** Youthful red-purple; clean, fresh cherry/red berry fruit of moderate intensity and just a hint of oak on the bouquet leads into a palate with an excellent volume of cherry fruit, soft tannins and subtle oak. **rating:** 85

best drinking 2000–2003 **best vintages** NA **drink with** Meat pie • $9.90

Deakin Estate Alfred Shiraz

1997 marked the inaugural release of Deakin Estate's Alfred Shiraz, paired with Alfred Chardonnay as the flag-bearers for Deakin Estate. It is a blend of 90 per cent Shiraz and 10 per cent Cabernet Sauvignon, matured in a mix of American (55 per cent) and French (45 per cent) oak hogsheads. One-third of the barrels are new, the remainder one and two years old, and the wine spends 14 months in barrel. It is an extremely impressive example of a wine made solely from fruit grown on the banks of the Murray River in northwestern Victoria — in other words, the Riverland.

▼▼▼▼ **1998** Has abundant ripe plummy/cherry fruit aromas and a lively, fruit-driven palate with just a touch of oak from its time in (real) barrels. **rating:** 87

best drinking 2000–2001 **best vintages** NA **drink with** Braised lamb shanks • $12.90

de bortoli ★★★★

De Bortoli Road, Bilbul, NSW 2680 **region** Riverina

phone (02) 6964 9444 **fax** (02) 6964 9400 **open** Mon–Sat 9–5.30, Sun 9–4

winemaker Darren De Bortoli **production** 3 million **est.** 1928

product range ($4.90–42.50 CD) Noble One Botrytis Semillon is the flagship wine; Premium varietals under Deen De Bortoli label, and a low-priced range of varietal and generic wines under the Sacred Hill label. Substantial exports in bulk; Montage White and Red.

summary Famous among the cognoscenti for its superb Botrytis Semillon, which in fact accounts for only a minute part of its total production, this winery turns around low-priced varietal and generic wines which are invariably competently made and equally invariably of value for money. Financial and marketing acumen made De Bortoli one of the fastest-growing large wineries in Australia in the 1990s. Exports to the UK, the US and Europe.

De Bortoli Deen De Bortoli Vat 7 Chardonnay

A wine which has on occasions been astonishingly good given its price, and the volume in which it is made. It is produced almost entirely from Griffith region grapes, but reflects careful selection of the best available material.

▼▼▼▼ **1999** Light green-yellow; the bouquet is gently complex with mineral/earthy overtones to gentle fruit and subtle oak. The palate is smooth, with gentle peach/nectarine flavours, and has some length. **rating:** 87

best drinking 2000–2003 **best vintages** '90, '92, '93, '99 **drink with** Pasta marinara • $9.90

De Bortoli Noble One Botrytis Semillon

A classic wine, without question the foremost example of barrel-fermented, wood-matured Botrytis Semillon in Australia. Every vintage made has won at least one trophy and innumerable gold medals.

▼▼▼▼▼ 1998 Brilliant, glowing yellow-green; a rich, complex and luscious bouquet with butterscotch, citrus and subliminal oak is followed by a lively, fresh, peach, honey and lemon-flavoured palate; perfect acidity on the finish. **rating:** 96

best drinking 2001–2010 **best vintages** '82, '84, '87, '90, '91, '92, '93, '94, '95, '96, '97, '98 **drink with** Crème brûlée • $25

de bortoli (victoria)   ★★★★★

Pinnacle Lane, Dixons Creek, Vic 3775 **region** Yarra Valley
phone (03) 5965 2271 **fax** (03) 5965 2442 **open** 7 days 10–5
winemaker Stephen Webber, David Slingsby-Smith, David Bicknell **production** 200 000 **est.** 1987
product range ($12–70 R) At the top comes the premium Melba (Cabernet blend), followed by Yarra Valley Semillon, Gewurztraminer, Chardonnay, Pinot Noir, Shiraz, Cabernet Sauvignon, Cabernet Merlot; then comes the intermediate Gulf Station range of Riesling, Chardonnay, Pinot Noir and Cabernet Sauvignon; the Windy Peak range of Riesling, Chardonnay, Pinot Noir, Cabernets, Prestige Cuvée.
summary The quality arm of the bustling De Bortoli group, run by Leanne De Bortoli and husband Stephen Webber, ex-Lindeman winemaker. The top label (De Bortoli), the second (Gulf Station) and the third label (Windy Peak) offer wines of consistently good quality and excellent value — the complex Chardonnay is of outstanding quality. Shares the same amazing split of export markets with its parent. Exports to the UK, Europe and the US.

De Bortoli Gulf Station Riesling

The middle tier in the De Bortoli range; made from 100 per cent Yarra Valley riesling.

▼▼▼▼ 1997 Medium to full yellow-green; good bottle-developed riesling aromas, quite powerful, with petrol and toast characters. The palate lacks the intensity of the bouquet, but is well balanced and flavoursome. **rating:** 86

best drinking 2000–2003 **best vintages** NA **drink with** Artichoke with hollandaise sauce • $14

De Bortoli Windy Peak Riesling

Made primarily from riesling grown in the Strathbogie Ranges and the Yarra Valley, often with a small percentage of Yarra Valley Gewurztraminer included. First made in 1989, the wine has garnered a stream of gold medals in national wine shows from that time.

▼▼▼▼ 1999 Light yellow-green; the bouquet is quite full and fragrant, with some tropical fruit aromas. The palate is tighter and crisper, and more citrus than tropical; has good length and acidity and will age well. **rating:** 88

best drinking 2000–2004 **best vintages** '90, '92, '94, '95, '96, '97, '99 **drink with** Fresh asparagus • $12

De Bortoli Gulf Station Semillon Sauvignon Blanc

One of a handful of such blends produced in the Yarra Valley.

▼▼▼▽ 1999 Light green-yellow; the bouquet is clean, fresh and crisp but tending light. The palate is similarly fresh, light and undeveloped, but gives the promise of flowering with time in bottle. **rating:** 84

best drinking 2002–2007 **best vintages** NA **drink with** Shellfish • $14

De Bortoli Gulf Station Chardonnay

Achieved immediate fame for De Bortoli when it swept all before it at the 1996 Adelaide Wine Show. This range, named after the historic Gulf Station on the outskirts of Yarra Glen, shows the winemaking skills of Stephen Webber to full advantage. It also shows just what can be achieved with American oak, a technique previously employed to full advantage by Yarra Ridge.

▼▼▼▽ 1999 Light to medium yellow-green; the bouquet is clean, with melon/fig fruit with subtle oak. The palate is very light and clean but lacking the weight of previous vintages. May develop in bottle. **rating:** 82

best drinking 2000–2003 **best vintages** '95, '96, '97, '98 **drink with** Yabbies • $14

De Bortoli Windy Peak Chardonnay

Sourced from vineyards in Victoria, but always containing a significant proportion of southern Victorian material, including the Yarra Valley. Over the years has consistently out-performed far more expensive wines in wine shows and has always represented exceptionally good value for money. Some barrel-ferment and lees contact, together with the very clever use of American oak, are all contributors. Smart new packaging introduced since the 1997 vintage does the wine justice, making it appear far above its class.

YYYY 1999 Light to medium green-yellow; the bouquet is clean and light, with slightly sawdusty oak. There is fair palate weight, with some melon fruit running through to the finish. **rating:** 82

best drinking 2000–2002 **best vintages** '90, '92, '93, '94, '97 **drink with** Sashimi • $12

De Bortoli Noble Traminer
A wine De Bortoli has had tucked away in its museum reserve, and which is quite fascinating.

YYYY 1986 Golden; the bouquet is gently spicy, with mandarin peel aromas merging into a moderately sweet palate with flavours of citrus, biscuit, almond and spice. **rating:** 88

best drinking 2000–2003 **best vintages** NA **drink with** Hazlenuts or almonds • $NA

De Bortoli Cabernet Rosé
Made by running juice away from the cabernet sauvignon skins immediately after pressing.

YYYY 1999 Light but vivid colour; the bouquet is fresh and lively, with attractive floral red fruit aromas. The palate is lively, but just a fraction uncertain in its balance and direction. **rating:** 83

best drinking Drink now **best vintages** NA **drink with** Any summer food • $12

De Bortoli Gulf Station Pinot Noir
A recent addition to the Gulf Station range of wines, produced entirely from Yarra Valley-grown grapes and using the full range of winemaking techniques including cold maceration before fermentation, the incorporation of whole bunches, hot fermentation temperature and some barrel-fermentation.

YYYY 1999 Light to medium red-purple; the bouquet is light but quite fragrant, with spicy/leafy pinot noir varietal character. The palate is well balanced in a very light, drink-now style. **rating:** 81

best drinking 2000–2001 **best vintages** NA **drink with** Roast pigeon • $15

De Bortoli Windy Peak Pinot Noir
Arguably, the best-value Pinot Noir produced in Australia today. Said to be produced from Victorian-grown grapes, but usually contains a high proportion of Yarra Valley material.

YYYY 1998 Light to medium red-purple; there are slight confectionary/boiled/jammy overtones to the ripe cherry and strawberry fruit of the bouquet. The palate is light and fresh, again with slight confection flavours. Best consumed slightly chilled; very good value at the price. **rating:** 85

best drinking 2000–2001 **best vintages** NA **drink with** Chinese dry-fried shredded beef • $12

De Bortoli Yarra Valley Pinot Noir
In the manner of Socrates dissatisfied, Stephen Webber once pronounced himself unhappy with the De Bortoli Pinot Noirs. However, the '95 won the prestigious Wine Press Club trophy for Best Mature Pinot Noir at the National Wine Show, and both the '96 and '97 wines are better than the '95. Partial cold maceration prior to fermentation, and partial barrel-fermentation in 100 per cent French oak are key techniques which have led to the improvement in style. The '97 was a multiple trophy winner, including the 1999 Sydney Royal Wine Show.

YYYY 1998 Medium red-purple; the bouquet is clean, and seems to be going through a slightly closed transition phase, with some plummy fruit evident. It is more accessible on the palate, with plum/cherry fruit and significant tannins. **rating:** 88

best drinking 2001–2005 **best vintages** '95, '96, '97 **drink with** Duck casserole • $36

De Bortoli Gulf Station Shiraz
To successfully ripen shiraz in the Yarra Valley a warm, north-facing slope is all-important.

YYYY 1998 Medium purple-red; the bouquet offers bright, fresh, juicy cherry with some charry American oak; there are similar flavours on the palate, which has quite good length but a fractionally tough finish. **rating:** 84

best drinking 2001–2005 **best vintages** NA **drink with** Stir-fried beef • $14

De Bortoli Yarra Valley Shiraz
There are surprisingly few Yarra Valley varietal Shirazes on the market, and the fruit flavours vary significantly from one maker to the next, ranging from strong spice and pepper through to more minty aromas and flavours. The De Bortoli wine can fit in either category according to the vintage.

YYYY 1998 Medium red-purple; the fragrant bouquet offers a mix of spice, berry and leaf; the fruit flavours are brought together with beautifully handled sweet vanilla oak and fine tannins on the palate. Elegant. **rating:** 90

best drinking 2002–2008 **best vintages** '88, '90, '91, '92, '94, '97, '98 **drink with** Grilled calf's liver • $29

De Bortoli Melba Barrel Select

First made in the 1992 vintage, when winemaker Stephen Webber selected the very best parcels of grapes available in that vintage to make tiny quantities of the wine, named after Dame Nellie Melba, whose family home was in the heart of the Yarra Valley. It is a blend of Cabernet Sauvignon, Shiraz, Cabernet Franc and Merlot which spends 27 months in 100 per cent new French oak and two years in bottle prior to release. Between 550 and 750 cases are made each year.

▼▼▼▼▽ **1995** Medium red-purple; the fine, elegant cedary/savoury/spicy aromas of the bouquet lead logically into an elegant palate with a subtle interplay of gentle dark berry and cedary flavours; finishes with fine tannins.

rating: 93

best drinking 2001–2011 **best vintages** '93, '94, '95 **drink with** Yarra Valley venison • $70

De Bortoli Gulf Station Cabernet Sauvignon

There are several schools of thought about the suitability of cabernet to the Yarra Valley, but not in vintages like 1998.

▼▼▼▼▽ **1998** The wine has excellent colour, seductive sweet cassis and cedar aromas of medium intensity, and a singularly attractive palate with ripe blackcurrant fruit, fine tannins and no green characters. **rating:** 90

best drinking 2002–2010 **best vintages** NA **drink with** Parmesan or aged cheddar • $14.90

De Bortoli Yarra Valley Cabernet Sauvignon

Like the Shiraz, made from both estate-grown and purchased grapes. A 100 per cent Cabernet Sauvignon (a Cabernet Merlot is also marketed) made using what might be described as traditional French techniques and matured in a mix of new and used French barriques for 18 months before bottling. Can be outstanding; the 1995 vintage won five trophies and six gold medals in various Victorian wine shows.

▼▼▼▼ **1997** Medium red-purple; a fragrant array of leafy/cedary/earthy aromas introduce a gentle, civilised wine with soft cedary oak on the palate. **rating:** 87

best drinking 2002–2007 **best vintages** '88, '90, '91, '92, '94, '95, '97 **drink with** Beef casserole • $29

deep dene vineyard   NR

36 Glenisla Road, Bickley, WA 6076 **region** Perth Hills
phone (08) 9293 0077 **fax** (08) 9293 0077 **open** By appointment
winemaker Celine Rousseau (Contract) **production** 4000 **est.** 1994
product range ($25–28 R) Pinot Noir, Shiraz.
summary Deep Dene is the largest of the Perth Hills vineyards, with French-born and trained Celine Rousseau as winemaker. It draws upon 4 hectares of pinot noir and half a hectare of shiraz, continuing the near obsession of the Perth Hills vignerons with pinot noir in a climate which, to put it mildly, is difficult for the variety.

deep woods estate   NR

Lot 10 Commonage Road, Yallingup, WA 6282 **region** Margaret River
phone (08) 9756 6066 **fax** (08) 9756 6066 **open** Tues–Sun 11–5, 7 days during holidays
winemaker Candy Jonsson, Ben Gould **production** 10 000 **est.** 1987
product range ($16–28 CD) Semillon, Sauvignon Blanc, Verdelho, Late Harvest (Verdelho), Cabernet Sauvignon, Reserve Cabernet Sauvignon.
summary The substantial-sized Deep Woods Estate has a convoluted history, with a number of changes of ownership since the first vines were planted in 1987. It is now owned by Malcolm and Margaret Gould who, with assistance from their children, are running both Deep Woods Estate and the Margaret River Marron Farm. In all, there are 24 hectares of vineyard planted to 14 different varieties. A winery was erected in 1998, and as from 1999 Mark Lane, former computer software designer-turned winemaker (with a vintage at Coldstream Hills), will be in charge of winemaking.

de iuliis   ★★★☆

Lot 1 Lovedale Road, Keinbah, NSW 2321 **region** Lower Hunter Valley
phone (02) 4930 7403 **fax** (02) 4968 8192 **open** By appointment
winemaker David Hook, Michael De Iuliis **production** 10 000 **est.** 1990
product range ($14–22 CD) Semillon, Verdelho, Chardonnay Shiraz, Cabernet Merlot.
summary Three generations of the De Iuliis family have been involved in the establishment of their 40-hectare vineyard at Keinbah in the Lower Hunter Valley. The family acquired the property in 1986 and planted the first vines in 1990, selling the grapes from the first few vintages to Tyrrell's but retaining small amounts of grapes for

release under the De Iuliis label. Michael De Iuliis, the third-generation family member involved, is completing postgraduate studies in oenology at the Roseworthy Campus of Adelaide University and assists David Hook (a long-term Hunter winemaker) in making the wine. The overall quality of the wines is good and, at this juncture, are only available by mail order or cellar door.

De Iuliis Semillon
Produced from 4 hectares of estate plantings, and cold-fermented in stainless steel, followed by early bottling in the classic manner. Well-balanced with 11 degrees alcohol.

TTTY **1999** Light straw green-yellow; the bouquet is clean, crisp and very light, with a mix of faint herb and lime. The palate is crisp, quite intense, and has good acidity; seems to have all the requisites for ageing but demands patience.   **rating:** 84

best drinking 2004–2009 **best vintages** NA **drink with** Pan-fried scallops • $13

De Iuliis Show Reserve Chardonnay
Chardonnay has the lion's share of the plantings and produces both a varietal and Show Reserve Chardonnay. The Show Reserve is whole-bunch pressed, barrel-fermented in new French oak, and spends nine months in barrel on lees.

TTTT **1999** Medium yellow-green; the bouquet is clean, smooth, of light to medium intensity, and, surprisingly, the oak is subtle. The palate is elegant, relatively undeveloped, and again with subtle oak influence. It has good length and offers the prospect of good development in bottle.   **rating:** 86

best drinking 2001–2004 **best vintages** NA **drink with** Chicken pasta • $16.60

De Iuliis Cabernet Merlot
The Cabernet Sauvignon component of the wine is made from purchased grapes; the Merlot comes from 2 hectares of estate plantings.

TTTY **1998** Medium to full red-purple; a powerful oaky/earthy bouquet is followed by a relatively rich and sweet palate, with very pronounced oak but (just) enough berry fruit to sustain that oak. The finish is pleasant and well balanced.   **rating:** 83

best drinking 2003–2008 **best vintages** NA **drink with** Leg of lamb with rosemary • $22

delacolline estate   ★★★
Whillas Road, Port Lincoln, SA 5606 **region** Other Wineries of SA
phone (08) 8682 5277 **fax** (08) 8682 4455 **open** Weekends 9–5
winemaker Andrew Mitchell (Contract) **production** 650 **est.** 1984
product range ($10–15 R) Riesling, Fumé Blanc, Cabernet Sauvignon.
summary Joins Boston Bay as the second Port Lincoln producer; the white wines are made under contract in the Clare Valley. The 3-hectare vineyard, run under the direction of Tony Bassett, reflects the cool maritime influence, with ocean currents that sweep up from the Antarctic.

delamere   ★★★
Bridport Road, Pipers Brook, Tas 7254 **region** Northern Tasmania
phone (03) 6382 7190 **fax** (03) 6382 7250 **open** 7 days 10–5
winemaker Richard Richardson **production** 2500 **est.** 1983
product range ($12–24 CD) Chardonnay, White Pinot Noir, Pinot Noir (Standard, Dry Red and Reserve), Sparkling.
summary Richie Richardson produces elegant, rather light-bodied wines that have a strong following. The Chardonnay has been most successful, with a textured, complex, malolactic-influenced wine with great, creamy feel in the mouth. The Pinots typically show pleasant varietal fruit, but seem to suffer from handling problems with oak and a touch of oxidation. Retail distribution through fine wine outlets in Tasmania, Melbourne, Sydney and Brisbane.

Delamere Reserve Pinot Noir
Made in typical Delamere style, much lighter and more savoury than most of its Tasmanian counterparts.

TTTY **1997** Light to medium red-purple; some savoury/foresty aromas on a quiet bouquet are followed by a palate which is pleasant but unequivocally light bodied.   **rating:** 80

best drinking 2000–2002 **best vintages** NA **drink with** Grilled salmon • $24

delaney's creek winery NR

70 Hennessey Road, Delaneys Creek, Qld 4514 **region** South Burnett and Other Wineries of Qld
phone (07) 5496 4925 **fax** (07) 5496 4926 **open** Mon–Fri 10–4, weekends and public holidays 10–5
winemaker Brian Wilson **production** 3000 **est.** 1997
product range ($9.50–14.50 CD) Verdelho, Marsanne Blanc, Muscat Rosé, Cabernet Franc, Shiraz Cabernet
Franc, Fortifieds.
summary Tom Weidmann established Delaney's Creek Winery in 1997 and by doing so has expanded the
vineyard map of Queensland yet further. Delaney's Creek is situated near the town of Woodford, itself not far
northwest of Caboolture. In 1998 Weidmann planted an exotic mix of 1 hectare each of shiraz, chardonnay,
sangiovese, touriga nacional and verdelho. In the meantime he is obtaining his grapes from 4 hectares of
contract-grown fruit, including cabernet sauvignon, cabernet franc, merlot, shiraz, chardonnay, marsanne and
verdelho.

delatite ★★★★

Stoneys Road, Mansfield, Vic 3722 **region** Central Victorian Mountain Country
phone (03) 5775 2922 **fax** (03) 5775 2911 **open** 7 days 10–4
winemaker Rosalind Ritchie **production** 14 000 **est.** 1982
product range ($18–35 CD) Unoaked Chardonnay, Chardonnay, Sauvignon Blanc, Riesling, Late Picked
Riesling, Dead Man's Hill Gewürztraminer, Delmelza Pinot Chardonnay, Pinot Noir, Shiraz, Merlot, Malbec,
Dungeon Gully, Devil's River (Cabernet Sauvignon Malbec Shiraz), Fortifieds.
summary With its sweeping views across to the snow-clad alps, this is uncompromising cool-climate viticulture,
and the wines naturally reflect the climate. Light but intense Riesling and spicy Traminer flower with a year or two
in bottle, and in the warmer vintages the red wines achieve flavour and mouthfeel, albeit with a distinctive
mintiness.

Delatite Riesling

Apart from being one of the first wineries to dispense with the word 'Rhine' from the label, Delatite has always
produced fine, delicate Rieslings which blossom with age.
▼▼▼▼ 1999 Light green-yellow; a delicate bouquet with some floral/spice aromas is followed by a similarly light
and fresh palate, with a touch of passionfruit adding to the appeal; finishes with good acidity.   **rating:** 86
best drinking 2000–2006 **best vintages** '82, '86, '87, '93, '97, '99 **drink with** Grilled fish • $18

Delatite Sauvignon Blanc

Produced from 2 hectares of fully mature estate plantings. Warm years like 1999 are particularly good in ultra-cool
areas such as Mansfield.
▼▼▼▼ 1999 Light yellow-green; the aromas are clean, fresh and crisp, with quite intense herb and citrus characters.
The palate is refreshingly crisp, with similar herb and citrus flavours; a well-balanced, fresh finish.   **rating:** 86
best drinking 2000–2002 **best vintages** '82, '86, '87, '93, '94, '99 **drink with** Fresh oysters • $20

Delatite Chardonnay

The 2 hectares of estate plantings produce a wine in mainstream Delatite style, far lighter than the usual run of
Chardonnays, even from cool-climate regions. Matured in a mix of new and one-year-old French oak barriques.
▼▼▼▼ 1998 Light green-yellow; while the bouquet is light, it is quite fragrant and floral, with the fruit supported
by subtle, spicy oak. The palate has pleasant mouthfeel and balance, with light peach and cashew flavours.
                                                                                                           rating: 86
best drinking 2001–2005 **best vintages** '88, '91, '92, '98 **drink with** Crab • $23

Delatite Merlot

A blend of 90 per cent Merlot and 10 per cent Cabernet Franc.
▼▼▼▽ 1997 Light to medium red-purple; the bouquet is clean and relatively light, with aromatic savoury/leafy
aromas. Similar savoury characters run through the palate, which sharpens up somewhat on the finish. **rating:** 81
best drinking 2001–2006 **best vintages** NA **drink with** Milk-fed veal • $27.50

demondrille vineyards NR

RMB 97, Prunevale Road, Kingsvale, NSW 2587 **region** Hilltops
phone (02) 6384 4272 **fax** (02) 6384 4292 **open** Fri–Mon 10–5, weekends 10.30–5 or by appointment
winemaker Pamela Gillespie, Tambourlaine (Contract) **production** NA **est.** 1979

product range ($15–20 CD) The Dove (Sauvignon Blanc Semillon), Purgatory (Pinot Noir), The Raven (Shiraz) and Black Rosé (Cabernet Sauvignon Merlot Franc), together with lesser quantities of cellar-door-only wines (from the 'Tin Shed' range).

summary Pamela Gillespie and Robert Provan purchased the former Hercynia Vineyard and winery in 1995. Pam Gillespie has an Associate Diploma in Winemaking and Marketing from Adelaide University, Roseworthy, and has been in the hospitality industry since 1989. Her partner had a remarkable career and is part way through a Bachelor of Science degree at Sydney University (as a mature-age student) majoring in agriculture. Most of the wines from Demondrille are made at Charles Sturt University, with smaller quantities made on site. Purgatory, though far from a great wine, is not so bad as to deserve its (bizarre) name. Specially created food platters featuring local produce are available at the winery each weekend.

dennis ★★★☆

Kangarilla Road, McLaren Vale, SA 5171 **region** McLaren Vale
phone (08) 8323 8665 **fax** (08) 8323 9121 **open** Mon–Fri 10–5, weekends, holidays 11–5
winemaker Peter Dennis **production** 10 000 **est.** 1970
product range ($14–40 CD) Sauvignon Blanc, Chardonnay, Shiraz, Cabernet Sauvignon, Grenache, Merlot, Egerton Vintage Port, Old Tawny Port.
summary A low-profile winery which has, from time to time, made some excellent wines, most notably typically full-blown, buttery/peachy Chardonnay. However, in 1998 the pendulum swung towards the Shiraz and Cabernet Sauvignon.

Dennis Shiraz

Made in the mainstream of McLaren Vale style, but, happily, at the lower end of the alcohol and extract scale.
TTTT 1998 Dark, dense red-purple; a concentrated and powerful bouquet with dark plum and hints of earth is followed by a palate that provides all of the promised flavour, but is not at all extractive and should positively flower with time in bottle. **rating: 89**
best drinking 2003–2013 **best vintages** '98 **drink with** Lamb kebabs • $18

Dennis Cabernet Sauvignon

Like the Shiraz, in mainstream McLaren Vale style, but, in this instance, is towards the big end of town.
TTTY 1998 Medium to full red-purple; the bouquet is quite solid, with savoury blackberry/blackcurrant fruit and subtle oak. The palate is exceedingly rich and concentrated, almost soupy, in huge, McLaren Vale fruit style. Mercifully, it has not also been loaded up with American oak. **rating: 84**
best drinking 2003–2013 **best vintages** '98 **drink with** Barbecued T-bone • $18

d'entrecasteaux NR

Boorara Road, Northcliffe, WA 6262 **region** Pemberton, Warren Valley and Manjimup
phone (08) 9776 7232 **open** By appointment
winemaker Alkoomi (Contract) **production** 600 **est.** 1988
product range Chardonnay, Sauvignon Blanc, Pinot Noir, Cabernet Sauvignon.
summary Not to be confused with the now moribund Tasmanian winery of the same name but likewise taking its name from the French explorer Admiral Bruni D'Entrecasteaux, who visited both Tasmania and the southwest coast of Western Australia. Four hectares of estate vineyards, planted on rich Karri loam, produce grapes for the wines which are contract-made at Alkoomi.

derwent estate ★★★★

329 Lyell Highway, Granton, Tas 7070 **region** Southern Tasmania
phone (03) 6248 5073 **fax** (03) 6248 5073 **open** Not
winemaker Stefano Lubiana (Contract) **production** 300 **est.** 1993
product range ($17.50 ML) Riesling, Pinot Noir.
summary The Hanigan family has established Derwent Estate as part of a diversification programme for their 400-hectare mixed farming property. Five hectares of vineyard have been progressively planted since 1993, initially to riesling, followed by pinot noir.

Derwent Estate Riesling

Produced entirely from 1.5 hectares of estate plantings; typically picked at the end of the first week of May with yields of around 8 tonnes per hectare. Cold-fermented to dryness and early-bottled.

▼▼▼▽ **1999** Light to medium green-yellow; rather closed in its youth but with the herbal/grassy overtones typical of this vineyard. The palate is relatively austere, with a mix of mineral and herb flavours. Needs time to come into its own, which it will surely do.   **rating:** 82

best drinking 2003–2008 **best vintages** '98 **drink with** Fresh asparagus • $17.50

devil's lair   NR

Rocky Road, Forest Grove via Margaret River, WA 6286 **region** Margaret River
phone (08) 9757 7573 **fax** (08) 9757 7533 **open** By appointment
winemaker Janice McDonald **production** 14 000 **est.** 1985
product range ($22–38 R) Chardonnay, Pinot Noir, Cabernet Merlot; Fifth Leg Dry White and Dry Red.
summary Having rapidly carved out a high reputation for itself through a combination of clever packaging and marketing allied with impressive wine quality, Devil's Lair was acquired by Southcorp (Penfolds, etc) Wine Group in December 1996, and production projected to increase to over 50 000 cases after the turn of the century. Readers should be aware that from mid-1997 I had Group Winemaking responsibility (inter alia) for Devil's Lair, although Janice McDonald remained firmly in command of winemaking until her departure in mid-2000. Because of my involvement with the winery I do not give it, or its wines, a rating. Wines are available for sale at the Margaret River Regional Wine Centre.

diamond valley vineyards   ★★★★☆

2130 Kinglake Road, St Andrews, Vic 3761 **region** Yarra Valley
phone (03) 9710 1484 **fax** (03) 9710 1369 **open** Not
winemaker David Lance, James Lance **production** 6000 **est.** 1976
product range ($16–44 R) Estate Riesling, Chardonnay, Pinot Noir, Cabernets, Sparkling Diamond; Blue Label Sauvignon Blanc, Chardonnay, Pinot Noir, Cabernet Merlot; Close Planted Pinot Noir.
summary One of the Yarra Valley's finest producers of Pinot Noir and an early pacesetter for the variety, making wines of tremendous style and crystal-clear varietal character. They are not Cabernet Sauvignon look-alikes but true Pinot Noir, fragrant and intense. Much of the wine is sold through an informative and well-presented mailing list.

Diamond Valley Estate Chardonnay

Produced in very limited quantities from a little over 1 hectare of estate vines, and first released in 1990. Typically intense, the wine is fruit- rather than oak-driven. The wine has won numerous gold medals.

▼▼▼▼ **1998** Bright, light to medium yellow-green; the bouquet is tangy and complex, with slightly reductive/French characters. The palate has attractive nectarine and peach fruit, with very subtle oak, and has well-above-average length. There is just a touch of green to the wine, unusual for a '98 vintage wine.   **rating:** 86

best drinking 2001–2006 **best vintages** '90, '92, '94, '96 **drink with** Cold smoked trout • $30

Diamond Valley Blue Label Pinot Noir

The Diamond Valley Blue Label denotes wines made from grapes grown by others in the Yarra Valley, and is roughly half the price of the Estate version. It tends to be lighter in body and less complex than the Estate, but usually shows David Lance's sure touch with the variety.

▼▼▼▼ **1999** Light to medium red-purple; a fragrant and exotic bouquet with spice, clove and aniseed leads into a palate which exhibits the flavours of the bouquet together with plenty of fresh, cherry fruit. A really lovely, early-drinking style.   **rating:** 87

▼▼▼▼ **1998** Bright, clear purple-red; there are very stemmy/gamey canopy aromas which are repeated on the palate. All in all, a fairly challenging style.   **rating:** 86

best drinking 2000–2002 **best vintages** '91, '92, '94, '96, '97 **drink with** Seared salmon • $22

Diamond Valley Estate Pinot Noir

Deserves its recognition as one of the greatest of the Yarra Valley Pinot Noirs, invariably generously flavoured, and invariably showing strong varietal character, often in a ripe mould. A prolific trophy winner over the years, and seldom misses the mark. The secret lies in large part in the estate vineyard, with meticulous viticulture and low yields.

▼▼▼▼▼ **1998** Strong red-purple in the context of Pinot Noir colour; the bouquet is powerful and stylish, with concentrated fruit and oak nicely balanced. The palate is similarly intense, but not forced; plum fruit is neatly counterpoised by a slightly foresty/stemmy green cut.   **rating:** 94

best drinking 2000–2004 **best vintages** '86, '90, '91, '92, '93, '94, '96, '98 **drink with** Wild duck • $44

Diamond Valley Blue Label Cabernet Merlot

Blends such as this do best in warm vintages, and 1998 was such a year.

TTTT 1998 Medium red-purple; the bouquet is clean, with a mix of earth, leaf and berry fruit; the medium-bodied palate is soft, sweet and supple, finishing with soft, fine tannins. Delicious early-drinking style. **rating:** 85

best drinking 2000–2003 **best vintages** NA **drink with** Yearling steak • $20

diggers rest   NR

205 Old Vineyard Road, Sunbury, Vic 3429 **region** Sunbury
phone (03) 9740 1660 **fax** (03) 9740 1660 **open** By appointment
winemaker Peter Dredge **production** 1000 **est.** 1987
product range ($15–20 CD) Chardonnay, Pinot Noir, Shiraz, Cabernet Sauvignon.
summary Diggers Rest was purchased from the founders Frank and Judith Hogan in July 1998; the new owners, Elias and Joseph Obeid, intend to expand the vineyard resources and, by that means, significantly increase production.

djinta djinta winery   NR

10 Stevens Road, Kardella South, Vic 3950 **region** Gippsland
phone (03) 5658 1163 **fax** (03) 5658 1863 **open** Weekends and public holidays 10–5 or by appointment
winemaker Peter Harley **production** 170 **est.** 1991
product range ($15–21 CD) Semillon, Sauvignon Blanc, Marsanne, Cabernet Sauvignon.
summary Is one of a group of wineries situated between Leongatha and Korumburra, the most famous being Bass Phillip. Vines were first planted in 1986 but were largely neglected until Peter and Helen Harley acquired the property in 1991, set about reviving the 2 hectares of sauvignon blanc and a little cabernet sauvignon, planting an additional 3 hectares (in total) of merlot, cabernet franc, cabernet sauvignon, semillon, marsanne, roussane and viognier. The first vintage was 1995, during the time that Peter Harley was completing a Bachelor of Applied Science (Wine Science) at Charles Sturt University. They are deliberately adopting a low-technology approach to both vineyard and winery practices, using organic methods wherever possible. They hope to finish the winery building and a 40-seat restaurant at some stage during 2000. Naturally high levels of acidity may need watching, particularly on the evidence of the 1997 Semillon. The 1998 Sauvignon Blanc (84 points) is a nice wine with plenty of passionfruit flavour, the 1995 even better (86 points).

domaine chandon   ★★★★★

Maroondah Highway, Coldstream, Vic 3770 **region** Yarra Valley
phone (03) 9739 1110 **fax** (03) 9739 1095 **open** 7 days 10.30–4.30
winemaker Wayne Donaldson **production** 90 000 **est.** 1986
product range ($12.50–52 CD) Sparkling (Méthode Champenoise) specialist with five sparkling wines: Brut, Blanc de Blancs, Blanc de Noirs, Rosé, Yarra Valley Cuvée Riche; Green Point is export label, also used for still Pinot Noir (with a Reserve version now joining ranks) and Chardonnay; Colonnades is third label for table wines.
summary Wholly owned by Moet et Chandon, and the most important wine facility in the Yarra Valley, superbly located with luxurious tasting facilities (a small tasting charge is levied). The wines are exemplary, thought by many to be the best produced by Moet et Chandon in any of its overseas subsidiary operations, a complex blend of French and Australian style.

Domaine Chandon Green Point Chardonnay

The Green Point varietal table wines have slowly but steadily assumed greater significance in the Domaine Chandon winemaking portfolio. The Chardonnay and Pinot Noir are both sourced from the Yarra Valley, and predominantly (if not exclusively) from estate vineyards surrounding the winery. Right from the outset, the style has been generous and full flavoured.

TTTY 1998 Medium yellow-green; the bouquet is moderately intense, with typical, restrained Yarra melon fruit. However, the palate falls away somewhat on the finish, which is not what one would expect. **rating:** 83

best drinking 2000–2003 **best vintages** '92, '93, '96 **drink with** Veal in white sauce • $23

Domaine Chandon Blanc de Noirs

The converse of the Blanc de Blancs, made entirely from Pinot Noir; like the Blanc de Blancs, held on lees for over three years before disgorgement. Sourced from numerous southern Australian vineyards, notably the Yarra Valley and Tasmania.

TTTTY 1995 Pale salmon, it has distinctive raisin bread aromas; very fine strawberry flavours, distinctively Pinot Noir, run through a well-balanced palate without any harshness or hardness. **rating:** 93

best drinking 2000–2003 **best vintages** '90, '92, '94 **drink with** Hors d'oeuvres • $33

Domaine Chandon Green Point Pinot Noir

Unlike the Domaine Chandon sparkling wines, sourced entirely from the Yarra Valley and principally from the estate vineyards surrounding the winery. Generously flavoured, but perhaps still finding its way.

YYYY 1998 Medium red-purple; the bouquet offers very ripe, slightly jammy, cherry fruit; the palate is similarly very ripe, with cherry jam/plum jam flavours; all in all, made to a style.　　　　　**rating:** 87

best drinking 2000–2003　**best vintages** '96, '97　**drink with** Smoked quail　• $22

donnelly river wines　★★★

Lot 159 Vasse Highway, Pemberton, WA 6260　**region** Pemberton, Warren Valley and Manjimup
phone (08) 9776 2052　**fax** (08) 9776 2053　**open** 7 days 9.30–4.30
winemaker Blair Mieklejohn　**production** 4000　**est.** 1986
product range ($15–19 CD) Chardonnay, Mist (white blend), Sauvignon Blanc, Pinot Noir, Cabernet Sauvignon, Port.
summary Donnelly River Wines draws upon 16 hectares of estate vineyards, planted in 1986 and which produced the first wines in 1990. It has performed consistently well with its Chardonnay.

donovan　★★☆

Main Street, Great Western, Vic 3377　**region** Grampians
phone (03) 5356 2288　**open** Mon–Sat 10–5.30, Sun 12–5
winemaker Chris Peters　**production** 2000　**est.** 1977
product range ($12–17.50 CD) Riesling, Chardonnay, Shiraz, Cabernet Sauvignon, Chardonnay Brut.
summary Donovan quietly makes some attractively fragrant Riesling and concentrated, powerful Shiraz, most of which is sold cellar door and by mail order with considerable bottle age.

doonkuna estate　★★★☆

Barton Highway, Murrumbateman, NSW 2582　**region** Canberra District
phone (02) 6227 5811　**fax** (02) 6227 5085　**open** 7 days 11–3
winemaker Malcolm Burdett　**production** 2000　**est.** 1973
product range ($12–25 CD) Riesling, Gewurztraminer, Frost, Chardonnay, Pinot Noir, Shiraz, Cabernet Sauvignon Merlot, Sparkling.
summary Following the acquisition of Doonkuna by Barry and Maureen Moran in late 1996, the plantings have been increased from a little under 4 hectares to 20 hectares (in 1998). The cellar-door prices remain modest, and increased production will follow in the wake of the new plantings.

Doonkuna Estate Chardonnay

Usually the better of the two white Doonkuna wines, and often the best Chardonnay made in the Canberra district, though sometimes shaded by Lark Hill. Invariably well made, with skilled use of barrel-fermentation.

YYYY 1998 Medium to full yellow-green; the bouquet has nice weight and balance, with nectarine/fig fruit and subtle oak. The palate offers the same nectarine fruit running through to a moderately long finish; subtle oak.　　　　　**rating:** 85

best drinking 2000–2003　**best vintages** '88, '90, '91, '92, '95, '97, '98　**drink with** Snowy Mountains trout　• $20

Doonkuna Estate Shiraz

At the lighter end of the spectrum, sometimes a little too leafy and minty, but not always.

YYYY 1998 Medium to full yellow-green; the wine shows obvious bottle development, with some earthy aromas starting to emerge. A big, fleshy wine but with a fractionally hard finish. Not in the same category as the marvellous '97.　　　　　**rating:** 84

best drinking 2000–2004　**best vintages** '92, '96, '97　**drink with** Rack of lamb　• $12

dorrien estate　NR

Corner Barossa Valley Way/Siegersdorf Road, Tanunda, SA 5352　**region** Barossa Valley
phone (08) 8561 2200　**fax** (08) 8561 2299　**open** Not
winemaker S Adams, W Dutschke, J Schwartzkopff, N Badrice, A Hooper　**production** 750 000　**est.** 1982
product range ($13.99–32.99 CD) Produces a substantial number of wines under proprietary labels for the Cellarmaster Group; notable are Storton Hill Riesling, Di Fabio Shiraz and Mums Block Shiraz.
summary Dorrien Estate is the physical base of the vast Cellarmaster network which, wearing its retailer's hat, is by far the largest direct-sale outlet in Australia. It buys substantial quantities of wine from other makers either in bulk or as cleanskin (i.e. unlabelled bottles), or with recognisable but subtly different labels of the producers

concerned. It is also making increasing quantities of wine on its own account at Dorrien Estate. The Cellarmaster Group was acquired by Mildara Blass in 1997, and just how the winemaking activities of Dorrien Estate will be conducted in the future remains to be seen.

dowie doole   ★★★☆

182 Main Road, McLaren Vale, SA 5171   **region** McLaren Vale
phone (08) 8323 7314   **fax** (08) 8323 7305   **open** Not
winemaker Brian Light (Contract)   **production** 4500   **est.** 1996
product range ($15.50–21.50 R) Chenin Blanc, Semillon Sauvignon Blanc, Chardonnay, Merlot, Shiraz, Cabernet Sauvignon.
summary The imaginatively packaged and interestingly named Dowie Doole was a joint venture between two McLaren Vale grape growers: architect Drew Dowie and one-time international banker Norm Doole. Between them they have over 40 hectares of vineyards, and only a small proportion of their grapes are used to produce the Dowie Doole wines. In 1999 the partnership was expanded to include industry marketing veteran Leigh Gilligan, who returns to his native McLaren Vale after five years in Coonawarra. (Gilligan is also involved with Boar's Rock.) The wines have retail distribution in South Australia and the eastern States, and are exported to Ontario and British Columbia in Canada.

Dowie Doole Merlot

Produced from estate-grown grapes on Dowie Doole's Californian Road Vineyard. After five days fermentation on skins the wine is pressed, finishing its primary fermentation in 100 per cent new Seguin Moreau American oak hogsheads. It is then racked and returned to barrel for an additional eight months, with a final small parcel of Cabernet Sauvignon being incorporated to give additional texture and tannin.

♥♥♥♥ **1998** Deep red-purple; the bouquet is quite powerful, with a mixture of chocolate, leaf and berry aromas. The palate is nicely weighted and structured, with the chocolate, leaf, plum and cedar flavours following on logically from the bouquet.   **rating:** 87

best drinking 2002–2008   **best vintages** NA   **drink with** Grilled calf's liver   • $21.50

drayton's family wines   ★★★☆

Oakey Creek Road, Cessnock, NSW 2321   **region** Lower Hunter Valley
phone (02) 4998 7513   **fax** (02) 4998 7743   **open** Mon–Fri 8–5, weekends and public holidays 10–5
winemaker Trevor Drayton   **production** 100 000   **est.** 1853
product range ($7.50–50 CD) Several label ranges, including budget-priced Oakey Creek, New Generation and Premium; Vineyard Reserve Chardonnay, Semillon, Shiraz, Merlot; Sparkling and Fortifieds; top-of-the-range Limited Release Chardonnay, Shiraz, Susanne Semillon, William Shiraz, Joseph Shiraz and Bin 5555 Shiraz.
summary A family-owned and run stalwart of the Valley, producing honest, full-flavoured wines which sometimes excel themselves and are invariably modestly priced. The size of the production will come as a surprise to many but it is a clear indication of the good standing of the brand. It is not to be confused with Reg Drayton Wines; national retail distribution with exports to New Zealand, the US, Japan, Singapore, Taiwan, Samoa and Switzerland.

drews creek wines   NR

558 Wollombi Road, Broke, NSW 2330   **region** Lower Hunter Valley
phone (02) 6579 1062   **fax** (02) 6579 1062   **open** By appointment
winemaker David Lowe (Contract)   **production** 300   **est.** 1993
product range ($10–16 R) Chardonnay, Unoaked Chardonnay, Merlot.
summary Graeme Gibson and his partners are developing Drews Creek step by step. The initial planting of 2 hectares of chardonnay and 3 hectares of merlot was made in 1991, and the first grapes produced in 1993. A further 2.5 hectares of sangiovese were planted in September 1999. Most of the grapes have been sold to contract-winemaker David Lowe, but a small quantity of wine has been made for sale to friends and through the mailing list. A cellar door is due to be opened some time before the end of 2000, and ultimately several holiday cabins overlooking the vineyard and Wollombi Brook will be opened.

driftwood estate   ★★★★

Lot 13 Caves Road, Yallingup, WA 6282   **region** Margaret River
phone (08) 9755 6323   **fax** (08) 9755 6343   **open** 7 days 11–4.30
winemaker Lyndon Crockett, Nick Betts   **production** 14 000   **est.** 1989
product range ($14–25 CD) Classic White, Semillon, Sauvignon Blanc Semillon, Chardonnay, Unoaked Chardonnay, Cane Cut Semillon, Late Harvest, Shiraz, Merlot, Cabernet Sauvignon, Sparkling, Tawny Port.

summary Driftwood Estate is yet another remarkable new entrant onto the vibrant Margaret River scene. Quite apart from offering a brasserie restaurant capable of seating 200 people open seven days for lunch and dinner and a mock Greek open-air theatre, its wines feature striking and stylish packaging (even if strongly reminiscent of that of Devil's Lair) and opulently flavoured wines. The winery architecture is, it must be said, opulent but not stylish. The wines are exported to Japan, the UK and Malaysia.

dromana estate ★★★★

Corner Harrison's Road and Bittern–Dromana Road, Dromana, Vic 3936 **region** Mornington Peninsula
phone (03) 5987 3800 **fax** (03) 5981 0714 **open** 7 days 11–4
winemaker Garry Crittenden **production** 20 000 **est.** 1982
product range ($15–45 CD) Dromana Estate Sauvignon Blanc, Chardonnay, Reserve Chardonnay, Pinot Noir, Reserve Pinot Noir, Shiraz, Reserve Merlot, Cabernet Merlot; second label Schinus range of Riesling, Chenin Blanc, Sauvignon Blanc, Chardonnay, Melia, Merlot, Longest Lunch Brut, Rosé, Pinot Noir; and a newly packaged range of Italian generics Barbera, Dolcetto, Sangiovese, Granaccia, Riserva, Nebbiolo and Rosato under the Garry Crittenden i label.
summary Since it was first established, Dromana Estate has never been far from the headlines. The energetic marketing genius of Garry Crittenden has driven it hither and thither, launching a brief but highly successful foray into the UK market, and since then concentrating much of its efforts on a no less successful restaurant and cellar door with a kaleidoscopic array of wines — first under the Dromana Estate label, then under the Schinus label and in late 1995, a strikingly revamped range of Italian-accented wines, the i wines. Exports to the UK, the US and Asia.

Dromana Estate Sauvignon Blanc

An addition to the range for Dromana Estate; unlike the Schinus version, sourced entirely from the Mornington Peninsula.
ŸŸŸŸ **1999** Very pale colour, almost water white. The grassy, herbal bouquet has no tropical fruit characters whatsoever, and the palate is similarly bracing in a herbaceous mineral spectrum. **rating:** 83
best drinking 2000–2001 **best vintages** NA **drink with** Delicate shellfish • $15

Dromana Estate Schinus Sauvignon Blanc

No geographical claim of any description is made for this wine, but it is probable much of the wine comes from the King Valley.
ŸŸŸŸ **1999** Light green-yellow; a light but correct bouquet with mineral and herb aromas is followed by a pleasantly balanced, easy, commercial style, with just a hint of residual sugar. **rating:** 80
best drinking 2000–2001 **best vintages** NA **drink with** Fish and chips • $15

Garry Crittenden i Barbera

To my palate, one of the better of the five Italian-style releases under the striking 'i' label. It is made from barbera grown by Arnie Pizzini in the King Valley.
ŸŸŸŸ **1998** Light red; a clean bouquet with interesting aromas of grass, spice and herb intermingling is followed by a palate which shows more of those savoury, spicy, herb-accented flavours, finishing with soft tannins. **rating:** 84
best drinking 2000–2003 **best vintages** NA **drink with** Osso buco • $20

Garry Crittenden i Dolcetto

Produced from grapes grown (by growers of Italian descent) in the King Valley and from a small planting of very old dolcetto at Best's Great Western.
ŸŸŸŸ **1998** Bright red-purple; the aromas are not unlike those of young, earthy Shiraz with plenty of fruit at the core. The palate offers sweet cherry, aniseed and mint fruit flavours, rounded off with soft tannins. **rating:** 85
best drinking 1999–2003 **best vintages** NA **drink with** Pizza • $20

Schinus Merlot

The origin of the grapes is not stated, but is almost certainly wholly or partially the King Valley.
ŸŸŸŸ **1998** Medium red-purple; the bouquet is fragrant, with leafy/minty fruit aromas replicated on the palate with its mix of leaf, mint and spice fruit; a crisp finish to a wine which is effectively a cross between Rosé and light dry red. **rating:** 81
best drinking Drink now **best vintages** NA **drink with** Spaghetti bolognaise • $14

Dromana Estate Cabernet Merlot

As with all of the wines under the Dromana Estate label, entirely estate-grown (and, of course, made and bottled). A blend of 90 per cent Cabernet Sauvignon and 10 per cent Merlot.

▼▼▼▼ **1998** Medium purple-red; fresh and lively leafy minty berry aromas lead into a palate with pleasant, red berry/cassis fruit, with little or no green characters anywhere to be found. Fine tannins; more evidence of the success of the vintage for Bordeaux varieties in southern Victoria. **rating: 89**

best drinking 2001–2006 **best vintages** '91, '93, '97, '98 **drink with** Beef in red wine sauce • $26

dulcinea ★★★★

Jubilee Road, Sulky, Ballarat, Vic 3352 **region** Ballarat
phone (03) 5334 6440 **fax** (03) 5334 6828 **open** 7 days 9–5
winemaker Rod Stott **production** 800 **est.** 1983
product range ($14–18 CD) Chardonnay, Sauvignon Blanc, Pinot Noir, Shiraz, Cabernet Sauvignon.
summary Rod Stott is a part-time but passionate grape grower and winemaker who chose the name Dulcinea from 'The Man of La Mancha', where only a fool fights windmills. With winemaking help from various sources, he has produced a series of very interesting and often complex wines, the current releases being exceptionally impressive.

duncan estate ★★★

Spring Gully Road, Clare, SA 5453 **region** Clare Valley
phone (08) 8843 4335 **fax** (08) 8843 4335 **open** 7 days 10–4
winemaker John Duncan (previous) **production** 2500 **est.** 1968
product range ($11–15 CD) Riesling, Chardonnay, Semillon Sauvignon Blanc, Spätlese, Shiraz, Cabernet Merlot Shiraz.
summary The Duncan family began growing grapes in the Clare Valley in 1968 and first produced wines from its 7.4 hectares of vineyards in 1984. Over the years some attractive wines have been produced, with the Cabernet Merlot and Shiraz usually good. The property was sold in late 1999, but I have no knowledge of the intentions of its new owners.

dyson wines NR

Sherriff Road, Maslin Beach, SA 5170 **region** McLaren Vale
phone (08) 8386 1092 **fax** (08) 8327 0066 **open** 7 days 10–5
winemaker Allan Dyson **production** 2000 **est.** 1976
product range ($14–18 CD) Chardonnay, Ella Rosé Sauvignon Blanc Semillon, Cabernet Sauvignon, White Port.
summary Owned by district veteran Allan Dyson, drawing on 6.5 hectares of estate vineyard. Sauvignon Blanc Semillon to one side, full-bodied Chardonnay, typical of the region, is the most reliable wine.

east arm vineyard NR

111 Archers Road, Hillwood, Tas 7250 **region** Northern Tasmania
phone (03) 6334 0266 **fax** (03) 6334 1405 **open** By appointment
winemaker Andrew Hood, Bert Sundstrup, Nicholas Butler (Contract) **production** 650 **est.** 1993
product range ($16–19.80 R) Riesling, WJW Late Picked Riesling, Chardonnay, Pinot Noir.
summary East Arm Vineyard was established by Launceston gastroenterologist Dr John Wettenhall and partner Anita James, who also happens to have completed the Charles Sturt University Diploma in Applied Science (wine growing). The 2 hectares of vineyard which came into full production in 1998 are more or less equally divided between riesling, chardonnay and pinot noir. It is established on an historic block, part of a grant made to retired British soldiers of the Georgetown garrison in 1821, and slopes down to the Tamar River. The property is 25 hectares, and there are plans for further planting and, somewhere down the track, a winery.

East Arm Riesling

Produced from a small estate planting of about two-thirds of a hectare of riesling established in 1993. Tiny amounts of wine were made in 1996 and 1997, with the first commercial vintage coming in 1998. Both the 1998 and 1999 wines won gold medals in the Tasmanian Wines Show when 12 months old, the 1998 winning its second gold medal when two years old at the 2000 show.

▼▼▼▼▼ **1999** Light green-yellow; a clean, intense bouquet with a mix of mineral and citrus aromas. Literally explodes on the palate, lively, fresh and perfectly balanced, with lime, citrus and mineral flavours running through to a long, bell-clear finish. **rating: 95**

best drinking 2001–2010 **best vintages** '98, '99 **drink with** Scallops • $18

eastbrook estate   NR

Lot 3 Vasse Highway, Eastbrook, WA 6260   **region** Pemberton, Warren Valley and Manjimup
phone (08) 9776 1251   **fax** (08) 9776 1251   **open** Fri–Sun, public holidays 11–4
winemaker Kim Skipworth   **production** 2000   **est.** 1990
product range ($10–17 CD) Chardonnay, Pinot Noir, Cabernet Sauvignon, Port.
summary Established on part of the same former grazing property which also accommodates Salitage, Phoenicia, and Dr Bill Pannell's vineyard. A jarrah pole, limestone and cedar weatherboard winery and restaurant have been built on the site by former Perth real estate agent Kim Skipworth, who is also a shareholder in one of the major Margaret River cheese factories. The wines come from 7 hectares of estate plantings of pinot noir, chardonnay, sauvignon blanc and shiraz.

eastern peake   NR

Clunes Road, Coghills Creek, Vic 3364   **region** Ballarat
phone (03) 5343 4245   **fax** (03) 5343 4365   **open** 7 days 10–5
winemaker Norman Latta   **production** 1500   **est.** 1983
product range ($15–20 CD) Chardonnay, Alba, Persuasion (Pinot Rosé), Pinot Noir.
summary Norm Latta and Di Pym commenced the establishment of Eastern Peake, situated 25 kilometres northeast of Ballarat on a high plateau overlooking the Creswick Valley, almost 15 years ago. In the early years the grapes were sold to Trevor Mast of Mount Chalambar and Mount Langi Ghiran, but the 4.5 hectares of vines are now dedicated to the production of Eastern Peake wines. The Pinot Noir is on the wirey/minerally/stemmy side; earlier bottling might preserve more of the sweet fruit.

edenhope wines   NR

Whitton Stock Route, Yenda, NSW 2681   **region** Riverina
phone 0418 421 000   **fax** (02) 4285 3180   **open** Not
winemaker St Peters (at the Wilton Estate winery)   **production** 16 500   **est.** 1978
product range ($8–17 CD) Semillon Chardonnay, Chardonnay, Verdelho, Botrytis Semillon, Brut, Shiraz Mourvedre, Shiraz Cabernet Merlot.
summary This is a joint venture between Stephen Chatterton and Russell Badham, the latter a partner of Denis Gastin in Australian Prestige Wines. The modestly priced wines are exported to a number of countries.

eden valley wines   NR

Main Street, Eden Valley, SA 5235   **region** Eden Valley
phone (08) 8564 1111   **fax** (08) 8564 1110   **open** 7 days 10–5
winemaker Peter Thompson   **production** 4000   **est.** 1994
product range ($10–20 CD) Riesling, Old Butts Riesling, Chardonnay, Shiraz, Cabernet Sauvignon, White Port, Tawny Port.
summary Eden Valley Wines has waxed and waned over the years but seems now very much in the ascendant. The venture now has 30 hectares each of recently planted riesling, cabernet sauvignon and shiraz, with 5 hectares of much older mourvedre. A major part of the production is sold as grapes to others; the wines currently on sale have varied (non-estate) backgrounds.

Eden Valley Wines Riesling

Produced from the same vineyard as the Old Butts version, and has many things in common with that wine.
🍷🍷🍷🍷 1999 Glowing yellow-green; intense, concentrated lime and mineral aromas lead into a long, intense and powerful palate with layers of lime and mineral fruit.   **rating: 89**
best drinking 2004–2014   **best vintages** '99   **drink with** Mussels in saffron sauce   • $10

Eden Valley Wines Old Butts Riesling

Produced from 45-year-old vines, hence the name 'Old Butts'.
🍷🍷🍷🍷 1999 Bright green-yellow; the bouquet shows excellent varietal aroma, with intense, sweet lime together with touches of mineral and spice. The palate is intense and potent, with masses of lime, mineral and spice fruit flavour.   **rating: 88**
best drinking 2003–2013   **best vintages** '99   **drink with** Mussels in saffron sauce   • $15

edwards & chaffey ★★★★☆

Chaffey's Road, McLaren Vale, SA 5171   **region** McLaren Vale
phone (08) 8323 8250   **fax** (08) 8323 9308   **open** Mon–Fri 9–4.30, Sat 10–5, Sun 11–4
winemaker Fiona Donald   **production** NFP   **est.** 1850
product range ($9.50–35 R) Under the varietal range E&C Chardonnay, Shiraz and Cabernet Sauvignon; under the premium Edwards & Chaffey Section 353 label: a similar range; also Edwards & Chaffey sparkling; the Seaview range of Riesling, Verdelho, Chardonnay and Shiraz Grenache continues in existence, but is not produced from McLaren Vale grapes.
summary In an endeavour to reposition the brand and obtain recognition (in terms of price) for the quality, Seaview has all but been phased out, and henceforth the winery (and the leading brands) will travel under the Edwards & Chaffey label, a nice twist given that these are the names of the partners who founded the business prior to its (indirect) acquisition by Southcorp.

Seaview Riesling
Produced from grapes grown in the Barossa, Eden and Clare Valleys, together with Padthaway; a gold medal winner at the Royal Brisbane Wine Show.
▼▼▼▽ 1999 Light green-yellow; the bouquet is clean, with quite rich, gently tropical fruit; the palate follows logically on, with plenty of sweet fruit flavour which thickens up slightly on the finish. Typically good value.
rating: 83
best drinking 2000–2003   **best vintages** NA   **drink with** Marinated octopus   • $9.50

E&C Chardonnay
Barrel-fermented in French oak, with judicious use of malolactic fermentation; all the winemaking techniques have been used with sensitivity.
▼▼▼▼ 1999 Medium yellow-green; the bouquet is clean, with delicate melon and citrus fruit neatly offset with subtle oak. A nicely balanced, surprisingly delicate palate; understated yet sophisticated.   **rating: 87**
best drinking 2000–2003   **best vintages** NA   **drink with** Crustacea   • $15

Edwards & Chaffey Section 353 Unfiltered Chardonnay
The Chardonnay is 100 per cent barrel-fermented in a mix of new, one- and two-year-old French oak barriques, and undergoes malolactic fermentation. Since 1994 it has been unfiltered. A super-premium wine of undoubted quality and sophistication as its multi-gold medal (and trophy) show record attests.
▼▼▼▼▽ 1997 Medium yellow-green; the intense, clean bouquet has excellent fruit and oak balance and integration, and the palate lives up to the bouquet with moderately rich creamy/nutty/melon fruit and good length.   **rating: 90**
best drinking 2000–2003   **best vintages** '94, '95, '96, '97   **drink with** King George whiting   • $22

Edwards & Chaffey Seaview Gull Rock
In the millennium madness which has engulfed the packaging of sparkling wine around the world, this once avant-garde label now seems conservative.
▼▼▼▼ NV The bouquet is quite full, with genuine fruit complexity; there is plenty of depth on the palate, which is not oversweet. For the record, bottle-fermented.   **rating: 86**
best drinking Drink now   **best vintages** NA   **drink with** Aperitif   • $10

E&C Shiraz
The new name and package is a significant repositioning exercise for a grossly undervalued brand.
▼▼▼▼ 1998 Earthy/cherry fruit and oak are well balanced and integrated; an attractive mid-weight wine with nice red stone fruit flavours and neatly balanced oak.   **rating: 88**
best drinking 2000–2003   **best vintages** NA   **drink with** Corned beef   • $15

Edwards & Chaffey Section 353 Shiraz
First made in 1992, with no release in 1993, returning with the 1994 and 1995 vintages. Sourced entirely from premium McLaren Vale vineyards, the wine spends 17 months in 100 per cent new French oak — an interesting departure from the normal pattern of American oak for big, rich South Australian Shiraz. Right from the first vintage, a wine of exceptional quality. Since 1997 the wine has been repackaged and labelled, with Section 353 signifying the super-premium release.
▼▼▼▼▽ 1997 Medium red-purple; the bouquet is surprisingly light and elegant in style, as is the fine palate. Gently sweet chocolatey fruit is supported by ripe, sweet tannins and nicely judged oak.   **rating: 93**
best drinking 2002–2012   **best vintages** '92, '94, '95, '96, '97   **drink with** Leave it in the cellar   • $35

E&C Cabernet Sauvignon

Another impressive wine in the new E&C range, and one which makes an emphatic statement.

▼▼▼▼ **1998** Medium to full red-purple, there is a melange of sweet fruit, chocolate and a nice hint of vanilla oak on the bouquet; the palate has bombastic, mouth-puckering (but not green) cabernet fruit and tannin. **rating:** 89

best drinking 2003–2013 **best vintages** NA **drink with** Char-grilled rump steak • $15

Edwards & Chaffey Section 353 Cabernet Sauvignon

The sister wine to the Edwards & Chaffey Section 353 Shiraz, made from old, low-yielding McLaren Vale cabernet and matured in new French oak for 18 months. Over the relatively few years the wine has been in production, it has won numerous trophies and gold medals.

▼▼▼▼▼ **1997** Medium to full red-purple; both the bouquet and palate are very sophisticated, fine and subtle, with earthy/cedary notes on the bouquet flowing into perfectly ripened cassis berry on the palate, feathery tannins and excellent oak. **rating:** 94

best drinking 2002–2012 **best vintages** '92, '94, '96, '97 **drink with** Char-grilled rump • $35

elan vineyard NR

17 Turners Road, Bittern, Vic 3918 **region** Mornington Peninsula
phone (03) 5983 1858 **fax** (03) 5983 2821 **open** First weekend of month, public holidays 11–5 or by appointment
winemaker Selma Lowther **production** 600 **est.** 1980
product range ($13–16 CD) Olive's Paddock Riesling, Chardonnay, Shiraz, Gamay, Cabernet Merlot.
summary Selma Lowther, fresh from Charles Sturt University (as a mature-age student) made an impressive debut with her spicy, fresh, crisp Chardonnay. Most of the grapes from the 2.5 hectares of estate vineyards are sold; production remains minuscule.

elderton

3 Tanunda Road, Nuriootpa, SA 5355 **region** Barossa Valley
phone (08) 8562 1058 **fax** (08) 8562 2844 **open** Mon–Fri 8.30–5, weekends, holidays 11–4
winemaker James Irvine **production** 32 000 **est.** 1984
product range ($9.95–65 CD) Riesling, Chardonnay, Golden Riesling, Golden Semillon, Pinot Chardonnay, Merlot, Shiraz CSM, Cabernet Sauvignon; Tantalus White and Red; Command Shiraz is the flag-bearer.
summary The wines are based on some old, high-quality Barossa floor estate vineyards, and all are driven to a lesser or greater degree by lashings of American oak; the Command Shiraz is at the baroque end of the spectrum and has to be given considerable respect within the parameters of its style. National retail distribution, with exports to the UK, the US, Europe and Asia.

Elderton Command Shiraz

First made in 1984, and since that time has consistently been the flagship for the Elderton range of wines. Produced from estate vineyards planted variously in 1939 and 1947, with cropping levels less than 6 tonnes per hectare. The wine spends two years in American oak puncheons and is given 12 months bottle age prior to release.

▼▼▼▼ **1995** Medium red-purple; the bouquet is clean and only moderately intense. The wine swells and opens up on the palate, with sweet red berry/cherry fruit, some chocolate and pleasant vanilla flavours from the balanced and integrated American oak. Soft tannins. **rating:** 88

best drinking 2001–2011 **best vintages** NA **drink with** Veal chops • $65

Elderton CSM

First made in 1992; a blend of 60 per cent Cabernet Sauvignon, 30 per cent Shiraz and 10 per cent Merlot. Matured in a mix of French and American oak puncheons for between 18 months and two years.

▼▼▼▼ **1996** Medium red-purple; the moderately intense bouquet offers soft, earthy fruit, with some vanilla oak; there are similar flavours on the palate, together with hints of chocolate and liquorice (possibly from the Shiraz component), finishing with soft tannins and more of that smooth vanilla oak. **rating:** 85

best drinking 1999–2004 **best vintages** '95 **drink with** Wild duck • $33

Elderton Cabernet Sauvignon

The Elderton red wines have always been full flavoured, and have been consistent medal winners across the national show system. Made from estate-grown grapes on the banks of the North Para River. A seven-day fermentation is followed by maturation in French and American oak puncheons for 18 months to two years.

▼▼▼▼ **1997** Medium to full red-purple; the bouquet has pleasant fruit and oak balance, with predominantly briary/cedary aromas. On the palate there is sweet and plump fruit, soft but persistent tannins, and that well-worn oak overcoat which is the stamp of the Elderton wines. **rating: 89**

best drinking 1999–2005 **best vintages** NA **drink with** Venison • $21

eldredge ★★★☆

Spring Gully Road, Clare, SA 5453 **region** Clare Valley
phone (08) 8842 3086 **fax** (08) 8842 3086 **open** 7 days 11–5
winemaker Leigh Eldredge, Tim Adams (Consultant) **production** 6500 **est.** 1993
product range ($13–20 CD) Watervale Riesling, Semillon Sauvignon Blanc, Late Harvest Riesling, New Age Grenache, Blue Chip Shiraz, Cabernet Sauvignon, Sparkling, Port.
summary Leigh and Karen Eldredge have established their winery and cellar-door sales area in the Sevenhill Ranges at an altitude of 500 metres, above the town of Watervale. Contract-winemaking by Tim Adams has ensured a solid start to the business. The wines are distributed in Victoria and exported to Southeast Asia and Japan through Australian Prestige Wines, and through the remainder of the Australian States by Normans. Also exports to the UK.

Eldredge Watervale Riesling

The long experience of consultant winemaker Tim Adams shows through in this wine, grown in the heartland of Australia's riesling.
▼▼▼▼ **1999** Light to medium yellow-green; a pleasant, moderately aromatic bouquet with lime and passionfruit leads into a soft, but not spongy, early-drinking style on the palate. Reflects Tim Adams' winemaking style and philosophy. **rating: 85**

best drinking 2000–2005 **best vintages** '98 **drink with** Bruschetta • $14

Eldredge Cabernet Sauvignon

A blend of 87 per cent Cabernet Sauvignon and 13 per cent Shiraz. Had its moment of glory when the '95 won the Cabernet Sauvignon at the 1997 Royal Adelaide Wine Show.
▼▼▼▼ **1997** Medium red-purple; the moderately intense bouquet is clean, with a mix of earthy/savoury/cedary aromas. The palate has greater density and ripeness than the bouquet promises, with sweet berry and chocolate fruit, a touch of mint, and finishes with appealing ripe tannins. **rating: 87**

best drinking 2001–2007 **best vintages** '95 **drink with** Barbecued lamb • $19

eldridge estate NR

Red Hill Road, Red Hill, Vic 3937 **region** Mornington Peninsula
phone (03) 5989 2644 **fax** (03) 5989 2644 **open** Weekends, public holidays and January 1–26 11–5
winemaker David Lloyd **production** 700 **est.** 1985
product range ($20–30 CD) Semillon Sauvignon Blanc, Chardonnay, Pinot Noir, Cabernet Merlot, Sparkling.
summary The Eldridge Estate vineyard, with seven varieties included in its 3.5 hectares, was purchased by Wendy and David Lloyd in 1995. Major retrellising work has been undertaken, changing to Scott-Henry, and all of the wines will now be estate-grown and made. The wines are available at the Victorian Wine Centre and Richmond Hill Cellars in Melbourne, and a few leading restaurants in Melbourne and Sydney.

Eldridge Estate Chardonnay

Estate-grown; whole-bunch pressed, oxidatively handled, barrel-fermented and taken through full malolactic fermentation. Aged for up to 12 months in new and used French oak barriques with regular lees stirring.
▼▼▼▽ **1998** Light green-yellow; the bouquet is clean, with gentle malolactic fermentation characters and subdued fruit. The palate is similar; quite sophisticated, not showing much punchy fruit, but does hang together nicely. **rating: 82**

best drinking 2000–2003 **best vintages** NA **drink with** Poached fish • $30

elgee park NR

Wallaces Road, Merricks North, Vic 3926 **region** Mornington Peninsula
phone (03) 5989 7338 **fax** (03) 5989 7553 **open** One day a year — Sunday of Queen's Birthday weekend
winemaker Various (Contract) **production** 1500 **est.** 1972
product range ($12–25 R) Chardonnay, Pinot Noir, Cabernet, Cuvée Brut.
summary The pioneer of the Mornington Peninsula in its twentieth-century rebirth, owned by Baillieu Myer and family. The wines are now made at Stonier's, Elgee Park's own winery having been closed, and the overall level of activity decreased. Melbourne retail distribution through Flinders Wholesale.

eling forest winery   NR

Hume Highway, Sutton Forest, NSW 2577 **region** Other Wineries of NSW
phone (02) 4878 9499 **fax** (02) 4878 9499 **open** 4 days 10–5
winemaker Leslie Fritz **production** 3500 **est.** 1987
product range ($13.50–20 CD) Eling Forest Riesling, Traminer Riesling, Chardonnay, Chardonnay Blend, Catherine Hill, Botrytis Riesling, Furmint, Cabernet Sauvignon, Peach Brandy, Cherry Brandy, Peach Ambrosia, Cherry Ambrosia.
summary Eling Forest's mentally agile and innovative founder Leslie Fritz celebrated his 80th birthday not long after he planted the first vines at his Sutton Forest vineyard in 1987. He proceeded to celebrate his 88th birthday by expanding the vineyards from 3 hectares to 4, primarily with additional plantings of the Hungarian varieties. He has also developed a Cherry Port and is using the spinning cone technology to produce various peach-based liqueurs, utilising second-class peach waste. The '98 Riesling (84 points) follows in the footsteps of the '97, a good wine made in New Zealand off-dry style.

elmslie   ★★☆

Upper McEwans Road, Legana, Tas 7277 **region** Northern Tasmania
phone (03) 6330 1225 **fax** (03) 6330 2161 **open** By appointment
winemaker Ralph Power **production** 600 **est.** 1972
product range ($18 ML) Pinot Noir, Cabernet Sauvignon.
summary A small, specialist red winemaker, from time to time blending Pinot Noir with Cabernet. The fruit from the now fully mature vineyard (half a hectare of pinot noir and 1.5 hectares of cabernet sauvignon) has depth and character, but operational constraints mean that the style of the wine is often somewhat rustic.

elsewhere vineyard   ★★★★☆

40 Dillons Hill Road, Glaziers Bay, Tas 7109 **region** Southern Tasmania
phone (03) 6295 1509 **fax** (03) 6295 1509 **open** Not
winemaker Andrew Hood (Contract), Steve Lubiana (Contract) **production** 4000 **est.** 1984
product range ($15–25 ML) Riesling, No Regrets Traminer, Dry White, Chardonnay, Pinot Noir, Méthode Champenoise.
summary Eric and Jette Phillips' evocatively named Elsewhere Vineyard used to jostle for space with a commercial flower farm also run by the Phillips. It is a mark of the success of the wines that in 1993 some of the long-established flower areas made way for additional chardonnay and riesling, although it is Elsewhere's long-lived Pinot Noirs that are so stunning. The estate-produced range comes from 4 hectares of pinot noir, 3 hectares of chardonnay and 2 hectares of riesling which constitute the immaculately tended vineyard. In 1998 the Phillips sold Elsewhere to Kylie and Andrew Cameron, who have also acquired an adjoining property with the potential for another 16 hectares of vineyard.

Elsewhere Vineyard No Regrets Traminer

A story in itself. Although Eric and Jette Phillips sold Elsewhere in 1998, they leased it back until 30 June 2000. Thus the 1999 and 2000 vintages are theirs, but in the meantime they have established a new vineyard which will make the No Regrets label from 2001 and thereafter.
TTTY 1998 Light yellow-green; the bouquet abounds with strong spicy/lychee varietal character, which continues on unabated on the palate. Would have received much higher points were it not for the fairly vicious acid attack on the finish.   **rating:** 80
best drinking 2000–2005 **best vintages** NA **drink with** Spicy Asian • $20

Elsewhere Vineyard Pinot Noir

Looking at the overall performance of Elsewhere's Pinot Noirs since 1991, it has to be rated among the top three or four in Tasmania. The most extraordinary feature of the wine is the fruit complexity which comes straight from the vineyard, for the winemaking approach is fairly straightforward. The '98 vintage received (my) Chairman's Trophy at the Tasmanian Wines Show 2000.
TTTTT 1998 Medium to full purple-red; an exceptionally complex, rich and full bouquet with plum, spice and game. The palate offers the same glorious array of flavours in a wine of great length, intensity and style.   **rating:** 95
best drinking 2000–2005 **best vintages** '89, '91, '93, '95, '98 **drink with** Breast of duck with demi glaze • $25

eltham vineyards   ★★★

225 Shaws Road, Arthurs Creek, Vic 3099 **region** Yarra Valley
phone (03) 9439 4688 **fax** (03) 9439 5121 **open** By appointment
winemaker George Apted, John Graves **production** 850 **est.** 1990
product range ($14.95–18.95 ML) Chardonnay, Pinot Noir, Cabernet Sauvignon.
summary Drawing upon vineyards at Arthurs Creek and Eltham, John Graves (brother of David Graves of the illustrious Californian Pinot producer Saintsbury) produces tiny quantities of quite stylish Chardonnay and Pinot Noir, the former showing nice barrel-ferment characters.

elysium vineyard   NR

393 Milbrodale Road, Broke, NSW 2330 **region** Lower Hunter Valley
phone (02) 9664 2368 **fax** (02) 9664 2368 **open** By appointment
winemaker Tyrrell's (Contract) **production** 250 **est.** 1990
product range ($19.95 CD) Verdelho.
summary Elysium was once part of a much larger vineyard established by John Tulloch. John Tulloch (not part of the Tulloch operation owned by Southcorp) continues to look after the viticulture, with the 1 hectare of verdelho being vinified at Tyrrell's. The Elysium Vineyard cottage, large enough to accommodate six people, has won a number of tourism awards, and proprietor Victoria Foster conducts wine education weekends on request, with meals prepared by a chef brought in for the occasion. As at last advice, the cost per person for a gourmet weekend was $300.

emerald estate   NR

Main North Road, Stanley Flat, SA 5453 **region** Clare Valley
phone (08) 8842 3296 **fax** (08) 8842 2220 **open** Mon, Tues, Thurs, Fri 11–5, weekends 10–5
winemaker Tim Adams (Consultant), Frank Sheppard **production** 1670 **est.** 1990
product range ($9–15 CD) Riesling, Unwooded Chardonnay, Classic Dry White, Shiraz, Cabernet Sauvignon.
summary Don and Gwen Carroll purchased a 33-hectare property at Stanley Flat in 1990. A small existing vineyard was pulled out, and since 1990 20 hectares of vines have been established. Most of the production is sold to leading wineries in the region, a portion being retained for the Emerald Estate wine range, with limited retail distribution in Melbourne.

❦ ensay winery   NR

Great Alpine Road, Ensay, Vic 3895 **region** Gippsland
phone (03) 5157 3203 **fax** (03) 5157 3372 **open** Weekends, public and school holidays 11–5 or by appointment
winemaker David Coy **production** 1500 **est.** 1992
product range ($10–20 R) Chardonnay, Unoaked Chardonnay, Pinot Noir, Shiraz, Cabernet Sauvignon.
summary A weekend and holiday business for the Coy family, headed by David Coy, with 2 hectares of chardonnay, pinot noir, merlot, shiraz and cabernet sauvignon.

eppalock ridge   NR

633 North Redesdale Road, Redesdale, Vic 3444 **region** Bendigo
phone (03) 5425 3135 **fax** (03) 5425 3135 **open** 7 days 10–6 by appointment
winemaker Rod Hourigan **production** 1500 **est.** 1979
product range ($25 CD) Shiraz, Cabernet Merlot.
summary A low-key operation now focusing mainly on Shiraz produced from the 4 hectares of this variety, the other wine in the portfolio comes from the 2.7 hectares of cabernet sauvignon, merlot and cabernet franc.

ermes estate   NR

2 Godings Road, Moorooduc, Vic 3933 **region** Mornington Peninsula
phone (03) 5978 8376 **open** Weekends and public holidays 11–5
winemaker Ermes Zucchet **production** 500 **est.** 1989
product range ($10–15 CD) Riesling Malvasia, Chardonnay Pinot Grigio, Cabernet Merlot.
summary Ermes and Denise Zucchet commenced planting of the 2-hectare estate in 1989 with chardonnay, riesling, cabernet sauvignon and merlot, adding pinot gris in 1991. In 1994 an existing piggery on the property was converted to a winery and cellar-door area (in the Zucchets' words, 'the pigs having been evicted'), and the modestly priced wines are on sale during the weekends. No recent tastings.

⍟ ese vineyards NR

1013 Tea Tree Road, Tea Tree, Tas 7017 **region** Southern Tasmania
phone 0417 319 875 **fax** (03) 6272 5398 **open** 7 days 10–5
winemaker Michael Vishacki (Contract) **production** 500 **est.** 1994
product range ($20–25 CD) Chardonnay, Pinot Noir.
summary Elvio and Natalie Brianese are an architect and graphic designer couple with an extended family having centuries-old viticultural roots in the Veneto region of northern Italy. Ese has 2.5 hectares of vineyard, and got off to a flying start with a gold and silver medal for its 1997 Pinot Noir. Subsequent vintages have been less exhilarating, but there is no question the potential is there.

ese Vineyards Chardonnay

Made in a rich, no-holds-barred style with barrel fermentation, yeast lees stirring and full malolactic fermentation.
▼▼▼▽ **1998** Medium to full yellow-green; a very rich, concentrated and complex bouquet with a slightly sweaty breath leads into an even more concentrated and powerful palate which is bold and uncompromising, rather than accommodating. **rating:** 80
best drinking 2000–2001 **drink with** Washed-rind cheese • $20

ese Vineyards Pinot Noir

A gold medal winner at the 1999 Royal Hobart Wine Show and a silver medal at the Tasmanian Wines Show 2000. Quite a wine.
▼▼▼▽ **1997** Medium to full red-purple; the bouquet is unusually complex, with a mix of soft plum, forest, savoury and sweet spice aromas. These characters manifest themselves in a savoury/spicy/foresty palate. **rating:** 90
best drinking 2001–2007 **drink with** Peking duck • $25

eurunderee flats winery NR

Henry Lawson Drive, Mudgee, NSW 2850 **region** Mudgee
phone (02) 6373 3954 **fax** (02) 6373 3750 **open** Sun–Fri 10–4, Sat 9–5
winemaker Peter Knights **production** 1500 **est.** 1985
product range ($9–15 CD) Sauvignon Blanc, Chardonnay, Shiraz, Cabernet Sauvignon, Merlin Rouge, Liqueur Muscat, Tawny Port.
summary Sometimes called Knights Vines, although the wines are marketed under the Eurunderee Flats label. There are 5 hectares of vineyards producing white wines of variable quality, and rather better dry red table wines.

evans & tate ★★★★☆

Metricup Road, Willyabrup, WA 6280 **region** Margaret River
phone (08) 9755 6244 **fax** (08) 9755 6346 **open** 7 days 10.30–4.30
winemaker Brian Fletcher **production** 120 000 **est.** 1970
product range ($13–50 R) Gnangara Chardonnay and Shiraz; Redbrook Semillon, Chardonnay and The Red; and the Margaret River range of Margaret River Classic, Sauvignon Blanc, Sauvignon Blanc Semillon, Two Vineyards Chardonnay, Barrique 62 Cabernet Merlot, Cabernet Sauvignon, Merlot and Shiraz.
summary Single-handedly changed perceptions of the Swan Valley red wines in the '70s before opening its highly successful Margaret River operation, which goes from strength to strength. The most recent expansion has been the establishment of a large vineyard in the new Jindong subregion of the Margaret River, precipitating a flood of other arrivals in that area. The continuing rapid growth of the business has taken the edge off the wines which, while immaculately crafted and ever-reliable, lack the concentration and complexity of the very best wines of the region. National distribution; exports to Canada, the UK, New Zealand, Europe, Fiji, Zimbabwe, Hong Kong, Japan, Taiwan, Singapore, Thailand and Malaysia.

Evans & Tate Margaret River Redbrook Semillon

Has its own light but intensely flavoured style, away from the Margaret River mainstream. Has had conspicuous show success over the years.
▼▼▼▽ **1997** Light yellow-green; spicy nutmeg oak in typical style leads the bouquet. The palate simply doesn't have the fruit weight and intensity to justify the price. **rating:** 80
best drinking 2000–2002 **best vintages** '91, '92, '93, '94, '95 **drink with** Marron, yabbies • $30

Evans & Tate Margaret River Sauvignon Blanc Semillon

A blend of 60 per cent Sauvignon Blanc and 40 per cent Semillon from Evans & Tate's Redbrook and Lionel's Vineyards, fermented in stainless steel and early-bottled.

▼▼▼▼ **1999** Light green-yellow; the bouquet is bright, fresh and crisp with some mineral and passionfruit aromas; the palate is gentle, nicely balanced, although not particularly concentrated.　**rating: 87**

best drinking Drink now　**best vintages** NA　**drink with** Shellfish　• $16

Evans & Tate Margaret River Classic

Previously sourced from various vineyards throughout Western Australia, the 1998 Classic comes back to the Margaret River (hence the change in name) and, indeed, to largely estate-grown grapes from Evans & Tate's new venture at Jindong, where it has established Lionel's Vineyard. The area is fertile, and there is abundant water, resulting in vigorous growth and generous yields. While Jindong may not produce the same concentration as traditional Margaret River subregions, it is doubtless well suited to lighter, cheaper wines such as Margaret River Classic. For the record, the wine is predominantly Semillon and Sauvignon Blanc, with lesser amounts of Chardonnay and Verdelho.

▼▼▼▼ **1999** Light green-yellow; a highly aromatic, fragrant bouquet with tropical passionfruit aromas is followed by a light, fresh and vibrantly crisp palate with flavours in the same spectrum. Drink immediately.　**rating: 87**

best drinking 1999–2000　**best vintages** NA　**drink with** Asian seafood　• $18

Evans & Tate Margaret River Redbrook Chardonnay

Made using the full panoply of winemaking techniques, many borrowed from Burgundy. Part whole-bunch pressed, and part crushed, fermentation is initiated in stainless steel and then transferred to new French oak barriques for the remainder of fermentation. Twenty per cent of the wine is taken through malolactic fermentation, and the wine matured in a temperature-controlled coolroom, with prolonged lees contact and stirring. Notwithstanding all of these techniques, typically a more elegant and restrained style than one usually encounters in Margaret River.

▼▼▼▼ **1997** Light to medium yellow-green; rich peach/passionfruit/nectarine fruit aromas are bound with vanillin oak on the bouquet. The palate has more ripe, nectarine/passionfruit flavours with a moderately long finish; subtle oak.　**rating: 86**

best drinking 2000–2004　**best vintages** '95, '96, '97　**drink with** Marron or lobster　• $40

Evans & Tate Two Vineyards Chardonnay

Notwithstanding the brand name, since 1998 this wine has come entirely from Evans & Tate's estate-owned Lionel's Vineyard at Jindong. Here the rich soil and warmer climate provide high yields of ripe grapes, in a very different style from areas further south in Margaret River. Forty per cent of the wine is fermented in barrel, 30 per cent being taken through malolactic fermentation.

▼▼▼▽ **1999** Medium yellow-green; there is very strong oak on the bouquet, and while the fruit struggles to express itself on the palate, the oak wins the fight.　**rating: 83**

▼▼▼▼ **1998** Light to medium yellow-green; the bouquet is relatively light, with a fragrant mix of citrus, stone fruit and more mineral notes. The palate is delicate, fresh and quite elegant, with the sensitive use of oak, which does not obscure the pretty, light fruit.　**rating: 86**

best drinking 2000–2001　**best vintages** '91, '92, '93, '94, '95, '98　**drink with** Sugar-cured tuna　• $16

Evans & Tate Margaret River Shiraz

A 100 per cent estate-grown wine from the Redbrook Vineyard (using the Hermitage name until 1992, but of course made from shiraz). The Margaret River region has not done a great deal with Shiraz overall, preferring to concentrate on other varieties, but the wine shows the potential that the region has for this variety.

▼▼▼▼ **1998** Medium red-purple; the moderately intense bouquet has nice varietal character and appropriately subtle oak; the palate delivers more of the same, with fresh cherry-accented fruit; not especially complex but easy on the gums.　**rating: 88**

best drinking 2003–2008　**best vintages** '86, '88, '90, '91, '92, '93, '95, '96　**drink with** Strong red meat dishes • $25

Evans & Tate Redbrook

Simply labelled Redbrook, but in fact a blend of Merlot, Cabernet Sauvignon and Shiraz. Is now the flagship red for Evans and Tate.

▼▼▼▼▽ **1996** Medium purple-red; sweet, lively plum and blackcurrant fruit is accompanied by well-balanced and integrated oak on the bouquet; juicy blackcurrant fruit is picked up by excellent sweet, cedary oak on the palate.　**rating: 92**

best drinking 2000–2010　**best vintages** '96　**drink with** Fillet of lamb　• $50

Evans & Tate Barrique 61 Cabernet Merlot

Made from higher yielding vines in an easy early-drinking style at a moderate price.

TTTY 1998 Medium red-purple; the fruit is of light to medium intensity, cedary oak being rather more prominent on the bouquet. The palate has sweet berry fruit but is a little thin or hollow on the mid-palate.

rating: 83

best drinking 2000–2004 **best vintages** NA **drink with** Gourmet sausages • $16

evans family ★★★★☆

Palmers Lane, Pokolbin, NSW 2321 **region** Lower Hunter Valley
phone (02) 4998 7333 **fax** (02) 4998 7798 **open** By appointment
winemaker Contract **production** 3000 **est.** 1979
product range ($16–22.50 ML) Semillon, Pinchem Chardonnay, Howard Chardonnay, Statue Vineyard Sparkling Pinot, Chapel Gamay, Hillside Pinot Noir, Howard Shiraz.
summary In the wake of the acquisition of Rothbury by Mildara Blass, Len Evans' wine interests now focus on Evans Family (estate-grown and produced from vineyards around the family home), the Evans Wine Company (a quite different, part-maker, part-negociant business) and, most recently, Tower Estate. Len Evans continues to persist with the notion that the Hunter Valley can produce Gamay and Pinot Noir of quality and, irritatingly, occasionally produces evidence to suggest he may be half right. There is, of course, no such reservation with the Chardonnay.

Evans Family Howard Shiraz

Produced from grapes grown on one of the best vineyards in the Hunter Valley.

TTTT 1997 Excellent red-purple; the bouquet is quite aromatic, with slightly sappy/earthy regional overtones. The supple palate has nicely balanced tannins and oak and will develop well. **rating:** 89

best drinking 2003–2009 **best vintages** NA **drink with** Rare sirloin beef • $25

evelyn county estate NR

35 New Road, Kangaroo Ground, Vic 3097 **region** Yarra Valley
phone (03) 9437 1668 **fax** (03) 9437 1232 **open** By appointment
winemaker David Lance (Contract) **production** 810 **est.** 1994
product range ($17–25 CD) Black Paddock range of Sauvignon Blanc, Chardonnay, Pinot Noir, Merlot, Cabernet Sauvignon.
summary The 7-hectare Evelyn County Estate has been established by former Coopers & Lybrand managing partner Roger Male and his wife Robyn, who is currently halfway through a degree in Applied Science (Wine Science) at Charles Sturt University. David Lance (of Diamond Valley) is currently making the wines, and an architect-designed cellar-door sales and gallery is due to open in April 2001. As one would expect, the quality of the wines is good.

Evelyn County Estate Black Paddock Chardonnay

Picked very ripe (as almost all 1998 Yarra Valley Chardonnays were) at 13.5° baumé and barrel-fermented. Looks as if it may develop reasonably quickly.

TTTY 1999 Light to medium yellow-green; the bouquet is clean, of light to moderate intensity, with subtle barrel-ferment oak inputs. The palate offers more of the same, but at the extreme end of the elegance and subtlety scale. **rating:** 83

best drinking 2000–2002 **best vintages** NA **drink with** Yarra Valley trout • $20

excelsior peak NR

22 Wrights Road, Drummoyne, NSW 2047 (postal address) **region** Tumbarumba
phone (02) 6948 5102 **fax** (02) 6948 5102 **open** Not
winemaker Charles Sturt University (Contract) **production** 1150 **est.** 1980
product range ($18–22 ML) Chardonnay, Pinot Noir, Méthode Champenoise.
summary Excelsior Peak proprietor Juliet Cullen established the first vineyard in Tumbarumba in 1980. That vineyard was thereafter sold to Southcorp, and Juliet Cullen subsequently established another vineyard, now releasing wines under the Excelsior Peak label. Plantings total 9 hectares, with 6.5 hectares in production.

eyton-on-yarra ★★★★

Corner Maroondah Highway and Hill Road, Coldstream, Vic 3370 **region** Yarra Valley
phone (03) 5962 2119 **fax** (03) 5962 5319 **open** 7 days 10–5
winemaker Matthew Aldridge **production** 13 000 **est.** 1993
product range ($22–40 R) There are now three labels in the range: at the top NDC Reserve, a tribute to the late Newell Cowan, who effectively founded Eyton-on-Yarra; the main varietal range under the Eyton label; and the second label range of Dalry Road, the name of the second vineyard owned by Eyton.
summary Now owned and run by the energetic and innovative Deidre Cowan, overseeing an excellent and capacious restaurant, a sound shell for concerts of every shape and hue, and — of course — the winemaking side of a substantial business, which is able to draw on 40 hectares of estate vineyards. Winemaker Matt Aldridge has now found his feet, with a corresponding significant lift in quality and style. Retail distribution through Victoria, New South Wales and ACT.

Eyton-on-Yarra Chardonnay

Produced from estate-grown fruit; Eyton-on-Yarra draws on two substantial vineyards, one around the winery and the other some distance away on flatter country closer to the Yarra River. Much of the grape production has been sold to others, with the best reserved for the Eyton-on-Yarra label. The wine spends 18 months in French oak and is given partial malolactic fermentation.

▼▼▼▼ 1999 Medium yellow-green; quite complex and powerful barrel-ferment spicy oak dominates the bouquet, but the play on the palate is quite different; here rich melon and peach fruit, together with some cashew, have good weight and structure, providing the requisite balance. **rating:** 89

best drinking 2001–2007 **best vintages** '95, '99 **drink with** Smoked salmon pasta • $24

Eyton-on-Yarra Dalry Road Chardonnay

This is the second label of Eyton-on-Yarra, but still drawn from the very substantial vineyard resources available to Eyton. A small percentage is barrel-fermented; a reliable wine which shows the winemaking skills of Matt Aldridge to good advantage.

▼▼▼▽ 1999 Medium yellow-green; the bouquet has gentle melon, honey and fig fruit; the oak is imperceptible. A nicely put together wine on the palate, with plenty of flavour, although does tend to cloy ever-so-slightly on the finish. **rating:** 84

best drinking 2000–2003 **best vintages** NA **drink with** Snapper • $17

Eyton-on-Yarra Pinot Noir

Made using the full gamut of pinot noir techniques, with 30 per cent whole bunches in the ferment, and the wine pressed and transferred to barrel at 3° baumé for the balance of its fermentation. Notwithstanding the very difficult, wet vintage conditions in 1999, has significantly more structure and character than preceding vintages.

▼▼▼▼ 1999 Medium red, with just a touch of purple; the bouquet, while not powerful, is certainly complex, with a mix of forest, spice, cedar and ripe plum. These characters come through on a palate which has considerable flavour and extract; the only criticism is the slightly grippy tannins on the finish, which should soften with time. **rating:** 85

best drinking 2000–2004 **best vintages** NA **drink with** Smoked quail • $24

Eyton-on-Yarra NDC Reserve Shiraz

The NDC Reserve range (currently Merlot and Shiraz) was created in memory of Eyton's founder, Newell Cowan. The wines are considered to be premium selections, and spend 18 months in oak.

▼▼▼▼▽ 1997 Medium to full red-purple; the bouquet has lots of sweet vanilla oak, promising a richly textured palate which is duly delivered. Stacked with sweet flavour, part fruit, part oak, the palate is particularly luscious; not necessarily varietal but nigh on irresistible. **rating:** 90

best drinking 2002–2012 **best vintages** '97 **drink with** Braised beef • $40

Eyton-on-Yarra Cabernet Merlot

A blend of 75 per cent Cabernet Sauvignon and 25 per cent Merlot, matured in a mix of new and used French oak barriques.

▼▼▼▼ 1998 Medium red-purple; cool-climate, fragrant leaf and spice aromas on the bouquet precede a palate with rather more sweet berry fruit; soft tannins and subtle oak. **rating:** 86

best drinking 2002–2007 **best vintages** '98 **drink with** Roast veal • $24

Eyton-on-Yarra NDC Reserve Cabernet Sauvignon

The NDC Reserve, named after the late Newell Cowan who founded Eyton-on-Yarra, is intermittently produced in limited quantities, and only appears when the wine is clearly of superior quality.

ŢŢŢŢ 1998 Medium red-purple; an elegant bouquet with a mix of smooth red berry and more savoury notes; the palate opens with fine, elegant, cassis berry fruit followed by an unexpected twist of almost lemony acidity on the finish, which, strangely enough, does not upset the flow of the wine.   **rating: 87**

best drinking 2003–2013 **best vintages** '98 **drink with** Marinated leg of lamb • $40

fairfield vineyard   NR

Murray Valley Highway, Browns Plains via Rutherglen, Vic 3685 **region** Rutherglen and Glenrowan
phone (02) 6032 9381 **open** Mon–Sat 10–5, some Sun 12–5
winemaker Andrew Sutherland-Smith **production** 4200 **est.** 1959
product range ($8.50–15 CD) White Hermitage, Riesling, Moselle, Rosé, Light Red, Shiraz, Durif, Cabernet Sauvignon, Fortified.
summary Specialist in red and fortified wines made with nineteenth-century wine equipment housed in the grounds of the historic Fairfield Mansion built by G F Morris. A tourist must. Offers a wide range of back vintages.

faisan estate   NR

Amaroo Road, Borenore, NSW 2800 **region** Orange
phone (02) 6365 2380 **open** Not
winemaker Col Walker **production** 500 **est.** 1992
product range ($8–13 ML) Chardonnay, Canobolas Classic White, Pinot Noir, Britton's Block Cabernet Sauvignon, Old Block Cabernet Sauvignon.
summary Faisan Estate, within sight of Mount Canobolas and 20 kilometres west of the city of Orange, has been established by Trish and Col Walker. They now have almost 7 hectares of vineyards coming into bearing and have purchased grapes from other growers in the region in the interim. The 1998 Chardonnay (84 points) offers lots of flavour (both fruit and oak) at the bargain price of $12 per bottle.

farrell's limestone creek   ★★★☆

Mount View Road, Mount View, NSW 2325 **region** Lower Hunter Valley
phone (02) 4991 2808 **fax** (02) 4991 3414 **open** Weekends, public holidays 10–5
winemaker Neil McGuigan (Consultant) **production** 3000 **est.** 1982
product range ($12–22 CD) Semillon, Chardonnay, Late Harvest Verdelho, Shiraz, Merlot, Cabernet Sauvignon Merlot.
summary The Farrell family purchased 50 acres on Mount View in 1980 and gradually established 18 acres of vineyards planted to semillon, verdelho, chardonnay, shiraz, cabernet sauvignon and merlot. Most of the grapes are sold to McWilliam's, which contract-makes a small amount for cellar-door sales. The quality of the wines is as good as one would expect, with a range of back vintages available at cellar door.

felsberg winery   NR

Townsends Road, Glen Aplin, Qld 4381 **region** Granite Belt
phone (07) 4683 4332 **fax** (07) 4683 4377 **open** 7 days 9–5
winemaker Otto Haag **production** 2000 **est.** 1983
product range ($12–18 CD) Rhine Riesling, Traminer, Sylvaner, Chardonnay, Traminer Rosé, Merlot, Shiraz, Cabernet Sauvignon, Mead, Ruby Mead.
summary Felsberg has been offering wine for sale via cellar door made by former master brewer Otto Haag. I had problems with the first few vintages but, after a gap in tasting of several years, I renewed my acquaintance with Felsberg through the particularly attractive '97 vintage reds and now the '98 vintage wines.

Felsberg Merlot

Merlot is a relatively new arrival on the scene in the Granite Belt, but holds much promise if the wines of Adam Chapman's Violet Cane and this Felsberg version are anything to go by.

ŢŢŢŢ 1998 Light to medium red-purple; the bouquet is clean, with leafy savoury/spicy aromas, the palate correspondingly light, fresh and clean, with savoury/lemony flavours.   **rating: 82**

best drinking 2000–2002 **best vintages** NA **drink with** Veal ragout • $16

Felsberg Cabernet Sauvignon

Produced from 1.7 hectares of estate plantings and given fairly lavish maturation in American oak.

TTTT 1998 Medium red-purple; there is rich and ripe fruit but even more American oak on the bouquet, a pattern repeated on the palate, where sweet berry fruit is completely surrounded by milky/chewy American oak. Less would have been so much better. **rating: 82**

best drinking 2001–2004 **best vintages** NA **drink with** Big Mac •$16

ferguson falls estate   NR

Pile Road, Dardanup, WA 6236 **region** Geographe
phone (08) 9728 1083 **fax** (08) 9728 1083 **open** By appointment
winemaker James Pennington (Contract) **production** 1000 **est.** 1983
product range ($15–17 CD) Chardonnay, Cabernet Sauvignon.
summary Peter Giumelli and family are dairy farmers in the lush Ferguson Valley, 180 kilometres south of Perth. In 1983 they planted 3 hectares of cabernet sauvignon, chardonnay and merlot, making their first wines for commercial release from the 1995 and 1996 vintages. Both confirm the suitability of the region for the production of premium wine.

fergusson   ★★★★

Wills Road, Yarra Glen, Vic 3775 **region** Yarra Valley
phone (03) 5965 2237 **fax** (03) 5965 2405 **open** 7 days 11–5
winemaker Christopher Keyes, Peter Fergusson **production** 10 000 **est.** 1968
product range ($15.50–38.50 CD) There are two basic ranges: the lower-priced Tartan Range sourced from grapes grown outside the Yarra Valley, with Chardonnay, Semillon Sauvignon Blanc, Pinot Noir, Shiraz, Fine Old Tawny Port and Sangria; and the Estate Range: Victoria Chardonnay, Victoria Reserve Chardonnay, Blanc de Blanc, Jeremy Shiraz and Benjamyn Cabernet Sauvignon.
summary Best known as a favoured tourist destination, particularly for tourist coaches, and offering hearty fare in comfortable surroundings accompanied by wines of non-Yarra Valley origin. For this reason the limited quantities of its estate wines are often ignored, but should not be.

Fergusson Victoria Reserve Chardonnay

Like the varietal wine, named after the Fergussons' daughter, not the State. The Reserve Chardonnay is a barrel selection available both in bottle and in limited release magnums.

TTTT 1998 Medium yellow-green; the clean and smooth bouquet has abundant ripe peach and fig fruit supported by subtle, slightly smoky oak. The palate follows along the same track, not forced, with attractive peachy fruit; finishes with well-balanced acidity and again subtle oak. **rating: 88**

best drinking 2000–2004 **best vintages** NA **drink with** Free range chicken •$38.50

Fergusson Jeremy Shiraz

Named after Peter and Louise Fergusson's son Jeremy and made from estate-grown grapes. The '93 vintage was a knockout, and the '98 is better still. When the subject of Yarra Valley Shiraz comes up, Fergusson is more often than not forgotten. It should not be.

TTTTT 1998 Medium to full red-purple; rich, dense, ripe spicy black cherry and oak aromas lead into a quite luscious palate with fully ripe dark berry fruit and fine, ripe tannins. **rating: 94**

best drinking 2003–2013 **best vintages** '88, '91, '92, '93, '98 **drink with** Osso buco •$28.50

Fergusson Benjamyn Cabernet Sauvignon

Completes the trio of wines named after the Fergusson children. As with all the estate-grown wines, well-made.

TTTT 1998 Medium red-purple; the bouquet offers strong, earthy cabernet fruit married with attractive cigar box oak. The palate is medium-bodied, with a mix of red berry and earthy fruit, finishing with moderately weighted tannins. The oak is evident, but in restraint. **rating: 85**

best drinking 2003–2008 **best vintages** '88, '91, '92, '93 **drink with** Leg of lamb •$28.50

fermoy estate   NR

Metricup Road, Willyabrup, WA 6280 **region** Margaret River
phone (08) 9755 6285 **fax** (08) 9755 6251 **open** 7 days 11–4.30
winemaker Michael Kelly **production** 15 000 **est.** 1985
product range ($12–28 CD) Sauvignon Blanc, Sentinel (Sauvignon Blanc Semillon), Semillon, Chenin Blanc, Chardonnay, Reserve Chardonnay, Cabernet Sauvignon, Reserve Cabernet.

summary Consistently produces wines with a particular character and style, with the focus away from primary fruit and into secondary flavours, with strong structure; the Americans would call them 'food styles'. Quite deliberately out of the mainstream.

fern hill estate   ★★☆

Ingoldby Road, McLaren Flat, SA 5171 **region** McLaren Vale
phone (08) 8383 0167 **fax** (08) 8383 0107 **open** Mon–Fri 10–5, weekends 10–5
winemaker Grant Burge (Contract) **production** 5000 **est.** 1975
product range ($14.95–17.95 CD) Semillon, Chardonnay, Shiraz, Cabernet Sauvignon.
summary One suspects there have been significant changes since Wayne Thomas sold Fern Hill to the Hill International Group, and not all for the better. The wines are now exported to the UK, the US, Canada, Japan, New Zealand, Singapore and Switzerland.

fishburn & o'keefe   ★★★☆

16 Pioneer Avenue, New Norfolk, Tas 7140 **region** Southern Tasmania
phone (03) 6286 1234 **fax** (03) 6261 4029 **open** 7 days at Meadowbank Vineyard
winemaker Greg O'Keefe **production** 3000 **est.** 1991
product range ($15–25 CD) Riesling, Chardonnay, Trout White (White Pinot), Pinot Noir, Cabernet Sauvignon, Trout Brut.
summary Wine consultant and contract-winemaker Greg O'Keefe, one time winemaker at Normans, has joined forces with Hutchins schoolteacher Mike Fishburn to produce wines made from grapes purchased from various growers across Tasmania, but with an estate vineyard in the course of establishment. Greg O'Keefe also has an active consultancy and contract-winemaking business in his own right. Has also managed to produce a hard-to-find Sparkling Shiraz from grapes grown in the Tamar Valley.

🐌 572 richmond road   NR

572 Richmond Road, Cambridge, Tas 7170 (postal 44 Lambert St, Kangaroo Point, Qld, 4169) **region** Southern Tasmania
phone 0419 878 023 **fax** (07) 3391 4565 **open** At Craigow Fri–Sun 10–5
winemaker Andrew Hood, Julian Alcorso (Contract) **production** 250 **est.** 1994
product range ($18–22 ML) Riesling, Gewurztraminer, Chardonnay.
summary It hardly needs be said 572 Richmond Road is both the address and the name of the vineyard. It is owned by John and Sue Carney, medical professionals, and is situated adjacent to Andrew Hood's winery, hence becoming part of a spectacular vineyard development with various ownerships but all situated close to the winery.

572 Richmond Road Riesling

Produced from 0.6 hectare of estate plantings, and is likely to continue to be the most important wine in the portfolio, with a side bit on the Gewurztraminer. The '98 was a strongly supported bronze medal winner at the Tasmanian Wines Show 2000.

▼▼▼▼ 1998 Light to medium green-yellow; the bouquet has quite pungent tropical fruit showing signs of a very slow fermentation; the palate is rich with plenty of lime/tropical fruit.   **rating:** 85
best drinking 2000–2004 **drink with** Mussels • $20

572 Richmond Road Gewurztraminer

Notwithstanding the slightly idiosyncratic name of the producer, the packaging is excellent, with an attractive label set on an antique green bottle. These externalities to one side, this is a promising start for a first crop.

▼▼▼▽ 1999 Light green-yellow; the bouquet is quite powerful, with tropical fruit aromas which flow through to the quite luscious yet racey palate.   **rating:** 82
best drinking 2000–2003 **drink with** Chinese crystal prawns • $22

five oaks vineyard   ★★★☆

60 Aitken Road, Seville, Vic 3139 **region** Yarra Valley
phone (03) 5964 3704 **fax** (03) 5964 3064 **open** Weekends and public holidays 10–5 and by appointment
winemaker Wally Zuk **production** 2000 **est.** 1997
product range ($17–24 CD) Riesling, Chardonnay, Cabernet Merlot, Cabernet Sauvignon.
summary Wally and Judy Zuk purchased the Five Oaks Vineyard in Aitken Road, Seville, from Oakridge Estate, which has moved to its new premises on the other side of the Yarra Valley. Wally Zuk, with a background in

nuclear physics, has completed his Wine Science degree at Charles Sturt University. He has now retired from the nuclear science world and is devoting himself (with help from Michael Zitzlaff of Oakridge and his wife Judy) to running Five Oaks. The winery rating is given for the red wines; the white wines are less successful.

Five Oaks Vineyard Cabernet Merlot
The Seville subregion is a cooler part of the Yarra Valley, and with its own distinctive red soil. It flourishes in the warmer vintages.
TTTY 1998 Medium to full red-purple; the bouquet is clean, with ripe dark berry/cassis fruit which flows through onto the palate. The wine is a little unformed/underworked; time in bottle should help it soften and open up.   **rating:** 84
best drinking 2002–2007 **best vintages** NA **drink with** Steak and kidney pie • $22

Five Oaks Vineyard Cabernet Sauvignon
Produced from fully mature vines, a legacy of the Zitzlaffs. It spends 20 months in oak before being bottled.
TTTT 1998 Medium red-purple; the bouquet is clean, with ripe berry fruit and a nice touch of vanilla oak. The palate is pleasantly firm, with berry fruit balanced by nicely integrated oak and tannins.   **rating:** 85
best drinking 2003–2008 **best vintages** NA **drink with** Roast beef • $24

flinders bay   NR
Davis Road, Witchcliffe, WA 6286 **region** Margaret River
phone (08) 9757 6281 **fax** (08) 9757 6353 **open** Not
winemaker Clive Otto, Will Shields (Contract) **production** 12 000 **est.** 1995
product range ($17–26 R) Sauvignon Blanc Semillon, Verdelho, Chardonnay, Shiraz, Cabernet Sauvignon.
summary Flinders Bay is a joint venture between the Gillespie and Ireland families. The Gillespies have been grape growers and viticultural contractors in the Margaret River region for over 20 years, while Bill and Noel Ireland were very prominent retailers in Sydney from 1979 to 1996. All in all, a potent and synergistic combination. Fifty hectares of vines were planted between 1995 and 1998 at Karridale, an extremely cool subregion (possibly the coolest in Western Australia) with the climate influenced by both the Indian and Southern Oceans. The wines presently being produced are blends of grapes from the northern and central parts of the Margaret River with estate-grown grapes. Ultimately, all of the wines will be estate-produced. They are contract-made at Vasse Felix which also provides the cellar-door facility for Flinders Bay.

Flinders Bay Sauvignon Blanc Semillon
Produced from grapes grown at Karridale and Witchcliffe; made without the disruptive influence of oak.
TTTT 1999 Light green-yellow; the moderately intense and clean bouquet has very precise herb and citrus varietal fruit. The palate, likewise, has good varietal definition and is nicely balanced; needs just a touch more fruit intensity to lift it into top class points.   **rating:** 89
best drinking 2000–2002 **drink with** Oysters kilpatrick • $17

fonty's pool   NR
c/o Cape Mentelle Vineyards, PO Box 11, Margaret River, WA 6285 **region** Manjimup
phone (08) 9757 3266 **fax** (08) 9757 3233 **open** Not
winemaker Eloise Jarvis (Cape Mentelle) **production** 1000 **est.** 1998
product range ($20.60–24.90 R) Chardonnay, Pinot Noir, Shiraz.
summary Fonty's Pool is a joint venture between Cape Mentelle and Fonty's Pool Farms. The Fonty's Pool vineyards are part of the original farm owned by pioneer settler Archie Fontanini, who was granted land by the government in 1907. In the early 1920s, a large dam was created to provide water for the intensive vegetable farming which was part of the farming activities. The dam became known as Fonty's Pool, and to this day remains a famous local landmark and recreational facility. The first grapes were planted in 1989, and the vineyard is now one of the region's largest, supplying grapes to a number of leading West Australian wineries. Only a small part of the production is used for Fonty's Pool; the wines are made at Cape Mentelle by Eloise Jarvis, who is part of the Cape Mentelle winemaking team.

Fonty's Pool Chardonnay
A complex range of winemaking techniques sees a small portion of the juice taken directly to barrel for a natural (wild) ferment, with the balance inoculated with commercial yeast before being split into two halves, one being barrel-fermented, the other half tank-fermented. One-third of the barrels are new, the rest one-year-old; one-third of the blend undergoes malolactic fermentation in the following spring. The components are blended in December, and the wine then spends another eight months in stainless steel before being bottled 18 months after vintage.

▼▼▼▽ **1999** Medium yellow-green; the bouquet is uncompromisingly complex with what are frequently referred to as 'dirty French' characters. The palate is smoother, but nonetheless with some quite aggressive characters; all in all, far from the typical Manjimup style. I have to confess that I cannot relate the characters in the wine to the unconventional making techniques, however. **rating:** 83

best drinking 2000–2003 **drink with** Oyster soup • $20.60

Fonty's Pool Pinot Noir

Fermentation takes place in open fermenters, hand-plunged and with a peak temperature of 30°C, before being pressed and taken to barrel prior to the end of fermentation; malolactic fermentation is likewise completed in barrel. One-third new French oak, two-thirds used. Bottled ten months after vintage.

▼▼▼▼ **1998** Medium purple-red; the aromas of the bouquet are primarily in the cedary/spicy/oaky spectrum, but there is a lot of character and flavour on the palate, where plum, cedar and forest characters are supported by good tannins and structure. Picked one day before the heavy rain which fell in March in the region, but also reflects disciplined viticulture and, in particular, crop reduction. **rating:** 87

best drinking 2000–2003 **drink with** Coq au vin • $24.80

☙ fordwich estate   NR

390 Milbrodale Road, Fordwich, NSW 2330 **region** Lower Hunter Valley
phone (02) 9968 1764 **fax** (02) 9960 3454 **open** Not
winemaker Tony Bainton, Michael Crooks **production** 2500 **est.** 1998
product range ($12–20 ML) Wollemi Semillon and Chardonnay; Q Chambourcin and Pinot Noir.
summary The Bainton family, headed by eminent Sydney QC Russell Bainton, has 48 hectares of vineyard, currently selling most of the grapes but intending to steadily increase production in house.

fox creek wines   ★★★★☆

Malpas Road, Willunga, SA 5172 **region** McLaren Vale
phone (08) 8556 2403 **fax** (08) 8556 2104 **open** 7 days 11–5
winemaker Daniel Hills, Tony Walker **production** 20 000 **est.** 1995
product range ($15–45 CD) Verdelho, Sauvignon Blanc, Chardonnay, Botrytis Chenin Blanc, Vixen Sparkling Burgundy, Reserve Shiraz, JSM Shiraz Cabernets, Merlot, Reserve Cabernet Sauvignon.
summary Fox Creek has made a major impact since coming on-stream late in 1995. It is the venture of a group of distinguished Adelaide doctors (three of them professors), with particular input from the Watts family, which established the vineyard back in 1985 (selling the grapes) and whose daughter Sarah is now married to former winemaker Sparky Marquis. The Reserve red wines, and especially the Reserve Shiraz, are outstanding and have enjoyed considerable show success. As well as comprehensive distribution throughout Australia, the wines are exported to the UK, New Zealand, the US, Canada, Sweden, Germany, Switzerland, Belgium, The Netherlands, Thailand and Singapore.

Fox Creek Verdelho

Produced from roughly equal quantities of grapes grown respectively at the Coona Vineyard and the new Fox Creek home vineyard. One-third of the wine was barrel-fermented in new American oak for 20 days, the remaining two-thirds fermented in stainless steel. The oak input is very subtle.

▼▼▼▽ **1999** Light green-yellow; the bouquet is quite aromatic, with tropical fruit aromas; the palate has above-average flavour (which may be damning it by faint praise), again with tropical fruit salad character. **rating:** 83

best drinking 2000–2002 **best vintages** NA **drink with** Pasta • $15

Fox Creek Reserve Shiraz

Estate-grown; and made in a consistently heroic style which often captures the attention of the perhaps jaded palates of wine show judges.

▼▼▼▼ **1998** Dense purple-red; a wine in the massive magimix fruit and oak style with everything thrown into the blender, with huge American oak whipped up with dense berry fruit. Taste, don't drink (yet). **rating:** 90

best drinking 2005–2015 **best vintages** '96, '98 **drink with** Grilled beef • $42

Fox Creek Grenache Shiraz

At least on the evidence of the 1998 vintage, a wine on the fringe of conventionality.

▼▼▼▽ **1998** Medium to full red-purple; the bouquet is dead-set spearmint chewing gum; the fruit on the palate is wrapped inside the spearmint coating; I cannot recollect ever having tasted a wine with such pronounced spearmint characters. **rating:** 83

best drinking 2001–2003 **best vintages** NA **drink with** Spiced beef • $16

Fox Creek JSM Shiraz Cabernets

JSM are the initials of James Stanley Malpas (born 1873) and are cut into the stone lintel above the present-day tasting room, but which was his house after he had graduated from Roseworthy Agricultural College. The wine is a blend of Shiraz, Cabernet Sauvignon and Cabernet Franc, 70 per cent of which is matured for 12 months in second-use American oak and 30 per cent for 12 months in second-use French oak.

▼▼▼▼ **1998** Medium to full red-purple; there is an interesting blend of aromas on the bouquet, with the leafy/cedary characters of the cabernet franc and cabernet sauvignon (the latter not shown on the front label) coming through on the back of ripe shiraz. A young, juicy, berry style with very sweet fruit on the palate; needs a couple of years to sort itself out, and could then be delicious. **rating:** 85

best drinking 2003–2008 **best vintages** NA **drink with** Rib of beef • $20

frankland estate ★★★★

Frankland Road, Frankland, WA 6396 **region** Great Southern
phone (08) 9855 1544 **fax** (08) 9855 1549 **open** By appointment
winemaker Barrie Smith, Judi Cullam **production** 12 000 **est.** 1988
product range ($18–32 R) Under the Isolation Ridge label are Riesling, Sauvignon Blanc, Chardonnay, Shiraz, Cabernet Sauvignon; Olmo's Reward (Bordeaux-blend) is the flag-bearer.
summary A rapidly growing Frankland River operation, situated on a large sheep property owned by Barrie Smith and Judi Cullam. The 26-hectare vineyard has been established progressively since 1988, and a winery was built on the site for the 1993 vintage. The Riesling, Isolation Ridge and Olmo's Reward are consistently good. Exports to the US, the UK, Taiwan, Japan, Belgium, Switzerland, Denmark and Singapore.

Frankland Estate Isolation Ridge Riesling

Usually the best of the Frankland Estate wines. Its consistency has shone through, notwithstanding that between 1992 and 1995 it was made by different winemakers at different wineries. As always, meticulous viticulture is the key, with viticultural consultancy advice from Dr Richard Smart.

▼▼▼▼ **1998** Light green-yellow; the aromas are clean, crisp with slatey/minerally characters and a touch of herb. The palate is tight, with mineral/herb flavours, still to build fruit richness, which will come with time. **rating:** 87

best drinking 2003–2007 **best vintages** '92, '93, '94, '96, '98 **drink with** Antipasto • $19.75

Frankland Estate Chardonnay

As with all the wines from Frankland Estate, grown and made on the estate in a straightforward, no-nonsense style.

▼▼▼▼ **1997** Light to medium yellow-green; the bouquet is still quite youthful, with clean fruit and subtle oak; the palate, likewise, has gentle peach, honey and oak influences. Will never be especially complex but should nonetheless develop nicely from this point. **rating:** 85

best drinking 2000–2003 **best vintages** NA **drink with** Fresh prawns • $21.50

Frankland Estate Olmo's Reward

Named in honour of Dr Harold Olmo, the viticulturist to point to the potential of the Frankland River as far back as 1955. Now in his 80s, Dr Olmo lives in retirement in California, and it is fitting that his contribution to viticulture should be so remembered. The wine is a blend of Cabernet Franc, Merlot, Malbec and Cabernet Sauvignon, all estate-grown.

▼▼▼▼ **1996** Light to medium red-purple; the bouquet is cleaner and fresher than on prior encounters, with light berry, earth and cedar aromas. A restrained Bordeaux style which utterly belies its 14 degrees alcohol. Finishes with crisp acidity, and the oak is in no way a problem. **rating:** 88

best drinking 2001–2006 **best vintages** NA **drink with** Veal chops • $31

freycinet ★★★★★

Tasman Highway via Bicheno, Tas 7215 **region** Southern Tasmania
phone (03) 6257 8574 **fax** (03) 6257 8454 **open** Mon–Fri 9–5, weekends 10–5
winemaker Claudio Radenti, Lindy Bull **production** 7000 **est.** 1980
product range ($15–35 CD) Riesling Muller Thurgau, Riesling, Chardonnay, Pinot Noir, The Hazards Pinot Noir, Cabernet Franc, Radenti (Méthode Champenoise).
summary The 4-hectare Freycinet vineyards are beautifully situated on the sloping hillsides of a small valley. The soils are podsol and decaying granite with a friable clay subsoil, and the combination of aspect, slope, soil and heat summation produce red grapes of unusual depth of colour and ripe flavours. One of Australia's foremost producers of Pinot Noir, with a wholly enviable track record of consistency — rare with such a temperamental variety.

Freycinet Pinot Noir

The remarkable site climate of the Freycinet vineyard is primarily responsible for the outstanding quality of the Pinot Noir, although the experience and skills of Geoff Bull, daughter Lindy Bull, and Claudio Radenti ensure that the potential quality is maximised. Interestingly, the only red fermenter the winery possesses is a rotary fermenter, which in turn helps in the extraction of both colour and flavour. Year in, year out one of Australia's (let alone Tasmania's) best Pinot Noirs.

▼▼▼▼ 1999 Strong purple-red; strong, dark plummy fruit on the bouquet is repeated on the rich and powerful palate. Absolutely in the mainstream of the Freycinet style, and sure to age well. Yet another gold medal to Freycinet. **rating:** 93

▼▼▼▼▼ 1998 Medium to full red-purple; some gamey/foresty/briary/savoury nuances add to the complexity of both the bouquet and the palate; however, the core of the wine lies in its rich, sweet fruit, which runs through the stylish, long finish. **rating:** 95

best drinking 2001–2006 **best vintages** '91, '92, '94, '95, '96, '97, '98, '99 **drink with** Duck, hare, venison • $35

fyffe field NR

Murray Valley Highway, Yarrawonga, Vic 3730 **region** Goulburn Valley
phone (03) 5748 4282 **fax** (03) 5748 4284 **open** 7 days 10–5
winemaker David Traeger (Contract) **production** 1300 **est.** 1993
product range ($8–15 CD) Diamond White, Verdelho, Shiraz, Shiraz Petit Verdot, Touriga, Tokay, Muscat, Tawny Snort.
summary Fyffe Field has been established by Graeme and Liz Diamond near the Murray River between Cobram and Yarrawonga in a mudbrick and leadlight tasting room opposite an historic homestead. A highlight is the ornamental pig collection, a display set up long before Babe was born. Wine quality is adequate.

galafrey ★★★☆

Quangellup Road, Mount Barker, WA 6324 **region** Great Southern
phone (08) 9851 2022 **fax** (08) 9851 2324 **open** Mon–Sat 10–5
winemaker Ian Tyrer **production** 4000 **est.** 1977
product range ($12–22 CD) Riesling, Chardonnay, Muller, Semillon Sauvignon Blanc, Unoaked Chardonnay, Pinot Noir, Shiraz, Cabernet Sauvignon, Tawny Port.
summary Relocated to a new purpose-built but utilitarian winery after previously inhabiting the exotic surrounds of the old Albany wool store, Galafrey makes wines with plenty of robust, if not rustic, character, drawing grapes in the main from 12 hectares of estate plantings at Mount Barker. Exports to The Netherlands, Switzerland and Japan.

galah wine ★★★☆

Tregarthen Road, Ashton, SA 5137 **region** Adelaide Hills
phone (08) 8390 1243 **fax** (08) 8390 1243 **open** Available at Ashton Hills
winemaker Stephen George **production** 1000 **est.** 1986
product range ($7.50–35 ML) Barossa Valley Riesling, Barossa Valley Fume Blanc, Marlborough Chardonnay, McLaren Vale Shiraz, SE Aust Shiraz Cabernet, Barossa Valley Grenache, Clare Valley Cabernet Malbec, Clare Valley Shiraz, Sparkling Shiraz, Galah Brut, Vintage Port.
summary Over the years, Stephen George has built up a network of contacts across South Australia from which he gains some very high-quality small parcels of grapes or wine for the Galah label. These are all sold direct at extremely low prices for the quality.

garbin estate NR

209 Toodyay Road, Middle Swan, WA 6056 **region** Swan District
phone (08) 9274 1747 **fax** (08) 9274 1747 **open** 7 days 10.30–5.30
winemaker Peter Garbin **production** 2500 **est.** 1956
product range ($13–18 CD) Chenin Blanc, Chardonnay, Shiraz, Cabernet Merlot, Vigneron's Red, Dessert Wine, Ruby Port.
summary Peter Garbin, winemaker by weekend and design draftsman by week, decided in 1990 that he would significantly upgrade the bulk fortified winemaking business commenced by his father in 1956. The vineyards have been replanted, the winery re-equipped, and the first of the new generation wines produced in 1994.

garden gully vineyards ★★★★

Western Highway, Great Western, Vic 3377 **region** Grampians
phone (03) 5356 2400 **fax** (03) 5356 2400 **open** Mon–Fri 10.30–5.30, weekends 10–5.30
winemaker Brian Fletcher, Warren Randall **production** 2000 **est.** 1987
product range ($13–27 CD) Riesling, Grenache, Shiraz, Sparkling Chardonnay, Sparkling Pinot Noir, Sparkling Shiraz.
summary Given the skills and local knowledge of the syndicate which owns Garden Gully, it is not surprising that the wines are typically good: an attractive stone cellar-door sales area is an additional reason to stop and pay a visit. Shiraz produced from the 100-year-old vines adjoining the cellar door is especially good. The 3 hectares of shiraz is complemented by 3 hectares of riesling, providing another good wine.

Garden Gully Riesling

Produced from 3 hectares of mature riesling, which occupies half of the estate plantings.
▼▼▼▽ 1999 Light straw-green; the bouquet is very light, crisp and minerally, the lively, lemony palate lifted by a pretty strong dose of spritz (CO_2). Once this subsides the wine will no doubt merit higher points.   **rating:** 83
best drinking 2003–2009 **best vintages** '98 **drink with** Light seafood • $13

Garden Gully Sparkling Shiraz

Shares the 4 hectares of old, dry-grown shiraz plantings with the varietal release, in much the same fashion as Seppelt does with its Show Sparkling Shiraz. This wine spends 9-12 months on lees as opposed to the ten years given to the Seppelt wine. The quality of the fruit would support such an approach to this wine, but the bank manager doubtless would not.
▼▼▼▼ 1998 Medium to full red-purple; clean, ripe shiraz with no oak or other distractions on the bouquet leads into a palate where you can see the superior fruit waiting to develop complexity. The balance is good, being at the drier end of the spectrum. Time on cork may not be as effective as time on lees, but is still effective.   **rating:** 88
best drinking 2003–2013 **best vintages** '98 **drink with** Game soup • $27

Garden Gully Shiraz

Produced from the 4 hectares of old, dry-grown vineyards surrounding the attractive cellar door. Unquestionably the best of the Garden Gully range, year in, year out. It spends 12 months in American oak hogsheads.
▼▼▼▽ 1998 Very good purple-red; there is fresh plum and cherry fruit on the bouquet together with an edge of charry American oak. The tightly structured palate is driven by plum/cherry fruit and firm tannins, the oak not being the least intrusive.   **rating:** 90
best drinking 2003–2013 **best vintages** '91, '93, '95, '98 **drink with** Barbecued lamb • $21

gartelmann hunter estate ★★★☆

Lovedale Road, Lovedale, NSW 2321 **region** Lower Hunter Valley
phone (02) 4930 7113 **fax** (02) 4930 7114 **open** 7 days 10–5
winemaker Jane Wilson, David Lowe, Gary Reed (Contract — Monarch Services) **production** 7000 **est.** 1996
product range ($12–29 CD) Unoaked Chardonnay, Barrel-Fermented Chardonnay, Semillon, Chenin Blanc, Botrytis Chenin Blanc, Shiraz, Diedrich Shiraz.
summary In 1996 Jan and Jorg Gartelmann purchased what was previously the George Hunter Estate, established by Sydney restaurateur Oliver Shaul in 1970. They acquired 16 hectares of mature vineyards, producing a limited amount of wine under the Gartelmann label in 1997, and moving to full production in 1998.

Gartelmann Hunter Estate Semillon

Produced from estate-grown 30-year-old vines at Lovedale.
▼▼▼▼ 1999 Light yellow-green; the bouquet has distinct fruit and presence in a mineral/herb spectrum. The palate is tight and crisp, with good varietal character running through an intense, long palate. Well made and oozes potential.   **rating:** 88
best drinking 2004–2014 **drink with** Shellfish • $19

Gartelmann Hunter Estate Chardonnay

Produced from 27-year-old vines; 50 per cent of the wine is barrel-fermented.
▼▼▼▽ 1997 Glowing yellow-green; a full-on bouquet with developed toasty/honeyed regional fruit aromas. The palate opens with rich, peach and honey fruit in a bold mode, but finishes with very high acidity, possibly over-corrected.   **rating:** 82
best drinking 2000–2001 **drink with** Pasta • $12

Gartelmann Hunter Estate Diedrich Shiraz

Named in honour of Jorg Gartelmann's grandfather Diedrich, and comes from a single block of 30-year-old vines planted on red volcanic clay over limestone. The wine is fermented in open concrete vats and aged in French and American oak casks.

TTTY 1998 Light to medium red; the bouquet is light, with a range of gamey/earthy/savoury regional fruit characters. The palate, too, shows strongly earthy/regional fruit characters with quite obvious vanilla oak. **rating:** 81 **best drinking** 2000–2003 **drink with** Smoked lamb • $29

gecko valley NR

Bailiff Road, via 700 Glenlyon Road, Gladstone, Qld 4680 **region** Queensland Zone
phone (07) 4979 0400 **fax** (07) 4979 0500 **open** 7 days 10–5
winemaker Bruce Humphery-Smith (Contract) **production** 1500 **est.** 1997
product range ($12.50–18.50 CD) Lightly Oaked Chardonnay, Special Reserve Chardonnay, Special Reserve Verdelho, Lazy Lizard White, Lazy Lizard Red, Special Reserve Shiraz, Liqueur Shiraz, Liqueur Mead.
summary Gecko Valley extends the viticultural map of Queensland yet further, situated little more than 50 kilometres of the tropic of Capricorn in an area better known for sugar cane farming and mineral activities. The 3-hectare vineyard (1 hectare each of chardonnay, verdelho and shiraz) provides the base for the table wines made by the omnipresent Bruce Humphery-Smith, supplemented by a range of liqueurs, ports and muscats made several thousand kilometres further south. As one would expect, the facility caters for the general tourist with a café, and a gift shop with a wide range of merchandise.

geebin wines NR

3729 Channel Highway, Birchs Bay, Tas 7162 **region** Southern Tasmania
phone (03) 6267 4750 **fax** (03) 6267 5090 **open** 7 days 10–5
winemaker Andrew Hood (Contract) **production** 50 **est.** 1983
product range ($17 CD) Riesling, Cabernet Sauvignon.
summary Although production is minuscule, quality has been consistently high. The Riesling is well made, but the interesting wine from this far southern vineyard is Cabernet Sauvignon — clearly, the vineyard enjoys favourable ripening conditions. With 0.7 hectare of vineyards (including 0.3 hectare of chardonnay yet to come into bearing) Geebin claims to be the smallest commercial producer in Australia, but isn't: Scarp Valley and (temporarily) Jollymont are smaller.

gehrig estate ★★★

Corner Murray Valley Highway and Howlong Road, Barnawartha, Vic 3688 **region** Rutherglen and Glenrowan
phone (02) 6026 7296 **fax** (02) 6026 7424 **open** Mon–Sat 9–5, Sun 10–5
winemaker Brian Gehrig **production** 5000 **est.** 1858
product range ($8.50–29 CD) Chenin Blanc, Riesling, Chardonnay, Trebbiano, Autumn Riesling, Late Harvest Tokay, Pinot Noir, Shiraz, Cabernet Sauvignon, Fortifieds.
summary An historic winery and adjacent house are superb legacies of the nineteenth century. Progressive modernisation of the winemaking facilities and operations has seen the quality of the white wines improve significantly, while the red wines now receive a percentage of new oak. Another recent innovation has been the introduction of the Gourmet Courtyard, serving lunch on weekends, public holidays and Victorian school holidays. A wide-ranging tasting of dry white, red and fortified wines in March 1999 showed Brian Gehrig to be equally at home with all three styles, the wines very reasonably priced for their quality.

gembrook hill ★★★★

Launching Place Road, Gembrook, Vic 3783 **region** Yarra Valley
phone (03) 5968 1622 **fax** (03) 5968 1699 **open** By appointment
winemaker Ian Marks, Martin Williams **production** 2000 **est.** 1983
product range ($30 R) Sauvignon Blanc, Chardonnay, Pinot Noir.
summary The 6-hectare Gembrook Hill Vineyard is situated on rich, red volcanic soils 2 kilometres north of Gembrook in the coolest part of the Yarra Valley. The vines are not irrigated, with consequent natural vigour control. The Sauvignon Blanc is invariably good, sometimes outstanding.

Gembrook Hill Sauvignon Blanc

The wine for which Gembrook Hill first came into prominence, and suited (in terms of wine style) both to the site and climate. It has proved to be a difficult variety to grow, or at least to crop well, with a tiny production from the 2 hectares of vines. Devotees of the style are pleased that Dr Ian Marks has persevered.

▼▼▼▼ **1999** Medium yellow-green; light to moderately intense tropical/passionfruit/gooseberry aromas feed into a palate with life, freshness and near perfect acidity to offset the softer fruit. **rating:** 86
best drinking 2000–2001 **best vintages** '90, '92, '93, '94, '95, '98 **drink with** Lobster bisque • $30

Gembrook Hill Pinot Noir
Tends to reflect the very cool climate, and the rich, red volcanic soils rather more than the two white wines, but nonetheless has style and genuine appeal in a lighter mould.
▼▼▼▼▽ **1998** Medium red, with just a touch of purple; gently but immediately complex soft spice and sweet savoury aromas on the bouquet are followed by a medium-weight palate with attractive varietal cherry/plum fruit, barely perceptible oak and perfectly balanced acidity. Not a heavyweight, but the taste lingers. **rating:** 90
best drinking 2000–2003 **best vintages** '97, '98 **drink with** Asian seafood dishes • $30

❧ gemtree vineyards ★★★★
Kangarilla Road, McLaren Flat, SA 5171 **region** McLaren Vale
phone (08) 8383 0403 **fax** (08) 8383 0506 **open** Not
winemaker Mike Brown **production** 500 **est.** 1992
product range ($20–25 R) McLaren Vale Shiraz, Cabernet Sauvignon Merlot Petit Verdot.
summary The Buttery family, headed by Paul and Jill, and with the active involvement of Melissa as viticulturist for Gemtree Vineyards, has been actively involved as grape growers in McLaren Vale since 1980, when they purchased their first vineyard. Today the family owns a little over 110 hectares of vines, the oldest block of 25 hectares on Tatachilla Road at McLaren Vale, planted in 1970. The first release is an excellent debut.

Gemtree Vineyards McLaren Vale Shiraz
Selected from a small patch of the oldest vines of total plantings of 100 hectares, most of the production being sold to others. It takes its name from the Gemtree area at the foothills underneath the Adelaide Hills. Interestingly, ten per cent of the grapes were picked and separately fermented as whole bunches.
1998 Dense red-purple; a massive wine on the bouquet; dense and impenetrable, with more of the same on the palate, although the tannins are not harsh, and the wine should unfold its secrets over the next 20 years. **rating:** 89
best drinking 2005–2020 **drink with** Leave it in the cellar • $20

❧ geoff hardy wines ★★★★
c/o Pertaringa Wines, Corner Hunt and Rifle Range Roads, McLaren Vale, SA 5171 **region** Adelaide Hills
phone (08) 8323 8125 **fax** (08) 8323 7766 **open** At Pertaringa
winemaker Geoff Hardy, Ben Riggs **production** 2000 **est.** 1996
product range ($19–30 CD) Kuitpo Sauvignon Blanc, Shiraz, Cabernet.
summary Geoff Hardy wines come from 26 hectares of vines, with a large percentage of the grape production being sold to other makers. Retail distribution through South Australia, New South Wales, Victoria and Queensland; exports to the UK, the US, Canada and Denmark.

geoff merrill ★★★★
291 Pimpala Road, Woodcroft, SA 5162 **region** McLaren Vale
phone (08) 8381 6877 **fax** (08) 8322 2244 **open** Mon–Fri 10–5, Sun 12–5
winemaker Geoff Merrill, Goe DiFabio, Scott Heidrich **production** 120 000 **est.** 1980
product range ($9.95–35 R) A change in brand structure has resulted in the Geoff Merrill range becoming Geoff Merrill Reserve representing the ultra-premium wines; the former Premium range is now released under the Geoff Merill label; Who Cares The Whites and Who Cares The Reds; Mount Hurtle wines are sold exclusively through Vintage Cellars/Liquorland.
summary In 1998 the product range was rearranged into two tiers: premium (in fact simply varietal) and reserve, the latter being the older (and best) wines, reflecting the desire for elegance and subtlety of this otherwise exuberant winemaker. As well as national retail distribution, significant exports to the UK, Europe, the US and Asia.

Geoff Merrill McLaren Vale Unwooded Semillon
It's a strange world when it's necessary to say a Semillon is unwooded, for this is the case with the vast majority. However, in the absence of oak, it is necessary to be patient.
▼▼▼▼ **1997** Light to medium green-yellow; the bouquet is clean, still not particularly aromatic, but with very correct grassy/earthy varietal character. The palate has moderately good length, well balanced, and with some herbaceous grip. Will continue improving with further cellaring. **rating:** 85
best drinking 2000–2007 **best vintages** NA **drink with** King George whiting • $12

Geoff Merrill Museum Semillon Chardonnay

An outstanding example of bottle development, even if the blend is old-fashioned.

TTTT 1988 Full golden yellow; rich, toasty aromas are braced by a hint of mineral on the bouquet; the wine has good flavour and length, again with a mix of toast, honey and mineral. **rating:** 93

best drinking 2000–2003 **best vintages** NA **drink with** Veal parmagiana • $30

Geoff Merrill Chardonnay

A wine which has undergone major style changes in recent years, becoming finer yet retaining its capacity to age with grace.

TTTT 1996 The massive moustache (Merv Hughes eat your heart out) says much but not all about its owner-grower Geoff Merrill, philanthropist, fun-lover and maker of surprisingly elegant wines. Citrus, melon and peachy fruit runs through a lively fresh and flavoursome wine, remarkably so for its age. A bargain at this price. **rating:** 87

best drinking 1999–2003 **best vintages** '84, '85, '86, '89, '91 **drink with** Poultry, rabbit • $13.50

Geoff Merrill Premium Shiraz

The fruit source for this wine sometimes contains a portion of Goulburn Valley fruit, but is always predominantly based in McLaren Vale. In 1997 it was 78 per cent McLaren Vale and 22 per cent Goulburn Valley fruit and spent 18 months in American oak.

TTTT 1997 Clean, fresh, cherry fruit and sweet oak on the bouquet are logically followed by more cherry fruit and soft, fine tannins; American oak is present throughout but is well integrated and balanced. **rating:** 92

best drinking 2000–2005 **best vintages** '97 **drink with** Ragout of veal • $16

Geoff Merrill Merlot

A blend of McLaren Vale and Goulburn Valley fruit matured for 17 months in American oak, apparently not new.

TTT 1997 Light to medium red-purple; light leafy berry aromas are accompanied by some earthy notes and subtle oak on the bouquet. The palate is similar, not rich, but does have the supple, soft tannins appropriate for Merlot structure. **rating:** 83

best drinking 2000–2003 **best vintages** NA **drink with** Ragout of veal • $16

Geoff Merrill Cabernet Merlot

An 'I've been everywhere' wine, with 26 per cent Cabernet Franc, 22 per cent Cabernet Sauvignon and 8 per cent Merlot from McLaren Vale; 20 per cent Merlot and 11 per cent Cabernet Sauvignon from the Goulburn Valley; and 13 per cent Cabernet Sauvignon from Coonawarra. Wow.

TTTT 1997 Medium red-purple; the bouquet is quite fragrant and savoury, with clean, light leafy fruit. The palate has a soft and easy profile, with gently sweet berry on the mid-palate and then more savoury notes and fine tannins on the finish. **rating:** 86

best drinking 2000–2005 **best vintages** NA **drink with** Veal goulash • $16

geoff weaver ★★★★★

2 Gilpin Lane, Mitcham, SA 5062 **region** Adelaide Hills
phone (08) 8272 2105 **fax** (08) 8271 0177 **open** Not
winemaker Geoff Weaver **production** 4500 **est.** 1982
product range ($20–43 ML) Riesling, Chardonnay, Sauvignon Blanc, Pinot Noir, Cabernet Merlot.
summary This is now the full-time business of former Hardy Group chief winemaker Geoff Weaver. He draws upon a little over 11 hectares of vineyard established between 1982 and 1988; for the time being, at least, the physical winemaking is carried out by Geoff Weaver at Petaluma. He produces an invariably immaculate Sauvignon Blanc, and one of the longest-lived Chardonnays to be found in Australia, which has intense grapefruit and melon flavour. The beauty of the labels ranks supreme with that of Pipers Brook. The wines are exported to the US, the UK and to five European destinations.

Geoff Weaver Lenswood Riesling

Produced from 1 hectare of riesling planted in 1982 at an altitude of 540 metres. The wines are unequivocally long-lived.

TTTT 1999 Light green-yellow; the fresh, delicate and youthful palate is crisp and clean; the palate is more open, with good weight and sweet lime, nectarine fruit and an incipient touch of honey. **rating:** 87

best drinking 2001–2006 **best vintages** '90, '93, '94, '96, '98 **drink with** Fresh asparagus • $20

Geoff Weaver Stafford Ridge Sauvignon Blanc

Produced from 1.8 hectares of close-planted but very low-yielding sauvignon blanc planted in 1987. Right from the outset, the quality of this wine has been exceptional, with a purity and intensity of flavour equalled by few other Australian Sauvignon Blancs. It is not wooded, nor does it need to be.

▼▼▼▼ **1999** Light green-yellow; the bouquet is light, bright, fresh and crisp, with a mix of mineral and herb fruit. The palate has the same delicate herb and mineral fruit flavour, and not so much tropical fruit as in other years. For whatever reason, does not appear particularly intense, which runs counter to the usual Weaver style.   **rating:** 85

best drinking 2000–2002 **best vintages** '92, '93, '94, '96, '97 **drink with** Mussels   • $20

Geoff Weaver Lenswood Chardonnay

The 3.5 hectares of estate chardonnay are now over 15 years old, producing grapes with great intensity of flavour, but with a particular grapefruit citrus character which has been present since the very first vintage. The wine matures slowly and gracefully, and is released with several years bottle age.

▼▼▼▼▼ **1998** Medium yellow-green; a subtle, beautifully balanced bouquet with melon/stone fruit seamlessly married with oak. The palate is as beautifully proportioned as the bouquet suggests it will be, with melon and ripe apple fruit flavours dusted with a subliminal touch of spicy oak. Elegance personified.   **rating:** 94

▼▼▼▼▽ **1997** Medium yellow-green; the bouquet is clean, with ripe nectarine/citrus fruit and subtle barrel-ferment influences underneath. The palate is similar, with less overt grapefruit than usual, yet (happily) it is the fruit which does dominate the palate, with a slight minerally touch to the finish.   **rating:** 91

best drinking 2002–2008 **best vintages** '95, '97, '98 **drink with** Sweetbreads   • $33

Geoff Weaver Pinot Noir

1998 is the first release of Pinot Noir from Geoff Weaver, and is a more than promising start.

▼▼▼▼ **1998** Medium to full red-purple; a rich and complex bouquet with some unusual sweet leather aromas. On the palate, a rich, 'boots and all' style, full of character. A mile away from the usual understated, slow-developing Weaver wine style. Perhaps concentrated first crop fruit at work.   **rating:** 89

best drinking 2000–2003 **best vintages** NA **drink with** Rich game   • $43

Geoff Weaver Cabernet Merlot

A blend of 82 per cent Cabernet Sauvignon and 18 per cent Merlot.

▼▼▼▽ **1997** Medium purple-red; the bouquet is distinctly earthy with some tobacco overtones; a leafy, minty cool-climate style, which will appeal to some more than others.   **rating:** 84

best drinking 2000–2004 **best vintages** NA **drink with** Seared rib-eye of beef   • $33.20

giaconda   ★★★★★

McClay Road, Beechworth, Vic 3747 **region** Alpine Valleys and Beechworth
phone (03) 5727 0246 **fax** (03) 5727 0246 **open** By appointment
winemaker Rick Kinzbrunner **production** 1000 **est.** 1985
product range ($45–75 R) Chardonnay, Pinot Noir, Cabernet Sauvignon.
summary Wines which have a super-cult status and which, given the tiny production, are extremely difficult to find, sold chiefly through restaurants and mail order. All have a cosmopolitan edge befitting Rick Kinzbrunner's international winemaking experience. The Chardonnay and Pinot Noir are made in contrasting styles: the Chardonnay tight and reserved, the Pinot Noir usually opulent and ripe.

Giaconda Chardonnay

Four hundred and fifty cases of hand-crafted wines are produced from a little under 1 hectare of estate vineyard every year. The style of the wine is entirely different from mainstream Australian Chardonnay, relying far more on texture and structure and far less on primary fruit. An exceptionally distinguished and consistent wine, which is the very deliberate product of Rick Kinzbrunner's winemaking philosophy. The label bears the ultimate politically correct statement 'Unfiltered. Wild yeast.'

▼▼▼▼▼ **1998** Medium yellow-green; the bouquet is complex and high-toned, with strong charry barrel-ferment oak; there is a great volume of flavour on the palate, carrying through to an excellently balanced, long finish. Despite all that flavour, does not cloy.   **rating:** 94

best drinking 2000–2008 **best vintages** '86, '88, '90, '92, '93, '94, '95, '96, '97, '98 **drink with** Slow-roasted Tasmanian salmon   • $75

Giaconda Pinot Noir

As fastidiously produced and as full of character as the Chardonnay. It comes from a little over half a hectare of estate plantings and is made in tiny quantities. The style has been quite different from the Pinot Noirs of southern Victoria, being much fuller and more robust, with the obvious potential to age well. In recent vintages, the style and flavour has veered more towards Burgundy and has become better and better.

▼▼▼▼ **1998** Medium red; the bouquet is predominantly in the savoury/foresty spectrum, rather than fruity, but is not bitter. As ever, the palate has excellent structure and texture; it is simply that varietal fruit flavour/intensity is lacking. **rating:** 89

best drinking 2000–2004 **best vintages** '85, '86, '88, '90, '91, '92, '95, '96, '97 **drink with** Tea-smoked duck • $55

⬛ gidgee estate wines   NR

441 Weeroona Drive, Wamboin, NSW 2621 **region** Canberra District
phone (02) 6236 9506 **fax** (02) 6236 9070 **open** First weekend of each month or by appointment
winemaker David Madew, Andrew McEwin (Contract) **production** 300 **est.** 1996
product range ($13–16 CD) Riesling, Chardonnay, Ensemble (Cabernet blend).
summary Brett and Cheryl Lane purchased the 1-hectare vineyard in 1996; it had been planted to riesling, chardonnay, cabernet sauvignon, cabernet franc and merlot over a ten-year period prior to its acquisition, but had been allowed to run down, and had to be rehabilitated. The Lanes intend to double the vineyard size over the next two years, and have retained David Madew and Andrew McEwen as contract-winemakers. The 1998 Chardonnay is a full-bodied buttery/peachy style with balancing acidity (83 points), the Bordeaux-blend Ensemble lying at the other extreme, with leafy/minty green fruit characters.

gilberts   ★★★★☆

RMB 438 Albany Highway, Kendenup via Mount Barker, WA 6323 **region** Great Southern
phone (08) 9851 4028 **fax** (08) 9851 4021 **open** Wed–Mon 10–5
winemaker Plantagenet (Contract) **production** 3000 **est.** 1980
product range ($16–25 CD) Riesling, Alira (medium sweet), Chardonnay, Shiraz, Old Tawny.
summary A part-time occupation for sheep and beef farmers Jim and Beverly Gilbert but a very successful one. The now mature vineyard, coupled with contract-winemaking at Plantagenet, has produced small quantities of high-quality Riesling and Chardonnay; the small production sells out quickly each year, with retail distribution through New South Wales, Victoria and Western Australia, and exports to Canada and Asia through Inland Trading.

Gilberts Riesling

A wine with a long and distinguished history; has demonstrated time and again its ability to age with grace.

▼▼▼▼ **1999** Light green-yellow; a bright, fresh and pure lime-accented bouquet is followed by a clean, classic Riesling on the palate, although I wonder whether it is just a little soft. **rating:** 87

best drinking 2001–2006 **best vintages** '90, '92, '95, '96 **drink with** Asparagus with prosciutto • $16

Gilberts Chardonnay

Chardonnay, with a little under 2.5 hectares, accounts for the largest proportion of the Gilbert vineyard plantings, but invariably sells out first. It is made in a very disciplined style, without much new oak input, and with an unusual capacity to age gracefully.

▼▼▼▽ **1999** Light green-yellow; the bouquet does not show a great deal of aroma, but the palate has considerable grip and presence; the flavours are unusual for Chardonnay, a mix of citrus and mineral. This may surprise with age. **rating:** 82

best drinking 2002–2006 **best vintages** '90, '92, '94, '95, '97 **drink with** Grilled fish • $23

Gilberts Shiraz

All the wines of Gilbert are made in tiny quantities, none more so than the Shiraz — which is a pity.

▼▼▼▼ **1998** Medium red-purple; the moderately intense bouquet has a mix of leafy characters, with touches of cherry and spice. An elegant, lighter style on the palate, with a mix of cherry, spice and leaf supported by subtle oak. In stark contrast to the voluptuous '97. **rating:** 85

best drinking 2002–2006 **best vintages** '97 **drink with** Seared beef • $25

gilgai winery   NR

Tingha Road, Gilgai, NSW 2360 **region** Other Wineries of NSW
phone (02) 6723 1204 **open** 7 days 10–6
winemaker Keith Whish **production** 400 **est.** 1968
product range Semillon, Shiraz Cabernet, Chandelier (Fortified White), Port.
summary Inverell medical practitioner Dr Keith Whish has been quietly producing wines from his 6-hectare vineyard for almost 30 years. All of the production is sold through cellar door.

glaetzer wines   NR

34 Barossa Valley Way, Tanunda, SA 5352 **region** Barossa Valley
phone (08) 8563 0288 **fax** (08) 8563 0218 **open** Mon–Sat 10.30–4.30, Sunday and public holidays 1–4.30
winemaker Colin Glaetzer, Ben Glaetzer **production** 3000 **est.** 1995
product range ($16–45 CD) Bush Vine Semillon, Semillon Ratafia, Grenache Mourvedre; Sparkling Pinot Noir, Bishop Shiraz, Malbec Cabernet Sauvignon, Shiraz, Sparkling Shiraz.
summary Colin and Ben Glaetzer are almost as well known in South Australian wine circles as Wolf Blass winemaker John Glaetzer, and, needless to say, they are all related. Glaetzer Wines purchases its grapes from Barossa Valley growers and makes an array of traditional Barossa styles. National retail distribution; exports to the US, Germany, the UK, Belgium, Italy, The Netherlands and Canada.

glenara wines   ★★★☆

126 Range Road North, Upper Hermitage, SA 5131 **region** Adelaide Hills
phone (08) 8380 5277 **fax** (08) 8380 5056 **open** Mon–Fri 11–5 (closed public holidays)
winemaker Trevor Jones **production** 5000 **est.** 1971
product range ($15–24 CD) Riesling, Chardonnay, Sauvignon Blanc Semillon, Unwooded Chardonnay, Pinot Noir, Shiraz, Cabernet Rosé, Cabernet Merlot, Cabernet Sauvignon, Sparkling, Old Tawny Port.
summary Glenara has been owned by the Verrall family since 1924; the first vines were planted in 1971, the first wine made in 1975, and the winery built in 1988. Has proceeded to produce many good wines, particularly the full-flavoured Rieslings, but also with creditable full-bodied reds. The wines have limited retail distribution in all States, and are exported to Japan and Malaysia.

Glenara Adelaide Hills Riesling
A range of vintages is available at cellar door, showing significant variation in style and quality from one year to the next.
▼▼▼♀ **1998** Medium green-yellow; moderately intense bouquet is not particularly aromatic but is clean, the fruit coming through on the attractive palate with gentle lime juice flavours. Relatively early-drinking style. **rating:** 82
best drinking 2000–2005 **best vintages** '90, '92, '96 **drink with** Braised pork neck • $16

Glenara White Quartz
Described as a sparkling Rosé, an unusual name for blanc de noir, but nonetheless gives a good idea of the style and character of the wine.
▼▼▼♀ **1996** Pale straw-pink; a rich, plushy bouquet is followed by an equally rich and heavy palate. **rating:** 80
best drinking 2000–2001 **best vintages** NA **drink with** Aperitif or antipasto • $20

Glenara Adelaide Hills Shiraz
A wine which shows that Glenara is situated in the warmest part of the Adelaide Hills, and can achieve flavours not unlike those of the Barossa Valley with late-ripening varieties.
▼▼▼▼ **1996** Medium red-purple; the bouquet is solid and not particularly expressive, but clean and with further development in front of it. The palate is rich and full, with lots of weight, yet not over-extracted. **rating:** 86
best drinking 2002–2010 **best vintages** NA **drink with** Fillet mignon • $21

Glenara Adelaide Hills Merlot
A wine which received consistent points in the bronze medal range at the 1999 Adelaide Hills Wine Show. There seems little doubt that Merlot fits comfortably into the Hills climate.
▼▼▼♀ **1996** Medium red-purple; a clean bouquet with well-balanced fruit and oak leads into a relatively soft, well-balanced and extracted wine in true Merlot style. **rating:** 84
best drinking 2000–2004 **best vintages** NA **drink with** Pastrami • $22

Glenara Adelaide Hills Cabernet Sauvignon

In fact a blend of Cabernet Sauvignon, Merlot and Cabernet Franc, the latter two varieties having been planted on the estate in 1987 and 1988, respectively, making their first contribution to the wine in 1990. The Glenara vineyards are established on the western-facing slopes of the Adelaide Hills in one of the warmest site climates of the region. The 1996 Cabernet Sauvignon topped its class at the 1999 Adelaide Hills Wine Show, and although it only received a silver medal overall, scored gold medal points on both my score sheet and that of one other judge, Steve Pannell.

▼▼▼▼♡ **1996** Very good purple-red; strong, clean cassis/berry fruit on the bouquet leads into a palate with lots of fruit weight and flavours in an identical spectrum to that of the bouquet. Has loads of development potential.

rating: 93

best drinking 2001–2011 **best vintages** '96 **drink with** Squab • $24

glenayr ★★★☆

Back Tea Tree Road, Richmond, Tas 7025 **region** Southern Tasmania
phone (03) 6260 2388 **fax** (03) 6260 2691 **open** Mon–Fri 8–5
winemaker Andrew Hood **production** 500 **est.** 1975
product range ($18–20 CD) Riesling, Chardonnay, Pinot Noir, Cabernet Shiraz Merlot; Tolpuddle Vineyards Chardonnay and Pinot Noir.
summary The principal occupation of Chris Harrington is as viticultural manager of the substantial Tolpuddle Vineyard, the grapes of which are sold to Domaine Chandon. Tiny quantities of wine are made from an adjacent 1-hectare vineyard for mailing list sales under the GlenAyr label; chardonnay and pinot noir grapes are also purchased from Tolpuddle Vineyards.

GlenAyr Chardonnay

Like all the GlenAyr wines, made in limited quantities. I found the 1998 to be far more enjoyable than my fellow judges at the Tasmanian Wines Show 2000.

▼▼▼▼ **1998** Medium green-yellow; the bouquet is clean, with smooth nectarine and citrus fruit supported by good oak. The palate offers more of the same in a medium-bodied frame, long and smooth, and well balanced in terms of fruit and oak.

rating: 89

best drinking 2001–2004 **best vintages** '98 **drink with** Milk-fed veal • $19

glen erin vineyard retreat NR

Rochford Road, Lancefield, Vic 3435 **region** Macedon Ranges
phone (03) 5429 1041 **fax** (03) 5429 2053 **open** Weekends, public holidays 10–6
winemaker Brian Scales **production** 1500 **est.** 1993
product range ($16–26 CD) Gewurztraminer, Chardonnay, Pinot Noir, Mystic Park Macedon Sparkling, Cabernet Merlot.
summary Brian Scales acquired the former Lancefield Winery and renamed it Glen Erin. Wines are contract-made from Macedon grapes and elsewhere; the conference and function facilities are supported by 24 accommodation rooms.

glenfinlass NR

Elysian Farm, Parkes Road, Wellington, NSW 2820 **region** Other Wineries of NSW
phone (02) 6845 2011 **fax** (02) 6845 3329 **open** Sat 9–5 or by appointment
winemaker Brian G Holmes **production** 500 **est.** 1971
product range ($10 CD) Sauvignon Blanc, Shiraz, Hill Vineyard Shiraz Cabernet, Cabernet Sauvignon.
summary The weekend and holiday hobby of Wellington solicitor Brian Holmes, who has wisely decided to leave it at that. I have not tasted the wines for many years, but the last wines I did taste were competently made. Brian Holmes says that the wines are currently in unusually short supply owing to drought and frost damage, but there are usually three vintages of Shiraz available at cellar door.

glenguin ★★★☆

River Oaks Vineyard, Lot 8 Milbrodale Road, Broke, NSW 2330 **region** Lower Hunter Valley
phone (02) 6579 1009 **fax** (02) 6579 1009 **open** At Boutique Wine Centre, Broke Road, Pokolbin
winemaker Robin Tedder **production** 15 000 **est.** 1993
product range ($17.50–30 R) Individual Vineyard series of The Old Broke Block Semillon, Unwooded Chardonnay, Shiraz, Merlot, Cabernet Sauvignon.
summary Glenguin's vineyard has been established along the banks of the Wollombi Brook by Robin, Rita and Andrew Tedder, Robin and Andrew being the grandsons of Air Chief Marshal Tedder, made Baron of Glenguin by

King George VI in recognition of his wartime deeds. (Glenguin is also the name of a Scottish distillery which continues to produce a single malt but which is otherwise unconnected.) Glenguin has 16 hectares of vineyard at Broke and another 5 hectares at Orange (cabernet and merlot). The wines are imported into the UK by Bibendum.

Glenguin The Old Broke Block Semillon
I have no idea what marketing gurus would make of a tongue-twisting label such as this, but I do know it is a seriously good wine, which I assume comes from the 4 hectares of estate plantings.
▼▼▼▼♀ **1999** Light green-yellow; the bouquet is quite intense, with grassy varietal character and a whiff of SO₂, which will dissipate in time and help the wine along a lengthy maturation path. The palate has attractive herby/citrussy flavour, and the structure to develop into something special. **rating: 92**
best drinking 2004–2014 **best vintages** '99 **drink with** Nothing at the moment • $17.50

Glenguin Individual Vineyard Unwooded Chardonnay
While unwooded, the wine spent nine months on yeast lees which might well have helped it, although the impact is far from obvious.
▼▼▼♀ **1998** Medium to full yellow-green; the bouquet is clean, with citrus-tinged fruit, the palate firm and very much in that citrus, even herbaceous, end of the spectrum. Crisp acid adds to the overall flavour impact; from left of centre, but may surprise with age. **rating: 83**
best drinking 2000–2005 **best vintages** NA **drink with** Chinese-style steamed fish • $19.50

Glenguin Individual Vineyard Shiraz
Produced from old, dryland vines growing in the heart of Pokolbin.
▼▼▼▼ **1998** Dense red-purple; powerful blackberry, liquorice, leather and spice aromas on the bouquet are followed by a big, concentrated, powerful and quite tannic wine, which is unapproachable at this juncture.
rating: 85
best drinking 2005–2015 **best vintages** NA **drink with** Extreme discretion • $30

Glenguin Individual Vineyard Merlot
One of a series of Individual Vineyard wines from Glenguin, the white wines coming from the Hunter Valley and the reds variously from Mudgee and, in this case, from Orange. It comes from a vineyard situated close to the town of Orange at an altitude of 800 metres on a gravelly clay soil.
▼▼▼♀ **1998** Strong red-purple; there are quite rich, dark savoury chocolate notes on the bouquet, and lots of flavour and extract on the palate. A flavoursome dry red. **rating: 84**
best drinking 2003–2008 **best vintages** NA **drink with** Game pie • $30

gloucester ridge vineyard ★★★
Burma Road, Pemberton, WA 6260 **region** Pemberton, Warren Valley and Manjimup
phone (08) 9776 1035 **fax** (08) 9776 1390 **open** 7 days 10–5, later on Saturdays
winemaker Brenden Smith **production** 5000 **est.** 1985
product range ($16.50–25 CD) Semillon, Sauvignon Blanc, Chardonnay, Pinot Noir, Premium Reserve Pinot Noir, Cabernets, Cabernet Sauvignon.
summary Gloucester Ridge is the only vineyard located within the Pemberton town boundary, within easy walking distance. It is owned and operated by Don and Sue Hancock; quality has varied, but can be good.

Gloucester Ridge Premium Reserve Pinot Noir
One makes definitive statements about Pemberton at one's peril; today's truth becomes tomorrow's fallacy, there are so many variables in play.
▼▼▼♀ **1998** Medium red-purple; the bouquet opens with ripe, slightly jammy, cherry fruit, then moves into cigar box. The palate, too, is far from a straight line, with quite firm cherry fruit set in a brisk stemmy/savoury framework. Has character, but not the silky softness of the best Pinots. Perhaps time will help. **rating: 83**
best drinking 2001–2004 **best vintages** NA **drink with** Wild duck • $25

Gloucester Ridge Cabernet Sauvignon
This wine emphasises yet again the difficulty of sweeping statements about Pemberton. In contra-distinction to the Gloucester Ridge Cabernets from 1997 and '98, which are quite green, this wine shows attractive sweet fruit character.
▼▼▼▼ **1996** Medium red, with just a touch of purple; the bouquet shows clear cabernet varietal character with a mix of spice, earth and cassis. The palate offers the same gently sweet cassis fruit, supported with subtle oak and soft tannins. **rating: 85**
best drinking 2000–2005 **best vintages** NA **drink with** Rack of veal • $NA

gnadenfrei estate   NR

Seppeltsfield Road, Marananga via Nuriootpa, SA 5355 **region** Barossa Valley
phone (08) 8562 2522 **fax** (08) 8562 3470 **open** Tues–Sun 10–5.30
winemaker Malcolm Seppelt **production** 1500 **est.** 1979
product range ($12–20 CD) Riesling, Semillon, Traminer Riesling, Shiraz Grenache, Tawny Port, Sparkling.
summary A strictly cellar-door operation, which relies on a variety of sources for its wines but has a core of 2 hectares of estate shiraz and 1 hectare of grenache. A restaurant presided over by Joylene Seppelt is open for morning teas, lunches and afternoon teas. Small quantities of the wines make their way to Pennsylvania, USA.

golden grape estate   NR

Oakey Creek Road, Pokolbin, NSW 2321 **region** Lower Hunter Valley
phone (02) 4998 7588 **fax** (02) 4998 7730 **open** 7 days 10–5
winemaker Neil McGuigan (Consultant) **production** NFP **est.** 1985
product range ($14.95–29.90 CD) Premier Semillon, Gewurztraminer, Sauvignon Blanc, Semillon Verdelho, Happy Valley Chardonnay, Five Star (light fruity), Frizzante Rosé, Mount Leonard (Cabernet Sauvignon), Domaine Springton (Shiraz), Classic Red, Fortifieds.
summary German-owned and unashamedly directed at the tourist, with a restaurant, barbecue and picnic areas, wine museum and separate tasting room for bus tours. The substantial range of wines are of diverse origins and style. The operation now has over 42 hectares of Hunter Valley plantings.

golden grove estate   ★★★☆

Sundown Road, Ballandean, Qld 4382 **region** Granite Belt
phone (07) 4684 1291 **fax** (07) 4684 1247 **open** 7 days 9–5
winemaker Sam Costanzo **production** 10 000 **est.** 1993
product range ($10–15 CD) Accommodation Creek Classic White and Classic Dry Red, Muscadean, Rosé, Shiraz, Cabernet Merlot, Liqueur Muscat.
summary Golden Grove Estate was established by Mario and Sebastiana Costanzo in 1946, producing stone fruits and table grapes for the fresh fruit market. The first wine grapes (shiraz) were planted in 1972, but it was not until 1985, when ownership passed to son Sam Costanzo and wife Grace, that the use of the property started to change. In 1993 chardonnay and merlot joined the shiraz, followed by cabernet sauvignon, sauvignon blanc and semillon. Wine quality has steadily improved, with many medals in regional shows awarded up to 2000, leading to national (though limited) retail distribution.

✿ golden gully wines   NR

5900 Midwestern Highway, Mandurama, NSW 2792 **region** Orange
phone (02) 6367 5148 **open** Not
winemaker Murray Smith (Contract) **production** 60 **est.** 1994
product range ($14–17 ML) Shiraz, Merlot, Cabernet Sauvignon.
summary Still very much in the development phase, production rising to 60 cases in 1999 from 21 cases in 1998. Family and friends stuff, indeed. However, Kevin and Julie Bate have established over 5 hectares of vineyard (2 hectares cabernet sauvignon, 1.6 shiraz, 0.5 merlot and 0.5 each of semillon and sauvignon blanc planted in 1999). So production will increase to fully commercial levels in the not to distant future. When it does, you can enjoy a BYO picnic lunch along the Belubula River.

golders vineyard   ★★★☆

Bridport Road, Pipers Brook, Tas 7254 **region** Northern Tasmania
phone (03) 6395 4142 **fax** (03) 6395 4142 **open** By appointment
winemaker Richard Crabtree **production** 400 **est.** 1991
product range ($18 R) Pinot Noir.
summary The initial plantings of 1.5 hectares of pinot noir have been supplemented by 1.5 hectares of chardonnay. The quality of the Pinot Noir has been good from the initial vintage in 1995.

Golders Pinot Noir

Winemaking runs in the family, it seems, for Richard Crabtree is Robert Crabtree's (of Watervale in the Clare Valley) brother. First made in 1995, and has shown consistently well since that vintage.
▼▼▼♢ **1998** Medium to full purple-red, bright and strong; solid, dark plum fruit has slightly cooked overtones on the bouquet, translating to slightly jammy fruit on the palate. Obviously picked very ripe, and has plenty of flavour.   **rating:** 82
best drinking 2000–2005 **best vintages** '95, '96, '97 **drink with** Quail •$18

goona warra vineyard ★★★☆

Sunbury Road, Sunbury, Vic 3429 **region** Sunbury
phone (03) 9740 7766 **fax** (03) 9744 7648 **open** 7 days 10–5
winemaker John Barnier **production** 2500 **est.** 1863
product range ($18–23 R) Semillon, Chardonnay, Black Cygnet Chardonnay, Pinot Noir, Cabernet Franc, Black Cygnet Cabernets, Black Widow Brut, Tawny Port.
summary An historic stone winery, established under this name by a nineteenth-century Victorian premier. Excellent tasting facilities; an outstanding venue for weddings and receptions; Sunday lunch also served. Situated 30 minutes drive from Melbourne (10 minutes north of Tullamarine Airport). Berry Bros & Rudd import the wines into the UK.

goundrey ★★★☆

Muir Highway, Mount Barker, WA 6324 **region** Great Southern
phone (08) 9851 1777 **fax** (08) 9851 1997 **open** Mon–Sat 10–4.30, Sun 11–4.30
winemaker Keith Bown **production** 150 000 **est.** 1976
product range ($15.50–40 R) Chenin Blanc, Classic White, Unwooded Chardonnay, Late Picked Riesling, Shiraz Grenache, Cabernet Merlot; Reserve range of Riesling, Sauvignon Blanc, Chardonnay, Pinot Noir, Shiraz, Merlot, Cabernet Sauvignon; second label is Fox River.
summary Under the ownership of Perth businessman Jack Bendat, not to mention the injection of many millions of dollars into vineyard and winery expansion, Goundrey grows apace. There seems to be a widening gap between the quality of the Reserve wines (usually, but not invariably, outstanding) and the varietal range (workmanlike). This may be no bad thing from a commercial viewpoint, particularly if the differential is reflected in the price, but does make an overall rating difficult. The increase from a 900-tonne crush in 1996 to 3200 tonnes in 1999 seems to have spread the range of quality even further. National distribution; exports to the US, Asia, the UK and Europe.

Goundrey Reserve Riesling

The Reserve range of Goundrey hasn't always hit the expected jackpots, but the powerful Riesling is generally very good.
♥♥♥♥ **1998** Light green-yellow; the bouquet is still relatively reserved and closed, with mineral/slate characters. The palate confounds the bouquet, with surprising depth and development; lime/kerosene flavours in traditional style, with good fruit weight. **rating:** 88
best drinking 2000–2005 **best vintages** NA **drink with** Antipasto • $19.74

Goundrey Unwooded Chardonnay

One of the thundering herd of Unwooded Chardonnays, and reasonably typical of what one can expect from the style.
♥♥♥♡ **1999** Light to medium green-yellow; the bouquet is quite complex, with tangy fruit with slightly reductive/pongy aspects. The palate has flavours of grapefruit and quite good length. **rating:** 81
best drinking 2000–2002 **best vintages** NA **drink with** Light seafood • $15.50

Goundrey Reserve Chardonnay

A wine which has had considerable success over the years, hitting a high point with the '94 vintage. For a while it seemed to me to be unnecessarily oaky, and the 1997 vintage marked a return to better balance. The wine is matured in 80 per cent French and 20 per cent American Calistoga oak for 12 months, with six months on lees.
♥♥♥♡ **1998** Medium yellow-green; there are very pronounced medicinal yeast fermentation aromas, which take the wine off in thoroughly unconventional directions. The oak which comes through on the palate does not compensate. **rating:** 81
best drinking 2000–2001 **best vintages** '91, '94, '95 **drink with** Coquilles St Jacques • $32.80

Goundrey Late Picked Riesling

The name suggests the wine derives its sweetness from extended ripening rather than botrytis, yet in 1998 the bouquet in particular seems to show botrytised characters.
♥♥♥♥ **1998** Glowing yellow-green; the bouquet has intense lime aromas and shows obvious botrytis influence, but that influence diminishes somewhat on the powerful, ever-so-slightly broad, palate. Nonetheless, convincing stuff. **rating:** 89
best drinking 2000–2004 **best vintages** NA **drink with** Sara Lee • $NA

Goundrey Reserve Pinot Noir

There is no doubt that Pinot Noir in the Mount Barker region is an on-again, off-again affair, at least in terms of varietal character. Plantagenet succeeded in 1994, but not in 1996, in which year it was Goundrey's turn to do so, while 1998 was not particularly successful for either.

TTTY 1998 Medium red-purple; there is not much, if any, varietal character evident on the bouquet, although it is not short of substance. The palate is powerful, with fairly high tannin levels; there have been obvious attempts to invest the wine with complexity which, however, can't overcome the shortcomings in the fruit.   **rating: 82**

best drinking 2000–2002 **best vintages** '96 **drink with** Spiced quail   •$32.80

Fox River Shiraz

The Fox River range is Goundrey's second label, generally made in a no-nonsense, early-drinking style.

TTTY 1998 Light to medium red-purple; there is relatively soft fruit on the bouquet with some charry oak; the palate is pleasant, with soft cherry fruit and clever oak handling.   **rating: 82**

best drinking 2000–2004 **best vintages** NA **drink with** Corned beef   •$14.80

Goundrey Reserve Shiraz

A wine which has hit the heights from time to time; for example, the '92 Reserve won two trophies at the Perth Show. The viticultural base has broadened enormously since that time, but you can still see this is a genuine Reserve selection.

TTTT 1998 Medium red, with some purple hues remaining; earthy/spicy shiraz is accompanied by bacony, slightly greasy, oak on the bouquet; attractive cherry/berry fruit comes through on the palate although, once again, the oak is a little suspect.   **rating: 86**

best drinking 2002–2008 **best vintages** '81, '85, '87, '91, '92, '95, '97 **drink with** Osso buco   •$32.80

Goundrey Reserve Merlot

Estate-grown, and based on an initial field selection followed by barrel ageing in a higher percentage of new oak.

TTTT 1997 Medium red-purple; clean, moderately intense red berry fruit and sweet vanilla oak on the bouquet are followed by fresh berry fruit on the palate, with just a hint of mint and green leaf. Nice fruit-driven style.   **rating: 87**

best drinking 2001–2006 **best vintages** NA **drink with** Roast leg of lamb   •$40

Goundrey Cabernet Merlot

A blend which tends to vary in style and quality according to the vintage but which does reflect its modest price.

TTTY 1998 Medium red-purple; the bouquet is very leafy, with undertones of earth and mint; the palate has sweeter fruit flavours, but the promise is nipped in the bud by charry, resinous oak phenolics.   **rating: 81**

best drinking 2001–2004 **best vintages** NA **drink with** Smoked beef   •$16.50

Goundrey Reserve Cabernet Sauvignon

Over the past 20 years the wine which has performed most consistently has been Goundrey Cabernet Sauvignon. Generous, rich and long-lived, it typifies the region. The '96 was a gold medal and trophy winner at the 1997 Liquorland National Wine Show and was an excellent wine.

TTTY 1997 Starting to show distinct colour change from purple to brick-red; the bouquet is of light to medium intensity, with earthy/savoury aromas. The palate has quite good structure and balance, with fine tannins and nice oak, but fruit is lacking from the mid-palate. Nowhere near the class of the '96.   **rating: 83**

best drinking 2001–2005 **best vintages** '81, '85, '87, '90, '92, '95, '96 **drink with** Fillet steak   •$32.80

gralyn estate   ★★★★

Caves Road, Willyabrup, WA 6280 **region** Margaret River
phone (08) 9755 6245 **fax** (08) 9755 6245 **open** 7 days 10.30–4.30
winemaker Graham Hutton, Merilyn Hutton **production** 2000 **est.** 1975
product range ($15–40 CD) Reserve Riesling, Late Harvest Riesling, Shiraz, Old Vine Shiraz, Late Harvest Cabernet, Cabernet Nouveau, Shiraz Cabernet, Cabernet Sauvignon, and an extensive range of fortifieds, including White Port, Pink Port, Vintage Port and Tawny Port.
summary The move from primarily fortified wine to table wine production continues, and does so with considerable success. The red wines are made in a distinctively different style from most of those from the Margaret River region, with a softness and sweetness (in part from American oak) which is reminiscent of some of the better-made wines from the eastern States.

Gralyn Estate Shiraz Cabernet

Obviously enough, a blend of Shiraz and Cabernet Sauvignon matured in predominantly new French and American oak barrels. Won the silver medal in its class (remembering there is only one gold, one silver and one bronze awarded in each class) at the 1999 Sheraton Wine Awards.

TTTT 1998 Medium to full red-purple; rich, dark berry fruit is married with well-balanced, sweet vanillin American oak on the bouquet, but on the palate the oak is invasive both texturally and flavourwise. Less would have been ever so much better. **rating: 85**

best drinking 2003–2008 **best vintages** '95 **drink with** Smoked lamb • $40

Gralyn Estate Cabernet Sauvignon

Produced from 2.5 hectares of 20-year-old estate vines. The '98 is regarded by the Huttons as the best wine they have made, and it has had great appeal to the show circuit, winning a gold medal at the Mount Barker Wine Show and silver medals at the Royal Perth Show and Sheraton Wine Awards, all in 1999.

TTTT 1998 Medium purple-red; the bouquet is super-charged with American oak, as is the palate. Peeking out from the oak is marvellous blackberry/cassis fruit, but nothing much will change in the relative balance between fruit and oak as the wine ages. **rating: 85**

best drinking 2003–2008 **best vintages** NA **drink with** Marinated beef • $40

Gralyn Estate Vintage Port

Gralyn started life as a Vintage Port producer, and has continued to make the style notwithstanding how much easier it is to sell top quality Shiraz than Vintage Port. Here, at least, I find myself in agreement with the Perth and Mount Barker Shows which both gave it gold medals.

TTTTY 1999 Medium to full red-purple; clean spirit is woven through ripe, earthy berry shiraz fruit on the bouquet. The wine has excellent texture and structure on the palate, with cherry and chocolate flavours, finishing with soft, fine tannins. Best of all, not too sweet. **rating: 90**

best drinking 2001–2015 **best vintages** '99 **drink with** Coffee • $35

granite ridge wines   NR

Sundown Road, Ballandean, Qld 4382 **region** Granite Belt
phone (07) 4684 1263 **fax** (07) 4684 1250 **open** Fri–Tues 10–5
winemaker Dennis Ferguson, Juliane Ferguson **production** 1200 **est.** 1995
product range ($10–20 CD) Semillon Chardonnay, Unwooded Chardonnay, Chardonnay, Sweet Chardonnay, Topaz, Granite Garnet, Shiraz, Shiraz Cabernet, Cabernet Sauvignon, Liqueur Muscat.
summary Formerly known as Denlana Ferguson Estate Wines, Granite Ridge has had considerable success, with both the 1995 and 1996 Cabernet Sauvignon being judged Queensland's Best Cabernet (though quite by whom I am not sure); continues to be run by Dennis Ferguson.

grant burge   ★★★★☆

Jacobs Creek, Tanunda, SA 5352 **region** Barossa Valley
phone (08) 8563 3700 **fax** (08) 8563 2807 **open** 7 days 10–5
winemaker Grant Burge **production** 108 000 **est.** 1988
product range ($13.40–79.95 R) Has recently moved to a series of vineyard-designated varietal wines, including Thorn Vineyard Riesling, Kraft Vineyard Sauvignon Blanc, Zerk Vineyard Semillon, Barossa Ranges Chardonnay, Lily Farm Frontignac, Filsell Shiraz, Hillcott Merlot, and Cameron Vale Cabernet Sauvignon. Top-of-the-range reds are Meshach Shiraz, The Holy Trinity (Grenache Shiraz Mourvedre) and Shadrach Cabernet Sauvignon; also Rubycind and Virtuoso; RBS1 Semillon, RBS2 Semillon, MSJ1 Shiraz Cabernet. The budget-priced Barossa Vines range joined the band in late 1999.
summary As one might expect, this very experienced industry veteran makes consistently good, full flavoured and smooth wines chosen from the pick of the crop of his extensive vineyard holdings, which total an impressive 200 hectares; the immaculately restored/rebuilt stone cellar-door sales buildings are another attraction. The provocatively named The Holy Trinity (a Grenache Shiraz Mourvedre blend) joins Shadrach and Meshach at the top of the range. In late 1999 Grant Burge repurchased the farm from Mildara Blass by acquiring the Krondorf winery (not the brand) in which he made his first fortune. He has renamed it Barossa Vines. The wines are exported to the UK, Europe, the US, Canada and Asia.

Grant Burge Thorn Vineyard Riesling

The Thorn Vineyard is situated in the Eden Valley, one of South Australia's two classic riesling areas. Traditionally, Eden Valley Rieslings took many years to develop their characteristic lime aroma and flavour, but modern winemaking seems to be bringing out those characters earlier in the life of the wines.

♥♥♥♀ **1999** Light to medium green-yellow; the bouquet has weight but lacks fruit aromaticity; the palate, likewise, is full bodied but doesn't dance. **rating:** 81

best drinking 2000–2002 **best vintages** '88, '90, '92, '93, '94, '96, '98 **drink with** Smoked trout mousse • $13.40

Grant Burge RB Semillon

While the average oaked Barossa Valley Semillon is little short of abominable, this wine shows that Semillon can be manipulated successfully. Burge explains 'nearly a third of the juice was fermented using indigenous rather cultured yeasts, the wine was matured on lees in new French and American oak for six months, and nearly a third also underwent malolactic fermentation.'

♥♥♥♥ **1999** RBS2. Medium yellow-green; spicy barrel-ferment oak is evident on the bouquet but on the palate the oak influence is restrained and enhances the tangy lemony fruit. If only all barrel-fermented Barossa Semillons tasted like this. **rating:** 87

♥♥♥♀ **1998** RBS1. Medium to full yellow-green; not surprisingly, the bouquet shows lots of oak, but in a complex fashion to produce lemony/tangy aromas, leaving you uncertain where the fruit stops and the oak starts. You can see all of the winemaker inputs on the milky, soft, oaky palate, which definitely comes from left field. **rating:** 84

best drinking 2000–2003 **best vintages** NA **drink with** Fish in white sauce • $25

Grant Burge Kraft Vineyard Sauvignon Blanc

Produced from grapes grown at Val and Dennis Kraft's vineyard at Tanunda. Eighty-five per cent of the wine is cold-fermented in stainless steel, 15 per cent barrel-fermented and kept on yeast lees for three months prior to blending and release.

♥♥♥♥ **1999** Light to medium yellow-green; attractive, moderately intense, passionfruit and gooseberry aromas lead into a well-balanced, flavoursome yet not heavy palate. Continues the success of the '98. **rating:** 87

best drinking 2000–2001 **best vintages** '94, '98, '99 **drink with** Rich seafood • $13.45

Grant Burge Virtuoso

A blend of Sauvignon Blanc (around 55 per cent) and Semillon (around 45 per cent), with avant-garde packaging deliberately aimed at the brasserie market. The wine is cold-fermented in stainless steel, and relatively early-bottled. Arguably an altogether better wine than the jolly packaging suggests it will be. The 1998 won a gold medal in Class 2 at the 1999 Sydney Royal Wine Show.

♥♥♥♥ **1999** Light green-yellow; the bouquet is clean and crisp, with some tropical fruit touches. The palate, likewise, has a good mix of fruit flavours, backed up by good length and acidity. **rating:** 85

best drinking 2000–2003 **best vintages** '98 **drink with** Brasserie food • $14.95

Grant Burge Lily Farm Frontignac

As Grant Burge says, 'No grape variety produces a wine which tastes so much like crushed, ripe grapes in a glass'. It comes from the Lily Farm Vineyard, on the eastern slopes of the Barossa Ranges, appropriately situated next to Grant Burge's front door.

♥♥♥♀ **1999** Light green-yellow; the spicy, grapey aromas are pungent and fragrant; although the palate finishes with attractive lemony acidity, I cannot help but think the wine would have been better were it not so sweet. **rating:** 83

best drinking 2000–2001 **best vintages** NA **drink with** A summer's morning • $10.45

Grant Burge Barossa Vines Chardonnay

Part of the new range of wines made at the former Krondorf winery purchased by Grant Burge in late 1999.

♥♥♥♀ **1999** Medium green-yellow; there is quite good fruit and oak balance and integration on both the bouquet and the palate. At the price you could hardly expect more, but the fruit does lack concentration. **rating:** 84

best drinking 2000–2002 **best vintages** NA **drink with** KFC • $10.45

Grant Burge Barossa Vines Shiraz

Part of the newly introduced second label Barossa Vines series of wines with their own specific winery; all the wines are positioned in the $10–$15 range.

♥♥♥♀ **1998** Light red-purple; the bouquet is light, fresh and crisp; like the palate, it borders on Rosé in style. The palate is fresh and finishes crisply dry; a good summer wine, best served slightly chilled. **rating:** 84

best drinking Drink now **best vintages** NA **drink with** Cold rare roast beef • $13.45

Grant Burge Filsell Shiraz

Produced from grapes grown on the estate Filsell Vineyard situated in the Lyndoch Valley; it is planted predominantly with shiraz, with vines up to 80 years old. The wine is fermented in open fermenters with heading down boards, drained daily in a technique pioneered by Max Schubert in the early days of Grange. The wine is aged for 18 months in American oak hogsheads, 50 per cent new.

♥♥♥♥♡ **1997** Medium red-purple; the bouquet has a nicely balanced mix of chocolate-toned fruit and vanilla oak, swelling into soft, sweet dark cherry fruit on the well-balanced and flavoured palate. While the oak is very much part of the style, has been well controlled throughout. All in all, a lovely wine. **rating: 90**

best drinking 2002–2012 **best vintages** '97 **drink with** Pizza • $24.75

Grant Burge Meshach Shiraz

First made in 1988, and the signature wine of the Grant Burge range. Named in honour of Meshach William Burge, Grant Burge's great-grandfather. It is produced from 65-year-old vines grown on the Filsell Vineyard, which also gives its name to the gold and trophy-winning varietal wine that sits alongside Cameron Vale. A prolific show winner over the years.

♥♥♥♥♡ **1996** Medium to full red-purple; the bouquet is rich and complex, with lots of dark berry fruit and the oak under control. Dark cherry, plum and chocolat, flavours on the palate are once again married with well-balanced and integrated oak; finishes with fine tannins. The best Meschach made to date. **rating: 93**

♥♥♥♥♡ **1995** Medium to full red-purple; in typically full-frontal oaky style on the bouquet, but there is lots of fruit to justify that oak. The same play occurs on the palate, with a mix of expansively sweet berry fruit and creamy vanilla oak. Has continued to develop well since its Adelaide Wine Show trophy. **rating: 92**

best drinking 2001–2011 **best vintages** '88, '90, '91, '92, '95, '96 **drink with** Braised beef • $79.95

Grant Burge MS Shiraz Cabernet

1994 was the inaugural vintage of this wine, said to have been inspired by the great Penfolds varietal/regional red blends. It is a mix of 56 per cent Barossa Valley Shiraz and 44 per cent Coonawarra Cabernet Sauvignon, the Shiraz component being American oak-matured and the Cabernet component French oak-matured, in each case for 22 months. The '94 won the Rudi Komon Trophy for Best Medium Bodied Dry Red at the Royal Sydney Wine Show. Teasingly, there is no explanation for the bin name.

♥♥♥♥ **1996** MSJ2. Medium red, with just a touch of purple remaining; the bouquet is quite complex, with a mix of earth, chocolate and vanilla aromas which flow through onto the palate, where nice, ripe, soft tannins and gentle oak complete the picture. **rating: 87**

♥♥♥♥♥ **1994** MSJ1. Medium purple-red; the fragrant bouquet offers a seamlessly welded mix of sweet berry, mocha and chocolate aromas; the palate continues in a more or less uninterrupted line, with those sweet, faintly mocha/chocolate flavours and delicious, cedary oak and fine tannins on the finish. Truly sophisticated. **rating: 94**

best drinking 2001–2006 **best vintages** '94 **drink with** Rare, boned leg of lamb • $60

Grant Burge Hillcott Merlot

A blend of 90 per cent Merlot and 10 per cent Cabernet Sauvignon which finishes its primary fermentation in barrel.

♥♥♥♥ **1998** Medium red-purple; the aromas are in a savoury/leafy spectrum, with restrained oak. The palate has excellent texture and balance, the flavours again being in the leafy/savoury spectrum; sweet tannins give persuasive length to the finish. **rating: 87**

best drinking 2002–2006 **best vintages** NA **drink with** Veal saltimbocca • $15.95

Grant Burge RBM1 Merlot

Yet another new addition to the Grant Burge range of red wines which consistently show high-quality fruit embellished with just the right amount of oak.

♥♥♥♥ **1998** Medium red-purple; there are quite complex cedar, cigar box, earth and berry varietal aromas leading into a palate with sweet raspberry fruit plus a touch of chocolate; the feel, structure and acidity are all appropriate for Merlot. **rating: 87**

best drinking 2002–2008 **best vintages** '98 **drink with** Beef stroganoff • $NA

Grant Burge Cameron Vale Cabernet Sauvignon

Produced, as the name suggests, from the estate-owned Cameron Valley Vineyard, planted to cabernet sauvignon in 1971–72. The wine is fermented in the same way as the Filsell Shiraz in open fermenters with heading down boards. Towards the end of fermentation, and while the wine has two baumé of sugar, it is transferred to French (Nevers) oak for the completion of fermentation. Fifty per cent of the oak is new, the rest used, and the wine spends 18 months in barrel with periodic rackings.

▼▼▼▼ **1997** Medium red-purple, showing some development. The bouquet offers a pleasant mix of mint, dark berry and toasty vanilla oak. There are similar palate flavours to a wine of moderate length and intensity. **rating:** 86
best drinking 2002–2007 **best vintages** '92, '93 **drink with** Roast beef • $19.95

great lakes wines   NR

Herivals Road, Wootton, NSW 2423 **region** Hastings River
phone (02) 4997 7255 **fax** (02) 4997 7255 **open** 7 days 8.30–6
winemaker John Webb, Ian Lindeman (Consultant) **production** 1200 **est.** 1990
product range ($8–10 CD) Chardonnay, Semillon Classic Dry White, Mellow White, Chambourcin, Mellow Red, Cabernets.
summary John Webber and family began planting their vineyard on the mid-north coast of New South Wales in 1990. There is now approximately half a hectare each of chardonnay, semillon, verdelho, shiraz, cabernet sauvignon and chambourcin, and the Webbers are proud of the fact that (to use their words) 'we are a fair dinkum winery where we "grow the grapes" and "we make the wine"'. All of the wines on current release have won at least one medal in regional wine shows, the 1998 Chambourcin winning silver medals at both the 1998 Cowra Show and 1998 New South Wales Small Winemakers Show.

greenock creek cellars   NR

Radford Road, Seppeltsfield, SA 5360 **region** Barossa Valley
phone (08) 8562 8103 **fax** (08) 8562 8259 **open** Wed–Mon 11–5
winemaker Michael Waugh **production** 1500 **est.** 1978
product range ($13–16.50 CD) Chardonnay, Shiraz, Cabernet Sauvignon.
summary Michael and Annabelle Waugh are disciples of Rocky O'Callaghan of Rockford Wines and have deliberately accumulated a series of old dryland, low-yielding Barossa vineyards, aiming to produce wines of unusual depth of flavour and character. They have handsomely succeeded in this aim. They also offer superior accommodation in the ancient but beautifully restored two-bedroom cottage 'Miriam's'; Michael Waugh is a highly skilled stonemason.

green valley vineyard   NR

3137 Sebbes Road, Forest Grove, WA 6286 **region** Margaret River
phone (08) 9384 3131 **open** Weekends and public holidays 10–6 or by appointment
winemaker Keith Mugford **production** 3000 **est.** 1980
product range ($16.50–27.50 CD) Chardonnay, Riesling, Müller Thurgau, Dolce (Chenin Blanc), Cabernet Sauvignon.
summary Owners Ed and Eleanore Green commenced the development of Green Valley Vineyard in 1980. It is still a part-time operation, with the wines made by contract, but production has grown steadily from the 7.7 hectares of vines, and the Cabernet Sauvignon has been a consistent medal winner. Exports to Singapore.

grevillea estate   NR

Buckajo Road, Bega, NSW 2550 **region** Other Wineries of NSW
phone (02) 6492 3006 **fax** (02) 6492 5330 **open** 7 days 9–5
winemaker Nicola Collins **production** 2900 **est.** 1980
product range ($10–18 CD) Daisy Hill Riesling, Lunatic Hill Sauvignon Blanc, Unoaked Chardonnay, Peak Hill Chardonnay, Gewurztraminer, Traminer Riesling, Rougon, Grosse's Creek Merlot, Edmund Kirby Cabernet Sauvignon, Old Tawny Port.
summary A tourist-oriented winery which successfully sells all of its surprisingly large production through cellar door and to local restaurants. All of the wines have very attractive labels, but it has to be said wine quality is not good.

grey sands   ★★★☆

Frankford Highway, Glengarry, Tas 7275 **region** Northern Tasmania
phone (03) 6396 1167 **fax** (03) 6396 1153 **open** By appointment
winemaker Bob Richter, Greg O'Keefe (Contract) **production** 150 **est.** 1989
product range ($17–25 ML) Pinot Gris, Merlot.
summary Bob and Rita Richter began the slow establishment of Grey Sands in 1988, slowly increasing the plantings over the ensuing ten years to the present total of 2.5 hectares. The ultra-high density of 8900 vines per hectare partially reflects the experience gained by the Richters during a three-year stay in England during which

time they visited many vineyards across Europe, and partially Bob Richter's graduate diploma in wine from Roseworthy Agricultural College (1985/86). 1998 marked the first commercial bottling of 100 cases of Pinot Gris, and 50 cases of Merlot.

Grey Sands Pinot Gris

An interesting style, fermented in stainless steel, taken through 100 per cent malolactic fermentation and then given lees contact. All of this adds to the mouthfeel.

▼▼▼♀ **1999** Light green-yellow; the bouquet is clean, with a mix of predominantly mineral and slight honeysuckle fruit. The same flavours come through on the palate, but it is the mouthfeel which gives the wine most distinction. Definitely made in a Pinot Gris (in other words Alsatian) rather than Grigio (Italian) style.   **rating: 83**

best drinking 2000–2002 **drink with** Bocconcini • $17

Grey Sands Merlot

The long time taken to arrive at the first commercial vintage has paid off handsomely with this wine, with the promise of an equally good '99 vintage in store.

▼▼▼▼ **1998** Medium red-purple; the bouquet has attractive, medium-intensity berry fruit, the palate appropriately supple with sweet fruit and silky tannins, just what Merlot should provide.   **rating: 86**

best drinking 2001–2008 **drink with** Braised lamb • $25

grosset   ★ ★ ★ ★ ★

King Street, Auburn, SA 5451 **region** Clare Valley
phone (08) 8849 2175 **fax** (08) 8849 2292 **open** Wed–Sun 10–5 from 1st week of September for approx 6 weeks
winemaker Jeffrey Grosset **production** 8500 **est.** 1981
product range ($23.95–49 R) Watervale Riesling, Polish Hill Riesling, Semillon Sauvignon Blanc, Piccadilly Chardonnay, Gaia (a Cabernet blend), Noble Riesling, Reserve Pinot Noir.
summary Jeffrey Grosset served part of his apprenticeship at the vast Lindeman Karadoc winery, moving from the largest to one of the smallest when he established Grosset Wines in its old stone winery. He now crafts the wines with the utmost care from grapes grown to the most exacting standards; all need a certain amount of time in bottle to achieve their ultimate potential, not the least the Rieslings and Gaia, among Australia's best examples of their kind. At a Riesling Summit held in Hamburg in the latter part of 1998, Grosset was voted Riesling Winemaker of the Year. Exports to the UK, the US, Japan, Belgium and Germany mean a continuous shortage of the wines in all markets.

Grosset Polish Hill Riesling

A finer, crisper and more elegant wine than the Watervale, with more lime and citrus fruit, albeit less generous. Since 1985 the Molloy Vineyard has been the major source, but as from 1994 estate plantings also contribute. Like the Watervale, made with neutral yeasts and without the use of enzymes. Always brilliant.

▼▼▼▼▼ **1999** There is a quiet precision in Jeffrey Grossett's demeanour, wholly apposite to his mantle as heir-apparent to John Vickery, Australia's greatest Riesling maker. This wine is a classic, with far more lime and passionfruit than usual apparent at this early stage, providing a deliciously lingering finish.   **rating: 96**

best drinking 2000–2014 **best vintages** '82, '86, '87, '90, '93, '94, '96, '97, '98 **drink with** Grilled South Australian whiting • $32.50

Grosset Watervale Riesling

Made from hand-picked grapes grown on a single vineyard established on red clay over limestone at an altitude of 450 metres. It is a richer, fuller style than the Polish Hill River wine, and tends to be slightly earlier maturing. All of the recent vintages have been made bone-dry, with deliberately neutral yeast influence.

▼▼▼▼▼ **1999** Light to medium green-yellow; a crisp, clean bouquet which is utterly classic Clare Valley, minerally and less exuberant than the Polish Hill of the same year. The palate is lively and lingering, with more citrus fruit showing than in the bouquet; very good balance and length.   **rating: 94**

best drinking 2004–2014 **best vintages** '81, '86, '90, '93, '94, '95, '96, '97, '98, '99 **drink with** Thai soup • $26.50

Grosset Semillon Sauvignon Blanc

Other than the Tim Knappstein Fumé Blanc, which incorporates Lenswood fruit from the Adelaide Hills, this is by far the best example of its kind from the Clare Valley. Immaculate winemaking produces a very fine, elegant, crisp seafood style. Composed of Semillon from the Clare Valley and Sauvignon Blanc from the Adelaide Hills. Typically only 750 cases made.

▼▼▼▼▽ **1999** Brilliant light green-yellow; fragrant mineral and herb aromas are followed by a palate in a crisp, herbaceous style and a long finish. **rating:** 92

best drinking 2000–2003 **best vintages** '93, '94, '95, '96, '97, '99 **drink with** Shellfish • $26.50

Grosset Piccadilly Chardonnay

Since 1994 Jeffrey Grosset has sourced his Chardonnay from Piccadilly in the Adelaide Hills, labelling it as such. In a far finer style than the preceding Clare Valley wines, and — one would imagine — a longer future. Forty per cent of the wine is taken through malolactic fermentation.

▼▼▼▼▽ **1998** Bright, light green-yellow; the aromas are clean, fresh and delicate, a mix of nectarine and citrus. Immaculately made and balanced but needs a year or so for the palate to start filling out and opening up. **rating:** 92

best drinking 2001–2008 **best vintages** '96, '97 **drink with** Gravlax • $38.50

Grosset Pinot Noir

Produced from grapes grown on the Adelaide Hills vineyard of Lindsay and Carolyn Barratt, and made using the full array of Burgundian winemaking techniques, including whole-bunch maceration.

▼▼▼▼▽ **1998** Light red, with just a touch of purple, noticeably advanced. The bouquet is light but wonderfully fragrant with a mix of violets and forest floor; subtle oak. The palate is remarkably intense given the colour, with savoury overtones to ripe cherry and strawberry fruit; well-balanced acidity on a lingering finish. You can't tell a Pinot by its colour. **rating:** 91

best drinking 1999–2002 **best vintages** NA **drink with** Braised duck • $49

Grosset Gaia

A blend of 85 per cent Cabernet Sauvignon, 10 per cent Cabernet Franc and 5 per cent Merlot, typically made in amounts of less than 1000 cases. Shot to stardom with the initial vintage of 1990 and has not faltered since.

▼▼▼▼ **1997** Medium to full red-purple; complex, rich blackberry fruit, with a few savoury overtones and subtle oak on the bouquet, are followed by a palate which opens with abundant fruit, but then drying tannins come as a real shock in what is normally a wine of impeccable balance. Given the abundance of fruit, the tannins may soften enough to bring it into balance. **rating:** 86

best drinking 2002–2017 **best vintages** '90, '91, '92, '94, '95, '96 **drink with** Game pie • $49

⚘ grove estate   NR

Boorowa Road, Young, NSW 2594 **region** Hilltops
phone (02) 6382 6999 **fax** (02) 6382 4527 **open** Weekends 10–5 or by appointment
winemaker Monarch Winemaking Services, Greg Silkman (Contract) **production** 2000 **est.** 1990
product range ($14–21 CD) Hilltops Semillon, Murringo Way Chardonnay, The Cellar Block Shiraz, The Partners Cabernet Sauvignon.
summary Brian Mullany has established a 30-hectare vineyard planted to Semillon, Chardonnay, Merlot, Shiraz, Cabernet Sauvignon and Zinfandel. Most of the grapes are sold (principally to Southcorp) but a limited amount of wine is contract-made at Charles Sturt University for the Grove Estate label.

grove hill   NR

120 Old Norton Summit Road, Norton Summit, SA 5136 **region** Adelaide Hills
phone (08) 8390 1437 **fax** (08) 8390 1437 **open** Sunday 11–5
winemaker David Powell (Contract) **production** 500 **est.** 1978
product range ($22–30 ML) Riesling, Chardonnay, Marguerite Pinot Chardonnay.
summary Grove Hill is a heritage property established in 1846 with the original homestead and outbuildings and held by the same family since that time. Not entered in the Adelaide Hills Wines Show and no recent tastings.

haan wines   NR

Siegersdorf Road, Tanunda, SA 5352 **region** Barossa Valley
phone (08) 8562 4590 **fax** (08) 8562 4590 **open** Not
winemaker James Irvine (Contract) **production** 1250 **est.** 1993
product range ($7–77 ML) Viognier, Merlot Prestige, Cabernet Rosé, Shiraz Prestige, Merlot Prestige.
summary Hans and Fransien Haan established their business in 1993 when they acquired a 16-hectare vineyard near Tanunda. The primary focus is on Merlot and in particular on the luxury Merlot Prestige, and they understandably chose James Irvine as their contract-winemaker. There are no cellar-door sales; the wines are sold through distributors in the eastern States, with Australian Prestige Wines also acting as export distributor.

Haan Viognier

Only 83 cases of this wine were made in 1999. Half of the crop was removed at veraison, no doubt helping the concentration of the wine.

TTTT 1999 Light yellow-green; the aroma is very authentic, with that elusive fruit pastille and blossom character of the variety. The palate is likewise true to variety, both in terms of its richness and depth and in terms of the pastille and spice flavours. Overall, the wine does show some warmth from the alcohol. All in all, one of the best Viogniers yet produced from Australia.   **rating: 90**

best drinking 1999–2003 **best vintages** NA **drink with** Rich fish dishes • $NA

Haan Merlot Prestige

Contract/consultant-winemaker James Irvine was one of the first in Australia to realise the potential for varietal Merlot, and likewise to focus on the export, rather than the domestic, market. This is very much in the James Irvine Grand Merlot style, and the 1996 vintage was selected in the Top 100 in the 1999 Sydney International Wine Competition. It is estate-grown, and matured in a mix of new, once-used and twice-used French oak for 18 months. It is then held in bottle for a further six to 12 months before release.

TTTT 1997 Strong red-purple; the bouquet is complex, with a mix of ripe fruit and more savoury/earthy aromas. The palate is crammed with ripe, rich, sweet dark berry and dark chocolate flavours, supported by soft vanilla oak. A wine which is a lovely Australian red style, rather than being strongly varietal.   **rating: 92**

best drinking 2002–2007 **best vintages** '96 **drink with** Game pie • $20

habitat   NR

Old Canobolas Road, Nashdale, NSW 2800 **region** Orange
phone (02) 6365 3294 **fax** (02) 6365 3294 **open** At Ibis Wines
winemaker Phil Stevenson (Contract) **production** 200 **est.** 1989
product range ($16–20 CD) Pinot Noir, Merlot.
summary The 2.5-hectare Habitat vineyard is situated on the northern slope of Mount Canobolas on deep red basalt soil at an altitude of 1100 metres, making it one of the highest — if not the highest — vineyards in Australia. In prior vintages the grapes were sold to Charles Sturt University to make sparkling (and table) wines.

Habitat Merlot

The youngest wine on sale as at 2000, and also the best, coming from the high altitude Habitat vineyard.

TTTT 1998 Medium red-purple; a clean, moderately rich bouquet with berry and chocolate aromas which are slightly lifted. The palate offers similar flavours; both the tannins and oak are neatly balanced.   **rating: 82**

best drinking 2000–2004 **best vintages** NA **drink with** Something feathered • $20

haig   NR

Square Mile Road, Mount Gambier, SA 5290 **region** Mount Gambier
phone (08) 8725 5414 **fax** (08) 8725 5414 **open** 7 days 11–5
winemaker Katnook (Contract) **production** 500 **est.** 1982
product range ($12–15 CD) Chardonnay, Late Harvest Chardonnay, Pinot Noir, Shiraz Pinot.
summary The 4 hectares of estate vineyards are planted on the rich volcanic soils near the slopes of the famous Blue Lake of Mount Gambier. I have neither seen nor tasted the wines.

hainault   ★★★

255 Walnut Road, Bickley, WA 6076 **region** Perth Hills
phone (08) 9328 6728 **fax** (08) 9328 6895 **open** Weekends 10–5
winemaker Celine Rousseau, Gary Dixon **production** 2300 **est.** 1980
product range ($14–21 CD) The Terroir range of Gewurztraminer, Pinot Noir, Merlot, Shiraz; Barking Owl Sauvignon Blanc Semillon, Chardonnay, Fruity Muscat, Old Vine Red, Cabernets, Vineyard Port; and Talus Sparkling.
summary Under the energetic ownership of public affairs consultant and businessman Bill Mackey and wife Vicki, the changes have come thick and fast at Hainault. Plantings have increased to 11 hectares; Celine Rousseau, a highly qualified French-born and trained oenologist, has been installed as winemaker; and the Barking Owl range, attractively packaged, and sourced from Pemberton, the Bickley and Swan Valleys introduced to sit under the Hainault Terroir range. Limited distribution in Victoria and the ACT.

halcyon daze ★★★

19 Uplands Road, Lilydale, Vic 3140 **region** Yarra Valley
phone (03) 9726 7111 **fax** (03) 9726 7111 **open** By appointment
winemaker Richard Rackley **production** 500 **est.** 1982
product range ($20–30 ML) Riesling, Chardonnay, Pinot Noir, Cabernets; also Sparkling.
summary One of the lower-profile wineries with a small, estate-grown production which in fact sells the major part of its output of grapes from its 6.5 hectares of vines to others. Immaculate viticulture ensures that the grapes have a strong market.

half mile creek ★★★☆

George Campbell Drive, Mudgee, NSW 2850 **region** Mudgee
phone (02) 6372 3880 **fax** (02) 6372 2977 **open** 7 days 10–4
winemaker Rob Guadagnini **production** 20 000 **est.** 1918
product range ($10 R) Hunter Valley Verdelho, Cowra Chardonnay, Mudgee Shiraz, Mudgee Cabernet Merlot.
summary Half Mile Creek was once the Augustine Vineyard, established by the Roth family in the nineteenth century, and was purchased by Dr Thomas Fiaschi (one of the great unsung heroes of the Australian wine industry) in 1917. It has had a chequered career ever since but has a great history, and is still a substantial producer (and part of the Mildara Blass empire).

hamelin bay ★★★★

Brockman Highway, Karridale, WA 6288 **region** Margaret River
phone (08) 9758 5000 **fax** (08) 9389 6020 **open** 7 days 10–5
winemaker Philip Tubb **production** 15 000 **est.** 1992
product range ($14.99–23 CD) Sauvignon Blanc, Semillon Sauvignon Blanc, Chardonnay, Classic Rampant White, Merlot, Shiraz, Cabernet Sauvignon.
summary The 25-hectare Hamelin Bay vineyard, established by the Drake-Brockman family, has enjoyed outstanding success with its first wine releases from the 1996 and 1997 vintages. For the time being its wines are contract-made, but a winery with cellar-door sales facility is due to be opened in the year 2000. In the meantime, production has soared from 5000 to 15 000 cases.

Hamelin Bay Chardonnay

Between 25 per cent and 50 per cent of the wine is barrel-fermented in French oak, the remainder in stainless steel, lees contact and partial malolactic fermentation then follow. A light-bodied but well-constructed style.
♥♥♥♥ **1999** Medium yellow-green; the bouquet is clean and light, with gently ripe nectarine fruit. The palate is similarly light, clean, fresh and crisp, needing greater fruit concentration for higher points. **rating:** 81
best drinking 2000–2002 **best vintages** NA **drink with** Lemon chicken • $23

hamilton ★★★★

Main Road, Willunga, SA 5172 **region** McLaren Vale
phone (08) 8556 2288 **fax** (08) 8556 2868 **open** 7 days 10–5
winemaker Phillipa Treadwell **production** 36 000 **est.** 1837
product range ($12–45 R) Synergy Dry White, Chardonnay, Pinot Noir, Shiraz; Hamilton Almond Grove Chardonnay, Ayliffe's Orchard Sauvignon Blanc, Slate Quarry Riesling, The Chook Sauvignon Blanc, Lot 148 Merlot, Block Shiraz; Hamilton Reserve wines are Richard Hamilton Signature Chardonnay, Marion Vineyard Grenache Shiraz, Old Vines Shiraz, Egremeont Reserve Merlot, Burton's Vineyard Grenache Shiraz; also The Hills (Adelaide Hills) Chardonnay and Pinot Noir.
summary The quality and character of the Richard Hamilton wines have grown in leaps and bounds over the past five years or so, no doubt due to the skills of winemaker Phillipa Treadwell and former winemaker Ralph Fowler, with support from owner Dr Richard Hamilton. The wines are boldly styled, full of flavour and character. Exports to Canada, the US, Asia, the UK and Europe.

Hamilton Slate Quarry Riesling

This estate-grown wines comes not from a slate quarry but from riesling vines planted on the Hut Block back in 1947. This apart, it has been very well made.
♥♥♥♥ **1999** Light yellow-green; the bouquet is tight, with minerally/slatey aromas (the power of suggestion); the palate is quite intense, powerful and commendably long; overall, well above average for McLaren Vale. **rating:** 84
best drinking 2000–2002 **best vintages** NA **drink with** Summer salads • $13.95

Richard Hamilton Signature Chardonnay

As the name attests, sits at or near the top of the Hamilton white wines.

▼▼▼▼ **1998** Glowing yellow-green; discreet melon fruit with hints of citrus and minimal and a deft touch of oak lead into an elegant, unforced palate with similar citrus and melon fruit together with subtle oak.   **rating:** 89

best drinking 1999–2003   **best vintages** NA   **drink with** Abalone   • $19.95

Hamilton Gumprs's Block Shiraz

James Gumprs (spelt without an 'e') was the first licensee (in 1851) of the building which these days houses McLaren Vale's best and best-known restaurant, The Salopian Inn.

▼▼▼▽ **1998** Medium to full purple-red; a wholly idiosyncratic wine from start to finish, with a powerful, intense gamey bouquet and a similarly confrontational palate. Rather angular, and belies its 14 degrees alcohol. **rating:** 82

best drinking 2000–2005   **best vintages** NA   **drink with** Kebabs   • $20

Hamilton Lot 148 Merlot

As with pinot noir, merely planting the vines is not enough to provide a wine with good varietal character. Whether or not this is important may be a matter of debate.

▼▼▼▽ **1998** Full red-purple; a solid bouquet, with a mix of blackberry and raspberry fruit together with slightly gamey overtones. The medium- to full-bodied palate is quite tannic; there is no varietal character evident at any point.   **rating:** 83

best drinking 2001–2005   **best vintages** NA   **drink with** Grilled beef   • $19.95

hamiltons bluff   NR

Longs Corner Road, Canowindra, NSW 2804   **region** Cowra
phone (02) 6344 2079   **fax** (02) 6344 2165   **open** Weekends and holidays 10–4, Mon–Fri by appointment
winemaker Andrew Margan   **production** 2000   **est.** 1995
product range ($14–30 CD) Canowindra Grossi range of Unwooded Chardonnay, Devonian Red NV, Cabernet; Cowra Chardonnay, Méthode Champenoise, Chairman's Reserve Chardonnay.
summary Hamiltons Bluff is owned and operated by the Andrews family, which planted 45 hectares of vines in 1995. 1998 produced the first crop, and three different Chardonnays were contract-made by Andrew Margan. The Cowra Chardonnay and Canowindra grossi Chardonnay received medals at the 1998 Cowra Wine Show. Cellar-door sales opened in early 1999, heralding a new stage of development for the Cowra region.

hanging rock winery   ★★★☆

The Jim Jim, Jim Road, Newham, Vic 3442   **region** Macedon Ranges
phone (03) 5427 0542   **fax** (03) 5427 0310   **open** 7 days 10–5
winemaker John Ellis   **production** 25 000   **est.** 1982
product range ($12–48 CD) Macedon Cuvée V, Colemans Gully Riesling, The Jim Jim Sauvignon Blanc, Victoria Semillon Sauvignon Blanc, Victoria Chardonnay, Reserve Swan Hill Chardonnay, Late Harvest Riesling, Late Harvest Gewurztraminer, Macedon Rosé, Central Highlands Pinot Noir, Victoria Cabernet Merlot, Gralaine Merlot, Victoria Shiraz, Picnic Red and White.
summary The Macedon area has proved very marginal in spots, and the Hanging Rock vineyards, with their lovely vista towards the Rock, are no exception. John Ellis has thus elected to source additional grapes from various parts of Victoria to produce an interesting and diverse style of wines. The low-priced Picnic White and Picnic Red, with the striking label, have been particularly successful. Exports to the UK, the US, Asia, Italy and Japan.

Hanging Rock The Jim Jim Sauvignon Blanc

Produced from the 1.4 hectares of estate plantings of sauvignon blanc, and — right from the word go — has been a supremely impressive wine. The flavours are remarkably intense, reflecting the low yields of the relatively low vigour vineyard.

▼▼▼▼ **1999** Very light straw-yellow; the bouquet is crisp and clean, with grassy/minerally fruit, the palate fresh, lively, zingy and intense, finishing with bracing but not unpleasant acidity.   **rating:** 89

best drinking Drink now   **best vintages** '93, '95, '96, '99   **drink with** Oysters   • $22.95

Hanging Rock Victoria Semillon Sauvignon Blanc

A blend of Semillon grown in Geelong and the estate Jim Jim vineyard together with Sauvignon Blanc from the Strathbogie Ranges. Cool-fermented and early-bottled, it is by a considerable distance the best of the Victoria range released in 1999.

▼▼▼▽ **1998** Light green-yellow; a clean, light, neutral bouquet is followed by a palate in which the flavours are not particularly intense but are nicely balanced.   **rating:** 81

best drinking 2000–2001   **best vintages** NA   **drink with** Shellfish   • $15

Hanging Rock Macedon Rosé

Produced from pinot noir grown in the Macedon Ranges region, and the first released since 1995. Only made in those years when there is pinot noir surplus to the requirement for sparkling wine.

▼▼▼▽ **1999** Light pink; the bouquet is clean, with pleasant strawberry fruit aromas, the palate crisp, clean and bone-dry, finishing with high acidity. In the final analysis, I cannot help but think the balance would have been improved had a little residual sugar been left in the wine. **rating: 80**

best drinking 2000–2001 **best vintages** NA **drink with** Antipasto • $17

Hanging Rock Central Highlands Pinot Noir

Made from grapes at two vineyards near Bendigo, and a third near Ballarat. The Bendigo vineyards, and in particular that of the Norris family at Faraday, provide the ripe fruit, the Ballarat vineyard produces the vitality. In the winery, John Ellis uses sophisticated and complex winemaking techniques, including an extreme adaptation of the pre-fermentation maceration (cold-soak) advocated by the Lebanese oenologist, Guy Accad. All in all, a very interesting wine.

▼▼▼▼ **1998** Medium to full purple-red; quite attractive gamey overtones to a mix of sweet and more savoury fruit aromatics. Overall, quite sweet in the mouth, but certainly has varietal character and secondary characters will develop with further maturation. **rating: 88**

best drinking 2000–2005 **best vintages** '98 **drink with** Baked ham • $19.95

Hanging Rock Winery Heathcote Shiraz

Without question the most distinguished wine in the Hanging Rock portfolio, made from dry-grown, low-yielding vines in what many regard as one of Australia's best Shiraz regions.

▼▼▼▼ **1998** Medium purple-red; clean, moderately intense black cherry fruit is offset by slightly charry oak on the bouquet; a big, show-style palate with opulent black cherry fruit and well-handled but evident vanilla oak; as always, the tannins are quite soft. **rating: 88**

best drinking 2003–2013 **best vintages** '97, '98 **drink with** Roast venison • $42.50

hankin estate   NR

Johnsons Lane, Northwood via Seymour, Vic 3660 **region** Goulburn Valley
phone (03) 5792 2396 **fax** (03) 9353 2927 **open** Weekends 10–5
winemaker Dr Max Hankin **production** 600 **est.** 1975
product range ($7–22 CD) Semillon, Sauvignon Blanc, Premium Dry White, Rosé, Shiraz, Shiraz Cabernet Malbec, Cabernet Sauvignon.
summary Hankin Estate is now the principal occupation of Dr Max Hankin, who has retired from full-time medical practice. He has to contend with phylloxera, which decimated the original plantings, with the replanting process still underway.

hanns creek estate   NR

Kentucky Road, Merricks North, Vic 3926 **region** Mornington Peninsula
phone (03) 5989 7266 **fax** (03) 5989 7500 **open** 7 days 11–5
winemaker Tony Aubrey-Slocock **production** 1500 **est.** 1987
product range ($18–25 CD) Chardonnay, Rosé, Pinot Noir, Cabernet Shiraz, Cabernet Sauvignon.
summary Denise and Tony Aubrey-Slocock have established a 3-hectare vineyard on the slopes of Merricks North. After an uncertain start, with contract-winemaking moving around, Kevin McCarthy took control and wine style steadied.

⊗ hansen hilltops   NR

Barwang Ridge, 1 Barwang Road, Young, NSW 2594 **region** Hilltops
phone (02) 6382 6363 **fax** (02) 6382 6363 **open** Mon–Fri 10–6
winemaker Charles Sturt University (Contract) **production** 2200 **est.** 1979
product range ($16.75–25 CD) Riesling, Chardonnay, Shiraz, Cabernet Sauvignon.
summary The vineyard has 5 hectares of vines, 1 hectare each of riesling, chardonnay, shiraz, cabernet sauvignon, and a further hectare roughly split between semillon, merlot and malbec. The plantings date back to 1979, but the first wines were not made until the late 1990s.

hanson-tarrahill vineyard   ★★★

340 Old Healesville Road, Yarra Glen, Vic 3775 **region** Yarra Valley
phone (03) 9439 7425 **fax** (03) 9439 4217 **open** Not
winemaker Dr Ian Hanson **production** 800 **est.** 1983
product range ($18.99–19.99 R) Pinot Noir, Cabernets, Cabernet Franc, Cabernet Sauvignon.

summary Dental surgeon Ian Hanson planted his first vines in the late 1960s, close to the junction of the Yarra and Plenty Rivers; in 1983 those plantings were extended (with 3000 vines), and in 1988 the Tarrahill property at Yarra Glen was established with 10 further acres. Hanson is the name which appears most prominently on the newly designed labels; Tarrahill Vineyard is in much smaller type.

Hanson–Tarrahill Vineyard Pinot Noir

Estate-grown and competently made to provide plenty of complexity.

▼▼▼♈ **1998** Medium red-purple; the bouquet is savoury, with gentle foresty and slightly smoky aromas. The palate offers a similar array of spicy/savoury/foresty flavours, scoring particularly well for its length.   **rating: 84**

best drinking 2000–2003 **best vintages** NA **drink with** Coq au vin • $19.90

happs ★★★☆

Commonage Road, Dunsborough, WA 6281 **region** Margaret River
phone (08) 9755 3300 **fax** (08) 9755 3846 **open** 7 days 10–5
winemaker Erl Happ, Damian Grindley **production** 19 000 **est.** 1978
product range ($13–28 CD) Dry table wines are Classic (Semillon Chardonnay), Marrime (Semillon Chenin Blanc), Chardonnay, Margaret River Red, Shiraz, Merlot and Cabernet Merlot; sweet table wines are Fuschia, Topaz and Late Picked Verdelho; fortifieds are Fortis (Vintage Port), 10 Year Fortis (Tawny), Garnet (from Muscat à Petit Grains), Pale Gold (White Port) and Old Bronze (Muscat). In 1994 a Preservative Free Red was also made.
summary Former schoolteacher turned potter and winemaker Erl Happ is an iconoclast and compulsive experimenter. Many of the styles he makes are very unconventional, the future likely to be even more so: the Karridale vineyard planted in 1994 has no less than 28 different varieties established. Merlot has been a winery specialty for a decade. Limited retail distributed through New South Wales, Victoria and Queensland and, more recently, exports to Europe.

Happs Marrime

If anyone doubted that Erl Happ has an eclectic bent, this wine should put the matter beyond doubt. It is a blend of 47 per cent Semillon, 35 per cent Chenin Blanc, 11 per cent Furmint, 4 per cent Marsanne and 3 per cent Viognier. Fifty per cent of the wine is barrel-fermented to dryness, and the wine is two years old prior to release.

▼▼▼♈ **1998** Medium to full yellow-green; the bouquet is moderately rich, with ripe, honeyed fruit and subtle oak. The palate is rather big and broad, the 14.5 degrees alcohol showing through on the finish. It certainly makes a statement.   **rating: 80**

best drinking 2000–2002 **best vintages** NA **drink with** Strongly sauced pasta • $13

Happs Merlot

Erl Happ has energetically promoted Merlot with major annual tastings, although his role has now been usurped by Chris Cameron of Peppertree in the Hunter Valley. Ironic, given that the '98 vintage is the best yet from Happs.

▼▼▼▼ **1998** Medium red-purple; a clean bouquet with a classic array of spice, cedar, savoury and earth aromas. The palate has attractive red fruits to go with the more savoury characters of the bouquet, and is given structure by silky, ripe tannins. An elegant wine with excellent varietal character.   **rating: 88**

best drinking 2002–2008 **best vintages** NA **drink with** Saltimbocca • $25

Happs Cabernet Merlot

A blend of 65 per cent Cabernet Sauvignon and 35 per cent Merlot, sourced from two vineyards at the extreme ends of the Margaret River region at Dunsborough in the north and Karridale in the south.

▼▼▼▼ **1997** Medium red-purple; the bouquet is clean, with attractive cedary/cigar/savoury aromas, followed by a palate with good cassis-flavoured fruit, an echo of the savoury characters of the bouquet, finishing with soft tannins.   **rating: 88**

best drinking 2000–2005 **best vintages** '92, '97 **drink with** Game pie • $23

harcourt valley vineyards   NR

Calder Highway, Harcourt, Vic 3453 **region** Bendigo
phone (03) 5474 2223 **fax** (03) 5474 2293 **open** 7 days 11–6
winemaker John Livingstone **production** 1200 **est.** 1976
product range ($14–20 CD) Chardonnay, Riesling, Malbec, Barbara's Shiraz, Cabernet Sauvignon.
summary Traditional producer of rich, full-bodied red wines typical of the district, but sporadic (and largely outdated) tastings since ownership changed preclude evaluation. No recent tastings; however, 1996 Barbara's Shiraz has won two gold and two silver medals during 1997, strongly suggesting the quality of this lovely wine has been maintained.

Harcourt Valley Barbara's Shiraz

Named in honour of Barbara Broughton, one of the founders of Harcourt Valley; matured for 16 months in American oak.

TTTT 1998 Medium red-purple; the bouquet is solid, clean and ripe, with aromas in the mulberry spectrum. On the palate there is a mix of interesting five-spice fruit flavours and a touch of mint; a lively wine from start to finish. **rating: 87**

best drinking 2003–2008 **best vintages** NA **drink with** Spicy designer sausages • $20

Harcourt Valley Cabernet Sauvignon

Produced from 25-year-old estate vines, and fermented in a mix of open and closed fermenters. After a period of post-fermentation maceration, is taken to American oak where it remains for the next 18-20 months prior to bottling.

TTT♀ 1998 Youthful, medium to full purple-red; there are very ripe earthy/berry fruit aromas with minimal oak influence to the bouquet. The palate is fruit-driven, with sweet cassis fruit, but tails away somewhat on the finish. **rating: 83**

best drinking 2002–2007 **best vintages** NA **drink with** Lamb chump chops • $20

hardys ★★★★☆

Reynell Road, Reynella, SA 5161 **region** McLaren Vale
phone (08) 8392 2222 **fax** (08) 8392 2202 **open** 7 days 10–4.30
winemaker Peter Dawson, Stephen Pannell, Tom Newton, Ed Carr **production** NFP **est.** 1853
product range ($8–65 R) Starts with Old Castle Rhine Riesling, St Vincent Chablis; then McLaren Vale Hermitage, Classic Dry White; Nottage Hill Riesling, Chardonnay, Cabernet Sauvignon; then the generic Bird series; then Insignia Chardonnay Sauvignon Blanc, and Cabernet Sauvignon Shiraz; followed by Siegersdorf Chardonnay and Rhine Riesling. No Preservative Added Chardonnay and Cabernet Sauvignon are available for allergy sufferers. The Sir James range and the Bankside wines fill in the middle; at the very top Eileen Hardy Chardonnay, Shiraz and Thomas Hardy Cabernet Sauvignon. There is a full range of sparkling wines, superior quality brandies and ports, including Australia's finest Vintage Port.
summary Since the 1992 merger of Thomas Hardy and the Berri Renmano group, the business has flourished, and the shareholders have profited greatly. The merged group has confounded expectations by aggressively, and very successfully, pushing the premium end of the business, making a number of acquisitions and investments across the length and breadth of Australia, all aimed at the upper end of the market. A high level of winemaking expertise and commitment has been an essential part of this success. It is basically for these wines that the winery rating is given.

Hardys Nottage Hill Riesling

While the regional source of the wine is not specified, Group White Winemaker Glenn James says full-flavoured citrussy fruit is selected, rather than grapes which produce more floral characters. This is certainly reflected in the flavour of the wine, which represents outstanding value at the price.

TTTT 1999 Light yellow-green; the moderately intense bouquet has a mix of herb, mineral and citrus fruit, with slightly dusty overtones. On the palate it is lime/citrus which dominates a wine with good length and balance. Slightly broad, perhaps, but that is hardly a concern at the price. **rating: 85**

best drinking 2000–2003 **best vintages** '98 **drink with** Vegetarian • $8.95

Hardys Siegersdorf Riesling

A wine with a long and distinguished pedigree, going back to the early 1970s when a youthful Brian Croser briefly served as chief white winemaker. Then one of Hardys' premium wines, it is now mainstream commercial but holds its market share simply because it is a good wine at the price. It is made from Clare Valley and Padthaway grapes, both premium regions, the Clare Valley particularly noted for its Riesling.

TTTT 1999 Light yellow-green; the bouquet is firm, with dusty mineral aromas followed by riper citrus and passionfruit notes as the wine is swirled in the glass. It has good mouthfeel, rich but not heavy, and attractive mid-range fruit flavours. Most importantly, it has length and persistence of flavour. **rating: 88**

best drinking 2000–2005 **best vintages** '88, '90, '92, '93, '94, '96, '99 **drink with** Thai dishes • $10.95

Hardys Insignia Chardonnay Sauvignon Blanc

Legend has it that when Seppelt released the first Chardonnay Sauvignon Blanc some years ago, it represented an inadvertent blend emanating from a mistake in the winery. It proved so successful that not only did Seppelt follow up with further vintages, but the strange blend became part of the broader landscape.

🍷🍷🍷🍷 **1998** Light green-yellow; the bouquet is clean, essentially neutral, but does have some tangy edges. Herbal flavours from the Sauvignon Blanc dominate the palate, which is of light to medium weight and moderate length. **rating: 80**

best drinking 2000–2001 **best vintages** NA **drink with** Light seafood • $11.95

Hardys Nottage Hill Chardonnay
Given the price at which the Nottage Hill brand sells any criticism of style of quality seems utterly superfluous.
🍷🍷🍷🍷 **1999** Light to medium green-yellow; the bouquet is quite aromatic, with some citrus and peach fruit. The palate is pleasant, of light to medium weight, with a gentle touch of slightly chippy oak. Excellent value. **rating: 83**
best drinking 2000–2001 **best vintages** NA **drink with** Pasta • $8.95

Hardys Sir James Chardonnay
Produced from grapes grown in the Adelaide Hills and Padthaway, and partially barrel-fermented.
🍷🍷🍷🍷 **1998** Light to medium yellow-green; the moderately intense bouquet is clean, with fresh grapefruit aromas and minimal oak. The fresh, citrussy palate shows its cool-climate origins in no uncertain fashion, supported by subtle barrel-ferment notes. **rating: 87**
best drinking 2000–2004 **best vintages** NA **drink with** Salmon terrine • $13.95

Hardys Arras
Has burst onto the scene like new year's eve fireworks, successfully redefining the upper end of Australian sparkling wine, with winemaker Ed Carr in masterful command.
🍷🍷🍷🍷🍷 **1995** A striking and complex bouquet with spice, hay and bread aromas is followed by a taut, powerful palate with impeccable length and balance. **rating: 94**
best drinking 2000–2001 **best vintages** NA **drink with** Aperitif • $55

Hardys Eileen Hardy Shiraz
If one includes the 1970 in the range, a wine with a proud history. As is the case with Wynns Michael Hermitage, the reincarnation bears little or no resemblance to the original model, but in common with Michael Hermitage, reflects a determination to produce the best (some would say the biggest) possible wine. A blend of Padthaway and McLaren Vale Shiraz which spends two years in French and American oak and has been a prolific trophy and gold medal winner in wine shows in recent years.
🍷🍷🍷🍷🍷 **1996** Dense purple, very good for age; there is a distinct change in the character of the bouquet, with more savoury notes, and it is difficult to feel where the fruit stops and the oak starts. The answer comes on the palate; in relative terms, this is a fruit-driven — well, more fruit-driven — wine than all the others, with scented raspberry, chocolate, liquorice and black cherry fruit. The first of the Eileens to be matured in 100 per cent French oak, which certainly makes a contribution. **rating: 94**
best drinking 2001–2011 **best vintages** '70, '88, '91, '93, '95, '96 **drink with** Game pie • $65

Hardys Tintara Shiraz
A new superbly packaged and presented premium range from Hardys, simultaneously replacing and upgrading the now discontinued Bankside range. Made from McLaren Vale shiraz, open-fermented and basket-pressed, it spends two years in a combination of French and American oak.
🍷🍷🍷🍷 **1997** Medium to full purple-red; the bouquet is clean, led by strong blackberry and black cherry fruit. On the palate slightly dusty sweet oak is very much more evident than on the bouquet, and while the flavours are rich, less oak would have made an even better, if not great, wine. **rating: 91**
best drinking 2007–2022 **best vintages** '95, '96, '97 **drink with** Beef in black bean sauce • $27.95

Hardys Sir James Cabernet Shiraz Merlot
A continuation of the brand extension from the nucleus of Sir James sparkling wines, and now covering mid-priced table wines, both white and red. This is a blend of McLaren Vale, Coonawarra and Padthaway-grown grapes matured in a mix of French and American oak.
🍷🍷🍷🍷 **1997** Medium red-purple; the bouquet is quite complex, with a mix of berry, earth, chocolate and game. The palate opens up promisingly with an array of the same flavours, but a slightly green finish detracts from an otherwise good wine. **rating: 84**
best drinking 2000–2003 **best vintages** NA **drink with** Rack of lamb • $13.95

Thomas Hardy Cabernet Sauvignon
First launched in 1994 when the 1989 vintage was released. Initially a blend of predominantly Coonawarra and McLaren Vale material, it is now entirely sourced from Coonawarra. The wine spends 18 months in a mix of

French and American oak, and is given at least two years bottle age prior to release. A wine at the opulent end of the scale, not unlike Wynns John Riddoch in style, and a prolific trophy and gold medal winner.

▼▼▼▼ **1995** Dense purple-red; very rich, very ripe cassis blackberry fruit on a fruit-laden bouquet. The palate is no less rich and ripe, with masses of fruit and appropriate tannins. **rating:** 92

best drinking 2005–2015 **best vintages** '89, '90, '91, '92, '94, '95 **drink with** Rich red meat dishes • $60

hardys (padthaway)　　NR

Stonehaven Winery, Riddoch Highway, Padthaway, SA 5271 **region** Padthaway
phone (08) 8765 6140 **fax** (08) 8765 6137 **open** Not
winemaker Tom Newton, Duncan McGillivray, Robert Mann **production** NFP **est.** 1998
product range ($15–35 R) Unwooded Chardonnay, Stonehaven Vineyards Chardonnay, Limestone Coast Chardonnay, Stonehaven Shiraz, Stonehaven Limestone Coast Shiraz, Cabernet Merlot, Cabernet Sauvignon.
summary It is, to say the least, strange that it should have taken 30 years for a substantial winery to be built at Padthaway. However, when BRL Hardy took the decision, it was no half measure: $20 million has been invested in what is the largest greenfields winery built in Australia for more than 20 years.

Hardys Stonehaven Limestone Coast Chardonnay

A Limestone Coast Zone blend of grapes from Padthaway, Elgin Valley and Wrattonbully.

▼▼▼▼ **1998** Light green-yellow; the bouquet is clean and youthful but light and fairly neutral; there is just a waft of citrus. The palate is crisp and youthful, with a touch of nectarine fruit and good length. **rating:** 85

best drinking 2000–2004 **best vintages** NA **drink with** Fresh crab cakes • $25

Hardys Stonehaven Chardonnay

Part of the portfolio of initial releases from the new Stonehaven winery. It shows clear region character throughout.

▼▼▼▼ **1999** Light to medium yellow-green; the crisp and delicate bouquet has abundant, scented passionfruit, nectarine and grapefruit aromas, characters which translate into the palate, which has good length and subtle oak. An elegant, unforced wine with good development potential. **rating:** 88

best drinking 2000–2005 **best vintages** NA **drink with** Wok-fried prawns • $15

Hardys Stonehaven Limited Release Chardonnay

The top-of-the-range release from BRL Hardys' new state-of-the-art winery at Padthaway, and an appropriate flag-bearer.

▼▼▼▼ **1998** Light green-yellow; clean and fresh, with light citrus/melon fruit and a delicate touch of vanilla oak. A wine with generous flavour on the palate, featuring bright citrus fruit; excellent length and finish. **rating:** 89

best drinking 2000–2006 **best vintages** NA **drink with** Braised neck of pork • $35

Hardys Stonehaven Shiraz

The better of the two Shiraz-based wines in the Stonehaven range, produced entirely from Padthaway fruit.

▼▼▼▽ **1996** Medium red-purple; the aromas have a slightly gamey background to cherry, plum and mint. Minty berry flavours, with slightly green tannins, hint at a degree of overcropping leading to imperfectly ripened fruit. **rating:** 84

best drinking 2001–2004 **best vintages** NA **drink with** Carpaccio of beef • $15

Hardys Stonehaven Limestone Coast Shiraz

The second label Limestone Coast accurately reflects the difference between it and the premium range.

▼▼▼▽ **1996** Medium red-purple; light cherry fruit with slightly heavier oak on the bouquet is followed by a palate which opens with cherry fruit flavours and closes with persistent tannins. Here the oak plays a positive role, sweetening the mid-palate fruit. **rating:** 84

best drinking 2001–2006 **best vintages** NA **drink with** Traditional Aussie meat pie • $25

Hardys Stonehaven Cabernet Merlot

The first release from the brand new Stonehaven winery established by BRL Hardy at Padthaway. The wine is a blend of Coonawarra, Padthaway and Wrattonbully material.

▼▼▼▽ **1997** Medium to full red-purple; the bouquet is quite powerful, offering a mix of earthy and briary characters balanced by some red berry fruit. The palate seems ultra-extractive, with heavy tannins which overwhelm the fruit. **rating:** 81

best drinking 2002–2005 **best vintages** NA **drink with** Barbecued sausages • $NA

Hardys Padthaway Cabernet Sauvignon
An invariably pleasant wine, made without any artifice and which allows the fruit to walk the talk.
ŸŸŸŸ 1997 Medium red-purple; the bouquet is smooth, moderately intense, with chocolatey overtones. A straightforward, no-frills style with some simple but pleasant fruit sustaining the palate. **rating:** 83
best drinking 2002–2004 **best vintages** NA **drink with** Braised beef pie • $18.95

harewood estate ★★★☆

Scotsdale Road, Denmark, WA 6333 **region** Great Southern
phone (08) 9840 9078 **fax** (08) 9840 9053 **open** By appointment
winemaker John Wade (Contract) **production** 700 **est.** 1988
product range ($29–30 R) Chardonnay, Pinot Noir.
summary Keith and Margie Graham have established a showpiece vineyard at Binalong. The majority of the grapes are sold to Howard Park and Domaine Chandon, but gradually increasing amounts of wine are being made under the Harewood Estate label. The wines have retail distribution in Perth and are exported to the UK but are otherwise only available by mail order.

Harewood Estate Chardonnay
Immaculate viticulture, with a mixture of high-tech trellis systems (Scott-Henry, Smart Dyson and Geneva Double Curtain) and varied row orientation pay dividends in this lush vineyard setting. The wine is barrel-fermented and matured in French oak for ten months.
ŸŸŸŸ 1998 Medium yellow-green; the clean and moderately intense bouquet has attractive peach, fig and melon fruit supported by subtle oak. The palate has plenty of weight and flavour in the same taste spectrum. An excellent cool-climate style. **rating:** 90
best drinking 2001–2005 **best vintages** '97, '98 **drink with** Seafood risotto • $30

hartzview wine centre ★★☆

RSD 1034 Off Cross Road, Gardners Bay, Tas 7112 **region** Southern Tasmania
phone (03) 6295 1623 **open** 7 days 9–5
winemaker Andrew Hood (Contract), Robert Patterson **production** NFP **est.** 1988
product range ($18 CD) Chardonnay, Pinot Noir; also a range of Pig and Whistle Hill fruit wines.
summary A combined wine centre, offering wines from a number of local Huon Valley wineries, and also newly erected and very comfortable accommodation for six people in a separate, self-contained house. Hartzview table wines (produced from 3 hectares of estate plantings) are much to be preferred to the self-produced Pig and Whistle Hill fruit wines.

haselgrove ★★★★

Foggo Road, McLaren Vale, SA 5171 **region** McLaren Vale
phone (08) 8323 8706 **fax** (08) 8323 8049 **open** Mon–Fri 9–5, weekends 10–5
winemaker Nick Haselgrove **production** 156 000 **est.** 1981
product range ($9.99–45 R) McLaren Vale Pictures Series Sauvignon Blanc, Chardonnay, Grenache, Shiraz, Merlot Cabernet; Futures Shiraz; Bentwing Chardonnay, Shiraz, Cabernet Sauvignon; premium releases under 'H' Reserve label; Sparkling, Port; lesser priced varietals under Sovereign Series.
summary Haselgrove Wines became a wholly owned subsidiary of the publicly listed Cranswick Premium Wines Limited in mid-1997. Under Nick Haselgrove's direction, the premium red wines, and in particular the 'H' Reserve range, have gone from strength to strength, the 1996 'H' Reserve Shiraz winning multiple trophies, including Best Wine of Show, at the 1998 Sydney International Wine Competition (otherwise known as the 'Top 100'). Exports to the UK, New Zealand and the US.

Haselgrove 'H' Reserve Viognier
A prime example of a trendy variety attracting a ludicrously high price.
ŸŸŸŸ 1999 Medium yellow-green; the bouquet is quite rich and positive, with some honeycomb aromas; the palate is soft, with hints of spice and even tobacco. However, it lacks acidity and focus. **rating:** 84
best drinking 2000–2002 **best vintages** NA **drink with** Kasseler • $45

Haselgrove 'H' Reserve Chardonnay
The grapes for this wine come principally from Haselgrove's Wrattonbully Vineyards (80 per cent), the remaining portion coming from McLaren Vale. The wine is barrel-fermented in French oak with a mix of cultured and native yeasts. The wine spends eight months on lees during which time it undergoes malolactic fermentation.

ΫΫΫΫ **1998** Medium yellow-green; the bouquet is clean and smooth, with peachy fruit and subtle oak. The palate is pleasantly smooth but lacks intensity; the shortcomings would appear to lie in the vineyard rather than the winery. **rating:** 85

best drinking 2000–2003 **best vintages** NA **drink with** Avocado and prawn salad • $22.80

Haselgrove McLaren Vale Chardonnay

Made using techniques similar to those adopted for the 'H' Reserve, but in this instance sourced primarily from McLaren Vale, with only 10 per cent or so coming from Wrattonbully. While the winemaking techniques are similar, fruit selection accounts for the major difference in the quality of the wines.

ΫΫΫΫ **1998** Light to medium yellow-green; the bouquet is of moderate intensity, and is rather simple. The palate is likewise simple, clean and smooth, with just a touch of nectarine. **rating:** 80

best drinking Drink now **best vintages** NA **drink with** Roast spatchcock • $14.90

Haselgrove Bentwing Shiraz

Produced entirely from shiraz grown at Wrattonbully, and spends 15 months in oak. The name comes from the bent wing bats which roost in the Naracoorte Caves.

ΫΫΫΫ **1999** Medium red-purple; the bouquet is clean, of light to medium intensity, with smooth cherry/berry fruit and subtle oak. The palate has good structure with nicely ripened sweet cherry shiraz fruit, gentle tannins and gentle oak. **rating:** 85

best drinking 2000–2005 **best vintages** NA **drink with** Barbecued beef • $22

Haselgrove 'H' Reserve Shiraz

There is no question this wine is often at the baroque end of the spectrum of Australian red winemaking, a wine for a winter's night and rich food, and not to be taken lightly. Has collected multiple trophies over the past few vintages.

ΫΫΫΫΫ **1997** The aromas of dark cherry and blackberry fruit are almost essencey yet are not jammy. Has a rich, luscious dark berry and chocolate palate, fine tannins and well-controlled oak. **rating:** 95

best drinking 2002–2017 **best vintages** '91, '94, '96, '97 **drink with** Eye fillet • $45

Haselgrove Picture Series Merlot

Like all of the Picture Series wines, made from 100 per cent McLaren Vale-grown grapes, and matured in a mix of used French and American oak barrels.

ΫΫΫΫ **1999** Medium red-purple; the bouquet is moderately intense, quite sweet and appropriately oaked. The light- to medium-bodied palate has a mix of sweet and more savoury fruit showing gentle varietal character. Unpretentious and easy. **rating:** 83

best drinking 2000–2003 **best vintages** NA **drink with** Lighter meat dishes • $17

Haselgrove Picture Series Cabernet Sauvignon

Fermented in open fermenters and basket-pressed, the wine spends 18 months in oak, mainly used.

ΫΫΫΫ **1998** Medium to full red-purple; the bouquet has quite aromatic and clean cassis/berry fruit, oak playing a minor role. The palate is quite powerful, with the tannins threatening to unbalance the finish, but with a bit of luck will soften before the fruit dies. **rating:** 86

best drinking 2002–2007 **best vintages** NA **drink with** Lamb shanks • $17

hastwell & lightfoot   NR

Foggo Road, McLaren Vale, SA 5171 **region** McLaren Vale
phone (08) 8323 8692 **fax** (08) 8323 8098 **open** Not
winemaker Nick Haselgrove (Contract) **production** 1000 **est.** 1990
product range ($12 ML) Shiraz, Cabernet.
summary Hastwell & Lightfoot is an offshoot of a rather larger grape growing business, with the majority of the grapes from the 15 hectares of vineyard being sold to others; the vineyard was planted in 1988 and the first grapes produced in 1990. Until the advent of GST, the wines were under the small business sales tax exemption, hence the mouthwateringly low prices. Incidentally, the labels are once seen, never forgotten. Exports to Germany, the US and New Zealand.

Hastwell & Lightfoot Shiraz

Sourced from the very best part of 5 hectares of estate plantings, and well made, although it is a living example of wine being made in the vineyard.

❦❦❦❦❦ **1998** Medium red-purple; quite sweet cherry and spice fruit is supported by subtle oak leading into an utterly seductive palate where soft, dark cherry, mint and vanilla flavours intermingle with soft tannins. **rating:** 90
best drinking 2001–2011 **best vintages** '98 **drink with** Ravioli • $12

Hastwell & Lightfoot Cabernet
A blend of 86 per cent Cabernet Sauvignon and 14 per cent Cabernet Franc. The '96, the predecessor of this wine, won a gold medal at the 1998 Australian Small Winemakers Show.
❦❦❦❦ **1998** Medium to full red-purple; the powerful bouquet has a range of savoury/earthy/chocolatey fruit which flows into chocolate and blackberry fruit on the palate, fleshed out with lots of ripe tannins and nicely balanced oak. **rating:** 89
best drinking 2002–2012 **best vintages** '96, '98 **drink with** Wood-fired pizza • $12

hawley vineyard NR
Hawley Beach, Hawley, Tas 7307 **region** Northern Tasmania
phone (03) 6428 6221 **fax** (03) 6428 6844 **open** 7 days
winemaker Andrew Pirie (Contract) **production** 1000 **est.** 1988
product range ($18–25 R) Rubicon Chardonnay, Unwooded Chardonnay, Rubicon Pinot Noir.
summary Hawley Vineyard overlooks Hawley Beach and thence northeast to Bass Strait. It is established on an historic 200-hectare farming property, with Hawley House offering dining and accommodation in a grand style. There are no other vineyards in what is a unique winegrowing region, and few hoteliers-cum-viticulturists as flamboyant as owner Simon Hawley. Limited distribution in Sydney.

Hawley Vineyard Unwooded Chardonnay
Together with most other wine-writers and wine judges in Australia, I shrink at the very mention of unwooded Chardonnay, but every now and then one comes along which suggests the style has legitimacy. Prior vintages suggest this wine flowers remarkably given sufficient time in bottle.
❦❦❦❦ **1998** Medium to full yellow, with some green tinges. A generous, aromatic bouquet with tropical and dried fruit aromas leads into a palate with great complexity, but is far from pristine, strongly suggesting botrytis at work. **rating:** 82
best drinking 2001–2003 **best vintages** '97 **drink with** White-fleshed fish • $20

Hawley Vineyard Pinot Noir
A most interesting wine, which won gold medals at the 1999 Cowra Wine Show and the Tasmanian Wines Show 2000.
❦❦❦❦ **1997** Medium red-purple; a fruit-driven bouquet offering very ripe albeit smooth cherry and plum fruit leads into a striking palate with brandied cherry/berry flavours in a wholly individual spectrum. **rating:** 90
best drinking 2001–2005 **best vintages** '97 **drink with** Coq au vin • $20

hay shed hill ★★★☆
RSM 398 Harmans Mill Road, Willyabrup, WA 6280 **region** Margaret River
phone (08) 9755 6234 **fax** (08) 9755 6305 **open** 7 days 10.30–5
winemaker Peter Stanlake **production** 17 000 **est.** 1987
product range ($13–35 CD) Sauvignon Blanc, Semillon, Chardonnay, Cabernet Sauvignon (light, unwooded), Cabernet Sauvignon, Pinot Noir, Cabernet Franc; Pitchfork Pink (Rosé), Pitchfork White, Pitchfork Pop, Pitchfork Red.
summary A landmark on the Margaret River scene, with a striking 200-tonne winery, a carefully devised business plan by the Morrison family, energetic marketing, and innovative label design. Wine quality has been a touch inconsistent, but the 'sold-out' sign so often displayed speaks for itself. At their best, tangy and incisive. The wines are distributed through retail outlets in Perth, Melbourne and Sydney, and are exported to the UK and the US.

hayward's whitehead creek NR
Lot 18A Hall Lane, Seymour, Vic 3660 **region** Goulburn Valley
phone (03) 5792 3050 **open** Mon–Sat 9–6, Sun 10–6
winemaker Sid Hayward, David Hayward **production** 600 **est.** 1975
product range ($7.50–12.50 CD) Riesling, Shiraz, Cabernet Sauvignon.
summary The last tastings, some years ago, were of somewhat rustic but full-flavoured wines. The ultra-low-yielding vineyards (4.5 hectares) are used solely to produce the Whitehead Creek wines.

heathcote winery ★★★☆

183–185 High Street, Heathcote, Vic 3523 **region** Bendigo
phone (03) 5433 2595 **fax** (03) 5433 3081 **open** Thurs–Sun 11–5
winemaker Mark Kelly **production** 6000 **est.** 1978
product range ($19–33.50 CD) Heathcote Winery range of Viognier, Chardonnay, Cane Cut, Mail Coach
Shiraz, Violet; 7th Horse range of Chardonnay and Shiraz (early-drinking styles predominantly sourced from
Padthaway).
summary The Heathcote Winery is now back in business with a vengeance. The wines are being produced
predominantly from the 12 hectares of estate vineyard, and some from local growers under long-term contracts.

Heathcote 7th Horse Chardonnay

A blend of Padthaway and Heathcote Chardonnay.
▼▼▼▽ **1998** Light green-yellow; the plain, smooth, light bouquet is followed by a similarly weighted, inoffensive
palate. It is slow-developing, and might well gain some useful complexity in bottle. **rating:** 80
best drinking 2000–2001 **best vintages** NA **drink with** Weisswurst • $15

Heathcote 7th Horse Shiraz

Part of the rebirth of Heathcote Winery, and which had a dream debut with the '97 vintage winning a trophy at
the 1998 Royal Adelaide Wine Show. It is a blend of Bendigo and Padthaway Shiraz.
▼▼▼▽ **1998** Strong red-purple colour is followed by a rich, dense and concentrated bouquet, with ripe plum and
cherry fruit. The palate has lots of fruit flavour and tannin; however, slightly gamey characters intrude, and the
flavour profile dips unexpectedly on the mid-palate. All in all, a curate's egg. **rating:** 83
best drinking 2001–2004 **best vintages** '97 **drink with** Kebabs • $15

Heathcote Barrel Select Shiraz

A wine which started life as a project to demonstrate that French oak is more suited to Heathcote Shiraz than
American. The wine was spotted by Heathcote's US distributor, Peter Weygandt, who effectively bought it on the
spot to prevent it being back-blended with a larger quantity of Mail Coach Shiraz. Only 60 cases were sold in
Australia.
▼▼▼▽ **1997** Medium red-purple; green canopy characters detract both from the bouquet and palate; there are
some sweet, fresh fruit flavours, but they don't win the battle. **rating:** 81
best drinking 2000–2003 **best vintages** NA **drink with** Grilled sausages • $30

heathfield ridge wines NR

Corner Caves Road and Penola Highway, Naracoorte, SA 5271 **region** Wrattonbully
phone (08) 8762 4133 **fax** (08) 8762 0141 **open** Mon–Sat 10–5, Sun and public holidays 10–4.30
winemaker Pat Tocaciu, Neil Doddridge **production** 20 000 **est.** 1998
product range Riesling, Sauvignon Blanc, Chardonnay, Shiraz, Merlot and Cabernet Sauvignon.
summary Heathfield Ridge Wines is the major winery in the Naracoorte region. Opened in time for the 1998
vintage, its major function was a contract crush facility but it offers full winemaking facilities for others and will
also release wines under the Heathfield Ridge label. Exports to the UK.

heggies vineyard ★★★★

Heggies Range Road, Eden Valley, SA 5235 **region** Eden Valley
phone (08) 8565 3203 **fax** (08) 8565 3380 **open** At Yalumba
winemaker Hugh Reimers **production** 20 000 **est.** 1971
product range ($16–24 R) Riesling, Viognier, Chardonnay, Botrytis Riesling, Cabernets.
summary Heggies was the second of the high-altitude (570 metres) vineyards established by S Smith & Sons
(Yalumba), with plantings on the 120-hectare former grazing property commencing in 1973. The once simple
view of Heggies as a better white than red wine producer has become more complicated, with the pendulum
swinging backwards and forwards according to vintage. Exports to all major markets.

Heggies Viognier

While viognier has been grown on the Mornington Peninsula, at Elgee Park, for many years, Yalumba (with a
separate importation of clonal material) was the first to commercialise viognier in Australia. The early vintages
produced fairly thin, ordinary wines, the first signs of real progress coming with the '93, '95 and '97 vintages. It
seems to be an odd-year progression, but the '99 takes Viognier into another dimension, at last showing
unmistakable varietal character.

🍷🍷🍷🍷 **1999** Medium to full yellow-green, bright and clear; the bouquet is rich, with the exotic fruit aromas the variety exhibits in the northern Rhône Valley. The palate, likewise, represents another step forwards in style and weight, rich and viscous, with a mix of pastille, lemon custard, apricot and honeycomb flavours. **rating:** 93

best drinking 2000–2003 **best vintages** '93, '95, '97, '99 **drink with** Pork fillet • $24

Heggies Chardonnay

Made, needless to say, from 100 per cent estate-grown grapes, barrel-fermented and always given time in bottle before it is brought onto the market. The result is a complex, rich wine, often sweet and toasty.

🍷🍷🍷🍷 **1997** Light to medium yellow-green; a tangy bouquet, with citrus/melon fruit and a nice hint of barrel-fermentation. The palate offers more of that tangy/citrus fruit, supported by subtle oak. Good acidity and length; an attractive wine now and in the years to come. **rating:** 91

best drinking 2000–2003 **best vintages** '86, '91, '93, '97 **drink with** Veal, turkey • $22.95

Heggies Merlot

First made its mark with the '93 vintage, repeating the performance in even more splendid fashion in 1994, and following up with a solid wine in 1995, and an even better wine in 1996.

🍷🍷🍷 **1996** Medium red-purple; cedary/earthy/leafy/savoury aromas intermingle with sweet berry fruit on the bouquet. The palate has plenty of weight and depth, coruscating with savoury/chocolate characters on the one hand and spicy/leafy notes on the other. **rating:** 88

best drinking 2001–2006 **best vintages** '93, '95, '96 **drink with** Rack of veal • $24

helm ★★★☆

Butt's Road, Murrumbateman, NSW 2582 **region** Canberra District
phone (02) 6227 5953 **fax** (02) 6227 0207 **open** Thur–Mon 10–5
winemaker Ken Helm **production** 3000 **est.** 1973
product range ($16–30 CD) Riesling Classic Dry, Chardonnay (Non Oaked), Merlot, Cabernet Merlot, Cabernet Sauvignon, Helm (Cabernet blend).
summary Ken Helm is well known as one of the more stormy petrels of the wine industry and is an energetic promoter of his wines and of the Canberra district generally. His wines have been consistent bronze medal winners, with silvers and the occasional gold dotted here and there, such as the gold medal to the 1997 Cabernet Merlot at the 1999 Sydney Royal Wine Show. The wines have limited retail distribution in New South Wales, ACT and Victoria.

henke ★★☆

175 Henke Lane, Yarck, Vic 3719 **region** Central Victorian Mountain Country
phone (03) 5797 6277 **fax** (03) 5797 6277 **open** By appointment
winemaker Tim Miller, Caroline Miller **production** 250 **est.** 1974
product range ($20 CD) Shiraz, Shiraz Cabernet.
summary Produces tiny quantities of deep-coloured, full flavoured, minty red wines known only to a chosen few. Typically, a range of back vintages up to five years of age are available at cellar door.

henkell wines NR

Melba Highway, Dixons Creek, Vic 3775 **region** Yarra Valley
phone (03) 9417 4144 **fax** (03) 9419 8873 **open** Weekends 11–5
winemaker Contract **production** 500 **est.** 1988
product range ($12–20 CD) Under the Henkell label Trocken, Trocken Piccolo, Chablis, Riesling Spatlese, Gutedel/Müller Thurgau (Süd-Baden), Cabernet Grenache, Port; under Henkell Yarra Valley are Sauvignon Blanc, Chardonnay, Pinot Noir and Cabernet Sauvignon.
summary Hans Henkell started with a 57-variety Heinz mix in the vineyard, but has now rationalised it to a total of 18 hectares of sauvignon blanc, chardonnay, pinot noir and cabernet sauvignon. Most of the grapes are sold, with small amounts contract-made each year. And yes, Hans Henkell is part of the family.

henley park wines NR

149 Swan Street, West Swan, WA 6055 **region** Swan District
phone (08) 9296 4328 **fax** (08) 9296 1313 **open** Tues–Sun 10–5
winemaker Claus Petersen, Lisbet Petersen **production** 3500 **est.** 1935
product range ($9.95–15.95 CD) Semillon, Chenin Blanc, Classic White, Muscat Gordo Blanco (late picked), Autumn Harvest (Sauternes style), Mousse Rosé Brut (Méthode Champenoise), Shiraz, Cabernet Sauvignon, Shiraz Cabernet Merlot, Tawny Port.

summary Henley Park, like so many Swan Valley wineries, was founded by a Yugoslav family, but it is now jointly owned by Danish and Malaysian interests, a multicultural mix if ever there was one. Majority owner and winemaker Claus Petersen arrived in 1986 and had his moment of glory in 1990 when Henley Park was the Most Successful Exhibitor at the Mount Barker Wine Show. Much of the production is sold through cellar door (and exported to Denmark and Malaysia).

henschke ★★★★★

Henschke Road, Keyneton, SA 5353 **region** Eden Valley
phone (08) 8564 8223 **fax** (08) 8564 8294 **open** Mon–Fri 9–4.30, Sat 9–12, public holidays 10–3
winemaker Stephen Henschke **production** 40 000 **est.** 1868
product range ($14–200 R) From the Henschke Eden Valley sources, Sauvignon Blanc, Chardonnay, Chenin Blanc, Dry White Frontignac, Joseph Hill Gewurztraminer, Louis Semillon, Tilly's Vineyard, Julius Riesling, Keyneton Estate, Mount Edelstone, Cyril Henschke Cabernet Sauvignon, Hill of Grace. From the Lenswood Vineyard in the Adelaide Hills, Green's Hill Riesling, Croft Chardonnay, Giles Pinot Noir, Abbott's Prayer Cabernet Merlot, Henschke Johann's Garden Grenache Shiraz Mourvedre, Barossa Ranges Eden Valley Chardonnay.
summary Unchallenged as the best medium-sized red wine producer in Australia and has gone from strength to strength over the past 14 years or so under the guidance of Stephen and Prue Henschke. The red wines fully capitalise on the very old, low-yielding, high-quality vines and are superbly made with sensitive but positive use of new small oak; the same skills are evident in the white winemaking. Hill of Grace is second only to Penfolds Grange as Australia's red wine icon. Exports to the UK, the US, Canada, New Zealand, Switzerland, France, Germany, Denmark, The Netherlands, Austria and Japan.

Henschke Julius Eden Valley Riesling

In a distinctly different style from the Green's Hill (Adelaide Hills) Riesling, this wine having more concentration and power but arguably less fragrance. Stephen Henschke is not only a great red winemaker, he has also dared to bottle this wine with a Stelvin cap.
▼▼▼▼ 1999 Medium yellow-green; generous lime and citrus fruit with flecks of mineral running through the bouquet. A generously flavoured, almost solid wine on the palate but arguably lacking a little focus. **rating: 88**
best drinking 2004–2009 **best vintages** NA **drink with** Barramundi • $23.60

Henschke Louis Eden Valley Semillon

Semillon in South Australia is usually surrounded by a forest of ugly American oak; at least on this score, Henschke avoids the trap.
▼▼▼▽ 1998 Light to medium yellow-green; the bouquet is clean, solid but not particularly aromatic; a big wine on the palate, with a slightly tough finish. **rating: 84**
best drinking 2000–2002 **best vintages** NA **drink with** Stir-fried abalone • $24.60

Henschke Hill Of Grace

Made entirely from 100-year-old shiraz vines on the Hill of Grace Vineyard planted in the late 1860s by a Henschke ancestor, Nicholas Stanitzki. Is second only to Penfolds Grange, which it rivals in terms of quality, scarcity and (almost) price. The wine has never been entered in wine shows, nor will it ever be: it has its own standards. Its soaring retail price bears testament to the public esteem in which the wine is rightly held.
▼▼▼▼▼ 1996 Dense purple-red; exceptionally rich, ripe and lusciously sweet blackberry, blackcurrant and mint fruit aromas herald a great wine from a great vintage. There is a spectacular range of flavours on the palate, akin to an exotic version of the '86. Average winter rainfall after drought years was followed by a mild spring and a mild, cool but windy summer. A cool, dry autumn provided an exceptionally long, slow ripening period and very good flavour development. A high-yield, high-quality year similar to 1990. **rating: 97**
best drinking 2006–2026 **best vintages** '59, '61, '62, '66, '78, '82, '85, '86, '88, '90, '91, '93, '96 **drink with** Rich casserole dishes • $200

Henschke Mount Edelstone

Made entirely from shiraz grown on the Mount Edelstone Vineyard, planted in the 1920s and acquired by Henschke in 1974, although the wine was first made (and labelled as such) in 1952. A wine of tremendous character and quality. The price is rapidly being pulled upwards by the Hill of Grace, but, here too, the wine quality justifies the price.

▼▼▼▼ **1997** Medium red-purple; the bouquet is clean but rather light and slightly leafy, tending simple. The palate is rather better — light but quite well balanced, with red fruits and some touches of sweet vanilla oak. Uncharacteristic tasting notes, perhaps, for a wine going through a particularly difficult phase of its development.

rating: 87

best drinking 2004–2012 **best vintages** '52, '56, '61, '66, '67, '78, '82, '86, '88, '90, '92, '93, '94, '95, '96 **drink with** Beef bourguignon • $63

Henschke Johann's Garden Grenache Shiraz Mourvedre

A relatively new arrival on the scene for Henschke, although the vineyard resources have been there for decades. The wine is a blend of 65 per cent Grenache, 25 per cent Shiraz and 15 per cent Mourvedre.

▼▼▼▼▽ **1998** Medium purple-red; clean, sweet, juicy/spicy varietal fruit aromas lead into a very attractive, supple palate with sweet berry fruit, fine tannins and minimal oak.

rating: 93

best drinking 2000–2005 **best vintages** '98 **drink with** Coq au vin • $32

Henschke Abbott's Prayer Cabernet Merlot

The evocatively named Abbott's Prayer links the history, religion and pioneers of the Adelaide Hills. Right from the first vintage, this Merlot-dominant blend of Merlot, Cabernet Sauvignon and Cabernet Franc has been of exceptional quality. Unusually for Henschke, it is matured entirely in French oak.

▼▼▼▼▽ **1997** Medium red-purple; the bouquet is multifaceted, offering lovely savoury fruit with gently sweet oak; dark berry fruit with foresty notes and subtle oak are the best features of the palate; the lingering tannins are a little strong, but may well soften with further bottle age.

rating: 91

best drinking 2002–2007 **best vintages** '89, '90, '91, '92, '93, '94, '96, '97 **drink with** Guinea fowl in red wine sauce • $63

Henschke Cyril Henschke Cabernet

The 1978 vintage was the first release in 1980, made by Stephen Henschke in memory of his father who had died the previous year. A blend of 60 per cent Cabernet Sauvignon, 20 per cent Merlot and 20 per cent Cabernet Franc which spends 21 months in new French oak. A prolific trophy and gold medal winner at national wine shows. Undoubtedly one of the three top Henschke wines and among the best Cabernets in Australia.

▼▼▼▼▼ **1996** Medium purple-red; a marvellously fine, elegant and fragrant bouquet featuring perfectly ripened cassis redcurrant fruit. The palate does not disappoint, being equally elegant and fine, particularly the absolutely beautiful tannins and gentle oak. It is fascinating to see how the fruit in the wine has soaked up the new oak.

rating: 94

best drinking 2001–2015 **best vintages** '78, '80, '85, '86, '88, '90, '91, '92, '93, '94, '96 **drink with** Roast lamb • $91

henty brook estate   NR

Box 49, Dardanup, WA 6236 **region** Geographe
phone (08) 9728 1459 **fax** (08) 9728 1459 **open** By appointment
winemaker James Pennington (Contract) **production** 500 **est.** 1994
product range Semillon, Sauvignon Blanc, Shiraz.
summary One hectare each of shiraz and sauvignon blanc and half a hectare of semillon were planted in the spring of 1994 and are still coming into bearing. James Pennington is the contract-winemaker; the first releases will follow over the next few years.

heritage farm wines   NR

RMB 1005 Murray Valley Highway, Cobram, Vic 3655 **region** Goulburn Valley
phone (03) 5872 2376 **open** 7 days 9–5
winemaker Kevin Tyrrell **production** 5000 **est.** 1987
product range ($5–11 CD) Riesling, Traminer Riesling, Chardonnay are varietal releases; there are a considerable number of generic releases and fortified wines on sale at cellar door.
summary Heritage Farm claims to be the only vineyard and orchard in Australia still using horsepower, with Clydesdales used for most of the general farmwork. The winery and cellar-door area also boasts a large range of restored horse-drawn farm machinery and a bottle collection. All of the wines are sold by mailing list and cellar door.

heritage wines ★★★★☆

106a Seppeltsfield Road, Marananga, SA 5355 **region** Barossa Valley
phone (08) 8562 2880 **fax** (08) 8562 2692 **open** 7 days 11–5
winemaker Stephen Hoff **production** 6000 **est.** 1984
product range ($11.50–25 CD) Riesling, Semillon, Chardonnay, Shiraz, Cabernet Franc, Cabernet Malbec, Cabernet Sauvignon, Barossa Shiraz, Rossco's Shiraz.
summary A little-known winery which deserves a far wider audience, for Stephen Hoff is apt to produce some startlingly good wines. At various times the Chardonnay, Riesling (from old Clare Valley vines) and Rossco's Shiraz (now the flag-bearer) have all excelled, at other times not. The red wines were emphatically on song in the 1998 vintage. Limited exports to the UK through Australian Wine Agencies, and in New Zealand.

Heritage Wines Barossa Shiraz

Produced largely, if not entirely, from 6 hectares of estate plantings.
YYYY 1998 Medium to full red-purple; the bouquet offers ripe cherry and plum fruit with minimal oak input; the palate is well crafted and well structured and while it is, like the bouquet, fruit-driven, it has abundant flavour and length. **rating:** 89
best drinking 2002–2008 **best vintages** '98 **drink with** Steak and kidney pie • $18

Heritage Wines Rossco's Shiraz

The flag-bearer for Heritage Wines is not, as one might imagine, estate-grown, but comes from an old vineyard nurtured by Ross Kalleske — hence the name.
YYYYY 1998 Dense red-purple; the bouquet has concentrated dark fruit mixed with dark chocolate; oak is no doubt there, but you cannot see it. The palate has deep, structured dark berry fruit flavours and fine, persistent tannins. Fruit-driven, and while enormously rich and powerful, is not the least bit extractive. **rating:** 94
best drinking 2003–2013 **best vintages** '98 **drink with** Roast kid • $25

Heritage Wines Cabernet Sauvignon

Drawn in part from 1 hectare of estate plantings. Conventionally matured in a mix of new and used American oak barrels.
YYYYY 1998 Full red-purple; the clean, firm bouquet offers strongly delineated, ripe Barossa cabernet fruit, the palate in the same marvellous fruit-driven style, with excellent concentration and balance. **rating:** 94
best drinking 2003–2010 **best vintages** '98 **drink with** Barbecued beef • $19

heritage wines of stanthorpe ★★☆

Granite Belt Drive, Cottonvale, Qld 4375 **region** Granite Belt
phone (07) 4685 2197 **fax** (07) 4685 2112 **open** 7 days 9–5
winemaker Jim Barnes **production** 8000 **est.** 1992
product range ($10.50–22.50 CD) Semillon Chardonnay, Sauvignon Blanc, Classic White (Chardonnay Semillon Sauvignon Blanc), Chardonnay, Simply Red, Club Red, Shiraz, Fortified and flavoured wines.
summary A tourist-oriented venture, emphasised by the opening of a new cellar door at Mount Tambourine (corner Bartletto Road and The Shelf Road) in an old church converted into a tasting and sales area, with views over the Gold Coast hinterland; also incorporating a restaurant, barbecue area and art gallery. The estate plantings comprise chardonnay (2 hectares), merlot (2 hectares), shiraz (1 hectare) and cabernet sauvignon (1 hectare).

hermes morrison wines NR

253 Swan Ponds Road, Woodstock, NSW 2793 **region** Other Wineries of NSW
phone (02) 6345 0153 **fax** (02) 6345 0153 **open** 7 days 10–5 summer, winter weekends and public holidays
winemaker Jill Lindsay (Contract) **production** 600 **est.** 1990
product range ($12–15 CD) Riesling, Semillon, Sauvignon Blanc, Chardonnay, Pinot Noir, Shiraz Cabernet.
summary The Morrison family established their Hermes Pol Dorset Stud in 1972, which continues but has now been joined by Hermes Morrison wines. The cellar door has been established by the side of a large lake fed by cold, clear water welling up from subterranean caves, and a ten-minute walk takes you to the summit of Mount Palatine, one of the highest peaks in the shire and with a spectacular view of the Canobolas Mountains 80 kilometres away.

herons rise vineyard   NR

Saddle Road, Kettering, Tas 7155 **region** Southern Tasmania
phone (03) 6267 4339 **fax** (03) 6267 4245 **open** By appointment
winemaker Andrew Hood **production** 300 **est.** 1984
product range ($12.50–20 CD) Muller Thurgau, Dry White, Pinot Noir.
summary Sue and Gerry White run a small stone country guesthouse in the D'Entrecasteaux Channel area and
basically sell the wines produced from the surrounding 1 hectare of vineyard to those staying at the guesthouse.
The postal address for bookings is PO Box 271, Kettering, Tas 7155.

hesperos wines   NR

36 Elva Street, Margaret River, WA 6285 **region** Margaret River
phone (08) 9757 3302 **fax** (08) 9757 3302 **open** By appointment
winemaker Jürg Muggli **production** 1250 **est.** 1993
product range ($18.50–30 CD) Sauvignon Blanc, Shiraz.
summary Hesperos is the venture of Jürg Muggli and Sandra Hancock. It supplies Jürg Muggli's winemaking
skills to Xanadu, where Muggli has been resident winemaker for many years. It also has a 30-hectare property near
Witchcliffe between Cape Mentelle and Devil's Lair, with the potential of 15 hectares of vineyard; planting
commenced in the winter of 1999. In the meantime the Hesperos wines are made from purchased grapes; the first
wine produced under the Hesperos label was a 1993 Shiraz, followed by a 1995 Sauvignon Blanc. Shiraz and
Sauvignon Blanc have been produced in each successive vintage. Exports to Japan, Switzerland and Germany.

hewitson   ★★★★☆

16 McGowan Avenue, Unley, SA 5061 **region** Other Wineries of SA
phone (08) 8271 5755 **fax** (08) 8271 5570 **open** Not
winemaker Dean Hewitson **production** 4500 **est.** 1996
product range ($18–37 R) La Source Eden Valley Riesling, L'Oizeau Shiraz, Old Garden Mourvedre, Barossa
Valley Shiraz, Barossa Valley Grenache.
summary Dean Hewitson was a Petaluma winemaker for ten years, and during that time managed to do three
vintages in France and one in Oregon as well as undertaking his Masters at UC Davis, California. It is hardly
surprising that the Hewitson wines are immaculately made from a technical viewpoint. However, he has also
managed to source 30-year-old riesling from the Eden Valley and 70-year-old shiraz from McLaren Vale for his
first two releases, following on with a 1998 Barossa Valley Mourvedre produced from 145-year-old vines at
Rowland Flat, and a Barossa Valley Shiraz and Grenache, coming from 60-year-old vines at Tanunda. The
vineyards are now under long-term contracts to Ian Hewitson. Exports to New Zealand, China, Japan, Malaysia,
Singapore, the US, Canada, Finland, The Netherlands, Norway, Germany and the UK.

Hewitson La Source Eden Valley Riesling

Produced from grapes grown on two 30-year-old plantings in the Eden Valley, and does full justice to the quality
of the source.
▼▼▼▼♡ **1999** Light yellow-green; the bouquet is quite powerful and concentrated, with a mix of dry, slatey and
more citrussy aromas. An impressive palate, long, concentrated and lingering, with flavours of herb, mineral and
lime. Sure to age well.   **rating:** 90
best drinking 2003–2010 **best vintages** '98, '99 **drink with** Summer salads • $17

Hewitson Barossa Shiraz

Dean Hewitson has secured a ten-year option on the grapes from a vineyard planted in the 1920s near the banks
of the North Para River on the outskirts of Tanunda. After a seven-day fermentation, with a temperature peak of
around 30°C, and with malolactic fermentation already underway, the must is pressed and the wine taken direct to
barrel for the finish of both the alcoholic and malolactic fermentation. A complex programme of barrel maturation
follows until the wine is egg white-fined and bottled without filtration 16-18 months after vintage.
▼▼▼▼▼ **1998** Deep red, with some purple; there is abundant, solid, dark berry and chocolate fruit running
through the bouquet, with well-balanced oak. The richly textured palate has abundant dark fruit flavours, yet
avoids going over the edge into jammy territory. As with the bouquet, the oak is nicely handled.   **rating:** 94
best drinking 2003–2008 **best vintages** '98 **drink with** Kangaroo fillet • $37

Hewitson L'Oizeau Shiraz

Produced from dry-grown, 70-year-old vines in McLaren Vale. It takes its name from the brigantine *Josephine L'Oizeau* which was shipwrecked on the Fleurieu Peninsula in 1856, taking its cargo of wine, spirits and tobacco down with it. Why anyone would wish to be reminded of that, I don't know, but I am not a brand manager.

▼▼▼▼▽ **1997** Medium to full red-purple; ripe, concentrated plum, prune and earth fruit on the bouquet is repeated on the palate, with touches of mint. Overall, very ripe, and seemingly higher than the 13.5 degrees alcohol. To be hypercritical, a fraction extractive.   **rating:** 92

best drinking 2001–2007 **best vintages** NA **drink with** Hearty red meat dishes • $37

Hewitson Old Garden Mourvedre

Mourvedre (which is still often incorrectly called Mataro in Australia) is usually blended with Shiraz and/or Grenache. Once can see why, although this is an interesting wine.

▼▼▼▼ **1998** Medium to full red-purple; clean plum and savoury fruit with restrained oak on the bouquet is followed by a palate with plenty of plum and chocolate fruit, promising much until the tannins start to take over on the finish.   **rating:** 89

best drinking 2003–2008 **best vintages** NA **drink with** Smoked beef • $37

hickinbotham   NR

Nepean Highway (near Wallaces Road), Dromana, Vic 3936 **region** Mornington Peninsula
phone (03) 5981 0355 **fax** (03) 5981 0355 **open** 7 days
winemaker Andrew Hickinbotham **production** 5000 **est.** 1981
product range ($14–26 CD) King Valley Riesling, Chardonnay, Classic White, Taminga, Sparkling (Strawberry Kiss and Futures), Pinot Noir, Merlot, Shiraz, Cabernet Merlot.
summary After a peripatetic period and a hiatus in winemaking, Hickinbotham established a permanent vineyard and winery base at Dromana. It now makes only Mornington Peninsula wines, drawing in part on 10 hectares of estate vineyards, and in part on contract-grown fruit. The wines are principally sold through cellar door and mail order. 1998 The Taminga (84 points) is an interesting wine, unique to Hickinbotham, and an Australian-bred variety created by the CSIRO. Grapey, spicy, floral aromas and flavours are the key.

hidden creek   NR

Eukey Road, Ballandean, Qld 4382 **region** Granite Belt
phone (07) 4684 1383 **fax** (07) 4684 1355 **open** Mon–Fri 12–3, weekends 10–4
winemaker Adrien Kuffer **production** 1400 **est.** 1998
product range ($13.50–18 CD) Semillon, Chardonnay, Mountain Muscat, Shiraz, First Block Shiraz, Merlot.
summary A beautifully located vineyard and winery on a ridge overlooking the Ballandean township and the Severn River valley, separated from Girraween National Park by Doctors Creek. The granite boulder-strewn hills mean that the 70-hectare property will only provide a little over 6 hectares of vineyard, in turn divided into six different blocks. The two wines tasted ('97 Dry White and '95 Shiraz) were of modest but acceptable quality.

highbank   NR

Riddoch Highway, Coonawarra, SA 5263 **region** Coonawarra
phone (08) 8736 3311 **fax** (08) 8736 3122 **open** By appointment
winemaker Dennis Vice, Trevor Mast **production** 1200 **est.** 1986
product range ($20–25 CD) Chardonnay, Basket Pressed Cabernet Blend, Basket Pressed Cabernet Sauvignon.
summary Mount Gambier lecturer in viticulture Dennis Vice makes a tiny quantity of smooth, melon-accented Chardonnay and stylish Coonawarra Cabernet Blend of good quality which are sold through local restaurants and cellar door, with limited Melbourne distribution. The wines have retail distribution through the eastern States, and are exported to the US, Taiwan, Japan, Malaysia, Hong Kong, China, Singapore, Germany, Belgium, Luxembourg, The Netherlands, New Zealand and Canada.

highland heritage estate   ★★★☆

Mitchell Highway, Orange, NSW 2800 **region** Orange
phone (02) 6361 3612 **fax** (02) 6361 3613 **open** Mon–Fri 9–3, weekends 9–5
winemaker John Hordern, Rex D'Aquino **production** 3500 **est.** 1984
product range ($10–30 CD) Under the Mount Canobolas label: Chardonnay, Sauvignon Blanc, Pinot Noir; Gosling Creek Chardonnay; and the newly released Wellwood Estate label.
summary The estate plantings have increased from 4 hectares to over 15 hectares, with new plantings in 1995 and 1997 to come into full production by 2001. The tasting facility is unusual: a converted railway carriage overlooking the vineyard.

highway wines   NR

612 Great Northern Highway, Herne Hill, WA 6056 **region** Swan District
phone (08) 9296 4354 **open** Mon–Sat 8.30–6
winemaker Tony Bakranich **production** 4000 **est.** 1954
product range ($5–14.50 CD) Exclusively Fortified wines, of which 20 are available, including six different styles of Sherry, six Muscats, three Ports, and so forth.
summary A survivor of another era, when literally dozens of such wineries plied their business in the Swan Valley. It still enjoys a strong local trade, selling much of its wine in fill-your-own-containers, and 2-litre flagons, with lesser quantities sold by the bottle.

hill-smith estate   ★★★★

PO Box 10, Angaston, SA 5353 **region** Eden Valley
phone (08) 8561 3200 **fax** (08) 8561 3393 **open** At Yalumba
winemaker Robert Hill-Smith, Hugh Reimers **production** 6000 **est.** 1973
product range ($18 R) Sauvignon Blanc, Chardonnay.
summary Part of the Yalumba stable, drawing upon its own estate plantings comprising 23 hectares of chardonnay and sauvignon blanc. Over the years has produced some excellent wines, but quality does seem to vary significantly with vintage, and the winery rating is a compromise between the best and the least. Exports to all major markets.

Hill-Smith Estate Sauvignon Blanc

Made from estate-grown Sauvignon Blanc produced from the east-facing 'Grass Tree Block' situated at the northern end of the Adelaide Hills, 650 metres above sea level. From time to time the wine has been piercingly intense in varietal character, in other years a little more subdued. Some will prefer one extreme, some the other.
TTTT 1999 Medium yellow-green; the bouquet is rich and ripe, with gooseberry and tropical fruit; the fleshy, rich, soft tropical gooseberry fruit on the palate provides excellent mouthfeel in a generous style.   **rating:** 87
best drinking 2000–2001 **best vintages** '82, '84, '86, '92, '93, '94, '95, '96, '99 **drink with** Fresh mussels • $18

hills of plenty   NR

370 Yan Yean Road, Yarrambat, Vic 3091 **region** Port Phillip Zone
phone (03) 9436 2264 **fax** (03) 9436 2264 **open** Last Sun of each month 12–5
winemaker Karen Coulston **production** 400 **est.** 1998
product range ($13–18 ML) Riesling, Sauvignon Blanc, Chardonnay, Pinot Noir, Cabernet Sauvignon.
summary Hills of Plenty has been established just outside the Melbourne Metropolitan area, a few minutes drive north of Greensborough. There is a tiny 0.2-hectare vineyard of riesling, chardonnay and cabernet sauvignon around the winery, but most of the fruit is purchased from other regions, notably Geelong, Gippsland and Swan Hill. The tiny production means that the cellar door only opens once a month, but is turned into a festive occasion with live music, and picnics or barbecues welcome.

hillstowe   ★★★★☆

104 Main Road, Hahndorf, SA 5245 **region** Adelaide Hills
phone (08) 8388 1400 **fax** (08) 8388 1411 **open** 7 days 10–5
winemaker Chris Laurie **production** 14 000 **est.** 1980
product range ($15.95–45 R) A range of vineyard and varietal-designated wines of ascending price and quality, being Buxton Sauvignon Blanc, Chardonnay, Buxton Shiraz, Buxton Cabernet Merlot; and at the top end Adelaide Hills Udy's Mill Chardonnay, Udy's Mill Pinot Noir, Mary's Hundred Shiraz, Lenswood Merlot.
summary Founded by renowned viticulturist David Paxton and Chris Laurie, but now owned by the latter and his family. Its principal vineyard, Udy's Mill, at Lenswood has 17 hectares planted, supplementing McLaren Vale grapes coming from the Buxton Vineyard. The wines are exported to the UK, Canada, the US, Europe and Asia.

Hillstowe Sauvignon Blanc

McLaren Vale and its adjacent hills have proved to be the most consistent producers of quality Sauvignon Blanc in Australia. The maritime-cooled climate produces wines which retain good varietal character, grassier in the cooler vintages and more tropical in the warmer years. This wine is a good example of the district style.
TTTT 1999 Light green-yellow; the attractively aromatic bouquet offers passionfruit and gooseberry followed by a light- to medium-weight palate with crisp, clean fruit.   **rating:** 85
best drinking 2000–2001 **best vintages** '90, '93, '94, '96 **drink with** King George whiting • $15.95

Hillstowe Buxton Sauvignon Blanc

A blend of Adelaide Hills and McLaren Vale grapes, stainless steel-fermented and early-bottled.

♥♥♥♥♀ **1999** Light straw-green; voluminous passionfruit aromas are quite striking, and are not the least reductive or sweaty. Fresh passionfruit flavours run through the mid-palate, followed by a crisp, clean, dry, slightly minerally finish. Great stuff.   **rating: 90**

best drinking 2000–2002 **best vintages** '99 **drink with** Blue swimmer crab   • $15.95

Hillstowe Buxton Chardonnay

Produced from Hillstowe's Buxton Vineyard established on alluvial flats in the heart of McLaren Vale, and typically released with two to three years bottle age.

♥♥♥♥ **1998** Medium yellow-green; while the bouquet is not particularly intense, it does have quite complex nectarine, fig and cashew fruit; the medium-weight palate is fruit-driven and pleasantly flavoured.   **rating: 86**

best drinking 2000–2001 **best vintages** NA **drink with** Gnocchi   • $15.95

Hillstowe Udy's Mill Pinot Noir

After a series of pleasant but unremarkable wines, produced an absolute blockbuster in 1998. Made from estate plantings which are now approaching ten years of age.

♥♥♥♥♀ **1998** Excellent purple-red colour; the bouquet is concentrated and complex, with predominantly plummy fruit and some spicy overtones. The palate provides plum, forest and spice flavours in abundance; tasted on several occasions, with mixed outcomes for the weight and finish, sometimes over the top, sometimes not. Seems certain to age well.   **rating: 94**

best drinking 2000–2008 **best vintages** '98 **drink with** Rich game   • $34.50

Hillstowe Mary's Hundred Shiraz

Mary's Hundred has a history to put the most voluble of the d'Arenberg stories to shame. Mary Laurie has been fairly described as South Australia's first woman winemaker, taking over winemaking responsibility from her husband Buxton Laurie when he died in 1876, continuing that role until 1892 when she suffered a stroke. This wine, produced from very old vines (some more than 100 years old) at the Laurie family's McLaren Vale vineyard, is named in her honour.

♥♥♥♥♀ **1998** Strong red-purple; complex berry, spice and sweet leather aromas run through the rich bouquet; dark berry and chocolate flavours provide a flavoursome yet elegant wine with subtle oak and good length. A welcome relief from the heavy-hitting high-alcohol McLaren Vale style.   **rating: 91**

best drinking 2003–2013 **best vintages** '96, '97, '98 **drink with** Rack of lamb   • $45

Hillstowe Buxton Cabernet Merlot

A 100 per cent McLaren Vale wine; 60 per cent Cabernet Sauvignon and 40 per cent Merlot which spends 12 months in predominantly used French oak barriques.

♥♥♥♥ **1998** Medium red-purple; the bouquet is fruit-driven, with a mix of earthy and more chocolatey fruit aromas; the palate has clean, fresh, berry fruit with flecks of mint and chocolate, rounded off by slightly savoury tannins on the finish.   **rating: 88**

best drinking 2003–2008 **best vintages** '98 **drink with** Roast veal   • $19.50

&❧ hills view vineyards   NR

4 Farr Court, Para Hills West, SA 5096 **region** McLaren Vale
phone (08) 8260 5964 **fax** (08) 8260 5964 **open** Not
winemaker Brett Howard **production** 10 000 **est.** 1998
product range ($9.99–29.99 R) Three ranges of wines produced: Blewitt Springs Semillon, Chardonnay, Shiraz and Cabernet Sauvignon; Howard Fleurieu Semillon and Coonawarra Shiraz; Hills View Chardonnay Verdelho, Shiraz and Shiraz Cabernet.
summary District Veteran Brett Howard, with 20 years winemaking experience, is now employed as winemaker for Hills View Vineyards, producing the Hills View Vineyards range of wines, the Blewitt Springs range and the single wine under the Howard label. The latter is a Coonawarra Shiraz released only in the best vintages.

---

hjt vineyards   NR

Keenan Road, Glenrowan, Vic 3675 **region** Rutherglen and Glenrowan
phone (03) 5766 2252 **fax** (03) 5765 3260 **open** Fri, Sat, 10–5 and Sunday during school holidays
winemaker Wendy Tinson **production** 1200 **est.** 1979

product range ($11.50–17.50 CD) A varietal range, with occasional use of bin numbers denoting winemaking approaches, Bin 4 being more delicate, Bin 19 fuller-bodied. Wines include Riesling Bins 4 and 19, Chardonnay, Chenin Blanc Bin 19, Late Picked Riesling, Pinot Noir, Cabernet Pinot, Shiraz, Cabernet Sauvignon, Merlot, Tawny Port.

summary Founded by the late Harry Tinson after he left Baileys following a long and illustrious stewardship, and now run by his daughter Wendy Tinson, with tiny production all sold from the cellar door.

hoffmann's NR

Ingoldby Road, McLaren Flat, SA 5171 **region** McLaren Vale
phone (08) 8383 0232 **fax** (08) 8383 0232 **open** 7 days 10–5
winemaker Nick Holmes (Consultant) **production** 500 **est.** 1996
product range ($13–17 CD) Chardonnay, Shiraz, Cabernet Sauvignon.

summary Peter and Anthea Hoffmann have been growing grapes at their property in Ingoldby Road since 1978, and Peter Hoffmann has worked at various wineries in McLaren Vale since 1979. Both he and Anthea have undertaken courses at the Regency TAFE Institute in Adelaide, and (in Peter Hoffmann's words) 'in 1996 we decided that we knew a little about winemaking and opened a small cellar door'. Only small quantities of wine are made for the Hoffmann's label; the balance of the production is sold to Mildara Blass (for the Ingoldby label).

hollick ★★★★

Riddoch Highway, Coonawarra, SA 5263 **region** Coonawarra
phone (08) 8737 2318 **fax** (08) 8737 2952 **open** 7 days 9–5
winemaker Ian Hollick, David Norman **production** 30 000 **est.** 1983
product range ($12.20–51 CD) A very disciplined array of products with Sauvignon Blanc Semillon, Unoaked Chardonnay and Shiraz Cabernet Malbec at the lower end of the price range; Reserve Chardonnay and Cabernet Sauvignon Merlot in the middle, along with Sparkling Merlot; Ravenswood, the deluxe Cabernet Sauvignon at the top end. Also small range of limited cellar-door releases.

summary Hollick has, if it were possible, added to the reputation of Coonawarra since it released its first wines in the mid-1980s. Winner of many trophies (including the most famous of all, the Jimmy Watson), its wines are well crafted and competitively priced, although sometimes a little on the light side. National distribution in all States; exports to the UK, the US, New Zealand, Canada, Hong Kong, Singapore and Switzerland.

Hollick Riesling

Riesling occupies only a tiny part (1.5 hectares) of just under 100 hectares of estate plantings, and there are those who advocate its extermination from Coonawarra as a whole. Properly grown and made, it in fact produces delicious wine with a distinctive regional character.

▼▼▼▼ 1999 Light to medium yellow-green; the bouquet is moderately floral, with citrus and some mineral notes; the palate is particularly well balanced, with that almost filigreed delicacy of Coonawarra, and is perfectly balanced. **rating: 89**

best drinking 2000–2005 **best vintages** '99 **drink with** Light seafood • $12.10

Hollick The Nectar

Predominantly Riesling (78 per cent), the remainder Sauvignon Blanc and Semillon with what seems to be a moderate level of botrytis infection.

▼▼▼▽ 1999 Bright yellow-green; the bouquet is quite intense, ranging through apricot to pineapple. An attractive sweet wine on the palate, albeit a fraction simple in textural terms. The overall balance is quite good. **rating: 84**

best drinking 2000–2004 **best vintages** NA **drink with** Fruit tart • $17.50

Hollick Shiraz Cabernet

1998 may prove to be as good as 1996 for Coonawarra and elsewhere in South Australia, which is a pretty big call. The 1998 Hollick Shiraz Cabernet is but one of many examples;

▼▼▼▼ 1998 Strongly coloured; the bouquet has plenty of intensity, with a mix of savoury/earthy/berry aromas leading into a marvellously fleshy palate with lovely mouthfeel, sweet fruit and fine, ripe tannins. An uncomplicated wine at an uncomplicated price. **rating: 89**

best drinking 2001–2008 **best vintages** '98 **drink with** Lamb loin • $14.30

Hollick Coonawarra Cabernet Merlot

A blend of 80 per cent Cabernet Sauvignon and 20 per cent Merlot, matured in a mix of French and American oak barrels for a period of 12 months.

♈♈♈♈ 1998 Medium to full red-purple; the aromas of the bouquet open with earthy notes, then leaf and mint and finally berry; it is quite sweet and smooth red berry fruit which drives the palate, gently supported by a touch of oak and soft tannins.   **rating:** 85

best drinking 2003–2008 **best vintages** '84, '88, '90, '91, '94, '98 **drink with** Gently spiced Asian meat dishes
• $18.50

hollyclare   NR

Lot 6 Milbrodale Road, Broke, NSW 2330 **region** Lower Hunter Valley
phone (02) 6579 1193 **fax** (02) 6579 1269 **open** Weekends 10–5
winemaker Tamburlaine (Contract) **production** 2500 **est.** 1987
product range ($15–18.50 CD) Chardonnay, Unoaked Chardonnay, Chardonnay Semillon, Semillon, Shiraz.
summary John Holdsworth established the Hollyclare Vineyard (now totalling 3 hectares of chardonnay, semillon and shiraz) ten years ago, but the Hollyclare label is a relatively new one on the market. While the wines are made under contract at Tamburlaine, Hollyclare has its own dedicated wine tanks and all of the wines are estate-grown.

holm oak   ★★★☆

RSD 256 Rowella, West Tamar, Tas 7270 **region** Northern Tasmania
phone (03) 6394 7577 **fax** (03) 6394 7350 **open** 7 days 10–5
winemaker Nick Butler, Julian Alcorso **production** 3000 **est.** 1983
product range ($16–25 R) Riesling, Pinot Noir Chardonnay (still table wine), Tyrian Rosé, Pinot Noir, Cabernet Sauvignon.
summary The Butler family produces tremendously rich and strongly flavoured red wines from the vineyard situated on the banks of the Tamar River, and which takes its name from the grove of oak trees planted around the turn of the century and originally intended for the making of tennis racquets. Together with Marion's Vineyard, it suggests that this section of the Tamar Valley may even be too warm for pinot noir in some vintages (not '97); certainly it is best suited to cabernet sauvignon and chardonnay.

Holm Oak Riesling

The first commercial release of Riesling from Holm Oak, and available only at cellar door and in Tasmanian liquor outlets. Contract-made by Julian Alcorso at Tamar Ridge.
♈♈♈♈♈ 1999 Medium yellow-green; a marvellously fragrant and spicy bouquet with a mix of passionfruit and apple cake is followed by a palate full of high-toned flavour with a passionfruit core. Very well balanced, with sweetness and acidity neatly counterpoised.   **rating:** 90

best drinking 2000–2009 **best vintages** '99 **drink with** Sweet and sour pork • $20

Holm Oak Pinot Noir

Nothing known about the fermentation methods employed, but the wine is estate-grown and spends 11 months in barrel, being bottled just prior to the ensuing vintage. Since 1997 the quality and style of the Pinot Noir seems to have taken a giant stride forward.
♈♈♈♈ 1998 Excellent purple-red colour; attractively ripened, sweet plum and cherry varietal fruit is supported by subtle oak on the bouquet. The palate has more of that attractive plummy Pinot Noir varietal fruit; a little more structural complexity would have lifted the wine into the highest category. Retasted January 2000 with similar notes and points; developing nicely.   **rating:** 89

best drinking 2000–2003 **best vintages** '98 **drink with** Quail • $25

home hill   NR

73 Nairn Street, Ranelagh, Tas 7109 **region** Southern Tasmania
phone (03) 6228 0128 **fax** (03) 6264 1069 **open** Not
winemaker Michael Vishacki, Stefano Lubiana (Contract) **production** 1700 **est.** 1994
product range ($15–20 ML) Chardonnay, Kelly's Reserve Chardonnay, Dry White, Pinot Noir.
summary Terry and Rosemary Bennett planted their first half hectare of vines in 1994 on gentle slopes in the beautiful Huon Valley. The plantings were quickly extended to 3 hectares, with another hectare being planted in 1999. The 4 hectares are in production, providing significant quantities of wine in 1998, the first commercial release.

Home Hill Kelly's Reserve Chardonnay

Made by Stefano Lubiana from specially selected parcels of grapes from the 1.5 hectares of estate plantings.

▼▼▼▽ **1999** Medium yellow-green; the bouquet is clean, with gentle citrus/melon/mineral aromas. The palate is typically fresh, with brisk citrus fruit and slightly lemony acidity on the finish. Quintessential Tasmanian Chardonnay. **rating:** 81

best drinking 2001–2005 **best vintages** NA **drink with** Lobster • $20

---

honeytree estate NR

16 Gillards Road, Pokolbin, NSW 2321 **region** Lower Hunter Valley
phone (02) 4998 7693 **fax** (02) 4998 7693 **open** Fri–Mon 10–5
winemaker Garry Reed **production** 3600 **est.** 1970
product range ($12–20 CD) Semillon, Traminer, Semillon Chardonnay, Clairette, Old Vine Shiraz, Cabernet Sauvignon.
summary The Honeytree Estate vineyard was first planted in 1970, and for a period of time wines were produced under the Honeytree Estate label. It then disappeared but has since been revived. Its 10 hectares of vines are of shiraz, cabernet sauvignon, semillon and a little clairette, known in the Hunter Valley as blanquette, and a variety which has been in existence there for well over a century. Jancis Robinson comments that the wine 'tends to be very high in alcohol, a little low in acid and to oxidise dangerously fast', but in a sign of the times the first Honeytree Clairette sold out so quickly (in four weeks) that 2.2 hectares of vineyard has been grafted over to additional clairette.

---

hope estate NR

Cobcroft Road, Broke, NSW 2330 **region** Lower Hunter Valley
phone (02) 6579 1161 **fax** (02) 6579 1373 **open** 7 days 10–4
winemaker Peter Howland **production** 30 000 **est.** 1996
product range ($15–20 CD) Verdelho, Semillon, Unwooded Chardonnay, Chardonnay, Botrytised Semillon, Blanc de Noir, Merlot, Cabernet Merlot.
summary Hope Estate is the reborn Saxonvale Winery purchased by Michael Hope, a Broke/Fordwich grape grower, with 90 hectares of vineyards. Ever-increasing amounts of wine are made and sold under the Hope Estate label.

Hope Estate Merlot

Nothing known about the background of this wine other than the apparent quality of the grapes and the over-enthusiastic use of oak.

▼▼▼▽ **1998** Medium red with just a touch of purple; the first aromas encountered on the bouquet are of oak, followed by a light regional overlay. The palate has some nice, sweet berry fruit but the oak is overplayed, the oak tannins combining with those of the fruit to unbalance the wine. A lighter touch would have made a very good wine. **rating:** 80

best drinking 2001–2005 **best vintages** NA **drink with** Beef pie • $19.95

---

hoppers hill vineyards NR

Googodery Road, Cumnock, NSW 2867 **region** Other Wineries of NSW
phone (02) 6367 7270 **open** Weekends 11–5
winemaker Robert Gilmore **production** NFP **est.** 1990
product range ($10–12 CD) Chardonnay, Sauvignon Blanc, Dry White, Cabernet Franc Merlot, Cabernet Sauvignon.
summary The Gilmores planted their vineyard in 1980, using organic growing methods and using no preservatives or filtration in the winery, which was established in 1990. Not surprisingly, the wines cannot be judged or assessed against normal standards, but may have appeal in a niche market.

🐌 horndale NR

Fraser Avenue, Happy Valley, SA 5159 **region** McLaren Vale
phone (08) 8387 0033 **fax** (08) 8387 0033 **open** Mon–Sat 9–6, Sun and public holidays 10–5.30
winemaker Phil Albrecht **production** NFP **est.** 1896
product range ($8.90–17.90 CD) Riesling, Colombard Semillon Chardonnay, Semillon Chardonnay, Chardonnay, Shiraz Cabernet, Cabernet Merlot, Shiraz Grenache, Cabernet Sauvignon Cabernet Franc, Cabernet Sauvignon; a wide range of dessert and fortified wines.

summary Given that it was established in 1896, and has remained continuously in production in one way or another since that time, Horndale may seem a rather strange new entry, but there have been a number of changes of ownership and direction, and the wines are only available from the cellar door and mail order. A personal connection is the Horndale Brandy my father used to buy 50 years ago, although it no longer appears on the extensive price list. On the other hand, as at March 2000 Cabernet Sauvignon from both the 1990 and 1991 vintages was available for $17.90 and $16.90 respectively.

horseshoe vineyard   NR

Horseshoe Road, Horseshoe Valley via Denman, NSW 2328 **region** Upper Hunter Valley
phone (02) 6547 3528 **open** Weekends 9–5
winemaker John Hordern **production** NFP **est.** 1986
product range ($13–18 CD) Classic Hunter Semillon, Chardonnay Semillon, Chardonnay, Pinot Noir.
summary Seems to have fallen by the wayside after its wonderful start in 1986, with rich, full flavoured, barrel-fermented Semillons and Chardonnays. The '87 Semillon was exhibited in the Museum Class at the 1996 Hunter Valley Wine Show and was still drinking beautifully, winning a strong silver medal. Younger vintages do not have the same magic.

hotham valley estate   ★★★★

South Wandering Road, Wandering, WA 6308 **region** Other Wineries of WA
phone (08) 9884 1525 **fax** (08) 9884 1079 **open** By appointment
winemaker James Pennington, Garry Baldwin (Consultant) **production** 12 000 **est.** 1987
product range ($14.99–25.99 CD) Semillon, Semillon Sauvignon Blanc, Chenin Blanc, Dryandra White, Chardonnay, Cabernet Merlot, Sandalwood Red.
summary An impressive newcomer to the scene, situated in a region of its own making, 120 kilometres southeast of Perth. It has a continental climate with cold winters and hot summer days, but cool nights, tempered by the altitude of 350 metres. Some exceptionally good wines have been made by former science teacher and now Charles Sturt University graduate James Pennington, on whose family property Hotham Valley Estate is established, albeit by way of a subdivision with outside investment. A state-of-the-art winery was built in 1993. Further details for the expanding Hotham empire appear under the Wildwood (Margaret River) entry. James Pennington has also created considerable interest with a patented development of oak treatment using sandalwood. Exports to the UK.

houghton   ★★★★★

Dale Road, Middle Swan, WA 6056 **region** Swan District
phone (08) 9274 5100 **fax** (08) 9274 5372 **open** 7 days 10–5
winemaker Larry Cherubino **production** 300 000 **est.** 1836
product range ($9.90–65 R) At the bottom end come the Wildflower Ridge range; then White Burgundy, Chablis, Frankland River Riesling, Semillon Sauvignon Blanc, Cabernet Sauvignon are the basic wines; next the Crofters range introduced in 1996; at the top end Gold Reserve Verdelho, Chardonnay and Cabernet Sauvignon with occasional special releases of aged Show Reserve wines, including White Burgundy, Riesling and Verdelho, always of high quality. Finally, the super-premium Jack Mann (a Cabernet blend) was introduced in July 1997.
summary The five-star rating may seem extreme but is very deliberate, and is in no small measure justified by Houghton White Burgundy, one of Australia's largest-selling white wines — almost entirely consumed within days of purchase, but which is superlative with seven or so years bottle age. To borrow a phrase of the late Jack Mann, 'There are no bad wines here'. Former winemaker Paul Lapsley's abundant winemaking skills brought the Jack Mann red and the Houghton Reserve Shiraz to the very forefront of Australian wine quality.

Houghton Frankland River Riesling

Produced from Houghton's large Frankland River vineyard, and typically has a somewhat unusual passionfruit aroma, which puts it apart from many more conventional Rieslings.
1999 Light yellow-green; has quite flowery aromas, fresh and tinged with passionfruit; the palate is crisp, clean, minerally and with good length, but needs time for the suppressed fruit to open up.   **rating:** 86
best drinking 2001–2005 **best vintages** '97 **drink with** Salad • $10.95

Houghton Semillon Sauvignon Blanc

A hugely underrated wine, which has also suffered from something of an identity crisis, sometimes effectively being released as Semillon, other times as a Semillon Sauvignon Blanc. The blend has now settled down as a 50 per cent Semillon, 50 per cent Sauvignon Blanc blend from the Margaret River, Manjimup and Mount Barker regions.

ŸŸŸŸ **1999** Light green-yellow; tropical passionfruit aromas intermingle with slight burnt match characters. The palate is clean, but lacks the intensity of the better wines and better vintages of this style. **rating:** 81

best drinking 2000–2001 **best vintages** '94, '95, '97 **drink with** Coquilles St Jacques • $10.95

Houghton Crofters Semillon Sauvignon Blanc

The Crofters range of wines was first released in 1996. The name comes from the historic Houghton homestead built in 1863 by Dr John Fergusson and which resembles a Scottish 'crofters' farmhouse. This particular wine is sourced from the Margaret River and Frankland regions; a blend of 50 per cent Semillon and 50 per cent Sauvignon Blanc, with the Semillon component barrel-fermented in new French oak and given three months lees contact.

ŸŸŸŸ **1999** Light to medium yellow-green; the bouquet is powerful and potent, with a mix of herb, grass and hay; the palate starts with promise but then falls away on a relatively short finish. **rating:** 83

best drinking 2000–2002 **best vintages** '96 **drink with** Lemon chicken • $14.95

Houghton White Burgundy

A wine with an extraordinary pedigree over its 60-year history, made from a blend of Chenin Blanc, Muscadelle, Semillon, Verdelho and Chardonnay primarily grown in the Swan Valley and at Gingin. Released and almost entirely consumed within 12 months of vintage, it invariably matures wonderfully well in bottle over a six- to eight-year period, leading to tiny releases of the Show Reserve Wines which accumulate innumerable gold medals and trophies.

ŸŸŸŸ **1999** If ever a wine suffers from schizophrenia, this one does. Designed (and doomed) to be consumed within hours of purchase, it will however turn from frog to prince around 2005, kissing not required. Fragrant yet delicate tropical passionfruit aroma and flavour, beguiling now, will be transformed into honeyed, luscious complexity with time. **rating:** 87

best drinking 1999–2007 **best vintages** '83, '87, '89, '91, '93, '95, '99 **drink with** Fish, chicken, veal • $10.95

Houghton Show Reserve White Burgundy

A re-release of 500 cases of the best bottling of the standard Houghton White Burgundy of its vintage year, the wine is a blend of Chenin Blanc, Muscadelle, Semillon, Verdelho and Chardonnay.

ŸŸŸŸŸ **1995** Glowing golden yellow; the bouquet offers a mix of rich, honeyed tropical fruit and more herbal/nettle notes. The palate has a delicious blend of ripe, almost dried fruit flavours, a hint of toast and well-balanced acidity. **rating:** 90

ŸŸŸŸŸ **1992** Golden yellow; the bouquet is surprisingly reserved, with a mix of dried fruits and more herbal/nettle notes. The palate is quite solid, again with a mix of dried fruits and a hint of toast; finishes with good acidity. **rating:** 90

best drinking 2000–2001 **best vintages** '91, '95 **drink with** West Australian marron • $26.95

Houghton Crofters Chardonnay

Produced from chardonnay grown at Mount Barker and Harvey, with a portion of the chardonnay juice barrel-fermented in new and one-year-old French oak barriques, then spending nine months on yeast lees. The 1998 has won gold medals at Brisbane, Sydney and Cowra.

ŸŸŸŸ **1998** Medium to full yellow-green; the bouquet is clean, fruit-driven with white peach and melon characters, though the level of aromatics is subdued. The palate, likewise, is pleasant and fruit-driven, though not particularly complex. **rating:** 86

best drinking 1999–2002 **best vintages** NA **drink with** Crumbed brains • $21.95

Houghton Shiraz Cabernet Merlot

There is no claim of any Geographic Indication for the wine, which is drawn broadly from across West Australia.

ŸŸŸŸ **1998** Medium to full red-purple; there is quite powerful earthy cabernet varietal character on the bouquet, and the palate, while powerful, has distinct touches of green astringency; the wine seems to have been rushed to bottle. **rating:** 81

best drinking 2000–2003 **best vintages** NA **drink with** Grilled beef • $10.95

Houghton Jack Mann

Released in July 1997 in honour of the late, great Jack Mann. It is a blend of Cabernet Sauvignon, Malbec and Shiraz primarily sourced from Houghton's Frankland River vineyard, with a lesser component from the Mount Barker Omrah vineyard. It spent two years in a mix of Nevers and Allier French oak; I suspect the cooper was Dargaud & Jaegle. An absolutely superb wine in every respect.

♥♥♥♥♥ **1996** The bouquet is rich, complex and concentrated; abundant ripe dark berry and chocolate fruit, and sumptuous oak. The palate is flooded with sweet raspberry, redcurrant and blackcurrant fruit, balanced by tannins. **rating:** 95

best drinking 2001–2021 **best vintages** '94, '95, '96 **drink with** Fillet of lamb • $54.95

howard park ★★★★☆

Lot 377 Scotsdale Road, Denmark, WA 6333 **region** Great Southern
phone (08) 9848 2345 **fax** (08) 9848 2064 **open** 7 days 10–4
winemaker Michael Kerrigan, James Kellie **production** 100 000 **est.** 1986
product range ($15–70 R) Madfish Premium Dry White and Red provide low-priced volume; limited quantities of Howard Park Riesling, Chardonnay and Cabernet Merlot.
summary The changes have come thick and fast for Howard Park. John Wade has departed as executive winemaker, retaining a short-term consultancy role. A splendid new winery has been constructed in the Margaret River region (incorporating Feng Shui principles) to complement the (near new) Denmark winery. Michael Kerrigan has become chief winemaker, and it seems certain that new wines will join the product range.

Howard Park Riesling

First made in 1986, and in my view the greatest Riesling made in the Great Southern region, itself home of many of Australia's finest examples of the style. It ages superbly, the '86 still with years in front of it.
♥♥♥♥♥ **1999** There have been changes aplenty at Howard Park, but not to the price of this classic wine. Bright, light green-yellow, the delicately understated bouquet doesn't prepare you for the spotlessly clean, vibrantly lively palate with passionfruit, apple and lime flavours. A wine with an impeccable history, bred to stay. **rating:** 94

best drinking 2004–2019 **best vintages** '86, '87, '88, '91, '93, '94, '95, '96, '97, '98, '99 **drink with** Fresh asparagus, Asian seafood • $22

Howard Park Madfish Premium Dry White

The strikingly labelled and named Madfish was designed by Maxine Fumagalli, a Noongar artist who lives in Denmark, Western Australia. The name itself comes from a favourite fishing spot 15 kilometres west of Denmark. The white is an unwooded blend of predominantly Chardonnay, and small amounts of Sauvignon Blanc and (in some years) Semillon from the Great Southern region.
♥♥♥♀ **1999** Light green-yellow; the bouquet is fresh and light, with touches of citrus and flowers; the palate is fresh, clean, delicate and lively, light but refreshing. **rating:** 83

best drinking 2000–2001 **best vintages** NA **drink with** Chicken • $16

Howard Park Madfish Premium Dry Red

Produced from a blend of Cabernet Franc, Merlot, Cabernet Sauvignon and Shiraz, the percentages varying from year to year; the grapes grown in the Great Southern, Pemberton and Margaret River regions.
♥♥♥♀ **1998** Medium red; there are juicy and fresh sweet berry aromas on the bouquet which replicate themselves in the flavours of the palate. An easy-drinking café style. **rating:** 83

best drinking 2000–2002 **best vintages** '95 **drink with** Pasta, most Italian-accented dishes • $18

Howard Park Cabernet Sauvignon Merlot

Like the Riesling, first made in 1986. The regional and varietal mix has changed a little over the years, with the Cabernet component ranging from between 70 per cent and 85 per cent and the wine being labelled Cabernet Merlot. Quality has wobbled around since 1994.
♥♥♥♥ **1997** Medium red-purple; the bouquet is clean, without any untoward lift, but the fruit is quite light. An elegant style on the palate, with delicate fruit sustained by spicy Troncais oak; well-balanced, fine tannins. **rating:** 87

best drinking 2000–2012 **best vintages** '86, '88, '89, '90, '92, '93, '94, '96 **drink with** Lamb fillets, mature cheddar • $70

howards way vineyard NR

Cobcroft Road, Broke, NSW 2330 **region** Lower Hunter Valley
phone (02) 4998 1336 **fax** (02) 4938 3775 **open** Not
winemaker Andrew Margan (Contract) **production** 3500 **est.** NA
product range ($15–20 ML) Semillon, Pinot Noir, Shiraz.
summary Yet another of the dozens of new vineyards and labels that have appeared in the Hunter Valley in the latter part of the 1990s. Eight hectares of shiraz, 3 of pinot noir and 2 of semillon provide a substantial base, and retail distribution began in 1999.

howarth's pycnantha hill   NR

Benbournie Road, Clare, SA 5453   **region** Clare Valley
phone (08) 8842 2137   **fax** (08) 8842 2137   **open** Not
winemaker Jim Howarth   **production** 600   **est.** 1997
product range ($8.75–12 ML) Riesling, Chardonnay, Shiraz, Cabernet Sauvignon.
summary The Howarth family progressively established 2 hectares of vineyard from 1987, making its first commercial vintage ten years later in 1997. Acacia pycnantha is the botanic name for the golden wattle which grows wild over the hills of the Howarth farm, and they say it was 'a natural choice to name our vineyards Pycnantha Hill'. I am not too sure that marketing gurus would agree, but there we go. The 1997 Chardonnay won a silver medal at the Australian Small Winemakers Show at Stanthorpe in 1998, which certainly suggests that there are no problems with the quality of the wines, for this is a tough show at which to succeed. The tiny production (which will peak at around 1300 cases) is sold by mail order or wholesale on a first-come, first-served basis.

hugh hamilton   ★★★

McMurtrie Road, McLaren Vale, SA 5171   **region** McLaren Vale
phone (08) 8323 8689   **fax** (08) 8323 9488   **open** Mon–Fri 10–5, weekends and public holidays 11–5
winemaker Hugh Hamilton   **production** 8500   **est.** 1992
product range ($14.50–19.50 R) Chenin Blanc, Unwooded Chardonnay, Shiraz, Merlot, Cabernet Sauvignon, Sparkling Shiraz.
summary Hugh Hamilton is a member of the famous Hamilton winemaking family, there being an intensely (and well-known) competitive spirit existing between those various members — notably between Richard and Hugh — which can only be good for the consumer.

hugo   ★★★

Elliott Road, McLaren Flat, SA 5171   **region** McLaren Vale
phone (08) 8383 0098   **fax** (08) 8383 0446   **open** Sun–Fri 10.30–5, Sat 12–5
winemaker John Hugo   **production** 5000   **est.** 1982
product range ($17–19 R) Sauvignon Blanc, Chardonnay, Unwooded Chardonnay, Shiraz, Cabernet Sauvignon, Port.
summary A winery which came from relative obscurity to prominence in the late 1980s with some lovely ripe, sweet reds which, while strongly American-oak-influenced, were quite outstanding. Subsequent red releases have continued in the same style, albeit slightly less exciting. There are 32 hectares of estate plantings, with part of the grape production sold to others. The wines are exported to the US, Canada and Singapore.

hungerford hill   NR

McDonalds Road, Pokolbin, NSW 2321   **region** Lower Hunter Valley
phone 1800 187 666   **fax** (02) 4998 7682   **open** Mon–Fri 9–4.30, weekends 10–4.30
winemaker Ian Walsh   **production** 30 000   **est.** 1967
product range ($10–22.50 R) Tumbarumba Chardonnay, Tumbarumba Sauvignon Blanc, Tumbarumba Pinot Gris, Cowra Chardonnay, Cowra Verdelho, Young Chardonnay, Young Semillon, Late Picked Semillon, Late Picked Riesling, Cabernet Merlot, Hunter Shiraz, Hilltops Cabernet Sauvignon, Adelaide Hills–McLaren Vale Cabernet, Tumbarumba Pinot Noir.
summary Now purely a brand owned by Southcorp, with the wines being made at Tulloch. However, eye-catching new labels and a new range of regionally sourced wines (all from New South Wales) have substantially elevated the status of the brand on the ever parochial Sydney market and raised wine quality to a significant degree. It should be noted that between 1997 and May 2000 I had some responsibilities for this brand and hence rate neither the winery nor the wines, though will do so in the future.

Hungerford Hill Hilltops Shiraz

This is the first Hilltops Shiraz release by Hungerford Hill. It is matured in French oak barriques, 20 per cent new, for 12 months. Don't get distracted by the label (depicting an egg shell, a chess piece and the Loch Ness Monster) for this is serious wine at a modest price.
1997 Very good purple-red; the bouquet is clean and firm with strong varietal earth, spice and anise aromas. A powerful wine on the palate, with fruit (rather than oak) doing the talking; a long finish with appropriate tannins.
best drinking 2002–2007   **best vintages** NA   **drink with** Beef teriyaki   •$19

171

hunter ridge   NR

Hermitage Road, Pokolbin, NSW 2320   **region** Lower Hunter Valley
phone (02) 4998 7500   **fax** (02) 4998 7211   **open** 7 days 10–5
winemaker Stephen Pannell   **production** NFP   **est.** 1996
product range ($12.50–22 R) Semillon, Verdelho, Chardonnay, Shiraz, Cabernet Merlot Reserve, Cabernet Sauvignon.
summary Hunter Ridge is effectively a joint venture between BRL Hardy and McGuigan Wines Limited. The grapes come from the vineyards surrounding the Hunter Ridge cellar door and which are owned by McGuigan Wines. The wines are fermented and partially matured in the Hunter Valley but are finally blended, finished and bottled by BRL Hardy in South Australia.

Hunter Ridge Shiraz
An honest and well-priced wine with good regional style and character.
▼▼▼▼ 1997 Medium purple-red; distinctive, ripe Hunter Valley varietal fruit on the bouquet has clean earthy overtones. There is plenty of character to the palate, with pleasing medium-weight structure and gently sweet fruit flavours.   **rating:** 85
best drinking 2000–2005   **best vintages** NA   **drink with** Big Mac   • $12.95

Hunter Ridge Cabernet Merlot Reserve
A pretty good example of an instance in which several general dollops of oak do not paper over deficiencies in the fruit.
▼▼▼▽ 1997 Medium red-purple; somewhat pedestrian oak comes through strongly on the bouquet; a quite powerful wine on the palate, but definitely on the rustic side, with raspy tannin and extract.   **rating:** 80
best drinking 2002–2005   **best vintages** NA   **drink with** Steak Diane   • $12.95

huntington estate   ★★★★☆

Cassilis Road, Mudgee, NSW 2850   **region** Mudgee
phone (02) 6373 3825   **fax** (02) 6373 3730   **open** Mon–Fri 9–5, Sat 10–5, Sun 10–3
winemaker Susie Roberts   **production** 15 000   **est.** 1969
product range ($14–24 CD) Semillon, Semillon Chardonnay, Chardonnay Non Wooded, Rosé, sundry sweet whites; red wines are released under bin numbers (FB = full-bodied; MB = medium-bodied) comprising Shiraz, Cabernet Merlot and Cabernet Sauvignon.
summary The remarkable Roberts family members have a passion for wine which is equalled only by their passion for music, with the Huntington Music Festival a major annual event. The red wines of Huntington Estate are outstanding and sell for absurdly low prices. The wines are not exported; almost all are sold via cellar door and mailing list.

Huntington Estate Bin W2 Semillon
Estate-grown, cool-fermented in stainless steel and early-bottled, all in classic style. All that is needed is patience.
▼▼▼▽ 1999 Light yellow-green; the bouquet is crisp and clean, with some mineral characters but little obvious fruit. The palate, however, has some presence and should begin to show its wares as it matures in bottle.   **rating:** 81
best drinking 2002–2007   **best vintages** NA   **drink with** Smoked trout   • $11

Huntington Estate Shiraz
In very much the same style and quality class as the Cabernet Sauvignon, made from estate-grown grapes and producing wines of great longevity. As the wines age, cherry/berry fruits gradually soften and take on that typically, gently earthy Shiraz character, and the tannins soften at the same rate as the fruit rounds off and develops. Thus the balance of the wine is never threatened, and patience is rewarded.
▼▼▼▼ 1997 Bin FB37. Medium red-purple; in soft, typical Huntington mode with cedar, chocolate and vanilla aromas preceding the attractive plum and cherry fruit running through the palate; the hallmark soft tannins round off the finish.   **rating:** 90
best drinking 2001–2010   **best vintages** '74, '75, '78, '79, '84, '90, '91, '93, '94, '95, '97   **drink with** Kangaroo fillet   • $14

Huntington Estate Special Reserve Shiraz
Small parcels of wine which Susan Roberts considers to be superior have, in the past, been held back a number of years before release. There seems to have been a change in her approach, for these are now the same vintage as the varietal release, and are distinguished by a much more lavish use of American oak. It also may be, of course, that the telescoping of the vintages makes the new oak more obvious.

▼▼▼▼ 1997 Bin FB31. Full red-purple; the bouquet is concentrated, with lots of American oak floating on top of the sweet berry fruit. The same play occurs on the palate, which while richly flavoured, has a lot more oak than hitherto. **rating: 87**

best drinking 2003–2013 **best vintages** '93 **drink with** Venison •$24

Huntington Estate Cabernet Sauvignon

As with all of the Huntington Estate wines, made entirely from estate-grown grapes. Yields are low, and the fruit is tremendously powerful and concentrated, producing wines which age slowly but majestically. There is no particular artifice in the making, with American oak playing a minor role.

▼▼▼▼ 1997 Bin FB35. Medium red-purple; the bouquet has a range of cedar, earth and berry aromas; cassis and chocolate flavours are the staple of a rich, round palate finishing with ripe tannins. **rating: 89**

best drinking 2000–2010 **best vintages** '74, '79, '81, '84, '89, '90, '94, '95, '97 **drink with** Grilled rump steak •$14

Huntington Estate Special Reserve Cabernet Sauvignon

Precisely the same changes have occurred with the Reserve Cabernet Sauvignon as with the Reserve Shiraz. Time will tell whether this represents a permanent change or not.

▼▼▼▼ 1997 Bin FB33. Dense red-purple; on both bouquet and palate vanilla American oak surrounds the dense berry fruit. **rating: 86**

best drinking 2002–2012 **best vintages** NA **drink with** Rib of beef •$24

huntleigh vineyards ★★☆

Tunnecliffes Lane, Heathcote, Vic 3523 **region** Bendigo
phone (03) 5433 2795 **open** 7 days 10–5.30
winemaker Leigh Hunt **production** 425 **est.** 1975
product range ($14.50–16 CD) Riesling, Traminer, Shiraz, Cabernet Sauvignon; Leckie Shiraz.
summary A retirement hobby, with robust, rather astringent red wines which need time in bottle to lose some of the rough edges. Part of the production from the 5.2 hectares of vines is sold to others.

hunt's foxhaven estate NR

Canal Rocks Road, Yallingup, WA 6282 **region** Margaret River
phone (08) 9755 2232 **fax** (08) 9255 2249 **open** Weekends, holidays 11–5 or by appointment
winemaker David Hunt **production** 1000 **est.** 1978
product range ($12–15 CD) Riesling (dry and sweet), Semillon, Canal Rocks White, Yallingup Classic, Noble Riesling, Hunting Pink, Cabernet Sauvignon.
summary Draws upon 4 hectares of vines progressively established, the oldest being 20-year-old riesling. All of the wine is sold through cellar door and by mail order.

hurley vineyard NR

101 Balnarring Road, Balnarring, Vic 3926 **region** Mornington Peninsula
phone (03) 9608 8220 **fax** (03) 9608 7293 **open** Not
winemaker Contract **production** NA **est.** 1998
product range Pinot Noir.
summary Hurley Vineyard has been established by Melbourne Queen's Counsel, Kevin Bell. Four hectares of pinot noir were planted in 1998, and are yet to come into production.

ibis wines NR

239 Kearneys Drive, Orange, NSW 2800 **region** Orange
phone (02) 6362 3257 **fax** (02) 6362 5779 **open** Weekends and public holidays 11–5 or by appointment
winemaker Phil Stevenson **production** 1100 **est.** 1988
product range ($16–22 CD) Riesling, Chardonnay, Reserve Chardonnay, Pinot Noir, Kanjara Shiraz, Cabernet Sauvignon, Cabernet Franc.
summary Ibis Wines is located just north of Orange (near the botanic gardens) on what was once a family orchard. Planting of the vineyard commenced in 1988, and after interim winemaking arrangements a new winery was completed on the property in 1998. The grapes are sourced from the home vineyards at an altitude of 800 metres, from the Habitat Vineyard at 1100 metres on Mount Canobolas (pinot noir and merlot) and from the Kanjara Vineyard (shiraz). As at early 2000, 12 wines from 1993 to 1998 were available for sale at low prices. It has to be said that overall the style is pretty rustic.

indigo ridge NR

Icely Road, Orange, NSW 2800 **region** Orange
phone (02) 6362 1851 **fax** (02) 6362 1851 **open** By appointment
winemaker Jon Reynolds (Contract) **production** 1700 **est.** 1995
product range ($16–20 ML) Sauvignon Blanc, Cabernet Sauvignon, Ophir Gold.
summary The newly established Indigo Ridge has 2 hectares each of sauvignon blanc and cabernet sauvignon; production is still very small, and all of the wines are sold by cellar door and mail order.

Indigo Ridge Sauvignon Blanc

1999 was the first release of this wine, fermented in stainless steel and early-bottled for early consumption.
TTTY 1999 Very pale; the bouquet is powerful, with intense mineral aromas, even to the point of being slightly abrasive. The palate is minerally and edgy, but has considerable personality.　　**rating:** 84
best drinking 2000–2001 **best vintages** NA **drink with** Shellfish •$18

inglewood vineyards ★★★

Yarrawa Road, Denman, NSW 2328 **region** Upper Hunter Valley
phone (02) 6547 2556 **fax** (02) 6547 2546 **open** Not
winemaker Gary Reed (Contract) **production** 25 000 **est.** 1988
product range ($7.50–20 R) Atmosphere Coastal White and Inland Red; Two Rivers Stone's Throw Semillon, Wild Fire Unwooded Chardonnay, Hidden Hive Verdelho, Rocky Crossing Cabernet Sauvignon, Back Track Cabernets; Reserve Hunter Semillon, Hunter Chardonnay, Hunter Shiraz and McLaren Vale/Hunter Cabernet Sauvignon.
summary A significant addition to the viticultural scene in the Upper Hunter Valley, with almost 170 hectares of vineyards established, involving a total investment of around $7 million. Much of the fruit is sold to Southcorp under long-term contracts, but part is made under contract for the expanding winemaking and marketing operations of Inglewood. The emphasis is on Chardonnay and Semillon, and the wines have been medal winners in the wine show circuit.

ingoldby ★★★★

Kangarilla Road, McLaren Flat, SA 5171 **region** McLaren Vale
phone (08) 8323 8853 **fax** (08) 8323 8550 **open** 7 days 10–5
winemaker Charles Hargrave **production** 40 000 **est.** 1972
product range ($14–18 CD) Colombard, Hugo's Hill Riesling, Sauvignon Blanc, Shiraz, Grenache, Cabernet Sauvignon, Meteora Tawny Port.
summary Acquired by Mildara Blass in 1995, apparently for the grapes and grape contracts controlled by Ingoldby. Phil Reschke is making some excellent wines, just as he is for the Andrew Garrett label. Exports and distribution via Mildara Blass.

Ingoldby Chardonnay

A very cleverly made wine, sourced entirely from contract-grown fruit in McLaren Vale. It is largely cold-fermented in stainless steel, and then transferred to new French and American oak hogsheads at 5° baumé to finish the fermentation. A small proportion of the wine undergoes malolactic fermentation, and the wine is usually bottled six months after vintage. All in all, very clever and effective winemaking, including the use of oak.
TTTY 1999 Light green-yellow; fragrant tangy fruit is interwoven with slightly assertive French and American oak. The palate has nice tangy fruit and good length but, like the bouquet, is not helped by slightly phenolic oak.
rating: 84
best drinking 2000–2003 **best vintages** '96, '97 **drink with** Crab with mayonnaise •$14

Ingoldby Road Block Grenache

The garrulous back label chould have been written by Zar Brooks (of D'Arenberg) but I don't believe his moonlighting extends as far as Mildara Blass. We learn that Ingoldby Road is the eastern boundary of the block from which the grapes come, and that it peters out into an impassable sand track a bit further on.
TTTT 1997 Light to medium purple-red; the 70 per cent Grenache component provides juicy, jammy berry fruit aromas and flavours; all in all, a pleasant medium-weight fruit-driven style, lively, fresh and well balanced. An ultra-easy trattoria style.
rating: 85
best drinking 1999–2001 **best vintages** NA **drink with** Italian •$18

Ingoldby Cabernet Sauvignon

Over the years Ingoldby has produced some quite wonderful Cabernet Sauvignon. It seems too much to hope that the best material will continue to come out under the Ingoldby label, but this has been a more than half decent wine.

▼▼▼▼▽ **1998** A lovely wine, with strong red-purple colour, concentrated dark berry fruit on the bouquet and abundant, ripe cassis fruit on the palate. Tannins and oak are there in the background, seen but not heard. **rating:** 91

best drinking 2003–2008 **best vintages** '90, '91, '94, '95, '98 **drink with** Steak and kidney pie • $15

inigo wines NR

PO Box 1557, Coorparoo DC, Qld 4151 **region** Granite Belt
phone (07) 3397 6425 **fax** (07) 3397 5280 **open** Not
winemaker Janis Carter **production** NA **est.** NA
product range ($16 CD) Sauvignon Blanc, Cabernet Merlot.
summary The property and winery operate as a kind of home-stay operation, and anyone staying at the Chateau Bernard and St Ignatius Vineyard Retreat (Inigo's home) can help in the winery.

Inigo Cabernet Merlot

Devoid of a back label, and with the front label going nowhere near satisfying the technical labelling requirements in Australia, all I know about the wine is that the label design comes from the incredibly multicultural background of Janis Carter, co-proprietor with husband Bernard. For a semi-home brew, this is a pretty decent wine.

▼▼▼▽ **1998** Light to medium red-purple; the bouquet is clean, with red fruit aromatics and minimal oak. The palate is well put together with attractive sweet fruit; a lively, early-drinking style with little or no tannin and minimal oak input.

rating: 83

best drinking 1999–2000 **drink with** Simple food • $16

innisfail vineyards NR

Cross Street, Batesford, Vic 3221 **region** Geelong
phone (03) 5276 1258 **fax** (03) 5221 8442 **open** Not
winemaker Ron Griffiths **production** 1600 **est.** 1980
product range ($20–24 ML) Riesling, Chardonnay, Pinot Noir, Cabernet Sauvignon.
summary This 6-hectare vineyard released its first wines in 1988, made in a small but modern winery on site, with a chewy, complex Chardonnay from both 1989 and 1990 attesting to the quality of the vineyard. No recent tastings, however.

ironbark ridge vineyard NR

Middle Road Mail Service 825, Purga, Qld 4306 **region** South Burnett and Other Wineries of Qld
phone (07) 5464 6787 **fax** (07) 5464 6858 **open** By appointment
winemaker Mark Ravenscroft (Contract) **production** 250 **est.** 1984
product range ($18–25 ML) Chardonnay, Vintage Port.
summary Ipswich is situated on the coastal side of the Great Dividing Range, and the high summer humidity and rainfall will inevitably provide challenges for viticulture here. On the evidence of the '98 Chardonnay, Ironbark Ridge is capable of producing Chardonnay equal to the best from Queensland.

iron pot bay wines ★★★☆

West Bay Road, Rowella, Tas 7270 **region** Northern Tasmania
phone (03) 6394 7320 **fax** (03) 6394 7346 **open** By appointment
winemaker Andrew Hood, Jim Chatto (Contract) **production** 2000 **est.** 1988
product range ($20 R) Unwooded Chardonnay, Sauvignon Blanc, Pinot Grigio.
summary Iron Pot Bay is now part of the syndicate which has established Rosevears Estate, with its large, state-of-the-art winery erected on the banks of the Tamar. The vineyard takes its name from a bay on the Tamar River and is strongly maritime-influenced, producing delicate but intensely flavoured unwooded white wines.

ironwood estate NR

RMB 1288 Porongurup, WA 6234 **region** Great Southern
phone (08) 9853 1126 **fax** (08) 9853 1172 **open** By appointment
winemaker Robert Lee, John Wade (Consultant) **production** 1000 **est.** 1996
product range ($14–21 CD) Riesling, Chardonnay, Shiraz, Cabernet Sauvignon.
summary Ironwood Estate was established in 1996 when the first wines were made from purchased grapes. In the same year chardonnay, shiraz and cabernet sauvignon were planted on a northern slope of the Porongurup Range. The twin peaks of the Porongurups rise above the vineyard and provide the basis for the label design. The first estate-grown grapes were vinified at the new Porongurup Winery, erected for the 1999 vintage and jointly owned by Jingalla and Chatsfield Wines.

Ironwood Estate Chardonnay

Produced from 0.75 hectare of estate plantings, and made without the use of oak.

ΥΥΥΥ 1999 Light green-yellow; intense passionfruit with slightly smoky overtones suggests a rather slow ferment; similar passionfruit and nectarine flavours come through on a palate with good length. **rating: 83**

best drinking 2000–2002 **best vintages** NA **drink with** Summer salad • $15

Ironwood Estate Shiraz

Estate-grown on 0.75 hectare of estate vineyard; promises much for the future.

ΥΥΥΥ 1997 Medium red-purple; the bouquet is quite fragrant, with an array of gently sweet spice, liquorice, berry and plum aromas. The palate offers sweet berry fruit with a juxtaposition of faintly jammy characters on the one hand and spicy undertones on the other. Judicious oak adds to an interesting wine. **rating: 87**

best drinking 2000–2007 **best vintages** NA **drink with** Smoked lamb • $21

irvine ★★★★

Roeslers Road, Eden Valley, SA 5235 **region** Eden Valley
phone (08) 8564 1046 **fax** (08) 8564 1046 **open** Not
winemaker James Irvine **production** 7000 **est.** 1980
product range ($14–100 R) Under the cheaper Eden Crest label: Unwooded Chardonnay, Pinot Merlot, Merlot Cabernet, Zinfandel Merlot, Meslier Brut, Pinot Chardonnay Brut; under the premium James Irvine label: Brut Royale, Merlot Brut and (at the top of the tree) Grand Merlot.
summary Industry veteran Jim Irvine, who has successfully guided the destiny of so many South Australian wineries, quietly introduced his own label in 1991, although the vineyard from which the wines are sourced was commenced in 1980 and now comprises 1 hectare of petit meslier, 1 hectare of merlot and 7 hectares of chardonnay. Much of the production is exported to Germany, the US, Japan, Taiwan and Switzerland.

Irvine Eden Crest Chardonnay

An unwooded wine made from 4.8 hectares of estate plantings.

ΥΥΥΥ 1998 Light green-yellow; the bouquet is light and clean, with the slightly mono-dimensional fruit which seems part and parcel of the style. There is more of the same on the palate, with pleasant melon fruit, and just a touch of complexity coming from prolonged lees contact and malolactic fermentation. **rating: 82**

best drinking 2000–2002 **best vintages** NA **drink with** Pasta carbonara • $26

Irvine Eden Crest Merlot

Produced from grapes grown in the Eden and Barossa Valleys, matured in older oak for 15 months. Was previously called Petit Merlot, but has now graduated to adulthood.

ΥΥΥΥ 1998 Medium red-purple; the bouquet has a mix of leafy/biscuity/earthy/spicy fruit in typical varietal mode. The sweet and savoury palate has silky tannins which invest the wine with the appropriate structure. **rating: 84**

ΥΥΥΥ 1997 Medium red-purple; the bouquet is ripe and sweet, with almost raisiny fruit melded with sweet oak. The same very ripe raisiny fruit is apparent on the palate, which has pleasant structure, soft tannins and subtle oak. The only question mark about the wine is whether it shows (desirable) varietal character. **rating: 85**

best drinking 2001–2005 **best vintages** '97, '98 **drink with** Barossa sausage • $26

James Irvine Grand Merlot

First made in 1985, and has received various international accolades over the years. Produced from 4.7 hectares of estate plantings on the Springhill Vineyard in the Eden Valley. The wine spends an incredible three and a half years in oak before being bottled.

ΥΥΥΥ 1996 Medium to full red-purple; the bouquet is very concentrated and complex, with distinctly savoury notes to the dark, rich fruit. The palate offers abundantly ripe fruit, almost into plum, supported by fine, lingering tannins. As one might expect, the oak is well integrated. **rating: 90**

best drinking 2003–2013 **best vintages** '96 **drink with** Venison • $100

Irvine Eden Crest Merlot Cabernet

Produced from merlot grown in the Eden and Barossa Valleys, and from cabernet sauvignon from the Barossa Valley.

ΥΥΥΥ 1997 Medium red; aromas of leaf and mint on the bouquet have slightly smoky overtones; much riper, sweet fruit and chocolate flavours, soft tannins and nicely balanced spicy oak. **rating: 87**

best drinking 2000–2004 **best vintages** '97 **drink with** Rabbit in herbs and red wine • $26

island brook estate   NR

817 Bussell Highway, Metricup, WA 6280 **region** Margaret River
phone (08) 9755 7501 **fax** (08) 9755 7501 **open** 7 days 10–5
winemaker Stuart Pym **production** 700 **est.** 1985
product range ($15 CD) Semillon, Summer Garden (white).
summary Ken and Judy Brook operate a vineyard café offering brunch, lunch, cappuccinos and Devonshire teas throughout the day, with a most unusual maze (built with rammed earth walls) to occupy children (and perhaps adults). Much of the production from the 8-hectare estate is sold to other makers, with limited quantities of wine made for sale from the restaurant and cellar door.

ivanhoe wines   NR

Corner Oakey Creek and Marrowbone Roads, Pokolbin, NSW 2320 **region** Lower Hunter Valley
phone (02) 4998 7325 **fax** (02) 4998 7848 **open** 7 days 10–5
winemaker Stephen Drayton, Tracy Drayton **production** NA **est.** 1995
product range Various varietal wines under the Ivanhoe, Stephen Drayton Signature Series and Lancelot brands, including Chardonnay and Shiraz.
summary Stephen Drayton is the son of the late Reg Drayton and, with wife Tracy, is the third branch of the family to be actively involved in winemaking in the Hunter Valley. The property on which the vineyard is situated has been called Ivanhoe for over 140 years, and 25 hectares of 30-year-old vines provide high-quality fruit for the label. The plans are to build a replica of the old homestead (burnt down, along with much of the winery, in the 1968 bushfires) to operate as a sales area.

jackson's hill   ★★★

Mount View Road, Mount View, NSW 2321 **region** Lower Hunter Valley
phone (02) 4990 1273 **fax** (02) 4991 3233 **open** Thurs–Mon and public holidays 10–5
winemaker Mike Winborne **production** 1200 **est.** 1984
product range ($16–18 CD) Semillon, Oak Fermented Semillon, Late Harvest Semillon, Vin en Rosé, Cabernet Franc.
summary One of the newer arrivals on the spectacularly scenic Mount View Road, making tiny quantities of wine sold exclusively through the cellar door and specialising in Cabernet Franc. The '97 Semillon and Cabernet Franc were not exhilarating, but Jackson's Hill does produce the most marvellous home-made chocolates I have tasted in a long time.

jadran   NR

445 Reservoir Road, Orange Grove, WA 6109 **region** Perth Hills
phone (08) 9459 1110 **open** Mon–Sat 10–8, Sun 11–5
winemaker Steve Radojkovich **production** NFP **est.** 1967
product range ($6–12 CD) Riesling, Hermitage, generic red and white table wines, Sparkling, Fortifieds.
summary A quite substantial operation which basically services local clientele, occasionally producing wines of quite surprising quality from a variety of fruit sources.

james estate   ★★★☆

Mudgee Road, Baerami via Denman, NSW 2333 **region** Upper Hunter Valley
phone (02) 6547 5168 **fax** (02) 6547 5164 **open** 7 days 10–4.30
winemaker Peter Orr **production** 80 000 **est.** 1971
product range ($9.99–19.99 CD) Café Range Chardonnay, Cabernet Sauvignon shiraz; Compass Range Chardonnay, Late Harvest Sylvaner, Semillon, Verdelho, Merlot, Cabernet Shiraz; Reserve Range Chardonnay, Botrytis Semillon; Méthode Champenoise Chardonnay Pinot Noir.
summary A substantial viticultural enterprise with 60 hectares of vineyards equally divided between sylvaner, semillon, chardonnay, shiraz and cabernet sauvignon. Since a change of ownership in 1997 there have been many innovations, including the appointment of Peter Orr as winemaker after a winemaking career with McWilliam's Mount Pleasant and thereafter Allandale Wines, and the complete revamping and repackaging of the wines.

James Estate Reserve Chardonnay

A vineyard selection, fermented and matured in a mix of new and one-year-old French and American oak barrels. Lees contact with stirring for three months, and bottled after 12 months in oak.

❦❦❦❦ **1998** Medium to full yellow-green; the bouquet offers full, ripe melon and peach fruit with well-balanced and integrated oak. The palate follows logically on the path of the bouquet, with some nice creamy notes on the mid-palate followed by a touch of acidity on the finish to round the wine off. **rating:** 86

best drinking 2000–2003 **best vintages** NA **drink with** Grilled spatchcock • $19.99

James Estate Cabernet Shiraz

The Cabernet and Shiraz were separately fermented before finishing their fermentation in American oak barriques. The wine then spends 13 months in a mix of French and American oak, principally used.

❦❦❦❦ **1998** Medium red, with just a touch of purple; the moderately intense bouquet is clean, with quite sweet berry fruit and a touch of vanillin oak. The palate is pleasant, with slightly savoury/leafy flavours and a hint of vanilla oak. **rating:** 82

best drinking 2001–2006 **best vintages** NA **drink with** Shepherd's pie • $17.50

jane brook estate ★★★

229 Toodyay Road, Middle Swan, WA 6056 **region** Swan District
phone (08) 9274 1432 **fax** (08) 9274 1211 **open** 7 days 12–5
winemaker Julie White, David Atkinson **production** 20 000 **est.** 1972
product range ($8.40–45 CD) Wood Aged Chenin Blanc, Chardonnay, James Vineyard Verdelho, James Vineyard Chardonnay, Sauvignon Blanc, Late Harvest Cabernet Merlot, Mountjoy Cabernet Merlot, Shiraz, Elizabeth Jane Méthode Champenoise, Fortifieds.
summary An attractive winery which relies in part on substantial cellar-door trade and in part on varying export markets, with much work having been invested in the Japanese market in recent years. It is in the course of establishing vineyards in the Margaret River and also is now sourcing fruit from Pemberton. Exports to Japan, Malaysia, Singapore and Taiwan, with distribution in each of the Australian States.

Jane Brook Estate James Vineyard Chardonnay

Sourced from the Swan Valley, and shows much better selection and use of oak than in bygone years.

❦❦❦❦ **1999** Light green-yellow; the bouquet is quite complex, with tangy oak and stylish fruit; the palate offers well-balanced fruit, oak and acidity, the only criticism being a lack of intensity in the fruit. **rating:** 85

best drinking 2000–2001 **best vintages** NA **drink with** Grilled chicken • $17.50

Jane Brook Estate Mountjoy Cabernet Merlot

A trophy winner at the 1999 Swan Valley Wine Show, which is a fair indication of the difficulty of producing wines of this style in such a relentlessly hot climate.

❦❦❦❦ **1998** Light to medium red-purple; the bouquet is plain, light and clean, the palate likewise; there are faint leafy characters, but the main drawback is a lack of concentration. **rating:** 80

best drinking 2000–2002 **best vintages** NA **drink with** Asian meat dishes • $19.50

jardee NR

Old School House, Jardee, WA 6258 **region** Pemberton, Warren Valley and Manjimup
phone (08) 9777 1552 **fax** (08) 9777 1552 **open** Not
winemaker Barrie Smith **production** 510 **est.** 1994
product range ($18–22 R) Chardonnay, Pinot Noir.
summary Jardee is a pioneering mill town, the wines are in fact made in tiny quantities from purchased fruit, the operation being a part-time interest for proprietor Steve Miolin.

jasper hill ★★★★★

Drummonds Lane, Heathcote, Vic 3523 **region** Bendigo
phone (03) 5433 2528 **fax** (03) 5433 3143 **open** By appointment
winemaker Ron Laughton **production** 3000 **est.** 1975
product range ($17–66 R) Georgia's Paddock Riesling, Georgia's Paddock Shiraz, Emily's Paddock Shiraz Cabernet Franc.
summary The red wines of Jasper Hill are highly regarded and much sought after, invariably selling out at cellar door and through the mailing list within a short time after release. These are wonderful wines, reflecting the very low yields and the care and attention given to them by Ron Laughton. The oak is not overdone, the fruit flavours showing Central Victoria at its best. No tasting of the 1998 vintage wines since they were bottled.

jasper valley   NR

RMB 880 Croziers Road, Berry, NSW 2535 **region** Shoalhaven
phone (02) 4464 1596 **fax** (02) 4464 1596 **open** 7 days 9.30–5.30
winemaker Contract **production** 1100 **est.** 1976
product range ($4.20–12 CD) White Burgundy, Riesling, Traminer Riesling, Moselle, Summer Red, Cabernet Sauvignon, Port; also non-alcoholic fruit wines.
summary A strongly tourist-oriented winery with most of its wine purchased as cleanskins from other makers. Features about 1 hectare of lawns, barbecue facilities, and sweeping views.

jeanneret wines   ★★★☆

Jeanneret Road, Sevenhill, SA 5453 **region** Clare Valley
phone (08) 8843 4308 **fax** (08) 8843 4251 **open** Mon–Fri 11–5, weekends and public holidays 10–5
winemaker Ben Jeanneret **production** 6000 **est.** 1992
product range ($15–22 CD) Riesling, Semillon, Sparkling Grenache, Shiraz, Cabernet Sauvignon.
summary Jeanneret's fully self-contained winery has a most attractive outdoor tasting area and equally attractive picnic facilities situated on the edge of a small lake surrounded by bushland. While it did not open the business until October 1994, its first wine was in fact made in 1992 (Shiraz) and it has already established a loyal following. National wholesale distribution; export markets have been established in Canada, the UK and the US.

Jeanneret Riesling

The grapes are hand-harvested from vines in the heart of the Watervale subregion, the wine is slow-fermented at cool temperatures in stainless steel, and is early-bottled in traditional fashion.
♥♥♥♡ 1999 Light yellow-green; the bouquet is very closed and lacks aromatics; the palate, too, is subdued other than for its acidity. Not easy to tell how the wine will develop, but could pleasantly surprise.   **rating:** 80
best drinking 2000–2004 **best vintages** NA **drink with** Shellfish • $15

Jeanneret Semillon

Comes from one hectare of organically grown semillon on a dry-farmed vineyard, and hand-picked over a 20-day period. Twenty per cent of the wine is barrel-fermented in French oak, the remainder in stainless steel.
♥♥♥♥ 1999 Light to medium green-yellow; the bouquet is quite complex, the oak being evident but not assertive. The palate is firm and crisp, with flavours of herb and lemon and a touch of slatey grip. Could develop well.   **rating:** 85
best drinking 2000–2005 **best vintages** NA **drink with** Yabbies • $15

Jeanneret Shiraz

Produced from 1.5 hectares of organically grown estate plantings.
♥♥♥♡ 1998 Medium purple-red; the bouquet is solid, with savoury earthy characters merging with dark berry fruits. Much the same interplay occurs on the palate, with black cherry, mint and then some slightly stemmy notes; restrained oak and tannins.   **rating:** 84
best drinking 2003–2008 **best vintages** NA **drink with** Beef stew with olives • $20

Jeanneret Cabernet Sauvignon

The principal vineyard source is the Stanley Flat subregion, together with a small amount from the Sevenhill area. It is extended maturation in one- and two-year-old French oak.
♥♥♥♡ 1998 Medium red-purple; the bouquet has clear-cut cabernet varietal character in an earth/herb/leaf/savoury spectrum. The palate, too, is in a distinctly austere mode, with leafy/earthy flavours of some depth.   **rating:** 81
best drinking 2002–2008 **best vintages** NA **drink with** Leg of lamb • $19

jeir creek   ★★★

Gooda Creek Road, Murrumbateman, NSW 2582 **region** Canberra District
phone (02) 6227 5999 **fax** (02) 6227 5900 **open** Fri–Sun, holidays 10–5
winemaker Rob Howell **production** 4000 **est.** 1984
product range ($16–20 CD) Riesling, Late Harvest Riesling, Botrytis Semillon Sauvignon Blanc, Semillon Sauvignon Blanc, Sauvignon Blanc, Chardonnay, Pinot Noir, Shiraz, Cabernet Merlot.
summary Rob Howell came to part-time winemaking through a love of drinking fine wine and is intent on improving both the quality and consistency of his wines. It is now a substantial (and still growing) business, with the vineyard plantings increased to 11 hectares by the establishment of more cabernet sauvignon, shiraz and merlot.

jenke vineyards ★★★

Barossa Valley Way, Rowland Flat, SA 5352 **region** Barossa Valley
phone (08) 8524 4154 **fax** (08) 8524 5044 **open** 7 days 11–5
winemaker Kym Jenke **production** 8000 **est.** 1989
product range ($13.50–30 CD) Riesling, Semillon, Chardonnay, Late Harvest Riesling, Mourvedre, Merlot, Cabernet Franc, Cabernet Sauvignon, Shiraz, Sparkling Shiraz.
summary The Jenkes have been vignerons in the Barossa since 1854 and have over 25 hectares of vineyards; a small part of the production is now made and marketed through a charming restored stone cottage cellar door. Wholesale distribution in Victoria and New South Wales; exports to the UK, the US, Canada, Switzerland and Germany.

jester hill wines NR

Mount Stirling Road, Glen Aplin, Qld 4381 **region** Granite Belt
phone (07) 4683 4380 **fax** (07) 4683 4380 **open** Not
winemaker Adrien Kuffer **production** 600 **est.** 1993
product range ($10.50–16 CD) Chardonnay, Shiraz, Shiraz Cabernet Sauvignon, Cabernet Sauvignon Shiraz, Dysons Flat Fortified Shiraz.
summary John and Genevieve Ashwell have established a little under 5 hectares of vines, predominantly shiraz and cabernet sauvignon, with lesser amounts of sauvignon blanc, merlot and chardonnay. The first commercial vintage is expected to be made in 2000.

jim barry wines ★★★★☆

Main North Road, Clare, SA 5453 **region** Clare Valley
phone (08) 8842 2261 **fax** (08) 8842 3752 **open** Mon–Fri 9–5, weekends, holidays 9–4
winemaker Mark Barry **production** 40 000 **est.** 1959
product range ($6.50–120 R) Watervale Riesling, Lodge Hill Riesling, Personal Selection Semillon Sauvignon Blanc and Chardonnay, Semillon, Unwooded Chardonnay, Lavendar Hill, Cabernet Shiraz, Personal Selection Cabernet Sauvignon, McCrae Wood Shiraz and Cabernet Malbec, The Armagh (Shiraz).
summary The Armagh and the McCrae Wood range continue to stand out as the very best wines from Jim Barry, exceptionally concentrated and full flavoured. The remainder are seldom less than adequate but do vary somewhat from one vintage to the next. Has an exceptional viticultural resource base of 160 hectares of mature Clare Valley vineyards. Exports to the UK, much of Europe, North America, Japan and Southeast Asia.

Jim Barry Watervale Riesling

The often excellent quality of this wine can be attributed in part to skilled winemaking but more particularly to the acquisition by Jim Barry of the famed Florita Vineyard at Watervale, once a jewel in the Leo Buring crown, and sold during a dark period of the latter's history. Leo Buring's loss has been Jim Barry's gain.

▼▼▼▼ **1999** Medium to full yellow-green; there is plenty of weight and depth to the bouquet with a mix of lime, apple and mineral aromas. A big, solidly built palate with abundant flavour, albeit not much finesse. Excellent short-term drinking. **rating:** 87

best drinking 2000–2005 **best vintages** '83, '86, '89, '91, '94, '95, '99 **drink with** Ginger pork • $12

Jim Barry McCrae Wood Shiraz

Ranks second to The Armagh Shiraz in terms of price, and first released in 1992. As with The Armagh, it is based upon scrupulous fruit selection and shows the well-handled use of oak. Whereas The Armagh needs decades, this wine only needs ten years.

▼▼▼▼▽ **1997** Medium to full red-purple; the bouquet is of medium to full intensity, in the mainstream of the style, with luscious berry and prune fruit aromas and well-balanced and integrated oak. There is a touch of mint on the palate, but even more ripe, red berry fruit; well-balanced tannin and oak. **rating:** 90

best drinking 2002–2010 **best vintages** '92, '93, '94, '95, '97 **drink with** Jugged hare • $39.95

Jim Barry The Armagh

First made in 1985 from very old, unirrigated, low-yielding vines. Not produced in 1986, and not exhibited in wine shows until the 1987 vintage was made. Since that time every vintage since the '87 has received at least one gold medal. Unashamedly a Grange pretender, and succeeding well in its aim.

▼▼▼▼ **1997** Medium red-purple; the moderately intense bouquet has a mix of berry, spice and leaf, with well-controlled oak. The palate denies the 14.5 degrees alcohol the wine has, with cherry, spice and leaf flavours, gentle tannins and balanced oak. **rating:** 89

best drinking 2002–2012 **best vintages** '89, '90, '91, '92, '93, '95, '96 **drink with** The richest game dish possible • $120

Jim Barry McCrae Wood Cabernet Malbec

The blend of Cabernet and Malbec is a Clare Valley specialty, pioneered by Leasingham in the vinous dawn of time. Malbec flourishes in the Clare Valley as in few parts of Australia, adding a juicy sweetness to the formidable power of Clare Valley Cabernet.

▼▼▼▼ 1997 Dense red-purple; a very rich and powerful bouquet crammed with blackberry and chocolate fruit is followed by a palate with compellingly rich and sweet fruit, perfectly offset with ripe tannins and subtle oak.

rating: 93

best drinking 2002–2012 **best vintages** NA **drink with** Oxtail • $39.95

jindalee estate ★★★☆

265 Ballan Road, Moorabool, North Geelong, Vic 3215 **region** Geelong
phone (03) 5277 2836 **fax** (03) 5277 2840 **open** 7 days 10–5 (from October 2000)
winemaker Contract **production** 100 000 **est.** 1997
product range ($9.95–11.95 R) Chardonnay, Shiraz, Merlot, Cabernet Sauvignon.
summary Jindalee Wines made its debut with the 1997 vintage. It is part of the Littore Group, which currently has 400 hectares of premium-wine grapes in wine production and under development in the Riverland. Corporate offices are now at the former Idyll Vineyard, acquired by Jindalee in late 1997. Here 15 hectares of estate vineyards are being re-trellised and upgraded, and a premium Jindalee Estate range should be on the market by mid-2000. National distribution through FD&C Wine; exports to the UK, the US, Malaysia, Singapore and China.

Jindalee Estate Chardonnay

Comes from the Jindalee vineyards in the Murray Darling region. Both the 1998 and '99 vintages offer excellent value for money.

▼▼▼▼ 1999 Medium to full yellow-green; quite rich, solid stone fruit aromas are followed by generous peachy fruit on the palate; very clever use of oak chips provides just a hint of oak.

rating: 83

best drinking 2000–2001 **best vintages** NA **drink with** Takeaway chicken • $9.95

Jindalee Estate Shiraz

A brother to the Chardonnay, and, if anything, showing even greater winemaking skills. Once again the winemaking team has resisted the temptation of front end-loading the wine with American oak chips.

▼▼▼▼ 1999 Medium to full red-purple; the bouquet is quite complex, with faintly leathery varietal fruit character, and there is masses of flavour on the rich and complex palate. The tannins and the oak are as good as you will ever find in a wine at this price point.

rating: 86

best drinking 2000–2004 **best vintages** NA **drink with** Pizza, pasta • $9.95

jingalla ★★★★

RMB 1316 Bolganup Dam Road, Porongurup, WA 6324 **region** Great Southern
phone (08) 9853 1023 **fax** (08) 9853 1023 **open** 7 days 10.30–5
winemaker John Wade, Robert Lee (Consultant) **production** 3500 **est.** 1979
product range ($11–23 CD) Great Southern White and Red, Riesling, Semillon, Verdelho, Late Harvest, Botrytis Riesling Verdelho, Shiraz Reserve, Cabernet Rouge, Cabernet Sauvignon, Late Harvest Semillon, Tawny Port, Liqueur Muscat.
summary Jingalla is a family-run business, owned and run by Geoff and Nita Clarke and Barry and Shelley Coad, the latter the ever-energetic wine marketer of the business. The 8 hectares of hillside vineyards are low-yielding, with the white wines succeeding best. Consistently competent winemaking at Goundrey has resulted in a range of very reliable, positively flavoured wines. While best known for its wooded and unwooded whites, it also produces some lovely red wines. National distribution; exports to Japan, Germany and Taiwan.

Jingalla Riesling

Produced from 2 hectares of riesling, with two clones, including the so-called Geisenheim clone. Consistent performer, always exhibiting abundant fruit flavour. Sometimes helped by a touch of traminer.

▼▼▼▼ 1999 Medium yellow-green; powerful, very ripe passionfruit and pineapple fruit on the bouquet is repeated on a very ripe, slightly broad, palate.

rating: 82

best drinking 2000–2002 **best vintages** '84, '86, '90, '93, '96, '98 **drink with** Chinese or Thai cuisine • $15.50

Jingalla Shiraz Reserve

Produced from 2 hectares of low-yielding, dry-grown vines, and a selection of the best barrels, bottled after two years in wood. The remaining Shiraz is blended with Cabernet Sauvignon to produce Jingalla's Great Southern Red.

TTTTY 1998 Medium to full red-purple; the moderately intense bouquet has spicy, savoury aromas which have an underlying sweetness. The same interplay occurs on the intense palate, where those spicy savoury notes mingle with sweet plum and cherry fruit swelling on the back palate. Fine, gentle tannins complete a delicious wine.

rating: 91

best drinking 2003–2013 **best vintages** '94, '98 **drink with** Ox tail • $23

jinks creek winery NR

Tonimbuk Road, Tonimbuk, Vic 3815 **region** Gippsland
phone (03) 5629 8502 **fax** (03) 5629 8551 **open** By appointment
winemaker Andrew Clarke **production** NA **est.** 1981
product range ($14 CD) Sauvignon Blanc, Chardonnay, Pinot Noir.
summary Jinks Creek Winery is situated between Gembrook and Bunyip, bordering the evocatively named Bunyip State Park. While the winery was not built until 1992, planting of the 2.5-hectare vineyard started back in 1981 and all of the wines are estate-grown. The 'sold out' sign goes up each year.

joadja vineyards NR

Joadja Road, Berrima, NSW 2577 **region** Other Wineries of NSW
phone (02) 4878 5236 **fax** (02) 4878 5236 **open** 7 days 10–5
winemaker Kim Moginie **production** 2000 **est.** 1983
product range ($13–21 CD) Classic Dry White, Sauvignon Blanc, Chardonnay, Botrytis Autumn Riesling, Sauternes, Classic Dry Red, Cabernet Malbec, Christopher Tawny Port.
summary The strikingly labelled Joadja Vineyards wines, first made in 1990, are principally drawn from 7 hectares of estate vineyards situated in the cool hills adjacent to Berrima. Both the red and whites have a consistent eucalypt/peppermint character which is clearly a product of the climate and (possibly) soil. Joadja is well worth a visit.

john gehrig wines ★★☆

Oxley–Milawa Road, Oxley, Vic 3678 **region** King Valley
phone (03) 5727 3395 **fax** (03) 5727 3699 **open** 7 days 9–5
winemaker John Gehrig **production** 5600 **est.** 1976
product range ($9–25 CD) Oxley Dry White, Riesling, Chardonnay, Late Harvest Riesling, Sparkling, Oxley Rosé, Pinot Noir, King River Red, Merlot, Cabernet Merlot, Fortifieds.
summary Honest, if seldom exciting, wines; the occasional Chardonnay, Pinot Noir, Merlot and Cabernet Merlot have, however, risen above their station.

jollymont NR

145 Pullens Road, Woodbridge, Tas 7162 **region** Southern Tasmania
phone (03) 6267 4594 **fax** (03) 6267 4594 **open** Not
winemaker Andrew Hood (Contract) **production** 20 **est.** 1990
product range ($20–25 R) Chardonnay, Pinot Noir.
summary However briefly, Jollymont has displaced Scarp Valley as the smallest producer in Australia, its 1998 vintage (the first) producing 10 cases. The vines are not irrigated, nor will they be, and Peter and Heather Kreet do not intend to sell any wine younger than three to four years old. Their aim is to produce wines of maximum intensity and complexity.

jones winery NR

Jones Road, Rutherglen, Vic 3685 **region** Rutherglen and Glenrowan
phone (02) 6032 8496 **fax** (02) 6032 8495 **open** Fri–Sat 10–5, Sun and holidays 10–4
winemaker Mandy Jones **production** 7000 **est.** 1864
product range Chablis, Riesling, White Burgundy, Light Red, Dry Red, Fortifieds.
summary Late in 1998 the winery was purchased from Les Jones by Leanne Schoen and Mandy and Arthur Jones (nieces and nephew of Les). They are planning to redevelop the property in the next few years, but to concentrate on Shiraz and the styles of wine that the winery is known for. All wine is sold through the cellar door.

𝕚 juniper estate   NR

Harmans Road South, Cowaramup, WA 6284   **region** Margaret River
phone (08) 9755 9000   **fax** (08) 9755 9100   **open** 7 days 10–5
winemaker Mark Messenger   **production** 4900   **est.** 1998
product range ($14–19 R) Under the Juniper Crossing label are Semillon Sauvignon Blanc, Chenin Blanc, Late Harvest Riesling, Chardonnay, Shiraz; Juniper Estate Cabernet Sauvignon.
summary This is the reincarnation of Wrights, which was sold by founders Henry and Maureen Wright in 1998. The 10-hectare vineyard has been retrellised, and the last 1.5 hectares of plantable land has seen the key plantings of shiraz and cabernet sauvignon increase a little. A major building programme was completed in February 2000, giving Juniper Estate a new 250-tonne capacity winery, barrel hall and cellar-door facility. The Juniper family is a famous one in the Margaret River region, its strong artistic bent evident in the immaculate packaging and background material. So far only Juniper Crossing wines have been released using a mix of estate-grown and contract-purchased grapes from other Margaret River vineyards. The upcoming Juniper Estate releases will be made only from the 25-year-old estate plantings.

Juniper Estate Shiraz
Shiraz has been relatively slow in making its presence felt in the Margaret River region, but there are far more successes than there are failures with this variety. That of Juniper is emphatically in the former group.
▼▼▼▼ **1999** Excellent purple-red; there is rich, soft dark cherry fruit and attractive oak on the bouquet, leading into abundant black cherry, liquorice and sweet leather flavours on the palate; the tannins are quite persistent, but not aggressive.   **rating:** 88
best drinking 2003–2008   **drink with** Venison pie   • $19

kaesler   ★★★

Barossa Valley Way, Nuriootpa, SA 5355   **region** Barossa Valley
phone (08) 8562 2711   **fax** (08) 8562 2788   **open** 7 days 10–5
winemaker Contract   **production** 1000   **est.** 1990
product range ($9–30 CD) Prestige Semillon, Cottage Block White, Late Harvest Semillon, Bush Vine Grenache, Old Vine Shiraz, Beerenauslese, Prestige Cuvée, Méthode Champenoise, Old Vine Shiraz, Fortifieds.
summary Toby and Treena Hueppauff purchased Kaesler Farm, with its 12 hectares of vines, in 1985 and since 1990 have had the wines made under contract by others. The winery has an à la carte restaurant offering both indoor and outdoor dining; there is also accommodation. The wines are exported to California.

kaiser stuhl   ★★☆

Tanunda Road, Nuriootpa, SA 5355   **region** Barossa Valley
phone (08) 8560 9389   **fax** (08) 8562 1669   **open** Mon–Sat 10–5, Sun 1–5
winemaker Nigel Logos   **production** 1.3 million   **est.** 1931
product range ($4–12 R) Black Forest, generic whites under bin numbers, Claret Bin 33, Bin 44 Riesling, Bin 55 Moselle, Bin 66 Burgundy, Bin 77 Chablis, Sparkling; also extensive cask and flagon range.
summary Part of the Southcorp Wines empire but a shadow of its former self, with its once-famous Green Ribbon Riesling and Red Ribbon Shiraz no more. Essentially provides flagon-quality wines in bottles at competitive prices.

kalari vineyards   NR

120 Carro Park Road, Cowra, NSW 2794   **region** Cowra
phone (02) 6342 1465   **fax** (02) 6342 1465   **open** Thurs–Mon 10–4
winemaker Alan Kennett, Jill Lindsay (Contract)   **production** 1000   **est.** 1995
product range ($14–17 ML) Verdelho, Late Picked Verdelho, Chardonnay, Unwooded Chardonnay, Shiraz.
summary Kalari Vineyards is yet another of the new brands to appear in the Cowra region. Fourteen and a half hectares of vines have been established, with a Verdelho, Chardonnay and Shiraz being included in the initial release.

kangarilla road vineyard & winery   ★★★☆

Kangarilla Road, McLaren Vale, SA 5171   **region** McLaren Vale
phone (08) 8383 0533   **fax** (08) 8383 0044   **open** Mon–Fri 9–5, weekends 11–5
winemaker Kevin O'Brien   **production** 15 000   **est.** 1975
product range ($12–30 CD) Chardonnay, Zinfandel, Shiraz, Cabernet Sauvignon, Tawny Port, Vintage Port.
summary Kangarilla Road Vineyard & Winery was formerly known as Stevens Cambrai. Long-time industry identity Kevin O'Brien and wife Helen purchased the property in July 1997 and are continuing to sell the existing stocks of Cambrai wines but with the strikingly labelled Kangarilla Road brand to progressively replace it.

Kangarilla Road Shiraz

Produced from grapes grown on three McLaren Vale vineyards, the first in the hills behind Coriole, the second on sandy soil at Blewitt Springs, and the third (and latest-ripening) from Kangarilla Road's own vineyard. All the parcels are open-fermented, and were separately matured in various combination of American and French and American oak. The wine spends months in barrel before being bottled.

♥♥♥♥ 1998 Medium to full red-purple; the bouquet is quite complex, with cedar, spice and liquorice, the medium-weight palate moving into sweeter, and perhaps simpler, red berry fruit and nicely restrained oak.

rating: 85

best drinking 2003–2008 best vintages '97 drink with Barbecued beef • $19

Kangarilla Road Zinfandel

Graham Stevens planted zinfandel almost 30 years ago, sometimes releasing it as a straight varietal, but more often blending it with other reds. It has had an up and down career since being made and released as a varietal wine.

♥♥♥♡ 1998 Light red; the bouquet is intriguing, with wafts of bacony, smoky, charry oak and fruit. The palate is reminiscent of ripe Grenache, with jammy fruit balanced by some acidity towards the finish. My problem is the lack of continuity in the palate.

rating: 80

best drinking 2000–2001 best vintages '96 drink with Spiced Moroccan lamb • $30

Kangarilla Road Cabernet Sauvignon

Produced from estate-grown grapes, open-fermented and plunged or pumped over twice a day. The wine spends 12 months in a mix of new, one-year-old and two-year-old French and American oak hogsheads.

♥♥♥♡ 1998 Medium red, with just a touch of purple; the bouquet is clean, moderately intense, with nicely weighted sweet berry fruit; the palate offers similar straightforward, no tricks, cabernet fruit, the oak all but imperceptible.

rating: 83

best drinking 2002–2008 best vintages NA drink with Ox tongue • $19

kangaroo island vines   NR

c/o 413 Payneham Road, Felixstow, SA 5070 **region** Other Wineries of SA
phone (08) 8365 3411 **fax** (08) 8336 2462 **open** Not
winemaker Caj Amadio **production** 600 **est.** 1990
product range ($19–23 ML) Island Sting, Cabernet Merlot, Special Reserve Cabernet Merlot.
summary Kangaroo Island is another venture of Caj and Genny Amadio, with the wines being sold through the Chain of Ponds cellar door. The Amadios have been the focal point of the development of vineyards on Kangaroo Island, producing the wines not only from their own tiny planting of 450 vines on quarter of an acre, but buying grapes from other vignerons on the island. The tiny quantities of wine so far produced strongly support the notion that Kangaroo Island has an excellent climate for Bordeaux-style reds, particularly the excellent Special Reserve Cabernet Merlot.

kangderaar vineyard   NR

Melvilles Caves Road, Rheola, Vic 3517 **region** Bendigo
phone (03) 5438 8292 **fax** (03) 5438 8292 **open** Mon–Sat 9–5, Sun 10–5
winemaker James Nealy **production** 500 **est.** 1980
product range ($12–15 CD) Chardonnay, Vintage Reserve Chardonnay, Cabernet Sauvignon.
summary The 4.5-hectare vineyard is situated at Rheola, near the Melville Caves, said to have been the hideout of the bushranger Captain Melville in the 1850s, and surrounded by the Kooyoora State Park. It is owned by James and Christine Nealy.

kara kara vineyard   ★★★

Sunraysia Highway, St Arnaud, Vic 3478 (10 km sth St Arnaud) **region** Pyrenees
phone (03) 5496 3294 **fax** (03) 5496 3294 **open** Mon–Fri 10.30–6, weekends 9–6
winemaker John Ellis, Steve Szigmond **production** 2500 **est.** 1977
product range ($17–20 CD) Chardonnay, Sauvignon Blanc, Semillon, Fume Blanc, Late Harvest Semillon, Shiraz Cabernet.
summary Hungarian-born Steve Zsigmond comes from a long line of vignerons and sees Kara Kara as the eventual retirement occupation for himself and wife Marlene. The first step has been the decision to have their production contract-made (first by Mitchelton, then by John Ellis — previously the grapes were sold) with predictably consistent results over the first few years. Draws upon 9 hectares of estate plantings.

karina vineyard ★★★★

35 Harrisons Road, Dromana, Vic 3936 **region** Mornington Peninsula
phone (03) 5981 0137 **fax** (03) 5981 0137 **open** Weekends 11–5, 7 days in January
winemaker Gerard Terpstra **production** 1500 **est.** 1984
product range ($15–21 CD) Riesling, Sauvignon Blanc, Chardonnay, Cabernet Merlot, Bald Hill Creek (Cabernet Sauvignon).
summary A typical Mornington Peninsula vineyard, situated in the Dromana/Redhill area on rising, north-facing slopes, just 3 kilometres from the shores of Port Phillip Bay, immaculately tended and with picturesque garden surrounds. Fragrant Riesling and cashew-accented Chardonnay are its best wines.

karl seppelt ★★★☆

Ross Dewells Road, Springton, SA 5235 **region** Eden Valley
phone (08) 8568 2378 **fax** (08) 8568 2799 **open** 7 days 10–5
winemaker Karl Seppelt, Petaluma (Contract) **production** 2500 **est.** 1981
product range ($18–22 R) Riesling, Springton Chardonnay, Springton Cabernet Sauvignon, Langhorne Creek Shiraz, Chardonnay Brut, Sparkling Shiraz, Brut Sauvage, Fino Sherry, Vintage Port, Tawny Port.
summary After experimenting with various label designs and names, Karl Seppelt (former marketing director of Seppelt) has decided to discontinue the brand name Grand Cru (although retaining it as a business name) and henceforth market the wines from his estate vineyards under his own name. The quality is highly consistent across the range, and the wines are exported to Canada, Germany and Japan.

karrivale ★★★★☆

Woodlands Road, Porongurup, WA 6324 **region** Great Southern
phone (08) 9853 1009 **fax** (08) 9853 1129 **open** Wed–Sun 10–5
winemaker Gavin Berry (Contract) **production** 1170 **est.** 1979
product range ($12–18 CD) Riesling, Chardonnay.
summary A tiny Riesling specialist in the wilds of the Porongurups forced to change its name from Narang because Lindemans felt it could be confused with its Nyrang Shiraz brand; truly a strange world. The viticultural skills of owner Campbell McGready and ultra-competent contract-winemaking fulfil the promise of this beautifully sited vineyard and its long-lived Riesling.

karriview ★★★★

RMB 913 Roberts Road, Denmark, WA 6333 **region** Great Southern
phone (08) 9840 9381 **fax** (08) 9840 9381 **open** Summer school holidays 7 days 11–4, Feb–Dec Fri–Tues 11–4
winemaker Michael Kerrigan (Contract) **production** 800 **est.** 1986
product range ($23–28 CD) Chardonnay, Pinot Noir.
summary One hectare each of immaculately tended pinot noir and chardonnay on ultra-close spacing produce tiny quantities of two wines of remarkable intensity, quality and style. Available only from the winery, but worth the effort. There is some vintage variation; the winery rating is based upon the successes, not the disappointments. Typically, back vintages are available; with age, the Pinot Noir acquires strong foresty characters which are quite Burgundian.

Karriview Chardonnay

Due to the ultra-close spacing of the vineyard, with exceedingly narrow rows, all of the work is done by hand, but the quality of the wine makes the effort worthwhile.
 1998 Medium to full yellow-green; quite rich, ripe figgy fruit marries with subtle oak on the bouquet. The palate is rich and solid, with concentrated figgy fruit and again subtly spicy oak. **rating:** 89
best drinking 2001–2005 **best vintages** '90, '92, '93, '95, '98 **drink with** Marron, yabbies • $25

Karriview Pinot Noir

Normally, the wine is severe and stemmy, distinguished but slightly forbidding. The '98 breaks the mould.
 1998 Medium red-purple; very ripe plum fruit veers almost into prune on the bouquet, and the palate is likewise stacked with very ripe fruit. Slippery acidity on the finish comes to save the wine at the last breath. **rating:** 86
best drinking 2000–2003 **best vintages** '90, '91, '92, '94 **drink with** Quail salad • $28

katnook estate ★★★★☆

Riddoch Highway, Coonawarra, SA 5263 **region** Coonawarra
phone (08) 8737 2394 **fax** (08) 8737 2397 **open** Mon–Fri 9–4.30, weekends 10–4.30
winemaker Wayne Stehbens **production** 70 000 **est.** 1979
product range ($8.50–40 R) Under the premium Katnook label: Riesling, Sauvignon Blanc, Chardonnay, Botrytis Riesling, Cabernet Sauvignon, Merlot, Odyssey (super-premium Cabernet) and Chardonnay Brut; under the Riddoch label: Chardonnay, Sauvignon Blanc, Shiraz and Cabernet Shiraz Merlot; also Woolshed Chardonnay and Cabernet Shiraz Merlot.
summary Still the largest contract grape grower and supplier in Coonawarra, selling 60 per cent of its grape production to others. The historic stone woolshed in which the second vintage in Coonawarra (1896) was made and which has served Katnook since 1980 is being restored. Together with the 1997 launch of the flagship Odyssey, points the way for a higher profile for the winemaking side of the venture. Exports to the UK, Northern Ireland, the US, Canada, Switzerland, Hong Kong and the Philippines.

Katnook Estate Riesling

At one point of time there was more riesling planted in Coonawarra than either cabernet sauvignon or shiraz. Times have changed dramatically, but Coonawarra has always been capable of producing first class Riesling if enough care is taken. It has an elegance seldom achieved in other Australian regions.
▼▼▼▼ **1999** Light green-yellow; the bouquet is light, with dusty/minerally aromas, the palate fine and delicate, with light, lemony flavours. All of these characters come together surprisingly well, and the wine will undoubtedly improve with cellaring. **rating:** 86
▼▼▼▼▽ **1998** Light to medium yellow-green; the bouquet is fragrant, with a mix of passionfruit, lime and apple. The palate shows the same excellent fruit, with lime and apple flavours running through a long, crisp finish. Totally delicious; if it develops like the '97 has over the past year, will be significantly better in the future and no doubt deserve higher points still. **rating:** 93
best drinking 2000–2005 **best vintages** NA **drink with** Vegetable terrine •$17.95

Katnook Estate Chardonnay

Stands alongside Sauvignon Blanc as Katnook's most consistent wine, always elegant and always long-lived. Produced from the pick of 18 hectares of mature vineyards.
▼▼▼▼ **1997** Medium to full yellow-green; the bouquet is clean, predominantly in the nectarine/citrus spectrum but with a touch of herbaceous lemon zest. The palate is well balanced, although that hint of herbaceousness is a slight distraction; sensitive oak handling is a decided plus. **rating:** 89
best drinking 2000–2007 **best vintages** '84, '86, '90, '92, '94, '96, '97 **drink with** Poached salmon •$30

Riddoch Shiraz

The wine is matured in small American oak barrels (20 per cent new, 30 per cent one year old, the balance older) for 15 months.
▼▼▼▽ **1998** Medium red-purple; the bouquet has some spicy/leathery notes in varietal mode, the palate with pleasant, soft dark cherry and spicy fruit. Minimal oak. **rating:** 83
best drinking 2000–2005 **best vintages** NA **drink with** Barbecued steak •$15.90

Katnook Estate Merlot

Produced from 100 per cent estate-grown merlot. It is aged for 19 months in barriques principally from the Nevers and Troncais forests of France, 30 per cent new.
▼▼▼▼ **1997** Medium red-purple; the bouquet is at once subtle yet complex, with savoury/foresty aromas which flow through seamlessly to the palate, where they are a little more intense, backed by plummy fruit and supported by soft tannins. One of the many faces of Australian Merlot. **rating:** 89
best drinking 2001–2007 **best vintages** NA **drink with** Roast wing rib of beef with mushrooms •$35

Katnook Estate Cabernet Sauvignon

Made from the very best selection from 70 hectares of estate vineyards but took its time in establishing the style it has shown since 1990 and, in particular, the power and concentration one expects from a wine in this price category.
▼▼▼▼▼ **1997** Medium to full red-purple; cedar, leaf, earth and berry on the bouquet lead into a palate with surprisingly sweet and gentle cassis cabernet fruit; fine flavour and length; sophisticated oak handling. **rating:** 95
best drinking 2001–2011 **best vintages** '90, '91, '92, '94, '97 **drink with** Prime rib of beef •$40

kay bros amery ★★★

Kay Road, McLaren Vale, SA 5171 **region** McLaren Vale
phone (08) 8323 8211 **fax** (08) 8323 9199 **open** Mon–Fri 9–5, weekends and public holidays 12–5
winemaker Colin Kay **production** 6000 **est.** 1890
product range ($15–33 CD) Sauvignon Blanc, Late Harvest Frontignac, Chardonnay, Shiraz, Block 6 Shiraz, Grenache, Merlot, Cabernet Sauvignon; Port Liqueur, Muscat.
summary A traditional winery with a rich history and 16 hectares of priceless old vines; while the white wines have been variable, the red wines and fortified wines can be very good. Of particular interest is Block 6 Shiraz, made from 100-year-old vines; both vines and wine are going from strength to strength.

kellermeister ★★★

Barossa Valley Highway, Lyndoch, SA 5351 **region** Barossa Valley
phone (08) 8524 4303 **fax** (08) 8524 4880 **open** 7 days 9–6
winemaker Trevor Jones **production** 8000 **est.** 1970
product range ($8.50–26.50 CD) High Country Riesling, Show Reserve Riesling, Abendlese, Frontignan Spatlese and Auslese, Late Harvest Sylvaner, Cabernet Rosé, Black Sash Shiraz, Cabernet Sauvignon, Cabernet Shiraz, Sparkling and Fortifieds; also the Trevor Jones range (under his own label) of Virgin Chardonnay, Riesling, Cabernet Merlot and Dry Grown Barossa Shiraz.
summary Specialises in older vintage wines made in traditional fashion, an extraordinary array of which are on offer at enticing prices. There is always a range of vintages available; the wines are soft and generous, if very traditional, in style.

kellybrook ★★★☆

Fulford Road, Wonga Park, Vic 3115 **region** Yarra Valley
phone (03) 9722 1304 **fax** (03) 9722 2092 **open** Mon–Sat 9–6, Sun 11–6
winemaker Darren Kelly, Philip Kelly **production** 3000 **est.** 1960
product range ($16–24 CD) Chardonnay, Riesling, Gewürztraminer, Pinot Noir, Shiraz, Cabernet Merlot, Cabernet Shiraz, Méthode Champenoise, Champagne Cider, Apple Brandy, Liqueur Muscat, Old Vintage Tawny Port.
summary The 8-hectare vineyard is situated at Wonga Park at the entrance to the principal winegrowing areas of the Yarra Valley, replete with picnic area and a full-scale restaurant. As well as table wine, a very competent producer of both cider and apple brandy (in Calvados style). Retail distribution through Victoria, New South Wales, Queensland and South Australia.

Kellybrook Chardonnay
The Kellybrook vineyards are now fully mature, and are relatively low yielding; the concentration of fruit flavour shows in the wine in the best vintages.
▼▼▼♡ **1999** Medium yellow-green; the moderately complex bouquet has some malty/meady notes, the palate veering more to citrus and melon in a fruit-driven style. Should improve with some time in bottle. **rating:** 80
best drinking 2001–2004 **best vintages** NA **drink with** Yarra Valley yabbies • $18

Kellybrook Shiraz
A lovely wine made during the late Peter Draper's brief tenure as winemaker for Kellybrook. Quantities are limited, as there is less than 1 hectare of shiraz grapes on the estate, but the wine is yet further proof of the suitability of the Yarra Valley to this grape, which is in fact relatively sparsely grown in the region.
▼▼▼▼ **1998** Bright purple-red of medium depth. The palate is clean, with ripe plum and cherry fruit together with a touch of vanilla oak. On the palate intense spice and clove flavours come through; it is not easy to tell whether they are fruit- or oak-derived, but I incline to the former. A striking wine. The '99, incidentally, looked to have good potential prior to bottling. **rating:** 88
best drinking 2002–2008 **best vintages** '90, '93, '94, '98 **drink with** Rack of lamb • $21

🐌 kelly's creek ★★★★☆

RSD 226a Lower Whitehills Road, Relbia, Tas 7258 **region** Northern Tasmania
phone (03) 6234 9696 **fax** (03) 6231 6222 **open** Not
winemaker Andrew Hood (Contract) **production** 650 **est.** 1992
product range ($15–17 R) Riesling, Chardonnay, Pinot Noir, Cabernet Sauvignon.
summary Kelly's Creek draws on 1 hectare of riesling, and 0.2 hectare each of chardonnay, pinot noir and cabernet sauvignon. Its majority owner is Darryl Johnson, who runs the vineyard, with help from Guy Wagner

who describes himself as 'merely a marketing minion'. Small quantities of Riesling are made for Kelly's Creek; every vintage between 1995 and 1999 won medals at the 2000 Tasmanian Wines Show, the '97 leading the way with a gold medal, the '96 with a silver. Back vintages are still available from the winery.

Kelly's Creek Riesling

Riesling occupies the major part of the 1.2-hectare vineyard situated on the slope above the creek which gives the winery its name. There is a striking similarity in the aromas and flavours of the wines as they acquire bottle age, the mark of a great vineyard site.

TTTTT **1996** Medium yellow-green; a marvellously powerful wine with abundant structure and depth to both the bouquet and palate; a rich, strong lime and toast flavoured palate; great to drink now but will hold.   **rating:** 94
best drinking 2000–2006 **drink with** Carpaccio of salmon • $16.50

🐚 kenilworth bluff wines   NR

Lot 13 Bluff Road, Kenilworth, Qld 4574 **region** Other Wineries of Qld
phone (07) 5472 3723 **fax** (07) 5472 3723 **open** Fri–Sun 10–4 and by appointment
winemaker Bruce Humphery-Smith (Contract) **production** NA **est.** 1993
product range ($13–16 CD) Semillon, Chardonnay, Shiraz, Merlot, Cabernet Sauvignon.
summary Brian and Colleen Marsh modestly describe themselves as 'little more than hobbyists at this point in time' but also admit that 'our wines show tremendous promise'. They began planting the vineyards in 1993 in a hidden valley at the foot of Kenilworth Bluff, and now have 4 hectares (shiraz, cabernet sauvignon, merlot, semillon, chardonnay) coming into bearing. Presently the wines are made off site by Bruce Humphery-Smith, but one day the Marshes hope it will be feasible to establish an on-site winery.

kennedys keilor valley   NR

Lot 3 Overnewton Road, Keilor, Vic 3036 **region** Sunbury
phone (03) 9311 6246 **fax** (03) 9331 6246 **open** By appointment
winemaker Peter Dredge **production** 300 **est.** 1994
product range ($16 CD) Chardonnay.
summary A newly established estate-based Chardonnay specialist, producing its only wine from 1.8 hectares of relatively newly established vineyards.

kevin sobels wines   NR

Corner Broke and Halls Roads, Pokolbin, NSW 2321 **region** Lower Hunter Valley
phone (02) 4998 7766 **fax** (02) 4998 7475 **open** 7 days 10–5
winemaker Kevin Sobels **production** 5000 **est.** 1992
product range ($12–18 CD) Chardonnay, Semillon, Traminer, Pinot Noir.
summary Veteran winemaker Kevin Sobels has found yet another home, drawing upon 8 hectares of vineyards (originally planted by the Ross Jones family) to produce wines sold almost entirely through cellar door and mail order, with limited retail representation. The cellar door offers light meals and picnic and barbecue facilities.

🐚 kilgour estate   NR

85 McAdams Lane, Bellarine, Vic 3223 **region** Geelong
phone (03) 5251 2223 **fax** (03) 5251 2223 **open** Wed–Sun 10.30–6, 7 days in Jan
winemaker John Ellis (Consultant) **production** 2000 **est.** 1989
product range NA.
summary Kilgour Estate has 7 hectares of vines, and the wines are contract-made by John Ellis at Hanging Rock. Fruit-driven Pinot Noir and Chardonnay are winery specialties, the Pinot Noir having won at least one gold medal.

kilikanoon   ★★★★

Penna Lane, Penwortham, SA 5453 **region** Clare Valley
phone (08) 8843 4377 **fax** (08) 8843 4377 **open** Weekends and public holidays 11–5
winemaker Kevin Mitchell **production** 3000 **est.** 1997
product range ($15–23 CD) Morts Block Riesling, Blocks Road Riesling, Prodigal Grenache, Oracle Shiraz, Cabernet Sauvignon.
summary Kilikanoon has 6 hectares of estate vineyards at Leasingham and Penwortham. Wholesale distribution in South Australia, Victoria and Western Australia; exports to the US, Canada, the UK, Germany, New Zealand, Singapore and Hong Kong.

Kilikanoon Oracle Shiraz

Produced from 2 hectares of estate plantings, and matured in a mix of French and American oak.

▼▼▼▼▼ 1998 Medium to full red-purple; ripe, rich blackberry and chocolate fruit aromas lead into a gloriously rich palate offering the same flavours as the bouquet, untrammelled by oak, and finishing with soft, almost silky, tannins. Irresistible. **rating:** 94

best drinking 2002–2012 **best vintages** '98 **drink with** Roast shoulder of lamb • $23

Kilikanoon Cabernet Sauvignon

Comes from 2.5 hectares of estate plantings, and has all the character one expects of Clare Valley Cabernet.

▼▼▼▼ 1998 Medium red-purple; the bouquet is quite fragrant, with cedar, berry and hints of vanilla; sweet American oak is woven continuously through the fruit and tannin of the palate, pretty clever winemaking in a consistent style. **rating:** 86

best drinking 2003–2008 **best vintages** NA **drink with** Roast lamb • $21

killawarra ★★★★

Tanunda Road, Nuriootpa, SA 5355 **region** Barossa Valley
phone (08) 8560 9389 **fax** (08) 8562 1669 **open** See Penfolds
winemaker Steve Goodwin **production** 205 000 **est.** 1975
product range ($8.99–14.50 R) Only Sparkling wines: Non Vintage Brut, Vintage Brut, Brut Cremant, Premier Brut and Reserve Brut; also Non Vintage Sparkling Burgundy.
summary Purely a Southcorp brand, without any particular presence in terms of either vineyards or winery, but increasingly styled in a mode different from the Seaview or Seppelt wines. As one would expect, the wines are competitively priced, and what is more, regularly sweep all before them in national wine shows.

killerby ★★★☆

Lakes Road, Capel, WA 6230 **region** Geographe
phone 1800 655 722 **fax** 1800 679 578 **open** 7 days 10–4.30
winemaker Paul Boulden **production** 10 000 **est.** 1973
product range ($19–27 CD) Semillon, Semillon Sauvignon Blanc, Selection Sauvignon Blanc, Chardonnay, Shiraz, Cabernet Sauvignon and budget-priced April Classic White (Traminer Semillon Chardonnay blend) and April Classic Red (Shiraz Pinot Cabernet blend).
summary The members of the Killerby family are long-term residents of the southwest; Ben Killerby is the fourth generation. The 21 hectares of vines were established in 1973 by Ben's father, the late Dr Barry Killerby, and are now fully mature. The Chardonnay, in particular, is very highly rated by some critics, but I would like to see a little more succulence and concentration in the wines. Australian distribution through Lionel Sampson and The Main Domain Wine Company; exports to the US and Singapore.

Killerby Semillon

Produced from a little over 2 hectares of estate plantings; 25 per cent is fermented in stainless steel, and 75 per cent barrel-fermented in a mix of new, one-year-old and two-year-old French oak barriques.

▼▼▼▼ 1999 Medium yellow-green; the bouquet is complex, with the subtle but clever use of oak; the palate likewise shows the benefit of well-handled oak to provide both texture and flavour in a lemony through to spicy spectrum. **rating:** 86

best drinking 2000–2005 **best vintages** '99 **drink with** Grilled scampi • $19

Killerby Chardonnay

In recent years, the best of the Killerby wines. The wine has been given the ultimate rating of five gold stars by Robin Bradley. The wine is 100 per cent barrel-fermented in new and one-year-old French barriques and taken through malolactic fermentation.

▼▼▼▼♀ 1998 Light to medium yellow-green; the bouquet, early in the wine's life, is rather closed, with little fruit or oak showing. The palate, too, is delicate and restrained, with cashew through to mineral, and little primary fruit showing but with a quite creamy feel. Has literally gobbled up all the oak. **rating:** 90

best drinking 2001–2005 **best vintages** '89, '92, '93, '94, '97, '98 **drink with** Chicken supreme • $27

Killerby Shiraz

Produced from 4.5 hectares of estate plantings. The light, near-sand soils of the coastal plain normally produce relatively light-bodied wines, but it is possible to produce full-bodied reds if the conditions are right.

♥♥♥♥ **1998** Medium to full red-purple; the bouquet is concentrated, with spice, black cherry and a hint of gaminess. A solid, chunky wine on the palate with lots of dark fruits, and slightly grippy tannins needing to soften.

rating: 88

best drinking 2003–2013 **best vintages** '91, '92, '94, '98 **drink with** Game pie • $20

☙ kimbarra wines   NR

422 Barkly Street, Ararat, Vic 3377 **region** Grampians
phone (03) 5352 2238 **fax** (03) 5352 1950 **open** Mon–Fri 9–5
winemaker Peter Leeke **production** 3500 **est.** 1990
product range NA.
summary Peter and David Leeke have established 14 hectares of riesling, shiraz and cabernet sauvignon, the three varieties overall which have proved best suited to the Grampians region.

kings creek winery   ★★★★

237 Myers Road, Bittern, Vic 3918 **region** Mornington Peninsula
phone (03) 5983 2102 **fax** (03) 5983 5153 **open** 7 days 11–5
winemaker Brien Cole **production** 2000 **est.** 1981
product range ($16–24 R) Pinot Noir, Reserve Pinot Noir, Chardonnay, Cabernet Sauvignon; White Label Pinot Gris, Unwooded Chardonnay, Sauvignon Blanc, Pinot Noir.
summary Kings Creek is owned and operated by the Bell, Glover and Perraton families. Planting commenced in 1981, and the vines are now fully mature. Since 1990 the quality of the wines, particularly of the Pinot Noir and Chardonnay, has been beyond reproach. Limited retail distribution in New South Wales and Victoria.

Kings Creek Pinot Noir

Estate-grown, and vinified using a range of Burgundian techniques including 20 per cent whole bunches in the fermentation. Matured for ten months in French oak and, like the Chardonnay from Kings Creek, a wine of real complexity and style, with many medals to its credit. At $16 the wine is highly competitively priced.

♥♥♥♡ **1999** Light to medium red; the bouquet is light and fresh, with sappy strawberry fruit, and the identical flavours come through in the lively, fresh, drink-now palate.

rating: 83

best drinking 2000–2001 **best vintages** '88, '89, '91, '92, '94, '95, '97, '98 **drink with** Chinese duck with mushrooms • $16

Kings Creek Reserve Pinot Noir

This is the first vintage in which the Pinot Noir has been split into varietal and Reserve. The consequence has been a reduction in the price of the varietal, but also (understandably and inevitably) some diminution in quality. The payback comes in the form of this Reserve wine.

♥♥♥♥ **1999** Medium red-purple; the quite intense and complex bouquet has stylish tangy, savoury aromas which flow through into the palate. Here plum and strawberry fruit counterbalances the savoury characters of the bouquet; a long carry and finish is supported by fine tannins.

rating: 92

best drinking 2001–2005 **best vintages** '99 **drink with** Grilled duck breast • $24

kingsley   ★★★

6 Kingsley Court, Portland, Vic 3305 **region** Far South West Victoria
phone (03) 5523 1864 **fax** (03) 5523 1644 **open** 7 days 1–4
winemaker Contract **production** 1200 **est.** 1983
product range ($12–21 CD) Riesling, Botrytis Riesling, Late Harvest Riesling, Chardonnay, Cabernet Sauvignon.
summary Only a small part of the 10 hectares is made into wine under contract, the remainder being sold as grapes. Older vintages are usually available at cellar door. In early 1999, wines spanning the 1995 to 1998 vintages were on sale at low prices.

kingston estate   ★★★☆

PO Box 67, Kingston-on-Murray, SA 5331 **region** Riverland
phone (08) 8583 0500 **fax** (08) 8583 0505 **open** By appointment
winemaker Bill Moularadellis, Rod Chapman **production** 100 000 **est.** 1979
product range ($10–33 R) Verdelho, Chardonnay, Semillon Sauvignon Blanc, Shiraz, Cabernet Sauvignon, Merlot; Tessera (Cabernet blend), Sarantos (Soft Press Chardonnay); Special Releases of Saprian NV, Durif, Zinfandel and Viognier; Reserve range of Chardonnay, Shiraz, Merlot and Petit Verdot.

summary Kingston Estate is a substantial and successful Riverland winery, crushing 10 000 tonnes a year and exporting 80 per cent of its production. It is only in recent years that it has turned its attention to the domestic market with national distribution. In more recent years Kingston Estate has set up long-term purchase contracts with growers in the Clare Valley, Adelaide Hills, Langhorne Creek and Mount Benson. It also embarked on a programme of expanding its varietal range, and seems to have seized the opportunity of significantly increasing its prices.

Kingston Estate Limited Release Viognier
The first Viognier from Kingston Estate, produced from contract-grown grapes.
▼▼▼ 1999 Medium yellow-green; the bouquet is clean but absolutely neutral, with no distinctive fruit or varietal character. The same applies to the palate; perhaps better things lie around the corner as the vines mature. **rating:** 78
best drinking 2000–2001 **best vintages** NA **drink with** Sugar-cured tuna • $18

Kingston Estate Durif
Yet another rarely propagated variety from Kingston Estate, and one which works well in the warm climate, no surprise given its ancestry.
▼▼▼▼♀ 1998 Dense red-purple; the bouquet is concentrated, with dense, dark berry and chocolate fruit which streams through fluidly to the palate, which has exceptional concentration for Riverland material. The blackberry fruit has some quite attractive savoury overtones that prevent the wine from cloying. **rating:** 90
best drinking 2000–2005 **best vintages** '98 **drink with** Rich game • $20

Kingston Estate Reserve Petit Verdot
Yet another offbeat varietal from the Kingston Estate portfolio, but which may be well worth following.
▼▼▼♀ 1997 Medium red-purple; strong oak obliterates whatever fruit might be present on the bouquet, and largely obscures the core of fruit on the palate. However, ripe tannins on the finish are a varietal characteristic, and this late-ripening variety may surprise in the warm Riverland area. **rating:** 82
best drinking 2000–2004 **best vintages** NA **drink with** Marinated lamb • $33

Kingston Estate Zinfandel
Zinfandel is grown in every conceivable combination of climate and terroir in California, including areas similar to the Riverland. Its potential should not be judged only by reference to this vintage.
▼▼▼♀ 1998 Medium red-purple; typical juicy/jammy berry fruit; the palate has unusual fruit flavours which are difficult to pinpoint, although they may stem from Zinfandel's habit of producing green, unripe berries and raisiny overripe berries on the same bunch. **rating:** 80
best drinking 2000–2002 **best vintages** NA **drink with** Beef in red wine • $20

Kingston Estate Merlot
The highest-priced of the three bottom-rung varietal red wines, but nonetheless offers good value.
▼▼▼♀ 1999 Light to medium red; the bouquet is clean, relatively light, with hints of savoury and sweet leather; has pleasant, softly ripe, light berry fruit, and happily restrained oak. **rating:** 80
best drinking 2000–2002 **best vintages** NA **drink with** Tortellini • $14

Kingston Estate Tessera
A blend of Cabernet Sauvignon, Cabernet Franc, Merlot and Petit Verdot, a classic Bordeaux mix, which may or may not successfully migrate to the Riverland.
▼▼▼♀ 1999 Light to medium red; sweet raisiny/berry fruit on both the bouquet and palate are not what one normally expects from such a blend. The texture and the oak handling are good. **rating:** 81
best drinking 2000–2003 **best vintages** NA **drink with** Lamb shanks • $12.35

kingtree wines   NR
Kingtree Road, Wellington Mills via Dardanup, WA 6326 **region** Geographe
phone (08) 9728 3050 **fax** (08) 9728 3113 **open** 7 days 12–5.30
winemaker Contract **production** 1000 **est.** 1991
product range ($16–20 CD) Riesling, Sauvignon Blanc, Gerrasse White, Cabernet Merlot.
summary Kingtree Wines, with 2.5 hectares of estate plantings, is part of the Kingtree Lodge development, a four and a half-star luxury retreat in dense Jarrah forest.

kinvarra estate   NR

RMB 5141, New Norfolk, Tas 7140 **region** Southern Tasmania
phone (03) 6286 1333 **fax** (03) 6286 2026 **open** Not
winemaker Andrew Hood (Table Wine), Greg O'Keefe (Sparkling) **production** 90 **est.** 1990
product range ($13.50–15 ML) Riesling, Pinot Noir.
summary Kinvarra is the part-time occupation of David and Sue Bevan, with their wonderful 1827 homestead depicted on the label. There is only 1 hectare of vines, half riesling and half pinot noir, and most of the crop is sold to Wellington Wines and Fishburn & O'Keefe.

Kinvarra Estate Riesling
Yet another wine made by Andrew Hood; despite the technical difficulties of making wines such as this in tiny quantities, it is nigh on perfect.
TTTT 1999 Light to medium yellow-green; there is abundant lime and tropical fruit on the bouquet, followed by a powerful and rich palate with near-identical lime/tropical fruit.   **rating:** 87
best drinking 2000–2006 **best vintages** '89 **drink with** Gravlax • $13.50

kirkham estate   NR

3 Argyle Street, Camden, NSW 2570 **region** Other Wineries of NSW
phone (02) 4655 7722 **fax** (02) 4655 7722 **open** 7 days 11–5
winemaker Stan Aliprandi **production** 5000 **est.** 1993
product range ($9.50–15.50 CD) Traminer Riesling, Semillon, Semillon Chardonnay, Botrytis Semillon, Pinot Noir, Merlot, Cabernet Sauvignon, Tawny Port.
summary Kirkham Estate is one of six or so wine producers near Camden, a far cry from the 18 producers of the mid-nineteenth century but still indicative of the growth of vineyards and winemakers everywhere. It is the venture of Stan Aliprandi, a former Riverina winemaker with an interesting career going back over 30 years. It draws upon 10 hectares of vineyards, planted to chardonnay, semillon, shiraz, merlot, pinot noir and cabernet sauvignon, supplemented, it would seem, by grapes (and wines) purchased elsewhere.

knappstein wines   ★★★★☆

2 Pioneer Avenue, Clare, SA 5453 region Clare Valley
phone (08) 8842 2600 **fax** (08) 8842 3831 **open** Mon–Fri 9–5, Sat 11–5, Sun and public holidays 11–4
winemaker Andrew Hardy **production** 40 000 **est.** 1976
product range ($16–28 R) Riesling, Gewurztraminer, Chardonnay, Sauvignon Blanc Semillon, Botrytis Riesling, Shiraz, Enterprise Shiraz, The Franc (Cabernet Franc), Cabernet Merlot, Enterprise Cabernet Sauvignon.
summary The bell has tolled, and Tim Knappstein (together with wife Annie) are now involved full-time in their Lenswood Vineyard. Petaluma stalwart Andrew Hardy has been put in charge at Knappstein Wines and has placed his stamp on the brand. Clever label redesign and a subtle label name change (dropping the word 'Tim') are physical signs of the new order. Exports to the UK and much of Europe, Japan, Hong Kong and much of Asia.

Knappstein Hand Picked Riesling
The reputation of the Rieslings of the Clare Valley is (or was) as much due to Tim Knappstein as to any other winemaker, past or present. Tim Knappstein himself was the first to say that the quality and style of Riesling is in turn strongly dependent upon the terroir and climate, and that too is true. The combination of man, climate and variety in the outcome produced a classic wine.
TTTT 1999 Light yellow-green; a fragrant and spicy bouquet with some mineral and subliminal lime aromas. A wine which begs for time in the bottle, with a very tight mineral- and spice-flavoured palate and a dry finish.
                    rating: 86
best drinking 2004–2009 **best vintages** '77, '78, '79, '80, '83, '86, '90, '93, '94, '96, '97 **drink with** Salads of all kinds • $16.25

Knappstein Gewurztraminer
The Clare Valley seems a strange environment for gewurztraminer until you consider its track record with riesling; it is, however, true that the latter has a far higher success rate than does gewurztraminer.
TTTT 1999 Light yellow-green; the bouquet has quite pronounced spice/lychee varietal character, and the palate has the flavour promised by that bouquet; the wine is made even more attractive by the excellent finish, which avoids the phenolic trap of full-flavoured Gewurztraminer.   **rating:** 87
best drinking 2000–2003 **best vintages** '99 **drink with** Gently spiced Asian • $16.25

Knappstein Botrytis Riesling

Tim Knappstein produced some exceptional Botrytis Rieslings 20 years ago using the inoculation of grapes laid on trays in a specially constructed room with botrytis spores. The method was discontinued because it was too costly, and now the intermittent releases are made from naturally occurring botrytis in the vineyard. In 1999 it was triggered by 36 mm of rain on 21 March, the grapes being picked three weeks later at 18.5° baumé.

TTTT 1999 Brilliant green-yellow; clean, gentle lime juice aromas show excellent varietal character. The palate is intense and lively, with tangy lime juice flavours. **rating:** 87

best drinking 2000–2005 **best vintages** '80, '82, '86, '89, '92, '99 **drink with** Fruit tart • $NA

Knappstein Shiraz

Sourced from five small vineyards in four separate subdistricts of the Clare Valley, reflected in a five-week span in picking dates. Partly fermented in open fermenters, and part in closed (Potter) fermenters, with the wine in the latter being kept on skins for one month after the conclusion of fermentation. Fifteen per cent of the wine is matured in new Nevers oak, the balance in one- and two-year-old French oak; in all the wine spends between 12 and 15 months in wood before being bottled in or about October of the year following vintage.

TTTTY 1998 Medium to full red-purple; clean, dark berry fruit is complexed by touches of chocolate and more savoury notes on the bouquet; the palate has excellent texture and structure, with black cherry fruit and fine tannins contributing to a long, silky finish. **rating:** 90

best drinking 2003–2010 **best vintages** '98 **drink with** Moroccan lamb • $20.90

Knappstein Enterprise Shiraz

Enterprise is the flagship label for Knappstein, first introduced with the 1994 vintage. It comes from a single 34-year-old block of vines on the eastern slopes of the Clare Valley; the terra rossa soil produces small crops of intense fruit using minimal irrigation. The wine spends 15 months in a mix of one- and two-year-old French oak before being eggwhite-fined and bottled without filtration. The outstanding quality of the wine is a direct reflection of the vineyard and the minimalist winemaker intervention.

TTTTY 1997 Full red-purple; the bouquet is clean and concentrated, with the seamless integration of dark fruits and oak. The palate is powerful, but not aggressive, with plum and cherry fruit supported by fine tannins through a long finish. **rating:** 91

best drinking 2002–2012 **best vintages** '94, '96, '97 **drink with** Rich red meat dishes • $28

Knappstein Cabernet Merlot

A blend of 60 per cent Cabernet Sauvignon 26 per cent Merlot, the balance being provided by Cabernet Franc and Malbec, now entirely sourced from the Clare Valley. The wine is fermented in a mix of open and closed fermenters, and spends between 11 and 14 months in a mix of French oak and a small percentage of American oak.

TTTY 1998 Medium to full red-purple; the bouquet is gently ripe and smooth, with no green characters at all. On the palate, unexpected mint hits you between the eyes in full-frontal fashion. **rating:** 82

best drinking 2002–2007 **best vintages** NA **drink with** Roast veal • $20.90

Knappstein Enterprise Cabernet Sauvignon

This is the second Enterprise bottling of Cabernet Sauvignon, coming from the best parcels of cabernet grown on the Knappstein Vineyard which was planted in 1971. It also contains a small percentage of Malbec, a traditional Clare blend. It is fermented in a mix of open and closed fermenters, and spends between 18 and 24 months in oak, before being blended and bottled more than two years after vintage.

TTTY 1997 Medium red-purple; a firm bouquet with a range of leaf, spice, berry and earth aromas is, like some of the other Knappstein wines, followed by quite minty fruit on entry to the mouth, although savoury/earthy flavours bring up the rear. **rating:** 83

best drinking 2002–2010 **best vintages** '96 **drink with** Thick-cut lamb loin chops • $27.90

knight granite hills ★★★☆

1481 Burke and Wills Track, Baynton, Kyneton, Vic 3444 **region** Macedon Ranges
phone (03) 5423 7264 **fax** (03) 5423 7288 **open** Mon–Sat 10–6, Sun 12–6
winemaker Llew Knight **production** 7000 **est.** 1970
product range ($13.90–39.30 R) Riesling, Chardonnay, Pinot Noir, Shiraz, Cabernet Sauvignon, Sparkling; also MICA Riesling, Pinot Noir and Cabernet Shiraz.
summary Knight Granite Hills was one of the early pacesetters, indeed the first pacesetter, for cool-climate, spicy Shiraz and intense Riesling. Revived marketing in a buoyant market and the introduction of the lesser-priced MICA range have resulted in greater activity; plantings remain the same at 9 hectares of mature, low-yielding vineyards.

Knight Granite Hills Méthode Champenoise

An estate-grown blend of 50 per cent Chardonnay and 50 per cent Pinot Noir, which spends 30 months on yeast lees. ▼▼▼▼ 1995 Pale salmon pink, the Pinot Noir component obvious. The bouquet is clean and fresh, with a mix of strawberry and mineral aromas; the palate is fine, light and elegant, with the strawberry-accented Pinot Noir component making its presence felt. Crisp acidity promises a long life. **rating:** 87

best drinking 1999–2005 **best vintages** NA **drink with** Antipasto • $38

knowland estate NR

Mount Vincent Road, Running Stream, NSW 2850 **region** Mudgee
phone (02) 6358 8420 **fax** (02) 6358 8423 **open** By appointment
winemaker Peter Knowland **production** 250 **est.** 1990
product range ($12.50–18 CD) Mt Vincent Sauvignon Blanc, Orange Pinot Noir, Mt Vincent Pinot Noir, Wellington Cabernet.
summary The former Mount Vincent Winery, which sells much of its grape production from the 3.5 hectares of vineyards to other makers but which proposes to increase production under its own label.

kominos ★★★

New England Highway, Severnlea, Qld 4352 **region** Granite Belt
phone (07) 4683 4311 **fax** (07) 4683 4291 **open** 7 days 9–5
winemaker Tony Comino **production** 4000 **est.** 1976
product range ($10–13 CD) Riesling, Sauvignon Blanc, Chardonnay, Vin Doux, White Shiraz, Nouveau, Shiraz, Cabernet Merlot, Cabernet Sauvignon.
summary Tony Comino is a dedicated viticulturist and winemaker and, together with his father, he has battled hard to prevent ACI obtaining a monopoly on glass production in Australia, foreseeing many of the things which have in fact occurred. However, Kominos keeps a very low profile, selling all of its wine through cellar door and mailing list. No recent tastings.

kongwak hills winery NR

1030 Korumburra–Wonthaggi Road, Kongwak, Vic 3951 **region** Gippsland
phone (03) 5657 3267 **fax** (03) 5657 3267 **open** Weekends and public holidays 10–5
winemaker Peter Kimmer **production** 600 **est.** 1989
product range ($10–25 CD) Riesling, Pinot Noir, Shiraz, Cabernet Malbec.
summary Peter and Jenny Kimmer started the development of their vineyard in 1989 and now have half a hectare each of cabernet sauvignon, shiraz and pinot noir, together with lesser quantities of malbec, merlot and riesling. Most of the wines are sold at cellar door, with limited distribution in Melbourne through Woods Wines Pty Ltd of Fitzroy.

koppamurra wines ★★★☆

Joanna via Naracoorte, SA 5271 **region** Wrattonbully
phone (08) 8357 9533 **fax** (08) 8271 0726 **open** By appointment
winemaker John Greenshields **production** 3500 **est.** 1973
product range ($8.50–17.50 ML) Riesling, Autumn Pick Riesling, Botrytis Riesling, Chardonnay, Pinot Meunier, Shiraz, Cabernet Merlot, Merlot, Cabernet Sauvignon, Two Cabernets, McLaren Vale Muscat.
summary Which Hollywood actress was it who said 'I don't care what they say about me, as long as they spell my name right'? This might be the motto for Koppamurra Wines, which became embroiled in a bitter argument over the use of the name Koppamurra for the region in which its vineyards are situated and which, through what seems to be sheer bloody mindedness by various of the parties involved, is now known as Wrattonbully. The wines have limited retail distribution in the eastern States, and are exported to the US.

Koppamurra Cabernet Merlot

Made from a varying blend of Cabernet Sauvignon, Cabernet Franc and Merlot, with the Cabernet component ranging between a low of 60 per cent and a high of 88 per cent. Cabernet Merlot has always been the most frequently produced wine in the somewhat unpredictable Koppamurra stable, with wines coming and going, and is invariably a pleasant, if sometimes light, wine. ▼▼▼▼ 1998 Strong purple-red; concentrated, ripe dark berry fruit on the bouquet is backed up by the palate, where the rich fruit is accompanied by tannins coming along the mid to back palate. Should cellar very well, and in this day and age, a bargain at the price. **rating:** 86

best drinking 2003–2013 **best vintages** '82, '90, '91, '93, '96 **drink with** Light Italian food • $15

kraanwood   NR

8 Woodies Place, Richmond, Tas 7025 **region** Southern Tasmania
phone (03) 6260 2540 **open** Not
winemaker Frank van der Kraan **production** 150 **est.** 1994
product range ($16.20 ML) Schonburger, Montage, Unwooded Chardonnay, Pinot Noir.
summary Frank van der Kraan and wife Barbara established their half-hectare vineyard Kraanwood between 1994 and 1995, with approximately equal plantings of pinot noir, chardonnay and cabernet sauvignon. Frank van der Kraan also manages the 1-hectare Pembroke Vineyard, and procures from it small quantities of schonberger, chardonnay, riesling and sauvignon blanc.

Kraanwood Unwooded Chardonnay

A silver medal winner at the Tasmanian Wines Show 2000; its seems that Andrew Hood is also involved with part of the winemaking of the Kraanwood wines.
♥♥♥♥ 1998 Light yellow-green; the bouquet is light, fresh and delicate, the palate similarly delicate but very well balanced, with flavour flowing across the tongue to the finish.   **rating: 85**
best drinking 2001–2004 **best vintages** NA **drink with** Chinese short soup   •$NA

kulkunbulla   ★★★★

Postal: PO Box 6265, Silverwater DC, NSW 1811 **region** Lower Hunter Valley
phone (02) 9848 2103 **fax** (02) 9898 0200 **open** Opening in 2000
winemaker Rhys Eather, Gavin Lennard **production** 2600 **est.** 1996
product range ($16.50–25.50 ML) Hunter Valley Semillon, The Glandore Semillon, Hunter Valley Chardonnay, Nullarbor Chardonnay, The Brokenback Chardonnay.
summary Kulkunbulla is owned by a relatively small Sydney-based company headed by Gavin Lennard and which has purchased part of the Brokenback Estate in the Hunter Valley formerly owned by Rothbury. For the time being all Kulkunbulla's wines are sold by mail order with a sophisticated brochure entitled Vinsight. A cellar door is due to open in the second half of 2000. Retail distribution in New South Wales and Queensland.

Kulkunbulla Hunter Valley Semillon

Produced from three rows of hand-picked 30-year-old semillon; only the free-run juice is used, and cold-fermented in stainless steel.
♥♥♥♡ 1999 Medium yellow-green; a clean, firm bouquet with some lemon and herb together with crisper mineral notes. The palate is soft, with lemony fruit and medium length. Medium-term cellaring only.   **rating: 84**
best drinking 2000–2004 **best vintages** NA **drink with** Seafood salad   •$20

Kulkunbulla The Glandore Semillon

Glandore was the original name of the Brokenback vineyard in the 1940s before it went out of production. (It was replanted in the late 1960s and given its present name.) This is the top-end Semillon of Kulkunbulla.
♥♥♥♥ 1999 Medium yellow-green; the bouquet is quite rich and powerful, the palate having greater fruit depth, ranging through lemon/citrus to stone fruit. Avoids the phenolic trap, and has nice mouthfeel and balance.
rating: 89
best drinking 2002–2008 **best vintages** '98, '99 **drink with** Balmain bugs   •$25.50

Kulkunbulla Hunter Valley Chardonnay

Given the usual barrel-ferment and lees contact treatment. In fact, I prefer the balance of this wine to the more expensive The Brokenback Chardonnay.
♥♥♥♥ 1999 Medium yellow-green; the bouquet is rather closed, showing slightly dull oak, which suppresses the fruit aromatics. However, there is considerable fruit richness and sweetness on the mid-palate, and the wine finishes clean.   **rating: 85**
best drinking 2000–2002 **best vintages** '98 **drink with** Rich seafood   •$22

kyeema estate   ★★★★

43 Shumack Street, Weetangera, ACT 2614 **region** Canberra District
phone (02) 6254 7557 (ah) **fax** (02) 6254 7536 **open** Not
winemaker Andrew McEwin **production** 750 **est.** 1986
product range ($22 ML) Chardonnay, Shiraz, Merlot, Cabernet Merlot.
summary Part-time winemaker, part-time wine critic (with *Winewise* magazine) Andrew McEwin produces wines full of flavour and character; every wine released under the Kyeema Estate label has won a show award of some description. Limited retail distribution in Brisbane and exports to California (The Grateful Palate).

Kyeema Estate Shiraz

Since 1994 Kyeema Shiraz has won 15 trophies and 10 gold medals; every vintage (including the '98) has won at least one gold medal at Australian regional wine shows. It is produced from grapes sourced from a number of vineyards in the Canberra District.

▼▼▼▼▽ **1998** Medium to full red-purple; the bouquet is quite concentrated and complex, with dark berry/plum fruit and an array of more savoury/earthy notes. The palate has strong plum, mint, leaf and spice flavours allied with touches of cedar and cigar box. Moderately high acidity should help the wine age. **rating:** 90

best drinking 2003–2008 **best vintages** '87, '88, '89, '90, '92, '94, '96, '97, '98 **drink with** Braised beef • $22

Kyeema Estate Cabernet Merlot

Another much-decorated wine from Kyeema, with seven trophies and five gold medals awarded to the five vintages since 1994.

▼▼▼▼ **1997** Medium to full red-purple; there is abundant sweet blackcurrant fruit on the bouquet, with oak evident but not aggressive. The palate is solid, rich and concentrated, with fruit and oak contributing more or less equally. **rating:** 85

best drinking 2001–2006 **best vintages** '87, '88, '89, '90, '92, '94 **drink with** Diced lamb • $22

laanecoorie ★★★

Bendigo Road, Betley, Vic 3472 **region** Pyrenees
phone (03) 5468 7260 **fax** (03) 5468 7388 **open** Not
winemaker John Ellis (Contract) **production** 1500 **est.** 1982
product range ($20 R) A single Bordeaux-blend dry red of Cabernet Franc, Cabernet Sauvignon and Merlot in roughly equal proportions.
summary John McQuilten's 7.5-hectare vineyard produces grapes of consistently high quality, and competent contract-winemaking by John Ellis at Hanging Rock has done the rest.

la cantina king valley NR

King Valley **region** King Valley
phone (03) 5729 3615 **open** Weekends and holidays 10–5 and by appointment
winemaker Gino Corsini **production** 750 **est.** 1996
product range ($9–13 CD) Riesling, Dry Red, Shiraz, Cabernet Sauvignon.
summary Gino and Peter Corsini have 20 hectares of riesling, chardonnay, shiraz and cabernet sauvignon, selling most but making a small amount on site in a winery 'made of Glenrowan granite stone in traditional Tuscan style'. The wines are made without the use of sulphur dioxide; in other words, they are organic.

ladbroke grove NR

Coonawarra Road, Penola, SA 5277 **region** Coonawarra
phone (08) 8737 2082 **fax** (08) 8762 3236 **open** 7 days 10–4
winemaker Ken Ward **production** 800 **est.** 1982
product range ($8–14 CD) Riesling, Late Picked Riesling, Shiraz, Premium Shiraz.
summary Relaunched with both standard and Premium Shiraz after a hiatus; wine quality has been variable, but it does have 2 hectares of hand-pruned shiraz planted by John Redman in the 1960s upon which to draw.

lake barrington estate ★★★☆

1133–1136 West Kentish Road, West Kentish, Tas 7306 **region** Northern Tasmania
phone (03) 6491 1249 **fax** (03) 6334 2892 **open** Tues–Sun 10–5 (Nov–Apr)
winemaker Steve Lubiana (Sparkling), Andrew Hood (Table), both Contract **production** 600 **est.** 1988
product range ($18–30 CD) Riesling, Chardonnay, Pinot Noir, Alexandra Méthode Traditionelle.
summary Lake Barrington Estate is owned by the vivacious and energetic Maree Taylor and takes its name from the adjacent Lake Barrington, 30 kilometres south of Devonport, on the northern coast of Tasmania. There are picnic facilities at the vineyard, and, needless to say, the scenery is very beautiful.

Lake Barrington Estate Chardonnay

In recent years Lake Barrington has moved from a specialist sparkling wine producer into a broader range of table wines. This wine shows the sure touch winemaker Andrew Hood has with oak; but also harks back to the original choice of the site as sparkling wine producer with its high acidity. Scored gold medal points on my score sheet at the Tasmanian Wines Show 2000.

🍷🍷🍷🍷🍷 **1998** Medium green-yellow; the bouquet is clean, moderately intense, with slightly herbal tones to the fruit. Comes alive on the tight but smooth-flowing palate with excellent varietal fruit and oak balance and integration. My tolerance for high acidity no doubt led to my higher points than those of my fellow judges.

rating: 91

best drinking 2000–2006 **best vintages** '98 **drink with** Marinated octopus • $24

lake breeze wines ★★★★☆

Step Road, Langhorne Creek, SA 5255 **region** Langhorne Creek
phone (08) 8537 3017 **fax** (08) 8537 3267 **open** 7 days 10–5
winemaker Greg Follett **production** 10 000 **est.** 1987
product range ($10–35 CD) Chardonnay, White Frontignac, Grenache, Cabernet Sauvignon, Shiraz, Bernoota (Cabernet Shiraz), Tawny Port. The premium Winemaker's Selection range was introduced in 1996.
summary The Folletts have been farmers at Langhorne Creek since 1880, grape growers since the 1930s. Since 1987 a small proportion of their grapes has been made into wine, and a cellar-door sales facility was opened in early 1991. The quality of the releases has been exemplary, the new Winemaker's Selection red wines particularly striking. Retail distribution in Victoria, New South Wales and Queensland is now augmented by exports to the US, the UK and Switzerland.

Lake Breeze Winemaker's Selection Shiraz

The Winemaker's Selection range is the Reserve equivalent, with the best fruit complemented by sometimes enthusiastic use of new oak.
🍷🍷🍷🍷🍷 **1998** Dense red-purple; big, rich, concentrated ripe fruit with swathes of American oak on both bouquet and palate produce a wine of unashamed show style.

rating: 90

best drinking 2003–2013 **best vintages** '96, '98 **drink with** Leave it in the cellar • $35

Lake Breeze Cabernet Sauvignon

Originally the Lake Breeze flag-bearer but now supplanted by the Winemaker's Selection range. Nonetheless, continues to be an outstanding Cabernet.
🍷🍷🍷🍷 **1997** Medium red-purple; the bouquet wanders around a bit, with mint and berry aromas but also slightly dusty characters. The palate has much better structure than the bouquet would suggest, with dark, savoury berry flavours and fine but persistent tannins.

rating: 87

best drinking 2002–2007 **best vintages** '87, '88, '90, '95, '96 **drink with** Smoked kangaroo fillet • $22

Lake Breeze Winemaker's Selection Cabernet Sauvignon

Obviously enough, the sister wine to the Winemaker's Selection Shiraz. Only limited quantities are made, and, like the Shiraz, is principally sold through cellar door and by mailing list.
🍷🍷🍷🍷🍷 **1998** Dense red-purple; the bouquet is full and sweet, with lashings of cassis, berry and oak. A powerful, well-structured palate where the tannins hold the rich, ripe fruit together, the oak powerful but justified. **rating:** 90

best drinking 2005–2015 **best vintages** '96, '98 **drink with** Char-grilled rump • $35

lake george winery ★★★

Federal Highway, Collector, NSW 2581 **region** Canberra District
phone (02) 4848 0039 **fax** (02) 4848 0039 **open** Not
winemaker Dr Edgar F Riek **production** 500 **est.** 1971
product range ($25–27 R) Chardonnay, Semillon, Sauternes, Pinot Noir, Cabernet Sauvignon, Merlot, Fortifieds.
summary Dr Edgar Riek is an inquisitive, iconoclastic winemaker who is not content with his role as Godfather and founder of the Canberra district, forever experimenting and innovating. His fortified wines, vintaged in northeastern Victoria but matured at Lake George, are very good. By 1998, however, Edgar Riek was looking for a successor, and threatening to hang up his boots. We shall see.

🐌 lake moodemere vineyard NR

McDonalds Road, Rutherglen, Vic 3685 **region** Rutherglen and Glenrowan
phone (02) 6032 9449 **fax** (02) 6032 9449 **open** Fri–Mon 10–5
winemaker Michael Chambers **production** 3000 **est.** 1995
product range ($13.50–16 CD) Riesling, Chardonnay, Late Harvest Biancone, Shiraz, Cabernet Sauvignon.
summary Michael, Belinda, Peter and Helen Chambers are all members of the famous Chambers family of Rutherglen. They have 17 hectares of vineyards (tended by Peter), and Lake Moodemere Homestead is in its thirteenth year as a bed and breakfast facility.

lake's folly ★★★★★

Broke Road, Pokolbin, NSW 2321 **region** Lower Hunter Valley
phone (02) 4998 7507 **fax** (02) 4998 7322 **open** Mon–Sat 10–4
winemaker Stephen Lake **production** 5000 **est.** 1963
product range ($36 CD) Simplicity itself: Chardonnay and Cabernets.
summary The first of the weekend wineries to produce wines for commercial sale, long revered for its Cabernet Sauvignon and thereafter its Chardonnay. Very properly, terroir and climate produce a distinct regional influence and thereby a distinctive wine style. Some find this attractive, others are less tolerant. The winery continues to enjoy an incredibly loyal clientele, with much of each year's wine selling out quickly by mail order. A little of the wine finds its way to the UK. Lake's Folly has been sold, but Stephen Lake and family will continue in residence at the winery until the end of the year, and Stephen will consult for at least two years after that. Perth businessman Peter Fogarty is the purchaser. Mr Fogarty's family company has previously established Millbrook Winery in the Perth Hills, so is no stranger to the joys and agonies of running a small winery.

Lake's Folly Chardonnay

Only 1200 cases a year (with some seasonal variation) are made from estate-grown grapes. The wine is invariably correct in style and — unlike the Cabernets — should cause no discussion or argument, except that it seems to be getting better year by year.

TTTTY 1998 Medium yellow-green; tangy melon/stone fruit aromas are woven through subtle oak, complex but smooth. The palate lacks the final intensity promised by the bouquet; very neat handling, but does not quite follow through on the finish. Time may change my perspective. **rating:** 90

best drinking 2001–2007 **best vintages** '81, '82, '83, '84, '86, '89, '92, '94, '96, '97, '98 **drink with** Sweetbreads
• $36

Lake's Folly Cabernets

It is not a wine which can or should be judged by conventional standards; if it were to be so treated, the judgment would not do the wine justice. A slightly varying blend of 65 per cent Cabernet Sauvignon, 15 per cent Petit Verdot, 10 per cent Shiraz and 10 per cent Merlot. Cork taint affecting many older bottles is an unpredictable hazard.

TTTTT 1998 Healthy, full red-purple; a distinctly regional, gently earthy/savoury cast to the fruit will doubtless raise the question in the minds of some, but for me the wine is spotlessly clean. A perfectly made wine on the palate, with cassis fruit the anchor for both the texture and structure; exemplary tannin and oak handling completes the picture. **rating:** 94

best drinking 2003–2013 **best vintages** '69, '75, '81, '87, '89, '91, '93, '96, '97, '98 **drink with** Rabbit, hare
• $36

lamont wines ★★★☆

85 Bisdee Road, Millendon, WA 6056 **region** Swan District
phone (08) 9296 4485 **fax** (08) 9296 1663 **open** Wed–Sun 10–5
winemaker Mark Warren **production** 7000 **est.** 1978
product range ($9–25 CD) Riesling, Verdelho, Barrel Fermented Semillon, Chardonnay, Barrel Fermented Chardonnay, WB (White Burgundy), Sweet White, Light Red Cabernet, Cabernet, Shiraz, Merlot; Fortifieds, including Flor Fino, Amontillado and Reserve Sherry (Oloroso style).
summary Corin Lamont is the daughter of the late Jack Mann, and makes her wines in the image of those her father used to make, resplendent in their generosity. Lamont also boasts a superb restaurant, with a gallery for the sale and promotion of local arts.

Lamont Barrel Fermented Chardonnay

Jack Mann was big on fruit, but not so much on oak, and in particular, new oak. This wine, however, might well have got through his guard, as the oak has been sensitively handled (much more so than in the Semillon of the same vintage).

TTTT 1999 Medium yellow-green; the bouquet is complex and tangy, albeit slightly funky; the palate is really quite fine and elegant, particularly given its Swan Valley origins. The tangy flavours run through to a long finish. **rating:** 86

best drinking 2000–2002 **best vintages** '97, '99 **drink with** Corn-fed chicken • $16

langanook wines   NR

Faraday Road RSD 181, Castlemaine, Vic 3450 **region** Bendigo
phone (03) 5474 8250 **fax** (03) 5474 8250 **open** Not
winemaker Matt Hunter **production** 400 **est.** 1985
product range ($16–30 ML) Chardonnay, Cabernet Sauvignon, Reserve Caberent Sauvignon.
summary The Langanook vineyard was established back in 1985 (the first wines coming much later), at an altitude of 450 metres on the slopes of Mount Alexander. The wines are available through a mailing list and limited Victorian distribution through Rathdowne Cellars, Armadale Cellars, the Victorian Wine Centre and Castlemaine Cellars.

langmeil winery   ★★★☆

Corner Para and Langmeil Roads, Tanunda, SA 5352 **region** Barossa Valley
phone (08) 8563 2595 **fax** (08) 8563 3622 **open** 7 days 11–4.30
winemaker Paul Lindner **production** 10 000 **est.** 1996
product range ($10.50–45 CD) White Frontignac, Barossa Riesling, Semillon, Chardonnay, Cabernet Rosé, Shiraz, The Freedom Shiraz, Barossa Grenache, Selwin's Lot (Cabernet blend), Cabernet Sauvignon, Sparkling, Fortifieds.
summary Vines were first planted at Langmeil in the 1840s, and the first winery on the site, known as Paradale Wines, opened in 1932. In 1996 cousins Carl and Richard Lindner along with brother-in-law Chris Bitter formed a partnership to acquire and refurbish the winery and its 5-hectare vineyard planted to shiraz, including 2 hectares planted in 1846. This vineyard has now been supplemented by another vineyard acquired in 1998, taking total plantings to 14.5 hectares and including cabernet sauvignon and grenache. Distribution in New South Wales and Victoria; exports to Canada, France, Taiwan and the US.

Langmeil The Freedom Shiraz

A new super-premium for Langmeil, referring to the religious persecution in Silesia which drove the Auricht family to the Barossa Valley in the mid-1840s, where the family planted the first vineyard. A few acres still remain, dry-grown, hand-picked and hand-pruned, yielding less than 2 tonnes per acre. It is this vineyard which produced the grapes for this wine.
▼▼▼▽ 1997 Medium red-purple; dusty vanilla oak is the first impression on the bouquet, then cherry/raspberry fruit comes through. The palate has more substance to the varietal fruit flavour (and also length), but the slightly dusty American oak still doesn't do the wine justice.   **rating:** 84
best drinking 2002–2007 **best vintages** NA **drink with** Smoked Barossa sausage • $45

Langmeil Selwin's Lot

There is some exceedingly complex family history involved in the antecedents of Langmeil, a small part of which is honoured with the name of the wine, deriving from Selwin Ernest Auricht, from the founding family of the area. This apart, this somewhat improbable blend works quite well in an unpretentious but friendly wine. The blend is of Cabernet Sauvignon, Grenache and Shiraz; the Cabernet is said to provide light fruitiness; Grenache, intense flavour; and Shiraz, dry pepperiness.
▼▼▼▼ 1998 Medium red-purple; the bouquet has very strong chocolate aromas tinged with vanilla oak. The medium-weight palate runs through more of that sweet chocolate to spicy berry fruit to a hint of jammy fruit ex the Grenache. The firm tannins need to soften a touch, but the wine has real substance.   **rating:** 86
best drinking 2003–2008 **best vintages** '98 **drink with** Beef goulash • $14.50

Langmeil Cabernet Sauvignon

Another wine made in traditional Barossa fashion, with the primary emphasis on ripe fruit.
▼▼▼▼ 1998 Medium to full red-purple; strong blackberry/blackcurrant fruit with some vanilla oak provides an attractive bouquet. The palate has plenty of depth and richness to the chunky fruit, and the oak is in balance. Should develop well.   **rating:** 85
best drinking 2003–2008 **best vintages** NA **drink with** Barbecued sausages • $17.50

lark hill   ★★★★☆

RMB 281 Gundaroo Road, Bungendore, NSW 2621 **region** Canberra District
phone (02) 6238 1393 **fax** (02) 6238 1393 **open** Wed–Mon 10–5
winemaker Dr David Carpenter, Sue Carpenter **production** 4000 **est.** 1978
product range ($15–27 R) Riesling, Sauvignon Blanc Semillon, Chardonnay, Late Harvest (dessert wine), Pinot Noir, Cabernet Merlot, Exultation Cabernet, The Canberra Fizz Méthode Champenoise.

summary The Lark Hill vineyard is situated at an altitude of 860 metres, level with the observation deck on Black Mountain Tower and offering splendid views of the Lake George Escarpment. Right from the outset, David and Sue Carpenter have made wines of real quality, style and elegance but achieved extraordinary success at the 1997 Sydney Wine Show, topping two classes (with gold medals in each). At the 1998 Canberra Regional Wine Show, Lark Hill won two trophies, five silver and four bronze medals. All of the wines are sold ex winery.

latara   NR

Corner McDonalds and Deaseys Roads, Pokolbin, NSW 2320 region Lower Hunter Valley
phone (02) 4998 7320 open Sat 9–5, Sun 9–4
winemaker Iain Riggs (Contract) production 250 est. 1979
product range ($9.50–11 CD) Semillon, Cabernet Sauvignon, Shiraz.
summary The bulk of the grapes produced on the 5-hectare Latara vineyard, which was planted in 1979, are sold to Brokenwood. A small quantity is vinified for Latara and sold under its label. As one would expect, the wines are very competently made, and are of show medal standard.

laurel bank   ★★★★

130 Black Snake Lane, Granton, Tas 7030 region Southern Tasmania
phone (03) 6263 5977 fax (03) 6263 3117 open By appointment
winemaker Andrew Hood (Contract) production 800 est. 1987
product range ($17–22 R) Sauvignon Blanc, Pinot Noir, Cabernet Merlot.
summary Laurel (hence Laurel Bank) and Kerry Carland planted their 2-hectare vineyard in 1986. They delayed the first release of their wines for some years and (by virtue of the number of entries they were able to make) won the trophy for Most Successful Exhibitor at the 1995 Royal Hobart Wine Show. Things have settled down since; wine quality is solid and reliable. Retail distribution through Sutherland Cellars, Melbourne.

Laurel Bank Sauvignon Blanc
Produced from 1 hectare of estate plantings, and raises the question why more Sauvignon Blanc is not grown in Tasmania.
▼▼▼▼ 1999 Light to medium yellow-green; a classically understated wine, with a firm, minerally bouquet and perfectly balanced citrus mineral flavours on the palate.   rating: 86
best drinking 2000–2002 best vintages '98, '99 drink with Spring salad • $17

Laurel Bank Cabernet Sauvignon Merlot
Like the Pinot Noir, produced from half a hectare of estate plantings. The '98 is a marvellous wine which won a gold medal at the Tasmanian Wines Show 2000. Somewhat unusually, but as a tribute to the vintage, the grapes were picked at the same time and fermented together.
▼▼▼▼▼ 1998 Medium to full purple-red; the bouquet is absolutely delicious, smooth and very sweet. The wine is no less seductively smooth on the palate, with sweet juicy berry fruit, excellent oak and ripe tannins.   rating: 95
best drinking 2000–2015 best vintages '98 drink with Sautéed lamb fillets • $18

lauren brook   ★★★☆

Eedle Terrace, Bridgetown, WA 6255 region Blackwood Valley
phone (08) 9761 2676 fax (08) 9761 1879 open 7 days 11–4
winemaker Stephen Bullied production 1300 est. 1993
product range ($14.40–20.90 CD) Riesling, Bridgetown Blend, Fumé, Late Harvest, Shiraz, Cabernet Sauvignon, Fortissimo.
summary Lauren Brook is established on the banks of the beautiful Blackwood River, and is the only commercial winery in the Bridgetown subregion of Mount Barker. An 80-year-old barn on the property has been renovated to contain a micro-winery and a small gallery. There is 1 hectare of estate chardonnay, supplemented by grapes purchased locally.

lavender bay   NR

39 Paringa Road, Red Hill South, Vic 3937 region Mornington Peninsula
phone (03) 9869 4405 fax (03) 9869 4423 open Not
winemaker Garry Crittenden (Contract) production NA est. 1988
product range Chardonnay, Pinot Noir.
summary Marketing consultant Kevin Luscombe established Lavender Bay in 1988 on a spectacular 4-hectare property in Red Hill South, with its view of the Bay to Phillip Island. Tiny quantities of the first three vintages were progressively released onto the market in mid-1997, distributed through Flinders Wholesale Wines.

🐚 lawrence victor estate   NR

Penola Road, Naracoorte, SA 5271   **region** Wrattonbully
phone (08) 8739 7276   **fax** (08) 8739 7344   **open** Not
winemaker Neil Dodderidge (Contract)   **production** 1600   **est.** 1994
product range ($18–30 R) Shiraz, Cabernet Sauvignon.
summary Lawrence Victor Estate is part of a large South Australian company principally engaged in the harvesting and transportation of soft wood plantation logging. The company was established by Lawrence Victor Dohnt in 1932, and the estate has been named in his honour by the third generation of the family. Although a small part of the group's activities, the plantings (principally contracted to Southcorp) are substantial, with 11 hectares of shiraz and 20 hectares of cabernet sauvignon established between 1994 and 1999. An additional 12 hectares of cabernet sauvignon and 6 hectares of pinot noir are due to be planted in the year 2000. The first wines, contract-made by Neil Dodderidge at Heathfield Ridge, were due to be released in March of that year.

lawson's hill   ★★★

Henry Lawson Drive, Eurunderee, Mudgee, NSW 2850   **region** Mudgee
phone (02) 6373 3953   **fax** (02) 6373 3948   **open** Mon, Thurs, Fri, Sat 10–4.30, Sun 10–4
winemaker Various Contract and José Grace   **production** 3000   **est.** 1985
product range ($11–39 CD) Chardonnay, Verdelho, Sauvignon Blanc, Riesling, Traminer Riesling, Louisa Rosé, Cabernet Merlot, Pinot Noir Gamay, Reserve Dryland Cabernet Sauvignon, Port.
summary Former music director and arranger (for musical acts in Sydney clubs) José Grace and wife June run a strongly tourist-oriented operation situated nextdoor to the Henry Lawson Memorial, offering a kaleidoscopic array of wines, produced from 8 hectares of vineyard, and made under contract. The red wines are richly representative of the deeply coloured, flavoursome Mudgee style.

leasingham   ★★★★☆

7 Dominic Street, Clare, SA 5453   **region** Clare Valley
phone (08) 8842 2555   **fax** (08) 8842 3293   **open** Mon–Fri 8.30–5.30, weekends 10–4
winemaker Kerri Thompson   **production** 95 000   **est.** 1893
product range ($12–36 R) Classic Clare Riesling, Shiraz, and Cabernet Sauvignon at the top end; mid-range Bin 7 Riesling, Bin 37 Chardonnay, Bin 42 Semillon Sauvignon Blanc, Bin 56 Cabernet Malbec, Bin 61 Shiraz; finally low-priced Hutt Creek Riesling, Sauvignon Blanc, Shiraz Cabernet.
summary Successive big-company ownerships and various peregrinations in labelling and branding have not resulted in any permanent loss of identity or quality. With a core of high-quality, aged vineyards to draw on, Leasingham is in fact going from strength to strength under BRL Hardy's direction. The stentorian red wines take no prisoners, compacting densely rich fruit and layer upon layer of oak into every long-lived bottle.

Leasingham Classic Clare Bin 7 Riesling

The wine has a rich history; the vineyards were planted in the 1940s against contemporary thinking in the 1960s when a newly graduated Tim Knappstein arrived at Leasingham, and proceeded to make Bin 7 one of Australia's most highly rated white wines. Thirty years later, the 50-year-old vines have been reworked with a new trellis and vertical spur positioning to produce even better grapes. In 1999 joined the Richmond Grove Rieslings in being offered with a Stelvin screw-cap through Vintage Cellars.
▼▼▼▽ **1999** Very light straw-yellow; a light, minerally bouquet with not much fruit evident is followed by an ultra-delicate palate; with just a flick of residual sugar. All of its best years are in front of it, its cellaring future guaranteed by the Stelvin cap.   **rating:** 82
best drinking 2003–2010   **best vintages** NA   **drink with** Vegetable terrine   • $12

Leasingham Bin 37 Chardonnay

A wine which, yet again, shows the uneasy relationship between the Clare Valley and Chardonnay. Its main attraction lies in its modest price.
▼▼▼▽ **1997** Quite strong green-yellow colour is a promising start, but slightly hessian/hay characters on the bouquet quickly bring you back to reality. The palate is typically plain, though it does have some bottle-developed depth.   **rating:** 80
best drinking Drink now   **best vintages** NA   **drink with** Takeaway   • $12.95

Leasingham Bin 56 Cabernet Malbec

The blend of 85 per cent Cabernet Sauvignon and 15 per cent Malbec has been a Clare Valley specialty for decades; anyone lucky enough to have the '71 Bin 56 or virtually any of Wendouree's Cabernet Malbecs will need no persuasion of the merits of the blend. Its show record is second to none.

TTTT♀ **1997** Medium to full red-purple; the bouquet has masses of sweet dark berry/blackberry fruit, joined by some dark chocolate flavours on the palate. For once, fruit, not oak, is the major driver; easy to see how it won two trophies at the National Wine Show in 1998. **rating:** 92

best drinking 2002–2012 **best vintages** '88, '90, '91, '94, '95, '96, '97 **drink with** Jugged hare • $17.95

leconfield ★★★★☆

Penola Road, Coonawarra, SA 5263 **region** Coonawarra
phone (08) 8737 2326 **fax** (08) 8737 2285 **open** 7 days 10–5
winemaker Phillipa Treadwell **production** 16 000 **est.** 1974
product range ($16.95–30.95 CD) Riesling, Twelve Rows Commemorative Riesling, Noble Riesling, Chardonnay (wooded and unwooded), Merlot, Shiraz, Cabernet.
summary A distinguished estate with a proud, even if relatively short, history. Long renowned for its Cabernet Sauvignon, its repertoire has steadily grown with the emphasis on single varietal wines. The style overall is fruit-rather than oak-driven. Exports to Canada, the US, Asia, the UK and Europe.

Leconfield Twelve Rows Commemorative Riesling

All but 12 rows of riesling (planted in the 1970s) were removed in the early 1990s, but the 12 surviving rows make this wine.

TTTT 1998 Light green-yellow; obvious bottle-developed characters, with some toast and a touch of kerosene; a quite powerful entry to the palate with toasty kerosene characters, but the wine does not quite carry through to the finish. **rating:** 87

best drinking 2000–2003 **best vintages** NA **drink with** Seafood salad • $16.95

Leconfield Merlot

A relatively early entrant in the Merlot stakes; Coonawarra has the appropriate climate for the variety, but winemakers everywhere seem to have different ideas about style.

TTTT♀ **1998** Medium purple-red; nicely balanced fruit and oak, with some olivaceous/herbal varietal aromas, lead into a palate with admirable fine, silky texture. The flavours are in the juicy berry spectrum, which many see as prime varietal character. **rating:** 93

best drinking 2003–2008 **best vintages** '97, '98 **drink with** Duck casserole • $30.95

leeuwin estate ★★★★★

Stevens Road, Margaret River, WA 6285 **region** Margaret River
phone (08) 9757 6253 **fax** (08) 9757 6364 **open** 7 days 10–4.30
winemaker Bob Cartwright **production** 50 000 **est.** 1974
product range ($18.10–74.02 CD) Art Series Chardonnay, Riesling, Sauvignon Blanc, Pinot Noir, Cabernet Sauvignon; Prelude Classic Dry White, Chardonnay, Pinot Noir, Cabernet Sauvignon and Siblings Sauvignon Blanc Semillon are lower-priced alternatives, with a non-vintage Prelude blended white the cheapest wine on the list.
summary Leeuwin Estate's Chardonnay is, in my opinion, Australia's finest example based on the wines of the last 15 years. The Cabernet Sauvignon, too, is an excellent wine with great style and character. Almost inevitably, the other wines in the portfolio are not in the same Olympian class, although the Prelude Chardonnay and Sauvignon Blanc are impressive at their lower price level.

Leeuwin Estate Art Series Riesling

A wine which has always had a loyal band of followers and which sells quickly. There is no question 1999 was a very successful year for Riesling in the region.

TTTT♀ **1999** Light green-yellow; the moderately intense bouquet is in a predominantly citrus mould. The palate has nice flavour and weight, again citrus and lime; the best Art Series Riesling for many years. **rating:** 90

best drinking 2000–2005 **best vintages** '99 **drink with** Margaret River marron • $20.56

Leeuwin Estate Siblings Sauvignon Blanc Semillon

A newly introduced blend of estate-grown Sauvignon Blanc (52 per cent) and Semillon (48 per cent) and partially barrel-fermented.

▼▼▼▼ 1999 Light green-yellow; the bouquet is quite sophisticated, with some tropical fruit aromas and gentle oak. The palate moves more towards tangy/minerally flavours, again showing a well-handled touch of oak; needs a touch more fruit richness for higher points. **rating: 85**

best drinking 2000–2003 **best vintages** NA **drink with** Vichysoisse • $20.56

Leeuwin Estate Art Series Chardonnay

The core of the Art Series Chardonnay is Block 20 (one of five blocks on the estate) with yields never exceeding 2.5 tonnes to the acre, and frequently less than 2 tonnes. Barrel-fermentation in the finest French oak, and prolonged bottle maturation do the rest.

▼▼▼▼▼ 1997 Medium to full yellow-green; a complex array of melon, fig, cashew and cream aromas on the bouquet are followed by a multi-layered and textured palate with seamless integration of fruit and oak. Perfect balance for a wine which was produced from microscopic yields. **rating: 97**

▼▼▼▼▼ 1996 Medium yellow-green; a complex bouquet in which the barrel-ferment/new oak contribution does show up. The wine really comes into its own on the palate, with fine melon and fig fruit; finely balanced and flavoured, with the long, lingering finish which all great white wines share. **rating: 94**

best drinking 2002–2017 **best vintages** '80, '81, '82, '83, '85, '87, '89, '90, '92, '94, '95, '96, '97 **drink with** Richer veal, chicken dishes • $74.02

lefroy brook NR

Glauder Road, Pemberton, WA 6260 **region** Pemberton, Warren Valley and Manjimup
phone (08) 9386 8385 **open** Not
winemaker Peter Fimmel (Contract) **production** 350 **est.** 1982
product range ($21.95 R) Chardonnay, Pinot Noir.
summary Owned by Perth residents Pat and Barbara Holt, the former a graduate in biochemistry and microbiology working in medical research but with a passion for Burgundy. The 1.5 hectares of vines are now both netted and fenced with steel mesh, producing wines which, on tastings to date, are outside the mainstream.

legana vineyard NR

24 Vale Street, Prospect Vale, Tas 7250 **region** Tasmania
phone (03) 6344 8030 **fax** (03) 6343 2937 **open** By appointment
winemaker Richard Richardson (Contract) **production** NA **est.** 1994
product range ($21–23 R) Pinot Noir, Cabernet Sauvignon.
summary The Legana vineyard was the first established in the Tamar Valley, planted in 1966 by Graham Wiltshire, and provided the first Heemskerk wines. In 1983 Heemskerk moved to the Pipers River region, and Steven Hyde (Rotherbythe) leased the Legana vineyard until 1994. In May of that year Kurt and Kaye Beyer acquired the vineyard and began its rehabilitation, with rich dividends now being paid.

Legana Vineyard Pinot Noir

The vines are now over 30 years old, and the vineyard has consistently shown its ability to produce very ripe fruit.

▼▼▼▽ 1997 Medium to full red-purple; the bouquet is clean, with a mix of plum, spice and forest aromas; the palate has good fruit although the texture and structure is a little on the simple side; finishes with crisp acid. **rating: 84**

▼▼▼▼ 1998 Medium to full purple-red; ripe, powerful plummy fruit floods the bouquet, leading into a full-on, rich, ripe and powerful palate where plummy fruit and strong tannins compete for attention — and get it. **rating: 88**

best drinking 2003–2010 **drink with** Braised duck • $23

Legana Vineyard Cabernet Sauvignon

Produced from the oldest Tamar Valley vineyard, a 1-hectare planting which was the birthplace of Heemskerk.

▼▼▼▼▽ 1997 Medium to full purple-red; strong cassis/berry fruit drives the bouquet and likewise the medium weight, smooth palate with its sweet cassis fruit. **rating: 90**

▼▼▼▼▽ 1998 Deep purple-red; very dense, ripe cassis berry fruit aromas are followed by a flood of cassis/redcurrant flavour on the palate supported by sweet tannins and just a hint of oak. The kind of ripeness achieved only in years like 1998. **rating: 94**

best drinking 2005–2015 **drink with** Rare rump steak • $23

leland estate ★★★★

PO Lenswood, SA 5240 **region** Adelaide Hills
phone (08) 8389 6928 **open** Not
winemaker Robb Cootes **production** 1250 **est.** 1986
product range ($13–20 CD) Sauvignon Blanc, Pinot Noir, Adele (Sparkling).
summary Former Yalumba senior winemaker Robb Cootes, with a Master of Science degree, deliberately opted out of mainstream life when he established Leland Estate, living in a split-level, one-roomed house built from timber salvaged from trees killed in the Ash Wednesday bushfires. The Sauvignon Blanc is usually good. A tiny part of the production finds its way to Victoria, where it is distributed by Dilettare; also exported to California.

Leland Estate Sauvignon Blanc

Made by the reclusive Robb Cootes from one of the oldest, albeit small, vineyards of the Adelaide Hills.
▼▼▼▽ **1999** Medium yellow-green; a highly aromatic bouquet redolent of fruit salad/passionfruit leads logically into a similarly high-flavoured palate, which does, however, seem to broaden a little towards the finish. **rating:** 83
best drinking 2000–2001 **best vintages** NA **drink with** Angel hair pasta and salmon • $13

lengs & cooter ★★★☆

24 Lindsay Terrace, Belair, SA 5042 **region** Other Wineries of SA
phone (08) 8278 3998 **fax** (08) 8278 3998 **open** Not
winemaker Contract **production** 2500 **est.** 1993
product range ($14–24 ML) Watervale Riesling, Clare Valley Semillon, Old Bush Vines Grenache, Clare Valley Old Vines Shiraz, Victor (Grenache Shiraz), Swinton (Cabernet blend).
summary Carel Lengs and Colin Cooter began making wine as a hobby in the early 1980s. Each had (and has) a full-time occupation outside the wine industry, and it was all strictly for fun. One thing has led to another, and although they still possess neither vineyards nor what might truly be described as a winery, the wines have graduated to big boy status, winning gold medals at national wine shows and receiving critical acclaim from writers across Australia.

lenswood vineyards ★★★★★

Crofts Road, Lenswood, SA 5240 **region** Adelaide Hills
phone (08) 8389 8111 **fax** (08) 8389 8555 **open** By appointment
winemaker Tim Knappstein **production** 10 000 **est.** 1981
product range ($20.50–44.40 R) Gewurztraminer, Semillon, Sauvignon Blanc, Chardonnay, Pinot Noir, The Palatine, Cabernets.
summary Lenswood Vineyards is now the sole (and full-time) occupation of Tim and Annie Knappstein, Tim Knappstein having retired from the winery which bears his name, and having sold most of the Clare vineyards to Petaluma (along with the wine business). With 25.5 hectares of close-planted, vertically trained vineyards maintained to the exacting standards of Tim Knappstein, the business will undoubtedly add to the reputation of the Adelaide Hills as an ultra-premium area. Complex Chardonnay, intense Sauvignon Blanc and broodingly powerful yet stylish Pinot Noir are trailblazers. The wines are exported to the UK, the US, Germany, Canada, Japan, Belgium, New Zealand and Singapore.

Lenswood Vineyards Chardonnay

Produced from 2.2 hectares of estate vineyards planted in 1981 and 1984. Only the best wine is chosen for release under the Lenswood Vineyards label, the remainder being disposed of elsewhere. The releases to date have been of very high quality.
▼▼▼▼▽ **1998** Light to medium green-yellow; a powerful bouquet with strong nectarine fruit and quite prominent oak. The palate has abundant mouthfeel and presence, rich, full and ripe, yet not flabby nor having any sign of overripeness. **rating:** 92
best drinking 2000–2004 **best vintages** '93, '94, '95, '96, '97, '98 **drink with** Terrine of smoked salmon • $33.75

Lenswood Vineyards Pinot Noir

Since a stellar debut in 1990 has been quite outstanding and leaving no doubt that the Lenswood area will in time become a most important producer of Pinot Noir. As Tim Knappstein himself observes, the style is fuller, riper and more robust than that of the Yarra Valley. It has found much favour, and the Lenswood Pinots have established themselves as leading examples of the fuller style of Australian Pinot Noir.

♥♥♥♥♡ 1998 Medium red-purple; the bouquet is intense, with a mix of sappy/savoury/foresty aromas; the very Burgundian palate has similar intense sappy/savoury/plummy flavours running through to a long, lingering finish.

rating: 90

best drinking 2000–2004 **best vintages** '91, '93, '94, '95, '96, '97, '98 **drink with** Quail, hare • $42.50

lenton brae wines ★★★★

Willyabrup Valley, Margaret River, WA 6285 **region** Margaret River
phone (08) 9755 6255 **fax** (08) 9755 6268 **open** 7 days 10–6
winemaker Edward Tomlinson **production** 8000 **est.** 1983
product range ($16–26 CD) Chardonnay, Semillon Sauvignon Blanc, Sauvignon Blanc, Late Harvest, Margaret River (Cabernet Sauvignon), Cabernet Merlot.
summary Former architect, town-planner and political wine activist Bruce Tomlinson built a strikingly beautiful winery but would not stand for criticism of his wines. Son Edward is more relaxed and is in fact making wines which require no criticism. Eastern States distribution and exports to Canada.

Lenton Brae Chardonnay
One of a number of very impressive white wines coming from Lenton Brae over the past few years, benefiting both from mature vines and astute winemaking influences.
♥♥♥♥♡ 1999 Light green-yellow; the bouquet is clean, tight and sophisticated, with a seamless marriage of melon fruit and oak. The palate follows precisely down the same path, with touches of cream and cashew; everything in front of it. **rating:** 90
best drinking 2001–2006 **best vintages** '97, '99 **drink with** Smoked chicken • $23

Lenton Brae Margaret River
Previously known as Cabernet Sauvignon, but now simply called Margaret River, and a blend of 78 per cent Cabernet Sauvignon, 16 per cent Merlot and 6 per cent Petit Verdot.
♥♥♥♥ 1997 Medium red-purple; the bouquet offers a mix of cedary, leafy, earthy, savoury aromas; the elegant palate is long and in a distinctly savoury mould, but the tannins are ripe and sweet. **rating:** 86
best drinking 2002–2009 **best vintages** NA **drink with** Grilled beef • $26

leo buring ★★★★

Tanunda Road, Nuriootpa, SA 5355 **region** Barossa Valley
phone NA **fax** NA **open** Mon–Sat 10–5, Sun 1–5
winemaker Geoff Henriks **production** 25 000 **est.** 1931
product range ($9.90–31 R) A very much simplified range of Clare Valley Riesling, Late Picked Clare Valley Riesling, Clare Valley Chardonnay, Clare Valley Semillon and Barossa Valley Coonawarra Cabernet Sauvignon, all under the split label introduced in 1996; the Aged Show Releases are now under the Leonay Eden Valley label.
summary Earns its high rating by virtue of being Australia's foremost producer of Rieslings over a 30-year period, with a rich legacy left by former winemaker John Vickery. But it also has the disconcerting habit of bobbing up here and there with very good wines made from other varieties, even if not so consistently.

Leo Buring Clare Valley Riesling
Sourced from a range of vineyards in the Clare Valley, and extremely well priced.
♥♥♥♡ 1999 Light yellow-green; the bouquet offers a mix of mineral, citrus and lime, but is not particularly aromatic. The palate, too, is solid but lacking excitement; should improve with time. **rating:** 81
best drinking 2003–2008 **best vintages** NA **drink with** South Australian whiting • $10

Leo Buring Leonay Riesling
In a move seemingly directed to making the position of the Leo Buring brand as difficult as humanly possible to follow, there are now two levels of release. The first is the commercial Riesling simply called 'Leo Buring', typically released at around 9–12 months age. The other is the Leonay Riesling, either with Watervale or Eden Valley appended. This is typically released when five years old, and is in effect the Show Reserve of years gone by with the bin number omitted. In some years there is a dual release from both Watervale and the Eden Valley, in other years there is no release at all.
♥♥♥♥♡ 1997 Eden Valley. Light green-yellow; the aromatic bouquet offers a mix of lime, lemon and mineral; the palate is still delicate and youthful, with herb, lemon and lime flavours and nice length to the finish. **rating:** 90

♀♀♀♀♀ **1995** Medium yellow-green; a highly aromatic bouquet with strong, toasty fruit is followed by a powerful petrol and toast-flavoured palate. Unusual in two respects: first, the degree of development, and second, the essentially old-fashioned style. Big appeal to traditionalists.   **rating:** 92

best drinking 2002–2012 **best vintages** '70, '72, '75, '77, '79, '90, '91, '92, '94, '95, '97 **drink with** Asparagus and salmon salad • $31

Leo Buring Clare Valley Shiraz

Part of a regional net cast by the Leo Buring label, and which can often come up with a surprising catch.

♀♀♀♀ **1998** Medium purple-red; the clean, moderately intense bouquet ranges through dark chocolate to dark cherry; the well-made palate repeats those dark cherry/chocolate flavours; good balance and fine tannins. **rating:** 85

best drinking 2001–2006 **best vintages** '97 **drink with** Home-made hamburger • $31

liebich wein   NR

Steingarten Road, Rowland Flat, SA 5352 **region** Barossa Valley
phone (08) 8524 4543 **fax** (08) 8524 4543 **open** Weekends 11–5, Mon–Fri by appointment
winemaker Ron Liebich **production** 600 **est.** 1992
product range ($9–18 CD) Riesling of the Valleys (a blend of Barossa and Clare Valley Riesling), Riesling Traminer, Chardonnay, Cabernet Sauvignon, Bush Vine Grenache, Classic Old Barossa Tawny Port, Benno Port; bulk port constitutes major sales.
summary Liebich Wein is Barossa Deutsch for 'Love I wine'. The Liebich family have been grape growers and winemakers at Rowland Flat since 1919, with Ron 'Darky' Liebich one of the great local characters. He himself commenced making wine in 1969, but it was not until 1992 that he and his wife Janet began selling wine under the Liebich Wein label.

lillydale vineyards   ★★★☆

Lot 10, Davross Court, Seville, Vic 3139 **region** Yarra Valley
phone (03) 5964 2016 **fax** (03) 5964 3009 **open** 7 days 11–5
winemaker Jim Brayne **production** NFP **est.** 1976
product range ($14–19.95 R) Sauvignon Blanc, Chardonnay, Pinot Noir, Cabernet Merlot.
summary Acquired by McWilliam's Wines in 1994; Alex White has departed, and Max McWilliam is in charge of the business. With a number of other major developments, notably Coonawarra and Barwang, on its plate, McWilliam's has so far adopted a softly, softly approach to Lillydale Vineyards, although a winery restaurant was opened in February 1997.

Lillydale Sauvignon Blanc

Lillydale Vineyards was one of the first producers of Sauvignon Blanc in the Yarra Valley, finding the variety very difficult to handle from a viticultural viewpoint, with inconsistent and often very low yields. Production has increased somewhat in recent years, the wine normally being made without the use of oak. It is situated in a relatively cool subregion, and the wine has always been delicate.

♀♀♀♀ **1999** Light green-yellow; delicate passionfruit and gooseberry fruit on the bouquet introduces a palate which is crisp, clean and delicate, finishing with neat acidity.   **rating:** 87

best drinking Drink now **best vintages** '98, '99 **drink with** Delicate fish dishes • $15.95

Lillydale Pinot Noir

An attractive wine, very much in the family style though with (relatively speaking) a little more depth than the white wines.

♀♀♀♀ **1999** Light to medium red-purple; the bouquet is light, but has some pleasing spicy/savoury characters. There is rather more red fruit on the palate, ranging into strawberry and cherry; the barest hint of oak. A good outcome for the vintage.   **rating:** 86

best drinking 2000–2003 **best vintages** '96 **drink with** Chinese seafood • $19.95

Lillydale Vineyards Cabernet Merlot

Juggling cabernet sauvignon and merlot in any part of the Yarra Valley is a challenging task, even more so in the cooler subregions around Lillydale Vineyards.

♀♀♀♀ **1998** Medium red-purple; the clean, moderately intense, savoury bouquet precedes a palate where sweet berry fruit comes at the core, surrounded by more savoury characters; gentle tannins and oak.   **rating:** 87

best drinking 2001–2006 **best vintages** NA **drink with** Young veal • $19.95

lillypilly estate ★★★☆

Lillypilly Road, Leeton, NSW 2705 **region** Riverina
phone (02) 6953 4069 **fax** (02) 6953 4980 **open** Mon–Sat 10–5.30, Sun by appointment
winemaker Robert Fiumara **production** 8000 **est.** 1982
product range ($9.70–15.65 CD) Riesling, Chardonnay, Sauvignon Blanc, Pound Hill Classic Dry White, Tramillon® (Traminer Semillon), Noble Riesling, Noble Traminer, Noble Semillon, Noble Muscat of Alexandria, Red Velvet® (medium sweet red), Cabernet Sauvignon, Shiraz, Vintage Port.
summary Apart from occasional Vintage Ports the best wines by far are the botrytised white wines, with the Noble Muscat of Alexandria unique to the winery; these wines have both style and intensity of flavour and can age well. The Noble Semillon and Noble Traminer add strings to the bow.

lindemans (coonawarra) ★★★★

Main Penola–Naracoorte Road, Coonawarra, SA 5263 **region** Coonawarra
phone (08) 8736 2613 **fax** (08) 8736 2959 **open** 7 days 10–5
winemaker Phillip John, Greg Clayfield **production** 15 000 **est.** 1908
product range ($9.50–35 R) Under the new Coonawarra Vineyard label, Riesling, Sauvignon Blanc; then come the premium red trio of Pyrus (Cabernet blend), Limestone Ridge (Shiraz Cabernet), and St George (Cabernet Sauvignon).
summary Lindemans is clearly the strongest brand other than Penfolds in the Southcorp Group, with some great vineyards and a great history. The Coonawarra vineyards are of ever-increasing significance because of the move towards regional identity in the all-important export markets, which has led to the emergence of a new range of regional/varietal labels. Whether the fullest potential of the vineyards (from a viticultural viewpoint) is being realised is a matter of debate. Worldwide distribution.

Lindemans Limestone Ridge

Arguably the most distinguished of the Coonawarra trio. A variable blend of Shiraz and Cabernet Sauvignon, varying from as much as 80 per cent Shiraz to as little as 55 per cent. The wine is matured in new American oak barrels for 20 months and is given additional bottle age prior to release. The 1997 vintage was a multiple trophy winner at the 1999 Sydney Royal Wine Show.
TTTTT 1997 Medium to full red-purple; lusciously ripe plummy/cherry fruit is swathed in high-quality oak on the bouquet. The same ripe cherry and plum fruit runs through a seductive palate with a long, soft finish. Oak certainly makes its contribution but does so in balance and harmony with the fruit. **rating: 94**
best drinking 2002–2012 **best vintages** '86, '88, '90, '91, '93, '94, '96, '97 **drink with** Beef casserole • $36

Lindemans Pyrus

A label conjured up in the heat of the moment when the 1985 vintage bobbed up with the Jimmy Watson Trophy when Lindemans was least expecting it. It is a blend of Cabernet Sauvignon, Merlot, Malbec and Cabernet Franc; since 1985 the percentage of Cabernet Sauvignon has increased from 35 per cent in the early days to 70 per cent. It has come of age, with the fruit and 18 months new French oak maturation working to great effect.
TTTTY 1996 Medium to full red-purple; the bouquet is clean, with an intriguing mix of sweet berry fruit on the one hand and more savoury bitter chocolate and earth on the other. An elegant wine in the mouth, of light to medium intensity, nicely balanced and with the dominant savoury characters reflecting the Merlot Cabernet Franc components. Finishes with soft tannins appropriate to the weight of the wine. **rating: 90**
best drinking 2001–2006 **best vintages** '88, '90, '91, '96 **drink with** Entrecote of beef • $35

Lindemans St George

Made entirely from cabernet sauvignon grown on the 12-hectare St George Vineyard, first produced in 1973. A very distinguished label with an at-times brilliant show record, but which has seen style vary and quality fluctuate over the years. The oak can dominate in lighter vintages, not surprising given that it spends up to 25 months in new French hogsheads and barriques.
TTTTY 1996 Medium to full red-purple; the bouquet is quite earthy and relatively austere, raising a question mark about the particular bottle, although the palate came through strongly with ripe, rich chunky cassis-flavoured fruit backed up by plenty of tannin providing a sturdy structure. **rating: 92**
best drinking 2001–2011 **best vintages** '86, '88, '90, '91, '96 **drink with** Shoulder of lamb • $35

lindemans (hunter valley)   NR

McDonalds Road, Pokolbin, NSW 2320 **region** Lower Hunter Valley
phone (02) 4998 7684 **fax** (02) 4998 7682 **open** Mon–Fri 9–4.30, weekends and public holidays 10–4.30
winemaker Patrick Auld **production** 12 000 **est.** 1843
product range ($7.50–95 R) Standard wines under annually changing Bin numbers of Semillon, Chablis, White Burgundy, Semillon Chardonnay, Chardonnay, Shiraz Burgundy, Hermitage, deluxe releases under Reserve Bin label, individual vineyard label (e.g. Steven) and revitalised older Classic Release label.
summary I have to declare an interest in Lindemans Hunter Valley: not only did I cut my vinous teeth on it, but between 1997 and May 2000 I had group winemaker responsibility for it within Southcorp. I have long been on record in saying that its crown had slipped somewhat. A major winery upgrade in 1997–98 will help to restore things, as will the renovations to the historic Ben Ean facility. Worldwide distribution. As with Tulloch and Hungerford Hill, I rate neither the winery nor the wines with which I have been involved but will do so in the future.

lindemans (karadoc)   ★★★★

Edey Road, Karadoc via Mildura, Vic 3496 **region** Murray Darling
phone (03) 5051 3333 **fax** (03) 5051 3390 **open** 7 days
winemaker Phillip John (Chief) **production** 10 million **est.** 1974
product range ($7–40 R) Bin 23 Riesling, Bin 65 Chardonnay (one of the largest selling Chardonnay brands in the world), Bin 95 Sauvignon Blanc, Bin 99 Pinot Noir, Bin 50 Shiraz Cabernet, Bin 60 Merlot are the most important in terms of volume; Cawarra range of Colombard Chardonnay, Classic Dry White, Traminer Riesling and Shiraz Cabernet; also Nyrang Semillon and Shiraz. Karadoc also produces the great fortified wines, including the premium Fino, Amontillado and Oloroso Sherries, Old Liqueur Muscat, Tokay and Madeira and fine Tawny Ports.
summary Now the production centre for all of the Lindemans and Leo Buring wines, with the exception of special lines made in the Coonawarra and Hunter wineries. The biggest and most modern single facility in Australia, allowing all-important economies of scale, and the major processing centre for the beverage wine sector (casks, flagons and low-priced bottles) of the Southcorp empire. Its achievement in making several million cases of Bin 65 Chardonnay a year is extraordinary given the quality and consistency of the wines. Worldwide distribution.

Lindemans Bin 65 Chardonnay

A winemaking tour de force and one of the world's leading brands of Chardonnay. It is sourced from no less than 14 different wine-growing regions across southeastern Australia and shows no sign of buckling under the ever-increasing production volumes. It has been praised by wine critics around the world and is the only wine to have ever been rated a 'Best Buy' by the *Wine Spectator* for nine consecutive vintages. Notwithstanding the ever-increasing volume (2 million cases in 2000) the quality has been rigorously guarded.
▼▼▼♡ **1999** Light to medium green-yellow; the bouquet shows fairly obvious bacony oak chips, and although the wine has nice mouthfeel allied with some sophisticated nutty/creamy characters, the level and type of oak is a worry. Winemaker Phillip John believes the wine is the best yet in this series, but I need to be persuaded that this is so. Perhaps a little time in bottle, and subsequent blend releases, will rectify things.   **rating:** 80
best drinking 1999–2000 **best vintages** NA **drink with** Virtually anything you choose • $8.90

Lindemans Bin 99 Pinot Noir

Has been an export-only wine until now; made in impressively large quantities, particularly for this difficult variety.
▼▼▼♡ **1998** Medium red-purple; the bouquet is quite fragrant, with strawberry/cherry varietal fruit and barely evident oak. The wine has commendable flavour and structure; undoubtedly a step forwards in bringing the wine into everyday drinking.   **rating:** 82
best drinking 2000–2001 **best vintages** NA **drink with** Pizza or pasta • $NA

Lindemans Bin 45 Cabernet Sauvignon

Sourced from cabernet grown in numerous regions across southeastern Australia and, as with all of the Lindemans wines in this price and category bracket, cleverly made and blended.
▼▼▼▼ **1998** Medium red-purple; the clean bouquet is moderately intense, driven by dark berry fruit aromas. A nice commercial wine on the palate, with sweet berry fruit, soft tannins and just a hint of oak. Sits easily alongside its more famous sister wine, Bin 65 Chardonnay.   **rating:** 86
best drinking 1999–2002 **best vintages** NA **drink with** Shepherd's pie • $9.95

lindemans (padthaway) ★★★★☆

Naracoorte Road, Padthaway, SA 5271 **region** Padthaway
phone (08) 8765 5155 **fax** (08) 8765 5073 **open** Not
winemaker Phillip John, Greg Clayfield **production** 68 000 **est.** 1908
product range ($11–17.90 R) Sauvignon Blanc, Verdelho, Chardonnay, Pinot Noir, Cabernet Merlot, also
Winemakers Reserve Chardonnay, Limestone Coast Chardonnay, Limestone Coast Shiraz and Padthaway Merlot.
summary Lindemans Padthaway Chardonnay could be said to be the best premium Chardonnay on the market
in Australia, with an exceptional capacity to age. Back vintages win gold medals seemingly at will, the
performance of the '94 vintage winning the Aged Chardonnay Trophy at the Liquorland National Wine Show in
both 1996 and 1997 being quite remarkable. Worldwide distribution.

Lindemans Padthaway Chardonnay

A wine with a long and at times very illustrious history. The style has changed somewhat over the years, starting
off as a fruit-driven wine which aged well (winning a major national wine show trophy for mature Chardonnay
along the way) then becoming very oaky, but with the '94 vintage returning to its very best, and providing one of
the great bargains of 1995, before going on to win the most prestigious Chardonnay trophy in Australia at the
Liquorland National Wine Show for two years in succession (1996 and 1997), recalling the feats of Wolf Blass and
Cape Mentelle with the Jimmy Watson Trophy in Melbourne. For the record, it is entirely barrel-fermented in a
mix of new and one-year-old French (Allier and Troncais) oak, and given extended lees contact.

▼▼▼▼ **1998** Medium to full yellow-green; the bouquet is quite rich and complex, although the oak is a fraction
assertive at this point of time. The palate offers the usual abundant flavour, with nectarine and peach fruit
supported by oodles of oak. **rating:** 88

best drinking 1999–2003 **best vintages** '84, '85, '90, '94, '96, '97 **drink with** Chinese prawns with cashew nuts
• $15

Lindemans Padthaway Pinot Noir

Quite sophisticated Pinot Noir winemaking methods are used with this wine. The grapes were handpicked, and
part of the fruit placed in 400 kg shallow bins, and gently macerated by foot-stamping four times daily for
6–7 days. Other components of the blend are fermented in small fermenters, usually with a proportion of stalks
and whole bunches. The wine then spends ten months on yeast lees in new, one-year-old and two-year-old
French oak barrels. I cannot but express admiration for the company's background notes which would have one
believe that the wine was barrel-fermented for ten months.

▼▼▼▽ **1998** Medium to full purple-red; the bouquet is soft, with an array of dark berry and plum fruit aromas.
The palate is gentle, with dark plummy fruit, subtle oak and an altogether soft structure and finish. That it does
not show more of the winemaking techniques used is not the fault of the winemaker but the limitations of
Padthaway as a pinot noir region. **rating:** 84

best drinking 1999–2000 **best vintages** NA **drink with** Quail • $17

Lindemans Limestone Coast Shiraz

This wine follows in the footsteps of the 1997 Limestone Coast Chardonnay. Like the Chardonnay, it uses the
Zone name of Limestone Coast, rather than one or more of the regions within that Zone (being Padthaway,
Coonawarra, Mount Benson, Robe and the as-yet-undeclared Bordertown). The intention is that the wine will
come from some, but no by no means all, of those regions, with the components varying from year to year. The
first vintage comes primarily from Padthaway and Robe, and, as the wine proclaims, is in radically different style
from other Lindeman reds.

▼▼▼▽ **1998** Vivid, deep purple-red; the bouquet is clean, with touches of sweet, dark berry fruits together with
hints of liquorice and spice. The palate is bright and fresh, with black cherry/earthy fruit, but is relatively hollow
and doesn't fulfil the promise of the colour and bouquet. Nonetheless, good value at the price, and something
different. **rating:** 81

best drinking 1999–2003 **best vintages** NA **drink with** Barbecues • $11

Lindemans Padthaway Cabernet Merlot

A blend of about 70 per cent Cabernet Sauvignon and 30 per cent Merlot which shows that, if yields are
controlled, Padthaway can produce red wines of equivalent quality to its white wines. The wine was matured in a
mix of new and used French and American oak, and has an abundance of fruit substance and flavour.

▼▼▼▼ **1998** Medium red-purple; the bouquet is soft yet quite solid, with dark berry, vanilla and chocolate aromas.
The palate has good fruit weight and extract, with soft yet persistent tannins. The flavours are in the dark berry,
chocolate and mint spectrum, all making for easy drinking. **rating:** 87

best drinking 2001–2006 **best vintages** '91, '94, '95, '97 **drink with** Fillet steak • $17.90

lirralirra estate ★★★

Paynes Road, Lilydale, Vic 3140 **region** Yarra Valley
phone (03) 9735 0224 **fax** (03) 9735 0224 **open** Weekends and holidays 10–6, Jan 7 days
winemaker Alan Smith **production** 400 **est.** 1981
product range ($14–28 CD) Semillon, Wooded Semillon, Semillon Sauvignon Blanc, Sauvignon Blanc, Pinot Noir, Yarra Valley Cabernets.
summary Twenty years ago I wrote that the Yarra Valley was a viticultural Garden of Eden; little did I know. The trials and tribulations of Lirralirra over the past ten years have been awesome, yet Alan Smith retains a sense of proportion and faith in the future. All I can say is he deserves every success that comes his way.

Lirralirra Sauvignon Blanc

Reappears on the roster after two very low-yielding years in 1997 and 1998 meant that it had to be blended with Semillon.
ŢŢŢŢ 1999 Light straw-green; the bouquet is crisp and clean with a mix of herb and grass aromas. The palate is delicate, crisp and fresh, with lemony/grassy flavours and good acid. Unlike most Sauvignon Blanc, will actually benefit from a few years in bottle.   **rating: 83**
best drinking 2000–2003 **best vintages** '94 **drink with** Shellfish • $17

Lirralirra Pinot Noir

After a promising 1996 Pinot Noir, 1997 reduced the crop to a mere 600 kilograms, 500 kilograms of which had been presold to David Lance (of Diamond Valley). Then, at the end of 1997 frost removed 60 per cent of the potential crop from the '98 vintage. What was left produced a Reserve Pinot Noir.
ŢŢŢŢ 1998 Reserve. Medium red with a touch of purple; the bouquet is slightly subdued, with foresty/earthy/stemmy aromas, but there is much more fruit on the palate with ripe cherry and plum flavours. For some reason I can't quite identify, the finish seems slightly jagged but will hopefully settle down with age in bottle (and merit higher points).   **rating: 82**
best drinking 2000–2003 **best vintages** NA **drink with** Smoked quail • $28

little river wines   NR

Corner West Swan and Forest Roads, Henley Brook, WA 6055 **region** Swan District
phone (08) 9296 4462 **fax** (08) 9296 1022 **open** Fri–Wed 10–5
winemaker Bruno de Tastes **production** 4000 **est.** 1934
product range ($15.50–40 CD) Chenin Blanc, Viognier, Chardonnay, Cabernet Sauvignon, Old Vines Shiraz, Cabernet Sauvignon, Grenache Shiraz, Brut de Brut, Vin Doux Late Harvest, Noble Classic.
summary Following several quick changes of ownership (and of consultant winemakers) the former Glenalwyn now has as its winemaker the eponymously named Count Bruno de Tastes. I, however, have had no recent tastes.

little's winery ★★☆

Lot 3 Palmers Lane, Pokolbin, NSW 2321 **region** Lower Hunter Valley
phone (02) 4998 7626 **fax** (02) 4998 7867 **open** 7 days 10–4.30
winemaker Ian Little **production** 6000 **est.** 1984
product range ($12–23 CD) Chardonnay, Semillon, Gewurztraminer, Late Harvest Semillon, Pinot Noir Blanc de Noir, Shiraz, Cabernet Sauvignon, Vintage Port.
summary A successful cellar-door operation with friendly service and friendly wines: aromatic, fresh and sometimes slightly sweet white wines and light, inoffensive red wines.

Little's Gewurztraminer

Gewurztraminer is a relatively rare grape in the Hunter Valley, but suits Ian Little's style of winemaking which enhances the aromatics and leaves enough residual sugar to attract those who like a touch of distinct sweetness to their white wines.
ŢŢŢŢ 1998 Medium yellow-green; there is clean, spicy lychee varietal character on the light bouquet; a light and delicately framed wine on the palate, but is well made, and in particular is not too sweet.   **rating: 82**
best drinking 1999–2000 **best vintages** NA **drink with** Asian stir fry • $16

Little's Reserve Shiraz

The grapes come from the Daisy Hill Vineyard not far from Little's own plantings. Two-thirds of the wine is fermented in oak barriques with the heads removed and is hand-plunged. The remaining portion is fermented in 3-tonne Potter Fermenters. Post-fermentation maceration follows at low temperatures in a coolroom, and the wine is then pressed and run off to a mix of new and one-year-old American and French hogsheads for a further 16 months maturation.

ŦŦŦŦ **1998** Medium red-purple; there are slightly gamey overtones to the cherry/berry fruit of the bouquet; the palate has quite good fruit weight and subtle oak but is hard in the mouth.   **rating:** 81

best drinking 2000–2003 **best vintages** NA **drink with** Braised beef •$23

lochvie wines   NR

28 Lavender Park Road, Eltham, Vic 3095 **region** Yarra Valley
phone (03) 9439 9444 **open** Weekends 9.30–5.30, weekdays by appointment
winemaker John Lewis **production** NFP **est.** 1985
product range ($10 CD) Cabernet Merlot.
summary A tiny home winery producing a single 65 per cent/35 per cent Cabernet Merlot blend. Since 1993 the grapes have been sold to others, and no further wines made, but the '90 to '92 wines were available at cellar door on last advice.

ℰ logan wines   ★★★★☆

Ground Floor, 160 Sailor's Bay Road, Northbridge, NSW 2063 **region** Upper Hunter Valley
phone (02) 9958 6844 **fax** (02) 9958 1258 **open** Not
winemaker Peter Logan, Simon Gilbert (Contract) **production** NFP **est.** 1997
product range ($16–25 R) Ripe White, Ripe Red, Riesling, Reserve Chardonnay, Shiraz, Orange Cabernet Sauvignon.
summary Logan Wines is a family operation, founded by businessman Mal Logan assisted by three of his children: Peter, who just happens to be an oenology graduate from the University of Adelaide, Greg (advertising) and Kylie (office administrator). With assistance from Simon Gilbert, the team has made an exceptionally auspicious start.

Logan Riesling
The wine reflects the negociant side of the business, being sourced from the Clare Valley. A very well-made wine.
ŦŦŦŦŦ **1999** Light to medium yellow-green; the bouquet is attractive with fresh, clean lime juice aromas; a snappy wine in the mouth, with more of those lime juice flavours, and good length.   **rating:** 91
best drinking 2000–2007 **drink with** Calamari •$17

Logan Ripe White
An unwooded Chardonnay produced from grapes grown in the Orange district.
ŦŦŦŦ **1998** Medium yellow-green; the bouquet is clean and fresh, largely neutral but with a hint of melon. The sweet melon fruit on the palate is typical of unwooded Chardonnay in lacking bite, but it does have flavour.
                                                                                     rating: 81
best drinking 2000–2001 **drink with** Takeaway pasta •$16

Logan Reserve Chardonnay
Barrel-fermented, and spends seven months in French oak barriques during which time it undergoes partial malolactic fermentation.
ŦŦŦŦŦ **1998** Medium to full yellow-green; a clean, nicely balanced bouquet where melon fruit is integrated with subtle oak. The palate has good mouthfeel and weight, the flavours running through cashew and melon, the oak nicely restrained.   **rating:** 90
best drinking 2000–2004 **drink with** Pan-fried veal •$24

Logan Shiraz
Like the Cabernet Sauvignon, comes from three-year-old vines planted on the red volcanic soils of Mount Canobolas at an elevation of 810 metres. The wine spends 16 months in 90 per cent American and 10 per cent French oak (a mixture of new and used) during which time it undergoes malolactic fermentation.
ŦŦŦŦŦ **1997** Medium to full purple-red; earthy, ripe and rich fruit aromas are surrounded by strong American oak. The amazingly rich, ripe, sweet and luscious palate is enhanced by cinnamon/clove/smoky oak. **rating:** 90
best drinking 2002–2010 **drink with** Game •$25

Logan Orange Cabernet Sauvignon
Produced from three-year-old vines planted on deep volcanic soils on north-facing slopes of Mount Canobolas. The wine spends 16 months in a mix of new and used oak (90 per cent French, 10 per cent American), during which time it undergoes malolactic fermentation.

▼▼▼▼ **1997** Medium to full red-purple; the bouquet is rich, with an array of chocolate, vanilla, blackberry and earth aromas. Powerful and distinctive cabernet fruit runs through the palate, finishing with lingering tannins. **rating:** 88
best drinking 2002–2012 **drink with** Seasoned leg of lamb • $25

☙ london lodge estate　　　NR
Muswellbrook Road, Gungal, NSW 2333 **region** Upper Hunter Valley
phone (02) 6547 6122 **fax** (02) 6547 6122 **open** 7 days 10–9
winemaker Gary Reed **production** NA **est.** 1988
product range NA.
summary The 16-hectare vineyard of Stephen and Joanne Horner is planted to chardonnay, pinot noir, shiraz and cabernet sauvignon, and sold through a cellar door (and restaurant) with a full array of tourist attractions including arts and crafts.

long gully estate　　　★★★☆
Long Gully Road, Healesville, Vic 3777 **region** Yarra Valley
phone (03) 9510 5798 **fax** (03) 9510 9859 **open** Weekends, holidays 11–5
winemaker Peter Florance **production** 20 000 **est.** 1982
product range ($9–30 CD) Riesling, Chardonnay, Semillon, Sauvignon Blanc, Sauvignon Blanc Semillon, Merlot, Irma's Cabernet, Pinot Noir, Shiraz; Limited Edition Reserve Chardonnay, Ice Riesling, Merlot and Cabernet.
summary One of the larger (but by no means largest) of the Yarra Valley producers which have successfully established a number of export markets over recent years. Wine quality is consistent rather than exhilarating; it is able to offer a range of wines with two to three years bottle age. Recent vineyard extensions underline the commercial success of Long Gully.

Long Gully Estate Riesling
Produced from 2 hectares of estate plantings. By and large does nothing to change the view that, for whatever reason, riesling doesn't perform as well as might be expected in the cool Yarra Valley climate.
▼▼▼▽ **1997** Light yellow-green; the bouquet is clean, light, with talcy/minerally aromas, amazingly youthful and undeveloped. The palate is fairly tight and no less youthful; what the wine lacks is fruit on the mid-palate. **rating:** 81
best drinking 2000–2004 **best vintages** NA **drink with** Light salad • $12

Long Gully Estate Sauvignon Blanc Semillon
As well as a varietal Sauvignon Blanc, Long Gully also produces a Sauvignon Blanc Semillon, drawing upon 2 hectares of sauvignon blanc and 1 hectare of semillon. The wine is steel-fermented and does not receive oak.
▼▼▼▼ **1997** Light to medium yellow-green; the bouquet is crisp and minerally, still very youthful. The palate is tight and fresh, and seems to have been protected by plenty of CO_2, and may well have spent a considerable time in tank before being bottled. Whatever, the wine has nice length and balance. **rating:** 85
best drinking 2000–2003 **best vintages** NA **drink with** Crab • $13.50

Long Gully Estate Pinot Noir
The Long Gully plantings of 2 hectares of pinot noir are now fully mature; the wine is essentially made on the north-facing slopes of the vineyard.
▼▼▼▽ **1998** Medium red-purple; the bouquet is soft, with attractive plum and spice fruit; the palate ups the ante in terms of richness, with plum, spice and cedar flavours. **rating:** 84
best drinking 2000–2002 **best vintages** NA **drink with** Asian • $19

Long Gully Estate Irma's Cabernet
Effectively a special selection of cabernet sauvignon, merlot, cabernet franc and malbec, all estate-grown, of course.
▼▼▼▼▽ **1997** Medium to full red-purple; the bouquet is solid, with a mix of savoury and dark berry fruit aromas opening up into a sweet, smooth and supple palate with ripe dark berry fruit and largely incidental oak. Trophy winner Sydney Wine Show 2000. **rating:** 90
best drinking 2000–2005 **best vintages** '97 **drink with** Yarra Valley venison • $20

longleat　　　★★★☆
Old Weir Road, Murchison, Vic 3610 **region** Goulburn Valley
phone (03) 5826 2294 **fax** (03) 5826 2510 **open** Thurs–Mon 10–5
winemaker David Traeger (Contract) **production** 7000 **est.** 1975
product range ($13–17 CD) Riesling, Semillon, Chardonnay, Shiraz, Cabernet Sauvignon.

summary Longleat has long had a working relationship with Chateau Tahbilk, which makes the Longleat wines under contract, and buys significant quantities of grapes surplus to Longleat's requirements. The wines are always honest and full flavoured, and have been given a striking new label design which, if nothing else, catches the eye.

Longleat Riesling
The Goulburn Valley has seldom been regarded as a classic Riesling area, but the performance of Mitchelton's Blackwood Park over the years suggests the region deserves greater recognition. The Rieslings of Longleat and Chateau Tahbilk are in a slightly more robust style, but none the worse for that.

▼▼▼▽ 1998 Light to medium yellow-green; the aromas are rich and ripe, with abundant citrus and passionfruit; the same flavours appear on the palate, which has lots of raw power.   **rating: 84**
best drinking 2000–2004 **best vintages** '85, '86, '87, '93, '94, '98 **drink with** Antipasto • $13

Longleat Shiraz
The estate-grown grapes, from vines vines which are now around 25 years old, are fermented in a rotary fermenter, with the last part of fermentation taking place in American oak barrels, where the wine spends the next 18 months.

▼▼▼▽ 1998 Medium purple-red; the bouquet is firm, in typically earthy style, with some chocolate and savoury edges. The very firm, youthful and powerful palate has marked acidity but is not overly tannic; seems to have all of the requisites for improvement in bottle.   **rating: 84**
best drinking 2003–2008 **best vintages** NA **drink with** Roast beef • $17

Longleat Cabernet Sauvignon
Produced from 7 hectares of cabernet sauvignon grown on the 'home' vineyard situated at Murchison on the banks of the Goulburn River. The relatively warm climate produces wines of great depth of colour, flavour and extract.

▼▼▼▼ 1998 Medium red-purple; the bouquet is clean, with rich dark berry/savoury fruit and subtle oak. The palate has a most attractive opening, with blackberry/raspberry fruit, and although it does tighten up on the finish, the tannins are not extractive and the balance is good.   **rating: 89**
best drinking 2003–2013 **best vintages** '82, '84, '86, '91, '98 **drink with** Marinated beef • $17

longview creek vineyard   NR
150 Palmer Road, Sunbury, Vic 3429 **region** Sunbury
phone (03) 9744 1050 **fax** (03) 9744 1050 **open** Sunday 11–5
winemaker David Hodgson **production** 350 **est.** 1988
product range ($18–22 CD) Chardonnay, Chenin Blanc, Pinot Noir, Tarrango, Shiraz.
summary A relatively new arrival in the Sunbury subdistrict of the Macedon region, owned by Ron and Joan Parker. A total of 3.3 hectares of chardonnay, pinot noir and chenin blanc are in production with an additional 2 hectares of shiraz coming into bearing.

lost valley winery   NR
35 Yamby Road, Strath Creek, Vic 3658 **region** Central Victorian Mountain Country
phone (03) 5797 0212 **fax** (03) 9351 2005 **open** Not
winemaker Alex White (Contract) **production** 1200 **est.** 1995
product range ($25–35 ML) Verdleho, Shiraz, Merlot, Cortese.
summary Dr Robert Ippaso planted the Lost Valley vineyard at an elevation of 450 metres on the slopes of Mount Tallarook, with 1.25 hectares of shiraz and 0.85 hectare each of merlot, verdelho and cortese, the last the only such planting in Australia. It pays homage to Dr Ippaso's birthplace in Savoie in the Franco-Italian Alps, where cortese flourishes.

louis-laval wines   NR
160 Cobcroft Road, Broke, NSW 2330 **region** Lower Hunter Valley
phone (02) 6579 1105 **fax** (02) 6579 1105 **open** By appointment
winemaker Roy Meyer **production** 600 **est.** 1987
product range ($25 CD) Shiraz, Cabernet Sauvignon.
summary It is ironic that the winery name should have associations with Alfa Laval, the giant Swiss food and wine machinery firm. Roy Meyer runs an organic vineyard (using only sulphur and copper sprays) and is proud of the fact that the winery has no refrigeration and no stainless steel. The wines produced from the 2.5-hectare vineyard are fermented in open barrels or cement tanks, and maturation is handled entirely in oak. At its first entry into the Hunter Valley Small Winemakers Show, the 1998 Cabernet Sauvignon won a silver medal, and the 1998 Shiraz a bronze medal.

lovey's estate   NR

1548 Melba Highway, Yarra Glen, Vic 3775 **region** Yarra Valley
phone (03) 5965 2444 **fax** (03) 5965 2460 **open** Wed–Sun 12–5
winemaker Brian Love **production** 1000 **est.** 1989
product range ($15–24.50 CD) Sauvignon Blanc, Chardonnay, Muscadelle, Pinot Noir, Shiraz, Cabernet Sauvignon.
summary Lovey's Estate is part of a restaurant and accommodation complex situated prominently on the Melba Highway, just on the far side of Yarra Glen. The majority of the production from the 11-hectare vineyard is sold; part is made under contract at Tarrawarra and is available through cellar door and the restaurant.

lowe family wines   ★★★

9 Paterson Road, Bolwarra, NSW 2320 **region** Mudgee
phone (02) 4998 7121 **fax** (02) 4998 7393 **open** At Peppers Creek
winemaker David Lowe, Jane Wilson **production** 4000 **est.** 1987
product range ($18–25 ML) Semillon, Peacock Hill Chardonnay, Lawless Chardonnay, Peacock Hill Shiraz.
summary Former Rothbury winemaker David Lowe and Jane Wilson make the Lowe Family Wines at the Oakvale Winery, drawing upon 15 hectares of family-owned vineyards in Mudgee, supplemented by purchases from Orange and the Hunter Valley. Interestingly, the plantings include sangiovese, barbera and zinfandel. David and Jane also run an increasingly important contract-winemaking business.

Lowe Family Chardonnay

Made from grapes sourced from Orange, the Hunter Valley and Mudgee. The wine is whole-bunch pressed, and barrel-fermented with spontaneous (i.e. wild yeast) initiation of the ferment.
▼▼▼▼ 1998 Medium yellow-green; the bouquet is clean, with pleasantly ripe fruit of medium intensity supported by subtle oak. A restrained wine on the palate, almost Giaconda-like, and will repay cellaring.   **rating:** 85
best drinking 2001–2005 **best vintages** NA **drink with** Fried chicken • $22

lyre bird hill   ★★★

Inverloch Road, Koonwarra, Vic 3954 **region** Gippsland
phone (03) 5664 3204 **fax** (03) 5664 3206 **open** Weekends, holidays 10–5 or by appointment
winemaker Owen Schmidt **production** 1000 **est.** 1986
product range ($12–25 CD) Riesling, Traminer, Chardonnay (wooded and unwooded), Pinot Noir, Pinot Noir Cellar Reserve, Cabernet Sauvignon, Shiraz, Rhapsody (Sparkling), Phantasy (Sparkling).
summary Former Melbourne professionals Owen and Robyn Schmidt make small quantities of estate-grown wine (the vineyard is 2.4 hectares in size), offering accommodation for three couples (RACV four-star rating) in their newly built spacious house. The 1997 Pinot Noir Cellar Reserve won a gold medal at the 1999 Ballarat Wine Show, the first such recognition for Lyre Bird Hill.

❧ macaw creek wines   NR

Macaw Creek Road, Riverton, SA 5412 **region** Other Wineries of SA
phone (08) 8847 2237 **fax** (08) 8847 2237 **open** Sun and public holidays 11–4
winemaker Rodney Hooper, Miriam Hooper **production** 1500 **est.** 1992
product range ($10–29 CD) Riesling, Chardonnay, Late Harvest White Frontignac, Yoolang Preservative Free Shiraz Cabernet, Grenache Shiraz Mourvedre, Reserve Shiraz Cabernet, Tawny Port, Sparkling.
summary The property on which Macaw Creek Wines is established has been owned by the Hooper family since the 1850s, but development of the estate vineyards did not begin until 1995; 10 hectares have been planted since that time, with a further 20 hectares being planted in the winter/spring of 1999. Rodney and Miriam Hooper have established the Macaw Creek brand previously (in 1992) with wines made from grapes from other regions, including the Preservative-Free Yoolang Cabernet Shiraz. Rodney Hooper is a highly qualified and skilled winemaker with experience in many parts of Australia and internationally in Germany, France and the US.

Macaw Creek Grenache Shiraz Mourvedre

Rodney Hooper's winemaking skills shine through in this wine, which was entirely made in stainless steel, and yet which won a gold medal at the 1999 Brisbane Wine Show. Certainly an early-drinking style.
▼▼▼▽ 1999 Youthful light to medium red-purple; the bouquet is clean, light and fresh with lively juicy/berry fruit. The palate follows down the same track; everything to be gained from drinking it, and nothing from keeping it in the cellar.   **rating:** 84
best drinking 2000–2001 **drink with** Spicy chicken • $14

Macaw Creek Reserve Shiraz Cabernet

Follows in the footsteps of a 1993 Reserve Shiraz Cabernet; I do not know the reason for the large gap in vintages.
TTTT 1998 Medium to full red-purple; the bouquet is rich, full, ripe and complex, with lots of American oak. However, blackberry and plum fruit on the palate, together with touches of chocolate, brings the wine into balance, even though the oak still makes its presence felt. The tannins are nicely balanced to round off a pretty impressive wine.   **rating:** 89

best drinking 2003–2013 **drink with** Rich casserole   • $29

macquariedale estate   NR

40 Rusty Lane, Branxton, NSW 2335 **region** Lower Hunter Valley
phone (02) 4938 1408 **fax** (02) 4938 1408 **open** Not
winemaker Contract **production** 4000 **est.** 1993
product range ($15–20 ML) Semillon, Shiraz.
summary Macquariedale Estate dates back to 1993, when Ross McDonald commenced the planting of a small vineyard at Branxton. One thing led to another, and he and his family have moved from Sydney to the Hunter Valley and significantly extended the scope of the operations by purchasing a 25-year-old vineyard to supplement production from the home vineyard. The wines are contract-made and are sold through the mailing list and the Boutique Wine Centre in Broke Road, Pokolbin.

madew wines   NR

Westering, Federal Highway, Lake George, NSW 2581 **region** Canberra District
phone (02) 4848 0026 **open** Weekends, public holidays 11–5
winemaker David Madew **production** 2500 **est.** 1984
product range ($13–20 CD) Riesling, Reserve Riesling, Semillon, Chardonnay, Phoenix (Botrytis Chardonnay), Dry Red, Merlot, Cabernets.
summary Madew Wines bowed to the urban pressure of Queanbeyan and purchased the Westering Vineyard from Captain G P Hood some years ago. Plantings there have now increased to 9.5 hectares, with 1 hectare each of shiraz and pinot gris coming into bearing.

maglieri   ★★★★☆

Douglas Gully Road, McLaren Flat, SA 5171 **region** McLaren Vale
phone (08) 8383 0177 **fax** (08) 8383 0136 **open** Mon–Sat 9–4, Sun 12–4
winemaker John Loxton **production** 30 000 **est.** 1972
product range ($18–34.99 R) While still billing itself as the 'House of Lambrusco', and still producing a range of Italian-derived styles for specialty markets within Australia, is increasingly known for the quality of its varietal table wines, spearheaded by Semillon, Cabernet Sauvignon and Shiraz, the last released in two guises: as a simple varietal, and the top-end Steve Maglieri. Typically several vintages available at any one time.
summary One of the better-kept secrets among the wine cognoscenti but not among the many customers who drink thousands of cases of white and red Lambrusco every year, an example of niche marketing at its profitable best. It was a formula which proved irresistible to Mildara Blass, which acquired Maglieri in 1999. Its dry red wines are invariably generously proportioned and full of character, the Shiraz particularly so — and of the highest quality. It is for these wines that the winery rating is given. Exports and distribution via Mildara Blass.

Maglieri Shiraz

Sourced primarily from estate-grown grapes in McLaren Vale and Blewitt Springs, but from time to time incorporating a 10 per cent Coonawarra component. Matured in American oak, and invariably rich and full flavoured in style. A consistent gold medal winner over the years, particularly in the better vintages.
TTTTY 1998 Medium to full red-purple. The smooth, rich, dark cherry/berry fruit of the bouquet is backed by subtle oak; the palate is classic Maglieri, with concentrated cherry and bitter, dark chocolate fruit flavours. The oak is subtle and the tannins sweet.   **rating:** 93

best drinking 2003–2013 **best vintages** '90, '91, '93, '95, '96, '97, '98 **drink with** Ravioli   • $20

Maglieri Shark Block Shiraz

Sold only through Cellarmasters; takes its name from a vineyard block in which a six centimetre fossilised shark's tooth was found when the vineyard was being planted in 1989. Winner of the 1999 Great Australian Shiraz Challenge.
TTTTT 1997 Medium to full purple-red; an exceptionally concentrated and complex bouquet, with blackberry, plum, chocolate and more savoury/earthy nuances in the background. Powerful fruit has largely soaked up the oak on the palate; complex, rich and dense. A mere 14.5 degrees alcohol.   **rating:** 94

best drinking 2002–2017 **best vintages** '97 **drink with** Rich game dishes   • $34.90

main ridge estate ★★★★

80 William Road, Red Hill, Vic 3937 **region** Mornington Peninsula
phone (03) 5989 2686 **fax** (03) 5931 0000 **open** Mon–Fri 12–4, weekends 12–5
winemaker Nat White **production** 1000 **est.** 1975
product range ($32–39 CD) Chardonnay, Pinot Noir, Half Acre Pinot Noir, Cabernet Merlot.
summary Nat White gives meticulous attention to every aspect of his viticulture and winemaking, doing annual battle with one of the coolest sites on the Peninsula. The same attention to detail extends to the winery and the winemaking. Not surprisingly, Nat White took full advantage of the excellent, warm 1997 vintage. Incidentally, with such minuscule production, the wines are available only through cellar door and mail order.

Main Ridge Chardonnay

Since 1991 Nat White has moved away from conventional Australian techniques to a far more French-influenced regimen, using barrel-fermentation, malolactic fermentation and lees contact. As is inevitably the case in the Mornington Peninsula, style and quality reflect vintage variations, with the warmer, drier years tending to produce the best wines.

▼▼▼▼▽ **1998** Light green-yellow; fresh, lively citrus, melon and apple fruit aromas are complexed by cashew malolactic fermentation and subtle oak. The palate is similarly elegant and well balanced, with creamy/cashew mlf influences and subtle oak. **rating:** 90

best drinking 2000–2003 **best vintages** '91, '92, '94, '96, '97, '98 **drink with** Sweetbreads • $35

Main Ridge Half Acre Pinot Noir

The cold-climate Main Ridge vineyard does peculiar things to Pinot Noir, sometimes producing wines with spicy pepper characteristics which makes them look for all the world like light-bodied Shiraz. In other years the flavours are more towards the stalky/tobacco end; never does the wine become jammy or heavy. The wines are kept in barrel for 17–18 months, which I personally think is too long.

▼▼▼▼ **1998** Light to medium red, with just a touch of purple; the bouquet is quite fragrant with light, gently savoury strawberry and plum fruit. The palate is in the mainstream of the estate style, with foresty/savoury edges and soft, lingering tannins. Well bred but lacks intensity. **rating:** 86

best drinking 2000–2002 **best vintages** '97 **drink with** Grilled salmon • $39

majella ★★★★☆

Lynn Road, Coonawarra, SA 5263 **region** Coonawarra
phone (08) 8736 3055 **fax** (08) 8736 3057 **open** 7 days 10–4.30
winemaker Bruce Gregory **production** 8000 **est.** 1969
product range ($27–50 CD) Shiraz, Cabernet Sauvignon, Malleea (Shiraz Cabernet), Sparkling Shiraz.
summary Majella is one of the more important contract grape growers in Coonawarra, with 55 hectares of vineyard, principally shiraz and cabernet sauvignon, and with a little riesling and merlot in production and now fully mature. Common gossip has it that part finds its way into the Wynns John Riddoch Cabernet Sauvignon and Michael Shiraz, or their equivalent within the Southcorp Group. Production under the Majella label is increasing as long-term supply contracts expire. Production under the Majella label has increased substantially over the past few years, rising from 2000 to 8000 cases, with exports to Asia and the US.

Majella Shiraz

First made in 1991, although the estate vineyards are almost 30 years old. Has the pick of the crop, as it were, from 30 hectares of estate plantings.

▼▼▼▼▽ **1998** Very dense purple-red; the bouquet is rich and complex, with luscious fruit and plenty of oak in modern style. The palate is solid and chunky, with rich plum and mulberry fruit woven through generous oak. **rating:** 90

best drinking 2003–2013 **best vintages** '97, '98 **drink with** Lamb chops • $27

Majella The Malleea Shiraz Cabernet

A new prestige cuvée for Majella. If the gossip that some of the best grapes had been sold to Wynns for inclusion in John Riddoch Cabernet and Michael Shiraz is correct, this wine may well represent Majella's gain and Wynns' loss. In any event, it represents a singularly impressive debut for a new super-premium Coonawarra red. The ferment is finished in French oak, where it spends the next 22 months before bottling. The wine is a blend of 55 per cent Cabernet Sauvignon, 45 per cent Shiraz.

▼▼▼▼▼ **1998** Dense red-purple; very rich, dense, concentrated and voluptuous fruit with distinctive chocolate aromas is followed by a palate which out-Riddochs John Riddoch in terms of its concentration and opulence. Custom demands top points. **rating:** 94

♥♥♥♥♡ **1997** Dense red-purple; the bouquet is powerful, ripe and concentrated, with masses of blackcurrant fruit and well-balanced oak. The palate is firmer than the bouquet suggests, with bright cassis and plum fruit, fine tannins and subtle oak. A dyed-in-the-wool stayer. **rating:** 93

best drinking 2005–2015 **best vintages** '96, '97, '98 **drink with** Marinated beef • $50

Majella Cabernet Sauvignon

The '93 vintage was the first Cabernet to be released from Majella, produced from the House Block. Aged in French oak hogsheads for two years, and deservedly accumulated five gold medals. Since 1996 the quality has corresponded neatly with that of the overall vintage.

♥♥♥♥♡ **1998** Medium to full red-purple, bright and alluring. The bouquet is rich and dense, flooded with sweet cassis and mulberry fruit, not to mention oak. The palate offers all of the above, with heaps of concentration and extract. Built in heroic mode. **rating:** 92

best drinking 2005–2015 **best vintages** '93, '94, '96, '98 **drink with** Rack of lamb • $27

malcolm creek ★★★★

Bonython Road, Kersbrook, SA 5231 **region** Adelaide Hills
phone (08) 8389 3235 **fax** (08) 8389 3235 **open** Weekends, public holidays 11–5
winemaker Reg Tolley **production** 650 **est.** 1982
product range ($13–16 R) Chardonnay, Cabernet Sauvignon.
summary Malcolm Creek is the retirement venture of Reg Tolley, and keeps a low profile. However, the wines are invariably well made and age gracefully; they are worth seeking out.

Malcolm Creek Chardonnay

Produced from 0.6 hectare of chardonnay planted in 1982, with a further 0.2 hectare planted in 1996 and to come into bearing in future years. A wine which ages with considerable grace; and back vintages are usually available by mail or phone order.

♥♥♥♥ **1998** Medium yellow-green; the moderately intense bouquet has touches of biscuity/cashew/cream, suggesting some malolactic fermentation influence. A beautifully soft palate with nectarine fruit and a gently soft finish. **rating:** 88

best drinking 2000–2004 **best vintages** '88, '90, '91, '94, '95, '96, '98 **drink with** South Australian whiting • $16

Malcolm Creek Cabernet Sauvignon

A 100 per cent Cabernet Sauvignon produced from 0.6 hectare of vines planted in 1982, although the area was doubled in 1996.

♥♥♥♥ **1996** Medium red-purple; the bouquet is clean but powerful, with blackberry/earthy/chocolatey fruit. The palate has progressively opened up over the past few years, now showing real elegance and harmonious balance. Has made the improvement predicted for it a year ago. **rating:** 89

best drinking 2001–2006 **best vintages** '86, '88, '93, '96 **drink with** Yearling beef • $16

mann NR

105 Memorial Avenue, Baskerville, WA 6056 **region** Swan District
phone (08) 9296 4348 **fax** (08) 9296 4348 **open** Weekends 10–5 and by appointment from 1 Aug until sold out
winemaker Dorham Mann **production** 550 **est.** 1988
product range ($16 CD) Méthode Champenoise.
summary Industry veteran Dorham Mann has established a one-wine label for what must be Australia's most unusual wine: a dry, only faintly pink, sparkling wine made exclusively from cabernet sauvignon grown on the 2.4-hectare estate surrounding the cellar door. Dorham Mann explains, 'Our family has made and enjoyed the style for more than 30 years, although just in a private capacity until recently'.

mansfield wines NR

204 Eurunderee Road, Mudgee, NSW 2856 **region** Mudgee
phone (02) 6373 3871 **fax** (02) 6373 3708 **open** 7 days 10–5
winemaker Bob Heslop **production** 3300 **est.** 1975
product range ($6.50–25 CD) Chardonnay, Golden Gully (semi-sweet), Colonial Gold (sweet white), Sparkling Muscat, Cabernet Sauvignon Merlot, and a selection of Fortified wines.
summary Mansfield Wines is one of the old-style wineries, offering a mix of varietal and generic table wines at low prices, and an even larger range of miscellaneous fortified wines, not all of which are locally produced. Distribution is through cellar door and various regional outlets.

🌼 mantons creek vineyard   NR

Tucks Road, Main Ridge, Vic 3928 **region** Mornington Peninsula
phone (03) 5989 6264 **fax** (03) 5959 6060 **open** 7 days 10–5
winemaker Alex White (Contract) **production** 5000 **est.** 1998
product range ($15–25 CD) Sauvignon Blanc, Muscat, Pinot Gris, Chardonnay, Tempranillo, Pinot Noir.
summary The substantial Mantons Creek Vineyard was in fact established in the early 1990s, with the grapes from the first five years production being sold to other makers. Since that time events have moved quickly: the label was launched in 1998 and a restaurant-cum-tasting room was opened in December 1998 with two chefs with impeccable credentials. The 14-hectare vineyard includes 3 hectares of tempranillo which John Williams says grows well in the cool climate of the Mornington Peninsula, making a very rich style of wine with great flavour. I cannot wait to taste it.

margan family winegrowers   ★★★★

1238 Milbrodale Road, Broke, NSW 2330 **region** Lower Hunter Valley
phone (02) 6579 1317 **fax** (02) 6579 1317 **open** 9–5 Mon–Fri
winemaker Andrew Margan **production** 15 000 **est.** 1989
product range ($15–20 R) Semillon, Verdelho, Chardonnay, Merlot, Shiraz, Cabernet Sauvignon.
summary Andrew Margan followed in his father's footsteps by entering the wine industry 20 years ago and has covered a great deal of territory since, working as a Flying Winemaker in Europe, then for Tyrrell's, first as a winemaker then as marketing manager. His wife Lisa, too, has had many years of experience in restaurants and marketing. They now have 10 hectares of fully yielding vines at their 50-hectare Ceres Hill homestead property at Broke and lease the nearby Vere Vineyard of 13 hectares. The first stage of a 700-tonne on-site winery was completed in 1998, the first wines having been made elsewhere in 1997. Wine quality (and the packaging) is good.

Margan Family Semillon

The grapes come from two vineyards; the Ceres Hill Vineyard, which provides grassy, herbaceous flavours, and the Fordwich Hill Vineyard, with 30-year-old dryland vines cropping at 1 tonne to the acre and providing intense citrus flavours. The 1999 wine has an unusually high alcohol level of 11.8 degrees, low pH and excellent acidity.
▼▼▼▼ **1999** Light straw-green; the bouquet is clean and stylistically correct, with attractive young Semillon fruit aromas. The palate has both weight and depth to the flavours which flow on logically from the bouquet, and the wine could develop into an exceptional example over the medium term.   **rating:** 88
best drinking 2002–2007 **best vintages** '99 **drink with** Rich seafood • $15

Margan Family Shiraz

Like the Cabernet Sauvignon, produced from 30-year-old vines grown on the red podsolic clays of the estate Vere Vineyard. A small amount of mourvedre is interplanted in the block and doubtless adds complexity. The average yield is 1 tonne per acre. The wine is cool-fermented, and matured for eight months in used oak hogsheads.
▼▼▼▼ **1998** Medium red; the bouquet is quite complex, with some liquorice and tar aromas and minimal oak influence. The palate is luscious, with ripe jammy berry fruit, falling away slightly on a soft tannin finish.   **rating:** 85
best drinking 2003–2010 **best vintages** '98 **drink with** Braised lamb shanks • $18.50

Margan Family Cabernet Sauvignon

Produced from 30-year-old vines grown on the hard, podsolic clays of the Vere Vineyard in the Broke/Fordwich subregion. The wine is cool-fermented, and matured in new American oak barriques for eight months prior to egg-fining and filtration.
▼▼▼▼ **1998** Dense red-purple; the bouquet is rich, with a mix of berry, chocolate, earth and cassis aromas. The powerful flavours of the palate are essentially fruit-driven, with the oak evident but not aggressive. It would seem to have outstanding development potential.   **rating:** 87
best drinking 2004–2010 **best vintages** NA **drink with** Braised ox cheek • $18.50

marienberg   ★★★

2 Chalk Hill Road, McLaren Vale, SA 5171 **region** McLaren Vale
phone (08) 8323 9666 **fax** (08) 8323 9600 **open** 7 days 10–5
winemaker Grant Burge (Contract) **production** 30 000 **est.** 1966
product range ($9.95–24.95 R) Cottage Classic range of Riesling, Sauvignon Blanc Semillon, Unwooded Chardonnay, Cabernet Grenache Mourvedre; Reserve Chardonnay, Shiraz and Cabernet Sauvignon; Limeburner's Chardonnay, Botrytis Semillon, Cabernet Sauvignon; also Late Picked Frontignac, Nicolle Méthode Champenoise and Tawny Port.

summary The Marienberg brand was purchased by the Hill International group of companies in late 1991 following the retirement of Ursula Pridham. Releases under the new regime have been honest, if unashamedly commercial, wines. The newly introduced Reserve 1998 Chardonnay and 1996 Reserve Shiraz do offer a significant lift in quality above the basic range. The wines are exported to the UK, the US, Canada, Hong Kong, Germany, The Netherlands, New Zealand, Philippines, Switzerland and Thailand.

Marienberg Riesling

A fuller-bodied style of Riesling designed for consumption sooner rather than later.

▼▼▼♈ 1997 Light yellow-green; quite full bottle-developed aromas running through toast, lime and kerosene. The palate has plenty of flavour tracking the aromas of the bouquet but adding some remnants of citrus. Just a little heavy in the mouth. **rating: 83**

best drinking 2000–2003 best vintages NA drink with Fish and chips • $12

mariners rest NR

Jamakarri Farm, Roberts Road, Denmark, WA 6333 region Great Southern
phone (08) 9840 9324 fax (08) 9840 9324 open 7 days 10–5
winemaker Ron Cocking, Peter Cocking production 750 est. 1996
product range ($14.50–19.75 R) Chardonnay, Southern White, Autumn Gold, Autumn Red, Southern Red, Pinot Noir.
summary Mariners Rest is the reincarnation of the now defunct Golden Rise winery. A new 2.5-hectare vineyard was planted in the spring of 1997, and in the meantime some excellent wines from the Golden Rise days have been marketed under the Mariners Rest label.

marion's vineyard ★★★☆

Foreshore Drive, Deviot, Tas 7275 region Northern Tasmania
phone (03) 6394 7434 fax (03) 6394 7434 open 7 days 10–5
winemaker Mark Semmens, Marion Semmens production 2000 est. 1980
product range ($15–30 ML) Chardonnay, Müller Thurgau, Pinot Noir, Cabernet Sauvignon.
summary The irrepressible Mark Semmens and indefatigable wife Marion have one of the most beautifully situated vineyards and wineries in Australia on the banks of the Tamar River. As well as an outdoor restaurant and accommodation, there is a jetty and a stage — indeed, life is a stage for Mark Semmens.

maritime estate NR

Tucks Road, Red Hill, Vic 3937 region Mornington Peninsula
phone (03) 9848 2926 fax (03) 9882 8325 open Weekends and public holidays 11–5, Dec 27–Jan 26 7 days
winemaker T'Gallant (Contract) production 1000 est. 1988
product range ($17–26 CD) Unwooded Chardonnay, Chardonnay, Pinot Gris, Pinot Noir, Cabernet Sauvignon.
summary John and Linda Ruljancich have enjoyed great success since their first vintage in 1994, no doubt due in part to skilled contract-winemaking but also to the situation of their vineyard, looking across the hills and valleys of the Red Hill subregion. The '98 Pinot Noir is a pleasantly savoury, foresty wine.

markwood estate NR

Morris Lane, Markwood, Vic 3678 region King Valley
phone (03) 5727 0361 fax (03) 5727 0361 open 7 days 9–5
winemaker Rick Morris production 500 est. 1971
product range ($15–21 CD) Rhine Riesling, Cabernet Sauvignon, Shiraz, Muscat, Tokay, Port.
summary A member of the famous Morris family, Rick Morris shuns publicity and relies virtually exclusively on cellar-door sales for what is a small output. Of a range of table and fortified wines tasted in February 1997, the Old Tawny Port (a cross between Port and Muscat, showing more of the character of the latter than the former) and a White Port (seemingly made from Muscadelle) were the best. Agglomerate corks may present a threat for prolonged cellaring, however.

marribrook ★★★

Albany Highway, Kendenup, Frankland, WA 6323 region Great Southern
phone (08) 9851 4651 fax (08) 9851 4652 open Wed–Sun 10–4
winemaker Gavin Berry, Gordon Parker (Contract) production 2000 est. 1990
product range ($14.80–19.75 CD) Unwooded Chardonnay, Botanica Chardonnay, Reserve Chardonnay, Semillon Sauvignon Blanc, Marsanne, Cabernet Merlot, Cabernet Sauvignon, Cabernet Malbec.

summary The Brooks family purchased the former Marron View 5.6-hectare vineyard from Kim Hart in 1994 and renamed the venture Marribrook Wines. Those wines are now made by Gavin Berry at Plantagenet, having been made at Alkoomi up to 1994. The Brooks have purchased an additional property on the Albany Highway north of Mount Barker and immediately south of Gilbert's Wines. Cellar-door sales have moved to this location, and a dedicated cellar-door sales building encompassing a small restaurant and gallery is due for completion in September 2000, with great views out to the Stirling Range. Retail distribution in Victoria, Queensland and South Australia; exports to the UK.

Marribrook Marsanne

Marribrook has around 2 acres (0.8 hectares) of marsanne (out of total vineyard plantings of 5.3 hectares) and have made a specialty of the wine. A vertical tasting from 1995 to 1999 in March 2000 shows that it develops in much the same way as the wines of Chateau Tahbilk: very well in the good vintages, and not so well in others. Of the mature wines, the '97 Marsanne stood out like a beacon, a very good wine with a long future.

▼▼▼♡ **1999** Light yellow-green; the bouquet is neutral, clean and crisp, the palate much the same, but well made and well balanced and has the ingredients to develop and build on those honey/honeysuckle characters. **rating:** 80

best drinking 2003–2008 **best vintages** '97 **drink with** Sweeter seafood dishes • $14.80

marsh estate ★★★

Deasey Road, Pokolbin, NSW 2321 **region** Lower Hunter Valley
phone (02) 4998 7587 **fax** (02) 4998 7884 **open** Mon–Fri 10–4.30, weekends 10–5
winemaker Peter Marsh **production** 4000 **est.** 1971
product range ($18–25 CD) Semillon, Private Bin Semillon, Chardonnay (oaked and unoaked), Semillon Sauternes, Shiraz (Private Bin, Vat S and Vat R), Cabernet Sauvignon, Champagne Brut, Andrew IV Vintage Port.
summary Through sheer consistency, value-for-money and unrelenting hard work, the Marsh family (who purchased the former Quentin Estate in 1978) has built up a sufficiently loyal cellar-door and mailing list clientele to allow all of the considerable production to be sold direct. Wine style is always direct, with oak playing a minimal role, and prolonged cellaring paying handsome dividends.

martins hill wines NR

Sydney Road, Mudgee, NSW 2850 **region** Mudgee
phone (02) 6373 1248 **fax** (02) 6373 1248 **open** Not
winemaker Pieter Van Gent (Contract) **production** 700 **est.** 1985
product range ($13–16 R) Sauvignon Blanc, Pinot Noir.
summary Janette Kenworthy and Michael Sweeny are committed organic grape growers and are members of the Organic Vignerons Association. It is a tiny operation at the moment, with only half a hectare each of sauvignon blanc and pinot noir in production but with an additional hectare of cabernet sauvignon to produce its first grapes in the year 2000, and 1.5 hectares of shiraz in 2001. While there is no cellar door (only a mailing list), organic vineyard tours and talks can be arranged by appointment.

marybrook vineyards NR

Vasse–Yallingup Road, Marybrook, WA 6280 **region** Margaret River
phone (08) 9755 1143 **fax** (08) 9755 1112 **open** Fri–Mon 10–5, 7 days 10–5 school holidays
winemaker Contract **production** 2000 **est.** 1986
product range ($12.50–22.95 CD) Chardonnay, Verdelho, Classic White, Nectosia (sweet), Cabernets, Cabernet Franc, Temptation (sweet red), Jetty Port.
summary It is easy to confuse Marybrook Vineyards with Marybrook Estate; they are in fact separate operations. Marybrook Vineyards is owned by Aub and Jan House. Seven hectares of vineyards are in production. As at March 1999, five vintages of Cabernets or Cabernet Franc ('92–'96) were available cellar door.

massoni main creek ★★★★

Mornington–Flinders Road, Red Hill, Vic 3937 **region** Mornington Peninsula
phone (03) 5989 2352 **fax** (03) 5989 2014 **open** By appointment
winemaker Ian Home, Sam Tyrrell **production** 3000 **est.** 1984
product range ($17–35 R) Chardonnay, Pinot Noir, Ian Home Lectus Cuvée, Shiraz are the top wines; also Homes Chardonnay, Pinot Noir and Cabernet Merlot.
summary The changes have continued to flow after Ian Home (best known as the founder of Yellowglen) acquired the remaining 50 per cent of Massoni from former restaurateur Leon Massoni. There are now two ranges of wines, and (quite sensibly) the Shiraz and Cabernet Merlot releases are in whole or in part sourced from outside the Mornington Peninsula (from Langhorne Creek). The flagships continue to be the Chardonnay, Pinot Noir and Lectus Cuvée, supported by Shiraz. Exports to the US, Asia and Germany.

Massoni Main Creek Chardonnay

Produced from 1.5 hectares of estate plantings and made using the full gamut of barrel-fermentation, malolactic fermentation and lees contact. In many ways the most striking example of Mornington Peninsula Chardonnay, with tremendous character, body and richness.

TTTT **1998** Medium to full yellow-green; a clean, rich, smooth bouquet with that estate hallmark tangy melon/citrus/vegetal fruit; the palate is nicely balanced, with smooth and harmonious fruit, good mouthfeel and a typically long finish. Subtle oak. **rating: 92**

best drinking 2000–2004 **best vintages** '89, '90, '92, '93, '94, '96, '97, '98 **drink with** Veal, pork • $30

Massoni Main Creek Pinot Noir

The mirror image of the Chardonnay, always rich, full bodied and opulent, where so many of the Mornington wines — Pinot and Chardonnay alike — tend to be prettier and more elegant. Aged in 45 per cent new French oak barriques, 30 per cent one-year-old and 25 per cent two-year-old. Less than 900 cases made.

TTTT **1998** Very light red; the wine exhibits foresty Pinot Noir aromas but does not have the fruit intensity of some of the preceding vintages. The palate, while likewise exhibiting authentic Pinot flavour and structure, is light, and the wine should be consumed sooner rather than later. **rating: 88**

best drinking 1999–2000 **best vintages** '91, '92, '93, '94, '96, '97 **drink with** Breast of duck • $35

matilda's meadow ★★★

Eladon Brook Estate, RMB 654 Hamilton Road, Denmark, WA 6333 **region** Great Southern
phone (08) 9848 1951 **fax** (08) 9848 1957 **open** Wed–Mon 10–4
winemaker Brenden Smith **production** 1500 **est.** 1990
product range ($12.50–25 CD) Riesling, Late Picked Riesling, Unwooded Chardonnay, Semillon, Semillon Sauvignon Blanc, Chardonnay, Autumn Amethyst (light red), Pinot Noir, Cabernet Sauvignon Cabernet Franc.
summary Former hotelier Don Turnbull and oil-industry executive Pamela Meldrum have quickly established a thriving business at Matilda's Meadow, based on 6 hectares of estate plantings and with a restaurant offering morning and afternoon teas and lunches every day.

Matilda's Meadow Cabernet Sauvignon Cabernet Franc

Produced from unirrigated vineyards at Scottsdale, and a blend of 75 per cent Cabernet Sauvignon and 25 per cent Cabernet Franc. Notwithstanding the fact that it spends 15 months in French oak, it is a predominantly fruit-driven style.

TTTT **1998** Medium to full red-purple; very attractive ripe blackberry/blackcurrant fruit on the bouquet translates into a lovely palate with gently luscious cassis/blackberry fruit, nicely balanced oak and soft tannins. **rating: 92**

best drinking 2002–2008 **best vintages** '94, '95, '98 **drink with** Beef sirloin • $20

mawarra NR

69 Short Road, Gisborne, Vic 3437 **region** Macedon Ranges
phone (03) 5428 2228 **fax** (03) 9621 1413 **open** 7 days
winemaker John Ellis (Contract) **production** 1000 **est.** 1978
product range NA.
summary Bob Nixon has a little under 3 hectares of semillon, chardonnay and pinot noir, and the wines are made for him by Macedon specialist, John Ellis (of Hanging Rock).

mawson ridge NR

24–28 Main Road, Hahndorf, SA 5066 **region** Adelaide Hills
phone (08) 8362 7826 **fax** (08) 8362 7588 **open** By appointment
winemaker Nepenthe (Contract) **production** 400 **est.** 1998
product range ($18–30 R) Sauvignon Balnc, Chardonnay, Pinot Noir.
summary You might be forgiven for thinking the winery name carries the cool climate association a little bit too far. In fact, Sir Douglas Mawson was also a conservationist and forester, and arrived in the Lenswood region in the early 1930s, harvesting the native stringy barks for hardwood and replanting the cleared land with pine trees. A hut that Mawson built on the property still stands today on Mawson Road, which is the road to which the vineyard fronts. Here Raymond and Madeline Marin have established 3.5 hectares of vines, with contract-winemaking by Peter Leske of Nepenthe Vineyards. The first three releases are a 1998 Chardonnay, 1999 Sauvignon Blanc and 1999 Pinot Noir.

maxwell wines ★★★★

Olivers Road, McLaren Vale, SA 5171　**region** McLaren Vale
phone (08) 8323 8200　**fax** (08) 8323 8900　**open** 7 days 10–5
winemaker Mark Maxwell　**production** 16 000　**est.** 1979
product range ($10–24 R) Under the Maxwell Wines brand, Semillon, Sauvignon Blanc, Chardonnay, Cabernet Merlot, Reserve Shiraz; Ellen Street Shiraz and Lime Cave Cabernet Sauvignon; and excellent Honey Mead, Spiced Mead and Liqueur Mead.
summary Maxwell Wines has come a long way since opening for business in 1979 using an amazing array of Heath Robinson equipment in cramped surroundings. A state-of-the-art and infinitely larger winery was built on a new site in time for the 1997 vintage, appropriate for a brand which has produced some excellent white and red wines in recent years. Exports to the US, the UK, Switzerland, Austria, Hong Kong, Belgium, Singapore and New Zealand.

Maxwell Chardonnay

Both the quality and the style of the wine varied substantially during the latter part of the 1990s.
ᵀᵀᵀᵀ 1998 Light green-yellow; the bouquet is clean, light and fresh, with no oak evident. The palate is simple, light and fault-free other than for a slightly watery finish.　**rating:** 80
best drinking Drink now　**best vintages** '95, '96　**drink with** Grilled scampi　•$15.95

Maxwell Ellen Street Shiraz

There is in fact a Reserve Shiraz, which is in theory superior to the Ellen Street, but I have often preferred the latter wine for its outstanding varietal character. Once again, high-quality fruit does the work, with oak playing a pure support role.
ᵀᵀᵀᵀ 1997 Medium to full red-purple; powerful, youthful, earthy berry fruit on the bouquet is followed by a palate which has attractive, clean fruit, but the wine has not been worked enough in barrel and ends up rather angular and hard. May improve with time in bottle.　**rating:** 85
best drinking 2002–2010　**best vintages** '82, '88, '91, '92, '94　**drink with** Kangaroo　•$24

Maxwell Grenache

McLaren Vale Grenache has the same richness and generosity as Shiraz from the same region, particularly when sourced from old, dry-grown vineyards.
ᵀᵀᵀᵀ 1998 Medium to full red-purple; the bouquet is deep and solid, with just the faintest hint of oak. The palate is dense and concentrated, with strong structure surrounding the plum and earth flavours.　**rating:** 87
best drinking 2001–2006　**best vintages** '98　**drink with** Ox cheek　•$20

Maxwell Cabernet Merlot

Maxwell was one of the early experimenters with Merlot in McLaren Vale, blending it with Cabernet Sauvignon to produce a wine which is often powerful and full flavoured. Matured in a mix of French and American oak, but a fruit rather than oak-driven style.
ᵀᵀᵀᵀ 1998 Dark purple; very luscious, very ripe prune and plum fruit on the bouquet flows into the exceptionally ripe, dense and luscious palate, which is nonetheless neither tannic nor extractive. A strange wine, but a compelling one.　**rating:** 89
best drinking 2005–2015　**best vintages** '82, '88, '91, '92, '94, '98　**drink with** Scotch fillet　•$15.50

mcalister vineyards　NR

Golden Beach Road, Longford, Vic 3851　**region** Gippsland
phone (03) 5149 7229　**fax** (03) 5149 7229　**open** By appointment
winemaker Peter Edwards　**production** 550　**est.** 1975
product range A single wine, The McAlister, a blend of Cabernet Sauvignon, Cabernet Franc and Merlot.
summary The McAlister Vineyards actively shun publicity or exposure which, on the basis of prior tastings, is a pity.

mcivor creek　NR

Costerfield Road, Heathcote, Vic 3523　**region** Bendigo
phone (03) 5433 3000　**fax** (03) 5433 3456　**open** 7 days 10–5.30
winemaker Peter Turley　**production** 5000　**est.** 1973
product range ($9.95–14.95 CD) Riesling, Auslese Riesling, Shiraz, Cabernet Shiraz, Fine Old Tawny Port.

summary The beautifully situated McIvor Creek winery is well worth a visit and does offer wines in diverse styles of which the red wines are the most regional. Peter Turley has 5 hectares of cabernet sauvignon together with 2.5 hectares of cabernet franc and merlot and supplements his intake with grapes from other growers. No recent tastings.

mcmanus   NR

Rogers Road, Yenda, NSW 2681   **region** Riverina
phone (02) 6968 1064   **open** 7 days 9–5
winemaker Dr David McManus   **production** 500   **est.** 1972
product range ($4–8 CD) Chardonnay, Chardonnay Semillon, Malbec, Merlot, Shiraz, Pinot Malbec Shiraz; many named after family members.
summary An extremely idiosyncratic winery run by Griffith GP Dr David McManus, his sister and other family members. Natural winemaking methods lead to considerable variation in quality, but the prices are from another era, some of the vintages likewise.

mcpherson wines   ★★☆

PO Box 529, Artarmon, NSW 1570   **region** Goulburn Valley
phone (02) 9436 1644   **fax** (02) 9436 3144   **open** Not
winemaker Leigh Clarnette, Andrew Dean, Andrew McPherson   **production** 1 million   **est.** 1993
product range ($7–10 R) Semillon Chardonnay, Chardonnay, Shiraz.
summary McPherson Wines is little known in Australia, but is, by any standards, a substantial business. Its wines are almost entirely produced for the export market, with Dan Murphy being the sole (and exclusive) retail source in Australia. The wines are made at various locations from contract-grown grapes, and represent good value at their price point. The 1998 Shiraz (80 points) is a particularly good example. For the record, McPherson Wines is a joint venture between Andrew McPherson and Alister Purbrick of Chateau Tahbilk. Both have had a lifetime of experience in the industry.

mcwilliam's   ★★★★

Winery Road, Hanwood, NSW 2680   **region** Riverina
phone (02) 6963 0001   **fax** (02) 6963 0002   **open** Mon–Sat 9–5
winemaker Jim Brayne   **production** NFP   **est.** 1877
product range ($6–40 R) A disciplined and easy-to-follow product range (all varietally identified) commencing with Hillside casks; Inheritance range; Hanwood; Charles King; JJ McWilliams (first released 1996), finally Limited Release Hunter Valley Chardonnay, Eden Valley Riesling and JJ McWilliam Riverina Botrytis Semillon. Also superb fortified wines, including MCW11 Liqueur Muscat and 10-Year-Old Hanwood Tawny Port heading a much larger range of Sherries, which still form an important part of the business.
summary Some of the best wines to emanate from the Hanwood winery are from other regions, notably the Barwang Vineyard at Hilltops in New South Wales, Coonawarra and Eden Valley; on the other side of the coin as it were, the critical mass of the business continues to come from the Murrumbidgee Irrigation Area, which provides the bulk of the rapidly growing export business of the company. The rating is a compromise between the best and the least of the wide range. Exports to many countries, the most important being the UK, the US, Germany and New Zealand. (Exports currently account for 30 per cent of McWilliam's sales.)

McWilliam's Hanwood Chardonnay

Partial barrel-ferment and extended lees contact has worked well in a wine of theoretically humble origins. Gold medals at Brisbane, Griffith and Rutherglen have to be carefully interpreted; these are not front-rank shows.
▼▼▼▽ **1999** Light to medium yellow-green; the bouquet shows tangy fruit and a nice touch of complexity. The delicate, fresh palate does have some style, even if not a great deal of richness, texture or character. A bargain at the price, however.   **rating: 83**
best drinking 2000–2001   **best vintages** NA   **drink with** Takeaway   • $9.95

mcwilliam's mount pleasant   ★★★★★

Marrowbone Road, Pokolbin, NSW 2320   **region** Lower Hunter Valley
phone (02) 4998 7505   **fax** (02) 4998 7761   **open** 7 days 10–4.30
winemaker Phillip Ryan   **production** NFP   **est.** 1880
product range ($10–45 R) Much simplified and rationalised over the past year. The base range now comprises Mount Pleasant Elizabeth, Philip, Late Harvest Dessert Wine, Chardonnay and Verdelho; then individual vineyard wines, Rosehill Shiraz, Old Paddock & Old Hill Shiraz, Lovedale Semillon (previously known as Anne), then Maurice O'Shea Chardonnay and Shiraz; finally Museum releases of Elizabeth.

summary McWilliam's Elizabeth and the glorious Lovedale Semillon are now the only mature Hunter Semillons generally commercially available and are undervalued and underpriced treasures with a consistently superb show record. The three individual vineyard wines, together with the Maurice O'Shea memorial wines, add to the lustre of this proud name. Exports to many countries, the most important being the UK, the US, Germany and New Zealand.

McWilliam's Mount Pleasant Elizabeth

A wine with an exceptional pedigree and deserved reputation for consistency, yet chronically underpriced and hence underrated (or the reverse, I am not sure which). Changes to the packaging, notably the bottle shape, and the hand of McWilliam's chief executive Kevin McLintock may well see the wine gradually being repositioned in the market to assume its rightful place. Even without this, an undoubted classic, having won more than 13 trophies and 129 gold medals since 1981.

▼▼▼▼♀ **1996** Glowing yellow-green; the bouquet is rich and smooth, with a mix of lemon, citrus and honey aromas. The palate is particularly fresh, with some CO_2 still evident, enhancing the lively lemony/citrussy flavours. Overall, the palate is a lot more youthful than the bouquet suggests it will be.   **rating:** 92

▼▼▼▼▼ **1995** Finally, McWilliam's has plucked up the courage to increase the price of this undervalued classic, although I will bet no one actually has to pay $18.95. It is still very youthful, with only a hint of the toasty characters to come; the palate is equally immature, delicately herbaceous, with a clean, lingering finish.   **rating:** 94

best drinking 2000–2010 **best vintages** '75, '81, '82, '83, '86, '89, '90, '91, '93, '94, '95, '96 **drink with** Rich seafood • $18.95

McWilliam's Mount Pleasant Lovedale Semillon

Now named after the Lovedale Vineyard from which it comes, but in earlier times called 'Anne'. Only released when fully mature, and then only from exceptional vintages. The 1984 vintage, which has won innumerable trophies and gold medals, was not released until 1995, and will live for another decade at least. Simply a superb wine. The 1986 is another magnificent wine, festooned with trophies and gold medals. The '95 is the first release since 1986; for obscure reasons, the Lovedale material was incorporated into Elizabeth in the intervening years.

▼▼▼▼▼ **1995** Medium to full yellow-green, quite developed; the bouquet is powerful, intense and complex; both it and the palate show aromas of herb, lemon and honey but as yet no toast and, indeed, may never do so. Has excellent mouthfeel and weight, very much in the tradition of Lovedale. The one question was the dodgy-looking cork.   **rating:** 94

best drinking 2000–2015 **best vintages** '69, '72, '74, '75, '79, '84, '86, '95 **drink with** Fine fish dishes • $45

McWilliam's Mount Pleasant Chardonnay

An always reliable, generously flavoured wine without any pretensions to greatness.

▼▼▼♀ **1997** Glowing yellow-green; honey, peach and toast aromas merge with subtle oak on the bouquet; overall, a big, soft, peachy regional style.   **rating:** 84

best drinking 2000–2001 **best vintages** NA **drink with** Creamy pasta • $13.50

McWilliam's Mount Pleasant Sparkling Pinot Noir

Produced from pinot noir grown in the Hunter Valley, arguably the best use for this variety in this region. It spends five years on lees prior to disgorgement and release. It is also worth noting that the first sparkling burgundies were indeed made from pinot noir (in Burgundy).

▼▼▼▼ **1993** Medium red; there is quite ripe plummy pinot noir fruit on the bouquet and some oak apparent. A very interesting wine in the mouth, with ripe plum and cherry fruit and touches of spice. The wine has elegance as well as that sweet fruit. You could actually drink several glasses of this.   **rating:** 87

best drinking 1999–2003 **best vintages** NA **drink with** Game terrine • $NA

McWilliam's Mount Pleasant O'Shea (OP & OH) Shiraz

OP & OH is the sort of obscure designation which so delighted Maurice O'Shea. The letters in fact stand for Old Paddock and Old Hill, planted respectively in 1880 and 1920, and which provide the bulk of the grapes which go into this distinguished wine. To confuse matters a little, since 1987 it has been sold as O'Shea Hermitage, in honour of Maurice O'Shea, in outstanding vintage years. So sometimes you will see it sold as O'Shea, sometimes as OP & OH.

▼▼▼♀ **1997** OP & OH. Medium to full red-purple; the bouquet is clean and quite concentrated, with plummy fruit and a touch of mint. The palate offers more of the same in a more savoury/earthy cast but lacks depth and, in particular, the brilliant fruit of the '96.   **rating:** 83

best drinking 2002–2007 **best vintages** '65, '66, '67, '79, '85, '87, '90, '91, '94, '95, '96 **drink with** Roast veal • $35

McWilliam's Mount Pleasant Rosehill Shiraz

The Rosehill Vineyard shares a hill of terra rossa soil bisected in the middle by the Broke Road, with Lake's Folly on the opposite side to Rosehill. Over the years it has produced many great wines (the '59 is particularly memorable) and, it must be said, a few disappointments, too. Recent vintages have been more consistent.

TTTY 1998 Medium red-purple; the bouquet is clean and smooth, moderately intense, with gently regional cherry and earth aromas. The medium-bodied palate has a mix of savoury/earthy and sweeter fruit notes, although there is a tinge of green on the finish. Difficult to call; may improve dramatically with time in bottle.   **rating:** 84

TTTT 1997 Medium purple-red; a fragrant bouquet with spice, cherry and a hint of Hunter earth leads into a fairly tight, elegant palate with the moderate acidity likely to underpin the ageing of the wine. Needs time, and will likely merit much higher points in five years time.   **rating:** 87

best drinking 2003–2013   **best vintages** '59, '65, '66, '67, '75, '95, '96   **drink with** Marinated spatchcock • $29.50

McWilliam's Mount Pleasant Merlot

A gold medal winner at the 1998 Hunter Valley Wine Show; produced from grapes grown by Mount Pleasant winemaker Phil Ryan.

TTTY 1998 Medium to full red-purple; the moderately intense bouquet has a mix of tarry/earthy fruit aromas which are wholly regional. Some oak is evident, and the palate is quite full, robust and fairly tannic. Might be a sleeper.   **rating:** 81

best drinking 2003–2008   **best vintages** NA   **drink with** Roast veal • $14.95

meadowbank wines ★★★☆

'Meadowbank', Glenora, Derwent Valley, Tas 7410   **region** Southern Tasmania
phone (03) 6286 1234   **fax** (03) 6286 1133   **open** 7 days 11–5
winemaker Andrew Hood (Contract)   **production** 4000   **est.** 1974
product range ($17.50–26 CD) Riesling, Sauvignon Blanc, Chardonnay, Grace Elizabeth Chardonnay, Henry James, Pinot Noir, Cabernet Sauvignon, Mardi Méthode Champenoise.
summary Now an important part of the Ellis family business on what was once (but is no more) a large grazing property on the banks of the Derwent. Increased plantings are being established under contract to BRL Hardy. Exports to Germany.

Meadowbank Riesling

Produced from estate plantings on the banks of the Derwent River which are now more than 20 years old.

TTTT 1999 Light green-yellow; the aromas are fine and delicate, crisp and touched with lime. The wine gains power on the palate with lime-accented fruit, the acidity cleverly balanced by a flick of residual sugar.   **rating:** 89

best drinking 2000–2009   **best vintages** '99   **drink with** Asparagus • $18

Meadowbank Sauvignon Blanc

1999 was the first vintage of Sauvignon Blanc under the Meadowbank label, and made a very auspicious debut, being the highest-pointed wine in the Sauvignon Blanc classes at the 2000 Tasmanian Wines Show.

TTTT 1999 Light green-yellow; the aromas are exotic, with tropical passionfruit the driving force on both the bouquet and palate. Despite all this flavour the wine has elegance, albeit with full-on Tasmanian acidity on the finish.   **rating:** 87

best drinking 2002–2002   **best vintages** NA   **drink with** Care • $NA

Meadowbank Unwooded Chardonnay

A new departure for Meadowbank, which previously offered two oaked versions. The move to separate the wines with an unwooded version reflects the philosophy of Andrew Hood, the newly appointed contract-winemaker.

TTTY 1999 Light to medium yellow-green; a fragrant, tropical bouquet suggestive of some botrytis is followed by a remarkably powerful and intense palate with citrus juice flavours and nicely balanced acidity.   **rating:** 84

best drinking 2001–2004   **best vintages** NA   **drink with** Diced chicken • $17.50

Meadowbank Pinot Noir

The original Meadowbank vineyard plantings are now fully mature, and, as this wine shows, are capable of producing high-quality grapes.

TTTT 1998 Medium to full red-purple; powerful, concentrated dark plum aromas are followed by a well-balanced, stylish palate with rich but smooth plummy fruit. To be hypercritical, perhaps a fraction short.   **rating:** 89

best drinking 2001–2005   **best vintages** '98   **drink with** Roast squab • $18.50

Meadowbank Henry James Pinot Noir

This is the Reserve Pinot Noir from Meadowbank, named after the Ellis's male twin.

▼▼▼▼▼ **1998** Medium to full purple-red; very strong, rich and powerful plummy fruit is balanced by nice oak. A lovely, rich, glossy plummy palate in luxuriant style, bolstered by appropriate tannins, acidity and oak, and which will age very well. **rating:** 95

best drinking 2001–2005 **best vintages** '94, '98 **drink with** Ragout of duck • $20

Meadowbank Cabernet Sauvignon

The Derwent does not provide the most hospitable climate for cabernet sauvignon, but years such as 1998 more than compensate.

▼▼▼▽ **1998** Youthful purple-red; clean, bright and firm cassis fruit on the bouquet moves into quite luscious, ripe cassis fruit on the forepalate before somewhat abrasive tannins come on the finish. Time may or may not soften out those tannins before the fruit fades. **rating:** 83

best drinking 2005–2010 **best vintages** NA **drink with** Barbecued steak • $18

meerea park ★★★☆

2 Denton Close, Windella via Maitland, NSW 2321 **region** Lower Hunter Valley
phone 0417 693 310 **fax** (02) 4930 7100 **open** At The Boutique Wine Centre, Broke Road, Pokolbin 9–4.30
winemaker Rhys Eather **production** 10 000 **est.** 1991
product range ($17–45 CD) Sauvignon Blanc Semillon, Semillon, Lindsay Hill Verdelho, Lindsay Hill Viognier, Unoaked Chardonnay, Chardonnay, Forefathers Chardonnay, Alexander Munro Chardonnay, Alexander Munro Shiraz, The Aunts Shiraz, Cabernet Merlot, Cabernet Sauvignon.
summary An interesting operation, selling its substantial production primarily through The Boutique Wine Centre, Broke Road, Pokolbin, and by mailing list. All of the wines are produced from grapes purchased from growers, primarily in the Broke/Fordwich region, but also from as far afield as McLaren Vale, the Barossa Valley, Mudgee and Orange. It is the brainchild of Rhys Eather, great-grandson of Alexander Munro, a leading vigneron in the middle of the nineteenth century, and who makes the wine in Simon Gilbert's contract winery. Retail distribution through the principal States, and the wines are exported to the UK and Asia.

Meerea Park Lindsay Hill Verdelho

Sourced from the Lindsay Hill vineyard situated in the Upper Hunter, adjacent to Rosemount's Roxburgh Vineyard. Sixty per cent of the wine is cold-fermented in stainless steel; the remaining 40 per cent fermented in new Allier and Vosges hogsheads for three weeks.

▼▼▼▽ **1999** Light yellow-green; the bouquet offers fruit salad aromas which are varietal, although there is a mix of cosmetic and greener aromatics. The palate really does have some fruit presence and power; my only problem with the wine is the base variety, which I see as a slightly more trendy form of Chenin Blanc. **rating:** 82

best drinking 2000–2002 **best vintages** NA **drink with** Caesar salad • $19

Meerea Park The Aunts Shiraz

The intriguing name recognises the two ladies who presided over the Meerea Park homestead in the early nineteenth century. The grapes are purchased from a mature Pokolbin vineyard and the wine is made in open fermenters before spending 15 months in American oak.

▼▼▼▼ **1998** Medium to full red-purple; there is lots of power and extract to the bouquet, with deep, dark plum fruit flavour. The palate, too, has considerable length and flavour, with very good back palate tannins countered by a touch of sweet American oak. **rating:** 90

best drinking 2003–2013 **best vintages** NA **drink with** Devilled kidneys • $30

Meerea Park Cabernet Merlot

Produced from grapes grown as far afield as Mount Benson in the South Australian Limestone Coast Zone, McLaren Vale and Orange.

▼▼▼▽ **1998** Medium purple-red; there are quite fragrant aromas with a range of clean cherry, blackcurrant and mint. The palate is youthful, indeed too youthful; it shows somewhat undermade components and seems to have been taken out of barrel too soon. Had potential, which it may realise in part in bottle. **rating:** 83

best drinking 2002–2008 **best vintages** NA **drink with** Barbecued pork spare ribs • $20

merrebee estate ★★★☆

Lot 3339 St Werburghs Road, Mount Barker, WA 6234 **region** Great Southern
phone (08) 9851 2424 **fax** (08) 9851 2425 **open** Weekends and public holidays 10–4 and by appointment
winemaker Brenden Smith (Contract) **production** 3000 **est.** 1986
product range ($14–22 CD) Riesling, Chardonnay, Unwooded Chardonnay, Mount Barker Chardonnay, Shiraz.
summary The 3.5-hectare Merrebee Estate vineyards were established in 1985, and the first wines released from the 1995 and 1996 vintages. The wines are available from selected retailers in Western Australia and from Rathdowne Cellars, Melbourne, and Ultimo Wine Centre, Sydney. These and subsequent releases have, at the very least, been good, some excellent. Exports to the US, Canada and Sweden.

Merrebee Estate Riesling
More proof, if proof were needed, of the symbiotic relationship between riesling and the Great Southern, particularly when you take into account the youth of the vines.
♥♥♥♥ **1999** Light green-yellow; the bouquet is light but quite floral, with passionfruit blossom aromas. The palate is likewise light and crisp, with some mineral notes appearing which give some grip to the finish.   **rating:** 86
best drinking 2004–2009 **best vintages** NA **drink with** Vegetable terrine • $15

Merrebee Estate Mount Barker Chardonnay
Barrel-fermented and matured; a fledgling wine from a young vineyard.
♥♥♥♥ **1998** Medium yellow-green; the bouquet is tangy rather than rich, with obvious barrel-ferment inputs; the palate, likewise, is tangy to the point of bitterness, the character probably deriving from the oak.   **rating:** 80
best drinking 2000–2004 **best vintages** NA **drink with** Chinese prawns • $19

Merrebee Estate Shiraz
A nicely-handled wine which has not been forced to be something which it is not, either by over-extraction or the over-compensating use of oak.
♥♥♥♥ **1998** Medium red-purple; the bouquet is moderately intense, with some gamey varietal aromas and subtle oak. A light style in the mouth, which really needs more sweet fruit, but on the credit side the oak handling is sympathetic.   **rating:** 81
best drinking 2002–2005 **best vintages** NA **drink with** Veal chops • $23

merricks estate ★★★☆

Thompsons Lane, Merricks, Vic 3916 **region** Mornington Peninsula
phone (03) 5989 8416 **fax** (03) 9627 4035 **open** First weekend of each month in Jan and public holiday weekends 12–5
winemaker Michael Zitzlaff **production** 2500 **est.** 1977
product range ($20–27.95 CD) Chardonnay, Shiraz, Cabernet Sauvignon, Pinot Noir.
summary Melbourne solicitor George Kefford, together with wife Jacquie, runs Merricks Estate as a weekend and holiday enterprise as a relief from professional practice. Right from the outset it has produced distinctive, spicy, cool-climate Shiraz which has accumulated an impressive array of show trophies and gold medals.

Merricks Estate Chardonnay
Produced from 1 hectare of estate plantings; made in the mainstream of regional style.
♥♥♥♥ **1998** Medium to full yellow-green; the big, rich and ripe melon and peach fruit aromas of the bouquet are reminiscent of the baroque New Zealand style; the palate, likewise, is a rich and full, big, ballsy style.   **rating:** 85
best drinking 2000–2003 **best vintages** '98 **drink with** Chinese-style chicken • $NA

Merricks Estate Pinot Noir
Like so many other Mornington producers, has had the benefit of twin warm and dry vintages in 1997 and 1998.
♥♥♥♥ **1998** The quite intense bouquet has savoury/foresty/sappy aromas with just a fleck of green stemmy characters, all of which join with the lively cherry and plum fruit on the palate, which again shows that hint of green, but not to the detriment of the wine. Should come together nicely over the next few years.   **rating:** 88
best drinking 2001–2005 **best vintages** '97, '98 **drink with** Squab • $NA

Merricks Estate Shiraz

Always an intense and striking wine which, right from the word go, has shown strong cool-climate characteristics with lots of spice and lots of leafy characters in normal vintages (which 1998 was not).

TTTT? **1998** Medium red-purple; the bouquet is very ripe, with plum and prune fruit in abundance; these flavours are joined by a touch of cigar box on the rich and stylish palate. Flavoursome but elegant.   **rating:** 90

best drinking 2001–2006 **best vintages** '84, '88, '90, '93, '97, '98 **drink with** Risotto • $NA

merrivale wines   ★★★

Olivers Road, McLaren Vale, SA 5171 **region** McLaren Vale
phone (08) 8323 9196 **fax** (08) 8323 9746 **open** 7 days 11–5
winemaker Contract **production** 10 000 **est.** 1971
product range ($10–18 CD) Under the Tapestry label Riesling, Chardonnay, Spaetlese, Shiraz, Cabernet, Muscat of Alexandria, Old Tawny Port.
summary After a relatively brief period of ownership by Brian Light and family, was then acquired by the Gerard family, owners of Chapel Hill.

merum   NR

Hillbrook Road, Northcliffe, WA 6262 **region** Pemberton
phone (08) 9776 6011 **fax** (08) 9777 1543 **open** By appointment
winemaker Maria Melsom **production** 500 **est.** 1996
product range ($22–28 ML) Semillon, Shiraz.
summary Merum is owned by Maria Melsom (formerly winemaker at Driftwood Estate) and Michael Melsom (former vineyard manager for Voyager Estate, both in the Margaret River region). The first 6.3 hectares of vineyard (3.3 shiraz, 2 semillon, 1 chardonnay) was planted in 1996, and the first wine made in 1999. The wines to be released in 2000 will comprise a lightly-oaked Semillon/Chardonnay blend and a barrel-fermented Shiraz. An additional 2.6 hectares equally split between merlot and cabernet sauvignon are to be planted in the year 2000.

métier wines   NR

Tarraford Vineyard, 440 Healesville Road, Yarra Glen, Vic 3775 **region** Yarra Valley
phone (03) 5962 2461 **fax** (03) 5962 2194 **open** Not
winemaker Martin Williams **production** 1400 **est.** 1995
product range ($29.50–32 R) Tarraford Vineyard Chardonnay, Schoolhouse Vineyard Chardonnay, Tarraford Vineyard Pinot Noir.
summary Métier is the French word for craft, trade or profession; the business is that of Yarra Valley-based winemaker Martin Williams MW, who has an array of degrees and winemaking stints in France, California and Australia which are, not to put too fine a word on it, extraordinary. The focus of Métier will be to produce individual vineyard wines, initially based on grapes from the Tarraford and Schoolhouse Vineyards, both in the Yarra Valley. The quality of the initial releases of Pinot Noir and Chardonnay is extremely high.

Métier Schoolhouse Vineyard Chardonnay

A single vineyard wine which, as the tasting note indicates, has been given the works.

TTTT 1998 Medium yellow-green; a complex range of secondary aromas on the bouquet suggest the full range of winemaking inputs, including wild yeast/oxidative juice handling/malolactic fermentation. The palate is much fresher with melon and stone fruit flavours, a tweak of acidity on the finish, and subtle, well-integrated oak.   **rating:** 89

best drinking 2001–2006 **drink with** Veal scaloppine • $29.50

Métier Tarraford Vineyard Chardonnay

The wine is whole-bunch pressed, fermented entirely in French oak barriques (25 per cent new), 50 per cent wild or indigenous yeast-fermented, and 50 per cent taken through malolactic fermentation. The wine spends 12 months in barrel on lees with minimal stirring; the wine is pumped only twice in the course of its production, once as juice to barrel, the second as wine to bottle.

TTTT? **1997** Brilliant light to medium yellow-green; the melon and nectarine fruit aromas are clean and fresh, supported by subtle oak. The feel and texture of the wine is reminiscent of that of Giaconda; perfectly balanced and constructed, with great length, it should be long-lived.   **rating:** 94

best drinking 1999–2005 **drink with** Milk-fed veal • $29.50

Métier Tarraford Vineyard Pinot Noir

The wine is fermented in small open vats, with around 12 per cent whole bunches. Three days cold-soak is followed by the spontaneous initiation of fermentation before a Burgundy yeast strain is added to ensure completion. The wine is hand-plunged, and the temperature encouraged to peak over 30°C. Part finishes its fermentation in barrel, part is macerated post-fermentation. The wine is matured in French oak, 30 per cent new, and bottled after 17 months. It is eggwhite-fined and filtered once.

▼▼▼▼ **1997** Strong red-purple; the bouquet is complex, with dark plum and savoury fruit, and subtle oak. The controversial aspect of the wine is the degree of volatile acidity, which will offend some but not others. The palate is powerful and potent, with quite firm tannins; volatile acidity to one side, it should be long-lived.   **rating:** 89

▼▼▼▼ **1998** Medium to full purple-red; a complex and rich array of predominantly foresty/bready/savoury aromas introduce a palate with plenty of plummy fruit swathed in the foresty characters of the bouquet. Uncompromising approach to extract and tannins.   **rating:** 87

best drinking 2001–2007 **drink with** Wild game • $32

🐚 miceli   NR

60 Main Creek Road, Arthurs Seat, Vic 3936 **region** Mornington Peninsula
phone (03) 5989 2755 **fax** (03) 5989 2755 **open** First weekend each month 12–5, public holidays, and also every weekend and by appointment in Jan
winemaker Anthony Miceli **production** 800 **est.** 1991
product range ($17–31 CD) Chardonnay (Unoaked), Olivia's Pinot Noir, Lucy's Choice Pinot Noir, Reserve Pinot Noir.
summary This may be a part-time labour of love for general practitioner Dr Anthony Miceli, but this hasn't prevented him taking the whole venture very seriously. He acquired the property in 1989 specifically for the purpose of establishing a vineyard, carrying out the first plantings of 1.8 hectares in November 1991, followed by a further 1 hectare of pinot gris in 1997. Ultimately the vineyard will be increased to 5 hectares with a projected production of 2500 to 3000 cases a year. Between 1991 and 1997 Dr Miceli enrolled in and thereafter graduated from the Wine Science course at Charles Sturt University, and thus manages both vineyard and winery. Retail distribution through fine wine outlets and restaurants in Melbourne.

Miceli Reserve Pinot Noir

A thoroughly distinguished wine which reflects the low yields and, in particular, the small berry size of the '97 vintage. Winner of the Pinot Noir Trophy at the Cowra Wine Show 1999.

▼▼▼▼♡ **1997** Medium red-purple; exotic barrel-ferment oak (new) is the driving force of the bouquet; however, spicy/tobacco/forest flavours, together with spicy plum comes through on a palate with good structure, balance and length; the oak is certainly present, but not destructively so.   **rating:** 91

best drinking 2000–2003 **drink with** Rare duck breast • $31

---

michelini wines   NR

Great Alpine Road, Myrtleford, Vic 3737 **region** King Valley
phone (03) 5751 1990 **fax** (03) 5751 1410 **open** Thurs–Mon 10–5
winemaker Josephine Horn (Contract) **production** 3000 **est.** 1982
product range ($13.50–20.50 CD) Riesling, Unwooded Chardonnay, Chardonnay, Pinot Noir, Marziemo, Merlot, Shiraz, Cabernet Sauvignon.
summary The Michelini family are among the best known grape growers in the Buckland Valley of northeast Victoria. Having migrated from Italy in 1949, the Michelinis originally grew tobacco, diversifying into vineyards in 1982. A little over 42 hectares of vineyard have been established on terra rossa soil at an altitude of 300 metres, mostly with frontage to the Buckland River. The major part of the production is sold (to Orlando and others), but since 1996 an on-site winery has permitted the Michelinis to vinify part of their production. The winery in fact has capacity to handle 1000 tonnes of fruit, thereby eliminating the problem of moving grapes out of a declared phylloxera area. The quality of the initial releases was modest, but the area does have the potential to produce pleasant wine, and doubtless better things are in store.

---

middlebrook   NR

Sand Road, McLaren Vale, SA 5171 **region** McLaren Vale
phone (08) 8383 0600 **fax** (08) 8383 0557 **open** Mon–Fri 9–5, weekends 10–5
winemaker Walter (Bill) Clappis **production** 5000 **est.** 1947
product range ($14–20 CD) In the course of redevelopment, with a top-end range under the Walter Clappis label, and a mid-range under the Middlebrook label.

summary Middlebrook has been acquired and is being redeveloped by industry veteran Bill Clappis after his former winery, Ingoldby, was acquired by Mildara Blass. He has been renovating the Middlebrook winery and restaurant, which reopened in the second half of 1998 with an appropriate fanfare of trumpets.

middleton estate   NR

Flagstaff Hill Road, Middleton, SA 5213 **region** Other Wineries of SA
phone (08) 8555 4136 **fax** (08) 8555 4108 **open** Fri–Sun 11–5
winemaker Nigel Catt **production** 3000 **est.** 1979
product range ($9–16 CD) Riesling, Sauvignon Blanc, Semillon Sauvignon Blanc, Cabernet Hermitage.
summary Nigel Catt has demonstrated his winemaking skills at Andrew Garrett and elsewhere, so wine quality should be good; despite its decade of production, I have never seen or tasted its wines. A winery restaurant helps the business turnover.

milbrovale   NR

520 Milbrovale Road, Broke, NSW 2330 **region** Lower Hunter Valley
phone (02) 9362 4915 **fax** (02) 9363 5716 **open** Not
winemaker Michael Glover, Richard Owens **production** 11 500 **est.** 1995
product range ($15–30 R) Verdelho, Semillon, Chardonnay, Shiraz in three distinct label ranges: Milbrovale White Label, Milbrovale Seven Stones and Milbrovale MV2.
summary Sixty-one-year-old Richard Owens and wife Mary are in the course of investing $5 million in establishing Milbrovale, a 34-hectare vineyard at the foot of the Brokenback Range. Both were once pharmacists, but Richard Owens became chief executive of a very successful supermarket chain in Newcastle and the Hunter Valley, so successful that it was acquired by Bi-Lo. Finding the money, therefore, wasn't a problem, and Owens was able to turn his love affair with wine (he was a founding member of the Newcastle Beefsteak and Burgundy Club 40 years ago) into reality. A 500-tonne, 30 000-case winery will be erected on a newly acquired 40-hectare property in Broke Road, Pokolbin, not far from Tyrrell's. In the meantime, the wines have been made at Rothbury Estate (using Milbrovale's own equipment) and former Rothbury winemaker Michael Glover will become chief winemaker at Milbrovale, assisted by Stuart Davies in the vineyard. The wines are being released in three ranges: a basic varietal White Label at the bottom end; the Seven Stones series in the middle and small quantities of MV2 (sourced from premium regions outside the Hunter Valley) at the top.

milburn park   ★★★

Campbell Avenue, Irymple, Vic 3498 **region** Murray Darling
phone (03) 5024 6800 **fax** (03) 5024 6605 **open** Mon–Sat 10–4.30
winemaker David Martin, Gary Magilton **production** 385 000 **est.** 1977
product range ($5–13 R) Top-end wines under the Milburn Park label are Chardonnay and Cabernet Sauvignon, and under the Salisbury Estate label Show Reserve Chardonnay and Show Reserve Cabernet Sauvignon. Then comes the standard Salisbury Estate range of Rhine Riesling, Chardonnay Semillon, Sauvignon Blanc Semillon, Chardonnay, Cabernet Sauvignon, Cabernet Merlot; the Castle Crossing range is even cheaper, consisting of Fumé Blanc, Colombard Chardonnay, Spätlese Rhine Riesling, Chenin Blanc, Chambourcin, Shiraz Malbec Mourvedre, Claret; Acacia Ridge non-vintage generics bring up the rear, with two wines in the Tennyson Vineyard off to one side.
summary Part of a widespread group of companies owned by Cranswick Premium Wines Limited, with a strong export focus.

Salisbury Estate Chardonnay

Produced from Riverland grapes with the principal focus on price, but offering plenty of unpretentious flavour.
▼▼▼▽ **1998** Medium yellow-green; the bouquet is clean, quite firm and solid, with unobtrusive oak. A solid, honest wine on the palate, with pleasantly ripe chardonnay fruit. **rating:** 81
best drinking Drink now **best vintages** NA **drink with** Gnocchi • $9

mildara (coonawarra)   ★★★★

Penola–Naracoorte Road, Coonawarra, SA 5263 **region** Coonawarra
phone (08) 8736 3380 **fax** (08) 8736 3307 **open** Mon–Fri 9–4.30, weekends 10–4
winemaker David O'Leary, Scott Rawlinson **production** 200 000 **est.** 1955
product range ($10–40 R) The volume is driven by Jamiesons Run Red and Jamiesons Run Chardonnay, then comes Robertson's Well Chardonnay (in fact a blend of Yarra Valley and King Valley fruit) and Cabernet Sauvignon and Flanagan's Ridge Cabernet Sauvignon. Jamiesons Run has been 'brand-extended' with the introduction of a smartly packaged Reserve, but Alexanders remains the top-end wine for the time being.

summary The quality jewel in the crown of the Fosters Brewing Group's Mildara Blass wine empire but a jewel which has always been put to industrial use, with the emphasis on volume brands such as Jamiesons Run, Robertson's Well and so forth. For all that, it has to be said the quality of Jamiesons Run has been zealously protected, notwithstanding the growth in volume of its production (and the 1998 introduction of Jamiesons Run Reserve). Worldwide distribution.

Mildara Jamiesons Run Sauvignon Blanc

Part of the continuing brand expansion of Jamiesons Run both across varieties and in terms of price (with the Reserve Red).

ŦŦŦŶ **1999** Light yellow-green; the bouquet is modest, crisp and faintly herbal; however, the palate does have some length to grassy/herbal/mineral fruit flavours. Above-average example. **rating:** 84

best drinking 2000–2001 **best vintages** NA **drink with** Sautéed scallops • $15

Mildara Jamiesons Run Chardonnay

A no-frills Chardonnay, but at least the winemakers have resisted the temptation to fill it with chippy oak.

ŦŦŦŶ **1998** Medium yellow-green; clean, moderately intense, with some peachy fruit. A pleasant fault-free commercial Chardonnay, soothing rather than exciting. **rating:** 81

best drinking Drink now **best vintages** NA **drink with** Red Rooster • $15

Mildara Pepperjack Barossa Shiraz

A new label for Mildara, with 85 per cent Barossa and 15 per cent Eden Valley fruit, positioned at the premium end of the market.

ŦŦŦŦ **1996** Medium red-purple; the bouquet is clean and sweet, with red berry/cherry fruit and subtle oak. The palate is as clean, smooth and sweet as the bouquet suggests, replete with soft, velvety tannins. A most appealing commercial red wine. **rating:** 87

best drinking 2000–2005 **best vintages** '96 **drink with** Beef stew • $20

Mildara Robertson's Well Shiraz

Formerly a blend of Shiraz and Cabernet Sauvignon, and a few other varieties and puppy dogs' tails. Robertson's Well has now been split into two varietals: Shiraz and Cabernet Sauvignon.

ŦŦŦŦ **1998** The dense, dark red-purple colour stains the glass as the wine is swirled; as the colour suggests, a voluminous bouquet with dark berry fruits and a whack of American oak. There is excellent base wine but the oak and the other components are as yet disjointed and separated. Had it had a little work, could have been exceptional; as it is, should develop well in bottle. **rating:** 85

best drinking 2003–2013 **best vintages** NA **drink with** Braised oxtail • $20

Mildara Jamiesons Run Coonawarra Merlot

Everyone with Merlot is hopping onto the bandwagon, it seems. I am not too sure what to make of this brand extension for Jamiesons Run; one might have expected a better end use for Coonawarra Merlot.

ŦŦŦŦ **1998** Bright purple-red; the bouquet is clean, with some oak surrounding pleasant but nondescript red fruit. The palate is nicely weighted and structured; a light- to medium-bodied red wine which happens to be fashioned from Merlot. **rating:** 85

best drinking 2001–2005 **best vintages** NA **drink with** Pan-fried veal • $17

Mildara Pepperjack Barossa Cabernet Sauvignon

The Barossa Valley is capable of growing shiraz and cabernet sauvignon of exceptionally high quality; the Pepperjack range is designed to make full use of that fact.

ŦŦŦŦ **1997** Medium red-purple; soft, sweet cassis berry fruit and a hint of vanilla oak on the bouquet precede an attractive, soft, easy sweetly fruited palate. A Wolf Blass style without the oak. **rating:** 87

best drinking 2000–2005 **best vintages** NA **drink with** Lamb loin chops • $20

Mildara Robertson's Well Cabernet Sauvignon

The big brother of the Robertson's Well Shiraz; the first split vintage came in '97, the second in '98. The latter wine has won gold medals at Hobart, Melbourne and Brisbane.

ŦŦŦŦ **1998** Medium to full red-purple; there is strong, slightly dusty vanillin oak over ripe, cassis fruit on the bouquet; there is plenty of fruit weight and sweetness on the palate even if the oak is in a slightly different compartment. Time in bottle should help bring the components together. **rating:** 87

best drinking 2003–2013 **best vintages** NA **drink with** Lamb Provençale • $20

mildara (murray darling) ★★★

Wentworth Road, Merbein, Vic 3505 **region** Murray Darling
phone (03) 5025 2303 **fax** (03) 5025 3300 **open** Mon–Fri 9–5, weekends 10–4
winemaker Steve Guy **production** 150 000 **est.** 1888
product range ($8–10 R) Church Hill Chardonnay, Fumé Blanc, Cabernet Merlot; Jimmy Watson Chardonnay and Cabernet Sauvignon; also makes fine Sherries (Chestnut Teal, George and Supreme) and superb Pot Still Brandy.
summary A somewhat antiquated Merbein facility remains the overall group production centre following its acquisition of Wolf Blass, although all of its premium wines are sourced from and made at Coonawarra.

milford vineyard ★★★★

Tasman Highway, Cambridge, Tas 7170 **region** Southern Tasmania
phone (03) 6248 5029 **fax** (03) 6224 2331 **open** Not
winemaker Andrew Hood (Contract) **production** 200 **est.** 1984
product range ($20 R) Pinot Noir.
summary Given the tiny production, Milford is understandably not open to the public, the excellent Pinot Noir being quickly sold by word of mouth. The 150-hectare grazing property (the largest Southdown sheep stud in Australia) has been in Charlie Lewis's family since 1830. Only 15 minutes from Hobart, and with an absolute water frontage to the tidal estuary of the Coal River, it is a striking site. The vineyard is established on a patch of 5-foot-deep sand over a clay base with lots of lime impregnation.

Milford Vineyard Pinot Noir

Produced from a little over 1 hectare of estate-grown pinot noir, a size chosen by the partnership which runs the vineyard (with property owner Charlie Lewis) because it represents one day's picking — and only one day. Has acquitted itself well in wine shows over the past few years.
▼▼▼♀ **1998** Medium red with some purple remaining; the bouquet is clean but seems slightly thin and dilute; however, the palate has much more flavour and concentration, with a nice mix of plummy fruit and gently charry oak. **rating:** 84
best drinking 2000–2003 **best vintages** '96, '98 **drink with** Char-grilled salmon • $20

🐌 milimani estate NR

92 The Forest Road, Bungendore, NSW 2621 **region** Canberra District
phone (02) 6238 1421 **fax** (02) 6238 1424 **open** First weekend of each month, Sat 2–4, Sun 10–4
winemaker Lark Hill (Contract) **production** NA **est.** 1989
product range NA.
summary The Preston family (Mary, David and Rosemary) have established a 4-hectare vineyard at Bungendore planted to sauvignon blanc, chardonnay, pinot noir, merlot and cabernet franc. Contract-winemaking at Lark Hill should guarantee the quality of the wine.

millers samphire NR

Watts Gully Road, Corner Robertson Road, Kersbrook, SA 5231 **region** Adelaide Hills
phone (08) 8389 3183 **fax** (03) 8389 3183 **open** 7 days 9–5
winemaker Tom Miller **production** 80 **est.** 1982
product range ($9 CD) Riesling.
summary Next after Scarp Valley, one of the smallest wineries in Australia offering wine for sale; pottery also helps. Tom Miller has one of the more interesting and diverse CVs, with an early interest in matters alcoholic leading to the premature but happy death of a laboratory rat at Adelaide University and his enforced switch from biochemistry to mechanical engineering. The Riesling is a high-flavoured wine with crushed herb and lime aromas and flavours.

millinup estate NR

RMB 1280 Porongurup Road, Porongurup, WA 6324 **region** Great Southern
phone (08) 9853 1105 **fax** (08) 9853 1105 **open** Weekends 10–5
winemaker Gavin Berry (Contract) **production** 220 **est.** 1989
product range ($12–16 CD) Twin Peaks Riesling, Late Harvest Riesling, Cabernet Sauvignon Franc Merlot.
summary The Millinup Estate vineyard was planted in 1978, when it was called Point Creek. Owners Peter and Lesley Thorn purchased it in 1989, renaming it and having the limited production (from half a hectare each of riesling and merlot, supplemented by purchased cabernet sauvignon) vinified at Plantagenet.

minot vineyard   NR

PO Box 683, Margaret River, WA 6285 **region** Margaret River
phone (08) 9757 3579 **fax** (08) 9757 2361 **open** By appointment
winemaker Various Contract **production** 1000 **est.** 1986
product range ($14.50–23.50 R) Semillon Sauvignon Blanc, Cabernet Sauvignon.
summary Minot, which takes its name from a small chateau in the Loire Valley in France, is the husband and wife venture of the Miles family, producing just two wines from the 4-hectare plantings of semillon, sauvignon blanc and cabernet sauvignon.

mintaro wines   NR

Leasingham Road, Mintaro, SA 5415 **region** Clare Valley
phone (08) 8843 9046 **fax** (08) 8843 9050 **open** 7 days 9–5
winemaker Peter Houldsworth **production** 4000 **est.** 1984
product range ($9–20 CD) Dry Riesling, Late Picked Riesling, Shiraz, Shiraz Cabernet Franc Cabernet Sauvignon, Cabernet Sauvignon Cabernet Franc.
summary Has produced some very good Riesling over the years, developing well in bottle. The red wines are formidable, massive in body and extract, built for the long haul.

miramar   ★★★☆

Henry Lawson Drive, Mudgee, NSW 2850 **region** Mudgee
phone (02) 6373 3874 **fax** (02) 6373 3854 **open** 7 days 9–5
winemaker Ian MacRae **production** 8000 **est.** 1977
product range ($11–30 CD) Semillon, Chardonnay, Fumé Blanc, Riesling, Sauvignon Blanc, Eurunderee Rosé, Cabernet Sauvignon, Shiraz; Doux Blanc, Encore (Sparkling).
summary Industry veteran Ian MacRae has demonstrated his skill with every type of wine over the decades, ranging through Rosé to Chardonnay to full-bodied reds. All have shone under the Miramar label at one time or another, although the Ides of March are pointing more to the red than the white wines these days. A substantial part of the production from the 38 hectares of estate vineyard is sold to others, the best being retained for Miramar's own use.

Miramar Shiraz
Another slow-developing wine made from estate-grown grapes, moving progressively earthy, cedary characters as it ages. The oak contribution is typically subtle.
▼▼▼▽ **1998** Light to medium red-purple; the bouquet is slightly uncharacteristically light, with slightly lifted minty edges. Cherry and mint fruit flavours drive the palate, again with a slight suggestion of lift.   **rating:** 83
▼▼▼▼ **1997** Medium red-purple; the moderately intense bouquet is clean with cherry, leaf and game aromas. The palate offers a different register of fruit from either the '96 or '98, verging on blackberry at the core. Soft tannins and subtle oak.   **rating:** 85
best drinking 2000–2005 **best vintages** '86, '90, '94, '95, '97 **drink with** Braised oxtail or, better still, the ox •$17

Miramar Cabernet Sauvignon
Produced from 7.5 hectares of estate plantings. The '97 is a nice wine, but if the '99 makes the transition safely to bottle, it will be a knockout.
▼▼▼▽ **1997** Medium red-purple; the bouquet is clean, with savoury fruit of medium intensity. The palate runs through the same savoury/earthy cabernet spectrum; the oak is subtle, the tannins soft.   **rating:** 83
best drinking 2000–2004 **best vintages** '86, '90, '91 **drink with** Veal chops •$16

miranda wines (barossa)   ★★★☆

Barossa Highway, Rowland Flat, SA 5352 **region** Barossa Valley
phone (08) 8524 4537 **fax** (08) 8524 4066 **open** Mon–Fri 10.4.30, weekends 11–4
winemaker David Norman **production** NFP **est.** 1919
product range ($9–45 CD) Premium Late Harvest Riesling; the Grey Series of Riesling, Semillon, Sauvignon Blanc, Chardonnay, Shiraz; Bush Vine Grenache and Cabernet Sauvignon; followed by Show Reserve range of Chardonnay, Old Vine Shiraz and Shiraz Cabernet.
summary Increasingly absorbed into the Miranda Wine Group since its acquisition, drawing on grapes produced both in the Barossa Valley and throughout other parts of southeast Australia. The accent is on value for money, with consistent show success underlining the quality. Exports to Europe, the UK, Canada and Illinois.

miranda wines (griffith)　　★★★☆

57 Jondaryan Avenue, Griffith, NSW 2680 **region** Riverina
phone (02) 6960 3000 **fax** (02) 6962 6944 **open** 7 days 9–5
winemaker Doug Wilson **production** NFP **est.** 1939
product range ($6–24 R) Top of the range is Show Reserve Chardonnay, Old Vine Shiraz, Shiraz Cabernet; Golden Botrytis; followed by the High Country Series (from the King Valley) of Riesling, Chardonnay, Merlot, Shiraz and Cabernet; Mirool Creek Dry White, Chardonnay and Cabernet Shiraz; Somerton Riesling Traminer, Semillon Chardonnay and Shiraz Cabernet; also lower-priced Christy's Land and assorted varietals, generics, sparkling and ports.
summary Miranda Wines continues its aggressive and successful growth strategy, having opened a new winery in the King Valley in 1998 and previously expanded winemaking operations into the Barossa Valley. A veritable cascade of wines now appear under the various brand names, the majority representing good value for money. Exports to Europe, UK, Canada and Illinois.

Miranda Golden Botrytis

Made its debut in 1993 as a blend of botrytised Semillon and Riesling and over the ensuing years has come second only to De Bortoli Noble One in terms of the number of trophies and gold medals accumulated. By 1997 alone, the winner of four trophies and 12 gold medals, the wine had moved to a Semillon varietal base.
▼▼▼▼▼ **1997** Bright bronze; a super-intense and complex bouquet of cumquat and peach is followed by a fantastically complex and flavoursome palate with a long finish, courtesy of the excellent acidity.　　**rating:** 95
best drinking 2000–2005 **best vintages** '93, '94, '96, '97 **drink with** Fruit ice-cream, sweet pastries　•$15.95

Miranda Old Vine Shiraz

Produced from 100 per cent old vine Barossa shiraz, a winner of gold medals at both Brisbane and Adelaide Wine Shows in 1997.
▼▼▼▼▽ **1996** Medium red-purple; the bouquet is complex and rich, offering a traditional blend of sweet, dark cherry fruit together with vanilla smoothie oak. The palate shifts gear into a mix of glossy cherry and mint which often appears in ripe Barossa Shiraz. It is a flavour characteristic which I have always had some personal difficulty with, but this is a good wine.　　**rating:** 91
best drinking 2001–2011 **best vintages** NA **drink with** Lasagne　•$24

☙ miranda wines (king valley)　　★★★

Corner Snow and Whitfield Roads, Oxley, Vic 3768 **region** King Valley
phone (02) 6960 3016 **fax** (02) 6964 4135 **open** Not
winemaker Luis F Simian (Snr), Jeff Martin, Luis F Simian **production** NFP **est.** 1998
product range ($9.95–24 R) The High Country series of Riesling, Chardonnay, Merlot, Shiraz, Cabernet Sauvignon, Dark Horse Cabernet Franc Malbec.
summary Miranda now has three quite separate winemaking entities: the original (and largest) in Griffith; the next in the Barossa Valley; and the most recent in the King Valley. It is at the latter winery that the High Country range is made, using 35 hectares of estate vineyards, supplemented by grapes purchased from elsewhere, including the Kiewa.

mistletoe wines　　★★★☆

771 Hermitage Road, Pokolbin, NSW 2335 **region** Lower Hunter Valley
phone (02) 4998 7770 **fax** (02) 4998 7792 **open** Mon–Fri 10–6 or by appointment
winemaker Jon Reynolds (Contract) **production** 3000 **est.** 1967
product range ($16–20 CD) Semillon, Silvereye Semillon, Barrel Fermented Chardonnay, The Rosé, Shiraz.
summary Mistletoe Wines, owned by Ken and Gwen Sloan, can trace its history back to 1909, when a substantial vineyard was planted on what was then called Mistletoe Farm. The Mistletoe Farm brand made a brief appearance in the late 1970s but disappeared and has now been revived under the Mistletoe Wines label by the Sloans, with contract-winemaking by Jon Reynolds. No retail distribution, but worldwide delivery service available ex winery.

Mistletoe Semillon

Produced from 30-year-old dry-grown estate plantings. Classic winemaking with cold fermentation in stainless steel and relatively early-bottling. As at March 2000, four vintages (1996–'99 inclusive) were on sale at $16 for the younger wines and $17 for the older.
▼▼▼▽ **1998** Medium yellow-green; the moderately intense bouquet has clean citrus/lemon aromas with a mineral twang. The mid-weight palate has the same lemony fruit and has good balance, and is accessible now. Trophy

winner Boutique Wines of Australia 1999 for Best Semillon. Also has one silver and three bronze medals to its credit. **rating:** 84

▼▼▼▼ **1997** Medium to full yellow-green; the bouquet is developing nicely, with good grip and intensity offset by the first signs of honey and toast. The tight palate has lemon/citrus fruit and crisp acidity; on its way to something special. **rating:** 86

best drinking 2003–2008 **best vintages** '97 **drink with** Crab, Balmain bugs • $16

Mistletoe Shiraz

The grapes are hand-picked; unusually, they are fermented in old oak hogsheads and then transferred to American Bluegrass oak barriques until being bottled immediately prior to the following vintage.

▼▼▼▼ **1998** Medium to full red-purple; the bouquet offers a rich mix of vanilla oak, chocolate and dark berry fruit. The palate, too, is quite rich with nice blackberry/plum fruit and balanced tannins. The American oak is there, of course, but is far from dominant. **rating:** 85

best drinking 2003–2010 **best vintages** NA **drink with** Rare beef • $20

mitchell ★★★★

Hughes Park Road, Sevenhill via Clare, SA 5453 **region** Clare Valley
phone (08) 8843 4258 **fax** (08) 8843 4340 **open** 7 days 10–4
winemaker Andrew Mitchell **production** 25 000 **est.** 1975
product range ($15–23 CD) Watervale Riesling, Peppertree Vineyard Shiraz, The Growers Semillon, The Growers Grenache, Sevenhill Cabernet, Sparkling Peppertree.
summary For long one of the stalwarts of the Clare Valley, producing long-lived Rieslings and Cabernet Sauvignons in classic regional style but having extended the range with very creditable Semillon and Shiraz. A lovely old stone apple shed provides the cellar door and upper section of the compact winery. Production has increased by almost 50 per cent over the past few years and as well as national retail distribution, the wines are exported to the UK, the US, Canada, New Zealand, Switzerland and Hong Kong.

Mitchell Watervale Riesling

First made in 1977 and produced from the estate vineyards in the Watervale region. This is a classic Clare Riesling which can age magnificently for up to 15 years in good vintages.

▼▼▼▽ **1999** Light yellow-green; faint burnt fermentation aromas dull the bouquet, but the palate is much better, quite intense and long. Patience should be rewarding. **rating:** 84

best drinking 2003–2008 **best vintages** '78, '84, '90, '92, '93, '94, '95 **drink with** Grilled fish • $14

Mitchell Peppertree Vineyard Shiraz

Like the Semillon, first made in 1984; takes its name from the old peppertree which grows in the shiraz vineyard at Watervale. The wine is aged for 18 months in small French and American oak; in some years it shows minty characters, in other years more spice and cherry.

▼▼▼▽ **1998** Youthful purple-red; the young, juicy/earthy shiraz fruit of the bouquet is repeated exactly on the palate; seems to have been rushed into bottle. Time may help. **rating:** 81

best drinking 2002–2007 **best vintages** '84, '86, '87, '94, '95, '96 **drink with** Devilled kidneys • $23

Mitchell Sevenhill Cabernet Sauvignon

First made in 1976; from then to 1983 fashioned entirely from Cabernet Sauvignon, but between then and 1985 first Cabernet Franc and then Merlot were added, now contributing 5–15 per cent of the finished wine, which is aged in a mix of new and older French oak.

▼▼▼▽ **1997** Medium red-purple; there are slightly feral/gamey undertones to the bouquet, followed by firm blackberry fruit on entry to the mouth, and ultimately a trace of bitterness on the finish. **rating:** 82

best drinking 2002–2006 **best vintages** '78, '80, '84, '86, '90, '92, '94, '96 **drink with** Roast lamb • $23

mitchelton ★★★★

Mitchellstown via Nagambie, Vic 3608 **region** Goulburn Valley
phone (03) 5794 2710 **fax** (03) 5794 2615 **open** 7 days 10–5
winemaker Don Lewis **production** 200 000 **est.** 1969
product range ($12.95–49.95 CD) Top of the range is Print Label Red; then come Chardonnay, Cabernet Sauvignon, Marsanne; next Mitchelton III wines, White (Marsanne, Grenache, Viognier), Red (Shiraz, Grenache, Mourvedre); Chinaman's Bridge Merlot, Blackwood Park Riesling. Preece Chardonnay, Sauvignon Blanc, Merlot and Cabernet Sauvignon are volume sellers; Goulburn Valley Shiraz introduced in 1996. Finally, intermittent aged classic releases.

summary Acquired by Petaluma in 1994, having already put the runs on the board in no uncertain fashion with the gifted team of Stephen Shelmerdine and winemaker Don Lewis. Boasts an impressive array of wines across a broad spectrum of style and price, but each carefully aimed at a market niche. The wines are exported to 19 countries throughout the UK, Europe, Asia and the US.

Mitchelton Blackwood Park Riesling

Over the past few years Blackwood Park has laid claim to being the best commercial Riesling in Australia, even though its origins go back to 1978 under different labels. Since that time various vintages have won eight trophies, 51 gold, 66 silver and 102 bronze medals.

TTTT **1999** Light yellow-green; the fresh and gently fragrant bouquet runs through citrus and tropical fruit; the palate is delicate and clean, with attractive, gently tropical fruit running through from the mid to back palate.

rating: 89

best drinking 2000–2010 **best vintages** '85, '90, '91, '92, '94, '95, '96, '98, '99 **drink with** Sashimi • $14.95

Mitchelton Classic Release Riesling

This museum release of what was originally the Blackwood Park Riesling shows just how well the wine matures in bottle.

TTTT **1993** Deep golden yellow; the bouquet is aromatic with lots of honey and preserved fruit aromas, characters which flood through on the mid-palate, where the honeyed fruit flavours abound. Good acidity on the finish.

rating: 88

best drinking 2000–2003 **best vintages** NA **drink with** Cheese soufflé • $24.95

Mitchelton Preece Sauvignon Blanc

Sourced predominantly from the King Valley, with a small proportion coming from the high altitude (650-metre) Fernlea Vineyard in the Strathbogie Ranges. Harvested in two parcels: a small amount in mid-March to capture grassy asparagus characters, the remainder being allowed to ripen for a further three-four weeks for tropical fruit aromas and flavours.

TTTY **1999** Light green-yellow; quite good varietal character with an obvious mix of grassy and tropical fruit of light to medium intensity. A light- to medium-bodied wine, gently flavoured, but the varietal characters are precise; well balanced.

rating: 84

best drinking 2000–2001 **best vintages** NA **drink with** Dolmades and bocconcini • $14.95

Mitchelton Viognier Roussanne

A new and very interesting release from Mitchelton, held back for bottle maturation prior to release.

TTTT **1997** Full yellow; some honeysuckle/honey aromas, not particularly bright or fresh, and with the suggestion of some fermentation yeast overhang. The palate has soft, gentle honeysuckle and vanilla flavours, fairly low in acidity, and hints of spice.

rating: 87

best drinking 2000–2001 **best vintages** NA **drink with** Turkey breast • $24.95

Mitchelton Chardonnay

This wine has undergone a number of name changes (not necessarily coincident with the arrival of new brand managers) in the 1990s. First called Reserve Chardonnay, the name was then changed to Victoria Chardonnay, and now simply Chardonnay: it is the best and yet the only Chardonnay released under the Mitchelton label. The same changes have taken place with the Marsanne and Cabernet Sauvignon.

TTTY **1998** Medium yellow-green; the clean and smooth, moderately intense bouquet has clear melon fruit and subtle oak, characters repeated on the palate. A light- to medium-bodied wine, smooth and correct in every particular, but falls away slightly on the finish and is not in the class of the '97.

rating: 84

best drinking 2000–2001 **best vintages** '81, '85, '90, '91, '92, '97 **drink with** Crumbed brains • $21.95

Mitchelton Shiraz

Now simply called Mitchelton Shiraz (previously Goulburn Valley), the wine is made from a mix of estate-grown grapes and a portion from Shepparton, 50 kilometres to the north on the Murray River. Slightly less than 15 per cent of the wine is Mourvedre and Grenache, and the wine spends 18 months in two- to three-year-old French and American oak barrels.

TTTY **1997** Medium red-purple; the bouquet offers a mix of leather and spice alongside savoury red fruits. A pleasant, easy-drinking style with soft tannins though not over-much flesh.

rating: 83

best drinking 2000–2004 **best vintages** NA **drink with** Braised duck • $18.95

Mitchelton Print Label Shiraz

In 1981 Mitchelton conceived the idea of staging a Print Exhibition and making an annual purchase of the best print in the exhibition for subsequent use as the label of the best red wine of the vintage. Both the '90 and '91 vintages were outstanding, the former winning the Jimmy Watson Trophy. Having started life as a Cabernet Sauvignon, Shiraz has ruled the roost for most recent vintages. However, the best wine of the 1994 vintage was a Cabernet Sauvignon, but since 1995 the wine has reverted to Shiraz.

♥♥♥♥♥ **1996** Medium to full red-purple; the rich, full and ripe bouquet has cascades of sweet leather, briary, liquorice fruit; the palate, likewise, has real presence and power, the impact building progressively through the palate, with mulberry and chocolate flavours, closing with fine tannins. **rating: 94**

best drinking 2001–2011 **best vintages** '81, '82, '90, '91, '92, '95, '96 **drink with** Marinated venison • $49.95

Mitchelton Preece Merlot

The wine comes from contract growers in the King Valley, and from Mitchelton's vineyards in the Goulburn Valley. It is aged in two- to three-year-old oak barrels for 17 months prior to release.

♥♥♥♡ **1998** Medium red-purple; the light to moderately intense bouquet has gently savoury/leafy varietal fruit, the palate offering more weight and sweeter berry fruit flavours; fair tannins on the finish. **rating: 83**

best drinking 2000–2003 **best vintages** NA **drink with** Chicken yakitori • $NA

Mitchelton Cabernet Sauvignon

Sourced primarily from vineyards in Central Victoria, augmented by a small portion from the Yarra Valley. Fermentation takes place in a mix of rotary fermenters (Vinimatics) and static fermenters with heading down boards. It then spends 18 months in French oak prior to bottling.

♥♥♥♥♡ **1996** Medium red-purple; the clean and smooth bouquet has quite sweet berry fruit and gentle, well-integrated oak. The palate shows dark savoury blackberry fruit, persistent tannins and, as with the bouquet, good use of oak. **rating: 90**

best drinking 2000–2010 **best vintages** '96 **drink with** Lamb casserole • $24.95

molly morgan vineyard ★★★☆

Talga Road, Lovedale, NSW 2321 **region** Lower Hunter Valley
phone (02) 4930 7695 **fax** (02) 9235 1876 **open** Weekends, public holidays 10–5
winemaker Rhys Eather (Contract) **production** 3500 **est.** 1963
product range ($15–25 CD) Joe's Block Semillon, Old Vines Semillon, Semillon Chardonnay, Chardonnay, Shiraz.
summary Molly Morgan has been acquired by Andrew and Hady Simon, who established the Camperdown Cellars Group in 1971, becoming the largest retailer in Australia before passing on to other pursuits, and John Baker, one of Australia's best-known fine wine retailers, who owned or managed Quaffers, Double Bay Cellars, the Newport Bottler and Grape Fellas (Epping) at various times. The property is planted to 5.5 hectares of 25-year-old unirrigated semillon, which goes to make the Old Vines Semillon, 0.8 hectares for Joe's Block Semillon, 2.5 hectares of chardonnay and 1.2 hectares of shiraz. The wines are contract-made (as has always been the case, in fact, but to a high standard).

Molly Morgan Joe's Block Semillon

A single vineyard wine, named after the third husband of the redoubtable Molly Morgan. It would be hard to imagine a greater contrast in style between the '98 and '99 vintages, each legitimate, but in my view the '99 far preferable in terms of both style and, of course, longevity.

♥♥♥♥ **1999** Very pale straw-green; the bouquet is fine and delicate, with crisp, herbal archetypal semillon. The palate is fine, quite intense and minerally; everything in front of it. **rating: 89**

best drinking 2004–2009 **best vintages** '99 **drink with** Seafood • $19

Molly Morgan Old Vines Semillon

Produced from 25-year-old, unirrigated vines which provide the best grapes from the estate. As with Joe's Block, the '98 and '99 are polar opposites in terms of style.

♥♥♥♥♡ **1999** Very pale straw-green; the delicate, crisp, herbal aromas of the bouquet are followed by a slightly greater depth of citrus/mineral fruit on the palate. As with Joe's Block, all it needs is lots of time. **rating: 91**

best drinking 2004–2014 **best vintages** '98, '99 **drink with** Calamari • $19

Molly Morgan Chardonnay
Although I have no information one way or the other, this would appear to be unwooded.
▼▼▼▽ **1999** Medium yellow-green; the bouquet is clean, light, with faint melon fruit. The palate is pleasant, with gentle citrus/melon fruit; its best feature is the length of the finish.   **rating: 84**
best drinking 2000–2002 **best vintages** NA **drink with** Lighter pasta dishes   • $20

---

monbulk winery   ★ ★ ☆

Macclesfield Road, Monbulk, Vic 3793 **region** Yarra Valley
phone (03) 9756 6965 **fax** (03) 9756 6965 **open** Weekends and public holidays 12–5, or by appointment
winemaker Paul Jabornik **production** 800 **est.** 1984
product range ($10–15 CD) Chardonnay, Riesling, Pinot Noir, Cabernet Sauvignon, Shiraz; also Kiwifruit wines.
summary Originally concentrated on kiwifruit wines but now extending to table wines; the very cool Monbulk subregion should be capable of producing wines of distinctive style, but the table wines are (unfortunately) not of the same standard as the kiwifruit wines, which are quite delicious.

monichino wines   ★ ★ ☆

1820 Berrys Road, Katunga, Vic 3640 **region** Goulburn Valley
phone (03) 5864 6452 **fax** (03) 5864 6538 **open** Mon–Sat 9–5, Sun 10–5
winemaker Carlo Monichino, Terry Monichino **production** 14 000 **est.** 1962
product range ($8–22 CD) Riesling, Semillon Sauvignon Blanc, Sauvignon Blanc, (Strathbogie) Semillon Sauvignon Blanc, Botrytis Semillon, Orange Muscat, Lexia, Rosé Petals Spätlese, Shiraz, Merlot, Malbec, Cabernet Franc, Cabernet Sauvignon; various Ports and Fortifieds; bulk sales also available.
summary A winery which has quietly made some clean, fresh wines in which the fruit character is carefully preserved.

montagne view estate   NR

555 Hermitage Road, Pokolbin, NSW 2335 **region** Lower Hunter Valley
phone (02) 4998 7822 **fax** (02) 6574 7276 **open** 7 days 10–5
winemaker Greg Silkman (Contract) **production** 500 **est.** 1993
product range ($20–25 CD) Edith Margaret Chardonnay, Vivian Laurie Merlot.
summary The major investment and principal business of Montagne View is the eight-studio-suite guesthouse sitting among the 5 hectares of vines. There is also a high-quality restaurant (Brents) offering the prospect of all-inclusive gourmet weekends for around $550 per couple. The estate wines are sold through the restaurant and cellar door, with other local wines available in the restaurant.

montara   ★ ★ ★

Chalambar Road, Ararat, Vic 3377 **region** Grampians
phone (03) 5352 3868 **fax** (03) 5352 4968 **open** Mon–Sat 9.30–5, Sun 12–4
winemaker Mike McRae **production** NFP **est.** 1970
product range ($10–22 CD) New Wave Riesling, Chardonnay, Pinot Noir, Shiraz, Cabernet Sauvignon, Shiraz Port.
summary Achieved considerable attention for its Pinot Noirs during the 1980s, but other regions (and other makers) have come along since. A recent tasting of the currently available wines ('97 and '96 vintages) was interesting, with a number of the wines having fragrance and elegance but lacking richness and concentration. Smart new label designs do help. Limited national distribution; exports to the UK, Switzerland, Canada and Hong Kong.

Montara Chardonnay
Estate-grown, and aged in French oak barriques for five months.
▼▼▼▼ **1997** Light to medium yellow-green; the aromas are clean, fresh and youthful, with mainstream melon fruit and barely perceptible oak. The palate faithfully reproduces the bouquet; a strong point of the wine is the leisurely rate of its development.   **rating: 85**
best drinking 2000–2004 **best vintages** NA **drink with** Deep-fried calamari   • $20

Montara Pinot Noir
Montara was one of the early pace-setters with Pinot Noir. It is not that the quality of this wine has declined, rather that the range and quality of other Pinots has dramatically increased.

♥♥♥♥ **1997** Medium red, but tending to brown. The bouquet is quite intense and complex, with a mix of ripe fruit and more sappy/foresty characters. The palate shows why Montara made an early name for itself for it has undeniable varietal character. The Achilles Heel is the slightly burnt, jammy nature of the fruit flavour. **rating:** 83
best drinking 2000–2002 **best vintages** NA **drink with** Quail casserole • $22

---

montgomery's hill   NR
Hassell Highway, Lower King, Albany, WA 6330 **region** Great Southern
phone (08) 9844 7177 **fax** (08) 9844 1104 **open** Not
winemaker Steve Pester (Porongurup Winery) **production** 2000 **est.** 1996
product range Chardonnay, Cabernet Sauvignon Franc.
summary Montgomery's Hill is situated 16 kilometres northeast of Albany on a north-facing slope on the banks of the Kalgan River. The vineyard is situated on an area which was previously an apple orchard and is a diversification for the third generation of the Montgomery family which owns the property. Chardonnay, cabernet sauvignon and cabernet franc were planted in 1996, followed by sauvignon blanc, shiraz and merlot in 1997. The 1998 wines were contract-made by Brenden Smith at West Cape Howe Wines, but as from 1999 Montgomery's Hill will be made at the new Porongurup Winery.

montrose   ★★★☆
Henry Lawson Drive, Mudgee, NSW 2850 **region** Mudgee
phone (02) 6372 2208 **fax** (02) 6372 4464 **open** At Poet's Corner
winemaker Brett McKinnon **production** 50 000 **est.** 1974
product range ($9.95–20.95 R) Poet's Corner Semillon Sauvignon Blanc Chardonnay, Unwooded Chardonnay and Shiraz Cabernet Sauvignon Cabernet Franc are at the inexpensive end; premium varietals are Chardonnay, Barbera, Sangiovese, Black Shiraz and Cabernet Sauvignon.
summary A small piece of the Orlando/Wyndham empire, acting partly as a grape and bulk wine source for that empire and partly as a quality producer in its own right, making typically full-flavoured whites and deep-coloured reds. Poet's Corner always provides excellent value for money. Exports to the UK, the US and Asia.

Montrose Barbera
Montrose was established by Italian-born engineers Carlo Salteri and Franco Belgiorno-Nettis (of Transfield Corporation), who in turn hired Italian winemaker Carlo Corino as winemaker. Inevitably, Italian grape varieties were planted and were briefly made, but disappeared from the scene for over a decade (although the plantings were not removed). The Italian craze has led to their reappearance, and not before time.
♥♥♥♥♥ **1997** Medium purple-red; clean, complex briary/savoury/cherry fruit on the bouquet is followed by powerful, dark red fruit flavours on the palate; excellent structure and tannin weight and texture.   **rating:** 91
best drinking 2002–2007 **best vintages** NA **drink with** Bistecca fiorentina • $20.95

---

moondah brook   ★★★★
c/o Houghton, Dale Road, Middle Swan, WA 6056 **region** Swan District
phone (08) 9274 5372 **fax** (08) 9274 5372 **open** Not
winemaker Larry Cherubino **production** 90 000 **est.** 1968
product range ($10–17 R) Chardonnay, Chenin Blanc, Verdelho, Sauvignon Blanc, Shiraz, Cabernet Sauvignon, Maritime (Sparkling); also occasional Show Reserve releases of Chenin Blanc and Verdelho.
summary Part of the BRL Hardy Wine Group which has its own special character as it draws part of its fruit from the large Gingin vineyard, 70 kilometres north of the Swan Valley, and part from the Margaret River and Great Southern. In recent times it has excelled even its own reputation for reliability with some quite lovely wines, in particular honeyed, aged Chenin Blanc and finely structured Cabernet Sauvignon.

Moondah Brook Chenin Blanc
Stakes a strong claim as Australia's best Chenin Blanc. The wines are cold-fermented and then matured in new American oak for six months, and mature well in bottle.
♥♥♥♥ **1998** Light green-yellow; the bouquet is pleasant, with uncomplicated, gentle fruit salad aromas. The medium-bodied palate provides more of the same, well balanced but equally boring. A quirky gold medal at the Hobart Wine Show in 1998 says more about the show than the wine.   **rating:** 82
best drinking 2000–2002 **best vintages** '80, '87, '89, '91, '93, '94, '97 **drink with** Prosciutto and figs • $12.95

Moondah Brook Verdelho

Sourced predominantly from the Gingin Vineyard, but with a smaller contribution from the Margaret River. It is cold-fermented in stainless steel, and not given any oak maturation. The wine can develop wonderful secondary characters given time in bottle, with attractive tropical and citrus fruit aromas and flavours.

▼▼▼▽ **1999** Light green-yellow; the bouquet is quite fresh and fragrant, with a mix of tropical and passionfruit. The palate has fresh, zippy acid, which holds out the promise of attractive development in bottle.　**rating: 84**
best drinking 2000–2005　**best vintages** '80, '87, '89, '90, '91, '93　**drink with** Sugar-cured tuna　•$12.95

Moondah Brook Maritime Dry Red

Introduced to partner the longer-established Maritime Dry White. In both instances the wine is non-vintage, but is attractively packaged in what seems an expensive bottle for a wine at this price point. It uses all of the Houghton grape resources in Western Australia, running from Moondah Brook through to the Frankland River vineyard in Great Southern. Predominantly a blend of Cabernet Sauvignon and Shiraz.

▼▼▼▽ **NV** Medium to full red-purple; the bouquet is quite rich and relatively full, with ample dark berry fruit and no oak to speak of. The wine is lighter on the mid-palate, dipping somewhat, but proceeds through to a long berry and mint-flavoured finish. Well worth a look if you prefer fruit to oak in your red wine.　**rating: 81**
best drinking 1999–2002　**best vintages** NA　**drink with** Pizza　•$10

moonshine valley winery　　NR

374 Mons Road, Forest Glen, Buderim, Qld 4556　**region** South Burnett and Other Wineries of Qld
phone (07) 5445 1198　**fax** (07) 5445 1799　**open** 7 days 10–5
winemaker Frederick Houweling　**production** 1700　**est.** 1985
product range ($10.40–32.95 CD) A kaleidoscopic array of basically fruit-based wines, including Le Dry (Mulberries and Blueberries, oak-matured), Moonlight White (West Indian Limes), Sunshine Nouveau (locally grown Jaboticabas), Old Buderim Ginger (fortified base with Honey and Ginger added), Strawberry Wine, Exporto (Mulberry and Blueberry-based Port Wine).
summary Frederick Houweling brings a European background to his making of these fruit-based wines. The winery is situated on a large property among natural lakes and forest, and also offers a restaurant, cafeteria, and souvenir shop.

moorebank vineyard　　NR

Palmers Lane, Pokolbin, NSW 2320　**region** Lower Hunter Valley
phone (02) 4998 7610　**fax** (02) 4998 7367　**open** Fri–Mon 10–5 or by appointment
winemaker Iain Riggs (Contract)　**production** 2000　**est.** 1977
product range ($19.50–24.50 CD) Chardonnay, Summar Semillon, Gewurztraminer, Merlot, now sold in the narrow 500-ml Italian glass bottle known as Bellissima.
summary Ian Burgess and Debra Moore own a mature 5.5-hectare vineyard with a small cellar-door operation offering immaculately packaged wines in avant-garde style. The peachy Chardonnay has been a medal winner at Hunter Valley Wine Shows.

moorilla estate　　★★★★☆

655 Main Road, Berriedale, Tas 7011　**region** Southern Tasmania
phone (03) 6249 2949　**fax** (03) 6249 4093　**open** 7 days 10–5
winemaker Alain Rousseau　**production** 15 000　**est.** 1958
product range ($13.95–47 R) Riesling, Chardonnay, Gewurztraminer, Botrytis Riesling, Winter Collection Merlot, Cabernet Sauvignon, Vintage Brut; Pinot Noir in three tiers: White Label, Black Label and Reserve.
summary Moorilla Estate is an icon in the Tasmanian wine industry and is thriving. Alain Rousseau is an exceptionally gifted winemaker, producing better wines than have ever previously come from Moorilla (particularly Pinot Noir and Merlot), while the opening of the museum in the marvellous Alcorso house designed by Sir Roy Grounds adds even more attraction for visitors to the estate, a mere 15–20 minutes from Hobart.

Moorilla Estate Riesling

Over the years, consistently the best of the Moorilla Estate wines, with a long track record of excellence. Produced from 1.5 hectares of estate vineyards. In addition, the occasional releases of Botrytised Riesling (by mailing list and through cellar door) are sensational.

▼▼▼▽ **1999** Pale green-yellow; a crisp, fresh bouquet with pronounced herb and lime aromas is followed by a palate which is initially delicate yet builds fruit flavour progressively towards the finish, with a mix of apple, tropical and lime flavours; excellent acidity.　**rating: 90**
best drinking 2003–2009　**best vintages** '81, '82, '90, '91, '93, '94, '95, '97, '98, '99　**drink with** Asparagus　•$23

Moorilla Estate Gewurztraminer

A delicate, crisp wine which typically shows relatively little in its youth, but which fills out with time in bottle. For decades one of the most successful wines for Moorilla Estate. Always delicate but with distinctive varietal character. ▼▼▼▽ **1999** Pale straw-green; the fruit and varietal character initially masked by some SO_2 but progressively revealed itself as the wine sat in the glass. Then delicate spice, rose petal and lychee aromas and flavours progressively unfurled, and I have the feeling that had I consumed the wine over a meal I would have given it significantly higher marks. **rating:** 84

best drinking 2002–2007 **best vintages** NA **drink with** Chinese stir-fried prawns • $26

Moorilla Estate Botrytis Riesling

Over the years Moorilla Estate has produced some quite exhilarating Botrytis Rieslings, always in tiny quantities, and available only from the cellar door or by mail order, released in 375-ml bottles. These wines are great when young, but even better with bottle age. ▼▼▼▽ **1999** Something seems to have happened to the botrytis mould in 1999, for the wine has an odd, non-varietal, waxy aroma. The palate is certainly complex and well balanced, and prior vintages of this wine suggest it will mature very well in bottle, perhaps throwing off those errant aromas. **rating:** 81

best drinking 2004–2010 **best vintages** '82, '87, '91, '92, '96 **drink with** Poached fruit • $25

Moorilla Estate Black Label Pinot Noir

The third tier of the Moorilla Pinot Noir structure, coming underneath the White Label Pinot Noir and ultimately the Reserve Pinot, a three-tiered classification which was introduced in 1997. ▼▼▼▽ **1999** Medium red-purple; the bouquet has a mix of funky/gamey characters on the one hand and spicy/plummy on the other. The palate has plenty of character, but I, for one, find the gamey bits a little too strong for comfort. **rating:** 82

best drinking 2000–2003 **best vintages** NA **drink with** Game, of course • $22

Moorilla Estate Reserve Pinot Noir

First introduced into the Moorilla Estate range in 1996, and usually has been significantly superior to the varietal releases. ▼▼▼▽ **1998** Medium to full red-purple; the bouquet is redolent of spicy/gamey aromas strongly suggesting whole-bunch carbonic maceration, characters which come through stridently on the palate. Preference (and points) with a wine such as this will depend entirely on the personal tastes of the observer. For me, the carbonic maceration characters are overdone. **rating:** 82

best drinking 2000–2003 **best vintages** '96, '97 **drink with** Venison • $47

Moorilla Estate White Label Pinot Noir

As if to underline the vast changes for the better since the arrival of Alain Rousseau, the '98 was the top (and only) gold medal winner in the 1998 Pinot Noir Class at the 1999 Tasmanian Wines Show. The '99 is a worthy successor, if not quite in the same class. ▼▼▼▼ **1999** Light to medium red-purple; the bouquet is fragrant but clean, with gently sappy fruit replete with spicy edges. Lively, fresh, bright cherry and plum fruit leads the palate, with hints of the more savoury characters of the bouquet, which will evolve with time. **rating:** 88

best drinking 2001–2005 **best vintages** '84, '86, '90, '91, '92, '98 **drink with** Quail • $26

Moorilla Estate Cabernet Sauvignon

Deservedly, a gold and trophy winner at the Tasmanian Wines Show 2000, offering a degree of richness and sweetness seldom seen from Tasmanian Cabernet. A convincing demonstration of the all-round skills of Alain Rousseau. ▼▼▼▼▼ **1998** Excellent, bright but deep purple-red. The bouquet is rich and ripe with concentrated cassis fruit and barely perceptible oak. The palate is commensurately rich and ripe, oozing blackcurrant fruit and sustained by ripe tannins on the finish. **rating:** 95

best drinking 2003–2013 **best vintages** '98 **drink with** Marinated venison • $28

moorooduc estate ★★★★☆

501 Derril Road, Moorooduc, Vic 3936 **region** Mornington Peninsula
phone (03) 9696 4130 **fax** (03) 9696 2841 **open** First weekend each month 12–5
winemaker Dr Richard McIntyre **production** 7000 **est.** 1983
product range ($19–45 R) Sauvignon Blanc, Chardonnay, Pinot Noir, Cabernet; also Devil Bend Creek Chardonnay and Pinot Noir.

summary Dr Richard McIntyre regularly produces one of the richest and most complex Chardonnays in the region, with grapefruit/peach fruit set against sumptuous spicy oak, and that hallmark soft nutty/creamy/regional texture. As well as retail distribution, the wines are exported to Japan.

Moorooduc Estate Chardonnay

Dr Richard McIntyre has worked ceaselessly to refine the style of his Chardonnays; initially the malolactic fermentation was very evident but has now been reined in without sacrificing complexity.

▼▼▼▼ **1998** Medium yellow-green; the bouquet is clean and quite fragrant, with nectarine and white peach fruit sustained by subtle oak. The palate is typically restrained yet stylish, with minimal mlf influence; should develop well in bottle. **rating:** 90

best drinking 2001–2008 **best vintages** '88, '90, '91, '92, '93, '94, '95, '97, '98 **drink with** Grilled spatchcock • $30

Moorooduc Estate Devil Bend Creek Chardonnay

Effectively the third label for Moorooduc Estate, unwooded but made using relatively sophisticated techniques.

▼▼▼▼ **1998** Light to medium yellow-green; the bouquet is fragrant, with a mix of citrus, melon and grapefruit aromas; the palate has length, life and intensity, much better than the run-of-the-mill unwooded style. **rating:** 88

best drinking 2000–2004 **best vintages** NA **drink with** Pork chops • $19

Moorooduc Estate Wild Yeast Chardonnay

1998 was the first commercial release of a so-called 'wild yeast' ferment by Moorooduc, following successful trials in earlier vintages.

▼▼▼▼ **1998** Excellent green-yellow; the bouquet is clean, with slightly subdued fruit showing hints of nut and mineral; subtle oak. The magic of the wine is on the palate, where the subtle interplay of flavours makes it difficult to know whether the extra touch of class comes from superior grapes or the wild yeast ferment. **rating:** 92

best drinking 2002–2008 **best vintages** '98 **drink with** Grilled spatchcock • $45

Moorooduc Estate Devil Bend Creek Pinot Noir

This is an exceptionally good wine for what is, in effect, a second label, first introduced from the 1998 vintage.

▼▼▼▼ **1998** Light purple-red; the bouquet is clean and fresh, with a mix of strawberry and stemmy fruit. The palate is commensurately clean and fresh, with strawberry/cherry fruit in an uncomplicated early-drinking style. **rating:** 87

best drinking 2000–2001 **best vintages** NA **drink with** Pastrami/antipasto • $19

Moorooduc Estate Shiraz

Moorooduc has been experimenting with Shiraz for a number of years, finally moving to small-scale commercial production. Even in warm years such as 1998, the very cool climate impacts on the wine.

▼▼▼▼ **1998** Medium red-purple; fragrant, light leafy/spicy aromas lead logically into an ultra-cool-climate style on the palate, at the opposite end of the planet to the typical Australian Shiraz. **rating:** 86

best drinking 2002–2005 **best vintages** NA **drink with** Roast pigeon • $30

morning cloud wines   NR

15 Ocean View Avenue, Red Hill South, Vic 3937 **region** Mornington Peninsula
phone (03) 5989 2762 **fax** (03) 5989 2700 **open** By appointment
winemaker Lindsay McCall (Contract) **production** 300 **est.** 1983
product range ($18 R) Chardonnay, Cabernet Sauvignon.
summary Morning Cloud Wines (previously Cloud Valley) is a joint venture between Kathy and Bill Allen and Peter and Judy Maxwell. Each family has its own vineyard at Red Hill South, and the grapes are pooled and the wine made under contract at Stonier's Winery. The Cabernet Sauvignon tends to be very leafy in Chinon-style; the Chardonnay, medium-bodied crisp and citrus-tinged.

morningside wines   ★★★★

RMB 3002 Middle Tea Tree Road, Tea Tree, Tas 7017 **region** Southern Tasmania
phone (03) 6268 1748 **fax** (03) 6268 1748 **open** By appointment
winemaker Peter Bosworth **production** 500 **est.** 1980
product range ($13–20 ML) Riesling, Pinot Noir, Chardonnay, Cabernet Sauvignon.
summary The name 'Morningside' was given to the old property on which the vineyard stands because it gets the morning sun first — the property on the other side of the valley was known as 'Eveningside' — and,

consistently with the observation of the early settlers, the Morningside grapes achieve full maturity with good colour and varietal flavour. Production is as yet tiny but will increase as the 2-hectare vineyard matures. Retail distribution through Sutherland Cellars, Melbourne.

mornington vineyards estate   ★★★

Moorooduc Road, Moorooduc South, Vic 3933 **region** Mornington Peninsula
phone (03) 5974 2097 **fax** (03) 5974 2097 **open** Weekends and public holidays 11–5
winemaker Hugh Robinson **production** 1500 **est.** 1989
product range ($17–28 CD) Chardonnay, Sauvignon Blanc, Pinot Noir, Shiraz.
summary As with so many Mornington Peninsula vineyards, a high degree of viticultural expertise, care and attention is needed to get to first base. With a little over 20 hectares in production, it is one of the larger vineyards on the Peninsula but sells a significant portion of its grapes. The eternal problem of cork taint to one side, the wines tend to be on the light side.

morris   ★★★★★

Mia Mia Road, Rutherglen, Vic 3685 **region** Rutherglen and Glenrowan
phone (02) 6026 7303 **fax** (02) 6026 7445 **open** Mon–Sat 9–5, Sun 10–5
winemaker David Morris **production** NFP **est.** 1859
product range ($12.95–45 R) A limited range of table wines, sparingly distributed, the most important of which is the red wine Durif and also Shiraz; then fortified wines comprising Mick Morris Old Tawny Port, Liqueur Tokay, Old Premium Liqueur Tokay, Mick Morris Muscat, Old Premium Liqueur Muscat, Mick Morris Commemorative Liqueur Muscat; Old Premium Liqueur Muscat at the top end of the range; and tiny quantities of Show Reserve are released from time to time, mainly ex winery.
summary One of the greatest of the fortified winemakers, some would say the greatest. If you wish to test that view, try the Old Premium Muscat and Old Premium Tokay, which are absolute bargains given their age and quality and which give rise to the winery rating. The table wines are dependable, the white wines all being made by owner Orlando.

Morris Durif

Durif is an exceedingly obscure variety closely related to another grape of similar ilk, peloursin. It may or may not be the same as California's petite syrah; if it is not, Australia is the only country in the world producing wines from it. It is as much for its rarity and for its individuality as its ultimate quality that it is included in my Classic Wines of Australia book.
TTTTY 1997 Medium to full red-purple; the rich bouquet is redolent of dark berries and chocolate; the medium-bodied palate has wonderful texture, structure and flavour, although it would be stretching things to suggest it is elegant. The alcohol is 14 degrees, which, by the standards of the wine, is low but which helps provide the balance.   **rating: 90**
best drinking 2002–2012 **best vintages** '70, '72, '74, '80, '83, '86, '88, '90, '92, '94, '96, '97 **drink with** Biltong • $20

Morris Cabernet Sauvignon

No Geographic Indication is claimed for the wine, which in all probability comes from regions outside northeast Victoria.
TTTY 1997 Medium red, with just a touch of purple; the bouquet has minty/herbaceous characters but the palate is rather better, with substance provided by riper fruit and quite chewy tannins on the finish.   **rating: 80**
best drinking 2002–2007 **best vintages** NA **drink with** Beef pie • $14.95

moss brothers   ★★★☆

Caves Road, Willyabrup, WA 6280 **region** Margaret River
phone (08) 9755 6270 **fax** (08) 9755 6298 **open** 7 days 10–5
winemaker Jane Moss, David Moss **production** 14 000 **est.** 1984
product range ($13.95–27.95 CD) Semillon, Sauvignon Blanc, Unwooded Chardonnay, Barrel Fermented Chardonnay, Moses Rock White, Sauvignon Blanc, Verdelho, NV Maggies Creek Pinot Noir, Shiraz, Cabernet Merlot, Cellar Door Red, Moses Rock Red (the last two unusual blends, Moses Rock including Merlot, Pinot Noir, Grenache, and Cabernet Franc); Bona Vista Ruby.
summary Established by long-term viticulturist Jeff Moss and his family, notably sons Peter and David and Roseworthy graduate daughter Jane. A 100-tonne rammed-earth winery was constructed in 1992 and draws upon both estate-grown and purchased grapes. National wholesale distribution; exports to the UK, Singapore, Malaysia and Belgium.

Moss Brothers Semillon

A quite outstanding wine, the quality of which was largely determined in the vineyard, for it was made in the traditional style, stainless steel-fermented at 13 degrees, and bottled in July of the year of vintage. The '98 was justly rewarded with a gold medal at the 1998 Sheraton Wine Awards, a gold medal at the Sydney International Wine Competition, and was one of the top wines in the 1999 *Winewise* Small Makers Competiton. The '99 is another very good wine.

▼▼▼▼ 1999 Medium yellow-green; powerful, pungent, herbaceous/herb/lemon fruit. The palate is exceptionally powerful, almost painful, crammed with herb and citrus fruit, yet not phenolic.   **rating:** 89

best drinking 2000–2004 **best vintages** '98, '99 **drink with** Fried chicken • $21.95

Moss Brothers Sauvignon Blanc

Another very good wine for Moss Brothers, emphasising the difference between the best wines and the least wines from this winery. Like the Semillon, made without artifice or elaboration.

▼▼▼▼▽ 1999 Light to medium green-yellow; a highly aromatic, floral bouquet with a mix of gooseberry, herb and tropical fruits; these flow through to the flavoursome palate with pristine varietal character and lovely style.   **rating:** 92

best drinking 2000–2002 **best vintages** '99 **drink with** Calamari • $16.95

moss wood   ★★★★★

Metricup Road, Willyabrup, WA 6280 **region** Margaret River
phone (08) 9755 6266 **fax** (08) 9755 6303 **open** By appointment
winemaker Keith Mugford **production** 5500 **est.** 1969
product range ($25–75 R) Semillon, Wood Matured Semillon, Chardonnay, Cabernet Sauvignon, Pinot Noir.
summary Widely regarded as one of the best wineries in the region, capable of producing glorious Semillon (the best outside the Hunter Valley) in both oaked and unoaked forms, unctuous Chardonnay and elegant, gently herbaceous, superfine Cabernet Sauvignon which lives for many years. Exports to the UK, the US, Switzerland, Germany, Denmark, Belgium, France, Japan, Hong Kong, Indonesia, Malaysia, Singapore and New Zealand.

Moss Wood Semillon

As with all the Moss Wood wines, entirely estate-grown and produced from 1.35 hectares of fully mature vines (the first vintage was 1977). After many years of making both an oaked and unoaked version, Keith Mugford has settled for the unoaked wine and relied on the patience of his fanatically loyal band of customers.

▼▼▼▼ 1999 Light to medium yellow-green; the bouquet is clean, light and crisp, tending more to mineral than herbal citrus. The palate is well balanced and smooth, yet to open up its underlying fruit character.   **rating:** 89

best drinking 2003–2008 **best vintages** '81, '82, '83, '84, '86, '87, '92, '94, '95, '97, '98, '99 **drink with** Crab, lobster • $23.50

mountadam   ★★★★☆

High Eden Road, High Eden Ridge, SA 5235 **region** Eden Valley
phone (08) 8564 1101 **fax** (08) 8361 3400 **open** 7 days 11–4
winemaker Adam Wynn, Andrew Ewart **production** 35 000 **est.** 1972
product range ($12.25–60 R) Under the premium Mountadam label, Riesling, Chardonnay, Pinot Noir, The Red (50 per cent Merlot, 50 per cent Cabernet), Merlot, Cabernet Sauvignon, Pinot Noir Chardonnay Brut; under the David Wynn label Riesling, Sauvignon Blanc, Chardonnay, Pinot Noir, Shiraz, Patriarch Shiraz, Cabernet Sauvignon; under organically grown Eden Ridge label, Sauvignon Blanc, Cabernet Sauvignon; also Ratafia Riesling and Chardonnay.
summary One of the leading small wineries, founded by David Wynn and run by winemaker son Adam Wynn, initially offering only the Mountadam range at relatively high prices. The subsequent development of the three ranges of wines has been very successful, judged both by the winemaking and wine-marketing viewpoint. Mountadam has built up an extensive export network over many years, with the US, Canada, Hong Kong, Japan and the UK being the major markets, but extending across the breadth of Europe and most Asian markets.

Mountadam David Wynn Riesling

Produced from relatively low-yielding old vines situated high in the Eden Valley.

▼▼▼▽ 1998 Medium yellow-green; a very rich and potent bouquet with concentrated lime juice aromas is followed by a palate with abundant flavour which, however, hangs around on the finish.   **rating:** 84

best drinking 2000–2003 **best vintages** NA **drink with** Sugar-cured tuna • $13

Mountadam Pinot Noir

The high Eden Valley climate is very marginal for Pinot Noir; the handful of wines made from the variety have seldom shown much, if any, finesse.

▼▼▼▽ **1998** Medium purple-red; there are some gamey aspects to the aroma, but overall the style tends more to dry red than varietal Pinot. The palate has firm plummy fruit, but a slightly hard finish detracts. May soften with time, but so may the fruit. **rating: 83**

best drinking 2000–2003 **best vintages** NA **drink with** Rabbit pie •$36

Mountadam David Wynn Patriarch Shiraz

In my view, has been the outstanding red wine from Mountadam, year in, year out, other than the difficult 1995 vintage. The grapes are produced from low-yielding Eden Valley vineyards established on sandy soils, and the wine is matured in a mix of American and French oak barrels for 12 months.

▼▼▼▼ **1997** Medium to full red; the bouquet is quite intense, with dark cherry and plum fruit supported by a dash of sweet oak. The wine is soft and round in the mouth with seductive velvety mouthfeel the best part of an impressive wine. **rating: 89**

best drinking 2001–2006 **best vintages** '90, '91, '93, '94, '96, '97 **drink with** Barbecued beef •$37

Mountadam Merlot

Merlot has been planted at Mountadam since 1984, but in all vintages prior to 1996, the Merlot was blended into The Red. Increased plantings have now resulted in the release of a 100 per cent Merlot, aged for 12 months in French barriques and given additional maturation time prior to release.

▼▼▼▼▽ **1997** Medium to full red; a nice wine, with complex spicy/tobacco overtones to a core of sweet berry fruit to the bouquet. A soft though complex palate with sweet fruit dominant. Slightly forward, but I like the overall effect and texture. **rating: 90**

best drinking 2000–2005 **best vintages** NA **drink with** Roast veal •$60

Mountadam Cabernet Sauvignon

Estate-grown, and aged in French Troncais oak barriques for 18 months. After an excellent '96, the '97 is very ordinary.

▼▼▼▽ **1997** Light to medium red; the bouquet is quite leafy, even to the extent of a hint of lemon peel. The palate ranges through leafy, foresty and savoury flavours, with soft tannins on the finish. **rating: 80**

▼▼▼▽ **1996** Medium red-purple; pleasant berry and earth fruit aromas are replicated on the palate, with the addition of a touch of chocolate; ripe tannins and subtle oak handling throughout are additional features of a good wine. **rating: 91**

best drinking 2001–2005 **best vintages** '90, '91, '95, '96 **drink with** Lamb cutlets •$36

mountain creek wines   NR

Mountain Creek Road, Moonambel, Vic 3478 **region** Pyrenees
phone (03) 5467 2230 **fax** (03) 5467 2230 **open** Weekends, holidays 10–7
winemaker Contract **production** 500 **est.** 1973
product range ($10–16 CD) Sauvignon Blanc, Sparkling Passion, Cabernet Shiraz, Frontignac, Muscat.
summary Brian Cherry acquired the Mountain Creek Vineyard in 1975 and has extended it to a total of 13 hectares. The first wine was made in 1987, all or part of the grapes before and in some years since then were sold to other Pyrenees wineries. The wine is made under contract and shows all of the substance and weight for which the district is renowned.

mount alexander vineyard   ★★

Calder Highway, North Harcourt, Vic 3453 **region** Bendigo
phone (03) 5474 2262 **fax** (03) 5474 2553 **open** 7 days 10–5.30
winemaker Keith Walkden **production** 6000 **est.** 1984
product range ($10–14 CD) A wide range of various table wines, sparkling, fortifieds, meads and liqueurs.
summary A substantial operation with large vineyards with 17 hectares planted to all the right varieties. It is several years since I have tasted the wines, but a recent report gives me no reason to suppose they have changed much.

mount anakie wines ★★☆

Staughton Vale Road, Anakie, Vic 3221 **region** Geelong
phone (03) 5284 1452 **fax** (03) 5284 1405 **open** Tues–Sun 11–6
winemaker Otto Zambelli **production** 6000 **est.** 1968
product range ($10–18 R) Biancone, Riesling, Semillon, Chardonnay, Dolcetto, Shiraz, Cabernet Franc, Cabernet Sauvignon.
summary Also known as Zambelli Estate and once produced some excellent wines (under its various ownerships and winemakers), all distinguished by their depth and intensity of flavour. No recent tastings; prior to that, the wines tasted were but a shadow of their former quality. The level of activity seems relatively low.

mount avoca vineyard ★★★☆

Moates Lane, Avoca, Vic 3467 **region** Pyrenees
phone (03) 5465 3282 **fax** (03) 5465 3544 **open** Mon–Fri 9–5, weekends 10–5
winemaker Matthew Barry **production** 15 000 **est.** 1970
product range ($12.30–32 R) Sauvignon Blanc, Chardonnay, Rhapsody, Trioss, Shiraz, Cabernet; Reserve range of Merlot, Shiraz and Cabernet Franc.
summary A substantial winery which has for long been one of the stalwarts of the Pyrenees region, and is steadily growing, with 23.7 hectares of vineyards. There has been a significant refinement in the style and flavour of the red wines over the past few years. Suspect a lot of worthwhile work has gone into barrel selection and maintenance.

Mount Avoca Shiraz

Produced from a little over 6 hectares of relatively low-yielding estate plantings. The wine spends 8–12 months in a mix of older French and new American oak barrels.
▼▼▼▼ **1998** Medium red-purple; the moderately intense bouquet offers a smooth mix of berry, earth, vanilla and chocolate characters which carry on to the palate where they are joined by cherry/berry fruit, balanced tannins and subtle oak. A nice wine. **rating:** 86
best drinking 2002–2007 **best vintages** NA **drink with** Marinated beef • $17.60

Mount Avoca Reserve Shiraz

Part of the newly-introduced range of small parcels of ultra-premium wines released after extended barrel and bottle maturation, and only in years which warrant a special release.
▼▼▼▽ **1997** Medium red-purple; the bouquet is soft, with plenty of sweet vanilla aromas, part oak and part fruit. There is cherry and mint on entry to the mouth, but the wine toughens up on the slightly rough-edged finish. **rating:** 83
best drinking 2002–2007 **best vintages** NA **drink with** Braised ox cheek • $32

Mount Avoca Reserve Cabernet Franc

Much of the cabernet franc planted in Victoria in the 1970s and '80s was originally thought to be merlot. The main virtue of the variety is consistent berry set and generous yields, but this wine shows it can offer more than just quantity.
▼▼▼▼ **1996** Medium red; there is clearly recognisable varietal character on the cedary/leafy bouquet; the relatively light and soft body has some affinities with Cabernet Franc from the Loire Valley of France; sweet, fine tannins provide a particularly attractive finish. **rating:** 85
best drinking 2000–2005 **best vintages** '96 **drink with** Pan-fried veal • $32

Mount Avoca Cabernet

Produced from 4 hectares of estate-grown grapes. Since 1995 the wine has moved from a straight Cabernet Sauvignon to 85 per cent Cabernet Sauvignon with 15 per cent Merlot and Cabernet Franc included. This change has also coincided with the eradication of some errant barrel-derived characters.
▼▼▼▽ **1997** Medium red-purple; the bouquet tends to the earthy/leafy spectrum together with a dusting of spice. The palate has savoury sweetness and the back palate, in particular, has complexity and strength, with nice spicy tannins rounding off the finish. **rating:** 84
best drinking 2002–2010 **best vintages** '88, '90, '91, '92, '93, '95, '97 **drink with** Char-grilled steak • $20.60

mount beckworth ★★★☆

RMB 915 Learmonth Road, Tourello via Ballarat, Vic 3363 **region** Ballarat
phone (03) 5343 4207 **fax** (03) 5343 4207 **open** Weekends 10–6 and by appointment
winemaker Paul Lesock **production** 800 **est.** 1984
product range ($14–16 CD) Chardonnay, Pinot Noir, Shiraz, Cabernet Merlot, Cabernets.
summary The 4-hectare Mount Beckworth vineyard was planted between 1984 and 1985, but it was not until 1995 that the full range of wines under the Mount Beckworth label appeared. Until that time much of the production was sold to Seppelt Great Western for sparkling wine use. It is owned and managed by Paul Lesock, who studied viticulture at Charles Sturt University, and his wife Jane. The wines reflect the very cool climate. Limited Victorian retail distribution.

Mount Beckworth Pinot Noir

Produced from 1.2 hectares of estate plantings. The '96 was an impressive wine, winning well-deserved silver medals at the 1997 Ballarat and Hobart Wine Shows. The 1998 did even better, winning a gold medal at the Victorian Wines Show in the year of its vintage.

▼▼▼▼ **1998** Slightly opaque colour, suggesting the wine is not filtered. The bouquet is essentially in the sappy/foresty spectrum, going through a phase with diminished aromatics. On the other hand, the palate is surprisingly intense and long even if, like the bouquet, it is at the austere fruit end of the spectrum. It is a style which regularly polarises opinion. **rating:** 85

best drinking 2000–2002 **best vintages** '96, '98 **drink with** Venison ragout • $16

mount charlie winery NR

228 Mount Charlie Road, Riddells Creek, Vic 3431 **region** Macedon Ranges
phone (03) 5428 6946 **fax** (03) 5428 6946 **open** Sun by appointment
winemaker Trefor Morgan **production** 500 **est.** 1991
product range ($20 ML) Sauvignon Blanc, Chardonnay, Red (Cabernet Shiraz blend).
summary Mount Charlie's wines are sold principally through mail order and through selected restaurants. A futures programme encourages mailing list sales with a discount of over 25 per cent on the ultimate release price. Trefor Morgan is particularly pleased with the quality of the 1998 wines, the product of a great year in Macedon.

mount duneed ★★☆

Feehan's Road, Mount Duneed, Vic 3216 **region** Geelong
phone (03) 5264 1281 **fax** (03) 5264 1281 **open** Public holidays and weekends 11–5 or by appointment
winemaker Ken Campbell, John Darling **production** 1000 **est.** 1970
product range ($10–18 CD) Semillon, Sauvignon Blanc, Riesling, Botrytis Semillon, Malbec, Cabernet Malbec, Cabernet Sauvignon.
summary Rather idiosyncratic wines are the order of the day, some of which can develop surprisingly well in bottle; the Botrytis Noble Rot Semillon has, from time to time, been of very high quality. A significant part of the production from the 7.5 hectares of vineyards is sold to others.

✿ mount eyre vineyard NR

Wollombi Road, Broke, NSW 2330 **region** Lower Hunter Valley
phone (02) 6579 1087 **fax** (02) 6579 1087 **open** Tastings at Broke Store
winemaker Simon Gilbert (Contract) **production** NA **est.** 1996
product range NA.
summary The 20-hectare estate at Broke is planted to semillon, chardonnay, shiraz, cabernet franc and cabernet sauvignon, the wines being made by Simon Gilbert at Muswellbrook. The wines are available for tasting (and purchase) at the Broke Store.

mountford NR

Bamess Road, West Pemberton, WA 6260 **region** Pemberton, Warren Valley and Manjimup
phone (08) 9776 1345 **fax** (08) 9776 1345 **open** 7 days 10–4
winemaker Andrew Mountford **production** 3000 **est.** 1987
product range ($16.50–28.50 R) Sauvignon Blanc, Chardonnay, Blanc de Noir, Pinot Noir, Merlot Cabernet Sauvignon.
summary English-born and trained Andrew Mountford and wife Sue migrated to Australia in 1983, first endeavouring to set up a winery at Mudgee and thereafter moving to Pemberton with far greater success. Their strikingly packaged wines (complete with beeswax and paper seals) have been well received in eastern Australian markets, being produced from 6 hectares of permanently netted, dry-grown vineyards.

mount gisborne wines   NR

5 Waterson Road, Gisborne, Vic 3437 **region** Macedon Ranges
phone (03) 5428 2834 **fax** (03) 5428 2834 **open** By appointment
winemaker Stuart Anderson **production** 1200 **est.** 1987
product range ($10–24 CD) Chardonnay, Dessert Chardonnay, Pinot Noir, Pinot Noir Limited Release.
summary Mount Gisborne Wines is very much a weekend and holiday occupation for proprietor David Ell, who makes the wines from the 6-hectare vineyard under the watchful and skilled eye of industry veteran Stuart Anderson, now living in semi-retirement high in the Macedon Hills.

mount horrocks   ★★★★

The Old Railway Station, Curling Street, Auburn, SA 5451 **region** Clare Valley
phone (08) 8849 2243 **fax** (08) 8849 2243 **open** Weekends and public holidays 10–5
winemaker Stephanie Toole **production** 5000 **est.** 1982
product range ($21.95–35.95 R) Watervale Riesling, Chardonnay, Semillon, Semillon Sauvignon Blanc, Cordon Cut Riesling, Cabernet Merlot, Shiraz.
summary Mount Horrocks has well and truly established its own identity in recent years, aided by positive marketing and, equally importantly, wine quality which has resulted in both show success and critical acclaim. Exports to New Zealand, the UK, the US, Belgium and Japan.

Mount Horrocks Watervale Riesling

Mount Horrocks was originally the wine-production end of the Ackland Brothers' extensive vineyard holdings. The two have now effectively been split, and Mount Horrocks is dependent on contract-grown grapes through the Watervale region. Sourced from two growers in the Watervale subdistrict of the Clare Valley who continue to both hand-prune and hand-pick their vines.
▼▼▼▽ **1999** Light green-yellow; as almost always, I have trouble coming to grips with the slightly burnt fermentation aromas which seem to be the hallmark of this wine. There is solid flavour on the palate, but once again haunted by the ghost of fermentation.   **rating: 84**
best drinking 2000–2003 **best vintages** '86, '87, '90, '93, '94, '97 **drink with** Thai or Chinese soup • $21.95

mount ida   ★★★★

Northern Highway, Heathcote, Vic 3253 **region** Bendigo
phone NA **open** Not
winemaker Nick Walker **production** 3000 **est.** 1978
product range ($30 R) Shiraz.
summary Established by the famous artist Leonard French and Dr James Munro but purchased by Tisdall after the 1987 bushfires and thereafter by Mildara Blass when it acquired Tisdall. Up to the time of the fires, wonderfully smooth, rich red wines with almost voluptuous sweet, minty fruit were the hallmark. After a brief period during which the name was used as a simple brand (with various wines released) has returned to a single estate-grown wine, sharing similar packaging with Mount Helen.

Mount Ida Shiraz

A single-vineyard wine produced from an estate established by noted Australian artist Leonard French, but which was acquired by Tisdall in the 1980s. Produced in limited quantities but well worth the search. Smart new packaging, bringing it into line with the Mount Helen releases, was introduced in 1997. In that year the '96 vintage won four gold medals.
▼▼▼▼ **1997** Medium red-purple; the exceptionally aromatic bouquet assails you with lantana/flowery fruit with high-toned toasty oak. The palate is a reflection of the bouquet, with tangy, spicy/leafy fruit which seems to have some of the characters one associates with white wines, although there is no question it all comes from shiraz. Some interesting things must have happened in the vineyard.   **rating: 85**
best drinking 2002–2007 **best vintages** NA **drink with** Australian Parmesan • $NA

mountilford   NR

Mount Vincent Road, Ilford, NSW 2850 **region** Mudgee
phone (02) 6358 8544 **fax** (02) 6358 8544 **open** 7 days 10–4
winemaker Don Cumming **production** NFP **est.** 1985
product range ($10–22 CD) Rhine Riesling, Gewürztraminer, Chardonnay, Highland White, Windamere, Sylvaner, Jubilation Cabernet Shiraz, Pinot Shiraz, Sir Alexander Port.
summary Surprisingly large cellar-door operation which has grown significantly over the past few years. I have not, however, had the opportunity of tasting the wines.

mount langi ghiran vineyards ★★★★★

Warrak Road, Buangor, Vic 3375 **region** Grampians
phone (03) 5354 3207 **fax** (03) 5354 3277 **open** Mon–Fri 9–5, weekends 12–5
winemaker Trevor Mast, Andrew McLoughney **production** 25 000 **est.** 1969
product range ($18–52 R) Chardonnay, Riesling, Pinot Gris; under Langi label Shiraz and Cabernet Merlot.
summary A maker of outstanding cool-climate peppery Shiraz, crammed with flavour and vinosity, and very good Cabernet Sauvignon. The Shiraz points the way for cool-climate examples of the variety, for weight, texture and fruit richness all accompany the vibrant pepper-spice aroma and flavour. Now partly owned by Trevor Mast, and partly by German wine entrepreneur Riquet Hess; the most tangible sign of the partnership has been the erection of a totally new, state-of-the-art winery, not to mention the expansion of the estate vineyards to over 70 hectares and the establishment of an export network throughout the US, the UK, Asia, Europe, New Zealand and Canada.

Mount Langi Ghiran Riesling

Always generously flavoured with an extra degree of weight which compensates for any lack of finesse.
♥♥♥♡ **1998** Medium to full yellow-green; a solid bouquet but lacks varietal sparkle; a pleasant wine, solid, with no fault, but lacking the zip of the best wines in its price bracket. **rating:** 84

best drinking 2000–2003 **best vintages** NA **drink with** Rich seafood; Asian • $20

Mount Langi Ghiran Pinot Gris

Although the label is not absolutely explicit on the point, I assume it does come from estate-grown grapes at Mount Langi Ghiran. If so, it certainly extends the area in which pinot grigio can flourish, for this is a good wine.
♥♥♥♥ **1999** Medium yellow-green; the bouquet has intensity, with distinct mineral tones, the palate having the distinct fruit weight and intensity of the variety; some minerally flavours run through the moderately long finish. **rating:** 86

best drinking 2000–2004 **best vintages** NA **drink with** Antipasto • $22

Langi Cabernet Merlot

Another good, estate-grown wine from Mount Langi Ghiran, perhaps lacking the sheer brilliance of the Shiraz, but that is hardly surprising.
♥♥♥♥♡ **1997** Strong red-purple; a concentrated bouquet with savoury/earthy/berry aromas is followed by a strong, rich palate with ripe berry fruit, well-balanced and integrated oak, and excellent tannins on the finish. **rating:** 91

best drinking 2002–2012 **best vintages** '97 **drink with** Rare fillet of beef • $42

Mount Langi Ghiran Joanna Cabernet Sauvignon

Produced from some of the oldest vines in the Wrattonbully region; Joanna was one of the possible alternative names. The vineyard is under contract to Mount Langi Ghiran for 18 years, and 1997 was the inaugural vintage. The grapes are transported to Langi Ghiran, open-fermented and hand-plunged before being matured in French oak barriques for 12 months.
♥♥♥♡ **1997** Medium to full red-purple; ripe fruit on the bouquet runs through blackcurrant, prune, mulberry and herb aromas. A juicy, fruit-driven style on the palate, with lively spice, herb and blackcurrant flavours. **rating:** 84
best drinking 2002–2007 **best vintages** NA **drink with** Rare roast beef • $30.60

mt lofty ranges vineyard ★★★★

Harris Road, Lenswood, SA 5240 **region** Adelaide Hills
phone (08) 8389 8339 **fax** (08) 8389 8349 **open** Weekends 11–5
winemaker Nepenthe (Contract) **production** 800 **est.** 1992
product range ($14–20 CD) Five Vines Riesling, Sauvignon Blanc, Chardonnay, Old Pump Shed Pinot Noir.
summary Mount Lofty Ranges is owned by Alan Herath and Jan Reed, who have been involved from the outset in planting, training and nurturing the 4.5-hectare vineyard. Both have professional careers, but are intending to become full-time vignerons in the not too distant future. Skilled winemaking by Peter Leske at Nepenthe has already brought rewards and recognition to the vineyard.

Mt Lofty Ranges Vineyard Five Vines Riesling

The 1 hectare of estate plantings have five different clones of riesling, hence the slightly ambiguous (even misleading) name. The 1999 was the top gold medal winner in the Riesling class at the 1999 Adelaide Hills Wine Show, ironically edging out the Nepenthe Riesling (which also received a gold medal) for first place.

▼▼▼▼▽ **1999** Light green-yellow; classic, youthful Riesling, with restrained slatey/mineral and faintly spicy overtones, strongly reminiscent of young Clare Valley Riesling. The palate is crisp, dry and minerally, still delicate, but long in the mouth.   **rating:** 94

best drinking 2004–2009 **drink with** Vegetable terrine • $14

Mt Lofty Ranges Vineyard Old Pump Shed Pinot Noir

The 1.8 hectares of pinot noir is planted to no less than 12 different clones, including all of the new Burgundy clones from Dijon. This should ensure a fascinating resource to work with as the vines mature.

▼▼▼▼ **1998** Light to medium red-purple; cherry and plum fruit aromas of medium intensity are a pleasant opening, but it is on the palate that the wine shows its class, with beautifully balanced and stylish fruit and oak, and a long and powerful finish.   **rating:** 89

best drinking 2000–2005 **drink with** Braised ox cheek • $20

mount macedon   NR

Bawden Road, Mount Macedon, Vic 3441 **region** Macedon Ranges
phone (03) 5427 2735 **fax** (03) 5427 1071 **open** Mon–Fri 9–5, weekends 10–5
winemaker Ian Deacon **production** 1500 **est.** 1989
product range ($15–35 CD) Unwooded Chardonnay, Chardonnay, Winemaker's Reserve Chardonnay, Pinot Noir Saignee Rosé, Pinot Noir, Shiraz, Sparkling.
summary Don and Pam Ludbey have established a substantial operation at Mount Macedon drawing upon two separate vineyards, Mount Macedon and Hay Hill. In all, they have 12.5 hectares under vine and also operate a restaurant during the weekend. Ian Deacon has made wine in the Yarra Valley and surrounding cool regions for many years; his experience shows through in the wines which, while not particularly rich or full, have a touch of elegance.

Mount Macedon Winemaker's Reserve Chardonnay

Produced from estate plantings with three traditional clones of chardonnay, the vineyard now being over ten years old. A bronze medal winner at the 1999 Seymour Wine Show.

▼▼▼▽ **1998** Light to medium yellow-green; the bouquet is clean and fresh, with delicate citrus and nectarine fruit together with more minerally notes. The same interplay of flavours occurs on the light- to medium-bodied palate; oak handling has been appropriately restrained throughout.   **rating:** 83

best drinking 2000–2004 **best vintages** NA **drink with** Lighter fish dishes • $22

🐞 mount majura wines   ★★★★

RMB 311 Majura Road, Majura, ACT 2609 **region** Canberra District
phone (02) 9222 3100 **fax** (02) 9222 3124 **open** Not
winemaker Dr Roger Harris **production** 500 **est.** 1988
product range ($15–25 R) Chardonnay, Merlot.
summary The first vines were planted in 1988 by Dinny Killen on a site on her family property which had been especially recommended by Dr Edgar Riek; its attractions were red soil of volcanic origin over limestone, the reasonably steep east and northeast slopes providing an element of frost protection. The 1–hectare vineyard was planted to pinot noir, chardonnay and merlot in equal quantities; the pinot noir grapes were sold to Lark Hill and used in their award-winning Pinot Noir, while the Chardonnay and Merlot were made for Mount Majura by Lark Hill, both wines enjoying show success. In 1999 a private syndicate purchased the property, and retained Roger Harris of Brindabella Hills as winemaker and consultant. Another 5 hectares of vineyard was established in the spring of 1999. The quality of the 1998 wines (made at Lark Hill) is impressive to say the least. One can only imagine that even better things are in store for the future.

mount mary   ★★★★★

Coldstream West Road, Lilydale, Vic 3140 **region** Yarra Valley
phone (03) 9739 1761 **fax** (03) 9739 0137 **open** Not
winemaker Dr John Middleton, Mac Forbes **production** 3000 **est.** 1971
product range ($32–60 ML) Chardonnay, Triolet (Sauvignon Blanc, Semillon, Muscadelle), Pinot Noir, Cabernets Quintet (Bordeaux-blend).

summary Superbly refined, elegant and intense Cabernets and usually outstanding and long-lived Pinot Noirs fully justify Mount Mary's exalted reputation. The Triolet blend is very good, more recent vintages of Chardonnay likewise. However, John Middleton does not believe in wine critics, and least of all myself, so no (official) tastings. Limited quantities of the wines are sold through the wholesale/retail distribution system in Victoria, New South Wales, Queensland and South Australia.

mount panorama winery   NR

117 Mountain Straight, Mount Panorama, Bathurst, NSW 2795 **region** Other Wineries of NSW
phone (02) 6331 5368 **fax** (02) 6331 5368 **open** By appointment
winemaker Bill Stuart, Deborah Stuart **production** 600 **est.** 1991
product range ($11.50–20 CD) Forrest Elbow Riesling, Chase Chardonnay, Hell Corner Shiraz, The Esses Cabernet Sauvignon, The Cutting (Cabernet blend), Thunder Mountain Port.
summary For all the obvious reasons, Mount Panorama Winery makes full use of its setting on Mountain Straight after the 'Hell Corner' on the inside of the famous motor racing circuit. Bill and Deborah Stuart are wholly responsible for the production of the wine, from picking and using the hand-operated basket press through to bottling, labelling etc. The '97 wines have had some success at the local (Yass Valley) wine show. They are gradually extending both the size and scope of the cellar-door facilities to take advantage of the tourist opportunities of the site.

mount prior vineyard   ★★★

Gooramadda Road, Rutherglen, Vic 3685 **region** Rutherglen and Glenrowan
phone (02) 6026 5591 **fax** (02) 6026 5590 **open** 7 days 9–5
winemaker Richard Langford **production** 12 000 **est.** 1860
product range ($11–25 CD) Chardonnay, Chenin Blanc, Classic Ibis White, Semillon Chardonnay, Late Picked Riesling, Noble Gold, Classic Ibis Dry Red, Cabernet Merlot, Shiraz, Durif, Sparkling Shiraz/Durif, Brut Cuvée, Port, Muscat, Tokay.
summary A full-scale tourist facility, with yet more in the pipeline. Full accommodation packages at the historic Mount Prior House; a restaurant operating weekends under the direction of Trish Hennessy, with four consecutive *Age Good Food Guide* awards to its credit; picnic and barbecue facilities; and a California-style gift shop. The wines are basically sold through cellar door and an active mailing list. The already substantial 40 hectares of vineyards were expanded by a further 5 hectares of durif planted in 1998, a mark both of the success of Mount Prior and of the interest in Durif.

mount tamborine winery   NR

32 Hartley Road, Mount Tamborine, Qld 4272 **region** South Burnett and Other Wineries of Qld
phone (07) 5545 3981 **fax** (07) 5545 3311 **open** 7 days 10–4
winemaker Brett Hetherington **production** 22 000 **est.** 1993
product range ($9.50–32 ML) Sauvignon Blanc Chardonnay, Semillon, Sauvignon Blanc Semillon, Cedar Ridge Chardonnay, Merlot Emily Cuvée de Rouge, Cedar Ridge Blanc de Blanc, Flaxton Nouveau Shiraz, Tehembrin Merlot, Shiraz Cabernet Merlot, Mountain Muscat, Bush Turkey (Port).
summary Mount Tamborine Winery draws upon 3 hectares of estate plantings adjacent to the winery, 30 hectares in Stanthorpe, and also purchases wine from the King Valley, Cowra and the Riverland to produce a wide range of wine styles. The Chardonnay and Merlot have both had success in Queensland wine shows and competitions, and the wines are sold both locally and exported to Southeast Asia.

mount trio vineyard   ★★★☆

Corner Castle Rock and Porongurup Roads, Porongurup WA 6324 **region** Great Southern
phone (08) 9853 1136 **fax** (08) 9853 1120 **open** By appointment
winemaker Gavin Berry **production** 2000 **est.** 1989
product range ($13.50–18 R) Sauvignon Blanc, Chardonnay, Pinot Noir, Cabernet Merlot.
summary Mount Trio was established by Gavin Berry and Gill Graham shortly after they moved to the Mount Barker district in late 1988. Gavin Berry was assistant winemaker to John Wade, and Gill managed the cellar-door sales. Gavin is now senior winemaker and managing director of Plantagenet, and Gill is the mother of two young children. In the meantime they have slowly built up the Mount Trio business, based in part upon estate plantings of 2 hectares of pinot noir and half a hectare of chardonnay and in part on purchased grapes. An additional 6 hectares was planted in the spring of 1999, and plans are to ultimately increase production to around 5000 cases.

Mount Trio Chardonnay

Comes from a mere half a hectare of estate plantings. Barrel-fermented in French oak, but very much a fruit-driven style.

▼▼▼▼ **1999** Medium yellow green; the bouquet seems to have slightly reductive/slow ferment characters to the intense passionfruit aromas. The palate does not show any of those problems, with citrus, passionfruit and grapefruit flavours balanced by nice acidity. As with the '98, a difficult wine to point. **rating:** 85

best drinking 2001–2004 **best vintages** '98 **drink with** West Australian marron • $15.80

Mount Trio Cabernet Merlot

A blend of 90 per cent Cabernet Sauvignon and 10 per cent Merlot, which effectively replaces the prior Cabernet Shiraz Merlot blend.

▼▼▼▽ **1998** Medium red-purple; the moderately intense bouquet offers a mix of cassis berry fruit with slightly savoury overtones, and minimal oak. The palate is quite firm, with a touch of sweet cassis coming through on the mid-palate, before toughening up a little on the finish. **rating:** 84

best drinking 2003–2008 **best vintages** NA **drink with** Beef in red wine sauce • $17

mount view estate ★★★★

Mount View Road, Mount View, NSW 2325 **region** Lower Hunter Valley
phone (02) 4990 3307 **fax** (02) 4991 1289 **open** Mon–Fri 10–4, weekends, holidays 10–5
winemaker Phillipa Hambleton, Scott Wright **production** 3000 **est.** 1971
product range ($12–26 CD) Verdelho, Reserve Verdelho, Kester Chardonnay, Verdelho Chardonnay, Kester Shiraz, Reserve Shiraz, Cabernet Sauvignon, Cabernet Port, Liqueur Verdelho, Trophy Muscat.
summary Following the involvement of former Rothbury winemaker Keith Tulloch, the overall quality of the wines had improved considerably. Then, with little warning, the winery was sold in February 2000. (For a substantial sum, I understand.) As at the date of going to print, no news of its future direction was available.

mountview wines ★★★

Mount Stirling Road, Glen Aplin, Qld 4381 **region** Granite Belt
phone (07) 4683 4316 **fax** (07) 4683 4111 **open** Wed–Sun 9.30–4.30
winemaker Patrick Fogarty, Scott Wright **production** 1250 **est.** 1990
product range ($10–25 CD) Chardonnay Semillon Sauvignon Blanc, Chardonnay Royal (sparkling), Bianco (sweet white), Cerise (light red), Shiraz, Cabernet Merlot, Sparkling Shiraz.
summary Mountview Wines has changed hands and is now owned by Pauline Stewart. I have no reason to suppose the quality of the Shiraz (in particular) has diminished.

mount vincent mead NR

Common Road, Mudgee, NSW 2850 **region** Mudgee
phone (02) 6372 3184 **fax** (02) 6372 3184 **open** Mon–Sat 10–5, Sun 10–4
winemaker Jane Nevell **production** 2000 **est.** 1972
product range ($13.90–28.80 CD) Does make a Shiraz and a Liqueur Muscat, but is essentially a meadery, with White Box Honey Wine, Napunyah Dry Mead, White Box Dry Mead, Napunyah Medium Sweet, Stringy Bark Sweet, Thistle Sweet Metheglin and Stringy Bark Liqueur Mead. Each of these is vintage-dated.
summary Forget the table wines and concentrate on the meads, which can be absolutely outstanding, dramatically reflecting the impact of the different plants from which the bees have collected their honey.

mount william winery NR

Mount William Road, Tantaraboo, Vic 3764 **region** Macedon Ranges
phone (03) 5429 1595 **fax** (03) 5429 1998 **open** 7 days 11–5
winemaker Murray Cousins, Michael Cope-Williams (Contract) **production** 1500 **est.** 1987
product range ($15–25 CD) Bedbur's Riesling, Chardonnay Semillon, Chardonnay, Pinot Noir, Cabernet Franc, Louis Clare Sparkling Red.
summary Adrienne and Murray Cousins established 6 hectares of vineyards between 1987 and 1992, planted to pinot noir, cabernet franc, semillon and chardonnay. The wines are made under contract (Cope-Williams) and are sold through a stone tasting room cellar-door facility which was completed in 1992, and also through a number of fine wine retailers around Melbourne.

mudgee wines NR

Henry Lawson Drive, Mudgee, NSW 2850 **region** Mudgee
phone (02) 6372 2258 **open** Thur–Mon 10–5, holidays 7 days
winemaker Jennifer Meek **production** 1000 **est.** 1963
product range ($9–15 CD) Chardonnay, Gewurztraminer, Crouchen, Riesling, Rosé, Shiraz, Pinot Noir, Cabernet Sauvignon.
summary All of the wines are naturally fermented with wild yeasts and made without the addition of any chemicals or substances, including SO₂; a very demanding route, particularly with white wines. For some consumers, any shortcoming in quality will be quite acceptable.

munari wines ★★★★

1129 Northern Highway, Heathcote, Vic 3523 **region** Bendigo
phone (03) 5433 3366 **fax** (03) 5433 3095 **open** 7 days 10–5
winemaker Adrian Munari, Deborah Munari **production** 1000 **est.** 1993
product range ($22–25 CD) Ladys Creek Vineyard Chardonnay, Shiraz, Schoolhouse Red, Reserve Merlot, Reserve Malbec.
summary Adrian and Deborah Munari made a singularly impressive entry into the winemaking scene, with both their 1997 and 1998 vintage wines winning an impressive array of show medals. With a little over 6.8 hectares of estate vines, production will be limited, but the wines are well worth seeking out.

Munari Ladys Creek Vineyard Chardonnay

Another well-made wine to join the panoply of red wines from Munari. It is barrel-fermented, and matured in French oak for 12 months.
▼▼▼▼ 1998 Medium yellow-green; the clean, moderately intense bouquet offers honey, peach and citrus supported by subtle oak. The fresh, elegant citrus and stone fruit palate has a long finish and, once again, the oak has been well handled. **rating:** 89
best drinking 2000–2003 **best vintages** '98 **drink with** Barbecued yabbies • $22

Munari Shiraz

There is a powerful case for the proposition that Heathcote (which is to receive its own status under the Geographic Indications legislation) is the foremost area in Australia for the production of full-bodied Shiraz.
▼▼▼▼ 1998 Quite dense, full red-purple; the bouquet is very powerful, with slightly gamey overtones to the varietal shiraz. The palate seems to have gone feral, with the gamey flavours over the top. **rating:** 82
best drinking 2000–2003 **best vintages** NA **drink with** Barbecued lamb • $25

Munari Reserve Malbec

A new addition to the Munari range, first made in 1998.
▼▼▼▼ 1998 Medium to full red-purple; big, bold, sweet dark berry fruit floods the bouquet; the palate is richly structured, with glossy/jammy fruit, rather like a Grenache on steroids. Finishes with soft tannins. A gold medal winner at the 1999 Cowra Wine Show. **rating:** 88
best drinking 2002–2010 **best vintages** '98 **drink with** Game pie • $25

Munari Reserve Merlot

The most powerful of a powerhouse range of wines from Munari, obviously picked ripe and equally obviously, from very low-yielding vines. The only question mark is whether this wine really exhibits varietal character.
▼▼▼▼ 1998 Medium to full red-purple; the bouquet is potent, with an array of minty/earthy fruit aromas. The palate is dominated by that rich, Central Victorian mint flavour which appears in some years and not others, and which is regional rather than varietal. Soft, chewy tannins close a nice red wine which is in no sense varietal. **rating:** 84
best drinking 2001–2005 **best vintages** '97 **drink with** Lamb Provençale • $25

⚘ mundrakoona estate NR

Old Hume Highway, Welby via Mittagong, NSW 2575 **region** Other Wineries of NSW
phone (02) 4872 1311 **fax** (02) 4872 1322 **open** Weekends and public holidays
winemaker Anthony Balog **production** 2000 **est.** 1997
product range ($15–25 CD) Sauvignon Blanc, Chardonnay, Pinot Noir, Cabernet Sauvignon.
summary Anthony Balog has progressively planted during 1998 and 1999 3.2 hectares of pinot noir, sauvignon blanc and tempranillo at an altitude of 680 metres. He is using wild yeast ferments, hand-plunging and other

'natural' winemaking techniques with the aim of producing Burgundian-style Pinot and Chardonnay and Bordeaux-style Sauvignon Blanc and Cabernet Sauvignon. For the foreseeable future, estate production will be supplemented by grapes grown from local Southern Highlands vineyards.

🐚 murdoch hill   NR

Mapping Road, Woodside, SA 5244 **region** Adelaide Hills
phone (08) 8389 7081 **fax** (08) 8389 7991 **open** By appointment
winemaker Brian Light (Contract) **production** 1000 **est.** 1998
product range ($19.95–24.95 R) Sauvignon Blanc, Cabernet Sauvignon.
summary A little over 21 hectares of vines have been established on the undulating, gum-studded countryside of the Erinka property, owned by the Downer family, 4 kilometres east of Oakbank. In descending order of importance the varieties established are sauvignon blanc, shiraz, cabernet sauvignon and chardonnay. The wines are distributed by Australian Prestige Wines in Melbourne and Sydney.

Murdoch Hill Sauvignon Blanc
Produced from grapes grown in the Adelaide Hills and McLaren Vale respectively.
TTTY 1999 Light straw-yellow; there are mineral and more tropical aromas in the somewhat muted bouquet; the palate is not particularly intense, but does have gentle mineral-accented varietal fruit running through a wine of moderate length.   **rating:** 83
best drinking 2000–2001 **drink with** Grilled fish • $19.95

murray robson wines   NR

'Bellona' Old North Road, Rothbury, NSW 2335 **region** Lower Hunter Valley
phone (02) 4938 3577 **fax** (02) 4938 3577 **open** 7 days 9–5
winemaker Murray Robson **production** 10 000 **est.** 1970
product range ($18–24 CD) Traminer, Semillon, Chardonnay, Shiraz, Merlot Cabernet, Cabernet Sauvignon.
summary Like a phoenix from the ashes, Murray Robson Wines rises once again, having reopened in its new location in February 1997. Four hectares of estate plantings are supplemented by grapes purchased from other growers in the valley; the initial releases from 1996 were all produced in tiny quantities of 150 cases or less, produced and packaged with the irrepressible flair of Murray Robson and using the same label which appeared back in the early 1970s, each one hand-signed — as ever — by Murray Robson. Exports to the US, the UK and New Zealand.

murrindindi   ★★★★

Cummins Lane, Murrindindi, Vic 3717 **region** Central Victorian Mountain Country
phone (03) 5797 8217 **fax** (03) 5797 8422 **open** Not
winemaker Alan Cuthbertson, Hugh Cuthbertson **production** 2000 **est.** 1979
product range ($22 R) Chardonnay, Cabernets Merlot.
summary Situated in an unequivocally cool climate, which means that special care has to be taken with the viticulture to produce ripe fruit flavours. In more recent vintages, Murrindindi has succeeded handsomely in so doing. Limited Sydney and Melbourne distribution through Wine Source.

murrumbateman winery   NR

Barton Highway, Murrumbateman, NSW 2582 **region** Canberra District
phone (02) 6227 5584 **open** Thur–Mon 10–5
winemaker Duncan Leslie **production** 2000 **est.** 1972
product range ($12–25 CD) Sauvignon Blanc, Unoaked Chardonnay, Sally's Sweet White, Shiraz, Cabernet Sauvignon, Mead, Fortifieds and Sparkling.
summary Revived after a change of ownership, the Murrumbateman Winery draws upon 4.5 hectares of vineyards, and also incorporates an à la carte restaurant and function room, together with picnic and barbecue areas.

🐚 nandroya estate   NR

262 Sandfly Road, Margate, Tas 7054 **region** Southern Tasmania
phone (03) 6267 2377 **open** By appointment
winemaker Andrew Hood (Contract) **production** 250 **est.** 1995
product range ($16.60 CD) Sauvignon Blanc, Pinot Noir.

summary John Rees and family have established half a hectare each of sauvignon blanc and pinot noir, the wines being sold through the cellar door and to one or two local restaurants. The Rees regard it as a holiday and retirement project, and modestly wonder whether they deserve inclusion in this work. They certainly do, for wineries of this size are an indispensable part of the Tasmanian fabric.

narkoojee ★★★★

1110 Francis Road, Glengarry, Vic 3854 **region** Gippsland
phone (03) 5192 4257 **fax** (03) 5192 4257 **open** By appointment
winemaker Harry Friend, Axel Friend **production** 1000 **est.** 1981
product range ($12–28 CD) Chardonnay, Cabernets Merlot, The Rosé, The Athelstan Merlot.
summary Narkoojee Vineyard is within easy reach of the old goldmining town of Walhalla and looks out over the Strzelecki Ranges. The wines are produced from 4 hectares of estate vineyards. Harry Friend was an amateur winemaker of note before turning to commercial winemaking with Narkoojee, his skills showing through with all the wines.

Narkoojee Chardonnay
An opulently flavoured wine, showing the full range of winemaking techniques. In recent years, the style has been tightened somewhat, with the promise of greater longevity.
▼▼▼▼ 1998 Medium yellow-green; the moderately complex bouquet has a range of peach, butterscotch, cashew and nut on display; the nicely weighted and balanced flavours of the palate replicate those of the bouquet, and the oak plays a pure support role. **rating:** 86
best drinking 2001–2005 **best vintages** '87, '89, '92, '93, '94, '97 **drink with** Salmon pizza • $20

Narkoojee Cabernets
A blend of Cabernet Sauvignon, Cabernet Franc and Merlot, with the vines dating back to 1981.
▼▼▼▼ 1998 Medium red-purple; quite fragrant spicy/leafy/savoury aromas on the bouquet are followed by a pleasantly sweet palate with ripe berry and chocolate fruit, fine tannins and subtle oak. **rating:** 85
best drinking 2002–2008 **best vintages** NA **drink with** Gippsland lamb • $22

nashdale wines NR

Borenore Lane, Nashdale, NSW 2800 **region** Orange
phone (02) 6365 2463 **fax** (02) 6361 4495 **open** Weekends 2–6
winemaker Mark Davidson (Contract) **production** 1000 **est.** 1990
product range ($10–25 CD) Riesling, Sauvignon Blanc, Chardonnay, Pinot Noir, Cabernet Sauvignon.
summary Orange solicitor Edward Fardell commenced establishing the 10-hectare Nashdale Vineyard in 1990. At an elevation of 1000 metres, it offers panoramic views of Mount Canobolas and the Lidster Valley, with a restaurant-café open on weekends.

needham estate wines NR

Ingoldby Road, McLaren Flat, SA 5171 **region** McLaren Vale
phone (08) 8383 0301 **fax** (08) 8383 0301 **open** Not
winemaker Contract **production** 2800 **est.** 1997
product range ($17–25 R) Albertus Shiraz, White House Shiraz.
summary Clive Needham has two vineyards; the first of 4 hectares is newly planted and will come into full production in 2001. The second has less than half a hectare of 100-year-old shiraz vines which go to produce the White Horse Shiraz, with an annual production of only 120 cases.

nepenthe vineyards ★★★★☆

Vickers Road, Lenswood, SA 5240 **region** Adelaide Hills
phone (08) 8389 8039 **fax** (08) 8389 8019 **open** By appointment
winemaker Peter Leske **production** 12 000 **est.** 1994
product range ($15–38 R) Riesling, Sauvignon Blanc, Unwooded Chardonnay, Chardonnay, Pinot Gris, Pinot Noir, Zinfandel, The Fugue (Cabernet Merlot).
summary The Tweddell family established 21 hectares of close-planted vineyards at Lenswood between 1994 and 1997, with an exotic array of varieties reflected in the wines. In late 1996 it obtained the second licence to build a winery in the Adelaide Hills, Petaluma being the only other successful applicant back in 1978. A 500-tonne winery has been constructed, with Peter Leske in charge of winemaking. Nepenthe has quickly established itself as one of the most exciting new wineries in Australia. Distribution through most States, and exports to the UK.

Nepenthe Vineyards Lenswood Riesling

Produced from 1.2 hectares of estate vineyards, and almost inevitably well made in the highly disciplined Australian style.

▼▼▼▽ **1999** Light green-yellow; the bouquet is aromatic and crisp, with herbaceous/lime/mineral aromas. The palate is still fairly light overall, with flavours tracking the bouquet; will develop. Gold medal winner at the 1999 Adelaide Hills Wine Show. **rating:** 90

best drinking 2003–2009 **best vintages** '98, '99 **drink with** Sashimi • $20

Nepenthe Vineyards Semillon

As in the case of the Nepenthe Chardonnay, barrel-fermented in high-quality French oak. A great success in 1997, but not so convincingly in 1998.

▼▼▼▽ **1998** Medium yellow-green; spicy clove oak dominates the bouquet; tangy semillon fruit struggles to penetrate that oak on the palate and partially succeeds. Doubtless has time in front of it, and the balance may improve. **rating:** 84

best drinking 1999–2003 **best vintages** '97 **drink with** Sautéed veal • $21

Nepenthe Vineyards Sauvignon Blanc

Yet another high-class wine from Nepenthe, which has 4 hectares of estate plantings. The making of the 1999 Sauvignon Blanc was recorded on a day-by-day basis from the time the grapes started to ripen to the end of ferment in a diary which was then printed every week and sent to journalists and, I assume, retailers. It gave a supremely accurate picture of a very difficult vintage, the end result underlining Peter Leske's winemaking skills.

▼▼▼▼ **1999** Light green-yellow; a fairly light bouquet with herb and mineral notes dominant. A gentle tropical fruit with a hint of passionfruit swells the palate, although the wine is still medium bodied at best. **rating:** 85

best drinking 2000–2001 **best vintages** NA **drink with** Poached scallops in white sauce • $20

Nepenthe Vineyards Unwooded Chardonnay

Nepenthe, it seems, does not know how to make a bland, let alone a bad, wine. Unwooded Chardonnay does not come better than this. It would seem this is likely to establish a reputation for itself for its consistency of quality and style.

▼▼▼▼ **1999** Light to medium yellow-green; the bouquet was initially closed but came up in the glass with attractive citrussy fruit. The palate has above-average fruit weight and length; moderate cellaring prospects. **rating:** 86

best drinking 2000–2003 **best vintages** NA **drink with** Mussel soup • $15

Nepenthe Vineyards Chardonnay

Made from 5 hectares of estate-grown grapes, barrel-fermented, lees-contacted and taken through partial malolactic fermentation.

▼▼▼▽ **1998** Medium yellow-green, showing some development. Right from the initial bouquet to the finish of the palate the wine shows indelible winemaker thumbprints, with both barrel-ferment and malolactic-ferment influences woven through the sweet melon fruit. One is left to wonder whether less would have been better.

rating: 84

best drinking 2001–2004 **best vintages** NA **drink with** Chinese steamed fish • $25

Nepenthe Vineyards Pinot Noir

Produced from 5.2 hectares of estate vineyards planted to five different clones including 114, 115 and MV6.

▼▼▼▽ **1998** Medium red-purple; the bouquet is clean, moderately intense, with some sappy/foresty characters. The palate opens with quite silky structure and texture, with a mix of sappy and plummy flavours, but does fall away on the finish. **rating:** 84

best drinking 2000–2004 **best vintages** NA **drink with** Confit of duck • $28

Nepenthe Vineyards The Fugue

The first release of a Cabernet Merlot blend from Nepenthe.

▼▼▼▼ **1997** Medium red-purple; the aromas are of cedar, mint, blackberry and blackcurrant, which follow through onto a finely structured palate with cigar box, cedar and blackberry fruit; the well-controlled use of oak adds a separate note of sweetness; fine tannins round off a nice wine. **rating:** 87

best drinking 2001–2007 **best vintages** NA **drink with** Fillet of kangaroo • $28

newstead winery NR

Tivey Street, Newstead, Vic 3462 **region** Bendigo
phone (03) 5476 2733 **fax** (03) 5476 2536 **open** Weekends and public holidays 10–5
winemaker Ron Snep, Cliff Stubbs **production** 1500 **est.** 1994
product range ($15–16 CD) Welshman's Reef Semillon, Barrel Fermented Semillon, Unwooded Chardonnay, Cabernet Sauvignon; Burnt Acre Riesling, Shiraz.
summary Newstead Winery is established in the old Newstead Butter Factory, drawing upon two distinct vineyards at Welshman's Reef (near Maldon) and Burnt Acre Vineyard at Marong, west of Bendigo. Vineyard designations are used for each of the wines.

nicholson river ★★★★

Liddells Road, Nicholson, Vic 3882 **region** Gippsland
phone (03) 5156 8241 **fax** (03) 5156 8433 **open** 7 days 10–4 for sales, tastings only during holidays
winemaker Ken Eckersley **production** 3000 **est.** 1978
product range ($14–39 CD) Gippsland White (Semillon Riesling Chardonnay), Semillon, Sur-Lie Riesling, Cuvée, Gippsland Red (Pinot Shiraz), Montview Cabernet Merlot, Tawny Port. The Chardonnays come in four levels: at the bottom Gippsland, then Montview, then Montview Special, and finally Nicholson River.
summary The fierce commitment to quality in the face of the temperamental Gippsland climate and the frustratingly small production has been handsomely repaid by some stupendous Chardonnays, mostly sold through cellar door; a little is exported to the UK and the US. Ken Eckersley does not refer to his Chardonnays as white wines but as gold wines, and lists them accordingly in his newsletter.

ninth island ★★★★

Baxter's Road, Pipers River, Tas 7252 **region** Northern Tasmania
phone (03) 6382 7122 **fax** (03) 6382 7231 **open** 7 days 10–5
winemaker Andrew Pirie **production** 14 000 **est.** 1999
product range ($18.14–23.09 R) Riesling, Chardonnay, Sauvignon Blanc, Straits Dry White, Botrytis Riesling, Pinot Noir, Cuvée Tasmania, Tamar Cabernets.
summary This is the former Rochecombe Vineyard, the Rochecombe brand having been discontinued. There is a sharing of vineyards and of winery facilities within the Pipers Brook Group; the Ninth Island Wines, however, have their own identity.

Ninth Island Sauvignon Blanc

Unashamedly made in a style which will appeal to the broadest possible market.
▼▼▼▽ **1999** Light to medium yellow-green; there is a mix of gooseberry and herbal fruit on a clean, moderately intense bouquet. The palate offers quite positive flavours, with a flick of residual sugar sweetness; overall, well balanced and neatly made. **rating:** 84
best drinking 2000–2001 **best vintages** NA **drink with** Seafood • $19

Ninth Island Pinot Noir

Typically fragrant, but light bodied and delicate.
▼▼▼▽ **1999** Vivid, light purple-fuchsia; fragrant strawberry and cherry fruit aromas are faithfully repeated on the palate, with just a hint of the forest. Could surprise with its bottle development. **rating:** 84
best drinking 2000–2004 **best vintages** NA **drink with** Osso bucco • $23

noon winery ★★★★

Rifle Range Road, McLaren Vale, SA 5171 **region** McLaren Vale
phone (08) 8323 8290 **fax** (08) 8323 8290 **open** Weekends and public holidays 10–5
winemaker Drew Noon **production** 2000 **est.** 1976
product range ($14–21 CD) Solaire, One Night (Rosé), Twelve Bells, Eclipse (Grenache Shiraz), The Reles, Grenache Shiraz, Reserve Shiraz, Reserve Cabernet Sauvignon, Solaire Reserve Grenache, Chalice (Vintage Port).
summary Drew Noon has returned to McLaren Vale and purchased Noon's from his parents, having spent many years as a consultant oenologist and viticulturist in Victoria, thereafter as winemaker at Cassegrain. Some spectacular and unusual wines have followed, such as the 16.8 degrees alcohol Solaire Grenache, styled like an Italian Amarone. In 1998 Drew Noon gained the coveted Master of Wine (MW) award. Exports to the UK, the US, Germany, Switzerland and New Zealand.

Noon Eclipse Grenache Shiraz

Noon Winery has always made a specialty of very ripe, late-picked red wine styles, but it is hard to imagine anything eclipsing this Eclipse. A blend of 65 per cent Grenache and 35 per cent Shiraz, the alcohol hovers around 16 degrees, and the wine is unfiltered.

TTTT 1998 Medium to full red-purple; the bouquet is attractive, with distinctively ripe and juicy grenache leading the attack. The palate is brimming with rich, juicy ripe fruit dusted with spice. One of those 'two bottles in one' wines with a lethal number of standard drinks. **rating: 85**

best drinking 2001–2005 **best vintages** '97 **drink with** Venison • $17

Noon Reserve Cabernet Sauvignon

Another monster with 15.5 degrees alcohol. There are arguments for such levels with Shiraz and Grenache, but they are far less convincing in the case of Cabernet.

TTTY 1998 Dense, deep purple; the bouquet is very ripe, with a hint of aldehydes and earthy overtones. A huge wine on the palate, dauntingly extractive. A good drink for a sumo wrestler. **rating: 82**

best drinking 2003–2013 **best vintages** NA **drink with** Rich game • $19.50

normans ★★★☆

Grant's Gully Road, Clarendon, SA 5157 **region** McLaren Vale
phone (08) 8383 6138 **fax** (08) 8383 6089 **open** Mon–Fri 10–5, weekends and public holidays 11–5
winemaker Peter Fraser, Stuart Auld **production** 1.1 million **est.** 1853
product range ($8.95–35 R) A spread of wines starting with the Riverland-sourced Lone Gum range of Chardonnay and Shiraz Cabernet and Jesse's Blend White and Red; Chandlers Hill Chardonnay Semillon, Chenin Blanc, Fumé Blanc and Shiraz; Conquest and Pinot Noir Brut; then the White Label series of Bin number-identified Chardonnay, Verdelho, Merlot, Pinot Noir and Shiraz; and at the top of the scale Chais Clarendon Chardonnay, Shiraz and Cabernet Sauvignon; also kosher Chardonnay, Pinot Noir and Shiraz (mainly for export) under the Teal Lake label.
summary In late 1994 Normans raised $6 million in new share capital, joining the lists of Australian Associated Stock Exchanges. The issue reflected the success Normans has enjoyed in recent years in establishing its brand both in domestic and export markets. The quality of the Chais Clarendon range is exemplary. Exports to the UK, much of Europe, the US, Canada, Japan, Southeast Asia and New Zealand.

Normans Lone Gum Unwooded Chardonnay

The unwooded part of the name speaks for itself; the Lone Gum series of wines come from Normans' Riverland vineyards.

TTTY 1996 Medium yellow-green; a solid, buttery, faintly peachy bouquet is followed by a palate with plenty of flavour and quite good balance. What I might describe as a Kentucky Fried Chicken style. **rating: 80**

best drinking 1999–2000 **best vintages** NA **drink with** KFC • $8.95

Normans Lone Gum Merlot

A well-priced varietal from Normans' Riverland vineyard.

TTT 1999 Light to medium red-purple; the bouquet is light, fresh and sweet, the palate likewise offering gently sweet fruit which is varietally nondescript but which cannot possibly offend. **rating: 79**

best drinking 2000–2002 **best vintages** NA **drink with** Whatever you choose • $8.95

Normans Old Vine Grenache

Comes exclusively from Normans' Eringa Park vineyard at Kangarilla in McLaren Vale, purchased by Normans just prior to the 1998 vintage. There are nine blocks of 60- to 70-year-old bush vine grenache planted by the Smart family in the 1930s. The grapes are destemmed without crushing, and are fermented in open tanks with low rates of yeast. Malolactic fermentation occurs in barrel, and the wine is held on lees for three months, spending a further nine months in a mix of French and American oak for 12 months.

TTTY 1998 Medium to full red, with just a touch of purple; the bouquet is solid, with a mix of savoury/briary and sweeter berry fruit. The palate is right in the mainstream of ripe grenache flavour, strong and powerful, and with those distinctive juicy, jammy flavours. **rating: 84**

best drinking 2000–2003 **best vintages** NA **drink with** Rich meat pie • $22

nuggetty vineyard NR

Maldon–Shelbourne Road, Nuggetty, Vic 3463 **region** Bendigo
phone (03) 5475 1347 **fax** (03) 5475 1647 **open** Weekends and public holidays 10–4 or by appointment
winemaker Greg Dedman, Jackie Dedman **production** 1000 **est.** 1993

product range ($12–30 CD) Shiraz, Nil Desperandum Shiraz, Reserve Shiraz.
summary Draws upon 5 hectares of estate plantings, with mailing list and cellar door sales available while stocks last.

oakridge estate ★★★★

864 Maroondah Highway, Coldstream, Vic 3770 **region** Yarra Valley
phone (03) 9739 1920 **fax** (03) 9739 1923 **open** 7 days 10–5
winemaker Michael Zitzlaff, Paul Evans **production** 18 000 **est.** 1982
product range ($18–50 R) Riesling, Sauvignon Blanc, Chardonnay, Botrytis Riesling, Pinot Noir, Double Fermented Pinot Noir, Shiraz, Merlot, Cabernet Merlot; Reserve Chardonnay, Merlot and Cabernet Sauvignon.
summary The 1997 capital raising by Oakridge Vineyards Limited was successful, and a new winery was built and officially opened on 31 January 1998. Production of the Oakridge Estate wines is projected to increase in leaps and bounds into the first few years of the new millennium. Exports to the US, the UK, Switzerland and Sweden.

Oakridge Estate Riesling

A wine made in limited quantities for sale from the cellar door only.
♥♥♥♡ **1999** Light green-yellow; the bouquet is light, but has aromas of passionfruit and even nectarine. On the palate there is an unexpected minerally edge, together with a touch of passionfruit and a cleverly judged flick of residual sugar.   **rating:** 83
best drinking 2000–2003 **best vintages** NA **drink with** Smoked Yarra Valley trout • $20

Oakridge Chardonnay

A solid wine, not in the class of the Reserve, but then why should it be. Barrel-fermented in a mix of French and American oak, and given the usual winemaking treatment for quality Chardonnay, including malolactic fermentation.
♥♥♥♥ **1998** Medium to full yellow-green; smooth, peachy fruit is offset by slightly funky oak on the bouquet. The palate is a different proposition, with distinctly rich fruit which is well balanced, and no problems whatsoever come from the oak. Nice wine.   **rating:** 88
best drinking 2000–2005 **best vintages** NA **drink with** Sweet and sour pork • $20

Oakridge Reserve Chardonnay

The wine is barrel-fermented and matured in 100 per cent new French oak.
♥♥♥♥ **1998** Medium yellow-green; the bouquet is clean and smooth, quite powerful, yet not particularly expressive other than plenty of new oak. The palate delivers more power on the ground; spicy oak is the driver, but there is citrus/grapefruit flavour and good acidity helping to build a long palate.   **rating:** 86
best drinking 2000–2004 **best vintages** '95 **drink with** Scallops or fish in white sauce • $NA

Oakridge Estate Pinot Noir

A most unusual wine which was refermented over pinot noir skins from the following (1999) vintage, an Italian technique called 'ripasso'. The technique is arguably more interesting than the wine.
♥♥♥♡ **1998** Medium red-purple; the bouquet offers a range of secondary fruit aromas in a savoury/foresty/stemmy spectrum; some plummy fruit comes through on the palate, but most of the drive is in the savoury/foresty end, with a slightly grippy finish. May or may not soften.   **rating:** 82
best drinking 2000–2002 **best vintages** NA **drink with** Smoked duck • $20

Oakridge Estate Shiraz

Made from grapes grown on three vineyards; fermented in small open-topped fermenters plunged 4-6 times a day and pressed after 28 days skin contact. Matured in a mix of new and one-year-old French and American oak barriques for 14 months prior to bottling.
♥♥♥♥ **1998** Dense red-purple; clean, very concentrated black cherry fruit aromas are followed by a powerful and concentrated palate with dark berry fruit dominant. Tannins and oak crowd the finish somewhat, but the wine should soften as there is plenty there.   **rating:** 89
best drinking 2003–2013 **best vintages** '98 **drink with** Jugged hare • $25

Oakridge Estate Merlot

Oakridge has made a name for itself with Merlot, and it is not hard to see why.
♥♥♥♥♡ **1998** Medium red-purple; the bouquet is clean, moderately intense, with cedary/savoury aromas. Its strongest point is its excellent texture and structure in the mouth, with a mix of savoury, spicy/berry flavours supported by subtle oak.   **rating:** 90
best drinking 2001–2008 **best vintages** '98 **drink with** Roast veal • $25

Oakridge Reserve Cabernet Sauvignon

The Oakridge Cabernet Sauvignons have been reliable, those with the Reserve tag particularly so.

▼▼▼▼ 1997 Dense red-purple; a powerful bouquet with savoury/herbal elements which became progressively more dominant as the wine breathes. There is plenty of extract and concentration on the palate, where the wine proclaims its cool-grown origins. Whether that is a good thing rests in the eye of the beholder. **rating: 88**

best drinking 2002–2010 **best vintages** '88, '90, '91, '94, '95, '97 **drink with** Yarra Valley venison • $NA

oakvale ★★★

Broke Road, Pokolbin, NSW 2321 **region** Lower Hunter Valley
phone (02) 4998 7520 **fax** (02) 4998 7747 **open** 7 days 10–5
winemaker Barry Shields, David Lowe **production** 5000 **est.** 1893
product range ($16–25 CD) Peach Tree Semillon, Selections Chardonnay (unwooded), Peach Tree Unwooded Chardonnay, Frontignac, Peppercorn Shiraz, Cabernet Merlot and a handful of fortified wines.
summary Former Sydney solicitor Barry Shields seems content with the change in his lifestyle as he presides over the historic Oakvale winery which he purchased from the Elliott family over a decade ago. The emphasis is on Semillon, Chardonnay and a blend of the two in both oaked and unoaked versions, most of which are offered with three to five years bottle age, with deep yellow colour and rich, sometimes heavy, buttery/nutty flavours. The best wine, however, is the Peppercorn Shiraz.

o'keefe wines　　　NR

PO Box 1021, Launceston, Tas 7250 **region** Northern Tasmania
phone 0419 875 586 **open** Not
winemaker Greg O'Keefe **production** NA **est.** 1999
product range Pinot Gris, Unwooded Chardonnay.
summary O'Keefe Wines, owned and operated by winemaker Greg O'Keefe, is running alongside the far longer established Fishburn & O'Keefe. It is one of those operations with neither vineyards nor a single, permanent winemaking base: Greg O'Keefe's major business these days is operating a mobile contract-bottling line.

O'Keefe Unwooded Chardonnay

Made from grapes contract-grown in the Tamar Valley.

▼▼▼▼ 1998 Medium yellow-green; a complex and tangy citrus and nectarine bouquet which is powerful but not over-done. The palate does not quite live up to the exceptional promise of the bouquet with a slightly sweet and sour fruit character. Still, a pretty good wine. **rating: 85**

best drinking 2000–2004 **drink with** Suckling pig • $NA

old caves　　　NR

New England Highway, Stanthorpe, Qld 4380 **region** Granite Belt
phone (07) 4681 1494 **fax** (07) 4681 2722 **open** Mon–Sat 9–5, Sun 10–5
winemaker David Zanatta **production** 2200 **est.** 1980
product range ($7.50–13.50 CD) Chardonnay, Classic Dry White, Light Red, Shiraz, Cabernet Sauvignon and a range of generic wines in both bottle and flagon, including fortifieds.
summary Has a strictly local, relatively uncritical and evidently loyal clientele.

old kent river　　　★★★☆

Turpin Road, Rocky Gully, WA 6397 **region** Great Southern
phone (08) 9855 1589 **fax** (08) 9855 1660 **open** At South Coast Highway, Kent River Wed–Sun 9–5
winemaker Alkoomi (Contract), Michael Staniford **production** 3200 **est.** 1985
product range ($16–54 CD) Chardonnay, Sauvignon Blanc, Pinot Noir, Reserve Pinot Noir, Shiraz, Diamontina (Sparkling).
summary Mark and Debbie Noack have done it tough all of their relatively young lives but have earned respect from their neighbours and from the other producers to whom they sell more than half the production from the 10-hectare vineyard established on their sheep property. 'Grapes', they say 'saved us from bankruptcy'. Exports to Canada, the UK, The Netherlands and Hong Kong.

🐦 old station vineyard ★★★★

St Vincent Street, Watervale, SA 5452 **region** Clare Valley
phone 0414 441 925 **fax** (02) 9144 1925 **open** Not
winemaker Quelltaler (Contract) **production** 3000 **est.** 1926
product range ($12.50–22 R) Watervale Riesling, Free Run Rosé, Grenache Shiraz, Shiraz.
summary When Bill and Noel Ireland decided to retire from the Sydney retail scene in 1996 to go all the way up (or down) the production stream and become grape growers and winemakers, they did not muck around. In 1995 they had purchased a six-hectare, 70-year-old vineyard at Watervale, and formed an even significantly larger joint venture in the Margaret River region which has given birth to Flinders Bay wines. In their first year of shows the Old Station Vineyard wines won two gold, three silver and eight bronze medals, a reflection of the strength of old vines and the skills of contract-winemaking at Quelltaler. Now, I just wonder what Bill Ireland thinks about retailers who slash and burn the theoretical retail price of his wines.

Old Station Vineyard Watervale Riesling
Produced from a vineyard block planted in 1926; won five bronze medals in succession during the 1999 show year.
▼▼▼⊽ **1999** Medium yellow-green, very advanced for its age. The bouquet is solid, and at least at this juncture, lacks aromatics; the powerful palate has a mix of mineral and tropical fruit flavours, but finishes somewhat abruptly. **rating:** 81
best drinking 2000–2003 **drink with** Full-flavoured fish • $14

Old Station Vineyard Watervale Free Run Rosé
Made entirely from estate-grown grenache, the vines more than 70 years old.
▼▼▼⊽ **1998** Full pink/red; there is attractive cherry/berry fruit to the bouquet, and the palate has plenty of flavour without coarse phenolics, but does dry somewhat on the finish. **rating:** 83
best drinking 2000–2001 **drink with** Grilled pork • $12.50

Old Station Vineyard Grenache Shiraz
Produced from 80 per cent Grenache and 20 per cent Shiraz; a consistent show medal winner throughout 1999, culminating in a gold medal at the National Wine Show.
▼▼▼▼ **1998** Medium to full red-purple; the bouquet has an array of dark berry, chocolate and earthy fruit in abundance, yet avoids being jammy. Similarly, the sweet Grenache comes rocketing through the dark berry and plum palate which is stiffened up by the Shiraz on the finish, and avoids the squashy confectionery characters which can mar this style. **rating:** 88
best drinking 2000–2002 **drink with** Game casserole • $18

olive farm ★★★

77 Great Eastern Highway, South Guildford, WA 6055 **region** Swan District
phone (08) 9277 2989 **fax** (08) 9279 4372 **open** Mon–Tues and Thurs–Fri 10–5, weekends 11–3
winemaker Ian Yurisich **production** 4000 **est.** 1829
product range ($12.90–24.50 CD) Verdelho, Chenin Blanc, Classic White, Chardonnay, Gewurztraminer, Sauterne Style, Pinot Noir, Cabernet Sauvignon, Cabernet Shiraz Merlot, Sherry, Port, Sparkling.
summary The oldest winery in Australia in use today, and arguably the least communicative. The ultra-low profile tends to disguise the fact that wine quality is by and large good. The wines come from 12 hectares of estate plantings of 11 different varieties.

oliverhill NR

Seaview Road, McLaren Vale, SA 5171 **region** McLaren Vale
phone (08) 8323 8922 **open** 7 days 10–5
winemaker Stuart Miller **production** 1300 **est.** 1973
product range ($5–11 CD) Great Outdoors White and Red, Chardonnay, Shiraz Cabernet, Port, Muscat.
summary Oliverhill has changed hands but otherwise continues an operation aimed almost entirely at the local tourist trade.

olssens of watervale NR

Government Road, Watervale, SA 5452 **region** Clare Valley
phone (08) 8843 0065 **fax** (08) 8843 0065 **open** Fri–Mon and public holidays 11–5 or by appointment
winemaker Contract **production** 2000 **est.** 1994
product range ($13–19 CD) Riesling, Semillon, Botrytised Riesling, Cabernet Sauvignon Cabernet Franc Merlot.

summary Kevin and Helen Olssen first visited the Clare Valley in December 1986. Within two weeks they and their family decided to sell their Adelaide home and purchased a property in a small, isolated valley 3 kilometres north of the township of Watervale. Between 1987 and 1993 production from the 5-hectare vineyard was sold to other makers, but in 1993 the decision was taken to produce wine under the Olssen label. The 1998 Riesling (85 points) is the best of the current releases, intense, tight and long, and bound to repay cellaring.

orani vineyard   NR

Arthur Highway, Sorrel, Tas 7172   **region** Southern Tasmania
phone (03) 6225 0330   **fax** (03) 6225 0330   **open** Weekends and public holidays 9.30–6.30
winemaker Various Contract   **production** NA   **est.** 1986
product range ($15.60–18.35 R) Riesling, Chardonnay, Pinot Noir.
summary The first commercial release from Orani was of a 1992 Pinot Noir, with Chardonnay and Riesling following in the years thereafter. The solidly constructed '96 Orani Pinot Noir, with abundant plum and mint fruit, is the best yet, well deserving of its bronze medal at the 1998 Tasmanian Wines Show. Owned by Tony and Angela McDermott, the latter the President of the Royal Hobart Wine Show.

orlando   ★★★★☆

Barossa Valley Way, Rowland Flat, SA 5352   **region** Barossa Valley
phone (08) 8521 3111   **fax** (08) 8521 3100   **open** Mon–Fri 10–5, weekends 10–4
winemaker Philip Laffer   **production** NFP   **est.** 1847
product range ($7.90–52 R) The table wines are sold in four ranges: first the national and international best-selling Jacob's Creek Semillon Sauvignon Blanc, Chardonnay, Riesling, Shiraz Cabernet and Grenache Shiraz and special Limited Releases; then the Gramps range of Chardonnay, Botrytis Semillon, Grenache, Cabernet Merlot; next the Saint range, St Helga Eden Valley Riesling, St Hilary Padthaway Chardonnay, St Hugo Coonawarra Cabernet Sauvignon; finally the premium range of Steingarten Riesling, Jacaranda Ridge Cabernet Sauvignon and Lawsons Padthaway Shiraz. Also Russet Ridge Coonawarra Chardonnay and Cabernet Shiraz Merlot off to one side; sparkling wines under the Trilogy and Carrington labels.
summary Jacobs Creek is one of the largest-selling brands in the world and is almost exclusively responsible for driving the fortunes of this French- (Pernod Ricard) owned company. The super-premium wines in the range continue to improve; Orlando had conspicuous trophy success at the 1997 National Wine Show. A colossus in the export game, chiefly to the UK and Europe, but also to the US and Asia.

Orlando St Helga Eden Valley Riesling

Produced from grapes grown on Orlando's St Helga Vineyard in the Eden Valley and first made in 1980. That initial release was not put onto the market until it was four years old and was initially priced as a premium product. It is now conventionally marketed in the year of production, and in real terms the price has come down significantly.
▼▼▼▼ **1999** Light yellow-green; the bouquet is quite firm and intense, with typical Eden Valley lime juice aromas. The palate has a nice, tight structure, moving more towards mineral and needing time to build.   **rating:** 86
best drinking 2004–2009   **best vintages** '90, '92, '94, '95, '96   **drink with** Asian cuisine   • $14.95

Orlando Steingarten Riesling

In 1962 Colin Gramp, then Orlando's managing director, embarked on one of the great romantic follies: establishing a riesling vineyard on a vineyard entirely composed of rock schist (hence 'steingarten', or garden of stones) at a height of 490 metres on the East Barossa Ranges. Planted at a density of 6000 vines per hectare, the yields were nonetheless minuscule, and during the latter part of the '60s and '70s this was one of the most celebrated of all Rieslings. Commercial reality has since turned the wine into a brand, the back label freely admitting that Steingarten is used, where possible, as a base for the wine. In other words, in some years there may be a contribution from the Steingarten Vineyard, but in other years not necessarily so.
▼▼▼▽ **1999** Light green-yellow; the moderately aromatic bouquet has a mix of lime and light tropical aromas. As ever, quite pretty but seems somewhat dilute and to lack focus. May pick up with time.   **rating:** 84
best drinking 2001–2004   **best vintages** '98   **drink with** Sautéed prawns   • $21.95

Orlando Trilogy Semillon Sauvignon Blanc Muscadelle

This is the classic varietal mix of white Bordeaux, but is relatively rare in Australia. The grapes predominantly come from South Australia.
▼▼▼▽ **1999** Light yellow-green; the bouquet is clean, with moderate grassy/herbal notes. The palate is of moderate intensity and length, the fruit flavours tracking the bouquet. An interesting blend which may well surprise with time in bottle; at this price it won't hurt too much to find out one way or the other.   **rating:** 83
best drinking 2000–2004   **best vintages** NA   **drink with** Cold prawns   • $12.95

Orlando Gramp's Barossa Chardonnay

A wine which surprised everyone (including myself) with its performance at the 1999 Cowra Wine Show (gold medal) and its subsequent appearance in the Tri-Nations (Australia, New Zealand and South Africa) Chardonnay Challenge.

YYYY 1998 Medium yellow-green; the bouquet is clean, with melon and grapefruit aromas supported by subtle oak. The palate is smooth, and moderately complex, with slightly milky oak. **rating: 85**

best drinking 2000–2001 **best vintages** NA **drink with** Sweetbreads • $14.95

Orlando Jacob's Creek Chardonnay

Doubtless the most important white version of Jacob's Creek these days, notwithstanding the consistent and persistent success of the Riesling in Australian wine shows. Sourced from all over southeast Australia, and professionally put together.

YYYY 1999 In the absence of Lindemans Bin 65, this stood out as the best value budget-priced Chardonnay in my Top 100 tasting. The bouquet is clean, with gentle melon and citrus fruit, the oak subliminal. A modestly honest palate, with light melon-accented fruit; delicately handled oak. There has been no attempt to force the wine into something it is not. **rating: 85**

best drinking Drink now **best vintages** NA **drink with** KFC • $7.90

Orlando Centenary Hill Shiraz

A new Barossa-based Shiraz from very old, dry-grown vines from a single vineyard which had great success throughout 1998 and 1999 in Australian wine shows.

YYYYY 1995 Medium to full red-purple; smooth, dark small berry and plum fruit allied with a coating of vanilla and chocolate on the bouquet. The palate shows lots of American oak, but does have length and presence, and those dark, sweet fruit flavours are there. Although the '96 was previously reviewed, '95 is the current release. **rating: 91**

YYYYY 1994 Medium red-purple; there are interesting and unusual sweet and sour aromas on the bouquet, fruity yet almost citrussy; berry, mint and pine flavours on the palate more or less track the bouquet. To say the least, an unusual wine. **rating: 90**

best drinking 2000–2010 **best vintages** '94, '95, '96 **drink with** Braised quail • $50

Orlando Jacob's Creek Grenache Shiraz

Both the price and the palate make it abundantly clear this is produced from high-yielding, irrigated grenache, which in this context does no one any harm.

YYYY 1999 Light fuchsia colour; the bouquet is fresh, somewhere between that of a Rosé and a Beaujolais. The palate, similarly, offers easy, fresh summer drinking; serve slightly chilled. **rating: 82**

best drinking Drink now **best vintages** NA **drink with** Lasagne • $7.90

Orlando Jacob's Creek Shiraz Cabernet

The wine which launched a thousand (container) ships and which describes itself on television as Australia's Top Drop.

YYYY 1998 Light to medium red-purple; the bouquet is clean and quite fragrant; the palate offers fresh, clean fruit with a touch of spice and a subliminal hint of sweetness. As reliable as ever. **rating: 83**

best drinking Drink now **best vintages** NA **drink with** Ravioli • $7.90

Orlando Trilogy

A blend of Cabernet Sauvignon, Cabernet Franc and Merlot the wine is a trilogy of both varieties and regions.

YYYYY 1998 Strongly coloured, it opens with nicely ripened blackcurrant/blackberry fruit aromas; there is plenty of dark berry fruit and dark chocolate flavour supported by lingering tannins on the finish. **rating: 90**

best drinking 2000–2008 **best vintages** NA **drink with** Braised lamb shanks • $12.95

Orlando Gramp's Cabernet Merlot

Overall, Australian Cabernet Merlot blends have provided more disappointments than successes over the past ten years, but this is a consistent success, particularly at the price.

YYYY 1997 Medium red-purple; the bouquet is clean and fresh, with attractive raspberry/blackcurrant fruit. A substantial wine on the palate with lots of dark berry fruit flavours and persistent, chewy tannins auguring well for continuing development. **rating: 87**

best drinking 2002–2007 **best vintages** NA **drink with** Braised oxtail • $14.95

orlando (padthaway)　　NR

c/o Barossa Valley Way, Rowland Flat, SA 5352 **region** Padthaway
phone (08) 8521 3111 **fax** (08) 8521 3100 **open** Not
winemaker Philip Laffer **production** NFP **est.** NA
product range ($14.95–55 R) St Hilary Padthaway Chardonnay, Jacob's Creek Limited Release Chardonnay,
Lawsons Padthaway Shiraz.
summary While Padthaway serves the same purpose for Orlando as it does for the other major companies in the
region by providing good-quality wine for cross-regional blends, it also produces three of Orlando's most
distinguished wines. The first to appear was Lawson's Shiraz; St Hilary Chardonnay is a more recent arrival; the
special Jacob's Creek Limited Release Chardonnay even more noteworthy. Other than its large vineyard, Orlando
has no physical presence in Padthaway, but its Padthaway wines are sold at Padthaway Estate (and, of course,
through retail shops).

Orlando St Hilary Padthaway Chardonnay

A wine which has surged into prominence in recent years, based on premium Padthaway fruit, winning a series of
international awards.
▼▼▼▼ **1998** Medium yellow-green; there is fairly obvious charry oak on the bouquet, with light citrus fruit; quite
nice flavour overall, although the oak is slightly rough.　　　　　　　　　　　　　　　　**rating:** 87
best drinking 2002–2005 **best vintages** '96 **drink with** Veal •$16.95

Orlando Lawson's Padthaway Shiraz

Named after a nineteenth-century pioneer surveyor, Robert Lawson. It is matured for two years in new Nevers
oak hogsheads, with further bottle maturation before release. This expansive oak input made its mark on the wine:
the regular shower of gold and silver medals that descend on the wine shows that many judges did not regard the
input as excessive. I have to admit that the vintages of the 1990s seem to me to be getting better and better,
particularly so far as the oak regime is concerned, reaching a height of perfection with the '94 vintage.
▼▼▼▼▼ **1995** Medium red-purple; slightly more pronounced charry oak than usual, but there is strong fruit to
balance that oak, fruit which comes through strongly on the sweet minty/berry palate. That intense fruit pushes
the oak back into a proper perspective.　　　　　　　　　　　　　　　　　　　　**rating:** 90
best drinking 2001–2010 **best vintages** '88, '90, '91, '93, '94, '95 **drink with** Beef stroganoff •$55

osborns　　★★★★

RMB 5935 Foxeys Road, Tuerong, Vic 3926 **region** Mornington Peninsula
phone (03) 5989 7417 **fax** (03) 5989 7510 **open** By appointment
winemaker Richard McIntyre (Consultant) **production** 1200 **est.** 1988
product range ($20–23 CD) Chardonnay, Pinot Noir, Cabernet Merlot.
summary Frank and Pamela Osborn are now Mornington Peninsula veterans, having purchased the vineyard
land in Ellerina Road in 1988 and (with help from son Guy) planted the vineyard over the following four years.
The first release of wines in 1997 offered six vintages each of Chardonnay and Pinot Noir and five vintages of
Cabernet Sauvignon, quite a debut. Part of the production from the 5.5 hectares of vineyards is sold to others, but
increasing amounts are made and marketed under the Osborns label.

Osborns Chardonnay

Produced from 2.3 hectares of chardonnay situated on the north-facing slope of a small valley in the warmer part
of the Mornington Peninsula. The wine style is absolutely in the mainstream of Mornington Peninsula style, with
the hallmark malolactic influence. 100 per cent fermented in French oak, typically with wild yeast initiation, and
remains on lees for 12 months.
▼▼▼▼ **1998** Medium yellow-green; some bottle development is showing on the bouquet, enhancing the melon,
fig and cashew aromas with a substrate of mineral. An attractively smooth and even palate with textural complexity
and good balance; carries its 14 degrees alcohol very well.　　　　　　　　　　　　　**rating:** 89
best drinking 2001–2006 **best vintages** '97, '98 **drink with** Sautéed scallops •$20

☙ oyster cove vineyard　　NR

134 Manuka Road, Oyster Cove, Tas 7150 **region** Tasmania
phone (03) 6267 4512 **open** By appointment
winemaker Andrew Hood **production** 150 **est.** 1994
product range ($15–20 CD) Chardonnay, Pinot Noir.

summary The striking label of Oyster Cove, with a yacht reflected in mirror-calm water, coupled with the address of the winery (Snug), are wholly appropriate, for Jean and Rod Ledingham have been quietly growing tiny quantities of grapes from the 1 hectare of chardonnay and pinot noir since 1994.

Oyster Cove Vineyard Pinot Noir

Yet another tribute to the quality of Tasmanian Pinot Noir in the 1998 vintage and to the awesomely consistent success Andrew Hood has in making the wine.

♥♥♥♥♡ **1998** Medium to full red-purple; a complex and lively bouquet with a mix of spicy, stemmy and plummy aromas leads into an intense, rich and complex palate with fruit and oak neatly counterpoised. Great finish. **rating: 95**

best drinking 2001–2008 **drink with** Oven-roasted squab • $20

padthaway estate ★★★☆

Keith–Naracoorte Road, Padthaway, SA 5271 **region** Padthaway
phone (08) 8765 5039 **fax** (08) 8765 5097 **open** 7 days 10–4
winemaker Nigel Catt, Ulrich Grey-Smith **production** 6000 **est.** 1980
product range ($14.95–22 R) Eliza Pinot Chardonnay Cuvée, Eliza Pinot Noir Brut, Eliza Sparkling Burgundy, Eliza Chardonnay (wooded and unwooded); Chardonnay, Unwooded Chardonnay, Cabernet Sauvignon.
summary For many years, until the opening of Stonehaven, the only functioning winery in Padthaway, set in the superb grounds of the Estate in a large and gracious old stone woolshed; the homestead is in the Relais et Chateaux mould, offering luxurious accommodation and fine food. Sparkling wines are the specialty of the Estate. Padthaway Estate also acts as a tasting centre for other Padthaway-region wines. National retail distribution; exports to the UK.

Padthaway Estate Chardonnay

Estate-grown; 75 per cent barrel-fermented in French oak (Dargaud & Jaegle) with malolactic fermentation and lees contact.

♥♥♥♥ **1997** Medium yellow-green; the bouquet is quite fragrant, with plenty of melon fruit and the type of supple oak which only Dargaud & Jaegle can impart. The medium-bodied palate features ripe melon and stone fruit flavours harmoniously melded with gently spicy oak. **rating: 86**

best drinking 2001–2004 **best vintages** NA **drink with** Robe crayfish • $18.95

Padthaway Estate Eliza Pinot Chardonnay

A blend of 85 per cent Pinot Noir, 12 per cent Chardonnay and 3 per cent Pinot Meunier which may vary a little from one vintage to the next. It spends not less than two years on yeast lees, and is the flagship wine of the estate. It is named after Eliza Lawson, who arrived on the property with her husband in 1847 and who supervised the construction of the beautiful homestead completed in 1882.

♥♥♥♥ **1997** Light to medium yellow-green; the bouquet is clean, with a mix of fresh citrus and apple; the palate is similarly lively, crisp and clean, with faintly creamy notes adding to the texture. **rating: 87**

best drinking 2000–2004 **best vintages** NA **drink with** Aperitif • $22

palmara ★★★☆

1314 Richmond Road, Richmond, Tas 7025 **region** Southern Tasmania
phone (03) 6260 2462 **open** Summer 12–6
winemaker Allan Bird **production** 250 **est.** 1985
product range ($14.50–17.50 CD) Chardonnay, Semillon Ehrenfeltzer, Montage Blend, Exotica (Siegerrebe), Pinot Noir, Cabernet Sauvignon.
summary Allan Bird makes the Palmara wines in tiny quantities. (The vineyard is slightly less than 1 hectare in total.) The Pinot Noir has performed consistently well since 1990. The Exotica Siegerrebe blend is unchallenged as Australia's most exotic and unusual wine, with amazing jujube/lanolin aromas and flavours.

palmer wines ★★★★

Caves Road, Willyabrup, WA 6280 **region** Margaret River
phone (08) 9797 1881 **fax** (08) 9797 0534 **open** By appointment
winemaker Eddie Price, Amberley Estate (Contract) **production** 6000 **est.** 1977
product range ($12–30 R) Sauvignon Blanc, Semillon, Classic White, Chardonnay, Merlot, Shiraz Cabernet, Cabernet Sauvignon, Cabernet Merlot.

summary Stephen and Helen Palmer planted their first hectare of vines way back in 1977, but a series of events (including a cyclone and grasshopper plagues) caused them to lose interest and instead turn to thoroughbred horses. But with encouragement from Dr Michael Peterkin of Pierro, and after a gap of almost ten years, they again turned to viticulture and now have 15 hectares planted to the classic varieties. The Cabernet Merlot is especially good.

Palmer Merlot

Estate-grown, and has been one of the more consistent wines in the Palmer portfolio, even if it is at times so powerful and concentrated varietal character all but disappears.

▼▼▼▼ **1998** Full red-purple; the bouquet is full of very ripe chocolate and blackberry fruit, almost into prune. The palate is luscious and very ripe, repeating the flavours promised by the bouquet, and finishing with medium-weight tannins. An excellent Margaret River dry red wine. **rating:** 85

best drinking 2003–2008 **best vintages** NA **drink with** Game • $30

pankhurst NR

Old Woodgrove, Woodgrove Road, Hall, NSW 2618 **region** Canberra District
phone (02) 6230 2592 **fax** (02) 6230 2592 **open** Sundays, public holidays and by appointment
winemaker Sue Carpenter (Contract) **production** 4000 **est.** 1986
product range ($18–25 CD) Chardonnay, Semillon, Semillon Sauvignon Blanc, Pinot Noir, Cabernet Merlot.
summary Agricultural scientist and consultant Allan Pankhurst and wife Christine (with a degree in pharmaceutical science) have established a 3-hectare, split canopy vineyard. Tastings of the first wines produced showed considerable promise. In recent years Pankhurst has shared success with Lark Hill in the production of surprisingly good Pinot Noir — surprising given the climatic limitations. Says Christine Pankhurst, 'the result of good viticulture here and great winemaking at Lark Hill', and she may well be right.

Pankhurst Pinot Noir

Pankhurst has achieved consistent success with its Pinot Noir, the '96, '97 and '98 vintages all winning awards of some kind or other. It is produced from 1 hectare of estate plantings, and the sophisticated winemaking techniques used by Sue Carpenter are evident in the wine.

▼▼▼▼ **1999** Medium to full red, with just a touch of purple. The complex, tangy, savoury bouquet has clear varietal character, the palate likewise in a foresty/savoury/stemmy style. Some may like more red fruit flavours, but others will be perfectly happy with what they find here. **rating:** 85

best drinking 2001–2003 **best vintages** '96, '97, '98 **drink with** Tea-smoked duck • $25

Pankhurst Cabernet Merlot

A blend of 78 per cent Cabernet Sauvignon and 22 per cent Merlot and matured in French oak for 12 months. Every vintage between 1991 and 1997 has had show success.

▼▼▼▼ **1998** Medium red-purple; the bouquet is clean and firm, with a mix of berry, leaf and mint aromas. The corresponding flavours come through well on the palate, with pleasantly sweet, ripe fruit, fine tannins and subtle oak. **rating:** 86

best drinking 2001–2007 **best vintages** NA **drink with** Leg of lamb • $18

panorama ★★★

RSD 297 Lower Wattle Grove, Cradoc, Tas 7109 **region** Southern Tasmania
phone (03) 6266 3409 **fax** (03) 6266 3409 **open** 6 days 10–5
winemaker Michael Vishacki **production** 250 **est.** 1974
product range ($10–30 CD) Chardonnay, Sauvignon Blanc, Pinot Noir, Cabernet Sauvignon.
summary Michael and Sharon Vishacki purchased Panorama from Steve Ferencz two years ago, and have since spent considerable sums in building a brand new winery, an attractive cellar-door sales outlet, and in trebling the vineyard size.

paracombe wines ★★★★

Main Road, Paracombe, SA 5132 **region** Adelaide Hills
phone (08) 8380 5058 **fax** (03) 8380 5488 **open** Not
winemaker Paul Drogemuller (Overseeing Contract) **production** 2000 **est.** 1983
product range ($18.50–27.50 R) Chardonnay, Sauvignon Blanc, Pinot Noir, Shiraz, Cabernet Franc, Shiraz Cabernet, Pinot Chardonnay Méthode Champenoise, Sparkling Shiraz.
summary The Drogemuller family have established 12 hectares of vineyards at Paracombe, reviving a famous name in South Australian wine history. The wines are in fact contract-made at Petaluma and are sold by mail order and through retailers in South Australia. Paracombe Wines has had particular success with its Sauvignon Blanc (1997 Adelaide Wine Show trophy) but all of the wines in the range are worth chasing.

Paracombe Shiraz

Shiraz can and does perform excellently in the Adelaide Hills if site selection (and hence site climate) is appropriate.

TTTT 1997 Excellent purple-red colour; the bouquet is essentially driven by its smooth, sweet fruit, the palate offering a wider spectrum of berry, liquorice and spice flavours. There is a faint edge of green, which arguably adds to, rather than detracts from, the wine.   **rating: 85**

best drinking 2001–2006 **best vintages** NA **drink with** Moroccan lamb • $23

Paracombe Cabernet Franc

One of the few varietal Cabernet Francs being made in Australia, the others of note coming from Knappstein and Chatsfield.

TTTY 1998 Light to medium red-purple; the bouquet is light but with authentic leafy varietal character in the manner of the wines of Chinon in the Loire Valley. There are sweeter notes on the palate, almost certainly partially oak-driven; finishes with fine, soft tannins.   **rating: 83**

best drinking 2000–2004 **best vintages** NA **drink with** Pastrami • $23

paradise enough   NR

Stewarts Road, Kongwak, Vic 3951 **region** Gippsland
phone (03) 5657 4241 **fax** (03) 5657 4229 **open** Sun, public holidays 12–5
winemaker John Bell, Sue Armstrong **production** 600 **est.** 1987
product range ($13–25 CD) Chardonnay, Reserve Chardonnay, Pinot Noir, Cabernet Merlot, Pinot Chardonnay.
summary Phillip Jones of Bass Phillip persuaded John Bell and Sue Armstrong to establish their small vineyard on a substantial dairy and beef cattle property.

paringa estate   ★★★★★

44 Paringa Road, Red Hill South, Vic 3937 **region** Mornington Peninsula
phone (03) 5989 2669 **fax** (03) 5931 0135 **open** 7 days 11–5
winemaker Lindsay McCall **production** 4000 **est.** 1985
product range ($20–40 R) Chardonnay, White Pinot, Pinot Noir, Shiraz, Cabernet Sauvignon; PE Chardonnay, PE Pinot Noir.
summary No longer a rising star but a star shining more brightly in the Mornington Peninsula firmament than any other. As recent vintages have emphasised, the Mornington Peninsula region is sensitive to growing season conditions, with problems in 1995 and 1996, but having wonderful years in 1997 and 1998. Paringa shines most brightly in the warmer years. The restaurant is open seven days 10–3.

Paringa Estate Chardonnay

Produced entirely from half a hectare of estate plantings, and 100 per cent barrel-fermented in 100 per cent new Vosges and Allier French oak barriques of the highest quality. Typically, ten per cent (and no more) is taken through malolactic fermentation, and the wine spends almost a year on yeast lees before bottling. The style is normally opulent and concentrated.

TTTT 1998 Light green-yellow; the bouquet is clean, fresh and of light to moderate intensity; all in all very different from the normal Paringa voluptuousness. The palate is equally understated; fresh, but slightly hard on the finish.   **rating: 88**

best drinking 2001–2005 **best vintages** '91, '92, '93, '94, '96, '97 **drink with** Pan-fried veal with abalone mushrooms • $32

Paringa Estate PE Chardonnay

A newly introduced second label from non-estate growers and some first-crop from the estate, 100 per cent barrel-fermented in older oak.

TTTT 1998 Medium to full yellow-green; there is rich, peachy fruit in abundance, the oak giving as much contribution to the texture as to the aroma; the palate is quite rich, with well-balanced acidity. Cloys ever-so-slightly but is good value.   **rating: 88**

best drinking 2000–2003 **best vintages** NA **drink with** Marinated spatchcock • $20

Paringa Estate Pinot Noir

The most strikingly individual style in the Paringa range, and arguably the most controversial, although its formidable show record, strewn with trophies and gold medals, would not suggest any great element of controversy. It is very pungent, with herb and spice aromas and flavours attesting to the very cool climate, yet to my palate it has the requisite vinosity and sweet fruit.

TTTT1998 As so often happens with Paringa Estate, a chameleon, forever changing. Light to medium red-purple; high toast oak dominates the bouquet, but on the palate sappy, strawberry, plum whole-bunch flavours come through in the shadow of extravagant oak. Could head anywhere as it matures. **rating: 89**
best drinking 2000–2005 **best vintages** '88, '90, '91, '92, '93, '95, '97 **drink with** Wild duck, game • $40

Paringa Estate PE Pinot Noir
Produced partly from first-crop vines at Paringa and partly from two other Red Hill vineyards, in a deliberately fruit-driven style.
TTTT1998 Medium red; the bouquet is complex and stylish, moderately intense with appealing tangy/foresty overtones to strawberry/cherry fruit. The palate is no less stylish, with good length, and has not been overworked or overoaked. **rating: 89**
best drinking 2000–2003 **best vintages** NA **drink with** Baked ham • $22

Paringa Estate Shiraz
The Mornington Peninsula is an unlikely place to produce first class Shiraz, particularly given that it is usually picked on the Queen's Birthday in June. And indeed, this extremely late-harvest date indicates that the growing conditions must be good (and in particular, warm) for the wine to really succeed — as it did brilliantly in a run of vintages from '90 to '94 inclusive. In this time the wine won numerous gold medals and trophies, the most prestigious being the trophy for Best Australian Wine in the 1995 Australia v South Africa Wine Challenge. In '95 and '96 the less favourable growing conditions have made their mark; the '97 and '98 are back to near top form and will improve with time in bottle.
TTTT1998 Medium to full red-purple; the bouquet is clean and smooth, with abundant ripe briary/berry/cherry aromas. The wine has good structure with nice mid-palate fruit; the acid, however, is quite tart on the finish. **rating: 89**
best drinking 2003–2008 **best vintages** '91, '92, '93, '94, '97 **drink with** Stir-fried beef • $35

parker coonawarra estate ★★★★
Riddoch Highway, Coonawarra, SA 5263 **region** Coonawarra
phone (02) 9357 3376 **fax** (02) 9358 1517 **open** Not
winemaker Chris Cameron **production** 6000 **est.** 1985
product range ($25–65 R) Cabernet Sauvignon under two labels, Parker Coonawarra Estate First Growth and Parker Coonawarra Estate Terra Rossa.
summary Parker Coonawarra Estate is now a 50:50 joint venture between founder John Parker and family and James Fairfax. It is by this mechanism that Pepper Tree in the Hunter Valley (controlled by James Fairfax) has its Coonawarra stake. It has also led to the highly regarded wines being made by Pepper Tree winemaker Chris Cameron, albeit using the Balnaves winery in Coonawarra to do so. A maturation cellar and cellar-door sales facility in Coonawarra are planned to be functional in late 2000. Exports to the UK, Switzerland, Japan, Taiwan, Hong Kong, Singapore, Malaysia and Indonesia.

park wines NR
RMB 6291, Sanatorium Road, Allan's Flat, Yackandandah, Vic 3691 **region** Alpine Valleys and Beechworth
phone (02) 6027 1564 **fax** (02) 6027 1561 **open** Weekends and public holidays 10–5
winemaker Rod Park, Julia Park **production** NA **est.** 1995
product range NA.
summary Rod and Julia Park have a 6-hectare vineyard of riesling, chardonnay, merlot, cabernet franc and cabernet sauvignon, set in the beautiful hill country of the Ovens Valley. Part of the vineyard is still coming into bearing, and the business is still in its infancy.

passing clouds ★★★★☆
RMB 440 Kurting Road, Kingower, Vic 3517 **region** Bendigo
phone (03) 5438 8257 **fax** (03) 5438 8246 **open** 7 days 12–5 by appointment
winemaker Graeme Leith, Greg Bennett **production** 3000 **est.** 1974
product range ($15–30 CD) Red wine specialist; principal wines include Pinot Noir, Grenache, Shiraz, Shiraz Cabernet, Merlot, Graeme's Blend (Shiraz Cabernet), Angel Blend (Cabernet), Glenalbyn Cabernet; also Ondine (Sparkling Shiraz Cabernet); Chardonnay and Sauvignon Blanc from the Goulburn Valley.
summary Graeme Leith is one of the great personalities of the industry, with a superb sense of humour, and makes lovely regional reds with cassis, berry and mint fruit. His smiling, bearded face has adorned the front cover of many of the Victorian Tourist Bureau's excellent tourist publications over the past few years. The cellar in which he is seen dispensing wine is not his, incidentally; it is that of Chateau Tahbilk.

Passing Clouds Shiraz

Contrary to what one might expect, 1992 marked the first release of a 100 per cent Shiraz from Passing Clouds; prior to that time the Shiraz was used in the various Shiraz Cabernet blends. It was an extremely auspicious start, albeit from a very good vintage. Subsequent releases have continued to impress.

♥♥♥♥ **1998** Medium to full purple-red; the bouquet is concentrated, ripe and rich, with plenty of plum and blackberry fruit supported by just a hint of vanilla oak. The rich, juicy plum, cherry and (a little) mint fruit drives a palate with good balance and length. **rating:** 90

best drinking 2002–2010 **best vintages** '92, '94, '97, '98 **drink with** Oxtail • $23

Passing Clouds Graeme's Blend Shiraz Cabernet

The blend of 60 per cent Shiraz and 40 per cent Cabernet Sauvignon was first made in 1980, and has since become the linchpin in the Passing Clouds repertoire.

♥♥♥♥♥ **1998** Full red-purple; a rich and ripe bouquet with abundant dark cherry and blackberry fruit flows into a lovely palate with ripe, but not the least jammy, fruit where chocolate joins the primary berry fruit of the bouquet. Fine, lingering tannins and subtle oak complete the picture. **rating:** 93

best drinking 2003–2011 **best vintages** '81, '82, '86, '90, '91, '92, '94, '97, '98 **drink with** Yearling steak or veal • $23

Passing Clouds Cabernet Shiraz

A blend of 50 per cent Shiraz and 50 per cent Cabernet Sauvignon from low-yielding, unirrigated estate vineyards. Hand-plunged in open fermenters, with 20 per cent completing its fermentation in new American oak. Matured for 12 months in American oak puncheons before light egg white fining; the wine is not filtered.

♥♥♥♥ **1996** Medium to full red-purple; there are attractive aromas of berry and chocolate on the bouquet, together with some vanilla oak. The palate follows logically from the bouquet, with concentrated red and black cherry fruit flavours, attractive tannins and well-balanced and integrated oak. **rating:** 91

best drinking 2001–2007 **best vintages** NA **drink with** Braised beef • $NA

Passing Clouds Angel Blend

A blend of 90 per cent Cabernet Sauvignon and 5 per cent each of Cabernet Franc and Merlot aged in predominantly new American oak.

♥♥♥♥ **1998** Dark red-purple; voluminous wafts of mint seem to obscure the other aromas of the bouquet; the palate is as minty as the bouquet suggests, though not more so, and there is plenty of dark berry fruit underpinning the mint. Others will think the wine is marvellous; I am intolerant of mint. **rating:** 84

best drinking 2003–2009 **best vintages** '90, '91, '92, '94, '96, '97 **drink with** Wild duck • $30

paternoster NR

17 Paternoster Road, Emerald, Vic 3782 **region** Yarra Valley
phone (03) 5968 3197 **open** Weekends 10.30–5.30
winemaker Philip Hession **production** 600 **est.** 1985
product range ($12–30 CD) Semillon, Chardonnay, Pinot Noir, Shiraz, Cabernets, Vintage Port.
summary The densely planted, non-irrigated vines (at a density of 5000 vines to the hectare) cascade down a steep hillside at Emerald in one of the coolest parts of the Yarra Valley. Pinot Noir is the specialty of the winery, producing intensely flavoured wines with a strong eucalypt mint overlay reminiscent of the wines of Delatite. No recent tastings; there also seems to be some dispute as to whether Paternoster falls within the Yarra Valley.

patrick creek vineyard NR

Springfield Park, North Down, Tas 7307 **region** Northern Tasmania
phone (03) 6424 6979 **fax** (03) 6424 6380 **open** By appointment
winemaker Andrew Hood (Contract) **production** 350 **est.** 1990
product range ($15 CD) Semillon, Chardonnay, Classic Dry White, Pinot Noir.
summary Patrick Creek Vineyard came into being in 1990 when Pat and Kay Walker established high-density plantings of chardonnay, pinot noir, semillon and sauvignon blanc in a 1-hectare vineyard.

Patrick Creek Chardonnay

Made in tiny quantities by that magician Andrew Hood.

♥♥♥ **1999** Medium yellow-green; the bouquet is moderately intense, although the fruit doesn't quite carry the oak. A solid wine with more flavour than finesse; one suspects there may have been only a single barrel made. **rating:** 83

best drinking 2000–2003 **best vintages** NA **drink with** Cheese soufflé • $NA

Patrick Creek Pinot Noir

Patrick Creek has consistently produced strongly flavoured and structured Pinot Noirs which have equally consistently been medal winners at the Tasmanian Wines Show. The 1999 is the best yet.

TTTT 1999 Medium red-purple; the bouquet runs primarily in the savoury/briary/woody spectrum, but the palate moves convincing into sweet plummy fruit; some of the savoury characters add complexity, and the wine has good length. **rating:** 85

best drinking 2001–2004 **best vintages** '99 **drink with** Smoked quail • $NA

patritti wines ★★☆

13–23 Clacton Road, Dover Gardens, SA 5048 **region** Other Wineries of SA
phone (08) 8296 8261 **fax** (08) 8296 5088 **open** Mon–Sat 9–6
winemaker G Patritti, J Patritti **production** 65 000 **est.** 1926
product range ($4.50–8 CD) A kaleidoscopic array of table, sparkling, fortified and flavoured wines (and spirits) offered in bottle and flagon. The table wines are sold under the Blewitt Springs Estate, Patritti and Billabong Wines brands.
summary A traditional, family-owned business offering wines at modest prices, but with impressive vineyard holdings of 40 hectares in Blewitt Springs and another 40 hectares at Aldinga.

pattersons ★★★☆

St Werburghs Road, Mount Barker, WA 6234 **region** Great Southern
phone (08) 9851 2063 **fax** (08) 9851 2063 **open** Sun–Wed 10–5
winemaker Plantagenet (Contract) **production** 2000 **est.** 1982
product range ($17–27 CD) Chardonnay, Unwooded Chardonnay, Pinot Noir, Shiraz, Sparkling Shiraz.
summary Schoolteachers Sue and Arthur Patterson have grown chardonnay, shiraz and pinot noir and grazed cattle as a weekend relaxation for a decade. The cellar door is in a recently completed and very beautiful rammed-earth house, and a number of vintages are on sale at any one time. Good Chardonnay and Shiraz have been complemented by the occasional spectacular Pinot Noir. Retail distribution in New South Wales, Victoria and West Australia.

Pattersons Unwooded Chardonnay

It is difficult to say much about unwooded Chardonnay in general; this wine, however, does have that little bit extra.
TTTY 1999 Medium yellow-green; the bouquet is quite aromatic, with pronounced melon and stone fruit; the palate, likewise, has plenty of fruit flavour and depth. **rating:** 84
best drinking 2000–2002 **best vintages** NA **drink with** Roast pork • $17

Pattersons Pinot Noir

Produced from a little under 1 hectare of estate plantings, with part of the output sold to Plantagenet, and which indeed formed part of the much-awarded 1994 Plantagenet Pinot Noir. The '94 vintage of Pattersons was a marvellous wine in its own right, easily winning a gold medal at the 1995 Mount Barker Wine Show. However, vintages since 1994 have proved that a year like that is a once or twice a decade proposition.
TTTY 1998 Medium red-purple; the moderately intense bouquet is quite complex, with an array of ripe savoury/leathery aromas. The palate is tending more to generic dry red than Pinot Noir, but does have a pleasant, relatively long finish. **rating:** 83
best drinking 2000–2003 **best vintages** NA **drink with** Smoked duck • $25

Pattersons Shiraz

Together with the Chardonnay, has been the most consistent performer for Pattersons. In bygone years, two or three vintages were available for sale at cellar door, but no more.
TTTT 1998 Medium red-purple; the smooth, moderately intense bouquet ranges through cherry, mint and vanilla, which neatly translate into the flavours on the nicely weighted and structured palate, finishing with fine tannins. **rating:** 85
best drinking 2000–2006 **best vintages** '90, '91, '93, '94, '98 **drink with** Duck casserole • $24

paul conti ★★★☆

529 Wanneroo Road, Woodvale, WA 6026 **region** Swan District
phone (08) 9409 9160 **fax** (08) 9309 1634 **open** Mon–Sat 9.30–5.30, Sun by appointment
winemaker Paul Conti, Jason Conti **production** 8000 **est.** 1948
product range ($12–23 CD) Chenin Blanc, Chardonnay, Carabooda Chardonnay, Late Harvest Muscat, Pinot Noir, Grenache, Grenache Shiraz, Shiraz, Mariginiup Shiraz, Cabernet Sauvingon, White Port, Reserve Port, Sparkling Shiraz.

summary Third-generation winemaker Jason Conti has now assumed day-to-day control of winemaking, although father Paul (who had succeeded his father in 1968) remains interested and involved in the business. Over the years Paul Conti challenged and redefined industry perceptions and standards; the challenge for Jason Conti will be to achieve the same degree of success in a relentlessly and increasingly competitive market environment.

Paul Conti Mariginiup Shiraz

Made from vines planted in the Mariginiup Vineyard in 1958, which have produced many fine vintages over the years stretching back into the 1960s. The style is not elaborate but does age well, attested to by the fact that the wine is sold with between two to three years bottle age.

▼▼▼▼ 1997 Medium red-purple; the bouquet is clean, moderately intense, with aromas of chocolate, dark cherry and earth. The medium-bodied palate has similarly attractive fresh fruit, with just a trace of lift. In true Conti style, the wine has not been ambushed by American oak.   **rating:** 85

best drinking 2001–2007 **best vintages** '88, '89, '91, '93, '94 **drink with** Grilled steak • $23

paulett ★★★★

Polish Hill Road, Polish Hill River, SA 5453 **region** Clare Valley
phone (08) 8843 4328 **fax** (08) 8843 4202 **open** 7 days 10–5
winemaker Neil Paulett **production** 14 000 **est.** 1983
product range ($14–40 CD) Riesling, Sauvignon Blanc, Chardonnay, Late Harvest Riesling, The Quarry Mourvedre, Shiraz, Andreas Shiraz, Cabernet Merlot, Trillians (Sparkling Riesling).
summary The completion of the winery and cellar-door sales facility in 1992 marked the end of a development project which began back in 1982 when Neil and Alison Paulett purchased a 47-hectare property with a small patch of old vines and a house in a grove of trees (which were almost immediately burnt by the 1983 bushfires). The beautifully situated winery is one of the features of the scenic Polish Hill River region, as is its Riesling and its Cabernet Merlot. Exports to New Zealand and the UK.

paul osicka ★★★★

Majors Creek Vineyard at Graytown, Vic 3608 **region** Bendigo
phone (03) 5794 9235 **fax** (03) 5794 9288 **open** Mon–Sat 10–5, Sun 12–5
winemaker Paul Osicka **production** NFP **est.** 1955
product range ($14–25 CD) Chardonnay, Riesling, Cabernet Sauvignon, Shiraz.
summary A low-profile producer but reliable, particularly when it comes to its smooth but rich Shiraz. The wines are distributed in Melbourne and Sydney by Australian Prestige Wines, with exports to the UK, Hong Kong and Japan.

Paul Osicka Shiraz

Produced from non-irrigated, 40-year-old vines grown on sandy gravel soils. Matured in American oak hogsheads (one-third new, two-thirds second and third fill) for 14 months.

▼▼▼▼ 1998 Medium to full red-purple; most attractive plum and cherry fruit with just a hint of liquorice is supported on the bouquet by carefully balanced oak. The medium- to full-bodied palate is, like the bouquet, driven by the dark cherry and plum fruit; savoury tannins and a touch of vanilla oak round off an impressive wine.
                                                                         rating: 87

best drinking 2003–2008 **best vintages** '96, '98 **drink with** Kangaroo fillet • $23

peacock hill vineyard NR

Corner Branxton Road and Palmers Lane, Pokolbin, NSW 2320 **region** Lower Hunter Valley
phone (02) 4998 7661 **fax** (02) 4998 7661 **open** Fri–Mon, public and school holidays, 10–5, or by appointment
winemaker David Lowe, Jane Wilson-Lowe **production** 2000 **est.** 1969
product range ($13.50–28 CD) Absent Friends Chardonnay, Reserve Chardonnay, Untamed Chardonnay, Jaan Shiraz, Cabernet Sauvignon.
summary The Peacock Hill Vineyard was first planted in 1969 as part of the Rothbury Estate, originally being owned by a separate syndicate but then moving under the direct control and ownership of Rothbury. After several further changes of ownership as Rothbury sold many of its vineyards, George Tsiros and Silvi Laumets acquired the 8-hectare property in October 1995. Since that time they have rejuvenated the vineyard and built a small but attractive accommodation lodge for two people, and have a tennis court and petanque rink for their exclusive enjoyment. Over the years, Peacock Hill has been a consistent medal winner in local wine shows.

pearson vineyards NR

Main North Road, Penwortham, SA 5453 **region** Clare Valley
phone (08) 8843 4234 **fax** (08) 8843 4141 **open** Mon–Fri 11–5, weekends 10–5
winemaker Jim Pearson **production** 800 **est.** 1993
product range ($13–18 CD) Riesling, Late Harvest Riesling, Cabernet Franc, Cabernet Sauvignon.
summary Jim Pearson makes the Pearson Vineyard wines at Mintaro Cellars. The 1.5-hectare estate vineyards surround the beautiful little stone house which acts as a cellar door and which appears on the cover of my book, *The Wines, The History, The Vignerons of the Clare Valley*.

peel estate ★★★★

Fletcher Road, Baldivis, WA 6171 **region** South West Coast
phone (08) 9524 1221 **fax** (08) 9524 1625 **open** 7 days 10–5
winemaker Will Nairn **production** 8000 **est.** 1974
product range ($13.50–34 R) Chardonnay, Wood Matured Chenin Blanc, Medium Dry Chenin Blanc, Unwooded Chardonnay, Classic White, Verdelho, Shiraz, Zinfandel, Cabernet Sauvignon.
summary The winery rating is given for its Shiraz, a wine of considerable finesse and with a remarkably consistent track record. Every year Will Nairn holds a Great Shiraz tasting for six-year-old Australian Shirazes, and pits Peel Estate (in a blind tasting attended by 60 or so people) against Australia's best. It is never disgraced. The white wines are workmanlike, the wood-matured Chenin Blanc another winery specialty, although not achieving the excellence of the Shiraz. At five years of age it will typically show well, with black cherry and chocolate flavours, a strong dash of American oak, and surprising youth. There is limited retail distribution through each Australian state, and exports to Ireland.

peerick vineyard NR

Wild Dog Track, Moonambel, Vic 3478 **region** Pyrenees
phone (03) 9817 1611 **fax** (03) 9817 1611 **open** Weekends 11–4
winemaker Contract **production** 1300 **est.** 1990
product range ($12.75–19.50 CD) Sauvignon Blanc, Semillon Sauvignon Blanc, Shiraz, Cabernet Sauvignon.
summary Peerick is the venture of Melbourne lawyer Chris Jessup and wife Meryl. They have mildly trimmed their Joseph's coat vineyard by increasing the plantings to 5.95 hectares and eliminating the malbec and semillon, but still manage to grow cabernet sauvignon, shiraz, cabernet franc, merlot, sauvignon blanc, and viognier. Don't ask me where the semillon for the Semillon Sauvignon Blanc blend comes from; I don't know. The '98 Sauvignon Blanc (85 points) is a clean, elegant light-bodied wine with nice varietal character.

☙ pembroke NR

Richmond Road, Cambridge, Tas 7170 **region** Southern Tasmania
phone (03) 6248 5139 **fax** (03) 6234 5481 **open** Not
winemaker Andrew Hood (Contract) **production** 100 **est.** 1980
product range ($18.75–20 ML) Pinot Noir.
summary The 1-hectare Pembroke vineyard was established in 1980 by the McKay and Hawker families, and is still owned by them. It is predominantly planted to pinot noir, with tiny quantities of chardonnay, riesling and sauvignon blanc.

pendarves estate ★★★☆

110 Old North Road, Belford, NSW 2335 **region** Lower Hunter Valley
phone (02) 6574 7222 **fax** (02) 9970 6152 **open** Weekends 11–5, Mon–Fri by appointment
winemaker Greg Silkman (Contract) **production** 10 000 **est.** 1986
product range ($16–20 CD) An unusual portfolio of Verdelho, Sauvignon Blanc, Semillon, Chardonnay, Pinot Noir, Chambourcin, Shiraz, Merlot Malbec Cabernet.
summary The perpetual-motion general practitioner and founder of the Australian Medical Friends of Wine, Dr Philip Norrie, is a born communicator and marketer as well as a wine historian of note. He also happens to be a passionate advocate of the virtues of Verdelho, inspired in part by the high regard held for that variety by vignerons around the turn of the century. His ambassadorship for the cause of wine and health in both Australia and overseas has no doubt indirectly contributed to the significant rise in production, and to the establishment of export markets in Singapore, and the UK (as well as national distribution).

penfolds ★★★★★

Tanunda Road, Nuriootpa, SA 5355 **region** Barossa Valley
phone (08) 8560 9408 **fax** (08) 8562 2494 **open** Mon–Fri 10–5, Sat, Sun and public hols 11–5
winemaker John Duval **production** 1.4 million **est.** 1844
product range ($9–250 R) Kalimna Bin 28 Shiraz, 128 Coonawarra Shiraz, 389 Cabernet Shiraz, 407 Cabernet Sauvignon, 707 Cabernet Sauvignon and Special Show Bin reds. Brands include Minchinbury Sparkling; Rawson's Retreat Semillon Chardonnay and Cabernet Shiraz; Penfolds The Valleys Chardonnay, Old Vine Barossa Valley Semillon and Old Vine Barossa Valley Shiraz Grenache Mourvedre; Koonunga Hill Shiraz Cabernet, Semillon Sauvignon Blanc and Chardonnay; Magill Estate; Clare Estate and Clare Estate Chardonnay; St Henri Cabernet Shiraz; Yattarna, Grange. Also various export-only labels. Finally, Grandfather Port and Great Grandfather Port.
summary Senior among the 17 wine companies or stand-alone brands in Southcorp Wines and undoubtedly one of the top wine companies in the world in terms of quality, product range and exports. The consistency of the quality of the red wines and their value for money can only be described as breathtaking. In 1998 it released its long-awaited super-premium white wine, Yattarna Chardonnay, intended to sit alongside Grange, Australia's greatest red wine. It is also increasingly giving a regional identity to its fighting varietal brands. Worldwide distribution.

Penfolds Eden Valley Reserve Riesling

A new label for Penfolds, signifying its continuing push into ultra-premium white wine territory.
♥♥♥♥♡ **1999** Light to medium green-yellow; the bouquet is clean and intense, with lime, herb and a hint of spice. The palate is clean, moderately intense and with attractive lime-accented fruit. It won the trophy for Best White Wine at the 2000 Royal Sydney Wine Show. **rating:** 90
best drinking 2004–2012 **best vintages** NA **drink with** Mussells in white wine • $25

Penfolds Adelaide Hills Semillon

This wine was developed as part of Penfolds' on-going search for a long-lived white wine to sit alongside Grange. It demonstrates that the Penfolds team was, at least toying with the idea of using semillon as the base. The Adelaide Hills, and the higher ridges of McLaren Vale adjacent to the Adelaide Hills, produce a distinctive style of Semillon, closer to that of the Margaret River than the Hunter.
♥♥♥♥♡ **1998** Medium to full yellow-green; a rich, full bouquet with hints of herb and grass, and exceptionally subtle oak handling. That sophisticated but gentle oak handling is a feature of the rich texture and structure of the palate; finishes with good acidity. **rating:** 91
best drinking 2003–2008 **best vintages** NA **drink with** Rich seafood or veal • $26

Penfolds Barossa Valley Semillon Chardonnay

A wine with modest aspirations and priced accordingly. However, as each vintage passes, the oak treatment improves and the wine gains a little bit of extra finesse.
♥♥♥♡ **1999** Light green-yellow; the bouquet is plain, neutral and inoffensive. The palate has just sufficient weight to lift it from the ruck, and will evolve into an old-style, so-called white burgundy, with time in bottle. **rating:** 80
best drinking 2000–2002 **best vintages** NA **drink with** Pork chops • $12

Penfolds Adelaide Hills Chardonnay

Produced, as the name suggests, from grapes grown in the Adelaide Hills. It is the base of the pyramid, with Yattarna at the top, and shows why Yattarna has received such acclaim. The full gamut of Chardonnay winemaking techniques are, of course, applied, although with sophistication and restraint.
♥♥♥♥♡ **1998** Light green-yellow; the bouquet is wonderfully fresh and relatively light, with melon, cashew and fine, nutty oak. The wine is beautifully balanced on the palate, with a remarkably long, lingering finish. Will undoubtedly repay cellaring. **rating:** 93
best drinking 2001–2005 **best vintages** '95, '98 **drink with** Marron • $31

Penfolds Koonunga Hill Chardonnay

Produced from grapes grown across the whole of southeastern Australia, but with surprisingly high-quality criteria for inclusion in the wine.
♥♥♥♡ **1999** Medium yellow-green; the bouquet is moderately intense and quite complex; fruit-driven. The palate has fair length but there is not over much character on the mid-palate. **rating:** 82
best drinking Drink now **best vintages** NA **drink with** Everyday food • $11

Penfolds Rawson's Retreat Chardonnay

Launched with the 1998 vintage, and a signpost for the direction in which the 'surplus' of Australian Chardonnay is headed. It also shows Penfolds' growing skill in white winemaking, being far less heavy-handed than earlier wines at this price point. Drawn from vineyard resources spread across the whole of southeastern Australia, but with McLaren Vale and the Riverland making the major contributions. A small amount of Sauvignon Blanc may be added according to the vintage.

▼▼▼▽ **1999** Medium yellow-green; the moderately intense bouquet features good oak and fruit balance and integration; plenty there. There is quite full peach and melon fruit on the palate supported by a well-handled flick of oak. A supremely honest wine with plenty of overall flavour; a bargain at the price (which will often be discounted below the theoretical level). **rating:** 84

best drinking 2000–2001 **best vintages** NA **drink with** KFC • $10

Penfolds Reserve Bin Chardonnay

This is the most important spin-off from the development programme which led to the birth of Yattarna in the 1995 vintage. The Adelaide Hills has exceptional site diversity which gives full scope to the Penfolds winemakers' skill at synergistically blending parcels of wine from varied sources.

▼▼▼▼▼ **1995** Bin 95A. Received three trophies at the 1999 Royal Adelaide Wine Show, including Best Wine of Show. The pinnacle of sophistication, with all the elements seamlessly welded together in a flowing river of gently tangy fruit, soft cashew and fine spicy oak. Outstanding Chardonnay. **rating:** 97

best drinking 2000–2010 **best vintages** '94, '95, '96 **drink with** Smoked chicken • $90

Penfolds The Valleys Chardonnay

Made from chardonnay grown in the Clare and Barossa Valleys, and now 100 per cent barrel-fermented in a mixture of new and one-year-old French oak, in which it spends eight months. 'The Valleys' was added to the label name in late 1995, part of a broad-ranging move towards greater regional identification for the wines in this price bracket.

▼▼▼▽ **1998** Medium to full yellow-green; the bouquet is solid, if a little pedestrian, there is quite good fruit weight on the palate, but the wine lacks zip. At least the oak handling is appropriate. **rating:** 83

best drinking Drink now **best vintages** '93 **drink with** Pasta, chicken, turkey • $14

Penfolds Yattarna Chardonnay

In April 1998 the long-awaited 'White Grange' was finally released, the name Yattarna putting to rest forever the idea that there could possibly be a brand extension of what is, and always will be, a unique wine. It was a blend of 50 per cent Adelaide Hills and 50 per cent McLaren Vale Chardonnay, given Rolls Royce treatment from start to finish. The '96 and subsequent vintages have been produced almost entirely from Adelaide Hills grapes.

▼▼▼▼▼ **1996** Glowing yellow-green; the bouquet is intense, with perfectly balanced nectarine and fig fruit woven through with subtle oak. The palate is elegant, almost to the point of delicacy, with absolutely impeccable fruit and oak balance and integration. **rating:** 95

best drinking 2000–2010 **best vintages** '95, '96 **drink with** Richer white meat dishes of all kinds • $100

Penfolds Bin 128 Coonawarra Shiraz

Curiously, the only wine made by Penfolds every vintage from Coonawarra grapes and sold in the Australian market (there are some export labels). No less curious has been the lacklustre performance (by Penfolds standards and given the reputation of Coonawarra) of the wine over the years. However, since 1986 the wine has taken a distinct turn for the better, which is as it should be. It is one of the few wines in the Penfolds range which is matured entirely in French oak, 20 per cent new and 80 per cent one and two years old.

▼▼▼▼ **1997** Good medium to full red-purple; the bouquet is inevitably less concentrated than the '96, with cherry and hints of sweet shoe leather. A nice wine in the mouth, with attractive berry flavours together with hints of mint and leather; fine tannins; gives the impression it will develop quite quickly over the next five years. **rating:** 88

best drinking 2002–2007 **best vintages** '63, '66, '80, '86, '89, '90, '91, '93, '94, '96 **drink with** Veal; mild cheddar • $20

Penfolds Grange

Australia's greatest red wine, with a turbulent early history chronicled in Huon Hooke's book entitled *Max Schubert: Winemaker* in December 1995. The '94 comes from a relatively unheralded vintage; it will be interesting to see whether others think it is as great as I do.

▼▼▼▼▽ **1995** Strong red-purple; rich, ripe and black cherry fruit, sweet as it can be, matched with good oak on the bouquet. There is plenty of power and ripeness to the palate, with no sign of a lesser vintage; good tannins and length. **rating: 93**

best drinking 2005–2020 **best vintages** '52, '53, '55, '62, '66, '67, '71, '76, '78, '80, '85, '86, '90, '91, '92, '93, '94 **drink with** Rich game dishes • $250

Penfolds Kalimna Bin 28 Shiraz

A multi-region blend sourced from the Barossa and Clare Valleys, McLaren Vale and Langhorne Creek regions. There is a good argument to be made that it should be Bin 28, rather than Bin 389, which is 'Poor Man's Grange'. The emphasis is on the same lush fruit; the oak used is second- and third-use American barrels handed down through the Grange and Bin 389 programmes.

▼▼▼▼ **1997** Medium red-purple; youthful plummy fruit with some earthy/charry notes on the bouquet introduces a pleasant, indeed pretty, wine which lacks the intensity of the '96 and won't go on forever, but by any other comparison is a good wine. **rating: 89**

best drinking 2002–2010 **best vintages** '64, '66, '71, '80, '81, '83, '86, '90, '91, '94, '95, '96 **drink with** Lamb or beef casserole • $20

Penfolds Magill Estate

Made solely from the 5.2-hectare vineyard established on the site where Dr Christopher Rawson Penfold built his house in 1844. It is an estate wine in the fullest sense of the term, made at the historic Magill winery, which has been restored and refurbished. Situated within 10 minutes of the centre of Adelaide, Magill Estate will become one of Australia's foremost viticultural landmarks.

▼▼▼▼ **1997** Medium to full red-purple; a highly scented bouquet with very ripe, juicy berry fruit characters. The palate has more of those juicy berry flavours together with a hint of mint. A good wine, but not great. **rating: 87**

best drinking 2002–2007 **best vintages** '83, '86, '89, '90, '91, '93, '95, '96 **drink with** Rack of lamb • $39.95

Penfolds Bin 389 Cabernet Shiraz

First made in 1960, and promptly dubbed 'Poor Man's Grange'. A blend of 50 per cent to 60 per cent Cabernet Sauvignon and 40 per cent to 50 per cent Shiraz from the Barossa Valley, Coonawarra, Padthaway, McLaren Vale, Langhorne Creek and the Clare Valley. Matured in a mixture of new (20 per cent) and older American oak barrels.

▼▼▼▼ **1997** Medium red-purple; surprisingly well integrated and balanced fruit and oak with lively cassis accents. The palate, too, offers attractive mint and berry flavours plus a slice of vanilla courtesy of the oak. **rating: 89**

best drinking 2002–2012 **best vintages** '66, '70, '71, '86, '90, '93, '94, '96 **drink with** Double lamb loin chops • $26

Penfolds Rawson's Retreat Cabernet Shiraz

Introduced in the mid-1990s to fill the volume gap underneath Koonunga Hill, and made in very substantial quantities. One of Australia's top-selling red wines under $10 and, for this reason if no other, cannot be ignored. A blend of Shiraz, Ruby Cabernet and Cabernet Sauvignon drawn from many parts of southeast Australia, predominantly from the Riverland, Barossa Valley and McLaren Vale districts. The touch of oak evident in the wine is derived from maturation in older, small oak barrels.

▼▼▼▽ **1998** Dark red; the bouquet is quite rich, with dark chocolate overtones to the berry fruit, and minimal oak. The palate, likewise, offers plenty of fruit flavour in a dark berry spectrum, finishing with attractive, soft tannins. Surprisingly good structure; very good value for money. **rating: 83**

best drinking 1999–2003 **best vintages** NA **drink with** Pizza • $9

Penfolds Bin 707 Cabernet Sauvignon

First made in 1964, with a hiatus between 1969 and 1976 as scarce supplies of Cabernet Sauvignon were diverted to Bin 389. Now made from a blend of Coonawarra, Barossa and Eden Valley grapes, vinified in a fashion similar to Grange, with the fermentation finished in American oak barrels. The '94 vintage won three trophies at the 1997 Sydney Wine Show, including the Dr Gilbert Phillips Trophy for Best Red Wine of the Show. Not made in 1995. The '96 is destined for greatness even in the ranks of Bin 707.

▼▼▼▼ **1997** Dark purple-red; a wine which continues that high-toned, lusciously aromatic fruit of the '96, with some cedary oak. There is plenty of weight and stuffing to the palate, where cassis and vanilla intermingle, rounded off with lingering tannins. **rating: 92**

best drinking 2003–2018 **best vintages** '66, '80, '84, '86, '88, '90, '92, '93, '94, '96, '97 **drink with** Rare scotch fillet • $80

Penfolds Block 42 Kalimna Cabernet Sauvignon

A superb Special Bin wine produced from 120-year-old cabernet sauvignon vines on the Kalimna Vineyard.

▼▼▼▼▼ **1996** Medium to full red-purple; a paradigm of everything Cabernet Sauvignon should be: the fragrant cassis/redcurrant fruit and perfect oak integration of the bouquet is followed by an intensely flavoured yet elegant wine on a very long palate flooded with cassis and redcurrant fruit, and crowned with fine tannins on the finish. **rating: 96**

best drinking 2006–2026 **best vintages** '96 **drink with** Lamb Provençale • $200

Penfolds Grandfather Port

First released in the 1960s; made from Barossa Valley Shiraz and Mourvedre which is oak-matured in old barrels for decades, and which is finally blended from selection of very old and much younger material. Penfolds has always kept a tight rein on production, thus preserving the all-important old material which forms the base of the wine.

▼▼▼▼▼ **NV** Medium to full tawny-red; exceedingly complex, with strong barrel-aged rancio characters and attractively earthy spirit. A long and richly flavoured wine, with the cleansing, drying finish which is so essential to the style. **rating: 90**

best drinking 2000–2010 **best vintages** NA **drink with** Coffee • $NA

Penfolds Great Grandfather Port

First released in 1994 to celebrate the 150th birthday of Penfolds. In a neat marketing gimmick, 1994 bottles were blended and bottled, utilising the very oldest and best stocks, dating back to the early years of the twentieth century. The concentration and power of the wine is reminiscent of the very old Seppelt Liqueur Tawny Ports.

▼▼▼▼▼ **NV** Deep tawny with an olive-green rim; both the bouquet and palate are extraordinarily concentrated and rich, very much into the liqueur style of Port which is unique to Australia. Shows the Brandy spirit which was used in the fortifying process, and which adds yet extra complexity. **rating: 95**

best drinking 2000–2010 **best vintages** NA **drink with** Coffee • $150

penley estate ★★★★☆

McLeans Road, Coonawarra, SA 5263 **region** Coonawarra
phone (08) 8736 3211 **fax** (08) 8736 3124 **open** By appointment
winemaker Kym Tolley **production** 20 000 **est.** 1988
product range ($17–70 R) Chardonnay, Hyland Shiraz, Ausvetia Shiraz, Shiraz Cabernet, Merlot, Cabernet Sauvignon, Phoenix Cabernet Sauvignon, Pinot Noir Chardonnay.
summary Owner winemaker Kym Tolley describes himself as a fifth-generation winemaker, the family tree involving both the Penfolds and the Tolleys. He worked 17 years in the industry before establishing Penley Estate and has made every post a winner since, producing a succession of rich, complex, full-bodied red wines and stylish Chardonnays. Now ranks as one of the best wineries in Coonawarra, drawing upon 81 precious hectares of estate plantings. Exports to the UK, Switzerland, Germany, Austria, Luxembroug, California and Canada.

Penley Estate Hyland Shiraz

At least on the performance of the '98 vintage, offers excellent value for money, and is certainly the bargain in the Penley range.

▼▼▼▼ **1998** Medium to full red-purple; the bouquet is rich and quite voluptuous, with sweet berry and seamlessly integrated oak. The palate is no less impressive, with rich, sweet fruit, the only faint criticism being a slightly chewy finish. **rating: 89**

best drinking 2003–2008 **best vintages** NA **drink with** Fillet mignon • $17

Penley Estate Shiraz Cabernet Sauvignon

A blend of 50 per cent Shiraz and 50 per cent Cabernet Sauvignon, sourced from Coonawarra (65 per cent), the balance from McLaren Vale (25 per cent) and Barossa Valley (10 per cent). Matured for two years in a mix of 75 per cent American and 25 per cent French (Troncais) oak. Like the Cabernet Sauvignon, a prolific medal winner.

▼▼▼▼ **1997** Medium red-purple; the bouquet runs through cedar, vanilla and then more spicy savoury characters. The palate replicates those characters; not luscious but well-balanced and has good length. **rating: 86**

best drinking 2002–2007 **best vintages** '88, '90, '91, '92, '94, '96 **drink with** Soft ripened cheese • $29

Penley Estate Cabernet Sauvignon

Made from the pick of 38 hectares of estate-grown Cabernet Sauvignon, matured in a cleverly handled mix of American and French oak. Over the years, various vintages of the wine have won a quite extraordinary number of trophies and gold medals.

▼▼▼▼ **1997** Medium red-purple; a complex bouquet with some bottle-developed aromas starting to emerge, ranging through blackcurrant into more earthy/cedary regional notes; the palate reflects those flavours, with good tannin structure and length. Impressive for an intermediate vintage. **rating: 89**
best drinking 2002–2012 **best vintages** '89, '90, '91, '92, '94, '96 **drink with** Rare beef • $56

penny's hill vineyards   NR

Main Road, McLaren Vale, SA 5171 **region** McLaren Vale
phone (08) 8362 1077 **fax** (08) 8362 2766 **open** By appointment
winemaker Ben Riggs (Contract) **production** 4300 **est.** 1988
product range ($23–26 R) Chardonnay, Shiraz, Specialized (Shiraz Cabernet Merlot).
summary Penny's Hill is a major new vineyard and winery operation in McLaren Vale owned by Adelaide advertising agency businessman Tony Parkinson and wife Susie. The Penny's Hill vineyard is 25 hectares and, unusually for McLaren Vale, is close-planted with a thin vertical trellis/thin vertical canopy, the work of consultant viticulturist David Paxton. The innovative red dot packaging was the inspiration of Tony Parkinson, recalling the red dot sold sign on pictures in an art gallery.

Penny's Hill Shiraz
The Wirra Wirra style of winemaking shows through to the full advantage of this elegant wine.
▼▼▼▼ **1997** Medium purple-red; the moderately intense bouquet is clean and smooth, with gentle, dark berry fruit and just a whisper of chocolate. The palate is supple and soft, with savoury chocolate and earth overtones to the fruit; nicely finished with fine tannins. **rating: 88**
best drinking 2002–2007 **best vintages** '97 **drink with** Lamb shanks • $NA

pennyweight winery   NR

Pennyweight Lane, Beechworth, Vic 3747 **region** Alpine Valleys and Beechworth
phone (03) 5728 1747 **fax** (03) 5728 1704 **open** Thur–Tues 10–5
winemaker Stephen Newton Morris **production** 1000 **est.** 1982
product range ($13–30 CD) A fortified specialist but also producing limited table wines, including Trebbiano Riesling, Pinot Noir and Shiraz; the primary focus is on Fino and Amontillado Sherries, a range of Ports from Old Tawny to Ruby, Vintage Port, White Port and Muscat.
summary Pennyweight was established by Stephen Morris, great-grandson of G F Morris, founder of Morris Wines. The 3 hectares of vines are not irrigated and are moving towards organic certification. The business is run by Stephen, together with his wife Elizabeth and assisted by their three sons; Elizabeth Morris says, 'It's a perfect world', suggesting Pennyweight is more than happy with its lot in life.

penwortham wines   NR

Government Road, Penwortham, SA 5453 **region** Clare Valley
phone (08) 8843 4345 **open** Sat 10–5, Sun, holidays 10–4
winemaker Richard Hughes **production** 1000 **est.** 1985
product range ($13–16 CD) Riesling, Cabernet Sauvignon, Shiraz.
summary Richard Hughes has progressively established 12 hectares of riesling, semillon, verdelho, shiraz and cabernet sauvignon, selling most of the grapes and making restricted quantities of wine from the remainder.

peppers creek   NR

Broke Road, Pokolbin, NSW 2321 **region** Lower Hunter Valley
phone (02) 4998 7532 **fax** (02) 4998 7531 **open** Wed–Sun 10–5
winemaker Peter Ireland **production** 700 **est.** 1987
product range ($20–25 CD) Enzo Bianco, Enzo Rosé, Semillon, Unwooded Chardonnay, Chardonnay, Enzo Rosso, Merlot, Yacht Squadron Port.
summary A combined winery and antique shop which sells all its wine through the cellar door and runs the Cafe Enzo. The red wines previously tasted were clean and full flavoured, the Merlot coming from the hectare of estate vineyards. No recent tastings.

pepper tree ★★★★

Halls Road, Pokolbin, NSW 2321 **region** Lower Hunter Valley
phone (02) 4998 7539 **fax** (02) 4998 7746 **open** 7 days 9–5
winemaker Chris Cameron, Chris Archer **production** 40 000 **est.** 1993
product range ($10–30 CD) Sundial White and Red; Chardonnay, Shiraz, Cabernet Franc; Reserve range of Semillon, Chardonnay, Sauvignon Blanc, Traminer, Verdelho, Muscat, Malbec, Coonawarra Merlot and Cabernet Sauvignon.
summary The Pepper Tree winery is situated in the complex which also contains The Convent guesthouse and Roberts Restaurant. The company which now owns Pepper Tree is headed by Chris Cameron, chief winemaker since 1991. It made a decisive move in 1996, formalising the acquisition of a major interest in the Parker (Coonawarra) Estate vineyards, having previously purchased some of the fruit from those vineyards. Pepper Tree has made a determined, and quite successful, effort to establish its reputation as one of Australia's leading producers of Merlot.

☙ perrini estate NR

Bower Road, Meadows, SA 5201 **region** Adelaide Hills
phone (08) 8388 3210 **fax** (08) 8388 3210 **open** Wed–Sun and public holidays 10–5
winemaker Antonio Perrini **production** 2200 **est.** 1997
product range ($10.50–18 CD) Unwooded Chardonnay, Semillon, Merlot, Shiraz, Cabernet Sauvignon, Tony's Blend, Tawny Port.
summary Perrini Estate is very much a family affair; Tony and Connie Perrini had spent their working life in the retail food business, and Tony purchased the land in 1988 as a hobby farm and retirement home (or so Tony told Connie). In 1990 Tony planted his first few grapevines, began to read everything he could about making wine, and thereafter obtained vintage experience at a local winery. Next came highly successful entries into amateur winemaker competitions, and that was that. Together the family established the 6 hectares of vineyard, and built the winery and cellar door, culminating in the first commercial releases of the 1997 vintage, which had sold out within months of release.

pertaringa ★★★★

Corner Hunt and Rifle Range Roads, McLaren Vale, SA 5171 **region** McLaren Vale
phone (08) 8323 8125 **fax** (08) 8323 7766 **open** Mon–Fri and public holidays 10–4
winemaker Geoff Hardy, Ben Riggs **production** 5000 **est.** 1980
product range ($15–25 R) Semillon, Sauvignon Blanc, Shiraz, Liqueur Frontignac, Cabernet Sauvignon.
summary The Pertaringa wines are made from part of the grapes grown by by leading viticulturists Geoff Hardy and Ian Leask. The Pertaringa vineyard of 33 hectares was acquired in 1980 and rejuvenated; establishment of the ultra-cool Kuitpo vineyard in the Adelaide Hills began in 1987 and now supplies leading makers such as Southcorp, Petaluma and Shaw & Smith. Retail distribution through South Australia, New South Wales, Victoria and Queensland; exports to the UK, the US, Canada and Denmark.

Pertaringa Shiraz

A classic example of McLaren Vale shiraz, coming from fully mature vines. It is fruit, rather than oak, which provides the flavour.
▼▼▼▼▼ 1998 Dark red-purple; strong, concentrated blackberry and cherry fruit on the bouquet leads into a lovely sweet palate with berry fruit and complex hints of liquorice and game; nice oak handling and soft tannins.
best drinking 2003–2013 **best vintages** '97, '98 **drink with** Beef casserole • $24 **rating:** 94

Pertaringa Cabernet Sauvignon

Produced from 2 hectares of estate plantings; prior to 1998 it was the Shiraz which attracted most attention, but it was emphatically the turn of Cabernet Sauvignon in that (1998) year.
▼▼▼▼▼ 1998 Medium to full red-purple; the bouquet has sweet blackberry/blackcurrant fruit supported by subtle oak; the wine really shines on the palate, where quite delicious cassis/berry fruit is cradled in softly spicy oak.
best drinking 2003–2013 **best vintages** '89, '90, '91, '98 **drink with** Boned leg of lamb • $22 **rating:** 94

petaluma ★★★★★

Spring Gully Road, Piccadilly, SA 5151 **region** Adelaide Hills
phone (08) 8339 4122 **fax** (08) 8339 5253 **open** See Bridgewater Mill
winemaker Brian Croser **production** 30 000 **est.** 1976
product range ($19–49 R) Riesling, Chardonnay, Coonawarra (Cabernet Blend), Croser (Sparkling); Second label Sharefarmers White and Red. Bridgewater Mill is another second label — see separate entry.

summary The Petaluma empire continues to flourish, now taking in both Knappstein Wines and Mitchelton. While running a public-listed group, Brian Croser has never compromised his fierce commitment to quality, and doubtless never will. The Riesling is almost monotonously good; the Chardonnay is the big mover, going from strength to strength; the Merlot another marvellously succulent wine to buy without hesitation.

Petaluma Riesling

A 100 per cent estate-produced wine from Petaluma's Hanlins Hill Vineyard in the Clare Valley, one of the classic Australian Riesling regions. The wine is made with iron discipline and is a crystal-pure reflection of the interaction of climate, soil and variety. As the notes indicate, it ages with grace.

♥♥♥♥♥ **1999** Light yellow-green; a highly floral and striking bouquet with herb, grass, spice and lime aromas erupting from the glass. The palate is similarly intense and striking, with herb, grass, mineral and spice flavours. One to watch at is develops.   **rating: 94**

best drinking 2004–2011   **best vintages** '80, '85, '86, '88, '90, '92, '93, '94, '95, '97   **drink with** Sashimi • $22.95

Petaluma Sharefarmers White Semillon Sauvignon Blanc

Produced from grapes grown on Petaluma's Sharefarmers Vineyard, the eye in the centre of the storm revolving around the drawing of the borders of Coonawarra. The wine is fermented in stainless steel and early-bottled.

♥♥♥♥ **1998** Light green-yellow; the bouquet is clean and not particularly aromatic, making one wonder why it was left for a year before release in mid-1999. The palate is pleasant, crisp and clean, with the length of flavour its strong point. Can legitimately claim to be a food style.   **rating: 87**

best drinking 1999–2001   **best vintages** NA   **drink with** All fish and white meats   • $18.80

Petaluma Chardonnay

One of the more elegant and refined Australian Chardonnays which has, however, radically changed its geographic base since it was first made in 1977, starting in Cowra then moving to Coonawarra, then partly to the Clare Valley, and ultimately (since 1990) being made from Piccadilly Valley grapes. The style of the wine has been refined over the period, but has remained remarkably consistent given the quite radically changing regional base.

♥♥♥♥ **1998** Light to medium green-yellow; a clean, finely balanced bouquet with nectarine, fig, a touch of cashew and a hint of mineral all present. A refined style, with gentle creamy/cashew flavours and subtle oak. Delicate and understated; will develop.   **rating: 89**

best drinking 2002–2008   **best vintages** '87, '90, '91, '92, '95, '96   **drink with** Slow-roasted Tasmanian salmon • $31

Petaluma Croser

It was the desire to make a great sparkling wine which primarily drew Brian Croser to the Piccadilly Valley in the first instance. The climate is very cool, and ideally suited to the production of the fine base wine for Croser. First made in 1984 from 100 per cent Chardonnay, but quickly moved to its current mix of approximately 50 per cent Chardonnay and 50 per cent Pinot Noir, although the mix between the two varies from 35 per cent–65 per cent (either side) according to the vintage.

♥♥♥♥♡ **1997** Has abundant fine mousse; the bouquet is restrained, with obvious Pinot Noir influence in its bready/minerally profile. Delicacy is the key word for a super-refined, perfectly balanced palate and a dry, but lingering, finish.   **rating: 93**

best drinking 2000–2001   **best vintages** '86, '88, '90, '92, '94, '96, '97   **drink with** Caviar   • $34

Petaluma Coonawarra

A logical counterpart to the Chardonnay in the sense that it is far more elegant and refined than the more typical South Australian (and in particular, Coonawarra) Cabernet. Its regional base has remained the same since 1979, but the varietal composition has changed significantly, moving from Shiraz and Cabernet in '79 through to a Cabernet-dominant blend with around 15 per cent Merlot. As with the Chardonnay, the more recent vintages are best.

♥♥♥♥♥ **1998** Very youthful purple-red; sweet, smooth and luscious casis/blackberry/plum fruit together with subtle oak on the bouquet leads into a medium- to full-bodied palate, very concentrated yet perfectly balanced, with cassis and chocolate flavours supported by ripe, soft, yet persistent, tannins. Without any question, the best Petaluma Coonawarra so far.   **rating: 95**

♥♥♥♥♥ **1997** Youthful purple-red; the clean bouquet offers cassis, mulberry and blackberry fruit supported by impeccable oak handling. Good fruit in the cassis/blackberry spectrum runs throughout a palate distinguished by fine, ripe tannins, subtle oak and considerable length. This really is a successful Petaluma Coonawarra.   **rating: 94**

best drinking 2003–2018   **best vintages** '79, '86, '88, '90, '91, '92, '95, '97, '98   **drink with** Saddle of lamb   • $49

peter lehmann ★★★☆

Para Road, Tanunda, SA 5352 **region** Barossa Valley
phone (08) 8563 2500 **fax** (08) 8563 3402 **open** Mon–Fri 9.30–5, weekends, holidays 10.30–4.30
winemaker Peter Lehmann, Andrew Wigan, Peter Scholz, Leonie Lange, Ian Hongell **production** 200 000
est. 1979
product range ($11–55 CD) Eden Valley Riesling, Barossa Semillon, Barossa Chenin Blanc, Semillon
Chardonnay, Chardonnay, Clancy's Classic Dry White, Botrytis Riesling, Noble Semillon, Grenache, Seven
Surveys Dry Red, Barossa Shiraz, Barossa Cabernet Sauvignon, Clancys Red, and Bin AD 2015 Vintage Port.
Premium wines are Reserve Riesling, Reserve Chardonnay, Mentor, Stonewell Shiraz, Eight Songs Shiraz, Black
Queen Sparkling Shiraz.
summary Public listing on the stock exchange has not altered the essential nature of the company, resolutely and
single-mindedly focused on Peter Lehmann's beloved Barossa Valley. Some of the top-of-the-range wines are
seriously good, the base range reliable rather than inspiring. Exports to the UK through its own subsidiary; also to
New Zealand, Asia, the South Pacific and the US.

Peter Lehmann Semillon Chardonnay

A wine which is said to be barrel-fermented, which would be an outstanding achievement for a $12 wine.
▼▼▼▼ **1999** Light green-yellow; oak is certainly there on both bouquet and palate, and has added to the flavour
and character of the wine, but it is certain to develop and broaden quickly. **rating:** 81
best drinking Drink now **best vintages** NA **drink with** Barossa smoked meats • $12

Peter Lehmann Clancy's Classic Dry White

Brand extension is the name of the game these days, and so the Clancy's Classic Dry White had to come sooner or
later. A blend of Semillon, Chardonnay and Sauvignon Blanc, it is refreshingly free of oak.
▼▼▼▽ **1999** Light green-yellow; the bouquet is fresh, clean and crisp; there is pleasant palate-feel, with gentle fruit
flavour uncomplicated by oak. **rating:** 80
best drinking 2000–2001 **best vintages** NA **drink with** Seafood pasta • $12

Peter Lehmann Shiraz

The blood brother, as it were, to the Peter Lehmann Riesling. A traditional Barossa style, as honest as the day is
long but also reflecting the multitude of vineyard sources available to Peter Lehmann through his long association
with the Valley.
▼▼▼▽ **1998** Medium to full purple-red; strong vanilla oak on the bouquet is followed by some nice berry fruit.
The flavours of both fruit and oak on the palate are less intense than the bouquet, but the balance of the wine is
pleasant. **rating:** 83
best drinking 2001–2005 **best vintages** '89, '90, '91, '92, '94 **drink with** Spiced Barossa sausage • $18

Peter Lehmann Eight Songs Shiraz

Created out of the marvellous 1996 vintage, which might seem enough in itself; however, the packaging, the story
behind the packaging and the labels are, quite simply, utterly remarkable. Shortly put, they are the eight songs
attributed to Mad King George III, the poetry of Australian Randolph Stowe, and the incomparable art of Barossa
resident Rod Schubert. The wine is sold in boxes of eight, the labels each reproducing a different Schubert
painting.
▼▼▼▼▽ **1996** Medium red-purple; tangy lemon and vanilla oak leads the singing on the bouquet, with the fruit
coming in as the basses on the palate, even if the melody remains with the oak. The wine has excellent texture,
structure and balance. **rating:** 90
best drinking 2006–2016 **best vintages** '96 **drink with** Four and twenty pie • $45

Peter Lehmann Stonewell Shiraz

The wine is made solely from low-yielding old vineyards of the Stonewell, Ebenezer and Moppa subdistricts of
the Barossa Valley. The fermentation is finished in new American oak in which it is then matured for two years
prior to bottling. It is then given three years bottle-age before release. The wine has a supremely illustrious show
record, with many major trophies to its credit.
▼▼▼▼ **1995** Dense red-purple; a rich, concentrated cherry and blackberry-accented bouquet is followed by a
palate with dense, ripe fruit. Just when you are poised to give the wine gold medal points, powerful tannins grip
the finish, taking no prisoners. The wine may come into balance, but I really think the tannins will outlive the
fruit. **rating:** 85
best drinking 2005–2015 **best vintages** '80, '89, '91, '92, '93, '94 **drink with** Kangaroo fillet • $55

Peter Lehmann Clancy's

A blend of Barossa-grown Shiraz, Cabernet Sauvignon, Cabernet Franc and Merlot, spiced with the American oak which is so much part of the Peter Lehmann style. Right from the outset, an unqualified success in the marketplace simply because it represents such good value for money, and because it is ready to drink when released.

ΨΨΨΨ 1998 Bright medium purple-red; clean, red berry fruit aromas, together with a touch of mint, lead into a palate in which mint comes through quite strongly; soft tannins and minimal oak. **rating: 85**

best drinking 2000–2003 **best vintages** '91, '92, '94, '96, '98 **drink with** Pasta with tomato or meat sauce • $14

Peter Lehmann Grenache

Peter Lehmann is among the ever-swelling band of producers of Grenache, appropriate given the long history of the variety in the Barossa Valley.

ΨΨΨ⅂ 1999 Light to medium purple-red; the bouquet is quite fragrant, with a mix of earthy/berry and spicy aromas. There are surprising tannins on the finish of an otherwise sweetly fruited wine. **rating: 83**

best drinking 2000–2003 **best vintages** NA **drink with** Italian cuisine • $12

Peter Lehmann Mentor

This wine is based predominantly on Cabernet Sauvignon, blended with Malbec, Merlot and Shiraz in varying proportions which fluctuate from year to year. Fermentation is finished in barrel and then matured for a further two and a half years in French and American oak hogsheads prior to bottling. Incidentally, Mentor is the new label for what was previously styled 'Cellar Collection Cabernet Blend'.

ΨΨΨΨ 1996 Medium red-purple; berry, leaf, mint, vanilla and earth all intermingle on the moderately intense bouquet; the palate is rather more powerful and chunky, with chocolate, berry and vanilla flavours; the tannins tremble on the brink. **rating: 89**

best drinking 2006–2016 **best vintages** '80, '89, '91, '93, '94, '95, '96 **drink with** Spiced beef • $35

Peter Lehmann Cabernet Sauvignon

Made in typical modern Barossa Valley style, with sweet, ripe cabernet fruit swathed in a gown of American vanilla-accented oak, and the tannins held in restraint.

ΨΨΨ⅂ 1998 Medium red-purple; a mix of lemony vanilla oak floats over the fruit on the bouquet, but sweet blackcurrant flavours come through on the smooth, soft palate, with both tannins and oak in relative restraint. **rating: 84**

best drinking 2003–2008 **best vintages** NA **drink with** Steak and kidney pie • $20

peter rumball wines　　NR

55 Charles Street, Norwood, SA 5067 **region** Other Wineries of SA
phone (08) 8332 2761 **fax** (08) 8364 0188 **open** Mon–Fri 9–5
winemaker Peter Rumball **production** 6000 **est.** 1988
product range ($12.90–49.90 R) Sparkling Shiraz, Vintage Pinot Noir Chardonnay Brut, The Pink.
summary Peter Rumball has been making and selling sparkling wine for as long as I can remember, but has led a somewhat peripatetic life, starting in the Clare Valley but now operating what I can only describe as a 'warehouse winery' operation, with neither vineyards nor winery of his own. The grapes are purchased and the wines made at various places under the supervision of Peter Rumball. His particular specialty has always been Sparkling Shiraz, and was so long before it became 'flavour of the month'. National retail distribution through Tucker Seabrook, and exports to Southeast Asia and the US.

peterson champagne house　　NR

Corner Broke and Branxton Roads, Pokolbin, NSW 2320 **region** Lower Hunter Valley
phone (02) 4998 7881 **fax** (02) 4998 7882 **open** 7 days 9–5
winemaker Gary Reed **production** 10 000 **est.** 1994
product range ($14–28 CD) Sparkling whites include First Creek, Sparkling Ambrosia, Chardonnay Pinot Noir, Semillon Pinot, Chardonnay Blanc de Blanc Millennium, Pinot Noir Chardonnay Pinot Meunier; sparkling reds, Sparkling Shiraz, Sparkling Chambourcin, Rouge Ambrosia and Sparkling Merlot; also table wine Chardonnay and Pinot Noir.
summary Prominently and provocatively situated on the corner of Broke and Branxton Roads as one enters the main vineyard and winery district in the Lower Hunter Valley. It is an extension of the Peterson family empire and, no doubt, very deliberately aimed at the tourist. While the dreaded word 'Champagne' has been retained in the business name, the wine labels now simply say Peterson House, which is a big step in the right direction. Almost all of the wine is sold through cellar door and through the wine club mailing list.

petersons ★★★☆

Mount View Road, Mount View, NSW 2325 **region** Lower Hunter Valley
phone (02) 4990 1704 **fax** (02) 4991 1344 **open** Mon–Sat 9–5, Sun 10–5
winemaker Colin Peterson **production** 15 000 **est.** 1971
product range ($15–40 CD) Semillon, Shirley Chardonnay, Verdelho, Back Block Pinot Noir, Back Block Shiraz, Cabernet Sauvignon, Botrytis Semillon, Muscat, Vintage Port, Sparkling; Back Block Cabernet Sauvignon, Ian's Selection Cabernet Sauvignon and Viognier are top of the range.
summary After a period in the doldrums, Petersons seems to be resurgent, although there has been no change in the team. Certainly it retains a high reputation in the marketplace, sustained by wines such as the splendidly rich and concentrated Back Block dry reds. Production continues to rise in line with domestic and export markets.

pewsey vale ★★★☆

PO Box 10, Angaston, SA 5353 **region** Eden Valley
phone (08) 8561 3200 **fax** (08) 8561 3393 **open** At Yalumba
winemaker Louisa Rose **production** 25 000 **est.** 1961
product range ($14–18 R) Riesling, Botrytis Riesling, Sauvignon Blanc, Cabernet Sauvignon.
summary Pewsey Vale was a famous vineyard established in 1847 by Joseph Gilbert, and it was appropriate that when S Smith & Son (Yalumba) began the renaissance of the high Adelaide Hills plantings in 1961, they should do so by purchasing Pewsey Vale and establishing 59 hectares of riesling and cabernet sauvignon. Once famous for its Riesling, recent vintages have not been inspiring, tending to be somewhat dilute and unfocused. Perhaps the '99 is a sign of better things to come. Exports to all major markets.

Pewsey Vale Riesling

In the late '60s and early '70s one of the great names in Australian Riesling, the '69 vintage still one to conjure with. After a succession of plain vintages, the '99 marks a distinct return to form.
▼▼▼▼ 1999 Bright, light green-yellow; a crisp, clean bouquet with distinct herb aromas together with lime. The palate follows on logically, crisp and clean, with herb, mineral and an underplay of lime flavours; tight structure. Should develop very well. **rating: 87**
best drinking 2004–2009 **best vintages** NA **drink with** Whiting • $11.95

pfeiffer ★★★

Distillery Road, Wahgunyah, Vic 3687 **region** Rutherglen and Glenrowan
phone (02) 6033 2805 **fax** (02) 6033 3158 **open** Mon–Sat 9–5, Sun 11–4
winemaker Christopher Pfeiffer **production** 15 000 **est.** 1984
product range ($12–15 R) Riesling, Chardonnay Semillon, Chardonnay, Frontignac, Ensemble (light Rosé-style), Gamay, Pinot Noir, Shiraz, Shiraz Cabernet, Cabernet Sauvignon, Vintage Port, Old Distillery Tawny, Old Distillery Liqueur Gold (Tokay).
summary Ex-Lindeman fortified winemaker Chris Pfeiffer occupies one of the historic wineries (built 1880) which abound in northeast Victoria and which is worth a visit on this score alone. The fortified wines are good, and the table wines have improved considerably over recent vintages, drawing upon 21 hectares of estate plantings. The winery offers barbecue facilities, children's playground, gourmet picnic hampers, and dinners (by arrangement). Exports to the UK, Canada, Singapore and Taiwan.

phillip island vineyard ★★★★

Berrys Beach Road, Phillip Island, Vic **region** Gippsland
phone (03) 5956 8465 **fax** (03) 5956 8465 **open** 7 days 11–7 (Nov–March) 11–5 (April–Oct)
winemaker David Lance, James Lance **production** 2500 **est.** 1993
product range ($14–30 CD) Sea Spray (Sparkling), Sauvignon Blanc, Cape Woolamai (Semillon Sauvignon Blanc), Summerland (Chardonnay), Newhaven (Riesling Traminer), The Pinnacles (Botrytis Riesling), The Nobbies (Pinot Noir), Berry's Beach (Cabernet Sauvignon), Western Port, Pyramid Rock.
summary A separate operation of Diamond Valley Vineyards, now coming into full flower. 1997 marked the first harvest from the 2.5 hectares of the Phillip Island vineyard, totally enclosed in the permanent silon net which acts both as a windbreak and protection against birds. The quality of the wines across the board must be especially pleasing to the Lance family; this is definitely not a tourist trap cellar door, rather a serious producer of quality wine. Exports to Southeast Asia.

Phillip Island Sauvignon Blanc

Sauvignon Blanc was the first wine to be made on Phillip Island, setting the scene for a string of beautifully crafted and ever elegant wines.

TTTT 1999 Light green-yellow; the bouquet is very light and fresh, with a mix of mineral and passionfruit aromas. The palate is equally fresh and crisp, tending minerally; moderate length. **rating: 88**

best drinking Drink now **best vintages** '97 **drink with** Fresh crab • $25

Phillip Island Vineyard Chardonnay

The first Phillip Island Vineyard estate-grown and produced Chardonnay was released in 1997, previous releases having come from the Yarra Valley. Given the expense of viticulture on the island, which necessitates the entire vineyard being covered by permanent netting, the wine is modestly priced.

TTTTY 1998 Light green-yellow; a fresh and lively bouquet with citrus, nectarine and melon fruit; barely perceptible oak. The palate is a replay of the bouquet, with subtle cashew and melon flavours and perfectly balanced and integrated oak. **rating: 92**

best drinking 2001–2006 **best vintages** NA **drink with** Sautéed prawns • $25

Phillip Island Vineyard The Nobbies

Made by the Lance family at Phillip Island from Leongatha grapes. The '96 won two trophies at the 1997 Victorian Wines Show, Best Pinot Noir and Best Wine of Show; the '98 a gold medal winner at the 1999 Royal Adelaide Wine Show

TTTTY 1998 Good colour; quite complex, sweet plum fruit aromas mingle with a hint of oak. A stylish wine with very good texture and structure; plum and forest flavours; long finish. **rating: 93**

best drinking 2000–2003 **best vintages** NA **drink with** Smoked quail • $22

Phillip Island Vineyard Cabernet Sauvignon

First produced in 1997, and is made entirely from estate-grown grapes. The '97 had abundant concentration, not unusual for first-crop vines, and in 1998 the wine was much lighter. It really is a challenging variety for a climate as unambiguously cool as this.

TTTY 1998 Medium red, with just a touch of purple; the bouquet is clean with cedar and savoury aromas which are quite elegant; much the same pattern evolves on the palate, with touches of mint into the bargain. A light, easy-drinking style which has almost no tannins and lacks structure. **rating: 82**

best drinking 2000–2003 **best vintages** '97 **drink with** Roast veal • $25

pibbin ~~~NR

Greenhill Road, Balhannah, SA 5242 **region** Adelaide Hills
phone (08) 8388 4794 **fax** (08) 8398 0015 **open** Weekends 11–5.30
winemaker Roger Salkeld **production** 1500 **est.** 1991
product range ($15–22 CD) Pinot Noir, Rosé Pinot Noir, White Pinot, Sparkling Pinot.
summary The 7-hectare Pibbin vineyard, near Verdun, is managed on organic principles; owners Roger and Lindy Salkeld explain that the name 'Pibbin' is a corruption of a negro-spiritual word for Heaven, adding that while the wines may not have achieved that lofty status yet, the vineyard has. Pibbin has made a name for itself for producing massive, dense Pinot Noir in a style radically different from that of the rest of the Adelaide Hills.

picardy ★★★★★

Corner Vasse Highway and Eastbrook Road, Pemberton, WA 6260 **region** Pemberton, Warren Valley and Manjimup
phone (08) 9776 0036 **fax** (08) 9776 0245 **open** By appointment
winemaker Bill Pannell, Dan Pannell **production** 4500 **est.** 1993
product range ($30 CD) Chardonnay, Pinot Noir, Shiraz, Cabernet Merlot.
summary Picardy is owned by Dr Bill Pannell and his wife Sandra, who were the founders of Moss Wood winery in the Margaret River region (in 1969). Picardy reflects Bill Pannell's view that the Pemberton area will prove to be one of the best regions in Australia for Pinot Noir and Chardonnay, but it is perhaps significant that the wines to be released include a Shiraz, and a Bordeaux-blend of 50 per cent Merlot, 25 per cent Cabernet Franc and 25 per cent Cabernet Sauvignon. Time will tell whether Pemberton has more Burgundy, Rhône or Bordeaux in its veins. It has lost no time in setting up national distribution, and exports to the UK, the US, Japan and Hong Kong.

Picardy Pinot Noir

The third release of this variety which continues to set the pace for Pinot Noir in the Pemberton region.

▼▼▼▼ **1998** Medium red-purple; attractive oak handling and obvious winemaking skills are evident on both the bouquet and palate; it is in the mouth that the varietal fruit, in a dark plum spectrum, makes more of a statement. Moderate length, fine tannins. **rating:** 88

best drinking 2000–2002 **best vintages** NA **drink with** Braised pheasant • $30

Picardy Shiraz

The second crop of Shiraz which, unfortunately, has been very heavily oaked.

▼▼▼▽ **1998** Youthful purple-red; a huge oak impact obliterates the bouquet and much of the palate. It is hard to see how the wine can come back into balance. **rating:** 80

best drinking 2000–2004 **best vintages** NA **drink with** Moroccan lamb • $30

Picardy Cabernet Merlot

Follows in the track of the first release in 1997; a blend of Cabernet Sauvignon, Merlot and Cabernet Franc.

▼▼▼▼ **1998** Medium red-purple; the bouquet is clean, with some leaf and olive fruit aromas supported by spicy oak. The palate has attractive, bright, cassis/redcurrant fruit; the oak is certainly present but doesn't overwhelm the wine. **rating:** 87

best drinking 2003–2008 **best vintages** NA **drink with** Rare beef • $30

piccadilly fields   NR

185 Piccadilly Road, Piccadilly, SA 5151 **region** Adelaide Hills
phone (08) 8370 8800 **fax** (08) 8232 5395 **open** Not
winemaker Sam Virgara **production** 3000 **est.** 1989
product range ($17.95 ML) Chardonnay, Merlot Cabernet Franc Cabernet Sauvignon.
summary Piccadilly Fields draws upon a very substantial vineyard, with much of the production being sold to Petaluma. The plantings include 10 hectares of pinot meunier, 8 hectares of pinot noir, 5 hectares each of chardonnay, merlot and sauvignon blanc, 2 hectares of cabernet franc and 1 hectare of cabernet sauvignon.

pierro

Caves Road, Willyabrup via Cowaramup, WA 6284 **region** Margaret River
phone (08) 9755 6220 **fax** (08) 9755 6308 **open** 7 days 10–5
winemaker Dr Michael Peterkin **production** 7500 **est.** 1979
product range ($24.90–49.50 R) Chardonnay, LTC Semillon Sauvignon Blanc, Fire Gully Semillon Sauvignon Blanc, Pinot Noir, Cabernets.
summary Dr Michael Peterkin is another of the legion of Margaret River medical practitioners who, for good measure, married into the Cullen family. Pierro is renowned for its stylish white wines, which often exhibit tremendous complexity. The Chardonnay can be monumental in its weight and complexity. The wines are exported to the UK, the US, Japan and Indonesia.

Pierro Semillon Sauvignon Blanc LTC

Made from relatively low-yielding estate-grown grapes; originally marketed under the 'Les Trois Cuvées' label, now abbreviated to LTC, which (coincidentally) can also stand for 'a little touch of Chardonnay'. The wine tastes as if it may have been wholly or partially barrel-fermented, though no mention of this is made on the label.

▼▼▼▼ **1999** Medium yellow-green; a solid bouquet in which the varieties are welded together, as they are on the palate; lots of dissolved CO_2 will ultimately help the development of the wine but introduces a dissonant note right now. **rating:** 86

best drinking 2001–2004 **best vintages** '87, '89, '90, '94, '95, '97 **drink with** Veal cutlets • $19.80

Pierro Fire Gully Semillon Sauvignon Blanc

While made for early consumption, partial barrel and partial malolactic fermentation help both the intensity of flavour and palate weight.

▼▼▼▼ **1999** Light green-yellow; the bouquet is clean, offering some herb and mineral aromas followed by a pleasant medium-weight wine with attractive mid-palate fruit and a relatively dry finish. **rating:** 86

best drinking 2000–2003 **best vintages** NA **drink with** Coquilles St Jacques • $17.80

Pierro Chardonnay

One of the most distinguished of a band of striking wines from the Margaret River region and which achieved great acclaim during the second half of the 1980s. The style is invariably complex, concentrated and powerful, with the emphasis on secondary rather than primary fruit characters.

▼▼▼▼ **1998** Medium yellow-green; the bouquet is at once firm, tight but powerful, with ripe figgy fruit and well-balanced oak. It is on the palate that the wine becomes difficult to handle, its high alcohol (14.5 degrees) very evident; I am not convinced the other components carry the burden of that alcohol. **rating:** 86

best drinking 2001–2005 **best vintages** '86, '87, '89, '90, '92, '94, '95, '96 **drink with** Seafood pasta • $44.80

Pierro Cabernet Merlot

A variety of fermentation techniques and partial barrel-fermentation and maturation in a mix of new and older French oak barrels are designed to add to the complexity of flavour.

▼▼▼▼ **1997** Medium red-purple; the bouquet is clean, moderately fragrant, with subtle oak. There is nicely ripened cassis berry fruit on the palate; the tannin structure and balance are excellent, and the cedary oak attractive. **rating:** 89

best drinking 2002–2010 **best vintages** NA **drink with** Lamb shoulder • $39.80

piesse brook   NR

226 Aldersyde Road, Bickley, WA 6076 **region** Perth Hills
phone (08) 9293 3309 **fax** (08) 9293 3309 **open** Sat 1–5, Sun, public holidays 10–5 and by appointment
winemaker Di Bray, Ray Boyanich (Michael Davies Consultant) **production** 1200 **est.** 1974
product range ($10–17.50 CD) Chardonnay, Shiraz, Merlot, Cabernet Sauvignon, Cabernet Merlot, Cabernet Shiraz, Cabernova (early-drinking style).
summary Surprisingly good red wines made in tiny quantities, and which have received consistent accolades over the years. The first Chardonnay was made in 1993; a trophy winning Shiraz was produced in 1995. Now has 4 hectares of chardonnay, shiraz, merlot and cabernet sauvignon under vine.

pieter van gent   ★★★

Black Springs Road, Mudgee, NSW 2850 **region** Mudgee
phone (02) 6373 3807 **fax** (02) 6373 3910 **open** Mon–Sat 9–5, Sun 11–4
winemaker Pieter van Gent, Philip van Gent **production** 10 000 **est.** 1978
product range ($9.50–16.90 CD) The only dry wines are the Chardonnay, Müller Thurgau, and Cabernet Sauvignon; the Frontignac, Rivaner, Angelic White and Sundance Soft Red all have varying degrees of sweetness; fortified wines are the specialty, including Pipeclay Port, Mudgee White Port, Cornelius Port, Mudgee Oloroso, Pipeclay Muscat, Mudgee Liqueur Frontignac, Pipeclay Vermouth.
summary Many years ago Pieter van Gent worked for Lindemans, before joining Craigmoor then moving to his own winery in 1979, where he and his family have forged a strong reputation and following for his fortified wines in particular, although the range extends far wider. The wines are seldom seen outside cellar door.

✿ piggs peake   NR

697 Hermitage Road, Pokolbin, NSW 2320 **region** Lower Hunter Valley
phone (02) 6574 7000 **fax** (02) 6574 7070 **open** 7 days 10–5
winemaker Steve Dodd, Lesley Minter **production** 8000 **est.** 1998
product range ($14–20 CD) Semillon, Unwooded Chardonnay, Premium Chardonnay, Verdelho, Botrytis Semillon, Shiraz; Rylstone Chardonnay and Pinot Noir.
summary The derivation of the name remains a mystery to me, and if it is a local landmark, I have not heard of it. Certain it is that it is one of the newest wineries to be constructed in the Hunter Valley, sourcing most of its grapes from other growers to complement the 1 hectare of estate plantings.

pikes   ★★★★

Polish Hill River Road, Sevenhill, SA 5453 **region** Clare Valley
phone (08) 8843 4370 **fax** (08) 8843 4353 **open** 7 days 10–4
winemaker Neil Pike **production** 30 000 **est.** 1984
product range ($15–22 R) Riesling, Reserve Riesling, Sauvignon Blanc, Chardonnay, Premio Sangiovese, Shiraz, Grenache Mourvedre, Shiraz, Reserve Shiraz, Cabernet Sauvignon.
summary Owned by the Pike brothers, one of whom (Andrew) was for many years the senior viticulturist with Southcorp, the other (Neil) a former winemaker at Mitchells. Pikes now has its own winery, with Neil Pike presiding. Generously constructed and flavoured wines are the order of the day. The wines are exported to the UK, the US, Canada, Japan, Switzerland, New Zealand, Malaysia and Belgium.

pinelli   NR

30 Bennett Street, Caversham, WA 6055 **region** Swan District
phone (08) 9279 6818 **fax** (08) 9377 4259 **open** 7 days 10–6
winemaker Robert Pinelli **production** 7000 **est.** 1979
product range ($5–16 CD) Limited table wine range centred on Chenin Blanc, Chardonnay, Shiraz and Cabernet Sauvignon, and an extensive range of fortified wines, including Cabernet-based Vintage Port. The wines have won a number of medals at the Perth Show in recent years.
summary Dominic Pinelli and son Robert — the latter a Roseworthy Agricultural College graduate — sell 75 per cent of their production in flagons but are seeking to place more emphasis on bottled-wine sales in the wake of recent show successes with Chenin Blanc.

pipers brook vineyard   ★★★★☆

Bridport Road, Pipers Brook, Tas 7254 **region** Northern Tasmania
phone (03) 6382 7527 **fax** (03) 6382 7226 **open** 7 days 10–5
winemaker Andrew Pirie **production** 60 000 **est.** 1974
product range ($23.50–55 R) Riesling, Gewurztraminer, Pinot Gris, Chardonnay, Reserve Chardonnay, Pellion, Reserve Pinot Noir, Opimium, Summit Vineyard Chardonnay and Pirie Cuvée.
summary The Pipers Brook Tasmanian empire has continued to grow apace. It now has 220 hectares of vineyard supporting the Pipers Brook, Heemskerk and Rochecombe labels, with the major focus, of course, being on Pipers Brook. The wines are exported to the UK, the US, Japan, Canada and Singapore, and are distributed throughout Australia by S Smith and Son. However, a considerable part of its sales are to its shareholders, who receive a substantial discount, and who have supported the company through to its public status on the Australian Stock Exchange. As ever, fastidious viticulture and winemaking, immaculate packaging and enterprising marketing constitute a potent and effective blend.

Pipers Brook Riesling

First made in 1979. The 3 hectares of riesling at the home Pipers Brook Vineyard are situated on the favourable north- and northeast-facing aspects and are now approaching 20 years of age. The wine is excellent and invariably develops well with prolonged cellaring.

▼▼▼▼▼ **1999** Whatever second thoughts Andrew Pirie has had about the suitability of Pipers Brook's foundation vineyard to certain varieties, he has none about Riesling. Fresh and zesty lime, apple and spice aromas are replicated in the delicious flavours of the palate. Will build complexity and richness as it slowly matures.   **rating:** 94
best drinking 2000–2014 **best vintages** '82, '91, '92, '93, '94, '98, '99 **drink with** Lemon chicken salad • $23.50

Pipers Brook Gewurztraminer

The wine comes from a single vineyard planted in 1974 at the original Pipers Brook vineyard. Meticulous care in the vineyard including total leaf removal around the fruiting zone allows the grapes to achieve full physiological and chemical ripeness.

▼▼▼▼ **1999** Light green-yellow; a potent, aromatic bouquet with classic lychee and spice aromas. The palate is really quite fine, repeating the flavours of the bouquet, which persist through to a dry finish. In no way shows its 14.2 degrees alcohol.   **rating:** 86
best drinking 2000–2005 **best vintages** '99 **drink with** Duck liver paté • $27.60

Pipers Brook Pinot Gris

Sourced from four vineyards located in the Pipers River region and a lesser amount from the Strathlynn Vineyard in the West Tamar Valley. The wine is cold-fermented in either tank or barrel; the barrel-fermented component does not impart oak flavour, but does add to the complexity and texture of the wine.

▼▼▼▽ **1999** Light green-yellow; the bouquet is clean, fresh and very neutral, with chalky mineral characters rather than any particular fruit showing at this point of time. The palate is well balanced and light bodied; it is near impossible to find any particular flavour, other than the tangy cut to the finish. More positive fruit will evolve over the next year or so.   **rating:** 83
best drinking 2000–2004 **best vintages** NA **drink with** Steamed fish, Chinese style • $23.50

Pipers Brook Reserve Chardonnay

A new release for Pipers Brook, fitting in between the varietal Chardonnay and Summit Chardonnay; 100 per cent estate-grown from older plantings.

▼▼▼▼▼ **1998** Excellent light to medium yellow-green; sophisticated, seamless fruit and oak blend in a creamy, nutty bouquet. The palate is super-elegant, long and restrained, the influence of partial malolactic fermentation is evident but by no means overwhelming. Shows much of the poise of the best Giaconda Chardonnays. **rating:** 94
best drinking 2000–2005 **best vintages** '98 **drink with** Salmon with sorrel cream sauce • $45

Pipers Brook Summit Vineyard Chardonnay

The Summit Chardonnay release is effectively the Pipers Brook reserve, made only in exceptional vintages and in small quantities.

♥♥♥♥♥ 1998 Bright green-yellow, stylish nectarine and citrus fruit floods the bouquet; the palate has an extra dimension of quality and flavour compared to the standard release. Great length and intensity; restrained oak.

rating: 96

best drinking 2000–2008 **best vintages** '97, '98 **drink with** Grilled Tasmanian lobster • $55

Pipers Brook Reserve Pinot Noir

The first Pinot Noir fitting between the varietal and Pellion release; from the north face of red soil blocks at the home Pipers Brook vineyard.

♥♥♥♥♡ 1998 Strong purple-red; warm, spicy oak with sweet cherry and herb fruit combine to give an enticing bouquet. The palate is quite firm and powerful, with dark cherry and some foresty/savoury characters which run through to a firm finish. Will undoubtedly improve with cellaring, and the prospect of significantly higher points when the wine softens.

rating: 90

best drinking 2003–2008 **best vintages** NA **drink with** Barbecued boned quail • $45

pirramimma ★★★★

Johnston Road, McLaren Vale, SA 5171 **region** McLaren Vale
phone (08) 8323 8205 **fax** (08) 8323 9224 **open** Mon–Fri 9–5, Sat 11–5, Sun, public holidays 11.30–4
winemaker Geoff Johnston **production** 30 000 **est.** 1892
product range ($10–21.50 R) Stock's Hill Semillon Chardonnay, Adelaide Hills Semillon, McLaren Vale Semillon, Hillsview Chardonnay, Stock's Hill Shiraz, Petit Verdot, Hillsview Cabernet Merlot, Cabernet Sauvignon, Ports.
summary An operation with large vineyard holdings of very high quality and a winery which devotes much of its considerable capacity to contract-processing of fruit for others. In terms of the brand, has been a consistent under-performer during the 1990s. The marketing of the brand does scant justice to the very considerable resources available to it, notably its gold medal Petit Verdot and fine elegant Chardonnay. Exports to the UK, New Zealand, Germany, Switzerland and the US.

Pirramimma Petit Verdot

Petit verdot is the least known of the principal Bordeaux red varieties, and is of declining importance there, partly because of difficulties with cropping, and partly because it ripens very late in the season. There is no problem with ripening in McLaren Vale (or in most regions of Australia, for that matter) but it is even rarer here than in Bordeaux. Amazing, but in a sense typically for Pirramimma, it planted petit verdot way back in 1983, and is the source for a number of other makers in the region. To my knowledge, this is the only varietal Petit Verdot commercially marketed in Australia. The '95 won a well-deserved gold medal at the 1997 Royal Adelaide Wine Show.

♥♥♥♥ 1996 Medium red-purple; the bouquet offers an integrated blend of vanilla (from the oak), a hint of bitter chocolate (the regional influence) and a hint of cedar (varietal). A powerful wine on the palate, with bitter chocolate, dark berry, a touch of mint, finishing with the powerful tannins expected of Petit Verdot. **rating:** 88

best drinking 2001–2011 **best vintages** NA **drink with** Grilled lamb chops • $21.50

pizzini NR

King Valley Road, Wangaratta, Vic 3768 **region** King Valley
phone (03) 5729 8278 **fax** (03) 5729 8495 **open** 7 days 12–4
winemaker Alfred Pizzini, Joel Pizzini, Mark Walpole **production** 4000 **est.** 1980
product range ($12–40 CD) Riesling, Sauvingon Blanc, Alfred Pizzini Chardonnay, Sangiovese, Nebbiolo, Alfred Pizzini Shiraz Cabernet, Cabernet.
summary Fred and Katrina Pizzini have been grape growers in the King Valley for over 20 years with over 60 hectares of vineyard. Grape growing (rather than winemaking) still continues to be the major focus of activity, but their move into winemaking has been particularly successful, and I can personally vouch for their Italian cooking skills. It is not surprising, then, that their wines should span both Italian and traditional varieties.

Pizzini Shiraz

Like all of the Pizzini wines, estate-grown, and reflects the ideal growing conditions in the '98 vintage in the King Valley.

♥♥♥♡ 1998 Medium red-purple; the moderately intense bouquet is clean, with a mix of berry and earth fruit aromas. Fresh, cherry/berry fruit on the palate has just the barest touch of oak, finishing with quite fine tannins. Easy-drinking style.

rating: 83

best drinking 2001–2005 **best vintages** NA **drink with** Ravioli • $20

Pizzini Sangiovese

Sangiovese, of course, is the grape of Tuscany, and is one of the Italian varieties which the grape growers of the King Valley of Italian extraction have planted with relish. Just because it has a link back home does not give it any inherent status, but this is a very nice wine.

▼▼▼▼ 1998 Medium red-purple; quite sweet berry fruit on the bouquet has that varietal tangy, almost lemony edge, together with the hint of spice. The palate, too, has those cherry pip flavours of sangiovese, with a touch of mint, finishing with soft tannins. **rating: 85**

best drinking 2002–2006 best vintages NA drink with Pizza, of course •$16

plantagenet ★★★★

Albany Highway, Mount Barker, WA 6324 **region** Great Southern
phone (08) 9851 2150 **fax** (08) 9851 1839 **open** Mon–Fri 9–5, weekends 10–4
winemaker Gavin Berry, Gordon Parker **production** 55 000 **est.** 1974
product range ($16.50–35 CD) Riesling, Omrah Sauvignon Blanc, Omrah Chardonnay (unoaked), Mount Barker Chardonnay, Fronti, Fine White, Fine Red, Pinot Noir, Shiraz, Henry II, Cabernet Sauvignon, Mount Barker Brut; Breakaway Fine White and Fine Red.
summary The senior winery in the Mount Barker region which is making superb wines across the full spectrum of variety and style — highly aromatic Riesling, tangy citrus-tinged Chardonnay, glorious Rhône-style Shiraz, ultra-stylish Cabernet Sauvignon and an occasional inspiring Pinot Noir. Exports to the US, the UK, Germany, Austria, Singapore, Japan, Switzerland and Hong Kong.

Plantagenet Mount Barker Riesling

Draws upon 6.2 hectares of estate vineyards, all of which are now fully mature and which (along with a similar amount of Cabernet Sauvignon) constitute the major estate plantings. First made in 1975, then one of the flagships not only for Plantagenet but for the region as a whole.

▼▼▼▽ 1999 Very pale straw-green; the bouquet is presently closed and stripped, with light mineral characters. A wine begging for time to resolve itself; lively acid on the finish adds strength to the cellaring argument. **rating: 83**

best drinking 2003–2007 best vintages '81, '83, '86, '92, '94, '95, '96, '98 drink with Most Asian dishes •$16.50

Plantagenet Omrah Sauvignon Blanc

The SS *Omrah* was a sailing ship built in 1899 which regularly sailed to Western Australia; as indicated elsewhere, it is now a Plantagenet brand (although, confusingly, also a Mount Barker vineyard). This wine is a blend of Mount Barker, Pemberton and Margaret River-sourced fruit.

▼▼▼▽ 1999 Light yellow-green; quite fragrant although light passionfruit aromas are followed by a palate which is very light on entry to the mouth, and then disappears altogether towards the finish. The finger of suspicion points at over-cropping. **rating: 81**

best drinking Drink now best vintages NA drink with Shellfish •$16.50

Plantagenet Omrah Chardonnay

The Omrah Chardonnay was one of the first unwooded Chardonnays to catch the eye of the public and wine-writers alike. Initially sourced from the Omrah Vineyard but is in fact a registered brand of Plantagenet, the Omrah Vineyard now having been purchased by BRL Hardy. Thus the fruit source has changed significantly; part of the fruit is still purchased from Hardys ex the Omrah Vineyard.

▼▼▼▼ 1999 Light to medium yellow-green; a quite fragrant and aromatic bouquet, rather like a Chardonnay Sauvignon Blanc cross. The palate does have life and length; to be consumed immediately while it still has that crisp freshness. **rating: 86**

best drinking Drink now best vintages NA drink with Scampi •$17

Plantagenet Mount Barker Pinot Noir

The '94 vintage of this wine proved emphatically that, if the vintage conditions are right, Mount Barker can produce excellent Pinot Noir. The following vintages have, quite frankly, been disappointing, although Goundrey did well in 1996, pointing to the extremely fickle nature of Pinot Noir in the region.

▼▼▼▽ 1998 Medium red; the bouquet is plain, with slight green fruit/canopy astringency. The palate shows some pinot noir varietal character but overall is a little hard. The essence of these wines should be softness in the mouth, which this wine doesn't have. **rating: 83**

best drinking 2000–2003 best vintages '94 drink with Char-grilled salmon •$25

Plantagenet Mount Barker Shiraz

It draws upon 4 hectares of estate plantings, the style varying with the vintage. In cooler years the vibrant pepper/spice characters are to the fore, in warmer years it tends more to liquorice, dark cherry and berry. The one consistent feature is the quality of the wine. Spends 18 months in 100 per cent French oak, the majority first and second use. In recent years has shown marked vintage variation.

▼▼▼⅄ **1997** Medium purple-red; the bouquet is quite firm, with some cherry and liquorice fruit, which is also present on the palate, where the effective use of oak helps add a little more complexity; finishes with good tannins.

rating: 83

best drinking 2000–2004 **best vintages** '82, '83, '85, '90, '91, '93, '94, '96 **drink with** Hare, squab • $35

Plantagenet Breakaway Fine Red

The Breakaway Vineyard is situated 15 kilometres south of Mount Barker; a blend of Cabernet Sauvignon, Grenache and Shiraz.

▼▼▼⅄ **1998** Light to medium red-purple; the bouquet is clean and quite brisk, with fresh berry, leaf and mint aromas. Overall the palate is quite sweet, including, I suspect, some residual sugar on the finish. **rating:** 80

best drinking Drink now **best vintages** NA **drink with** Pasta • $12

Plantagenet Omrah Merlot Cabernet

The only Geographic Indication claimed for the wine is West Australia, but it almost certainly comes from the same sources as the Omrah Sauvignon Blanc: Mount Barker, Pemberton and Margaret River.

▼▼▼⅄ **1998** Medium red-purple; quite leafy fruit is married with sweeter oak aromas on the bouquet; the palate is oak-driven, with milky/oaky tannins on the mid to back palate. **rating:** 82

best drinking 2001–2004 **best vintages** NA **drink with** Pizza • $17.50

Plantagenet Mount Barker Cabernet Sauvignon

First made in 1974 (in fact at Sandalford in the Swan Valley) and has established itself as one of the West Australian classics over the intervening years. While primarily based upon estate-grown Cabernet Sauvignon, Malbec, Cabernet Franc and Merlot have all contributed to the wine over the last decade, with the core of the wine coming from the Plantagenet Bouverie Vineyard at Denbarker.

▼▼▼▼ **1997** Medium red with some purple hues remaining. The moderately intense bouquet is clean, with earthy berry cabernet fruit and subtle oak. Some slightly green edges to the fruit appear on the palate, which finishes with firm tannins. **rating:** 86

best drinking 2002–2006 **best vintages** '81, '83, '85, '86, '90, '91, '94 **drink with** Rack of lamb • $28

platt's ★★☆

Mudgee Road, Gulgong, NSW 2852 **region** Mudgee
phone (02) 6374 1700 **fax** (02) 6372 1055 **open** 7 days 9–5
winemaker Barry Platt **production** 4000 **est.** 1983
product range ($9–12 CD) Chardonnay, Semillon, Gewurztraminer, Cabernet Sauvignon.
summary Inconsistent and often rather unhappy use of oak prevents many of the wines realising their potential.

plunkett ★★★

Lambing Gully Road, Avenel, Vic 3664 **region** Central Victorian Mountain Country
phone (03) 5796 2150 **fax** (03) 5796 2147 **open** 7 days 11–5
winemaker Sam Plunkett **production** 10 000 **est.** 1980
product range ($14–35 CD) The top-of-the-range wines are released under the Strathbogie Ranges label (Riesling, Chardonnay, Merlot, Cabernet Merlot); standard wines under the Blackwood Ridge brand of Riesling, Gewurztraminer, Unwooded Chardonnay, Sauvignon Blanc Semillon, and Shiraz; Reserve Shiraz.
summary The Plunkett family first planted grapes way back in 1968, establishing 3 acres with 25 experimental varieties. Commercial plantings commenced in 1980, with 100 hectares now under vine. While holding a vigneron's licence since 1985, the Plunketts did not commence serious marketing of the wines until 1992 and have now settled down into producing an array of wines which are pleasant and well-priced. Wholesale distribution to all States; exports to the US, the UK, Canada, Japan, Germany and Malaysia.

Plunkett Reserve Shiraz

The selection process starts in the vineyard with shoot thinning and tightly controlled irrigation; the grapes are fermented in a 10-tonne rotofermenter and then taken to a mix of predominantly new American oak and a small amount of second-use French.

ΨΨΨΨ **1998** Medium red-purple; the clean bouquet has attractive, varietal spicy liquorice aromas. These characters come through as the palate opens, providing a range of spicy, savoury, dark berry flavours; has length and concentration, finishing with fine tannins and subtle oak. **rating:** 90

best drinking 2003–2008 **best vintages** '98 **drink with** Rich Lebanese dishes • $35

poet's corner wines ★★★

Craigmoor Road, Mudgee, NSW 2850 **region** Mudgee
phone (02) 6372 2208 **fax** (02) 6372 4464 **open** Mon–Fri 9–4, weekends 10–4
winemaker Brett McKinnon **production** NFP **est.** 1858
product range ($12.95–13.95 R) Craigmoor Semillon, Chardonnay, Shiraz, Cabernet Sauvignon.
summary Poet's Corner is located in one of the oldest wineries in Australia to remain in more or less continuous production: Craigmoor (as it was previously known) was built by Adam Roth in 1858/1860, whose grandson Jack Roth ran the winery until the early 1960s. Notwithstanding the change of name, both Craigmoor and Poet's Corner are produced.

pokolbin estate ★★☆

McDonalds Road, Pokolbin, NSW 2321 **region** Lower Hunter Valley
phone (02) 4998 7524 **fax** (02) 4998 7765 **open** 7 days 10–6
winemaker Contract **production** 4000 **est.** 1980
product range ($15–40 CD) Semillon, Riesling, Pokolbin Horse Coaches Verdelho, Unwooded Chardonnay, Show Reserve Chardonnay, Pinot Noir, Shiraz Merlot, Shiraz; Port.
summary An unusual outlet, offering its own-label wines made under contract by Trevor Drayton, together with the wines of Lake's Folly, Peacock Hill and Pothana, and with cheap varietal 'cleanskins'. Wine quality under the Pokolbin Estate label is very modest, although the 1997 Hunter Riesling (perversely, true Riesling, not Semillon) won a silver medal and was the top-pointed wine in its class at the 1997 Hunter Valley Wine Show. No recent news.

poole's rock ★★★☆

Lot 41 Wollombi Road, Broke, NSW 2330 **region** Lower Hunter Valley
phone (02) 9667 1622 **fax** (02) 9667 1442 **open** Not
winemaker Philip Ryan (Contract) **production** 4000 **est.** 1988
product range ($20–24 R) Chardonnay.
summary Sydney merchant banker David Clarke has had a long involvement with the wine industry, including a directorship of McGuigan Brothers Limited. The 5-hectare Poole's Rock vineyard, planted purely to chardonnay, is his personal venture. The wine has retail distribution throughout Australia and is exported to the UK.

pooley wines NR

Cooinda Vale Vineyard, Barton Vale Road, Campania, Tas 7026 **region** Southern Tasmania
phone (03) 6224 3591 **fax** (03) 6224 3591 **open** Wed–Sun 10–5
winemaker Mat Pooley, Andrew Hood (Contract) **production** 1000 **est.** 1985
product range ($18–24 CD) Cooinda Vale Estate Riesling, Chardonnay, Cooinda Vale Estate Pinot Noir.
summary Three generations of the Pooley family have been involved in the development of the Cooinda Vale Estate; it was indeed under the Cooinda Vale label that the winery was previously known. After a tentative start on a small scale, plantings have now reached 4 hectares, and will continue to grow, on a property which covers both sides of the Coal River in a region which is substantially warmer and drier than most people realise. The wines have limited retail distribution in Victoria (Southern Fine Wines) and of course in Tasmania.

poplar bend NR

RMB 8655 Main Creek Road, Main Ridge, Vic 3928 **region** Mornington Peninsula
phone (03) 5989 6046 **fax** (03) 5989 6460 **open** Weekends and public holidays 10–5, also by appointment
winemaker David Briggs **production** 350 **est.** 1988
product range ($16–28 ML) Pineau Chloe, Cabernet Chloe, Sparkling Chloe, Pinot Noir, Cellar Reserve Pinot Noir, Cabernet Shiraz.
summary Poplar Bend was the child of Melbourne journalist, author and raconteur Keith Dunstan and wife, Marie, who moved into full-scale retirement in 1997, selling Poplar Bend to David Briggs. The changes are few; the label still depicts Chloe in all her glory, which could be calculated to send the worthy inhabitants of the Bureau of Alcohol, Tobacco and Firearms (of the US) into a state of cataleptic shock.

port phillip estate ★★★★☆

261 Red Hill Road, Red Hill, Vic 3937 **region** Mornington Peninsula
phone (03) 5989 2708 **fax** (03) 5989 2708 **open** Weekends and public holidays 12–5
winemaker Lindsay McCall (Contract) **production** 4000 **est.** 1987
product range ($18–35 R) Sauvignon Blanc, Chardonnay, Pinot Noir, Reserve Pinot Noir, Reserve Shiraz.
summary Established by leading Melbourne QC Jeffrey Sher, who, after some prevarication, sold the estate to Giorgio and Dianne Gjergja in February 2000. The Gjergjas are rightly more than content with the quality and style of the wines; the main change will be enhanced cellar-door facilities.

Port Phillip Estate Sauvignon Blanc

Yet another good wine from Port Phillip Estate, made without artifice and simply relying on the cool Mornington Peninsula climate. Cold-fermented in stainless steel, and bottled early to retain maximum fruit freshness.
▼▼▼▼ **1999** Light to medium yellow-green; the bouquet is clean and light, with gentle hints of tropical passionfruit aromas. While the flavours on the palate are light, they are pure, and the wine has length and persistence. **rating: 85**
best drinking 2000–2001 **best vintages** NA **drink with** Shellfish • $18

Port Phillip Estate Chardonnay

Produced from a little over 1.8 hectares of chardonnay planted in 1988. High natural acidity often forces Mornington Peninsula winemakers to rely on the malolactic fermentation to a considerable degree, and not always to the benefit of the wines. One of the attractions of this wine is that the malolactic characters are not overdone.
▼▼▼▼ **1998** Developed straw yellow; the bouquet is smooth and creamy, showing malolactic fermentation influences supported by subtle oak. The palate is rich, full and mouthfilling, with typical creamy/nutty Mornington style offset by a twist of acidity; these components were still coming together mid-1999. **rating: 89**
best drinking 2000–2004 **best vintages** '96, '97, '98 **drink with** Lobster, shellfish • $NA

Port Phillip Estate Reserve Pinot Noir

The '97 was a challenging but majestic wine which is a testament both to the exceptional quality of the '97 vintage in the Mornington Peninsula and to Lindsay McCall's skills as a winemaker. In the space of a few weeks it won two trophies at the 1999 Sydney Royal Wine Show including the Trophy for the Best 1997 Red Table Wine of Show, as well as the Trophy for the Best Table Wine Exhibited by a Small Producer. The '98 is a worthy successor, less challenging perhaps, but no less enjoyable.
▼▼▼▼▼ **1998** Light to medium red; a super-fragrant bouquet with ripe plum and cherry fruit leads into a quite lovely wine, with excellent texture and mouthfeel. The fruit is certainly sweet and ripe, but the wine has the requisite finesse and length. Should develop relatively quickly. **rating: 94**
best drinking 1999–2003 **best vintages** '97, '98 **drink with** Duck • $NA

portree ★★★☆

72 Powells Track via Mount William Road, Lancefield, Vic 3455 **region** Macedon Ranges
phone (03) 5429 1422 **fax** (03) 5429 2205 **open** Weekends and public holidays 10–5
winemaker Ken Murchison **production** 800 **est.** 1983
product range ($15–35 CD) Chardonnay, Greenstone, Damask (Cabernet Franc Rosé), Quarry Red (Cabernet Franc Merlot).
summary Owner Ken Murchison selected his 4-hectare Macedon vineyard after studying viticulture at Charles Sturt University and being strongly influenced by Dr Andrew Pirie's doctoral thesis. All of the wines show distinct cool-climate characteristics, the Quarry Red having clear similarities to the wines of Chinon in the Loire Valley. However, it is with Chardonnay that Portree has done best and which is its principal wine (in terms of volume). As from the 1998 vintage the wines were made at a newly constructed on-site winery.

port stephens wines NR

69 Nelson Bay Road, Bobs Farm, NSW 2316 **region** Other Wineries of NSW
phone (02) 4982 6411 **fax** (02) 4982 6766 **open** 7 days 10–5
winemaker Contract **production** 3500 **est.** 1984
product range ($10–21.50 CD) Chardonnay, Tri-Blend, Tomaree White, Late Harvest, Golden Sands, Shiraz, Cabernet Merlot, Cabernet Sauvignon, Sparkling and Fortifieds.
summary Planting of the quite substantial Port Stephens Wines vineyard began in 1984, and there are now 4 hectares of vines in production. The wines are made under contract by John Baruzzi at Wilderness Estate in the Hunter Valley but are sold through an attractive, dedicated cellar-door sales outlet on site.

pothana   NR

Carramar, Belford, NSW 2335 **region** Lower Hunter Valley
phone (02) 6574 7164 **fax** (02) 6574 7209 **open** By appointment
winemaker David Hook **production** 2000 **est.** 1984
product range Chardonnay, Semillon, Pinot Noir, Adina Pinot Grigio; The Gorge range of Unwooded Chardonnay, Classic Dry White, Chardonnay, Verdelho, Semillon and Shiraz.
summary Principally sold through Pokolbin Estate and by mailing list; the Chardonnay is a soft, buttery/toasty wine in mainstream Hunter Valley style.

potters clay vineyards   ★★★

Main Road, Willunga, SA 5172 **region** McLaren Vale
phone (08) 8556 2799 **fax** (08) 8556 2922 **open** Not
winemaker John Bruschi **production** 900 **est.** 1994
product range ($15.90–16.90 R) Chardonnay, Shiraz, Merlot Cabernet Franc.
summary John and Donna Bruschi are second-generation grapegrowers who assumed full ownership of the 16-hectare Potters Clay Vineyard in 1994 with the aim of establishing their own winery and label. In 1999 construction of stage one of a two-stage boutique winery was completed: stage one is a winery production facility, stage two is to be cellar, door, restaurant and garden/picnic area at some future date. At least this is in the correct order; all too often it is the cellar door and restaurant which come first. The first and second vintages (1998 and 1999) were made off site by John Bruschi, but future operations will be centralised. The clever packaging and high-quality promotional literature should do much to enhance sales.

Potters Clay Chardonnay

Draws upon 4.5 hectares of estate plantings. It is basket-pressed, fermented and left on yeast lees with prolonged barrel maturation in new American oak barrels.
▼▼▼▼ 1999 Medium green-yellow; the bouquet is quite rich, with ripe melon and fig fruit, and just a hint of vanilla oak. The palate has less weight and intensity, but is clean and quite well balanced. Surprisingly, the American oak is barely perceptible.   **rating:** 81
best drinking 2001–2003 **drink with** Creamy pasta • $15.90

Potters Clay Shiraz

Estate-grown and picked in typically ripe McLaren Vale fashion, with alcohol of around 14.5 degrees. The wine is basket-pressed, and spends 15 months in new American oak barrels.
▼▼▼▼ 1998 Bright medium red-purple; the bouquet is clean, with moderately intense fresh, simple fruit. The same dynamics apply to the bright, fresh, breezy palate made in an early-drinking style. Once again, I have no idea where the American oak went, but it's no loss.   **rating:** 84
best drinking 2000–2002 **drink with** Simple food • $16.90

🐚 powercourt vineyard   NR

2 McEwans Road, Legana, Tas 7277 **region** Northern Tasmania
phone (03) 6330 1225 **fax** (03) 6330 2161 **open** By appointment
winemaker Ralph Power **production** 1000 **est.** 1972
product range ($18 CD) Pinot Noir, Cabernet Pinot, Cabernet Sauvignon.
summary A long-established but ultra-low-profile winery with a mostly local clientele, also retail distribution in Canberra.

preston peak   NR

Old Wallangarra Road, Wyberba via Ballandean, Qld 4382 **region** South Burnett and Other Wineries of Qld
phone (07) 4630 9499 **fax** (07) 4630 9477 **open** At Wyberba Vineyard
winemaker Philippa Hambleton **production** 5500 **est.** 1994
product range ($9–26 CD) Sauvignon Blanc, Code Flag White, Chardonnay, Code Flag Red, Shiraz, Cabernets.
summary The spectacular growth plans of dentist owners Ashley Smith and Kym Thumpkin have seemingly slowed to a more realistic level, although production has doubled over the past year. Winemaking continues at Wyberba, with the proposed winery at Toowoomba on hold.

primo estate ★★★★★

Old Port Wakefield Road, Virginia, SA 5120 **region** Adelaide Plains
phone (08) 8380 9442 **fax** (08) 8380 9696 **open** June–Sept Mon–Fri 9–5, Sat, holidays 10–4.30
winemaker Joseph Grilli **production** 20 000 **est.** 1979
product range ($12–100 R) Colombard, La Magia Botrytis Riesling, Shiraz, Cabernet Merlot, Adelaide Shiraz, Joseph Moda Amarone Cabernet Merlot, Joseph Sparkling Red.
summary Roseworthy dux Joe Grilli has risen way above the constraints of the hot Adelaide Plains to produce an innovative and always excellent range of wines. The biennial release of the Joseph Sparkling Red (in its tall Italian glass bottle) is eagerly awaited, the wine immediately selling out. However, the core lies with the zingy, fresh Colombard, the velvet-smooth Adelaide Shiraz and the distinguished, complex Joseph Cabernet Merlot. National distribution through Negociants; exports to the UK, Asia, Europe and Japan.

Primo Estate La Biondina Colombard

Joe Grilli has always been able to conjure something quite magical from the 4.5 hectares of estate plantings of colombard. The variety is known for its capacity to hold its natural acidity in hot climates (and the Adelaide Plains are hot), but no one else seems to be able to invest the wine with the fruit freshness and crispness — almost Sauvignon Blanc-like — achieved by Joe Grilli.
ŸŸŸŸŸ 1999 Smart new packaging and an Italianesque name does not disguise the crisp, aromatic, tangy bouquet; followed by a delicate yet piercing gooseberry/tropical palate. Gold medal 1999 Royal Adelaide Wine Show. **rating:** 92
best drinking 1999–2000 **best vintages** NA **drink with** Oysters, shellfish • $12

Primo Estate Joseph Moda Amarone Cabernet Merlot

Although the front label does not make reference to it, the back label says 'moda amarone' — a modest claim which has brought the wrath of the Italians down on the head of Joe Grilli, and his promise to desist from using it. The wine does in fact use the amarone methods of partially drying the red grapes before fermentation. The blend varies between Coonawarra and McLaren Vale according to the vintage.
ŸŸŸŸŸ 1998 Full red-purple; the bouquet offers a subtle interplay of ripe plum, prune, cassis and oak; mouthfilling plum, prune, blackberry and bitter chocolate fruit flavours are surrounded by a web of silky tannins and subtle oak. **rating:** 94
best drinking 2003–2013 **best vintages** '81, '84, '86, '90, '91, '93, '94, '95, '96, '97, '98 **drink with** Bistecca Fiorentina • $45

prince albert ★★★★

100 Lemins Road, Waurn Ponds, Vic 3216 **region** Geelong
phone (03) 5241 8091 **fax** (03) 5241 8091 **open** By appointment
winemaker Bruce Hyett **production** 600 **est.** 1975
product range ($29 ML) Pinot Noir.
summary Australia's true Pinot Noir specialist (it has only ever made the one wine), which also made much of the early running with the variety: the wines always show good varietal character and have rebounded after a dull patch in the second half of the 1980s. In 1998 the vineyard and winery was certified organic by OVAA Inc. Apart from the mailing list, the wine is sold through fine wine retailers in Sydney and Melbourne, with a little finding its way to the UK.

Prince Albert Pinot Noir

The 2-hectare vineyard was planted in 1975 on a north-facing slope of terra rossa soil, 600 mm deep, on top of limestone/marle. The grapes are hand-picked; 50 per cent is crushed, the remainder left as whole bunches, and the wine is foot-stamped in open wax-lined concrete fermenters before being taken to Troncais oak for ten months.
ŸŸŸŸ 1999 Medium red-purple; the clean, smooth cherry fruit of the bouquet is complexed by touches of more savoury spicy characters, while the firm cherry fruit of the palate is followed by a crisp finish. Tasted when recently bottled and needs to loosen up to display the latent complexity. **rating:** 85
best drinking 2001–2005 **best vintages** '97, '98 **drink with** Game pie • $29

providence vineyards NR

236 Lalla Road, Lalla, Tas 7267 **region** Northern Tasmania
phone (03) 6395 1290 **fax** (03) 6395 1290 **open** 7 days 10–5
winemaker Andrew Hood (Contract) **production** 600 **est.** 1956

product range ($18.50–24.95 CD) Semillon, Botrytis Semillon, Chardonnay, Pinot Noir; in exceptional years may be released under the Miguet label.

summary Providence incorporates the pioneer vineyard of Frenchman Jean Miguet, now owned by the Bryce family, which purchased it in 1980. The original 1.3-hectare vineyard has been expanded to a little over 3 hectares, as well as grafting over unsuitable grenache and cabernet (left from the original plantings) to chardonnay and pinot noir and semillon. Miguet in fact called the vineyard 'La Provence', reminding him of the part of France from whence he came, but after 40 years the French authorities forced a name change to Providence.

Providence Chardonnay

Particularly when tasted in the company of mainland-grown Chardonnays, shrieks its cool-climate origins, but in a far from unattractive fashion. Indeed, one of the best unwooded Chardonnays to be found anywhere.

TTTT 1999 Light to medium yellow-green; the bouquet is of moderate to full intensity, with cashew, mineral and lees/malolactic component adding complexity. A nicely balanced wine on the palate with more texture than usual and good length. I gave this wine gold medal points on my score sheet at the 2000 Tasmanian Wines Show.

rating: 91

best drinking 2001–2004 **best vintages** '99 **drink with** Fresh abalone • $20

Providence Pinot Noir

Providence makes two Pinot Noirs, a Reserve model named Miguet in honour of Jean Miguet, the founder of the vineyard, and the other a simple varietal version. This is the latter, but a more than handy wine. The 1998 was a silver medal winner at the Tasmanian Wines Show 2000.

TTTT 1998 Medium red-purple; lifted, fragrant sweet cherry and plum aromas mix with charry oak on the bouquet; the palate offers similar characters in a light-bodied mode. **rating:** 83

best drinking 2000–2003 **best vintages** NA **drink with** Tasmanian venison • $20

punters corner ★★★★☆

Corner Riddoch Highway and Racecourse Road, Coonawarra, SA 5263 **region** Coonawarra
phone (08) 8737 2007 **fax** (08) 8737 2007 **open** 7 days 10–5
winemaker Peter Bissell (Contract) **production** 8000 **est.** 1988
product range ($17–45 CD) Chardonnay, Shiraz, Spartacus Reserve Shiraz, Cabernet Merlot, Cabernet Sauvignon.
summary The quaintly named Punters Corner started off life in 1975 as James Haselgrove but in 1992 was acquired by a group of investors who quite evidently had few delusions about the uncertainties of viticulture and winemaking, even in a district as distinguished as Coonawarra. The arrival of Peter Bissell as winemaker at Balnaves paid immediate (and continuing) dividends. Sophisticated packaging and label design add to the appeal of the wines. National retail distribution; exports to the US, Canada, Italy, Belgium, The Netherlands, Switzerland, Germany, Malaysia and Singapore.

Punters Corner Shiraz

Sourced from both the Victoria and Albert Block and the Punters Corner Cellardoor Block, and employing sophisticated winemaking techniques. The V & A component is fermented on skins for four days, followed by barrel-fermentation in new American oak, while the Cellardoor component is given extended post-fermentation maceration.

TTTT 1998 Medium to full red-purple; ripe, quite concentrated dark black cherry/blackberry/blackcurrant fruit marries with a touch of spicy oak on the bouquet. The palate has abundant, ripe black cherry fruit offset by just a touch of vanilla oak. **rating:** 89

best drinking 2002–2010 **best vintages** '97 **drink with** Mushroom risotto • $24

Punters Corner Spartacus Reserve Shiraz

Introduced in the excellent 1998 vintage; happily, the extra quality comes from the vineyard and not from the oak forest.

TTTT 1998 Dense red-purple; powerful, concentrated dark berry/cherry fruit with hints of earth flood the bouquet, oak making only a minor contribution. Another dimension of fruit depth is revealed on the palate, with dark cherry, chocolate and ripe, well-balanced tannins. **rating:** 92

best drinking 2003–2013 **best vintages** '98 **drink with** Game pie • $45

Punters Corner Cabernet Sauvignon

The sourcing and making of this wine is similar to the Shiraz. Part, coming from the V & A vineyard, is barrel-fermented; most comes from low-yielding old vines on the high-bank red soil on the Cellardoor Block, which is given extended maceration.

ŸŸŸŸŸ **1998** Strong, bright purple-red; a most attractive bouquet with ripe cassis fruit touched with cedary oak. The palate is concentrated, powerful and dense but is well balanced; simply needs patience. **rating:** 90

best drinking 2003–2013 **best vintages** '98 **drink with** Yearling beef • $26

queen adelaide ★★

Sturt Highway, Waikerie, SA 5330 **region** Barossa Valley
phone (08) 8541 2588 **fax** (08) 8541 3877 **open** Not
winemaker Nigel Logos **production** 800 000 **est.** 1858
product range ($6–8 R) Rhine Riesling, Chenin Blanc, Semillon Chardonnay, Chardonnay, Spatlese Lexia, Sauvignon Blanc, Regency Red.
summary The famous brand established by Woodley Wines and some years ago subsumed into the Seppelt and now Southcorp Group. It is a pure brand, without any particular home either in terms of winemaking or fruit sources, but is hugely successful; Queen Adelaide Chardonnay is and has for some time been the largest-selling bottled white wine in Australia. However, the use of agglomerate corks precludes assessment of the true quality of the wines because of the near-certainty of lesser or greater degrees of cork taint. The move to synthetic corks cannot come too soon; all the wines show agglomerate cork taint in some measure.

raleigh winery NR

Queen Street, Raleigh, NSW 2454 **region** Other Wineries of NSW
phone (02) 6655 4388 **fax** (02) 6655 4265 **open** 7 days 10–5
winemaker Lavinia Dingle **production** 1000 **est.** 1982
product range ($13–25 CD) Semillon Chardonnay, Traminer Riesling, Rouge (Rosé), Late Harvest, Shiraz Cabernet Merlot, Port.
summary Raleigh Winery lays claim to being Australia's most easterly vineyard. The vineyard was initiated in 1982 and was purchased by Lavinia and Neil Dingle in 1989, with the wine produced in part from 1 hectare of vines planted to no less than six varieties. The wines have won bronze medals at the Griffith Wine Show.

ralph fowler wines ★★★★

Limestone Coast Road, Mount Benson, SA 5265 **region** Mount Benson
phone (08) 8365 6968 **fax** (08) 8365 2516 **open** Mon–Fri 9–5
winemaker Ralph Fowler **production** 6500 **est.** 1999
product range ($18–38 R) Limestone Coast Sauvignon Blanc, Limestone Coast Shiraz, Limestone Coast Cabernet Sauvignon.
summary Ralph Fowler's career as a winemaker encompasses a lengthy period in the Hunter Valley, first at Hungerford Hill and then with Tyrrell's, before moving to Coonawarra and McLaren Vale, where he was chief winemaker for the Richard Hamilton/Leconfield Group until mid-1999. While keeping his hand in as consultant to some other producers, he has established a little over 13 hectares of vineyards at Mount Benson, planting shiraz, viognier and merlot, a thoroughly eclectic mix. This vineyard, together with grapes purchased from Coonawarra and McLaren Vale, will take production to 10 000 cases over the next few years, with a new winery to be constructed in time for the 2001 vintage. Retail distribution through all States; exports to the US, Singapore and Malaysia/Hong Kong.

Ralph Fowler Limestone Coast Sauvignon Blanc

A blend of 50 per cent Coonawarra material and 50 per cent Mount Benson made in traditional, unoaked style.
ŸŸŸŸ **1999** Light to medium yellow-green; the bouquet is quite fragrant, with gentle tropical fruit; the palate is nicely balanced, with a mix of herb, lime and tropical flavours; the strongest part of the wine is its persistence on a lingering finish. **rating:** 89

best drinking 2000–2001 **drink with** Calamari • $18

Ralph Fowler Limestone Coast Cabernet Sauvignon

A blend of 60 per cent Coonawarra and 40 per cent Mount Benson material, which spends 14 months in oak.
ŸŸŸŸŸ **1998** Medium red-purple; fresh mint, leaf and berry aromas run through both the bouquet and palate. The latter is well balanced, with gentle tannins, subtle oak and a clean finish. **rating:** 90

best drinking 2003–2008 **drink with** Rack of lamb • $27

ravenswood lane vineyard ★★★★

Ravenswood Lane, Hahndorf, SA 5245 **region** Adelaide Hills
phone (08) 8388 1250 **fax** (08) 8388 7233 **open** Not
winemaker Stephen Pannell (Red), Glenn James (White) at Hardys **production** 11 500 **est.** 1993
product range ($18–50 ML) Gathering Sauvignon Blanc, Beginning Chardonnay, Reunion Shiraz, 19th Meeting Cabernet; Starvedog Lane Sauvignon Blanc, Chardonnay and Shiraz.
summary With their sales and marketing background, John and Helen Edwards opted for a major lifestyle change when they began the establishment of the first of the present 28.1 hectares of vineyards in 1993. Initially, part of the production was sold to BRL Hardy, but now the wine is made for release under the Ravenswood Lane label. A second venture is Starvedog Lane, producing wines from a patchwork of vineyards throughout the Adelaide Hills.

Starvedog Lane Sauvignon Blanc

Produced from grapes grown in the Hahndorf and Kuitpo subregions of the Adelaide Hills, stainless steel-fermented and early fermented.
♥♥♥♡ **1999** Light to medium yellow-green; a clean, light bouquet with what appears to be a subliminal touch of oak is a quiet start to a wine which progressively unfolds its flavour as it moves through to a long finish. **rating:** 84
best drinking 2000–2001 **best vintages** NA **drink with** Marinated fish • $18

Ravenswood Lane The Gathering Sauvignon Blanc

Produced from 4 hectares of estate vineyards, with yields restricted to around 7 tonnes per hectares. The wine is barrel-fermented in a mix of new and one-year-old oak barrels, and briefly held in those barrels at the end of fermentation.
♥♥♥♥♡ **1999** Light to medium yellow-green; the bouquet is complex, changing as it evolves in the glass, with tropical fruit and a touch of oak intermingling. The same complex interaction of fruit and oak is evident on the palate, which has a particularly long, lingering finish. The only gold medal winner in the Sauvignon Blanc class at the 1999 Adelaide Hills Wine Show. **rating:** 90
best drinking 2000–2003 **best vintages** '99 **drink with** Coquilles St Jacques • $27

Starvedog Lane Chardonnay

The first release of Starvedog Lane Chardonnay won the Dinner at Eight Trophy for Best One Year Old Dry White Wine at the 1999 Brisbane Wine Show, going on to win the 1999 Hyatt Wine Awards White Wine of the Year Trophy.
♥♥♥♥ **1998** Medium to full yellow-green; the bouquet is complex, with spicy barrel-ferment and what appear to be malolactic fermentation-aromas woven through fine, melon fruit. The palate follows the bouquet, with toasty oak and long, quite intense fruit. For my money, the oak is just a little assertive for the fruit weight, but others have obviously rated the wine more highly. **rating:** 85
best drinking 2000–2003 **best vintages** '98 **drink with** Barbecued chicken • $25

Ravenswood Lane Starvedog Lane Shiraz

First produced in 1997. Fermented in open fermenters, interestingly including a proportion of whole bunches. Basket-pressed, with 30 per cent going into new oak, the balance into one-year-old barriques. Both the 1997 and 1998 wines are of high quality, the latter winning the only gold medal in the Shiraz class at the 1999 Adelaide Hills Wine Show.
♥♥♥♥♥ **1998** Medium to full red-purple; the bouquet is powerful, with fruit and oak interwoven. The concentrated palate has distinct Rhône Valley overtones, with spicy fruit coping with the oak. Has the potential to develop very well. **rating:** 94
♥♥♥♥♡ **1997** Abundant, smooth dark cherry, plum and blackberry fruit, with a hint of spice, is supported by well-handled, positive oak on both bouquet and palate. **rating:** 93
best drinking 2003–2010 **best vintages** '97, '98 **drink with** Turkish lamb pizza • $25

ray-monde NR

250 Dalrymple Road, Sunbury, Vic 3429 **region** Sunbury
phone (03) 5428 2657 **fax** (03) 5428 3390 **open** Sundays or by appointment
winemaker John Lakey **production** 770 **est.** 1988
product range ($25 CD) Pinot Noir.

summary The Lakey family has established a little under 4 hectares of pinot noir on their 230-hectare grazing property at an altitude of 400 metres. Initially the grapes were sold to Domaine Chandon, but in 1994 son John Lakey (who had gained experience at Tarrawarra, Rochford, Virgin Hills, Coonawarra plus a vintage in Burgundy) commenced making the wine — and very competently.

reads ★★

Evans Lane, Oxley, Vic 3678 **region** King Valley
phone (03) 5727 3386 **fax** (03) 5727 3559 **open** Mon–Sat 9–5, Sun 10–6
winemaker Kenneth Read **production** 1900 **est.** 1972
product range ($7.50–13 CD) Riesling, Chardonnay, Sauvignon Blanc, Crouchen, Cabernet Shiraz, Cabernet Sauvignon, Port.
summary Limited tastings have not impressed, but there may be a jewel lurking somewhere, such as the medal-winning though long-gone 1990 Sauvignon Blanc.

redbank winery ★★★★

Sunraysia Highway, Redbank, Vic 3467 **region** Pyrenees
phone (03) 5467 7255 **fax** (03) 5467 7248 **open** Mon–Sat 9–5, Sun 10–5
winemaker Neill Robb **production** 58 000 **est.** 1973
product range ($9.90–66 CD) The range centres on a series of evocatively named red wines, with Sally's Paddock the flagship, followed by Cabernet Sauvignon and Cabernet Franc; then Hard Hill Cabernet Sauvignon, Fighting Flat Shiraz and Spud Gully Pinot; and various specialties available cellar door. Long Paddock Shiraz, Long Paddock Chardonnay and Emily Brut are cheaper, larger-volume second labels.
summary Neill Robb makes very concentrated wines, full of character; the levels of volatile acidity can sometimes be intrusive but are probably of more concern to technical tasters than to the general public. Sally's Paddock is the star, a single vineyard block with an esoteric mix of Cabernet, Shiraz and Malbec and which over the years has produced many great wines.

🐚 red clay estate NR

269 Henry Lawson Drive, Mudgee, NSW 2850 **region** Mudgee
phone (02) 6372 4569 **fax** (02) 6372 4596 **open** Jan–Sept 7 days 10–5, Oct–Dec Mon–Fri 10–5 or by appointment
winemaker Ken Heslop **production** NA **est.** 1997
product range NA.
summary Ken Heslop and Annette Bailey are among the most recent arrivals in Mudgee, with a 2.5-hectare vineyard planted to a diverse range of varieties. The wines are exclusively sold through cellar door and by mail order.

red edge ★★★★★

Golden Gully Road, Heathcote, Vic 3523 **region** Bendigo
phone (03) 9370 9565 **fax** (03) 9370 9565 **open** Not
winemaker Peter Dredge **production** 300 **est.** 1971
product range ($23–29 R) Shiraz, Cabernet Sauvignon.
summary Red Edge is a new name on the scene, but the vineyard dates back to 1971, at the renaissance of the Victorian wine industry. In the early 1980s it produced the wonderful wines of Flynn & Williams and has now been rehabilitated by Peter and Judy Dredge, producing two quite lovely wines in their inaugural 1997 vintage. For the time being, at least, Peter Dredge continues to keep body and soul together by making the wines at Wildwood and at Witchmount Estate, Rockbank. Trying to eke a living out of 300 cases of what in these days are moderately priced wines is simply not possible.

Red Edge Shiraz

Produced from unirrigated and very low-yielding estate vineyards planted in 1971. The wine is neither fined nor filtered, and is deliberately not overoaked.
▼▼▼▼▽ **1998** Dense, opaque purple-red; there is luscious, dense and ripe black cherry fruit which oozes from the bouquet, and more of the same on the intensely fruit-driven palate. Not surprisingly, the oak is barely perceptible. **rating: 93**

best drinking 2003–2013 **best vintages** '97, '98 **drink with** Beef stroganoff • $29

Red Edge Cabernet Sauvignon

Like the Shiraz, produced from low-yielding, unirrigated estate vines. A minimalist handling approach has been adopted, leaving the powerful fruit to express its own personality. It is neither fined nor filtered.

TTTT 1998 The almost impenetrable colour stains the glass as the wine is swirled. The powerful bouquet is full of ripe blackcurrant and blackberry fruit; the power-packed and dense palate with abundant blackberry fruit; the tannins are not aggressive.   **rating:** 94

best drinking 2003–2013 **best vintages** '97, '98 **drink with** Roast lamb • $25

redgate   ★★★☆

Boodjidup Road, Margaret River, WA 6285 **region** Margaret River
phone (08) 9757 6488 **fax** (08) 9757 6308 **open** 7 days 10–5
winemaker Andrew Forsell **production** 10 000 **est.** 1977
product range ($14–32.50 CD) Sauvignon Blanc Reserve, Chardonnay, Semillon, Chenin, Late Harvest Riesling, Pinot Noir, Cabernet Franc, Cabernet Sauvignon, White Port.
summary Twenty hectares of vineyard provide the base for one of the larger wineries of the Margaret River region, which probably has a lower profile than it deserves. The wines do have limited distribution in the eastern States, and export markets in Singapore, Hong Kong, Canada, Japan, Taiwan, Denmark and Switzerland have been established.

red hill estate   ★★★★

53 Redhill–Shoreham Road, Red Hill South, Vic 3937 **region** Mornington Peninsula
phone (03) 5989 2838 **fax** (03) 5989 2855 **open** 7 days 11–5
winemaker Michael Kyberd **production** 20 000 **est.** 1989
product range ($15–36 CD) Particular emphasis on Méthode Champenoise, but also producing Unoaked Chardonnay, Chardonnay, Riesling, Sauvignon Blanc, Hill Block Pinot (Rosé), Pinot Noir and Cabernet Sauvignon; also Muscat (from Rutherglen material) available cellar door only.
summary Sir Peter Derham and family completed the construction of an on-site winery in time for the 1993 vintage, ending a period in which the wines were made at various wineries under contract arrangements. The 10-hectare vineyard is one of the larger plantings on the Mornington Peninsula, and the tasting room and restaurant have a superb view across the vineyard to Westernport Bay and Phillip Island. Production continues to surge, and the winery goes from strength to strength.

Red Hill Estate Chardonnay

An almost startlingly different style from that normally encountered from the Mornington Peninsula, normally bracingly crisp, clean and direct. Years such as '96, however, impose their own imperative (in the form of botrytis), balanced by perfect vintages such as '98. 1999 was somewhere in the middle.

TTT 1999 Medium yellow-green; the bouquet is quite subtle, with melon fruit complexed by hints of fig and honey. The fairly crisp palate has length and brightness, though not overmuch intensity.   **rating:** 83

best drinking 2000–2003 **best vintages** '98 **drink with** Seafood • $25

Red Hill Estate Pinot Noir Chardonnay

A variable blend of Chardonnay and Pinot Noir, sometimes with the Chardonnay dominant, on other occasions (as in 1997) the Pinot Noir. Given a minimum of 15 months on lees and six months on cork after disgorgement.

TTTT 1997 Light straw-pink; a yeasty/bready pinot-driven bouquet with a touch of (deliberate) aldehyde is followed by a stylish palate, with strawberry/bready/yeasty flavours and good balance.   **rating:** 85

best drinking 2000–2002 **best vintages** NA **drink with** Aperitif • $28

Red Hill Estate Pinot Noir

The Red Hill Pinot Noir is sourced from three different vineyards at Merricks, Red Hill and Main Ridge. To add additional complexity, four clones (MV6, D2V5, G5V15 and D5V12, often grown on different canopies such as Geneva Double Curtain or Scott-Henry) are used. Each parcel is picked separately and processed separately with both pre- and post-fermentation maceration.

TTTT 1999 Medium red-purple; an aromatic and sweet bouquet with complex berry and plum fruit is followed by a palate with excellent varietal character and structure. Here plum fruit provides a nice core of sweetness surrounded by hints of forest and subtle oak.   **rating:** 90

best drinking 2000–2005 **best vintages** '99 **drink with** Tea-smoked duck • $30

Red Hill Estate Shiraz

1999 was the first vintage of Shiraz for Red Hill Estate but, in the words of Sir Peter Derham 'It will most definitely not be the last'.

TTTT 1999 Medium red-purple; the bouquet offers quite rich, dark fruit aromas, the light- to medium-bodied palate with attractive cherry and spice flavours and subtle oak. Tasted immediately after bottling it was slightly angular, and the points may prove to be miserly. **rating:** 86

best drinking 2002–2007 **best vintages** NA **drink with** Braised lamb • $25

Red Hill Estate Cabernet Sauvignon

A wine which breaks many of the rules or preconceptions about the suitability of the Mornington Peninsula for Cabernet Sauvignon. Whether future vintages will achieve the same magic remains to be seen, but 1999 could by no stretch of the imagination be classed as easy.

TTTT 1999 Medium red-purple; the bouquet is clean, amazingly without any vegetal/dimethyl sulphide aromas. Instead there is nice dark berry fruit with touches of mint and savoury earth. The palate has red berry fruit, with a touch of mint and a splash of vanilla oak. Despite its relatively early bottling (February 2000) does not appear unfinished. **rating:** 87

best drinking 2001–2010 **best vintages** '99 **drink with** Kraft parmesan cheese • $25

redman ★★★

Riddoch Highway, Coonawarra, SA 5253 **region** Coonawarra
phone (08) 8736 3331 **fax** (08) 8736 3013 **open** Mon–Fri 9–5, weekends 10–4
winemaker Bruce Redman, Malcolm Redman **production** 18 000 **est.** 1966
product range ($13–25.95 R) Shiraz (formerly labelled as Claret), Cabernet Merlot (the first new wine in 26 years), Cabernet Sauvignon.
summary After a prolonged period of mediocrity, the Redman wines are showing sporadic signs of improvement, partly through the introduction of modest amounts of new oak, even if principally American. It would be nice to say the wines now reflect the full potential of the vineyard, but there is still some way to go.

Redman Shiraz

First released in 1966, the wine of that year, 1969 and 1970 all being very good, and still showing well. Those wines were made from the Arthur Hoffman Block, planted around the turn of the century; a number of things happened thereafter which led to a distinctly more diffuse style. There have been intermittent signs of a recovery since 1990.

TTTY 1998 Good red-purple colour; the bouquet isn't lush but it is clean, with dark cherry fruit and slightly regional earthy overtones. The palate has pleasant dark cherry fruit and balanced tannins; not complex or weighty. Gold medal Rutherglen Show 1999. **rating:** 84

best drinking 2001–2005 **best vintages** '66, '69, '70, '90, '91, '93, '98 **drink with** Pasta • $13.95

Redman Cabernet Sauvignon Merlot

Introduced into the Redman range in the early 1990s, and since that time has been one of the few bright lights in the Redman stable.

TTTT 1996 Medium red-purple; clean blackberry/blackcurrant fruit with a hint of varietal/regional cabernet earth and subtle oak leads into a palate with pleasing red berry fruit in a light- to medium-bodied frame. The best Redman wine for some years. **rating:** 86

best drinking 2001–2006 **best vintages** '93, '94, '96 **drink with** Shoulder of lamb • $25.95

🐾 red rock winery NR

RMB 5059 East West Road, Barongarook, Vic 3249 **region** Geelong
phone 015 231 190 **fax** (03) 9380 9711 **open** Weekends and public holidays 11–5 or by appointment
winemaker Rohan Little **production** NA **est.** 1981
product range NA.
summary The former Barongvale Estate, with 5 hectares of riesling, semillon, chardonnay, pinot noir, merlot and cabernet sauvignon; a part-time occupation for Rohan Little, with wines sold under both the Red Rock and Ottway Vineyards labels.

reedy creek vineyard NR

Reedy Creek, via Tenterfield, NSW 2372 **region** Other Wineries of NSW
phone (02) 6737 5221 **fax** (02) 6737 5200 **open** 7 days 9–5
winemaker Bruce Humphery-Smith (Contract) **production** 2300 **est.** 1971
product range ($12–23 CD) Bianco Alpino, Chardonnay, Rosso Alpino, Shiraz Mourvedre, Old Vine Shiraz, Shiraz, Valambrossa Liqueur, Muscat Liqueur, Port.

summary Like so many Italian settlers in the Australian countryside, the De Stefani family has been growing grapes and making wine for its own consumption for over 30 years at its Reedy Creek property near Tenterfield, in the far north of New South Wales. What is more, like their compatriots in the King Valley, the family's principal activity until 1993 was growing tobacco, but the continued rationalisation of the tobacco industry prompted the De Stefanis to turn a hobby into a commercial exercise. The vineyard has now been expanded to 6.1 hectares, and the first commercial vintage of Shiraz was made in 1995, with Chardonnay following in 1998. The wines are made by the incredibly industrious Bruce Humphery-Smith at Rimfire Vineyards at MacLagan and are sold cellar door from the maturation cellar opened in 1997.

reg drayton wines ★★★☆

Corner Pokolbin Mountain and McDonalds Roads, Pokolbin, NSW 2321 **region** Lower Hunter Valley
phone (02) 4998 7523 **fax** (02) 4998 7523 **open** 7 days 10–5
winemaker Tyrrell's (Contract) **production** 3000 **est.** 1989
product range ($17–25 CD) Lambkin Semillon, Lambkin Verdelho, Pokolbin Hills Chardonnay, Pokolbin Hills Chardonnay Semillon, Three Sons Shiraz, Pokolbin Hills Shiraz, Pokolbin Hills Cabernet Shiraz, Port.
summary Reg and Pam Drayton were among the victims of the Seaview/Lord Howe Island air crash in October 1984, having established Reg Drayton Wines after selling their interest in the long-established Drayton Family Winery. Their daughter Robyn (a fifth-generation Drayton and billed as the Hunter's first female vigneron) and husband Craig continue the business, which draws chiefly upon the Pokolbin Hills Estate but also takes fruit from the historic Lambkin Estate vineyard. The wines are made for them at Tyrrell's.

reilly's wines NR

Corner Hill and Burra Streets, Mintaro, SA 5415 **region** Clare Valley
phone (08) 8843 9013 **fax** (08) 8337 4111 **open** 7 days 10–5
winemaker Justin Ardill **production** 5000 **est.** 1994
product range ($13–35 CD) Watervale Riesling, Late Picked Riesling, Chardonnay, Semillon, Sparkling Grenache, Old Bushvine Grenache, Clare Valley Shiraz, Dry Land Shiraz, Cabernet Sauvignon, Port.
summary Justin and Julie Ardill are among the newest arrivals in the Clare Valley, with just a handful of vintages under their belt. An unusual sideline of Reilly's Cottage is the production of an Extra Virgin Olive Oil; unusual in that it is made from wild olives found in the Mintaro district of the Clare Valley. Retail distribution in South Australia, Victoria and New South Wales.

renmano ★★★★

Sturt Highway, Renmark, SA 5341 **region** Riverland
phone (08) 8586 6771 **fax** (08) 8586 5939 **open** Mon–Sat 9–5
winemaker Glenn James, Tony Ingle **production** 1.6 million **est.** 1914
product range ($14.95 R) Chairman's Selection Chardonnay; River Breeze is a second label.
summary Part of the BRL Hardy Group. A radical change in winemaking technique and philosophy in 1996 has wrought miracles with the Chairman's Selection Chardonnay, now the only premium wine under the Renmano label.

Renmano Chairman's Selection Reserve Chardonnay

For years made in a totally distinctive, fast-maturing, over-the-top style, loaded with peachy/buttery fruit and oak which could look hugely attractive when very young, but which became fat and blowsy after a year or two. A change in the winemaking team led to a finer wine style, though still not destined for long cellaring.
▼▼▼▼ 1997 Medium to full yellow-green; the bouquet is full and complex, with some spicy/charry/chippy oak; as usual, has ripe, mouthfilling peachy fruit. However, the fruit and oak phenolics toughen up the finish; best enjoyed within a year of vintage. **rating: 85**
best drinking Drink now **best vintages** '89, '94, '96 **drink with** Braised pork • $14.95

reynell ★★★★☆

Reynell Road, Reynella, SA 5161 **region** McLaren Vale
phone (08) 8392 2222 **fax** (08) 8392 2202 **open** 7 days 10–4.30
winemaker Stephen Pannell **production** NFP **est.** 1838
product range ($37.95 R) Basket Pressed Shiraz, Basket Pressed Merlot, Basket Pressed Cabernet Sauvignon.
summary Reynell is the name under which all wines from the historic Reynella winery (once called Chateau Reynella) are released. What is more, the range of wines has been compressed and taken into the super-premium category with the initial release in July 1997 of three multi-award-winning wines, all effectively Show Reserve releases.

Reynell Basket Pressed Shiraz

The initial release of this wine (the '94) had won seven gold medals prior to its release, and is the type of wine which will continue to amass gold medals so long as it is exhibited in wine shows. Hugely powerful and concentrated, it was matured in American oak for 24 months. Initially that oak is married well with the wine but does gradually build-up on retasting, and ultimately threatens the balance of the wine. Those more tolerant of the flavour of American oak will find no problem with it, however.

▼▼▼▼▼ **1996** Deep colour; savoury, spicy notes are woven through the intense dark berry fruit of the bouquet; rich and powerful, but not over the top; controlled oak and good tannin structure accompany the luscious, savoury berry fruit. **rating:** 94

best drinking 2001–2016 **best vintages** '94, '95, '96 **drink with** Barbecued rump steak • $37.95

reynolds wine company ★★★★

Yarraman Road, Wybong, NSW 2333 **region** Upper Hunter Valley
phone (02) 6547 8127 **fax** (02) 6547 8013 **open** Mon–Sat 10–4, Sun, public holidays 11–4
winemaker Jon Reynolds, Nic Millichip **production** 20 000 **est.** 1967
product range ($15–25 CD) From the Hunter Valley: Semillon, Chardonnay, Shiraz; from Orange: Chardonnay, Cabernet Sauvignon; Cabernet Merlot is a blend from both the Hunter Valley and Orange.
summary With the Orange region steadily assuming greater importance for Reynolds, wine quality (and consistency) likewise continues to increase, although the Semillons will of course remain Hunter Valley-sourced. The skills of Jon Reynolds as a winemaker have never been in doubt, and as the size and maturity of the Orange vineyards grow, it seems certain that even better wines will appear in the future. The wines are exported to the UK, the US, Europe and Asia.

Reynolds Orange Sauvignon Blanc

The first release by Reynolds of a Sauvignon Blanc from Orange; as one would expect, Sauvignon Blanc is infinitely better-suited to Orange than the Hunter Valley.

▼▼▼▽ **1999** Light straw-green; the bouquet is clean and fresh, with light citrus blossom aromas; delicate, crisp lemony fruit runs through the palate; fair length and a good finish. **rating:** 84

best drinking 2000–2001 **best vintages** NA **drink with** Seafood • $16

Reynolds Orange Chardonnay

The two most distinguished wines in the Reynolds portfolio now come not from the Upper Hunter but from Orange, whence Jon Reynolds has sourced increasing amounts of fruit over the recent years. The Chardonnay was the first 100 per cent Orange district wine made by Jon Reynolds; barrel-fermented in French oak, with the full range of malolactic fermentation and lees contact. It comes from the Bloodwood and Bantry Grove vineyards.

▼▼▼▼ **1998** Deep yellow-green; an intriguing mix of butter and peach fruit together with mineral notes on the bouquet. The palate is quite complex, well structured, but lacks a little vinosity on the mid-palate. May fill out with time in bottle. **rating:** 86

best drinking 2000–2003 **best vintages** '97 **drink with** Sautéed veal • $22.50

Reynolds Orange Merlot

Like the Sauvignon Blanc, an inaugural vintage which promises much for the future.

▼▼▼▼ **1998** Medium red-purple; quite complex savoury/leafy/berry/earthy aromas are mirrored by the flavours of the palate. The wine has good weight, texture and style; a touch of sweet oak is a plus, as are soft tannins. **rating:** 88

best drinking 2002–2008 **best vintages** '98 **drink with** Braised veal • $25

ribbon vale estate ★★★☆

Lot 5 Caves Road, Willyabrup via Cowaramup, WA 6284 **region** Margaret River
phone (08) 9755 6272 **fax** (08) 9755 6337 **open** Weekends, holidays 10–5
winemaker Mike Davies **production** 4000 **est.** 1977
product range ($15–29 CD) Semillon, Semillon Sauvignon Blanc, Sauvignon Blanc, Cabernet Merlot, Merlot, Cabernet Sauvignon.
summary Made crisp, herbaceous Semillon and Sauvignon Blanc (and blends), ideal seafood wines, and austere, very firm Cabernets all in mainstream regional style. Retail distribution in Western Australia, New South Wales and Victoria. However, major changes are in store following the acquisition of the estate by Moss Wood in early 2000.

richfield vineyard   NR

Bruxner Highway, Tenterfield, NSW 2372 **region** Other Wineries of NSW
phone (02) 6737 5588 **fax** (02) 6737 5598 **open** Not
winemaker Contract **production** NA **est.** 1997
product range Chardonnay, Shiraz, Merlot, Cabernet Sauvignon.
summary Richfield Vineyard points to the tyranny of State boundaries. Established at the instigation of Denis Parsons of Bald Mountain vineyards in the Granite Belt (Queensland), Richfield is little more than 30 kilometres south of Bald Mountain vineyards as the crow flies. A little over 11 hectares were planted in 1997, with plans for future expansion.

richmond grove   ★★★★

Para Road, Tanunda, SA 5352 **region** Barossa Valley
phone (08) 8563 2184 **fax** (08) 8563 2804 **open** Mon–Fri 10–5, weekends 10–4
winemaker John Vickery **production** NFP **est.** 1977
product range ($9.95–19.95 R) Eden Valley Traminer Riesling, Watervale Riesling, Barossa Riesling, Oak Matured Chablis, Cowra Chardonnay, Cowra Verdelho, French Cask Chardonnay, Hunter Valley Classic Dry White, Marlborough Sauvignon Blanc, Barossa Shiraz, Cabernet Merlot.
summary Richmond Grove now has two homes, including one in the Barossa Valley where John Vickery presides. It is owned by Orlando Wyndham and draws its grapes from diverse sources. The Richmond Grove Barossa Valley and Watervale Rieslings made by John Vickery represent the best value for money (for Riesling) year in, year out. If these were the only wines produced by Richmond Grove, it would have five-star rating. Exports to the UK.

Richmond Grove Barossa Riesling

A twin to the Watervale Riesling, likewise made by John Vickery, and a supremely honest wine offering plenty of flavour from a young age.
▼▼▼▼ 1999 Medium yellow-green; the moderately intense bouquet is clean, with gentle, citrus-tinged fruit. The perfectly balanced and modulated palate really comes alive, adding authority to the bouquet.   **rating:** 89
best drinking 2002–2012 **best vintages** '94, '95, '96, '97, '99 **drink with** Pasta, white meat dishes   • $14.95

Richmond Grove Watervale Riesling

With John Vickery's vast experience and impeccable contacts, it is not surprising that Richmond Grove Rieslings should be as exceptionally good as they are, although only ferocious attention to detail can produce such consistently excellent wines.
▼▼▼▼▽ 1999 The spotlessly clean bouquet offers splashes of citrus, herb, mineral, ripe apple and passionfruit; the perfectly balanced palate is less exuberant flavourwise but is intense and powerful.   **rating:** 92
best drinking 1999–2019 **best vintages** '94, '96, '97, '98 **drink with** Asparagus with hollandaise sauce   • $14.95

Richmond Grove Hunter Valley Semillon

The wheel comes full circle with this wine, for Richmond Grove started its life in the Hunter Valley, however well known it may now be for its South Australian Rieslings.
▼▼▼▽ 1999 Light yellow-green; the bouquet is light, fresh and clean, with a correct touch of herbaceous varietal character. The palate follows along the same track but lacks intensity on the finish.   **rating:** 82
best drinking 2000–2003 **best vintages** NA **drink with** Chicken breast   • $14.95

Richmond Grove French Cask Chardonnay

Marketers are strange; they can't resist fiddling with a highly successful label, yet can persist in holding on to relics of the past. The name of this wine certainly falls in the latter category.
▼▼▼▼ 1999 Light to medium yellow-green; a cleverly made wine with good balance and integration of fruit and oak on both bouquet and palate. Ripe nectarine flavours sit easily with a gentle touch of oak.   **rating:** 85
▼▼▼▼ 1998 Light to medium yellow-green; highly scented fruit and oak on the bouquet is followed by quite positive, ripe apple and melon fruit on the palate. The oak is well balanced and integrated.   **rating:** 86
best drinking 2000–2003 **best vintages** NA **drink with** Pan-fried veal   • $12

Richmond Grove Barossa Shiraz

The wine is made using a variety of techniques, all adding up to sophistication. Varying temperatures are used during fermentation, and while the majority of the wine is given post-fermentation maceration (or skin contact) part completed its primary fermentation in barrel. The pressings are back-blended, and the partly clarified wine is placed in American oak barrels where it spends the next 18 months. The '97 won a gold medal at the Brisbane Wine Show in 1999.

▼▼▼▼ **1997** Medium red-purple; a thoroughly traditional style, with berry fruit and vanilla American oak on the bouquet. The medium-bodied palate has pleasant fresh fruit flavours; the oak is just a fraction disjointed but should settle down with time. **rating:** 86

best drinking 2002–2007 **best vintages** NA **drink with** Rib of beef • $18

Richmond Grove Coonawarra Cabernet Sauvignon

The initial release of Coonawarra Cabernet Sauvignon under the Richmond Grove label, matured in a mix of French and American oak casks for 18 months before blending and bottling. It is a wine of light to medium intensity, not surprising given its modest price.

▼▼▼▼ **1997** Medium red, with just a touch of purple; the bouquet is clean, moderately intense, with neatly balanced fruit and oak. A solid commercial red wine on the palate with ripe fruit bolstered by plenty of vanillin oak and soft tannins. **rating:** 85

best drinking 2001–2007 **best vintages** '94, '96 **drink with** Lamb cutlets • $18

🦡 richmond park vineyard   NR

Logie Road, Richmond, Tas 7025 **region** Southern Tasmania
phone (03) 6265 2949 **fax** (03) 6265 3166 **open** Not
winemaker Andrew Hood (Contract) **production** 600 **est.** 1989
product range ($9–15ML) Chardonnay, Pinot Noir.
summary A small vineyard owned by Tony Park which gives the clue to the clever name.

Richmond Park Vineyard Pinot Noir

Quaintly, said to be Product of Australia, but I cannot imagine it is a blend of Tasmanian and mainland fruit. A surprise silver medal winner at the Tasmanian Wines Show 2000.

▼▼▼▼ **1997** Medium purple-red; the smooth, ripe, plummy bouquet leads into a palate with voluminous, ripe plummy fruit. Given the fruit freshness, should develop well in bottle. **rating:** 89

best drinking 1999–2003 **drink with** Spiced quail • $9

rimfire vineyards   ★★★☆

Bismarck Street, MacLagan, Qld 4352 **region** South Burnett and Other Wineries of Qld
phone (07) 4692 1129 **fax** (07) 4692 1260 **open** 7 days 10–5
winemaker Tony Connellan **production** 6000 **est.** 1991
product range ($9–16 CD) Settlers Blend, Estate Chardonnay, Oak Matured Chardonnay, Estate Colombard, Pioneer White, Verdelho, Shiraz, Colonial Cabernet, Light Fruity Red; Fortifieds.
summary The Connellan family (parents Margaret and Tony and children Michelle, Peter and Louise) began planting the 12-hectare, 14-variety Rimfire Vineyards in 1991 as a means of diversification of their very large (1500-hectare) cattle stud in the foothills of the Bunya Mountains, 45 minutes drive northeast of Toowoomba. Rimfire has had one success after another in Queensland wine shows and on this yardstick has to be regarded as one of the best producers in Queensland.

Rimfire Chardonnay

Estate-grown, and, barrel-fermented in new French oak, this wine has led the way for Rimfire since its debut in 1996, winning the *Courier-Mail*/Sheraton Wine Award for Best Queensland Dry White Wine, and moving to even greater heights with the 1997, which won the first-ever gold medal for a Queensland wine in the Australian Small Winemakers Show. The 1999 performed with considerable distinction in the 2000 *Winewise* Small Makers Competiton.

▼▼▼▼ **1999** Light to medium yellow-green; the bouquet is bright and fresh, with subtle oak and light nectarine fruit. The palate is similarly bright, with a mix of creamy cashew and nectarine fruit, fine acidity and subtle oak. **rating:** 85

best drinking 2000–2003 **best vintages** '96, '97, '99 **drink with** Rack of veal • $16

rivendell   ★★★

Lot 328 Wildwood Road, Yallingup, WA 6282 **region** Margaret River
phone (08) 9755 2235 **fax** (08) 9755 2295 **open** 7 days 10–5
winemaker Mike Davies, Jan Davies (Contract) **production** 2750 **est.** 1987
product range ($12.50–14.50 CD) Semillon Sauvignon Blanc, Honeysuckle Late Harvest Semillon, Verdelho, Shiraz Cabernet.

summary With 13.5 hectares of vineyards coming into bearing, production for Rivendell will increase significantly over the coming years. The cellar-door sales facility is in a garden setting, complete with restaurant. An unusual sideline is the sale of 50 types of preserves, jams and chutneys. No recent tastings.

riverbank estate   NR

126 Hamersley Road, Caversham, WA 6055 **region** Swan District
phone (08) 9377 1805 **fax** (08) 9377 2168 **open** Weekends and public holidays 10–5
winemaker Robert James Bond **production** 3500 **est.** 1993
product range ($12–16 CD) Semillon, Verdelho, Chenin, Chardonnay, Cabernet.
summary Robert Bond, a graduate of Charles Sturt University and a Swan Valley viticulturist for 20 years, established RiverBank Estate in 1993. He draws upon 11 hectares of estate plantings and, in his words, 'The wines are unashamedly full bodied, produced from ripe grapes in what is recognised as a hot grape growing region'.

riverina wines   ★★★★☆

700 Lidman Way, Griffith, NSW 2680 **region** Riverina
phone (02) 6962 4122 **fax** (02) 6962 4628 **open** 7 days 9–5.30
winemaker Sam Trimboli **production** 220 000 **est.** 1969
product range ($7.50–14.50 CD) An extensive range of varietal wines under the Ballingal Estate, Ridgewood Estate and Warburn Estate labels, the former being slightly higher priced, each including Chardonnay, Semillon, Semillon Chardonnay, Shiraz, Cabernet Sauvignon and Cabernet Merlot, with a few additions under the Ballingal Estate label. There is also a range of sparkling wines and fortifieds in both bottle and cask.
summary One of the large producers of the region, drawing upon 1100 hectares of estate plantings. While much of the wine is sold in bulk to other producers, selected parcels of the best of the grapes are made into table wines, with quite spectacular success. At the 1997 National Wine Show, Riverina Wines won an astonishing six gold medals, topping no less than four classes. That success has, it seems, given rise to the introduction of the Show Reserve wines, and while the 1997 success has not been equalled since, the Show Reserve wines continue to justify their label. Exports to the UK.

riversands vineyards   NR

Whytes Road, St George, Qld 4487 **region** South Burnett and Other Wineries of Qld
phone (07) 4625 3643 **fax** (07) 4625 5043 **open** Mon–Sat 8–6, Sunday 9–4
winemaker Ballandean Estate (Contract) **production** 2000 **est.** 1990
product range ($9–15 CD) Sauvignon Blanc Semillon, Chardonnay, Major Mitchell White, Three Rivers Red, Dr Seidel's Soft Red, Ellen Meacle Merlot, Golden Liqueur Muscat, Gaolhouse Port.
summary Riversands is situated on the banks of the Balonne River near St George in the southwest corner of Queensland. It is a mixed wine grape and table grape business, acquired by present owners Alison and David Blacket in 1996. The wines are very competently made under contract at Ballandean Estate and have already accumulated a number of silver and bronze medals. The Chardonnay is particularly meritorious.

✿ roberts estate wines   NR

Game Street, Merbein, Vic 3505 **region** Murray Darling and Swan Hill
phone (03) 5024 2944 **fax** (03) 5024 2877 **open** Not
winemaker Ian McElhinney **production** 80 000 **est.** 1998
product range ($8–10 R) Chardonnay, Merlot, Shiraz, Cabernet Sauvignon; under the Denbeigh label Chardonnay, Semillon Chardonnay, Colombard Chardonnay, Shiraz, Cabernet Sauvignon, Shiraz Cabernet.
summary A very large winery acting as a processing point for grapes grown up and down the Murray River. Over 10 000 tonnes are crushed each vintage; much of the wine is sold in bulk to others, but some is exported under the Denbeigh and Kombacy labels.

robinsons family vineyards   ★★★

Curtin Road, Ballandean, Qld 4382 **region** Granite Belt
phone (07) 4684 1216 **fax** (07) 4684 1216 **open** 7 days 9–5
winemaker Craig Robinson **production** 3000 **est.** 1969
product range ($14–20 CD) Sauvignon Blanc Semillon, Chardonnay, Unwooded Chardonnay, Lyra Dry White, Traminer, Late Harvest Traminer, Shiraz, Shiraz Cabernet, Cabernet Sauvignon, Sparkling.
summary The conjunction of a picture of a hibiscus and 'cool climate' in prominent typeface on the labels is a strange one, but then that has always been the nature of Robinsons Family Vineyards. The red wines can be very good, particularly when not overly extracted and tannic.

Robinsons Family Cabernet Sauvignon

The first wine made by solicitor/founder John Robinson in 1975 was a gold medal winning Cabernet Sauvignon. Over the intervening years this has always been the best of the Robinson wines, its at times awesome power reflecting the low-yielding vines crouching between great granite boulders.

▼▼▼▼ **1998** Medium to full red-purple; rich blackberry/blackcurrant fruit is supported by subtle oak on the bouquet. An extremely concentrated and powerful palate which will still be flexing its muscles in ten years time.

rating: 86

best drinking 2003–2013 **best vintages** NA **drink with** Roast beef • $20

robinvale

Sea Lake Road, Robinvale, Vic 3549 **region** Murray Darling
phone (03) 5026 3955 **fax** (03) 5026 1123 **open** Mon–Fri 9–6, Sun 1–6
winemaker Bill Caracatsanoudis **production** 15 000 **est.** 1976
product range ($8.50–20 CD) A kaleidoscopic array of wines, including five preservative-free wines, white wines which run from Retsina through to Auslese Muscat Hamburg, Dry Marsanne, red wines which encompass Lambrusco, Scarlet Bliss, Cabernet Sauvignon/Franc, Kokkineli, Fruity Rosé; and fortified wines ranging from Mavrodaphne to Cream Marsala, with a few Vintage Ports thrown in for good measure.
summary Robinvale was one of the first Australian wineries to be fully accredited with the Biodynamic Agricultural Association of Australia. Most, but not all, of the wines are produced from organically grown grapes, with certain of the wines made preservative-free. Production has increased dramatically, no doubt reflecting the interest in organic and biodynamic viticulture and winemaking. Exports to the UK and Japan.

rochford ★★★☆

Romsey Park, Rochford, Vic 3442 **region** Macedon Ranges
phone (03) 5429 1428 **fax** (03) 5429 1066 **open** By appointment
winemaker David Creed **production** 2500 **est.** 1983
product range ($19–32 R) Chardonnay, Pinot Noir, Cabernet Sauvignon; Romsey Park is second label.
summary In February 1998 Helmut Konecsny and Yvonne Lodoco-Konecsny acquired Rochford. David Creed continues as winemaker, and it is the Konecsnys' intention to leave wine style unchanged, with the emphasis on Chardonnay and Pinot Noir, and gradually increase production.

Rochford Pinot Noir

Pinot has consistently been the outstanding wine from Rochford, typically exhibiting both complexity and richness of flavour and helping establish the reputation of the Macedon region as yet another area suited to this fickle variety.

▼▼▼▼ **1998** Medium to full red-purple; the bouquet is solid but rather closed at the moment, with some dark fruit aromas escaping. The palate is similarly solid, with plummy fruit, but needing to develop light and shade; this may come with time.

rating: 85

best drinking 2000–2004 **best vintages** '91, '92, '93, '95, '96, '98 **drink with** Jugged hare • $30

rockford ★★★★

Krondorf Road, Tanunda, SA 5352 **region** Barossa Valley
phone (08) 8563 2720 **fax** (08) 8563 3787 **open** Mon–Sat 11–5
winemaker Robert O'Callaghan, Chris Ringland **production** 19 000 **est.** 1984
product range ($10.50–45 CD) Eden Valley Riesling, Local Growers Semillon, Alicante Bouchet, White Frontignac, Basket Press Shiraz, Sparkling Black Shiraz, Dry Country Grenache, Cabernet Sauvignon, Tawny Port.
summary The wines are sold through Adelaide retailers only (and cellar door) and are unknown to most eastern Australian wine-drinkers, which is a great pity because these are some of the most individual, spectacularly flavoured wines made in the Barossa today, with an emphasis on old, low-yielding dry-land vineyards. This South Australian slur on the palates of Victoria and NSW is exacerbated by the fact that the wines are exported to Switzerland, the UK and New Zealand; it all goes to show we need proper authority to protect our living treasures.

Rockford Black Shiraz

This, quite simply, is a great sparkling Shiraz, inspired by the Sparkling Burgundies of Colin Preece at Great Western, and made using fundamentally the same techniques. The base wine is matured in large old wood for three years before being tiraged, and then left on lees for a year before disgorgement and further cellaring prior to release. This particular bottle was part of the September '96 disgorgement. Almost impossible to procure; sold only through Adelaide retailers and by mailing list and cellar door, and sells out almost overnight with a limit of six bottles per customer. The unique personality of Robert O'Callaghan comes rocketing through the newsletter, which at the end of the day is probably the best way of getting hold of these scarce wines.

▼▼▼▼▼ NV Dark red, but with some brick hues evident. There is an attractive mix of spice and earth aromas on the bouquet, but the palate is something else, with that fine, faintly spicy, faintly earthy taste of mature Shiraz of the old Great Western style. It is neither heavy nor sweet, and has tremendous balance and length. **rating: 94**

best drinking 2000–2020 **best vintages** NA **drink with** Needs no accompaniment • $45

romavilla NR

Northern Road, Roma, Qld 4455 **region** South Burnett and Other Wineries of Qld
phone (07) 4622 1822 **fax** (07) 4622 1822 **open** Mon–Fri 8–5, Sat 9–12, 2–4
winemaker David Wall, Richard Wall **production** 2500 **est.** 1863
product range ($12–40 CD) An extensive range of varietal and generic table wines and fortified wine styles, including Madeira and Tawny Port, are on sale at the winery; the Very Old Tawny Port is made from a blend of material ranging in age from 10 to 25 years.
summary An amazing historic relic, seemingly untouched since its nineteenth-century heyday, producing ordinary table wines but still providing some extraordinary fortifieds, including a truly stylish Madeira made from Riesling and Syrian (the latter variety originating in Persia). David Wall has now been joined by son Richard in the business, which will hopefully ensure continuity for this important part of Australian wine history.

rosabrook estate NR

Rosa Brook Road, Margaret River, WA 6285 **region** Margaret River
phone (08) 9757 2286 **fax** (08) 9757 3634 **open** 7 days 10–4
winemaker Simon Keall **production** 4000 **est.** 1980
product range ($15–22 CD) Semillon Sauvignon Blanc, Chardonnay, Autumn Harvest Riesling, Botrytis Riesling, Shiraz, Cabernet Merlot.
summary The 14-hectare Rosabrook Estate vineyards have been established progressively since 1980, with seven varieties planted. The cellar-door facility is housed in what was Margaret River's first commercial abattoir, built in the early 1930s, with a new winery constructed in 1993. Limited retail distribution in New South Wales, Victoria and West Australia; exports to the US.

Rosabrook Estate Semillon Sauvignon Blanc

A blend of 60 per cent Semillon and 40 per cent Sauvignon Blanc, cold-fermented and having no contact with oak.

▼▼▼▼ 1999 Very pale straw-green; the bouquet is crisp and clean, with a mix of high-toned lemon and passionfruit aromas which flow through to the palate in identical fashion. A neat, light-bodied early-drinking style. **rating: 85**

best drinking 2000–2001 **best vintages** NA **drink with** Pan-fried garfish • $15

rosemount estate (hunter valley) ★★★★★

Rosemount Road, Denman, NSW 2328 **region** Upper Hunter Valley
phone (02) 6549 6400 **fax** (02) 6549 6499 **open** Mon–Sat 10–4; Sun summer 10–4, winter 12–4
winemaker Philip Shaw **production** 2.5 million **est.** 1969
product range ($8.99–55.99 R) A very large range of wines which in almost all instances are varietally identified, sometimes with the conjunction of vineyards at the top end of the range, and which in the case of the lower-priced volume varietals increasingly come from all parts of southeast Australia. Names and label designs change regularly but the emphasis remains on the classic varietals. Roxburgh Chardonnay is the white flag-bearer; Mountain Blue Shiraz Cabernet the real leader. Chardonnay, Shiraz and Cabernet Sauvignon under the standard labels consistently excellent at the price. In 1997 a Yarra Valley Chardonnay was added to the regional range, which also encompasses Coonawarra, Orange and Mudgee (Hill of Gold).
summary Rosemount Estate has achieved a miraculous balancing act over the past years maintaining — indeed increasing — wine quality while presiding over an ever-expanding empire and ever-increasing production. The wines are consistently of excellent value; all have real character and individuality; not a few are startlingly good.

Rosemount Estate Hunter Valley Semillon

Notwithstanding Rosemount's domicile in the Upper Hunter, this is one of the few commercial wines produced by Rosemount which has a Hunter Valley appellation. That, of course, is no accident, and simply reflects the fact that there is a true synergy between the region and the variety. Just for the record, this wine won two gold medals in the year of its making.

❦❦❦❦ **1999** Light green-yellow; a light, clean and fresh bouquet but not much character showing yet. The palate, however, has good length and persistence and bodes well for medium-term cellaring. **rating:** 86

best drinking 2002–2006 **best vintages** '96, '99 **drink with** Mussels • $16.90

Rosemount Estate Show Reserve Semillon

Rosemount's Show Reserve label means what it says: this really is a carefully selected wine of well-above-average quality, sourced from Rosemount's best vineyards in the Hunter Valley.

❦❦❦❦ **1998** Medium yellow-green; the bouquet is purely fruit-driven, gently herbaceous, yet quite complex. That complexity manifests itself with very good mouthfeel, the palate offering a mix of ripe citrus and more grassy flavours, finishing with good acidity. Held in stainless steel only, but probably on yeast lees. **rating:** 90

best drinking 2001–2008 **best vintages** NA **drink with** Breast of turkey • $27

Rosemount Estate Sauvignon Blanc

While made by Rosemount for many years, took a new (and better) turn with the 1997 vintage, which incorporates the first harvest from Rosemount's new The Range Vineyard in the Adelaide Hills, first planted in 1994 and dedicated to the production of sauvignon blanc. The '97 vintage was a blend of 60 per cent Hunter Valley and 40 per cent Adelaide Hills fruit, but with the latter component providing the character the wine has. It is a reasonable assumption that the percentage of Adelaide Hills material will increase in future years, although it will be interesting to see whether Rosemount makes a separate, higher-priced release.

❦❦❦❦ **1999** Light green-yellow; the bouquet is clean and minerally, but not particularly fragrant or fruity; a straight line palate follows; a pleasant, neutral food style. **rating:** 84

best drinking Drink now **best vintages** NA **drink with** Pan-fried prawns • $16.90

Rosemount Estate Semillon Sauvignon Blanc

Neither the region(s) nor the varietal percentage are provided by Rosemount, but it seems to be predominantly Upper Hunter and traditionally cold-fermented without the use of oak.

❦❦❦❦ **1999** Light green-yellow; clean, gentle but correct varietal character in a grassy/citrus/mineral spectrum is followed logically by an admirably balanced, crisp and clean palate with good length. Well above the normal ruck for a wine of this price. **rating:** 86

best drinking 2000–2001 **best vintages** NA **drink with** Deep-fried fish • $12

Rosemount Estate Semillon Chardonnay

Drawn from vineyards across southeastern Australia, and made with the usual flair one comes to expect from Rosemount Estate. Prior vintages have been gold medal winners.

❦❦❦❦ **1999** Medium yellow-green; the bouquet is soft with touches of melon and grass, the light- to medium-weight palate clean but somewhat plain and amorphous. **rating:** 80

best drinking 2000–2001 **best vintages** NA **drink with** Takeaway • $12

Rosemount Estate Chardonnay

Sourced from vineyards in the Hunter Valley, McLaren Vale and Murray River Valley. A proportion of the wine undergoes malolactic fermentation while ageing in French oak; the major part is fermented and retained on lees in stainless steel prior to being blended.

❦❦❦❦ **1999** Light to medium yellow-green; the moderately intense bouquet has melon and peach fruit and a hint of chippy oak; the medium-weight palate has similar flavours, but the oak is slightly resiny and threatens the fruit. Not as cleverly made as most Rosemount wines. **rating:** 84

best drinking Drink now **best vintages** '84, '86, '87, '90, '93, '95 **drink with** Veal parmigiana • $16.90

Rosemount Estate Giants Creek Chardonnay

The wine comes from a single vineyard of the same name near Sandy Hollow in the upper reaches of the Hunter Valley; like Roxburgh, it is owned by Rosemount. The grapes are whole-bunch pressed and the free-run is taken directly to barrel without settling, with spontaneous fermentation from the indigenous cellar population of natural yeast. Spontaneous malolactic fermentation also takes place in the barrels, which are a mix of one- and two-year-old French Allier, with small proportion of new oak. The wine is held in barrel for ten months prior to fining, clarification and bottling.

❦❦❦❦ **1997** Light green-yellow; the bouquet is surprisingly youthful, but there is a bitter, green edge which runs both through the bouquet and the palate. The wine did not seem corked, but perhaps those green, bitter edges are not typical. **rating:** 81

best drinking 2000–2002 **best vintages** NA **drink with** Pork loin • $20.90

Rosemount Estate Rosé Label Orange Vineyard Chardonnay

The vineyard was planted in 1989 at an elevation of 900 metres. The planting density is high, and a high-wall vertical trellis is used. The wine undergoes barrel-fermentation and usually undergoes 100 per cent malolactic fermentation. Has an excellent show record.

♥♥♥♥ 1998 Light to medium yellow-green; a crisp and clean bouquet with light melon fruit and subtle oak flows into a palate with melon and citrus/grapefruit flavours which are still tight and locked-in. Needs time, and on the track record of the wine, will develop very well. **rating: 85**

best drinking 2001–2005 best vintages '92, '95, '96, '97 drink with Oyster soup • $25

Rosemount Estate Roxburgh Chardonnay

Since 1983 the flagship of Rosemount Estate and, at least in some quarters, regarded as the premier Australian white. Throughout the 1980s the style was quite controversial but has become more conventional in the 1990s as more emphasis has been placed on fresh fruit. It is a single-vineyard wine, most of the fruit coming from two 3.5-hectare blocks at the top of the Roxburgh Vineyard planted on limestone-impregnated terra rossa soil. I am left to ponder whether time has passed the style by.

♥♥♥♥♥ 1997 Once claimed the position as the Chardonnay equivalent of Grange, but the competition is now too strong and Yattarna has entered the fray. As ever, in its own idiom, with nutty, creamy aromas and plenty of oak. Has good power, length and grip, with ripe nectarine/peach fruit on the mid-palate. **rating: 94**

best drinking 2000–2003 best vintages '86, '87, '89, '91, '92, '93, '95, '97 drink with Veal, pork • $55.90

Rosemount Estate Show Reserve Chardonnay

The grapes for this wine are sourced from favoured blocks on two of Rosemount's principal Hunter Valley vineyards — Roxburgh and Giants Creek. The winemaking methods are nothing if not complex, with the Giants Creek component being processed in a quite different fashion from that of the Roxburgh fruit. Likewise, the juices were cold-settled for periods ranging between six and 48 hours, deliberately giving different levels of solids in the musts. Most of the wine was transferred straight to barrel for the initiation of fermentation, with 60 per cent French Allier and 40 per cent American oak being used. The malolactic fermentation occurs spontaneously.

♥♥♥♥ 1998 Medium yellow-green; lemony, tangy fruit shows through some spicy barrel-ferment oak on the bouquet; the palate is pleasant but lacks the intensity of the very best Chardonnays; short-term cellaring will help. **rating: 87**

best drinking 2000–2003 best vintages NA drink with Pan-fried veal • $26.90

Rosemount Estate Pinot Noir

The grapes are grown on estate vineyards in McLaren Vale and Mudgee, an unlikely regional base; very clever winemaking, with carefully considered components, produces an excellent wine at its price point.

♥♥♥▽ 1998 Medium red; the bouquet immediately tells you there is something extra, with plum, cedar and spice aromas which follow through into a palate with surprising complexity and structure. **rating: 84**

best drinking 2000–2002 best vintages NA drink with Quail in red wine sauce • $16

Rosemount Estate Hill of Gold Mudgee Shiraz

After a warm fermentation, the wine is kept on skins for around ten days of post-fermentation maceration. It then spends 15 months in a mix of French and American oak.

♥♥♥♥ 1998 Dense red-purple; the rich bouquet is flooded with ripe, sweet plum and prune fruit, the palate likewise extremely rich and concentrated, yet not extractive, adding dark chocolate to the range of flavours. Trophy and gold medal Mudgee Wine Show 1999 and gold Rutherglen Wine Show 1999. **rating: 88**

best drinking 2003–2008 best vintages '98 drink with Rib of beef • $20

Rosemount Estate Grenache Shiraz

Sixty-five per cent Grenache and 35 per cent Shiraz from the riverlands of northeast Victoria are fermented separately, the Grenache at 30°C, the Shiraz at 22°C.

♥♥♥▽ 1999 Light to medium red-purple; the bouquet is soft, ripe and slightly jammy; the palate is sweet, with slightly jammy grenache varietal character strongly expressing itself; next to no tannins. **rating: 81**

best drinking 2000–2001 best vintages NA drink with Big Mac • $12

Rosemount Estate Shiraz Cabernet

A blend of 65 per cent Shiraz and 35 per cent Cabernet Sauvignon drawn across southeast Australia. Rosemount has consistently achieved more with this early-release, early-drinking red wine than any other Australian producer. The wine shows no sign of having been rushed into bottle, but is usually released within six months of vintage.

▼▼▼▼ **1999** Medium to full red-purple; the bouquet is clean, with soft cherry, plum and even a hint of liquorice; the palate has plenty of flavour and ample structure, with generic dark berry fruit flavours and enough tannins to do the job. Clever making; does not see oak. **rating:** 87

best drinking 2000–2002 **best vintages** '96, '98, '99 **drink with** Lasagne • $12

Rosemount Estate Mountain Blue Shiraz Cabernet

The first regional release by Rosemount from Mudgee, but doubtless not the last. The Rosemount jigsaw puzzle continues to spread across the premium wine-growing regions of Australia, but without any compromise on quality, as evidenced by the trophy and seven gold medals which this wine has won. A blend of 90 per cent Shiraz and 10 per cent Cabernet Sauvignon, much of the Shiraz coming from the 40-year-old shiraz planted on the Mountain Blue vineyard, and which is low yielding. Matured in a mix of French and American oak for 18 months, 100 per cent new. Hit the ground running with its first release and hasn't looked back, with show successes galore.

▼▼▼▼▼ **1997** The smooth power and balance of the bouquet flows into a satiny/velvety palate with succulent, ripe berry fruit and seamlessly integrated French and American oak; the tannins are equally soft and ripe. Liquid seduction. **rating:** 95

best drinking 2002–2012 **best vintages** '95, '96, '97 **drink with** Barbecued beef • $51.90

Rosemount Estate Cabernet Merlot

First introduced into the varietal blend range in 1999; a blend of 55 per cent Cabernet Sauvignon and 45 per cent Merlot grown in various southeast Australian regions including Mudgee and McLaren Vale.

▼▼▼▽ **1999** Light to medium red-purple; the bouquet is clean, with light, bright fresh fruit uncomplicated by oak. The palate is similarly light and fresh, with juicy berry fruit; another tour de force of winemaking to produce a wine which is engineered for immediate consumption. **rating:** 84

best drinking 2000–2001 **best vintages** NA **drink with** Chinese meat dishes • $NA

Rosemount Estate Cabernet Sauvignon

Produced from grapes principally grown in McLaren Vale, Langhorne Creek and Mudgee, but with the net thrown over the whole of southeast Australia to supplement the core. Clever winemaking gives the wine the smoothness and mouthfeel of extended barrel maturation.

▼▼▼▽ **1998** Medium red-purple; the bouquet is quite unusual, with ripe, almost essencey fruit. There is more of the same on the early to mid-palate, before drying off on the finish. Curiously compartmentalised. **rating:** 81

best drinking 2001–2006 **best vintages** '86, '88, '90, '92, '93, '94, '96 **drink with** Rare sirloin steak • $16.90

Rosemount Estate Coonawarra Show Reserve Cabernet Sauvignon

Rosemount's first move outside of the Hunter Valley was into Coonawarra, establishing its Kirri Billi vineyard on the outskirts of the town of Penola around the time of the second wave of vineyard planting in the region. The vines are now fully mature and consistently produce grapes of the highest quality.

▼▼▼▼ **1997** Medium red-purple; the bouquet is moderately intense, with clean, red berry fruit, but is not complex until you get to the palate, where intriguing spicy characters to the fruit add a novel and unexpected dimension; soft tannins. **rating:** 86

best drinking 2000–2012 **best vintages** NA **drink with** Steak with mushrooms • $29

Rosemount Estate Hill of Gold Mudgee Cabernet Sauvignon

Almost identical winemaking methods are used for this wine as for the Hill of Gold Shiraz, the only difference being an extra three months in oak.

▼▼▼▼ **1998** Dense purple-red; the voluminous bouquet has a mix of blackcurrant, earth and cedary oak. A no-holds-barred palate with tannins which coat the mouth, the fruit dipping slightly towards the back palate. Needs a bit more time to soften and come together. Gold medal Melbourne 1999. **rating:** 86

best drinking 2003–2008 **best vintages** '98 **drink with** Double-cooked veal shank • $20

Rosemount Estate Rosé Label Orange Vineyard Cabernet Sauvignon

Produced from vines planted in 1989, and which yielded their first crop in 1993. The wine is warm-fermented and then left to macerate for ten days to maximise the extraction of soft tannins. The pressings are blended back into the wine, which spends 20 months in new French and American oak barrels.

♥♥♥♥♡ **1996** Medium to full red-purple; a fragrant bouquet with berry and chocolate fruit interwoven with cedar and cigar box aromas. The palate shows elegant Cabernet flavours, with a long, lingering, gently tannic finish. In an austere mode, which will particularly appeal to those who like the wines of Bordeaux. **rating: 92**
best drinking 2001–2006 **best vintages** '96 **drink with** Roast lamb shoulder • $25

rosemount estate (mclaren vale)   ★★★★★

Ingoldby Road, McLaren Vale, SA 5171 **region** McLaren Vale
phone (08) 8383 0001 **fax** (08) 8383 0456 **open** Mon–Fri 10–5, weekends 11–5
winemaker Charles Whish **production** 100 000 **est.** 1888
product range ($20–69.99 CD) Ryecroft Unwooded Chardonnay, Balmoral Syrah, Show Reserve Shiraz, GSM (Grenache Shiraz Mourvedre blend), Traditional (Cabernet blend), Ryecroft Cabernet Shiraz.
summary The specialist red wine arm of Rosemount Estate, responsible for its prestigious Balmoral Syrah, Show Reserve Shiraz and GSM.

Rosemount Estate Show Reserve Shiraz

Rosemount has been making a Reserve Shiraz from low-yielding McLaren Vale vines for many years now. It in fact pre-dates the acquisition of the Ryecroft vineyard and winery which now constitutes the Rosemount base in McLaren Vale. It also pre-dates the development of the super-premium Balmoral Syrah, which uses similar (albeit the very top) fruit sources. The majority of the vines are between 50 and 100 years of age. It is matured in a mix of new and one-year-old American oak barrels for 20 months.
♥♥♥♥ **1996** Medium to full red-purple; abundant, high toast barrel-ferment oak characters dominate the bouquet and to a lesser extent the palate, where more fruit is evident. The 1996 vintage is a winner of four gold medals at national wine shows, and the oak may have caught me on a bad day. **rating: 89**
best drinking 2001–2006 **best vintages** '90, '91, '93, '94, '95 **drink with** Marinated beef • $27

Rosemount Estate Balmoral Syrah

The name comes from the 1852 Hunter Valley homestead of the Oatley family, founders of the Rosemount Estate. Tastings of all the wines so far released ('89 to '94) have shown an incredible consistency of style, with the 100-year-old vines at Rosemount's Ryecroft Vineyard in McLaren Vale at the heart of the wine. Less than 2000 cases are made each year, 50 per cent being exported to the US.
♥♥♥♥♡ **1997** Medium to full red-purple; the bouquet is potent, with voluminous cherry/plum fruit and spicy vanilla oak. The rich, complex palate is expansive in every way — fruit, oak and tannins. All it needs is time. **rating: 93**
best drinking 2005–2015 **best vintages** '86, '87, '88, '89, '91, '93, '95, '96, '97 **drink with** Char-grilled rump • $69.90

Rosemount Estate GSM

Grenache (typically 50 per cent), shiraz (typically 40 per cent) and mourvedre (typically 10 per cent) grapes are selected from old, low-yielding vines drawn from vineyards across McLaren Vale, and are separately fermented in a mix of traditional open fermenters and vinomatics (rotary fermenters). The wines are matured for 18 months in a mix of new and used American oak, and a final blend decision taken shortly prior to bottling, the blend components varying slightly according to the outcome of vintage. A wine which adds lustre to the cornucopia of Rhône-style wines from McLaren Vale.
♥♥♥♥ **1997** Medium red-purple; strong charry oak tends to overwhelm the fruit on the bouquet but is less assertive on the palate, allowing sweet fruit with regional chocolate overtones to come up. **rating: 89**
best drinking 2002–2007 **best vintages** '94, '95, '96 **drink with** Beef with olives • $28.90

Rosemount Estate Traditional

When Rosemount acquired the Ryecroft winery in 1991, Ryecroft had a brand simply called 'Traditional'. Rosemount has continued using the name, applying it to, what in Bordeaux, France would be described as a 'traditional blend of Cabernet Sauvignon, Merlot and Petit Verdot'. As with the GSM, the percentage will vary from one year to the next, but is typically 70 per cent Cabernet Sauvignon, 20 per cent Merlot and 10 per cent Petit Verdot. Likewise as with the GSM, the components are separately fermented and matured, blending taking place after oak maturation.
♥♥♥♥♡ **1997** Medium red-purple; there is a range of cedar, chocolate and savoury aromas on the bouquet, complexed by subtle oak. The palate is rich and round, with chocolate and dark berry fruit in classic regional style; soft tannins and nice oak complete the picture. **rating: 92**
best drinking 2001–2010 **best vintages** '91, '94, '95, '96, '97 **drink with** Char-grilled beef • $24.90

🐝 rosevears estate NR

1a Waldhorn Drive, Rosevears, Tas 7277 **region** Northern Tasmania
phone (03) 6330 1800 **fax** (03) 6330 1810 **open** 7 days 10–4
winemaker James Chatto **production** 10 000 **est.** 1999
product range ($18–24 CD) Riesling, Sauvignon Blanc, Unwooded Chardonnay, Rosé, Notley Gorge
Cabernet Sauvignon.
summary The multi-million-dollar Rosevears Estate winery and restaurant complex was opened by the Tasmanian
premier in November 1999. Built on a steep hillside overlooking the Tamar River, it is certainly to make a lasting
and important contribution to the Tasmanian wine industry. It is owned by a syndicate of investors headed by Dr
Mike Beamish, and incorporates both Notley Gorge and Ironpot Bay. The inaugural winemaker is the youthful Jim
Chatto, who brought with him large winery experience gained in the Hunter Valley and an extremely acute palate.

Rosevears Estate Unwooded Chardonnay

Confidently produced from grapes deemed not suitable for the oaked version, but reflecting excellent vineyard
work which kept disease completely at bay.
▼▼▼▽ **1999** Light green-yellow; the bouquet is moderately intense, clean and tending minerally; the palate picks
up on this with herbal/green apple fruit, redeemed by its liveliness and its length. **rating:** 84
best drinking 2000–2002 **drink with** Cold seafood • $18

Rosevears Estate Notley Gorge Cabernet Sauvignon

The 1998 was the first vintage to be made by Jim Chatto at the new Rosevears Estate winery.
▼▼▼▼ **1998** Very good purple-red; a powerful mix of cassis and more earthy/oaky notes on the bouquet leads
into a mouthfilling wine full of sweet cassis fruit and outstanding potential. **rating:** 90
best drinking 2003–2013 **drink with** Rare eye fillet • $NA

rosewhite vineyards NR

Happy Valley Road, Rosewhite via Myrtleford, Vic 3737 **region** Alpine Valleys and Beechworth
phone (03) 5752 1077 **open** Weekends and public holidays 10–5, 7 days January
winemaker Joan Mullett **production** 700 **est.** 1983
product range ($10 CD) Traminer, Chardonnay, Pinot Noir, Shiraz, Cabernet Sauvignon, Tawny Port.
summary After careers with the Victorian Department of Agriculture, agricultural scientists Ron and Joan
Mullett began the establishment of Rosewhite in 1983 and have since established a little over 2 hectares of
vineyards at an altitude of 300 metres.

rossetto ★★☆

Farm 576 Rossetto Road, Beelbangera, NSW 2686 **region** Riverina
phone (02) 6963 5214 **fax** (02) 6963 5542 **open** Mon–Sat 8.30–5.30
winemaker Eddy Rossi **production** 500 000 **est.** 1930
product range ($5.50–22 R) Several ranges, the commercial Wattle Glen series ($5.50), the Silky Oak range
($8.50–$9.50), the Rossetto premium varietals ($9–$16) and the Promenade Range of Riverina Chardonnay,
Watervale Riesling and Riverina Cabernet Merlot ($12.50–$20); also fortifieds.
summary Another family-owned and run Riverina winery endeavouring to lift the profile of its wines, although
not having the same spectacular success as Riverina Wines. Rossetto does have distributors in each State, but of
course much of the total production is sold in bulk to other makers.

Rossetto Family Reserve Promenade Chardonnay

A Leviathan style; for reasons not immediately obvious, recently selected for Qantas business class flights.
▼▼▼▽ **1998** Deep yellow; the bouquet is in full-frontal style, with obvious skin contact and somewhat raspy
American oak. The palate is quite simply huge, with 14.6 degrees alcohol more than slightly obvious. To be fair,
the wine won silver medals at Brisbane, Melbourne and Cowra. **rating:** 80
best drinking 2000–2001 **best vintages** NA **drink with** KFC • $13.90

Rossetto Silky Oak Saint Mac

Produced from a rare Bordeaux variety, St Macaire.
▼▼▼▽ **1998** Medium purple-red; the bouquet is (quite properly) dominated by ripe fruit, with just a hint of
French and American oak. The palate shows similar ripe fruit, which dips on the back palate before tannins come
through on the finish. An interesting wine, but probably better employed as a blend component. **rating:** 80
best drinking 2000–2002 **best vintages** NA **drink with** Designer sausages • $12

rothbury estate ★★★

Broke Road, Pokolbin, NSW 2321 **region** Lower Hunter Valley
phone (02) 4998 7555 **fax** (02) 4998 7553 **open** 7 days 9.30–4.30
winemaker Rob Cuadagnini, Alan Harris **production** 100 000 **est.** 1968
product range ($8.90–22 R) At the top comes the Individual Vineyard range of Hunter Valley Semillon, Chardonnay and Shiraz; next the Hunter Valley range of varietals; and finally varietals from Mudgee and Cowra.
summary Rothbury celebrated its 30th birthday in 1998, albeit not quite in the fashion that founder and previous chief executive Len Evans would have wished. After a protracted and at times bitter takeover battle, it became part of the Fosters/Mildara empire. Exports and distribution via Mildara Blass.

Rothbury Estate Chardonnay
The regional source is not stated, but most probably a blend of Hunter Valley and Cowra material; a (lucky) gold medal winner at the Adelaide Wine Show 1998.
▼▼▼♀ **1998** Medium yellow-green; a solid wine with good fruit and oak balance on the bouquet; the palate is likewise well balanced, albeit rather less concentrated, showing light melon and peach fruit. **rating:** 83
best drinking 2000–2001 **best vintages** NA **drink with** Wiener schnitzel • $8.90

Rothbury Estate Mudgee Cabernet Merlot
A commercial red wine made to a price, and says little about true Mudgee red wine style.
▼▼▼♀ **1998** Medium red-purple; the bouquet has a mix of juicy berry fruit and slightly chippy oak, characters which are faithfully reproduced on the palate. Overall, lacks the concentration one expects from Mudgee. **rating:** 81
best drinking 2000–2002 **best vintages** NA **drink with** Takeaway • $13

🐂 rothbury ridge NR

Talga Road, Rothbury, NSW 2320 **region** Lower Hunter Valley
phone (02) 4930 7122 **fax** (02) 4930 7198 **open** Mon–Sat 9–5, Sun 10–5
winemaker Peter Jorgensen **production** 10 000 **est.** 1988
product range ($15–28 ML) Stanleigh Park Reserve Semillon, Mary FDW Chablis Style, Anne Chardonnay Semillon, Steven FBW Chardonnay, Mount Royal Reserve Durif, Early Release Chambourcin, Edgar Chambourcin, James Shiraz Chambourcin, Mount Royal Reserve Chambourcin, Joye Cabernet Sauvignon, Mount Royal Méthode Champenoise.
summary Rothbury Ridge has an extraordinarily eclectic choice of varieties planted, with between 1.2 hectares and 2.4 hectares each of chardonnay, semillon, verdelho, chambourcin, durif, shiraz and cabernet sauvignon.

rotherhythe ★★★★☆

Hendersons Lane, Gravelly Beach, Exeter, Tas 7251 **region** Northern Tasmania
phone (03) 6394 4869 **open** By appointment
winemaker Steven Hyde **production** 1600 **est.** 1976
product range ($16–26.95 CD) Chardonnay, Pinot Noir, Cabernet Sauvignon, Pinot Chardonnay.
summary At the 1996 Tasmanian Wines Show Rotherhythe swept all before it, winning trophies for Most Successful Exhibitor, Best Light to Medium Bodied Red Wine, Best Full Bodied Red Wine and Best Wine of Show. Ironically, two days later Dr Steven Hyde sold the vineyard, although he has retained all of the existing wine stocks and will remain involved in the winemaking for some time to come. In both 1997 and again in 1998 Rotherhythe was awarded the trophy for Most Successful Exhibitor at the Tasmanian Wines Show. Retail distribution in Melbourne.

🐂 rothvale vineyard ★★★★☆

Deasy's Road, Pokolbin NSW 2321 **region** Lower Hunter Valley
phone (02) 4998 7290 **fax** (02) 4998 7290 **open** 7 days 10–5
winemaker Max Patton, Luke Patton **production** 5000 **est.** 1978
product range ($18–35 CD) Semillon, Semillon Chardonnay, Unwooded Chardonnay, Lightly Oaked Chardonnay, Reserve Chardonnay A (American Oak), Reserve Chardonnay F (French Oak), Annie's Dry Red, Tilda's Shiraz, Cabernet Sauvignon.
summary Owned and operated by the Patton family, headed by Max Patton who has the fascinating academic qualifications of BVSc, MSc London, BA Hons Cantab, the scientific part of which has no doubt come in useful

for his winemaking. The wines are sold only through cellar door and direct to an imposing list of restaurants in the Hunter Valley and Sydney. Rothvale also has four vineyard cottages available for bed and breakfast accommodation. The wines have already accumulated an impressive array of medals, including a gold medal for the 1998 Reserve Chardonnay at the 1999 Hunter Valley Wine Show.

Rothvale Vineyard Barrel Fermented Semillon
Barrel-fermented for four weeks in one-year-old French oak before being removed to stainless steel and bottled.
▼▼▼♀ **1999** Medium yellow-green; the bouquet is moderately intense, quite complex, but with slightly funky/reductive aromas. The sensitively used oak is barely perceptible on the palate, where lemony/citrussy fruit drives the wine. If it shakes off the slightly uncertain aromas, will rate even higher points.　　**rating: 84**
best drinking 2001–2005　**drink with** Blue swimmer crab　• $25

Rothvale Vineyard Unwooded Chardonnay
Produced from 27-year-old vines, and vividly reflects a long, cold fermentation of clear juice.
▼▼▼▼ **1999** Light green-yellow; a highly aromatic, perfumed bouquet with seductive passionfruit and peach aromas leads onto a fresh, light peachy wine, with a touch of spritz and well-balanced acidity.　　**rating: 85**
best drinking 1999–2000　**drink with** Eggplant and capsicum terrine　• $18

Rothvale Vineyard Lightly Oaked Chardonnay
A blend of stainless steel-fermented Chardonnay and wine barrel-fermented in French oak. Like all of the Rothvale Chardonnays, produced from 27-year-old vines.
▼▼▼▼♀ **1999** Medium yellow-green; a highly fragrant and stylish bouquet with grapefruit and melon supported by the promised subtle oak. A classy wine, with lots of grapefruit flavour and a nice touch of oak coming through on the finish.　　**rating: 91**
best drinking 2000–2002　**drink with** All seafood　• $18

Rothvale Vineyard Reserve Chardonnay A
'A' denotes the one-year-old American oak barriques in which the wine was fermented and matured. The wine spends nine months in barrel on lees.
▼▼▼▼ **1999** Medium yellow-green; the bouquet is less aromatic than that of the Lightly Oaked Chardonnay, although the oak is not oppressive. Vanilla oak is much more evident on the palate, a smooth raincoat wrapped around the grapefruit/melon/nectarine fruit.　　**rating: 89**
best drinking 2000–2003　**drink with** Roast pork　• $25

Rothvale Vineyard Reserve Chardonnay F
Here, as the name implies the oak is French, from the Troncais, Allier and Boutes forests. The wine is barrel-fermented with nine months maturation on lees.
▼▼▼▼♀ **1999** Light yellow-green; the bouquet is at once subtle yet complex, with gentle tangy fruit and nutty oak. The powerful, mouthfilling and complex palate has a mix of melon and riper fruit flavours investing it with considerable length. Near the top of the Chardonnay tree in the Hunter Valley.　　**rating: 93**
best drinking 2000–2004　**drink with** Sautéed veal　• $28

Rothvale Vineyard Tilda's Shiraz
Draws upon 6 hectares of 30-year-old estate plantings, and matured in a mix of new and one-year-old American oak barriques.
▼▼▼▼♀ **1999** Dense red-purple; the bouquet is concentrated and full of ripe, dark berry fruit which largely obscures the oak. The palate is typical of very powerful, young Shiraz; is moderately extractive, but should age well if given enough time.　　**rating: 90**
best drinking 2004–2014　**drink with** Leave it in the cellar　• $35

Rothvale Vineyard Annie's Dry Red
Made from 65 per cent Shiraz from 30-year-old vines, and 35 per cent Cabernet Sauvignon from similarly aged vines. Matured for a little under a year in a mix of new and one-year-old American oak barriques.
▼▼▼▼ **1999** Medium to full red-purple; the bouquet is complex, with lots of American oak but also plenty of fruit. The same interplay occurs on the palate, where vanillin American oak and strong tannins mark the start and the finish, with the spicy blackberry fruit poking its head up on the mid-palate.　　**rating: 87**
best drinking 2004–2014　**drink with** High-flavoured red meat dishes　• $30

rouge homme ★★★☆

Riddoch Highway, Coonawarra, SA 5263 **region** Coonawarra
phone (08) 8736 3205 **fax** (08) 8736 3250 **open** 7 days 10–5
winemaker Paul Gordon **production** 64 000 **est.** 1954
product range ($10–40 R) Semillon, Chardonnay, Unoaked Chardonnay, Pinot Noir, Reserve Pinot Noir, Shiraz Cabernet, Cabernet Merlot, Cabernet Sauvignon.
summary From time to time I have described Rouge Homme as the warrior brand of the Lindeman Group Coonawarra operations. In recent times it has proved a formidable warrior, most surprisingly with its Pinot Noir but also with its Cabernet and Cabernet blend wines.

Rouge Homme Unoaked Chardonnay

Unoaked Chardonnays are very much a creation of the 1990s, in part reflecting a move away from excessive oak, in part a deliberate move to present another style of Chardonnay, and in part to offer a cheaper alternative. Winemakers (and wine critics) have both learned that high-quality chardonnay has to be used for the style to succeed, simply because there is no oak present to paper over the cracks or deficiencies in lesser quality wine.
▼▼▼▼ **1998** Light to medium yellow-green; the bouquet and the palate are both of medium intensity, exhibiting very correct citrus, melon and nectarine fruit aromas and flavours. The palate is clean, soft and finishes dry.   **rating:** 86
best drinking 2000–2003 **best vintages** NA **drink with** Creamy chicken • $NA

Rouge Homme Pinot Noir

Coonawarra, despite its limestone-based soil, has utterly resisted attempts to produce Pinot Noir with adequate, let alone good, varietal character. Winemaker Paul Gordon used all the techniques in making this wine, and it had its moment of glory when awarded the trophy as Champion Wine at the Hobart Wine Show in 1999 by departing chairman Max Lake. Charity begins somewhere other than home, it seems.
▼▼▼▼ **1998** Medium red-purple; the bouquet is clean, smooth but shows no desirable varietal character. A nice medium-bodied red wine on the palate, with soft plummy fruit and nicely handled oak.   **rating:** 83
best drinking 2000–2005 **best vintages** '93, '94 **drink with** Saddle of hare • $17

Rouge Homme Shiraz Cabernet

This is the descendant of Rouge Homme Claret, for long the mainstay of the Rouge Homme brand. Originally made entirely from Shiraz, it is now a 50/50 blend of Shiraz and Cabernet Sauvignon matured in French and American oak barrels for an average period of 12 months.
▼▼▼▼ **1998** Medium to full red-purple; there is attractive, sweet, ripe blackberry/blackcurrant fruit on the bouquet leading into a fresh, fruit-driven and lively palate with subtle oak and soft tannins.   **rating:** 87
best drinking 2002–2008 **best vintages** '88, '90, '91, '92, '94, '98 **drink with** King Island cheddar • $14

Rouge Homme Cabernet Sauvignon

While in price terms the flagship of the range, does not seem to have the quality edge over the other wines that one might expect. Certainly it is well made, coming as it does from 100 per cent Coonawarra cabernet sauvignon, and being matured in French oak hogsheads for 15 months. The weight and concentration of the wine has increased significantly in recent vintages. The '96 was a gold medal winner at the 1997 Liquorland National Wine Show.
▼▼▼▼ **1997** Medium purple-red; the bouquet is clean, with gentle cassis fruit and subtle oak; the medium-bodied palate has pleasant, ripe cassis and chocolate fruit, good tannins running through its length; balanced oak.   **rating:** 87
▼▼▼▼ **1996** Medium to full red-purple; a rich bouquet with concentrated blackberry/cassis fruit, supported by a deft touch of oak. There is more cassis/blackberry fruit on the palate, together with some more minty characters; finishes with soft tannin.   **rating:** 88
best drinking 2002–2007 **best vintages** '88, '90, '91, '94, '96 **drink with** Roast leg of lamb • $17

ruker wines   NR

Barton Highway, Dickson, ACT 2602 **region** Canberra District
phone (02) 6230 2310 **fax** (02) 6230 2818 **open** Weekends, public holidays 10–5
winemaker Richard Ruker **production** 500 **est.** 1991
product range ($15 CD) Riesling, Gewurztraminer.
summary Barbara and Richard Ruker, with the assistance of eldest daughter Niki, planted 2 hectares of riesling and traminer in 1984. The cellar door-cum-winery is a farmshed subsequently converted to an office and then to its present function of winery and restaurant; it is finished with heavy wooden beams salvaged from a railway bridge near Tarago and clad with the remains of an old slab hut, while the tables are made from huge red and yellow box trees cut down when the vineyard was planted.

rumbalara ★★☆

Fletcher Road, Fletcher, Qld 4381 **region** Granite Belt
phone (07) 4684 1206 **fax** (07) 4684 1299 **open** 7 days 9–5
winemaker Bob Gray **production** 1500 **est.** 1974
product range ($11.50–19.50 CD) Barrel Fermented Semillon, Granitegolde, Light Shiraz, Cabernet Sauvignon, Pinot Noir, Cabernet Shiraz and a range of Fortified wines, Cider and Vermouth.
summary Has produced some of the Granite Belt's finest honeyed Semillon and silky, red berry Cabernet Sauvignon, but quality does vary. The winery incorporates a spacious restaurant, and there are also barbecue and picnic facilities.

ryland river NR

RMB 8945 Main Creek Road, Main Ridge, Vic 3928 **region** Mornington Peninsula
phone (03) 5989 6098 **fax** (03) 9899 0184 **open** Weekends and public holidays 10–5 or by appointment
winemaker John W Bray **production** 2000 **est.** 1986
product range ($15–30 CD) Semillon Sauvignon Blanc, Chardonnay, Cabernet Sauvignon, Jack's Delight Tawny Port and Muscat.
summary John Bray has been operating Ryland River at Main Ridge on the Mornington Peninsula for a number of years, but not without a degree of controversy over the distinction between Ryland River wines produced from Mornington Peninsula grapes and those produced from grapes purchased from other regions. A large lake with catch-your-own trout and a cheese house are general tourist attractions.

rymill ★★★☆

The Riddoch Run Vineyards, Coonawarra, SA 5263 **region** Coonawarra
phone (08) 8736 5001 **fax** (08) 8736 5040 **open** 7 days 10–5
winemaker John Innes **production** 50 000 **est.** 1970
product range ($12–25 R) Sauvignon Blanc, Chardonnay, March Traminer, June Traminer, Shiraz, Merlot Cabernets, Cabernet Sauvignon and Sparkling.
summary The Rymills are descendants of John Riddoch and have long owned some of the finest Coonawarra soil, upon which they have grown grapes since 1970, with present plantings of 140 hectares. Peter Rymill made a small amount of Cabernet Sauvignon in 1987 but has long since plunged headlong into commercial production, with winemaker John Innes presiding over the striking winery portrayed on the label. Australian distribution is through Negociants Australia; exports go to all of the major markets in Europe, North America and Asia.

Rymill June Traminer 375 ml
Rymill has only 2 hectares of gewurztraminer (out of total vineyard holdings of 154 hectares) and can afford to take the risks associated with leaving the grapes on the vine until very late in the season. The result is a thoroughly unusual but often appealing wine.
▼▼▼▼ 1998 Orange-yellow; an exotic bouquet of marmalade, spice and honey follows through into a rich palate of marmalade and gingerbread flavours. **rating: 86**
best drinking 2000–2004 **best vintages** NA **drink with** Cakes or rich tarts • $12

Rymill Shiraz
Produced entirely from estate-grown grapes and matured in a mix of new and used French and American oak barrels.
▼▼▼▼ 1997 Medium red-purple; the bouquet has abundant dark berry fruit with some more earthy, savoury overtones, and the palate lives up to the promise of the bouquet, with much more weight and concentration than previous releases. Soft, chewy tannins complete a wine with lots of development potential. **rating: 88**
best drinking 2002–2012 **best vintages** '90, '91, '92, '95, '97 **drink with** Stuffed eggplant • $20

Rymill Merlot Cabernets
A blend of 40 per cent Merlot, 30 per cent Cabernet Sauvignon and 30 per cent Cabernet Franc.
▼▼▼▽ 1997 Medium red-purple; the wine has that recurrent streak of green which for reasons I don't understand appears in so many Australian Cabernet Merlot blends. The palate has good texture, with silky tannins and quite pronounced acidity, the latter picking up on that edge of green from the bouquet. **rating: 81**
best drinking 2000–2003 **best vintages** NA **drink with** Marinated beef • $18

saddlers creek ★★★☆

Marrowbone Road, Pokolbin, NSW 2320 **region** Lower Hunter Valley
phone (02) 4991 1770 **fax** (02) 4991 2482 **open** 7 days 9–5
winemaker John Johnstone **production** 15 000 **est.** 1989
product range ($16–40 CD) Marrowbone Chardonnay, Pinot Noir, Bluegrass Merlot, Cabernet Sauvignon; Equus Hunter Shiraz, McLaren Shiraz; Premium Chardonnay, Verdelho, Classic Hunter Semillon, Reserve Selection Sauvignon Blanc, Unwooded Chardonnay, Sauvignon Blanc Semillon, Botrytis Semillon, Botrytis Tokay, Liqueur Muscat; Single Vineyard Hunter Shiraz, Langhorne Reserve Cabernet.
summary Made an impressive entrance to the district with consistently full flavoured and rich wines. Marrowbone Chardonnay and Equus Hunter Shiraz are its best wines. Limited retail distribution in New South Wales, Queensland and Victoria. At the time of going to press, the winery was being offered for sale.

Saddlers Creek Single Vineyard Hunter Shiraz

Saddlers Creek is not averse to introducing new wines into its portfolio, and has followed the pattern of Brokenwood and others in sourcing material from McLaren Vale and, more recently Langhorne Creek.
▼▼▼▼ **1998** Quite strong red-purple; the bouquet offers a harmonious range of plum/cherry/savoury/spicy aromas. Those sweet fruit aromas provide the core of the palate, supported by more savoury/regional characters. Well-balanced oak and tannin. **rating:** 87
best drinking 2002–2008 **best vintages** NA **drink with** Rack of lamb • $NA

Saddlers Creek Langhorne Reserve Cabernet

This is the inaugural vintage of the wine and is part of an interesting trend; small winemakers around the country are quietly dipping into the vast pool of Langhorne Creek grapes, and coming up with some impressive results.
▼▼▼▼ **1998** Medium purple-red; the bouquet is clean and sweet, with blackberry/cassis fruit supported by subtle oak; the palate is generous, with lots of blackberry and chocolate fruit flavours before vanilla oak builds on the finish. **rating:** 85
best drinking 2002–2007 **best vintages** NA **drink with** Wood-fired oven pizza • $NA

st gregory's NR

Bringalbert South Road, Bringalbert South via Apsley, Vic 3319 **region** Far South West Victoria
phone (03) 5586 5225 **open** By appointment
winemaker Gregory Flynn **production** NFP **est.** 1983
product range ($14 ML) Port.
summary Unique Port-only operation selling its limited production direct to enthusiasts (by mailing list).

st hallett ★★★★☆

St Hallett's Road, Tanunda, SA 5352 **region** Barossa Valley
phone (08) 8563 2319 **fax** (08) 8563 2901 **open** 7 days 10–4
winemaker Stuart Blackwell, Cathy Spratt **production** 65 000 **est.** 1944
product range ($10.95–44.95 CD) Poacher's Blend (White), Eden Valley Riesling, Semillon Sauvignon Blanc, Semillon Select, Sweet Meredith, Chardonnay, Gamekeeper's Reserve (Red), Faith Shiraz, Blackwell Shiraz, Grenache, Cabernet Merlot, Old Block Shiraz, Cabernet Sauvignon, Cabernet Reserve.
summary Nothing succeeds like success, and St Hallett continues to grow, significantly expanding the range of its Shiraz-based wines but also coming up with wines such as the multiple gold medal and trophy winning 1997 Eden Valley Riesling. One has to say that some of the wines (even Old Block Shiraz) don't seem to have quite the intensity (or is it excitement?) they once had. Elegant and smooth, yes, but with a certain sameness about the wines. It has established its own distribution network in the UK, and actively exports to Europe, North America and Asia.

St Hallett Semillon Select

The Barossa Valley and Semillon are uneasy partners at the best of times, and this wine reflects that unease even if, mercifully, it hasn't been hit with a sledge hammer of American oak.
▼▼▼▽ **1998** Medium yellow-green; starts promisingly with a complex bouquet but seems prematurely aged on the palate, lacking mid-palate flesh and with a rather phenolic finish. **rating:** 81
best drinking Drink now **best vintages** NA **drink with** Takeaway • $18.95

St Hallett Poacher's Blend

The wine is stainless steel-fermented and early-bottled. A shotgun was pointed at this poacher to produce a marriage of Chenin Blanc, Semillon, Sauvignon Blanc and Riesling.

▼▼▼▼ **1998** Medium yellow-green; the tangy fruit shows bottle-developed richness. The palate has quite substantial flavours, smooth and rich; a wine which shows the Barossa Valley habit of submerging white wines in inferior American oak is not necessary. **rating: 85**

best drinking 2000–2001 **best vintages** NA **drink with** Mussel and saffron soup • $10.95

St Hallett Blackwell Shiraz

Blackwell Shiraz, named after long-term winemaker Stuart Blackwell, fits in between Faith Shiraz and Old Block.

▼▼▼▼ **1996** Light to medium red-purple; the bouquet is clean but rather simple, lacking intensity. The palate, likewise, has pleasant cherry/berry fruit and nicely balanced oak and tannin. I just wish there was a bit more there. **rating: 85**

best drinking 2001–2006 **best vintages** NA **drink with** Lamb shanks • $28.95

St Hallett Faith Shiraz

Introduced in the mid-1990s as part of a three-tier structure for St Hallett Shiraz, Faith at the bottom, Blackwell in the middle, and Old Block at the top.

▼▼▼▽ **1998** Medium red-purple; aromatic and quite intense cherry/berry fruit plus a coat of American oak leads into a lively juicy berry-flavoured palate. Needed a touch more barrel work, but there is nothing wrong with the base material. **rating: 84**

best drinking 2001–2005 **best vintages** NA **drink with** Italian • $18.95

St Hallett Old Block Shiraz

A wine which has propelled St Hallett into international stardom, and which is responsible for the overall winery rating. Made from 60 to 100-year-old dry-grown Barossa vines, with the addition of new American oak making its impact since 1988.

▼▼▼▼▽ **1997** Medium red-purple; the bouquet is complex, with a mix of cedar, vanilla and chocolate over the red berry fruit; the flavours are quite intense though far from heavy, offering cherry and the faintest hint of mint, closing with fine tannins. **rating: 90**

▼▼▼▼▽ **1996** Medium red-purple; there are distinct minty notes to the fruit, which come and go in ripe Barossa Shiraz. The palate has soft, easy cherry/mint fruit, nicely handled oak and fine tannins. Elegant, but once again, I would have hoped for a touch more concentration. **rating: 90**

best drinking 2002–2012 **best vintages** '80, '84, '87, '88, '90, '91, '93, '94, '96, '97 **drink with** Kangaroo, game • $44.95

St Hallett Cabernet Sauvignon Merlot

A blend of Cabernet Sauvignon, Merlot and a touch of Cabernet Franc, all Barossa Valley-sourced, and matured in a mix of American and French oak. The best yet under this label.

▼▼▼▼ **1997** Light to medium red-purple; the bouquet is light, with some fragrance in a leafy/minty/earthy spectrum. The palate has a nice core of sweet, redcurrant fruit; the tannins are just a fraction assertive. **rating: 85**

best drinking 2000–2007 **best vintages** '90, '91, '93 **drink with** Lamb kebabs • $18.95

St Hallett Cabernet Reserve

A new wine on the St Hallett roster, its birth doubtless helped by the excellent '96 vintage. St Hallett hasn't done it by halves, pricing it at the same level as the iconic Old Block Shiraz.

▼▼▼▼ **1998** Medium red-purple; the moderately intense bouquet offers a mix of savoury cassis berry and attractive, faintly spicy oak. The palate has particularly good structure and balance, with soft cassis/mulberry fruit sustained by supple tannins. There just seems to be a touch of acid prickle on the finish. **rating: 87**

best drinking 2001–2011 **best vintages** '98 **drink with** Beef tenderloin • $44.95

st huberts ★★★★

Maroondah Highway, Coldstream, Vic 3770 **region** Yarra Valley
phone (03) 9739 1118 **fax** (03) 9739 1096 **open** Mon–Fri 9–5, weekends 10.30–5.30
winemaker Fiona Purnell **production** 30 000 **est.** 1966
product range ($20–30 R) Roussanne, Chardonnay, Pinot Noir, Cabernet Sauvignon, Cabernet Merlot; under the second label Rowan Sauvignon Blanc, Chardonnay, Shiraz, Pinot Noir, Cabernet Merlot.

summary The changes have come thick and fast at St Huberts, which is now part of the Mildara Blass (Rothbury Estate) Group. It has produced some quite lovely wines, notably Chardonnay and Cabernet Sauvignon. Plans are afoot for the rebuilding of the ornate nineteenth-century winery on its original (recently repurchased) site.

St Huberts Roussanne

The Yarra Valley was famous for its Marsanne in the nineteenth century, and St Huberts' neighbour Yeringberg reintroduced that grape to the Valley in the 1970s, following with small plantings of roussanne, paralleled by plantings at St Huberts. This is one of the rarest wines in Australia; the 1994 marked the first release from St Huberts; cellar door is the best bet to find the wine.

ᵀᵀᵀᵀ 1999 Light to medium yellow-green; the bouquet is clean and fresh, with ripe fruit aromas running through into the nicely made and balanced palate; the problem is that the fruit lacks any particular varietal character. **rating:** 87

best drinking 2000–2002 **best vintages** NA **drink with** Pork with apple or peach • $20

St Huberts Chardonnay

An estate-grown wine with a very good track record of show success. Is usually (but not always) at the riper, more concentrated end of the Yarra Valley Chardonnay spectrum.

ᵀᵀᵀᵀ 1999 Light to medium green-yellow; a restrained, quite stylish bouquet with melon, citrus and mineral aromas; subtle, tangy oak. The fruit is even more restrained on the palate, with slightly nutty/mealy/minerally characters, needing a touch more intensity. Gold medal winner Victorian Wine Show 1999. **rating:** 84

ᵀᵀᵀᵀ 1997 Full yellow-green; concentrated, ripe melon and fig fruit with subtle oak on the bouquet leads on to a rich, concentrated and full-flavoured palate, where the flavours veer slightly more towards yellow peach. Fine oak throughout. **rating:** 90

best drinking 2001–2005 **best vintages** '88, '90, '91, '92, '93, '94, '95, '97 **drink with** Yabbies • $19

St Huberts Cabernet Sauvignon

Almost 50 per cent of the 20 hectares of estate plantings at St Huberts are cabernet sauvignon, some of it original plantings, and more grafted over from other varieties. The '77 St Huberts Cabernet caused a sensation at the time, both for its quality and its then astronomically high price of $17 a bottle. Clever winemaking continues to produce rich, smooth wines 20 years later, selling at much the same price.

ᵀᵀᵀᵀ 1998 Medium red-purple; a solid bouquet with quite ripe redcurrant fruit with more savoury cedary/tobacco notes. The palate opens with cassis blackberry fruit but seems to have some slightly fluffy, soapy edges. **rating:** 84

best drinking 2001–2006 **best vintages** '77, '88, '90, '91, '92, '96, '97 **drink with** Rich casserole dishes • $25

st leonards ★★★☆

Wahgunyah, Vic 3687 **region** Rutherglen and Glenrowan
phone (02) 6033 1004 **fax** (02) 6033 3636 **open** 7 days 11–5
winemaker Peter Brown **production** NFP **est.** 1860
product range ($11–35 CD) Kalara Red and White; Muscadello, Semillon, Wahgunyah Shiraz; the Carlyle range of Riesling, Chardonnay, Durif, Cabernet Sauvignon.
summary An old favourite, relaunched in late 1997 with a range of three premium wines cleverly marketed through a singularly attractive cellar door and bistro at the historic winery on the banks of the Murray. All Saints and St Leonards are now wholly owned by Peter Brown; the vast majority of the wines are sold through cellar door and by mailing list.

St Leonards Carlyle Riesling

Not a style which one normally associates with northeast Victoria, but does show good bottle-developed character.

ᵀᵀᵀᵀ 1995 Medium yellow-green; the bouquet is quite rich, with toasty bottle-developed characters evident; the palate has fair flavour, being slightly hollow, but again having the advantage of some bottle-developed complexity. **rating:** 82

best drinking 2000–2003 **best vintages** NA **drink with** Lebanese food • $14.50

St Leonards Carlyle Durif

Produced from vines planted immediately in front of the winery castle in 1996. It spends 18 months in French and American oak barriques (70 per cent new, 30 per cent four-year-old) and has had minimal filtration and handling. Very highly commended at the 1999 Rutherglen Wine Show.

▼▼▼▼ **1998** Dense red-purple; rich, concentrated blackberry and chocolate fruit on the bouquet provides an enticing start, but then the massive tannins on the palate hit you the moment you take the wine into your mouth. Those Rutherglen judges must have had mouthguards. If those tannins ever soften, the wine will merit substantially higher points. **rating: 80**

best drinking 2010–2020 **best vintages** NA **drink with** Don't dare open it • $30

st mary's ★★★★

V & A Lane, via Coonawarra, SA 5277 **region** Limestone Coast Zone
phone (08) 8736 6070 **fax** (08) 8736 6045 **open** 7 days 10–4
winemaker Barry Mulligan **production** 4000 **est.** 1986
product range ($12–22 CD) Riesling, Chardonnay, Shiraz, House Block Cabernet Sauvignon.
summary Established by the Mulligan and Hooper families in 1986, but with Tyrrell's Vineyards purchasing the Hooper interest in the vineyards (though not the brand name St Mary's) in 1995. The winemaking operation continues as a separate entity, now wholly owned by the Mulligans. National distribution through agents in each State; exports to the US, Canada and the UK.

St Mary's Shiraz
Produced from vines planted in 1986, now reaching maturity.
▼▼▼▼▼ **1998** Medium red-purple; the bouquet is solid, with a complex array of dark berry, leather, liquorice, earth and spice aromas all intermingling. The palate delivers the promise of the bouquet, with all of the flavours rippling through to the finish. **rating: 90**

best drinking 2002–2010 **best vintages** '98 **drink with** Lamb fillets • $22

St Mary's House Block Cabernet Sauvignon
Like the Shiraz, comes from the first plantings in 1986, and is the product of a well-made wine from a good vintage.
▼▼▼▼ **1998** Medium to full red-purple; the aromas of the bouquet run through cedar, earth, berry and spice, oak making only a minor contribution. The medium-bodied palate has attractive cassis/raspberry fruit, with a clean finish supported by crisp acidity. **rating: 88**

best drinking 2002–2010 **best vintages** '98 **drink with** Aged parmesan • $22

st matthias ★★★☆

113 Rosevears Drive, Rosevears, Tas 7277 **region** Northern Tasmania
phone (03) 6330 1700 **fax** (03) 6330 1975 **open** 7 days 10–5
winemaker Alain Rousseau **production** 4000 **est.** 1983
product range ($13–21 CD) Riesling, Chardonnay, Pinot Noir, Cabernet Sauvignon Merlot, Brut, Cuvée Printemps Dry White, Cuvée Printemps Dry Red.
summary After an uncomfortable period in the wilderness following the sale of the vineyard to Moorilla Estate, and the disposal of the wine made by the previous owners under the St Matthias label, Moorilla has re-introduced the label, and markets a full range of competitively priced wines which are in fact made at Moorilla Estate.

St Matthias Riesling
Grown on the banks of the Tamar River; a classic Tasmanian Riesling with a long cellaring future.
▼▼▼▼▼ **1999** Light green-yellow; the bouquet is light, fresh and crisp, with a mix of lime, mineral and green apple aromas. The palate has excellent fruit intensity; the lime and apple of the bouquet comes through in a delightfully sweet form (fruit sweet, not sugar sweet) before the wine finishes with typical Tasmanian acidity. **rating: 92**

best drinking 2002–2009 **best vintages** '97, '99 **drink with** Gravlax • $17

st peters winery & distillery ★★★

Whitton Stock Route, Yenda, NSW 2681 **region** Riverina
phone (02) 6968 1303 **fax** (02) 6968 1328 **open** Mon–Fri 9–5
winemaker Dave Wilson **production** 20 000 **est.** 1977
product range ($8–17 CD) A wide variety of wines under the St Peters and Wilton Estate labels.
summary Wilton Estate draws grapes and wine from various parts of southern Australia and New South Wales for its dry table wines, but is having outstanding success with its Botrytis Semillon from locally grown fruit. It shares the winemaking facilities at St Peters. The wines are sold in the UK by separate distributors for the Yenda Vineyards label and for the Wilton Estate label.

salem bridge wines   NR

Salem Bridge Road, Lower Hermitage, SA 5131 **region** Adelaide Hills
phone (08) 8380 5240 **fax** (08) 8380 5240 **open** Not
winemaker Barry Miller **production** NFP **est.** 1989
product range ($16–18 R) Cabernet Franc, Shiraz, Cabernet Sauvignon.
summary Barry Miller acquired the 45-hectare Salem Bridge property in the Adelaide Hills of South Australia in 1988. A little under 2 hectares of cabernet franc were planted in 1989, and cabernet franc has been the only commercial release prior to 1999. However, a further 13 hectares have been planted to cabernet sauvignon, shiraz and merlot, with a Shiraz and Cabernet Sauvignon release in the pipeline. The wine is made off site by contract-winemaking, with input from Barry Miller.

salitage   ★★★☆

Vasse Highway, Pemberton, WA 6260 **region** Pemberton, Warren Valley and Manjimup
phone (08) 9776 1771 **fax** (08) 9776 1772 **open** 7 days 10–4
winemaker Patrick Coutts **production** 15 000 **est.** 1989
product range ($16–34 R) Chardonnay, Unwooded Chardonnay, Sauvignon Blanc, Pinot Noir, Cabernet Merlot, Pemberton (Cabernet blend); Treehouse range Chardonnay Verdelho, Pinot Noir, Shiraz and Cabernets.
summary Salitage is the showpiece of Pemberton. If it had failed to live up to expectations, it is a fair bet the same fate would have befallen the whole of the Pemberton region. The quality and style of Salitage has varied substantially, presumably in response to vintage conditions and yields. It still remains the key producer in the Pemberton region but the variability is a little unsettling, as is the propensity to age quickly. Key retail distribution in all States, and exports to the UK, Germany, Switzerland, the US, Canada, Hong Kong, Japan, Singapore, Taiwan and New Zealand.

Salitage Unwooded Chardonnay

The opulent use of oak in what might loosely be called the 'normal' Salitage Chardonnay serves to highlight the difference between the two wines, with quality of the underlying fruit very evident from this wine. Unwooded Chardonnays work when the fruit quality is there, and don't when it is not. This one does work.
▼▼▼♀ **1999** Light to medium green-yellow; the bouquet is clean, with citrus and nectarine fruit aromas; the wine has pleasant entry and mid-palate flavours but a relatively short finish.   **rating:** 84
best drinking Drink now **best vintages** '97 **drink with** Vegetarian dishes • $18

Salitage Chardonnay

Estate-grown and produced, always with strong barrel-ferment and oak influences. As with the Pinot Noir, has tended to develop fairly quickly.
▼▼▼▼♀ **1998** Medium straw-yellow; there are some honeyed notes to the bouquet, and a whisper of burnt fermentation yeast; the oak is relatively restrained. After an uncertain start, the wine gains some stature on the palate, which has ripe fig/melon fruit of good length and intensity, helped by a touch of spicy oak. Emphatic drink now.   **rating:** 90
best drinking Drink now **best vintages** '98 **drink with** Turkey breast • $30

Salitage Pinot Noir

Pemberton has had various prophets, notably Dr John Gladstones and Gerard Potel, co-owner of the distinguished Burgundy producer Domaine de la Pousse d'Or, not to mention Salitage's owner and founder John Horgan. The jury is emphatically out on the whole subject of Pemberton/Warren Valley and its suitability for Pinot Noir. Rapid ageing seems a common problem across many producers, regardless of soil type.
▼▼▼▼ **1998** Medium red-purple; moderately intense fruit shows some stemmy carbonic maceration characters underneath positive oak. The palate is a mix of sweet and sour, sappy and boiled fruit flavours on the palate, which are not unattractive. However, drink soon.   **rating:** 85
best drinking 2000–2001 **best vintages** '93, '94 **drink with** Barbecued quail • $34

Salitage Pemberton

Simply (and confusingly) called Pemberton, this is a Bordeaux-blend of 60 per cent Cabernet Sauvignon, 22 per cent Merlot, 14 per cent Cabernet Franc and 4 per cent Petit Verdot. It is yet another wine to suggest that, contrary to original belief and opinion, the Pemberton region may be more suited to the Bordeaux varieties, than to those of Burgundy.
▼▼▼♀ **1998** Medium red-purple; strong savoury/oaky aromas are followed by a soft, rounded palate in which the vanillin oak is a major contributor to flavour, the structure coming from soft tannins. Made in the high oak style favoured by winemaker Patrick Coutts.   **rating:** 84

ΨΨΨΨ **1996** Developed medium red; the bouquet is likewise developed, with secondary/foresty/savoury aromas to the fore. The palate builds on the interest of the bouquet, with cedar/cigar box/savoury flavours and nicely balanced soft, ripe tannins. A very interesting wine. **rating:** 91

best drinking 2000–2003 **best vintages** '96 **drink with** Rolled shoulder of lamb • $32

saltram ★★★★

Angaston Road, Angaston, SA 5353 **region** Barossa Valley
phone (08) 8564 3355 **fax** (08) 8564 2209 **open** 7 days 10–5
winemaker Nigel Dolan **production** 150 000 **est.** 1859
product range ($10–49.95 R) At the top is No. 1 Shiraz; then Mamre Brook, now 100 per cent Barossa and comprising Chardonnay, Shiraz and Cabernet Sauvignon; Metala Black Label and White Label; and the Saltram Classic range sourced from southeast Australia.
summary There is no doubt that Saltram has taken giant strides towards regaining the reputation it held 30 or so years ago. Under Nigel Dolan's stewardship, grape sourcing has come back to the Barossa Valley for the flagship wines, a fact of which he is rightly proud. The red wines, in particular, have enjoyed great show success over the past few years, with No. 1 Shiraz, Mamre Brook and Metala leading the charge. Exports to the UK, the US, Southeast Asia and New Zealand.

Saltram Classic Semillon

A wine made in typical Barossa style which was awarded a trophy at the Royal Perth Wine Show in 1998 for reasons best known to the judges.
ΨΨΨΨ **1998** Medium to full yellow-green; the bouquet is pungent and rich with masses of oak and rather less fruit. A big, broad rapidly ageing wine in yesterday's style. Its strongest point is its price. **rating:** 81

best drinking 2000–2001 **best vintages** NA **drink with** Deep-fried chicken • $10

Saltram Mamre Brook Chardonnay

On the face of it, bringing the source for a top-flight Chardonnay back to the Barossa adds a degree of difficulty which might easily be avoided by looking either to the Adelaide Hills, Eden Valley or McLaren Vale. However, this wine shows just what can be done.
ΨΨΨΨ **1999** Medium to full yellow-green; the bouquet is clean and quite well balanced, with tangy citrus/melon fruit and oak. The medium-bodied palate shows up to be a little hollow and just a tad green; nice oak handling, though. **rating:** 83

best drinking 2000–2002 **best vintages** '98 **drink with** Cold Barossa mettwurst • $17

Saltram Classic Shiraz

The Classic range, despite its slightly pretentious name, typically offers a bang for your buck.
ΨΨΨΨ **1998** Medium red-purple; the moderately intense bouquet is clean and fresh, with touches of fruit spice and subtle oak. Dark cherry and plum fruit on the palate are followed by a firm finish which needs to soften a touch, and will do so. **rating:** 85

best drinking 2003–2008 **best vintages** '98 **drink with** Pie floater • $20

Saltram Mamre Brook Shiraz

As from the 1996 vintage, the Mamre Brook Red has split itself from a Cabernet Shiraz blend into its two component parts, with a Mamre Brook Shiraz and a Mamre Brook Cabernet Sauvignon. It has also reverted to a 100 per cent Barossa origin. The wine is made in the old, open fermenters of the Saltram winery with heading down boards used to encourage extraction. The wine spends 18 months in a mix of American (60 per cent) and French (40 per cent) oak.
ΨΨΨΨ **1998** Strong red-purple; a complex, rich bouquet with a rainbow of aromas running through liquorice, leather, berry, vanilla and mint. The palate offers all of the above together with a delicious dollop of chocolate. **rating:** 90

best drinking 2002–2012 **best vintages** '98 **drink with** Grilled calf's liver • $20

Saltram Metala Shiraz Cabernet

Draws upon a century-old block of vines at Metala Creek, and first made by present winemaker Nigel Dolan's father, Brian, in 1959. The 1961 vintage won the inaugural Jimmy Watson Trophy, adding to the lineage of one of Australia's enduring brands. A blend of 65 per cent Shiraz and 35 per cent Cabernet Sauvignon; the standard release under the famous Metala label with its striking script-like printing and numbered bottles.
ΨΨΨΨ **1998** Very good purple-red; the moderately intense red berry/cherry fruit of the bouquet is supported by subtle vanilla oak. Attractively sweet mid-palate fruit is followed by faintly dusty/dry tannins, but I fancy there is enough fruit there to provide time for those tannins to settle down. **rating:** 86

best drinking 2002–2008 **best vintages** '96 **drink with** Italian • $16.50

sandalford ★★★★

West Swan Road, Caversham, WA 6055 **region** Swan District
phone (08) 9374 9374 **fax** (08) 9274 2154 **open** 7 days 10–5
winemaker Bill Crappsley, Severine Dombret **production** 70 000 **est.** 1840
product range ($12.95–35 R) At the bottom end under the Caversham label Chenin Verdelho, Late Harvest Cabernet Shiraz; then the 1840 Collection of Semillon Sauvignon Blanc, Chardonnay and Cabernet Merlot; under the premium range Margaret River Mount Barker Riesling, Margaret River Verdelho, Mount Barker Margaret River Chardonnay, Mount Barker Margaret River Shiraz, Mount Barker Margaret River Cabernet Sauvignon; plus excellent fortifieds, notably Sandalera; also the new Element brand, including Chenin Verdelho, Chardonnay and Cabernet Shiraz.
summary The arrival of Bill Crappsley as winemaker, coupled with the refurbishment of the winery, has heralded major changes at Sandalford. Wine quality has improved year by year, with Chenin Blanc and Chardonnay leading the way but not alone. The quality of the labelling and packaging has also taken a giant leap forwards. Exports to the UK, Switzerland, US, Japan, Singapore and Hong Kong.

Sandalford Reserve Semillon

A new addition to the Sandalford range, both by virtue of its name and the quality of the wine in the glass, at the top echelon. Presumably produced from the 1.5 hectares of semillon in the Margaret River vineyards of Sandalford.
▼▼▼▼ **1999** Light green-yellow; the bouquet has light lemony/grassy aromas which are varietal and do not suggest unripe fruit. The palate shows a clever touch of barrel-ferment reminiscent of the better Evans & Tate wines; the influence is subtle, and the wine should develop well.   **rating:** 86
best drinking 2000–2005 **best vintages** NA **drink with** Calamari • $NA

Sandalford Reserve Chenin

Sandalford has chenin blanc planted in more or less equal quantities (2.5 hectares) in both its Margaret River and Caversham vineyards. This wine has been barrel-fermented in the style pioneered by Houghton, and which has shown the capacity to age well in bottle.
▼▼▼▼ **1999** Medium yellow-green; a powerful bouquet with lots of spicy barrel-ferment French oak aromas is followed, logically enough, by a generously proportioned palate with lots of tangy fruit and spicy oak. Will cellar well if you like this bigger style.   **rating:** 85
best drinking 2000–2005 **best vintages** '99 **drink with** Cassoulet • $NA

Sandalford Sandalera 375 ml

A famous old fortified wine including Verdelho and Chenin Blanc and made using a solera system with an average age of over 15 years.
▼▼▼▽ **NV** Olive-brown; the intensely spicy Christmas cake bouquet leads into a long, complex palate with a distinctly biscuity aftertaste. In a style all of its own.   **rating:** 90
best drinking 2000–2010 **best vintages** NA **drink with** Coffee and biscuits • $35

Sandalford Element Shiraz Cabernet

The Element range of three wines (Chenin Verdelho, Chardonnay and Cabernet Shiraz) are the lowest-priced in the Sandalford portfolio. This is a particularly attractive wine at the price.
▼▼▼▼ **1999** Medium to full red-purple; there is some depth to the slightly earthy, firm fruit of the bouquet; the palate is softer, with pleasantly ripe sweet cherry/plum/raspberry fruit flavours; as with the bouquet, the oak is barely perceptible.   **rating:** 85
best drinking 2001–2004 **best vintages** NA **drink with** Pizza • $12.95

Sandalford Cabernet Sauvignon

A blend of the best grapes coming from 27 hectares of cabernet in the Margaret River vineyard and 19 hectares at Mount Barker.
▼▼▼▼ **1998** Medium red-purple; the moderately intense bouquet has fresh, red berry fruit and just a light touch of mint. The palate, like the bouquet, is fruit-driven but has plenty of structure and weight, finishing with persistent tannins. An elegant but powerful style which should develop particularly well in bottle.   **rating:** 87
best drinking 2003–2013 **best vintages** NA **drink with** Roast leg of lamb • $23.95

sandalyn wilderness estate   NR

Wilderness Road, Rothbury, NSW 2321 **region** Lower Hunter Valley
phone (02) 4930 7611 **fax** (02) 4930 7611 **open** 7 days 10–5
winemaker Adrian Sheridan (Contract) **production** 4000 **est.** 1988

product range ($16–22 CD) Semillon, Verdelho, Semillon Verdelho, Chardonnay, Semillon Late Harvest, Pinot Noir, Conservatory Shiraz, Sparkling.

summary Sandra and Lindsay Whaling preside over the picturesque cellar-door building of Sandalyn on the evocatively named Wilderness Road, where you will find a one-hole golf range and views to the Wattagan, Brokenback and Molly Morgan ranges. The estate has 8.85 hectares of vineyards.

sand hills vineyard ★★☆

Sandhills Road, Forbes, NSW 2871 region Other Wineries of NSW
phone (02) 6852 1437 fax (02) 6852 4401 open Mon–Sat 9–5, Sun 12–5
winemaker John Saleh, Jill Lindsay production 1200 est. 1920
product range ($10–13 CD) Classic Dry White, Chardonnay, Colombard Semillon, Shiraz, Shiraz Cabernet, Lucien Tawny Port.

summary Having purchased Sand Hills from long-term owner Jacques Genet, the Saleh family has replanted the vineyard to appropriate varieties, with over 3 hectares of premium varieties having been established between 1989 and 1995. Winemaking duties are split between John Saleh at Sand Hills (Pinot Noir and fortifieds) and Jill Lindsay of Woodonga Hill (white wines).

🐄 sandhurst ridge ★★★

156 Forest Drive, Marong, Vic 3515 region Bendigo
phone (03) 5435 2534 fax (03) 5435 2548 open Weekends 12–5 and by appointment
winemaker John, Paul, Silvano and George Greblo production 1200 est. 1990
product range ($22–26 R) Sauvignon Blanc, Chardonnay, Shiraz, Cabernet Sauvignon.

summary The four Greblo brothers, with combined experience in business, agriculture, science and construction and development, began the establishment of Sandhurst Ridge in 1990 with the planting of the first 2 hectares of shiraz and cabernet sauvignon. Those plantings have now been increased to 6.6 hectares, principally cabernet and shiraz, but with small amounts of merlot, sauvignon blanc and chardonnay. The fully equipped winery was completed in 1996 with a cellar capacity of 400 barriques.

sandstone ★★★

CMB Carbunup River, WA 6280 region Margaret River
phone (08) 9755 6271 fax (08) 9755 6292 open Not
winemaker Mike Davies, Jan Davies production 750 est. 1988
product range ($18–22 R) Semillon, Cabernet Sauvignon.

summary The family operation of consultant-winemakers Mike and Jan Davies, who also operate very successful mobile bottling plants. The wines are made at Ribbonvale, where the Davies work as consultants and contract-winemakers for others.

🐄 sandy farm vineyard NR

RMB 3734 Sandy Farm Road, Denver via Daylesford, Vic 3641 region Macedon Ranges
phone (03) 5348 7610 open Weekends 10–5 or by appointment
winemaker Peter Comisel production 800 est. 1988
product range ($15–20 CD) Pinot Noir, Merlot, Cabernet Sauvignon.

summary Peter Covell has a small, basic winery in which he makes preservative-free Cabernet Sauvignon, Merlot and Pinot Noir which has a loyal local following.

🐄 sarsfield estate NR

345 Duncan Road, Sarsfield, Vic 3875 region Gippsland
phone (03) 5156 8962 fax (03) 5156 8970 open Not
winemaker Dr Suzanne Rutschmann production 600 est. 1995
product range ($15 CD) Pinot Noir, Cabernet Sauvignon Shiraz.

summary The property is owned by Suzanne Rutschmann, who has a PhD in Chemistry, a Diploma in Horticulture and is in Year 4 of the Charles Sturt University BSc (Wine Science) course and by Swiss-born Peter Albrecht, a civil and structural engineer, who has also undertaken various courses in agriculture and viticulture. For a part-time occupation, these are exceptionally impressive credentials. Their 2-hectare vineyard was planted between 1991 and 1998; the first vintage made at the winery was 1998, the grapes being sold in previous years to others.

scarborough ★★★★

Gillards Road, Pokolbin, NSW 2321 **region** Lower Hunter Valley
phone (02) 4998 7563 **fax** (02) 4998 7786 **open** 7 days 9–5
winemaker Ian Scarborough **production** 10 000 **est.** 1985
product range ($18.50–30 CD) A Chardonnay specialist, making token quantities of Pinot Noir.
summary Ian Scarborough put his white winemaking skills beyond doubt during his years as a consultant, and his exceptionally complex and stylish Chardonnay is no disappointment. Vintage conditions permitting, Ian Scarborough makes two styles: a rich, traditional buttery White Burgundy version for the Australian market (exemplified by the 1995 with its mustard-gold label) and a lighter, more elegant Chablis style (under a blue-silver label) for the export market. Exports to the UK and the US.

Scarborough Chardonnay

Produced from 9 hectares of estate plantings, invariably made in a big, rich full-bodied style which has a strong following. Active marketing is barely necessary.
▼▼▼▼ **1998** Glowing medium yellow-green; the bouquet is complex and rich, with ripe peach/stone fruit aromas and minimal oak. The palate, while rich, is not phenolic, with smooth and nicely balanced stone fruit flavours and a clean finish.   **rating:** 87
▼▼▼▼ **1996** Glowing, full yellow-green. The bouquet is rich, with peach and honey aromas, yet is not blowsy. Medium- to full-bodied palate in classic regional style, but has developed exceptionally well. Great with rich food.   **rating:** 87
best drinking 2000–2004 **best vintages** '87, '89, '91, '94, '96, '98 **drink with** Rich white meat dishes • $18.50

scarpantoni estate ★★★☆

Scarpantoni Drive, McLaren Flat, SA 5171 **region** McLaren Vale
phone (08) 8383 0186 **fax** (08) 8383 0490 **open** Mon–Fri 10–5, weekends 11–5
winemaker Michael Scarpantoni, Filippo Scarpantoni **production** 15 000 **est.** 1979
product range ($5.50–20 CD) Block 1 Riesling, Sauvignon Blanc, Unwooded Chardonnay, Chardonnay, Fleurieu Brut, Gamay, Fiori, School Block (Cabernet Shiraz Merlot), Block 3 Shiraz, Cabernet Sauvignon, Botrytis Riesling, Tawny Port, Vintage Port.
summary While an erratic producer at times, and not helped by the earlier use of agglomerate corks, has made some excellent wines in recent years which — if repeated — would earn the winery an even higher rating.

scarp valley ★★★★

6 Robertson Road, Gooseberry Hill, WA 6076 **region** Perth Hills
phone (08) 9454 5748 **open** By appointment
winemaker Hainault (Contract) **production** 25 **est.** 1978
product range ($15 ML) Hermitage.
summary Owner Robert Duncan presides over what has to be one of the smallest producers in Australia, with one-quarter acre of shiraz and 30 cabernet sauvignon vines producing a single cask of wine each year if the birds do not get the grapes first.

schmidts tarchalice NR

Research Road, Vine Vale via Tanunda, SA 5352 **region** Barossa Valley
phone (08) 8563 3005 **fax** (08) 8563 0667 **open** Mon–Sat 10–5, Sun 12–5
winemaker Christopher Schmidt **production** 1500 **est.** 1984
product range ($8.50–19.75 CD) Barossa Riesling, Eden Valley Riesling, Barossa Chardonnay, Barossa Semillon, Auslese Riesling, Shiraz Cabernet/Cabernet Franc, four different Ports and Old Liqueur Frontignac.
summary Typically has a range of fully mature wines at low prices available at cellar door.

scotchmans hill ★★★★

190 Scotchmans Road, Drysdale, Vic 3222 **region** Geelong
phone (03) 5251 3176 **fax** (03) 5253 1743 **open** 7 days 10.30–4.30
winemaker Robin Brockett **production** 30 000 **est.** 1982
product range ($15.50–26.50 R) Riesling, Sauvignon Blanc, Chardonnay, Pinot Noir, Cabernet Sauvignon Merlot; Spray Farm is the second label with Sauvignon Blanc, Chardonnay and Pinot Noir.
summary Situated on the Bellarine Peninsula, southeast of Geelong, with a well-equipped winery and first class vineyards. It is a consistent performer with its Pinot Noir and has a strong following in both Melbourne and Sydney for its astutely priced, competently made wines. A doubling in production has seen the establishment of export markets to the UK and The Netherlands. The second label of Spray Farm takes its name from a National

Trust property with panoramic views of Port Phillip Bay and Melbourne, which has also been planted to vines by the Brown family and is run as a distinct vineyard and brand operation. The same four varieties are produced but at a lower price-point across the range.

Spray Farm Chardonnay

Fifty per cent of the wine is barrel-fermented in a mix of first and second use French barriques, with five months maturation in barrel; 50 per cent is tank-fermented, and 30 per cent of the total blend taken through malolactic fermentation.

▼▼▼♀ **1999** Medium to full yellow-green; the bouquet has slightly nutty/hessiany overtones to the apple cake fruit; on the palate, a mix of melon and apple come through, investing the wine with fruit sweetness. The oak influence is barely perceptible. **rating: 82**

best drinking 2000–2003 **best vintages** NA **drink with** Light seafood • $17

scotts brook   NR

Scotts Brook Road, Boyup Brook, WA 6244 **region** Blackwood Valley
phone (08) 9765 3014 **fax** (08) 9765 3015 **open** Weekends, school holidays 10–5 or by appointment
winemaker Aquila Estate (Contract) **production** 2000 **est.** 1987
product range ($11–19 CD) Riesling, Autumn Harvest White, Chardonnay, Cabernet Sauvignon.
summary The Scotts Brook winery at Boyup Brook (equidistant between the Margaret River and Great Southern regions) has been developed by local schoolteachers Brian Walker and wife Kerry — hence the opening hours during school holidays. There are 17.5 hectares of vineyards, but the majority of the production is sold to other winemakers, with limited quantities being made by contract.

sea winds vineyard   NR

RMB 9020, Main Creek Road, Main Ridge, Vic 3928 **region** Mornington Peninsula
phone (03) 5989 6204 **fax** (03) 5989 6204 **open** Not
winemaker Kevin McCarthy (Contract) **production** NA **est.** 1990
product range NA.
summary Ron Matson has developed 3 hectares of sauvignon blanc, chardonnay and pinot noir; the wines are made for him by Kevin McCarthy at T'Gallant.

seldom seen vineyard   NR

Craigmoor Road, Mudgee, NSW 2850 **region** Mudgee
phone (02) 6372 4482 **fax** (02) 6372 1055 **open** 7 days 9.30–5
winemaker Barry Platt **production** 4500 **est.** 1987
product range ($11–16 CD) Semillon (wooded and unwooded), Chardonnay Semillon, Chardonnay, Traminer.
summary A substantial grape grower (with 18 hectares of vineyards) which reserves a proportion of its crop for making and release under its own label. No recent tastings.

seppelt   ★★★★★

Seppeltsfield via Nuriootpa, SA 5355 **region** Barossa Valley
phone (08) 8568 6200 **fax** (08) 8562 8333 **open** Mon–Fri 10–5, Sat 10.30–4.30, Sun 11–4
winemaker James Godfrey, Jonathan Ketley **production** NFP **est.** 1851
product range ($8–3000 R) The great wines of Seppeltsfield are first and foremost Para Liqueur Port, Show Tawny Port DP90, Seppeltsfield Fino Sherry and Dorrien Cabernet Sauvignon. The other wines in the Seppelt portfolio are handled at Great Western. The 100 Year Old Para Liqueur Port is the $500 a bottle (375 ml) jewel in the crown, the current vintage being the 1900.
summary A multi-million-dollar expansion and renovation programme has seen the historic Seppeltsfield winery become the production centre for the Seppelt wines, adding another dimension to what was already the most historic and beautiful major winery in Australia. It is now home to some of the world's unique fortified wines, nurtured and protected by the passionate James Godfrey. Worldwide distribution.

Seppelt Rutherglen Show Tokay DP57

A very old Tokay from Rutherglen; here the winemaking trick is to keep the wine fresh without taking away from the predominantly aged characteristics of the wine.

▼▼▼▼▼ **NV** Mahogany gold; complex, sweet and rich tea-leaf, raisin and plum pudding aromas are followed by an equally complex, multiflavoured palate which leaves the mouth fresh, thanks to its perfect balance. **rating: 94**

best drinking 2000–2019 **best vintages** NA **drink with** Fine, dark chocolate • $24.95

Seppelt Show Reserve Muscat DP63

An extraordinary show reserve wine of great age which invariably scores high gold medal points every time I taste it. The following note (and points) were made in March 1999.

TTTTT NV Deep mahogany brown, with a mix of gold and green on the rim. Rich, raisined, spicy plum pudding aromas are lifted by perfectly balanced and integrated spirit. The powerful, complex and rich palate — plum pudding and Christmas cake — has a very long, lingering finish.   **rating:** 96

best drinking 2000–2001 **best vintages** NA **drink with** Dried fruits • $24.95

Seppelt Amontillado Sherry DP116

Just as winemaker James Godfrey is forever seeking ways to make the Show Fino finer and more delicate (without losing character) so he believes in fine Amontillados with sweetness on the mid-palate, but a cleansing, dry finish.

TTTTT NV Bright mid-gold; the bouquet has a lovely touch of honey over the bite of the rancio; the very elegant, very fresh palate finishes distinctly dry after the mellowness of the bouquet and mid-palate. This is as it should be.   **rating:** 94

best drinking 2000–2001 **best vintages** NA **drink with** A great winter aperitif • $NA

Seppelt Show Fino Sherry DP117

DP117 has reigned supreme in the Australian show circuit for decades. It is made using the traditional solera system, resulting in a seamless blend of wines of varying age, protected by the flor yeast which floats on the surface of the wine and is responsible for its unique taste. This driest-of-all Sherries is also the finest, and recent changes in the law have allowed Seppelt winemaker James Godfrey to make the wine even finer by reducing the alcohol content from around 17 per cent to around 15.5 per cent. There is nothing better than a chilled glass of Fino on a hot summer's day. It is essential, incidentally, that the stock be fresh, and that the bottle be kept in the refrigerator after it is opened, and consumed within two or three days of opening.

TTTTT NV Brilliant green-yellow; the bouquet is strong and stylish, with that faintly nutty, faintly tangy cut which is the hallmark of Fino Sherry. The palate is intense and racy, the flavour lingering in the mouth long after the wine is swallowed, but not so long to stop you taking the next mouthful.   **rating:** 96

best drinking 2000–2001 **best vintages** NA **drink with** Olives, tapas • $NA

Seppelt Show Oloroso Sherry DP38

The sweetest of the Seppelt Sherries, yet even here (in the Spanish tradition) sweetness and dryness are delicately balanced.

TTTTT NV Golden brown; nutty rancio complexity, with just a hint of sweetness, introduce a finely balanced palate with a constant interplay between nutty, honeyed sweetness and drier, rancio characters.   **rating:** 95

best drinking 2000–2001 **best vintages** NA **drink with** Sweet biscuits • $NA

Seppelt Show Tawny Port DP90

DP90 has an average age of 21 years, blended from the reserve stocks of very old Tawny Port made from Barossa Valley Shiraz and Grenache, with a little Cabernet Sauvignon. Between 1968 and 1991 alone DP90 won 30 trophies and 106 gold medals at Australian wine shows, making it the most-awarded wine of any style. It is intermittently released in limited quantities. No other Australian Tawny challenges the sheer complexity and finesse of DP90. It is a blend of wines that span more than 100 years, aged in all kinds of barrels (none new, of course) and only a limited quantity is bottled each year to preserve the balance of very old material in the blend.

TTTTT NV The tawny hues are rimmed with olive-green, immediately proclaiming the age of the wine. The bouquet is fine, fragrant and penetrating, much closer to the Tawny Ports of Portugal than most Australian wines. The palate offers flavours of spice, butterscotch and more nutty characters, but it is the length of flavour and finish which is absolutely remarkable. Given its age, arguably the most undervalued wine on the Australian market today.

rating: 97

best drinking 2000–2019 **best vintages** NA **drink with** Dried fruits and nuts • $88.50

seppelt great western ★★★★★

Moyston Road, Great Western, Vic 3377 **region** Grampians
phone (03) 5361 2239 **fax** (03) 5361 2200 **open** 7 days 10–5
winemaker Ian McKenzie (Chief) **production** NFP **est.** 1865
product range ($5.95–51 R) Méthode Champenoise comprising (from the bottom up) Brut Reserve, Imperial Reserve, Rosé Reserve, Grande Reserve, Sunday Creek Pinot Noir Chardonnay, Fleur de Lys, Harpers Range, Rhymney Sparkling Sauvignon Blanc, Original Sparkling Shiraz and Salinger; table wines include Moyston Unoaked Chardonnay and Cabernet Shiraz; Sheoak Riesling; Terrain Series Chardonnay and Cabernet Sauvignon; Eden Valley Botrytis Gewurztraminer, Corella Ridge Chardonnay, Harpers Range Cabernet Sauvignon, Chalambar Shiraz, Sunday Creek Pinot Noir, Drumborg Riesling, Partalunga Vineyard Chardonnay,

Great Western Shiraz, and Drumborg Cabernet Sauvignon. Great Western Hermitage and Show Reserve Sparkling Burgundy are the flag-bearers alongside Salinger.

summary Australia's best-known producer of sparkling wine, always immaculate in its given price range but also producing excellent Great Western-sourced table wines, especially long-lived Shiraz and Australia's best Sparkling Shirazes. Now the production centre for many Southcorp Group brands, with a vast new bottling plant and attendant warehouse facilities. Worldwide distribution.

Seppelt Drumborg Riesling

An interesting wine, not made every year, and by no means released in vintage sequence. The time of release depends entirely on winemaker Ian McKenzie's judgment, and thus the '93 was not released until late 1998, followed quickly by the '98 vintage in 1999.

▼▼▼▼▼ **1998** Light green-yellow; a fragrant bouquet with a very distinctive spicy lift is followed by a quite lovely juicy, grapey appley palate, finishing with lively acidity; quite distinctive.   **rating: 94**

best drinking 2001–2006 **best vintages** '98 **drink with** Chinese prawns with cashews • $22.50

Seppelt Mornington Peninsula Pinot Gris

1998 marks the initial release by Seppelt of a Mornington Peninsula Pinot Gris. As Seppelt chief winemaker Ian McKenzie observes, it has been made in the Alsace style rather than the Italian, hence the Pinot Gris rather than the Pinot Grigio label.

▼▼▼▼ **1998** Light to medium yellow-green; the bouquet has some fruit richness with tropical fruit and hints of guava. The palate has good fruit flavour and varietal character, with attractive minerally notes on the finish.

rating: 85

best drinking 1999–2001 **best vintages** NA **drink with** Shellfish • $15

Seppelt Corella Ridge Chardonnay

First made in 1991, utilising grapes grown in premium cool-climate Victorian regions, and 100 per cent barrel-fermented in new and one-year-old French oak barriques. Matured on its yeast lees for nine months. In general the grapes came from Great Western, Strathbogie Ranges and Drumborg. A much underrated and under-appreciated wine, offering exceptional value at its price.

▼▼▼▼ **1998** Light green-yellow; clean, fresh citrus fruit is married with subtle, spicy oak. The palate is delicate, crisp and well balanced, with melon fruit flavours, good acidity and length.   **rating: 87**

best drinking 2000–2003 **best vintages** '96, '97 **drink with** Fish mornay • $13.50

Seppelt Drumborg Pinot Noir

Seppelt has taken a long time to come to terms with its Drumborg vineyard, with most of the pinot noir being used in its sparkling wines. Warmer vintages, however, can and do produce high-quality table wines.

▼▼▼▼ **1998** Strong, youthful purple-red; the bouquet is aromatic, with some savoury/foresty notes; there is ripe plummy fruit on the mid-palate, but the wine falls away slightly on the finish.   **rating: 88**

best drinking 2000–2004 **best vintages** NA **drink with** Rare duck breast • $42

Seppelt Great Western Shiraz

A wine made intermittently by Colin Preece (who was much given to blending) and which disappeared altogether between 1975 and 1983 inclusive. Since its reappearance, it has been sourced principally from the 70-year-old block of shiraz adjacent to the winery, which produces wine of tremendous style.

▼▼▼▼▽ **1995** Medium purple-red; high-toned black cherry fruit marries with soft French oak on the bouquet; the palate offers cherry, mint and berry fruit flavours, with those utterly distinctive, hallmark fine tannins of Great Western.   **rating: 91**

best drinking 2001–2015 **best vintages** '54, '56, '60, '63, '71, '84, '85, '86, '91, '93 **drink with** Herbed rack of lamb • $36.50

Seppelt Chalambar Shiraz

Part of the Seppelt Victorian portfolio, using grapes grown predominantly at Great Western but including components from the Ovens Valley, Strathbogie Ranges and Bendigo, all premium areas. It is matured in a mix of new and one-year-old French and American oak casks for 12 months but is fruit- rather than oak-driven. It has been a prolific gold medal and trophy winner over the past seven years.

▼▼▼▼▽ **1998** Medium red-purple; the intense bouquet is full of sweet dark chocolate, cherry and spice aromas, the palate with excellent depth and structure; fine tannins run throughout and the oak handling is assured.

rating: 92

best drinking 2003–2013 **best vintages** '53–63, '91, '93, '94, '95, '96, '97, '98 **drink with** Braised game dishes • $19.80

Seppelt Harpers Range Cabernet Sauvignon

Produced from grapes grown entirely in premium Victorian regions, typically the Mornington Peninsula, Strathbogie Ranges, Yarra Valley and Drumborg. It usually contains a percentage of Merlot, sometimes a little Cabernet Franc or Malbec. It is matured in new and one-year-old French and American oak barrels for 17 months. While it seems to languish in the shade of Chalambar Shiraz, is consistently reliable.

▼▼▼♀ 1998 Medium red-purple; the moderately intense bouquet has spice, savoury and dark berry/blackberry aromas supported by subtle oak. On the palate blackberry, mint and a touch of chocolate with savoury overtones and fine tannins round off a nicely balanced wine. **rating: 84**

best drinking 2002–2007 **best vintages** NA **drink with** Stir-fried beef • $16.40

serventy ★★☆

Valley Home Vineyard, Rocky Road, Forest Grove, WA 6286 **region** Margaret River
phone (08) 9757 7534 **fax** (08) 9757 7534 **open** Fri–Sun, holidays 10–4
winemaker Peter Serventy **production** 1500 **est.** 1984
product range ($15 CD) Chardonnay, Pinot Noir, Shiraz.
summary Peter Serventy is nephew of the famous naturalist Vincent Serventy and son of ornithologist Dominic Serventy. It is hardly surprising, then, that Serventy should practise strict organic viticulture, using neither herbicides nor pesticides. The wines, too, are made with a minimum of SO_2, added late in the piece and never exceeding 30 parts per million.

settlers ridge NR

54b Bussell Highway, Cowaramup, WA 6284 **region** Margaret River
phone (08) 9755 5388 **fax** (08) 9755 5388 **open** 7 days 10–5
winemaker Wayne Nobbs **production** NFP **est.** 1998
product range ($13–25 CD) Chenin Blanc, Chenin Sauvignon Blanc, Sauvignon Blanc, Shiraz, Shiraz Cabernet Sauvignon, Cabernet Sauvignon.
summary Wayne and Kaye Nobbs have established what they say is the only winery in Western Australia with organic certification and the only winery in Australia with dual classification from NASA (National Association for Sustainable Agriculture) and OVAA (Organic Vignerons of Australia). They have 6.4 hectares of vineyard in bearing, with an additional hectare of merlot coming into production. All of the wines are distributed direct from cellar door.

settlers rise montville NR

249 Western Avenue, Montville, Qld 4560 **region** Queensland Zone
phone (07) 5478 5558 **fax** (07) 5478 5558 **open** 7 days 10–6
winemaker Peter Scudamore-Smith (Contract) **production** 4000 **est.** 1998
product range ($12.50–22 CD) Queensland Classic White, Sauvignon Blanc Semillon Chardonnay, Cabernet Sauvignon Shiraz.
summary Settlers Rise is located in the beautiful highlands of the Blackall Range, 75-minutes drive north of Brisbane and 20 minutes from the Sunshine Coast. 1.5 hectares of chardonnay, verdelho, shiraz and cabernet sauvignon have been planted at an elevation of 450 metres on the deep basalt soils of the property. First settled in 1887, Montville has gradually become a tourist destination, with a substantial local arts and crafts industry, with a flourishing bed and breakfast and lodge accommodation infrastructure.

sevenhill cellars ★★★★

College Road, Sevenhill via Clare, SA 5453 **region** Clare Valley
phone (08) 8843 4222 **fax** (08) 8843 4382 **open** Mon–Fri 9.30–4.30, Sat, public holidays 10–4
winemaker Brother John May, John Monten **production** 20 000 **est.** 1851
product range ($8–22 CD) St Aloysius (Chenin Blanc, Chardonnay, Verdelho blend), Semillon, Riesling, College White, Verdelho, Semillon, Gewurztraminer, St Ignatius (Cabernet Sauvignon, Malbec, Franc and Merlot blend), Kranewitter, Shiraz, Cabernet Sauvignon, Fortifieds, Sacramental Wine.
summary One of the historical treasures of Australia; the oft-photographed stone wine cellars are the oldest in the Clare Valley, and winemaking is still carried out under the direction of the Jesuitical Manresea Society and in particular Brother John May. Quality is very good, particularly that of the powerful Shiraz, all the wines reflecting the estate-grown grapes from old vines. Extensive retail distribution throughout all States; exports to New Zealand, Switzerland and the US.

Sevenhill Cellars St Aloysius

Packaged in the distinctive ceramic glass bottle, and an unusual blend of Chardonnay, Chenin Blanc and Verdelho, the latter one of the larger plantings on the Sevenhill Cellars vineyards.

ŸŸŸŸ **1999** Light to medium yellow-green; the bouquet has quite rich fruit and just a subliminal suggestion of oak. The palate has quite good depth of flavour; again there is a suggestion of slightly chippy oak. **rating:** 82

best drinking 2000–2002 **best vintages** '92, '93, '94, '95, '96 **drink with** Grilled spatchcock • $15

Sevenhill Cellars St Ignatius

A blend of Cabernet Sauvignon, Malbec, Cabernet Franc and Merlot, all of which are estate-grown. The policy has always been to pick the grapes very ripe, thus producing a densely coloured and massively flavoured wine which really needs much time to soften and mature. The '96 topped its class at the 1997 Liquorland National Wine Show.

ŸŸŸŸ **1998** Excellent, deep purple-red; a highly fragrant, scent, essencey minty/berry bouquet is followed by a palate oozing with minty/berry fruit. I just wish it had had more time and work in barrel. **rating:** 88

best drinking 2003–2008 **best vintages** '80, '87, '89, '91, '92, '96, '98 **drink with** Strong cheese or red meat • $22

Sevenhill Cellars Cabernet Sauvignon

As with all of the Sevenhill reds, made in an heroic style. It is taken from just under 10 hectares of estate vineyards, with mature and relatively low-yielding vines adding to the authority of the wine which needs patience.

ŸŸŸŸŸ **1998** Medium to full red-purple; clean, perfectly ripened blackcurrant fruit on the bouquet leads into a wine with excellent structure and richness, full but not extractive, persistent but not abrasive tannins. However, overall the oak is just a fraction assertive. **rating:** 90

best drinking 2003–2013 **best vintages** '80, '87, '89, '91, '92, '96, '98 **drink with** Leave it in the cellar • $20

severn brae estate   NR

Lot 2 Back Creek Road (Mount Tully Road), Severnlea, Qld 4352 **region** Granite Belt
phone (07) 4683 5292 **fax** (07) 3391 3821 **open** Weekends 9–5 or by appointment
winemaker Bruce Humphery-Smith **production** 300 **est.** 1990
product range ($14–16 ML) Chardonnay, Shiraz, Liqueur Muscat.
summary Patrick and Bruce Humphery-Smith have established 5.5 hectares of chardonnay with relatively close spacing and trained on a high two-tier trellis. Winery and cellar-door facilities were completed in time for the 1995 vintage. Prior to that time, the Chardonnay was made at Sundown Valley winery.

seville estate   ★★★★☆

Linwood Road, Seville, Vic 3139 **region** Yarra Valley
phone (03) 5964 2622 **fax** (03) 5964 2633 **open** Not
winemaker Iain Riggs **production** 5000 **est.** 1970
product range ($12–25 ML) Chardonnay, Chardonnay Sauvignon Blanc, Pinot Noir, Shiraz, Cabernet Sauvignon; new GP label of Chardonnay Semillon and Cabernet Sauvignon in honour of winery founder Dr Peter McMahon.
summary In February 1997 a controlling interest in Seville Estate was acquired by Brokenwood (of the Hunter Valley) and interests associated with Brokenwood. I was one of the founding partners of Brokenwood, and the acquisition meant that the wheel had turned full circle. This apart, Seville Estate will add significantly to the top-end of the Brokenwood portfolio, without in any way competing with the existing styles.

shantell   ★★★★

1974 Melba Highway, Dixons Creek, Vic 3775 **region** Yarra Valley
phone (03) 5965 2264 **fax** (03) 5965 2331 **open** Thurs–Mon 10.30–5
winemaker Shan Shanmugam, Turid Shanmugam **production** 2000 **est.** 1980
product range ($15–30 CD) Semillon, Chardonnay, Glenlea Chardonnay, Pinot Noir, Shiraz, Cabernet Sauvignon, Sparkling.
summary The substantial and now fully mature Shantell vineyards provide the winery with a high-quality fruit source; part is sold to other Yarra Valley makers, the remainder vinified at Shantell. In January 1998 Shantell opened a new cellar door situated at 1974 Melba Highway, 50 metres along a service road from the highway proper. Chardonnay, Semillon and Cabernet Sauvignon are its benchmark wines, sturdily reliable, sometimes outstanding (witness the 1997 Chardonnay). Domestic and international distribution through Australian Prestige Wines.

Shantell Semillon

There is not a great deal of semillon grown in the Yarra Valley but what there is produces some attractive wines. In most vintages, as one would expect, the wine has a distinctly herbaceous feel akin to Sauvignon Blanc but enough intensity not to require oak. The Shantell wine is made in this fashion from half a hectare of 20-year-old vines.

▼▼▼♀ **1999** Extremely pale colour; the bouquet is light and crisp, with minerally overtones. The palate has some length but needs much time. It is almost certain it will develop excellently and merit much higher points when mature. **rating:** 83

best drinking 2003–2010 **best vintages** '88, '90, '91, '92, '93, '97 **drink with** Abalone • $15

Shantell Chardonnay

The Shantell vineyard has been producing high-quality chardonnay grapes for well over a decade, producing elegant fruit-driven wines which age with grace.

▼▼▼▼ **1998** Inevitably not quite in the same class as the '97, but a useful wine. Glowing yellow-green; the bouquet is clean, with a fine mix of melon and nectarine fruit. An elegant, fruit-driven wine with melon flavours and minimal oak influence. **rating:** 88

best drinking 2001–2008 **best vintages** '90, '92, '94, '97, '98 **drink with** Yarra Valley smoked trout • $24

Shantell Shiraz

Estate-grown, made and bottled; the vines are over 20 years old.

▼▼▼▼ **1998** Medium purple-red; the bouquet is clean, fresh, moderately intense, with dark cherry and plum fruit and just a touch of earth. The palate doesn't quite deliver the promise of the bouquet, lacking textural complexity at this relatively early stage of its life. May well improve if given the chance. **rating:** 86

best drinking 2003–2008 **best vintages** NA **drink with** Spiced lamb • $24

sharmans ★★★☆

Glenbothy, 175 Glenwood Road, Relbia, Tas 7258 **region** Northern Tasmania
phone (03) 6343 0773 **fax** (03) 6343 0773 **open** Weekends by appointment
winemaker James Chatto **production** 900 **est.** 1987
product range ($15–18 ML) Riesling, Sauvignon Blanc, Chardonnay, Pinot Noir.
summary Mike Sharman has very probably pioneered one of the most promising wine regions of Tasmania, not far south of Launceston but with a distinctly warmer climate than (say) Pipers Brook. Ideal north-facing slopes are home to a vineyard now approaching 3 hectares, most still to come into bearing. The few wines produced in sufficient quantity to be sold promise much for the future.

shaw & smith ★★★★★

Lot 4 Jones Road, Balhannah, SA 5242 **region** Adelaide Hills
phone (08) 8398 0500 **fax** (08) 8398 0600 **open** Not
winemaker Martin Shaw, Willy Lunn **production** 22 000 **est.** 1989
product range ($20–30 R) Sauvignon Blanc, Unoaked Chardonnay, Reserve Chardonnay, Incognito Merlot.
summary Has progressively moved from a contract grape growing base to estate production with the development of a 40-hectare vineyard at Woodside in the Adelaide Hills. Wine quality has been exemplary throughout, and the wines have wide international distribution including the UK, Italy, Japan, the US, Canada, Hong Kong and Malaysia.

Shaw & Smith Sauvignon Blanc

Since 1997 this has been an estate-grown wine from Shaw & Smith Woodside Vineyard but has been a leader in its category since 1992.

▼▼▼▼♀ **1999** Light green-yellow; the bouquet is light but fragrant, with a mix of gooseberry and more minerally notes. A perfectly weighted and balanced wine on the palate, with flavours tracking those of the bouquet and good length. **rating:** 93

best drinking 2000–2001 **best vintages** '92, '93, '95, '97, '99 **drink with** Grilled whiting • $20

Shaw & Smith Reserve Chardonnay

First made in 1992 and undoubtedly merits the Reserve designation. Using fruit from Geoff Hardy's vineyard, winemaker Martin Shaw applies the full gamut of Burgundian techniques of barrel-fermentation, extended time on yeast lees and partial malolactic fermentation, using only finest French oak. A mini vertical tasting in January 1997 of all four vintages then released underlined how well these wines mature in bottle.

▼▼▼▼ **1998** Excellent, bright medium green-yellow; the bouquet is stylish and smooth, with perfectly balanced and integrated fruit and oak. A medium-bodied, elegant wine on the palate, essentially fruit-driven, with melon and cashew flavours. **rating:** 94

best drinking 2000–2005 **best vintages** '92, '94, '95, '96, '97, '98 **drink with** Baked schnapper • $27

Shaw & Smith Incognito Merlot

1998 was the inaugural release from the 2 hectares of merlot established at the Woodside Vineyard in the Adelaide Hills. Very clever packaging gives a sophisticated, Italianate feel to the bottle.

▼▼▼▽ **1998** Medium red-purple; the moderately intense savoury/berry/leafy bouquet has obvious varietal character. The palate, however, is on another plane, with ripe, silky tannins giving the texture and structure of first class Merlot. The gently sweet savoury berry flavours are supported by positive oak. An impressive debut. **rating:** 91

best drinking 2002–2008 **best vintages** '98 **drink with** All things Italian • $25

shottesbrooke ★★★★

Bagshaws Road, McLaren Flat, SA 5171 **region** McLaren Vale
phone (08) 8383 0002 **fax** (08) 8383 0222 **open** Mon–Fri 10–4.30, weekends and public holidays 11–5
winemaker Nick Holmes **production** 8000 **est.** 1984
product range ($15–19.50 CD) Fleurieu Sauvignon Blanc, Chardonnay, Eliza Shiraz, Shiraz, Merlot, Cabernet Merlot Malbec.
summary Now the full-time business of former Ryecroft winemaker Nick Holmes; the grapes grown on his vineyard at Myoponga, at their best, show clear berry fruit, subtle oak and a touch of elegance. A compact, handsome new winery was erected prior to the 1997 vintage. Exports to the UK and the US supplement distribution through all Australian States.

Shottesbrooke Fleurieu Sauvignon Blanc

Unwooded and with masses of fruit flavour.

▼▼▼▼ **1999** Light green-yellow; the bouquet is clean and crisp, with herb aromas; the palate is in typical Shottesbrooke style, herbaceous, not flamboyant, but well balanced. **rating:** 86

best drinking 2000–2001 **best vintages** '95, '98 **drink with** Baby octopus • $15

Shottesbrooke Chardonnay

Produced from 3.6 hectares of estate plantings. The fruit is distinctive, citrussy to the point of Sauvignon Blanc, but lends itself to the Chablis-style subtle oak treatment, apparently with partial barrel-fermentation.

▼▼▼▼ **1999** Medium yellow-green; the bouquet is quite complex but in a gentle, laid-back fashion, with fruit and oak balanced and integrated, sliding into a gentle fig, melon and cashew-flavoured palate. **rating:** 86

best drinking 2000–2003 **best vintages** NA **drink with** King George whiting • $15.50

Shottesbrooke Merlot

A wine which has been part of the Shottesbrooke portfolio for some years now, but, for whatever reason, has not featured in prior tastings.

▼▼▼▼ **1999** Medium red-purple; the bouquet has clean, ripe fruit but is not particularly distinctive; the palate, however, is excellent, with plenty of ripe, sweet fleshy berry fruit offset by nicely balanced and flavoured oak. Scores particularly well for its overall structure and weight. **rating:** 89

best drinking 2002–2009 **best vintages** '99 **drink with** Baked ham • $15.50

🐌 silk hill NR

324 Motor Road, Deviot, Tas 7275 (postal) **region** Northern Tasmania
phone (03) 6394 7385 **fax** (03) 6326 2350 **open** Not
winemaker Gavin Scott **production** NA **est.** 1990
product range Pinot Noir.
summary Pharmacist Gavin Scott has been a weekend and holiday viticulturist for many years, having established the Glengarry Vineyard which he sold, and then establishing the half-hectare Silk Hill (formerly Silkwood Vineyard) in 1989, planted exclusively to pinot noir. Growing and making Pinot Noir and fishing will keep him occupied when he sells his pharmacy business.

Silk Hill Pinot Noir

Phil Laing in his book *Tasmanian Wines* quotes Gavin Scott as saying 'basically I'm a hobbyist trying to make Pinot Noir I like. Texture is crucial; Pinot Noir can have richness but it should retain charm.' As Scott himself also notes, the '98 vintage is a return to the class of the '94 and '95 vintages.

▼▼▼▼ 1998 Medium purple-red; attractive, spiced plum fruit aromas are woven through oak; the palate is quite racy, with great style and length. Just a tad more sweetness to the mid palate fruit would have justified even higher points.   **rating:** 85

best drinking 2000–2003 **drink with** Rabbit pie • $NA

silvan winery   NR

Lilydale–Silvan Road, Silvan, Vic 3795 **region** Yarra Valley
phone (03) 9737 9392 **open** Weekends, public holidays 11–6
winemaker John Vigliaroni **production** 500 **est.** 1993
product range ($8 CD) Chardonnay, Pinot Noir, Cabernet, Cabernet Shiraz Merlot, Merlot.
summary One of the newest and smallest of the Yarra Valley wineries; tastings are held in the Vigliaronis' spacious Italian villa.

simon hackett   ★★★☆

Budgens Road, McLaren Vale, SA 5171 **region** McLaren Vale
phone (08) 8323 7712 **fax** (08) 8323 7713 **open** Wed–Sun 11–5
winemaker Simon Hackett **production** 14 000 **est.** 1981
product range ($12–35 R) Barossa Valley Semillon, Barossa Valley Chardonnay, McLaren Vale Shiraz, McLaren Vale Anthony's Reserve Shiraz, McLaren Vale Old Vine Grenache, McLaren Vale Cabernet Sauvignon, McLaren Vale Foggo Road Cabernet Sauvignon.
summary In 1998 Simon Hackett acquired the former Taranga winery in McLaren Vale, which has made his winemaking life a great deal easier. He also has 8 hectares of estate vines and has contract growers in McLaren Vale, the Adelaide Hills and the Barossa Valley, with another 32 hectares of vines.

Simon Hackett Barossa Valley Semillon
One of those relatively rare Barossa Valley Semillons made without American oak, and with little evidence of skin contact and/or lees contact.
▼▼▼♀ 1999 Light green-yellow; the bouquet is clean and crisp, with spicy herb aromas; the palate has clear varietal character in a light-bodied frame, and has length and persistence.   **rating:** 82

best drinking 2000–2003 **best vintages** NA **drink with** Summer salads • $12

Simon Hackett McLaren Vale Shiraz
A wine made in the 'what you see is what you get' mould.
▼▼▼♀ 1998 Medium red-purple, bright and clear; the bouquet offers fresh, clean ripe cherry fruit and subtle oak, the palate ripe, sweet and fresh. The wine gives the impression of having spent some time on stainless steel and should soften and open up with a few years in bottle.   **rating:** 84

best drinking 2002–2007 **best vintages** NA **drink with** Lamb cutlets • $15

Simon Hackett McLaren Vale Anthony's Reserve Shiraz
A special bottling named in memory of Simon Hackett's late brother. Appropriately, significantly the best of the current releases from Simon Hackett.
▼▼▼▼ 1998 Medium to full red-purple; a big, concentrated and ripe bouquet with sweet leather and liquorice fruit supported by vanilla American oak. The palate is firm, with slightly grippy tannins on the finish, but has enough fruit to carry the wine until the tannins soften. Well-handled oak is another positive.   **rating:** 89

best drinking 2003–2013 **best vintages** '98 **drink with** Kangaroo fillet • $25

sinclair wines   NR

Graphite Road, Glenoran, WA 6258 **region** Pemberton, Warren Valley and Manjimup
phone (08) 9421 1399 **fax** (08) 9421 1191 **open** By appointment
winemaker Brenden Smith **production** 2500 **est.** 1993
product range ($10–22 CD) Sauvignon Blanc, Chardonnay, Unwooded Chardonnay, Cabernet Sauvignon.
summary Sinclair Wines is the child of Darelle Sinclair, a science teacher, wine educator and graduate viticulturist from Charles Sturt University, and John Healy, a lawyer, traditional jazz musician and graduand wine marketing student of Adelaide University, Roseworthy Campus. Five hectares of estate plantings are coming into production, with the first wines released in August 1998.

Sinclair Glenoran Sauvignon Blanc

A promising wine from first-crop vines.

♥♥♥♡ 1999 Light straw with a suspicion of a touch of pinking; the palate is light, clean and faintly tropical; the palate is light, with some mineral/dusty characters, but also has surprising persistence. **rating:** 82

best drinking 2000–2001 **best vintages** NA **drink with** Shellfish • $14

Sinclair Glenoran Cabernet Sauvignon

Likewise, a first release for Sinclair Wines; a winner of three bronze medals.

♥♥♥♡ 1998 Medium red-purple; the bouquet is fresh, with earthy/leafy fruit and a hint of charry oak. The palate is dominated by its fairly high acidity, and given its 12.2 degrees alcohol, seems to have been picked before optimum ripeness. **rating:** 80

best drinking 2000–2003 **best vintages** NA **drink with** Veal sausages • $18.50

sittella wines NR

100 Barrett Road, Herne Hill, WA 6056 **region** Swan District
phone (08) 9296 2600 **fax** (08) 9296 2600 **open** Thurs–Sun and most public holidays 11–4
winemaker Candy Johnsson (Contract) **production** 1000 **est.** 1998
product range ($11.95–14.95 CD) Chenin Blanc, Semillon, Verdelho, Chardonnay, Shiraz, Tawny Port.
summary Perth couple Simon and Maaike Berns acquired a 7-hectare block at Herne Hill, making the first wine in February 1998 and opening the most attractive cellar-door facility later in the year. They also own the Wildberry Springs Estate vineyard in the Margaret River region, which commenced to provide grapes from the 1999 vintage.

s kidman wines NR

Riddoch Highway, Coonawarra, SA 5263 **region** Coonawarra
phone (08) 8736 5071 **fax** (08) 8736 5070 **open** 7 days 9–5
winemaker John Innes (Contract) **production** 7000 **est.** 1984
product range ($11–18 CD) Riesling, Sauvignon Blanc, Cabernet Sauvignon, Shiraz.
summary One of the district pioneers, with a 16-hectare estate vineyard which is now fully mature. No recent tastings; limited retail distribution in Melbourne and Adelaide.

skillogalee ★★★★

Off Hughes Park Road, Sevenhill via Clare, SA 5453 **region** Clare Valley
phone (08) 8843 4311 **fax** (08) 8843 4343 **open** 7 days 10–5
winemaker Dave Palmer **production** 7000 **est.** 1970
product range ($13.50–24.50 CD) Riesling, Late Picked Riesling, Gewurztraminer, Chardonnay, Sparkling Riesling, Shiraz, The Cabernets, Fortifieds.
summary David and Diana Palmer purchased the small hillside stone winery from the George family at the end of the 1980s and have capitalised to the full on the exceptional fruit quality of the Skillogalee vineyards. The winery also has a well-patronised lunchtime restaurant. All of the wines are generous and full flavoured, particularly the reds.

Skillogalee Riesling

The principal wine of Skillogalee, produced from 8 hectares of estate grapes which wind up and down the steep hills of the Skilly Valley and which are now fully mature. This particular wine comes from the highest slopes of the vineyard at around 500 metres; the vines are hand-pruned and the grapes hand-picked. The style is consistently at the fuller end of the Clare Valley spectrum, honest, generous and relatively quick-maturing.

♥♥♥♥ 1999 Medium yellow-green; a powerful bouquet ranging through mineral, herb and lime introduces a big-framed wine with lots of citrus/lime fruit, closing with a touch of grip. Winner of a gold and two silver medals at 1999 wine shows. **rating:** 88

best drinking 2000–2006 **best vintages** '80, '84, '87, '90, '92, '97, '99 **drink with** Quiche Lorraine • $15

Skillogalee Shiraz

The hillside vineyards of Skillogalee, now over 20 years old, should by rights produce very concentrated and powerful red wines. Has been a consistent gold medal winner.

♥♥♥♥♡ 1997 Excellent bright but deep red-purple; there is typically concentrated Clare fruit on the bouquet, quite plummy, and oak in support. An excellent young wine on the palate, fruit-driven and not extractive. The oak is subtle, the tannins well balanced. **rating:** 90

best drinking 2005–2012 **best vintages** NA **drink with** Rich game • $24.50

Skillogalee The Cabernets

Predominantly Cabernet Sauvignon, with a small percentage of estate-grown Cabernet Franc and Malbec making up the blend. The style is relatively light bodied, often with distinctly minty overtones, balanced by a touch of American oak. The '96 has won three gold medals (Perth, Rutherglen and Brisbane).

♥♥♥♥ 1997 Medium red-purple; the bouquet is moderately intense, with gentle berry aromas and a hint of chocolate. A wine which swells nicely in the mouth; blackberry and chocolate flavours, nicely balanced tannins and subtle oak do the job nicely.   **rating: 89**

best drinking 2002–2009 **best vintages** '84, '87, '90, '93, '96, '97 **drink with** Yearling steak • $24.50

smithbrook   ★★★☆

Smith Brook Road, Middlesex via Manjimup, WA 6258 **region** Pemberton, Warren Valley and Manjimup
phone (08) 9772 3557 **fax** (08) 9772 3579 **open** By appointment
winemaker Michael Symons **production** 12 000 **est.** 1988
product range ($15–28 R) Sauvignon Blanc, Chardonnay, Early Release Chardonnay, Merlot, Cabernet Merlot, Cabernet Sauvignon.
summary Smithbrook is a major player in the Pemberton region, with 60 hectares of vines in production. A majority interest was acquired by Petaluma in 1997 but will continue its role as a contract grower for other companies, as well as supplying Petaluma's needs and making relatively small amounts of wine under its own label. Perhaps the most significant change has been the removal of Pinot Noir from the current range of products, and the introduction of Merlot. National distribution through Negociants; exports to the UK and Japan.

Smithbrook Sauvignon Blanc

First made in 1998; stainless steel-fermented and early-bottled, in a no-frills style.

♥♥♥�♀ 1999 Medium yellow-green; the bouquet is soft, tending tropical, even with a hint of banana; the palate is pleasant but lacks intensity until kicking into slightly sharp acidity on the finish.   **rating: 82**

best drinking Drink now **best vintages** NA **drink with** Sashimi • $15

Smithbrook Cabernet Sauvignon

A blend of 88 per cent Cabernet Sauvignon, 7 per cent Petit Verdot and 5 per cent Cabernet Franc.

♥♥♥♀ 1998 Bright purple-red; the bouquet is very youthful, fresh and seems slightly unfinished, as if it had spent considerable time in stainless steel. The palate has good fruit in a bright red berry spectrum but again feels curiously undermade.   **rating: 84**

best drinking 2002–2007 **best vintages** NA **drink with** Lamb fillet • $23

☙ smithleigh vineyard   NR

53 Osborne Road, Lane Cove, NSW 2066 (postal) **region** Lower Hunter Valley
phone 0418 411 382 **fax** (02) 9420 2014 **open** Not
winemaker Andrew Margan (Contract) **production** 4000 **est.** 1997
product range ($11.50–14 ML) Old Vine Hunter Semillon, Verdelho, Chardonnay, Shiraz.
summary As the name suggests, a partnership between Rod and Ivija Smith and John and Jan Leigh, which purchased the long-established vineyard from Southcorp in 1996. A lot of work in the vineyard, and skilled contract-winemaking by Andrew Margan, brought immediate results with the 1998 Old Vine Semillon, which won a silver medal at both the Hunter Valley and Cowra Wine Shows, demonstrating very considerable power and flavour.

snowy river winery   NR

Rockwell Road, Berridale, NSW 2628 **region** Other Wineries of NSW
phone (02) 6456 5041 **fax** (02) 6456 5005 **open** 7 days 10–5
winemaker Contract **production** 2500 **est.** 1984
product range ($10–20 CD) Alpine Dry White, Semillon, Sauvignon Blanc, Semillon Chardonnay, Müller Thurgau Sylvaner, Sieger Rebe [sic], Rhine Riesling Auslese, Snow Bruska, Port.
summary Claimed the only Eiswein to have been made in Australia, picked on 8 June 1990 after a frost of −8°C. Also makes a Trocken Beeren Auslese [sic] picked mid-May from the vineyard situated on the banks of the Snowy River, one hour from Mount Kosciusko. One suspects many of the wines are purchased from other makers.

somerset hill wines   NR

891 McLeod Road, Denmark, WA 6333 **region** Great Southern
phone (08) 9840 9388 **fax** (08) 9840 9394 **open** 7 days 11–5
winemaker Brenden Smith (Contract) **production** 2000 **est.** 1995
product range ($19.50–24 CD) Sauvignon Blanc, Chardonnay (Unwooded), Semillon, Harmony (Chardonnay, Semillon, Sauvignon Blanc), Pinot Noir.

summary Graham Upson commenced planting 9 hectares of pinot noir, chardonnay, semillon, merlot and sauvignon blanc in 1995, and Somerset Hill Wines duly opened its limestone cellar-door sales area with sweeping views out over the ocean. It has to be said the packaging and labelling does not do justice to the quality of the wines.

Somerset Hill Semillon
Produced from a little under 1 hectare of estate plantings, and a striking first vintage.
TTTT 1999 Light to medium green-yellow; a highly aromatic bouquet with a mix of flowers, herbs and passionfruit leads into a potent, lively and striking herb/grass-flavoured palate. **rating:** 84
best drinking 2000–2003 **best vintages** NA **drink with** Stuffed capsicum • $21

Somerset Hill Sauvignon Blanc
A little over 2 hectares of sauvignon blanc have been planted, second only to chardonnay (more than 5 hectares). Made in similar style to the Semillon.
TTTT 1999 Light to medium yellow-green; the bouquet is quite fragrant, with tropical passionfruit aromatics; the palate offers a mix of passionfruit and some crushed leaf flavours; a little different from the run of the mill. **rating:** 83
best drinking 2000–2001 **best vintages** NA **drink with** Spicy calamari • $22

sorrenberg   NR
Alma Road, Beechworth, Vic 3747 **region** Alpine Valleys and Beechworth
phone (03) 5728 2278 **fax** (03) 5728 2278 **open** Mon–Fri by appointment, most weekends 1–5 (phone first)
winemaker Barry Morey **production** 1500 **est.** 1986
product range ($22–34 CD) Sauvignon Blanc Semillon, Chardonnay, Gamay, Cabernet Sauvignon, Havelock Hills Shiraz.
summary Barry and Jan Morey made their first wines in 1989 from the 2.5-hectare vineyard situated on the outskirts of Beechworth. No recent tastings, but the wines have a good reputation and loyal clientele.

southern grand estate   NR
c/o 111 Goulburn Street, Sydney, NSW 2333 **region** Upper Hunter Valley
phone (02) 9282 0987 **fax** (02) 9211 8130 **open** Not
winemaker Jon Reynolds (Contract) **production** 1600 **est.** 1997
product range ($16.50–19.95 R) Semillon, Chardonnay, Cabernet Sauvignon.
summary Southern Grand Estate is the successor of the long-lost Hollydene Estate, the label of which (though not the vineyards) disappeared almost 20 years ago. The Kho family purchased the Hollydene vineyard from Orlando Wyndham in 1997 and, using their long involvement in the Australian hospitality and hotel industry, are planning to build a holiday and convention resort on the property. In the meantime, winemaking is in the capable hands of Jon Reynolds.

spring vale vineyards   ★★★☆
Spring Vale, Swansea, Tas 7190 **region** Southern Tasmania
phone (03) 6257 8208 **fax** (03) 6257 8598 **open** Weekends, holidays 10–5
winemaker Andrew Hood (Contract) **production** 3000 **est.** 1986
product range ($19.50–29.50 CD) Gewurztraminer, Chardonnay, Pinot Gris, Pinot Noir.
summary Rodney Lyne has progressively established 1.5 hectares each of pinot noir and chardonnay and then added half a hectare each of gewurztraminer and pinot gris; the latter produced a first crop in 1998. After frost problems, Spring Vale is now enjoying the fruits of two excellent vintages in 1997 and 1998.

Spring Vale Chardonnay
Produced from a little over 1 hectare of estate plantings which have recovered from two years of very low yields.
TTTT 1998 Strong green-yellow; complex powerful fruit on the bouquet is followed by a strongly flavoured, rich palate, albeit without the superb structure of the '97. **rating:** 86
best drinking 2001–2005 **best vintages** '97 **drink with** Veal or pork • $25

Spring Vale Pinot Noir
Through both conviction and necessity, Andrew Hood (the Spring Vale contract-winemaker) destems and conventionally ferments the Pinot Noirs he makes, thereby excluding whole bunches. One can hardly argue with the approach, particularly when the grapes come from Tasmania's east coast, one of the most favoured spots for pinot noir in Australia.

▼▼▼▼ **1998** Excellent red-purple colour; strong, ripe plummy fruit with some spicy notes is followed by a palate on which those spicy characters seem to gain in intensity. The wine has good balance, mouthfeel and length; all four judges at the Tasmanian Wines Show 2000 gave it identical silver medal points (17/20). Another tasting note from another occasion gave a wildly inconsistent view of the wine (green characters), for which I have no explanation. **rating: 85**

best drinking 2001–2005 **best vintages** NA **drink with** Roast duck • $29.50

springviews wine NR

Woodlands Road, Porongurup, WA 6324 **region** Great Southern
phone (08) 9853 2088 **fax** (08) 9853 2098 **open** 7 days 10–5
winemaker Howard Park (Contract) **production** NA **est.** 1994
product range ($15–18 CD) Riesling, Chardonnay, Cabernet Sauvignon.
summary Andy and Alice Colquhoun planted their 5-hectare vineyard (2 hectares each of chardonnay and cabernet sauvignon and 1 hectare of riesling) in 1994. The wine is made at Howard Park by John Wade and is sold through the cellar door and mailing list.

stanley brothers ★★★

Barossa Valley Way, Tanunda, SA 5352 **region** Barossa Valley
phone (08) 8563 3375 **fax** (08) 8563 3758 **open** 7 days 9–5
winemaker Lindsay Stanley **production** 10 000 **est.** 1994
product range ($11–25 CD) Sylvaner, Full Sister Semillon, Chardonnay Pristine, John Hancock Shiraz, Thoroughbred Cabernet, Cabernet Shiraz, Late Harvest Sylvaner; NV Black Sheep; Sparkling, Fortifieds.
summary Former Anglesey winemaker and industry veteran Lindsay Stanley established his own business in the Barossa Valley when he purchased (and renamed) the former Kroemer Estate in late 1994. As one would expect, the wines are competently made. Twenty-one hectares of estate plantings have provided virtually all of the grapes for the business. Exports to Canada, France, Hong Kong, Singapore and the US.

stanton & killeen wines ★★★★☆

Jacks Road, Murray Valley Highway, Rutherglen, Vic 3685 **region** Rutherglen and Glenrowan
phone (02) 6032 9457 **fax** (02) 6032 8018 **open** Mon–Sat 9–5, Sun 10–5
winemaker Chris Killeen **production** 20 000 **est.** 1875
product range ($11.50–37.50 CD) A red wine and fortified wine specialist, though offering Chardonnay, Riesling, White Frontignac and Dry White as well as Cabernet Sauvignon, Shiraz, Durif. Fortified wines include Rutherglen White Port, Ruby Port, Muscat and Vintage Port; the Classic range of Rutherglen Tawny Port, Tokay, Muscat and Grand Muscat are now available in 500-ml bottles.
summary Chris Killeen has skilfully expanded the portfolio of Stanton & Killeen but without in any way compromising its reputation as a traditional maker of smooth, rich reds, some of Australia's best Vintage Ports, and attractive, fruity Muscats and Tokays.

Stanton & Killeen Durif

A rare grape variety brought to northeast Victoria about the turn of the century, and which may or may not be the same as California's petite syrah. Wherever grown, it makes a massively dense and potent wine, characteristics enhanced by the climate of northeast Victoria, to which it is ideally suited. Yet another example of the all-round winemaking skills of Chris Killeen, topping the Other Red Class at the 1999 *Winewise* Small Makers Competition, and doing so by a wide margin.
▼▼▼▼♡ **1998** Strong red-purple; the rich and savoury/briary/earthy overtones to the chocolate, mint and berry aromas of the bouquet lead into a very ripe, luscious and slightly jammy palate; happily, the tannins are nicely balanced. Gold medals Melbourne and Ballarat 1999. **rating: 90**

best drinking 2003–2013 **best vintages** '97 **drink with** Two-inch-thick rump steak • $25.50

staughton vale vineyard NR

20 Staughton Vale Road, Anakie, Vic 3221 **region** Geelong
phone (03) 5284 1229 **fax** (03) 5284 1229 **open** Fri–Mon and public holidays 10–5 or by appointment
winemaker Paul Chambers **production** 1800 **est.** 1986
product range NA.
summary Paul Chambers has 6 hectares of grapes, with the accent on the classic Bordeaux mix of cabernet sauvignon, merlot, cabernet franc and petit verdot, although chardonnay and pinot noir are also planted. Weekend lunches available at the Staughton Cottage Restaurant.

steels creek estate   NR

1 Sewell Road, Steels Creek, Vic 3775 **region** Yarra Valley
phone (03) 5965 2448 **fax** (03) 5965 2448 **open** Weekends and public holidays 10–6
winemaker Simon Peirce **production** 400 **est.** 1981
product range ($15–20 CD) Colombard, Chardonnay, Shiraz, Cabernet Sauvignon.
summary While only a tiny operation, with 1.7 hectares of vineyard planted at various times between 1981 and 1994, Steels Creek Estate has an on-site winery where the wines are made with assistance from consultants, but increasingly by Simon Peirce, who has completed his associate diploma in Applied Science (Winegrowing) at Charles Sturt University. Steels Creek 1996 Cabernet Sauvignon won a silver medal at the Southern Victorian Wine Show in 1998, an excellent outcome for what was an extremely difficult vintage with the late-ripening varieties.

stefano lubiana   ★★★★

60 Rowbottoms Road, Granton, Tas 7030 **region** Southern Tasmania
phone (03) 6263 7457 **fax** (03) 6263 7430 **open** 7 days 9–5 (closed public holidays)
winemaker Steve Lubiana **production** 8000 **est.** 1990
product range ($17–35 CD) Chardonnay, Riesling, Pinot Noir, Vintage Brut; also Primavera label are Riesling, Sauvignon Blanc, Chardonnay and Pinot Noir.
summary Steve Lubiana has moved from one extreme to the other, having run Lubiana Wines at Moorook in the South Australian Riverland for many years before moving to the Tamar Valley region of Tasmania to set up a substantial winery which acts as both contract-maker and maker for its own label wines, and which was also known as Granton Vineyard. He has progressively grown his contract-winemaking business, and in particular the sparkling wine side. For the past three years, has made the trophy-winning sparkling wine at the Tasmanian Wines Show, first for Barrington Estate and (in 1998) for Elsewhere Vineyard. The estate-produced Stefano Lubiano wines come from 5.5 hectares of beautifully located vineyards sloping down to the Derwent River.

Stefano Lubiana Primavera Sauvignon Blanc

Produced from estate-grown grapes in a moist, cool vintage.
♥♥♥♡ **1999** Light green-yellow; an unusual bouquet, almost raisiny/grapey and showing the influence of botrytis. There are some sweet fruit flavours on the palate but overall seems to lack focus, doubtless due to the impact of a degree of botrytis.   **rating:** 81
best drinking 2000–2001 **best vintages** NA **drink with** Smoked salmon •$20

Stefano Lubiana Chardonnay

Estate-grown on the backs of the Derwent, and made with a skilled, gentle touch.
♥♥♥♥ **1998** Medium to full yellow-green; the bouquet is quite complex, with the dual influence of barrel-fermentation and malolactic fermentation investing the wine with cashew characters. The medium-bodied palate is well balanced, with good length and subtle oak.   **rating:** 86
best drinking 2000–2005 **best vintages** NA **drink with** Chinese prawns •$20

Stefano Lubiana Pinot Noir

First made in the 1996 vintage from estate-grown grapes. It is fermented partly in an open vat and partly in a closed tank, predominantly using wild (or native) yeasts. Around 350 cases made.
♥♥♥♥♡ **1998** Deep purple-red; the bouquet is redolent of very ripe, deep plummy fruit, even to the point of raisin. The palate is extremely rich and powerful, with more of that ultra-ripe fruit flavour. It trembles on the brink of over-ripeness, and it will be fascinating to watch the development of the wine.   **rating:** 92
best drinking 1999–2004 **best vintages** '98 **drink with** Jugged hare •$32

Stefano Lubiana Primavera Pinot Noir

Estate-grown and wild yeast-fermented at relatively high temperatures.
♥♥♥♥♡ **1999** Excellent, strong purple-red; very positive varietal character in the plum and cherry spectrum comes through on the bouquet; a tightly structured and youthful Pinot Noir with good length and excellent development potential. Competitively priced.   **rating:** 90
best drinking 2002–2006 **best vintages** '99 **drink with** Breast of squab •$20

steins   ★★★

Pipeclay Lane, Mudgee, NSW 2850 **region** Mudgee
phone (02) 6373 3991 **fax** (02) 6373 3709 **open** 7 days 10–4.30
winemaker Robert Stein, Phil Kerney **production** 6000 **est.** 1976

product range ($10–16.50 CD) Semillon, Semillon Riesling, Traminer, Chardonnay, Late Harvest Riesling, Rosé, Mt Buckaroo Dry Red, Shiraz, Cabernet Sauvignon and a range of Muscats and Ports; Robert Stein range of Semillon, Chardonnay, Shiraz, Cabernet Shiraz, Cabernet Sauvignon.

summary The sweeping panorama from the winery is its own reward for cellar-door visitors. Right from the outset Steins has been a substantial operation but has managed to sell the greater part of its production direct from the winery by mail order and cellar door, with limited retail distribution in Sydney, but nowhere else. Wine quality has been very good from time to time, with the Shiraz and Chardonnay variously coming out on top.

Robert Stein Chardonnay

A reliable wine which, in years such as 1995, reaches unexpected heights. Usually sold at cellar door with between two and three years bottle age.

🍷🍷🍷🍷 **1997** Medium yellow-green; the bouquet is quite complex, with nutty butterscotch vanilla aromas, characters which come through on the light- to medium-bodied palate, which does thin out a little on the finish.

rating: 82

best drinking 2000–2003 **best vintages** '95 **drink with** Rack of veal • $15

Robert Stein Shiraz

Like the Chardonnay, sometimes soars above its station. Estate-produced from 25-year-old vines.

🍷🍷🍷🍷 **1998** Medium red-purple; there is lots of American oak on the bouquet which is possibly derived from innerstaves or chips, both perfectly legal. The palate opens with a mix of cherry, berry and plum fruit, but is then overtaken by oak on the finish. A pity, because there is some very good base wine here.

rating: 83

best drinking 2003–2008 **best vintages** '91 **drink with** Lamb • $15

stephen john wines   ★★★

Government Road, Watervale, SA 5452 **region** Clare Valley
phone (08) 8843 0105 **fax** (08) 8843 0105 **open** 7 days 11–5
winemaker Stephen John **production** 5000 **est.** 1994
product range ($10–40 CD) Watervale Riesling, Watervale Pedro Ximinez, Chardonnay, Clare Valley Shiraz, Estate Reserve Shiraz, Merlot, Clare Valley Cabernet Sauvignon, Estate Reserve Cabernet Sauvignon, Traugott Cuvée Sparkling Burgundy.
summary The John family is one of the best-known names in the Barossa Valley, with branches running Australia's best cooperage (AP John & Sons) and providing the chief winemaker of Lindemans (Philip John) and the former chief winemaker of Quelltaler (Stephen John). Stephen and Rita John have now formed their own family business in the Clare Valley, based on a 6-hectare vineyard overlooking the town of Watervale and supplemented by modest intake from a few local growers. The cellar-door sales area is housed in an 80-year-old stable which has been renovated and is full of rustic charm. The significantly increased production has led to the appointment of distributors in each of the eastern States, and to limited exports to the US.

Stephen John Estate Reserve Shiraz

Sits alongside a newly introduced Estate Reserve Cabernet Sauvignon. Shiraz has always been the best wine in the Stephen John stable, and this Reserve version is no exception to the rule.

🍷🍷🍷🍷 **1998** Medium red-purple; the moderately intense bouquet is fruit-driven, with sweet berry and chocolate aromas; the palate, too, derives its character from the quite sweet dark cherry and plum fruit, again with a hint of chocolate; the oak is subtle, the tannins soft.

rating: 85

best drinking 2003–2008 **best vintages** NA **drink with** Moussaka • $40

sterling heights   ★★★★

Faulkners Road, Winkleigh, Tas 7275 **region** Northern Tasmania
phone (03) 6396 3214 **fax** (03) 6396 3214 **open** By appointment
winemaker Moorilla Estate (Contract) **production** 400 **est.** 1988
product range ($11–19 CD) Riesling, Chardonnay, Breton Rosé, Pinot Noir.
summary With just over 1.5 hectares of vines, Sterling Heights will always be a small fish in a small pond. However, the early releases had considerable success in wine shows, and the quality is all one could expect.

stone ridge   ★★★

Limberlost Road, Glen Aplin, Qld 4381 **region** Granite Belt
phone (07) 4683 4211 **fax** (07) 4683 4211 **open** 7 days 10–5
winemaker Jim Lawrie, Anne Kennedy **production** 1950 **est.** 1981
product range ($10–40 CD) Under the Stone Ridge label Semillon, Chardonnay, Shiraz, Cabernet Malbec; under the Mount Sterling label Dry Red Shiraz.

summary Spicy Shiraz is the specialty of the doll's-house-sized winery, but the portfolio has progressively expanded over recent years to include two whites and the only Stanthorpe region Cabernet Malbec (and occasionally a straight varietal Malbec). No recent tastings.

stoney vineyard   NR

Campania, Tas 7026 **region** Southern Tasmania
phone (03) 6260 4174 **fax** (03) 6260 4390 **open** Mon–Fri 9–4, weekends by appointment
winemaker Peter Althaus **production** 5000 **est.** 1973
product range ($18–60 CD) Domaine A is the top label with Cabernet Sauvignon and Pinot Noir; second label is Stoney Vineyard with Aurora (wood-matured Sylvaner), Sauvignon Blanc, Pinot Noir, Cabernet Sauvignon.
summary The striking black label of the premium Stoney Vineyard wine, dominated by the single, multicoloured 'A', signified the change of ownership from George Park to Swiss businessman Peter Althaus. The NR rating for the winery is given in deference to Peter Althaus, who has no faith whatsoever in Australian wine judges or critics, and profoundly disagrees with their ratings. If I were bold enough to give a rating, it would not be less than four and a half stars. Retail distribution in Melbourne, Sydney and Perth; exports to Switzerland, China, the US and Singapore.

Stoney Vineyard Sauvignon Blanc

Produced, as are all the Stoney Vineyard wines, from estate-grown grapes picked very ripe. Destemmed, then crushed, and fermented in stainless steel.
▼▼▼▽ **1999** Light to medium yellow-green; there is plenty of ripe, solid fruit to the bouquet, the palate rich, with well-above-average texture. Small vines and low yields give this level of concentration.   **rating:** 82
best drinking 2000–2001 **best vintages** NA **drink with** Gravlax • $25

Stoney Vineyard Domaine A Pinot Noir

The concentration evident in the wine is no doubt due to the ultra-close spacing of the vines and their maturity.
▼▼▼▼ **1998** Medium to full red-purple; the bouquet is smooth and concentrated, with plummy fruit; the palate is likewise dense and concentrated, with layers of fruit. The wine is still locked up but should develop complexity as it ages. A wine which split opinions at the Tasmanian Wines Show 2000.   **rating:** 89
best drinking 2003–2008 **best vintages** NA **drink with** Ragout of venison • $60

stonier wines   ★★★★★

362 Frankston–Flinders Road, Merricks, Vic 3916 **region** Mornington Peninsula
phone (03) 5989 8300 **fax** (03) 5989 8709 **open** 7 days 12–5 (summer 11–5)
winemaker Tod Dexter **production** 22 000 **est.** 1978
product range ($18–39 CD) Chardonnay, Pinot Noir and Cabernet under the Stonier and Stonier Reserve labels.
summary Looked at across the range, Stonier is now the pre-eminent winery in the Mornington Peninsula; its standing is in turn based more or less equally on its Chardonnay and Pinot Noir under the Reserve label. The acquisition of a 70 per cent interest by Petaluma in 1998 has given both Stonier's (and the Mornington Peninsula as a whole) even greater credibility than hitherto. Exports to the UK and Asia.

Stonier Reserve Chardonnay

Produced from 3.5 hectares of estate-grown grapes and made using the full gamut of Burgundian techniques, including barrel-fermentation, lees contact and malolactic fermentation. The wines are exceptionally complex and stylish; successive vintages have all received accolades.
▼▼▼▼▽ **1998** Light green-yellow; there are perfumed, lifted barrel-ferment aromas together with high toast oak on the bouquet. The wine has good length, with ripe nectarine and cashew flavour; not particularly intense but is very well balanced.   **rating:** 92
best drinking 2000–2004 **best vintages** '86, '88, '91, '93, '94, '95, '96, '97, '98 **drink with** Milk-fed veal • $36

Stonier Reserve Pinot Noir

A wine of genuine style and complexity, partly created in the vineyard and partly in the winery. It is thus inevitably influenced by the variable Mornington Peninsula climate.
▼▼▼▽ **1998** Light to medium red-purple; there seemed to be distinct green tinges to the fruit on the bouquet, and the same characters come again on the palate. A major disappointment; was this a bad bottle?   **rating:** 83
best drinking 2000–2004 **best vintages** '90, '91, '92, '94, '95, '97 **drink with** Coq au vin • $39

stratherne vale estate   NR

Campbell Street, Caballing, WA 6312 **region** Other Wineries of WA
phone (08) 9881 2148 **fax** (08) 9881 3129 **open** Not
winemaker James Pennington (Contract) **production** 600 **est.** 1980
product range A single red wine made from a blend of Cabernet Sauvignon, Zinfandel, Merlot and Shiraz.
summary Stratherne Vale Estate stretches the viticultural map of Australia yet further. It is situated near Narrogin, which is north of the Great Southern region and south of the most generous extension of the Darling Ranges. The closest viticultural region of note is at Wandering, to the northeast.

strathkellar   NR

Murray Valley Highway, Cobram, Vic 3644 **region** Goulburn Valley
phone (03) 5873 5274 **fax** (03) 5873 5270 **open** 7 days 10–6
winemaker Chateau Tahbilk (Contract) **production** 2000 **est.** 1990
product range ($9–15 CD) Chenin Blanc, Chardonnay, Late Picked Chenin Blanc, Shiraz, Muscat, Tokay, Putters Port, Sparkling.
summary Dick Parkes planted his 5.5-hectare vineyard to chardonnay, shiraz and chenin blanc in 1990, and has the wine contract-made at Chateau Tahbilk by Alister Purbrick. The fact that the wines are made at Chateau Tahbilk is a sure guarantee of quality, and the prices are modest.

straws lane   NR

Corner Mount Macedon Road and Straws Lane, Hesket, Vic 3442 **region** Macedon Ranges
phone (03) 9654 9380 **fax** (03) 9663 6300 **open** Not
winemaker Stuart Anderson, Hanging Rock, Cope-Williams (Contract) **production** 1000 **est.** 1987
product range ($21–35 ML) Gewurztraminer, Macedon Blanc de Noirs, Pinot Noir.
summary The Straws Lane vineyard was planted 12 years ago, but the Straws Lane label is a relatively new arrival on the scene; after a highly successful 1995 vintage, adverse weather in 1996 and 1997 meant that little or no wine was made in those years, but the pace has picked up again with the excellent 1998 vintage. Stuart Anderson guides the making of the Pinot Noir, Hanging Rock Winery handles the Gewurztraminer and the sparkling wine base, and Cope-Williams looks after the tiraging and maturation of the sparkling wine. It's good to have co-operative neighbours.

stringy brae   NR

Sawmill Road, Sevenhill, SA 5453 **region** Clare Valley
phone (08) 8843 4313 **fax** (08) 8843 4319 **open** Weekends and public holidays 10–5, weekdays refer to road sign
winemaker Contract (Mitchell) **production** 1500 **est.** 1991
product range ($14–40 CD) Riesling, Shiraz, Sir Lancelot Shiraz, Mote Hill, Cabernet Sauvignon.
summary Donald and Sally Willson have established over 8 hectares of vineyards that since the 1996 vintage have produced all the grapes for their wines. (Previously grapes from Langhorne Creek were used.) The Australian domestic market is serviced direct by mail order, but the wines are exported to the UK, Singapore and the US.

stuart range estates   ★★★☆

67 William Street, Kingaroy, Qld 4610 **region** South Burnett and Other Wineries of Qld
phone (07) 4162 3711 **fax** (07) 4162 4811 **open** 7 days 9–5
winemaker Charles Williams **production** 5000 **est.** 1997
product range ($8–15 CD) Chardonnay, Goodger Vineyard Chardonnay, South Burnett Chardonnay, Range White and Range Red (both semi-sweet), Shiraz (unwooded), Cabernet Merlot.
summary Stuart Range Estates is a prime example of the extent and pace of change in the Queensland wine industry, coming from nowhere in 1997 to crushing just under 120 tonnes of grapes in its inaugural vintage in 1998, producing 7000 cases. The crush for 1999 was around 11 000 cases, the grapes being supplied by seven growers in the South Burnett Valley with 52 hectares planted by 1996. A state-of-the-art winery has been established within an old butter factory building. The barrel-fermented Chardonnay won the trophy for the Best Queensland White Wine in the annual *Courier-Mail* Top 100 Wine Competition. Very much a case of watch this space.

Stuart Range Estates Goodger Vineyard Chardonnay

Barrel-fermented in a mix of American and French barriques to good effect. There is very competent winemaking at work here.

🍷🍷🍷🍷 **1999** Medium yellow-green; a complex and stylish bouquet with strong barrel-ferment inputs giving a nutty cashew overlay to melon fruit on the bouquet. The fruit on the palate is lighter, showing how cleverly the oak has in fact been used, for it is not overly assertive and does allow the length of the fruit to express itself.

rating: 87

best drinking 2000–2002 **best vintages** NA **drink with** Char-grilled salmon • $15

Stuart Range Estates South Burnett Chardonnay

A cunning blend of stainless steel-fermented and unwooded Chardonnay with another portion barrel-fermented in French and American oak.

🍷🍷🍷🍷 **1999** Very light green-yellow; the aromas are light and fresh, with citrus and nectarine fruit and only the barest hint of oak. The palate is similarly lively, fresh and crisp, especially the bright acidity on the finish. Utterly belies its 13.5 degrees alcohol.

rating: 82

best drinking 1999–2002 **best vintages** NA **drink with** Thai food • $NA

stumpy gully ★★★☆

1247 Stumpy Gully Road, Moorooduc, Vic 3933 **region** Mornington Peninsula
phone (03) 5978 8429 **fax** (03) 5978 8419 **open** Weekends 11–5
winemaker Frank Zantvoort, Wendy Zantvoort **production** 2000 **est.** 1988
product range ($16–22 CD) Riesling, Sauvignon Blanc, Chardonnay, Encore Chardonnay, Marsanne, Pinot Grigio, Pinot Noir, Merlot Cabernet, Merlot Shiraz, Cabernet Sauvignon, Sangiovese.
summary Frank and Wendy Zantvoort have progressively established 9 hectares of vineyard planted to chardonnay, marsanne, sauvignon blanc, pinot noir, cabernet sauvignon and merlot, electing to sell 80 per cent of the production to local winemakers, and vinifying the remainder, with impressive results. The '97 Cabernet Sauvignon (84 points) neatly reflected the warm, dry vintage.

🐛 suckfizzle augusta NR

Lot 14 Kalkarrie Drive, Augusta, WA 6290 (PO Box 570, Margaret River, WA 6285) **region** Margaret River
phone (08) 9758 0303 **fax** (08) 9758 03040 **open** Not
winemaker Stuart Pym **production** 1500 **est.** 1997
product range ($30–40 R) Semillon Sauvignon Blanc, Cabernet Sauvignon.
summary First things first. The back label explains 'the name Suckfizzle has been snaffled from the fourteenth century monk and medico turned writer Rabelais and his infamous character the great lord Suckfizzle'. Suckfizzle is the joint venture of two well-known Margaret River winemakers who, in deference to their employers, do not identify themselves on any of the background material or the striking front and back labels of the wines.

Suckfizzle Augusta Semillon Sauvignon Blanc

Estate-grown and made in restricted quantities, using sophisticated oak handling techniques.

🍷🍷🍷🍷 **1997** Medium to full yellow-green; a very rich, opulent and ripe bouquet with a mix of gooseberry and nectarine fruit supported by subtle oak leads into a powerful, long and complex palate, the flavours repeating those of the bouquet. Positive, high-quality French oak adds to the attraction of the wine.

rating: 93

best drinking 2001–2007 **drink with** Marron • $32

summerfield ★★★★

Main Road, Moonambel, Vic 3478 **region** Pyrenees
phone (03) 5467 2264 **fax** (03) 5467 2380 **open** 7 days 9–6
winemaker Ian Summerfield, Mark Summerfield **production** 2300 **est.** 1979
product range ($14–29 CD) Sauvignon Blanc, Chardonnay, Trebbiano, Shiraz, Reserve Shiraz, Cabernet Shiraz, Cabernet Sauvignon, Reserve Cabernet.
summary A specialist red wine producer, the particular forte of which is Shiraz. The wines since 1988 have been consistently excellent, luscious and full bodied and fruit-driven but with a slice of vanillin oak to top them off.

Summerfield Sauvignon Blanc

Notwithstanding Summerfield's reputation as a red wine producer, it can do quite nicely with its straightforward Sauvignon Blanc.

🍷🍷🍷🍷 **1999** Very pale straw-green; the bouquet is light, crisp and delicate, with faint lemon and gooseberry aromas. The palate follows in precisely the same track, clean, light and sustained by just a flick of residual sugar. The only lack is of varietal fruit intensity.

rating: 83

best drinking 2000–2001 **best vintages** NA **drink with** Light seafood • $16.50

Summerfield Shiraz

Produced from a little over 3.5 hectares of estate plantings, with various label convolutions now in the past. There are simply two wines: a varietal Shiraz and a Reserve Shiraz.

▼▼▼▼ **1998** Medium red with a touch of purple. The bouquet is quite rich, opening with savoury notes but then moving through to berry and mint. It is the latter flavours that come through on the palate in typical central Victorian style, running through to a reasonably long finish. **rating: 85**

best drinking 2003–2008 best vintages '88, '90, '91, '92, '93, '94, '96, '97 drink with Beef stew • $23

Summerfield Reserve Shiraz

In a sign of the times, the Reserve Shiraz sells out on the mailing list before it even gets to cellar door, let alone retail outlets. You have to be quick.

▼▼▼▼♀ **1998** Dense red-purple; very concentrated berry and chocolate fruit on the bouquet leads into a commensurately ripe and concentrated palate with dark berry fruit predominant, and just a touch of mint. Fruit-driven; don't worry about the oak. **rating: 90**

best drinking 2002–2012 best vintages '98 drink with Venison pie • $29

Summerfield Reserve Cabernet

Sits alongside the Reserve Shiraz and is similarly priced, but inevitably does not scale quite the same heights.

▼▼▼▼ **1998** Medium red-purple; the bouquet is quite sweet, with redcurrant fruit flecked with leaf and mint. The palate oscillates between concentrated mint and berry fruit, finishing with firmish tannins. **rating: 85**

best drinking 2003–2013 best vintages NA drink with Osso bucco • $29

surveyor's hill winery   NR

215 Brooklands Road, Wallaroo, NSW 2618 **region** Canberra District
phone (02) 6230 2046 **fax** (02) 6230 2048 **open** Weekends and public holidays or by appointment
winemaker Hardys (Contract) **production** 1000 **est.** 1986
product range ($13–25 R) Riesling, Estate Dry White, Alexandra's Block Chardonnay, Touriga Dry Red, Shiraz, Cabernet Sauvignon.
summary Surveyor's Hill has 7.5 hectares of vineyard, but most of the grapes are sold to Hardys, which vinifies the remainder for Surveyor's Hill — which should guarantee the quality of the wines sold.

sutherland   ★★☆

Deasey's Road, Pokolbin, NSW 2321 **region** Lower Hunter Valley
phone (02) 4998 7650 **fax** (02) 4998 7603 **open** 6 days 10–4.30
winemaker Neil Sutherland, Nicholas Sutherland **production** 7000 **est.** 1979
product range ($15–40 CD) Chardonnay, Chenin Blanc, Chenin Cremant, Shiraz, Cabernet Shiraz, Cabernet Sauvignon.
summary With substantial and now fully mature vineyards to draw upon, Sutherland is a more or less consistent producer of generous, mainstream Hunter whites and reds, albeit with a high level of phenolic extraction.

sutherland smith wines   NR

Corner Falkners Road and Murray Valley Highway, Rutherglen, Vic 3685 **region** Rutherglen and Glenrowan
phone (03) 6032 8177 **fax** (03) 6032 8177 **open** Weekends 10–5 or by appointment
winemaker George Sutherland Smith **production** 1000 **est.** 1993
product range ($10.90–16.50 CD) Riesling, Josephine (Riesling Traminer), Chardonnay, Merlot, Cabernet Shiraz, Port.
summary George Sutherland Smith, for decades managing director and winemaker at All Saints, has opened up his own small business at Rutherglen, making wine in the refurbished Emu Plains winery, originally constructed in the 1850s. He draws upon fruit grown in a leased vineyard at Glenrowan and also from grapes grown in the King Valley.

⚘ symphonia wines   ★★★☆

Boggy Creek Road, Myrrhee, Vic 3732 **region** King Valley
phone (03) 5729 7579 **fax** (03) 5729 7519 **open** By appointment
winemaker Peter Read **production** 500 **est.** 1998
product range ($9–14 CD) Chardonnay Plus Viognier & Petit Manseng, Pinot Grigio, Quintus, Dry Red Bin 5, Merlot, Cabernet Plus Tannat & Merlot, Merlot Plus Cabernet & Tempranillo, Pinot Chardonnay Méthode Champenoise.

summary Peter Read and his family are veterans of the King Valley, commencing the development of their vineyard in 1981 to supply Brown Brothers. As a result of extensive trips to both Western and Eastern Europe Peter Read embarked on an ambitious project to trial a series of grape varieties little known in this country. The process of evaluation and experimentation continues, but Symphonia released the first small quantities of wines in mid-1998, and will slowly build on that start. A number of the wines have great interest and not a little merit.

Symphonia Pinot Chardonnay Méthode Champenoise
Made from grapes grown partly on the Whitlands plateau at an elevation of 800 metres and partly from Peter Read's Myrrhee Hills vineyard, 400 metres lower down. The wine is tiraged and disgorged at Anderson Wines, and spends over three years on yeast lees prior to disgorgement. It is an impressive wine.
▼▼▼▼ 1996 Glowing yellow-green; the bouquet offers a range of complex bready/yeasty/minerally aromas, the palate in tight, citrussy style, lively and long. **rating:** 86
best drinking 2000–2004 **drink with** Oysters • $14

Symphonia Quintus
A blend of Merlot and Cabernet Sauvignon, together with lesser quantities of Tannat, Saperavi and Tempranillo, all grown on the Myrrhee Hills vineyard. The winery notes suggest that tannat gives the wines of France's southwest their particular tannin and red fruit character; sapervai, the most widely planted red variety in Russia for its very deep colour; and tempranillo, of Spain, giving Riojan wines their fruit and flavour.
▼▼▼▽ 1997 Medium red-purple; the bouquet is clean, with a mix of ripe plum, spice and clove aromas. The light to medium-bodied palate is well balanced, and has a touch more concentration than the '98; gently ripe fruit with some spicy characters contribute most; oak and tannin are largely insignificant. **rating:** 84
▼▼▼▽ 1998 Medium purple-red; the bouquet is ripe, with slightly fuzzy plum fruit and touches of leaf and spice. The palate is likewise ripe, with sweet berry and plum fruit; light to medium bodied and well balanced. **rating:** 82
best drinking 2001–2003 **drink with** Pasta with meat sauce • $14

Symphonia Cabernet Plus Tannat & Merlot
In this wine the influence of Tannat, most famous in the wines of the Madiran region of southwest France, makes its presence felt, more than offsetting the softness of the Merlot.
▼▼▼▽ 1998 Medium to full red-purple; the moderately intense bouquet has savoury overtones to the core of red and dark berry fruit aromas. The palate is quite powerful, with a mix of dark berry/savoury/earthy flavours which are all fruit-derived. **rating:** 84
best drinking 2002–2008 **drink with** Mediterranean dishes • $14

tait wines   NR
Yaldara Drive, Lyndoch, SA 5351 **region** Barossa Valley
phone (08) 8524 5000 **fax** (08) 8524 5220 **open** Weekends 10–5 and by appointment
winemaker Contract **production** 500 **est.** 1994
product range ($12–18 CD) Chardonnay, Bush Vine Grenache, Shiraz, Cabernet Sauvignon.
summary The Tait family has been involved in the wine industry in the Barossa for over 100 years, making not wine but barrels. Their recent venture into winemaking has been extremely successful, with four of the five wines on release in early 1998 having won either a silver or gold medal. Retail distribution through single outlets in Melbourne, Adelaide and Sydney.

talijancich   NR
26 Hyem Road, Herne Hill, WA 6056 **region** Swan District
phone (08) 9296 4289 **fax** (08) 9296 1762 **open** Sun–Fri 11–5
winemaker James Talijancich **production** 10 000 **est.** 1932
product range ($17–135 CD) Verdelho, Voices Dry White, Grenache, Shiraz, Julian James White Liqueur, Julian James Red Liqueur, Liqueur Tokay.
summary A former fortified wine specialist (a 1969 Liqueur Tokay was released in November 1999) now making a broad range of table wines, with particular emphasis on Verdelho: on the third Saturday of August each year there is a tasting of fine three-year-old Verdelho table wines from both Australia and overseas. Also runs an active wine club and exports to China, Japan and Hong Kong.

Talijancich Liqueur Tokay 375 ml
This wine has the distinction of being the most expensive Liqueur Tokay (or Muscat) in Australia. Winemaker James Talijancich has watched its evolution since 1977, when he was first employed at his family's winery, and is rightly proud of the resulting wine.

♥♥♥♥♀ 1969 Dark brown, with the typical olive rim of a barrel-aged wine. The bouquet is very complex, showing its age, but is not stale and has good rancio character. The palate has powerful chocolate/cake/biscuit flavours, but is not as luscious as aged Rutherglen Tokay. Perhaps the point of difference is all to the better.   **rating:** 91
best drinking Drink now **best vintages** '69 **drink with** Preserved fruits, nuts or chocolate • $135

tallara   NR

Cassilis Road, Mudgee, NSW 2850 **region** Mudgee
phone (02) 6372 2408 **fax** (02) 6372 6924 **open** Not
winemaker Simon Gilbert (Contract) **production** 1800 **est.** 1973
product range ($15 ML) Chardonnay, Cabernet Sauvignon.
summary Tallara's large, 54-hectare vineyard was first established in 1973 by KPMG partner Rick Turner. Only a fraction of the production has ever been made into wine, currently by Simon Gilbert. It is sold principally through a mailing list, with a little local distribution.

tallarook   ★★★★

Ennis Road, Tallarook, Vic 3659 **region** Central Victorian Mountain Country
phone (03) 9818 3455 **fax** (03) 9818 3646 **open** Not
winemaker Martin Williams (Contract) **production** 2000 **est.** 1987
product range ($23–28 R) Chardonnay, Marsanne, Pinot Noir.
summary TallarooK has been established on a property between Broadford and Seymour at an elevation of 200–300 metres. 10.7 hectares of vines have been planted since 1987, the three principal varieties being chardonnay, shiraz and pinot noir. The retainer of Martin Williams as winemaker in the 1998 vintage brought a substantial change in emphasis, and the subsequent release of an impressive Chardonnay. It is mainly sold by mail order, but three of Melbourne's most distinguished restaurants have listed it, and it is also available through Philip Murphy Wines & Spirits.

TallarooK Chardonnay

Sophisticated winemaking including barrel-fermentation in French oak, partial malolactic fermentation and extended lees contact has paid appropriate dividends.
♥♥♥♥ 1998 Light to medium yellow-green; some slightly charry barrel-ferment oak surrounds gentle, creamy/nutty-accented fruit. The palate is clean and fresh, with melon/nectarine/citrus fruit and more of those creamy/nutty characters of the bouquet; subtle but sustained oak.   **rating:** 89
best drinking 2000–2004 **drink with** Pan-fried veal • $26

taltarni   ★★★☆

Taltarni Road, Moonambel, Vic 3478 **region** Pyrenees
phone (03) 5467 2218 **fax** (03) 5467 2306 **open** 7 days 10–5
winemaker Shane Clohesy, Chris Markell, David Crawford **production** 70 000 **est.** 1972
product range ($10–28 R) Sauvignon Blanc, Blanc des Pyrenees, Rosé, Reserve des Pyrenees, Merlot Cabernet, Shiraz, Cabernet Sauvignon, Merlot; Sparkling Blanc de Blanc Tete de Cuvée, Cuvée Brut, Brut Tache.
summary In the shadow of the departure (on the best of terms) of long-serving winemaker and chief executive Dominique Portet, Taltarni seems to have backed off the high levels of tannin and extract evident in the older vintage wines, which ought really to be a step in the right direction but (perversely) seems to have robbed the red wines of some of their (formidable) character. A rock and a hard place, it seems. Exports to all the major markets, including the UK, the US, Canada, Japan, Hong Kong, Switzerland, Sweden and extensively thoughout Southeast Asia and Western Europe.

talunga   NR

Adelaide to Mannum Road (PO Box 134), Gumeracha, SA 5233 **region** Adelaide Hills
phone (08) 8389 1222 **fax** (08) 8389 1233 **open** Wed–Sun and public holidays 10.30–5
winemaker Vince Scaffidi **production** 3000 **est.** 1994
product range ($11–22.50 CD) Sauvignon Blanc, Semillon, Chardonnay, Yearling Blend, Shiraz, Sangiovese Franc, Sangiovese Merlot, Pinot Noir, Cabernet Merlot, High Block Cabernet Sauvignon.
summary Talunga owners Vince and Tina Scaffidi have a one-third share of the 67-hectare Gumeracha Vineyards, and it is from these vineyards that the Talunga wines are sourced.

Talunga Sauvignon Blanc

Estate-grown; made in a no-frills fashion, cold-fermented in stainless steel and early-bottled. Needs time to develop.
▼▼▼▽ **1999** Very pale colour; light minerally fruit and a crisp, dry palate in uncompromising seafood style. Seems to have been early-picked, and is not as rich as the '98. **rating:** 80
best drinking 2000–2002 **best vintages** NA **drink with** Oysters • $16.80

Talunga Cabernet Sauvignon

A vineyard block selection from the Gumeracha vineyards of the Scaffidi family, holding considerable promise for the future.
▼▼▼▼ **1997** Medium red-purple; chocolate and vanilla aromas surround sweet berry fruit on the bouquet, a flavour mix repeated on the complex palate, which has particularly good structure. **rating:** 88
best drinking 2001–2006 **best vintages** '97 **drink with** Steak and kidney pie • $22.50

Talunga High Block Cabernet Sauvignon

Came equal second in its class at the 1999 Adelaide Hills Wine Show.
▼▼▼▽ **1998** Medium purple-red; very strong oak accompanies the rich, dark berry fruit on both the bouquet and palate. Both of my fellow judges at the Show were more forgiving of the level of oak than I. **rating:** 84
best drinking 2003–2008 **best vintages** NA **drink with** Char-grilled rump steak • $16.95

tamar ridge ★★★★

Auburn Road, Kayena, Tas 7270 **region** Northern Tasmania
phone (03) 6334 6208 **fax** (03) 6334 6050 **open** 7 days 10–5
winemaker Julian Alcorso **production** 15 000 **est.** 1994
product range ($15–21.10 CD) Riesling, Sauvignon Blanc, Chardonnay, Pinot Noir, Sparkling; second label Devil's Corner Dry White, Chardonnay, Dry Red.
summary Tamar Ridge is the most recent venture into wine production of grass-fed-beef magnate Joe Chromy. When he sold Heemskerk and Rochecombe to Pipers Brook in 1998, he retained a substantial vineyard in the Tamar Valley which presently has 28 hectares in bearing and which is to be increased to 70 hectares over the next two to three years. The new winery, situated on the edge of a large dam (or lake, for that is what it looks like) is a striking piece of architecture, and a large restaurant is in the plans for the future. The quality of the early releases is impressive; if maintained will lead to an even higher winery rating.

Tamar Ridge Riesling

A wine which reflects the very cool climate in which the grapes are grown, and, in particular, the retention of high levels of natural acidity. Estate-grown, and of high quality. The 1999 was a trophy winner at the Tasmanian Wines Show 2000.
▼▼▼▼▼ **1999** Medium yellow-green; both the bouquet and palate have intense, lifted passionfruit and lime flavours, which give the wine great impact. The palate is long and has excellent balance. **rating:** 95
▼▼▼▼▽ **1998** Light to medium yellow-green; a highly scented, rich, lime and tropical fruit bouquet leads into a palate with abundant, lime, apricot and apple fruit, with some suggestion of a touch of botrytis. Good acidity sustains a long, lingering finish. **rating:** 90
best drinking 2000–2010 **best vintages** '99 **drink with** Sashimi • $16.80

Tamar Ridge Chardonnay

Skilfully made by Julian Alcorso in a winery then being built around his ears.
▼▼▼▼▽ **1998** Medium yellow-green; the bouquet is complex and quite concentrated, with nuances of barrel-fermentation and creamy/nutty malolactic-fermentation inputs. The palate has excellent fruit weight and intensity, the flavours running through melon to nectarine; there is pronounced acidity on the finish, but not sufficient to unbalance the wine. **rating:** 91
best drinking 2000–2005 **best vintages** '98 **drink with** Slow-cooked Tasmanian salmon • $19.95

Tamar Ridge Devil's Corner Chardonnay

Yet another example of a Tasmanian winemaker, in this case Julian Alcorso, preferring to make an unoaked Chardonnay at the lower end of the price range, rather than throwing in a bucket of oak chips.
▼▼▼▼ **1999** Light to medium green-yellow; a clean, moderately intense bouquet with some minerally/stony notes, the palate offering finely balanced melon fruit and a long finish. **rating:** 85
▼▼▼▽ **1998** Medium yellow-green; the bouquet is quite intense and solid, with a mix of mineral and citrus aromas. The wine has plenty of length and good balance on the palate, although it is slightly sweet. **rating:** 84
best drinking 2000–2002 **best vintages** NA **drink with** Crayfish • $15

Tamar Ridge Pinot Noir

Predominantly sourced from the estate vineyard retained by Joe Chromy when he sold the remainder of his earlier wine investments to Pipers Brook.

▼▼▼▼ 1998 Medium red-purple; plum, cedar, forest and spice aromas weave their way through the bouquet; the palate is in no sense a heavyweight but is quite silky, with good texture and mouthfeel. The flavours are of sweet plum and spice supported by subtle oak. **rating:** 89

best drinking 2000–2003 **best vintages** NA **drink with** Spiced quail • $19.95

tamburlaine ★★★☆

McDonalds Road, Pokolbin, NSW 2321 **region** Lower Hunter Valley
phone (02) 4998 7570 **fax** (02) 4998 7763 **open** 7 days 9.30–5
winemaker Mark Davidson **production** 48 000 **est.** 1966
product range ($14–22 CD) Semillon, Verdelho, Sauvignon Blanc, 3 Parishes Chardonnay, The Chapel Reserve Chardonnay, Late Harvest Verdelho, Botrytis Semillon, Petite Fleur (Sparkling), Cabernet Merlot Malbec, The Chapel Reserve Red, Barrique Blend Petite Sirah, Old Muscat.
summary A thriving business which, notwithstanding the fact that it has doubled its already substantial production in recent years, sells over 90 per cent of its wine through cellar door and by mailing list (with an active tasting club members' cellar programme offering wines which are held and matured at Tamburlaine). Unashamedly and deliberately focused on the tourist trade (and, of course, its club members).

Tamburlaine The Chapel Reserve Chardonnay

As the name suggests, the top-of-the-range Chardonnay release from Tamburlaine. It is drawn from numerous small vineyards (Tamburlaine owns no vineyards of its own) and is both barrel-fermented and taken through malolactic fermentation in American oak.

▼▼▼▽ 1999 Medium yellow-green; the bouquet has ripe peach fruit with subtle oak and mlf inputs. The palate is user-friendly, smooth, and well balanced, but not too much zip. **rating:** 84

best drinking 2000–2002 **best vintages** NA **drink with** Pork chops • $22

tanglewood downs NR

Bulldog Creek Road, Merricks North, Vic 3926 **region** Mornington Peninsula
phone (03) 5974 3325 **fax** (03) 5974 4170 **open** Sun–Mon 12–5
winemaker Ken Bilham, Wendy Bilham **production** 1200 **est.** 1984
product range ($25 CD) Riesling, Gewurztraminer, Chardonnay, Pinot Noir, Cabernet Sauvignon, Cabernet Franc Merlot.
summary One of the smaller and lower-profile wineries on the Mornington Peninsula, with Ken Bilham quietly doing his own thing on 2.5 hectares of estate plantings. Winery lunches and dinners are available by arrangement.

tannery lane vineyard NR

174 Tannery Lane, Mandurang, Vic 3551 **region** Bendigo
phone (03) 5439 5011 **fax** (03) 5439 5891 **open** By appointment
winemaker David Anderson (Contract) **production** 200 **est.** 1990
product range ($15–23 CD) Sangiovese, Shiraz, Merlot, Cabernet Merlot.
summary Ray and Anne Moore established their tiny vineyard in 1990, gradually establishing a total of 2 hectares of shiraz, cabernet sauvignon, cabernet franc, sangiovese, merlot and nebbiolo. Their Sangiovese is the only such wine coming from the Bendigo region at the present time. The micro-production is sold through cellar door only and then only while stocks last, which typically is not for very long. A phone call will quickly establish whether or not wine is available.

tantemaggie NR

Kemp Road, Pemberton, WA 6260 **region** Pemberton, Warren Valley and Manjimup
phone (08) 9776 1164 **fax** (08) 9776 1810 **open** By appointment
winemaker Contract **production** 3600 **est.** 1987
product range ($15–22 CD) Verdelho, Cabernet Sauvignon.
summary Tantemaggie was established by the Pottinger family with the help of a bequest from a deceased aunt named Maggie. It is part of a mixed farming operation, and by far the greatest part of the 20 hectares is under long-term contract to Houghton. The bulk of the plantings are cabernet sauvignon and verdelho, the former producing the light-bodied style favoured by the Pottingers.

tarrawarra estate ★★★★☆

Healesville Road, Yarra Glen, Vic 3775 **region** Yarra Valley
phone (03) 5962 3311 **fax** (03) 5962 3887 **open** 7 days 10.30–4.30
winemaker Clare Halloran **production** 8200 **est.** 1983
product range ($22–46 R) Chardonnay and Pinot Noir each released under the Tarrawarra Estate and second label Tunnel Hill; also Kidron Chardonnay (kosher).
summary Slowly evolving Chardonnay of great structure and complexity is the winery specialty; robust Pinot Noir also needs time and evolves impressively if given it. The second label Tunnel Hill wines are more accessible when young, and better value for those who do not wish to wait for the Tarrawarra wines to evolve. National retail distribution; exports to the UK, Switzerland and Belgium.

Tarrawarra Chardonnay

Produced from 11.5 hectares of estate-grown grapes in a state-of-the-art winery, using a complex range of viticultural and winemaking techniques, including multiple picking of the grapes at different maturity levels, barrel-fermentation of partly clarified juice, lees contact and malolactic fermentation. The style is always very complex, with much of the emphasis placed on structure and texture; the resulting style is quite different from most other wines of the Yarra Valley.
▼▼▼▼▼ 1998 Light green-yellow; the bouquet is quite complex, although the high toast barrel-ferment characters are on the ascendant. There is a nice, creamy textured palate thanks to some mlf contribution; fair length, but does need a tad more fruit. **rating:** 90
▼▼▼▼ 1997 Medium to full yellow-green; the bouquet is powerful, concentrated and complex in typical '97 Yarra Valley style. The palate has well-balanced and well-integrated oak; strangely and unexpectedly, the fruit dips slightly on the back palate. **rating:** 87
best drinking 2000–2005 **best vintages** '87, '88, '90, '92, '93, '94, '97, '98 **drink with** Pheasant, turkey • $38

Tarrawarra Estate Kidron Chardonnay

A kosher for passover mevushal Chardonnay.
▼▼▼▼ 1999 Light green-yellow; the bouquet offers light fruit with pronounced spicy oak, and the palate is rather light in fruit terms, with peaky acidity. **rating:** 81
best drinking 2000–2003 **best vintages** NA **drink with** Kosher food • $22

Tarrawarra Pinot Noir

Produced from 6.5 hectares of estate plantings of several different clones. As with the Chardonnay, much attention is paid to style and structure: the grapes are picked when very ripe, and the winemaking techniques are designed to gain maximum extraction of colour and flavour from the grapes. The wines are often awkward when young, powerfully impressive with age and have won a significant number of trophies in Australian wine shows in recent years.
▼▼▼▼ 1998 Medium to full red-purple; a clean bouquet with smooth plummy fruit showing a gentle hand, and not forced. The palate has excellent structure and length, with savoury plummy fruit, lingering tannins and subtle oak. A particularly good outcome for the vintage. **rating:** 91
best drinking 2000–2004 **best vintages** '88, '90, '91, '92, '94, '95, '96, '98 **drink with** Squab • $46

Tarrawarra Tunnel Hill Pinot Noir

The second label is not simply a selection of those barrels of Tarrawarra Pinot which have been less successful, but at least part of the wine is deliberately made in a different fashion right from the outset, placing less emphasis on structure, more on fruit and using less new oak. Quite deliberately designed to make a simpler style.
▼▼▼▼ 1998 Excellent red-purple colour; the moderately intense bouquet is clean, with light plum/strawberry fruit not aspiring to complexity. There is in fact rather more to the palate, which has quite good structure and nice plummy fruit; good short-term development potential. **rating:** 89
best drinking 2000–2002 **best vintages** '91, '92, '94, '96, '97, '98 **drink with** Poached Tasmanian salmon • $22

tarwin ridge NR

Wintles Road, Leongatha South, Vic 3953 **region** Gippsland
phone (03) 5664 3211 **fax** (03) 5664 3211 **open** Weekends and holidays 10–5
winemaker Brian Anstee **production** 700 **est.** 1983
product range ($16–27 CD) Sauvignon Blanc, White Merlot, Pinot Noir, Pinot Noir Premium, Cabernet Merlot.
summary For the time being Brian Anstee is making his wines at Nicholson River under the gaze of fellow social worker Ken Eckersley; the wines come from 2 hectares of estate pinot and half a hectare each of cabernet and sauvignon blanc.

tatachilla ★★★★☆

151 Main Road, McLaren Vale, SA 5171 **region** McLaren Vale
phone (08) 8323 8656 **fax** (08) 8323 9096 **open** Mon–Sat 10–5, Sundays and public holidays 11–5
winemaker Michael Fragos, Justin McNamee **production** 150 000 **est.** 1901
product range ($11.95–45 CD) Clarendon Vineyard Riesling, Late Harvest Riesling, Adelaide Hills, Sauvignon Blanc, Growers (Chenin Blanc Semillon Sauvignon Blanc), Padthaway Chardonnay, Bluestone Brut, Sparkling Malbec, Merlot, Foundation Shiraz, Keystone (Grenache Shiraz), Padthaway Cabernet Sauvignon, Partners (Cabernet Sauvignon Shiraz), Tawny Port.
summary Tatachilla was reborn in 1995 but has an at-times tumultuous history going back to 1901. For most of the time between 1901 and 1961 the winery was owned by Penfolds but was closed in that year before being reopened in 1965 as the Southern Vales Co-operative. In the late 1980s it was purchased and renamed The Vales but did not flourish, and in 1993 it was purchased by local grower Vic Zerella and former Kaiser Stuhl chief executive Keith Smith. After extensive renovations, the winery was officially reopened in 1995 and has won a number of tourist awards and accolades. The star turns are Keystone (Grenache Shiraz) and Foundation Shiraz, bursting with vibrant fruit. It has 771 hectares of vineyards, and the expanding production services markets throughout Europe, Hong Kong and Taiwan.

Tatachilla Adelaide Hills Sauvignon Blanc

No-frills, straightforward winemaking; it remains to be seen how much downwards pressure New Zealand will place on the price of wines such as this.
TTTT 1999 Light green-yellow; some estery grassy fruit over a mineral base is followed by a palate which starts quietly but builds intensity on the back palate and through to the finish. **rating:** 88
best drinking 2000–2001 **best vintages** '99 **drink with** Calamari •$18.95

Tatachilla Adelaide Hills Chardonnay

Sourced from the Pendle Hill Vineyard at Hahndorf, and the Golding Vineyard at Lenswood, the free-run press material being fermented in a combination of 30 per cent new, 35 per cent one-year-old and 35 per cent two-year-old French oak where it spends 11 months on yeast lees prior to bottling.
TTTT 1998 Medium yellow-green; quite a rich wine on the bouquet, with strong honey peach fruit and subtle oak. The palate, likewise, offers solidly sweet peachy fruit, with a nice touch of oak to add interest. **rating:** 87
best drinking 2000–2003 **best vintages** NA **drink with** Creamy pasta •$19.95

Tatachilla Padthaway Chardonnay

Both the price and the palate suggest this is an unoaked wine which shows distinctive regional flavour.
TTTY 1999 Light to medium green-yellow; the bouquet is quite fragrant, with citrus/grapefruit/melon aromas. The palate has good length, but a slightly sharp finish detracts. **rating:** 82
best drinking Drink now **best vintages** NA **drink with** Richer fish dishes •$15.95

Tatachilla Foundation Shiraz

Foundation Shiraz is Tatachilla's flag-bearer, taking its name from the foundation stone of the winery which was laid in place in 1901 by founder Cyril Pridmore. open fermentation, using a mixture of heading down boards and plunging, is followed by partial barrel-fermentation, before the wine is matured in a mix of predominantly American (70 per cent new) oak for 18 months. Has had considerable show success.
TTTTT 1997 Deep, inky purple-red. The richly layered and ripe bouquet has abundant glossy, dark cherry fruit and balanced oak. While the palate is powerful, intense and concentrated, it cleverly avoids heaviness; the oak is subtle and the acidity beautifully balanced. **rating:** 94
best drinking 2002–2012 **best vintages** '95, '97 **drink with** Kangaroo fillet •$45

Tatachilla McLaren Vale Shiraz

Produced from vineyards spread across McLaren Vale; matured in 30 per cent new American oak, the remainder a mix of previously used French and American oak.
TTTT 1998 Dense purple-red; an extremely rich and concentrated bouquet, with masses of savoury chocolatey fruit and oak signals a huge wine in Battlestar Galactica style. A wine for heroes and a large rump steak. Trophy winner 1999 McLaren Vale Wine Show. **rating:** 87
best drinking 2005–2015 **best vintages** '98 **drink with** Rump steak •$22.95

Tatachilla Clarendon Vineyard Merlot

1995 was the first vintage under this label, produced from grapes grown at an altitude of 215 metres above the floor of McLaren Vale. The wine is made in open fermenters, part being pressed before dryness, and matured in oak, half new and half used. This is an archetypal show style, both the '97 and '98 being trophy and gold medal winners. How much the style reflects (desirable) varietal character is a different question.

▼▼▼▽ **1998** Dense red-purple; very powerful fruit and oak on the bouquet are matched by enormous flavour and extract on the palate. A Merlot on steroids which takes up where the '97 left off.   **rating:** 90

best drinking 2005–2010 **best vintages** '96, '97, '98 **drink with** Rare rump steak • $40

Tatachilla Partners Cabernet Sauvignon Shiraz

First made in 1996, and in that and the two following vintages won gold medals (and a trophy) at significant wine shows, making it an outstanding bargain.

▼▼▼▽ **1999** Medium red, with a touch of purple; fresh, youthful cassis berry aromas on the bouquet continue onto the minty berry palate. Not a bad wine, but not up to the quality of prior vintages.   **rating:** 84

best drinking 2002–2007 **best vintages** '96, '97, '98 **drink with** Marinated beef • $13.95

Tatachilla Padthaway Cabernet Sauvignon

A brother to the Padthaway Chardonnay; like others of the Tatachilla reds, a large-scale wine bottled early.

▼▼▼▽ **1998** Dense purple-red; the bouquet is youthful and powerful, with raw oak asserting itself. There is lots of fruit on the palate, but the oak and extract are raw and unformed; a wine which may or may not settle down and which seems to have been bottled too early.   **rating:** 84

best drinking 2003–2008 **best vintages** NA **drink with** Beef pie • $20.95

☙ tawonga vineyard   NR

2 Drummond Street, Tawonga, Vic 3697 **region** Alpine Valleys
phone (03) 5754 4945 **fax** (03) 5754 4945 **open** By appointment
winemaker John Adams **production** 300 **est.** 1994
product range ($12.50 CD) Chardonnay, Shiraz, Shiraz Cabernet, Cabernet Sauvignon.
summary Diz and John Adams made their first wine in 1995, but it was not until 1998 that they finally received their producer's licence entitling them to sell the wine they had made. With a planned maximum production of 10 tonnes in 2001 (650 cases or thereabouts) Tawonga has been able to take advantage of the small business sales tax exemption. Understandably, they look forward to the brave new world of GST and WET with more than a little apprehension. In the meantime the prices for their handcrafted wines (virtually all of which have won show medals) remains at a magically low $12.50.

taylors   ★★★☆

Taylors Road, Auburn, SA 5451 **region** Clare Valley
phone (08) 8849 2008 **fax** (08) 8849 2240 **open** Mon–Fri 9–5, Sat and public holidays 10–5, Sun 10–4
winemaker Adam Eggins, Graig Grafton **production** 200 000 **est.** 1972
product range ($8.50–50 R) The premium range consists of Chardonnay, Clare Riesling, Gewurztraminer, White Clare, Promised Land Unwooded Chardonnay, Pinot Noir, Merlot, Shiraz and Cabernet Sauvignon; the lower-priced Clare Valley range consists of Dry White, Sweet White and Dry Red; also St Andrew Chardonnay and Cabernet Sauvignon.
summary Taylors continues to flourish and expand, with yet further extensions to its vineyards. Now totalling almost 500 hectares, by far the largest holding in Clare Valley. There have also been substantial changes on the winemaking front, both in terms of the winemaking team and in terms of the wine style, the latter moving to fresher, earlier-release wines. Change always brings a measure of pain, but I wonder whether Taylors has not gone from one extreme to the other. Widespread national distribution, with exports to New Zealand, Germany, Northern Ireland, the US, Thailand, Fiji, Hong Kong, China, Malaysia and Singapore.

Taylors St Andrews Chardonnay

A new ultra-premium range of wine for Taylors under the St Andrews label. Against all the odds, the Chardonnay is the most impressive.

▼▼▼▼ **1997** Glowing yellow-green; a rich and complex bouquet with strong inputs from barrel-fermentation using high-quality oak. There is abundant, ripe peachy fruit on the palate, again with smoky/toasty high-quality oak.   **rating:** 89

best drinking 2000–2005 **best vintages** '97 **drink with** Coquilles St Jacques • $32

Taylors St Andrews Cabernet Sauvignon

An unconventional oak regime, with the first 12 months spent in old oak and the next 12 months spent in an equal mix of American and French hogsheads, has only partially succeeded.

♥♥♥♡ **1996** Medium red-purple; the bouquet is very oaky and does not have the integration one would hope for. The palate has rich chocolate and berry fruit but, once again, the oak is assertive. **rating:** 83

best drinking 2000–2006 **best vintages** NA **drink with** Braised beef • $50

temple bruer ★★★☆

Milang Road, Strathalbyn, SA 5255 **region** Langhorne Creek
phone (08) 8537 0203 **fax** (08) 8537 0131 **open** Mon–Fri 9.30–4.30
winemaker Nick Bruer **production** 14 000 **est.** 1980
product range ($12.80–23.70 R) Riesling, Verdelho, Viognier, Chenin Blanc, Botrytis Riesling, Cornucopia Grenache, Cabernet Merlot, Reserve Merlot, Shiraz Malbec, Sparkling Cabernet Merlot.
summary Always known for its eclectic range of wines, Temple Bruer (which also carries on a substantial business as a vine propagation nursery) has seen a sharp lift in wine quality. Clean, modern redesigned labels add to the appeal of a stimulatingly different range of red wines. Part of the production from the 24 hectares of estate vineyards is sold to others, the remainder being made under the Temple Bruer label. All of the 24-hectare vineyard is now certified organic.

Temple Bruer Shiraz Malbec

A blend of 74 per cent Shiraz and 26 per cent Malbec from the 1.5 hectares of shiraz and half a hectare of malbec, both estate plantings. A traditional Langhorne Creek blend which works very well. The wine is made in old-style open fermenters, and matured in American oak, but without that oak making more than a subliminal contribution, which is all to the good.

♥♥♥♥ **1997** Youthful, medium purple-red; the bouquet is fresh and bright, showing plum with touches of spice and barely perceptible oak. The palate is equally firm, fresh and extremely youthful; one is left to wonder whether it spent some time in tank to preserve that freshness prior to being bottled. **rating:** 85

best drinking 2000–2004 **best vintages** '81, '83, '87, '89, '90, '91, '96 **drink with** Grilled steak • $16.10

Temple Bruer Reserve Merlot

The Langhorne Creek area should provide excellent merlot because of its (the region's) propensity towards soft, silky fruity red wines — which is what Merlot should be.

♥♥♥♡ **1997** Medium red-purple; the bouquet is quite fragrant, light and with a haunting mix of leaf, lemon and spice. The palate is far more conventional, with gently sweet berry fruit, a fleeting hint of mint, and is harmonious and well balanced. **rating:** 83

best drinking 2000–2004 **best vintages** NA **drink with** Escalope of veal • $23.60

templer's mill NR

Orange Agricultural College, Leeds Parade, Orange, NSW 2800 **region** Orange
phone (02) 6360 5509 **fax** (02) 6360 5698 **open** Friday 2–5 or by appointment
winemaker Jon Reynolds **production** 4000 **est.** 1997
product range ($16–18 CD) Chardonnay.
summary Templer's Mill is a most interesting alliance of winemaker (Jon Reynolds), businessman-entrepreneur-cum-vigneron (Gary Blom of Barrington Estate in the Upper Hunter Valley) and the Orange Agricultural College, which is part of the University of Sydney. Together they are erecting a substantial winery which will cater not only for the needs of the joint venture partners but also other growers in the district, as well as providing a teaching facility for the College. It looks a very promising venture.

tempus two wines ★★★☆

Hermitage Road, Pokolbin, NSW 2321 **region** Lower Hunter Valley
phone (02) 9818 7222 **fax** (02) 9818 7333 **open** 7 days 10–5
winemaker Peter Hall **production** 30 000 **est.** 1997
product range ($18–35 R) Varietal range of Verdelho, Semillon Sauvignon Blanc, Cowra Chardonnay, Shiraz, Merlot, Cabernet Shiraz; Heart range of Broke Chardonnay, Sparkling Chardonnay, Sparkling Shiraz, Mudgee Merlot, Hollydene Cabernet Sauvignon, Vine Vale Shiraz; Reserve range of Clare Riesling, Cabernet Merlot and Botrytis Semillon.
summary Tempus Two is the new name for Hermitage Road Wines, a piece of doggerel akin to that of Rouge Homme, except that it is not Franglais, but a mix of Latin (Tempus means time) and English. I should not be too critical, however; the change was forced on the winery by the EU Wine Agreement and the prohibition of the use of the word 'hermitage' on Australian wine labels. Nor should the fracas over the labels disguise the fact that some very attractive wines have appeared so far, and will do so in the future, no doubt.

Tempus Two Botrytis Semillon 375 ml

Produced from grapes grown in the Riverina, unchallenged as Australia's best region for this style. Packaged in what can only be described as phallic-shaped bottle which is also remarkably unstable.

TTTT 1998 Glowing yellow-green; the bouquet is clean, with a mix of tinned fruit aromas and citrus; a clean, easy style in the mouth, with yellow peach and some spicy notes coming from the subtle oak. **rating: 83**

best drinking 2000–2004 **best vintages** NA **drink with** Home-made ice-cream • $18

Tempus Two Vine Vale Shiraz

With its Barossa Valley background, this wine emphasises the reach of the Tempus Two Wines portfolio, but leads one to wonder how it could ever be given a coherent identity or brand focus, no matter how good the wine quality.

TTTT 1998 Medium to full red-purple; the bouquet is quite intense, with rich and complex dark berry, spice, leaf and plum aromas. The fruit-driven palate is flooded with juicy berry flavours, the oak being just a little edgy. **rating: 85**

best drinking 2002–2008 **best vintages** NA **drink with** Braised steak • $28

terrace vale ★★★☆

Deasey's Lane, Pokolbin, NSW 2321 **region** Lower Hunter Valley
phone (02) 4998 7517 **fax** (02) 4998 7814 **open** 7 days 10–4
winemaker Alain Leprince **production** 8000 **est.** 1971
product range ($14.50–19 CD) Bin 1 Semillon, Bin 2 Chardonnay, Semillon Chardonnay, Gewurztraminer, Elizabeth Sauvignon Blanc, Sauvignon Blanc Semillon, Fine Hunter White, Pinot Noir, Bin 6 Shiraz, Fine Hunter Red, Cabernet Merlot, Bin 7 Cabernet Sauvignon, Sparkling, Vintage Port.
summary Long-established but relatively low-profile winery heavily dependent on its cellar-door and local (including Newcastle) trade. Smart new packaging has lifted the presentation, and as always there are one or two very good wines among the portfolio.

Terrace Vale Bin 1 Semillon

Newly packaged with the bold 'T' design label of Terrace Vale, but made in traditional-style from vines now approaching 30 years of age. Has the capacity to develop marvellously given time.

TTTT 1999 Light green-yellow; tight, light, clean and crisp, with savoury mineral characters on the bouquet; the palate has unexpected impact, with tangy, almost sweet lemony fruit and a jab of CO_2. It could well be this wine will follow down the track of the '98, although possibly a few years in advance. **rating: 84**

TTTTT 1998 Light to medium yellow-green; the bouquet is light, clean and crisp, in utterly correct varietal style. The palate is similarly light, clean and crisp; there is something which makes me super-confident that this will age superbly; it is rated more for what it will be than what it is. **rating: 90**

best drinking 2002–2010 **best vintages** '98 **drink with** Shellfish • $15

Terrace Vale Bin 6 Shiraz

Like the Semillon, produced from old vines in an unostentatious fashion.

TTTT 1998 Full red-purple, excellent for the region; the bouquet is clean, with rich dark cherry fruit touched with liquorice and earth. The medium- to full-bodied palate is fresh, with sweet cherry fruit and nicely balanced oak. Has won several silver medals, including a silver medal at the 1999 Hunter Valley Wine Show. **rating: 88**

best drinking 2003–2013 **best vintages** '98 **drink with** Whole roasted ox kidney • $19

t'gallant ★★★★☆

Mornington Road, Red Hill, Vic 3937 **region** Mornington Peninsula
phone (03) 5989 6565 **fax** (03) 5989 6577 **open** 7 days 10–5
winemaker Kathleen Quealy, Kevin McCarthy **production** 10 000 **est.** 1990
product range ($14–26 R) An ever-changing list of names (and avant-garde label designs) but with Unwooded Chardonnay and Pinot Gris at the centre. Labels include Chardonnay, Lot 2 Chardonnay, The T'Gallant Chardonnay, Flag Pinot Grigio, Tribute Pinot Gris, Celia's White Pinot, Cape Schanck Pinot Grigio, IO McCabe Late Harvest Pinot Gris, Holystone, Cyrano Pinot Noir, Juno Pinot Noir and a range of wines under the Lyncroft label.
summary Husband and wife consultant-winemakers Kathleen Quealy and Kevin McCarthy are starting to carve out an important niche market for the T'Gallant label, noted for its innovative label designs and names. The acquisition of a 15-hectare property, and the planting of 10 hectares of pinot gris gives the business a firm

geographic base, as well as providing increased resources for its signature wine. The yearly parade of new (usually beautiful and striking, it is true) labels designed by Ken Cato do not make my life at all easy. No sooner is the database built up than it is discarded for next year's rash of labels. La Baracca Trattoria is open seven days for lunch and for specially booked evening events.

T'Gallant Cape Schanck Pinot Grigio Chardonnay

A new and interesting direction for T'Gallant, very obviously aimed at the smart café and brasserie market, designed to go at the top of the list and into the value category. This, I venture to say, is not only the sole Australian Chardonnay Pinot Grigio blend, but the only one in the world. It has to be said that rarity is not a magic wand when it comes to quality.

▼▼▼▽ **1999** Distinct straw tinges; the bouquet is clean and neutral, as is the palate; strange varietal bedfellows indeed, and the palate does not have the textural richness of the preceding vintage. **rating:** 82

best drinking 2000–2002 **best vintages** '98 **drink with** Virtually anything • $15

T'Gallant Pinot Grigio

A wine the name of which seems to change with the direction of the wind; in 1997 the word 'Flag' was part of the label, but in '98 not. The key is the use of the name 'Pinot Grigio' (the Italian version) as opposed to Pinot Gris (the French). The Pinot Grigio is always lighter, crisper and less opulent than the Pinot Gris.

▼▼▼▽ **1999** Light green-yellow; the bouquet is very muted indeed, the palate with some mineral and herb flavours, which the makers describe as akin to licking the inside of an oyster shell. Hmm. **rating:** 80

best drinking 2000–2002 **best vintages** NA **drink with** Smoked salmon • $19

T'Gallant Tribute Pinot Gris

An extraordinarily powerful and complex wine at its best, sometimes nearing 15 degrees alcohol. The grapes come from the vineyard of Madeleine and Patrick McCabe. The Tribute for the 1999 vintage is to the late Mark Shield.

▼▼▼▼ **1999** Medium yellow-green; the bouquet is right in the slot for the T'Gallant style, with elusive hints of spice but an extra degree of richness from the alcohol. The palate is moderately intense, with hints of spice, peach and mineral, the alcohol simply providing roundness to the mouthfeel. **rating:** 86

best drinking 2000–2005 **best vintages** '94, '95, '97 **drink with** Gravlax • $26

The T'Gallant Chardonnay

Resolutely unwooded, with the grapes coming from up to 15 contract growers across the peninsula. In 1999 the average yield from these vineyards was less than 1 tonne to the acre.

▼▼▼▼ **1999** Light yellow-green; clean, fresh melon, citrus and white peach aromas are followed on a clean, well-balanced and intense bouquet with considerable length. A particularly good example of unoaked Chardonnay.

rating: 87

best drinking 2000–2004 **best vintages** NA **drink with** Rich seafood • $19

T'Gallant Triumph Late Harvest Pinot Gris

The second Late Harvest Pinot Gris made from grapes grown on the McCabe Vineyard. In 1999 part of the harvest was fermented dry (McCable Vineyard Late Harvest) with an alcohol of 17 degrees (84 points). The other portion (which is Triumph) was left with residual sugar, like the '98, and had a better balanced outcome. For all that, and like the Vendage Tardive wines of Alsace, are often easier to respect than to love, the labelling of byzantine complexity.

▼▼▼▼ **1999** Light green-yellow; the bouquet offers fragrant pear and apple aromas, the palate rich, with tropical/poached pear flavours and good acid balance. **rating:** 86

best drinking 2000–2006 **best vintages** '98, '99 **drink with** Goose • $25

thalgara estate   NR

De Beyers Road, Pokolbin, NSW 2321 **region** Lower Hunter Valley
phone (02) 4998 7717 **fax** (02) 4998 7774 **open** 7 days 10–5
winemaker Steve Lamb **production** 3000 **est.** 1985
product range ($15–30 CD) Chardonnay, Show Reserve Chardonnay, Semillon Chardonnay, Shiraz, Show Reserve Shiraz, Shiraz Cabernet.
summary A low-profile winery but given to surprising show success, never more so than at the 1997 Hunter Valley Wine Show when it won the Doug Seabrook Memorial Trophy for Best Dry Red of Show with its 1995 Show Reserve Shiraz.

🐝 the belgenny vineyard   NR

92 DeBeyers Road, Pokolbin, NSW 2320 **region** Lower Hunter Valley
phone (02) 9247 5300 **fax** (02) 9247 7273 **open** Not
winemaker Monarch Winemaking Services (Contract) **production** 7000 **est.** 1992
product range ($15.85–26.65 R) Semillon, Unwooded Chardonnay, Chardonnay, Proprietor's Reserve Chardonnay, Merlot, Shiraz, Blanc de Blanc.
summary The Belgenny Vineyard was established by Norman Seckold with the planting of 5.8 hectares of chardonnay, 1.2 of semillon, 4.5 of shiraz and 2.1 of merlot. The wines are being contract-made, and cellar door and function rooms were opened in January 2000.

The Belgenny Vineyard Proprietor's Reserve Chardonnay

By a considerable distance, the best of the Belgenny wines, thoroughly deserving its Proprietor's Reserve status.
▼▼▼▼ 1999 Brilliant green-yellow; complex barrel-ferment oak is woven through moderately rich melon/peach fruit on the bouquet. The palate is elegant, the melon fruit neatly counterbalanced by well-handled oak; nice mouthfeel.   **rating:** 88

best drinking 2000–2002 **drink with** Roast chicken • $NA

🐝 the blok estate   NR

Riddoch Highway, Coonawarra, SA 5263 **region** Coonawarra
phone (08) 8737 2734 **fax** (08) 8737 2994 **open** 7 days 10–4
winemaker Contract **production** 1200 **est.** 1999
product range ($15–24 CD) Riesling, Chardonnay, Shiraz, Cabernet Sauvignon
summary Di and John Blok have owned a tiny vineyard planted to cabernet sauvignon for the past five years. They have now decided to take the production from this and from contract-grown grapes elsewhere in Coonawarra for release under their own label. The cellar door is situated in an old stone home which has recently been renovated and surrounded by newly landscaped gardens.

🐝 the fleurieu   NR

Main Road, McLaren Vale, SA 5171 **region** McLaren Vale
phone (08) 8323 8999 **fax** (08) 8323 9332 **open** 7 days 9–5
winemaker Mike Farmilo **production** 800 **est.** 1994
product range ($17–30 CD) Shiraz, released under the Fleurieu and Stump Hill labels.
summary A specialist shiraz producer, with 6.5 hectares of estate vineyards, and contract winemaking by the former long-serving Seaview/Edwards & Chaffey winemaker Mike Farmilo. Limited New South Wales distribution through Busby Wine Co; otherwise serves the local market.

🐝 the gap   ★★★☆

Pomonal Road, Halls Gap, Vic 3381 **region** Grampians
phone (03) 5356 4252 **fax** (03) 5356 4645 **open** Wed–Sun 10–5, 7 days during school holidays
winemaker Trevor Mast, Andrew McLoughney **production** 1600 **est.** 1969
product range ($16–30 CD) Chardonnay, Late Harvest Riesling, Shiraz Cabernet Sauvignon; Four Sisters Sauvignon Blanc Semillon; Billi Billi Creek Shiraz Grenache Cabernet, Shiraz Chardonnay.
summary The Gap is the reincarnation of Boroka, a spectacularly-situated vineyard 5 kilometres east of Halls Gap, with the slopes of the Mount William Range forming a backdrop. The vineyard was planted in 1969, but following its acquisition by Mount Langi Ghiran has been rehabilitated, and extensive renovations have been made to the cellar-door sales area, which offers estate-grown 'The Gap' wines and a selection of Mount Langi Ghiran and Four Sisters wines.

The Gap Shiraz

A blend of Langi Ghiran-grown shiraz supplemented by grapes from Dalkins Westgate Vineyard near Great Western.
▼▼▼▼ 1997 Medium red-purple; the bouquet is clean, with nice berry/cherry fruit but seems slightly unformed. The palate restores the balance with cherry fruit and the clever use of sweet vanilla oak; soft tannins on the finish.   **rating:** 85

best drinking 2002–2006 **drink with** Spiced chicken • $23

The Gap Billi Billi Creek Shiraz Grenache Cabernet

Made from grapes grown in McLaren Vale, Langhorne Creek and the Langi estate, matured in one-year-old French and American oak barrels.

ㅜㅜㅜㅅ **1998** Strong red-purple; the bouquet is quite rich with a mix of sweet and more savoury fruit; the moderately weighted palate has soft plum flavours and commensurately soft tannins; well put together as a drink-now style.   **rating:** 84

best drinking 2000–2002 **drink with** Bistro food • $16

The Gap Shiraz Cabernet

The first release under The Gap label entirely grown on the estate. It spends 12 months in French and American oak before bottling. A blend of 80 per cent Shiraz and 20 per cent Cabernet Sauvignon.

ㅜㅜㅜㅜ **1998** Medium purple-red; the bouquet is rich, with a mix of spicy, juicy, berry/plum fruit. The palate follows down the same flavour track, adding liquorice; finishes with fine, soft tannins and subtle oak, and shows the elegance of the region.   **rating:** 86

best drinking 2003–2008 **drink with** Grilled venison fillet • $26

the green vineyards   ★★★★

1 Alber Road, Upper Beaconsfield, Vic 3808 **region** Yarra Valley
phone (03) 5944 4599 **fax** (03) 5944 4599 **open** Weekends by appointment
winemaker Sergio Carlei **production** 2000 **est.** 1994
product range ($12–25 CD) Yarra Valley Riesling, Mornington Sauvignon Blanc, Yarra Valley Chardonnay, Sunbury Pinot Noir, Heathcote Shiraz, Yarra Valley Cabernets.
summary The Green Vineyards has come a long way in a little time, with Sergio Carlei graduating from home winemaking in a suburban garage to his own (real) winery in Upper Beaconsfield, which happens to fall just within the boundaries of the Yarra Valley. As the product range attests, many of the wines come from grapes grown by others for Green Vineyards, but Carlei does have 2.25 hectares of pinot noir and his preferred source is the Yarra Valley. He has already produced a number of remarkably stylish wines, with more in the pipeline.

the gurdies   NR

St Helier Road, The Gurdies, Vic 3984 **region** Gippsland
phone (03) 5997 6208 **fax** (03) 5997 6511 **open** 7 days 10–5
winemaker Peter Kozik **production** 1000 **est.** 1991
product range ($15–18 R) Riesling, Pinot Noir, Shiraz, Cabernet Sauvignon.
summary The only winery in the southwest Gippsland region, established on the slopes of The Gurdies hills overlooking Westernport Bay and French Island. Plantings of the 3.5-hectare vineyard commenced in 1981, but no fruit was harvested until 1991 owing to bird attack. A winery has been partially completed, and it is intended to increase the vineyards to 25 hectares and ultimately build a restaurant on site.

the melbourne wine company   ★★★☆

PO Box 74, Bannockburn, Vic 3331 **region** Port Phillip Zone
phone (03) 5281 7477 **fax** (03) 5281 7377 **open** Not
winemaker Scott Ireland, Martin Williams **production** 3000 **est.** 1995
product range ($15–30 R) Riesling, Pinot Gris, Chardonnay, Pinot Noir; premium range under the Provenance label.
summary The Melbourne Wine Company was originally conceived by Donleavy Fitzpatrick but is now owned by five partners, headed by winemakers Scott Ireland and Martin Williams. The concept is to source grapes from the four major grape-growing regions encircling Melbourne: the Yarra Valley, Macedon, Geelong and the Mornington Peninsula. The principal range of wine places the emphasis on light, fresh styles which do not need cellaring. The most distinctive feature of distinctive packaging is the use of crown seals, yet another solution to cork taint. The initial releases precisely fulfilled the partners' aims, offering simple enjoyment.

The Melbourne Wine Company Chardonnay

The winemaking team of Scott Ireland and Martin Williams took grapes from the Geelong and Alpine regions of Victoria (a reasonable assumption is that the King Valley is included in the term Alpine regions), to make this easy-drinking style.

ㅜㅜㅜㅅ **1999** Light to medium green-yellow; the bouquet is clean, tending neutral, with slightly green fruit aspects. Fresh melon fruit does, however, come through on the palate, with what seems to be the barest hint of oak.   **rating:** 82

best drinking 2000–2002 **best vintages** NA **drink with** Seafood • $16.45

The Melbourne Wine Company Provenance Chardonnay

Seventy per cent of the grapes come from Geelong, 30 per cent from Mansfield.

▼▼▼▼ **1998** Medium yellow-green; the bouquet has attractive grapefruit and melon complexed by tangy barrel-ferment inputs. The palate has pleasant, sweet melon fruit, subtle oak and good length. **rating: 88**

best drinking 2000–2004 **best vintages** NA **drink with** Baked ham • $30

The Melbourne Wine Company Pinot Noir

Sourced from a varying array of vineyards in Geelong, the Yarra Valley, the Macedon Ranges, the Goulburn Valley and Ballarat. The regions vary from one year to the next.

▼▼▼▽ **1999** Medium red-purple; the bouquet is primarily in the gamey/foresty/woody spectrum, although there is some plum fruit evident. The palate suggests over-extraction, which makes the finish somewhat hard; a masculine, macho style. **rating: 82**

best drinking 2000–2002 **best vintages** NA **drink with** Spicy Asian dishes • $19.75

The Melbourne Wine Company Provenance Pinot Noir

A superior wine coming entirely from the Kurabana Vineyard in Geelong; the full gamut of Pinot Noir winemaking techinques have been used.

▼▼▼▼ **1998** Medium red-purple; the bouquet is very full, with complex, ripe plummy/gamey fruit. The palate, likewise, is full, ripe and rich, with abundant plummy fruit and considerable extract. Some will like the no-holds-barred character of the wine, others might prefer a lighter touch. **rating: 89**

best drinking 2000–2003 **best vintages** NA **drink with** Peking duck • $30

The Melbourne Wine Company Provenance Merlot

Sourced from vineyards near Mansfield in the Central Victorian Mountain Country.

▼▼▼▽ **1998** Medium red; light earthy/savoury aromas flow through to a palate which has some varietal character but not a lot of substance. **rating: 80**

best drinking 2000–2002 **best vintages** NA **drink with** Thinly sliced calf's liver • $30

✿ the mews NR

84 Gibson Street, Kings Meadows, Tas 7249 **region** Northern Tasmania
phone (03) 6344 2780 **fax** (03) 6343 2076 **open** Not
winemaker Graham Wiltshire **production** 300 **est.** 1984
product range Chardonnay.
summary Robin and Anne Holyman have established 0.4 hectare of pinot noir and 9.2 hectares of chardonnay at Kings Meadows, only 4 kilometres from the centre of Launceston. Industry veteran Graham Wiltshire acts as winemaker, and the wines are sold by direct contact with the Holymans.

the minya winery NR

Minya Lane, Connewarre, Vic 3227 **region** Geelong
phone (03) 5264 1397 **open** Public holidays and by appointment
winemaker Susan Dans **production** 1330 **est.** 1974
product range ($10–20 CD) Gewurztraminer, Chardonnay, Unwooded Chardonnay, Grenache, Cabernet Shiraz Merlot.
summary Geoff Dans first planted vines in 1974 on his family's dairy farm, followed by further plantings in 1982 and 1988. I have not tasted any of the wines.

the silos estate NR

Princes Highway, Jaspers Brush, NSW 2535 **region** Shoalhaven
phone (02) 4448 6082 **fax** (02) 4448 6246 **open** Wed–Sun 10–5
winemaker Gaynor Sims, Kate Khoury **production** 1000 **est.** 1985
product range ($13–18 CD) Traminer Riesling, Semillon, Chardonnay, Sauvignon Blanc, Wileys Creek Brut, Mostly Malbec, Softly Shiraz, Tawny Port, Liqueur Muscat.
summary Since 1995, Gaynor Sims and Kate Khoury, together with viticulturist Jovica Zecevic, have worked hard to improve the quality of the wine, starting with the 5 hectares of estate vineyards but also in the winery. The winery continues to rely on the tourist trade, however, and the wines do not appear in normal retail channels.

the warren vineyard   NR

Conte Road, Pemberton, WA 6260 **region** Pemberton/Warren Valley Manjimup
phone (08) 9776 1115 **fax** (08) 9776 1115 **open** 7 days 11–5
winemaker Andrew Forsell **production** 600 **est.** 1985
product range ($17–25 CD) Chardonnay, Riesling, Merlot, Cabernet Merlot, Cabernet Sauvignon, Vintage Port.
summary The 1.4-hectare vineyard was established in 1985 and is one of the smallest in the Pemberton region, coming to public notice when its 1991 Cabernet Sauvignon won the award for the Best Red Table Wine from the Pemberton region at the 1992 SGIO Western Australia Winemakers Exhibition.

the willows vineyard   ★★★

Light Pass Road, Light Pass, Barossa Valley, SA 5355 **region** Barossa Valley
phone (08) 8562 1080 **fax** (08) 8562 3447 **open** 7 days 10.30–4.30
winemaker Peter Scholz, Michael Scholz **production** 5000 **est.** 1989
product range ($10–24 CD) Riesling, Semillon, Shiraz, Cabernet Sauvignon, Sparkling.
summary The Scholz family have been grape growers for generations and have a little over 37 hectares of vineyards, selling part and retaining part of the crop. Current generation winemakers Peter and Michael Scholz could not resist the temptation to make smooth, well-balanced and flavoursome wines under their own label. These are all marketed with some years bottle age.

the yarrahill   ★★★★

886 Maroondah Highway, Coldstream, Vic 3770 **region** Yarra Valley
phone (03) 5962 2988 **fax** (03) 5964 9314 **open** Not
winemaker Rob Dolan **production** 5000 **est.** 1999
product range ($18–30 R) Semillon, Sauvignon Blanc, Chardonnay, Shiraz.
summary The YarraHill brings together a syndicate headed by Rob Dolan (as winemaker) and Malcolm Fell as viticulturist. The venture has been in the pipeline for several years, the wines having been made (under contract) at Yarra Ridge, where Rob Dolan was chief winemaker for a decade. It has two Yarra Valley vineyards totalling 56.5 hectares, part fully owned, and part owned by partners; the principal vineyard is ten years old. The venture has purchased a site on the Maroondah Highway next to Eyton-on-Yarra, and plans to have the cellar door operational by 2001; its own Yarra Valley winery should come on-stream around the same time. In the meantime the wines will be made at the new, large Dominion Wines winemaking facility in the Strathbogie Ranges near Avenel.

The YarraHill Chardonnay
The wine is fermented in stainless steel and then transferred to a mix of French and American oak for eight months during which time partial malolactic fermentation occurs.
▼▼▼▽ **1998** Medium yellow-green; quite complex, assertive, charry oak dominates the bouquet; on the palate, some melon fruit is to be found hiding in the oak thickets. May settle down with a little more time in bottle. **rating:** 83
best drinking 2002–2006 **drink with** Pork chops • $30

The YarraHill Shiraz
The grapes are hand-picked and fermented in both open-topped fermenters with hand plunging and in static enclosed red fermenters. The wine is matured in new and seasoned American oak for 12 months.
▼▼▼▼ **1998** Medium red-purple; the moderately intense bouquet offers ripe, sweet cherry fruit and vanilla oak. The medium-weight palate is clean, with sweet cherry fruit and soft tannins, the oak nicely balanced. **rating:** 85
best drinking 2002–2008 **drink with** Yearling steak • $23

thistle hill   ★★★☆

McDonalds Road, Mudgee, NSW 2850 **region** Mudgee
phone (02) 6373 3546 **fax** (02) 6373 3540 **open** Fri–Tues 10–4
winemaker David Robertson **production** 4000 **est.** 1976
product range ($12–22 CD) Riesling, Semillon, Chardonnay, Pinot Noir, Merlot, Cabernet Sauvignon.
summary David and Leslie Robertson produce supremely honest wines, always full of flavour and appropriately reflecting the climate and terroir. Some may be a little short on finesse but never on character. Chardonnay and Cabernet Sauvignon lead the way and age well.

thomas NR

23–24 Crowd Road, Gelorup, WA 6230 **region** Geographe
phone (08) 9795 7925 **open** By appointment
winemaker Gill Thomas **production** 600 **est.** 1976
product range ($4.50–25 CD) Pinot Noir, Cabernet Sauvignon.
summary I have not tasted the elegant wines of Bunbury pharmacist Gill Thomas for several years; they are only sold to a local clientele.

thornhill/the berry farm NR

Bessel Road, Rosa Glen, WA 6285 **region** Margaret River
phone (08) 9757 5054 **fax** (08) 9757 5116 **open** 7 days 10–4.30
winemaker Eion Lindsay **production** NFP **est.** 1990
product range ($11.50–25 CD) Under the Thornhill label Classic Dry Semillon, Sauvignon Blanc, Cabernet Sauvignon, Tickled Pink (Sparkling Cabernet Sauvignon), Still Tickled Pink (Light Cabernet Sauvignon). Under The Berry Farm label a range of fruit-based wines, including Sparkling Strawberry and Plum Port.
summary Although I have not enjoyed the Thornhill table wines, the fruit wines under The Berry Farm label are extraordinarily good. The sparkling strawberry wine has intense strawberry flavour; the plum port likewise, carrying its 16 degrees alcohol with remarkable ease.

🦐 three moon creek NR

Waratah Vineyard, Mungungo, via Monto, Qld 4630 **region** South Burnett
phone (07) 4166 5161 **fax** (07) 3876 9311 **open** 7 days 10–5
winemaker Andrew Hickinbotham (Contract) **production** 500 **est.** 1998
product range ($13–16 R) Queensland White, Queensland Shiraz Cabernet Sauvignon.
summary The Waratah Vineyard of Three Moon Creek is situated at the northern end of the South Burnett region, with 3.2 hectares of vineyard planted to chardonnay, verdelho, semillon, marsanne, viognier, shiraz, merlot and petit verdot, an exotic mix if ever there was one.

tilba valley NR

Glen Eden Vineyard, Corunna Lake via Tilba, NSW 2546 **region** Other Wineries of NSW
phone (02) 4473 7308 **open** Mon–Sat 10–5, Sun 11–5
winemaker Barry Field **production** 1400 **est.** 1978
product range ($10–14 CD) Traminer Riesling, Semillon, Chardonnay, Cabernet Hermitage.
summary A strongly tourist-oriented operation, serving a ploughman's lunch daily from noon to 2 pm. Has 5 hectares of estate vineyards; no recent tastings.

tim adams ★★★★

Warenda Road, Clare, SA 5453 **region** Clare Valley
phone (08) 8842 2429 **fax** (08) 8842 3550 **open** Mon–Fri 10.30–5, weekends 11–5
winemaker Tim Adams **production** 15 000 **est.** 1986
product range ($14–32.50 CD) Riesling, Semillon, Botrytis Semillon, Botrytis Riesling, The Fergus (Grenache), Shiraz, Aberfeldy Shiraz, Cabernet.
summary Tim and Pam Adams have built a first class business since Tim Adams left his position as winemaker at Leasingham in 1985. Eleven hectares of estate vineyards increasingly provide the wine for the business, supplemented by grapes from local growers. Tim Adams has consistently produced wines of exceptional depth of flavour and he also makes significant quantities of wine under contract for others in the district. Extensive distribution through all Australian States; exports to the UK and the US.

Tim Adams Riesling

Tim Adams is an immensely experienced winemaker, and now a veteran of the Clare Valley. Since establishing his own label, his forté has been full-bodied wooded whites and reds, but this wine shows that his skills most certainly extend to Riesling — where he started off many years ago at Leasingham.
▼▼▼▼ **1999** Light to medium yellow-green; the bouquet is powerful, tight and minerally, the palate likewise, with abundant grip and concentration, indeed, so much so that for the time being the fruit is locked up. **rating: 86**
best drinking 2004–2009 **best vintages** NA **drink with** Seafood salad • $14

Tim Adams Shiraz

Produced from 7 hectares of shiraz owned by the Adams and Crawley families.
ŦŦŦŦ 1998 Medium red-purple; the fragrant bouquet offers a complex array of cedar, cigar box, earth and leaf; a pleasant medium-bodied palate with a mix of cherry/plum and more savoury flavours. Both the tannins and oak are integrated and balanced. **rating:** 85
best drinking 2002–2007 **best vintages** '86, '88, '90, '92, '93, '96 **drink with** Spit roast lamb • $18

Tim Adams Cabernet

As the abbreviated name suggests, in fact a blend of 87 per cent Cabernet Sauvignon, 8 per cent Malbec and 5 per cent Cabernet Franc.
ŦŦŦŦ 1998 Medium to full red-purple; powerful, ripe blackberry/cassis/earth/chocolate aromas run into an equally rich, ripe and concentrated palate, literally flooded with sweet, juicy cassis/berry fruit; tannins and oak are there in the background. **rating:** 93
best drinking 2003–2013 **best vintages** '86, '88, '90, '92, '94, '98 **drink with** Char-grilled rump steak • $18

tim gramp ★★★★

Mintaro Road, Watervale, SA 5452 **region** Clare Valley
phone (08) 8431 3338 **fax** (08) 8431 3229 **open** Weekends and holidays 10.30–4.30
winemaker Tim Gramp **production** 5000 **est.** 1990
product range ($15.60–26.30 R) Watervale Riesling, McLaren Vale Shiraz, McLaren Vale Grenache, Watervale Prism Cabernet Sauvignon.
summary Tim Gramp has quietly built up a very successful business with a limited product range, and — by keeping overheads to a minimum — provides good wines at modest prices. The operation is supported by 2 hectares of cabernet sauvignon around the cellar door.

Tim Gramp McLaren Vale Shiraz

The wine is made in a full-throated, full-blooded style, using low-yielding dry-grown grapes and lots of American oak, and works to perfection. The wine is sourced from Willunga (in McLaren Vale) and spends 14 months in oak.
ŦŦŦŦŦ 1998 Dense but bright red-purple; the rich and complex bouquet oozes dark berry fruit and vanilla oak, while on the palate it is the rich, generous and complex fruit which leads the way, although oak is still there in support. A really excellent example of McLaren Vale Shiraz, particularly given its moderate alcohol of only 13 degrees. **rating:** 94
best drinking 2003–2013 **best vintages** '91, '92, '94, '96, '97, '98 **drink with** Barbecued, marinated steak • $26.30

Tim Gramp Watervale Cabernet Sauvignon

Produced from the 2 hectares of estate plantings which surround the winery and which are now fully mature.
ŦŦŦŦ 1998 Medium red-purple; very strong vanilla American oak thrusts its way through the bouquet; the wine has fair structure and balance, but the fruit is overwhelmed by that oak. **rating:** 81
best drinking 2002–2007 **best vintages** NA **drink with** Barbecued beef • $19.60

🥂 tinderbox vineyard NR

Tinderbox, Tas 7054 **region** Southern Tasmania
phone (03) 6229 2994 **fax** (03) 6229 2994 **open** By appointment
winemaker Andrew Hood (Contract) **production** 170 **est.** 1994
product range ($25 CD) Pinot Noir.
summary Lis McGown is a Hobart nurse who has established her 1-hectare vineyard on the slope beneath her house overlooking the entrance to the Derwent River and the D'Entrecasteaux Channel. The attractive label was designed by Barry Tucker, who was so charmed by Lis McGown's request that he waved his usual (substantial) fee.

Tinderbox Vineyard Pinot Noir

The first vintage from the vineyard, and a most auspicious debut, winning a silver medal at the Tasmanian Wines Show 2000.
ŦŦŦŦ 1998 Medium red-purple; ripe, slightly stewy cherry fruit aromas are effectively replicated on the very ripe flavoured palate. Some savoury notes and tannins add interest and structure to a well-balanced wine. **rating:** 84
best drinking 2001–2004 **drink with** Braised quail • $25

tingle-wood ★★★★★

Glenrowan Road, Denmark, WA 6333 **region** Great Southern
phone (08) 9840 9218 **fax** (08) 9840 9218 **open** 7 days 9–5
winemaker Brenden Smith (Contract) **production** 1000 **est.** 1976
product range ($15–20 CD) Yellow Tingle (Riesling), Late Harvest Yellow Tingle, Tree Top Walk, Red Tingle (Cabernet Shiraz), Ruby Tingle (Port-style).
summary An intermittent producer of Riesling of extraordinary quality, although birds and other disasters do intervene and prevent production in some years.

⚘ tinklers vineyard NR

Pokolbin Mountains Road, Pokolbin, NSW 2330 **region** Lower Hunter Valley
phone (02) 4998 7435 **fax** (02) 4998 7529 **open** By appointment
winemaker Ian Tinkler **production** NA **est.** 1997
product range NA.
summary Ian and Usher Tinkler own a large (32-hectare) vineyard on the slopes of the Pokolbin Mountain Road; most of the production is sold, a small amount being contract-made for cellar door sales.

tinlins NR

Kangarilla Road, McLaren Flat, SA 5171 **region** McLaren Vale
phone (08) 8323 8649 **fax** (08) 8323 9747 **open** 7 days 9–5
winemaker Warren Randall **production** 30 000 **est.** 1977
product range ($1.50–3.40 CD) Generic table, fortified and flavoured wines sold for $1.50 for table wines and $3.40 for fortified wines.
summary A very interesting operation run by former Seppelt sparkling winemaker Warren Randall, drawing upon 100 hectares of estate vineyards, which specialises in bulk-wine sales to the major Australian wine companies. A small proportion of the production is sold direct through the cellar door at mouthwateringly low prices to customers who provide their own containers and purchase by the litre. McLaren Vale's only bulk-wine specialist.

tinonee vineyard NR

Milbrodale Road, Broke, NSW 2330 **region** Lower Hunter Valley
phone (02) 6579 1308 **fax** (02) 6579 1146 **open** Weekends and public holidays 11–4
winemaker Andrew Margan, Ray Merger (Contract) **production** 1000 **est.** 1997
product range ($15–18 CD) Chardonnay, Chardonnay Semillon, Verdelho, Merlot, Shiraz.
summary Ian Craig has established 14 hectares of vineyards on a mix of red volcanic and river flat soils at Broke. Part were in production, with the remainder coming into bearing by the end of the last decade, ultimately producing 5000 cases of wine per year.

tintilla wines NR

725 Hermitage Road, Pokolbin, NSW 2335 **region** Lower Hunter Valley
phone 0411 214 478 **fax** (02) 9767 6894 **open** By appointment
winemaker Jon Reynolds (Contract) **production** 3000 **est.** 1993
product range ($15–30 CD) Semillon, Sangiovese, Sangiovese Merlot, Shiraz, Reserve Shiraz, Merlot.
summary The Lusby family has established a 7.5-hectare vineyard (including 1 hectare of sangiovese) on their northeast-facing vineyard, with its red clay and limestone soil. They have also established an olive grove producing four different types of olives, which are cured and sold on the estate. The first wine release promises much for the future.

Tintilla Shiraz

Ten per cent of the wine is fermented using the carbonic maceration technique, the remaining part a 'natural' fermentation. The wine spends a little under 12 months in American oak. The 1997 was a tentative start, the '98 in a different league altogether, and the '99 somewhere in between.
▼▼▼▽ **1999** Medium to full red-purple; the rich bouquet has dark cherry, chocolate and lots of vanilla oak. The palate provides more of the same, looking very youthful and very slightly unfinished. On the other hand, it was bottled only days before it was tasted, and the judgment may prove a little harsh. **rating:** 84
best drinking 2003–2009 **best vintages** '98 **drink with** Rare scotch fillet • $22.95

tipperary hill estate   NR

Alma–Bowendale Road, Alma via Maryborough, Vic 3465 **region** Bendigo
phone (03) 5461 3312 **fax** (03) 5461 3312 **open** Weekends 10–5, or by appointment
winemaker Paul Flowers **production** 300 **est.** 1986
product range ($16–24 CD) Shiraz, Pinot Noir, Cabernets.
summary All of the wine is sold through the cellar door and on-site restaurant, open on Sundays. Says Paul Flowers, production depends 'on the frost, wind and birds', which perhaps explains why this is very much a part-time venture. Situated 7 kilometres west of the city of Maryborough, Tipperary Hill Estate is the only winery operating in the Central Goldfields Shire. Winemaker Paul Flowers built the rough-cut pine winery and the bluestone residential cottage next door with the help of friends. Together with wife Margaret he also operates a restaurant.

tizzana   ★★☆

518 Tizzana Road, Ebenezer, NSW 2756 **region** Other Wineries of NSW
phone (02) 4579 1150 **fax** (02) 4579 1216 **open** Weekends, holidays 12–6
winemaker Peter Auld **production** 300 **est.** 1887
product range ($9.50–17 CD) From Tizzana vineyards Rosso di Tizzana (a light, dry Cabernet Sauvignon), Waterloo Shiraz, Cabernet Sauvignon, Sackville Tawny, Vintage Port and Old Liqueur Sweet White; the Tizzana Selection from other regions of Traminer Riesling, White Port, Sherry (the latter two from Stanton & Killeen) and then two wines from South Australia under the Hawkesbury History Heritage 2001 Committee (a strange combination), including Federation Semillon Chardonnay and Federation Tawny Port.
summary Tizzana has been a weekend and holiday occupation for Peter Auld for many years now, operating in one of the great historic wineries built (in 1887) by Australia's true renaissance man, Dr Thomas Fiaschi. The wines may not be great, but the ambience is.

tollana   ★★★★

Tanunda Road, Nuriootpa, SA 5355 **region** Barossa Valley
phone (08) 8560 9408 **fax** (08) 8562 2494 **open** Mon–Sat 10–5, Sun 1–5
winemaker Neville Falkenberg **production** 30 000 **est.** 1888
product range ($10–20 R) Eden Valley Riesling, Eden Valley Chardonnay, Coonawarra Botrytis Riesling, Hermitage, Show Reserve Shiraz, Eden Valley Adelaide Hills Cabernet Sauvignon Bin TR222.
summary As the Southcorp Wine Group moves to establish regional identity for its wines, Tollana is emphasising its Eden Valley base. Seemingly as a by-product of Penfolds development of Yattarna and related wines, the Tollana Chardonnay style has become more elegant, now standing comfortably alongside the flavoursome Riesling and Shiraz.

Tollana Eden Valley Shiraz

While it has been the Show Reserve Shiraz which has been featured in prior editions, the base varietal from 1998 is a commendable wine.

▼▼▼▼ **1998** Medium red-purple; the bouquet is quite fragrant yet smooth, with an attractive twist of lemon vanilla oak. Dark cherry fruit leads the way on the palate, although that savoury/tangy oak is evident in a positive and not aggressive fashion; vanilla tones and soft, fine tannins appear on the finish.   **rating:** 86
best drinking 2002–2008 **best vintages** '98 **drink with** Grilled T-bone • $20

Tollana Cabernet Sauvignon Bin TR222

Another Tollana classic with a proud history. Made entirely from Eden Valley Cabernet Sauvignon, it is matured in new and one-year-old American and French oak for 12 months. Like the Riesling, it has been a prolific and consistent gold medal winner. The wine comes from the Woodbury Vineyard, which has 60 hectares of fully mature cabernet sauvignon, the best parcels going to produce this wine which has been a prolific gold medal winner over the years.

▼▼▼▼▽ **1998** Medium purple-red; the bouquet is quite sweet, with blackberry and blackcurrant fruit to the fore, and far less of the savoury/leafy characters one often finds in this wine. The palate is similarly moulded, with blackberry, blackcurrant and dark chocolate flavours supported by fine, sweet tannins and attractive oak. Really delicious.   **rating:** 91
▼▼▼▼ **1997** Medium red-purple; the bouquet is moderately intense, with a good balance between dark berry fruit and spicy oak. The palate is quite elegant and restrained, with a mix of red and dark berry fruit flavours, and finishes with soft tannins. A winner of gold medals at the Perth and Barossa wine shows.   **rating:** 85
best drinking 2003–2013 **best vintages** '86, '88, '90, '91, '92, '93, '95, '96, '98 **drink with** Braised lamb • $20

❧ tom's waterhole wines   NR

Felton, Longs Corner Road, Canowindra, NSW 2804 **region** Cowra
phone (02) 6344 1819 **fax** (02) 6344 2172 **open** Weekends 10–5
winemaker Graham Kerr **production** 300 **est.** 1997
product range ($7–15 ML) TWW Semillon, Humpers Shiraz, TWW Vat 7 Shiraz, TWW Vat 12 Cabernet.
summary Graham Timms and Graham Kerr started the development of Tom's Waterhole Wines in 1997, progressively establishing 2 hectares of shiraz, and 1 hectare each of cabernet sauvignon, merlot and semillon, the planting programme to be completed in the year 2000. A decision has been taken to bypass the use of irrigation, and the yields will be low, with an expectation that the small on-site winery will crush around 20 tonnes per year.

toorak estate   NR

Toorak Road, Leeton, NSW 2705 **region** Riverina
phone (02) 6953 2333 **fax** (02) 6953 4454 **open** Mon–Sat 9–5
winemaker Robert Bruno **production** 10 000 **est.** 1965
product range ($7–14 CD) Rhine Riesling, Traminer Riesling, Colombard Chardonnay, Semillon, Chardonnay, Autumn Harvest, Lambrusco Red and White, Leeton Shiraz, Shiraz Cabernet, Ruby Cabernet, Cabernet Sauvignon, Sparkling, Fortifieds.
summary A traditional, long-established Riverina producer with a strong Italian-based clientele around Australia. Production has been increasing significantly, utilising 65 hectares of estate plantings and grapes purchased from other growers.

torbreck vintners   ★★★★☆

Roenfeldt Road, Marananga, SA 5352 **region** Barossa Valley
phone (08) 8562 4155 **fax** (08) 8562 4195 **open** Not
winemaker David Powell **production** 400 **est.** 1994
product range ($24–55 ML) The Steading (Grenache Mataro Shiraz), RunRig (Shiraz Viognier), Juveniles, Descendants.
summary Torbreck has made a major impact since its first releases in 1997 of a 1995 RunRig and 1996 The Steading. David Powell's family has assembled small patches of old vine shiraz, grenache and mourvedre in the Barossa Valley which they are sharefarming, complementing a small vineyard of their own. The two vintages of each of the red wines so far released have been of very high quality, opulently concentrated and rich. The '97 releases were tasted shortly prior to the book going to print; Murphy's Law has led to the loss of my notes, but the wines were every bit as good as, if not better than, the previous releases.

❧ tower estate   ★★★★☆

Corner Broke Road/Hall Road, Pokolbin, NSW 2320 **region** Lower Hunter Valley
phone (02) 4998 7879 **fax** (02) 4998 7798 **open** Sun–Fri 1–5, Sat 10–6
winemaker Dan Dineen **production** 8000 **est.** 1999
product range ($18–25 CD) Clare Valley Riesling, Adelaide Hills Sauvignon Blanc, Hunter Valley Semillon, Hunter Valley Verdelho, Hunter Valley Shiraz, Barossa Valley Shiraz, Coonawarra Cabernet Sauvignon.
summary Tower Estate is a joint venture headed by Len Evans, featuring a luxury conference centre and accommodation. I have in fact tasted the wines informally during an early visit to Tower Estate in the course of its construction, and each was exemplary. However, retasting on a formal basis was not possible prior to publication.

trafford hill vineyard   NR

Lot 1 Bower Road, Normanville, SA 5204 **region** Other Wineries of SA
phone (08) 8558 3595 **open** By appointment
winemaker John Sanderson, Allan Dyson (Consultant) **production** 300 **est.** 1996
product range ($11–17 ML) Riesling, Monique Family Reserve Blend.
summary Irene and John Sanderson have established 1.25 of vineyard at Normanville, on the coast of the Fleurieu Peninsula near to its southern extremity. Irene carries out all the viticulture, and John Sanderson makes the wine with help from district veteran Allan Dyson. Distribution is through local restaurants, the remainder through mail order and cellar door.

treehouse vineyard ★★★★

257 Richmond Road, Cambridge, Tas 7170 **region** Southern Tasmania
phone (03) 6248 5367 **fax** (03) 6248 4175 **open** Wed–Sun 10–5
winemaker Andrew Hood (Contract) **production** 500 **est.** 1991
product range Riesling, Chardonnay, Pinot Noir.
summary Gradon and Margaret Johnstone established Treehouse in 1991 with the planting of their first grapes. Restaurant meals and casual food is available at the Treehouse Wine Centre, and all of the wines are sold through the cellar door and by mail order. Treehouse was purchased by Gillian Christian and her husband in 1999.

Treehouse Vineyard Riesling

A typical Tasmanian Riesling, with good acidity and the promise of cellaring well. Produced in tiny quantities, normally a difficult challenge for delicate white wines, but no problem for the experienced contract-winemaker Andrew Hood.
▼▼▼▼▽ **1999** Light green-yellow; a clean, delicate but fragrant bouquet with a mix of lime juice and passionfruit aromas expands into an intense, powerful and lingering palate, with herbal notes adding yet further interest. Gold medal winner 2000 Tasmanian Wines Show. **rating:** 93
best drinking 2000–2007 **best vintages** '99 **drink with** Caesar salad • $NA

Treehouse Vineyard Chardonnay

First made in 1996, and quickly established its high quality. The 1998 vintage topped its class at the 1999 Tasmanian Wines Show, while the 1999 ended up with a silver medal, receiving gold medal points on my score sheet at the 2000 show.
▼▼▼▼▽ **1999** Very good green-yellow colour; a marvellously complex and aromatic bouquet with tangy, citrussy fruit leads into a palate with equally good length and intensity; here the fruit is supported by just a hint of delicate oak. **rating:** 91
best drinking 2001–2007 **best vintages** '98, '99 **drink with** Pan-fried veal • $NA

treen ridge estate NR

Packer Road, Pemberton, WA 6260 **region** Pemberton, Warren Valley and Manjimup
phone (08) 9776 1131 **fax** (08) 9776 0442 **open** Wed–Fri 11–5, weekends 10–5
winemaker Andrew Mountford (Contract) **production** NFP **est.** 1992
product range ($12–18 CD) Riesling, Late Harvest Riesling, Sauvignon Blanc, Springfield, Springfield Shiraz, Shiraz, Cabernet Sauvignon.
summary The Treen Ridge vineyard and three-room accommodation is set between the Treen Brook state forest and The Warren national park and is operated by Mollie and Barry Scotman.

Treen Ridge Estate Springfield Shiraz

Deliberately made in a lighter style with reduced skin contact; the intention is to provide a wine for those who do not like conventional tannic reds.
▼▼▼▽ **1999** Medium purple-red; the bouquet is firm, with distinct herbal notes, but riper cherry fruit comes through on the smooth palate with nicely balanced acidity. As intended, the tannins are very soft. **rating:** 83
best drinking 2000–2002 **best vintages** NA **drink with** Red meat of all kinds • $18

treeton estate ★★★

North Treeton Road, Cowaramup, WA 6284 **region** Margaret River
phone (08) 9755 5481 **fax** (08) 9755 5051 **open** 7 days 10–6
winemaker David McGowan **production** 3000 **est.** 1984
product range ($15–17 R) Chardonnay, Riesling, Estate White, Petit Rouge, Shiraz, Liqueur Muscat.
summary In 1982 David McGowan and wife Corinne purchased the 30-hectare property upon which Treeton Estate is established, beginning to plant the vines two years later. David has done just about everything in his life, and in the early years was working in Perth, which led to various setbacks for the vineyard. The wines are light and fresh, sometimes rather too much so.

trentham estate ★★★☆

Sturt Highway, Trentham Cliffs, NSW 2738   **region** Murray Darling
phone (03) 5024 8888   **fax** (03) 5024 8800   **open** Mon–Fri 8.30–5, weekends 9.30–5
winemaker Anthony Murphy, Shane Kerr   **production** 50 000   **est.** 1988
product range ($8.50–15 R) Riesling, Sauvignon Blanc, Colombard Chardonnay, Viognier, Chardonnay, Noble Taminga, Pinot Noir, Merlot, Grenache Shiraz, Shiraz, Burke & Wills Tawny Port; Tresoli White and Red, Falling Leaf Autumn White and Red.
summary Remarkably consistent tasting notes across all wine styles from all vintages since 1989 attest to the expertise of ex-Mildara winemaker Tony Murphy, now making the Trentham wines from his family vineyards. Indeed, Trentham seems to be going from strength to strength with each succeeding vintage, exemplified by the Tresoli White and Red wines. The winery restaurant is also recommended. National retail distribution; exports to the US, Canada, the UK and Europe.

Trentham Estate Viognier

The spread of viognier continues, however uncertain some of the resulting wines are; this wine offers promise.
▼▼▼▼ 1999 Medium to full yellow-green; the bouquet is quite rich, with honey and pastille aromas in authentic varietal mode. The palate is rich and quite weighty, with honey, peach, lychee and apricot flavours all evident. Very creditable result.   **rating:** 85
best drinking 2000–2002   **best vintages** NA   **drink with** Creamy pasta   • $15

Trentham Estate Chardonnay

Produced from 6 hectares of estate-grown grapes, which account for 20 per cent of the total plantings of around 30 hectares. Skilfully made, using predominantly French oak; the '98 was a gold medal winner at the Brisbane Wine Show in 1999.
▼▼▼▼ 1998 Glowing yellow-green; the bouquet is solid, with buttery/peachy fruit and a hint of French oak. The palate has good fruit intensity and length, with ripe peachy fruit typical of the best riverland fruit; mercifully, the oak handling is subtle.   **rating:** 89
best drinking 2000–2001   **best vintages** '89, '90, '92, '94, '95, '98   **drink with** Stir-fried abalone   • $12.50

trevor jones ★★★★☆

Barossa Valley Highway, Lyndoch, SA 5351   **region** Barossa Valley
phone (08) 8524 4303   **fax** (08) 8524 4880   **open** 7 days 9–6
winemaker Trevor Jones   **production** 2000   **est.** 1996
product range ($15–25 CD) Riesling, Virgin Chardonnay, Dry Grown Shiraz, Cabernet Merlot.
summary Trevor Jones is an industry veteran, with vast experience in handling fruit from the Barossa Valley, Eden Valley and Adelaide Hills. He has finally taken the step of introducing his own strikingly designed label, using grapes purchased from various contract growers, with the first wines going on sale in 1996, although including earlier vintages.

trio station NR

17–21 Piper Street, Kyneton, Vic 3444   **region** Macedon Ranges
phone (03) 5422 7444   **fax** (03) 5422 7400   **open** Weekends 10–6 or by appointment
winemaker David Watson   **production** 15 000   **est.** 1998
product range ($13.95-24.95 R) Trio Station Dry Riesling, Chardonnay, Shiraz Cabernet.
summary Trio Station is one of the businesses of Vincorp Wineries Limited, a listed company (the other, and very important, winery is Virgin Hills). It is situated in an historic building in the heart of the township of Kyneton, Victoria, and was established in co-operation with the Macedon Ranges Shire Council. It draws upon 28 hectares of vineyard in the Geographe region of Western Australia and a further 40 hectares at the nearby Glenhope Vineyard in the Macedon Ranges.

Trio Station Reserve Chardonnay

Produced from grapes grown on the Fryerstown Road Vineyard at Taradale, north of Kyneton. The wine is pressed and taken direct to new French oak for fermentation, with the malolactic fermentation also completed in oak.
▼▼▼▽ 1998 Medium yellow-green; the bouquet is quite stylish, with obvious barrel-ferment oak influences and inputs; that oak comes through on the palate to completely subjugate the elegant fruit. Might conceivably come back into better balance with more age.   **rating:** 83
best drinking 2000–2003   **best vintages** NA   **drink with** Wiener schnitzel   • $24.95

Trio Station Three Steps Chardonnay

Produced from grapes grown in northwest and central Victoria, predominantly fermented in stainless steel, part in oak.

▼▼▼⟟ 1999 Medium to full yellow-green; the bouquet is very rich and full, promising to develop quickly. The palate, likewise, has lots of extract and flavour. Red alert: drink immediately. **rating: 83**

▼▼▼▼ 1998 Medium yellow-green; the bouquet is quite rich and complex, the palate with rich, peachy fruit, balancing acidity and good length. Surprisingly impressive. **rating: 87**

best drinking Drink now **best vintages** '97 **drink with** Breast of chicken • $13.95

tuck's ridge ★★★★

37 Red Hill–Shoreham Road, Red Hill South, Vic 3937 **region** Mornington Peninsula
phone (03) 5989 8660 **fax** (03) 5989 8579 **open** 7 days 12–5
winemaker Daniel Greene **production** 13 000 **est.** 1988
product range ($14–45 CD) Semillon, Riesling, Altera Semillon Sauvignon Blanc, Chardonnay, Pinot Noir, Altera Pinot Noir, Reserve Pinot Noir, Merlot, Cabernet Sauvignon Merlot, Vues Méthode Champenoise.
summary After an initial burst of frenetic activity following its launch in July 1993, Tuck's Ridge has slowed down a little. Nonetheless, plantings have been increased to a little over 25 hectares, making it one of the largest vineyards in production on the Mornington Peninsula.

Tuck's Ridge Chardonnay

Made using all of the politically correct techniques, including 'wild' (naturally occurring) malolactic fermentation, lees contact and minimal filtration.

▼▼▼▼ 1999 Medium yellow-green; a quite rich bouquet with cashew, peach and honey is followed by a palate with intense nectarine, citrus and peach flavours, with good length and persistence. The oak is appropriately subtle.

rating: 89

best drinking 2001–2005 **best vintages** '99 **drink with** Thai cuisine • $24

Tuck's Ridge Pinot Noir

Produced from 10 hectares of estate plantings and now released in three modes: Reserve, varietal and the far cheaper third label of Altera.

▼▼▼▼ 1999 Medium red-purple; the bouquet is already quite complex, with a mix of spicy/foresty/stemmy/dusty aromas intertwined around sweet cherry. On the palate, lively, fresh cherry fruit comes to the fore, finishing crisp and clean. Will undoubtedly flower over the next few years. **rating: 86**

best drinking 2001–2005 **best vintages** '94, '97 **drink with** Grilled Atlantic salmon • $27

Tuck's Ridge Altera Pinot Noir

Although made as an early release style, has above-average character, and is a highly competitive Pinot at its price point.

▼▼▼⟟ 1999 Medium red-purple; ripe, juicy, spicy fruit on the bouquet is followed by a palate in which quite strong carbonic maceration stem/spice characters come through. **rating: 84**

best drinking 2000–2003 **best vintages** '99 **drink with** Ragout of wild mushrooms • $18

Tuck's Ridge Reserve Pinot Noir

A new arrival on the scene, utilising the best available fruit, and given longer time in barrel and bottle prior to release. Deserves its Reserve status and price.

▼▼▼▼⟟ 1998 Medium to full red-purple; a richer and deeper version of the varietal wine, with powerful savoury/foresty aromas. The palate is rich and complex, with a mix of plum, savoury and spice flavours; good balance and structure; a sophisticated wine. **rating: 92**

best drinking 2000–2006 **best vintages** '98 **drink with** Braised duck • $45

tulloch NR

'Glen Elgin', De Beyers Road, Pokolbin, NSW 2321 **region** Lower Hunter Valley
phone (02) 4998 7580 **fax** (02) 4998 7682 **open** Mon–Fri 9–4.30, weekends 10–4.30
winemaker Greg Jarrat **production** 20 000 **est.** 1895
product range ($11.20–13.80 R) Unoaked Chardonnay, Classic Hunter White, Semillon Chardonnay, Verdelho, Justina (Fruity White), Classic Rich Red, Cabernets, Hector of Glen Elgin (Hermitage), Fortifieds.
summary A once-great name and reputation which suffered enormously under multiple ownership changes with a loss of identity and direction. In production terms at least, it has found its feet, for it is now the centre of winemaking activities in the Hunter Valley for the Lindeman, Hungerford Hill and Tulloch brands, the last suckling at the breast of the Verdelho, and doing very nicely. Once again, a disclosure of interest, as for Lindemans and Hungerford Hill. It should be noted that between 1997 and May 2000 I had some responsibilities for this brand and hence rate neither the winery nor the wines, though will do so in the future.

tumbarumba wine cellars   NR

Sunnyside, Albury Close, Tumbarumba, NSW 2653 **region** Tumbarumba
phone (02) 6948 3055 **fax** (02) 6948 3055 **open** Weekends and public holidays, or by appointment
winemaker Charles Sturt University (Contract) **production** 600 **est.** 1990
product range ($15–25) Chardonnay, Pinot Noir and Pinot Chardonnay sparkling wines under the Black Range label, with further individual labels likely for the future.
summary Tumbarumba Cellars has taken over the former George Martins Winery (itself established in 1990) to provide an outlet for wines made from Tumbarumba region grapes. It is essentially a co-operative venture, involving local growers and businessmen, and with modest aspirations to growth.

tumbarumba wine estates   NR

Maragle Valley via Tumbarumba, NSW 2653 **region** Tumbarumba
phone (02) 6948 4457 **fax** (02) 6948 4457 **open** Not
winemaker Charles Sturt University (Contract) **production** NA **est.** 1995
product range Chardonnay, Pinot Chardonnay Sparkling.
summary Having established his vineyards progressively since 1982, Frank Minutello decided to seek to add value (and interest) to the enterprise by having a small proportion of his production vinified at Charles Sturt University, commencing with the 1995 vintage. The wines are sold by mail order and from The Elms Restaurant in Tumbarumba.

turkey flat   ★★★★☆

Bethany Road, Tanunda, SA 5352 **region** Barossa Valley
phone (08) 8563 2851 **fax** (08) 8563 3610 **open** 7 days 11–5
winemaker Peter Schulz **production** 10 000 **est.** 1990
product range ($11.99–42 R) Semillon, Rosé, Grenache Noir, Butchers Block, Shiraz, Cabernet Sauvignon.
summary The establishment date of Turkey Flat is given as 1990 but it might equally well have been 1870 (or thereabouts), when the Schulz family purchased the Turkey Flat vineyard, or 1847, when the vineyard was first planted to the very shiraz which still grows today. In addition there are 6 hectares of very old grenache and 10.5 hectares of much younger semillon and cabernet sauvignon, together with 2 hectares each of mourvedre, dolcetto and (a recent arrival) marsanne. A significant part of the output is sold to some of the best-known Barossa Valley makers, not the least being Charles Melton, St Hallett, and Rockford. Retail distribution in Adelaide, Melbourne and Sydney; exports to the US, the UK, Belgium and Switzerland.

Turkey Flat Rosé

A quite delicious wine, made from a blend of 80 per cent Grenache, 10 per cent Cabernet Sauvignon and 10 per cent Shiraz. The addition of the Cabernet Sauvignon and Shiraz components in fact takes the wine from a conventional Rosé-style towards a light-bodied dry red, an elusive goal for most winemakers.
▼▼▼▼ 1999 Light, vivid fuchsia; clean and fresh rose petal aromas are followed by a palate with that extra degree of length; very clever manipulation of residual sugar and acidity. **rating:** 88
best drinking Drink now **best vintages** '99 **drink with** Nothing or anything • $11.90

Turkey Flat Shiraz

Based upon a precious patch of 150-year-old vines at the heart of the Turkey Flat Vineyard. Right from the outset it has been an exceptional wine, praised by all who have tasted and written about it.
▼▼▼▼▼ 1998 Medium to full red-purple; the powerful, ripe bouquet ranges through blackberry, spice and plum aromas, supported by subtle oak. The palate has very concentrated flavours tracking the bouquet, yet is not extractive; all the power comes from the dark plum and blackberry fruit. **rating:** 95
best drinking 2003–2018 **best vintages** '90, '92, '93, '94, '98 **drink with** Smoked kangaroo • $42

Turkey Flat Grenache Noir

Peter Schulz, who effectively runs Turkey Flat, is a vigneron, not a winemaker, and from the word go has had the Turkey Flat wines made by experts. The Grenache is made by Chris Ringland of Rockford and right from its first release has been a cult wine.
▼▼▼▽ 1998 Light to medium red-purple; the bouquet is clean, fresh and lively, one step up from Rosé. The palate follows logically; all in all, a very different manifestation of Barossa Grenache. **rating:** 81
best drinking Drink now **best vintages** '91, '92, '93 **drink with** Maggie Beer's game pie • $14.50

Turkey Flat Cabernet Sauvignon

Made in the generously proportioned and fruity style which has gained Turkey Flat such a loyal band of followers.
TTTY 1998 Medium to full red-purple; the solid berry fruit with hints of leather and earth on the bouquet is accompanied by lots of vanilla oak. The moderately intense palate has the hallmark cassis berry fruit, but is going through a transition phase at the moment, making it a little hard. There is no problem with the oak, and the wine should merit higher points in the years ahead. **rating:** 84

best drinking 2002–2007 **best vintages** '97 **drink with** Roast leg of lamb • $38

turramurra estate ★★★★

RMB 4327 Wallaces Road, Dromana Vic 3926 **region** Mornington Peninsula
phone (03) 5987 1146 **fax** (03) 5987 1286 **open** 12–5 first weekend of the month or by appointment
winemaker David Leslie **production** 7000 **est.** 1989
product range ($26–40 CD) Sauvignon Blanc, Chardonnay, Pinot Noir, Shiraz, Cabernet Sauvignon.
summary Dr David Leslie gave up his job as a medical practitioner after completing the Bachelor of Applied Science (Wine Science) at Charles Sturt University to concentrate on developing the family's 10-hectare estate at Dromana. Wife Paula is the viticulturist. Limited retail distribution in Melbourne and Sydney; exports to the UK.

Turramurra Estate Pinot Noir

Estate-grown; very complex winemaking techniques used; unfined and unfiltered.
TTTTY 1998 Medium red-purple; the bouquet is uncompromisingly complex, with a range of secondary, savoury/spicy aromas mingling with plum and cherry fruit. The palate is smooth and rounded, with delicious plummy fruit at its core; good acidity and length. **rating:** 90

best drinking 2000–2004 **best vintages** '97, '98 **drink with** Double-cooked veal shank • $40

Turramurra Estate Cabernet

A blend of 90 per cent Cabernet Sauvignon, and 5 per cent each of Merlot and Cabernet Franc. A moderately warm ferment is followed by 22 months maturation in French oak barriques, 50 per cent new, 50 per cent second use or older.
TTTT 1997 Medium to full red-purple; the bouquet is full and complex, with slightly gamey overtones which are climate-derivative, not winemaking. The palate has plenty of sweet berry fruit, touches of mint and leaf, and finishes with soft tannins. An outstanding achievement for Mornington Peninsula cabernet, obviously attributable to the ideal growing conditions. **rating:** 86

best drinking 2001–2005 **best vintages** '97 **drink with** Roast veal • $33

12 acres ★★☆

Nagambie–Rushworth Road, Bailieston, Vic 3608 **region** Goulburn Valley
phone (03) 5794 2020 **fax** (03) 5794 2020 **open** Thurs–Mon 10–6, July weekends only
winemaker Peter Prygodicz, Jana Prygodicz **production** 700 **est.** 1994
product range ($16 CD) Shiraz, Merlot, Cabernet Sauvignon.
summary The charmingly named 12 Acres is a red wine specialist, with Peter and Jana Prygodicz making the wines on site in a tiny winery. The wines could benefit from renewal of the oak in which they are matured, for they are all quite astringent.

twin bays NR

Lot 1 Martin Road, Yankalilla, SA 5203 **region** Other Wineries of SA
phone (08) 8267 2844 **fax** (08) 8239 0877 **open** Weekends and holidays
winemaker Bruno Giorgio, Alan Dyson **production** 1000 **est.** 1989
product range ($10–19 CD) Riesling, Light Red, Rosado, Wild Grenache, Shiraz, Cabernet Sauvignon, Fortifieds.
summary Twin Bays operates the first winery in the Yankalilla district, one hour's drive south of Adelaide on the Fleurieu Peninsula. Two hectares of estate plantings have been established, but until these and future plantings come into bearing, the wines are made by district veteran Alan Dyson and Adelaide doctor and specialist Bruno Giorgio from grapes partly estate-grown and partly purchased from McLaren Vale. Retail distribution in Sydney, Melbourne and Adelaide.

twin valley estate NR

Hoffnungsthal Road, Lyndoch, SA 5351 **region** Barossa Valley
phone (08) 8524 4584 **fax** (08) 8524 4978 **open** Weekends 10–5
winemaker Fernando Martin, Kay Martin **production** 3500 **est.** 1990
product range ($9–18 CD) Traminer, Frontignac Spätlese, Eden Valley Rhine Riesling, Semillon Chardonnay, Cabernet Sauvignon Franc, Classic Burgundy, Pinot Cabernet, White Port, Martin's Mead.
summary While Fernando Martin has always had his sights set firmly on the tourist trade, the Twin Valley Estate wines are more than acceptable, the spicy, limey Frontignac Spätlese being a particularly good example of its kind.

2 bud spur NR

Unit 2, 8 Binney Court, Sandy Bay, Tas 7005 (postal) **region** Southern Tasmania
phone (03) 6225 0711 **fax** (03) 6233 3477 **open** Not
winemaker Michael Vishacki **production** 100 **est.** 1996
product range ($18–28 ML) Sauvignon Blanc, Chardonnay, Pinot Noir.
summary Phil Barker and Anne Lasala commenced establishing 2.5 hectares of vineyard in 1996. Phil Barker has the most extraordinary qualifications, having worked as a chef for over ten years after acquiring a PhD in Botany, and is now a botanist with the Tasmanian Parks and Wildlife Department. There is still much agonising about the name; originally named Latitude, it has now become 2 Bud Spur, a term viticulturists are very familiar with, but which will completely confuse the average wine drinker.

tyrrell's ★★★★★

Broke Road, Pokolbin, NSW 2321 **region** Lower Hunter Valley
phone (02) 4993 7000 **fax** (02) 4998 7723 **open** Mon–Sat 8–5
winemaker Andrew Spinaze **production** 750 000 **est.** 1858
product range ($7–50 R) At the bottom end the large-volume Long Flat White and Red; next in price is Old Winery Chardonnay, Semillon, Chardonnay Semillon, Semillon Sauvignon Blanc, Riesling, Pinot Noir, Shiraz, Cabernet Merlot; next the Individual Vineyard range of wines, including Shee-Oak Chardonnay, Stevens Semillon, Lost Block Semillon, Brookdale Semillon, Fordwich Verdelho, Eclipse Pinot Noir, Moon Mountain Chardonnay, Brokenback Shiraz, Stevens Shiraz; at the very top Vat 1 Semillon, Vat 6 Pinot Noir, Vat 9 Shiraz, Vat 47 Chardonnay.
summary A quite extraordinary family winery which has grown up from an insignificant base in 1960 to become one of the most influential mid-sized companies, successfully competing with wines running all the way from cheap, volume-driven Long Flat White up to the super-premium Vat 47 Chardonnay, which is one of Australia's best. There is a similar range of price and style with the red wines, and in recent years Tyrrell's has simply never faltered within the parameters of price and style. Exports to all of the major markets throughout North America, Europe and Southeast Asia.

Tyrrell's Lost Block Semillon

The Lost Block is in fact part of the famous HVD Vineyard, and was so named after the 1993 vintage when the grapes were mistakenly allowed to ripen longer than normal, i.e. someone forgot about them. Smart new label designs were introduced in 2000 for the '99 and subsequent vintages.
▼▼▼▼ 1999 Light green-yellow; the bouquet has that extra level of intensity yet hard-to-define fruit; you know what will develop with age, but right now you can't pinpoint the characters. The palate doesn't disappoint, with lively sweet lemon, grass and a subliminal touch of honey. **rating:** 88
best drinking 2004–2010 **best vintages** '93, '94, '96, '97, '99 **drink with** Calamari • $18

Tyrrell's Old Winery Semillon

Comes at or near the base of the Tyrrell's Semillon hierarchy, but is always made with skill and in years such as 1999 can provide exceptional value.
▼▼▼▼♡ 1999 Light green-yellow; the bouquet is light but quite fragrant, with classic, crisp minerally semillon fruit. The palate is long and intense, with a great finish; bursting with life. **rating:** 93
best drinking 2004–2014 **best vintages** '99 **drink with** Cold seafood • $14

Tyrrell's Stevens Semillon

An individual vineyard (Stevens) wine which is always of high quality.
▼▼▼▼▼ 1996 Light green-yellow; very tight and youthful, with just a hint of toast starting to build; the palate is tight, lively and lemony, still a baby, braced by excellent, fresh acidity. **rating:** 94
best drinking 2001–2011 **best vintages** '96 **drink with** Balmain bugs • $22

Tyrrell's Vat 1 Semillon

One of the great, classic Hunter Valley Semillons, produced from unirrigated vines which, because of their superior soils, do in fact yield well. Released as a young wine through the Tyrrell's mailing list and cellar door but re-released through the retail trade at various intervals according to the vintage. Vat 1 Semillons have won 20 trophies, 101 gold, 110 silver and 109 bronze medals since 1971. Never looked better than at the 1998 National Wine Show where the '91 won three trophies, including the Len Evans Trophy for Best Wine of Show.

♥♥♥♥♥ **1995** Glowing yellow-green; a superbly smooth bouquet with honey, lemon and faintly buttered toast all coalescing. The same flavours appear on a palate with great length, flavour and balance.　**rating:** 96

best drinking 2001–2011　**best vintages** '75, '76, '77, '86, '87, '89, '90, '91, '92, '93, '94, '95　**drink with** Pan-fried veal　• $35

Tyrrell's Long Flat Chardonnay

In a sign of the times, the Long Flat range now extends to Chardonnay.

♥♥♥♀ **1998** Medium yellow-green; a clever commercial style with sweet fruit and a touch of chippy oak. The palate is likewise cleverly made with peachy fruit and the same touch of chippy oak.　**rating:** 80

best drinking 2000–2002　**best vintages** NA　**drink with** Takeaway　• $7

Tyrrell's Old Winery Chardonnay

A wine which is as much a testament to the production skills of the Tyrrell's winemaking team as to the vast storehouse of accumulated knowledge in handling this variety. It is deliberately made in a richer, earlier-maturing style than Vat 47, and perhaps for this reason is often very nearly as well-treated in wine shows as a young wine, being a prolific medal winner. The message is, drink it, don't cellar it. The wine is a blend of Hunter Valley, Liverpool Plains (Camden, NSW) and McLaren Vale fruit, 30 per cent barrel-fermented.

♥♥♥♀ **1998** Very light green-yellow; scented, slightly chippy oak on the bouquet is followed by a palate with some life and length, though not over-much weight.　**rating:** 83

best drinking Drink now　**best vintages** '97　**drink with** Turkey breast　• $13

Tyrrell's Shee-Oak Chardonnay

The Shee-Oak Vineyard, with its sandy flats, was purchased in 1981, and the vines planted in 1982. This is classic Hunter white country, and it shows through in the wine. Unoaked Chardonnay has quickly gained a dreadful reputation as vapid and lollyish, but as Cole Porter said, it ain't necessarily so.

♥♥♥♥ **1999** Light green-yellow; fresh and quite fragrant melon and nectarine aromas of the bouquet are followed by a lively, fresh palate with a little extra CO_2 and acid to emphasise the freshness.　**rating:** 86

♥♥♥♥ **1998** Medium yellow-green; has built up considerable weight since being bottled, although still has a slight minerally edge. The palate is quite lively and flavoursome, with nectarine and peach fruit balanced by crisp acidity.　**rating:** 87

best drinking 2000–2003　**best vintages** '97　**drink with** Steamed fish　• $18

Tyrrell's Vat 47 Pinot Chardonnay

First made in the appalling vintage of 1971, sharing with the Craigmoor wine of the same year the honour of being the first Chardonnay labelled as such and sold this century. Has since unequivocally stamped itself as one of the great marques, enjoying a more or less unending stream of trophies and gold medals.

♥♥♥♥♥ **1999** Light to medium yellow-green; the bouquet is elegant yet complex, with particularly harmonious oak integration through the melon and nectarine fruit. The palate has that extra dimension and length which immediately sets this wine apart from all of its peers.　**rating:** 95

♥♥♥♥♀ **1998** Medium yellow-green; quite obvious charry barrel-ferment oak is followed by gentle, white peach fruit on the bouquet. A stylish wine, cleverly made, even if the oak component needs time to settle down; has good length and acidity.　**rating:** 93

best drinking 2001–2002　**best vintages** '82, '84, '85, '89, '91, '94, '95, '96, '97, '98, '99　**drink with** Fresh, slow-cooked salmon　• $50

Tyrrell's Old Winery Shiraz

Sourced entirely from Hunter Valley Shiraz, and made in the traditional fashion in the old, wax-lined concrete vats at Tyrrell's, hand-plunged, then matured in large oak casks for 12 months before being given a brief period in one- and two-year-old French oak barriques prior to bottling. Always a complex wine; and usually great value.

♥♥♥♥ **1997** The bouquet is quite complex, with dark berry fruit, chocolate and earth; the light- to medium-bodied palate has good feel and texture, with nice acidity and fine tannins.　**rating:** 88

best drinking 2000–2005　**best vintages** '81, '83, '87, '91, '92　**drink with** Smoked cheese　• $14

Tyrrell's Rufus Stone Shiraz

Part of a new and imaginatively-packaged range from Tyrrell's featuring regions outside the Hunter Valley (Coonawarra, Heathcote and McLaren Vale), with various vintages introduced onto the market in 1998.

TTTTϒ **1998** McLaren Vale. Full purple-red; the bouquet is rich, concentrated and ripe, with sweet, dark cherry fruit and subtle oak. The mouthfilling palate is flooded with similar dark cherry/berry/chocolate flavours, finishing with soft, lingering tannins. **rating:** 93

best drinking 2003–2013 **best vintages** '96, '97, '98 **drink with** Lasagne • $22

Tyrrell's Stevens Shiraz

One of the Individual Vineyard wines of Tyrrell's, sourced from one of the great old shiraz vineyards in the Pokolbin region, owned by George and Neil Stevens. 1993 was the first vintage made by Tyrrell's from this prime source.

TTTϒ **1996** Medium red-purple; the bouquet is of light to medium intensity, and a fraction plain and earthy. The palate is relatively light-bodied and, all in all, the wine appears to be in a thoroughly closed phase of its development. **rating:** 83

best drinking 2001–2006 **best vintages** '94, '95 **drink with** Moroccan lamb • $22

Tyrrell's Vat 8 Shiraz Cabernet

The incredibly baroque, old-fashioned label with a dozen different typefaces is a blast from the past, even if the blend of 65 per cent Hunter Valley Shiraz and 35 per cent Coonawarra Cabernet Sauvignon is not.

TTTTϒ **1997** Medium red-purple; a powerful bouquet with tarry, earthy berry fruit and toasty oak is followed by a rich, full, flavoursome palate which has very good balance and structure. Given ten years in the cellar this could be a great classic in traditional style. **rating:** 92

TTTT **1996** Medium red-purple; a mix of leathery/earthy/savoury aromas followed by an elegant, fruit-driven palate, fine tannins and a fresh finish. **rating:** 89

best drinking 2005–2015 **best vintages** '97 **drink with** Barbecued lamb fillets • $40

undercliff NR

Yango Creek Road, Wollombi, NSW 2325 **region** Lower Hunter Valley
phone (02) 4998 3322 **fax** (02) 4998 3322 **open** Weekends 10–4 or by appointment
winemaker Keith Tulloch (Contract) **production** 1200 **est.** 1990
product range ($12–18 CD) Semillon, Shiraz, Sparkling Shiraz.
summary Peter and Lesley Chase now own Undercliff, but it continues to function as both winery cellar door and art gallery. The wines, produced from 2.5 hectares of estate vineyards, have won a number of awards in recent years at the Hunter Valley Wine Show and the Hunter Valley Small Winemakers Show. All of the wine is sold through cellar door.

upper reach vineyard NR

77 Memorial Avenue, Baskerville, WA 6056 **region** Swan District
phone (08) 9296 0078 **fax** (08) 9296 0278 **open** Weekends and public holidays 11–5
winemaker Derek Pearse, Dorham Mann **production** 1000 **est.** 1996
product range ($13–18 CD) Unwooded Chardonnay, Reserve Chardonnay, Shiraz, Cabernet Sauvignon.
summary The 10-hectare property, situated on the banks of the upper reaches of the Swan River, was purchased by Laura Rowe and Derek Pearse in 1996. Four hectares of 12-year-old chardonnay made up the original vineyard, being expanded with 1.5 hectares of shiraz and 1 hectare of cabernet sauvignon, with plans for trials of merlot, zinfandel and barbera in the pipeline. The partners also own 4 hectares of vineyard in the Margaret River region planted to shiraz, cabernet sauvignon, merlot and semillon, but the releases so far have been drawn from the Swan Valley vineyards. The fish on the label, incidentally, is black bream, which can be found in the pools of the Swan River during the summer months.

van de scheur NR

O'Connors Lane, Pokolbin, NSW 2321 **region** Lower Hunter Valley
phone (02) 4998 7789 **fax** (02) 4998 7789 **open** Weekends 10–5
winemaker Kees Van De Scheur **production** 2000 **est.** 1995
product range ($16.50 CD) Semillon, Chardonnay, Shiraz.
summary Kees Van De Scheur is a Hunter Valley veteran, having spent the last 25 years in the Hunter Valley, first with the Robson Vineyard and then Briar Ridge, before leaving in November 1993 to establish his own winery and label. He has purchased part of the historic Ingleside property established by vigneron Frederick Ingle in 1872.

After a hiatus of 60 years, vines have returned, with an initial planting of a little over 1 hectare (semillon, chardonnay and shiraz) increasing to 4 hectares by 1997. In the meantime, grapes purchased within the Hunter Valley provide the base for the Van De Scheur Wines.

✿ varrenti wines   NR

Glenheather, Blackwood Road, Dunkeld, Vic 3294 **region** Western Victoria Zone
phone (03) 5577 2368 **fax** (03) 5577 2367 **open** 7 days 12–3
winemaker Ettore Varrenti **production** NA **est.** 1999
product range NA.
summary Ettore Varrente has established 4 hectares of pinot noir, malbec, shiraz and cabernet sauvignon at the extreme southern end of the Grampians National Park. It is remote from any other winery, and appears to fall just outside the Grampians region.

vasse felix   ★★★★★

Corner Caves Road and Harmans Road South, Willyabrup, WA 6284 **region** Margaret River
phone (08) 9755 5242 **fax** (08) 9755 5425 **open** 7 days 10–5
winemaker Clive Otto, Will Shields **production** 100 000 **est.** 1967
product range ($12–50 R) Classic Dry White, Theatre White and Red, Forest Hill Riesling, Semillon, Chardonnay, Noble Riesling, Classic Dry Red, Shiraz, Flinders Bay Cabernet Sauvignon, Sparkling Brut, Heytesbury.
summary The 1999 vintage will see Vasse Felix wines produced in a brand new 2000-tonne winery situated 200 metres to the west of the current facility; the old winery will be dedicated entirely to the restaurant and tasting rooms. A new 140-hectare vineyard at Jindong in the north of the Margaret River will supply a large part of the increased fruit intake. National Australian distribution; exports to the UK, the US, Switzerland, Singapore and Hong Kong.

Vasse Felix Semillon
Drawn primarily from 4 hectares of estate plantings. A very richly structured wine with an unusual depth of flavour, enhanced by 100 per cent barrel-fermentation in mainly new French oak and five months in barrel thereafter.
TTTT 1999 Very pale green-yellow; strong, spicy clove oak rockets out of the glass; there is light, crisp fruit there, but the clove oak is simply too much for the fruit, no matter what the quality of the oak may indeed be. **rating:** 85
best drinking 2001–2004 **best vintages** '92, '93, '95, '96 **drink with** Coquilles St Jacques • $22.50

Vasse Felix Chardonnay
Draws upon 22 hectares of estate plantings, and made in a powerful style, not far short of that of Heytesbury.
TTTT 1998 Medium to full yellow-green; the powerful bouquet shows lots of winemaker inputs into sweet, tangy grapefruit base wine. The palate is in similar bold style, with slightly canned fruit flavours; subtle oak. **rating:** 85
best drinking 2000–2005 **best vintages** NA **drink with** Pork chops • $22.50

Vasse Felix Heytesbury Chardonnay
One of the super-premium wines from Vasse Felix, made entirely from grapes grown on the Forest Hill Vineyard planted in 1978. Is given both oak barrels.
TTTTY 1998 Medium to full yellow-green; a very rich and opulent style, with sweet, ripe figgy fruit and lots of oak input to the bouquet; this is followed by a huge mouthful of fruit and oak; not too much subtlety here, but it certainly makes a statement. **rating:** 91
best drinking 2000–2004 **best vintages** '97, '98 **drink with** Rich seafood • $35

Vasse Felix Shiraz
Draws upon a little under 7 hectares of estate plantings and over the years has produced some outstanding wines. Since 1991 the quality of the wine has often been outstanding, at other times inexplicably disappointing.
TTTTY 1998 Medium red-purple; raw oak sits on top of the fruit on the bouquet and likewise the palate; there is fruit there but it is very difficult to imagine it will ever stand up to the oak. **rating:** 81
best drinking 2005–2008 **best vintages** '83, '85, '88, '90, '91, '92, '94, '96 **drink with** Rich casseroles • $33

Vasse Felix Cabernet Sauvignon
For decades the flag-bearer of Vasse Felix, and traditionally made in a lighter, more elegant style than most of the big names in the Margaret River, and none the worse for that. In recent years, the style has become more powerful and hence more typical of the region as a whole.

♟♟♟♟ **1998** Medium red-purple; the bouquet is in typical savoury/earthy Cabernet mode, and the oak is well balanced. A strong, powerful wine on the palate with lots of redcurrant/cassis fruit, but the tannins are on the hard side. Patience is required.   **rating:** 83

best drinking 2003–2010 **best vintages** '85, '88, '90, '91, '94, '95, '96 **drink with** Lamb cutlets • $30

veritas ★★★☆

94 Langmeil Road, Tanunda, SA 5352 **region** Barossa Valley
phone (08) 8563 2330 **fax** (08) 8563 3158 **open** Mon–Fri 9–5, weekends 11–5
winemaker Rolf Binder, Christa Deans **production** 14 000 **est.** 1955
product range ($10–30 CD) Riesling, Semillon, Chardonnay, Cabernet Shiraz, Cabernet Merlot, Binder's Bull's Blood, Shiraz Mourvedre Pressings, Fortifieds.
summary The Hungarian influence is obvious in the naming of some of the wines, but Australian technology is paramount in shaping the generally very good quality. Veritas has 28 hectares of estate vineyards to draw on. A near-doubling of production has coincided with the establishment of export markets to the UK, Germany, Switzerland, Belgium, The Netherlands and the US.

🐂 verona vineyard NR

Small Winemakers Centre, McDonalds Road, Pokolbin, NSW 2321 **region** Lower Hunter Valley
phone (02) 4998 7668 **fax** (02) 4998 7430 **open** 7 days 10–5
winemaker Greg Silkman, Gary Reed (Contract) **production** NA **est.** 1972
product range NA.
summary Verona has had a chequered history, and is still a significant business acting, as it does, as a sales point for a number of other Hunter Valley winemakers from its premises in McDonalds Road, directly opposite Brokenwood. The Verona wines come from 22 hectares at Muswellbrook, and 5 hectares surrounding the winery.

vicarys ★★☆

Northern Road, Luddenham, NSW 2745 **region** Other Wineries of NSW
phone (02) 4773 4161 **fax** (02) 4773 4411 **open** Mon–Fri 9–5, weekends 10–5
winemaker Chris Niccol **production** 1700 **est.** 1923
product range ($12–36 CD) Chardonnay, Semillon, Riesling, Gewurztraminer, Fumé Blanc, Cabernet Sauvignon, Shiraz Cabernet Merlot, Sparkling, Fortifieds.
summary Vicarys justifiably claims to be the Sydney region's oldest continuously operating winery, having been established in a very attractive, large, stone shearing shed built about 1890. Most of the wines come from other parts of Australia, but the winery does draw upon 1 hectare of estate traminer and 3 hectares of chardonnay for those wines, and has produced some good wines of all styles over the years.

vico NR

Farm 1687 Beelbangera Road, Griffith, NSW 2680 **region** Riverina
phone (02) 6962 2849 **open** Mon–Fri 9–5
winemaker Ray Vico **production** 1200 **est.** 1973
product range ($5–15 CD) Semillon, Late Harvest Semillon, Barbera, Cabernet Sauvignon, Liqueur Muscat.
summary Ray Vico has been growing grapes for many years with 9 hectares of vines, more recently deciding to bottle and sell part of the production under the Vico label. At $60 to $70 a dozen for the table wines and $15 per bottle for the 1984 Liqueur Muscat, the prices are positively mouthwatering — the more so given that 1997 Barbera, 1996 Cabernet Sauvignon and 1984 Liqueur Muscat all won silver medals at the Australian Small Winemakers Show, the '97 Semillon collecting a bronze medal.

victorian alps wine co NR

Great Alpine Road, Gapsted, Vic 3737 **region** King Valley
phone (03) 5751 1992 **fax** (03) 5751 1368 **open** Fri–Sun 10–4.30
winemaker Shayne Cunningham, Michelle Cope-Williams **production** 20 000 **est.** 1996
product range ($10–25 R) The High Canopy range of Chardonnay, Durif, Merlot, Shiraz, Cabernet Franc Merlot.
summary Victorian Alps Wine Co is primarily a contract grape crushing and fermenting facility, processing grapes grown in the King and Ovens Valleys and adjacent regions for wineries spread across various parts of Australia. Its total crush in 1998 was 2400 tonnes, of which only a small part will find its way onto the market as branded, bottled wine. Indeed, the first commercial release (and unveiling of the brand name and packaging) was made in September 1999.

villa primavera   NR

Mornington–Flinders Road, Red Hill, Vic 3937 **region** Mornington Peninsula
phone (03) 5989 2129 **fax** (03) 5931 0045 **open** Weekends, public holidays 10–5 and 7 days from Dec 26 to end January
winemaker Gennaro Mazzella **production** 300 **est.** 1984
product range ($18–30 CD) Chardonnay, Pinot Noir, Limoncello, Méthode Champenoise.
summary A most unusual operation, which is in reality a family Italian-style restaurant at which the wine is principally sold and served, and which offers something totally different on the Mornington Peninsula. A consistent winner of tourism and food awards, it is praised by all who go there, particularly for the concerts staged throughout January each year.

vincorp   NR

58 Piper Street, Kyneton, Vic 3444 **region** Macedon Ranges
phone (03) 5422 7444 **fax** (03) 5422 7400 **open** 7 days 10–6
winemaker David Watson **production** NA **est.** 1996
product range ($8.95–27.95 R) The 'One' range of White One (Sauvignon Blanc from Western Australia), Red One (unoaked Shiraz from Victoria and New South Wales), and Grand One (premium Cabernet Merlot from Central Victoria).
summary A smartly packaged but curiously named trio of wines from Vincorp, which joined the lists of the Stock Exchange in 1998 and also owns — but runs as separate ventures — Virgin Hills and Trio Station. Where the range will head in the future remains to be seen; it had a somewhat uncertain start.

☙ vinden estate   NR

17 Gillards Road, Pokolbin, NSW 2320 **region** Lower Hunter Valley
phone (02) 4998 7410 **fax** (02) 4998 7421 **open** NA
winemaker John Baruzzi (Contract) **production** 750 **est.** 1998
product range ($18.50–19.50 CD) Semillon, Chardonnay, Shiraz.
summary Sandra and Guy Vinden have bought their dream home with landscaped gardens in the foreground and 2.5 hectares of vineyard with the Brokenback mountain range in the distance. The initial releases of Semillon and Chardonnay were made from contract-grown grapes, with contract-winemaking by John Baruzzi. The wines are available through the cellar door and also via a wine club which offers buying advantages to members. An estate-grown Merlot will be released in the year 2000; the inaugural 1998 Semillon and 1998 Chardonnay were both competently made and will improve with time in bottle.

vintina estate   NR

1282 Nepean Highway, Mount Eliza, Vic 3930 **region** Mornington Peninsula
phone (03) 9787 8166 **fax** (03) 9775 2035 **open** 7 days 9–5
winemaker Jim Filippone, Kevin McCarthy (Consultant) **production** 400 **est.** 1985
product range ($12–14 CD) Chardonnay, Semillon, Pinot Gris, Pinot Noir, Cabernet Sauvignon.
summary The initial releases of Vintina (the only wines tasted to date) were mediocre. With competent contract-winemaking, improvement can be expected. However, no recent tastings.

violet cane vineyard   NR

13 Wallace Court, Glen Aplin, Qld 4381 **region** Granite Belt
phone 0418 739 257 **fax** (07) 4162 5328 **open** Not
winemaker Adam Chapman **production** 60 **est.** 1994
product range ($22–40 ML) Semillon, Merlot, Sparkling.
summary The intriguingly named Violet Cane Vineyard, and no less startlingly labelled wine, is the tiny personal business of Ballandean winemaker Adam Chapman, who is also a Flying Winemaker travelling to Europe each Australian spring. It is perhaps fitting that Adam Chapman should have married Elle Sigurdardottir in her native Iceland in June 1998.

virage   ★★★

13B Georgette Road, Gracetown, WA 6284 **region** Margaret River
phone (08) 9755 5318 **fax** (08) 9755 5318 **open** Not
winemaker Bernard Abbott **production** 1000 **est.** 1990
product range ($13–20 R) Sauvignon Blanc, Semillon Chardonnay, Traminer Riesling, Cabernet Shiraz Zinfandel, Cabernet Merlot.

summary Former Vasse Felix winemaker Bernard Abbott, together with wife Pascale, acquired (under long-term lease) the former government research station vineyard at Bramley Estate in 1990. Bernard Abbott makes the wines at a local Margaret River winery and sells them by mailing list and direct to retailer and restaurants in Perth, Melbourne and Sydney.

virgin hills ★★★★★

Salisbury Road, Lauriston West via Kyneton, Vic 3444 **region** Macedon Ranges
phone (03) 5422 7444 **fax** (03) 5422 7400 **open** By appointment
winemaker Mark Sheppard, David Watson **production** 4000 **est.** 1968
product range ($39.95 R) A single Cabernet Sauvignon Shiraz Merlot Blend called Virgin Hills; occasional limited Reserve release.
summary Virgin Hills has now become part of the public-listed Vincorp Group, a turn of events which has seen the return of Mark Sheppard (assisted by David Watson) to the role he held for so many years as winemaker. All eyes will be focused on what is in many ways an icon winery which constantly faces the climatic odds with its late-ripening varieties in an unequivocally cool region.

Virgin Hills

An entirely estate-grown blend (in descending order) of Cabernet Sauvignon, Shiraz, Merlot, Malbec and occasionally a touch of Pinot Noir. Not only are the grapes organically grown, but between 1988 and 1995 the wine was made without the use of added SO_2. It was a brave move which makes world's best preservative-free red; only time will tell how these wines age over a decade. Small amounts of sulphur are now added.
▼▼▼▼ 1997 Medium red-purple; the fragrant bouquet offers spicy fruit with a touch of mint together with smoky/cigar box oak. The palate has red berry, cherry and mint flavours which are much less dense than the barrel sample previously tasted. All in all, shows the low alcohol of 11.3 degrees. **rating:** 86
best drinking 2000–2005 **best vintages** '74, '75, '76, '80, '82, '85, '88, '90, '91, '92, '95 **drink with** Duck • $39.95

voyager estate ★★★★☆

Lot 1 Stevens Road, Margaret River, WA 6285 **region** Margaret River
phone (08) 9757 6354 **fax** (08) 9757 6494 **open** 7 days 10–5
winemaker Stuart Pym, Cliff Royle **production** 25 000 **est.** 1978
product range ($19–70 R) Chenin Blanc, Sauvignon Blanc Semillon, Tom Price Sauvignon Blanc Semillon, Semillon, Marsanne, Chardonnay, Shiraz Grenache, Cabernet Merlot, Tom Price Cabernet Merlot.
summary Formerly Freycinet Estate, renamed after its purchase (in May 1991) from Western Australian viticulturist Peter Gherardi. Much money has been spent on the property by new owner, the mining magnate Michael Wright (including the expansion of the vineyards to over 51 hectares), although the winery itself remains in strictly utilitarian form. The wines are rich and opulent, particularly the white wines.

Voyager Estate Semillon

Produced from 7.5 hectares of estate plantings, and right from the outset has proved itself a very distinguished wine. Partial barrel-fermentation in a mix of French and American oak has been skilfully employed to add a dimension to the wine, but without taking away from the varietal fruit character.
▼▼▼▼ 1998 Light green-yellow; a very pungent, assertive bouquet with some slightly reductive, smoky aromas. The palate is powerful, concentrated and tangy; held back from higher points by the hint of reduction. **rating:** 87
best drinking 2000–2005 **best vintages** '95, '96 **drink with** Chicken • $22

Voyager Estate Sauvignon Blanc Semillon

Voyager Estate regularly produces high class Sauvignon Blanc and Semillon (the latter also offered as a straight varietal) from its now fully mature vineyards.
▼▼▼▼ 1999 Light to medium yellow-green; the bouquet is initially curiously closed and inexpressive, although some tropical/guava aromas can be coaxed out. The palate has considerable weight, but not as positive as prior vintages of what is normally an excellent wine. **rating:** 85
best drinking 2000–2001 **best vintages** '95, '97 **drink with** Marinated octopus • $19

Voyager Estate Tom Price Sauvignon Blanc Semillon

A blend of 60 per cent Sauvignon Blanc and 40 per cent Semillon from the oldest part of the vineyard at Voyager Estate. It was inspired by winemaker Stuart Pym's vintage at Domaine de Chevalier in 1995 (retrospectively reinforced by visits to Chateau Haut Brion and Leville Haut Brion). Only 300 cases of the wine were made; future vintages of Tom Price will be predominantly Semillon, but Stuart Pym believes this wine will continue to develop for another ten years at least.

▼▼▼▼▽ **1996** Medium yellow-green; the bouquet is rich and complex with obvious spicy barrel-ferment oak and a mix of ripe fruit aromas. The palate, likewise, shows strong oak influences, but the layered fruit, ranging from nectarine to herbs and grass, stands up to the oak. Most significantly, the phenolics have not become coarse, nor will they do so in the future. Stands alongside the best of Cullen, Yarra Yarra and Mount Mary.　　**rating:** 91
best drinking 2001–2010　**best vintages** NA　**drink with** Rich seafood　• $45

Voyager Estate Marsanne
From a small planting at Voyager Estate.
▼▼▼▼ **1998** Medium yellow-green; the bouquet has quite pronounced fruit with a mix of ripe citrus and more savoury hay characters. The palate, likewise, has strong fruit flavour with some interesting characters; also has good length.　　**rating:** 88
best drinking 2000–2003　**best vintages** NA　**drink with** Pan-fried veal　• $19

Voyager Estate Chardonnay
In the majority of vintages Voyager Estate produces a Chardonnay of complexity, style and verve typical of the Margaret River at its very best.
▼▼▼▼▼ **1997** Medium yellow-green; there is intense, ripe melon and fig fruit smoothly married with quality oak on the bouquet. The tight structure of the palate promises longevity; nectarine and a touch of grapefruit are beautifully balanced with subtle oak.　　**rating:** 96
best drinking 2000–2007　**best vintages** '92, '93, '95, '96, '97　**drink with** Braised pork neck　• $28

Voyager Estate Cabernet Sauvignon Merlot
A classic Bordeaux-blend of 75 per cent Cabernet Sauvignon, 20 per cent Merlot, 4 per cent Cabernet Franc and 1 per cent Petit Verdot. The wine is fermented in closed fermenters with pump-over, and 40 per cent is given post-fermentation maceration. It spends two years in small French oak barriques prior to bottling.
▼▼▼▼ **1996** Medium to full red-purple; complex berry, leaf and earth fruit aromas are nicely offset by a touch of sweet oak. The palate, too, is nicely balanced and rich, with cassis and chocolate followed by a touch of varietal astringency on the finish.　　**rating:** 88
best drinking 2001–2010　**best vintages** '91, '93　**drink with** Beef in red wine sauce　• $35

Voyager Estate Tom Price Cabernet Merlot
A super-premium reserve wine which spent 30 months in French oak. Only 2496 bottles were produced.
▼▼▼▼▼ **1992** Medium to full red-purple; the bouquet is extremely powerful, with a mix of secondary-developed savoury/earthy aromas. The palate is equally concentrated and powerful, with a core of sweet, dark berry fruit which (just) sustains the considerable oak contribution.　　**rating:** 94
best drinking 2002–2017　**best vintages** '92　**drink with** Grain-fed beef　• $70

wa-de-lock　　★★★
76 Tyers Street, Stratford, Vic 3862　**region** Gippsland
phone (03) 5145 7050　**fax** (03) 5145 7030　**open** Mon–Thurs 10–6, Fri–Sun 10–8
winemaker Graeme Little　**production** 2000　**est.** 1987
product range ($9.50–22 R) Chameleon White Pinot, Chardonnay, Reserve Chardonnay, Sauvignon Blanc, Avon Valley Spatlese Lexia Pinot Noir, Cabernet Merlot, Avon Valley Tawny Port.
summary The initial plantings of pinot noir, cabernet sauvignon and sauvignon blanc in 1987 have been progressively expanded by increases in those varieties and the addition of chardonnay, nebbiolo, shiraz, merlot and durif, with 12 hectares under vine, some of it still coming into production. The quality of the wines has improved steadily as Graeme Little's handling of oak has become more assured, and the range of wines has increased. The wines have distributors in Melbourne, Sydney, Tasmania and Perth.

wallington wines　　NR
Nyrang Creek Vineyard, Canowindra, NSW 2904　**region** Cowra
phone (02) 6344 7153　**fax** (02) 6344 7153　**open** By appointment
winemaker Blair Duncan, Murray Smith (Contract)　**production** 2000　**est.** 1992
product range ($14–20 CD) Chardonnay, Shiraz, Cabernet Sauvignon.
summary Anthony and Margaret Wallington commenced the development of their Nyrang Creek Vineyard with a little over 2 hectares of cabernet sauvignon in 1992, followed by 7 hectares of chardonnay in 1994, then shiraz (2.5 hectares) and semillon (0.75 hectare) in 1995 and ultimately 0.75 hectare each of cabernet franc and pinot noir in 1998. Most of the production is sold, but Don Buchanan at Arrowfield makes the Wallington Chardonnay and Murray Smith of Canobolas-Smith Wines at Orange makes the Cabernet Sauvignon and Shiraz. The quality of the wines is such that exports to the US have already commenced.

walsh family wines   NR

90 Walnut Road, Bickley, WA 6076 **region** Perth Hills
phone (08) 9291 7341 **fax** (08) 9291 7341 **open** 7 days 9–5
winemaker Celine Rousseau (Contract) **production** 420 **est.** 1995
product range ($14.50 CD) Shiraz.
summary Walsh Family Wines is aptly named: it is a partnership of the Walshes and their eight children. One of those children is establishing a vineyard near Bridgetown in the Great Southern, the grapes from which will ultimately form part of the Walsh Family winery intake.

wandering brook estate   NR

PO Box 32, Wandering, WA 6308 **region** Other Wineries of WA
phone (08) 9884 1064 **fax** (08) 9884 1064 **open** Weekends 9.30–6
winemaker Steve Radikovich **production** 2000 **est.** 1989
product range ($10–14.95 CD) Verdelho, Chardonnay, Unwooded Chardonnay, Soft Red and White, Cabernet Sauvignon, Sparkling Verdelho, Port.
summary Laurie and Margaret White have planted 10 hectares of vines on their 130-year-old family property in a move to diversify. Up to 1994 the wines were made at Goundrey, currently at Jadran. Renamed Wandering Brook Estate late in 1994; up till then known as Redhill Estate.

wandin valley estate   ★★★★

Wilderness Road, Rothbury, NSW 2321 **region** Lower Hunter Valley
phone (02) 4930 7317 **fax** (02) 4930 7814 **open** 7 days 10–5
winemaker To be appointed **production** 8000 **est.** 1973
product range ($13.50–25 R) Pavilion Range Dry White, Classic White and Dry Red; Estate Range of Semillon, Chardonnay, Cabernet Sauvignon, Shiraz, Ruby Cabernet and Muscat; top of the range WVE Cabernet Brut Champagne, Reserve Chardonnay, Bridie's Shiraz and Reserve Cabernet Sauvignon.
summary The former Millstone vineyard, now owned by the producer of Australian television's classic 'A Country Practice'. Rapidly developing Chardonnays have been the focal point of Wandin Valley's considerable show success. The estate also boasts a Cope-Williams-type village cricket oval and extensive cottage accommodation. Limited Victorian retail distribution; exports to Ontario, Canada.

Wandin Valley WVE Reserve Chardonnay

The Reserve Chardonnay was introduced with effect from the 1994 vintage, and was a gold medal winner at the 1994 Australian National Wine Show in Canberra. Part of the wine is barrel-fermented in a mix of French and American oak barriques, and part is fermented in stainless steel. The two portions are then blended.
▼▼▼▼ 1998 Medium to full yellow-green; the bouquet is strong and rich, with nutty/buttery/peachy fruit. The palate is nicely balanced and composed, again buttery/peachy and not over the top. The excess American oak of prior years seems to have been banished.   **rating:** 85
best drinking 2000–2002 **best vintages** '94, '97 **drink with** Barbecued spatchcock • $18

Wandin Valley Estate Bridie's Shiraz

Whether James and Phillipa Daverne's granddaughter came first, I am not sure, but I suspect the wine was named in her honour. Whatever be the answer, a most attractive wine.
▼▼▼▼ 1998 Medium red-purple; the bouquet has a mix of cherry and plum spun through more obvious savoury/earthy/spicy aromas. The palate is in typical savoury Hunter mode, which does have length and intensity, and creeps up on you, with the plum fruit coming through on a long finish.   **rating:** 85
best drinking 2002–2008 **best vintages** NA **drink with** Moroccan lamb • $20

waninga   ★★★★

Hughes Park Road, Sevenhill via Clare, SA 5453 **region** Clare Valley
phone (08) 8843 4395 **fax** (08) 8843 4395 **open** 7 days 10–5
winemaker Tim Adams, Jeffrey Grosset (Contract) **production** 1500 **est.** 1989
product range ($12.50–30 CD) Skilly Hills Riesling, Late Picked Riesling, Chenin Blanc, Chardonnay, Ninnes, Shiraz, Reserve Shiraz, Cabernet Sauvignon, Hilary Port.
summary The large (37.5 hectares) vineyards owned by Waninga were established in 1974, but it was not until 1989 that a portion of the grapes was withheld from sale and vinified for the owners. Since that time, Waninga has produced some quite lovely wines, having wisely opted for very competent contract-winemaking.

wansbrough wines   NR

Richards Road, Ferguson, WA 6236   **region** Geographe
phone (08) 9728 3091   **fax** (08) 9728 3091   **open** Weekends 10–5
winemaker Willespie Wines (Contract)   **production** 250   **est.** 1986
product range ($12–18 CD) Riesling, Semillon, Sauvignon Blanc, Constantia (late-picked Semillon), Shiraz Cabernet, Port.
summary Situated east of Dardanup in the picturesque Ferguson Valley, Wansbrough enjoys views of the distant Geographe Bay and the nearer State forest with the Bibblemun Track running along its northern and eastern borders. To taste the wine you need either to order by mail or visit the Wansbrough restaurant on weekends.

wantirna estate   NR

Bushy Park Lane, Wantirna South, Vic 3152   **region** Yarra Valley
phone (03) 9801 2367   **fax** (03) 9887 0225   **open** By appointment
winemaker Reg Egan, Maryann Egan   **production** 1000   **est.** 1963
product range ($33–40 CD) Isabella Chardonnay, Lily Pinot Noir, Amelia Cabernet Merlot.
summary Situated well within the boundaries of the Melbourne metropolitan area, Wantirna Estate is part of a nature reserve. The only retail outlet for the wine is Richmond Hill Cellars; all the remainder is sold through mail order to selected restaurants and to a few overseas customers. In deference to Reg Egan's very firmly held views on the subject, neither the winery nor the wines are rated.

wards gateway   ★★☆

Barossa Valley Highway, Lyndoch, SA 5351   **region** Barossa Valley
phone (08) 8524 4138   **open** 7 days 9–5.30
winemaker Ray Ward (plus Contract)   **production** 800   **est.** 1979
product range ($7.50–17 CD) Riesling, Frontignac, Chardonnay, Frontignac Spatlese, Barossa Shiraz, Cabernet Sauvignon, Port.
summary The very old vines surrounding the winery produce the best wines, which are made without frills or new oak and sold without ostentation.

warrabilla   NR

Murray Valley Highway, Rutherglen, Vic 3685   **region** Rutherglen and Glenrowan
phone (02) 6035 7242   **fax** (02) 6035 7242   **open** 7 days 10–5
winemaker Andrew Sutherland-Smith   **production** 6000   **est.** 1986
product range ($12–19 CD) Chardonnay, Brimin Series Cabernet Shiraz, Glenrowan Cabernet Sauvignon, Glenrowan Shiraz, Merlot, Vintage Port, Liqueur Muscat; Reserve Shiraz, Reserve Durif.
summary Former All Saints winemaker Andrew Sutherland-Smith has leased a small winery at Corowa to make the Warrabilla wines from a 4-hectare vineyard developed by himself and Carol Smith in the Indigo Valley. The red table wines are rated highly by others. Exports to the US.

warramate   ★★★☆

27 Maddens Lane, Gruyere, Vic 3770   **region** Yarra Valley
phone (03) 5964 9219   **fax** (03) 5964 9219   **open** 7 days 10–6
winemaker Jack Church, David Church   **production** 900   **est.** 1970
product range ($18-28 CD) Riesling, Shiraz, Cabernet Sauvignon.
summary Wine quality has been variable in recent years; it would seem that the oak in some of the older barrels is questionable. At their best, reflect the distinguished site on which the vineyard sits.

Warramate Shiraz

Produced from just under half a hectare of estate-grown plantings, typically providing about 200 cases of wine. The plantings are not irrigated and enjoy a prime north-facing slope.

 1998 Medium to full red-purple; firm, dark berry fruit with slightly savoury overtones on the bouquet leads into a palate with good weight and richness; here sweet fruit on the mid-palate is followed by gentle tannins; long and balanced.   **rating:** 92

▼▼▼▼ **1997** Medium red-purple; the bouquet is clean, quite firm and still youthful, with savoury berry aromas. An elegant palate, with spicy savoury fruit and minimal oak, which is developing nicely.   **rating:** 89

best drinking 2003–2013   **best vintages** '88, '92, '93, '97, '98   **drink with** Spiced lamb   • $28

Warramate Cabernet Sauvignon

Produced from 0.8 of a hectare of cabernet sauvignon, with a little merlot included in the plantings. Like the Shiraz, the vines are not irrigated and are consequently low-yielding.

▼▼▼♀ **1998** Medium to full red-purple; there is rather too much oak on the bouquet and palate alike; the ripe fruit does makes its presence felt on the palate, but it would have been far better if it did not have to fight for expression. **rating: 83**

best drinking 2003–2008 **best vintages** '88, '95 **drink with** Mature cheddar • $25

warraroong estate   NR

Wilderness Road, Lovedale, NSW 2321 **region** Lower Hunter Valley
phone (02) 4930 7594 **fax** (02) 4930 7199 **open** 7 days 10–5
winemaker Adam Rees, Greg Silkman (Consultant) **production** 2000 **est.** 1988
product range ($15–25 CD) Semillon, Sauvignon Blanc, Chenin Blanc, Chardonnay, Shiraz, Malbec.
summary Warraroong Estate was formerly Fraser Vineyard and adopted its new name after it changed hands in 1997. The name 'Warraroong' is an Aboriginal word for hillside, reflecting the southwesterly aspect of the property looking back towards the Brokenback Range and Watagan Mountains. The label design is from a painting by local Aboriginal artist Kia Kiro who, while coming from the Northern Territory, is living and working in the Hunter Valley.

warrenmang vineyard   ★★★☆

Mountain Creek Road, Moonambel, Vic 3478 **region** Pyrenees
phone (03) 5467 2233 **fax** (03) 5467 2309 **open** 7 days 9–5
winemaker Luigi Bazzani **production** 17 000 **est.** 1974
product range ($11–50 CD) Bazzani Chardonnay Chanin Blanc, Cabernet Shiraz Dolcetto, Saluté (Méthode Champenoise), Vintage Port; Valley of the Kings Chardonnay Chenin Blanc, Cabernet Shiraz; Warrenmang Late Harvest Traminer, Vintage Port; flagship wine is a limited release of a once-only bottling of 1991–1997 Luigi Riserva (Cabernet blend).
summary Warrenmang is now the focus of a superb accommodation and restaurant complex created by former restaurateur Luigi Bazzani and wife Athalie, which is in much demand as a conference centre as well as for weekend tourism. The striking black Bazzani label is gradually overtaking the Warrenmang label in importance, and is responsible for the growth in the volume of production. It is partially sourced from contract-growers; the estate wines are, as their name suggests, estate-grown.

🐌 warrina wines   NR

Back Road, Kootingal NSW 2352 **region** Other wineries of NSW
phone (02) 6760 3985 **fax** (02) 6765 5746 **open** Not
winemaker David Nicholls **production** 100 **est.** 1989
product range ($5–12 ML) Sauvignon Blanc, Semillon, Chardonnay, Shiraz, Cabernet Sauvignon.
summary David Nicholls has progressively established a total of 2 hectares of sauvignon blanc, semillon, chardonnay, shiraz and cabernet sauvignon at his vineyard 15 kilometres northeast of Tamworth. Wine prices are low, but the production has see-sawed wildly over the years.

water wheel   ★★★☆

Bridgewater-on-Loddon, Bridgewater, Vic 3516 **region** Bendigo
phone (03) 5437 3060 **fax** (03) 5437 3082 **open** Mon–Sat 9–5, Sun 12–5
winemaker Peter Cumming, Bill Trevaskis **production** 25 000 **est.** 1972
product range ($13–17 R) Chardonnay, Riesling, Sauvignon Blanc, Pinot Noir, Shiraz, Cabernet Sauvignon; grapes from other districts under premium Wing Fields label.
summary Peter Cumming gained great respect as a winemaker during his four-year stint with Hickinbotham Winemakers, and his 1989 purchase of Water Wheel was greeted with enthusiasm by followers of his work. Recent releases have been of consistent quality and modest price, being distributed throughout Australia and with export markets in New Zealand, Asia, the UK and Europe, and the US and Canada.

Water Wheel Bendigo Sauvignon Blanc

A pleasant wine which, however, suggests that Bendigo is more suited to red wines.

▼▼▼ **1999** Medium yellow-green; the bouquet is clean but tending plain, with slightly flabby tropical aromas. A pleasant, commercial style on the palate, with gently tropical fruit balanced by crisp acidity. Any shortcomings derive from the vineyard, not the winemaking. **rating: 79**

best drinking 2000–2001 **best vintages** NA **drink with** Asian seafood • $14

Water Wheel Chardonnay

Peter Cumming has always made generously flavoured and constructed wines, and the Chardonnay is very much in the mainstream of his style. The high alcohol often gives the wine a particular sweetness and richness, and it is the fruit (not the oak) which drives the wine. For the record, air-dried American oak is used.

ᵀᵀᵀᵼ **1999** Light yellow-green; the bouquet is clean and fresh, but tending neutral. The palate flavours are in the citrus/mineral spectrum, the American oak almost invisible. A plain, no-frills wine at a no-frills price. **rating:** 82

best drinking 2000–2003 **best vintages** NA **drink with** Roast pork • $13

Water Wheel Bendigo Shiraz

The Shiraz is always presented in a way which encourages early consumption, for the wines are never tannic or extractive, and put the emphasis on fresh fruit. However, in many vintages there is the substance for medium-term cellaring.

ᵀᵀᵀᵀᵼ **1998** Dense red-purple; the bouquet is rich and ripe, with a cascade of blackberry, bitter chocolate and more savoury/earthy varietal nuances. The palate is very rich and full bodied, with masses of dark berry fruit and appropriate tannins; outstanding value and cellaring potential. **rating:** 93

best drinking 2003–2013 **best vintages** '94, '96, '97, '98 **drink with** Rich meat dishes • $17

Water Wheel Bendigo Cabernet Sauvignon

Produced predominantly from plantings of cabernet sauvignon established when the Cumming family took over control of Water Wheel. Right from the outset these plantings produced wines with intense fruit flavours. A small percentage (15 per cent) of Cabernet Franc and Merlot adds complexity. Often in the same class as the Shiraz, but not in 1998.

ᵀᵀᵀᵼ **1998** Light to medium red-purple; light, cedary/leafy/earthy aromas are followed by a palate which does have some cassis fruit but which is still in a rather dry savoury/earthy mode. All in all, a total contrast to the Shiraz.

rating: 82

best drinking 2001–2004 **best vintages** '90, '91, '92, '97 **drink with** Yearling steak • $17

waybourne   NR

60 Lemins Road, Waurn Ponds, Vic 3221 **region** Geelong
phone (03) 5241 8477 **fax** (03) 5241 8477 **open** By appointment
winemaker David Cowburn (Contract) **production** 730 **est.** 1980
product range ($12–16 ML) Riesling, Trebbiano, Pinot Gris, Cabernet Sauvignon.
summary Owned by Tony and Kay Volpato, who have relied upon external consultants to assist with the winemaking. No recent tastings.

wayne thomas wines   NR

26 Kangarilla Road, McLaren Vale, SA 5171 **region** McLaren Vale
phone (08) 8323 9737 **fax** (08) 8323 9737 **open** 7 days 12–5
winemaker Wayne Thomas **production** 4500 **est.** 1994
product range ($12–30 ML) Sauvignon Blanc, Chardonnay, Shiraz, Cabernet Sauvignon, Sparkling Cabernet Franc.
summary Wayne Thomas is a McLaren Vale veteran, having commenced his winemaking career in 1961, working for Stonyfell, Ryecroft and Saltram before establishing Fern Hill with his wife Pat in 1975. When they sold Fern Hill in April 1994 they started again, launching the Wayne Thomas Wines label, using contract-grown grapes sourced from throughout McLaren Vale. The wines are exported to the UK and to California, as well as enjoying limited retail distribution through all Australian States except WA.

wellington   ★★★★☆

Corner Richmond and Denholms Roads, Cambridge, Tas 7170 **region** Southern Tasmania
phone (03) 6248 5844 **fax** (03) 6248 5855 **open** By appointment
winemaker Andrew Hood **production** 3000 **est.** 1990
product range ($18–24 R) Riesling, Iced Riesling, Chardonnay, Pinot Noir, Ruby Port.
summary Consultant-winemaker Andrew Hood (ex-Charles Sturt University) and wife Jenny have constructed a state-of-the-art winery on land leased from the University of Tasmania. The 2000-case production of Wellington is dwarfed by the 4500 cases contract-made for others, but the wines are always flawlessly crafted, particularly the Chardonnay.

Wellington Riesling

Another wine from the Wellington stable to repay cellaring, and, as with the other wines, immaculately made. Sourced not from southern Tasmania, but from a vineyard at Relbia, on the outskirts of Launceston. Each of the last four vintages has been a gold medal winner

▼▼▼▼♀ **1999** Medium yellow-green; a powerful bouquet with more herb and mineral aromas than many wines from this vintage. The palate, too, has a definite and different personality, mixing some herbal fruit with citrus/lime. **rating:** 90

▼▼▼▼ **1998** Bright green-yellow; the bouquet is crisp, with a mix of piercing mineral and citrus aromas. The palate is quite special, with flowery, lively spice and crushed rose petal nuances woven through a more conventional structure. A gold medal wine on my score sheet at the 2000 Tasmanian Wines Show. **rating:** 89

best drinking 2001–2010 **best vintages** '96, '97, '98, 99 **drink with** Sautéed prawns • $20

Wellington Chardonnay

Andrew Hood is nothing if not economical in his back label description of this wine as 'a dry, lightly wooded wine made from fruit grown mainly in northern Tasmania'. Over the years these wines have proved their great ageing potential. The '97 was a gold medal winner at the 1998 Tasmanian Wines Show, and when it reappeared at the 2000 show, scored gold medal points on my score sheet.

▼▼▼▼♀ **1999** Medium to full yellow-green; the bouquet offers a mix of mineral and citrus fruit with subtle oak, the immaculately balanced palate offering the same spectrum of flavours. Yet another impeccable wine from Andrew Hood. **rating:** 92

▼▼▼▼▼ **1997** Light green-yellow; light, fresh melon, apple and citrus aromas are followed by a well-structured palate with melon, fig and apple flavours. Subtle French oak has not been allowed to overwhelm the wine's delicacy. Retasted January 2000 showing all of the positive characteristics of the wine when young, simply adding a degree of complexity. **rating:** 94

best drinking 2000–2005 **best vintages** '92, '95, '96, '97, '98, '99 **drink with** Gravlax • $24

Wellington Iced Riesling 375 ml

Produced using freeze concentration of the unfermented juice in a stainless steel tank. Water freezes first, and is removed in solid form, lifting the sugar, acidity (and flavour) of the remaining juice which is then conventionally cold-fermented. Never less than good, and on occasions reaches trophy standard.

▼▼▼▼ **1999** Light green-yellow; there are slightly reductive edges to the aroma, but the palate delivers the intense, moderately sweet and very long flavours which have always been the mark of this wine. **rating:** 88

best drinking 2002–2007 **best vintages** '97, '98, '99 **drink with** Sorbet • $20

Wellington Pinot Noir

Produced from grapes grown near Cambridge in the Coal River Valley close to Andrew Hood's winery, with most vintages in the top echelon of Tasmanian Pinots. It consistently shows strong, dark plum fruit reminiscent of the east coast Pinot Noirs, and quite different from those of northern Tasmania. Winemaker Andrew Hood takes a deliberately simple approach to the fermentation of the Wellington Pinot Noir, in part due to the constraints of a very busy winery, and in part to a belief that the Pinot Noir he works with does not need more complexity.

▼▼▼▼♀ **1998** Medium red-purple; a fresh, clean, lively bouquet with plum and spice aromas is followed by an elegant, lively palate with fresh, sweet plummy fruit and a perfectly constructed finish. Great drinking now or later. **rating:** 93

best drinking 2000–2005 **best vintages** '94, '98 **drink with** Tasmanian salmon • $24

☙ wells parish wines   NR

Benerin Estate, Sydney Road, Kandos, NSW 2848 **region** Mudgee
phone (02) 6379 4168 **fax** (02) 6379 4996 **open** By appointment
winemaker Pieter Van Gent **production** 500 **est.** 1995
product range ($17–18 CD) Chardonnay, Cabernet Sauvignon, Strayleaves Vintage Port.
summary Richard and Rachel Trounson, with help from father Barry Trounson, have established 16 hectares of vineyards at Benerin Estate since 1995. Most of the grapes are sold to Southcorp, but small quantities of wine are made for sale under the Wells Parish label. The vineyards are situated at the eastern extremity of the Mudgee region, near Rylstone, and both the soils and climate are distinctly different from those of the traditional Mudgee area.

wendouree ★★★★★

Wendouree Road, Clare, SA 5453 **region** Clare Valley
phone (08) 8842 2896 **open** By appointment
winemaker Tony Brady **production** 2500 **est.** 1895
product range ($26–30 ML) Shiraz Malbec, Shiraz Mataro, Cabernet Malbec, Cabernet Sauvignon, Muscat of Alexandria.
summary The iron fist in a velvet glove best describes these extraordinary wines. They are fashioned with passion and yet precision from the very old vineyard with its unique terroir by Tony and Lita Brady, who rightly see themselves as custodians of a priceless treasure. The 100-year-old stone winery is virtually unchanged from the day it was built; this is in every sense a treasure beyond price.

west cape howe wines   NR

PO Box 548, Denmark, WA 6333 **region** Great Southern
phone (08) 9848 2959 **fax** (08) 9848 2903 **open** 7 days 10–5
winemaker Brenden Smith, Dave Cleary **production** 3000 **est.** 1997
product range ($14.50–24.50 CD) Semillon Sauvignon Blanc, Unwooded Chardonnay, Chardonnay, Late Picked Riesling, Cabernet Sauvignon, Muscat.
summary Brenden Smith was senior winemaker at Goundrey Wines for many years and has branched into business on his own with a contract-winemaking facility for growers throughout the Great Southern region.

West Cape Howe Unwooded Chardonnay

Comes from 3 vineyards in the Denmark and Pemberton/Manjimup subregions with a spread of picking ripeness from 12.8° baumé to 14° baumé.
♥♥♥♀ 1999 Light to medium yellow-green; the bouquet is quite aromatic, with melon and citrus; the clean, fresh palate with nectarine and citrus flavours running through to a moderately long finish.   **rating:** 82
best drinking 2000–2002 **best vintages** NA **drink with** Pan-fried flathead fillets • $14.50

West Cape Howe Chardonnay

Produced from several vineyards in the Mount Barker region. Barrel-fermented and left on its yeast lees for eight months, with stirring every two months.
♥♥♥♥ 1999 Medium to full yellow-green; quite complex nectarine and grapefruit aromas are woven through subtle oak on the bouquet; the quite full and well-balanced palate offers similar fruit flavours joined by hints of cashew and spice.   **rating:** 87
best drinking 2000–2003 **best vintages** '99 **drink with** Roast pork • $18

westend ★★★☆

1283 Brayne Road, Griffith, NSW 2680 **region** Riverina
phone (02) 6964 1506 **fax** (02) 6962 1673 **open** Mon–Fri 9–4.30
winemaker William Calabria, James Ceccato **production** 117 000 **est.** 1945
product range ($5.90–19.95 CD) Outback Traminer Riesling, Semillon Colombard, Sauvignon Blanc, Shiraz; Richland Semillon Chardonnay, Chardonnay, Cabernet Sauvignon, Cabernet Merlot, Shiraz, Merlot; Port and Liqueur Muscat; then comes the 3 Bridges range of Chardonnay, Shiraz, Cabernet Sauvignon and Golden Mist Botrytis Semillon.
summary Along with a number of Riverina producers, West End is making a concerted move to lift both the quality and the packaging of its wines, spearheaded by the 3 Bridges range, which has an impressive array of gold medals to its credit since being first released in April 1997. It has also ventured into the export market, with distribution in the UK, the US and Switzerland.

Westend 3 Bridges Golden Mist Botrytis Semillon

Yet another botrytised Semillon from Griffith. It is 100 per cent estate-grown at Hanwood, and has been made each year since 1995. As one would expect, a prolific winner of trophies and gold medals, even in the highly competitive botrytised Semillon wine show classes of Australia. The '98 vintage achieved its mandatory gold medals at the Perth and Rutherglen Shows in 1999.
♥♥♥♥ 1998 Glowing golden-yellow; rich honey and peach aromas and subtle oak lead into similar flavours on the palate, where quite well-balanced acidity braces the finish. Not overly complex.   **rating:** 85
best drinking 2000–2004 **best vintages** NA **drink with** Fruit tart • $19.95

Westend 3 Bridges Shiraz

1998 3 Bridges Shiraz joined the prior releases of Cabernet Sauvignon, Chardonnay and Botrytis Semillon (from the 1997 vintage) by virtue of winning a gold medal at the Perth Wine Show; it is a self-imposed requirement that each wine released under the 3 Bridges label should have won at least one gold medal.

▼▼▼▼ **1998** Medium red-purple; there is lots of sweet, chocolatey red berry fruit on the bouquet, with oak evident but controlled. Distinct spicy notes, almost into cinnamon, run through the medium-weight palate, where the oak handling has once again succeeded. **rating: 86**

best drinking 2000–2003 **best vintages** '98 **drink with** Pasta with meat sauce • $19.95

Westend 3 Bridges Cabernet Sauvignon

A wine which had considerable show success over the years, the '97 continuing that record with a gold medal at Perth in 1998 and a very highly commended at Rutherglen in 1997, the '98 winning a trophy at Griffith and golds at that show and at Perth.

▼▼▼▽ **1998** Medium red-purple; obvious American oak on the bouquet is accompanied by soft berry fruit; the medium-bodied palate is oak-driven, but blackberry fruit manages to makes its presence felt. **rating: 84**

best drinking 2001–2005 **best vintages** '95, '96, '97 **drink with** Roast beef • $19.95

westfield ★★★☆

Corner Memorial Avenue and Great Northern Highway, Baskerville, WA 6056 **region** Swan District
phone (08) 9296 4356 **fax** (08) 9296 4356 **open** 7 days 10–5.30
winemaker John Kosovich **production** 11 000 **est.** 1922
product range ($17–22 CD) Verdelho, Sauvignon Blanc, Unwooded Chardonnay, Chardonnay, Bronze Wing Chardonnay, Chenin Blanc, Semillon, Riesling, Verdelho, Bronze Wing Verdelho, Bronze Wing Merlot, Shiraz, Cabernet Sauvignon, Vintage Port, Liqueur Muscat, Sparkling.
summary Consistent producer of a surprisingly elegant and complex Chardonnay; the other wines are more variable, but from time to time has made attractive Verdelho and excellent Cabernet Sauvignon. 1998 saw the first release of wines partly or wholly coming from the family's new planting at Pemberton, those being Swan/Pemberton blends released under the Bronze Wing label. Limited retail distribution in Perth, Melbourne and Sydney.

wetherall NR

Naracoorte Road, Coonawarra, SA 5263 **region** Coonawarra
phone (08) 8737 2104 **fax** (08) 8737 2105 **open** 7 days 10–4
winemaker Michael Wetherall **production** 1600 **est.** 1991
product range ($16–25 CD) Chardonnay, Cabernet Sauvignon, Shiraz, Sparkling Cabernet.
summary The Wetherall family has been growing grapes in Coonawarra for more than 30 years, and Michael Wetherall (a Roseworthy graduate) has been responsible for overseeing wine production since Wetherall extended its operations into winemaking in 1991. Most of the grapes are still sold; no recent tastings.

wharncliffe NR

Summerleas Road, Kingston, Tas 7050 **region** Southern Tasmania
phone (03) 6229 7147 **fax** (03) 6229 2298 **open** Not
winemaker Andrew Hood (Contract) **production** 32 **est.** 1990
product range ($20 ML) Chardonnay.
summary With total plantings of 0.75 hectare, Wharncliffe could not exist without the type of contract-winemaking service offered by Andrew Hood, which would be a pity, because the vineyard is beautifully situated on the doorstep of Mount Wellington, the Huon Valley and the Channel regions of southern Tasmania.

whispering hills NR

54 Gibbs Road, Majorca, Vic 3465 **region** Bendigo
phone (03) 5964 6070 **fax** (03) 5964 6231 **open** Not
winemaker Murray Lyons, Ron Snep **production** 500 **est.** 1994
product range ($22 ML) Chardonnay, Cabernet Sauvignon.
summary The minuscule production of Whispering Hills is limited to one wine (a Cabernet Sauvignon), which is sold by mail order and word of mouth.

whisson lake NR

PO Box 91, Uraidla, SA 5142 **region** Adelaide Hills
phone (08) 8390 1303 **fax** (08) 8390 3822 **open** By appointment
winemaker Roman Bratasiuk (Contract) **production** 300 **est.** 1985
product range ($27.50–31.50 CD) Pinot Noir.
summary Mark Whisson is primarily a grape grower, with 4.5 hectares of close-planted, steep-sloped north-facing vineyard. A small quantity of the production is made for the Whisson Lake label by Roman Bratasiuk, best known as the owner/winemaker of Clarendon Hills. Tiny quantities are exported to the US and the UK; as at March 2000 both '95 and '96 Pinot Noirs were available but seemed to have passed their 'best by' date.

whitehorse wines NR

4 Reid Park Road, Mount Clear, Vic 3350 **region** Ballarat
phone (03) 5330 1719 **fax** (03) 5330 1288 **open** Weekends 11–5
winemaker Noel Myers **production** 900 **est.** 1981
product range ($10–18 CD) Riesling, Riesling Müller Thurgau, Chardonnay, Pinot Noir, Cabernet Shiraz.
summary The Myers family has moved from grape growing to winemaking, utilising the attractive site on its sloping hillside south of Ballarat. Four hectares of vines are in production, with pinot noir and chardonnay the principal varieties.

wignalls wines ★★★★

Chester Pass Road (Highway 1), Albany, WA 6330 **region** Great Southern
phone (08) 9841 2848 **fax** (08) 9842 9003 **open** 7 days 12–4
winemaker Bill Wignall **production** 5000 **est.** 1982
product range ($12–32 R) Chardonnay, Sauvignon Blanc, Late Harvest Frontignac, Pinot Noir, Reserve Pinot Noir, Cabernet Sauvignon, Tawny Port, White Port.
summary A noted producer of Pinot Noir which has extended the map for the variety in Australia. The Pinots have tremendous style and flair, but do age fairly quickly. The white wines are elegant, and show the cool climate to good advantage. A new winery was constructed and opened for the 1998 vintage, utilising the production from the 16 hectares of estate plantings.

wild dog NR

South Road, Warragul, Vic 3820 **region** Gippsland
phone (03) 5623 1117 **fax** (03) 5623 6402 **open** 7 days 10–5
winemaker John Farrington **production** 2500 **est.** 1982
product range ($12–18 CD) Riesling, Chardonnay, Rosé, Pinot Noir, Shiraz, Cabernet Sauvignon.
summary An aptly named winery which produces somewhat rustic wines from the 11.5 hectares of estate vineyards; even the Farringtons say that the Shiraz comes 'with a bite', also pointing out that there is minimal handling, fining and filtration. Be warned.

wild duck creek estate NR

Spring Flat Road, Heathcote, Vic 3523 **region** Bendigo
phone (03) 5433 3133 **fax** (03) 5433 3133 **open** By appointment
winemaker David Anderson **production** 5000 **est.** 1980
product range ($16–45 CD) Springflat Shiraz, Shiraz Pressings, Alan's Cabernets, Alan's Cabernets Pressings, The Blend, Duck Muck (which rivals Demondrille's Purgatory in the contest for the worst wine name).
summary The first release of Wild Duck Creek Estate from the 1991 vintage marks the end of 12 years of effort by David and Diana Anderson. They commenced planting the 4.5-hectare vineyard in 1980, made their first tiny quantities of wine in 1986, the first commercial quantities of wine in 1991, and built their winery and cellar-door facility in 1993. Exports to Belgium, Switzerland, Canada, the US and Germany.

wilderness estate NR

Branxton Road, Pokolbin, NSW 2321 **region** Lower Hunter Valley
phone (02) 4998 7755 **fax** (02) 4998 7750 **open** 7 days 9–5
winemaker John Baruzzi, Josef Lesnik **production** 25 000 **est.** 1986
product range ($16.30–17.80 CD) The premium varietal range of Unwooded Chardonnay, Reserve Chardonnay, Unwooded Semillon, Individual Block Semillon, Shiraz, Cabernet Merlot and Merlot is under the Wilderness Estate label; the second Black Creek label encompasses a similar range of lower-priced varietals.

summary Long-term Wyndham Estate winemaker John Baruzzi has formed a 50:50 joint venture with Joe Lesnik, resulting in the former Lesnik Family Winery now renamed Wilderness Estate. The Lesnik label will be phased out, with all wines from the '95 vintage and onwards being released either under the Wilderness Estate label or under the Black Creek label. The '97 Reserve Chardonnay is a good wine with plenty of fruit and balanced use of what appears to be American oak. National distribution through Normans is supplemented by exports to the US, Canada and the UK.

wildwood ★★★★☆

St John's Lane, Wildwood, Bulla, Vic 3428   **region** Sunbury
phone (03) 9307 1118   **fax** (03) 9331 1590   **open** 7 days 10–6
winemaker Dr Wayne Stott, Peter Dredge   **production** 2000   **est.** 1983
product range ($15–30 CD) Chardonnay, Viognier, Chenin Blanc, Cabernets, Merlot Cabernet Franc, Pinot Noir, Shiraz.
summary Wildwood is situated just 4 kilometres past Melbourne airport. The vineyard and cellar door are situated at an altitude of 130 metres in the Oaklands Valley, which provides unexpected views back to Port Phillip Bay and the Melbourne skyline. Plastic surgeon Wayne Stott has taken what is very much a part-time activity rather more seriously than most by undertaking (and completing) the Wine Science degree at Charles Sturt University. The rating is given for the 1998 red wines; it has to be said the white wines are far less impressive.

Wildwood Pinot Noir

The progress of Pinot Noir in both Sunbury and the Macedon Ranges reminds me strongly of its first decade or so in Tasmania: in theory the climate was perfect, but with the odd exception, Pinot simply failed to live up to expectations. Then, all of a sudden, the variety (and its makers) started to feel at home. So it is proving in Sunbury. ▼▼▼▼▽ **1998** Medium red-purple; the bouquet opens with slightly dusty oak, but sappy/plummy fruit then starts to manifest itself. This progression is even more marked on the palate, which has intensity, a racy style and length, with an excellent balance of savoury flavours.   **rating:** 91
best drinking 2000–2005   **best vintages** '98   **drink with** Duck breast   • $30

Wildwood Shiraz

Given the reverence with which Craiglee Shiraz is greeted, it should be no surprise to find Wildwood coming up with a lovely wine in a vintage made to measure for the variety in the Sunbury region.
▼▼▼▼▽ **1998** Dark red-purple; a very fragrant and warmly spiced, seductive bouquet is followed by a luscious, ripe palate with very sweet cherry/berry fruit neatly complemented by oak and tannins.   **rating:** 93
best drinking 2003–2013   **best vintages** '97, '98   **drink with** Coq au vin   • $25

Wildwood Cabernets

Started with a bang back in 1993, but has wandered around before hitting form with successive vintages in 1997 and 1998.
▼▼▼▼▽ **1998** Medium to full red-purple; a very concentrated and ripe bouquet with rivulets of dark berry, dark chocolate and herb is followed by a high-flavoured palate with spice, chocolate, raspberry and herb flavours all intermingling.   **rating:** 90
best drinking 2003–2010   **best vintages** '93, '97, '98   **drink with** Oxtail   • $25

☙ wildwood winery   NR

Caves Road, Yallingup, WA 6282   **region** Margaret River
phone (08) 9755 2066   **open** Sun–Fri 11–4
winemaker James Pennington, John Wade (Consultant)   **production** 12 000   **est.** 1984
product range Chardonnay, Semillon, Sauvignon Blanc, Chenin Blanc, Shiraz, Cabernet Merlot.
summary Wildwood Winery is part of the spectacularly expanding Hotham Valley Estate empire, which now includes a 33-hectare property at Chapman Brook with 5 hectares under vine, the Bridgeland Vineyard, a 207-hectare property with 97 hectares under vine, and Wildwood, with 56 hectares accommodating a restaurant, cellar door and accommodation, with 6 hectares under vine, all in the Margaret River region. These complement the original property at Wandering which has 15 hectares and a state-of-the-art winery completed in 1993. All of this will see current production of 12 000 cases skyrocket to 100 000 cases in the years ahead, with Wildwood Winery no doubt providing the principal cellar door sales outlet.

willespie ★★★☆

Harmans Mill Road, Willyabrup via Cowaramup, WA 6284 **region** Margaret River
phone (08) 9755 6248 **fax** (08) 9755 6210 **open** 7 days 10.30–5
winemaker Michael Lemmes **production** 4000 **est.** 1976
product range ($15–35 R) Sauvignon Blanc, Semillon Sauvignon Blanc, Verdelho, Riesling, Shiraz, Cabernet Sauvignon, Merlot; Harmans Mill White and Harmans Mill Red are cheaper second-label wines.
summary Willespie has produced many attractive white wines over the years, typically in brisk, herbaceous Margaret River style. All are fruit- rather than oak-driven; the newer Merlot also shows promise. The wines have had such success that the Squance family (which founded and owns Willespie) has announced plans to substantially increase winery capacity, drawing upon an additional 25 hectares of estate vineyards in the course of establishment.

williams rest NR

Lot 195 Albany Highway, Mount Barker, WA 6324 **region** Great Southern
phone (08) 9367 3277 **fax** (08) 9367 3328 **open** Not
winemaker Contract **production** NA **est.** 1972
product range Granite Flats White and Red.
summary A long-established vineyard, planted way back in 1972, which is now part of the Selwyn Wine Group. The vineyard is named after Benjamin Williams, an eight-year-old boy who was accidentally killed by a mail coach in 1890.

willow bend ★★★☆

Lyndoch Valley Road, Lyndoch, SA 5351 **region** Barossa Valley
phone (08) 8524 4169 **fax** (08) 8524 4169 **open** Not
winemaker Wayne Dutschke **production** 1500 **est.** 1990
product range ($16–25 R) Chardonnay, Shiraz, Shiraz Merlot Cabernet, Shiraz Cabernet Merlot.
summary Wayne Dutschke has had ten years of winemaking experience with major wine companies in South Australia, Victoria and New South Wales but has returned to South Australia to join his uncle, Ken Semmler, a leading grape grower in the Barossa Valley and now in the Adelaide Hills. No recent tastings, simply because Willow Bend sells out of wine in less than six months each year. Annual release in August; there is limited retail distribution in Sydney and Melbourne.

willow creek ★★★★

166 Balnarring Road, Merricks North, Vic 3926 **region** Mornington Peninsula
phone (03) 5989 7448 **fax** (03) 5989 7584 **open** 7 days 10–5
winemaker Simon Black **production** 14 000 **est.** 1989
product range ($15–27 R) Sauvignon Blanc, Unoaked Chardonnay, Tulum Chardonnay, Pinot Noir, Shiraz, Cabernet Sauvignon, Sparkling Cuvée.
summary Yet another significant entrant in the fast-expanding Mornington Peninsula area, with 15 hectares of vines planted to cabernet sauvignon, chardonnay and pinot noir. The cellar-door sales area boasts picnic areas, barbecue facilities, trout fishing and bocce; lunches are served every day, and dinners by appointment. Expansion of the cellar door was completed by January 1998, with a winery constructed for the 1998 vintage. Exports to Singapore, the US and the UK.

Willow Creek Tulum Chardonnay

The estate-grown grapes are whole-bunch pressed, and fermented in French oak barriques, part being taken through malolactic fermentation. It spends 12 months in oak before being bottled.
▼▼▼▼ **1998** Light to medium yellow-green; the bouquet is clean, smooth and with well-balanced and integrated oak but not much sparkle. The palate has much more to it, with quite powerful grapefruit and melon flavours, the acid picking up on the finish and aiding the length of the wine. **rating:** 89
best drinking 1999–2003 **best vintages** '98 **drink with** Pan-fried flathead fillets • $25

Willow Creek Pinot Noir

The wine is made using a variety of techniques, with selected parcels undergoing barrel-fermentation, and others extended skin maceration. It can spend up to 18 months in new and used French oak barriques, as it did in 1997, a response to the low-yielding and intense vintage.
▼▼▼▼ **1998** Light to medium red; the bouquet is light, with a mix of earthy/foresty/cherry aromas. As with the Chardonnay, the palate moves immediately into another league; surprisingly intense and long, it has fine, silky tannins and good acidity. The oak, too, has been nicely judged. **rating:** 91
best drinking 1999–2003 **best vintages** '91, '94, '95, '97, '98 **drink with** Gently spiced Asian food • $25

🥀 willowvale wines   NR

Black Swamp Road, Tenterfield, NSW 2372   **region** Northern Slopes Zone
phone (02) 6736 3589   **fax** (02) 6736 3753   **open** 7 days 10–5
winemaker John Morley   **production** 1000   **est.** 1994
product range ($11.50–17.95 CD) Riesling, Chardonnay, Shiraz Grenache Pinot Noir, Merlot, Cabernet Merlot, Cabernet Sauvignon, Old Red Port, Ambrosia.
summary John Morley commenced establishing 2 hectares of vineyard of equal portions of chardonnay, merlot and cabernet sauvignon in 1994, and has further planting was scheduled for both 1999 and 2000. The vineyard is at an altitude of 940 metres, and was the first in the growing Tenterfield region. Advanced vineyard climatic monitoring systems have been installed, and a new winery building has been constructed which is planned to be equipped in time for the 2000 vintage. At this point winemaking will return to Willowvale, which will also offer contract-winemaking services for others; John Morley is currently attempting (his word) a wine science degree at Charles Sturt University and it is clear this is a serious attempt at diversification.

will taylor wines   ★★★★

1 Simpson Parade, Goodwood, SA 5034   **region** Other Wineries of SA
phone (08) 8271 6122   **fax** (08) 8271 6122   **open** By appointment
winemaker Various contract   **production** 1300   **est.** 1997
product range ($20 R) Clare Valley Riesling, Adelaide Hills Sauvignon Blanc, Hunter Valley Semillon, Pinot Noir.
summary Will Taylor is a partner in the leading Adelaide law firm Finlaysons and specialises in wine law. Together with Suzanne Taylor, he has established a classic negociant wine business, having wines contract-made to his specification. Moreover, he chooses what he considers to be the best regions for each variety and added a Geelong/Yarra Valley Pinot Noir in 2000. Most of the wine is sold to restaurants, with small volumes sold to a select group of fine wine stores and mail order. Exports to the US, Asia and Europe (but in small volumes).

wilmot hills vineyard   NR

407 Back Road, Wilmot, Tas 7310   **region** Northern Tasmania
phone (03) 6492 1193   **fax** (03) 6492 1193   **open** 7 days 9–7
winemaker John Cole, Ruth Cole   **production** NA   **est.** 1991
product range ($15–20 CD) Muller Thürgau, Pinot Noir, El Nino Pinot Noir, fruit wines and ciders.
summary The beautiful Wilmot Hills Vineyard is situated on the western side of Lake Barrington, not far from the Cradle Mountain road, with marvellous views to Mount Roland and the adjacent peaks. It is very much a family affair, established by John and Ruth Cole, and produces both wine and cider. John Cole spent 18 years in Melbourne participating in engineering design and some graphic art, Ruth working in the hospitality industry for ten years and making fruit wines for 20 years. The neat on-site winery was both designed and built by the Coles, as was much of the wine and cider-making equipment.

wilson vineyard   ★★★★

Polish Hill River, Sevenhill via Clare, SA 5453   **region** Clare Valley
phone (08) 8843 4310   **open** Weekends 10–4 May–Oct
winemaker John Wilson, Daniel Wilson   **production** 5000   **est.** 1974
product range ($13–26 CD) Gallery Series Riesling, Cabernet Sauvignon, Hippocrene Sparkling Burgundy, Chardonnay, Semillon, Zinfandel, Liqueur Gewurztraminer.
summary Dr John Wilson is a tireless ambassador for the Clare Valley and for wine (and its beneficial effect on health) in general. His wines were made using techniques and philosophies garnered early in his wine career and can occasionally be idiosyncratic but in recent years have been most impressive. The winemaking mantle has now passed to his son, Daniel. The wines are sold through cellar door and retail in Sydney, Melbourne, Brisbane and Adelaide; no mailing list.

Wilson Gallery Series Riesling

This powerful Riesling from the Polish Hill River vineyards is almost invariably at the upper end of the Clare Valley hierarchy. A bottle of 1991 tasted in January 1997 was magnificent, a great Riesling at the height of its power and complexity. The '99 should go down the same path; these are Rieslings with the capacity to age exceptionally well.

🍷🍷🍷🍷 1999 Medium green-yellow; the bouquet is clean, with nicely weighted lime juice aromas. A powerful, zesty palate with lime, mineral and herb flavours; attractive now but will improve yet further.   **rating:** 91
best drinking 2000–2007   **best vintages** '85, '90, '91, '92, '94, '96, '97, '99   **drink with** Japanese cuisine   •$17.50

� wimbaliri wines   NR

Barton Highway, Murrumbateman, NSW 2582 **region** Canberra District
phone (02) 6227 5921 **fax** (02) 6227 5921 **open** Weekends 11–5 and by appointment
winemaker John Andersen **production** 550 **est.** 1988
product range ($16–18 CD) Chardonnay, Pinot Noir, Cabernet Merlot.
summary John and Margaret Andersen moved to the Canberra district in 1987, and commenced the
establishment of their vineyard at Murrumbateman in 1988; the property borders two highly regarded Canberra
producers, Doonkuna and Clonakilla. The vineyard is close-planted with a vertical trellis system, with a total of
0.6 hectare of cabernet sauvignon, merlot and cabernet franc, the same amount of chardonnay and shiraz (the last
not yet bearing) and 0.2 hectare pinot noir. The 1995 Cabernet Merlot, the first wine made by John Andersen
from estate-grown fruit, won two silver and two bronze medals at local wine shows, and subsequent Cabernet-
based wines have all won awards, the 1997 just missing out on a trophy at the Canberra Regional Wine Show.

Wimbaliri Wines Cabernet Merlot
An estate-grown blend matured in cask for 20 months, and which shows competent winemaking.
🍷🍷🍷🍷 **1997** Medium red-purple; the soft, gently earthy/leathery fruit of the bouquet is offset by a touch of sweet
oak; those sweet notes come through on the palate both as fruit and as vanilla-accented oak; finishes with soft
tannins.   **rating:** 86
best drinking 2000–2004 **drink with** Grilled steak • $18

� windarra   NR

DeBeyers Road, Pokolbin, NSW 2321 **region** Lower Hunter Valley
phone (02) 4998 7648 **fax** (02) 4998 7648 **open** Tues–Sun 10–5
winemaker Tom Andresen **production** NA **est.** NA
product range NA.
summary The Andresen family has 6 hectares of semillon, chardonnay and shiraz; the wines are contract-made.

windowrie estate   NR

Windowrie, Canowindra, NSW 2804 **region** Cowra
phone (02) 6344 3234 **fax** (02) 6344 3227 **open** 7 days 10–6
winemaker Tobias Ansted **production** 42 000 **est.** 1988
product range ($14–30 CD) Chardonnay, Botrytis Sauvignon Blanc, Cabernet Sauvignon; the Mill range of
Chardonnay, Sauvignon Blanc, Shiraz and Shiraz Cabernet.
summary Windowrie Estate was established in 1988 on a substantial grazing property at Canowindra, 30
kilometres north of Cowra and in the same viticultural region. Most of the grapes from the 240-hectare vineyard
are sold to other makers, with increasing quantities being made for the Windowrie Estate and The Mill labels, the
Chardonnays enjoying show success. The cellar door is situated in a flour mill built in 1861 from local granite. It
ceased operations in 1905 and lay unoccupied for 91 years until restored by the O'Dea family.

Windowrie Estate The Mill Chardonnay
Plenty of flavour but a lighter touch with the oak would have been better.
🍷🍷🍷🍷 **1999** Medium yellow-green; obvious oak (almost certainly chips) swamps the bouquet; the palate has ripe
melon and banana fruit, and the oak is less heavy-handed.   **rating:** 80
best drinking 2000–2001 **best vintages** NA **drink with** Pasta • $14

windy ridge vineyard   ★★★

Foster–Fish Creek Road, Foster, Vic 3960 **region** Gippsland
phone (03) 5682 2035 **open** Holiday weekends 10–5
winemaker Graeme Wilson **production** 300 **est.** 1978
product range ($20–25 CD) Traminer, Pinot Noir, Cabernet Sauvignon Malbec, Vintage Port, Georgia's
Liqueur Pinot Noir, Graeme's Late Bottled Vintage Port.
summary The 2.8-hectare Windy Ridge Vineyard was planted between 1978 and 1986, with the first vintage
not taking place until 1988. Winemaker Graeme Wilson favours prolonged maturation, part in stainless steel and
part in oak, before bottling his wines, typically giving the Pinot Noir three years and the Cabernet two years
before bottling. The '97 Cabernet Malbec (70 per cent/30 per cent) was an austere and powerful wine, with cedar,
tobacco and powerful tannins which seem likely to outlive the fruit, but which is nonetheless interesting.

winewood   NR

Sundown Road, Ballandean, Qld 4382 **region** Granite Belt
phone (07) 4684 1187 **fax** (07) 4684 1187 **open** Weekends, public holidays 9–5
winemaker Ian Davis **production** 1000 **est.** 1984
product range ($15–20 CD) Chardonnay, Chardonnay Marsanne, Shiraz Marsanne, MacKenzies Run (Cabernet blend), Muscat.
summary A weekend and holiday activity for schoolteacher Ian Davis and town-planner wife Jeanette; the tiny winery is a model of neatness and precision planning. The use of marsanne with chardonnay and semillon shows an interesting change in direction. Has a little over 3 hectares of estate plantings. All wine sold through cellar door.

winstead   ★★★★☆

75 Winstead Road, Bagdad, Tas 7030 **region** Southern Tasmania
phone (03) 6268 6417 **fax** (03) 6268 6417 **open** By appointment
winemaker Andrew Hood (Contract) **production** 750 **est.** 1989
product range ($17–20 CD) Riesling, Ensnared Riesling, Pinot Noir.
summary The good news about Winstead is the outstanding quality of its extremely generous and rich Pinot Noirs, rivalling those of Freycinet for the abundance of their fruit flavour without any sacrifice of varietal character. The bad news is that production is so limited, with only half a hectare each of riesling and pinot noir being tended by fly-fishing devotee Neil Snare and wife Julieanne. Retail distribution in Melbourne.

Winstead Riesling

Produced from a little over half a hectare of estate plantings. One of the most consistent Tasmanian Rieslings, and which richly repays cellaring, not to mention service with trout caught by Winstead owner Neil Snare.
TTTY 1999 Light to medium yellow-green; the bouquet is firm, with a mix of mineral (predominant) and citrus aromas. The palate is still classically austere and undeveloped; will blossom with time in bottle. **rating: 84**
best drinking 2002–2009 **best vintages** '98 **drink with** Pan-fried trout • $17

Winstead Ensnared Riesling

Owner Neil Snare makes two wines 'for fun'. The first is Pinot Noir, the second (since 1998) a botrytised Riesling. It is very late harvested (around the first day of winter) and is, in Neil Snare's words 'wildly uneconomic because so many berries have fallen off the bunch onto the ground due to extreme ripeness'. This is technically a very difficult style of wine to make, and the exceptional quality of this trophy-winning vintage (1999) must have been extremely satisfying for Neil Snare.
TTTTT 1999 Glowing yellow-green; the bouquet is as complex as it is intense, with essence of lime juice aromas; the palate is fine, intense and long, with citrus/lime fruit and perfectly balanced acidity. **rating: 94**
best drinking 2001–2015 **best vintages** '99 **drink with** Poached fruit • $20

Winstead Pinot Noir

Like the Riesling, produced from a little over half a hectare of estate plantings. Going from strength to strength as the vines mature, with a now consistently produced depth and richness of flavour not far removed from that of Freycinet. Very much a Pinot to watch (and buy); it is just a pity there is not more of it.
TTTTY 1998 Light to medium red-purple; a brilliantly clean and fragrant wine with crystal clear varietal character on both bouquet and palate. There is a mix of cherry and spice, the oak playing a pure support role. An intriguing wine, for it is a little simple in terms of structure but very pure and long in terms of its fruit. **rating: 91**
best drinking 2001–2005 **best vintages** '95, '96, '97, '98 **drink with** Saddle of hare • $20

winters vineyard   NR

Clarke Road, O.B. Flat via Mount Gambier, SA 5290 **region** Mount Gambier
phone (08) 8726 8255 **fax** (08) 8726 8255 **open** 7 days 10–5
winemaker Bruce Gregory (Contract) **production** 500 **est.** 1988
product range ($10–14 CD) Chardonnay, Cabernet Sauvignon.
summary Former restaurateurs Martin and Merrilee Winter have established 8 hectares of vineyards 6 kilometres south of Mount Gambier and about 60 kilometres south of Coonawarra proper. The wines are contract-made, with an ultimate production target of 2500 cases. Light, leafy but pleasant Cabernet Sauvignon shows the cool climate but is well made, with a nice touch of cedary vanillin oak.

wirilda creek   ★★★

PO Box 215, McLaren Vale, SA 5171   **region** McLaren Vale
phone (08) 8323 9688   **fax** (08) 8323 9260   **open** 7 days 10–5
winemaker Kerry Flanagan   **production** 2000   **est.** 1993
product range ($13–25 CD) Verdelho, Grape Pickers (Riesling Chardonnay Semillon), Sauvignon Blanc, Trinity — The Blend (Cabernet Malbec Shiraz), Cabernet Merlot, Shiraz, Rare Shiraz, Cabernet Sauvignon Rare, Evening Shadow (Sparkling Shiraz), Fortifieds.
summary Wirilda Creek may be one of the newer arrivals in McLaren Vale but it offers the lot: wine, lunch every day (Pickers Platters reflecting local produce) and accommodation (four rooms opening onto a private garden courtyard). Co-owner Kerry Flanagan (with partner Karen Shertock) has had great experience in the wine and hospitality industries: a Roseworthy graduate (1980) he has inter alia worked at Penfolds, Coriole and Wirra Wirra and also owned the famous Old Salopian Inn for a period of time. A little under 4 hectares of McLaren Vale estate vineyards have now been joined with a little over 3 hectares of vineyards planted at Antechamber Bay, Kangaroo Island. Limited retail distribution in New South Wales and South Australia; exports to Canada and the US.

Wirilda Creek Vine Pruners Cabernet Blend

A blend of 60 per cent Shiraz, 35 per cent Cabernet Sauvignon and 5 per cent Merlot, presently sourced from the estate vineyards in McLaren Vale and from Langhorne Creek material until the Kangaroo Island plantings come into bearing.
▼▼▼▽ 1998 Medium red-purple; the moderately intense bouquet ranges through mint, leaf and earth as well as blackberry fruit. The palate focuses more on sweet, small berry and plum fruit; the tannins are not too raspy but do tighten up on the finish.   **rating:** 83
best drinking 2003–2008   **best vintages** NA   **drink with** Moussaka   • $15

Wirilda Creek Cabernet Sauvignon Rare

As the name implies, a reserve selection, the lesser Cabernet being used in the Cabernet Merlot blend and in Vine Pruners.
▼▼▼▽ 1997 Medium red-purple; the bouquet is in a leafy, woody, spicy spectrum; the palate is warmer than expected, with pleasant savoury, chocolatey fruit in a strongly regional mode, finishing with soft tannins.   **rating:** 84
best drinking 2002–2007   **best vintages** NA   **drink with** Marinated beef   • $25

wirra wirra   ★★★★☆

McMurtie Road, McLaren Vale, SA 5171   **region** McLaren Vale
phone (08) 8323 8414   **fax** (08) 8323 8596   **open** Mon–Sat 10–5, Sun 11–5
winemaker Benn Riggs   **production** 75 000   **est.** 1969
product range ($13–69 R) The Cousins (Sparkling), Hand Picked Riesling, Late Picked Riesling, Semillon Sauvignon Blanc, Scrubby Rise Semillon, Sauvignon Blanc, Scrubby Rise Semillon Sauvignon Blanc Chardonnay, Chardonnay, Wood Matured Semillon Sauvignon Blanc, The Angelus Cabernet Sauvignon, Pinot Noir, Church Block (Cabernet Shiraz Merlot), RSW Shiraz, Original Blend (Grenache Shiraz), Fortifieds.
summary Long-respected for the consistency of its white wines, Wirra Wirra has now established an equally formidable reputation for its reds. Right across the board, the wines are of exemplary character, quality and style, The Angelus Cabernet Sauvignon and RSW Shiraz battling with each other for supremacy. Long may the battle continue.

Wirra Wirra Hand Picked Riesling

When, well over a decade ago, Wirra Wirra incorporated the words 'Hand Picked' into its Riesling label, it was regarded as another example of owner Greg Trott's notorious sense of humour. In the intervening years it has come to represent a statement of individuality for one of the region's better Rieslings (all things being relative). Typically, a blend of 80 per cent McLaren Vale and 20 per cent Clare Valley material.
▼▼▼▼ 1999 Light yellow-green; the bouquet is quite complex, with a mix of citrus and savoury herbal notes. The palate is more delicate, but very fresh, and will richly repay cellaring.   **rating:** 86
best drinking 2003–2009   **best vintages** '82, '89, '91, '92, '94, '96, '97   **drink with** South Australian whiting • $14.95

Wirra Wirra Sauvignon Blanc

One of the pioneers of quality Sauvignon Blanc in McLaren Vale. Wine quality is never less than good, excelling in the cooler vintages. Draws principally upon 3.5 hectares of estate plantings.
▼▼▼▽ 1999 Light to medium yellow-green; a clean, somewhat pedestrian bouquet with some herbal notes is followed by a palate which has weight but which is not particularly focused.   **rating:** 84
best drinking 1999–2000   **best vintages** '91, '92, '94, '96, '97   **drink with** Blue swimmer crab   • $16.95

Wirra Wirra Scrubby Rise

A blend of Semillon, Sauvignon Blanc and Chardonnay, all sourced from McLaren Vale.

▼▼▼▽ **1999** Light green-yellow; the bouquet is clean and crisp, with gentle sweet fruit; in the mouth there is a pleasant, well-balanced commercial dry white wine made without oak interference. **rating:** 83

best drinking 2000–2002 **best vintages** NA **drink with** Smoked cod • $14.50

Wirra Wirra Chardonnay

A blend of McLaren Vale and Adelaide Hills fruit, barrel-fermented in a mix of new, one-year-old and two-year-old barrels coming respectively from the Vosges, Allier and Troncais forests. If this were not enough, a portion was stainless steel-fermented and back-blended. The wine was given partial lees contact for eight months. In other words, it had the full book thrown at it in the winery.

▼▼▼▼ **1998** Medium yellow-green; a solid bouquet with nectarine/peach fruit and nicely balanced and integrated oak. The palate is a carbon copy of the bouquet, with good depth of flavour. **rating:** 86

best drinking 2000–2003 **best vintages** '82, '89, '91, '92, '94, '96, '97 **drink with** Wiener schnitzel • $24

Wirra Wirra RSW Shiraz

RSW Shiraz is named after Robert Strangways Wigley, who founded Wirra Wirra in 1894. While The Angelus has brought much recognition to Wirra Wirra, it is arguable that, viewed since 1994, RSW Shiraz is its best wine. It is a beautifully elegant, constructed and structured wine, showing a particular sensitive use of French (80 per cent) and American (20 per cent) oak.

▼▼▼▼ **1997** Medium red-purple; the bouquet is laden with sweet, luscious minty berry fruit; oak is certainly present but is not obtrusive. The palate is much more elegant in its youth than preceding vintages, with lovely, sweet black cherry and red cherry fruit; once again, the oak is restrained. **rating:** 88

best drinking 2002–2017 **best vintages** '94, '95, '97 **drink with** Smoked beef • $38.50

Wirra Wirra Original Blend Grenache Shiraz

The first red wine produced by cousins Greg and Roger Trott in 1972 was a blend of Grenache and Shiraz grown on one of Greg Trott's vineyards which became known as the Church Block. In time that vineyard was replanted to cabernet and merlot (retaining some shiraz) and it was not until 1992 that another Grenache appeared under the Wirra Wirra label, bearing the name 'Original Blend'. Now a blend of approximately two-thirds Grenache and one-third Shiraz, it has become an important part of the Wirra Wirra stable.

▼▼▼▼ **1998** Medium red-purple; bright, fresh fruit of light to medium intensity drives both the bouquet and palate, where sweet berry fruit and soft, ripe tannins coalesce. A few years in bottle will bring good complexity. **rating:** 87

best drinking 2003–2008 **best vintages** '96, '98 **drink with** Kangaroo tail stew • $20.50

Wirra Wirra Church Block Cabernet Shiraz Merlot

Church Block, typically a blend of around 50 per cent Cabernet Sauvignon, 30 per cent Shiraz and 20 per cent Merlot, was the first of the Wirra Wirra red wines to catch the eye, although quality did wander around somewhat for a while.

▼▼▼▽ **1998** Medium red-purple; the bouquet is quite firm and surprisingly earthy, but the palate is much riper and richer, with cassis and dark chocolate flavours leading the way. A touch of the earth of the bouquet lingers but does not detract from the wine. **rating:** 90

best drinking 2003–2008 **best vintages** '90, '91, '94, '98 **drink with** Pasta bolognaise • $16.50

Wirra Wirra The Angelus Cabernet Sauvignon

Named after a one-tonne bell which used to ring at St Ignatius Church, Norwood; a Trott whimsy for The Angelus is only made in 'ring the bell' vintages — four in total up to 1992, including the '91 which received national acclaim as the top wine at the 1992 Sydney International Wine Competition. The precise source varies from year to year, typically 65 per cent McLaren Vale and 35 per cent Coonawarra material. It spends 20 months in French oak.

▼▼▼▼▼ **1997** Medium red-purple, it has a mix of red berry, earth and cedary oak on the bouquet. The palate is soft and rounded, with smooth berry fruit fine tannins and a wonderful finish. **rating:** 94

best drinking 2002–2012 **best vintages** '86, '90, '91, '92, '95, '96, '97 **drink with** Fillet of beef • $38.50

wise wines   NR

Lot 4 Eagle Bay Road, Dunsborough, WA 6281 **region** Margaret River
phone (08) 9756 8627 **fax** (08) 9756 8770 **open** 7 days 10.30–4.30
winemaker Siobhan Lynch **production** 36 000 **est.** 1986
product range ($17–35 R) Sauvignon Blanc Semillon, Aquercus Chardonnay (Unwooded), Leaf Chardonnay, Classic White, Late Harvest (Chenin Blanc, Semillon, Muscat), Pinot Noir, Classic Soft Red, Eagle Bay Shiraz, Shiraz Merlot, Cabernet Sauvignon, Tawny Port.
summary Wise Wines, headed by Perth entrepreneur Ron Wise, brings together the 20.5-hectare Eagle Bay Vineyard at Meelup, the 10.3-hectare Donnybrook Valley Vineyard at Donnybrook, and the 4-hectare Bramley Estate Vineyard at Margaret River. The appointment of Siobhan Lynch, formerly winemaker at Chatsfield, has coincided with a sharp increase in production, and exports to the US.

witchmount estate   NR

557 Leakes Road, Rockbank, Vic 3335 **region** Sunbury
phone (03) 9747 1047 **open** Wed–Sun
winemaker Peter Dredge **production** 2000 **est.** 1991
product range ($10–30 CD) Semillon, Sauvignon Blanc, Chardonnay, Nebbiolo, Shiraz, Cabernet Sauvignon.
summary Gaye and Matt Ramunno operate Witchmount Estate in conjunction with its on-site Italian restaurant and function rooms which are open from Wednesday to Sunday inclusive for lunch and dinner. Twelve hectares of vines have been established since 1991, with a further 9 hectares currently being planted. Varieties include nebbiolo and the rare northern Italian white grape picolit. Another variety new to the region will be tempranillo.

Witchmount Estate Shiraz

By the time the new planting programme is completed, shiraz and cabernet sauvignon will be the principal varieties. Winemaker Peter Dredge has followed convention, it would seem, by using American oak with this wine.
TTTT 1998 Medium red-purple; quite sweet plum and cherry fruit mixes with smooth vanilla American oak on the bouquet; fresh cherry/berry fruit is the driver of the light to medium-bodied palate, with nicely balanced tannins; American oak provides the wheels.   **rating:** 84
best drinking 2002–2007 **drink with** Ravioli • $30

Witchmount Estate Nebbiolo

Made from an existing planting of a little under 1 hectare, and a very interesting wine. It seems there are no plans to increase the size of the planting.
TTTT 1998 Medium red, with the first signs of brick starting to appear. The bouquet is incredibly fragrant and lifted with spicy/leafy/cigar box aromas. The palate, likewise, has remarkable intensity and length, with green leaf and spice flavours; far from luscious but full of interest.   **rating:** 84
best drinking 2000–2004 **drink with** Osso bucco • $30

Witchmount Estate Cabernet Sauvignon

The Ramunnos are clearly pleased with the performance of cabernet sauvignon, for it represents the largest single planting in the existing vineyards (3.5 hectares) with another 2.5 hectares being planted. If the '98 vintage is the least bit typical, it is not hard to understand their enthusiasm.
TTTT 1998 Medium to full red-purple; the bouquet is essentially savoury, with a mix of berry and earth; cabernet in a classic mould. Any sweetness lacking in the bouquet is compensated for by the smooth, sweet cassis/blackberry-flavoured palate, replete with soft tannins and subtle oak.   **rating:** 86
best drinking 2003–2008 **drink with** Bistecca fiorentina • $30

wolf blass   ★★★★

Bilyara Vineyards, Sturt Highway, Nuriootpa, SA 5355 **region** Barossa Valley
phone (08) 8562 1955 **fax** (08) 8562 4127 **open** Mon–Fri 9.15–4.30, weekends 10–4.30
winemaker John Glaetzer (Red), Wendy Stuckey (White), Caroline Dunn **production** 150 000 **est.** 1966
product range ($11–100 R) White wines under White, Yellow, Green and Gold labels, with emphasis on Riesling and blended Classic Dry White; red wines under Red, Yellow, Brown, Grey and Black labels with emphasis on Cabernet Sauvignon, Shiraz and blends of these. Also sparkling and fortified wines. The Eaglehawk now roosts here, too. The Blass range, with its red, minimalist labels in stark contrast to the usual baroque designs so loved by Wolf, is a relatively recent addition.

summary Although merged with Mildara and now under the giant umbrella of the Fosters Brewing Group, the brands (as expected) have been left largely intact, and — so far at least — the style of the wines has changed little. The red wines continue to be very oaky and, to my palate at least, increasingly old-fashioned. The white wines (made by Wendy Stuckey) are particularly impressive, none more so than the Gold Label Riesling. Worldwide distribution via Mildara Blass International.

Blass Clare Valley Red Label Riesling

1999 marks the second release under the Blass Red Label, the fruit source on this occasion being 100 per cent Clare Valley from vineyards in the Watervale and Sevenhill regions. Cold settling of the juice prior to fermentation, followed by cool fermentation and early bottling are the standard winemaking techniques.

 1999 Medium green-yellow; a highly scented, aromatic bouquet with tropical lime fruit is followed by a wine with plenty of rich fruit flavour on the palate; well-balanced, but seems to be an early-developing style.

rating: 90

best drinking 2000–2004 **best vintages** NA **drink with** Crab mornay • $18

Eaglehawk Riesling

Now made at Wolf Blass by Wendy Stuckey, and uses grapes grown in various parts of southeast Australia.

 1999 Medium yellow-green; a solid and quite rich mix of tropical, lime, mineral and toast aromas. The palate is generous, but doesn't have the length or finesse of the very best wines. For all that, excellent value.

rating: 85

best drinking 2000–2005 **best vintages** '90, '92, '93, '96 **drink with** Terrine of scallops • $11

Wolf Blass Gold Label Riesling

Has been a prolific gold medal and trophy winner in national wine shows over the past four or five years, winning trophies and multiple gold medals. A blend of Eden Valley and Clare Valley material.

 1999 Light green-yellow; the bouquet is clean and fresh but lacks the aromaticity of the Clare Riesling of the same vintage. The palate is pleasant, well balanced but a little soft, and not up to the scintillating quality of prior vintages. May, however, confound my judgment with age.

rating: 89

best drinking 2000–2005 **best vintages** '90, '92, '95, '96, '97, '98 **drink with** Salad Niçoise • $16

Wolf Blass Semillon Sauvignon Blanc

A gold medal winner at the National Wine Show in Canberra 1998, but seems to have lost the character it then had.

 1998 Light green-yellow; there is tangy, complex fruit on the bouquet, suggestive of the use of some oak, but there is in fact none. A pleasant but unremarkable wine on the palate which was better when younger.

rating: 83

best drinking Drink now **best vintages** NA **drink with** Fried fish • $15

Wolf Blass Chardonnay

A southeastern Australian blend competently made for the legion of Wolf Blass followers.

 1999 Light to medium yellow-green; there is light fruit on the bouquet with slightly dusty, green oak. The palate is basically inoffensive and unremarkable, and won't frighten the horses.

rating: 80

best drinking Drink now **best vintages** NA **drink with** Pork fillet • $15

Wolf Blass Green Label Shiraz

A blend of Langhorne Creek, Wolf Blass's old stamping ground, Barossa Valley and McLaren Vale fruit.

 1998 Medium to full red-purple; the bouquet is powerful, with some foresty/gamey/pine notes; sweeter fruit comes through on the palate, where American oak is also certainly part of the picture but under relative restraint.

rating: 83

best drinking 2000–2004 **best vintages** NA **drink with** Takeaway • $17

Wolf Blass Grey Label Cabernet Sauvignon Shiraz

Produced from grapes grown entirely in Langhorne Creek, which has always been the preferred supply region for the Wolf Blass wines. Chosen in the Sydney International Wine Competition Top 100 in 1999.

 1996 Medium red-purple; the bouquet shows typical traditional Blass-style strong American oak influence, with overall richness. The palate has plenty of flavour in that sweet fruit and strong vanillin American oak style. You certainly know what you are going to get when you choose a bottle of Wolf Blass red wine.

rating: 86

best drinking 2000–2006 **best vintages** NA **drink with** Beef bordelaise • $29

Wolf Blass Eaglehawk Cabernet Sauvignon

Made from grapes grown in the company's own plantings in the Clare Valley and from unspecified vineyard areas elsewhere in southeast Australia. The wine is fermented in stainless steel before maturation in American oak hogsheads for 12 months.

▼▼▼▽ **1998** Medium red-purple; the bouquet is clean, fresh with direct redcurrant fruit and minimal oak. The fruit flavours on the palate are pleasant but, as the bouquet hints, the structure is somewhat hollow with that classic doughnut hole in the middle.   **rating:** 82

best drinking 2000–2004 **best vintages** NA **drink with** Steak and kidney pie • $12

woodend winery   NR

82 Mahoneys Road, Woodend, Vic 3442 **region** Macedon Ranges
phone (03) 5427 2183 **fax** (03) 5427 4007 **open** Weekends 10–6
winemaker Howard Bradfield **production** 600 **est.** 1983
product range ($15–30 CD) Unwooded Chardonnay, Pinot Noir, Cabernet Franc.
summary Woodend Winery (for a while known as Bluestone Bridge, a name which had to be relinquished due to trademark problems) draws upon 2.5 hectares of vineyard established way back in 1983, although the winemaking is of much more recent origin. The wines are available at cellar door but are also distributed through wholesaler Australian Prestige Wines.

woodlands   NR

Corner Caves and Metricup Roads, Willyabrup via Cowaramup, WA 6284 **region** Margaret River
phone (08) 9755 6226 **fax** (08) 9321 6385 **open** Weekends by appointment
winemaker David Watson, Dorham Mann (Consultant) **production** 1000 **est.** 1973
product range ($20–30 CD) Chardonnay, Pinot Noir, James Cabernet, Emily Cabernets.
summary Burst on the scene with some superlative Cabernet Sauvignons early on but did not manage to maintain the momentum; and indeed made no red wine in 1988, 1989 or 1991. The 1992 red wines marked a return to form, but no recent tastings.

woodonga hill   NR

Cowra Road, Young, NSW 2594 **region** Hilltops
phone (02) 6382 2972 **fax** (02) 6382 2972 **open** 7 days 9–5
winemaker Jill Lindsay **production** 4000 **est.** 1986
product range ($12.50–21 CD) Dry Rhine Riesling, Sauvignon, Chardonnay, Botrytis Semillon, Auslese Gewurztraminer, Meunier, Shiraz, Vintage Port, Cherry Liqueur Port.
summary Early problems with white wine quality appear to have been surmounted. The wines have won bronze or silver medals at regional wine shows in NSW and Canberra, and Jill Lindsay is also a successful contract-winemaker for other small producers.

wood park   NR

RMB 1139 Bobinawarrah–Whorouly Road, Milawa, Vic 3678 **region** King Valley
phone (03) 5727 3367 **fax** (03) 5727 3682 **open** By appointment
winemaker John Stokes, Rick Kinzbrunner **production** 1800 **est.** 1989
product range ($15–30 CD) Meadow Creek Chardonnay, Shiraz Cabernet.
summary The first vines were planted at Wood Park in 1989 by John Stokes as part of a diversification programme for his property at Bobinawarrah in the hills of the Lower King Valley to the east of Milawa. The bulk of the 8-hectare production is sold to Brown Brothers, with a further 8 hectares of vineyard being established for Southcorp. In an unusual twist, Stokes acquires his chardonnay from cousin John Leviny, one of the King Valley pioneers, who has his vineyard at Meadow Creek. To complicate matters further, all four vintages of Chardonnay ('95 to '98) were made by Rick Kinzbrunner. 1995 Cabernet Shiraz won a silver medal at the Victorian Wines Show in 1996, the '96 and '97 Shiraz following suit in 1997.

🐌 woodsmoke estate   NR

Lot 2 Kemp Road, Pemberton, WA 6260 **region** Pemberton
phone (08) 9776 0225 **fax** (08) 9776 0225 **open** By appointment
winemaker Julie White **production** 1500 **est.** 1992
product range ($18–25 CD) Sauvignon Blanc, Semillon, Cabernet blend.
summary The former Jimlee Estate was acquired by the Liebeck family in July 1998, and renamed to WoodSmoke Estate. The current plantings of a little over 2 hectares of semillon, sauvignon blanc, cabernet franc and cabernet sauvignon are to be expanded with a further 6 acres of cabernet franc and merlot planted in 2000.

woodstock ★★★★☆

Douglas Gully Road, McLaren Flat, SA 5171 **region** McLaren Vale
phone (08) 8383 0156 **fax** (08) 8383 0437 **open** Mon–Fri 9–5, weekends, holidays 12–5
winemaker Scott Collett **production** 20 000 **est.** 1974
product range ($9.95–33 CD) Riesling, Semillon, Chardonnay, Douglas Gully Semillon, Semillon Sauvignon Blanc, Botrytis Sweet White, Five Feet (Dry Red), Grenache, Cabernet Sauvignon, Shiraz, Vintage Port, Tawny Port and Muscat. The Stocks Shiraz is a recently introduced flagship.
summary One of the stalwarts of McLaren Vale, producing archetypal, invariably reliable full-bodied red wines and showing versatility with spectacular botrytis sweet whites and high-quality (14-year-old) Tawny Port. Also offers a totally charming reception-cum-restaurant, which understandably does a roaring trade with wedding receptions. Has recently supplemented its 22 hectares of McLaren Vale vineyards with 10 hectares at its Wirrega Vineyard near Bordertown in the Limestone Coast Zone. The wines are exported to the UK, Canada, New Zealand, Philippines and Taiwan.

Woodstock Shiraz

Previously made entirely from McLaren Vale vineyards, but now two-thirds comes from Woodstock's Wirrega Vineyard near Bordertown, in the Limestone Coast Zone.
▼▼▼▽ **1998** Medium red-purple; pleasant, smooth berry and chocolate aromas on the bouquet are followed by a light- to medium-bodied palate, with more of that smooth shiraz and nicely balanced oak and tannins. A slick commercial style. **rating:** 83
best drinking 2001–2005 **best vintages** '82, '84, '91, '92, '93, '94 **drink with** Steak in black bean sauce • $17

Woodstock The Stocks Shiraz

First made in the 1991 vintage and released in late 1994. It is made from century-old (99-year-old, to be precise) vines, and matured in new American oak hogsheads. The subsequent vintages continue the line: very ripe, concentrated fruit with positive use of new American oak.
▼▼▼▼ **1997** Medium to full red-purple; cubic metres of American oak encase quite sweet cherry/plum fruit on the bouquet, and the palate is an exact replay of the bouquet. Whereas the fruit in '96 was able to soak up the oak, the less-dense fruit of '97 hasn't been able to work the same magic. **rating:** 85
best drinking 2002–2007 **best vintages** '91, '94, '95, '96 **drink with** Barbecued steak • $30

Woodstock Five Feet

An interesting blend of Cabernet Sauvignon, Petit Verdot and Shiraz from the Wirrega Vineyard in the Limestone Coast Zone and McLaren Vale. The back label is a clone of d'Arenberg, but, happily, rather more abbreviated as we learn about the five leg-holes in a set of stocks.
▼▼▼▽ **1998** Medium red-purple; the bouquet is clean, with savoury accents to the dark plum/blackberry fruit. The palate is quite concentrated but is a little callow, suggesting that the wine needed more handling during its time in barrel. **rating:** 84
best drinking 2003–2008 **best vintages** NA **drink with** Beef bourguignon • $16

Woodstock McLaren Vale Grenache

Produced from 80-year-old vines in the best region for this variety, complexed by the inclusion of 10 per cent Shiraz.
▼▼▼▼▽ **1998** The deep red-purple colour announces a wine which is entirely built around dark plum, prune and spice fruit on both bouquet and palate; silky tannins provide excellent structure. **rating:** 91
best drinking 2000–2003 **best vintages** NA **drink with** Kangaroo fillet • $14

woody nook ★★★★

Metricup Road, Busselton, WA 6280 **region** Margaret River
phone (08) 9755 7547 **fax** (08) 9755 7547 **open** 7 days 10–4.30
winemaker Neil Gallagher **production** 3000 **est.** 1982
product range ($14–17 CD) Chenin Blanc, Sauvignon Blanc, Classic Dry White, Late Picked Chenin Blanc, Late Harvest Semillon, Merlot, Cabernet Sauvignon; Gallagher's Choice Cabernet Sauvignon is top of the range.
summary This improbably named and not terribly fashionable winery has produced some truly excellent wines in recent years, with its Classic Dry White and Cabernet Sauvignon both starring at the 1999 *Winewise* Small Makers Competition, having put in a similar performance at prior *Winewise* competitions, and likewise at the Mount Barker Wine Show.

wyanga park ★★★

Baades Road, Lakes Entrance, Vic 3909 **region** Gippsland
phone (03) 5155 1508 **fax** (03) 5155 1443 **open** 7 days 9–5
winemaker Graeme Little **production** 5000 **est.** 1970
product range ($8–20 CD) Riesling Traminer, Estate Grown Sauvignon Blanc, Colombard, Estate Grown Chardonnay, Miriam's Fancy Chardonnay, Rosé, Boobialla (medium-sweet white), Shiraz, Shiraz Cabernet Sauvignon, Fortifieds.
summary Offers a broad range of wines of diverse provenance directed at the tourist trade; one of the Chardonnays and the Cabernet Sauvignon are estate-grown. Winery cruises up the north arm of the Gippsland Lake to Wyanga Park are scheduled four days a week throughout the entire year. The best of the current releases are, without question, the two Chardonnays.

wyldcroft estates   NR

98 Stanleys Road, Red Hill South, Vic 3937 **region** Mornington Peninsula
phone (03) 5989 2646 **fax** (03) 5989 2646 **open** Weekends and public holidays 10–5
winemaker Philip Jones (Contract) **production** 700 **est.** 1987
product range ($18–21 CD) Chardonnay, Unwooded Chardonnay, Pinot Noir, Cabernet Sauvignon.
summary Richard Condon and Sharon Stone commenced planting Wyldcroft Estates in 1987, extending the plantings in 1993 and 1996 to the present total of just over 3 hectares, constructing a mudbrick winery and cellar door in 1995.

wyndham estate ★★★

Dalwood Road, Dalwood, NSW 2335 **region** Lower Hunter Valley
phone (02) 4938 3444 **fax** (02) 4938 3422 **open** Mon–Fri 9.30–5, weekends 10–4
winemaker Robert Paul **production** NFP **est.** 1828
product range ($6.95–24.95 R) In ascending order: Bin TR2 Classic White and Classic Red; Chablis Superior Semillon Sauvignon Blanc, Bin 777 Semillon Chardonnay; Bin 222 Chardonnay, Bin 111 Verdelho, Bin 333 Pinot Noir, Bin 555 Shiraz; Oak Cask Chardonnay, Bin 444 Cabernet Sauvignon, Bin 888 Cabernet Merlot; Show Reserve Semillon and Shiraz, 1828 Cabernet Sauvignon Shiraz, Ruby Cabernet.
summary An absolutely reliable producer of keenly priced mid-range table wines which are smoothly and precisely aimed at those who enjoy wine but don't wish to become over-involved in its mystery and intrigue. Every now and then it comes up with a wine of surprising quality, although there does seem to be some variation between different batch bottlings.

Wyndham Estate Bin 555 Shiraz

A gold medal winner at the 1999 Pacific Rim Wine Competition. No Geographic Indication claim; southeast Australian.
▼▼▼▽ **1997** Light to medium red-purple; the bouquet is fairly light, with fresh, clean juicy berry fruit; the palate is very youthful indeed, with sweet fruit and a sweet, sugar-tinged finish. **rating:** 81
best drinking Drink now **best vintages** NA **drink with** Whatever you wish • $10

Wyndham Estate Show Reserve Shiraz

One of only two Show Reserve wines (the other is Semillon) made by Wyndham Estate, and held for at least five years before release.
▼▼▼▼ **1995** Medium red-purple; the bouquet is ripe, with distinctly gamey varietal character supported by subtle oak. The palate is interesting, with soft, ripe plummy/gamey fruit and very soft, fine tannins. A genuine Show Reserve, even if it does fall away slightly on the finish. **rating:** 89
best drinking 2000–2010 **best vintages** NA **drink with** Game pie • $24.95

Wyndham Estate 1828 Cabernet Sauvignon Shiraz Ruby Cabernet

A cunningly wrought varietal and regional blend, the type of wine which has brought Australia such conspicuous success in export markets around the world — simply great value. 1828, incidentally, refers to the year George Wyndham planted his first vines.
▼▼▼▼ **1998** Light to medium red-purple; the bouquet is light and fresh, with small berry/strawberry fruit. There is quite surprising texture on the palate, with soft sweet tannins. Really quite attractive, especially at its price. **rating:** 85
best drinking Drink now **best vintages** NA **drink with** Cheddar • $7

Wyndham Estate Bin 888 Cabernet Merlot

No Geographic Indication claimed; apparently a widely-sourced blend from southeastern Australia.

TTTT **1996** Medium red-purple; the bouquet is quite light, with leafy/savoury/earthy/berry aromas. The palate is distinctly sweeter, with some chocolate notes; finishes with fine tannins and subtle oak. **rating:** 86

best drinking 2000–2005 **best vintages** NA **drink with** Wood-fired pizza • $18

wynns coonawarra estate ★★★★★

Memorial Drive, Coonawarra, SA 5263 **region** Coonawarra
phone (08) 8736 3266 **fax** (08) 8736 3202 **open** 7 days 10–5
winemaker Sue Hodder **production** NFP **est.** 1891
product range ($8–80 R) Riesling, Chardonnay, Shiraz, Cabernet Shiraz Merlot, Black Label Cabernet Sauvignon, Michael Shiraz, John Riddoch Cabernet Sauvignon; also Ovens Valley Shiraz (not sourced from Coonawarra).
summary The large-scale production has in no way prevented Wynns from producing excellent wines covering the full price spectrum from the bargain basement Riesling and Shiraz through to the deluxe John Riddoch Cabernet Sauvignon and the more recently introduced Michael Shiraz. Even with recent price increases, Wynns offers extraordinary value for money.

Wynns Coonawarra Estate Riesling

Arguably the best value Riesling in the country — a label revamp has slightly lifted the cachet of the wine, however much I personally disapprove of the new label. Extensive vertical tastings of the wines show that the better vintages can live for 20 years or more, becoming great classics in the course of so doing.

TTTTT **1999** A gold medal winner at September's Royal Adelaide Wine Show. Both bouquet and palate are tight, with herb/lime fruit. The crisp, dry, classical restraint is the hallmark of a wine certain to age very well. **rating:** 91

best drinking 1999–2019 **best vintages** '90, '91, '93, '95, '96, '98, '99 **drink with** Tiger prawns • $11

Wynns Coonawarra Estate Chardonnay

A wine which has evolved dramatically over the years. 1985 was the first vintage to utilise barrel-fermentation; in 1992 winemaking was moved back to Coonawarra from McLaren Vale, and French oak was introduced (previously German and American were used). By 1995 only French oak was being employed, and in 1996 the barrel size had started to change from puncheon to barrique, with tight-grained French oak. All of these changes have progressively tightened and refined a wine which deserves greater recognition from critics and consumers — it has, in fact, done very well in wine shows in recent years.

TTTTT **1999** Surely a pea and thimble trick: a wine with so much class and breed has no business being sold at this price. Its bouquet shows the sophisticated and subtle use of oak and malolactic fermentation, seamlessly welded fruit and oak. The fig and cashew palate, with its creamy texture, has great length and balance. **rating:** 93

best drinking 2000–2003 **best vintages** '92, '93, '94, '96, '97, '98, '99 **drink with** Robe lobster • $14

Wynns Coonawarra Estate Shiraz

Estate means what it says; this is 100 per cent estate-grown Coonawarra Shiraz, a wine which vies with Penfolds Koonunga Hill dry red for the title of best-value red wine in Australia. A vertical tasting in March 1997 climaxed with the magnificent '53, '54 and '55 vintages. While the new generation wines may not last for 40 years, those made in the 1990s are the best since the 1950s, and the recommended drinking range should be regarded as strictly nominal. Well-corked and well-cellared, the wines have almost indefinite life.

TTTTT **1998** Medium purple-red; the moderately intense bouquet is clean and smooth, with excellent mulberry fruit and oak integration and balance. There is plenty of sweet, dark berry/cherry fruit on the palate, with soft tannins contributing to a well-structured wine. **rating:** 90

best drinking 2001–2011 **best vintages** '54, '55, '62, '65, '70, '85, '86, '89, '90, '91, '92, '93, '94, '95, '96, '98 **drink with** Spiced lamb • $16

Wynns Coonawarra Estate Cabernet Shiraz Merlot

A blend of Cabernet and Shiraz, with a little Merlot added since the end of the 1980s. It is aged in a mixture of new and used American and French barrels for 15 months, and the aim is to produce a more elegant and slightly lighter earlier-drinking style of red wine than that offered by the other red wines under the Wynns label.

TTTT **1997** Medium red-purple; the moderately intense bouquet has a mix of earthy, leafy, minty and spicy fruit. The palate has real pretensions to elegance, with savoury/spicy/dark berry fruit well balanced and integrated with the oak. **rating:** 85

best drinking 2000–2004 **best vintages** '86, '88, '90, '91, '92, '96 **drink with** Yearling beef • $17

Wynns Coonawarra Estate Black Label Cabernet Sauvignon

Given the volume in which this wine is made (said to be over 40 000 cases) it has to be the most important Cabernet in Australia, a powerful testament to the synergy between Coonawarra and Cabernet Sauvignon. Another dyed-in-the-wool classic with a magnificent history.

TTTT♀ **1997** Medium red-purple; the bouquet is quite fragrant, with cassis berry fruit, a touch of mint and subtle oak. The palate offers nicely ripened black and redcurrant fruit, neatly handled oak, and soft tannins. Not a '96 but a useful wine nonetheless. **rating: 91**

best drinking 2002–2017 **best vintages** '53, '57, '58, '62, '82, '86, '88, '90, '91, '94, '95, '96, '97 **drink with** Roast beef • $23

Wynns Coonawarra Estate John Riddoch Cabernet Sauvignon

First made in 1982, and only vintaged in the best years, and then from the finest material available. It is matured in new French and American oak hogsheads for 12–15 months, and is a wine of enormous concentration and power. Vertical tastings over the past few years have shown that at somewhere about seven years of age the wine typically undergoes a remarkable transformation, opening up almost overnight. We are still to see how long the ensuing plateau will last, for none of the wines back to 1982 have started to decline. Not made in 1995.

TTTTT 1997 Deep purple-red; sweet cassis fruit and powerful but integrated oak on the bouquet lead into a power-packed palate, rich and deep, with tannins providing a sledgehammer finish. History shows that the tannins will in fact soften. **rating: 94**

best drinking 2005–2015 **best vintages** '82, '85, '86, '88, '90, '91, '94, '96, '97 **drink with** Leave it in the cellar • $80

xanadu wines ★★★★

Terry Road, Margaret River, WA 6285 **region** Margaret River
phone (08) 9757 2581 **fax** (08) 9757 3389 **open** 7 days 10–5
winemaker Jürg Muggli **production** 16 000 **est.** 1977
product range ($13.50–165 R) Semillon, Chenin Blanc, Chardonnay, Unwooded Chardonnay, Secession (Semillon Sauvignon Blanc Chenin Blanc), Semillon, Late Harvest Riesling, Featherwhite (Rosé), Shiraz, Merlot, Cabernet Franc, Cabernet Sauvignon, Cabernet Reserve.
summary Samuel Taylor Coleridge would thoroughly approve of the labels on the Xanadu wines and, one imagines, would be equally pleased with wine quality — quality which can be excitingly variable, but is more often good than not. A capital raising via a prospectus issued in 1999 will fund a major explansion of the business.

Xanadu Semillon Sauvignon Blanc

A portion of the Semillon component is whole-bunch pressed and barrel-fermented.
TTTT 1999 Light green-yellow; a soft, moderately intense bouquet with just a hint of oak is followed by a palate with quite ripe flavours, and a touch of fruit salad balanced by good acidity on the finish. **rating: 88**
best drinking 2000–2003 **best vintages** NA **drink with** Pan-fried scallops • $18

Xanadu Chardonnay

A stylish, restrained style using many of the same techniques employed by Xanadu to produce its Semillon. The wine is whole-bunch pressed, barrel-fermented and given lees contact, and gives the impression of having at least some malolactic fermentation, although none is mentioned in the background material furnished by the winery.
TTTT 1998 Light green-yellow; there are some interesting nuances to the bouquet which are difficult to categorise, but which is overall sophisticated and subtle; the palate has been fined by whole-bunch pressing, but once again, the nuances and components are subtle and sophisticated. All in all, seems to be a wine which will flower with time in bottle. **rating: 89**
best drinking 2000–2005 **best vintages** NA **drink with** White-fleshed fish • $23.50

yaldara wines ★★★

Gomersal Road, Lyndoch, SA 5351 **region** Barossa Valley
phone (08) 8524 4200 **fax** (08) 8524 4678 **open** 7 days 9–5
winemaker Robert Ruediger **production** 500 000 **est.** 1947
product range ($4–90 R) A kaleidoscopic array of wines under (in ascending order) the Ducks Flat, Lyndoch Valley, Acacia Hill, Lakewood, Julians, and the super-premium The Farms labels. The Lakewood range is the largest, covering all major wine styles and varietals. There is also a substantial range of sparkling, non-alcoholic and fortified wines.

summary Two days before Christmas 1999 Yaldara was purchased by the publicly listed Simeon Wines, which is embarking on a $10 million upgrade of the winery with the intention of allowing it to bottle 2 million cases of wine per year. Long-serving Southcorp winemaker Robert Ruediger has been appointed to oversee the winemaking; only part of the wine will be premium Barossa, the rest coming through from the parent Simeon. It is expected that the wine style and quality will change markedly, $1.5 million of substandard wine having been written off.

yalumba ★★★★☆

Eden Valley Road, Angaston, SA 5353 **region** Barossa Valley
phone (08) 8561 3200 **fax** (08) 8561 3393 **open** Mon–Fri 8.30–5, Sat 10–5, Sun 12–5
winemaker Brian Walsh, Alan Hoey, Louis Rose **production** 950 000 **est.** 1849
product range ($7.95–65 R) Under the Yalumba label (in ascending order) Oxford Landing range, Galway Hermitage, and Christobels Dry White; Family Selection range, Virgilius Viognier, The Menzies Cabernet Sauvignon, The Signature Collection and Octavius Shiraz. Separate brand identities for Hill-Smith Estate, Pewsey Vale and Heggies, with strong emphasis on key varietals Riesling, Chardonnay, Semillon and Cabernet Sauvignon. Angas Brut is a leader in the sparkling wine market, with Jansz and Yalumba D at the top end of the quality tree.
summary Family-owned and run by Robert Hill-Smith; much of its prosperity in the late 1980s and early 1990s turned on the great success of Angas Brut in export markets, but the company has always had a commitment to quality and shown great vision in its selection of vineyard sites and brands. In particular, it has always been a serious player at the top end of full-bodied (and full-blooded) Australian reds. Exports to all major markets.

Yalumba Oxford Landing Limited Release Semillon
Made from grapes produced from Yalumba's large Riverland vineyard; reliable value.
▼▼▼▽ **1998** Medium yellow-green; the bouquet is clean enough, but there isn't much character. The wine shifts up a gear on the palate, which is cleverly put together, apparently with some malolactic fermentation or other agency leading to creamy/nutty flavours. There is also what may be an illusion of a whisper of oak. **rating: 83**
best drinking 2000–2002 **best vintages** NA **drink with** Everyday food • $9.95

Yalumba Oxford Landing Sauvignon Blanc
A wine without any pretensions of any kind but is none the worse for that.
▼▼▼▽ **1999** Light yellow-green; the bouquet is light but does have some identifiable sauvignon blanc aromas. The palate offers more of the same in a crisp, dry style; it has to be said the fruit does not threaten, but the wine does represent good value. **rating: 81**
best drinking Drink now **best vintages** NA **drink with** Everyday food • $7.95

Yalumba Christobels Dry White
An interesting, unwooded varietal blend which, when first introduced, incorporated Viognier, but is now made from Semillon, Sauvignon Blanc and Marsanne. It has also been mirrored by an up-market version at twice the price — the strikingly labelled Antipodean.
▼▼▼▼ **1999** The varietal composition of this wine has wandered around over the years, with exotic components such as Viognier. A simple Sauvignon Blanc Semillon recipe has produced the goods this year, with intense, attractively herbaceous fruit aroma and flavour from the Sauvignon Blanc and good mouthfeel from the Semillon. **rating: 87**
best drinking 2000–2001 **best vintages** '94, '99 **drink with** Seafood salad • $10.95

Yalumba Growers Limited Release Viognier
Yalumba was the first winery in South Australia (and the second in Australia, the first being Elgee Park in the Mornington Peninsula) to commercially grow and make Viognier. Planted in the East Barossa Ranges, it is perhaps a mark of the long learning curve through which Yalumba has gone that this is the first occasion on which a wine entry has appeared in the *Wine Companion*. That learning curve has finally led to the conclusion that viognier has to be allowed to ripen way beyond the normal point, with flavour changes occurring well after sugar accumulation has ceased — a unique characteristic.
▼▼▼▼ **1998** Medium yellow-green; the bouquet is plain and gives no hint of the palate, which has some of the sweet pastille fruit expected of the variety. **rating: 85**
best drinking 2000–2001 **best vintages** '96 **drink with** Peach-fed pork • $20

Yalumba Antipodean Unwooded Chardonnay
Sourced from the Eden Valley, but that is about all that can be said about it.
▼▼▼▽ **1999** Medium to full yellow-green; the bouquet is solid, but not aromatic; there are melon and citrus flavours to be found on the no-fault palate but, as with so many of these wines, seriously boring. **rating: 82**
best drinking Drink now **best vintages** NA **drink with** Takeaway • $15.95

Yalumba Barossa Growers Chardonnay

Part of a mid-priced range of wines which acknowledge the grape growers who have been part of the extended Yalumba family for generations.

▼▼▼♀ **1998** Medium yellow-green; the bouquet has solid fruit but, overall, is a little plain. The palate has pleasant mouthfeel and weight, with nicely balanced fruit and oak. **rating:** 82

best drinking 2000–2001 **best vintages** NA **drink with** Cassoulet (unfermented) • $14.95

Yalumba Family Reserve Chardonnay

Sits underneath the Show Reserve Chardonnay; both are very well priced, but as with the Christobels/Antipodean contrast, one has to say that the Family Reserve offers the best value for money.

▼▼▼♀ **1997** Light to medium yellow-green; the bouquet is of light to moderate intensity, clean, but tending plain; the palate follows precisely in the track of the bouquet; for those who like maturity and not too much fruit. **rating:** 83

best drinking 2000–2003 **best vintages** '90, '91, '92, '93 **drink with** Calamari • $25

Yalumba Oxford Landing Chardonnay

The first wine to appear under the Oxford Landing label, which has subsequently been expanded across most major varieties.

▼▼▼♀ **1999** Medium to full yellow-green; the bouquet has surprising depth and is really quite complex; the palate, too, has more weight on the palate than the majority in its price category, even if it is slightly pedestrian. Overall, excellent value. **rating:** 83

best drinking Drink now **best vintages** NA **drink with** Everyday food • $7.95

Jansz

The Jansz brand was acquired by Yalumba in 1998 (from Pipers Brook) and the wines made before that time have Yalumba's imprint on disgorgement and dosage, but are otherwise inherited.

▼▼▼▼ **1995** Light straw-yellow; an extremely complex bouquet with strong autolysis characters and some of the wet dog encountered from time to time in champagne. The palate is equally complex, with the usual biting acidity which is the Jansz hallmark. There seems to be something going on in this wine that I don't quite understand. **rating:** 87

best drinking 1999–2003 **best vintages** NA **drink with** Shellfish • $28

Yalumba Barossa Growers Shiraz

Part of a range of Yalumba wines released in 1997. Predominantly Barossa Valley fruit, with a lesser component from the Eden Valley. Has been a trophy winner.

▼▼▼▼ **1997** Medium to full red-purple; a traditional earthy/oaky/leathery bouquet but founded on a core of fruit. The palate has good flavour and structure, with the tannins running right through the palate; ideal red meat food style. **rating:** 87

best drinking 2000–2007 **best vintages** '95, '97 **drink with** Rare beef fillet • $14.95

Yalumba Octavius Shiraz

Octavius is the super-premium Yalumba red. The first vintage was 1988 (Coonawarra Cabernet) but the two subsequent vintages have been of old Barossa Shiraz, and this is where the future of the wine will lie. The distinguishing feature of the wine is its opulent oak treatment: it is matured in barrels made at Yalumba's own cooperage from American oak from Missouri which was seasoned for eight years before being made into barrels. More is not always best, but in this instance it is. Incidentally, the barrels are unusually small (octaves) which increases the potential impact of the oak.

▼▼▼▼♀ **1996** Dark, dense red-purple; aromas leap from the glass, ranging through vanilla, chocolate and mint, all in mega-mode. The palate simply oozes black cherry/berry fruit; lusciously concentrated but not extractive or, amazingly, over-oaked. **rating:** 92

best drinking 2001–2021 **best vintages** '88, '90, '92, '93, '95, '96 **drink with** The biggest steak imaginable • $65

Yalumba Reserve Barossa Shiraz

Produced from old, low-yielding vines with open canopies which deal well with the more difficult vintages. Aged in barrels made from French oak air-dried for five years before being coopered at Yalumba. Thirty per cent of the oak is new, the balance one or two years old; the wine spends just under two years in oak.

▼▼▼▼♀ **1993** Medium to full red-purple; the aromas are rich, full and complex, with classic sweet leather, berry and spice aromas. The palate has abundant fruit flavour moving into the prune spectrum, with nicely balanced tannins. The oak is restrained and stylish. **rating:** 90

best drinking 1999–2009 **best vintages** NA **drink with** Venison • $25

Yalumba Reserve Clare Valley Shiraz

Part of a trio of premium wines from Yalumba, also including a Reserve Clare Valley Cabernet Sauvignon and a Reserve Eden Valley Chardonnay. These rank on a par with The Menzies Coonawarra Cabernet Sauvignon, and are second only after The Octavius and The Signature.

▼▼▼▼ **1998** Medium to full red-purple; the bouquet is very concentrated indeed, with lots of small dark berry fruit and equally abundant American oak. The palate follows on logically, concentrated and full bodied, oozing blackberry and blackcurrant fruit and vanilla oak. **rating:** 87

▼▼▼▼ **1996** Medium red-purple; the bouquet is moderately intense, clean and pleasant, in the mainstream of traditional Australian red. The wine builds significantly on the palate with ripe plum and berry fruit, a touch of mint, and perfectly balanced and integrated oak. **rating:** 86

best drinking 2003–2013 **best vintages** '98 **drink with** Braised ox cheek • $25

Yalumba Oxford Landing Merlot

The most recent varietal release to join the Oxford Landing brand; what do they say about sow's ears and silk purses?

▼▼▼▽ **1998** Medium red-purple; the bouquet is distinctly green and leafy, but the palate shows rather riper, sweeter fruit, although leaf and mint flavours are certainly present. **rating:** 80

best drinking Drink now **best vintages** NA **drink with** Whatever you wish • $9.95

Yalumba Growers Bush Vine Grenache

Produced from 70-year-old vines grown by the Anderson, Burgmeister, Habermann and Wachter families. Most releases have tended to be jammy yet dilute, which may seem to be a contradiction in terms; perhaps I am suggesting they lack structure.

▼▼▼▽ **1998** Medium red-purple; the bouquet is fresh, with juicy berry fruit which flows through into the palate, joining a touch of chocolate and soft, sweet tannins. Despite the flavour the wine offers, there is not much structure. **rating:** 80

best drinking Drink now **best vintages** '97 **drink with** Ravioli • $14.95

Yalumba Barossa Growers Cabernet Merlot

Part of a mid-priced range of wines which acknowledge the grape growers who have been part of the extended Yalumba family for generations.

▼▼▼▼ **1997** Light to medium red-purple; the bouquet is fresh and clean, with minty/berry fruit; the palate, too, has quite attractive red berry fruit flavours supported by gentle but persistent ripe tannins. **rating:** 85

best drinking 2000–2005 **best vintages** NA **drink with** Ragout of kidneys • $14.95

Yalumba Signature Cabernet Shiraz

An Australian Classic, dating back to 1962, but deriving from Sir Robert Menzies' declaration at a lunch in Adelaide that the '61 Special Vintage Galway Claret was 'the finest Australian wine I have ever tasted'. A blend of 65 per cent Coonawarra Cabernet Sauvignon and 35 per cent old-vine Barossa Shiraz; it spends 24 months in American oak prior to bottling but never seems to be overwhelmed by it.

▼▼▼▼ **1996** Medium to full red-purple; the bouquet opens with sweet, rich dark chocolate and plum, then moves through to plentiful American oak. The palate has red berry, dark plum and vanilla flavours in abundance, neatly cradled by soft tannins. **rating:** 88

best drinking 2001–2011 **best vintages** '62, '66, '75, '81, '85, '88, '90, '91, '92, '93, '95, '96 **drink with** Rare roast beef • $35

Yalumba Reserve Clare Valley Cabernet Sauvignon

Part of a trio of premium wines from Yalumba, also including a Reserve Clare Valley Shiraz and a Reserve Eden Valley Chardonnay. These rank on a par with The Menzies Coonawarra Cabernet Sauvignon, and are second only after The Octavius and The Signature.

▼▼▼▼ **1998** Strong red-purple; savoury/foresty/earthy cabernet fruit is sweetened by touches of dark chocolate and spicy vanilla oak on the bouquet. The palate offers more immediate and obvious blackcurrant fruit together with all of the complexity of the bouquet; ripe tannins give authority and structure to the finish. **rating:** 85

best drinking 2003–2008 **best vintages** NA **drink with** Wild mushroom risotto • $25

Yalumba The Menzies Cabernet Sauvignon

The Menzies is a 20-hectare vineyard established by Yalumba in Coonawarra, planted on terra rossa soil within the heart of the Coonawarra region. Its name derives from the particular affection Sir Robert Menzies had for the wines of Yalumba. The '96 is the 10th vintage of The Menzies Coonawarra Cabernet, originally made from contract-grown grapes but now predominantly from Yalumba's own 40 hectares of red soil vineyards. Matured in French hogsheads (33 per cent new) for 23 months.

▼▼▼▼ **1996** Medium red-purple; the bouquet ranges through earthy, leafy and far sweeter Cabernet aromas, backed by subtle oak. The wine comes alive on the palate, with clean raspberry/redcurrant/cassis fruit on a very long and lingering finish, sustained by soft acid. **rating:** 89

best drinking 2003–2010 **best vintages** '90, '91, '94, '96 **drink with** Topside steak • $25

🐾 yandoit hill vineyard NR

Nevens Road, Yandoit Creek, Vic 3461 **region** Bendigo
phone (03) 9379 1763 **fax** (03) 9379 1763 **open** By appointment (special open days for mail list customers)
winemaker Colin Mitchell **production** 300 **est.** 1988
product range ($17 R) Arneis, Nebbiolo Cabernet Sauvignon, Cabernets.
summary Colin and Rosa Mitchell commenced the development of Yandoit Hill with the first plantings in 1988 with merlot, and a little under a hectare each of cabernet franc and cabernet sauvignon followed by half a hectare each of arneis (the first planting in Australia), and nebbiolo in 1995. The vineyard is situated 20 kilometres north of Daylesford, roughly halfway from Ballarat to Bendigo, and, although situated on the north-facing slope of Yandoit Hill, is in an uncompromisingly cool climate. Colin Mitchell has already discovered that nebbiolo won't ripen to his satisfaction in most years, but in vintages like 1988 makes a successful wine. The Cabernet Franc blends made between 1994 and the first commercial vintage in 1998 all show pronounced cool-climate characteristics.

Yandoit Hill Nebbiolo Cabernet Sauvignon

A rare blend of estate-grown grapes made in minuscule quantities.
▼▼▼▼ **1998** Medium red-purple; the bouquet is clean, with gently sweet blackberry fruit. The palate has very attractive and ripe fruit in a blackberry/plum/cedar range with a touch of mint, finishing with fine tannins.
rating: 87

best drinking 2002–2008 **drink with** Italian • $17

Yandoit Hill Cabernets

An estate-grown blend of Cabernet Franc, Cabernet Sauvignon and Merlot.
▼▼▼▼ **1998** Medium red-purple; the bouquet shows very ripe berry fruit, the palate with extraordinarily minty, almost mint essence, fruit. One of the most extreme examples of the Central Victorian mint character I have come across. **rating:** 87

best drinking 2001–2005 **drink with** Strong cheese • $17

---

yarrabank ★★★★★

42 Melba Highway, Yarra Glen, Vic 3775 **region** Yarra Valley
phone (03) 9730 2188 **fax** (03) 9730 2189 **open** 7 days 10–5
winemaker Claude Thibaut, Tom Carson, Darren Rathbone **production** 2000 **est.** 1993
product range ($30 R) Thibaut & Gillet Cuvée Brut, Cuvée Rosée.
summary The 1997 vintage saw the opening of the majestic new winery established as part of a joint venture between the French Champagne House Devaux and Yering Station, and which adds another major dimension to the Yarra Valley. Until 1997 the Yarrabank Cuvée Brut was made under Claude Thibaut's direction at Domaine Chandon, but henceforth the entire operation will be conducted at Yarrabank. Four hectares of dedicated 'estate' vineyards have been established at Yering Station; the balance of the intake comes from other growers in the Yarra Valley and southern Victoria. Wine quality has been quite outstanding, the wines having a delicacy unmatched by any other Australian sparkling wines.

Yarrabank Brut Cuvée

The first release of Yarrabank is a blend of 50 per cent Pinot Noir and 50 per cent Chardonnay, half of each variety coming, respectively, from the Yarra Valley and Mornington Peninsula. It spent three years on yeast lees prior to disgorgement. The rating of the '93 previously appearing was erroneous; it should have been five glasses (or 94 points), the same as for the 1994 (and 1995) vintages.
▼▼▼▼▼ **1995** Great mousse and colour, there are fine autolysis characters underlying the tight, crisp minerally bouquet; the crisp citrussy flavours of the palate linger and tingle on the fine finish. **rating:** 95

best drinking 2002–2007 **best vintages** '93, '94, '95 **drink with** Aperitif, shellfish • $30

yarra burn ★★★★

Settlement Road, Yarra Junction, Vic 3797 **region** Yarra Valley
phone (03) 5967 1428 **fax** (03) 5967 1146 **open** 7 days 10–5
winemaker Tom Newton, Ed Carr, Stephen Pannell **production** 4500 **est.** 1975
product range ($17.95–45 R) Sauvignon Blanc Semillon, Chardonnay, Pinot Noir, Shiraz, Cabernet Sauvignon, Sparkling Pinot, Chardonnay Pinot; Bastard Hill Chardonnay, Bastard Hill Pinot Noir.
summary Acquired by BRL Hardy in 1995 and destined to become the headquarters of Hardy's very substantial Yarra Valley operations, the latter centring on the 1000-tonne production from its Hoddles Creek vineyards. The new brand direction is slowly taking shape, though not helped by the very difficult 1995 and 1996 Yarra Valley vintages; the Bastard Hill Reserve wines are by far the most significant signs of change.

Yarra Burn Sauvignon Blanc Semillon

Since 1995, a well-put-together blend of Yarra Valley and King Valley fruit; comparisons with the Sauvignon Blanc of Yarra Ridge are inevitable, and Yarra Burn comes off better in that comparison. No Geographic Indication is claimed for this wine, which is in all likelihood a Victorian blend.
▼▼▼▼ 1999 Light green-yellow; the bouquet is of light to medium intensity, crisp, with some lifted citrus and gooseberry aromas. The palate has good intensity and length, with lemon zest flavours. No regional claim of any description is made.　　　　　　　　　　　　　　　　　　　　　　　　　　　**rating:** 85
best drinking 2000–2001 **best vintages** NA **drink with** Light seafood • $18

Yarra Burn Chardonnay

The label is ambiguous, implying Yarra Valley appellation without directly saying so.
▼▼▼▼ 1997 Medium yellow-green; the bouquet is quite complex, with tangy fruit and charry barrel-ferment oak. The palate, however, has slightly less weight than expected from this vintage, and acid which is just a little sharp.　　　　　　　　　　　　　　　　　　　　　　　　　　　　　　　　　　**rating:** 86
best drinking 2000–2003 **best vintages** NA **drink with** Grilled scampi • $17.95

Yarra Burn Cabernet Sauvignon

The Yarra Burn vineyards are in some of the coolest parts of the Yarra Valley and often struggle to produce ripe flavours in Cabernet Sauvignon.
▼▼▼▽ 1997 Medium to full red-purple; the bouquet is quite complex, with savoury/foresty/briary aromas repeated on the palate, which is quite tannic into the bargain. Not a wine to cuddle up to.　　　　　**rating:** 80
best drinking 2002–2005 **best vintages** NA **drink with** Marinated beef • $19.95

yarra edge ★★★☆

PO Box 390, Yarra Glen, Vic 3775 **region** Yarra Valley
phone (03) 9730 1107 **fax** (03) 9739 0135 **open** At Yering Station
winemaker Tom Carson, Darren Rathbone **production** 2000 **est.** 1984
product range ($27.50–28.50 CD) Chardonnay, Cabernets.
summary Now leased to Yering Station, which makes the wines but continues to use the Yarra Edge brand for grapes from this estate. Tom Carson, the Yering Station winemaker, was briefly winemaker/manager at Yarra Edge and knows the property intimately, so the rich style can be expected to continue.

Yarra Edge Chardonnay

Made entirely from estate-grown fruit and now produced at Yering Station. The style is usually rich and concentrated.
▼▼▼▼▽ 1998 Medium to full yellow-straw; the bouquet is quite complex, with a mix of barrel-ferment and nutty/creamy/figgy/bready fruit, all suggestive of wild yeast fermentation. The palate has interesting cashew/mealy flavours and texture, with some alcohol-derived sweetness.　　　　　　　　　　　　　　　　　　**rating:** 91
best drinking 2000–2005 **best vintages** '92, '93, '94, '97, '98 **drink with** Smoked salmon pasta • $27.50

yarra ridge ★★★★

Glenview Road, Yarra Glen, Vic 3755 **region** Yarra Valley
phone (03) 9730 1022 **fax** (03) 9730 1131 **open** 7 days 10–5
winemaker Nick Walker **production** 90 000 **est.** 1983
product range ($16–40 R) Chardonnay, Sauvignon Blanc, Botrytis Semillon, Pinot Noir, Reserve Pinot Noir, Merlot, Shiraz, Cabernet Sauvignon; Mount Tanglefoot has been introduced as a second range expressly made from grapes grown in regions other than the Yarra Valley.

summary Now under the sole ownership and control of Mildara Blass, with a winery which is strained to its limits. Recent vineyard plantings in the Yarra Valley, and continued purchasing of Yarra Valley grapes, mean that the majority of the wines will continue to be Yarra Valley-sourced. Sometimes it is not easy to tell which are and which aren't, even if one has a master's degree in label reading and interpretation.

Yarra Ridge Sauvignon Blanc

This is the wine which launched the Yarra Ridge ship, but both time and volume of production seem to have caught up with it. The back label now tells us that it is 'grown in the renowned Yarra Valley with small parcels of Sauvignon Blanc selected from other cooler regions of Victoria'. I don't think the writer means regions which are cooler than the Yarra Valley, and does mean to include the King Valley.

▼▼▼▼ **1999** Light green-yellow; the bouquet is clean, light and fresh, with touches of gooseberry; the palate similarly light, clean and pleasant, but far from challenging. **rating:** 85

best drinking Drink now **best vintages** NA **drink with** Fish and chips • $18

Yarra Ridge Mount Tanglefoot Shiraz

The grapes are grown at Mount Helen and at Baileys, Glenrowan.

▼▼▼▼ **1998** Medium red, with a touch of purple; the sweet berry fruit of the bouquet has some spice and leather aromas supported by subtle oak. Smooth cherry fruit glides across the tongue with just a twist of American oak; a pretty smart wine. **rating:** 88

best drinking 2002–2008 **best vintages** NA **drink with** Prime rib of beef • $17

Yarra Ridge Mount Tanglefoot Victorian Cabernet Franc

Part of a new range of Yarra Ridge wines sourced from regions outside the Yarra Valley. The Cabernet Franc comes from the Strathbogie Ranges.

▼▼▼▼ **1998** Strong red-purple; attractive, sweet, gently spicy/juicy blackcurrant fruit on the bouquet tracks through to the palate, where touches of mint also appear. Soft tannins; a particularly good example of the style. **rating:** 86

best drinking 1999–2002 **best vintages** NA **drink with** Stir-fried beef • $16

❧ yarra track wines ★★★★

Viggers Vineyard, 518 Old Healesvile Road, Yarra Glen, Vic 3775 **region** Yarra Valley
phone (03) 9730 1349 **fax** (03) 9730 1349 **open** Weekends and public holidays 10–5
winemaker Martin Williams (Contract) **production** 400 **est.** 1989
product range ($22–25 CD) Chardonnay, Pinot Noir.
summary Jim and Diana Viggers began the establishment of their vineyard back in 1989; it now has 3.1 hectares of chardonnay and 3.4 hectares of pinot noir. The Viggers have chosen very competent winemakers (Tom Carson 1997 and 1998 and Martin Williams from 1999), and intend to increase wine production progressively while selling part of the grape production in the meantime. The wine is sold only through cellar door and through local restaurants.

Yarra Track Chardonnay

Estate-grown, and 100 per cent barrel-fermented. Made in an ebullient style, but still retains distinctive regional character.

▼▼▼▼ **1997** Medium yellow-green; obvious barrel-ferment oak aromas dominate the bouquet, but the fruit comes through on the palate with that elegance and intensity of Yarra Chardonnay. Crisp citrus flavours are supported by pronounced, perhaps too pronounced, acidity. **rating:** 85

best drinking 2000–2004 **drink with** Pan-fried veal • $25

Yarra Track Pinot Noir

Like the 1997 Chardonnay, made by Tom Carson at Yering Station. A particularly impressive wine from the 1998 vintage.

▼▼▼▼♀ **1998** Medium red-purple; the bouquet is quite complex, with moderately intense forest floor and plum aromas. The palate has good presence, with nice plummy fruit sliding into a long finish with fine, silky tannins. **rating:** 90

best drinking 2000–2003 **drink with** Smoked quail • $25

yarra valley hills ★★★★☆

Delaneys Road, Warranwood, Vic 3134 **region** Yarra Valley
phone (03) 5962 4173 **fax** (03) 5962 4059 **open** Weekends, public holidays 11–5
winemaker Martin Williams (Consultant) **production** 10 000 **est.** 1989
product range ($18–27 CD) Warranwood Riesling, Log Creek Sauvignon Blanc, Kiah Yallambee Chardonnay,
Log Creek Pinot Noir, Log Creek Cabernet Sauvignon.
summary Former schoolteacher Terry Hill has built up a very successful empire in a short period of time
through leasing two substantial vineyards and principally acting as a grape supplier to others, with a small
proportion of the grapes being contract-made by a range of Yarra Valley winemakers.

Yarra Valley Hills Log Creek Sauvignon Blanc Semillon

As the name suggests, produced from grapes grown at the Log Creek Vineyard near Coldstream Hills, which has
been under long-term contract to Yarra Valley Hills. Selected in the 1999 Sydney International Wine Competiton
Top 100.
▼▼▼▽ **1998** Light to medium yellow-green; the bouquet is fairly neutral, with just a hint of herbaceousness. The
palate is light and delicate, with the flavours seemingly closer to Semillon than Sauvignon Blanc. Crisp and
delicate but far from complex.   **rating:** 83
best drinking 1999–2000 **best vintages** NA **drink with** Bouillabaisse •$20

Yarra Valley Hills Kiah Yallambee Chardonnay

From the Kiah and Yallambee vineyards. Shows authentic Yarra Valley cool-climate fruit flavours, and should
mature quite well.
▼▼▼▼ **1999** Medium yellow-green; a very rich and complex bouquet with ripe melon, peach and fig aromas is
followed by a palate which, while smooth, has less weight and less complexity; subtle oak and good acidity on the
finish are the good parts of a curate's egg wine.   **rating:** 87
best drinking 2000–2005 **best vintages** '93, '94, '96 **drink with** Crab, lobster •$25

Yarra Valley Hills Warranwood Pinot Noir

Warranwood, like Log Creek has been under long-term lease to Yarra Valley Hills. The vines are now over 15
years old, and are capable of producing high-quality fruit.
▼▼▼▼ **1997** Medium red, with very slightly opaque edges; the bouquet is interesting, with a slight decayed/gamey
edge to the forest floor aromas. The palate is a mix of plummy, foresty and slightly gamey fruit; curiously, I
personally like the combination, although it may not appeal to everyone.   **rating:** 88
best drinking 1999–2002 **best vintages** NA **drink with** Wild game •$27

yarra yarra ★★★★★

239 Hunts Lane, Steels Creek, Vic 3775 **region** Yarra Valley
phone (03) 5965 2380 **fax** (03) 9830 4180 **open** By appointment
winemaker Ian Maclean **production** NFP **est.** 1979
product range ($30–45 CD) Semillon Sauvignon Blanc, Merlot, Cabernets.
summary Notwithstanding its tiny production, the wines of Yarra Yarra have found their way onto a veritable
who's who listing of Melbourne's best restaurants. This has encouraged Ian Maclean to increase the estate plantings
from 2 hectares to over 7 hectares during the 1996 and 1997 seasons. The demand for the wines will only be
intensified by the quality of the current releases.

Yarra Yarra Semillon Sauvignon Blanc

A blend of 70 per cent Semillon, fermented and aged for 15 months in 30 per cent new, the remainder in older,
French oak barriques. A number of different yeasts including wild yeasts are used and the wine is left on lees and
stirred regularly.
▼▼▼▼ **1998** Light to medium yellow-green; that typically rich, powerful and complex mix of tangy fruit and a
hint of spicy oak is followed by a quite fleshy palate, much fatter than the usual style, no doubt thanks to the
relentless heat of the '98 vintage. Spicy nutmeg oak does help the finish.   **rating:** 87
▼▼▼▼▼ **1997** Light to medium green-yellow; once again, there is a seamless marriage of both fruit and oak on
the bouquet, with hints of honey and caramel. The palate is potent, dense and concentrated, but with the same
excellent balance of all constituents: fruit, oak and acidity.   **rating:** 94
best drinking 2000–2004 **best vintages** '97 **drink with** Wiener schnitzel •$30

Yarra Yarra Cabernet

Produced from 4 hectares of cabernet sauvignon, cabernet franc and merlot grown on a north-facing slope, and which are not irrigated. The final wine (a blend of 80 per cent Cabernet and 13 per cent Cabernet Franc and 7 per cent Merlot) reflects the low-yielding vines, and is not released every year. Basket-pressed, and incorporating the pressings fraction. Aged for two years in 40 per cent new French oak barriques.

▼▼▼▼▼ 1997 Excellent full red-purple; a clean and concentrated bouquet with blackcurrant fruit and a touch of well-integrated spicy oak is followed by a powerful, concentrated palate with lots of blackcurrant/cassis fruit and ripe but potent tannins which are quite different from those of any other wine in the line-up. Like a big Bordeaux from a ripe year. **rating: 95**

best drinking 2002–2017 **best vintages** '84, '86, '89, '90, '92, '95, '97 **drink with** Osso bucco • $45

Yarra Yarra Reserve Cabernet Sauvignon

Ian Maclean runs one of the lowest-profile, top-quality Yarra Valley wineries, selling to restaurants and by mail list only.

▼▼▼▼▼ 1997 Bright purple-red; the bouquet is fragrant with berry and cedar. A truly lovely wine in the mouth, with ripe cassis fruit, sweet in the mouth; fine-grained tannins and high-quality oak. **rating: 94**

best drinking 2002–2017 **best vintages** '97 **drink with** Braised beef • $40

yarra yering ★★★★★

Briarty Road, Coldstream, Vic 3770 **region** Yarra Valley
phone (03) 5964 9267 **fax** (03) 5964 9239 **open** Sat, public holidays 10–5, Sun 12–5
winemaker Bailey Carrodus **production** 6000 **est.** 1969
product range ($49–100 CD) Dry White No. 1 (Sauvignon Blanc Semillon), Chardonnay, Pinot Noir, Dry Red No. 1 (Bordeaux-blend), Dry Red No. 2 (Rhône-blend), Merlot (tiny quantities at $100 a bottle), Underhill Shiraz, Underhhill 3 Year Cask Shiraz, Portsorts. The portfolio continues to expand, with Dry Red No. 3, Sangiovese and Viognier all making an appearance from the 1998 and/or '99 vintages.
summary Dr Bailey Carrodus makes extremely powerful, occasionally idiosyncratic wines from his 30-year-old, low-yielding unirrigated vineyards. Both red and white wines have an exceptional depth of flavour and richness, although my preference for what I believe to be his great red wines is well known.

Yarra Yering Pinot Noir

Made in a no-holds-barred style from low-yielding, unirrigated vines. Long on power but not necessarily finesse.

▼▼▼▼▽ 1998 Medium red-purple; the bouquet is rich, with a range of spicy/savoury/foresty aromas. The palate has excellent texture and structure, with lovely sweet, plummy fruit unfurling on the mid to back palate. The best for years. **rating: 92**

best drinking 2002–2010 **best vintages** '97, '98 **drink with** Squab • $68

Yarra Yering Underhill Shiraz

Made entirely from the former Prigorje Vineyard, which adjoins that of Yarra Yering and is now, indeed, part of the Yarra Yering estate — and has been so for some years. Here, too, the vines are mature, low-yielding and unirrigated.

▼▼▼▼▽ 1998 Medium red-purple; the intense bouquet exudes ripe, sweet leather, liquorice, spice and savoury aromas. Opulent, sweet fruit on the palate, with a range of liquorice, blood plum and sweet spice flavours, has eaten up the oak. Fine tannins add to the attraction. **rating: 93**

best drinking 2003–2015 **best vintages** '91, '92, '93, '97 **drink with** Victorian Parmesan cheese • $68

Yarra Yering Underhill 3 Year Cask Shiraz

Dr Bailey Carrodus has never been afraid to experiment; this wine spent three years in French oak barriques.

▼▼▼▼ 1996 The colour is still strong red-purple; the bouquet has strong cedary/cigar box/spice aromas, together with touches of leaf. It seems to me a slight green thread runs through the wine, but it is still fresh and, against all the odds, the oak is contained. **rating: 89**

best drinking 2001–2007 **best vintages** NA **drink with** Venison pie • $77

Yarra Yering Dry Red No 2

Predominantly Shiraz, with a little Viognier and a few scraps of other things from time to time. Entirely estate-grown, of course, and produced from vines which are now over 25 years old.

▼▼▼▼▼ 1998 Medium to full red-purple; the bouquet is strongly savoury/spicy, with touches of roasted hazelnuts surrounding the lovely sweet cherry and plum fruit which comes through strongly in the mouth. Sweet, soft and ripe tannins round off the finish; once again, the oak has been absorbed by the fruit. **rating: 94**

best drinking 2005–2015 **best vintages** '80, '81, '86, '89, '90, '91, '92, '93, '96, '97, '98 **drink with** Beef bourguignon • $68

Yarra Yering Dry Red No 1

Predominantly cabernet sauvignon, with small quantities of merlot, cabernet franc and malbec and a tiny contribution of petit verdot. Entirely estate-grown from low-yielding, unirrigated vines and matured in high-quality 100 per cent new French oak. It is a sign of truly great wine produced anywhere in the world if it is matured in new oak without showing any obvious signs of having been so made.

▼▼▼▼▽ **1998** Medium to full red-purple; there is more slightly charry oak evident on the complex bouquet with its sea of dark berry fruit. Quite firm berry fruit, and a touch of mint that needs time to evolve, and the oak is more restrained on the palate. **rating:** 91

best drinking 2005–2015 **best vintages** '80, '81, '86, '89, '90, '91, '93, '94, '96, '97, '98 **drink with** Roast leg of lamb • $68

Yarra Yering Portsorts

Only Bailey Carrodus could come up with a name such as this for his Vintage Port, made from the classic Portuguese varieties planted on a single, dedicated vineyard immediately abutting his original plantings. When I first came to the Yarra Valley and planted Coldstream Hills in 1985, Bailey suggested to me I should plant the port varieties. I thought he was joking. Now I know he was not.

▼▼▼▼▼ **1998** Dense red-purple; a fragrant and spicy bouquet runs through briary and sweet leather aromas backed by subtle spirit. Very complex fruit flavours on the palate include spice, chocolate, leather, liquorice, mint and vanilla; the finish is pleasantly dry, the spirit subtle. **rating:** 94

best drinking 2000–2020 **best vintages** '96, '97, '98 **drink with** As many friends as possible • $68

yass valley wines NR

9 Crisps Lane, Murrumbateman, NSW 2582 **region** Canberra District

phone (02) 6227 5592 **fax** (02) 6227 5592 **open** Wed–Sun and public holidays 11–5 or by appointment

winemaker Michael Withers **production** 6000 **est.** 1979

product range ($14 CD) Riesling, Traminer, Chardonnay, Chardonnay Semillon, Shiraz, Cabernet Merlot, Merlot.

summary Michael Withers and Anne Hillier purchased Yass Valley in January 1991 and have subsequently rehabilitated the existing run-down vineyards and extended the plantings. Mick Withers is a chemist by profession and has completed a Wine Science degree at Charles Sturt University; Anne is a registered psychologist and has completed a Viticulture diploma at Charles Sturt. No recent tastings.

yaxley estate NR

31 Dransfield Road, Copping, Tas 7174 **region** Southern Tasmania

phone (03) 6253 5222 **fax** (03) 6253 5222 **open** 7 days 10–6.30

winemaker Andrew Hood (Contract) **production** 230 **est.** 1991

product range ($18.50 CD) Pinot Gris, Sauvignon Blanc, Chardonnay, Pinot Noir.

summary While Yaxley Estate was established back in 1991, it was not until 1998 that it offered each of the four wines from its vineyard plantings, which total 1.7 hectares. Once again, the small batch handling skills (and patience) of contract-winemaker Andrew Hood have made the venture possible.

Yaxley Estate Pinot Gris

Produced from half a hectare of estate plantings, and made in conventional style, fermented in stainless steel and early-bottled. The 1998 won a silver medal at the 1999 Tasmanian Wines Show. And the '99 was a worthy follow-on, winning a strong bronze medal at the 2000 Tasmanian Wines Show.

▼▼▼▽ **1999** Light straw-green; a quite intense, aromatic bouquet leads invitingly into an intense and powerful palate. The acidity is too high; had it been lower the wine would have been in gold medal territory. **rating:** 84

best drinking 2000–2003 **best vintages** NA **drink with** Summer salads • $18.50

yellowglen ★★★☆

Whites Road, Smythesdale, Vic 3351 **region** Ballarat

phone (03) 5342 8617 **fax** (03) 5333 7102 **open** Mon–Fri 10–5, weekends 11–5

winemaker Charles Hargrave **production** 300 000 **est.** 1975

product range ($10–25 R) Brut Cremant, Brut Pinot Chardonnay, Brut Rosé, Cuvée Victoria, Vintage Pinot Chardonnay, Y, Yellow, Yellow Chardonnay.

summary Just as the overall quality of Australian sparkling wine has improved out of all recognition over the past five or so years, so has that of Yellowglen. Initially the quality lift was apparent at the top end of the range but now extends right to the non-vintage commercial releases.

Yellowglen Vintage Pinot Chardonnay Brut

A blend of Pinot Noir and Chardonnay sourced from cool regions across southeastern Australia, but predominantly Coonawarra, Eden Valley, Yarra Valley and Ballarat. Some good wines have appeared under this label over the last decade.

▼▼▼▽ 1997 Light straw-green; a tight minerally/citrussy bouquet leads into a lively, fresh and quite long palate; not at all complex, but could not be faulted as an aperitif style. **rating: 83**

best drinking 2000–2001 **best vintages** '88, '90, '92, '94 **drink with** Aperitif or oysters • $21

yeringberg ★★★★★

Maroondah Highway, Coldstream, Vic 3770 **region** Yarra Valley
phone (03) 9739 1453 **fax** (03) 9739 0048 **open** By appointment
winemaker Guill de Pury **production** 1400 **est.** 1863
product range ($30–45 CD) Chardonnay, Yeringberg White (Marsanne/Roussanne), Pinot Noir, Yeringberg Red (Cabernet blend).
summary Makes wines for the next millennium from the low-yielding vines re-established on the heart of what was one of the most famous (and infinitely larger) vineyards of the nineteenth century. In the riper years, the red wines have a velvety generosity of flavour which is rarely encountered, yet never lose varietal character, while the Yeringberg White takes students of history back to Yeringberg's fame in the nineteenth century. The wines are exported to the UK, the US, Switzerland and Germany.

Yeringberg Marsanne/Roussanne

In fact simply labelled 'Yeringberg' (as is the dry red) in the tradition of the nineteenth-century label, which is faithfully reproduced. The wine is predominantly Marsanne with just a touch of Roussanne, and in the warmer years ('94, '97, '98) achieved a level of flavour and richness which one imagines the great wines of the nineteenth century possessed.

▼▼▼▼ 1999 Light straw-yellow; the clean and fresh bouquet is light and faintly floral; the palate has a distinct mineral grip, with touches of herb and spice. Back to a less opulent level than the preceding couple of vintages. **rating: 85**

best drinking 2003–2011 **best vintages** '94, '97, '98 **drink with** Snowy Mountains trout • $30

Yeringberg Chardonnay

Produced from the half-hectare of estate plantings and made in necessarily very limited quantities. This restricts its opportunity for show entries, but it has been a consistent trophy and gold medal winner at the Lilydale Wine Show.

▼▼▼▼ 1999 Light to medium yellow-green; in classic Yeringberg style, clean, with a mix of melon, mineral and cashew supported by subtle oak. Citrussy/lemony fruit builds towards the finish of a wine which is still quite tight. **rating: 87**

best drinking 2002–2010 **best vintages** '88, '90, '91, '92, '93, '94, '97, '98 **drink with** Sweetbreads • $30

Yeringberg Pinot Noir

Estate-grown, and usually at the fuller end of the Pinot Noir spectrum, with the capacity to age better than most of its counterparts.

▼▼▼▼ 1998 Medium red-purple; the conventional bouquet is clean, with moderately ripe, gentle plummy fruit. The palate follows down the same track, soft and clean, with sweet plummy fruit and a touch of spice; neither particularly concentrated nor complex, following the usual vintage pattern for Pinot from '98. **rating: 86**

best drinking 2000–2005 **best vintages** '97 **drink with** Squab • $45

Yeringberg Dry Red

Produced from an estate-grown blend of Cabernet Sauvignon, Merlot, Cabernet Franc and Malbec (with Cabernet Sauvignon dominant, and the other components in descending order as listed). The vineyard is established on the precise site of the great nineteenth-century plantings, albeit but a fraction of the size of those vineyards, enjoying a prime north-facing slope.

▼▼▼▼▽ 1998 Medium red-purple; the bouquet is moderately intense, clean, with gently ripe blackberry/blackcurrant fruit and a hint of spice. In typical fashion, there is far greater depth and richness to the fruit on the palate, flooded with sumptuous flavours of cassis, blackberry and blackcurrant. Every bit as good as the '97. **rating: 93**

best drinking 2003–2013 **best vintages** '85, '86, '88, '90, '91, '93, '94, '97, '98 **drink with** Yarra Valley venison • $45

yering farm   NR

St Huberts Road, Yering, Vic 3770 **region** Yarra Valley
phone (03) 9735 4161 **fax** (03) 9735 4012 **open** Weekends 10–5
winemaker Alan Johns **production** 3000 **est.** 1989
product range ($18–25 ML) Chardonnay, Pinot Noir, Merlot, Cabernet.
summary Alan and Louise Johns established their 12-hectare vineyard in 1989 on the site of the original Yeringa winery built by the Deschamps family in the last century. Between 1992 and 1998 the wines were made by Alan Johns, and since then at Yarra Ridge, which purchases most of the production from the vineyard.

yering grange vineyard   NR

14 McIntyre Lane, Coldstream, Vic 3770 **region** Yarra Valley
phone (03) 9739 1172 **fax** (03) 9739 1172 **open** By appointment
winemaker John Ellis (Contract) **production** 300 **est.** 1989
product range ($15 CD) Cabernet Sauvignon.
summary Yering Grange has 2 hectares of cabernet sauvignon under vine, part being sold and part made under the Yering Grange label by John Ellis at Hanging Rock. The tiny production is sold through a mailing list.

yering station   ★★★★☆

Melba Highway, Yering, Vic 3770 **region** Yarra Valley
phone (03) 9730 1107 **fax** (03) 9739 0135 **open** Thur–Sun 10–5
winemaker Tom Carson, Darren Rathbone, Paul Kaan, Dan Buckle **production** 45 000 **est.** 1988
product range ($12.50–42 CD) Baraks Bridge Chardonnay, Pinot Noir, Shiraz, Cabernet Sauvignon, Botrytis Semillon; Yering Station Sauvignon Blanc, Chardonnay, Pinot Noir Rosé ED, Pinot Noir, Cabernet Merlot; Reserve range of Chardonnay, Pinot Noir and Shiraz; also Verjuice in 375-ml bottles.
summary The historic Yering Station (or at least the portion of the property on which the cellar-door sales and vineyard are established) was purchased by the Rathbone family in January 1996 and is now the site of a joint venture with the French Champagne House Devaux. A spectacular and very large winery has been erected which handles the Yarrabank sparkling wines and the Yering Station and Yarra Edge table wines. Has immediately become one of the focal points of the Yarra Valley, particularly with the historic Chateau Yering next door. Here, luxury accommodation and the finest dining in the Yarra Valley is available.

Yering Station Chardonnay

1996 marked the transition from the old regime at Yering Station to the new, following its acquisition in the middle of 1996 by the Rathbone family. Tom Carson was installed as winemaker and is responsible for taking the wine through to bottle. As from 1997, all winemaking has been and will be carried out in the large, state-of-the-art winery part-completed in time for the 1997 vintage.
▼▼▼▼ 1998 Light to medium yellow-green; the bouquet is understated and takes time to develop, with melon showing initially, followed by citrus notes. The palate is delicate and youthful and will develop, although may ultimately be held back by a lack of concentration in fruit flavour.   **rating:** 88
best drinking 2000–2004 **best vintages** '97, '98 **drink with** Poached Tasmanian salmon • $19.50

Yering Station Barak's Bridge Chardonnay

Sourced from grapes grown in the Hastings Valley, the King Valley and the Yarra Valley, and for this reason, if no other, unique.
▼▼▼▽ 1998 Medium yellow-green; the bouquet has some depth, but is slightly broad; a well-put-together commercial wine on the palate, with mouthfeel its strongest point.   **rating:** 81
best drinking 2000–2001 **best vintages** NA **drink with** Takeaway • $12.50

Yering Station Pinot Noir Rosé

The juice is given 12 to 18 hours maceration or skin contact, and then barrel-fermented, and left in oak for four months before bottling. Either way, it works well, and is the very model of a modern-day brasserie wine, catching the wave (how long will it last?) of enthusiasm for all things Rosé.
▼▼▼▽ 1999 Salmon; the bouquet offers distinctive sappy/stemmy pinot varietal character, which follows through onto the palate, resulting in a somewhat idiosyncratic style.   **rating:** 82
best drinking Drink now **best vintages** NA **drink with** Seafood, Singapore noodles — you name it • $17.50

407

Yering Station Pinot Noir

The standard release of Yering Station Pinot, and one of the winery's flag-bearers.

▼▼▼▼ 1998 Medium red; light, sappy/gamey fruit aromas are followed by a lively palate, again with some foresty/sappy characters; neatly handled oak helps a wine which will become quite Burgundian over the next few years. **rating:** 86

best drinking 2000–2003 **best vintages** '91, '94, '96, '97 **drink with** Smoked quail • $21

Yering Station Barak's Bridge Pinot Noir

If nothing else, proves the difficulty of making a cheap, second label Pinot Noir which is accessible and enjoyable.

▼▼▼▽ 1998 Light to medium red-purple; the bouquet is clean but does not have over-much character. The palate opens well enough, nice pinot varietal character, but then has a rather stalky, bitter finish. **rating:** 82

best drinking Drink now **best vintages** NA **drink with** Pastrami • $14.50

Yering Station Barak's Bridge Shiraz

A blend of Cowra and King Valley grapes fermented and aged in older French oak barriques.

▼▼▼▽ 1998 Medium purple-red; the bouquet is clean, moderately intense, with cherry and a touch of chocolate. The palate opens with attractive sweet fruit but does fall away quite markedly on the finish. **rating:** 80

best drinking Drink now **best vintages** NA **drink with** Designer meat pie • $14.50

Yering Station Cabernet Sauvignon

Produced from some of the original (late 1980s) plantings on Yering Station.

▼▼▼▼ 1998 Medium purple-red; fresh, youthful raspberry/blackberry fruit on the bouquet is followed by a smooth palate with pleasant dark berry fruits, soft tannins and subtle oak. **rating:** 85

best drinking 2001–2008 **best vintages** NA **drink with** Rack of lamb • $22

🐀 yunbar estate   NR

Light Pass Road, Vine Vale, SA 5352 **region** Barossa Valley
phone (08) 8564 0114 **fax** (08) 8564 0164 **open** 7 days 10–4.30
winemaker Vicky-Louise Bartier **production** 2000 **est.** 1998
product range ($16–25 CD) Eden Riesling, Semillon, Chardonnay, Sinners Shiraz, Merlot.
summary The intriguingly-named Sinners Shiraz, the Merlot, Semillon and Chardonnay are produced from a total of 8 hectares of estate-grown grapes, the Eden Riesling is made from contract-grown grapes.

yungarra estate   NR

Yungarra Drive, Dunsborough, WA 6281 **region** Margaret River
phone (08) 9755 2153 **fax** (08) 9755 2310 **open** 7 days 10–5
winemaker Erland Happ (Contract) **production** 1450 **est.** 1988
product range ($10.50–12 CD) Semillon, Sauvignon Blanc, Quartet (Semillon, Sauvignon Blanc, Chenin Blanc, Verdelho), Chenin Blanc Verdelho, Pink Opal (sweet red table wine made from Cabernet and Merlot), Springtime (sweet Sauvignon Blanc, Verdelho), Cabernet Sauvignon, Cabernet Merlot, Royale.
summary Yungarra Estate is a combined tourist lodge and cellar-door facility set on a 40-hectare property overlooking Geographe Bay. The 9-hectare vineyard was first planted in 1988, producing its first wines in 1992, contract-made by Erland Happ. Cellar-door sales commenced in 1993, and there are five bed and breakfast cottages on the Yungarra Estate property.

zappacosta estate   NR

Farm 161 Hanwood Road, Hanwood, NSW 2680 **region** Riverina
phone (02) 6963 0278 **fax** (02) 6963 0278 **open** By appointment
winemaker Judy Zappacosta, Dino Zappacosta **production** 20 000 **est.** 1996
product range ($12 CD) Riesling, Semillon, Dry White, Shiraz.
summary Zappacosta Estate, briefly known as Hanwood Village Wines, is a relatively new business, with the first release from the 1996 vintage.

zarephath wines   NR

Moorialup Road, East Porongurup, WA 6324 **region** Great Southern
phone (08) 9853 1152 **fax** (08) 9841 8124 **open** 7 days 9–4
winemaker Brenden Smith **production** 300 **est.** 1994
product range ($15–20 CD) Riesling, Chardonnay, Pinot Noir, Shiraz, Cabernet Sauvignon.

summary The Zarephath vineyard is owned and operated by Brothers and Sisters of The Christ Circle, a Benedictine community. They say the most outstanding feature of the location is the feeling of peace and tranquillity which permeates the site, something I can well believe on the basis of numerous visits to the Porongurups.

zema estate ★★★★☆

Riddoch Highway, Coonawarra, SA 5263 **region** Coonawarra
phone (08) 8736 3219 **fax** (08) 8736 3280 **open** 7 days 9–5
winemaker Matt Zema, Nick Zema **production** 10 000 **est.** 1982
product range ($18–45 CD) Shiraz, Cabernet Sauvignon, Family Selection Cabernet Sauvignon, Cluny (Cabernet blend).
summary Zema is one of the last outposts of hand-pruning and hand-picking in Coonawarra, the various members of the Zema family tending a 40-hectare vineyard progressively planted between 1982 and 1994 in the heart of Coonawarra's terra rossa soil. Winemaking practices are straightforward; if ever there was an example of great wines being made in the vineyard, this is it.

Zema Estate Shiraz

Zema Estate's very conservative approach to viticulture has paid big dividends, with outstanding wines produced consistently over the past 15 years. Matured for 16 months in a mix of French and American oak, mostly used.
▼▼▼▼▼ 1998 Dense purple-red; the rich blackberry, plum and chocolate fruit of the bouquet is followed by a dense and powerful palate with masses of blackberry and plum fruit, supported by quite persistent tannins. Simply needs time in typical Zema style. **rating:** 94
best drinking 2003–2013 **best vintages** '84, '86, '88, '92, '94, '96, '97, '98 **drink with** Bistecca Fiorentina • $18

Zema Estate Family Selection Cabernet Sauvignon

A reserve selection of the best grapes; unlike many such wines does not rely on an extra shipload of oak to give it status.
▼▼▼▼▼ 1998 Medium to full red-purple; the bouquet is solid but complex, with ripe blackberry/blackcurrant fruits coupled with some more savoury earthy characters in typical Coonawarra style. The palate is rich, with abundant mulberry/blackcurrant/blackberry fruit and those slightly savoury overtones. Entirely fruit-driven; fine tannins to close. **rating:** 94
best drinking 2006–2016 **best vintages** '97, '98 **drink with** Game • $45

zuber estate NR

Northern Highway, Heathcote, Vic 3523 **region** Bendigo
phone (03) 5433 2142 **open** 7 days 9–6
winemaker A Zuber **production** 450 **est.** 1971
product range ($10–12 CD) Chardonnay, Pinot Noir, Shiraz, Cabernet Sauvignon.
summary A somewhat erratic winery, which is capable of producing the style of Shiraz for which Bendigo is famous but does not always do so. No recent tastings.

new zealand

wineries and wines

akarangi   NR

River Road, Havelock North, Hawke's Bay **region** Hawke's Bay
phone (06) 877 8228 **fax** (06) 877 2200 **open** Weekends, public holidays and summer 9–5
winemaker Morton Osborne **production** 800 **est.** 1988
product range ($12–18 CD) Sauvignon Blanc, Riesling Late Harvest, Chardonnay, Cabernet Merlot.
summary Former contract grape growers now making and selling tiny quantities cellar door and through one or two local shops. Morton and Vivien Osborne have 5 hectares of vineyards and operate the cellar-door sales through a century-old Presbyterian church moved onto the property.

alana estate   ★★★★

Puruatanga Road, Martinborough **region** Wairarapa
phone (06) 306 9784 **fax** (06) 306 9784 **open** Mon–Thurs 1–3, Fri–Sun 11–5
winemaker John Kavanagh **production** 2500 **est.** 1995
product range ($17–36 CD) Riesling, Sauvignon Blanc, Chardonnay, Pinot Noir.
summary Ian and Alana Smart acquired their prime vineyard site, situated between Dry River and Te Kairanga in 1995, no mean feat given the scarcity of such sites on the Martinborough terraces. It came after a decade of living in London and travelling incessantly, and is now their permanent home. Twenty hectares of vineyard were established between 1995 and 2000. A completed stage one of a gravity-fed winery has been built into the side of a hill, and production is projected to increase to about 12 000 to 15 000 cases by 2002. Winemaker John Kavanagh has joined Alana Estate from Palliser Estate, bringing both industry and local knowledge with him.

Alana Estate Pinot Noir

The first vintage for Alana Estate, promising much for the future. The wine is picked very ripe, and spends 12 months in French oak, which it has promptly eaten up.
TTTTY **1998** Youthful purple-red; a rich, very ripe bouquet with a mix of plum and prune fruit; the palate is dense and succulent, with ripe plum fruit and some tannins to give structure on the finish. Needs time, but is full of promise in a baroque style.   **rating: 92**
best drinking 2001–2005 **best vintages** '98 **drink with** Ragout of venison • $36

🐌 alan mccorkindale   ★★★☆

PO Box 29 338, Christchurch **region** Waipara
phone (03) 351 4924 **fax** (03) 351 4925 **open** Not
winemaker Alan McCorkindale **production** 3000 **est.** 1996
product range ($19.90–29.90 R) Riesling, Sauvignon Blanc, Chardonnay, Millennium Brut, Pinot Noir.
summary Alan McCorkindale established a reputation as one of New Zealand's finest winemakers during his ten-year stint as Corbans (and Stoneleigh) winemaker before deciding to do his own thing in 1996. During his time with Corbans, he had begun the development of a small, close-planted vineyard in Waipara, North Canterbury planted to specially selected clones of pinot noir, chardonnay and meunier. This vineyard provides the base wine for the Millennium Brut; the riesling, sauvignon blanc, chardonnay and pinot noir all come from Marlborough.

Alan McCorkindale Millennium Brut

A blend of 78 per cent Pinot Noir, 20 per cent Chardonnay and 2 per cent Pinot Meunier grown in North Canterbury and made according to the Bollinger charter of quality including hard-harvesting, whole-bunch pressing, use of the first pressing cut (the cuvée fraction) and fermentation in oak. Held for three years on lees before disgorging in October 1999.
TTTT **NV** Medium yellow-green; a complex bouquet with some spice and also a touch of wet dog. The palate is quite well balanced, with bready/cakey notes and pronounced flavour persistence. Finishes with relatively high acidity.   **rating: 85**
best drinking 2000–2005 **drink with** Aperitif • $29.80

Alan McCorkindale Pinot Noir

Produced from the Johnson vineyard in Marlborough's Waihopai Valley, all clone 10/5. The grapes are hand-harvested, crushed and destemmed, and then cold macerated for six days at 8 to 11°C. Fermentation follows in open vats, peaking at 33°C, and the wine taken to barrel at the completion of fermentation to French oak, 50 per cent new and 50 per cent one-year-old where it spends 15 months before bottling.

♥♥♥♡ **1998** Light red; light, fresh, clean cherry aromas lead into a relatively light spicy, cherry-flavoured palate. There is an interesting conundrum here; on the one hand, the oak is not overdone, and yet on the other, the fruit seems light. A standard explanation would be over-cropping, but that is inherently improbable, given Alan McCorkindale's obsession with quality. **rating:** 84

best drinking 2000–2003 **drink with** Guinea fowl • $29.80

alexander vineyard   NR

Dublin Street Extension, Martinborough (PO Box 87) **region** Wairarapa
phone (06) 306 9389 **open** Not
winemaker Elise Montgomery **production** 500 **est.** 1991
product range ($15–30 ML) Dusty Road Dry Red, Pinot Noir, Alexander Cabernet Sauvignon Merlot.
summary The Alexanders share with Benfield & Delamere the conviction that Martinborough is best-suited to the Bordeaux varieties of cabernet sauvignon, cabernet franc and merlot, which they have planted on a high-density, low-trellis, guyot-pruned configuration. The first small vintage was in 1994; an on-site winery was built for the 1996 vintage.

allan scott wines   ★★★★

Jacksons Road, RD3, Blenheim **region** Marlborough
phone (03) 572 9054 **fax** (03) 572 9053 **open** 7 days 9.30–4.30
winemaker Paddy Borthwick **production** 30 000 **est.** 1990
product range ($14–28 R) Marlborough Sauvignon Blanc, Marlborough Riesling, Autumn Riesling, Chardonnay, Marlborough Pinot Noir; Prestige range of Sauvignon Blanc, Marlborough Brut Méthode Champenoise, Cabernet Sauvignon.
summary The collapse of Vintech in 1995 accelerated former Corbans' chief viticulturist Allan Scott's plans for his own winery and full-time winemaker (previously the wines were contract-made at Vintech). Thus from 1996 a winery joined the attractive cellar-door sales and restaurant open seven days a week from noon to 4 pm), utilising 63 hectares of estate vineyards. Wine quality is all one could ask for.

Allan Scott Marlborough Riesling

Drawn from about 8 hectares of estate plantings. A wine with a distinguished show history going back to the '92 vintage.

♥♥♥♥ **1999** Light green-yellow; the bouquet is crisp, clean and minerally, with touches of herb and spice. The palate is near-dry, crisp, tight and refreshing. **rating:** 88

best drinking 2000–2004 **best vintages** '92, '93, '97, '99 **drink with** Fresh asparagus • $15

Allan Scott Marlborough Sauvignon Blanc

Given normal vintage conditions this is a classic example of Marlborough Sauvignon Blanc, reflecting the viticultural skills and experience of Allan Scott and the maturity of the estate vineyards.

♥♥♥♥ **1999** Light green-yellow; the bouquet is spotlessly clean and quite delicate, with a mix of passionfruit and more minerally characters. The palate follows down the same track, perhaps more mineral than tropical, but with echoes of the passionfruit running through a long palate with pleasant grip on the finish. **rating:** 86

best drinking 2000–2001 **best vintages** '92, '94, '97, '98 **drink with** Sugar-cured tuna • $18

Allan Scott Prestige Cabernet Sauvignon

Part of a new super-premium range of wines released in 1999, taking full advantage of the great 1998 vintage.

♥♥♥♥ **1998** Dense red-purple; high-toned berry and herb aromas on the bouquet lead into an exceptionally luscious palate, crammed with sweet berry fruit, and finishing with soft tannins. **rating:** 89

best drinking 2002–2010 **best vintages** '98 **drink with** Rare venison • $28

alpha domus   NR

1829 Maraekakaho Road, RD1, Bridge Pa, Hastings **region** Hawke's Bay
phone (06) 879 6752 **fax** (06) 879 6952 **open** Mon–Fri 10–4, summer 7 days 10–5
winemaker Evert Nijzink **production** 12 000 **est.** 1996
product range ($14–45 CD) Chardonnay, Semillon Sauvignon Blanc, Sauvignon Blanc, Leonarda Late Harvest Semillon, Rosé, Pinot Noir, Cabernet Merlot, The Navigator (Merlot blend); AD Selection Barrel Fermented Semillon, Barrel Fermented Chardonnay, Noble Selection, Cabernet Merlot Malbec Franc.
summary An estate-based operation drawing upon 16 hectares of vineyards and enjoying significant growth in production. The wines have attracted considerable favourable comment in New Zealand, with export markets in The Netherlands and the UK presently under development.

🐦 anapai river ★★★☆

Couts Island Road, Christchurch **region** Christchurch
phone NA **open** Not
winemaker Alan McCorkindale **production** NA **est.** NA
product range Marlborough Sauvignon Blanc, Canterbury Pinot Noir.
summary A Negociant business using the skills of Alan McCorkindale to produce wines from contract-grown grapes initially aimed at the export markets of the UK and Australia.

Anapai River Marlborough Sauvignon Blanc

Made from grapes grown in Marlborough's Wairau Valley; it is cold-fermented in stainless steel tanks and aged on light lees for three months prior to bottling.
🍷🍷🍷🍷 **1999** Light green-yellow; the bouquet is clean and firm, with dry minerally characters, but the palate has rather more fruit than the bouquet suggests, with tangy lemony/grapefruit/gooseberry flavours; nicely balanced with subliminal residual sugar. **rating:** 87
best drinking 2000–2001 **drink with** Pan-fried John Dory • $NA

Anapai River Canterbury Pinot Noir

Hand-picked fruit is cold-macerated for one week prior to the commencement of fermentation in small open vats with hand plunging. The wine undergoes malolactic fermentation while maturing in French oak barrels for six months.
🍷🍷🍷🍷 **1998** Light to medium red, with just a touch of purple; the quite fragrant bouquet has aromas of cherry and spice, the palate light but moderately intense cherry and five-spice flavours. An attractive, lighter style of Pinot. **rating:** 86
best drinking 2000–2003 **drink with** Chinese duck • $NA

arahura vineyard NR

Ness Valley Road, Clevedon **region** Auckland Area
phone (09) 292 8749 **fax** (09) 292 8749 **open** 10–4 summer
winemaker Ken Mason, Tim Mason **production** 850 **est.** 1991
product range ($15–25 CD) Arahura Merlot Cabernet Sauvignon is the leader; the Ness Valley Malbec Cabernet Sauvignon and Cabernet Sauvignon Merlot are on a lower price level.
summary Retired judge Ken Mason and wife Dianne are following in the footsteps of Tony Molloy QC by venturing into a new viticultural area and specialising in a single Bordeaux-style red (the plantings also include a little cabernet franc and merlot). A micro-winery was built in 1997 to handle the production from the 2 hectares of vineyards. If the Masons are as successful as Tony Molloy (of St Nesbit) they will have done well.

ashwell vineyards ★★★☆

Kitchener Street, Martinborough **region** Wairarapa
phone (04) 472 0519 **fax** (04) 389 8748 **open** Not
winemaker John Phipps **production** 500 **est.** 1989
product range ($17.50–28 R) Sauvignon Blanc, Chardonnay, Pinot Noir, Cabernet Merlot.
summary Vivienne and John Phipps planted 2 hectares of vines in 1989, only to suffer severe frost damage in 1991. Undaunted, they doubled plantings in 1994 and were appropriately rewarded with silver medals for both their 1997 Pinot Noir and Sauvignon Blanc at the 1998 Air New Zealand Wine Awards. The Pinot Noir also received a five-star rating from Australia's *Winestate* magazine in March 1999.

Ashwell Vineyards Chardonnay

Made in small quantities by a winery whose primary focus is on Pinot Noir.
🍷🍷🍷♀ **1998** The deep yellow, slightly bronze colour is ominous for such a young wine. The bouquet opens with strong oak with lifted tropical fruit to follow. Tangy tropical/peachy fruit jumps up and down on the palate, suggesting some botrytis. At least there is plenty of flavour; drink sooner rather than later. **rating:** 83
best drinking Drink now **best vintages** NA **drink with** KFC • $19.50

askerne NR

267 Te Mata–Mangateretere Road, Havelock North **region** Hawke's Bay
phone (06) 877 6085 **fax** (06) 877 2089 **open** Sat 10–5, Sun 10.30–4.30, weekends summer 10–5
winemaker Sorrelle Pearson, Jenny Dobson (Consultant) **production** 1500 **est.** 1993
product range ($15.50–25 CD) Riesling, Semillon, Semillon Sauvignon Blanc, Sauvignon Blanc, Chardonnay, Botrytised Riesling.
summary Askerne is the venture of John Loughlin, son of Dr John Loughlin of Waimarama Estate, who has named his vineyard after the Yorkshire town which was his wife's birthplace. It runs counter to conventional Hawke's Bay wisdom by having its 5.6-hectare vineyard planted entirely to white varieties: in descending order sauvignon blanc, riesling, semillon, chardonnay, gewurztraminer and optima.

ata rangi ★★★★★

Puruatanga Road, Martinborough **region** Wairarapa
phone (06) 306 9570 **fax** (06) 306 9523 **open** 7 days Oct–Mar, 1–3 midweek, 11–5 weekends
winemaker Clive Paton, Oliver Masters **production** 6000 **est.** 1980
product range ($16–40 CD) Craighall Chardonnay, Petrie Chardonnay, Dalnagairn Chardonnay (Hawke's Bay), Summer Rosé, Pinot Noir, Celebre (Cabernet, Syrah, Merlot blend).
summary Consistently ranks among the best wineries in New Zealand, let alone Martinborough. Both the Pinot Noir and Celebre are remarkable for their depth of colour and sweetness of fruit, showing the impact of full physiological ripeness. A splendid new winery was commissioned for the 1996 vintage, handling the grapes from the 19 hectares of estate plantings as well as the grapes purchased from other regions. The wines are exported to Australia, the UK and the US.

Ata Rangi Craighall Chardonnay

Made from grapes grown on the Craighall Vineyard in Martinborough which, interestingly enough, is jointly owned by Ata Rangi and Dry River. Like all the Ata Rangi wines, opulently power-packed.

🍷🍷🍷🍷🍷 **1998** Medium to full yellow-green; the bouquet is rich and full, with complex barrel-ferment/malolactic-ferment influences on honey and peach fruit. The palate is full and complex, reflecting the entire range of winemaker inputs, and is well balanced despite its 14 degrees alcohol. **rating:** 92

best drinking 2000–2005 **best vintages** '92, '94, '98 **drink with** Smoked chicken • $32

Ata Rangi Petrie Chardonnay

First made in 1997, coming from Hawke's Bay grapes grown by Neil Petrie. A beautifully sculpted wine, with only partial malolactic fermentation.

🍷🍷🍷🍷🍷 **1998** Medium yellow-green; a seamless bouquet introduces a wine with greater elegance than the Craighall, the palate with lovely citrus and melon fruit, perfectly balanced acidity, and a long, clean finish. **rating:** 94

best drinking 2000–2008 **best vintages** '98 **drink with** Slow-cooked salmon • $28

Ata Rangi Pinot Noir

Made in a very different style from the other consistently great Pinot Noir from the Wairarapa, that of Martinborough Vineyard. Ata Rangi is bigger, richer and more fleshy; that of Martinborough tighter and perhaps more elegant. There should not be a question of choice between the two styles: both should be in your cellar.

🍷🍷🍷🍷🍷 **1998** Medium to full red-purple; the bouquet is rich and sweet with complex plummy fruit; the immediate presence of long, tannins mark the opening of the palate; dark berries and some savoury characters then appear, followed by slightly hot alcohol on the finish. Phyll Pattie says, 'it is one of the biggest we've made', and I wouldn't quarrel with that. **rating:** 93

best drinking 2003–2008 **best vintages** '86, '88, '89, '90, '91, '92, '93, '94, '96, '97, '98 **drink with** New Zealand venison • $40

Ata Rangi Celebre

A blend of Cabernet Sauvignon, Syrah, Merlot and Cabernet Franc, with the 15 per cent of Syrah always making a major contribution. Typically, the wine shows ripe and robust fruit flavours, a light-year removed from the thin, weedy, and grassy red wines of lesser makers (and regions). Like the Pinot Noir, is the creation of Clive Paton.

🍷🍷🍷🍷 **1998** Medium red-purple; the bouquet offers a complex mix of spice, leaf and cedar, flavours which dominate the palate. It seems to run slightly counter to most of the '98 New Zealand red wines, having a slightly green edge to the finish. **rating:** 83

best drinking 2000–2004 **best vintages** '91, '94 **drink with** Barbecued lamb • $30

babich ★★★★

Babich Road, Henderson **region** Auckland Area
phone (09) 833 7859 **fax** (09) 833 9929 **open** Mon–Fri 9–5, Sat 9–6, Sun 11–5
winemaker Neill Culley **production** 80 000 **est.** 1916
product range ($10–33.50 R) The Patriarch Chardonnay, Cabernet Sauvignon; Irongate Chardonnay, Cabernet Merlot; Mara Estate Chardonnay, Sauvignon, Merlot, Cabernet Sauvignon, Syrah; also varietal/regional wines such as Marlborough Sauvignon Blanc, Hawke's Bay Sauvignon Blanc, East Coast Chardonnay.
summary Continues to uphold the reputation it gained in the 1960s, but has moved with the times in radically changing its fruit sources and wine styles. Particularly given the volume of production, quality is admirably consistent, with the expanded Mara Estate range leading the way, and strong support from Irongate Chardonnay. It now has 114 hectares of estate vineyards, with 57 hectares in the Gimblett Road region of Hawke's Bay, 42 hectares in the Awatere Valley of Marlborough and the remainder around the Henderson winery. Wines are exported throughout Europe, Asia and North America.

Babich Marlborough Riesling

Produced from grapes grown in the Pigou Vineyard in the Rapaura district of Marlborough, from vines which were crop-thinned during the growing season to enhance the flavour development. Only free-run and light-press juice is used in the wine, with a very cold fermentation to capture the maximum riesling flavour. The residual sweetness of 15 grams per litre is on the generous side.
♥♥♥♡ **1999** Light to medium yellow-green; the bouquet is solid, with mineral, toast and lime aromas, followed by a well-balanced palate in unabashed commercial off-dry style. **rating:** 82
best drinking 2000–2003 **best vintages** NA **drink with** Chinese • $15

Babich Winemaker's Reserve Sauvignon Blanc

Introduced in 1999 utilising grapes grown on the Wakefield Downs Vineyard in the Awatere Valley of Marlborough. Fermentation of the major part is in stainless steel, and a lesser portion in French oak barriques.
♥♥♥♥♡ **1999** Light green-yellow; the bouquet is firm and clean, although not particularly aromatic; a hint of the oak does come through. However, on the palate the clever use of barrel-fermentation adds a delicate touch of spice to a wine which shows sophisticated winemaking from start to finish. **rating:** 90
best drinking 2000–2001 **best vintages** '99 **drink with** Seafood paella • $18

Babich Marlborough Pinot Gris

A new direction for Babich, first made in 1998 from grapes grown by the Pigou family. Produced from fully ripe grapes, pressed quickly and then slowly fermented in stainless steel at low temperatures.
♥♥♥♡ **1999** Light green-yellow; the bouquet is fresh and delicate, but not with over-much varietal character or intensity. The palate is quite well balanced, soft but not flabby, with stone fruit flavours, and a hint of spice. Does finish somewhat short. **rating:** 83
best drinking 2000–2003 **best vintages** NA **drink with** Seafood • $13.50

Babich Irongate Chardonnay

Produced from relatively low-yielding vineyards on the shingle soils to the west of Hastings, and rated as a classic by both Bob Campbell and Michael Cooper. The wine receives the full winemaking treatment, being barrel-fermented (50 per cent new) and held on lees for nine months, with evident malolactic fermentation.
♥♥♥♥♡ **1998** Medium yellow-green; the bouquet is smooth and rich with nicely balanced and integrated oak; the surprisingly delicate and lively palate has excellent nectarine fruit flavours and a nice, bright finish. **rating:** 91
best drinking 2000–2002 **best vintages** '94, '95, '96, '98 **drink with** Tortellini • $26

🐌 banks peninsula wines NR

French Farm Valley Road, RD2, French Farm **region** Canterbury
phone (03) 304 5870 **fax** (03) 304 5870 **open** Not
winemaker Mark Leonard **production** 1000 **est.** 1996
product range ($15–20 R) The wines are released under the Akaroa Harbour brand and comprise Riesling, Chardonnay, Pinot Noir and Merlot.
summary To quote from a small leaflet of Banks Peninsula Wines '150 years ago French settlers grew grapes at French Farm. In 1991 a small vineyard called Sunnybrae was established on the western side of Akaroa Harbour. Sunnybrae Vineyard overlooks the beautiful bay and valley of French Farm'. Thus we have Sunnybrae, French Farm, Akaroa Harbour and Banks Peninsula all co-existing as place names, and another winery called French Farm which started out life as a winery, then became a restaurant and subsequently reverted to a winery. In any event, you can sort the mystery out by visiting the Banks Peninsula.

benfield & delamere   NR

Cambridge Road, Martinborough **region** Wairarapa
phone (06) 306 9926 **fax** (06) 306 9926 **open** By appointment
winemaker Bill Benfield, Sue Delamere **production** 350 **est.** 1987
product range ($25–38 ML) 'Martinborough', a single Cabernet Sauvignon Merlot Cabernet Franc blend. The
second label is 'A Song for Osiris'.
summary Wellington architect Bill Benfield and partner librarian Sue Delamere have single-mindedly set about
recreating Bordeaux, with an ultra-high density, very low-trellised vineyard and utilising 'conservative' techniques
of the kind favoured by the Bordelaise. All of the tiny production is sold by mailing list and limited exports to the
UK and the US.

bentwood wines   NR

Akaroa Highway, Tai Tapu, Canterbury **region** Canterbury
phone (03) 329 6191 **fax** (03) 329 6192 **open** By appointment
winemaker Grant Whelan **production** 500 **est.** 1991
product range ($14–17 CD) Riesling, Gewurztraminer, Pinot Blanc, Pinot Noir.
summary Ray Watson has established a 2-hectare vineyard on the Banks Peninsula, his interest in wine fired after
a 12-month sojourn living on a vineyard in France. The first wines were released from the 1995 vintage; the Pinot
Blanc is already a silver medal winner.

bilancia   ★★★★

2396 State Highway 50 (PO Box 2508, Stortford Lodge), Hastings **region** Hawke's Bay
phone (06) 877 8288 **fax** (06) 877 8288 **open** Not
winemaker Warren Gibson, Lorraine Leheny **production** 1000 **est.** 1997
product range ($24–34 R) Pinot Grigio, Pinot Grigio Reserve, Chardonnay, Merlot.
summary Warren Gibson and Lorraine Leheny are husband and wife winemakers at Trinity Hill, and in 1997
made their first wines under the Bilancia label, using the Trinity Hill facilities to do so. (John Hancock is a very
broadminded and generous employer.) So far Bilancia has relied on purchased grapes (again with John Hancock's
good graces) but in 1998 began establishing their own 6-hectare vineyard at Roys Hill.

Bilancia Pinot Grigio Reserve
Six barrels of the wine were made, following on from the inaugural vintage of 1998. Whole-bunch pressed before
being barrel-fermented in older oak and held for six months on lees.
▼▼▼▼ **1999** Light to medium yellow-green; the bouquet is quite intense and rich, yet it is difficult to describe any
particular aroma other than hints of spice and (perhaps) stone fruit. The palate tells you it is all to do with texture
and structure, for here the richness and roundness of the wine comes to the fore.   **rating:** 88
best drinking 2001–2005 **drink with** Roast veal • $30

Bilancia Chardonnay
Hand-picked and whole-bunch pressed before being barrel-fermented and aged in French oak for 12 months.
▼▼▼▼ **1998** Medium yellow-green, bright and clear; the bouquet is rich, with a mix of cashew and fig supported
by subtle oak. A bold, rich palate with lots of cashew, fig and stone fruit.   **rating:** 87
best drinking 2000–2003 **drink with** Roast pheasant • $34

Bilancia Merlot
The grapes are hand-picked, and fermented in open fermenters with hand-plunging, before being pressed and
matured for 12 months in one-year-old French oak barriques.
▼▼▼▼▽ **1998** Medium red-purple; the bouquet is wonderfully ripe, with savoury/spicy fruit together with
touches of earth and vanilla. The ripe raspberry and redcurrant fruit floods the palate, supported by fine, ripe
tannins. Happily, the oak was used to enhance the flavour and provide texture, which is as it should be.**rating:** 91
best drinking 2002–2008 **drink with** Pot-roasted lamb • $34

black ridge   ★★★★

Conroys Road, Earnscleugh, Alexandra **region** Otago
phone (03) 449 2059 **fax** (03) 449 2597 **open** 7 days 10–5
winemaker Tim Wardell **production** 3000 **est.** 1981
product range ($12.50–35 R) Otago Gold, Riesling, Chardonnay, Gewurztraminer, Pinot Noir, Cabernet
Sauvignon.

summary The formidable, rocky vineyard site at Black Ridge is legendary even in New Zealand, where toughness is taken for granted. The 8-hectare vineyard will always be low-producing, but the wines produced to date have all had clear and bracing varietal character. The outstanding Pinot Noir is a particularly good example of what the site can produce. Exports to the UK and the US.

Black Ridge Riesling

Estate-grown on steep, rocky slopes such as those of the great estates in the Mosel Valley of Germany. Low yields and intense flavours are the order of the day.

TTTT 1999 Light to medium green-yellow; the bouquet is fine, crisp and intense with the lemon, lime and apple characters which appear with equal intensity on the palate. There is no evidence of botrytis in the wine, and although it is technically in the medium, off-dry category, the acidity masks the sweetness (or is it vice versa?).

rating: 86

best drinking 2001–2007 best vintages '99 drink with Fresh artichoke in hollandaise sauce • $16

bladen ★★★☆

Conders Bend Road, Renwick, Marlborough region Marlborough
phone (03) 572 9417 fax (03) 572 9217 open 7 days 12–5 Labour weekend to Easter weekend, then by appointment
winemaker Simon Waghorn (Contract) production 1500 est. 1997
product range ($15–21 R) Riesling, Gewurztraminer, Pinot Gris, Sauvignon Blanc, Sauvignon Blanc Oak Aged.
summary The McDonald family began establishing the Bladen vineyard in 1989, inspired by travels through Europe in the mid-1980s. The name has two derivations: the burial place of Sir Winston Churchill, and a combination of the names of the McDonald children, Blair and Deni. Initially all of the grapes were sold to Grove Mill, but since 1997 part of the 6-hectare vineyard production has been vinified by contract-winemaker Simon Waghorn. Exports to the UK.

Bladen Marlborough Riesling

First made in 1997, and has shown some variation in style and quality in its first three vintages.

TTTT 1999 Medium green-yellow; the bouquet is initially masked by strong SO_2 and some reduced characters, although there is quite intense fruit underneath. The palate is in typical New Zealand spätlese style, tending to be a fraction heavy. One is left to wonder why this style is so common. rating: 83

best drinking 2002–2004 best vintages NA drink with Pasta marinara • $15

Bladen Gewurztraminer

Skilled handling of grapes from a relatively mature vineyard shows through in a wine of excellent varietal character.

TTTT 1999 Light green-yellow; the bouquet is quite concentrated, with a mix of lychee and spice; the palate reflects the very ripe grapes and high (14.5 degrees) alcohol, which provides both a fruit and alcohol-driven sweetness and lusciousness. A wine with considerable presence and character. rating: 88

best drinking 2000–2004 best vintages '99 drink with Fresh fruit • $20

Bladen Sauvignon Blanc

Produced from ten-year-old vines and made in classic Marlborough fashion and, appropriately enough, producing a classic Marlborough wine.

TTTT 1999 Light to medium yellow-green; the bouquet is clean and crisp, with a mix of mineral and tropical fruit aromas. The palate is quite lively and crisp, with good balance and length, repeating the spread of mineral and tropical flavours; crisp, clean finish. rating: 87

best drinking 2000–2001 best vintages NA drink with Shellfish • $16

Bladen Pinot Gris

The wine is fermented and briefly matured in older oak barrels which contribute to the texture of the wine, but not to its flavour — which is no bad thing.

TTTT 1999 Light to medium yellow-green; a clean, crisp bouquet of light to medium intensity with delicate aromas of mineral, herb and spice. The palate, likewise, is of moderate weight, but has fruit grip and length, and a pleasantly dry finish. rating: 87

best drinking 2000–2003 best vintages '99 drink with Crab salad • $20

bradshaw estate NR

291 Te Mata Road, Havelock North **region** Hawke's Bay
phone (06) 877 8017 **fax** (06) 876 5494 **open** 7 days 10–5
winemaker Wayne Bradshaw, Murray McGill **production** 2500 **est.** 1994
product range ($16–29.95 CD) Sauvignon Blanc, Non-wooded Chardonnay, Merlot Cabernet.
summary Wayne and Judy Bradshaw established their operation on the historic Vidal's No. 1 Vineyard and Homestead and in 1996 opened a new winery with an attendant restaurant on the vineyard. The winery restaurant is open Friday to Sunday and every day throughout January.

briar vale estate NR

Kelliher Lane, Alexandra, Central Otago **region** Otago
phone (03) 448 8221 **fax** (03) 448 8221 **open** 7 days 10–5
winemaker John Currie, Judy Currie **production** 250 **est.** 1990
product range ($15–25 CD) Riesling, Chardonnay, Pinot Blanc, Pinot Noir.
summary Alsace was the inspiration for the varieties chosen by John and Judy Currie when they established their 1.75-hectare vineyard on a steep north-facing slope above their cherry orchard. The cool climate carries the threat of spring frosts, however, and until the installation of frost protection (via overhead sprinklers) the crops were significantly reduced; better things are now on the way.

Briar Vale Estate Pinot Noir

Up to 1999 the wine was contract-made by Dean Shaw, but it is likely Briar Vale Estate will secure a more permanent home in the future.
♟♟♟♟ **1998** Bright, light red-purple; a clean, light and fresh cherry-accented bouquet is precisely repeated on the palate; a mid-point between Rosé and dry table red. **rating:** 80
best drinking 2000–2002 **best vintages** NA **drink with** Vegetarian • $22

brick bay NR

PO Box 28270, Remuera, Auckland **region** Auckland Area
phone (09) 524 2831 **fax** (09) 524 2831 **open** Not
winemaker Anthony Ivicevich of West Brook (Contract) **production** 340 **est.** NA
product range ($22 ML) Pinot Gris.
summary A brand new producer which made a dramatic entrance with its gold medal-winning Pinot Gris, which remains the only wine in production from 0.75 hectares of bearing vineyard. However, a further 2 hectares of cabernet sauvignon, cabernet franc, merlot and malbec have been planted by proprietors Christine and Richard Didsbury.

brookfields vineyards ★★★★☆

Brookfields Road, Meeanee, Napier **region** Hawke's Bay
phone (06) 834 4615 **fax** (06) 834 4622 **open** 7 days 10.30–4.30
winemaker Peter Robertson **production** 10 000 **est.** 1937
product range ($16–48 R) Chardonnay, Reserve Chardonnay, Gewurztraminer, Barrel Fermented Sauvignon Blanc, Fumé Blanc, Pinot Gris, Cabernet Sauvignon, Reserve Cabernet Merlot.
summary Peter Robertson has worked hard since acquiring Brookfields in 1977, producing stylish Sauvignon Blanc, lightly oaked, understated Chardonnay and — best of all — the powerful, structured Gold Label Cabernet Merlot, now his highly regarded top-of-the-range release. A particular feature of his wines is their ability to age with grace. Exports to Brazil, Japan, Singapore and Canada.

Brookfields Barrel Fermented Sauvignon Blanc

The wine is fermented in predominantly used oak, which keeps the impact of that oak under control, and the approach works excellently.
♟♟♟♟♟ **1999** Light to medium yellow-green; the bouquet is crisp, clean with a mix of mineral and herb aromas offset by just a touch of oak. An attractive, fine, very long palate leaves the mouth looking for more, for many a rare feature with Sauvignon Blanc. Restrained, not extroverted. **rating:** 90
best drinking 2000–2003 **best vintages** '99 **drink with** Rich fish dishes • $18

Brookfields Pinot Gris

Produced from vines grown on the stony river flats of Ohiti Estate, and typically harvested mid-April. Stainless steel-fermented and early-bottled.

♥♥♥♡ **1999** Light yellow-green; the bouquet is clean, with some mineral but also a touch of fruit spice. The palate is, as expected, delicate, with hints of apple, pear and spice; has mouthfeel. **rating: 84**

best drinking 2000–2003 **best vintages** '96, '98, '99 **drink with** Antipasto • $18

Brookfields Reserve Cabernet Merlot

Produced from grapes grown on the hillside vineyard of Tukituki, across the road, as it were, from Te Mata. Not produced in lesser years (none made in '92, '93 or '96), with production typically ranging between 300 and 500 cases in the top years. The wine spends 18 months in 95 per cent new Nevers oak, and is eggwhite-fined but not filtered. Previously called Gold Label; it is a blend of 85 per cent Cabernet Sauvignon, 10 per cent Merlot and 5 per cent Cabernet Franc.

♥♥♥♥♡ **1998** Medium to full purple-red; a smooth, rich and unequivocally ripe bouquet, packed with blackcurrant and blackberry fruit. An elegant wine on the palate, more savoury/oliveceous than the bouquet suggests, but this in no way detracts; closer to Bordeaux than to Australia. **rating: 90**

best drinking 2003–2013 **best vintages** '95, '98 **drink with** Fine New Zealand lamb • $48

Brookfields Cabernet Sauvignon

In another label and product change, Peter Robertson has discontinued the Reserve Cabernet Sauvignon, and used that material to lift the quality of what was previously called Estate Cabernet. 1998 was the first vintage for the change, and, as one would expect, was highly successful.

♥♥♥♥ **1998** Medium purple-red; a clean, solid bouquet with a mix of savoury dark berry fruit aromas is followed by a palate which again offers a mix of savoury blackberry and blackcurrant fruit, again showing some of the temperament of a good Bordeaux. **rating: 87**

best drinking 2003–2008 **best vintages** NA **drink with** Prime rib of beef • $18

cairnbrae wines ★★★★

Jacksons Road, RD3, Blenheim **region** Marlborough
phone (03) 572 8048 **fax** (03) 572 7018 **open** 7 days 9–5
winemaker Matt Thomson, Kim Crawford (Consultant) **production** 14 000 **est.** 1981
product range ($17–25 R) Riesling, Reserve Riesling, Old River Riesling, Noble Riesling, Semillon, Sauvignon Blanc, Barrel Fermented Sauvignon Blanc, Pinot Gris, Chardonnay, Reserve Chardonnay.
summary The Brown family (Daphne, Murray and Dion) established 18 hectares of vineyard progressively from 1981, selling the grapes to Corbans until 1992, when part of the production was made for them by Kim Crawford, and the label was launched with immediate success. A fast-growing label to watch, with Pinot Noir and Pinot Gris in the pipeline, likewise exports to Australia, the US, Hong Kong, The Netherlands, Denmark and Canada.

Cairnbrae Marlborough Old River Riesling

Produced from fruit grown on the Cairnbrae Jacksons Road Vineyard, complemented by grapes from the Ellin Vineyard at the confluence of the Omaka and Wairau Valleys.

♥♥♥♥ **1999** Light to medium green-yellow; the quite intense bouquet has attractively lifted lime/lemon/herb aromas, the mid-weight palate with very attractive overall flavour and feel, the residual sugar being nicely judged. **rating: 88**

best drinking 2002–2006 **best vintages** '98, '99 **drink with** Vegetarian • $17

Cairnbrae The Stones Sauvignon Blanc

Estate-grown, and made without artifice. The wine has had considerable show success over the years. A wine developed for the export market; Cairnbrae also produces a wood-aged Sauvignon Blanc, and most observers agree the stainless steel-fermented wine is the better.

♥♥♥♥ **1999** Light green-yellow; appropriately enough given the name, minerally/stony characters define the bouquet. The palate is pleasant, clean and well balanced, with attractive gooseberry fruit. **rating: 85**

best drinking 2000–2001 **best vintages** '93, '94, '97, '99 **drink with** Grilled flounder • $17

Cairnbrae Chardonnay

Since 1998 the wine has been fermented and matured in American oak, with full malolactic fermentation. Some see this as a major step forward, but I am in the minority which don't.

♥♥♥♡ **1999** Medium yellow-green; obvious, slightly sawdusty, barrel-ferment oak comes through strongly on the bouquet; on the palate the fruit struggles to keep up with the oak, escaping at the very end to allow its ripe citrussy flavours to appear. **rating: 84**

best drinking 2000–2001 **best vintages** NA **drink with** Smoked pork • $21

Cairnbrae Noble Riesling 375 ml

Made only in those years when there is a strong infestation of botrytis.

♥♥♥♥♀ **1999** Light green-yellow; the bouquet is intense, with quite spiky lime/lemon aromas due to the presence of some volatility. The palate is very intense, with lingering, piercing acidity but with enough sweetness to provide balance. I like the wine; so did the judges at the Royal Easter Wine Show 2000, who gave it a gold medal. **rating: 91**

best drinking 2000–2005 **best vintages** '99 **drink with** Crème brûlée • $25

canadoro NR

New York Street, Martinborough **region** Wairarapa
phone (04) 387 9761 **fax** (04) 387 9761 **open** Via The Grape Vine
winemaker Chris Lintz, Greg Robins **production** 400 **est.** 1993
product range ($25–28 CD) Chardonnay, Cabernet Sauvignon.
summary A weekend operation for Wellington residents Greg and Lesley Robins. The 1.25-hectare vineyard is planted to cabernet sauvignon and chardonnay but is due to be expanded over the next few years; Greg Robins makes the wine with assistance from Chris Lintz.

Canadoro Cabernet Sauvignon

One of the small Wellington/Wairarapa vineyards which supports the minority view that the region is as well suited to Cabernet Sauvignon as it is to Pinot Noir. The '96 vintage won two silver medals in New Zealand wine shows which, I suppose, adds weight to the argument. For the record, the wine spends just under 12 months (46 weeks, to be precise) in French oak.

♥♥♥♥ **1998** Dense red-purple; very ripe plum and prune fruit on the bouquet leads into a big, rich wine with plenty of tannin on the palate, although it does dip ever-so-slightly on the back palate. **rating: 88**

best drinking 2003–2008 **best vintages** '98 **drink with** Game pie • $28

canterbury house vineyards ★★★★

780 Glasnevin Road, RD3, Amberley **region** Canterbury
phone (03) 314 6700 **fax** (03) 314 6905 **open** 7 days 10–4
winemaker Mark Rattray **production** 17 500 **est.** 1994
product range ($16.90–23.90 CD) Riesling, Sauvignon Blanc, Chardonnay, Pinot Gris, Pinot Noir, Merlot, Cabernet Sauvignon.
summary Californian Michael Reid (and his wife) came to New Zealand for a vacation and are now engaged in a most ambitious vineyard and winery development in the Waipara region. The first of five planned stages of winery construction was completed in time for the 1998 vintage; when the final phase is completed it will have a production capacity of 150 000 cases. The first 40 hectares of vineyard have been established, with a further 110 hectares due to be planted over the coming years. If that is not the most expensive vacation ever taken, I don't know what is.

Canterbury House Pinot Noir

A wine which shows the experience Mark Rattray has had over the years in making Pinot Noir, although the style is distinctly lighter than the style he makes at Floating Mountain.

♥♥♥♥ **1998** Light to medium red-purple; the light to moderately intense bouquet has fragrant aromas of plum; the light but elegant palate offers plum, spice and cedar flavours; not forced to be something it is not. **rating: 85**

best drinking 2000–2003 **best vintages** '98 **drink with** Smoked chicken • $23.80

cellier le brun ★★★★

Terrace Road, Renwick **region** Marlborough
phone (03) 572 8859 **fax** (03) 572 8814 **open** 7 days 9–5
winemaker Allan McWilliams **production** 18 000 **est.** 1985
product range ($14–40 CD) Méthode Champenoise specialist with a large range of both vintage and non-vintage wines, including the Daniel Le Brun range of Brut, Brut Taché, Vintage, and Blanc de Blancs. Small quantities of Sauvignon Blanc, Chardonnay and Pinot Noir table wine also made and sold under the Terrace Road label.
summary For almost a decade has produced some of New Zealand's highly rated sparkling wines, initially somewhat erratic but now much more consistent in style — a style which tends to the baroque but which seems to be exactly what New Zealanders like and want. The Courtyard Café restaurant is open seven days from 9 am to 5 pm. A doubling of production over the past few years bears eloquent testimony to the quality of the wines, which are now also exported to the UK and the US.

🐝 central hawke's bay wines   NR

RD 3 Takapau, Central Hawke's Bay   **region** Hawke's Bay
phone (06) 855 8318   **fax** (06) 855 8318   **open** Not
winemaker Evert Nijnk   **production** NA   **est.** 1996
product range ($10.50–22 R) Three Sisters Chenin Blanc, Riesling, Gewurztraminer, Pinot Noir; Richard Harrison Sauvignon Blanc, Chardonnay Chenin and Pinot Noir.
summary A most interesting small-scale operation which combines the output from five small vineyards, the wines being released under the Richard Harrison and Three Sisters labels. Sir Richard Harrison heads the consortium, overseeing the making of wines in a relatively austere, European style.

chancellor wines of waipara   ★★★

133 Mount Cass Road, Waipara   **region** Canterbury
phone (03) 314 6834   **fax** (03) 314 6894   **open** By appointment
winemaker Kym Rayner   **production** 4300   **est.** 1982
product range ($16–25 R) Mount Cass Waipara Riesling, Sauvignon, Chardonnay and Cabernet Sauvignon; Nor'Wester Marlborough Chardonnay, Marlborough Cabernet Merlot.
summary Having been grape growers for 15 years Anthony and Helen Willy took the plunge of establishing the Chancellor Wines brand in 1995 and also almost doubling the estate plantings to 11 hectares; Pinot Noir will be added to the portfolio in the near future. A winery, cellar door and restaurant are all planned for the future. Wines are exported to Australia, the UK and the US.

Chancellor Mount Cass Waipara Sauvignon Blanc

There are no frills to the fermentation in stainless steel tanks and early bottling, but to my palate this is a quite lovely wine which I gave gold medal points to at the Royal Easter Wine Show 2000 (in contra-distinction to my fellow judges).
▼▼▼▼▽ 1999 Light straw-green; mineral, herb and gooseberry aromas and flavours run through a wine with excellent balance, length and intensity of flavour.   **rating:** 92
best drinking 2000–2002   **best vintages** '99   **drink with** Grilled white-fleshed fish   • $18

chard farm   ★★★★☆

Chard Road, RD1, Gibbston   **region** Otago
phone (03) 442 6110   **fax** (03) 441 8400   **open** 7 days 11–5
winemaker Duncan Forsyth, Rob Hay   **production** 21 000   **est.** 1987
product range ($18–39 R) Riesling, Gewurztraminer, Sauvignon Blanc, Pinot Gris Sur Lie, Judge and Jury Chardonnay, Closeburn Chardonnay, Southern Lakes Chardonnay, River Run Pinot Noir, Finla Mor Pinot Noir, Bragato Pinot Noir, Arcadia Special Cuvée Brut, Perrelle Grand Cuvée.
summary Perched precariously between sheer cliffs and the fast-flowing waters of the Kawarau River, Chard Farm is a tribute to the vision and courage of Rob and Gregory Hay. At a latitude of 45 degrees, viticulture will never be easy, but Chard Farm has made every post a winner to date, supplementing production from the 20-hectare vineyard with grapes purchased from Marlborough. The Chardonnay and Pinot Noir are superb, especially the intermittent prestige releases.

Chard Farm Riesling

Sourced from vineyards in the Bannockburn and Cromwell regions. Rob Hay says that 1999 is the greatest year for riesling since 1991, the grapes being hand-harvested in excellent condition; for the record, the wine was de-acidified.
▼▼▼▼▽ 1999 Light green-yellow; intense lime juice and more floral aromas follow through into a beautifully balanced and wonderfully fresh palate, with a long, sliding finish.   **rating:** 91
best drinking 2000–2009   **best vintages** '99   **drink with** Fresh asparagus   • $18

Chard Farm Sauvignon Blanc

Another wine to uncompromisingly reflect the cool climate (and for that matter craggy beauty) of Chard Farm. It takes up where Marlborough Sauvignon Blanc leaves off; piercingly crisp in style in cooler years, richer and riper in outstanding vintages. It is produced from grapes grown on four different vineyards giving a spread of flavour and maturity. Classically made with no oak or other intervention.
▼▼▼▼ 1999 Light green-yellow; voluminous, zesty passionfruit and gooseberry aromas come through strongly on both the bouquet and palate. Overall, a very accessible, soft easy-drinking style.   **rating:** 87
best drinking 2000–2001   **best vintages** '91, '93, '95, '99   **drink with** Calamari   • $18

Chard Farm Pinot Gris Sur Lie

These days the wine is tank-fermented and kept on its lees in small tanks, with regular stirring.

▼▼▼▼ **1999** Light green-yellow; both the bouquet and palate are highly aromatic and rich, with strongly structured fruit which seems quite sweet on the palate, but the wine in fact has less than 6 grams per litre of residual sugar. **rating:** 87

best drinking 2000–2004 **best vintages** NA **drink with** Antipasto • $21

Chard Farm Closeburn Chardonnay

Only partially barrel-fermented, the majority being fermented in tank but then kept on lees with weekly stirring. One hundred per cent malolactic fermentation.

▼▼▼▼ **1998** Light to medium yellow-green; the bouquet has attractive aromatic qualities, with a mix of nectarine and citrus, and barely perceptible oak. A gentle wine, with nice mouthfeel, the flavours tracking the bouquet. **rating:** 86

best drinking 2000–2003 **best vintages** NA **drink with** Sweetbreads • $19.50

Chard Farm Judge And Jury Chardonnay

Strikingly packaged in one of the new generation rocket missile-shaped dark green Italian glass bottles, and taking its name from the prominent outcrops of rock across the Kawarau Gorge. There is a great deal more to the wine than innovative (and no doubt expensive) packaging. Produced from low-yielding (heavily thinned) vines from selected sites planted with the Mendoza clone. Barrel-fermented in predominantly new French oak.

▼▼▼▼▽ **1998** Medium yellow-green; complex, nutty, mealy bouquet leads into what can only be described as a sophisticated wine on the palate, with fine melon and cashew flavours and a long, well-balanced finish. **rating:** 92

best drinking 2000–2005 **best vintages** '98 **drink with** Calamari • $29.50

Chard Farm Bragato Pinot Noir

Named in honour of the visionary viticulturist Romeo Bragato who came to New Zealand from Victoria at the end of the nineteenth century and momentarily took the New Zealand industry by the scruff of the neck, propelling it in the direction in which it has finally headed over 90 years later. He departed, and his vision was lost but not entirely forgotten. This is a fitting tribute to his memory, even more fittingly packaged in an exotic Italian glass bottle.

▼▼▼▼▽ **1998** Medium to full purple-red; spotlessly clean, fine plum and cherry fruit aromas are followed by a well-structured, relatively firm palate with plum and cherry fruit again the driving force, finishing with appropriate tannins. Good now, but has real improvement in front of it. **rating:** 91

best drinking 2000–2005 **best vintages** '91, '93, '98 **drink with** Spiced quail • $39

🐌 charles wiffen ★★★★☆

1639 Parnassus Road, Cheviot, North Canterbury **region** Marlborough
phone (03) 319 2826 **fax** (03) 319 2829 **open** Not
winemaker Anthony Ivicevich **production** 2500 **est.** 1997
product range ($15–30 R) Riesling, Sauvignon Blanc, Chardonnay, Late Harvest Riesling.
summary The Wiffen family conducts farming operations both in Marlborough (since 1907) and in North Canterbury, the latter being the principal base of operations. The Marlborough vineyard, with 8.7 hectares of sauvignon blanc, 2.5 hectares of riesling, 4.2 hectares of chardonnay and 1.6 hectares of merlot was established in 1980, but it was not until 1997 that the Wiffens moved from grape growing to winemaking, with immediate success. The 1998 Riesling was a gold medal winner, the Chardonnay from that year receiving four stars from *Cuisine* magazine.

Charles Wiffen Sauvignon Blanc

Produced from estate-grown grapes in Marlborough which are now 20 years old.

▼▼▼▼▽ **1999** Medium yellow-green; a super-intense and concentrated citrus and gooseberry bouquet is followed by a long, intense and lingering palate with concentrated and ripe fruit flavours; this is a very interesting wine. **rating:** 93

best drinking 2000–2001 **drink with** Bouillabaisse • $17.95

Charles Wiffen Chardonnay

Fermented and matured for three months in a mix of new and used French oak, with partial malolactic fermentation and lees stirring during its time in oak. An early maturing-style.

▼▼▼▼ **1999** Advanced medium to full green-yellow; the bouquet is big and bold, with tangy melon fruit which expands into almost essencey fruit on the palate. An altogether interesting style which demands early drinking. **rating:** 89

best drinking 2000–2000 **drink with** Pasta carbonara • $21

Charles Wiffen Late Harvest Riesling

Packaged in 500 ml bottles, which is a sensible compromise for wines such as this. The grapes were picked very ripe, but with relatively little botrytis.

▼▼▼▼ 1999 Glowing green-yellow' the bouquet is firm and clean, rather less aromatic than many of the more spectacular New Zealand late harvest styles. The palate, however, has plenty of mandarin and lime juice flavour, is moderately intense and well balanced. For many this will make it more approachable. Gold medal at the Royal Easter Wine Show 2000.   **rating:** 91

best drinking 2000–2004 **drink with** Home-made ice cream • $30

chateau waimarama   NR

PO Box 8638, Havelock North **region** Hawke's Bay
phone (06) 877 4822 **fax** (06) 877 2980 **open** Not
winemaker Elise Montgomery (Consultant) **production** 3000 **est.** 1988
product range ($27.95 R) Syrah, Cabernet Sauvignon, Cabernet Merlot, Dessert Cabernet; Undercliffe is the second label.
summary Waimarama Estate was purchased by a Japanese company in 1999, and virtually all of the wine produced now goes to that company in Japan. Tiny quantities of '97 Cabernet Sauvignon and Syrah may be found in New Zealand at $27.95.

chifney wines   ★★★

Huangarua Road, Martinborough **region** Wairarapa
phone (06) 306 9495 **fax** (06) 306 9493 **open** 7 days 11–5 (usually)
winemaker Sue Chifney **production** 1800 **est.** 1980
product range ($18–27 CD) Bottle Fermented Chiffonnay (Sparkling Chenin Blanc), Chenin Blanc, Chardonnay, Chenin Chardonnay Reserve, Enigma (Cabernet Merlot blend), Cabernet Sauvignon, Tawny Port.
summary A final entry for Chifney; it is in the course of being sold to nextdoor neighbour Margrain Vineyard, four years after the death of Stan Chifney the family has decided it is time to let the business go.

church road winery   ★★★★☆

150 Church Road, Taradale **region** Hawke's Bay
phone (06) 844 2053 **fax** (06) 844 3378 **open** 7 days 9–5
winemaker Tony Prichard **production** NFP **est.** 1897
product range ($18.35–35 R) Church Road Sauvignon Blanc, Chardonnay, Noble Semillon, Cabernet Sauvignon Merlot; Church Road Reserve Chardonnay, Merlot, Cabernet Sauvignon Merlot; Twin Rivers Cuvée Brut; super-deluxe Cabernet Cuvée released 1997.
summary Montana's acquisition of the historic McDonald Winery in 1989 and its investment of $2 million on refurbishment, followed by the announcement of the Cordier joint venture together with the acquisition of premium Hawke's Bay vineyards, signalled Montana's determination to enter the top end of the market with high-quality Chardonnay and Cabernet Sauvignon. Legal squabbles have forced the adoption of the Church Road name for the wine label.

c j pask winery   ★★★★☆

1133 Omahu Road, Hastings **region** Hawke's Bay
phone (06) 879 7906 **fax** (06) 879 6428 **open** Mon–Fri 9–5, Sat and public holidays 10–5, Sun 11–4
winemaker Kate Radburnd **production** 35 000 **est.** 1985
product range ($14.50–32.50 R) Under the Gimblett Road label are Sauvignon Blanc, Chenic Blanc, Chardonnay, Pinot Noir, Merlot, Cabernet Merlot, Cabernet Sauvignon, Reserve Chardonnay, Merlot and Cabernet Sauvignon; Roy's Hill White and Red are second label.
summary Ex-cropduster pilot Chris Pask became one of the most highly regarded grape growers in Hawke's Bay; his coup in securing former Vidal winemaker Kate Radburnd (née Marris) has paid the expected dividends. Production has increased rapidly, and the wines have had significant and consistent success in New Zealand and international wine shows thanks to the complexity of the Chardonnays and the supple, sweet fruit of its Cabernet Merlots and Reserve Cabernet Sauvignons. The wines find their way to Australia, Canada, the US, Japan, Thailand, the UK and The Netherlands.

C J Pask Gimblett Road Sauvignon Blanc

Chris Pask was the first vigneron to plant vines in the now famous Gimblett Road region when he moved there in 1982. The deep gravel soils always produce wines with an extra dimension of flavour. Gifted winemaker Kate Radburnd uses an interesting approach for the Sauvignon Blanc, relying on multiple pickings between 18.5 and 21.5° brix to give a range of fruit flavours and a balance of acidity. The wine is cold-fermented in stainless steel and retains around 4 grams per litre of residual sugar.

TTTT 1999 Light green-yellow; there are distinct lemony/lemon rind aromas, and the palate has some power in a similar citrussy/lemony spectrum; fair length. **rating: 86**

best drinking 2000–2001 **best vintages** NA **drink with** Shellfish • $15

C J Pask Chardonnay

The experience of Kate Radburnd shows through in this wine, as does her philosophy that it should be the fruit to shine through, rather than complicated oak handling. Produced from a mix of Mendoza (50 per cent) and clones 6 and 15. The wine is not given any skin contact, but is crushed direct into press and is then tank fermented, employing innerstaves and/or oak chips. No malolactic fermentation, of course.

TTTT 1999 Light to medium yellow-green; the bouquet is moderately intense, with citrus fruit and a slightly leesy overhang. The palate is crisp and clean, with citrus/melon fruit and fairly high acidity. Happily, the oak is barely perceptible. **rating: 83**

best drinking 2000–2002 **best vintages** '95, '96 **drink with** White-fleshed fish • $19.50

C J Pask Reserve Chardonnay

As with all the C J Pask wines, estate-grown. The wine is entirely barrel-fermented in French oak, and portions are given varying amounts of lees contact before the wine is finally blended after ten months in barrel. Interestingly, and consistently with all of the Pask Chardonnays, does not undergo malolactic fermentation.

TTTTT 1998 Medium yellow-green; complex nutty French oak marries with moderately intense fruit on the bouquet. The refined palate exudes class, with long and intense citrus and melon fruit, oak playing a pure support role. The low pH and good acidity suggest a longer than usual life in bottle. **rating: 94**

best drinking 2000–2005 **best vintages** '95, '96, '98 **drink with** Blue-lipped mussels in sauce • $26.95

C J Pask Gimblett Road Pinot Noir

While the warm and dry 1998 vintage was obviously manna from Heaven for the Bordeaux varieties in Hawke's Bay, it is really difficult to understand why it should have produced a superior Pinot Noir. It has to be said that the fermentation in tank with pump-over, and with fermentation temperatures between 24 and 28°C only compound the mystery. However, you can't argue with the result.

TTTT 1998 Medium red-purple; the bouquet is solid, with soft, ripe plummy fruit and sensible oak. The same smooth plummy fruit, with plenty of depth, is neatly balanced with soft tannins on the finish. A silver medal at the International Wine & Spirit Competition and a gold medal at the Air New Zealand Wine Awards 1999, followed by a silver medal at the Royal Easter Wine Show 2000. **rating: 89**

best drinking 2000–2003 **best vintages** '98 **drink with** Smoked quail • $28.95

C J Pask Gimblett Road Merlot

Machine harvested from a number of different estate sites which include some new Bordeaux clones. The fermentation is in closed fermenters with regular pumping-over at warm temperatures. The wine then spends 14 months in a mix of French and American oak barrels.

TTTTT 1998 Full purple-red; there is gloriously rich fruit on the bouquet with a cascade of dark plum, spice, prune and chocolate aromas. The palate is wonderfully supple, with sweet fruit, fine tannins, subtle oak and an elegant finish. A richly deserved gold medal at the 1999 Air New Zealand Wine Awards. **rating: 94**

best drinking 2000–2008 **best vintages** '95, '98 **drink with** Devilled kidneys • $22

C J Pask Reserve Merlot

Selected from a single site with 15-year-old ungrafted, low-yielding vines. The primary fermentation takes place in closed fermenters at warm temperatures; part is then finished in new oak, the other portion being left in stainless steel for two to three weeks post-fermentation maceration. The wine spends 17 months in new French and American oak.

TTTTT 1998 Dense red-purple; the bouquet is rich and complex, with abundant fruit and equally abundant oak. The palate has length, power and presence, crammed with ripe blackberry and chocolate fruit and luscious oak. A classic show style, although you might wonder whether it has as much to do with Cabernet Sauvignon as Merlot. It is not hard to see why this ('98) vintage won gold medals at the 1999 Air New Zealand Wine Awards and the Royal Easter Wine Show 2000. **rating: 94**

best drinking 2003–2010 **best vintages** '97, '98 **drink with** Grilled calf's liver • $28

C J Pask Gimblett Road Cabernet Merlot

A blend of 80 per cent Cabernet Sauvignon and 20 per cent Merlot fermented in closed fermenters with pump-over at moderately warm temperatures. A small proportion finished its fermentation in new barriques, the remainder given post-fermentation maceration before being taken to a mix of one- and two-year-old French and American oak barriques for 15 months maturation.

TTTTY **1998** Medium red-purple; the moderately intense bouquet initially shows some gamey/savoury characters before dark berry fruit and tinges of earth start to express themselves. Sweet, redcurrant/cassis fruit floods the palate; the wine has admirably fine texture, and the oak is subtle. **rating:** 92

best drinking 2002–2008 **best vintages** '98 **drink with** Whole roasted fillet of beef • $24.95

C J Pask Gimblett Road Cabernet Sauvignon

Estate-grown and machine picked. Straightforward fermentation in closed fermenters with pump-over, followed by three weeks post-fermentation maceration during which time the malolactic fermentation was completed. Pressed and then matured for 15 months in French and American oak.

TTTTT **1998** Medium to full red-purple; ripe cassis and blackberry fruit of the bouquet is complexed by hints of sweet leather. The palate is flooded with intense, pure cassis/blackberry fruit; a lovely wine, which is a tribute to the vineyard and the vintage, with the winemaker happy to stand back. **rating:** 94

best drinking 2003–2013 **best vintages** '98 **drink with** Fillet mignon • $20

claddagh vineyards NR

Puruatanga Road, Martinborough **region** Wairarapa
phone (06) 306 9264 **fax** (06) 306 9264 **open** By appointment
winemaker Russell Pearless **production** 300 **est.** 1991
product range ($14.95–25 R) Pinot Noir, Cabernet Sauvignon.
summary Presently a weekend and holiday occupation for computer industry executives Russell and Suzanne Pearless, but when the 4-hectare vineyard (also planted to chardonnay and sauvignon blanc) comes into full bearing, the level of involvement will doubtless increase.

clearview estate ★★★★★

Clifton Road, RD2, Te Awanga **region** Hawke's Bay
phone (06) 875 0150 **fax** (06) 875 1258 **open** 7 days Labour weekend to Easter, winter Fri–Sun 10–5
winemaker Tim Turvey **production** 4000 **est.** 1989
product range ($12–70 CD) Beach Head Chardonnay, Reserve Chardonnay, Black Reef Riesling, Te Awanga Sauvignon Blanc, Fumé Blanc, Reserve Fumé Blanc, Reserve Cabernet Franc, Reserve Merlot, Reserve The Old Olive Block (Cabernet Sauvignon Merlot), Cape Kidnappers Cabernet, Basket Press Cabernet, Blush, Sea Red (dessert red wine), Noble 51 (botrytised Chardonnay).
summary Clearview Estate is situated on a shingly site first planted by Anthony Vidal in 1916 on the coast of Te Awanga; it has been replanted since 1988 with chardonnay, cabernet sauvignon, cabernet franc and merlot, with grapes also coming from a neighbouring vineyard. All of the wines to date have been of exceptional quality, especially the magically concentrated and complex Chardonnay. The icing on the cake is an outstanding restaurant, rated by Bob Campbell as Hawke's Bay's best.

Clearview Estate Reserve Te Awanga Sauvignon Blanc

Fifty per cent of the wine is barrel-fermented, the other half in stainless steel. The components are blended fairly quickly, and the oak influence is much less marked than in previous vintages (sold under the Fumé Blanc name).

TTTT **1998** Medium yellow-green; the bouquet is intense, with citrus/lemon/peach aromas and subtle oak. The palate repeats those ripe, almost tropical flavours, and has good intensity, balance and length. Here, too, the oak does not intrude too strongly. **rating:** 88

best drinking 2000–2001 **best vintages** '98 **drink with** Fresh salmon • $16

Clearview Estate Reserve Chardonnay

Tim Turvey makes the most spectacular Chardonnays in New Zealand. A mini vertical tasting of the '93 to '96 Chardonnays in September 1997 was overwhelmingly impressive. These are monumental wines, whether one looks at the alcohol consistently exceeding 14 degrees, or the sheer volume and complexity of flavour. For the record, 30 per cent to 50 per cent is given between six and eight hours skin contact, and the rest is whole-bunch pressed. The wine is barrel-fermented in a coolroom at 11°C for up to six weeks, and around 20 per cent is taken through malolactic fermentation. Only a tiny fraction of the total production makes the Reserve label.

TTTTT **1998** Brilliant light to medium yellow-green; yet another wine with an extremely oaky bouquet, and inevitably makes an emphatic statement on the palate. However, the longer the wine sat in the glass, and the more often it was retasted, the more evident did the grapefruit, peach and nectarine fruit which lies at the core of the wine become evident. And whatever else, it is certainly in the mainstream of the baroque Clearview style. **rating:** 94

best drinking 2000–2003 **best vintages** '94, '95, '96, '98 **drink with** Sweetbreads • $30

Clearview Estate Reserve Cabernet Franc

Outside of the Chinon region of the Loire Valley, only a few brave souls attempt to make a varietal wine from cabernet franc, a variety often somewhere between cabernet sauvignon and merlot, but without the best features of either. Clearview, however, shows that a high-quality wine can be made from the grape when conditions are favourable. None was made in 1995 or 1996.

▼▼▼▼ 1998 Medium red-purple; the oak surrounds the nice fruit of the bouquet; the wine has a marvellously delicate structure on the palate with well-balanced tannins; the problem is you are mainly tasting the oak. **rating:** 87

best drinking 2002–2006 **best vintages** '94, '97, '98 **drink with** Steak and kidney pie • $30

Clearview Estate Reserve Merlot

The Clearview vineyards are planted on a free-draining shingle which always limits the yield and protects against dilution through wet weather. The wine is made from low-yielding vines and exhibits tremendous concentration and power. It spends 18 months in predominantly French Nevers oak with a touch of Seguin Moreau American oak. A consistent gold medal winner over the years.

▼▼▼▼▽ 1998 Medium red-purple; dark fruits, sweet leather and savoury/oaky aromas swirl through a complex bouquet; the powerful and intense palate offers a mix of dark berry and more savoury flavours. The tannins are well balanced and the oak well integrated. **rating:** 93

best drinking 2001–2007 **best vintages** '94, '95, '98 **drink with** Smoked lamb • $30

Clearview Estate Reserve Old Olive Block Cabernet Sauvignon Merlot Cabernet Franc

A blend of 60 per cent Cabernet Sauvignon, 30 per cent Merlot, 9 per cent Cabernet Franc and 1 per cent Malbec barrel-aged for 14 months in a mix of new French (60 per cent) and new American (40 per cent) oak. A gold medal winner at both the 1999 Liquorland Top 100 and 1999 Air New Zealand Wine Awards.

▼▼▼▼ 1998 Medium purple-red; lashings of dusty cedar vanilla oak obscure anything else there may be on the bouquet. On the palate there are lots of attractive fruit flavours, and the structure and balance of the fruit is good. I simply do not understand why it has been walloped with oak. **rating:** 89

best drinking 2003–2010 **best vintages** '95, '98 **drink with** Barbecued T-bone • $30

clifford bay estate ★★★★☆

26 Rapaura Road, Blenheim **region** Marlborough
phone (03) 572 7148 **fax** (03) 572 7138 **open** 7 days 9–5
winemaker Glen Thomas (Vavasour Wines — Contract) **production** 10 500 **est.** 1994
product range ($14.95–18.95 R) Single Vineyard Riesling, Sauvignon Blanc and Chardonnay.
summary Clifford Bay made the most spectacular entry onto the scene imaginable, winning two gold medals (Air New Zealand Wine Awards and Christchurch Show) with its first wine, a 1997 Sauvignon Blanc, and hasn't looked back since. It is the venture of Eric and Beverley Bowers, Graham and Thelma Cains and Chris Wilson. Viticultural advice has come from Richard Bowling, and the wine is made by the masterful Glen Thomas. Twenty hectares of sauvignon blanc, chardonnay and riesling are under vine. The wines are exported to Australia, the UK and the US.

Clifford Bay Riesling

First made in 1999; the grapes are late harvested, hand-picked and whole-bunch pressed. Conventional low temperature fermentation in stainless steel follows, with early bottling.

▼▼▼▼▽ 1999 Light green-yellow; the bouquet is firm and intense, with lime and mineral aromas. The palate is even and clean, with more of those firm mineral lime flavours promised by the bouquet; seems to need a touch more zest for absolute top points. **rating:** 90

best drinking 2001–2007 **best vintages** '99 **drink with** Asparagus • $15.95

Clifford Bay Sauvignon Blanc

Grown on river terraces adjoining the Awatere River, and late-picked. Fifteen per cent of the wine is barrel-fermented in new French oak barriques, the remainder in stainless steel.

▼▼▼▼▽ 1999 Light green-yellow; a firm, powerful bouquet with mineral and herb notes dominant. The palate is similarly intense and powerful, with good length; all in all, a masculine style. **rating:** 90

best drinking 2000–2001 **best vintages** '97, '99 **drink with** Sugar-cured tuna • $16.95

cloudy bay ★★★★★

Jacksons Road, Blenheim **region** Marlborough
phone (03) 520 9140 **fax** (03) 520 9040 **open** 7 days 10–4.30
winemaker Kevin Judd **production** 100 000 **est.** 1985
product range ($24.95–42 R) Sauvignon Blanc, Chardonnay, Pinot Noir, Cabernet Merlot, Pelorus NV and
Pelorus Vintage (sparkling); also Te Koko (barrel-fermented, bottle-aged Sauvignon Blanc).
summary The other arm of Cape Mentelle, masterminded by David Hohnen and realised by Kevin Judd, his
trusted lieutenant from day one. A marketing tour de force, it became a world-recognised brand in only a few
years, but the wine quality and style should not be underestimated: Hohnen and Judd may share a great sense of
humour, but they are perfectionists in every way, the wines consistently great. A warped New World view,
perhaps, but I rate the Sauvignon Blanc the best in the world, all vintages taken into account. Kevin Judd,
incidentally, could as easily earn a living as a photographer; he has a rare talent. The wines are available in Australia,
Japan, the US, Singapore, Canada, Thailand, Hong Kong, Indonesia, South Africa and most parts of Europe.

Cloudy Bay Sauvignon Blanc

The most famous New World Sauvignon Blanc, with an international reputation second to none. The creative
team of David Hohnen and Kevin Judd are disarmingly modest about the wine, however correctly they may point
to the perfect marriage between the variety and the climate and soil of Marlborough. There is also the attention to
detail, the discipline and the creative intelligence required to make a wine of such distinction with such
consistency.

♥♥♥♥♥ **1999** Brilliant light green-yellow colour; an elegant, multifaceted bouquet with fruit aromas that refuse to
be pinned down into one type, and a subliminal touch of oak. The palate positively sparkles with life, with lively
citrus and gooseberry flavours running through to a long, intense lingering finish. Just great summer drinking.

rating: 94

best drinking 1999–2003 **best vintages** '92, '94, '96, '98, '99 **drink with** Virtually any seafood dish • $25

Cloudy Bay Chardonnay

The extensive chardonnay plantings of Cloudy Bay (almost 35 hectares in total) are partially directed to the
production of Pelorus, with the newer plantings dedicated to this purpose. However, Cloudy Bay produces a
Chardonnay of real stature and complexity, made using prolonged yeast lees contact, malolactic fermentation and
ageing in French oak. About 70–80 per cent of the wine is barrel-fermented, 20 per cent in new French oak.

♥♥♥♥♡ **1998** Medium to full yellow-green; rich and tangy fruit on the bouquet is supported by clear but
controlled barrel-ferment characters. The palate is remarkably rich, the fruit continuing to build in waves on an
intense, long finish. **rating: 92**

best drinking 2001–2003 **best vintages** '87, '91, '93, '94, '95, '97, '98 **drink with** Sweetbreads • $33

collards ★★★★☆

303 Lincoln Road, Henderson, Auckland **region** Auckland Area
phone (09) 838 8341 **fax** (09) 837 5840 **open** Mon–Sat 9–5, Sun 11–5
winemaker Bruce Collard, Geoff Collard **production** 20 000 **est.** 1910
product range ($7.70–25 CD) Riesling, Queen Charlotte Riesling, Chardonnay (Rothesay, Hawke's Bay,
Marlborough, Blakes Mill), Chenin Blanc, Sauvignon Blanc (Rothesay, Marlborough), Barrique Fermented
Semillon, Queen Charlotte Marlborough Pinot Noir, Marlborough Syrah, Rothesay Cabernet Sauvignon,
Cabernet Merlot, Tawny Port.
summary A family-owned and run business which is a bastion of conservatism, adopting a low promotional
profile, but which consistently produces fastidiously crafted wines of excellent quality, and which has moved with
the times in developing new wines and labels. Exports to Singapore, Japan, the UK, Germany, The Netherlands,
Denmark and Hong Kong.

coopers creek ★★★★

State Highway 16, Huapai **region** Auckland Area
phone (09) 412 8560 **fax** (09) 412 8375 **open** Mon–Fri 9–5.30, weekends 10.30–5.30
winemaker Simon Nunns **production** 50 000 **est.** 1980
product range ($10–27 CD) Hawke's Bay Riesling, Chardonnay, Pinot Noir, Merlot, Cabernet Sauvignon
Franc; Semillon Chardonnay, First Edition, Marlborough Sauvignon Blanc, Gisborne Chardonnay and Huapai
Cabernet Merlot; the Reserve range of Hawke's Bay Reserve Riesling, Reserve Oak Aged Sauvignon Blanc,
Swamp Reserve Chardonnay, Wild Ferment Chardonnay, Late Harvest Riesling, Coopers Gold, Hawke's Bay

Reserve Pinot Noir, Hawke's Bay Reserve Merlot, Hawke's Bay Reserve Merlot Cabernet Franc, Hawke's Bay Reserve Cabernet Merlot, Hawke's Bay Reserve Cabernet Sauvignon and Huapai Reserve Cabernet Merlot.
summary A long-term producer of stylish white wines sourced from Gisborne, Hawke's Bay and Marlborough, respectively. They are full of character and flavour but avoid the heavy, coarse phenolics which were once so much part of the white wine scene in New Zealand.

Coopers Creek Reserve Marlborough Sauvignon Blanc
Produced from grapes grown on the Eilin family vineyard at the entrance to the Omaka Valley. The wine was conventionally made, with a long, cool ferment in stainless steel.
▼▼▼▼ **1999** Medium green-yellow; a big, solid bouquet with slightly heavy fruit is followed by a similarly solid palate. The wine certainly has flavour, but doesn't have the crisp brightness of the best wines. **rating:** 85
best drinking 2000–2001 **best vintages** NA **drink with** Vegetable terrine • $20

Coopers Creek Swamp Reserve Chardonnay
The somewhat off-putting name should not mislead you; this is the flagship of the excellent Coopers Creek white wine range. One hundred per cent barrel-fermentation in all tight-grain, heavy toast French oak (from Francois Freres and Dargaud & Jaegle), 70 per cent of which is new, with malolactic fermentation and ten months in barrel produce a wine which is never to be denied. Not made in poor vintages, incidentally.
▼▼▼▼▽ **1998** Medium to full yellow-green; the oak tends to dominate on the bouquet and to a lesser degree on the palate. On the other hand, the wine has abundant tropical fruit, which runs right through the palate, all adding up to a pretty delicious mouthful. Gold medal Air New Zealand Wine Awards 1999. **rating:** 92
best drinking 2000–2002 **best vintages** '92, '94, '95, '96, '98 **drink with** Creamy pasta • $25

Coopers Creek Hawke's Bay Reserve Pinot Noir
Produced from two Hawke's Bay vineyards, with brief cold maceration and maturation in a mix of French and American one-year-old barriques for ten months. Does nothing to suggest that Hawke's Bay is particularly suited to Pinot Noir.
▼▼▼▽ **1998** Medium red-purple; some interest is provided by smoky oak characters which come through on the stalky/smoky cherry and strawberry flavoured palate. **rating:** 84
best drinking 2000–2003 **best vintages** NA **drink with** Smoked chicken • $27

Coopers Creek Hawke's Bay Reserve Merlot
Sourced from five Hawke's Bay vineyards, and incorporating a small amount of Cabernet Franc. The grapes from one coastal vineyard, which comprised the bulk of the blend, were so impressive they were macerated on skins for an unprecedented six weeks. The wine spent 12 months in oak, 15 per cent new American and 15 per cent new French, the balance older oak.
▼▼▼▼ **1998** Medium to full red-purple; opulent berry fruit with striking five-spice overtones, a touch of game and a dressing of oak provide a complex bouquet. There is rather more oak on the palate, and the tannins, even though ripe, dominate the finish. Does have the potential to improve as those tannins soften, for there is enough fruit there. **rating:** 87
best drinking 2003–2008 **best vintages** '98 **drink with** Lamb casserole • $25

Coopers Creek Hawke's Bay Reserve Merlot Cabernet Franc
A blend of 80 per cent Merlot and 20 per cent Cabernet Franc picked from a single, young vineyard site at Te Awanga. The wine is cold-soaked for three days before inoculation, and towards the end of fermentation 15 per cent of the wine was drawn off to finish its fermentation in a mix of new and used French oak. The remaining wine was left on skins for six weeks post-fermentation maceration, during which time it underwent mlf. It is then taken to a mix of new and used French and American oak for 12 months. The 1998 has received a gold medal at the 1999 Air New Zealand Wine Awards and 5 stars from Bob Campbell.
▼▼▼▼ **1998** Medium to full red, with just a touch of purple suggesting fairly rapid colour change. The bouquet is essentially savoury with a mix of leafy/gamey aromas; the palate has excellent texture and stucture, but I really can't get swept away by the flavours. **rating:** 86
best drinking 2001–2005 **best vintages** NA **drink with** Veal goulash • $27

Coopers Creek Hawke's Bay Reserve Cabernet Merlot
The grapes come from four vineyards located around Havelock North, a blend of 75 per cent Cabernet, 20 per cent Merlot and 5 per cent Cabernet Franc. These components are vinified and barrel-aged separately in 40 per cent new French oak, the remainder a mixture of used French and American. The blend is made and the wine bottled after 12 months in barrel.

♥♥♥♡ **1998** Medium red, with some purple, showing some early development. The bouquet is in the gamey/leafy/savoury spectrum, the palate moderately intense with a slight twist of bitterness to the fruit flavours towards the finish. **rating: 82**

best drinking 2001–2004 **best vintages** NA **drink with** Game sausages •$27

Coopers Creek Hawke's Bay Reserve Cabernet Sauvignon

Produced from a single vineyard on an elevated terrace overlooking Te Awanga. A long post-ferment maceration was followed by 12 months in new American oak with four barrel to barrel rackings during this time.

♥♥♥♡ **1998** Medium red, with just a touch of purple; lighter than most, and suggesting reasonably quick development. There is a mix of cedar and vanilla oak (dominant) and light, earthy fruit on the bouquet; sweet fruit and even sweeter oak follow on the palate; a nicely constructed wine but where did the fruit intensity go? **rating: 84**

best drinking 2000–2004 **best vintages** NA **drink with** Eye rib of beef •$27

corbans

320 Ti Rakau Drive, East Tamaki, Auckland **region** Auckland Area
phone (09) 273 4800 **fax** (09) 273 4844 **open** Not
winemaker Michael Kluczko **production** 1.5 million **est.** 1902
product range ($11–36 R) The Corbans wines are now marketed under five sub-brands, each with their separate price range: Cottage Block ($25–35), Private Bin ($20–26), Select ($14–16), Estate ($12–14) and White Label ($8–10); also Amadeus and Verde (sparkling). There are then the quasi-independent and stand-alone brands of Longridge (Hawke's Bay) and Stoneleigh (Marlborough), which have their own entries.
summary New Zealand's second largest wine group with a turnover exceeding $NZ100 million, 500 hectares of estate vineyards and another 500 hectares of contracted vineyards. Wine quality is exemplary, setting the pace for others to follow. The wines are exported to Europe, Asia, the US, Canada and Iceland.

Corbans Select Marlborough Sauvignon Blanc

Introduced in 1998 as part of the complete overhaul of the brand structure. The wine comes from the Stoneleigh Vineyard, with 5 per cent barrel-fermented.

♥♥♥♥ **1999** Medium yellow-green; a huge in-your-face style with masses of gooseberry and herb fruit on both bouquet and palate, the latter having tremendous intensity of flavour. **rating: 89**

best drinking 2000–2001 **best vintages** '99 **drink with** Roasted red capsicum •$17

Corbans Select Merlot Cabernet Sauvignon

A blend of Marlborough and Hawke's Bay grapes; the 1998 vintage was doubtless a great base to work from, but this wine offers exceptional value for money.

♥♥♥♡ **1998** Strong red-purple; the bouquet is quite powerful, with a mix of sweet berry and more savoury characters, supported by pleasant oak. The palate offers more of the same, with sweet berry fruit on the mid-palate moving through to lingering but gentle tannins on the finish. **rating: 90**

best drinking 2002–2008 **best vintages** '98 **drink with** New Zealand lamb •$16

cottle hill winery NR

Corner State Highway 10 and Cottle Hill Drive, Kerikeri **region** Northland and Matakana
phone (09) 407 5203 **fax** (09) 407 6808 **open** 7 days 10–5
winemaker Simone Parker **production** 1000 **est.** 1997
product range ($14–29 CD) Sauvignon Blanc, Chardonnay, Bay Breeze (Sauvignon Blanc Chardonnay), Pinotage, Cabernet Sauvignon.
summary Michael and Barbara Webb are fugitives from 'the southern California rat-race'. They first arrived in the Bay of Islands on their yacht in 1992 and have now returned to establish Cottle Hill Winery.

covell estate NR

Troutbeck Road, Galatea, RD1, Murupara **region** Waikato and Bay of Plenty
phone (07) 366 4827 **fax** (07) 366 4071 **open** 7 days 10–4 by appointment
winemaker Bob Covell, Robert Covell Jnr, Norm Iles **production** 1000 **est.** NA
product range ($12–20 CD) Riesling, Chardonnay, Pinot Noir, Rata (Cabernet Merlot).
summary Owners Bob and Desarei Covell have established this vineyard using strict biodynamic organic standards; they mature their wines for extended periods in oak, and give them further time in bottle before release.

crab farm NR

125 Main Road, Bay View, Hawke's Bay **region** Hawke's Bay
phone (06) 836 6678 **open** 7 days 10–5
winemaker Hamish Jardine **production** 3900 **est.** 1989
product range ($10–17 CD) Gewurztraminer, Sauvignon Blanc, Chardonnay, Pinot Noir, Merlot, Cabernet Sauvignon.
summary Hamish Jardine has worked at both Chateau Reynella and Matawhero; the family vineyards were planted in 1980 and are now mature, so given the equable Hawke's Bay climate there is no reason why the wines should not succeed. A seafood restaurant has recently been added, open from the end of October to Easter seven days a week 11.30–3. Exports to the UK, Taipai and the US.

🦀 craggy range vineyards ★★★★☆

The Tin Shed, 18 Napier Road, Havelock North (office) **region** Hawke's Bay
phone 0508 CRAGGY **fax** (09) 534 9794 **open** Not
winemaker Steve Smith MW **production** 3500 **est.** 1998
product range ($18–30 R) Rapaura Road Vineyard Marlborough Riesling, Old Renwick Vineyard Marlborough Sauvignon Blanc, Apley Road Vineyard Hawkes Bay Chardonnay, Strugglers Flat Vineyard Marlborough Pinot Noir.
summary A major arrival on the scene in New Zealand, major vineyard developments hinged around a 40-hectare site on Gimblett Road and a 70-hectare site in Martinborough. A spectacular winery has been designed for the Hawke's Bay site with a circular red wine fermentation cellar and underground barrel hall, wine and culinary school, guest house and restaurant; the winery will be completed by March 2002, which will coincide with the first vintages from the estate vineyards. In the meantime, single-vineyard wines (a cornerstone of the winery's philosophy) have been made from selected sites in Marlborough and Hawke's Bay.

cross roads winery ★★★★

State Highway 50, Korokipo Road, Fernhill, Napier **region** Hawke's Bay
phone (06) 879 9737 **fax** (06) 879 6068 **open** 7 days 10–5
winemaker Malcolm Reeves, Andrea Paterson **production** 8500 **est.** 1990
product range ($10–35 CD) Gewurztraminer, Dry Riesling, Late Harvest Riesling, Chardonnay, Reserve Chardonnay, Oak Aged Sauvignon, Sauvignon, Rosé, Pinot Noir, Syrah, Cabernet Merlot, Reserve Cabernet Merlot, Talisman, Stormy Ports.
summary A very successful partnership between Malcolm Reeves, wine journalist and Massey University lecturer, and computer entrepreneur Lester O'Brien. Right from the first vintage, the wines have received widespread critical acclaim and have enjoyed great success in wine shows. Draws in part on 5 hectares of various red vinifera varieties which go to produce the super-premium Talisman red. The identity of those varieties (and hence the blend) is deliberately kept confidential. Exports to California, Germany and Scotland.

Cross Roads Chardonnay

As might be expected, this wine has even less barrel-ferment and malolactic-ferment influences than the Reserve, and in my view is none the worse for that. The '98 was a silver medal winner at the 1999 Air New Zealand Wine Awards.
▼▼▼▼ 1998 Medium yellow-green; there is a seamless integration of and balance between fruit and oak on the bouquet; the palate is equally harmonious with ripe melon and fig fruit leading the way, although it does tail off structurally on the finish. You can't have your Chardonnay and eat it, it would seem. **rating:** 87
best drinking 2000–2001 **best vintages** NA **drink with** Milk-fed veal • $18

Cross Roads Reserve Chardonnay

As one would expect, has distinctly more weight and complexity than the varietal release, benefiting from better fruit and obvious winemaker inputs through the full cavalcade of barrel-ferment, lees contact and malolactic fermentation.
▼▼▼▼ 1997 Medium to full yellow-green; the bouquet offers rich, ripe, sweet peachy fruit, with the malolactic influence kept to a bare minimum. Sweet peachy fruit and relatively subtle oak is the mark of a fruit-driven style that has pleasing delicacy. **rating:** 88
best drinking 2000–2002 **best vintages** '97 **drink with** Kassler • $22

Cross Roads Shiraz

Not the highest-rated New Zealand Syrah by any means, but does help the proposition that Hawke's Bay may prove best suited to the variety. It is matured in a mix of new and used French and American oak barriques.

▼▼▼▼ **1998** Medium red-purple; the moderately intense bouquet offers ripe plum and mint fruit together with vanilla oak; the light- to medium-bodied palate has similar plum and mint fruit and subtle oak but lacks concentration. **rating:** 83

best drinking 2000–2004 **best vintages** NA **drink with** Rabbit pie • $21

Cross Roads Reserve Cabernet Merlot

A blend of around 40 per cent Cabernet Sauvignon, 40 per cent Merlot and 20 per cent Cabernet Franc which spends up to two years in French oak.

▼▼▼▼ **1997** Medium red-purple; a quite complex bouquet has a mix of cedar, vanilla and cinnamon spice over red berry fruit. The palate offers more savoury characters, with cedar and mint both evident, and I prefer the wine to the Talisman of the same vintage. **rating:** 84

best drinking 2000–2004 **best vintages** NA **drink with** Marinated lamb • $22

daniel schuster ★★★★

192 Reeces Road, Omihi Valley, RD3, Amberley **region** Canterbury
phone (03) 314 5901 **fax** (03) 314 5902 **open** By appointment
winemaker Danny Schuster, Mark Neville **production** 5000 **est.** 1986
product range ($19–30 R) Canterbury Chardonnay, Petrie Vineyard Selection Chardonnay, Canterbury Pinot Noir, Reserve Pinot Noir.
summary Austrian-born, German-trained Danny Schuster must now rank as one of the leading consultant viticulturists in the world, his clients ranging from Stag's Leap, Neibaum Coppola, Moraga and Spotswoode in the Napa Valley to Antinori in Tuscany. The mix is all the more fascinating when one considers that the Napa Valley makers are all producing powerful and dense Cabernet-based red wines; that the climate of Tuscany is as far removed from that of Canterbury as one could imagine; and that at home Danny Schuster is known for his pioneering work in the production of Pinot Noir from the Canterbury/Waipara region. Truly a man for all seasons, producing wines of equally variable (seasonal) quality, at times exhilarating, at times depressing. Exports to Australia, Belgium, The Netherlands, Italy and the US.

Daniel Schuster Omihi Hills Selection Pinot Noir

The 1998 is unlikely to be released much before the end of 2001, but is the best wine Danny Schuster has produced since 1982, and will be well worth the wait.

▼▼▼▼▼ **1998** Medium to full red-purple; the bouquet is rich, with abundant plum, cherry and spice fruit, backed by subtle oak. The voluptuously rich palate has superb dark fruits in a plush texture, with tannins, acidity and oak simply doing their job. **rating:** 96

best drinking 2002–2010 **best vintages** '98 **drink with** Rare squab • $NA

darjon vineyards NR

North Eyre Road, Swannanoa, North Canterbury **region** Canterbury
phone (03) 312 6045 **fax** (03) 312 6544 **open** Weekends and most public holidays 12–5
winemaker John Baker **production** 500 **est.** 1992
product range ($16–22 CD) The minute estate-produced Swannanoa range of Pinot Noir and Riesling is supplemented by wines from Marlborough and from other New Zealand and Australian boutique producers.
summary A new arrival on the Christchurch scene, run by former amateur winemaker John Baker and his wife Michelle. The restaurant was opened on site in 1994, coinciding with the first production from the 2 hectares estate plantings of riesling and pinot noir, and all of the Darjon wine will be sold through the restaurant, mail list and cellar-door sales.

de gyffarde NR

Giffords Road, Rapaura, RD3, Blenheim **region** Marlborough
phone (03) 572 8189 **fax** (03) 572 8178 **open** At Marlborough Vintners, Rapaura Road, Blenheim
winemaker Graeme Paul **production** 4500 **est.** 1995
product range ($16–18 CD) Sauvignon Blanc, Chardonnay under both de Gyffarde and Lofthouse labels.
summary English-born owners Di and Rod Lofthouse were 20-year veterans of the film and television industry before establishing their 6-hectare vineyard in 1989 and moving into winemaking from 1995. They have now taken the process one step further by becoming part-owners of Marlborough Vintners Limited. This operates the

new winery, commissioned for the 1998 vintage, which makes the wine for de Gyffarde and three other similar-sized Marlborough wineries. The wines are now sold in New Zealand under the Lofthouse label, which is also used for some exports along with de Gyffarde. Exports to the UK and the US.

delegat's wine estate ★★★★☆

Hepburn Road, Henderson **region** Auckland Area
phone (09) 836 0129 **fax** (09) 836 3282 **open** Mon–Fri 10–5, weekends 10–6
winemaker Michael Ivicevich **production** NFP **est.** 1947
product range ($18.50–25 R) Estate label of Chardonnay, Sauvignon Blanc and Cabernet Merlot; top-of-the-range Reserve Hawke's Bay label of Chardonnay, Fumé Blanc, Cabernet Sauvignon and Merlot. Also vineyard-designated Chardonnay from Hawke's Bay, Oyster Bay Chardonnay and Sauvignon Blanc, and Sauvignon Blanc from Marlborough.
summary Delegat's now sources most of its grapes from Hawke's Bay, utilising its own vineyards there and contract growers. The quality of the wines is seldom less than good, with a number of excellent wines, conspicuously the Chardonnay. In July 1999 Delegat's successfully floated a new company, Oyster Bay Marlborough Vineyards Limited, to continue the development of the Oyster Bay label. Delegat's owns 30 per cent of that company.

Oyster Bay Sauvignon Blanc

The first vintage of Oyster Bay Sauvignon Blanc, made from two-year-old vines, had extraordinary success in winning the Marquis de Goulaine Trophy for Best Sauvignon Blanc at the International Wine and Spirit Competition in London in July 1991. It is made in a classic, no-frills, bracingly direct Marlborough style.
▼▼▼▼ **1999** Light to medium yellow-green; the bouquet abounds with rich, tropical fruit, which almost necessarily blurs the needle-sharp focus of the greatest Sauvignon Blancs. There is a similarly abundant level of flavour on the palate, with an appealing range of tropical/melon fruit flavours. **rating:** 89
best drinking 2000–2001 **best vintages** '90, '91, '92, '94, '97, '99 **drink with** Oysters, mussels • $18.50

Oyster Bay Chardonnay

The partner to Oyster Bay Sauvignon Blanc, both so prominently branded and well known that they have secured a life independent of Delegat's. Seventy-five per cent of the wine undergoes barrel-fermentation in new oak and spends six months thereafter on yeast lees. Significantly, none of the wine goes through malolactic fermentation, producing a style which (to my palate, at least) works brilliantly well.
▼▼▼▼ **1999** Light to medium green-yellow; a clean, fresh and lively bouquet with light citrus and nectarine fruit flows logically into a palate with all of the same virtues. Fresh, uncomplicated wine with sensitive oak handling. **rating:** 88
▼▼▼▽ **1998** Medium yellow-green; the bouquet is clean, with relatively restrained fruit and oak. The palate runs along the same tracks, nicely balanced, particularly with the fruit/acid ratio. **rating:** 84
best drinking 2000–2002 **best vintages** '92, '94, '97, '98, '99 **drink with** Sugar-cured tuna • $20

Delegat's Reserve Chardonnay

Made from hand-harvested, estate-grown grapes; 50 per cent is barrel-fermented in a mixture of new and one-year-old French oak barriques, and a sensibly restrained 25 per cent undergoes malolactic fermentation. Consistently one of the highest-rated New Zealand Chardonnays, although in some years I prefer the more direct appeal of the Oyster Bay style.
▼▼▼▼▽ **1998** Medium to full yellow-green; a complex and rich bouquet showing the sophisticated use of oak, with the same impact coming through on the palate. However, there is also plenty of tangy fruit, and good acidity on the finish. Retasted January 2000 with similar notes and points. **rating:** 90
best drinking 1999–2000 **best vintages** '86, '89, '91, '92, '94, '96 **drink with** Smoked salmon • $25

Delegat's Reserve Hawkes Bay Merlot

Previously labelled Proprietor's Reserve and changed to Reserve Hawkes Bay from the 1997 vintage. The wine is made using a variety of pump-over techniques throughout fermentation, and a portion of the ferment is completed in new French oak barriques, followed by the malolactic fermentation. It is matured in 100 per cent French oak and is eggwhite-fined prior to bottling. For around $20 the wine is outstanding value.
▼▼▼▼▽ **1998** Medium to full purple-red; very rich and ripe dark berry, dark chocolate and earth aromas on the bouquet flow into a palate with sweet, dark plum and spice fruit, with lingering, ripe tannins. The oak is present but unobtrusive. **rating:** 92

❦❦❦❦❦ **1997** Medium red-purple; there are quite complex, savoury characters running through the attractive fruit of the bouquet; the wine has good length and structure, with savoury, dark berry fruits and (at least by New Zealand standards) ripe tannins. It is easy to enjoy a wine such as this.   **rating:** 90

best drinking 2002–2010 **best vintages** '86, '89, '91, '92, '94, '96, '97, '98 **drink with** Seared venison   • $20

Delegat's Reserve Cabernet Sauvignon

The wine is made using a variety of pump-over techniques during fermentation, with part completed in new French oak barriques followed by malolactic fermentation. Matured in a mix of new and one-year-old French oak barriques. Eggwhite-fining prior to bottling.

❦❦❦❦❦ **1998** Medium to full red-purple; the bouquet offers a neat marriage between dark berry and chocolate fruit, with some savoury hints on the one hand and sweet oak on the other. A generous, ripe and harmonious palate, with dark berry and dark chocolate fruit flavours sustained by gently spicy oak.   **rating:** 92

best drinking 2002–2007 **best vintages** '91, '94, '98 **drink with** Rare roast beef   • $20

de redcliffe estates   ★★★☆

Lyons Road, Mangatawhiri Valley, Bombay Hills, near Auckland **region** Waikato and Bay of Plenty
phone (09) 302 3325 **fax** (09) 303 3726 **open** 7 days 9.30–5
winemaker Mark Compton, Daryl Solijan **production** 40 000 **est.** 1976
product range ($13–20 R) Mangatawhiri Chardonnay, Estates Chardonnay, Semillon Chardonnay, Hawke's Bay Estates Cabernet Merlot, Hawke's Bay Cabernet Merlot Franc, Marlorough Estates Riesling, Marlborough Estates Sauvignon Blanc, Estates Tawny Port.
summary The Waikato's answer to the Napa Valley, with the $7 million Hotel du Vin, luxury restaurant, wine tours, lectures, the lot; briefly listed on the Stock Exchange but now Japanese-owned. Production continues to increase, and De Redcliffe now has vineyards in both Hawke's Bay and Marlborough. Increasing production has not prevented winemaker Mark Compton from making some very good wines. Exports to the UK, Europe, Hong Kong, China, Japan.

De Redcliffe Marlborough Estates Riesling

Sourced from de Redcliffe's Marlborough vineyard, and agreed on all sides to be the most reliable and best of the De Redcliffe.

❦❦❦❦❦ **1999** Light green-yellow; the fragrant lemon/lime bouquet leads into a lively, crisp palate, with lemony/lime juice flavours and a perfectly balanced finish that is neither sweet nor dry. Marginally unlucky to only receive a silver medal at the Royal Easter Wine Show 2000.   **rating:** 90

best drinking 2000–2005 **best vintages** '91, '92, '94, '99 **drink with** Grilled aubergine   • $15

De Redcliffe Marlborough Estates Sauvignon Blanc

Contains a little under 15 per cent Semillon which is aged in a mix of German and French oak barrels. The Sauvignon Blanc component is slow-fermented in stainless steel at low temperatures.

❦❦❦❦❦ **1999** Light green-yellow; very ripe, full-on tropical fruit, almost into pineapple. The palate is rich and full of tropical/gooseberry fruit; notwithstanding the abundance of flavour, has a bracingly clean finish that pulls the wine back into excellent balance. Gold medal winner Royal Easter Wine Show 2000.   **rating:** 91

best drinking 2000–2001 **best vintages** '99 **drink with** Shellfish   • $15

domaine georges michel   NR

Vintage Lane, RD3, Blenheim **region** Marlborough
phone (03) 572 7230 **fax** (03) 572 7231 **open** By appointment
winemaker Guy Brac de la Pi, John McGinlay **production** NA **est.** 1998
product range ($16–19.50 CD) Sauvignon Blanc, Chardonnay.
summary Domaine Georges Michel is the new incarnation of Merlen Estate. Georges Michel, a French native of the Island of Reunion, has widespread business interests including a Chateau in Beaujolais. Michel has invested several million dollars in upgrading and expanding the winery and in the acquisition of additional vineyards, with the aim of increasing production to 20 000 cases.

Domaine Georges Michel Sauvignon Blanc

Made in the conventional manner, cool-fermented in stainless steel, but the fruit characters add a touch of complexity.

❦❦❦❦ **1999** Light yellow-green; the bouquet is elegant, yet quite complex with almost subliminal spice; the palate moves into riper lime and passionfruit flavours, but without losing that touch of delicacy.   **rating:** 82

best drinking 2000–2001 **drink with** Shellfish   • $16

🐛 dry gully vineyard   NR

Earnscleugh Road, RD1, Alexandra   **region** Otago
phone (03) 449 2030   **fax** (03) 449 2030   **open** By appointment
winemaker Rudi Bauer (Contract)   **production** 150   **est.** 1997
product range ($29 R) Pinot Noir.
summary Sibylla and Bill Moffitt purchased what was then an apricot orchard in the late 1970s. The trees were old and unproductive, so they were removed and a little over 1.5 hectares of pinot noir was planted. The first commercial vintage was 1997, and the wine was rewarded with a gold medal, a dream start for the vineyard. Winemaking by Rudi Bauer at the Central Otago Wine Company no doubt plays its part.

drylands estate winery   ★★★★☆

Hammerichs Road, Rapaura   **region** Marlborough
phone (03) 570 5252   **fax** (03) 570 5272   **open** Mon–Sun 10–5
winemaker Darryl Woolley   **production** NFP   **est.** 1934
product range ($9–35 CD) Under the Selaks Drylands Marlborough label: Riesling, Sauvignon Blanc, Chardonnay; under the Selaks Premium Selection label: Riesling, Sauvignon Blanc, Chardonnay; and under the Selaks Founders Reserve: Sauvignon Blanc, Chardonnay. Also made is a Riesling Gewurztraminer Ice Wine.
summary In 1998 Nobilo acquired Selaks, and in so doing acquired the state-of-the-art winery recently built by Selaks at its Rapaura vineyard. While Selaks has been removed from the name of the Marlborough Estate, production of the Selaks-branded wines continues alongside that of Nobilo.

Drylands Estate Dry Riesling

First made in 1998 from a new vineyard planting, and has performed marvellously well right from the outset.
▼▼▼▼▼ 1999 Light green-yellow; a perfectly balanced and composed wine on both bouquet and on the soft, satin-smooth palate with its citrus flavours. A well-deserved gold medal at the Royal Easter Wine Show 2000.   **rating:** 94
best drinking 2001–2005   **best vintages** '99   **drink with** Asian seafood   • $16.95

Selaks Premium Selection Riesling

Produced from grapes grown on Selaks Matador Vineyard. Typically picked very ripe, with some botrytis, and left with moderately high residual sugar.
▼▼▼▼ 1999 Medium yellow-green; the voluminous bouquet with its tropical lime aromas is virtually repeated on the richly sweet lime/tropical palate; these flavours are neatly balanced by crisp acidity on the finish.   **rating:** 86
best drinking 2000–2005   **best vintages** '98, '99   **drink with** Fresh fruit   • $13.95

Drylands Estate Marlborough Sauvignon Blanc

Made at the Marlborough winery, with the skill accumulated over 20 years of handling the variety. It is one of Selak's flagship wines.
▼▼▼▼ 1999 Light straw-yellow; the bouquet is lively and tangy, with a mix of gooseberry and passionfruit aromas in classic Sauvignon Blanc style. The palate is powerful, with some unexpected dried fruit flavours running through to a back palate which has grip and flavour.   **rating:** 89
best drinking 1999–2000   **best vintages** '97, '98   **drink with** Stir-fried vegetables   • $16.95

dry river   ★★★★★

Puruatanga Road, Martinborough   **region** Wairarapa
phone (06) 306 9388   **fax** (06) 306 9275   **open** Not
winemaker Neil McCallum   **production** 3500   **est.** 1979
product range ($25–40 CD) Craighall Amaranth Riesling, Botrytis Selection Riesling, Chardonnay, Gewurztraminer, Sauvignon Blanc, Pinot Gris, Pinot Noir, Arapoth Amaranth Syrah.
summary Winemaker/owner Neil McCallum is a research scientist with a Doctorate from Oxford University, with winemaking very much a part-time occupation. He has justifiably gained an international reputation for the exceptional quality of his wines, which he jealously guards and protects. Each is made in tiny quantities and sells out immediately on release, but minuscule quantities are now making their way to Australia. Some rate Dry River as New Zealand's best winery, and I'm not sure I would disagree. Limited exports to the UK (London and Edinburgh).

Dry River Craighall Riesling

Produced from the Craighall Vineyard, part-owned by Dry River and in every respect a remarkable wine, year in, year out.

❥❥❥❥❥ **1999** Medium yellow-green; an exceptionally intense and powerful bouquet ranging through lime, toast and a touch of kerosene. The palate is, quite simply, imperious, long and with a near bone-dry finish. **rating:** 94
best drinking 2000–2008 **best vintages** '93, '96, '97, '98, '99 **drink with** Cold smoked salmon •$25

Dry River Marlborough Gewurztraminer
Yet another masterpiece from Neil McCallum. Between 70 and 200 cases are produced each year from the half hectare of estate plantings.
❥❥❥❥❥ **1999** Brilliant green-yellow; the bouquet is intensely aromatic, with spice almost verging on liquorice; the palate is rich, intense and luscious, with perfectly balanced sugar and acid. Takes Gewurztraminer onto another plane. **rating:** 94
best drinking 2000–2006 **best vintages** '92, '94, '96, '98, '99 **drink with** Gently spiced Asian dishes •$30

Dry River Arapoff Amaranth Syrah
First made its appearance in 1997, and then in minuscule quantities. A rare but fascinating wine.
❥❥❥❥❥ **1998** Dark red-purple; the bouquet is packed with dense, dark chocolate fruit with hints of black cherry. The palate is rich, ripe and concentrated, with dark chocolate, black cherry and prune flavours. An extremely interesting, if idiosyncratic, rendition of Shiraz from a freak vintage. **rating:** 93
best drinking 2005–2015 **best vintages** '98 **drink with** Marinated venison •$40

eskdale winegrowers   NR
Main Road, Eskdale **region** Hawke's Bay
phone (06) 836 6302 **open** Mon–Sat 9–5
winemaker Kim Salonius **production** 1500 **est.** 1973
product range ($25 R) Gewurztraminer, Chardonnay, Cabernet Merlot.
summary Having gained winemaking experience at McWilliam's, Canadian-born Kim Salonius and family have established a small 4-hectare estate operation, making wines in very small quantities, sold cellar door, which have gained a strong reputation for consistency of style, the Chardonnay being barrel-aged for two years and bottle-aged for a further three years, the Cabernet Merlot being oak-aged for three years.

esk valley estate   ★★★★☆
745 Main Road, Bay View, Napier **region** Hawke's Bay
phone (06) 836 6411 **fax** (06) 836 6413 **open** 7 days 9–5.30 summer, 9–5 winter
winemaker Gordon Russell **production** 30 000 **est.** 1933
product range ($15.95–75 CD) Black Label Chenin Blanc, Riesling, Chardonnay, Merlot Rosé, Merlot; Reserve Chardonnay, Late Harvest Chenin Blanc, Merlot Malbec Cabernet Sauvignon; also The Terraces, a super-premium single estate vineyard Bordeaux-blend sold by mail order only, when two years old.
summary The little brother in the Villa Maria-Vidal family, but with the ultra-premium The Terraces standing boldly in the top echelon of New Zealand reds and making the winery rating difficult. Which is not to say that some of the other wines in the portfolio aren't impressive; they are. Exports to the UK, Ireland, Canada, Hong Kong, Thailand and Singapore.

Esk Valley Reserve Chenin Blanc
Produced from the stoniest section of the Wicken Vineyard on Omahu Road, was harvested separately and barrel-fermented in a mix of older and new French oak. A specially selected Vouvray yeast was used for fermentation, and the wine left on lees for seven months. A small portion of heavily botrytised wine from a later pick was blended to the finished wine.
❥❥❥❥ **1998** Very good green-yellow; the bouquet is clean and smooth but does not reflect the special care which went into the making of the wine. The palate is very well made, the oak subtle, but if it is ever going to convince, will only do so four or five years down the track. **rating:** 84
best drinking 2004–2010 **best vintages** NA **drink with** Sweetbreads •$20

Esk Valley Reserve Chardonnay
The grapes are sourced from a variety of Hawke's Bay vineyards and a range of clones and soil types. The grapes are whole-bunch pressed and the juice is run to barrel for fermentation after minimal settling. A mix of 60 per cent new and one-year-old French oak barriques are used, and 45 per cent of the wine undergoes malolactic fermentation. Blended after nine months in oak, and bottled in March.

❦❦❦❦ **1998** Medium to full yellow-green; the oak is quite assertive on the bouquet, although some fruit is there. The fruit fights back to a degree on the palate with a mix of melon and cashew malolactic fermentation inputs. I have endeavoured to restrain my personal prejudices allotting points for the wine. **rating:** 89

best drinking 2000–2005 **best vintages** '94, '95, '96, '98 **drink with** Chinese pork with cashew nuts • $28

Esk Valley Chenin Blanc Botrytis Selection 375 ml

Very ripe-picked chenin blanc (38–40 brix), with a strong botrytis infection, is the base; the wine is barrel-fermented at low temperatures and spends 11 months in French oak.

❦❦❦❦ **1998** Light green-yellow; oak dominates the bouquet, despite quite complex fruit with apricot and honey flavours, but the oak is really overdone. A pity. **rating:** 83

best drinking 2001–2004 **best vintages** NA **drink with** Rich fruit tart • $40

Esk Valley Reserve Merlot Malbec Cabernet Sauvignon

A blend of 48 per cent Merlot, 28 per cent Malbec, 16 per cent Cabernet Sauvignon and 8 per cent Cabernet Franc, fermented in open fermenters and then aged in new and one-year-old French oak barriques for 17 months before blending and bottling.

❦❦❦❦❦ **1998** Dense red-purple; a particularly concentrated and powerful bouquet, with dark berry, chocolate and more savoury notes. The wine expands into lusciously sweet fruit on the forepalate before good, ripe tannins frame the finish. **rating:** 95

best drinking 2003–2013 **best vintages** '96, '98 **drink with** Aged beef • $39.95

Esk Valley The Terraces

A blend of 35 per cent Merlot, 45 per cent Malbec and 20 per cent Cabernet Franc drawn from a single small terraced vineyard adjacent to the winery. Originally terraced in the 1940s, it was replanted with the Bordeaux varietal mix in 1988. Its spends 18 months in new French barriques. Made in tiny quantities (as little as 200 cases) and principally sold through cellar door. The Terraces was not made in either 1996 or 1997.

❦❦❦❦❦ **1998** Medium to full purple-red; a very smooth and suave bouquet, concentrated but not flashy, is followed by a palate with rich, ripe, sweet and dense fruit balanced by wholly appropriate tannins. The ultimate fist in the velvet glove. **rating:** 96

best drinking 2004–2015 **best vintages** '95, '98 **drink with** Char-grilled rump • $75

fairhall downs estate ★★★★☆

814 Wrekin Road, RD2, Brancott Valley, Marlborough **region** Marlborough
phone (03) 572 8356 **fax** (03) 572 8357 **open** By appointment
winemaker Ken Small, John Forrest (Contract) **production** 10 000 **est.** 1996
product range ($15.95–24 R) Sauvignon Blanc, Pinot Gris, Chardonnay.
summary Ken Small and Stuart Smith have been grape growers in Marlborough since 1982, supplying Montana and Villa Maria from their 20-hectare vineyard at the top of the Brancott Valley Road. In 1996 they launched their own label, with John Forrest as contract-winemaker and using the Forrest Estate winery facility. Instant success followed, with both the 1996 and 1998 Sauvignon Blancs winning trophies. The wines are exported to Australia, the UK, the US, Canada, Brazil and Hong Kong.

Fairhall Downs Estate Sauvignon Blanc

Draws upon 10 hectares of estate sauvignon blanc and 2.25 hectares of estate semillon; it represents only a small part of the vineyard output. Cold-fermented in stainless steel, the wine has 4–9 per cent (depending on the vintage) Semillon included to add structure. A 20-day spread in harvest dates is also used to maximise fruit complexity.

❦❦❦❦ **1999** Light to medium yellow-green; the bouquet is quite aromatic, with lemony/gooseberry aromas. The palate is very attractive, fruit-sweet rather than sugar-sweet; this is a really pretty wine. Top 100 Sydney International Wine Competition 2000. **rating:** 93

best drinking 2000–2001 **best vintages** '98, '99 **drink with** Tempura • $15.95

Fairhall Downs Estate Chardonnay

Produced from grapes grown at the head of the Brancott Valley, and 20–25 per cent barrel-fermented in American oak, the remainder held in stainless steel and back-blended. A wine which has consistently shown it has the capacity to improve in bottle.

❦❦❦❦ **1999** Light to medium yellow-green; the bouquet offers a range of citrus and cashew aromas in a subtle, elegant mould. The spicy/vanilla American oak does make its presence felt on the palate, but it has length and elegance. Gold medal winner Royal Easter Wine Show 2000. **rating:** 91

best drinking 2000–2003 **best vintages** '97, '99 **drink with** Wok-fried king prawns • $17.95

fairmont estate   NR

Gladstone Road, RD2, Gladstone, Wairarapa **region** Wairarapa
phone (06) 379 8498 **fax** (06) 379 5498 **open** 7 days 9–5
winemaker Jon McNab **production** 2000 **est.** 1996
product range ($10–30 CD) Riesling, Sauvignon Blanc, Chardonnay, Young Vines Pinot Noir, Old Vines Pinot Noir.
summary Jon McNab started his wine career at Martinborough Vineyard 'as a general dogsbody', working for Larry McKenna for two years before taking up an assistant winemaker position in Germany. Thereafter he commuted between Germany and Martinborough Vineyard for several years before coming back to Fairmont Estate and its first on-site vintage in 1997. (The initial vintage was made off site by Chris Lintz at Lintz Estate.) Fairmont is in the Gladstone subregion of Wairarapa, situated on the free-draining alluvial Ruamahanga River terrace.

felton road wines   ★★★★★

Bannockburn, RD, Central Otago **region** Otago
phone (03) 445 0885 **fax** (03) 445 0881 **open** 7 days 11–5 Nov–Apr, Mon–Fri 11–5 May–Oct
winemaker Blair Walter **production** 6500 **est.** 1991
product range ($16.50–38 CD) Dry Riesling, Riesling, Riesling Block 1, Barrel Fermented Chardonnay, Pinot Noir, Pinot Noir Block 3.
summary Overnight Felton Road has become a major player in the Central Otago wine scene. Twelve hectares of vines were established between 1992 and 1994. The grapes from the first two vintages (1995 and 1996) were sold to Gibbston Valley, the first Felton Road wines being produced from the '97 vintage. Winemaker Blair Walter has had an impeccable apprenticeship for making Pinot Noir and Chardonnay, including a lengthy stint at Giesen, followed by Sokol Blosser (Oregon), Tarrawarra (Yarra Valley), Rippon Vineyard (Central Otago) and Domaine de L'Arlot (Nuits St Georges, France). He has designed and built a 200-tonne winery drawing upon this varied yet specialised experience; not surprisingly, Felton Road wines have made a major impact in both New Zealand and Australia with the complex, concentrated Pinot Noir leading the way. Small quantities are already being exported to Australia, the US and the UK.

Felton Road Riesling

Yes, of course, this is the wine with around 25 grams per litre of residual sugar, sweetness which is sustained by the fruit and effortlessly balanced by the acidity.
▼▼▼▼▽ **1999** Light to medium green-yellow; the moderately intense and decidedly firm bouquet has the same mix of mineral and citrus as its sister wine. The intense, lingering Germanic palate has some flesh added by the residual sugar, but the acidity still runs through the long, penetrating finish. Another wine for the cellar. **rating:** 93
best drinking 2003–2013 **best vintages** NA **drink with** Pan-fried scallops • $19.95

Felton Road Dry Riesling

Blair Walter conforms to the New Zealand standards in naming his two Rieslings. Both this and its sister are truly formidable wines, estate-grown on a particularly fine vineyard.
▼▼▼▼▽ **1999** Light green-yellow; the spotlessly clean and firm bouquet offers a mix of mineral and citrus, albeit still in its infancy. The intense, long, clean palate has challenging acidity on the finish, reminiscent of some of the Giesen wines of years gone by. It really isn't made for drinking now. **rating:** 91
best drinking 2005–2015 **best vintages** '99 **drink with** Leave it in the cellar • $19.95

Felton Road Pinot Noir

A wine which immediately shows how much Blair Walter has learned about handling Pinot Noir. Certainly, the vineyard site is a very good one, but — contrary to public belief — Pinot Noir like this does not come off the vines ready for bottling.
▼▼▼▼▼ **1998** Medium red-purple; the bouquet is very stylish, tangy and intense, with a mix of cherry/savoury/sappy aromas. The palate is as stylish as it is seductive, with exceptional tannin structure and subtle oak handling all supporting gorgeous fruit. **rating:** 95
best drinking 2001–2007 **best vintages** '98 **drink with** Jugged hare • $37.95

Felton Road Pinot Noir Block 3

Produced from a small section of the vineyard adjacent to the winery which has consistently provided grapes with that intangible extra degree of quality and flavour. There is no magic in the clone: it is the fairly common 10/5.
▼▼▼▼▼ **1998** Medium to full red-purple; the bouquet is wondrously complex, stylish and savoury, simply offering an extra dimension. The palate has seldom-encountered length and concentration, with a rainbow of sappy/savoury/truffle/plum/spice flavours. Quite simply, world class. **rating:** 97
best drinking 2001–2008 **best vintages** '98 **drink with** Rare breast of squab • $38

fenton twin bays vineyard ★★★★★

56 Korora Road, Oneroa, Waiheke Island **region** Waiheke Island
phone (09) 372 2441 **fax** (09) 372 7037 **open** By appointment
winemaker John Hancock **production** 600 **est.** 1989
product range ($46 CD) Premium label is Fenton Cabernet Merlot; second label is The Red (only produced in lesser vintages).
summary Despite its tiny size (2 hectares) Twin Bays has already made its contribution to the international reputation enjoyed by Waiheke Island, for the 1994 Stonyridge Airfield Cabernet Merlot which won the trophy for Best New Zealand Cabernet Merlot Blend at the Air New Zealand Wine Awards was made from Twin Bays grapes. Since 1998 the wine has been made by John Hancock at Trinity Hills; not surprisingly, the '98 is a wonderful wine.

fiddler's green ★★★☆

Georges Road, Waipara **region** Waipara
phone (03) 314 6979 **fax** (03) 314 6978 **open** Mon–Sat 11.30–5
winemaker Peter Evans (Contract) **production** 2700 **est.** 1994
product range ($15–16 CD) Riesling, Sauvignon Blanc.
summary Fiddler's Green has been established by Christchurch lawyer Barry Johns and his wife Jenny; 30 hectares have been established — 20 hectares of vines (5 hectares each of sauvignon blanc and semillon, 4 hectares each of riesling and pinot noir, and 2 hectares of chardonnay). New Burgundian clones of both chardonnay and pinot noir have been chosen, and the expectation is that Pinot Noir will be the flagship wine.

Fiddler's Green Waipara Riesling

Estate-grown, and conventionally cold-fermented in stainless steel, followed by early bottling.
▼▼▼▼ 1999 Light green-yellow; the bouquet is slightly subdued, but the wine comes into its own on the palate — long, crisp and intense, with a lovely balance of lemon, lime and mineral flavours, finishing dry. **rating:** 89
best drinking 2001–2005 **best vintages** '99 **drink with** Seafood antipasto • $16

🐌 floating mountain NR

418 Omihi Road, Waipara **region** Canterbury
phone (03) 314 6710 **fax** (03) 314 6710 **open** Weekends by appointment
winemaker Mark Rattray **production** 3000 **est.** 1992
product range ($39 R) Pinot Noir.
summary The Maori name for Mount Grey, the peak of which rises above the winter mists, is Maukatere; the English translation of that name is Floating Mountain. It is the poetic new name for the previous prosaically-named Mark Rattray Vineyards.

Floating Mountain Pinot Noir

Everyone seems agreed: this is a Pinot Noir made in utterly heroic style which demands to be cellared. My notes come from the Royal Easter Wine Show 2000, but are utterly consistent with the reviews of others who have tasted the wine outside of the show circuit.
▼▼▼▼ 1998 Dark red-purple; an intense and complex savoury plum bouquet is followed by an equally powerful and complex palate; it is the tannins which, for the time being, tell against it and hold it out of gold medal territory. **rating:** 87
best drinking 2003–2008 **drink with** Leave it in the cellar • $39

forrest estate ★★★★★

Blicks Road, Renwick, Marlborough **region** Marlborough
phone (03) 572 9084 **fax** (03) 572 9084 **open** Mon–Sun 10–5 Sept–May
winemaker John Forrest **production** 20 000 **est.** 1988
product range ($14.95–29.95 R) Marlborough Chardonnay, Sauvignon Blanc, Semillon, Riesling, Gibsons Creek (Cabernet blend), Indian Summer Late Harvest, Botrytis Riesling, Merlot.
summary Former biochemist and genetic engineer John Forrest has had considerable success since his first vintage in 1990, relying initially on purchased grapes but with a 30-hectare vineyard now planted. Wine quality has been exemplary right across the range, perhaps reflecting John Forrest's strong grounding in chemistry. Exports to the US, Australia, the UK, Denmark, The Netherlands, Canada.

Forrest Estate Estate Dry Riesling

First produced in 1990, and for winemaker John Forrest is not only his favourite wine, but the best variety for the region. He also notes he has picked it as early as April 14 and as late as June 14; the Estate Dry is the flagship Riesling from a series of four wines ranging from dry to the very sweet botrytised style.

▼▼▼▼ 1999 Light green-yellow; a clean, crisp chalky/minerally bouquet is not dissimilar to that of a young Clare Valley Riesling. The crisp, firm though not aggressively dry palate has excellent length and is guaranteed to mature with grace. **rating: 88**

best drinking 2003–2010 **best vintages** '90, '91, '92, '99 **drink with** Summer salad • $19

Forrest Estate Gewurztraminer

Leapt to stardom with its initial vintage (1999) with a well deserved trophy and gold medal at the Royal Easter Wine Show 2000.

▼▼▼▼▽ 1999 Bright, light green-yellow; voluminous spice and lychee aromas leap from the glass. The palate faithfully reproduces the fruit character of the bouquet, beautifully balanced, intense and with no hint of the oily phenolics which can so easily disfigure Gewurztraminer. The hint of sweetness adds to, rather than detracts from, the wine. **rating: 93**

best drinking 2000–2004 **best vintages** '99 **drink with** Gently spiced Asian dishes • $20

Forrest Estate Sauvignon Blanc

An interesting wine in which a small or greater portion of Semillon is used in the blend, a small proportion in the cooler years and a higher proportion in the warmer years; overall ranges between 4 per cent and 15 per cent. Part of the wine is taken through malolactic fermentation. John Forrest is forever looking for ways to add weight and complexity to his Sauvignon Blanc, including multiple pickings over varying degrees of ripeness.

▼▼▼▼▽ 1999 Light to medium green-yellow; a complex bouquet with the spread of aroma inputs reflecting the painstaking approach to the making of the wine. The palate is especially long, with flavours running all the way from passionfruit to a hint of vanilla and then to capsicum/herb. So rich it almost gives the impression of sweetness, but the residual sugar is only slightly above threshold at 5.7 grams per litre. **rating: 93**

best drinking 2000–2001 **best vintages** '91, '92, '94, '95, '97, '98, '99 **drink with** Fresh schnapper • $15.95

Forrest Estate Botrytised Semillon Sauvignon Blanc

So far as I can determine, first made in 1999, and then in tiny quantities. A luscious blend of 80 per cent Semillon (the Barossa Valley clone) and 20 per cent Sauvignon Blanc.

▼▼▼▼▽ 1999 Medium yellow-green, showing some development. The bouquet is very rich and full of botrytis character in an apricot/peach spectrum. A voluptuously rich and complex palate is well balanced by a nice twist of acidity on the finish. **rating: 93**

best drinking 2000–2003 **best vintages** '99 **drink with** Poached peaches • $27

Forrest Estate Merlot

Made from hand-picked fruit, with oak nicely restrained and contained.

▼▼▼▼▼ 1998 Medium to full purple-red; a mix of blackberry, dark chocolate, savoury and earthy aromas lead into a lively and intense palate with dark berry fruit predominant; well-balanced acidity and appropriate tannins sustain a long finish. **rating: 94**

best drinking 2001–2006 **best vintages** '98 **drink with** Venison • $25

foxes island wines ★★★★

PO Box 1039, Blenheim **region** Marlborough
phone (03) 578 6221 **fax** (03) 578 4482 **open** 7 days 10–5 at Wairau River Wine Shop
winemaker John Belsham **production** 3000 **est.** 1992
product range ($30–32 CD) Chardonnay, Pinot Noir.
summary Former Hunter's winemaker John Belsham runs Rapaura Vintners contract-winemaking business (formerly Vintech), but since 1992 has made small quantities of wine under the Foxes Island label. He has established 2.5 hectares each of chardonnay and pinot noir, giving the wines an estate base. Exports to Japan and the US.

Foxes Island Chardonnay

John Belsham deliberately adopts a very low profile for Foxes Island, emphasising that his main business is the contract-making of wine for others through Rapaura Vintners (formerly Vintech) and emphatically not Foxes Island.

❦❦❦❦❦ **1998** Light to medium yellow-green; a sophisticated and subtle bouquet with cashew, melon and citrus is followed by a particularly well-focused and balanced palate in which the barrel-ferment and malolactic-ferment inputs have been handled with great finesse. **rating:** 94

best drinking 2000–2003 **best vintages** '94, '96, '97, '98 **drink with** Blanquette of veal • $32

Foxes Island Pinot Noir

A light-bodied style which spends ten months in French oak, 30 per cent new.

❦❦❦❦ **1997** Medium red headed to tawny; a complex bouquet with sappy spicy berry aromas is followed by a palate which does not have a lot of weight, although the sappy flavours and structure will appeal to some. **rating:** 83

best drinking 2000–2002 **best vintages** NA **drink with** Quail • $30

framingham ★★★★

Conders Bend Road, Marlborough **region** Marlborough
phone (03) 572 8884 **fax** (03) 572 9884 **open** 7 days 11–5
winemaker Ant Mackenzie **production** 17 000 **est.** 1982
product range ($15–28 CD) Classic Riesling, Dry Riesling, Noble Selection, Sauvignon Blanc, Chardonnay, Merlot, Méthode Traditionelle.
summary Rex and Paula Brooke-Taylor established their 13-hectare vineyard in 1981, being content to sell the grapes in the intervening years to various makers, most conspicuously Grove Mill and Corbans. Since 1994 a rapidly increasing proportion of their grape production has been vinified under the Framingham label, with exports to Australia, the UK, Denmark, The Netherlands, Ireland, Switzerland, Israel and the US.

Framingham Dry Riesling

The Dry Riesling in fact has over 7 grams per litre of residual sugar, which would exclude it from any Australian dry Riesling class; however, the balance with the acid at a similar level is entirely logical. If you see the Classic Riesling, you will know it is distinctly sweeter.

❦❦❦❦ **1999** Medium green-yellow; the bouquet is clean, firm and solid but has yet to develop aromatics. The palate, likewise, offers a mix of mineral and citrus/lime flavours which are as yet largely bound together. Will richly repay cellaring; the points are given for the wine today, not what it will become tomorrow. **rating:** 84

best drinking 2003–2009 **best vintages** NA **drink with** Asparagus • $17

Framingham Gewurztraminer

1999 is the inaugural vintage for this wine, a particularly successful debut.

❦❦❦❦❦ **1999** Light yellow-green; a fresh and fragrant bouquet with classic spice and lychee aromas leads into a crisp, clean, well-balanced palate with similar flavours; no sign of phenolics, and perfect sugar/acid balance. **rating:** 90

best drinking 2000–2003 **best vintages** '99 **drink with** Light Thai dishes • $16

🦃 fraser river estate NR

280 Earnscleugh Road, Alexandra **region** Otago
phone (03) 449 2690 **fax** (03) 449 2200 **open** Not
winemaker Karen Hitchcock, Shayne Hitchcock **production** 100 **est.** 1997
product range ($20 R) Chardonnay, Cabernet Merlot.
summary Karen and Shayne Hitchcock have established half a hectare of chardonnay and half a hectare of cabernet sauvignon and merlot on a rough, rocky hillside which was covered in thyme before the vines were planted. The northern aspect allows the low-yielding vines to produce fully-ripe grapes.

🦃 french farm vineyards NR

12 Winery Road, French Farm, Akaroa Harbour **region** Canterbury
phone (03) 304 5784 **fax** (03) 304 5785 **open** 7 days 10–5
winemaker Mark Leonard **production** NA **est.** 1998
product range ($18–24 R) Chardonnay, Rosé, Pinot Noir.
summary Has had a short but complicated history, which seems par for the course on the Banks Peninsula. Established as a winery-cum-restaurant, later becoming a restaurant only (leasing out the winery portion) before once again venturing back into winemaking (in 1998) and building an outdoor pizza and barbecue facility for good measure.

French Farm Vineyards Pinot Noir
The first release of Pinot Noir after the resurrection of French Farm as a winery, and an auspicious one at that.
▼▼▼▼ **1999** Medium red-purple; there is attractive, fresh plummy fruit on the bouquet and on the light to medium-bodied palate; made in a clean, unforced style with the plummy fruit supported by subtle oak. **rating:** 85
best drinking 2000–2002 **drink with** Roast turkey • $24

fromm winery ★★★★☆

Godfrey Road, RD2, Blenheim **region** Marlborough
phone (03) 572 9355 **fax** (03) 572 9366 **open** Sat 11–5, summer holidays Tues–Sat 11–5
winemaker Hatsch Kalberer, George Fromm **production** 6000 **est.** 1992
product range ($15–42 R) Released under the La Strada Reserve label are Pinot Noir, Merlot, Syrah, and Malbec; under the La Strada label are Riesling, Riesling Auslese, Chardonnay, Syrah, Pinot Noir and Cabernet Sauvignon; and under Fromm Vineyard label is Marlborough Pinot Noir.
summary Swiss-born and resident George Fromm, wife Ruth, and former Matawhero winemaker Hatsch Kalberer have formed a dynamic team to produce exceptionally full-flavoured wines, with the emphasis on red wines. Fromm has 21 hectares of estate vineyards coming into maturity and, while the emphasis remains on Pinot Noir, produces an utterly eclectic range of wines, with Sangiovese in the pipeline. Exports to Australia, the UK, Hong Kong, Austria and (of course) Switzerland.

fullers NR

86 Candia Road, Swanson, Auckland **region** Auckland Area
phone (09) 833 7026 **fax** (09) 832 1778 **open** Mon–Sat 9–6, Sun 11–6
winemaker Ray Allen **production** 300 **est.** NA
product range ($6–18 CD) Sauvignon Blanc, Cabernet Merlot and a range of sparkling and fortified wines.
summary A west Auckland landmark specialising in functions for up to 240 people at a time, year round, with all of the estate-produced wine sold through this outlet.

gatehouse wines NR

Jowers Road, RD6, Christchurch **region** Canterbury
phone (03) 342 9682 **fax** (03) 342 9682 **open** Mon–Sat 10–5 Nov–Feb, Sat 10–5 Mar–Oct
winemaker Peter Gatehouse **production** 500 **est.** 1989
product range Chardonnay, Gewurztraminer, Riesling, Pinot Noir, Merlot, Cabernet Sauvignon.
summary The Gatehouse family made its first wines in 1989 from estate plantings commenced in the early 1980s. The initial release was under the Makariri label, but subsequent releases have been under the Gatehouse label.

gibbston valley ★★★★★

State Highway 6, Gibbston, RD1, Queenstown **region** Otago
phone (03) 442 6910 **fax** (03) 442 6909 **open** 7 days 10–5.30
winemaker Grant Taylor **production** 15 000 **est.** 1989
product range ($18.50–48 R) Riesling, Gewurztraminer, Central Otago Sauvignon Blanc, Marlborough Sauvignon Blanc, Pinot Gris, Greenstone (unoaked Chardonnay), Chardonnay, Pinot Noir, Gold River (Pinot Noir), Reserve Pinot Noir.
summary A highly professional and attractive winery, restaurant and cellar-door sales facility situated near Queenstown which has been an outstanding success since the day it opened. The rapid expansion of the Central Otago area, and the development of vineyards in a range of meso-climates, has allowed Gibbston Valley to both lift production and simultaneously lift the quality of its wines, and particularly Pinot Noir, to the highest level. The role of winemaker Grant Taylor, a Pinotphile, has also been pivotal. The wines are distributed throughout Australia by Negociants; also exports to the UK and Japan.

Gibbston Valley Central Otago Pinot Gris
The grapes are grown on a number of vineyards in the Central Otago region and are typically hand-picked over a period of two weeks. The wine is fermented in stainless steel at low temperatures, and is deliberately made in an off-dry style, although Gibbston Valley does not specify how much residual sugar is left in the wine.
▼▼▼▼▽ **1999** Light to medium yellow-green; a very perfumed and intense bouquet with lemon, pear and mineral aromas is followed by an equally striking palate with admirable mouthfeel, and sweet apple and spice flavours. The residual sugar is balanced by bracing acidity but is, of course, evident. **rating:** 90
best drinking 2000–2005 **best vintages** '99 **drink with** Salmon risotto • $19

Gibbston Valley Central Otago Chardonnay

Produced from grapes grown at Gibbston Valley, Lowburn, Bannockburn and Wanaka, whole-bunch pressed and then fermented and aged in French oak for ten months with regular lees stirring. One hundred per cent malolactic fermentation.

TTTT 1998 Light to medium yellow-green; the bouquet is clean and fresh, with distinct herb/nettle aromas set against a touch of spicy oak. The palate is fruit-driven, and seems to have a hint of sweetness on the finish, an almost mandatory touch to balance the acidity of just under 10 grams per litre. In theory will age well. **rating: 87**

best drinking 2000–2004 **best vintages** '98 **drink with** Spicy calamari • $25

Gibbston Valley Pinot Noir

The grapes for this wine come from vineyards in the Gibbston, Lowburn, Wanaka and Bannockburn subregions. Each parcel of grapes is kept separate, and after cold maceration for five days, is fermented in open-topped tanks for about seven days, using a combination of yeasts and fermentation techniques, including differing whole-bunch percentages. Fermentation temperatures peaked at 30°C; after pressing, the wine is matured for 11 months in French oak.

TTTTY 1998 Medium purple-red; the bouquet is quite fragrant and complex, showing the sophisticated use of oak. The wine has excellent length and intensity, with a mix of savoury and berry flavours supported by lingering tannins. This is the winemaker leading the Pinot Noir, not vice versa. **rating: 91**

best drinking 2000–2005 **best vintages** '94, '96, '97, '98 **drink with** Spiced quail • $29

Gibbston Valley Home Block Pinot Noir

1998 was the inaugural vintage of this wine, made, as the name suggests, from the pinot noir plantings immediately surrounding the winery.

TTTT 1998 Medium purple-red; the wine has a slightly higher level of charry barrel-ferment oak flavours than does the varietal version; precisely the same balance is struck on the palate, and I would prefer to see less oak and a little more fruit. **rating: 87**

best drinking 2001–2005 **best vintages** '98 **drink with** Saddle of hare • $35

Gibbston Valley Reserve Pinot Noir

Californian-trained winemaker Grant Taylor came to Gibbston Valley in 1993, but returned to Oregon for the 1995 and 1996 vintages, and to Domaine Dujac in Burgundy for the '97 vintage. Two vintages a year working with Pinot Noir attest to Taylor's passion; the Reserve Pinots from Gibbston Valley attest to his skill. They are outstanding wines. The wine spends 11 months in 100 per cent new French oak, but the strength of the fruit is such that the oak plays no more than a support role.

TTTTT 1998 Medium to full purple-red; a complex and fragrant array of plum, spice and savoury aromas lead into a powerful, structured palate, with luscious fruit balanced by lingering tannins and spicy oak. **rating: 96**

best drinking 2000–2008 **best vintages** '96, '97, '98 **drink with** Venison • $48

giesen estate ★★★★★

Burnham School Road, Burnham **region** Canterbury
phone (03) 347 6729 **fax** (03) 347 6450 **open** Mon–Sat 10–5
winemaker Andrew Blake **production** 60 000 **est.** 1981
product range ($11–35 CD) Riesling, Late Harvest Riesling, Reserve Riesling, Marlborough Sauvignon Blanc, Canterbury Burnham School Road Chardonnay, Reserve Chardonnay, Pinot Noir and Reserve Pinot Noir (in each case both from Canterbury and Marlborough); Merlot; Selwyn River Chenin Chardonnay and Pinot Noir.
summary Determination, skill and marketing flair have seen Giesen grow from obscurity to one of the largest family-owned and run wineries in New Zealand. Given the Giesens' Rhine Valley origins it is not surprising that they have done so well with aromatic, non-wooded white wines, but they have also gained acclaim for impressive Chardonnay and Pinot Noir. The ever-increasing production has allowed distribution throughout Europe, the US and Canada, and the Pacific including Australia through Negociants.

Giesen Canterbury Riesling

Sourced from several Canterbury vineyards, and the most widely available Canterbury Riesling in New Zealand. The majority of the juice, with some botrytis influence, is fermented to dryness, while the balance of the blend, using fully botrytised fruit, is fermented to the desired sugar level then blended with the dry portion to produce a final balance of 15 grams per litre and 7.85 titratable acidity. Some winemaking magic at work here.

TTTTT 1999 Light to medium green-yellow; a very intense bouquet with lime juice, apple and apple blossom aromas leads into a similarly intense palate, with fruit flavours tracking the bouquet; excellent length and acid/residual sugar balance. This is an extraordinary bargain. **rating: 94**

best drinking 2000–2005 **best vintages** '99 **drink with** Vegetarian • $14

Giesen Canterbury Riesling Reserve Selection

1998 marked the first release of this wine. Two particularly good batches of grapes were kept separate, and fermented slowly over five weeks to the desired sugar level, followed by time on yeast lees to develop balance and structure.

▼▼▼▼▽ **1998** Striking, glowing green-yellow; the bouquet offers intense lime aromas with fleeting glimpses of spice and honey. The palate has excellent balance, although at this juncture it doesn't have quite the length and authority promised by the bouquet and the colour. There is every likelihood this will come with further time in bottle. **rating:** 91

best drinking 2003–2013 **best vintages** '98 **drink with** Sugar-cured tuna • $21

Giesen Marlborough Sauvignon Blanc

In recent years Giesen has established its own vineyards in Marlborough, and this wine now comes from its Dillon's Point Vineyard. In typical Giesen fashion, it is also fermented dry, using partial skin contact and extended lees contact to add both complexity and balance.

▼▼▼▼▽ **1999** Light green-yellow; the clean and crisp bouquet is quite aromatic, with gentle gooseberry fruit; the palate is very cleverly balanced, with attractive gooseberry fruit, not particularly intense, but what is there is spot on. **rating:** 92

best drinking 2000–2001 **best vintages** '97, '98, '99 **drink with** Full-flavoured Asian seafood • $16

Giesen Canterbury Reserve Chardonnay

Produced from three vineyard sites in Canterbury, most coming from the 15-year-old vines at Burnham. The wine is barrel-fermented in 45 per cent new French oak barriques, the balance in one- to three-year-old barriques, with 75 per cent undergoing malolactic fermentation and lees stirring until blending and bottling in March.

▼▼▼▼ **1998** Medium to full yellow-green; complex barrel-ferment and malolactic-ferment inputs into the cashew-accented bouquet flow through into a soft palate that doesn't appear to have the fruit to adequately carry all the inputs. **rating:** 87

best drinking 2000–2003 **best vintages** '96, '97, '98 **drink with** Crab mornay • $30

Giesen Canterbury/Marlborough School Road Chardonnay

Made from grapes grown on three vineyard sites in Canterbury and Marlborough with approximately 50 per cent from each region. Sixty per cent of the wine is fermented in French oak barriques, and 40 per cent in stainless steel; half is taken through malolactic fermentation. In all, the wine spends eight months in oak with regular yeast lees stirring.

▼▼▼▼▼ **1998** Medium yellow-green; an elegant and quite intense bouquet, with melon, citrus and herb fruit aromas supported by subtle oak. An elegant, refined wine, with beautifully handled acidity contributing to a long, clean and fresh finish. An exceptional bargain. **rating:** 94

best drinking 2000–2005 **best vintages** '98 **drink with** Scampi • $18

Giesen Reserve Marlborough Chardonnay

The grapes are selected from two low-yielding Marlborough vineyards. Approximately 25 per cent is barrel-fermented in new French oak, 25 per cent in one- and two-year-old barriques, with the balance in older oak. Fermentation temperatures are controlled to between 13 and 16°C. Fifty per cent of the blend undergoes malolactic fermentation, and the wine spends 12 months in barrel before selection and bottling. Not made in 1995 or 1996.

▼▼▼▼▼ **1998** Medium yellow-green; a sophisticated and seamless mix of fruit, oak and malolactic influences on the bouquet flow into an impeccably balanced palate; here fig, cashew and a touch of melon provide the flavour. **rating:** 96

best drinking 2000–2005 **best vintages** '94, '97, '98 **drink with** Fresh Tasmanian salmon • $21

Giesen Voyage

A méthode champenoise wine produced from 100 per cent Pinot Noir sourced partly in Canterbury and partly in Marlborough. Seems to have been given an extended period of time on lees.

▼▼▼▼▽ **NV** Medium yellow-green with good mousse; the bouquet is quite rich, with attractive nuances of bread, cake and toffee. The palate is attractive, with distinctly sweet pinot noir fruit followed by a drier finish and good acid balance. **rating:** 91

best drinking Drink now **best vintages** NA **drink with** Aperitif • $21

Giesen Canterbury Pinot Noir Reserve Barrel Selection

Hand-picked, fully destemmed but with a large proportion of whole berries. Eight days pre-fermentation cold maceration in open vats was followed by fermentation peaking at 33°C with hand-plunging three to four times a day. Post-fermentation maceration for two days followed before the wine was pressed and taken to a mix of new and one-year-old French barriques for just over 12 months.

TTTTY 1998 Light to medium red-purple; there is a mix of fragrant savoury, earthy, spicy aromas on the bouquet which are quite delicate. The palate is in similar vein, with spicy cherry fruit and subtle oak. Has elegance; the intensity creeps up on you, and it is very different from the bigger Pinots of 1998. Gold medal winner at the Royal Easter Wine Show 2000. **rating:** 92

best drinking 2000–2003 **best vintages** '94, '96, '98 **drink with** Peking duck • $33

gillan wines ★★★★

454B Rapaura Road, Blenheim, Marlborough **region** Marlborough
phone (03) 572 9979 **fax** (03) 572 9980 **open** 7 days 10.30–5 spring, summer and autumn, and by appointment in winter
winemaker Sam Weaver, Ian Marchant **production** 2500 **est.** 1992
product range ($15.95–27.95 CD) Eastfields Sauvignon Blanc, Single Vineyard Chardonnay, Merlot, Brut Reserve.
summary Gillan Wines is a partnership between English-born Toni and Terry Gillan and local vignerons Hamish and Anne Young. A white, Mediterranean-style wine cellar and restaurant (serving tapas-style food) opened in December 1996. While being Mediterranean in style, architect Neil Charles-Jones believes it is also a building 'which belongs in the Marlborough landscape while quietly alluding to the great Champagne cellars of France'. That is quite an achievement. Exports to the UK and Germany.

gladstone vineyard ★★★★☆

Gladstone Road, RD2, Carterton, Wairarapa **region** Wairarapa
phone (06) 379 8563 **fax** (06) 379 8563 **open** Tues–Sun 11–5
winemaker Christine Kernohan **production** 2000 **est.** 1987
product range ($11–30 CD) Riesling, Sauvignon Blanc, Pinot Gris, Chardonnay, Cabernet Merlot; occasional releases of Reserve Merlot and Late Harvest Riesling. Red Label and Cafe Red are cheaper second labels.
summary Gladstone Vineyard was acquired from founder Dennis Roberts by Christine and David Kernahan in February 1996, with Christine now in charge of winemaking. That the transition has been without pain is handsomely demonstrated by the quality of the Sauvignon Blanc.

Gladstone Riesling

There are no tricks in the winemaking here, simply tank-fermented at low temperatures. The '99 vintage does suggest a slightly slow, attenuated fermentation, however.

TTTY 1999 Light green-yellow; while the primary aromas are of herb and mineral/stone, there is a slightly reductive edge to the bouquet. The palate basically throws the reductive characters away, dry but soft and nicely balanced. **rating:** 83

best drinking 2000–2004 **best vintages** '90, '91, '94 **drink with** Lebanese bread and dips • $17

Gladstone Sauvignon Blanc

Made from estate plantings established in 1984 on an ancient riverbed with sandy clay loam over river gravels. Complex winemaking techniques see part of the wine tank-fermented, part barrel-fermented and taken through malolactic fermentation. Superb Sauvignon Blanc has been produced since 1992. The wine always seems to possess an extra degree of richness, without ever being coarse, phenolic or aggressive.

TTTTT 1999 Pale straw-green; the bouquet immediately tells of the sophisticated winemaking, with both the barrel-ferment and malolactic-ferment inputs evident yet not obtrusive. The palate is almost creamy yet retains the essence of Sauvignon Blanc. It is extremely difficult to attain this point of balance; the wine richly deserved the gold medal it received at the Royal Easter Wine Show 2000. **rating:** 95

best drinking 2000–2002 **best vintages** '92, '94, '97, '99 **drink with** Mussels • $19

Gladstone Pinot Gris

A new wine in the Gladstone portfolio, and on the evidence to date, a worthwhile one.

TTTT 1999 Light straw-green; the bouquet is in typical mode, clean, fresh and basically neutral, with just a hint of that elusive flowery spice varietal character. The palate is particularly well balanced between the textural sweetness of Pinot Gris on the one hand and a nicely crisp finish on the other. You can take it that I abhor the numerous sweet Pinot Gris peddling their wares around New Zealand. **rating:** 88

best drinking 2000–2003 **best vintages** NA **drink with** Fish soup • $20

glenmark wines ★★☆

Mackenzies Road, Waipara **region** Waipara
phone (03) 314 6828 **fax** (03) 314 6828 **open** 7 days 11–5
winemaker Kym Rayner **production** 2000 **est.** 1981
product range ($11–22 CD) Waipara White, Triple Peaks Dry, Triple Peaks Medium, Riesling Dry, Riesling Medium, Weka Plains Riesling, Gewurztraminer, Chardonnay, Waipara Red, Late Harvest Riesling.
summary Much of the wine is sold cellar door, with the Weka Plains Wine Garden offering a full restaurant service and wine by the glass from October through to April. Bookings are essential. Owner John McCaskey has put the property on the market, and it may well be sold by the time you read these words.

glover's vineyard ★★☆

Gardner Valley Road, Upper Moutere **region** Nelson
phone (03) 543 2698 **open** 7 days 10–6
winemaker David Glover **production** 1900 **est.** 1984
product range ($15–34 CD) Sauvignon Blanc, Riesling, Late Harvest Riesling, Nelson Pinot Noir, Moutere Pinot Noir Back Block, Moutere Pinot Noir Front Block, Springgrove Shiraz, Cabernet Sauvignon.
summary David Glover studied winemaking and viticulture at Charles Sturt University in southern New South Wales during a 17-year stay in Australia. He returned with wife Penny to establish their own vineyard in 1984, struggling with birds and other predators before producing their first wines in 1989. The quality of the white wines has been good, although the muscular, brawny Pinot Noir has pleased others more than it has me.

Glover's Moutere Pinot Noir — Front Block

David Glover is utterly unrepentant about his love affair with tannins. In his own words 'grippy tannins are the hallmark of the Glover style'. The Back Block Pinot Noir is fearsome, the Front Block relatively speaking more approachable. It spends one month maceration post-fermentation which explains where the tannins come from.
▼▼▼▽ 1997 Medium red, with a touch of purple; the bouquet is powerful, with abundant, somewhat brawny foresty character. The palate takes up where the bouquet leads off, youthfully raw and very grippy; time alone will tell whether it will loosen its grip before the fruit fades. **rating: 84**
best drinking 2002–2007 **best vintages** NA **drink with** Char-grilled venison • $34

goldwater estate ★★★★★

18 Causeway Road, Putiki Bay, Waiheke Island **region** Waiheke Island
phone (09) 372 7493 **fax** (09) 372 6827 **open** 7 days 11–4 summer while stocks last
winemaker Kim Goldwater, Nicholai St George **production** 26 000 **est.** 1978
product range ($19.95–90 R) Marlborough Roseland Chardonnay, Zel Waiheke Island Chardonnay, Dog Point Marlborough Sauvignon Blanc, Waiheke Island Esslin Merlot, Waiheke Island Cabernet Sauvignon Merlot.
summary Goldwater Estate goes from strength to strength. Having initially forged a reputation for its Waiheke Island Cabernet Merlot Franc, it has built on that with its superb Waiheke Island Esslin Merlot and a range of beautifully crafted wines made from Marlborough grapes, with the limited volume Waiheke Island-sourced Delamore Chardonnay providing additional support. The wines come from 13 precious hectares on Waiheke Island and 35 hectares in Marlborough. The wines are exported to Australia (DWS), the US, the UK, Europe, Brazil, Singapore, Israel and the Philippines.

Goldwater Estate Dog Point Marlborough Sauvignon Blanc

Produced from the 11-hectare Dog Point Vineyard in Marlborough, established by Goldwater Estate some years ago. A luscious and striking wine; Kim Goldwater may be without technical training, but certainly knows how to make wine. A small portion of the wine is barrel-fermented to add complexity.
▼▼▼▼▼ 1999 Light to medium green-yellow; as ever, a beautifully crafted wine, with gentle gooseberry fruit and a bracing touch of mineral to the bouquet. A very stylish and bone-dry palate, with an extra degree of finesse and length. **rating: 94**
best drinking 2000–2003 **best vintages** '96, '98, '99 **drink with** New Zealand whitebait • $20

greenhough vineyard ★★★★

Patons Road, RD1, Richmond, Nelson **region** Nelson
phone (03) 542 3868 **fax** (03) 542 3462 **open** Mon–Sat 10–5 Dec–Mar
winemaker Andrew Greenhough **production** 2000 **est.** 1991
product range ($16–32 CD) Riesling, Sauvignon Blanc, Chardonnay, Pinot Noir, Hope Vineyard Pinot Noir.

summary Yet another name change for what was initially Ranzau, then Pelorus and now Greenhough — the last change a sensible one, dictated by the confusion with the Pelorus Méthode Champenoise of Cloudy Bay. Under whatever name, Andrew Greenhough makes appealing wines, notably the Sauvignon Blanc and Riesling.

Greenhough Vineyard Nelson Riesling

Sophisticated winemaking sees 30 per cent of the grapes destemmed and crushed followed by six hours skin contact, and 70 per cent whole-bunch pressed, followed by the usual ultra-cool fermentation for up to six weeks. In the manner of so many New Zealand Rieslings, has much higher residual sugar than one would expect in Australia, typically between 25 and 30 grams per litre.

▼▼▼▼ 1999 Light green-yellow; a fine, delicate bouquet with tight and crisp lime aromas leads logically into a palate which has good length and balance, retaining the delicacy and finesse of the bouquet. **rating:** 89

best drinking 2002–2007 **best vintages** '93, '94, '99 **drink with** Vegetable terrine • $NA

🏵 greenstone point   NR

Weedons Ross Road, RD 5, Christchurch **region** Canterbury
phone (03) 347 9060 **fax** (03) 347 8225 **open** Not
winemaker Dayne Sherwood **production** NA **est.** 1999
product range ($14–16) Sauvignon Blanc, Chardonnay, Pinot Noir.
summary Greenstone Point owns three vineyards situated in the Rapaura region of the the Wairau Valley in Marlborough. The wine, however, is made by Dayne Sherwood at his Christchurch Winery.

Greenstone Point Marlborough Sauvignon Blanc

Sixty per cent is crushed, 40 per cent whole-bunch pressed, followed by cold-fermentation in stainless steel.

▼▼▼▼ 1999 Light green-yellow; the bouquet is light, very crisp and tending minerally rather than fruity. The palate is spotlessly clean and quite intense; it is feel rather than flavour which gives the wine its impact. Very interesting. **rating:** 86

best drinking 2000–2001 **drink with** Oysters • $14

Greenstone Point Chardonnay

Thirty per cent of the wine is barrel-fermented, the remainder fermented in stainless steel. Thirty-five per cent is taken through malolactic fermentation, and the wine is blended and bottled relatively early in the piece.

▼▼▼▽ 1999 Light green-yellow; the bouquet offers attractive tangy citrussy stone fruit aromas with just a touch of oak. The palate is very herby/citrussy/tangy, the oak once again subtle. Overall, made in a very alternative style which may surprise with time in bottle. **rating:** 84

best drinking 2000–2003 **drink with** Calamari • $16

grove mill   ★★★★☆

Waihopai Valley Road, Marlborough **region** Marlborough
phone (03) 572 8200 **fax** (03) 572 8211 **open** 7 days 11–5
winemaker David Pearce, Sarah Hennessy **production** 60 000 **est.** 1988
product range ($12.95–30 R) Marlborough Sauvignon Blanc, Chardonnay, Riesling and Pinot Noir, Winemakers Reserve Pinot Noir, Merlot; Lansdowne Chardonnay; also lower-priced Sanctuary Sauvignon Blanc, Chardonnay and Pinotage.
summary Has firmly established itself as a producer of wines of consistently high quality in substantial volumes. Its success in wine shows both in New Zealand and elsewhere (particularly Australia) underlines the continuing achievements of the winemaking team headed by David Pearce. The wines are now distributed through New Zealand by Eurowine, Australia by Fesq & Co, and are also found in Hong Kong, the US, Canada, Singapore, Japan, the UK and The Netherlands.

Grove Mill Marlborough Riesling

Made from grapes grown principally on the Framingham vineyard and given top ranking by Michael Cooper (five stars), Keith Stewart (*Fine Wines of New Zealand*), and Bob Campbell (*Wine Annual*). The extraordinary feature of the wine is the way it carries its residual sugar, which typically varies between 18 and 30 grams per litre, almost into spätlese levels, yet always seems balanced.

▼▼▼▼ 1999 Light green-yellow; the bouquet is firm, with quite toasty/minerally fruit, but there is a slightly blurred edge to it. An easy-drinking style on the palate, with the usual skilful use of residual sugar to create a harmonious wine. **rating:** 89

best drinking 2001–2010 **best vintages** '91, '92, '93, '94, '96, '98, '99 **drink with** Salad of snow peas • $17

Grove Mill Sanctuary Riesling

Sanctuary is the lowest price range from Grove Mill and, as this wine demonstrates, can offer exceptional value for money.

▼▼▼▼ 1999 Light green-yellow; the elegant but intense bouquet, redolent of lime juice, is followed by an intense but smooth palate with more of those citrus/lime flavours; excellent balance. A silver medal winner at the Royal Easter Wine Show 2000, and very nearly gold. **rating: 89**

best drinking 2000–2003 **best vintages** '99 **drink with** Lemon chicken • $13

Grove Mill Winemakers Reserve Riesling

Another of the offbeat experimental wines of Grove Mill. Amazingly, the grapes were harvested before any other white varieties came into the winery, yet on the other hand, the wine was the last fermentation to be completed (by filtration) leaving the wine with 24 grams per litre of residual sugar. The resultant alcohol is below 10 degrees and the pH well below 3.

▼▼▼▼♀ 1999 Bright green-yellow; a range of interesting aromas, with touches of spice and high SO_2. The palate is intense, the sweetness balanced by even more powerful acidity. Whatever points are awarded today are superfluous; the success or failure of this wine will be determined in ten years time. **rating: 92**

best drinking 2009–2015 **best vintages** '99 **drink with** Leave it in the cellar • $20

Grove Mill Marlborough Sauvignon Blanc

This is a long way from the straightforward, no-frills, cut-throat Marlborough Sauvignon Blanc style, utilising partial oak ageing, partial malolactic fermentation, some Semillon if the year is right and, generally speaking, a lot of thought. Increasingly recognised as a classic wine, even if very occasionally (as in 1999) it comes back to earth.

▼▼▼▼ 1999 Light green-yellow; the bouquet is clean and crisp, with a mix of mineral, herb and gooseberry aromas. The palate follows precisely down the track of the bouquet, classically flavoured but not particularly intense, particularly when tasted in the context of mid-range Australian Sauvignon Blancs (and also at the Auckland Royal Easter Wine Show 2000). **rating: 85**

best drinking 2000–2001 **best vintages** '92, '94, '96, '97, '98 **drink with** Wairau River trout • $19

Grove Mill Pinot Gris

The wine is cold-fermented at 10°C fermentation taking between three and four weeks. It is then taken through 100 per cent malolactic fermentation to add palate weight, and a hefty 14.5 grams per litre of residual sugar is another way of adding to the palate flavour.

▼▼▼▼ 1999 Medium yellow-green; the bouquet is clean and fresh, with a pleasantly complex mix of citrus and mineral aromas. The full palate is fleshed out by the creamy notes from the malolactic fermentation but, most of all, by an unabashed level of sweetness. Trophy winner Royal Easter Wine Show 2000, but not on my score sheet. **rating: 89**

best drinking 2000–2003 **best vintages** NA **drink with** Blue cheese • $22

Grove Mill Marlborough Chardonnay

A lower-priced version, partially barrel-fermented in French and American oak, and part stainless steel, the wine does not appear to have undergone any malolactic fermentation. Prolonged fermentation for over two months at 12°C was followed by 13 months in French barrels on yeast lees.

▼▼▼▼ 1998 Excellent green-yellow; slightly abrasive/dusty/dirty oak obscures the bouquet, but sweet, peachy fruit takes over on the generously proportioned palate. It is quite possible the off characters of the bouquet were due to cork taint. **rating: 86**

best drinking 2000–2002 **best vintages** NA **drink with** Slow-cooked salmon • $18

Grove Mill Winemakers Reserve Chardonnay

In one of the more Irish marketing manoeuvres, the Winemakers Reserve range are experimental wines and the label is not intended to imply a quality differential. The wines are made irregularly and are not released through national distribution channels, being available by mail order and direct sales only. The grapes for this particular wine were harvested very late at over 25° brix; only 15 per cent of the wine was barrel-fermented, the rest being fermented in stainless steel, and the wine did not undergo malolactic fermentation. I can but plead with New Zealand's winemakers to take note.

▼▼▼▼▼ 1998 Medium green-yellow; the bouquet is much finer and more intense than the varietal Grove Mill, with aromas of melon, fig and citrus and the barest touch of oak. The palate is elegant yet intense, with lovely melon fruit running through to a long finish, the oak being purely incidental. These tasting notes were written before I had any background information on the wine, by the way. **rating: 95**

best drinking 2000–2005 **best vintages** '98 **drink with** Fresh lobster • $22

Grove Mill Marlborough Merlot

Hand-harvested from vines which have been bunch-thinned to one cluster per shoot. Both pre- and post-fermentation maceration and a percentage of barrel-fermentation is employed, followed by 18 months in a mix of French oak barriques from various cooperages and forests.

TTTT 1998 Medium red-purple; the fragrant bouquet shows raspberry/plummy fruit and cedary/vanillin/dusty oak. The palate has the even flow and softness one expects to find in first class Merlot; the vintage has ensured the fruit flavours are ripe. **rating:** 89

best drinking 2001–2005 **best vintages** '98 **drink with** Veal chops • $22

gunn estate   NR

85 Ohiti Road, RD9, Hastings **region** Hawke's Bay
phone (06) 874 3250 **fax** (06) 874 3256 **open** By appointment
winemaker Denis Gunn **production** 2000 **est.** 1994
product range ($18–25 R) With effect from the 1998 vintage, only two wines will be produced, Skeetfield Chardonnay and Woolshed Merlot Cabernet Sauvignon.
summary Denis and Alan Gunn have been contract grape growers since 1982, with 15 hectares of vines providing grapes for many of the best-known names in the Hawke's Bay region. In the interim, Denis Gunn graduated from Roseworthy College, Australia, and became assistant winemaker at Villa Maria in 1993, moving to Kemblefield in 1995, where the 1995 Gunn Estate wines were made. In 1996 production moved to a newly constructed on-site winery.

harrier rise vineyard   ★★★★

748 Waitakere Road, RD1, Kumeu **region** Auckland Area
phone (09) 412 7256 **fax** (09) 412 7256 **open** Weekends 12–6
winemaker Tim Harris **production** 3700 **est.** 1986
product range ($16–20 CD) Kumeu Merlot, Kumeu Cabernet Franc, Uppercase Merlot.
summary The project of Auckland lawyer and wine-writer Tim Harris and wife Alix. The resolution of some complicated vineyard ownership arrangements in 1996 has led to the change of name from Waitakere Road to Harrier Rise, and to the Harrises acquiring full ownership of the 4-hectare Harrier Rise Vineyard, replete with 15-year-old cabernet sauvignon, merlot and cabernet franc. Wine quality is impressive, with ripe flavours and tannins. Exports to Hong Kong.

hawkesbridge wines   ★★★★

Hawkesbury Road, Renwick, Marlborough **region** Marlborough
phone (03) 572 8024 **fax** (03) 572 9489 **open** 7 days 10.30–4.30 Dec–Apr
winemaker Contract **production** 3500 **est.** 1991
product range ($17–28 R) Willowbank Vineyard Sauvignon Blanc, Sophie's Vineyard Chardonnay, Sophie's Vineyard Chardonnay Reserve, Pinot Noir, Cabernet Merlot, Merlot.
summary Hawkesbridge Wines and Estates (to give it its full name) is presently chiefly a contract grape grower, but export demand for its wines is likely to see half the production from its 16 hectares of vines vinified under the Hawkesbridge label. Exports to Australia, Hong Kong, Ireland, The Netherlands and the UK.

Hawkesbridge Willowbank Vineyard Sauvignon Blanc

First made in 1994, and very well received. After an indifferent 1995 — not surprising given the vintage — bounced back with the '96 and '97, but the '99 is the best yet.

TTTTT 1999 Light to medium yellow-green; fragrant, spotlessly clean passionfruit and gooseberry aromas on the bouquet flow into a marvellously bright and fresh palate with utterly seductive fruit, good balance and acidity. Sauvignon Blanc at its simple best. **rating:** 94

best drinking 2000–2001 **best vintages** '94, '96, '97, '99 **drink with** Seafood • $17

Hawkesbridge Sophie's Vineyard Chardonnay

Produced from Mendoza clone chardonnay grapes; the wine spends eight months on lees in used American oak, and undergoes 100 per cent malolactic fermentation.

TTTT 1999 Light to medium yellow-green; the fruit is subdued but quite complex, with some cashew aromas joining subtle oak. Light fruit on the palate is once again complexed by cashew malolactic fermentation flavours, and there is a hint of sweetness on the finish, which actually works quite well. **rating:** 87

best drinking 2000–2002 **best vintages** NA **drink with** Salmon pizza • $19

heron's flight ★★★★☆

Sharp Road, Matakana **region** Northland and Matakana
phone (09) 422 7915 **fax** (09) 422 7915 **open** 7 days 10–6
winemaker David Hoskins **production** 1500 **est.** 1987
product range ($17–50 CD) La Volee (Chardonnay), Barrique Fermented Matakana Chardonnay, La Cerise (Merlot), Sangiovese, Montepulciano, Matakana Cabernet Sauvignon Merlot, Cabernet Merlot.
summary Having established a small vineyard in 1987, David Hoskins and Mary Evans leased the defunct Antipodean Winery which was the scene of so much marketing hype and excitement in the mid-1980s. (The Antipodean has built a new winery since.) The first Heron's Flight wine (a densely coloured and flavoured Cabernet Sauvignon) was produced from the 1991 vintage and was a gold medal winner. The '94 Cabernet Merlot was, if anything, even better, but no wines were made in either 1995 or 1996. In deference to David Hoskins' wishes I have not rated the new releases received as this was going to print.

Heron's Flight Barrique Fermented Matakana Chardonnay

Produced from 100 per cent estate-grown grapes, barrel-fermented in French oak, taken entirely through malolactic fermentation, and given extensive lees contact during 12 months oak maturation.
1998 Bright yellow-green; appealing melon/nectarine/peach fruit leads the bouquet, supported by subtle oak. A rich, ripe mouthfilling wine with lots of glycerol and sweet peachy fruit. The oak is subtle, as is the malolactic fermentation influence.
best drinking 2000–2002 **best vintages** '98 **drink with** Rich pasta • $27

Heron's Flight Montelpulciano

New Zealand's only Sangiovese, matured in new oak for 12 months. In future David Hoskins intends to call the wine Brunello, but I am not sure whether the Italian producers of Brunello will be too pleased about that.
1998 Youthful purple-red; the bouquet is clean, the new oak having been eaten up by the rich, spicy, plummy fruit. The palate is similarly clean but curiously devoid of mid-palate fruit; the tannins on the finish are inevitably obvious, but are ripe, and the acid is balanced. It will be interesting to see whether the mid-palate builds with age as the other limbs of the wine soften.
best drinking 2004–2010 **best vintages** '98 **drink with** Leave it in the cellar • $50

hidden valley vineyard NR

Moiki, RD1, Greytown **region** Wairarapa
phone (06) 306 9287 **fax** (06) 306 8315 **open** By appointment
winemaker James Francis, Clare Kennet **production** NA **est.** 1997
product range ($18–22 R) Semillon, Chardonnay, Shiraz.
summary James Francis and Clare Kennet have established 1 hectare of vines in an out-of-the-way spot near Martinborough, so out of the way that Hidden Valley seemed the logical name. To add further spice, the tiny winery has been constructed out of straw bales.

Hidden Valley Vineyard Semillon

Extends both the viticultural map of Martinborough and the range of wine styles; holds much promise.
▼▼▼▼ **1998** Bright, light green-yellow; the bouquet is clean, with good varietal fruit showing a mix of herbaceous and more citrussy characters. The palate has good flavour, length and acidity, and hence excellent development potential. **rating:** 87
best drinking 2003–2010 **drink with** Vegetable terrine • $19.50

highfield estate ★★★☆

Brookby Road, RD2, Blenheim **region** Marlborough
phone (03) 572 8592 **fax** (03) 572 9257 **open** 7 days 10–5
winemaker Alistair Soper **production** 25 000 **est.** 1990
product range ($13.95–53 CD) Under the Highfield label are Riesling, Sauvignon Blanc, Chardonnay and Merlot; under the premium Elstree range: Vintage Cuvée, Millennium Brut, Riesling, Sauvignon Blanc, Reserve Chardonnay, Optima Chardonnay, Botrytised Semillon Sauvignon Blanc, Pinot Noir and Merlot.
summary Highfield Estate was purchased by an international partnership in late 1991, the English and Japanese limbs of which are associated with the French Champagne house Drappier. The ornate Tuscan-style winery which has since been built is Marlborough's answer to some of the more bizarre edifices of the Napa Valley. Exports to Australia, the UK, Ireland, Japan, the US, South Africa and Canada.

Highfield Estate Marlborough Riesling

Has vacillated between Marlborough and Waipara for its grape source; in 1998 a blend of the two regions, but in 1999 coming back to Marlborough.

▼▼▼♀ **1999** Light green-yellow; the bouquet is light, clean and fresh, with gentle citrus/lime aromas. Contrary to the '98 the palate seems sweeter than is necessary, and without the fruit to justify it. **rating: 82**

best drinking 2000–2003 **best vintages** NA **drink with** Smoked ham hock • $16.50

Highfield Estate Sauvignon Blanc

A wine which has had its ups and downs over the years but had particular success with its '99 vintage winning a gold medal at the 1999 Air New Zealand Wine Awards, the toughest school of all.

▼▼▼▼ **1999** Light yellow-green; the bouquet is moderately intense, with gentle tropical and passionfruit aromas. The palate is similarly light, gentle and pleasant, with soothing passionfruit and gooseberry flavours. To me, lacks intensity for gold medal points. **rating: 88**

best drinking 2000–2001 **best vintages** '99 **drink with** Marinated octopus • $17

Highfield Estate Elstree Reserve Sauvignon Blanc

First introduced in 1997, a year in which it was understandably better than the varietal release. Unless I am much deceived, this is not the case in 1999.

▼▼▼▼ **1999** Light green-yellow; the bouquet is clean, though not aromatic, hinting at concentration to come on the palate. Here, however, the flavours seem slightly diffuse and unfocused, with a grippy, minerally finish. **rating: 86**

best drinking 2000–2001 **best vintages** NA **drink with** Fresh asparagus with hollandaise sauce • $30

Highfield Estate Elstree Millennium Brut

An extremely distinguished wine made from a whole-bunch pressed blend of 50 per cent Pinot Noir and 50 per cent Chardonnay, held on yeast lees for 33 months prior to disgorgement.

▼▼▼▼▼ **NV** Glowing yellow-green; the bouquet has undoubted complexity and concentration, with a powerful mix of bread, citrus and overall autolysis. The palate is no less powerful and intense, with apple cake and citrus flavours braced by good acidity within a convincing structure. **rating: 95**

best drinking 2000–2005 **best vintages** NA **drink with** Seafood antipasto • $37

Highfield Estate Elstree Reserve Pinot Noir

Follows on the heels of a very good inaugural vintage of 1997, and marks another step forward.

▼▼▼▼▼ **1998** Medium to full red-purple; very ripe plummy fruit is supported by neatly balanced and integrated oak on the bouquet. Similarly, rich, ripe plummy fruit is counterbalanced by sweet fruit and oak tannins on the finish; the acidity, too, is spot on. **rating: 94**

best drinking 2000–2005 **best vintages** '97, '98 **drink with** Game • $53

huia ★★★★

Rapaura Road, RD3, Blenheim **region** Marlborough
phone (03) 572 8326 **fax** (03) 572 8331 **open** 7 days 10–4.30
winemaker Claire Allan, Mike Allan **production** 8500 **est.** 1996
product range ($17–30 CD) Gewurztraminer, Riesling, Sauvignon Blanc, Chardonnay, Pinot Gris, Pinot Noir, Marlborough Brut.
summary Owners Claire and Mike Allan bring a wealth of experience to Huia. Both are winemakers and both have had outstanding careers in Marlborough, variously working at Cloudy Bay, Corbans Marlborough, Rapaura Vintners, Lawsons Dry Hills and Vavasour Wines — as well as working an 'extended stage' in Champagne, France. They acquired their vineyard in Rapaura Road in late 1990 and have now planted 12 hectares of vines, with new Dijon (Burgundy) clones of pinot noir and chardonnay which came into full production in 1999. Exports to Australia, the UK, Ireland and the US.

Huia Gewurztraminer

Huia's gewurztraminer vineyard, named Traminer View, is located on the clay run-off of the Wither Hills. The variety and the vineyard are usually very low-yielding, but is sometimes bunch-thinned. Part of the crop is hand-picked and whole-bunch pressed, part machine harvested for a small level of skin contact.

▼▼▼▼ **1999** Light green-yellow; the bouquet is intense, but more towards lime juice than spice or lychee. The palate is also intense, but with touches of spice; the bone-dry finish in a wine in which the 13.5 degrees alcohol shows the no compromise approach. **rating: 86**

best drinking 2000–2004 **best vintages** NA **drink with** Gently-spiced Asian dishes • $20

Huia Sauvignon Blanc

Both the viticultural and winemaking approach for this wine vary from year to year according to the conditions. Typically, the vineyard will be picked at different times according to the state of ripeness of the grapes, part undergoing indigenous yeast fermentation in a large French oak vat, the remainder using cultured yeasts for stainless steel tank fermentation in traditional Marlborough style. The care taken pays substantial dividends.

▼▼▼▼ **1999** Medium yellow-green; the bouquet is clean and tight, with aromas that range all the way from mineral to passionfruit and gooseberry. The palate is similarly powerful and tight, with texture and structure that set the wine apart and turn it into a food style.   **rating:** 88

best drinking 2000–2002 **best vintages** NA **drink with** Shellfish • $18

Huia Chardonnay

1998 marked the first crop from Huia's estate plantings. The major portion is a newly imported Burgundy clone 95, together with lesser amounts of clone 15 and clone 96. The grapes are whole-bunch pressed, with wild yeast fermentation initiated in stainless steel tanks before being transferred to a mix of new and one-year-old French oak puncheons. Malolactic fermentation was allowed to start, but then stopped early to retain natural acidity.

▼▼▼▼▽ **1998** Light green-yellow; a very clean bouquet offers a mix of citrus, herb and mineral, together with just a hint of perfectly integrated oak. The palate is fruit-driven, quite intense, with more of the citrus/melon flavours promised by the bouquet; good length.   **rating:** 91

best drinking 2000–2003 **best vintages** '97, '98 **drink with** Full-flavoured fish • $23

Huia Marlborough Brut

A blend of 56 per cent Chardonnay and 44 per cent Pinot Noir, with the base wines aged in small, old oak and coming from the 1995 and '96 vintages. Spends three years on yeast lees.

▼▼▼▼ **NV** Medium to full yellow; the bouquet is rich and smooth, with sweet, citrus aromas and no aldehydes. The palate is lively and crisp, with lemony/citrussy fruit, and no sign of any oak flavour, which is no doubt what Claire and Mike Allan intended.   **rating:** 85

best drinking 2000–2003 **best vintages** NA **drink with** Shellfish • $NA

hunter's wines   ★★★★★

Rapaura Road, Blenheim **region** Marlborough
phone (03) 572 8489 **fax** (03) 572 8489 **open** 7 days 9.30–4.30
winemaker Gary Duke **production** 40 000 **est.** 1980
product range ($15.95–32 R) Chardonnay, Gewurztraminer, Sauvignon Blanc, Oak Aged Sauvignon Blanc, Riesling, Pinot Noir, Merlot, Cabernet Merlot, Brut, Miru Miru Brut; Spring Creek is a newly introduced second label.
summary Hunter's goes from strength to strength, consistently producing flawless wines with tremendous varietal character. Given the quantity and quality of its production it is a winery of world standing, and certainly among the top dozen in Australasia: it is hard to choose between its long-lived Riesling, Sauvignon Blanc, Oak Aged Sauvignon Blanc (a tour de force) and subtly complex Chardonnay.

Hunter's Riesling

Not a major item in the Hunter's line-up, but an attractive wine, showing typical New Zealand (or, rather, Marlborough) elegance. It ages with grace, showing no tendency to toughen up or coarsen. Part of the grapes, incidentally, are grown by the noted journalist-turned-grape grower Ted Reynolds in the Awatere Valley.

▼▼▼▼▽ **1999** Light to medium green-yellow; delicate, floral apple, lime and citrus aromas introduce a clean, moderately intense and well-balanced wine on the palate which, mercifully, is relatively dry.   **rating:** 90

best drinking 2000–2005 **best vintages** '90, '91, '94, '99 **drink with** Asparagus with hollandaise sauce • $16

Hunter's Gewurztraminer

Sourced from two vineyards harvested at different levels of ripeness, the parcels being fermented and kept separate until blending. The wine is filtered prior to fermentation at low temperatures, and is virtually, though not quite, dry.

▼▼▼▼ **1999** Light green-yellow; the bouquet is clean and crisp, though lacking overt varietal character. The palate is fresh, lively and limey, seemingly showing more riesling than gewurztraminer characters, but at the end of the day, this may broaden its appeal.   **rating:** 86

best drinking 2000–2002 **best vintages** NA **drink with** Chinese • $17

Hunter's Sauvignon Blanc

Unchallenged as one of New Zealand's benchmark Sauvignon Blancs. Drawn from a number of vineyards in the Wairau Valley, each parcel is fermented separately in stainless steel tanks at low temperatures, the fermentation taking four weeks. The blending of the components takes place shortly prior to bottling in mid-year.

▼▼▼▽ **1999** Light green-yellow; the bouquet is bright, fresh and clean, of light to medium intensity, showing a mix of gooseberry, passionfruit and herb. The elegant, flowing palate runs through gooseberry and faintly tropical flavours; stylish and well-balanced. **rating:** 92

best drinking 2000–2001 **best vintages** '88, '89, '91, '92, '94, '96, '99 **drink with** All seafood • $18

Hunter's Oak Aged Sauvignon Blanc

Having decided to put Sauvignon Blanc in oak, Jane Hunter and her winemaking/consulting team have not done anything by half measures. It is barrel-fermented with a substantial percentage of new wood making a pronounced impact on the wine. Whether it is a better wine than the unoaked version really depends on one's personal view of oak and, for that matter, of Sauvignon Blanc. Universally accepted as a five-star/classic wine.

▼▼▼▽ **1998** Medium yellow-green; a typical, complex and powerful bouquet, with tangy lemony aromas woven through the oak. There is plenty of weight and flavour on the palate, with a mix of lemon, gooseberry, capsicum and spicy oak. Impossibly conservative on such matters, I prefer the unoaked style. **rating:** 90

best drinking 2000–2004 **best vintages** '88, '89, '91, '93, '94, '96, '97, '98 **drink with** Grilled spatchcock • $22

Hunter's Winemakers Reserve Sauvignon Blanc

A relatively new arrival on the scene; it is a single vineyard wine picked in a single day, rather than the multi-vineyard, two-week spread for the standard wine. It is also picked much later than the standard wine, although the sugar was no higher.

▼▼▼▼ **1999** Light green-yellow; the bouquet is clean, firm and concentrated, not showy or splashy. The palate has another dimension of concentration and power; classic, restrained fruit definition running through passionfruit and gooseberry to a zesty finish. **rating:** 94

best drinking 2000–2003 **best vintages** '99 **drink with** Seafood antipasto • $25

Hunter's Chardonnay

Just as the Sauvignon Blanc is so often at the head of the field in New Zealand, so is the Chardonnay. After a slight wobble in '93, bounced back with a vengeance in '94, following up with a marvellous '95 in the face of a challenging vintage. The '96 and '97 are in the same class.

▼▼▼▼ **1997** Medium yellow-green; a complex array of aromas, with citrussy fruit neatly combining with touches of cashew and oak on the bouquet; is followed by a tangy, intense and long palate; here grapefruit and citrus flavours are gently supported by spicy oak. **rating:** 94

best drinking 2001–2005 **best vintages** '90, '91, '92, '94, '95, '96, '97 **drink with** Honey prawns • $22

Hunter's Winemakers Reserve Chardonnay

A new development for Hunter's, using a selection of the best grapes available, and given Rolls Royce treatment in the winery.

▼▼▼▼ **1998** Medium yellow-green; while the bouquet is complexed by barrel-fermented and malolactic-ferment inputs, it all works, with lovely cashew aromas. The promise of the bouquet is fulfilled with the beguiling texture of the palate — round, soft and almost silky, with a harmonious blend of fruit, mlf and oak flavours which individually either defy or do not need description. **rating:** 94

best drinking 2000–2003 **best vintages** '98 **drink with** Milk-fed veal • $29.50

Hunter's Brut

A blend of approximately 50 per cent Pinot Noir, 40 per cent Chardonnay and 10 per cent Pinot Meunier (the percentages vary slightly from one year to the next). As with the Miru Miru, no SO_2 is used with the intention of allowing the formation of trace aldehydes, and the wine spends 33 months on yeast lees prior to disgorgement.

▼▼▼▽ **1996** Medium yellow-green; has much fuller bouquet than Miru Miru, rich, with some biscuity/bready characters. While still fine, has richer mouthfeel and weight, with some attractive bready notes. **rating:** 92

best drinking Drink now **best vintages** '96 **drink with** Bluff oysters • $32

Hunter's Miru Miru Marlborough Brut

A blend of approximately 60 per cent Chardonnay and 40 per cent Pinot Noir (the percentages vary fractionally from year to year) fermented in stainless steel and taken through full malolactic fermentation before spending two years on yeast lees prior to disgorgement.

❡❡❡❡ **1997** Light to medium yellow-green; fine, crisp citrus aromas with not a great deal of bready autolysis or other characters to provide complexity. The palate is fine, crisp and tight, with the accent on fruit, and a fairly brisk finish. **rating:** 87

best drinking Drink now **best vintages** NA **drink with** Aperitif • $28

Hunter's Pinot Noir

A wine with quite a long history but which has never hit the heights. Given the sophistication of the winemaking, and the continuing quest for better wine, I can only assume the limitations come from the vineyard, with clonal problems and crop levels the most likely culprits.

❡❡❡❦ **1998** Slightly dull reddish; the bouquet is light, with foresty/savoury/woody aromas; there is rather more cherry and ripe plum fruit on the palate, but once again, the intensity is lacking. **rating:** 84

best drinking 2000–2003 **best vintages** NA **drink with** Saddle of hare • $22

Hunter's Merlot

A blend of 90 per cent Merlot and 10 per cent Cabernet Sauvignon which spends 16 months in a mix of new and used French oak barriques.

❡❡❡❡ **1998** Medium red-purple; the bouquet is clean, with sweet berry fruit and subtle oak; the palate follows down the same path, soft, indeed gentle, with silky, fine tannins and gently savoury fruit. **rating:** 85

best drinking 2000–2004 **best vintages** '98 **drink with** Guinea fowl • $22

huthlee estate   NR

Montana Road, RD5, Hastings, Hawke's Bay **region** Hawke's Bay
phone (06) 879 6234 **fax** (06) 879 6234 **open** Mon–Sat 10–5, Sun 11–4
winemaker Devon Lee **production** 1500 **est.** 1991
product range ($15–30 R) Pinot Gris, Sauvignon Blanc, Rosé, Kaweka Red, Cabernet Franc, Cabernet Sauvignon Merlot, Merlot Cabernet Franc, Cabernet Sauvignon.
summary Devon and Estelle Lee commenced planting their 6-hectare vineyard in 1984 and established an on-site cellar door in 1992. The majority of the grapes are sold to other producers; the best is reserved for their own label.

🐝 hyperion wines   NR

Tongue Farm Road, Matakana, North Auckland **region** Northland and Matakana
phone (09) 422 9375 **fax** (09) 422 9375 **open** Weekends and holidays 10–5
winemaker John Crone **production** 1500 **est.** 1994
product range ($13.50–27 CD) Helios Chardonnay, Selene Chardonnay Pinot Gris, Phoebe Pinot Gris, Eos Pinot Noir, Gaia Merlot, Kronos Cabernet Merlot, Millennios Cabernet Sauvignon.
summary Jill and John Crone were enthusiastic wine drinkers for many years before they began the establishment of Hyperion Wines in 1994 by planting vines on a site near the Providence Vineyard. In 1996 they purchased part of the renowned Antipodean Farm (of the warring Vuletic family). The Crones now live on the vineyard at Matakana. The 1998 Phoebe Pinot Gris has some positive varietal fruit, even if the finish is a little papery.

Hyperion Gaia Merlot

I am not too certain whether the Clare Valley's Jeffrey Grosset will be pleased with the adoption of the Gaia name, but he would surely approve of the wine.

❡❡❡❡❡ **1998** Very good red-purple; rich, sweet red berry fruit has just the faintest touch of forest around the edges; the palate has fine savoury red berry fruit perfectly framed by the silky tannins running through to a long finish. A unanimous gold medal at the Royal Easter Wine Show 2000. **rating:** 96

best drinking 2000–2008 **drink with** Osso bucco • $27

🐝 inverness estate   NR

Ness Valley Road, Clevedon, Manukau City **region** Auckland Area
phone (09) 292 8710 **fax** (09) 292 8714 **open** By appointment
winemaker Anthony Ivicevich **production** 500 **est.** 1993
product range ($18–24 R) Ness Valley Chardonnay, Cabernet Franc, Reserve Cabernet Franc.
summary Yo and John Robinson purchased the 35-hectare property on which Inverness Estate is established in 1993. Situated in the Ness Valley, grape growing is but part of a larger hospitality complex with an Andalusian horse stud and equestrian activities together with native and exotic forests, complete with a stream which meanders through the garden surrounding the house which offers four double rooms, each with an en suite. The 2.8-hectare vineyard is planted to cabernet franc, chardonnay and semillon and the first wines were released in 1999. With the skill of Anthony Ivicevich as contract-winemaker, quality should be assured.

isabel estate ★★★★☆

Hawkesbury Road, Renwick, Marlborough **region** Marlborough
phone (03) 572 8300 **fax** (03) 572 8383 **open** By appointment
winemaker Jeff Sinnott **production** 22 000 **est.** 1982
product range ($18.95–28.95 R) Sauvignon Blanc, Chardonnay, Pinot Noir.
summary The 54-hectare Isabel Estate Vineyard was planted in 1982 and until 1994 was purely and simply a grape growing enterprise (and the largest external supplier to Cloudy Bay). In that time it built up a considerable reputation for the quality of its grapes and in 1994 introduced the Isabel Estate label. It has now taken a further critical step, constructing a 300-tonne winery, which was commissioned for the 1998 vintage, and employing a full-time winemaker, of course. Stage 2 will see the construction of an underground cellar for 500 barrels. The wines are exported to Australia, Canada, Japan, Hong Kong, the US, the UK and The Netherlands.

Isabel Estate Marlborough Sauvignon Blanc

Unusually complex winemaking techniques are used to produce this wine, which is made up of a number of different components. The majority is cold-fermented with a neutral yeast and aged on lees for three months. Fifteen per cent of the wine is fermented in French oak barriques and underwent a partial malolactic fermentation. A small portion was whole-bunch pressed directly to barrel and fermented warm. The finished wine has over 7 grams of acid and very low residual sugar. A classy act.
▼▼▼▼▽ **1999** Medium yellow-green; the fragrant bouquet has abundant tropical, gooseberry and stone fruit aromas which lead into a wine that is full of flavour right through the length of the palate, juicy but not the least heavy. Truly delicious. **rating:** 93
best drinking 2000–2001 **best vintages** '94, '97, '98, '99 **drink with** Sugar-cured tuna • $19

Isabel Estate Marlborough Chardonnay

Thirty per cent of the wine is fermented in new and used French oak barriques, then aged on lees with stirring for 14 months. The balance is cool-fermented in tank, aged on lees, and allowed to go through a natural malolactic fermentation.
▼▼▼▼▽ **1998** Medium yellow-green; the bouquet is quite tight and restrained, with a mix of mineral and more nutty/figgy characters; the palate opens with a creamy texture, the flavours in a nutty/figgy spectrum, a twist of citrus on the finish providing length; restrained oak throughout. **rating:** 90
best drinking 2000–2003 **best vintages** '97, '98 **drink with** Crumbed brains • $25

Isabel Estate Marlborough Pinot Noir

Hand-picked fruit is hand-sorted and destemmed, before being fermented in an open fermenter with hand-plunging and natural (wild) yeast activity. Pressed after dryness, and matured in oak (20 per cent new) for 15 months.
▼▼▼▼▽ **1998** Light to medium red-purple; fresh, savoury, spice, game, forest and plum aromas are all wound up in the bouquet, which leads into a savoury/foresty/plummy palate with fine-grained tannins running through the latter part and into the finish. Stylish, cerebral. **rating:** 91
best drinking 2000–2003 **best vintages** '97, '98 **drink with** Smoked quail • $29

jackson estate ★★★★☆

Jacksons Road, Blenheim **region** Marlborough
phone (03) 572 8287 **fax** (03) 572 9500 **open** At Jackson Estate shop, Blenheim airport 9–7.30 or by appointment
winemaker Martin Shaw (Consultant) **production** 22 000 **est.** 1988
product range ($10.55–29 ML) Riesling, Dry Riesling, Sauvignon Blanc, Chardonnay, Botrytis Riesling, Méthode Traditionelle, Pinot Noir. A top-line maker of Sauvignon Blanc and Chardonnay.
summary Long-term major grape growers John and Warwick Stichbury, with leading viticulturist Richard Bowling in charge, own substantial vineyards in the Marlborough area and have now established their own winery and brand. The wines are exported to Australia, the UK, the US and France.

Jackson Estate Riesling

As with the Sauvignon Blanc, estate-grown (from 4 hectares of vines) and, again as with the Sauvignon Blanc, showing an unusual degree of ripeness and softness. Perhaps some of these fruit characters derive from the fact that the vines are not irrigated, although the impeccable balance with low residual sugar also plays a role.

▼▼▼▼ **1999** Light green-yellow; the aromas are light, first faintly spicy and then with a twist of lemon peel. The palate is crisp and dry, with ripe apple joining the flavour spectrum, and finishing with fairly brisk acidity. **rating:** 88
best drinking 2000–2006 **best vintages** '92, '94, '98, '99 **drink with** Steamed mussels • $15

Jackson Estate Sauvignon Blanc

Produced from 15 hectares of estate plantings established in 1988, and producing the first vintage in 1991. The vines are not irrigated, are hand-pruned and utilise the Scott-Henry trellis. The quality of the fruit is beyond dispute, and the winemaking skills of international flying winemaker Martin Shaw add the final touch. The most striking feature of this wine is that in all except the most extreme years it is perfectly weighted and proportioned.
▼▼▼▼▽ **1999** Very pale green; pungent, lifted gooseberry and more tropical fruit aromas are followed by a powerful, dry palate where a number of fruit flavours manifest themselves, predominantly gooseberry but also a touch of melon. **rating:** 91
best drinking 2000–2001 **best vintages** '91, '92, '93, '94, '97, '99 **drink with** Calamari • $17

Jackson 2000

A single vineyard blend of 60 per cent Pinot Noir and 40 per cent Chardonnay, picked in the cool 'Pinatubo' vintage. The wine was held on yeast lees for five years prior to disgorgement between the end of 1999 and 2000.
▼▼▼▼ **1994** Medium to full yellow-green; a powerful bouquet with a mix of bready yeast-derived characters and dried fruit aromas. The palate again offers these powerful dried apple/pear/citrus fruit flavours before closing with a brisk finish. **rating:** 89
best drinking Drink now **best vintages** '94 **drink with** Parmigiana and nashi pear • $25

Jackson Estate Pinot Noir

A relatively recent arrival on the scene, part of a rush to turn the variety into table (as opposed to sparkling) wine. Open-fermented, hand-plunged and, of course, matured in French oak.
▼▼▼▼ **1998** The colour is deep but slightly dull; the bouquet is primarily in the foresty/savoury spectrum, but there is certainly some plum present. Plum, chocolate, savoury, spicy flavours run along the palate, finishing with slightly dry tannins. **rating:** 85
best drinking 2000–2003 **best vintages** NA **drink with** Mushroom risotto • $19

johanneshof cellars NR

State Highway 1, Koromiko, RD3, Blenheim **region** Marlborough
phone (03) 573 7035 **fax** (03) 573 7034 **open** Tues–Sun 10–4
winemaker Edel Everling, Warwick Foley **production** 2500 **est.** 1991
product range ($15–32 R) Riesling, Gewürztraminer, Sauvignon Blanc, Botrytised Sauvignon Blanc Chardonnay, Müller Thurgau, Emmi Méthode Champenoise, Pinot Noir.
summary Marlborough district winemaker Warwick Foley met his wife-to-be Edel Everling in New Zealand and followed her back to Germany (where her family has a winemaking history) to spend five years studying and working, inter alia at Geisenheim. The couple have returned to New Zealand to make European-style wines in an underground cellar blasted into a hillside between Blenheim and Picton.

Johanneshof Emmi

A méthode champenoise blend of Chardonnay and Pinot Noir given extended yeast lees contact.
▼▼▼▼ **1994** Medium yellow-green; the first impression on the bouquet comes from spicy characters followed by more conventional yeasty/bready notes of medium intensity. The palate is fairly light bodied, but has appealing bready complexity and a delicate finish. **rating:** 87
best drinking Drink now **best vintages** NA **drink with** Aperitif • $32

john mellars of great barrier island NR

Okupu Beach, Great Barrier Island **region** Northland and Matakana
phone (09) 429 0361 **fax** (09) 429 0370 **open** By appointment
winemaker John Mellars **production** 100 **est.** 1990
product range ($35 R) Great Barrier Cabernet.
summary The winery's full name is John Mellars of Great Barrier Island, and indeed the hectare of vines planted on a steep, stony slope facing the nearby sea is the only planting on the island. Output is tiny and likely to remain so, perhaps fortunate given that access to the cellar door is either a ten-minute beach and track walk or by dinghy from a boat. Judging by the newsletter, those who make the effort will be rewarded by a delightfully eccentric and humorous John Mellars in person.

☙ kaikoura wine company ★★★★

State Highway 1, Kaikoura **region** South Island
phone (03) 319 4440 **fax** (03) 319 4441 **open** 7 days 10–5.30
winemaker Mike Just **production** 1650 **est.** 1998
product range ($12–24.95 CD) Reisling, Gewurztraminer, Sauvignon Blanc, Chardonnay (unoaked), Rosé, Pinot Noir, Méthode Champenoise.
summary Conceived and founded by Kaikoura-born Ross Lawson, a direct descendant of Luke and Anne Abraham, the first Europeans to settle at Kaikoura, halfway between Blenheim and Christchurch. The brand new 150-tonne winery, with 5 hectares of surrounding vineyard, is situated on a limestone bluff with views of snow-capped mountain ranges on one side and the Pacific ocean on the other. Its six shareholders are all involved in various aspects of the business, which is buying grapes from Marlborough until its own vineyards and local contract growers fill the breach.

Kaikoura Riesling

Made in what New Zealanders call an off-dry style, in which residual sugar of 12.5 grams per litre is offset against titratable acidity of 7.8 grams per litre. Well done, as in this case, the result is impressive.
▼▼▼▼▽ **1999** Light to medium yellow-green; the bouquet opens quietly, with faintly tropical fruit, a twist of lime, but seemingly lacking intensity. The palate, however, picks up the pace, with an attractive mix of citrus and mineral fruit and impeccable residual sugar/acid balance; a very nice wine in every respect.   **rating:** 93
best drinking 2000–2005 **drink with** Prosciutto and melon   • $15.60

Kaikoura Gewurztraminer

Produced from contract-grown gewurztraminer from Marlborough.
▼▼▼▽ **1998** Medium to full yellow-green; the bouquet is powerful, with spice, ginger and peach aromas which flow into a generously proportioned, quite succulent, palate. The rate of development, however, suggests it should be drunk sooner rather than later.   **rating:** 83
best drinking 2000–2001 **drink with** Singapore noodles   • $17

Kaikoura Sauvignon Blanc

Produced from grapes grown on a number of vineyard sites in Marlborough, cold-fermented in stainless steel and taken through to dryness.
▼▼▼▼▽ **1999** Light green-yellow; the fragrant bouquet is clean, with attractive gooseberry fruit, and it is near-identical gooseberry and passionfruit flavours which come through on the nicely balanced palate; finishes with good acidity.   **rating:** 92
best drinking 2000–2001 **drink with** Poached breast of chicken   • $17.50

☙ kaimira estate winery NR

121 River Terrace Road, RD1, Bridgewater, Nelson **region** Nelson
phone (03) 542 3431 **fax** (03) 542 3431 **open** By appointment
winemaker Jane Cooper **production** 4000 **est.** 1997
product range ($16–18 R) Golden Bay Gewurztraminer, Brightwater Sauvignon Blanc, Golden Bay Chardonnay, Golden Bay Pinot Noir.
summary The husband and wife team of Ian Miller and June Hamilton planted the Kaimira Estate vineyard in 1997 and built a 12 000-case winery in time for the 1999 vintage. Kaimira Estate will act as a contract-winemaker until such time as its own vineyards come into full bearing, and is supplementing its own label production with limited amounts of contract-grown grapes.

kaituna valley ★★★★

230 Kaituna Valley Road, RD2, Christchurch **region** Canterbury
phone (03) 329 0110 **fax** (03) 329 0113 **open** Not
winemaker Grant Whelan, Helen Whelan **production** 1000 **est.** 1993
product range ($17–30 R) Awatere Vineyard Sauvignon Blanc, Pinot Noir.
summary Grant and Helen Whelan bring considerable skills to this tiny venture: Grant Whelan was a tutor in Wine Science and Viticulture at Lincoln University before becoming winemaker for Rossendale Wines in Christchurch, while Helen has a PhD in plant pathology. The vineyard is established on the Banks Peninsula on a north-facing, non-irrigated slope; extensive canopy work paid dramatic dividends with the first vintage (1993), which won the gold medal and trophy for Champion Pinot Noir at the 1995 Liquorland Royal Easter Wine Show.

Kaituna Valley Awatere Vineyard Sauvignon Blanc

Estate-grown on the stony river terraces of the Awatere Valley, with a high-density planting. Ten per cent of the wine was fermented in new oak and aged on yeast lees for three months; the remainder was treated conventionally.

▼▼▼▼ **1999** Medium green-yellow; the bouquet is firm and quite intense, with herb and gooseberry aromas. The impact of the barrel-fermented portion is particularly noticeable on the mid-palate, which has a sweet, fleshy profile. All in all, a very interesting wine. **rating: 88**

best drinking 2000–2001 **best vintages** '99 **drink with** Chinese wantons or dumplings • $17

Kaituna Valley Pinot Noir

The grapes are hand-picked from 20-year-old unirrigated vines planted on basaltic clay soils of a north-facing slope in the Kaituna Valley. Yields are typically very low. Right from the outset, the wine has been of very high quality. A consistent medal winner at the Royal Easter Wine Show.

▼▼▼▼▼ **1998** Medium to full red-purple; sweet, ripe and smooth plummy fruit with an exotic dusting of spice on the bouquet leads into a very good palate, where ripe, plummy fruit is supported by soft, supple tannins on the finish. **rating: 94**

best drinking 2000–2005 **best vintages** '93, '94, '97, '98 **drink with** Grilled spatchcock • $30

kanuka forest wines   NR

Moore Road, Thornton, RD2, Whakatane **region** Waikato and Bay of Plenty
phone (07) 304 9963 **fax** (07) 304 9963 **open** Weekends 10–6, Tues–Fri 3–6
winemaker Tony Hassall **production** 500 **est.** 1992
product range ($12.50–20 CD) Rangitaiki River Sauvignon Blanc, Whale Island Cabernet Sauvignon Merlot.
summary Tony and Julia Hassall commenced the establishment of their 3-hectare vineyard in 1989, offering their first wine for sale at the end of 1994. The winery and vineyard enjoy spectacular views of the eastern Bay of Plenty. It is the eastern Bay of Plenty's only commercial wine producer; the wines are made exclusively from grapes grown at Thornton.

kawarau estate   NR

Cromwell–Wanaka Highway, SH6, Cromwell **region** Otago
phone (03) 445 1315 **fax** (03) 218 7657 **open** By appointment
winemaker Dean Shaw (Contract) **production** 1400 **est.** 1992
product range ($13–28 CD) Sauvignon Blanc, Chardonnay, Reserve Chardonnay, Pinot Noir, Reserve Pinot Noir.
summary Kawarau Estate is owned by four partners: Wendy Hinton and Charles Finney, and Geoff Hinton and Nicola Sharp-Hinton; Geoff is the vineyard manager and Nicola the marketing and sales manager. The 7-hectare Dunstan Vineyard at Lowburn, 10 kilometres north of Cromwell, which is managed according to strict organic principles, has been the principal source of grapes. All of the wines on the 1998 price list have been medal winners at New Zealand wine shows. Exports to Australia and the US.

Kawarau Estate Pinot Noir

Produced from the full organic Bio-Gro™ vineyard of Kawarau Estate. It is the second crop from the vineyard, which is planted to the 10/5 clone.

▼▼▼▽ **1999** Light to medium purple-red; light but sweet cherry aromas lead into a light, cherry-flavoured palate, which does have a little more texture and structure than the colour or the bouquet suggest, but is halfway between a conventional Pinot Noir and a Rosé. **rating: 82**

best drinking 2000–2002 **best vintages** NA **drink with** Guinea fowl • $28

kemblefield estate   ★★★☆

Aorangi Road, RD1, Hastings **region** Hawke's Bay
phone (06) 874 9649 **fax** (06) 874 9457 **open** Mon–Fri 9–5 (all year), weekends 11–3 September to May (rest of year by appointment)
winemaker John Kemble **production** 18 000 **est.** 1993
product range ($15.95–24.95 CD) Gewürztraminer, Sauvignon Blanc, Reserve Sauvignon Blanc, Chardonnay, Cabernet Merlot, Merlot; also Terrace View range of Sauvignon Blanc, Chardonnay and Cabernet Merlot.
summary With 8.6 hectares of sauvignon blanc, 15 hectares of chardonnay, 14.6 hectares of merlot and 8.3 hectares of cabernet sauvignon together with other varieties, lifting the total to 59 hectares, Kemblefield Estate has accelerated out of the blocks since it graduated from grape growing to winemaking in 1994. John Kemble, incidentally, is a graduate of UC Davis, and worked in California for 15 years before moving to Hawke's Bay. Exports to the UK, the US, Switzerland, Sweden, Canada and Germany.

Kemblefield Estate Sauvignon Blanc

The major part is fermented in stainless steel, the lesser portion fermented in French oak and left on lees for five months.

▼▼▼▼ 1998 Medium yellow-green; a complex and tangy bouquet which has life and lift, and is not heavy. The palate is quite long and lively; the oak complements rather than dominates. **rating: 88**

best drinking 2000–2002 **best vintages** NA **drink with** Blue swimmer crab • $20

Kemblefield Estate Terrace View Sauvignon Blanc

Terrace View is Kemblefield's second label; the wine is self-evidently fermented in stainless steel and early-bottled without any pretensions to complexity.

▼▼▼▼ 1999 Medium yellow-green; lifted, light citrus blossom aromas lead into a fresh, crisp and lively palate; high acidity slightly unbalances the finish of a pretty attractive wine. **rating: 85**

best drinking 2000–2001 **best vintages** NA **drink with** Shellfish • $15.95

Kemblefield Estate Chardonnay

Produced from the small-berried Mendoza clone of chardonnay grown near the Tutaekuri River. It is 100 per cent barrel-fermented in French oak, 25 per cent new. Seventy-five per cent undergoes malolactic fermentation, and is kept on lees for nine months prior to bottling, with fortnightly lees stirring.

▼▼▼▼ 1998 Medium yellow-green; the bouquet is complex, with barrel-ferment oak obvious but within bounds; overall, a nice mix of cashew, melon and fig. The palate is relatively restrained and delicate, and nicely balanced. The fruit seems to have been toned down by malolactic fermentation and (possibly) by oxidative juice handling. **rating: 89**

best drinking 2000–2003 **best vintages** NA **drink with** Sautéed veal • $24.95

Kemblefield Estate Terrace View Chardonnay

Terrace View is the second label of Kemblefield, and while made in a distinctively different style, I actually rate it marginally higher.

▼▼▼▼▽ 1998 Light to medium yellow-green; a clean, uncomplicated bouquet with restrained citrus/melon fruit is followed by a lively palate with attractive citrus, yellow peach and passionfruit flavours, all with plenty of length. Little or no oak evident. **rating: 90**

best drinking 2000–2003 **drink with** Mussels in saffron sauce • $16.95

Kemblefield Estate Merlot Cabernet

Typically contains up to 15 per cent of Cabernet Sauvignon and Cabernet Franc, and aged for over 12 months in French oak, mainly used.

▼▼▼▼▽ 1998 Full purple-red; the bouquet exudes lusciously ripe fruit, almost into prune, with dark chocolate and spice also present. The palate is precisely as the bouquet suggests it will be, with cassis, spice and prune flavours supported by ripe tannins. Over the top, but wow. Perhaps the sort of wine which will appeal to Australian palates. Postscript: it did just that at the *Winewise* 2000 Small Winemaker Awards, topping its class. **rating: 92**

best drinking 2003–2008 **best vintages** '98 **drink with** Barbecued venison • $16.95

kenley vineyard   NR

Earnscleugh Road, RD, Alexandra **region** Otago
phone (03) 449 2674 **fax** (03) 440 2064 **open** Not
winemaker Rudi Bauer (Contract) **production** 300 **est.** 1989
product range ($12–20 R) Riesling, Gewurztraminer, Sauvignon Blanc, Pinot Noir.
summary Ken and Bev Boddy have taken the slow boat in establishing their 1-hectare Kenley Vineyard. Ken Boddy became interested in the possibility of growing grapes in the Central Otago region in the mid-1960s during his time as a staff bacteriologist at the Oamaru Hospital. He corresponded with institutions around the world as well as New Zealand's Te Kauwhata Research Station, the latter giving him scant encouragement but eventually supplying him with grape cuttings which formed the nucleus of a back garden nursery vineyard. Another 20 years were to pass before the Boddys acquired their present vineyard site (in 1989), planting half a hectare of pinot noir and half a hectare of gewurztraminer. They have 10 hectares available for planting, and Ken Boddy is currently evaluating the potential for scheurebe and viognier through trial plantings of each. Even after this long time, they appear to be in no great hurry.

kerr farm vineyard   NR

48 Dysart Lane, Kumeu, Auckland **region** Auckland Area
phone (09) 412 7575 **fax** (09) 412 7575 **open** Thurs–Sat 11–6 or by appointment
winemaker Contract **production** 2800 **est.** 1989
product range ($14.95–23 CD) Semillon, Sauvignon Blanc, Chardonnay, Limited Release Kumeu Chardonnay, Pinotage, Cabernet Sauvignon.
summary Jason and Wendy Kerr have established 7.5 hectares of vines on the site of an old Corbans vineyard; their first wines were made in 1995.

kim crawford wines   ★★★★☆

Clifton Road, RD2, Hastings, Hawke's Bay **region** Hawke's Bay
phone (09) 630 6263 **fax** (09) 630 6293 **open** Summer 7 days, Winter Thur–Mon 11–6
winemaker Kim Crawford **production** 22 000 **est.** 1996
product range ($15–40 R) Marlborough Riesling, Marlborough Sauvignon Blanc, Awatere Sauvignon, Marlborough Unoaked Chardonnay, Tietjen Gisborne Chardonnay, Hawke's Bay Reserve Chardonnay, Hawke's Bay Merlot, Taine Hawke's Bay Merlot Cabernet Franc and Wicken Hawke's Bay Cabernet Franc.
summary Kim Crawford first made his reputation as winemaker at Coopers Creek, then as consultant winemaker for a number of vineyards, and now as the producer of a number of very good wines under his own label (as well as wines made for others), sourced from vineyards in Marlborough, Hawke's Bay and Gisborne. Exports to Australia, the UK, the US, Canada and Hong Kong. Wine sales and tastings at Clifton Road, RD2, Hastings, Hawke's Bay.

Kim Crawford Marlborough Sauvignon Blanc

Produced from grapes grown in Marlborough's Awatere Valley, emanating from low-yielding vines. Straightforward cold fermentation in stainless steel and early-bottling followed, the wine quality coming principally from the vineyard selection, and partly from the choice of yeast strain.
▼▼▼▼ 1999 Very pale; the bouquet is pungent, with grassy/herbal notes in traditional style. The palate explores the same crisp, herbal/grass flavours, without any tropical overtones. Crisp, dry finish.   **rating:** 85
best drinking 2000–2001 **best vintages** '97 **drink with** Salmon terrine • $16.95

kingsley estate   NR

PO Box 1100, Hastings **region** Hawke's Bay
phone (025) 454 780 **fax** (08) 326 9463 **open** Not
winemaker Kingsley Tobin **production** 400 **est.** 1991
product range ($29–39 ML) Merlot, Cabernet Sauvignon.
summary Kingsley Tobin has established a 6-hectare vineyard in Gimblett Road with certified Bio-Gro™ status. Most of the grapes are sold; a small portion is made by C J Pask winemaker Kate Radburnd, but Tobin does have plans to establish his own storage facility at the vineyard and to expand production. The very highly rated but tiny production of Merlot and Cabernet Sauvignon is sold by mail order, with a few cases being exported to Boutique Vineyards, Sydney and the US.

🐚 konrad & conrad wines   NR

Waihopai Valley Road, Renwick, Marlborough **region** Marlborough
phone (03) 572 4110 **fax** (03) 572 4113 **open** Not
winemaker Contract **production** NFP **est.** 1999
product range ($17.90–19.90 R) Marlborough Riesling, Sigrun Noble Riesling, Marlborough Sauvignon Blanc.
summary A father and son partnership which has established two vineyards at the extreme upper end of the Waihopai Valley. Twenty hectares have been planted in total, with 10 hectares of sauvignon blanc on each vineyard block, together with 5 hectares of riesling and 5 of pinot noir. Reflecting their Australian domicile, the partners are initially marketing the wines in Australia and overseas, with New Zealand distribution left for the future.

Konrad & Conrad Marlborough Riesling

Produced from hand-picked grapes harvested on April 10; conventionally fermented in stainless steel at low temperatures.
▼▼▼▼ 1999 Light green-yellow; the bouquet is lively and crisp, with quite pungent herb, spice, lime and talc aromas. The palate opens with high acidity then moves into sweet fruit, the reverse of what one often encounters; the sweetness comes from the fruit and not residual sugar, for the wine is dry.   **rating:** 88
best drinking 2000–2005 **drink with** Baby clams • $17.80

Konrad & Conrad Marlborough Sauvignon Blanc
Produced from estate-owned vineyards in the Waihopai and Wairau Valleys.

▼▼▼♀ **1999** Light green-yellow; a minerally bouquet with deliberately subdued fruit aromatics. The palate has nice mouthfeel, but constructed in its own (quasi-European) style. Perhaps I have been hard on it.　**rating:** 82

best drinking 2000–2002　**drink with** Antipasto　• $19.80

Konrad & Conrad Sigrun Noble Riesling (375 ml)
Very late harvested with the picking brix ranging between 27° and 32°. It was left on skins for some time before being pressed, and while this may threaten the long-term life, adds to the immediate flavour.

▼▼▼▼♀ **1999** Light to medium green-yellow; intense varietal lime/apricot aromas on the bouquet lead into a gloriously rich and lingering palate, which has perfect acid/sugar balance.　**rating:** 92

best drinking 2000–2005　**drink with** Poached fruit　• $19.80

koura bay wines　　　NR
7 Nursery Road, Seddon　**region** Marlborough
phone (03) 578 3882　**fax** (03) 578 3771　**open** By appointment
winemaker Simon Waghorn　**production** 2000　**est.** 1992
product range ($14.95–18.95 R) Whalesback Sauvignon Blanc, Mount Fyffe Chardonnay.
summary Geoff and Dianne Smith have established 21 hectares of vineyard; they initially sold their grapes to Nobilo and gained recognition for their quality when the 1996 Nobilo Grand Reserve Marlborough Sauvignon Blanc won a gold medal at the Braggato Awards (the medal went to the vineyard, not the winery). This no doubt prompted the Smiths to have part of their production vinified for sale under the Koura Bay label; since 1998 Whitehaven Wines has fulfilled that task. Exports to Australia, Ireland and the UK.

Koura Bay Wines Whalesback Sauvignon Blanc
Koura is a Maori word for crayfish, and the vineyard is on the banks of the Awatere River, which does not number whales among its population, nor even crayfish. Name quibbles to one side, Koura Bay produces classy Sauvignon Blanc.

▼▼▼▼ **1999** Light green-yellow; the bouquet is firm and crisp, with a mix of herbal/nettle aromas. The palate virtually replicates the bouquet, clean and crisp, again showing herbal/nettle flavours before a nice, fresh finish.　**rating:** 86

best drinking 2000–2001　**best vintages** NA　**drink with** Lightly poached oysters　• $18.95

Koura Bay Mount Fyffe Chardonnay
The grapes are machine harvested and lightly pressed without intervening skin contact. The greater portion is barrel-fermented in a mix of new and predominantly older oak, the balance in stainless steel. Sixty per cent is taken through malolactic fermentation.

▼▼▼▼ **1998** Light green-yellow; the bouquet offers quite attractive citrus/melon fruit, slightly simple but nonetheless appealing. The palate offers nicely handled fruit flavours, with well-judged creamy cashew mlf on a light-bodied wine.　**rating:** 87

best drinking 2000–2002　**best vintages** NA　**drink with** Stir-fried prawns　• $18.95

kumeu river wines　　　★★★★★
550 Highway 16, Kumeu　**region** Auckland Area
phone (09) 412 8415　**fax** (09) 412 7627　**open** Mon–Fri 9–5.30, Sat 11–5.30
winemaker Michael Brajkovich　**production** 20 000　**est.** 1944
product range ($14–33 CD) At the top end come the limited production Maté Vineyard Chardonnay; then follow the Kumeu River range of Chardonnay and Merlot Cabernet; the less expensive wines come under the Brajkovich Signature range, with Chardonnay, Cabernet Merlot, Merlot Malbec Cabernet Franc and Cabernet Franc.
summary The wines of Michael Brajkovich defy conventional classification, simply because the highly trained, highly skilled and highly intelligent Brajkovich does not observe convention in crafting them, preferring instead to follow his own French-influenced instincts and preferences. The wines enjoy strong export markets in the US, the UK, Hong Kong, Singapore, Belgium, Denmark, Taiwan, Switzerland and Australia.

Kumeu River Pinot Gris
Once again, the viticultural and winemaking skills of Michael Brajkovich are impressively displayed, because the Auckland region has no business producing a Pinot Gris of this quality. First produced in 1998.

TTTTY **1999** Light green-yellow; the bouquet is spotlessly clean with very good varietal fruit definition accompanied by the slightly steely chalky edge of gris. The palate is truly excellent, with faint citrus and spice flavours in a wine of outstanding balance and rounded mouthfeel which avoids going over the edge into oily territory. **rating:** 90

best drinking 2000–2003 **best vintages** '99 **drink with** Rich fish dishes • $22

Kumeu River Melba

A new super-premium release to go alongside Maté's Vineyard Chardonnay. It is a blend of Merlot, Malbec and Cabernet Franc, all grown on the estate vineyards.

TTTT **1998** Medium red-purple; the bouquet has a mix of savoury/cedary aromas with some degree of lift. The palate features a raft of secondary flavours, all more or less savoury, and way outside the mainstream. Not an easy wine to rate, so different is it. **rating:** 85

best drinking 2001–2008 **best vintages** NA **drink with** Veal with rosemary • $27

lake chalice wines ★★★★

Vintage Lane (Box 66), Renwick **region** Marlborough
phone (03) 572 9327 **fax** (03) 572 9327 **open** Mon–Sat 10.30–4.30
winemaker Matt Thomson, Chris Gambitsis **production** 6000 **est.** 1989
product range ($15.95–27.95 R) The Black Label range of Marlborough Riesling, Marlborough Sauvignon Blanc, Oak Aged Sauvignon Blanc, Marlborough Chardonnay, Marlborough Botrytised Riesling; and the Platinum range of Chardonnay, Merlot and Cabernet Sauvignon.
summary Lake Chalice Wines is a partnership of three long-time friends, Chris Gambitsis, Ron Wichman and Phil Binnie. In 1989 they purchased the 11.5-hectare Falcon Vineyard; the name of the winery comes from a wilderness lake situated in the Richmond Range, which borders the northern side of Marlborough's Wairau Plain. The first wine release was in 1993; the first red wine was released in 1997. Exports to Australia and the US.

Lake Chalice Marlborough Botrytised Riesling 375 ml

Picked on April 24 at 40 brix and grown on the Falcon Vineyard. After fermentation the wines was matured in used French oak for three months, for what precise reason I do not know, although it certainly did not harm the wine.

TTTTT **1999** Glowing yellow-green; the bouquet exudes intense botrytis but has retained great varietal character, with strong lime juice in Germanic mode. The palate lives up to the promise of the bouquet, long and clean, with a pure essence of sweet lime and apricot flavours. Impeccable acid balance rounds the wine off. If this wine were indeed from Germany it would cost many times the price. **rating:** 95

best drinking 2000–2010 **best vintages** '99 **drink with** Or without, it really doesn't matter • $19.95

Lake Chalice Platinum Cabernet Sauvignon

1998 was the debut vintage for this wine; it may be a while before a better wine comes along.

TTTY **1998** Medium red-purple; the bouquet is clean, with earthy cabernet fruit, not as luscious as some of the wines from this vintage, but there is more red berry fruit, allied with a touch of chocolate and charry oak, on the palate. The tannins are a fraction dry, but should soften with bottle age. **rating:** 84

best drinking 2002–2007 **best vintages** '98 **drink with** Roast beef • $23.95

🦢 landmark estate wines NR

132 Bruce McLaren Road, Henderson, Auckland **region** Auckland Area
phone (09) 838 8459 **fax** (09) 837 4939 **open** Not
winemaker Zlatomir Vitasovich **production** NA **est.** 1937
product range ($12–30 R) Headed by the infrequently released Earls label; then Landmark Estate ($11–17) with Chardonnay and Gewurztraminer from Gisborne, Sauvignon Blanc, Chenin Blanc and Cabernet Sauvignon from Hawke's Bay; the Albatross Point label ($11–14) comes at the bottom of the pyramid with a series of blended and varietal wines.
summary One of the long-established Auckland wineries which has moved with the times and now sources almost all of its grapes from Gisborne and Hawke's Bay.

Landmark Estate Hawke's Bay Cabernet Sauvignon

A nicely made wine with restrained oak allowing the varietal fruit (and the vintage) to express itself.

TTTT **1998** Medium to full red-purple; a solid bouquet, with moderately sweet fruit and quite pronounced dark chocolate aromas is followed by a medium-bodied, smooth palate with gently sweet cassis fruit, rounded off with subtle oak. **rating:** 85

best drinking 2003–2008 **drink with** Steak and kidney pie • $17

langdale estate NR

Langdale Road, West Melton, Christchurch **region** Canterbury
phone (03) 342 6266 **fax** (03) 342 4059 **open** Tues–Thur 11–5, Fri–Sat 11–late, Sun 11–6
winemaker Carol Bunn **production** 3000 **est.** 1989
product range ($12.95–31.95 R) Riesling, Marlborough Sauvignon Blanc, Pinot Gris, Chardonnay, Breidecker, Pinot Noir, Melton Hills Pinot Noir.
summary Based upon 4.5 hectares of estate vineyards planted to pinot noir, riesling, breidecker and pinot gris, with plantings commencing in 1989 and expanded since. Most of the wine is sold through the cellar door and restaurant and wedding function centre on site.

Langdale Estate Sauvignon Blanc
Produced not from Canterbury-region grapes, but from Marlborough. Competently made in a no-frills fashion.
▼▼▼▽ **1999** Medium yellow-green; the bouquet is moderately intense, with soft gooseberry fruit aromas which translate directly into the attractive palate with moderately ripe tropical/gooseberry fruit.   **rating:** 84
best drinking 2000–2001 **best vintages** NA **drink with** Stir-fried chicken and snow peas •$15.95

larcomb vineyard ★★★☆

Larcombs Road, RD5, Christchurch **region** Canterbury
phone (03) 347 8909 **open** Tues–Sun 11–5 Nov–March, Fri–Sun 11–5 Apr–Oct
winemaker Alan McCorkindale **production** 1300 **est.** 1985
product range ($14–19 CD) Riesling, Breidecker, Gewurztraminer, Pinot Gris, Chardonnay, Pinot Noir.
summary Following its acquisition by Michelle and Warren Barnes in 1995, the winery has apparently obtained a reputation for itself as 'home of Rattle the Rafters Barn Dance', which — if nothing else — is something different.

lawson's dry hills ★★★★★

Alabama Road, Blenheim **region** Marlborough
phone (03) 578 7674 **fax** (03) 578 7603 **open** 7 days 10–5
winemaker Mike Just **production** 25 000 **est.** 1992
product range ($17–24 R) Gewurztraminer, Sauvignon Blanc, Chardonnay, Riesling, Late Harvest Riesling, Pinot Noir.
summary Lawson's Dry Hills is situated on the Wither Hills, which in turn take their name from their parched midsummer look. It is part-owned by Barbara and Ross Lawson, recently joined by three shareholders who have contributed vineyards, giving a total of 22 hectares. The partners have all graduated from being grape growers to winemakers with conspicuous success, and production is steadily rising. Exports to Australia, the UK, the US, Brazil, The Netherlands, Italy, Ireland, France, Denmark, Switzerland, Singapore and Hong Kong.

Lawson's Dry Hills Riesling
Produced from grapes grown in the Hutchison Vineyard in the Wairau Valley.
▼▼▼▼▽ **1998** Medium green-yellow; intense, flowery lime/lemon/citrus aromas lead into a richly flavoured and structured palate, again with abundant flavour, and with a neat juxtaposition of a flick of residual sugar with crisp acidity. Has very good mouthfeel.   **rating:** 90
best drinking 2000–2005 **best vintages** '94, '98 **drink with** Asparagus with hollandaise sauce •$17

Lawson's Dry Hills Sauvignon Blanc
Another classic Marlborough wine made with skill and discipline. A portion of the wine is fermented in French oak barriques and undergoes malolactic fermentation and is then back-blended with the major component, which is conventionally fermented in stainless steel. The 1999 ignited the landscape in much the same way as the 1998 Wither Hills Pinot Noir, sweeping all other Sauvignon Blancs before it at the 1999 Air New Zealand Wine Awards and elsewhere.
▼▼▼▼▼ **1999** Light green-yellow; an explosively aromatic bouquet with waves of passionfruit and gooseberry leads into a wonderfully vibrant palate with no less intense passionfruit and gooseberry flavours, finishing with lilting acidity. Vinous poetry indeed.   **rating:** 97
best drinking 2000–2001 **best vintages** '94, '97, '99 **drink with** Crayfish •$17

leaning rock vineyard   NR

Hillview Road, Alexandra **region** Otago
phone (03) 448 9169 **fax** (03) 448 9169 **open** By appointment
winemaker Mark Hesson, Dhana Pillai **production** 1200 **est.** 1991
product range ($18–28 CD) Riesling, Gewurztraminer, Chardonnay, Pinot Noir.
summary Notwithstanding bare gravel soils and a northerly slope, spring frosts proved a major problem for geologist owners Mark Hesson and Dhana Pillai, curtailing production until sprinklers were installed prior to the 1996 growing season. Small quantities of strongly flavoured wines were then produced, with gradually increasing quantities (particularly Pinot Noir) expected over coming vintages.

Leaning Rock Vineyard Riesling
Estate-grown and produced in small quantities; made in an off-dry style which seems to suit the high acidity of the Otago region.
▼▼▼▼ **1999** Light green-yellow; the bouquet is crisp, lively and minerally, the palate likewise but with some citrus elements on the mid to back palate, finishing with some emphasis.   **rating:** 84
best drinking 2000–2005 **best vintages** NA **drink with** Fish soup •$18

Leaning Rock Vineyard Pinot Noir
Estate-grown and made in micro quantities, but nonetheless gained headlines when its 1997 vintage won a gold medal at the Air New Zealand Wine Awards in 1998. The 1998 vintage is a worthy follow-up.
▼▼▼▼ **1998** Medium red, with just a touch of purple; the sweet cherry fruit of the bouquet has slightly gamey overtones which the elegant, medium-bodied palate offsets by cherry fruit with savoury nuances, finishing with long, fine tannins.   **rating:** 87
best drinking 2001–2005 **best vintages** '97, '98 **drink with** Braised duck Chinese style •$28

limeburners bay   NR

112 Hobsonville Road, Hobsonville **region** Auckland Area
phone (09) 416 8844 **open** Mon–Sat 9–6
winemaker Alan Laurenson **production** 3500 **est.** 1978
product range ($7–19.95 CD) Müller Thurgau, Semillon Chardonnay, Sauvignon Blanc, Chardonnay, Cabernet Merlot, Cabernet Sauvignon.
summary Initially established a reputation for itself in the 1980s with some good Cabernet Sauvignon, but with more variable outcomes in the 1990s. No recent tastings.

lincoln vineyards   ★★☆

130 Lincoln Road, Henderson **region** Auckland Area
phone (09) 838 6944 **fax** (09) 838 6984 **open** Mon–Fri 9–5.30, weekends 10–6
winemaker Joseph Papesch **production** 35 000 **est.** 1937
product range ($9.50–57 CD) Chardonnay (under a series of labels, including Vintage Selection, Gisborne, Show Reserve and Parklands Vineyard), Sauvignon Blanc, Chenin Blanc, Riesling, Müller Thurgau, Cabernet Sauvignon, Merlot. Presidents Selection is newly introduced flagship.
summary A substantial family-owned operation drawing its grapes from Auckland, Gisborne and Hawke's Bay. The labels are avant-garde, but the wines have been variable, good at best but sometimes disappointing, even if the prices are competitive. Exports to the UK, Australia, the Pacific Islands, Japan and Canada.

linden estate   NR

Napier–Taupo Road, SH5, Eskdale **region** Hawke's Bay
phone (06) 836 6806 **fax** (06) 836 6586 **open** 7 days 10–5
winemaker Nick Chan **production** 12 000 **est.** 1971
product range ($15–32 R) Sauvignon Blanc, Chardonnay Esk Valley, Reserve Chardonnay, Merlot Esk Valley, Cabernet Esk Valley.
summary This is the project of retired civil engineer and long-term grape grower Wim van der Linden and family, son John being a tutor in viticulture at the Polytechnic in Hawke's Bay. The estate vineyard was replanted in 1989 to 25 hectares of premium varieties, including a 2.5-hectare hillside planting producing a Reserve wine first released in 1996. The wines are distributed in New Zealand (Eurowine), Denmark, Canada, and the US.

Linden Estate Esk Valley Merlot

The use of the name Esk Valley is not as provocative as might appear at first sight, for this is precisely where the vineyard is situated.

TTTT 1998 Medium red-purple; the bouquet is complex, with a mix of ripe plum, dark berry and spice aromas. The palate has very good weight and feel, with a mix of savoury dark berry and cedar flavours, finishing with fine tannins. A prime example of Merlot in varietal mode. **rating:** 88

best drinking 2001–2006 **best vintages** '88 **drink with** Roast veal • $18

lintz estate   NR

Kitchener Street, Martinborough **region** Wairarapa
phone (06) 306 9174 **fax** (06) 306 9175 **open** By appointment while stocks last
winemaker Chris Lintz **production** 5800 **est.** 1989
product range ($20–65 CD) Chardonnay Barrique, Sauvignon Blanc, Riesling, Gewurztraminer, Sauvignon Blanc Barrique, Auxerrois, Saint Anthony, Pinot Noir #1, Pinot Noir #2, Moy Hall Pinot Noir, Cabernet Merlot, Cabernet Merlot #1, Franc Merlot, Renaissance, Chardonnay Late Harvest, Riesling Late Harvest, Optima Noble Selection.
summary New Zealand-born Chris Lintz comes from a German winemaking family and graduated from Geisenheim. The first stage of the Lintz winery, drawing grapes from the 9-hectare vineyard, was completed in 1991. Since 1996 Lintz Estate has enjoyed much show success, winning numerous gold medals across the full range of wines, both white and red, success which briefly underpinned a public issue of shares in 1998.

lombardi wines   NR

298 Te Mata Road, Havelock North **region** Hawke's Bay
phone (06) 877 7985 **fax** (06) 877 7816 **open** 7 days 10–5
winemaker Tracy Haslam **production** 1000 **est.** 1948
product range ($13.95–28 CD) Chardonnay, Barrel Fermented Sauvignon Blanc, Reserve Merlot Cabernet, Cabernet Sauvignon, Dessert Cabernet.
summary The Australian Riverland transported to the unlikely environment of Hawke's Bay, with a half-Italian, half-English family concentrating on a kaleidoscopic array of Vermouths and sweet, flavoured fortified wines. A change of ownership at the end of 1994 has not signalled any fundamental change in direction — except for a desire to have fun while making better wines.

longbush wines   NR

State Highway 2, Manutuke, Gisborne **region** Gisborne
phone (06) 862 8577 **fax** (06) 867 8012 **open** Tues–Sun 10–5 Oct–Easter
winemaker John Thorpe **production** 15 000 **est.** 1992
product range ($11.95–25 R) Woodlands Chardonnay; the Longbush range of Rhine Riesling, Chardonnay, Sauvignon Blanc, Botrytis Riesling, Pinot Noir, Merlot, Kahurangi; Nicks Head Sauvignon Blanc, Muller Muscat, Sea Breeze Classic Dry, Chardonnay, and Merlot.
summary Part of the ever-changing circus of winemaking and brand ventures of the Thorpe Brothers Group. Woodlands is the premium label; Longbush the principal (and mid-range) label; Nicks Head is the third and lowest priced.

longridge wines   ★★★★☆

91 Thames Street, Napier **region** Hawke's Bay
phone (06) 835 4333 **fax** (06) 835 9791 **open** Not
winemaker Kirsty Walton **production** NA **est.** 1944
product range ($12–13 R) Gewurztraminer, Sauvignon Blanc, Chardonnay and Merlot Cabernet.
summary Longridge Wines is the Hawke's Bay brand of Corbans, with its own distinct identity and price point, with all of the products line-priced.

Longridge Hawke's Bay Chardonnay

Sourced from vineyards in the Omaranui district; it spends six months in a mix of new and used American oak barrels, and is a soft, easy-drinking style.

TTTT 1998 Medium yellow-green; melon/cashew fruit is supported by a hint of spicy oak on the bouquet; the wine is gentle, round and soft in the mouth with supple melon/cashew flavour. As honest as they come. **rating:** 87

best drinking 2000–2001 **best vintages** '83, '89, '90, '91, '94, '98 **drink with** Takeaway • $13

longview estate NR

State Highway 1, Whangarei **region** Northland and Matakana
phone (09) 438 7227 **fax** (09) 438 7224 **open** Summer Mon–Sat 8.30–6; winter Sat 8.30–5.30, Sun 9–5
winemaker Mario Vuletich **production** 2800 **est.** 1969
product range ($12–27 CD) Unwooded Chardonnay, Barrique Chardonnay, Reserve Chardonnay, Gewurztraminer, Northern White, White Diamond, Scarecrow Cabernet Sauvignon, Mario's Merlot, Hawke's Bay Merlot, Gumdigger's Port, Golden Sherry, Dry Sherry.
summary Mario and Barbara Vuletich have been involved in viticulture and winemaking since 1969; they have replanted the 6-hectare vineyard on elevated slopes overlooking Whangarei harbour with the four principal Bordeaux varieties (and shiraz) with the intention of making full-bodied dry reds. That they have succeeded handsomely in so doing is evident by the fact that both the Cabernet Sauvignon and the Merlot have received four stars in *Cuisine* magazine for the '93, '94 and '96 vintages.

loopline vineyard NR

Loopline Road, RD1, Masterton **region** Wairarapa
phone (06) 377 3353 **fax** (06) 378 8338 **open** 7 days 10–6
winemaker Frank Parker **production** 700 **est.** 1994
product range ($16.50–29.50 CD) Chasselas, Riesling, Chardonnay, Sauvignon Blanc, Chasselas Chenin Blanc, Waipipi Red, Joseph's (Red).
summary Frank and Bernice Parker are pioneer viticulturists on the Opaki Plains, 5 kilometres north of Masterton. They have established 1 hectare of riesling and a quarter of a hectare of chasselas, supplementing their intake with limited quantities of grapes grown by other producers in the region.

lynskeys wairau peaks NR

36 Godfrey Road, RD2, Blenheim **region** Marlborough
phone (03) 572 7180 **fax** (03) 572 7181 **open** Summer Wed–Sun 11–5, winter by appointment
winemaker Graeme Paul (Contract) **production** 2000 **est.** 1998
product range ($17–30 CD) Sauvignon Blanc, Gisborne Mendoza Chardonnay, Pinot Noir.
summary Ray and Kathy Lynskey bring diverse backgrounds to their newly established business. Kathy Lynskey has moved between Sydney and New Zealand at various times and established her first vineyard in 1989, providing contract-grown chardonnay. She now has a distribution business in Sydney (Lynskeys New Zealand Wine Cellars) selling not only the Lynskey wines but those of Lake Chalice, Le Grys and de Gyffarde. Ray Lynskey is an airline pilot based in Blenheim, flying gliders for relaxation so successfully that he won the world gliding championships at Omarama in 1995. Their 8.7-hectare vineyard is now in production; the wine is made at Marlborough Vintners. Exports to the US and Canada.

Lynskeys Wairau Peaks Sauvignon Blanc

1998 was the inaugural vintage from Lynskeys Wairau Peaks vineyard. Both vintages have shared characteristics which one would have thought came in the winery, but may in fact be reflections of the young vines.
TTTT 1999 Light green-yellow; the bouquet seems to have an SO₂ edge, which gives bite; the palate has length, although it dips up and down a bit along the way; subliminal sweetness fills out the back palate. Silver medal 1999 Air New Zealand Wine Awards. **rating: 87**
best drinking 2000–2001 **best vintages** '99 **drink with** Crab cakes • $17

margrain vineyard ★★★

Ponatahi Road (PO Box 97), Martinborough **region** Wairarapa
phone (06) 306 9292 **fax** (04) 569 2698 **open** Weekends and holidays 11–5
winemaker Strat Canning **production** 500 **est.** 1992
product range ($18–30 CD) Riesling, Chardonnay, Pinot Noir, Merlot.
summary Graham and Daryl Margrain planted their first vines in 1992 and produced the first wine (Chardonnay) in 1994. The vineyard is now planted to a total of 24 hectares of chardonnay, pinot noir, merlot and pinot gris; eight luxury accommodation villas have been built on an adjoining ridge, and a woolshed has been converted into a conference facility and tasting room. An underground cellar was constructed in 1994, and a winery (including a restaurant) was commissioned for the 1996 vintage, followed by the acquisition of Chifney in early 2000. And what did the Margrains do before they established Margrain Vineyard? They spent 25 years in the building industry, of course.

martinborough vineyard ★★★★★

Princess Street, Martinborough **region** Wairarapa
phone (06) 306 9955 **fax** (06) 306 9217 **open** 7 days 11–5
winemaker Claire Mulholland **production** 10 000 **est.** 1980
product range ($16.50–40 CD) Riesling, Riesling Late Harvest, Gewurztraminer, Pinot Gris, Sauvignon Blanc, Chardonnay, Pinot Noir, Pinot Noir Reserve.
summary After almost 15 years of devoted service to Martinborough Vineyards, during which time he lifted its profile to the highest level in both the domestic and international markets, Larry McKenna was effectively squeezed out and is actively developing his own vineyard and consultancy interests in both New Zealand and Australia. Incoming winemaker Claire Mulholland has big shoes to fill, but if she fails to do so, it won't be because of lack of commitment. And for the time being, the five-star rating remains.

matariki wines ★★★★

Gimblett Road, Havelock North **region** Hawke's Bay
phone (06) 877 8002 **fax** (06) 877 8004 **open** Mon–Fri 9–5 or by appointment
winemaker John O'Connor, Greg Foster **production** 2500 **est.** 1981
product range ($19.95–27.50 CD) Sauvignon Blanc, Chardonnay, Syrah, Anthology (Bordeaux-blend), Blanc de Blanc Méthode, Late Harvest Riesling.
summary John and Rosemary O'Connor purchased their Gimblett Road property in 1981 and are now the owners of the largest individual vineyard in that area, with 30 hectares (of a total 60 hectares) under vine, with syrah and sauvignon blanc planted on pure shingle, and cabernet franc, cabernet sauvignon, malbec, merlot, semillon and chardonnay on terraces with a greater amount of soil. They have also more recently purchased a limestone terrace property below Te Mata Peak, which is cooler and which has been planted to chardonnay. Currently they share the Trinity Hill winery with John Hancock, which houses their own winemaking equipment, but have plans for a large two-storey winery already drawn up. The quality of the wines released to date has been impressive, Anthology outstanding. Exports to the UK, and the US.

Matariki Sauvignon Blanc

1999 Matariki Sauvignon Blanc has made a considerable impression since its debut vintage in 1997. It is a blend of 85 per cent Sauvignon Blanc and 15 per cent Semillon part barrel-fermented.
▼▼▼▼ **1999** Medium yellow-green; the barrel-ferment oak characters are obvious on both bouquet and palate, but there is sufficient ripe fruit ranging through tropical to gooseberry to stone fruit to carry that oak.
rating: 87
best drinking 2000–2001 **best vintages** '97, '99 **drink with** Fish or shellfish with velouté sauce • $19.95

Matariki Anthology

A complex blend of 50 per cent Merlot, 30 per cent Cabernet Sauvignon, 13 per cent Syrah and 7 per cent Cabernet Franc which spends ten months in French oak, two-thirds of which are new. A gold medal winner at the 1999 Air New Zealand Wine Awards.
▼▼▼▼▼ **1998** Medium to full purple-red; an entrancing array of savoury, cedary, earthy, blackcurrant aromas slide into an elegant, smooth and rounded palate where sweet juicy berry fruit, fine tannins and subtle oak all add up to a high-class wine.
rating: 95
best drinking 2003–2008 **best vintages** '98 **drink with** Roast leg of lamb • $27.50

matawhero wines ★★☆

Riverpoint Road, Matawhero **region** Gisborne
phone (06) 868 8366 **fax** (06) 867 9856 **open** Mon–Sat 9–5
winemaker Denis Irwin **production** 6000 **est.** 1975
product range ($15–25 CD) Gewurztraminer, Riesling, Chardonnay, Reserve Chardonnay, Sauvignon Blanc, Chenin, Pinot Noir, Syrah, Cabernet, Bridge Estate.
summary The wines have always been cast in the mould of Matawhero's unpredictable founder and owner, Denis Irwin: at their best, in the guise of the Gewurztraminer from a good vintage, they are quite superb, racy and powerful; at their worst, they are poor and exhibit marked fermentation problems.

matua valley ★★★★

Waikoukou Road, Waimauku **region** Auckland Area
phone (09) 411 8301 **fax** (09) 411 7982 **open** Mon–Fri 9–5, Sat 10–5, Sun 11–4.30
winemaker Ross Spence, Mark Robertson **production** 125 000 **est.** 1974
product range ($11–34 CD) A the bottom end of the market are three Settlers Series wines ($11); next are a regional series of wines comprising Hawke's Bay Chardonnay, Hawke's Bay Sauvignon Blanc and Hawke's Bay Cabernet Merlot ($14.95); then an estate series from the Matheson Vineyard in Hawke's Bay of Chardonnay, Reserve Sauvignon Blanc, Cabernet Merlot and Cabernet Sauvignon; next is the Innovator Series ($22–25) for experimental wines, currently including Wairarapa Pinot Noir; and at the very top the intermittent releases from exceptional vintages of Ararimu Chardonnay.
summary One of the stalwarts of the New Zealand wine industry, producing a wide range of wines of good quality. The Shingle Peak label has been particularly successful, while the presentation of the Ararimu Chardonnay and Cabernet Sauvignon (not to mention the quality of the wines) set new standards of excellence for New Zealand. There are substantial exports to the UK, the US, Western Europe, Canada, Hong Kong, Japan and Australia.

Matua Valley Matheson Sauvignon Blanc

An interesting wine made in a style which is the polar opposite of that of Marlborough. The Hawke's Bay fruit is oxidatively handled as juice, partially barrique-fermented and largely wood-aged, and a small amount is taken through malolactic fermentation. The 1998 version was Michael Cooper's Best Buy of the Year.
TTTT 1999 Medium yellow-green; a complex bouquet with obvious lemony barrel-ferment oak leads into a soft, oaky and fruit-sweet (not residual sugar) palate. There is no doubting the sophistication and, for that matter, the success of the winemaking methods; the problem for me is that it ends up looking like a poor man's Chardonnay.
rating: 89
best drinking 2000–2003 **best vintages** NA **drink with** Veal fricassee • $17

Matua Valley Matheson Chardonnay

Hand-picked grapes are whole-bunch pressed and, after cold settling, the juice is racked and fermented in French oak barriques where it spends the next 12 months or so.
TTTT 1998 Deep yellow-green; the bouquet is smooth, of moderate to full intensity, with buttery peach and fig fruit supported by positive oak. The palate is extremely rich; were it not for the 14.3 degrees alcohol, which really makes its presence felt, this would be a more than useful wine.
rating: 85
best drinking 2000–2001 **best vintages** NA **drink with** Roast pork • $30

Matua Valley Innovator Wairarapa Pinot Noir

Part of the experimental series of Matua Valley. Ten tonnes of fruit were purchased from the Petrie Vineyard in Wairarapa and the wine was divided into six lots, each treated in slightly different ways; the major part was cold-macerated with high SO_2 and acid additions with a long post-ferment maceration, with other components using whole-bunch hot ferments. The radically different components were then blended and bottled after eight months in oak.
TTTT 1998 Medium red-purple; potent fruit with slightly stemmy/woody overtones on the bouquet leads into a palate of great complexity and power. There is plenty of plummy fruit there, but the stemmy/woody/oaky characters consistently challenge that fruit. Fascinating.
rating: 89
best drinking 2001–2005 **best vintages** NA **drink with** Rich game • $25

Matua Valley Dartmoor Merlot

The wine takes its name from the Dartmoor Valley in Hawke's Bay; made in typical Matua Valley style without the over-use of oak.
TTTT 1998 Medium to full red-purple; the bouquet ranges through cedary, savoury notes among pleasantly sweet fruit; the moderately intense palate has cedar, spice and blackberry flavours running through a long finish with soft tannins.
rating: 85
best drinking 2002–2007 **best vintages** '98 **drink with** Veal chops • $24

mazuran's vineyard NR

255 Lincoln Road, Henderson **region** Auckland Area
phone (09) 838 6945 **open** Mon–Sat 9–6
winemaker Rado Hladilo **production** 1400 **est.** 1938
product range ($12–350 CD) Sherries and Ports.
summary A Sherry and Port specialist, still surviving on the reputation built for its wines by George Mazuran, who died in 1980. The business is continued by his son and son-in-law. The $350, incidentally, is not a typographical error; it is the price of a 1942 Madeira.

๖ mccashin's ★★★★

660 Main Road, Stoke, Nelson **region** Nelson
phone (03) 547 5357 **fax** (03) 547 6876 **open** 7 days 9.30–6
winemaker Craig Gass **production** 10 000 **est.** 1999
product range ($16–35 R) Canterbury Riesling, Marlborough Sauvignon Blanc, Marlborough Chardonnay, Marlborough Pinot Noir, Méthode Traditionelle.
summary Normally, brewers and spirit merchants simply go out and acquire wineries created by others. In this instance, McCashin's has done it from scratch, harnessing the unstoppable energy of winemaker Craig Gass.

McCashin's Marlborough Sauvignon Blanc

What you see is what you get; this first vintage is an excellent example of ripe but not over-ripe Marlborough Sauvignon Blanc.
▼▼▼▼ **1999** Light to medium yellow-green; the bouquet is clean and ripe, with light touches of passionfruit and gooseberry. The palate has abundant varietal flavour and mouthfeel, weighty, but not cloying.   **rating:** 87
best drinking 2000–2001 **drink with** New Zealand whitebait • $19

McCashin's Marlborough Pinot Noir

1998 was the debut vintage for this wine, produced from a low-yielding vineyard (1.5 tonnes to the acre) and matured in oak for 11 months. It was my top-pointed wine in its class at the Royal Easter Wine Show 2000, a judgment radically different from that of the judges in the class. Why, I do not know.
▼▼▼▼▽ **1998** Medium red-purple; the bouquet is rich, with a mix of sweet plum and more savoury aromas. The palate has excellent flavour, style and balance, with plum, spice and soft but sustaining tannins on the finish.
rating: 95
best drinking 2000–2005 **drink with** Rare roasted squab • $30

melness wines NR

1816 Cust Road, Cust, North Canterbury **region** Canterbury
phone (03) 312 5402 **fax** (03) 512 5466 **open** Summer 7 days 10–6, winter Thurs–Sun 10–4.30
winemaker Mathew Donaldson, Lynette Hudson **production** 1000 **est.** NA
product range ($10–30 CD) Gewurztraminer, Riesling, Chardonnay (spray free), Floral (spray free), Rosé, Pinot Noir.
summary Melness' s vineyards are run organically, which makes the utilisation of what is claimed to be the only Lyre Trellis system on the South Island all the more understandable as it maximises sunlight and wind penetration. Owners Colin and Norma Marshall have established the winery with a café in a garden setting. Exports to Taiwan.

Melness Pinot Noir

Has made a name for itself with its Pinot Noirs, which are contract-made by Matthew Donaldson and Lynette Hudson at Pegasus Bay; the Pegasus Bay philosophy seems to show through in the 1998 vintage.
▼▼▼▼ **1998** Dark red-purple; a potent, ripe and concentrated bouquet with plum and prune aromas is followed logically enough by a rich plummy/pruney palate; the tannins are in balance and, although very ripe, the wine avoids over-extraction.   **rating:** 88
best drinking 2002–2007 **best vintages** '98 **drink with** Rich game • $30

mills reef winery ★★★★★

Moffat Road, Bethlehem, Tauranga **region** Bay of Plenty
phone (07) 576 8800 **fax** (07) 576 8824 **open** 7 days 8–5
winemaker Paddy Preston, Tim Preston **production** 40 000 **est.** 1989
product range ($11–32.50 CD) Under the Moffat Road/Mere Road labels: Riesling, Sauvignon Blanc, Chardonnay, Pinot Blush and Cabernet Sauvignon; then comes the Reserve range of Riesling, Sauvignon Blanc, Chenin Blanc, Chardonnay, Pinot Noir and Ice Wine Riesling; the top of the range is the Elspeth range of Riesling, Sauvignon Blanc, Chardonnay, Cabernet Sauvignon and Cabernet Merlot; Méthode Champenoise comprises Charisma NV and Vintage.
summary Mills Reef has recently completed a new winery, situated on an 8-hectare chardonnay vineyard within five minutes of Tauranga, incorporating wine tasting and display rooms, a restaurant and a conference/meeting room, together with usual winemaking facilities. The initial releases from Mills Reef were impressive, and after a wobbly period the flagship Elspeth range is among New Zealand's best. With its Hawke's Bay base, it is able to span Chardonnay, Cabernet-based reds and Méthode Champenoise with equal ease. Exports to the UK, the US, Japan, Hong Kong, The Netherlands and Germany.

Mills Reef Elspeth Syrah

The first Mills Reef Syrah, and one of a handful of such wines in New Zealand. Grown on the Mere Road Vineyard and made according to the Mills Reef formula also, it is said.

▼▼▼▼ **1998** Full red-purple; very sweet, inky fruit and sweet oak coalesce on the bouquet; there are interesting, lifted fruit flavours on the fine and vaguely lemony palate; fine tannins and controlled oak. **rating:** 88

best drinking 2001–2007 **best vintages** NA **drink with** Moroccan lamb • $32.50

Mills Reef Elspeth Merlot

The grapes are grown on the Mere Road Vineyard, Hawke's Bay. Borrowing a practice widely used for pinot noir, the grapes are crushed and then cold macerated prior to fermentation in open fermenters. After pressing it spends 16 months in French oak.

▼▼▼▼▽ **1998** Full red-purple; gorgeous, lusciously ripe plum, cassis and berry fruit aromas are followed by lively, rippling flavours of cassis and plum on the palate. The only Bordeaux-style from Mills Reef not to win a gold medal at the 1999 Air New Zealand Wine Awards (it received a silver), which seems a miscarriage of justice; perhaps the generous serving of tannins on the finish was held against it. **rating:** 92

best drinking 2001–2011 **best vintages** '98 **drink with** Rack of lamb • $32.50

Mills Reef Elspeth Merlot Cabernet Syrah

The wine is a blend of 36 per cent Merlot, 36 per cent Cabernet Sauvignon and 28 per cent Syrah, all estate-grown on the Mere Road Vineyard of Mills Reef in Hawke's Bay. The wine is made according to the Mills Reef formula, cold macerated prior to fermentation in open fermenters, and then 16 months in French oak.

▼▼▼▼▼ **1998** Medium to full red-purple; the gloriously complex bouquet with buckets of oak but the spicy, dark berry fruit to accommodate that oak. A high-toned, youthful and luscious palate with juicy berry fruit and twists of spice. Still a baby; great future. Trophy for Best Cabernet and/or Merlot predominant blend Air New Zealand Wine Awards 1999. **rating:** 94

best drinking 2004–2014 **best vintages** '98 **drink with** Braised venison • $32.50

Mills Reef Elspeth Cabernet Merlot

A blend which varies slightly from one vintage to the next, but is typically around 70 per cent Cabernet Sauvignon and 30 per cent Merlot. The grapes are cold macerated prior to fermentation in open fermenters, and the wine spends 16 months in French oak before being bottled.

▼▼▼▼▽ **1998** Medium red-purple; fragrant, scented dark berry fruit is woven through sweet oak on the bouquet. The palate opens with wonderfully sweet blackcurrant and plum fruit, quite gorgeous, before quite assertive tannins come on the finish. There is so much fruit in the wine I have little doubt the tannins will soften before the fruit fades. Gold medal Air New Zealand Wine Awards 1999. **rating:** 93

best drinking 2005–2015 **best vintages** '97, '98 **drink with** Rack of lamb • $30

Mills Reef Elspeth Cabernet Sauvignon

Made from grapes grown exclusively on the Mere Road Vineyard, and like so many of the gold medal and trophy-winning wines from Mills Reef in the 1998 vintage, made according to the cold soak, open fermenter, French oak regime.

▼▼▼▼▼ **1998** Outstanding deep and youthful purple-red; creme de cassis fruit with sweet, spicy oak on the bouquet moves into a lusciously sweet forepalate, then a long, fine finish with significant acid. Trophy for Champion Cabernet Sauvignon 1999 Air New Zealand Wine Awards. **rating:** 95

best drinking 2005–2015 **best vintages** '97, '98 **drink with** Beef with olives • $30

millton vineyard ★★★★☆

Papatu Road, Manutuke, Gisborne **region** Gisborne
phone (06) 862 8680 **fax** (06) 862 8869 **open** By appointment
winemaker James Millton **production** 12 000 **est.** 1984
product range ($15–60 CD) Barrique Fermented Chardonnay, Clos de Ste Anne Chardonnay, Chenin Blanc, Tete du Cuvée (botrytised Chenin Blanc), Te Arai River Sauvignon Blanc, Riesling Opou Vineyard, Clos de Ste Anne Pinot Noir, Te Arai River Cabernet Merlot.
summary The first of the increasing number of registered organic vineyards in New Zealand using biodynamic methods and banning insecticides and herbicides; winemaking methods are conventional but seek to limit the use of chemical additives wherever possible. The white wines, particularly botrytised, can be of the highest quality; the Germanic, lime-flavoured Riesling Opou Vineyard is almost always outstanding, while James Millton is doing some of the most exciting things with Chenin Blanc anywhere in the world outside the Loire Valley. Exports to Australia, Belgium, Germany, Japan, Singapore, Hong Kong and the UK.

miro   NR

Browns Road, Waiheke Island **region** Waiheke Island
phone (09) 372 7854 **fax** (09) 372 7056 **open** By appointment
winemaker Stephen White, Barnett Bond **production** 500 **est.** 1994
product range ($20–70 R) Chardonnay, Archipelago (Bordeaux-blend second label) and Miro (super-premium Bordeaux-blend).
summary Dr Barnett Bond and wife Cate Vosper are the most recent arrivals on the beautiful Waiheke Island scene, planting their first vines in 1994 and extending the vineyard to 3 hectares in 1996. A luxury holiday cottage on site is available, overlooking the steep north-facing slopes of the vines looking out to the Onetangi Bay.

mission estate winery   ★★★☆

Church Road, Taradale **region** Hawke's Bay
phone (06) 844 2259 **fax** (06) 844 6023 **open** Mon–Sat 8.30–5.30, Sun 11–4
winemaker Paul Mooney **production** 74 000 **est.** 1851
product range ($12.95–33 CD) Mission Estate range of Gewurztraminer, Riesling, Pinot Gris, Sauvignon Blanc, Chardonnay, Merlot, Cabernet Merlot, Cabernet Sauvignon, Botrytised Semillon and Iced Wine; Mission Reserve range of Riesling, Semillon, Pinot Gris, Sauvignon Blanc, Chardonnay, Cabernet Merlot, Cabernet Sauvignon; and the premium Jewelstone Selection range of Chardonnay, Noble Riesling, Gimblett Road Syrah and Gimblett Road Cabernet Merlot.
summary New Zealand's oldest winemaker, owned by the Society of Mary. Once content to make honest, basically unpretentious wines at modest prices, it has developed some top-end wines since 1992, notably the Jewelstone range. Production has been increased by 50 per cent in recent years, partly reflecting the buoyancy of the New Zealand wine industry but also the quality of the Mission Estate wines.

Mission Estate Hawke's Bay Riesling

Since 1998 this wine has been relegated to second place behind a Reserve Riesling, but does not appear to have suffered.
▼▼▼▼ **1999** Light to medium yellow-green; a solid bouquet with lots of depth and character, although the fruit has a slightly muffled character. The no-holds-barred palate is rich and full of character, with a mix of lime and kerosene flavours. Silver medal winner Royal Easter Wine Show 2000.   **rating:** 87
best drinking 2000–2003 **best vintages** NA **drink with** Fish and chips • $15

Mission Estate Reserve Cabernet Sauvignon

Estate-grown and sits in terms of price just under the Jewelstone range. Vintages such as 1998 do not deserve to come second.
▼▼▼▼▽ **1998** Dark red-purple; the bouquet is quite fragrant, with a mix of dark fruits and more earthy/leafy varietal character. The palate has abundant cassis and blackberry fruit, with touches of chocolate and earth, before finishing with powerful tannins which will sustain the wine for many years.   **rating:** 91
best drinking 2003–2013 **best vintages** '98 **drink with** Charcoal-grilled rump steak • $25

montana wines   ★★★★

171 Pilkington Road, Glen Innes, Auckland **region** Auckland Area
phone (09) 570 5549 **fax** (09) 527 1113 **open** 7 days 9.30–5.30
winemaker Jeff Clarke (Chief) **production** 35 000 tonnes (2.25 million case equivalent) **est.** 1977
product range ($9.95–26.95 R) A vast range headed by Marlborough Sauvignon Blanc, Riesling, Chardonnay and Cabernet Sauvignon; Renwick Estate Chardonnay, Timara Riesling, Brancott Estate Sauvignon Blanc, Fairhall Estate Cabernet Sauvignon, Saints Sauvignon Blanc (also all from Marlborough); Patutahi Gewurztraminer Ormond Estate Chardonnay (Gisborne); important sparkling wines headed by Deutz Marlborough Cuvée (Brut and Blanc de Blanc) and Lindauer (Special Reserve Brut de Brut, Brut, Sec and Rosé); large volume Wohnsiedler Müller Thurgau, Blenheimer and Chablisse; Church Road Chardonnay and Cabernet Sauvignon are top-of-the-range. The bright blue bottle of Azure Bay was a colourful (and commercially significant) addition in 1996.
summary Has a more dominant position than does Southcorp through Seppelts-Penfolds-Lindemans in Australia, as it produces 50 per cent of New Zealand's wine. Having parted company with Seagram many years ago, it formed joint ventures with Deutz for sparkling winemaking and Cordier with its Church Road winery offshoot. As one might expect, the wines are invariably well crafted right across the range, even if most attention falls on its Marlborough Sauvignon Blanc. It has recently decided to tackle the difficult Australian market in earnest and deserves to succeed. However, it would be good if they could manage to respond to journalists' requests for information and samples.

Montana Patutahi Gewurztraminer
Grown in Gisborne, late-harvested, and often (as in 1998) with some botrytis.
🍷🍷🍷🍷 **1998** Glowing yellow-green; the bouquet is incredibly rich, almost essencey, with lychee/peach/tropical fruit aromas. The palate is similarly exotically rich and power-packed, though not excessively. Not for the timorous.   **rating:** 89
best drinking 1999–2002 **best vintages** NA **drink with** Spicy Asian food • $25

morton estate ★★★★
State Highway 2, RD2, Kati Kati **region** Waikato and Bay of Plenty
phone (07) 552 0795 **fax** (07) 552 0651 **open** 7 days 10.30–5
winemaker Evan Ward **production** 90 000 **est.** 1978
product range ($11.95–33 CD) At the top end is the Black Label range of Chardonnay, Pinot Noir, Merlot, Late Harvest Chardonnay and Méthode Champenoise; next is the White Label range of Chardonnay, Sauvignon Blanc and Cabernet Merlot (all Hawke's Bay); then follows the Stone Creek range of Riesling, Sauvignon Blanc and Chardonnay; and the budget-priced Mill Road range of Chardonnay, Sauvignon Blanc, Dry White, Müller Thurgau, Dry Red and Cabernet Merlot, with Boars Leap Dry White bringing up the rear.
summary Now owned by John Coney, with Evan Ward in charge of winemaking, long-term winemaker John Hancock having left to head up his new Hawke's Bay winery. It will be interesting to watch the development of wine style; it seems probable that the more restrained approach of recent years will continue. Exports to the UK, the US, The Netherlands, Singapore, Fiji and Japan.

morworth estate NR
Shands Road, Christchurch **region** Canterbury
phone (03) 349 5014 **fax** (03) 349 4419 **open** By appointment
winemaker St Helena (Contract) **production** 4000 **est.** 1995
product range ($9–17 CD) Riesling, Breidecker, Sauvignon Blanc, Pinot Noir.
summary Leonie and Chris Morkane have established 13 hectares of vines on the outskirts of Christchurch, predominantly planted to pinot noir (6 hectares) and riesling (3 hectares), with lesser quantities of breidecker, pinot gris and gewurztraminer. The Morkanes intend to erect a 200-tonne winery-cum-art gallery and functions centre on the property in the near future.

Morworth Estate Sauvignon Blanc
In 1999 winemaking moved from Sherwood to St Helena, putting Alan McCorkindale in charge, and producing immediate dividends.
🍷🍷🍷🍷🍸 **1999** Light green-yellow; the moderately intense bouquet offers a mix of herb, lemon and mineral aromas, and the palate more than lives up to the promise of the bouquet, quite intense and long; plenty of action.
                                                                                          rating: 91
best drinking 2000–2001 **best vintages** '99 **drink with** Mud crab • $15

🐌 mt difficulty wines ★★★★
Felton Road, RD 2, Bannockburn, Cromwell **region** Otago
phone (03) 445 1054 **fax** (03) 445 1052 **open** Not
winemaker Grant Taylor **production** 5000 **est.** 1998
product range ($19–33 R) Sauvignon Blanc, Pinot Gris, Chardonnay, Pinot Noir.
summary Mt Difficulty is a rare beast in the wine world: a joint venture between five grape growers who have banded together to have the wine made under a single brand, giving economies of scale otherwise impossible. The vineyards will produce the equivalent of 25 000 cases annually once they are in full production, which won't be too many years away. The difficulty comes from the 'my grapes are better than yours' syndrome which, whether true or not, tends to thwart ventures such as this. It is to their credit that the joint venturers have worked around the problem, and equally that they have secured the services of Grant Taylor as contract-winemaker. Exports to the UK.

mount edward NR
Coalpit Road, Gibbston, Queenstown **region** Otago
phone (03) 442 6113 **fax** (03) 442 9119 **open** By appointment
winemaker Alan Brady, Grant Taylor **production** 700 **est.** 1995
product range ($18–35 CD) Riesling, Pinot Noir.

summary Alan Brady was the driving force behind the establishment and success of Gibbston Valley winery. In 1998 he retired as general manager of Gibbston Valley and commissioned Queenstown architect Michael Wyatt to design a new small winery on Brady's private vineyard in Coalpit Road. Here 1 hectare of riesling is planted, which he supplements with pinot noir (his continuing passion) purchased from growers in the Otago region. Tastings — and tutored tastings — are by appointment only and are always conducted by Alan Brady in person. Exports to the UK.

mountford vineyard   NR

434 Omihi Road, Waipara, North Canterbury **region** Canterbury
phone (03) 314 6819 **fax** (03) 314 6820 **open** By appointment
winemaker C P Lin (Consultant) **production** 1000 **est.** 1991
product range ($30–35 CD) Chardonnay, Pinot Noir.
summary Michael and Buffy Eaton have established 4 hectares of vines on an east-facing slope of the Waipara Valley, producing the first tiny vintage in 1996; full production began in 1999. An on-site winery has been constructed, as has a lodge with up-market accommodation. The wines have all been highly rated by Bob Campbell and Michael Cooper.

mount riley   ★★★☆

Old Renwick Road, Blenheim **region** Marlborough
phone (09) 486 0286 **fax** (09) 486 0643 **open** By appointment
winemaker Bill 'Digger' Hennessy **production** 20 000 **est.** 1995
product range ($14–29 R) Riesling, Sauvignon Blanc, Chardonnay, Seventeen Valley Chardonnay, Pinot Noir, Cabernet Merlot, Sparkling Sauvignon Blanc Savée.
summary Mount Riley is a joint venture between Auckland-based businessmen and wine enthusiasts Steve Hotchin and John Buchanan and Marlborough vigneron and winemaker Allan Scott. Mount Riley owns three vineyards in the Wairau Valley and has developed a fourth vineyard in Seventeen Valley, 10 kilometres south of Blenheim, planted to clonally selected pinot noir. In all, Mount Riley owns 50 hectares of vineyards and is in no sense a second label of Allan Scott, even though it shares winemakers and wine facilities with Allan Scott Wines. If there were a value rating, Mount Riley would receive five stars. Exports to Australia, the UK, Canada, Scandinavia and Hong Kong.

Mount Riley Riesling

Arguably provides the best value of all of the attractively priced Mount Riley range of wines.
▼▼▼▼ 1999 Light green-yellow; the intense bouquet is flooded with lime juice aromas which underpin but do not over-weight the stylish, elegant palate. The crisp, firm finish provides the balance needed.   **rating:** 89
best drinking 2001–2006 **best vintages** '99 **drink with** Salmon and asparagus terrine •$14

Mount Riley Sauvignon Blanc

Made in a classically uncomplicated fashion, night-harvested by machine and cold-fermented in stainless steel at low temperatures for three weeks. Both at juice and wine stage minimal intervention and maximum fruit protection pays handsome dividends.
▼▼▼▼ 1999 Light green-yellow; the bouquet is of light to medium intensity, clean and crisp, minerally and just a hint of citrus. Much the same things happen on the palate, although it does build intensity towards the back palate, which in turn invests the wine with good length.   **rating:** 85
best drinking 2000–2001 **best vintages** NA **drink with** Clams •$15

Mount Riley Chardonnay

Sixty per cent of the wine is barrel-fermented and aged on lees in a mix of French and American oak (two-thirds new); the rest is stainless steel-fermented and matured. Deliberately made in a fresh, drink-now style.
▼▼▼▼ 1999 Light yellow-green; the bouquet is fresh and crisp, with light citrussy fruit and even a touch of mineral. The palate follows down the same track, fresh, light and uncomplicated, but with enough there to satisfy.   **rating:** 86
best drinking 2000–2003 **best vintages** NA **drink with** Crab cakes •$17

Mount Riley Seventeen Valley Chardonnay

Mount Riley's super-premium Chardonnay, 60 per cent of which is barrel-fermented in a mix of French and American oak (two-thirds new) where it spends eight months on yeast lees.

❦❦❦❦ **1998** Medium to full yellow-green; lots of barrel-ferment oak inputs tend to swamp the fruit on the bouquet and to a large measure on the palate. It is only on the finish that the low-cropping Mendoza clone Chardonnay can really express itself. It is remotely possible that time will improve the balance. **rating:** 83

best drinking 2001–2005 **best vintages** NA **drink with** Swiss-style veal •$29

Mount Riley Pinot Noir

Low-priced, early-drinking Pinot Noir is always a tricky wine to make; it can so easily descend to the level of a light cordial with incidental alcohol. This wine succeeds in beating the bogie.

❦❦❦❦ **1999** Light to medium red-purple; fresh, bright and simple cherry fruit on the bouquet is likewise the focal point of the palate, although there is some texture and style there. Overall, to be enjoyed rather than analysed. **rating:** 81

best drinking 2000–2002 **best vintages** NA **drink with** Light Italian dishes •$19

Mount Riley Cabernet Merlot

An open-fermented and hand-plunged blend of 80 per cent Cabernet Sauvignon matured in new American oak and 20 per cent Merlot matured in used French oak. An early-release, early-drinking style which works very well and represents excellent value.

❦❦❦❦ **1999** Youthful, dense purple-red; the bouquet is solid with a mix of blackberry and blackcurrant fruit, the oak being surprisingly subtle. Full of fresh, lively fruit on the palate; very much in the style of the early release Rosemount Estate red wines. **rating:** 88

best drinking 2000–2003 **best vintages** '99 **drink with** Any red meat •$17

moutere hills vineyard ★★★☆

Sunrise Valley, RD1, Upper Moutere, Nelson **region** Nelson
phone (03) 543 2288 **fax** (03) 543 2288 **open** October–Easter 11–6
winemaker Simon Thomas **production** 2500 **est.** 1996
product range ($14.50–18.50 CD) Nelson Riesling, Barrique Fermented Sauvignon Blanc, Chardonnay, Sunrise Valley Red (Rosé), Merlot, Cabernet Merlot.
summary Moutere Hills winery was established in an old shearing shed by owners Simon and Alison Thomas. Overlooking the Moutere Valley, it draws upon 3 hectares of estate vineyards supplemented by small quantities of grapes purchased from local growers. Wines are available by the glass, matched by light meals.

mudbrick vineyard NR

Church Bay Road, Oneroa, Waiheke Island **region** Waiheke Island
phone (09) 372 9050 **fax** (09) 372 9052 **open** 7 days summer, lunch and dinner (reduced hours in winter)
winemaker Simon Lampen **production** 1600 **est.** 1992
product range ($25–35 CD) Chardonnay, Cabernet Sauvignon Merlot Malbec Cabernet Franc, Croll Vineyard Cabernet Syrah.
summary The metamorphosis from accountancy to winemaking and restaurateurs/hoteliers is about as radical as they come, but Nick and Robyn Jones have accomplished it. Their 8-hectare vineyard is planted to chardonnay, cabernet sauvignon, syrah, cabernet franc and malbec. Mudbrick also offers a restaurant and accommodation.

muddy water ★★★★

434 Omihi Road, Waipara **region** Canterbury
phone (03) 377 7123 **fax** (03) 377 7130 **open** Not
winemaker Belinda Gould **production** 4500 **est.** 1992
product range ($14–30 CD) Sauvignon Blanc, Waipara Chardonnay, Pinot Noir.
summary I must say, I don't think I could ever be persuaded to call my winery (least of all my wines) Muddy Water, even if it does happen to be the literal translation of the Maori word 'Waipara'. However, Michael East, a Christchurch doctor, and his wife Jane, who studied viticulture at Lincoln University, had different ideas when they established Muddy Water in 1992. They already have 11 hectares of vineyard planted, with another 4 hectares on the drawing board, and room for a total of 25 hectares. Exports to the UK.

Muddy Water Waipara Riesling

The absence of the word 'dry' on the label is indicative of some sweetness; in a game of Russian roulette (if you are at a restaurant, say) you are left to find out the hard way. It would be nice if New Zealand's winemakers could agree on some system to help consumers.

▼▼▼▼ 1999 Light green-yellow; lime juice aromas come through on a moderately intense bouquet, which also has a touch of mineral, and perhaps the faintest suggestion of a touch of reduction. The palate is nicely balanced, moderately sweet, drinking well now but will do no less well in the future. **rating:** 88

best drinking 2000–2006 **best vintages** NA **drink with** Artichokes and hollandaise sauce • $16

Muddy Water Waipara Dry Riesling

First made in 1996; that wine is still intense and powerful with Germanic lime juice characters, but the biting acidity on the finish will never soften. The 1999 is much better balanced.

▼▼▼▼ 1999 Light green-yellow; a clean and quite intense bouquet with lime juice aromas leads into a fresh, delicate crisp wine with lime juice flavours and a lingering finish. **rating:** 89

best drinking 2000–2007 **best vintages** NA **drink with** Chinese stir-fried prawns • $21

Muddy Water Waipara Chardonnay

Produced from very low-yielding estate vineyards (1.5 tonnes per acre) and fermented and matured in French oak barriques, 25 per cent of which are new.

▼▼▼▽ 1998 Medium to full yellow-green; a gently complex bouquet with creamy cashew and mineral aromas introduces an elegant wine, harmonious and well balanced in a lighter style, and possessing a particularly good finish. **rating:** 91

best drinking 2000–2003 **best vintages** '98 **drink with** Milk-fed veal • $24

Muddy Water Waipara Pinot Noir

First came to notice with its 1997 Pinot Noir at the 1999 Liquorland Royal Easter Wine Show. The 1998 is a somewhat uncertain follow-on, with what I perceive to be technical problems.

▼▼▼▽ 1998 Medium to full red-purple; the powerful plum fruit of the bouquet is elevated by volatile acidity; similarly, the dense plummy/savoury fruit of the palate exudes character but is sharpened off by what seems to me to be volatile acidity. **rating:** 82

best drinking 2000–2002 **best vintages** '97 **drink with** Char-grilled salmon • $24

mud house ★★★☆

197 Rapaura Road, Renwick, Marlborough **region** Marlborough
phone (03) 572 9490 **fax** (03) 572 9491 **open** 7 days 10–5
winemaker Graeme Paul, Matt Thomson (Consultant) **production** 21 000 **est.** 1993
product range ($16–31 CD) Sauvignon Blanc, Chardonnay, Pinot Noir offered both under the Le Grys and Mud House labels.
summary Mud House marks the end of an odyssey dating back to 1066; Jennifer Joslin's family name (Le Grys) dates back to that time, and the Marlborough vineyard was purchased by John and Jennifer Joslin at the end of a six-year sailing trip around the world. A mudbrick guesthouse built in 1995 is ultimately to be followed by a mudbrick tasting room and cellar. Production has almost trebled over the past few years, and the wines are distributed (through separate agencies for Mud House and Le Grys respectively) in the UK, Australia, the US, Hong Kong and China.

Mud House Sauvignon Blanc

The source and composition of this wine, even the reasons for the existence of this and the Le Grys label, are enough to give a wine writer a migraine. Suffice it to say that in 1999 the wine is (apparently) 100 per cent Sauvignon Blanc from the Jocelyn Vineyard.

▼▼▼▼ 1999 Light yellow-green; the bouquet is delicate and fine, with flashes of tropical/passionfruit aroma. The palate is quite light and crisp, with a delicate mid-palate, before moving through to a slightly minerally grip to the finish. This note and rating give the benefit of the doubt on the level of volatile acidity in the wine. **rating:** 87

best drinking 2000–2001 **best vintages** NA **drink with** Summer salad • $16

Le Grys Sauvignon Blanc

The Le Grys label is simply an alternative label to Mud House, initially created for distribution reasons, but now having a genuinely independent existence. That difference stems from the different fermentation techniques, with 10 per cent fermented in new French oak, and 30 per cent undergoing malolactic fermentation. The varietal base of 86 per cent Sauvignon Blanc and 14 per cent Semillon (until further notice).

▼▼▼▼♡ **1999** Light green-yellow; the bouquet is clean and delicate, the similarly delicate palate finely focused, with gooseberry and herb fruit; good length and acidity underpin a classy wine which won a double gold at the Sydney International Wine Competition 2000. Once again, ignores whatever level of volatile acidity the wine has.

rating: 91

best drinking 2000–2001 **best vintages** '97, '99 **drink with** Tortellini • $16

Le Grys Chardonnay

Predominantly sourced from the Le Grys estate vineyard, but with 10 per cent coming from the Beatrice estate. Made in a fairly direct style, with some lees contact but not a great deal of oak.

▼▼▼♡ **1998** Medium green-yellow; the bouquet is faintly reductive, with slightly cosmetic-scented oak; there is pleasant fruit on the palate, and the oak does not present the same challenges as it does on the bouquet. **rating: 81**

best drinking 2000–2002 **best vintages** '98 **drink with** Seafood pasta • $20.50

Mud House Marlborough Pinot Noir

Another wine to come, as it were, out of nowhere, but underlining the enormous potential the vast expanses of Marlborough have for high-quality pinot noir.

▼▼▼▼▼ **1998** Medium red-purple; the bouquet is clean, with some attractively savoury edges to light to moderately intense plum fruit on the bouquet. The palate creeps up on you, its intensity and length building as you retaste it. Plum and forest flavours intermingle with excellent oak and tannin handling. Subtlety, not power, is the exercise. **rating: 94**

best drinking 2000–2004 **best vintages** '98 **drink with** Braised duck • $31

Mud House Merlot

Aged for one year in French oak, runs counter to the general flow of 1998 reds, with the sort of herbal characters encountered in other years.

▼▼▼♡ **1998** Medium red-purple; there is a degree of complexity to the bouquet, but leafy/gamey aromas are foremost. The palate is lively but altogether lacking the plush ripeness of the best wines of the year. If it were not from the '98 vintage, would in all probability receive higher points. **rating: 84**

best drinking 2001–2004 **best vintages** NA **drink with** Veal ragout • $28

muirlea rise ★★☆

50 Princess Street, Martinborough **region** Wairarapa
phone (06) 306 9332 **open** Fri–Mon 10–6
winemaker Willie Brown **production** 700 **est.** 1987
product range ($18–40 CD) Pinot Noir, Justa Red, Apres Wine Liqueur, Sibbald (Rhône-style Cabernet Sauvignon).
summary Former Auckland wine distributor Willie Brown has established a 2.5-hectare vineyard. Since the first wine release of a 1991 Pinot Noir, the accent has remained on that variety, but with an extraordinarily eclectic gaggle of other wines which are decidedly left-of-centre in style and, for that matter, quality.

murdoch james estate ★★★☆

c/o Barbara Turner, 15 Cologne Street, Martinborough **region** Wairarapa
phone (06) 306 9193 **fax** (06) 306 9120 **open** Not
winemaker Chris Buring **production** 2100 **est.** 1986
product range ($16–45 R) Unoaked Chardonnay, Pinot Noir, Cabernet Franc, Shiraz, Tres Ami Pinot Noir Cabernet Sauvignon Cabernet Franc.
summary The origin of Murdoch James Estate goes back to 1986 when Roger and Jill Fraser planted 2.5 hectares of shiraz and pinot noir. The Frasers' plans were interrupted in 1989 when Roger was transferred to Melbourne by his employer, and the decision was made to sell the grapes rather than make wine. Between 1993 and 1998 only tiny quantities of wine were made, but the estate then purchased Blue Rock Vineyard, giving 11 hectares of estate vines and triggering construction of underground barrel storage tunnels and a new tasting room.

nautilus wines ★★★★

12 Rapaura Road, Marlborough **region** Marlborough
phone (09) 572 9364 **fax** (09) 572 9374 **open** 7 days 10.30–4.30
winemaker Clive Jones **production** 50 000 **est.** 1985
product range ($19.95–31.95 R) Chardonnay, Reserve Chardonnay, Sauvignon, Pinot Noir, Cabernet Sauvignon Merlot, Cuvée Marlborough Brut; Twin Islands is the second label, sold only in NZ.

summary Nautilus is ultimately owned by Yalumba of Australia. Until 1996 the wines were made by Yalumba winemaker Alan Hoey at Matua Valley, but from that vintage most were made at Rapaura Vintners (of which Nautilus is now a part-owner) under the direction of former Brokenwood (Australia) winemaker Matt Harrop, now replaced by Clive Jones. Draws both upon 15.5 hectares of estate vineyards and contract-grown grapes. Given its parentage, with Yalumba itself having a major agency export business around the world, it is not surprising that Nautilus is exported through much of Europe, Asia, the Pacific Islands, the US and Canada.

Nautilus Marlborough Sauvignon

Sauvignon Blanc was the first wine to be released under the striking and beautiful Nautilus label, and remains the most important wine in terms of quantity; invariably clearly defined. Principally made from vineyards situated in the Awatere Valley, the remainder from two vineyards in the Wairau Valley.

▼▼▼▼ **1999** Light green-yellow; the bouquet is moderately aromatic, with notes of herb, gooseberry and passionfruit. The palate is nicely balanced, with attractive, gentle gooseberry/tropical fruit; a user-friendly style.

rating: 89

best drinking 2000–2001 **best vintages** '89, '90, '91, '94, '98, '99 **drink with** Crayfish • $20

Nautilus Marlborough Chardonnay

Sophisticated winemaking includes partial wild yeast ferment, barrel-fermentation in French oak barriques (20 per cent new) with part fermented in stainless steel, and malolactic fermentation.

▼▼▼▼▽ **1998** Light to medium yellow-green; while the barrel-ferment and malolactic-ferment inputs are obvious, they do not overwhelm the fruit on the bouquet, and the spicy/nutty characters are indeed attractive. The palate appeals to me greatly, hanging together really well, with creamy cashew and melon flavours and texture interwoven.

rating: 90

best drinking 2000–2004 **best vintages** '91, '94, '98 **drink with** Scallops in cream sauce • $24

Nautilus Cuvée Marlborough Brut

Made from 75 per cent Pinot Noir and 25 per cent Chardonnay, all Marlborough-sourced. As one would expect, 100 per cent malolactic fermentation precedes secondary fermentation and 18 months on yeast lees prior to disgorgement.

▼▼▼▽ **NV** Medium yellow-green; the bouquet offers somewhat unusual waxy/flowery aromas, presumably deriving from the fruit rather than yeast, but it is difficult to tell. The palate has more conventional strawberry-accented fruit and is surprisingly delicate. Not an easy wine to assess.

rating: 84

best drinking Drink now **best vintages** NA **drink with** Aperitif • $29.50

neudorf vineyards ★★★★★

Neudorf Road, Upper Moutere, Nelson **region** Nelson
phone (03) 543 2643 **fax** (03) 543 2955 **open** 7 days 10–5 September–May
winemaker Tim Finn **production** 7500 **est.** 1978
product range ($16.90–35 CD) The Moutere label is reserved for estate-grown wines, notably Chardonnay and Pinot Noir; Nelson typically indicates a mix of estate-grown and locally purchased grapes from the Nelson region; the second label is Neudorf Village. Wines encompass Chardonnay, Sauvignon Blanc, Semillon, Riesling, Pinot Noir and Cabernet Sauvignon.
summary Tim Finn has produced some of Australasia's most stunningly complex and rich Chardonnays, outstanding in any class. But his skills do not stop there, spanning all varieties consistently to show medal standard. Exports to Australia, the UK, the US, France, Denmark and Singapore. The restaurant is open 27 December to 31 January.

Neudorf Moutere Chardonnay

Entirely estate-grown, hand-picked (of course) and whole-bunch pressed, the wine is fermented in a half and half mix of new and one-year-old French oak barriques. Seventy per cent is typically taken through malolactic fermentation, and the wine spends a year in barrel before being cleaned up, blended and bottled. A monumental style, the South Island's answer to Hawke's Bay Clearview.

▼▼▼▼▽ **1998** Medium to full yellow-green; an exceedingly complex bouquet with obvious barrel-ferment and malolactic-ferment inputs is followed by an explosion of flavour on the palate with a mix of tropical/figgy fruit, butterscotch and spicy oak.

rating: 92

best drinking 2000–2003 **best vintages** '87, '89, '91, '92, '93, '94, '96, '97, '98 **drink with** Veal, pasta • $35

Neudorf Nelson Chardonnay

This is the second-tier Chardonnay from Neudorf, initially released (1994) under the 'Village' label, but now simply called 'Nelson'. Second tier it may be, but a useful wine by any standards. Barrel-fermented and lees-aged, but entirely in one- to three-year-old barrels and, I suspect, with minimal malolactic fermentation. A marvellous wine to drink when young.

TTTTY 1999 Glowing green-yellow; a very fine and elegant mix of nectarine, peach, fig and cashew on the bouquet leads into a lovely wine, not the least bit overworked, and all of the components balanced and integrated.

rating: 93

best drinking 2000–2002 best vintages '99 drink with Abalone • $23

nevis bluff ★★★☆

PO Box 2012, Wakatipu, Queenstown **region** Otago
phone 0800-4-PINOT **fax** (02) 178 8909 **open** Not
winemaker Contract **production** 2256 **est.** 1995
product range ($18–28 R) Pinot Gris, Chardonnay, Osteiner, Pinot Noir.
summary Yet another impressive Central Otago label. Owned by Dunedin chartered accountant Bill Dawson. Nevis Bluff presently has 7 hectares of estate vineyards which huddle in a mountain-flanked valley, sheltered by the spectacularly steep and jagged Nevis Bluff.

Nevis Bluff Pinot Gris

Both the 1998 and 1999 vintages of this wine reaffirm the symbiosis between Central Otago and pinot gris.

TTTT 1999 Pale straw-green; the bouquet is clean, with hints of citrus, pear, apple and mineral, all fleeting and delicate. The palate is lively, crisp and long, with that typical cut of Pinot Gris on the finish. **rating: 88**

best drinking 2000–2003 best vintages '98, '99 drink with Fresh shellfish • $25

Nevis Bluff Pinot Noir

Four clones of pinot noir have been established on the Nevis Bluff vineyard. The wine is made using what are described as traditional Burgundian techniques.

TTTT 1998 Light to medium red-purple; the aromas are predominantly of cherry, with some light gamey/foresty undertones. The clean and fresh palate is likewise driven by the cherry-flavoured fruit, supported by a touch of sweet oak; a well-balanced, early-drinking, easy-on-the-gums style. **rating: 88**

best drinking 2000–2003 best vintages NA drink with Game terrine • $28

newton forrest estate ★★★★

Corner State Highway 50 and Gimblett Road, Hawke's Bay **region** Hawke's Bay
phone (06) 879 4416 **fax** (06) 876 6020 **open** At Forrest Estate, Blicks Road, Renwick
winemaker John Forrest (Contract) **production** 3300 **est.** 1988
product range ($32.95 ML) Cornerstone Cabernet Merlot; also Cabernet Sauvignon.
summary Newton Forrest is a joint venture between Hawke's Bay grape grower Bob Newton and Marlborough winemaker and vigneron John Forrest of Forrest Estate. It has produced the super-premium Cornerstone Cabernet Merlot each year since 1994; more recently a small quantity of Cabernet Sauvignon has been made. The remainder of the production from the 30 hectares of vines is sold to the Villa Maria/Vidal/Esk Valley for their Reserve wines.

Newton Forrest Cornerstone Cabernet Merlot

Estate-grown from a vineyard which has cabernet sauvignon, merlot, cabernet franc and malbec planted, the latter, too, making minor contributions to the blend.

TTTT 1998 Medium to full red-purple; luscious dark chocolate and cassis fruit is tempered by a slightly savoury/earthy edge on the bouquet. There is excellent fruit on entry to the mouth but very powerful tannins on the finish. Would have been outstanding had it been fined more heavily than it evidently was. I am far from convinced that time will address the problem, but you can always hope. **rating: 89**

best drinking 2004–2010 best vintages NA drink with Char-grilled rump • $32.95

ngatarawa wines ★★★★

Ngatarawa Road, Bridge Pa, RD5, Hastings **region** Hawke's Bay
phone (06) 879 7603 **fax** (06) 879 6675 **open** 7 days 11–5
winemaker Alwyn Corban, Peter Gough **production** 35 000 **est.** 1981
product range ($12.95–60 R) The top wines under the Glazebrook label include Chardonnay and Cabernet Merlot; the lesser-priced Stables range comprises Chardonnay, Sauvignon Blanc, Classic White, and Cabernet Merlot. Also Alwyn Chardonnay, Noble Botrytis.

summary Alwyn Corban is a highly qualified and highly intelligent winemaker from a famous New Zealand wine family who has elected to grow vines organically and make wines which sometimes (but certainly not always) fall outside the mainstream. Challenging and interesting, and not to be taken lightly. The wines are exported to the UK, Europe, Asia, the US and Canada.

Ngatarawa Glazebrook Sauvignon Blanc

The quality of the 1999 (and 1998) vintages led to the inclusion of Sauvignon Blanc in the Glazebrook range for the first time.

YYYY 1999 Light to medium yellow-green; the bouquet is clean, firm and not aromatic; on the other hand, the palate has nice mouthfeel and weight, propelling it firmly in the direction of food.　　　　**rating:** 87

best drinking 2000–2002　**best vintages** NA　**drink with** NA　• $17

Ngatarawa Alwyn Chardonnay

Just as Sauvignon Blanc joined the Glazebrook range, so was the 1998 Chardonnay elevated to join the super-premium Alwyn label (previously only used for the Noble Harvest).

YYYYY 1998 Medium yellow-green; the bouquet is complex, with layers of nut, fig and a little more oak than usual. The palate is particularly well balanced and constructed, with a range of nutty/figgy/cashew flavours folding into a clean, dry finish.　　　　**rating:** 90

best drinking 2000–2003　**best vintages** '98　**drink with** Corn-fed chicken　• $35

Ngatarawa Glazebrook Chardonnay

Estate-grown, hand-picked grapes are barrel-fermented in 100 per cent new French oak, with extended time on yeast lees. Eighty per cent of the wine is taken through malolactic fermentation. The aim of Alwyn Corban is to take the wine into secondary flavours and textures, and he succeeds admirably in his aim.

YYYY 1998 Medium to full yellow-green; another complex wine, more oaky and at once more open than the Alwyn. The palate shows the impact of the malolactic fermentation, which takes the edge off that fruit and lessens its intensity.　　　　**rating:** 87

best drinking 2000–2003　**best vintages** NA　**drink with** Smoked salmon　• $NA

Ngatarawa Alwyn Noble Harvest

Not made every year, but when it is made and when conditions are right, scales the ultimate heights. The grapes are allowed to hang on the vines for long after normal harvest, with a mix of botrytis and raisining lifting the sugar levels over 40° brix. Unusually, the wine is barrel-fermented and held in oak for 18 months, yet shows no sign either of oak or oxidation. Some of the great German botrytis wines are made this way, but relatively few in the New World.

YYYYY 1994 Re-released. Golden yellow; the wine has developed a very particular cinnamon/cardamom spice aroma, the palate with honey on cinnamon toast followed by lingering acidity on the finish. Unusual but compelling.　　　　**rating:** 97

best drinking 2000–2005　**best vintages** '92, '94, '96　**drink with** Dappled sunlight　• $NA

Ngatarawa Alwyn Merlot Cabernet

The first time the Alwyn brand has been extended beyond the Botrytis Riesling, prompted by what Alwyn Corban describes as the best vintage he has experienced in 18 years at Ngatarawa. The wine is a blend of 82 per cent Merlot and 18 per cent Cabernet Sauvignon taken from vines crop-thinned to less than 2 tonnes per acre. The wine is matured for 18 months in new French oak barriques.

YYYYY 1998 Medium red-purple showing slight signs of development; the bouquet is off on its own, with a mix of savoury, sweet leather, herb and spice aromas; the palate opens with lovely chocolatey, savoury fruit, finishing with soft, fine tannins and subtle oak.　　　　**rating:** 91

best drinking 2002–2010　**best vintages** '98　**drink with** Grilled calf's liver　• $NA

nga waka vineyard　★★★★

Kitchener Street, Martinborough　**region** Wairarapa
phone (06) 306 9832　**fax** (06) 306 9832　**open** Weekends 1–5 while stocks last
winemaker Roger Parkinson　**production** 3000　**est.** 1988
product range ($20–35 R) Riesling, Sauvignon Blanc, Chardonnay, Pinot Noir.
summary Roseworthy-trained Roger Parkinson produces the Nga Waka wines from 4 hectares of estate plantings in the heart of the Martinborough Terraces. The early promise of the vineyard came into full flower in the unlikely environment of the 1995 vintage with the performance of the 1995 Sauvignon Blanc at the Air New Zealand Wine Awards of that year. Subsequent vintages have been good but not quite so exciting as the '95. Exports to Australia, Japan and the US.

Nga Waka Riesling

Estate-grown, and typically an intense, long-lived style.

TTTT 1998 Light green-yellow; a lively, pungently intense bouquet of lime and more minerally characters is followed by a highly flavoured palate, with lime/tropical fruit counterbalanced by crisp mineral acidity on the finish. **rating:** 88

best drinking 2002–2008 **best vintages** '98 **drink with** Mussels • $20

nobilo ★★★★

Station Road, Huapai **region** Auckland Area

phone (09) 412 6666 **fax** (09) 412 7124 **open** Mon–Fri 9–5, Sat 10–5, Sun 11–4

winemaker Darryl Woolley **production** 375 000 **est.** 1943

product range ($8.95–34.95 R) At the bottom the White Cloud range ($8.95–9.95); then Fernleaf Sauvignon Blanc, Chardonnay and Cabernet Sauvignon ($9.95); then Fall Harvest Sauvignon Blanc, Chardonnay, Cabernet Shiraz and Merlot ($11.95); next Marlborough Sauvignon Blanc and Poverty Bay Chardonnay ($12.95); then Icon Sauvignon Blanc, Riesling, Gewurztraminer and Chardonnay ($17.95); and finally Grand Reserve Sauvignon Blanc ($22.95) and Grand Reserve Chardonnay ($34.95).

summary One of the more energetic and effective wine marketers, with production heavily focused on white wines sourced from Gisborne, Hawke's Bay and Marlborough. Significantly increased the critical mass of its business with the acquisition of Selaks, giving it secure access to Marlborough. A long-time exponent of flamboyant label and packaging redesign, but the quality of the top-of-the-range Grand Reserve wines leaves nothing to be desired. Exports to the UK, much of Europe, North America and Singapore.

Nobilo Icon Riesling

A well-made and consistently reliable mid-price wine produced from Marlborough grapes.

TTT 1999 Light green-yellow; gentle tropical/lime aromas flow into a gentle palate with Germanic lime juice flavours; good balance and good length. **rating:** 84

best drinking 2000–2003 **best vintages** NA **drink with** Avocado mousse • $17.95

Nobilo White Cloud Chardonnay

The wine primarily destined for the export market and exceptionally well-priced given its quality. A silver medal winner at the Royal Easter Wine Show 2000.

TTTT 1999 Light to medium yellow-green; the bouquet is effusive, with generous nectarine and peach fruit. Any oak present is incidental. The palate is on the sweet side, no doubt engineered to be so, but does have above-average length. **rating:** 87

best drinking 2000–2001 **best vintages** NA **drink with** Kentucky Fried Chicken • $9.95

obsidian NR

Te Makiri Road, Onetangi, Waiheke Island **region** Waiheke Island

phone (09) 372 6100 **fax** (09) 372 6100 **open** Not

winemaker Simon Nunns **production** 1500 **est.** 1993

product range ($45 R) A single red wine made from about 70 per cent Cabernet Sauvignon and 30 per cent Merlot, with just a dash of Malbec and Cabernet Franc.

summary Although still in its infancy (the first vintage was 1997), destined to be an important part of the Waiheke Island scene. A partnership between Andrew Hendy, owner of Coopers Creek, winemaker Kim Crawford and businessman Lindsay Spilman, it brings together the formidable winemaking skills of Crawford and the largest (7.3-hectare) vineyard on Waiheke Island, established in a natural amphitheatre. The wine is initially offered en primeur by mailing list, and then to selected on-premise outlets on Waiheke Island. Exports to UK via Farr Vintners.

Obsidian

An estate-grown blend of 67 per cent Cabernet Sauvignon, 30 per cent Merlot, 2 per cent Cabernet Franc and 1 per cent Malbec which spends 12 months in a mix of American and French oak barriques, half of which are new, the other half older.

TTTT 1998 Slightly disappointing medium red colour, with just a touch of purple. The bouquet offers light fruit driven more by cedary vanilla oak than fruit. A pleasant wine on the palate, with easy berry fruit and plenty of soft, sexy oak. Nowhere near meeting the hype. **rating:** 86

best drinking 2001–2005 **best vintages** NA **drink with** Osso bucco • $45

odyssey wines   NR

6D, 50 Keeling Road, Henderson **region** Auckland Area
phone (09) 837 5410 **fax** (09) 837 5409 **open** Not
winemaker Rebecca Salmond **production** 4500 **est.** 1994
product range ($16–28 R) Marlborough Sauvignon Blanc, Gisborne Pinot Gris, Gisborne Chardonnay, Hawke's Bay Reserve Cabernet Sauvignon. Within New Zealand the flagship wines carry the Reserve Illiad label.
summary Rebecca Salmond is winemaker for Pleasant Valley and makes the wines for her Odyssey brand at that facility. There are no cellar-door sales; the wines are sold via retail and mail order. Within New Zealand the winery is known as Odyssey Wines, but owing to a legal dispute with the Wingarra Group in Australia, the wines are sold under the Rebecca Salmond label.

ohinemuri estate   NR

Moresby Street, Karangahake **region** Waikato and Bay of Plenty
phone (07) 862 8874 **fax** (07) 862 8847 **open** 7 days 10–6
winemaker Horst Hillerich **production** 1000 **est.** 1989
product range ($15.50–20 CD) Riesling, Gewurztraminer, Chardonnay, Pinotage.
summary German-born, trained and qualified winemaker Horst Hillerich came to New Zealand in 1987, first working at Totara before establishing Ohinemuri Estate. An atmospheric restaurant was duly opened at the newly constructed winery in the Karangahake Gorge in 1993; Hillerich has produced some highly regarded Gewurztraminer and Sauvignon Blanc. All of the grapes, incidentally, are purchased from growers in Hawke's Bay, the Waikato and Gisborne.

okahu estate   NR

Okahu Road, Kaitaia **region** Northland and Matakana
phone (09) 408 2066 **fax** (09) 408 2686 **open** 7 days 10–6 Oct–June, Mon–Fri July–Sept
winemaker Michael Bendit **production** 5000 **est.** 1984
product range ($16.95–45 CD) In more or less ascending order: Shipwreck Bay Riesling, Lightly Oaked Chardonnay, Red; Clifton Riesling and Chardonnay; Ninety Mile Semillon Chardonnay and Cabernet Merlot; Adelines Blanc de Blanc Méthode Traditionelle; and at the top of the range Kaz Semillon, Shiraz and Cabernet; also sundry fortified and sweet wines.
summary The 90 Mile wines (respectively blends of Chardonnay, Semillon and Arnsburger, and Cabernet Merlot, Pinotage and Pinot Noir) signal the location of Okahu Estate at the bottom end of New Zealand's well-known 90 Mile Beach. Recently the focus of the estate plantings of 2.5 hectares has switched to semillon and shiraz, which are said to show considerable promise; the plethora of other wines are made from grapes purchased from other regions.

Okahu Estate Kaz Cabernet

An estate-grown wine, which spends 18 months in a mix of French (70 per cent) and American (30 per cent) oak, 60 per cent new. Although from the 1997 vintage, and sandwiched between the spectacular 1998 wines, performed with considerable credit at the Royal Easter Wine Show 2000.
TTTY 1997 Medium red, with some purple hues remaining; the moderately intense bouquet offers cassis/berry fruit with hints of savoury spice. The palate runs along the same track, with soft berry fruit accompanied by leafy/savoury edges, finishing with fine tannins.   **rating: 84**
best drinking 2000–2005 **best vintages** NA **drink with** Spring lamb • $45

olssen's of bannockburn   NR

306 Felton Road, Bannockburn, Central Otago **region** Otago
phone (03) 445 1716 **fax** (03) 445 0050 **open** 7 days 10–4
winemaker Duncan Forsythe **production** 2000 **est.** 1989
product range ($17.95–37.50 CD) Riesling, Gewurztraminer, Sauvignon Blanc, Chardonnay, Pinot Noir, Slapjack Creek Reserve Pinot Noir.
summary Heather McPherson and John Olssen began the establishment of their 10-hectare vineyard (and now 5 hectares of rural garden and outdoor eating sites) in 1989. For the first three years after the vineyard came into bearing the grapes were sold to Chard Farm, but in 1997 the first wines were made under the Olssen's of Bannockburn label. A new but substantial enterprise in the Central Otago scene. Exports to the UK.

Olssen's of Bannockburn Pinot Noir

Fully ripe grapes and 12 months in French oak are the only known details, other than a very low pH which may well be the reason why the wine is rather hard.

▼▼▼▼ 1998 Medium red-purple; the bouquet is slightly hard and closed, with woody notes. Plum and cherry fruit is revealed on the palate, though that hardness persists; the wine needs time to soften and open up, although the window of peak drinkability may not be large. Curiously, I still like the wine. **rating: 87**

best drinking 2002–2004 **best vintages** NA **drink with** Stuffed mushrooms • $28

omaka springs estate ★★★

Kennedys Road, RD2, Blenheim, Marlborough **region** Marlborough
phone (03) 572 9933 **fax** (03) 572 9934 **open** 7 days 12–5
winemaker Ian Marchant **production** 19 600 **est.** 1992
product range ($7.99–16 R) Riesling, Semillon, Sauvignon Blanc, Chardonnay, Pinot Noir, Merlot, Cabernet Merlot.
summary Omaka Springs is a substantial operation with their state-of-the-art winery, built at the end of 1994, now reaching capacity (20 000 cases) and drawing upon 38 hectares of estate vineyards. The wines are exported to Australia, the UK, Sweden, the US, Canada, Hong Kong and Ireland.

Omaka Springs Sauvignon Blanc

Made in mainstream Marlborough style, unoaked but with up to 13 per cent Semillon incorporated to give a little more complexity and depth.

▼▼▼▼ 1999 Light green-yellow; there are nicely balanced fruit aromas in the mid-range of ripeness. Curiously, the floral characters increase on the palate, which is very fruity, with supple passionfruit flavours and a clean finish. **rating: 87**

best drinking 2000–2002 **best vintages** '94, '97, '99 **drink with** Sautéed scallops • $13

Omaka Springs Pinot Noir

A new arrival for Omaka Springs, using the Dijon Burgundy clones 115 and 116. The wine is given seven days pre-fermentation cold soak, with 15 per cent stalks returned to the ferment, which is then conducted at warm temperatures with pump-over.

▼▼▼▽ 1998 Light to medium red-purple; a clean, cherry-accented bouquet is followed by a palate with cherry, herb and spice flavours together with some grip to the finish. Overall a little simple notwithstanding the winemaking techniques used; it would seem young vines (or high yields?) are holding the wine back. **rating: 81**

best drinking 2001–2004 **best vintages** NA **drink with** Baked ham • $16

Omaka Springs Merlot

Yet another wine to capitalise on the wonderful vintage of 1998.

▼▼▼▼ 1998 Medium red-purple; the bouquet offers very pretty, ripe plummy fruit. The fresh palate has juicy berry flavours in an elegant, uncomplicated mode. **rating: 85**

best drinking 2000–2004 **best vintages** '98 **drink with** Yearling steak • $16

opihi vineyard NR

Gould's Road, Opihi, Pleasant Point, South Canterbury **region** Canterbury
phone (03) 614 7232 **fax** (03) 614 7234 **open** Vineyard Cafe is open Tues–Sun 11–4 and longer during daylight saving tel (03) 614 8308
winemaker Alan McCorkindale (Contract) **production** 1000 **est.** 1991
product range ($10–22 CD) Riesling, Müller Thurgau, Chardonnay, Pinot Gris, Pinot Noir.
summary Plantings at Opihi Vineyard commenced in 1991 with half a hectare each of müller thurgau, riesling, pinot noir and chardonnay, followed the next year by 2 hectares of pinot gris. The vineyard is established on a north-facing slope of Timaru clay loam with superb views across to the snow-clad Two Thumb Range. The tiny production is chiefly sold by mail order, with limited South Canterbury regional distribution.

Opihi Vineyard Chardonnay

A generous, full, fleshy fruit-driven style which, so far as I can tell, has not been barrel-fermented.

▼▼▼▽ 1999 Medium yellow-green; rich nectarine fruit aromas are followed by a flavoursome, albeit very fruit-sweet, palate with abundant nectarine and fig flavour. **rating: 82**

best drinking 2000–2001 **best vintages** NA **drink with** Peach-fed pork • $19.95

pacific vineyards ★★★

90 McLeod Road, Henderson **region** Auckland Area
phone (09) 838 9578 **fax** (09) 838 9578 **open** Mon–Sat 9–6
winemaker Steve Tubic **production** 7000 **est.** 1936
product range ($12.50–20 CD) Under the Phoenix label come Gisborne Gewurztraminer, Marlborough Riesling, Marlborough Sauvignon Blanc, Gisborne Chardonnay, Merlot, Cabernet Sauvignon; at the top of the range come Minnie's Merlot and Genesis Chardonnay.
summary One of the more interesting New Zealand wineries, notwithstanding its low profile, which has at various times produced very large quantities of wine (sold in cask and bulk) but is now refocusing on its bottled wine production (in more limited quantities) utilising grapes from Marlborough, Hawke's Bay and Gisborne, and on the other side of the fence has ventured into beer brewing.

palliser estate ★★★★☆

Kitchener Street, Martinborough **region** Wairarapa
phone (06) 306 9019 **fax** (06) 306 9946 **open** 7 days 10–4
winemaker Allan Johnson **production** 20 000 **est.** 1989
product range ($16–32 CD) Chardonnay, Sauvignon Blanc, Riesling, Noble Riesling, Méthode Champenoise, Pinot Noir; Pencarrow Sauvignon Blanc, Chardonnay and Pinot Noir.
summary Palliser Estate has produced a series of highly regarded and highly awarded wines from its state-of-the-art winery, right from its first vintage in 1989, and which has grown rapidly in recent years. My tasting notes indicate high scores across the full range of the wines produced, with the perfumed silky Pinot Noir to the fore. The wines are distributed in Australia through Negociants; other exports to the UK, Denmark, Switzerland, Canada, Bermuda, Singapore, Hong Kong and Thailand.

Palliser Estate Riesling

Produced both as a dry Riesling (as in this case) with occasional delectable late-harvest, botrytised versions. The '93, '96 and '98 were all gold medal winners in major wine shows, and there is no questioning the class of the wine.
▼▼▼▼ **1999** Medium yellow-green; the usual effusive bouquet with ripe citrus, pear and tropical fruit aromas; the palate has good intensity and length, with more of those ripe fruit flavours and its usual generosity. **rating:** 88
best drinking 2000–2006 **best vintages** '93, '96, '97, '98 **drink with** Lightly poached asparagus • $17

Palliser Estate Sauvignon Blanc

The Wellington/Wairarapa region seems to produce excellent Sauvignon Blanc year in, year out, a capacity underlined by the success the region has had in the annual Air New Zealand Wine Awards. Palliser Estate has been one of the most consistent and impressive performers, even if the '99 seems off-song.
▼▼▼☆ **1999** Light yellow-green; fragrant passionfruit aromas are promptly followed by reductive, sweaty, dead match characters, the palate with lively fruit but overshadowed by the reduction. The same problem exists with the Marlborough- and Martinborough-sourced wines, and I can only assume was due to the errant behaviour of yeasts during the 1999 vintage. **rating:** 83
best drinking 2000–2001 **best vintages** '91, '92, '94, '95, '96, '97, '98 **drink with** Grilled fish • $20

Palliser Estate Pencarrow Sauvignon Blanc

The second label of Palliser; quite obviously, has had a long and very slow ferment. The grapes, incidentally, come not from Martinborough but from Marlborough.
▼▼▼▼ **1999** Light to medium yellow-green; very fragrant passionfruit aromas are marred by a touch of reduction; a high-flavoured, intense palate has exactly the same strength and weakness, marred by the reduced characters evident on the bouquet. A pity. **rating:** 85
best drinking 2000–2001 **best vintages** NA **drink with** Barbecued prawns • $17

Palliser Estate Chardonnay

An exercise in restraint in anyone's language, and most particularly that of New Zealand. It is barrel-fermented, but only a little over 20 per cent new oak is used; while left on lees, the lees are not stirred; and less than half the wine is taken through malolactic fermentation.
▼▼▼▼☆ **1998** Light to medium green-yellow; a delicate and refined bouquet with crisp citrus and melon fruit supported by subtle oak is followed by an admirably restrained palate, the flavours harmoniously blending and providing a wine which is at once seamless and very long. **rating:** 93
best drinking 2000–2005 **best vintages** '91, '92, '93, '94, '98 **drink with** Fresh New Zealand whitebait • $30

Palliser Estate Pencarrow Chardonnay

Pencarrow is the second label, but a strange one because it so faithfully copies the design of the premium version.

TTTY 1998 Medium yellow-green; there is obvious, slightly coarse, oak input on the bouquet, but the fruit strikes back on the palate, with quite good length. **rating:** 84

best drinking 2000–2002 **best vintages** NA **drink with** Pan-fried chicken • $18

Palliser Estate Noble Riesling

Estate-grown and selectively picked heavily botrytised riesling has resulted in a wine with 10.4 degrees alcohol and 180 grams per litre of residual sugar.

TTTTY 1999 Glowing golden green; intense apricot and peach fruit aromas seem to have a hint of plasticene lurking behind them. However, the palate throws off any suggestion of ignoble rot, with more of those apricot and peach flavours in a luscious mouthful; the acidity is not abrasive. **rating:** 90

best drinking 2000–2004 **best vintages** NA **drink with** Crispy apple tart • $20

Palliser Estate Pinot Noir

Once somewhat lighter than the biggest wines from Wellington/Wairarapa but always showing bell-clear varietal character. A change in philosophy has seen the introduction of extended pre-fermentation cold-soak, a warm primary fermentation and then extended post-fermentation maceration. Matured for 12 months on light lees in a mix of new and older French oak casks.

TTTTT 1998 Medium red-purple; a clean and stylish bouquet offering a mix of tangy fruit and foresty/oaky notes in the background. The palate has particular good intensity and length, finishing with firm but not overdone tannins. For long one of my favourite Pinot Noirs, and this year is no exception. **rating:** 94

best drinking 2000–2005 **best vintages** '89, '91, '94, '96, '98 **drink with** Duck risotto • $32

Palliser Estate Pencarrow Pinot Noir

Unlike its sister wine, the Pencarrow Chardonnay, made from Martinborough grapes. Pre-fermentation and post-fermentation maceration are both used, although the used oak in which it was matured is noticeable.

TTTT 1998 Light to medium red-purple; a light bouquet with foresty notes and some passing glue paste aromas from previously used oak barrels. The palate is light, but authentically Pinot Noir, in a predominantly stemmy/foresty/savoury spectrum. **rating:** 85

best drinking 2000–2003 **best vintages** NA **drink with** Pork with rosemary potato wedges • $24

parker mc   NR

91 Banks Street, Gisborne **region** Gisborne
phone (06) 867 6967 **fax** (06) 867 6967 **open** 7 days 9.30–6
winemaker Phil Parker **production** 1000 **est.** 1987
product range ($15–32 R) Dry Flint, Classical Brut, Rosé Brut, Firstlight Red, Firstlight Fortified.
summary A Méthode Champenoise specialist which has caused much interest and comment. Firstlight Red is a blend of Merlot and Pinotage and is billed as being the world's first light red wine each year; unless it is picked on 1 January it is unlikely that claim will stand unchallenged. Has not entered the show ring and I have not tasted the wines. The winery also has a restaurant open for lunch and dinner every day of the week.

park estate winery   NR

2087 Pakowhai Road, RD3, Napier **region** Hawke's Bay
phone (06) 844 8137 **fax** (06) 844 6800 **open** 7 days 10–5.30
winemaker Owen Park **production** 5000 **est.** 1992
product range ($9–25 CD) Riesling, Gewurztraminer, Sauvignon Blanc, Chardonnay, Merlot, Cabernet Sauvignon, Sparkling Sauvignon Cuvée, Late Harvest Muscat; Bell Tower is cheaper second label.
summary Owen and Dianne Park run a thriving and varied enterprise offering both fruit and grape-based wines (and 35 different types of fudge) from a large mission-style winery and restaurant. Wine production (from grapes, that is) constitutes a modest part of the business. Exports to Australia, Singapore, Hong Kong, Japan, The Netherlands, Germany and the US.

pegasus bay   ★★★★☆

Stockgrove Road, Waipara, RD2, Amberley **region** Canterbury
phone (03) 314 6869 **fax** (03) 314 6869 **open** 7 days 10–5
winemaker Matthew Donaldson, Lynette Hudson **production** 15 000 **est.** 1986
product range ($18.95–37.95 CD) Chardonnay, Sauvignon Blanc Semillon, Riesling, Aria (Reserve Riesling), Pinot Noir, Maestro (Bordeaux-blend), Finale (Reserve Noble Chardonnay); Main Divide is second-label range of Aged Riesling, Riesling, Marlborough Sauvignon Blanc, Merlot Cabernet, Pinot Noir.

summary Leading wine-writer and wine judge Professor Ivan Donaldson (a neurologist) has, together with his wife and family, established the largest winery in Waipara, with 20 hectares of vineyards in bearing and a large and striking cathedral-like winery. Son Matthew is a Roseworthy graduate, and in every respect this is a serious operation. A winery restaurant adds to the attraction for visitors. Wine quality is consistently good, the wines with style and verve. Exports to Australia, the US and Japan.

Pegasus Bay Riesling

Made in the typically adventurous Pegasus Bay fashion, given eight months on lees, and incorporating a varying percentage of botrytised grapes.

▼▼▼▼ **1999** Light to medium green-yellow; voluminous, fragrant flowery aromas lead into a full-flavoured palate. Here the problem is that even by the standards of New Zealand, the sweetness seems well over the top for the (apparent) acidity, but there is no shortage of character.   **rating:** 88

best drinking 2001–2005 **best vintages** '98 **drink with** Prosciutto and melon   • $18.95

Pegasus Bay Canterbury Pinot Noir

Pegasus Bay has produced astonishing rich, deeply coloured and full-bodied Pinot Noirs right from the outset. An extremely impressive wine which proclaims its unfiltered origins. The Donaldson family has also worked very hard in evaluating fermentation and maturation techniques for the variety, all of which have paid off.

▼▼▼▼▽ **1998** Very strong purple-red colour; a powerful and complex bouquet with plum and spice leads into a typically powerful and concentrated palate with dark plum and prune at the sweet end of the spectrum and a touch of herb/stem at the other end. The tannins test the depth of the fruit, but the wine remains in balance (just).   **rating:** 91

best drinking 2001–2006 **best vintages** '93, '94, '95, '97, '98 **drink with** Rare breast of squab   • $34.95

peninsula estate ★★★★

52A Korora Road, Oneroa, Waiheke Island **region** Waiheke Island
phone (09) 372 7866 **fax** (09) 372 7840 **open** Weekends 1–4
winemaker Christopher Lush **production** 1400 **est.** 1986
product range ($13–35 CD) The top-of-the-line release is Peninsula Estate Cabernet Merlot; the intermittent second label is Oneroa Bay Cabernet Merlot. Both in fact include a small percentage of Cabernet Franc and Malbec. Since 1998 has also included Chardonnay and Syrah.
summary The Peninsula Estate Cabernet Merlot comes from a 5.5-hectare estate vineyard situated on a peninsula overlooking Oneroa Bay. The spectacular vineyard has produced some equally spectacular wines. The expansion to the range of wines came in the wake of forming a joint venture with its nextdoor neighbours, Robert and Emerald Gilmour, doubling the size of vineyards and making a little Chardonnay and rather more Syrah available. No recent tastings, however.

perrelle lake hayes NR

c/o Chard Farm, Chard Road, RD 1, Queenstown **region** Otago
phone (03) 442 6110 **fax** (03) 441 8400 **open** Not
winemaker Rob Hay, Duncan Forsyth **production** 3000 **est.** 1995
product range ($20–30 R) Cuvée de Prestige, Grand Cuvée Brut, Blanc de Blancs, Arcadia Lake Hayes Special Cuvée Brut.
summary Perrelle Lake Hayes is a specialist sparkling wine producer and a joint venture between John Derby (who is the general manager of the business) and Rob Hay, long-time Chard Farm owner-winemaker. Back in 1989 they identified an outstanding vineyard site at Gibbston, which was purchased and then subdivided and sold as vineyard lots. Part of the grapes for Perrelle come from these vineyards, but future growth will come from new plantings on the Amisfield Vineyard near Cromwell, where 120 hectares will be developed by 2004. Perrelle Lake Hayes has a major holding in this venture.

pleasant valley wines ★★★

322 Henderson Valley Road, Waitakere **region** Auckland Area
phone (09) 838 8857 **fax** (09) 838 8456 **open** Mon–Sat 9–6, Sun 11–6
winemaker Rebecca Salmond **production** 10 000 **est.** 1902
product range ($9.80–21.95 CD) Gewurztraminer, Sauvignon Blanc, Chenin Chardonnay, Chardonnay, Riesling, Pinotage, together with a range of fortified wines, chiefly Sherries but also Port.
summary A former moribund fortified winemaker, revitalised since 1984 and now complementing its stocks of old fortified wines with well-made table wines sourced from Hawke's Bay, Gisborne and Marlborough, supplementing a 7-hectare estate vineyard at Henderson. Exports to Japan.

✿ pleiades vineyard   NR

RD 6, Blenheim **region** Marlborough
phone (03) 572 4841 **fax** (03) 572 4842 **open** Not
winemaker Winston Oliver **production** 300 **est.** 1993
product range ($28 R) Maia (Merlot Malbec blend).
summary Pleiades Vineyard has been established as a partnership between Maggie Dewar, a clinical psychologist in real life, and Winston Oliver, who has had ten years experience in the Marlborough wine industry, including the Marlborough viticultural course and practical winery experience. The vineyard is situated in the Waihopai Valley (one of the offshoots of the Wairau Valley) with clay-rich loam over very deep gravels. Merlot, malbec and pinot gris are planted with more pinot noir and pinot gris planned, which will lift the total plantings to 5 hectares. The 1998 Pleiades Maia is a brilliant debut for the winery.

ponder estate   ★★★☆

New Renwick Road, Blenheim **region** Marlborough
phone (03) 572 8642 **fax** (03) 572 9034 **open** 7 days 10–4.30
winemaker Graham Paul **production** 12 000 **est.** 1987
product range ($16.50–45 CD) Classic Riesling, Marlborough Sauvignon Blanc, Chardonnay, Artist's Reserve Pinot Noir.
summary With 25 hectares of vineyard and olive grove, Ponder Estate is primarily a grape grower (supplying chardonnay, sauvignon blanc and riesling to Matua Valley for its Shingle Peak label) but is rapidly increasing the amount vinified for its own label. It also has a press house for its own olive oil production. Exports to Australia, the UK and the US.

Ponder Estate Marlborough Sauvignon Blanc

Produced from 8.5 hectares of estate planting. Marlborough Sauvignon Blanc seems to have veered between two extremes in 1998 (heavy and truculent) and 1999 (delicate and feminine). This wine is no exception.
▼▼▼▼ 1999 Light green-yellow; the bouquet is moderately intense, with a mix of gooseberry/tropical fruit and more herbal characters. The moderately intense palate is the mirror image of the bouquet; overall delicate and seemingly lacking concentration.   **rating:** 85
best drinking 2000–2001 **best vintages** '94, '97 **drink with** Shellfish • $16.50

Ponder Estate Chardonnay

A wine made without pretension, designed to be consumed when young and fresh, and with minimal oak influence.
▼▼▼▽ 1999 Light to medium yellow-green; the bouquet is clean and crisp, with light citrus/melon fruit and the barest hint of oak. A refreshing, light style on the palate, with no claim to complexity.   **rating:** 84
best drinking 2000–2001 **best vintages** NA **drink with** Antipasto • $20

pouparae park   NR

Bushmere Road, Gisborne **region** Gisborne
phone (06) 867 7931 **fax** (06) 867 7909 **open** 7 days 10–6
winemaker Alec Cameron **production** 500 **est.** 1994
product range ($7.50–15 R) Riesling, Chardonnay, Solstice Blanc (Müller Thurgau, Dr Hogg Muscat blend), Pinotage.
summary Pouparae Park was established on the family's property by Alec and Rachel Cameron in 1994. 'Pouparae' means 'high vantage point'.

Pouparae Park Chardonnay

The minuscule production does not prevent the Camerons from fashioning a rich, full-flavoured Chardonnay which is a good example of quality Gisborne fruit.
▼▼▼▽ 1998 Medium to full yellow-green; the bouquet is softly attractive, with melon, peach and cashew; the cashew flavours build somewhat on the palate, but are not compounded by oak, leaving the fruit for all to see and enjoy.   **rating:** 82
best drinking 2000–2001 **best vintages** NA **drink with** Crumbed brains • $14

purple heights estate   NR

Main West Coast Road, RD6, Christchurch **region** Canterbury
phone (03) 358 2080 **fax** (03) 325 3843 **open** Not
winemaker Dayne Sherwood (Contract) **production** NA **est.** 1996
product range Riesling, Noble Riesling.
summary Partners Delwyn and John Mathieson and David and Diana Jackson named their vineyard after the colour of the nearby foothills, planting 2 hectares to riesling. Having sold the grapes to other makers for many years, the partners ventured into winemaking (via contract at Sherwood Estate) in 1996. There are no sales to the public; all wine is sold wholesale to retailers and restaurants.

quarry road estate   NR

Waerenga Road, RD1, Te Kauwhata **region** Waikato and Bay of Plenty
phone (07) 826 3595 **fax** (07) 826 3595 **open** 7 days 8–6
winemaker Toby Cooper, Jenny Gander, Nikki Cooper **production** 3500 **est.** 1996
product range ($6.50–22 R) Grape juices, table wines, sparkling wines, fortified wines and liqueurs. The table wines are Sauvignon Blanc, Chardonnay and Cabernet Sauvignon Merlot. Wines are also purchased in bulk from Bazzard Estate.
summary 1996 is a nominal year of establishment, for this is the former Aspen Ridge, acquired by the Cooper family in that year. With the aid of consultancy advice, they intend to move more towards the production of premium table wines and to expand the cellar-door facilities.

quartz reef   ★★★★☆

PO Box 63, Cromwell, Central Otago **region** Otago
phone (03) 445 1135 **fax** (03) 445 1180 **open** By appointment
winemaker Rudi Bauer **production** 1500 **est.** 1996
product range ($21–33 R) Pinot Gris, Pinot Noir, Chauvet Méthode Champenoise.
summary Quartz Reef is a joint venture between Rudi Bauer and Clotilde Chauvet, both of whom are Rippon winemakers. Three hectares have been planted to pinot noir and chardonnay, with plantings intended to extend to 9 hectares of pinot noir and 1 hectare of pinot gris.

Quartz Reef Pinot Gris

Rudi Bauer is a dedicated maker (and consumer) of Pinot Gris, partially due, no doubt, to his Austro-Germanic upbringing.
▼▼▼▼♀ **1999** Light to medium yellow-green; the bouquet is quite complex, with lemon, lemon blossom and lemon peel aromas. A tight, lively, crisp and long palate is enhanced by the flavours which run right through its length. The only gold medal winner in the dry 1999 Pinot Gris class at the Royal Easter Wine Show 2000.
rating: 92
best drinking 2000–2005 **best vintages** '99 **drink with** Quiche Lorraine • $20

Quartz Reef Chauvet

A blend of 80 per cent Pinot Noir and 20 per cent Chardonnay grown not in Central Otago but in Marlborough. It spends 24 months on yeast lees before disgorgement.
▼▼▼▼♀ **NV** Medium yellow-green; the bouquet is clean, with quite soft citrus fruit, a hint of bready yeast, and no apparent aldehydes. The wine has a welcoming mouthfeel with a mix of citrus, pear and ripe apple fruit flavours, supported by a singularly well-balanced finish.
rating: 93
best drinking Drink now **best vintages** NA **drink with** Aperitif • $23

Quartz Reef Pinot Noir

Rudi Bauer established his credentials as a Pinot Noir maker during his time with Rippon, and has since built on that reputation to the point where he was voted Champion Winemaker of the Year at the 1999 Liquorland Royal Easter Wine Show for his role in shaping and making so many of the Cental Otago Pinot Noirs to be awarded medals at that show. All of his skills come through on this wine, which spent 11 months in French oak before being bottled. The grapes come from the Pisa Range Estate Vineyard, owned by Jenny and Warrick Hawker.
▼▼▼▼♀ **1998** Medium red-purple; spicy oak is somewhat dominant on the bouquet but does not obscure the attractive dark fruit underneath. The palate opens with attractive savoury/plummy fruit, spicy oak still being evident but less assertive than on the bouquet. The wine has good texture and tannins.
rating: 92
best drinking 2000–2005 **best vintages** '98 **drink with** Wild boar • $33

rabbit ridge   NR

407 Taylor Road, Waimauku **region** Auckland Area
phone (09) 411 8556 **fax** (09) 411 8556 **open** By appointment
winemaker Matua Valley (Contract) **production** 210 **est.** 1990
product range ($19.95 R) Chardonnay, Cabernet Sauvignon Merlot.
summary Former architect and now leading New Zealand fine wine wholesaler and importer Paul Mitchell (of
Wine Direct Imports) is indulging in a little poaching at Rabbit Ridge. He established a 1-hectare vineyard 30
minutes from the centre of Auckland, with his house situated in the middle of the vineyard; it is sufficiently
elevated for him to see rabbits feeding in the vineyard from the lounge. The wines are contract-made at Matua
Valley, and Paul Mitchell has no intention of hopping into a fermenter at vintage time. However, he does concede
there are plans to build a small cellar-door sales and barrel storage area; in the meantime the wines are available
from Wine Direct or by mail order.

Rabbit Ridge Burrow Cabernet Sauvignon Merlot

Produced from the 1-hectare planting of a mix of cabernet sauvignon, merlot, cabernet franc and malbec.
▼▼▼▽ **1997** Medium red; the bouquet is quite fragrant in a quite leafy/spicy spectrum. The palate, likewise, runs
in the spicy/savoury/leafy spectrum, finishing with slightly green tannins. Not forced to be something it isn't, but
one hopes for better things with the '98.   **rating:** 82
best drinking 2001–2004 **best vintages** NA **drink with** Rabbit in red wine, of course • $19.95

✿ ransom wines   NR

Valerie Close, Warkworth **region** Northland and Matakana
phone (09) 425 8862 **fax** (09) 360 5539 **open** Weekends 10–6 summer, 11–5 winter or by appointment
winemaker Robin Ransom **production** 800 **est.** 1996
product range ($16–24 R) Gumfield Chardonnay, Barrique Chardonnay, Clos de Valerie Pinot Gris, Dark
Summit Cabernet Sauvignon.
summary Robin and Marion Ransom are in the course of establishing a 6-hectare vineyard, south of
Warkworth, with north-facing slopes and relatively free-draining soils. Their weekend and holiday relaxation
through Ransom Wines was the result of a trip to Tuscany and some subsequent vintage experience in Nelson.

redmetal vineyards   NR

2006 Maraekakaho Road, RD1, Bridge Pa, Hastings **region** Hawke's Bay
phone (06) 879 6567 **fax** (06) 879 6717 **open** Not
winemaker Grant Edmonds **production** 1500 **est.** 1992
product range ($24–39 R) Rosé, Merlot, Basket Press Merlot Cabernet.
summary A joint venture between the vastly experienced winemaker Grant Edmonds, wife Sue, and Diane and
Gary Simpson, with initial plantings of 4.5 hectares (on an 8-hectare block) on an alluvial silt over gravel soil
known locally as red metal. The wines are exported to the UK. No recent tastings.

rippon vineyard   ★★★★

Mount Aspiring Road, Lake Wanaka **region** Otago
phone (03) 443 8084 **fax** (03) 443 8084 **open** 7 days 11.30–5 Dec–Apr, 1.30–4 July–Nov, May–June by
appointment
winemaker Russell Lake **production** 5000 **est.** 1975
product range ($14.50–35 CD) Riesling, Sauvignon Blanc, Hotere White, Osteiner, Chardonnay,
Gewurztraminer, Rosé, Emma Rippon Sparkling, Pinot Noir, Merlot Syrah.
summary Claimed, with some justification, to be the most beautifully sited vineyard in the world, situated on
the edge of Lake Wanaka (which is responsible for the remarkable site climate), with the snow-clad New Zealand
Alps painting a striking backdrop. Right across the range, Rippon has produced some outstanding wines, none
more so than the Pinot Noir. In recent years, Rippon has moved to Bio-Gro™ certified organic status. The wines
are exported to Australia, the UK, Brazil and Japan.

Rippon Vineyard Pinot Noir

Eighty per cent of the fruit is destemmed, 20 per cent fermented as whole bunches, with foot stamping (pigeage).
The wine spends 11 months in French oak and is racked once, with no filtration prior to bottling.
▼▼▼▼ **1998** Light to medium red, with just a touch of purple; the bouquet is clean, firm and fresh, with
moderately intense cherry fruit the driver. The medium-weight palate has good length and texture, with
appropriate acidity on the finish; once again, it is the cherry fruit which is doing the work.   **rating:** 86
best drinking 2001–2004 **best vintages** '90, '92, '93, '95 '96, '98 **drink with** Coq au vin • $35

🐦 riverline vineyard   NR

State Highway 83, Georgetown, North Otago **region** Otago
phone (03) 431 1737 **fax** (03) 431 1737 **open** 7 days 12–6
winemaker Graeme Thorn **production** 8 **est.** 1994
product range ($15–20 CD) Riesling, Gewurztraminer, Pinot Noir.
summary Graeme and Pip Thorn preside over a micro vineyard and winery in North Otago (the only winery in this region). Experimental plantings of half a hectare of pinot noir and a quarter of a hectare each of gewurztraminer and riesling produced 100 bottles of wine in 1999, sold through the shop on site which also offers other New Zealand wines and beer. It also offers the only taxidermy showroom I have ever encountered as part of a winery cellar door.

riverside wines   ★★☆

Dartmoor Road, Puketapu, Napier **region** Hawke's Bay
phone (06) 844 4942 **fax** (06) 844 4671 **open** Summer 7 days 11–5, winter by appointment
winemaker Russell Wiggins **production** 12 000 **est.** 1989
product range ($12–28 CD) Dartmoor Sauvignon Blanc, Barrel Fermented Sauvignon Blanc, Dartmoor Chardonnay, Stirling Chardonnay, Reserve Chardonnay, Rosé, Merlot, Cabernet Merlot.
summary Ian and Rachel Cadwallader have established 14 hectares of vines on their farm which are coming progressively into production. The wine is made on site in the small winery above the Dartmoor Valley. It has to be said that overall wine quality was far from exciting, but the arrival of Russell Wiggins as winemaker in late 1998 is almost certain to rectify matters. In the meantime, exports to the US and Thailand are under way.

rockwood cellars   NR

James Rochford Place, RD5, Hastings **region** Hawke's Bay
phone (06) 879 8760 **fax** (06) 879 4158 **open** By appointment
winemaker Tony Bish **production** 10 000 **est.** 1995
product range ($15 R) Sauvignon Blanc, Chardonnay, Cabernet Merlot.
summary Rockwood Cellars aims primarily at the export market, with a varied range of modestly priced wines all selling for less than $15 and is in fact part of the Sacred Hill Wine Group, albeit with its separate brand identity.

rongopai wines   ★★★★

Te Kauwhata Road, Te Kauwhata **region** Waikato and Bay of Plenty
phone (07) 826 3981 **fax** (07) 826 3462 **open** Mon–Fri 9–5, Sat 10–5, Sun 11–4
winemaker Tom van Dam **production** 15 000 **est.** 1985
product range ($11.50–35.50 R) Sauvignon Blanc, Sauvignon Blanc The Knoll, Sauvignon Blanc Vintage Reserve, Riesling, Chardonnay, Chardonnay Single Vineyard, Chardonnay Vintage Reserve, Chardonnay Swan Road, Pinot Noir, Merlot Cabernet and Botrytised Selection.
summary Now owned solely by Tom van Dam and wife Faith but going from strength to strength, it would seem. The reputation of Rongopai rests fairly and squarely upon its spectacular botrytised wines, which enjoyed equal quantities of show success and critical acclaim throughout most of the 1990s. Both Chardonnay and the more conventional Riesling are used in these wines; the minimal use of chemicals and herbicides in the vineyards promotes late-season botrytis, countered by vine-trimming, leaf-plucking and bunch-thinning for the conventional table wines. All grapes are hand-picked. No recent tastings

rosebank estate   NR

Corner Johns and Groynes Drive, Belfast, Christchurch **region** Canterbury
phone (03) 323 8539 **fax** (03) 323 8538 **open** 7 days 10–5
winemaker Kym Rayner **production** 1200 **est.** 1993
product range ($6.95–15.95 CD) Riesling, Sauvignon Blanc, Chardonnay, Marlborough Chardonnay, Canterbury Chardonnay, Reserve Canterbury Chardonnay, Müller Thurgau, Directors' White, Sparkling Sekt, Pinot Noir, Cabernet Shiraz.
summary Situated only minutes from the city centre and six minutes from Christchurch airport, this is as much an entertainment centre as it is a winery, with a beautiful garden setting containing hundreds of roses, rhododendrons and camellias; lunch is served from the restaurant each day, and à la carte dinner from Wednesday to Sunday from 6 pm. The Waipara vineyard will ultimately provide 50 per cent of the production; in the meantime most of the grapes are being sourced from Marlborough. In 1996 a cricket ground was established at Rosebank in village-green style. No recent tastings.

rossendale wines   NR

150 Old Tai Tapu Road, Christchurch **region** Canterbury
phone (03) 322 7780 **fax** (03) 332 9272 **open** 7 days 10–5
winemaker Grant Whelan **production** 6000 **est.** 1987
product range ($12–22 CD) Chardonnay, Barrel Selection Chardonnay, Riesling, Sauvignon Blanc, St Helena Pinot Noir, Lancaster Pinot Noir.
summary Rossendale is the highly successful venture of beef exporter Brent Rawstron, who ventured into viticulture on his farm in 1987. A 120-year-old gatekeeper's lodge on the farm has been converted into a restaurant and sales area, nestling in a century-old forest. All this, and situated only 15 minutes from the centre of Christchurch, making it the closest winery to that city. Exports to the UK and Ontario.

ruby bay winery   ★★☆

Korepo Road, RD1, Upper Moutere, Nelson **region** Nelson
phone (03) 540 2825 **fax** (03) 540 2105 **open** 7 days 11–6
winemaker Anita Ewart-Croy **production** 750 **est.** 1976
product range ($15–22.50 CD) Nelson Sauvignon Blanc, Marlborough Chardonnay, Nelson Pinot Noir.
summary The beautifully sited former Korepo winery, purchased by the Moore family in 1989, is well known for its restaurant. The winery changed hands in 1999, and it seems that positive changes are under way even though the volume of production has been sharply cut back. No recent tastings.

sacred hill   ★★★★☆

Dartmoor Road, RD6, Napier **region** Hawke's Bay
phone (06) 844 0138 **fax** (06) 844 3271 **open** 7 days Jan, weekends 11–4 Mar–Apr, winter by appointment
winemaker Tony Bish **production** 19 500 **est.** 1986
product range ($14.95–35 R) There are three ranges of wines; at the very top come intermittent releases of special selection wines, including 1995 Rifleman's Chardonnay and Brokenstone Merlot; then comes the Reserve range, although not necessarily carrying that word in the name (just to confuse the unwary, typically being described as barrel-fermented or basket press); and at the bottom the Whitecliff range.
summary The Mason family are pastoralists-turned-grape growers and thereafter winemakers (Mark Mason is a Roseworthy graduate). Sacred Hill has had its ups and downs since it was founded in 1986 but has steadied significantly since 1995. The top-of-the-range Rifleman's Chardonnay, Brokenstone Merlot, and Basket Press Cabernet Sauvignon are high-quality wines. Exports to the UK, The Netherlands and the US.

Sacred Hill Reserve Barrel Fermented Chardonnay
Produced from the small-berried Mendoza clone, which is a far more controllable clone in Hawke's Bay than it is in Marlborough, and which provides greater intensity and density of fruit than Clone 5. It also lends itself to the whole-bunch pressing technique used to make this wine, which is fermented in new French oak.
▼▼▼▼♀ 1999 Medium yellow-green; a complex bouquet with the generous use of barrel-fermentation and malolactic fermentation to push the wine along. The palate is long and quite intense, with fig and cashew flavours, the fruit supporting the winemaking inputs.   **rating:** 90
best drinking 2000–2001 **best vintages** '99 **drink with** Pasta carbonara •$22

Sacred Hill Rifleman's Chardonnay
The top-of-the-range Chardonnay from Sacred Hill, given the Full Monty of winemaker's tricks; hand-picked, whole-bunch pressed, barrel-fermented with some wild yeast, and left on lees for 12 months. A mix of new and one-year-old French oak barriques are used, and the grapes are the small-berried Mendoza clone.
▼▼▼▼ 1998 Medium to full yellow-green; the complex bouquet swirls with fruit, oak and nut aromas, leading into an opulently textured palate with quite pronounced malolactic-fermentation inputs, the cashew being balanced by ripe melon and grapefruit flavours. Stylish, albeit oaky, stuff.   **rating:** 89
best drinking 2000–2001 **best vintages** '97, '98 **drink with** Turkey •$35

Sacred Hill Basket Press Merlot
The lesser of two Merlots produced by Sacred Hill with Brokenstone the senior partner. In years such as 1998 the junior status seems largely irrelevant.
▼▼▼▼ 1998 Medium to full red-purple; the bouquet is complex, with quite ripe fruit and cedary oak. Overall, the palate is relatively restrained but again has that ripe fruit, with sweet tannins coming partly from the oak and partly from the fruit.   **rating:** 89
best drinking 2002–2007 **best vintages** '98 **drink with** Grilled T-bone steak •$20

Sacred Hill Brokenstone Reserve Merlot

1995 was the inaugural vintage of this wine, which was a blend of 80 per cent Merlot and 20 per cent Malbec. It is given post-fermentation maceration for 21 days, and spends 15 months in new French barriques.

♥♥♥♥♀ **1998** Dense red-purple; a concentrated, rich bouquet which takes some time to open up, but does so revealing powerful, ripe berry fruit which spills over into the sweet, smooth palate with touches of liquorice and spice. Very long but, like some of the other Hawke's Bay Merlots of the vintage, seems to stray into Cabernet Sauvignon territory. **rating:** 91

best drinking 2003–2013 **best vintages** '95, '98 **drink with** Ragout of venison • $35

Sacred Hill Whitecliff Vineyards Merlot

Unconventionally made without the use of oak, and designed as an early-drinking style. Producing a wine such as this is not as easy as might appear at first sight, as many of the reductive, sweaty Chilean wines show. This is as good as they come.

♥♥♥♥♀ **1999** Light to medium red-purple; clean, fresh and delicate red berry aromas lead into a gentle red berry-flavoured palate with just a hint of savoury spice; excellent structure, feel and balance. **rating:** 90

best drinking 2000–2001 **best vintages** '99 **drink with** Whatever takes your fancy • $15

saint clair estate ★★★★☆

156 New Renwick Road, RD2, Blenheim **region** Marlborough
phone (03) 578 8695 **fax** (03) 578 8696 **open** At Country Life Craft Shop, Aberharts Road, Blenheim
winemaker Kim Crawford (Consultant), Matt Thomson **production** 28 000 **est.** 1978
product range ($15–26 R) The Marlborough range consists of Riesling, Sauvignon Blanc, Unoaked Chardonnay, Chardonnay and Merlot; the Reserve range comprises Awatere Sauvignon Blanc, Omaka Chardonnay, Rapaura Merlot and Doctors Creek Noble Botrytis.
summary Neal and Judy Ibbotson followed the tried-and-true path of growing grapes for 15 or so years before venturing into wine production, which they did with spectacular success in 1994. Since that year, ever-increasing quantities of grapes from their 56 hectares have been vinified, with the exceptional skills of Kim Crawford leading to a cascade of show awards. The wines are exported to 21 countries across Europe, North America, Asia and the Pacific Region, including Australia.

Saint Clair Estate Marlborough Riesling

Since 1997 estate-grown; made by consultant winemaker Kim Crawford in a typically flamboyant style.

♥♥♥♥♀ **1999** Light to medium green-yellow; the bouquet is fragrant and intense, with citrus aromas running into the tropical end. A full-on wine in a complex spätlese style, with lots of tropical/citrus fruit to carry the sweetness, helped by balanced acidity. **rating:** 92

best drinking 2000–2004 **best vintages** '99 **drink with** Fresh fruit • $15

Saint Clair Estate Marlborough Sauvignon Blanc

Produced from the Saint Clair Estate vineyards in the Wairau and Awatere Valleys. The 1994 vintage was a triumphant introduction and did much to establish the reputation of Saint Clair. Subsequent vintages have been good rather than great but certainly offer excellent value.

♥♥♥♥♀ **1999** Light to medium yellow-green; the bouquet is slightly dull and muted, though without fault. The palate, likewise, has varietal fruit flavour but lacks the sparkle and zip of the best wines. **rating:** 84

best drinking 2000–2001 **best vintages** '94, '96, '97 **drink with** Sashimi • $16

Saint Clair Estate Marlborough Chardonnay

Fifty per cent of the wine is barrel-fermented in a mix of new and used American oak and then aged on its lees for eight months. The balance was cool-fermented in stainless steel tanks and retained there, with two-thirds of the total wine undergoing malolactic fermentation.

♥♥♥♥♀ **1999** Light to medium yellow-green; the bouquet is quite tight and elegant, with citrus and melon fruit together with a whiff of cashew. The palate is similarly fresh and elegant, with sensitive oak handling; a lighter style with a clean finish. However, drink as quickly as possible. **rating:** 90

best drinking 2000–2001 **best vintages** '99 **drink with** Grilled fish • $17

Saint Clair Estate Doctors Creek Noble Botrytis 375 ml

First made in 1996, with follow-on vintages in 1998 and 1999; only made in those years when there is a clean infection of botrytis in the vineyard.

🍷🍷🍷🍷🍷 **1999** Light green-yellow; a gloriously intense bouquet with Germanic lime juice aromas. The palate is equally intense, with superb lime juice flavours and great balance. Desperately unlucky not to win a gold medal at the Royal Easter Wine Show 2000; it certainly did on my score sheet.   **rating:** 94

best drinking 2001–2009 **best vintages** '99 **drink with** Millefeuille of strawberries • $26

Saint Clair Estate Marlborough Merlot

Like its Reserve counterpart, made from grapes grown in the Rapaura Road district. Apart from (presumed) differences in the fruit quality, the considerable gap which exists between the wines comes through oak handling. Whereas the Reserve is heavily oaked, this wine is only briefly oak aged. Perhaps that is why I (controversially) prefer this to its illustrious brother.

🍷🍷🍷🍷 **1998** Very good purple-red; the bouquet is quite intense, with sweet, juicy berry fruit aromas. The palate is fine and lively, with spicy savoury fruit, crisp acidity and just the barest flick of oak.   **rating:** 93

best drinking 2001–2006 **best vintages** '98 **drink with** Lamb fillets • $19

Saint Clair Estate Rapaura Reserve Marlborough Merlot

Produced from the best grapes grown on the Mere Road Vineyard. It spends 12 months in a mix of new and used American oak barriques. Once again, it fairly and squarely raises the question of the level of oak, an issue made more pointed by the choice of American barrels.

🍷🍷🍷🍷 **1998** Medium red-purple; strong, dusty vanilla oak utterly dominates the bouquet; the fruit is a little more evident on the palate, and has good length and intensity.   **rating:** 89

best drinking 2001–2006 **best vintages** '98 **drink with** Duck confit • $26

st helena estate ★★★☆

Coutts Island Road, Christchurch **region** Canterbury
phone (03) 323 8202 **fax** (03) 323 8252 **open** Mon–Sat 10–4.30, Sun 12–5
winemaker Alan McCorkindale **production** 10 000 **est.** 1978
product range ($7.50–30 CD) Riesling, Canterbury Plains Müller Thurgau, Southern Alps Dry White, Chardonnay, Reserve Chardonnay, Noble Bacchus, Pinot Gris, Pinot Blanc, Pinot Noir, Reserve Pinot Noir, Port Hills Dry Red, Peers Port.
summary Whether in its moments of success or otherwise, controversy has never been far from St Helena's door. After a spectacular debut for its Pinot Noir in 1982, there has been a roller-coaster ride since, but much work in the vineyard (and also winery) is starting to pay dividends. The arrival of the immensely talented Alan McCorkindale as winemaker has seen the expected lift in quality, and the wines are now exported to Australia, the UK and Canada.

St Helena Marlborough Sauvignon Blanc

1999 marked the first vintage from St Helena's newly acquired Marlborough plantings in the Wairau Valley. Three pickings over a period of 12 days were made, and the wine was cold-fermented in stainless steel. A portion of the blend was fermented in French oak, and a small percentage of Semillon is also included.

🍷🍷🍷🍷 **1999** Light to medium yellow-green; a delicate and elegant wine, perfectly balanced and beautifully made but which, in the final analysis, lacks distinctive character. I am at a loss to explain the reason.   **rating:** 83

best drinking 2000–2002 **best vintages** NA **drink with** Delicate seafood • $14

St Helena Estate Marlborough Chardonnay

The first release from its Marlborough vineyard, acquired in 1999. part of the wine is barrel-fermented in French oak and all undergoes malolactic fermentation and ageing on yeast lees with regular barrel stirring for a period of six months.

🍷🍷🍷🍷 **1999** Medium yellow-green; a quite complex bouquet, with cashew, vanilla and fig coming through from the barrel-ferment and mlf regime is followed by a palate which is lighter and more delicate than the bouquet suggests, fruit-driven with fresh citrus flavours and a faintly creamy mouthfeel.   **rating:** 88

best drinking 2000–2002 **best vintages** '99 **drink with** Salmon tartare • $16

St Helena Estate Reserve Canterbury Chardonnay

Estate-grown and whole-bunch pressed before fermentation in a mixture of French and American oak barrels. The wine undergoes full malolactic fermentation and is aged on lees in barrel for 12 months with regular stirring.

🍷🍷🍷🍷 **1998** Medium yellow-green; clean, with light to medium intensity, generally giving the impression of being underplayed. The same impression is given on the palate, one of the possibilities being that there was a lack of flavour ripeness in the grapes, notwithstanding the excellent vintage. It is quite probable the wine will build character with bottle age.   **rating:** 84

best drinking 2001–2005 **best vintages** NA **drink with** Light fish soup • $23

st jerome wines NR

219 Metcalfe Road, Henderson **region** Auckland Area
phone (09) 833 6205 **fax** (09) 833 6205 **open** Mon–Sat 9–6, Sun 12–5
winemaker Davorin Ozich, Miro Ozich **production** 7000 **est.** 1968
product range ($14.50–36 CD) Riesling, Sauvignon Blanc, Chardonnay, Chablis, Gewurztraminer, Cabernet Merlot, Port.
summary The Cabernet Merlots made by Davorin Ozich between 1987 and 1991 reflect his Master of Science degree and practical training at Chateau Margaux and Chateau Cos d'Estournel in Bordeaux. They were hugely powerful wines, the 1991 in particular. It was rated number two in New Zealand's Top Ten Reds of the Year in the September 1994 edition of *Cuisine* magazine but did not impress the judges at the 1995 Sydney International Wine Competition, being described as 'harsh and over-extractive'. Herein lies the rub: these are wines which demand cellaring and a certain degree of understanding. No recent tastings.

st nesbit NR

Hingaia Road, RD1, Papakura **region** Auckland Area
phone (09) 379 0808 **fax** (09) 376 6956 **open** Not
winemaker Dr Tony Molloy QC **production** 800 **est.** 1980
product range ($37 CD) A single Cabernet Merlot (Cabernet Sauvignon, Cabernet Franc, Merlot, Malbec, Petit Verdot) Bordeaux-blend has been supplemented more recently by a Rosé, the result of indifferent vintages in 1992 and 1993 and of the effects of leaf roll virus.
summary Tony Molloy is a leading tax lawyer with a weekend passion; his Bordeaux-blend is revered in New Zealand and very well regarded elsewhere. His outstanding Cabernet Merlot is always produced in tiny quantities, but the last indication of the quality of the vineyard was in 1991. Since that time there has been a much troubled replanting of the 4-hectare vineyard, and the next wine is unlikely to be released much before 2004.

sandihurst wines ★★★☆

Main West Coast Road, West Melton, Canterbury **region** Canterbury
phone (03) 347 8289 **fax** (03) 347 8289 **open** 7 days 11–5 mid-Oct–Apr
winemaker Alan McCorkindale **production** 4200 **est.** 1992
product range ($13–28 CD) Riesling, Reserve Gewurztraminer, Pinot Gris, Pinot Gris Reserve, Chardonnay, Breidecker, Pinot Noir.
summary Yet another of the ever-expanding number of wineries in the Christchurch region, releasing its first wines in November 1993. It is a substantial operation, with 16 hectares of vineyards in bearing. However, production (and winemaking) has fluctuated, the best wines undoubtedly being the Pinot Noir and Pinot Gris.

seibels NR

113 Sturges Road, Henderson **region** Auckland Area
phone (09) 836 6113 **fax** (09) 836 6205 **open** Mon–Fri 11–6 or by appointment
winemaker Norbert Seibel **production** 3500 **est.** 1988
product range ($11.95–19.95 CD) Limited Edition Hawke's Bay Chardonnay, Hawke's Bay Sauvignon Blanc, Select Noble Late Harvest Chardonnay lead the roster; then come Scheurebe, Barrel Fermented White Riesling, Late Harvest White Riesling, Barrel Fermented Chenin Blanc, Semi-Dry Gewurztraminer, Medium Dry Riesling, Cabernet Franc Merlot Cabernet Sauvignon.
summary Significantly increased production shows that Norbert Seibel is doing well; the wine styles have been described as innovative and those I have tasted have been outside the mainstream. No recent tastings. Exports to Denmark, Taiwan and the US.

seifried estate ★★★★

PO Box 7020, Nelson **region** Nelson
phone (03) 544 5599 **fax** (03) 544 5522 **open** 7 days 11–5
winemaker Hermann Seifried, Daniel Schwarzenbach **production** 80 000 **est.** 1973
product range ($13–25 R) Under the Seifried Estate range: Riesling, Riesling Dry, Gewurztraminer, Sauvignon Blanc, Chardonnay, Pinot Noir, Cabernet Merlot, Cabernet Sauvignon and Sekt (Sparkling); under the Winemaker's Collection label: Riesling, Gewurztraminer Dry, Barrique Fermented Chardonnay, Botrytis Riesling and Riesling Ice Wine.

summary With 56 hectares of vineyards established progressively between 1973 and 1988 and a crush in excess of 900 tonnes, Seifried Estate is by far the largest of the Nelson wineries. The production is heavily biased towards white wines, which are of wholly admirable consistency of style and quality. Just prior to vintage in 1996 Seifried moved to its new winery situated in its picturesque Appleby Vineyard. Exports to the UK, the US, Canada, Germany, Austria and Hong Kong.

Seifried Estate Winemaker's Collection Gewurztraminer

Made in the off-dry fashion so popular in New Zealand with almost all the white wines.

▼▼▼▼ **1999** Light green-yellow; gently floral spice and lychee aromas leave no doubt about the varietal authenticity of the wine. These flavours come through on a gently sweet palate which has good length. **rating:** 86

best drinking 2000–2002 **best vintages** NA **drink with** Chinese prawns • $19.95

seresin estate ★★★★☆

Bedford Road, Renwick, Marlborough **region** Marlborough
phone (03) 572 9408 **fax** (03) 572 9850 **open** Summer 10–4.30
winemaker Brian Bicknell, Gordon Ritchie **production** 15 000 **est.** 1992
product range ($21.90–32.90 R) Riesling, Sauvignon Blanc, Pinot Gris, Estate Chardonnay, Reserve Chardonnay, Pinot Noir.
summary Seresin has charged into the Marlborough scene since New Zealand filmmaker Michael Seresin purchased a little over 60 hectares of prime alluvial terrace land adjacent to the Wairau River. Forty hectares of vineyard have been established, and the state-of-the-art winery designed by Ian Athfield (of Te Mata Estate fame) constructed. Brian Bicknell, one of New Zealand's most experienced Flying Winemakers (he has worked in New Zealand, Hungary, France and for three years in Chile) has been installed as chief winemaker. The first vintage in 1996 immediately established Seresin as one of the star performers in the Marlborough scene. Exports to Australia, the UK, Denmark, Switzerland, Belgium, The Netherlands, Ireland, Canada and the US.

Seresin Estate Sauvignon Blanc

To say sophisticated winemaking techniques have been used with what might seem a straightforward wine style is a masterly understatement. The wine is a blend of Sauvignon Blanc (90 per cent) and Semillon (10 per cent), with the sauvignon blanc picked over an extended period. Eleven per cent of the wine is barrel-fermented and lees aged in a mix of new and one-year-old French oak barriques. Part of the remaining wine is fermented using cultured yeasts, part relying upon indigenous yeast. If this were not enough, a small component of the barrel-fermented portion undergoes malolactic fermentation. All this, and yet the end result is a wine in which Marlborough Sauvignon Blanc, rather than winemaker's tricks, does the talking.

▼▼▼▼▼ **1999** Light green-yellow; the attractive bouquet is clean, clear and crisp, with flecks of lemon and gooseberry. It is the palate which ripples with complexity and texture. The flavours again with a slight lemony edge to gooseberry fruit; the wine has great length and a fraction of my tasting notes reads 'plenty happening'. **rating:** 94

▼▼▼▼ **1998** Light yellow-green; the bouquet is clean and relatively light, with hints of gooseberry and more tropical fruit. The palate does show a slightly grainy texture, which no doubt derives from the complex winemaking techniques; at the end of the day, the wine is a prisoner of the vintage. **rating:** 85

best drinking 2000–2003 **best vintages** '99 **drink with** Steamed crab • $21.80

Seresin Estate Pinot Gris

The grapes are whole-bunch pressed and fermented at low temperatures in stainless steel until the last stages of fermentation, when it is transferred to one-year-old French barriques to finish fermentation. Weekly battonage (stirring) and ageing on lees adds to the textural character of the wine; the oak has minimal impact on the flavour, which is as the makers would wish.

▼▼▼▼▽ **1999** Intense, glowing green-yellow; a complex bouquet with a mix of lemon rind, ripe pear and mineral leads into a palate with excellent structure, long and intense, with an almost creamy feel. **rating:** 90

best drinking 2000–2004 **best vintages** '99 **drink with** Smoked white-fleshed fish • $24.80

Seresin Estate Chardonnay

Typically picked over a two-week period, with 75 per cent fermented in French oak, the balance in stainless steel. Both indigenous and a range of cultured yeasts are used; the percentage taken through malolactic fermentation varies with the vintage but is normally not less than 50 per cent.

▼▼▼▼ **1998** Medium yellow-green; the moderately intense bouquet is clean, with an attractive hint of five-spice oak character and pleasant fruit. An elegant wine on the palate; the fruit is just a little weak. **rating:** 87

best drinking 2000–2003 **best vintages** NA **drink with** Steamed mussels • $21.80

Seresin Estate Chardonnay Reserve

The best of the estate-grown grapes are selected for the Reserve programme; the wine is barrel-fermented in 100 per cent new French oak barriques, and is all taken through malolactic fermentation, with the usual lees contact and stirring. Unusually, after spending a year in barrel, the wine is transferred to stainless steel for a further five months before being bottled.

TTTTY **1998** Much deeper yellow-green than the varietal; the bouquet is more complex, with nutty barrel-ferment and malolactic-ferment characters making a positive contribution to quite intense fruit. The palate does not let the wine down, with melon, fig and cashew flavours; intense and long. **rating:** 93

best drinking 2000–2004 **best vintages** '96, '98 **drink with** Corn-fed chicken • $29.80

Seresin Estate Pinot Noir

For the first time, includes a portion of new Dijon clone 115. The grapes are hand-picked, with a portion placed into the tank to give carbonic maceration characters; the remainder destemmed and pumped directly to the tank without crushing. Pre-fermentation cold-maceration followed, then a warm ferment, with the wine being pressed and taken straight to barrel at the end of fermentation.

TTTT 1998 Medium red-purple, ever-so-slightly dull. The bouquet is of moderate intensity, with plum fruit dominant complexed by some foresty notes. The palate is quite complex, with cherry/plum fruit and supporting spicy oak. Notwithstanding that the wine spent 15 months in barrel, seems to be compartmentalised, and needing to integrate. **rating:** 88

best drinking 2000–2004 **best vintages** '97 **drink with** Game • $32.80

settler winery   NR

Crownthorpe Settlement Road, RD9, Hastings **region** Hawke's Bay
phone (06) 874 3244 **fax** (06) 874 3244 **open** Not
winemaker Evert Nijzink **production** 400 **est.** 1993
product range ($14–20 R) Sauvignon Blanc, Chardonnay, Cabernet Merlot.
summary Evert Nijzink has established a 2.5-hectare biodynamically managed vineyard and since 1997 has relied entirely upon estate production. A cellar-door and café facility opened in late 1996.

shalimar estate   NR

RD2, Ngatapa Road, Gisborne **region** Gisborne
phone (06) 862 7776 **fax** (06) 862 7776 **open** 7 days 10–5
winemaker Alexander Stuart **production** 900 **est.** 1994
product range ($8–16 R) Sauvignon Blanc, Semillon, Chardonnay, Pinot Gris, Pinotage, Cabernet Merlot.
summary Having been grape growers for 25 years, the Stuart family took the plunge into winemaking in 1994, drawing upon a recently established (and in Gisborne, rare) terraced hillside vineyard. Alexander Stuart believes greater flavour and character will follow the lower than normal yields. Most of the production from the 8-hectare vineyard is, once again, being sold to others.

sherwood estate   ★★★★

Weedons Ross Road, Christchurch **region** Canterbury
phone (03) 347 9060 **fax** (03) 347 8225 **open** 7 days 11–5
winemaker Dayne Sherwood **production** 17 000 **est.** 1987
product range ($12–28 R) Canterbury Riesling, Müller Thurgau, Sauvignon Blanc, Chardonnay, Unoaked Chardonnay, Reserve Chardonnay, Estate Pinot Noir, Reserve Pinot Noir, Single Vineyard Selection Rivendell Pinot Noir, Cabernet Franc.
summary Sherwood Estate produced its first wines in 1990; situated close to Christchurch (15 minutes drive), it also offers a garden-setting tasting room with snacks and lunches available in the Vineyard Bar throughout summer. Production has risen significantly since the early days, making Sherwood Estate an important part of the Christchurch landscape. After a disappointing period, the quality of the wines has significantly improved. Exports to Australia, the UK, Europe, Asia and the US.

Sherwood Estate Canterbury Riesling

Estate-grown, and made in what is described in New Zealand as an off-dry or medium style.

TTTT 1999 Light yellow-green; the bouquet is still tight, crisp and shy, but the palate has easy lemony fruit neatly fleshed out with well-balanced sweetness on the finish. Silver medal at the Royal Easter Wine Show 2000. **rating:** 85

best drinking 2000–2003 **best vintages** NA **drink with** Whitebait fritters • $15

Sherwood Estate Sauvignon Blanc

Everyone was in agreement on this wine at the Royal Easter Wine Show 2000, scoring gold medal points from all the judges first up.

▼▼▼▼▼ **1999** Light green-yellow; vibrant and complex lemon and herb aromas are followed by a tightly constructed yet very flavoursome palate with near perfect balance and length. **rating: 94**

best drinking 2000–2001 **best vintages** '99 **drink with** Stronger-flavoured seafood • $17

🐌 shingle peak wines   ★★★☆

Corner Rapaura Road/State Highway 6, Blenheim **region** Marlborough
phone (09) 411 8301 **fax** (09) 411 7982 **open** at Matua Valley
winemaker Mark Robertson **production** 25 000 **est.** 1990
product range ($14–19 R) Riesling, Sauvignon Blanc, Chardonnay, Pinot Gris, Botrytis Riesling and Pinot Noir, Merlot.
summary Shingle Peak is the stand-alone Marlborough brand for Matua Valley. The wines are made at Rapaura Vintners, in which Matua Valley has a significant shareholding, and consistently offer excellent value for money.

sileni estates   ★★★★☆

Maraekakaho Road, Bridge Pa, Hastings **region** Hawke's Bay
phone (06) 879 8768 **fax** (06) 879 7187 **open** 7 days 10–5
winemaker Grant Edmonds, Nigel Davies, Eleanor Dodd **production** 15 000 **est.** 1997
product range ($26.50–35 R) Semillon, Chardonnay, Pinot Noir, Merlot Cabernets.
summary Sileni Estates is poised to become a major force in the Hawke's Bay region. The three partners are chief winemaker Grant Edmonds, Graeme Avery and Chris Cowper (and their families), who between them have winemaking, management and marketing and financial backgrounds and skills. With just under 100 hectares of vines planted, production has increased in leaps and bounds, and the quality has indeed proved to be excellent. Exports to the UK, France and the US through Louis Latour.

Sileni Estates Semillon

First made in 1999 from relatively young vines. Twenty-five per cent of the wine is barrel-aged for three months.

▼▼▼▽ **1999** Light yellow-green; the bouquet is clean and crisp, without any fault whatsoever, but not showing much varietal character. The palate is fresh, quite crisp and pleasantly balanced; if it follows the track of Australian Semillons, it could transform itself down the track but right now isn't showing a lot. **rating: 84**

best drinking 2003–2010 **best vintages** NA **drink with** White-fleshed fish • $27

Sileni Estates Chardonnay

A particularly impressive debut vintage, barrel-fermented and matured on lees in French oak for nine months. Where so many of New Zealand Chardonnays are at the opulent, baroque end of the scale, this is at the elegant end.

▼▼▼▼▼ **1998** Light to medium yellow-green; the bouquet is clean, with particularly restrained and sophisticated use of oak, which leaves the fruit untarnished. The palate is quite delicate yet intense, with citrus, melon and cashew flavours running through an admirably long finish. **rating: 94**

best drinking 2000–2004 **best vintages** '98 **drink with** Grilled scampi • $31.95

Sileni Merlot Cabernets

A blend of Merlot, Cabernet Sauvignon and Cabernet Franc which only serves to underline the promise of this signature estate.

▼▼▼▼ **1998** Dense red-purple; very ripe blackberry, mulberry, plum and chocolate aromas flood the bouquet; the palate is not quite as luscious as the bouquet suggests it will be but has a sweet entry and mid-palate before tailing off ever-so-slightly on the finish. Happily, the oak does not try to compensate. **rating: 90**

best drinking 2001–2007 **best vintages** '98 **drink with** Braised lamb • $35

🐌 sirocco wines   NR

The Settlement (11 Methven-Barrhill Road), Rakai **region** Canterbury
phone (03) 302 7252 **fax** (03) 302 7252 **open** 7 days 10–5
winemaker Paul Phillips **production** 500 **est.** 1997
product range ($12–16 CD) Riesling, Chardonnay, Pinot Noir.
summary Paul and Helena Phillips run a small but surprisingly diverse business on their property on the famous salmon and trout fishing Rakaia River. They produce cut flowers (gentians) for the export market, and Helena teaches decorative painting on the property. Paul Phillips was brought up in the Swan Valley, which prompted the other development of vines and winemaking. The first experimental varieties were planted 12 years ago, there

being no other local vineyards to point the way. In the outcome 2.5 hectares of chardonnay, riesling, sauvignon blanc and pinot noir have been taken to the point of commercial production, and all of the wines are made on site by Paul. The vineyard is moving towards Bio-Gro™ organic status, and the Phillips are the Canterbury representatives for the New Zealand Grapevine Improvement Group.

soljans wines   ★★★

263 Lincoln Road, Henderson **region** Auckland Area
phone (09) 838 8365 **fax** (09) 838 8366 **open** Mon–Sat 9–6, Sun 11–5
winemaker Simone Parker **production** 25 000 **est.** 1937
product range ($9–26 CD) White wines under the Ivory label include Müller Thurgau, Marlborough Riesling, Gisborne Gewurztraminer, Hawke's Bay Sauvignon Blanc, Hawke's Bay Unoaked Chardonnay, Barrique Reserve Chardonnay; red wines under the Ebony label are Pinotage, Barrique Reserve Merlot, Barrique Reserve Cabernet Merlot; also fortifieds and dessert wines; Legacy Méthode Traditionelle.
summary The traditional but immaculately maintained winery and vineyard constitute a major tourist attraction, and the well-made wines are sold at very modest prices. In 1993 Soljans made a heavy investment importing state-of-the-art sparkling winemaking equipment from France and is now a major contractor for New Zealand Méthode Traditionelle producers. Exports to the UK, the US, France, Denmark and Poland — the latter a considerable achievement.

solstone estate   NR

119 Solway Crescent, Masterton **region** Wairarapa
phone (06) 377 5505 **fax** (06) 337 7504 **open** Mon–Fri 8–5, weekends and public holidays 10.30–4.30
winemaker Luc des Bonnets **production** 3100 **est.** 1981
product range ($12–38 CD) Riesling, Rosé, Merlot, Cabernet Franc, Cabernet Merlot Franc.
summary Tiny quantities of the wines sold to date have been eagerly snapped up by the local clientele, but wines are now being distributed (sparingly) through Kitchener Wines. The wines draw upon 2 hectares of estate cabernet sauvignon and a single hectare of pinot noir, sauvignon blanc, merlot and cabernet franc.

spencer hill estate   ★★★★

Best Road, RD1, Upper Moutere, Nelson **region** Nelson
phone (03) 543 2031 **fax** (03) 543 2031 **open** Thurs–Sat 12–4 Dec–Feb
winemaker Philip Jones **production** 15 000 **est.** 1991
product range ($15–31 R) Spencer Hill is the top label from single vineyard sources; Tasman Bay is the second but main label made in larger volume. Chardonnay, Sauvignon Blanc, Pinot Noir, Pinot Gris, Riesling, Gewurztraminer, Pinotage, Merlot.
summary Philip Jones is a graduate in viticulture from UCLA Davis, California, and also undertook an oenology degree at Fresno State University. The ornately complex Spencer Hill Chardonnays have won a cascade of trophies and gold medals, joined by the Tasman Bay Chardonnay in 1997, in wine competitions running from New Zealand to London. There can be no doubt that Philip Jones is a highly talented winemaker and an equally accomplished marketer, with exports to Australia, the UK, Hong Kong, Germany and Japan.

Spencer Hill Tasman Bay Marlborough Sauvignon Blanc

Produced from Marlborough Sauvignon Blanc blended with a small amount of Gisborne Semillon which is barrel-fermented, then aged for four months in a mix of French and American oak barriques. Part of the wine is taken through malolactic fermentation, part not.
▼▼▼▼ 1998 Light to medium yellow-green; the bouquet is as complex as one would expect, with sensitive use of oak a feature. A well-made and balanced wine on the palate which, however, lacks the sharp definition one expects of Sauvignon Blanc. It does finish with good acidity and is doubtless made in precisely the style Phil Jones strives for.   **rating:** 85
best drinking 1999–2000 **best vintages** NA **drink with** Pan-fried scallops • $15

Spencer Hill Estate Pinot Gris

Not only Spencer Hill Estate's first Pinot Gris, but the first from the Nelson area. Fifty per cent of the wine was fermented and aged in older French oak puncheons for five months; the unoaked portion was taken through malolactic fermentation. The techniques have been used to increase complexity 'in a somewhat neutral-flavoured grape', says Philip Jones.
▼▼▼▼ 1998 Light straw, with the faintest tinge of pink. The bouquet is clean, with a mix of mineral and hints of spice. The palate has good length and grip, tangy and minerally, yet also having fruit flesh. Finishes dry. **rating:** 87
best drinking 2000–2003 **best vintages** '98 **drink with** Grilled scampi • $21

Spencer Hill Tasman Bay Pinot Noir

Nowhere mentioned in dispatches before the 1999 vintage, when it won a silver medal at the Royal Easter Wine Show 2000.

♥♥♥♥ **1999** Light to medium purple-red; the bouquet offers savoury spices together with plummy fruit and nicely balanced and integrated oak. The light- to medium-bodied palate has sweet plummy fruit, fine tannins and good length. **rating:** 88

best drinking 2000–2003 **best vintages** NA **drink with** Stuffed spatchcock • $NA

Spencer Hill Estate Pinotage

South Africa's Pinotage is world famous these days, and it is easy to forget that New Zealand once had very large plantings of pinotage when measured as a percentage of total red production. It has steadily withered away, perhaps due to over-cropping, and certainly a lack of public esteem. This wine comes from an experimental acre, on a hilltop in the Spencer Hill vineyards; a hot ferment of very ripe grapes using native or wild yeast was followed by ageing in old French and American oak for eight months.

♥♥♥♡ **1999** Light to medium red; light, spicy fruit with sweet, jammy aromas is followed by a light, very spicy palate, finishing with slightly sharp acidity. **rating:** 80

best drinking 2000–2001 **best vintages** NA **drink with** Yakitori chicken • $22

springvale estate NR

Dunstan Road, Alexandra **region** Otago
phone (03) 449 2995 **fax** (03) 449 2331 **open** 7 days 18 Dec–Apr, weekends and public holidays May–Dec
winemaker Rudi Bauer, Dean Shaw (Contract), production 1000 **est.** 1989
product range ($16.50–22 CD) Gewurztraminer, Sauvignon Blanc, Chardonnay, Pinot Noir, Cabernet Sauvignon.
summary Tony and Jo-Anne Brun planted their first hectare of vines in 1989, gradually increasing the area to its present level of just under 5 hectares. The neat restaurant caters for all tastes from nibbles to functions. The 1998 Pinot Noir was a marvellous wine, deserving its gold medal at the 1999 Royal Easter Wine Show. Rudi Bauer and Dean Shaw have inherited the winemaking responsibilities.

stonecroft vineyard NR

Mere Road, RD5, Hastings **region** Hawke's Bay
phone (06) 879 9610 **fax** (06) 879 9610 **open** Weekends, public holidays 11–5
winemaker Dr Alan Limmer **production** 2500 **est.** 1987
product range ($18–40 CD) Gewurztraminer, Gewurztraminer Late Harvest, Sauvignon Blanc, Chardonnay, Ruhani, Crofters II, Syrah, Aquilon.
summary Analytical chemist Dr Alan Limmer produces very full bodied, rich and ripe wines from his 3-hectare vineyard situated on free-draining, gravelly soils which promote early ripening. Most interesting is the almost unprocurable (mailing list only) Syrah, widely regarded as New Zealand's best. Not rated because there have been no tastings for several years. Exports to Australia and the UK.

stoneleigh vineyards ★★★★☆

Jacksons Road, RD3, Blenheim **region** Marlborough
phone (03) 572 8198 **fax** (03) 572 8199 **open** 7 days 10–4
winemaker Sam Weaver **production** NA **est.** 1988
product range ($11–36 R) Riesling, Sauvignnon Blanc, Chardonnay, Pinot Noir.
summary Stoneleigh is the Marlborough brand of Corbans. Like Longridge, it has its own largely separate existence and brand identity and, what is more, is open to visitors. It has its own separate price-point, pitched above that of Longridge.

Stoneleigh Marlborough Riesling

As most observers agree, this has been the best of the Stoneleigh range, and certainly provides a highly flavoured, easily-accessed commercial wine. As prior vintages (notably the multi-trophy winning '91) attest, ages superbly if vintage conditions are good.

♥♥♥♥ **1999** Light green-yellow; the bouquet has some intensity, with lime and tropical fruit aromas which lead logically into a full, soft, round lime/pineapple-accented palate. If there is a criticism, it is that the wine lacks length. **rating:** 85

best drinking 2001–2004 **best vintages** '91, '93, '97, '98 **drink with** Pan-fried sole • $14

Stoneleigh Marlborough Sauvignon Blanc

A no-frills but ever-reliable unwooded Marlborough Sauvignon Blanc that normally contains about 15 per cent Semillon. Produced from Corbans' Stoneleigh Vineyard, which gives the wine its brand name, and treated to traditional cold stainless steel fermentation. Typically has lower-than-threshold residual sugar.

▼▼▼▼ **1999** Light yellow-green; the bouquet is fresh and delicate, with just a flick of gooseberry. The palate offers more weight, with a mix of gooseberry and mineral flavours; has grip and length. **rating:** 86

best drinking 2000–2001 **best vintages** '92, '94, '96, '98 **drink with** Shellfish • $14

Stoneleigh Marlborough Chardonnay

Barrel-fermented and matured in French oak barriques for six months, with 75 per cent taken through malolactic fermentation.

▼▼▼▼ **1999** Light to medium yellow-green; the bouquet is quite tight, with some herb characters and subtle oak. The palate opens up with sweet cashew and melon providing attractive mouthfeel and length; the oak is pleasantly restrained. **rating:** 89

best drinking 2000–2002 **best vintages** '94, '98, '99 **drink with** Pan-fried veal • $15

Stoneleigh Marlborough Pinot Noir

Very much a sign of the times, with even the larger producers operating in a lower price band venturing into the Pinot Noir thickets — in this case with some success.

▼▼▼▽ **1998** Light to medium red-purple; the moderately intense bouquet is quite stylish, with cherry and spice aromas; the palate is tight and savoury, rather than lush, but does have some length; if you wish, a cerebral Pinot Noir, but not to be cellared. **rating:** 84

best drinking 2000–2001 **best vintages** NA **drink with** Cassoulet • $15

stonyridge vineyard ★★★★★

80 Onetangi Road, Waiheke Island **region** Waiheke Island
phone (09) 372 8822 **fax** (09) 372 8822 **open** 7 days 9–5
winemaker Stephen White **production** 1250 **est.** 1982
product range ($25–95 ML) The top label is Larose Cabernets; the second is Airfield Cabernets. Minuscule quantities of Que Sera Syrah are also grown, and a Hawke's Bay Merlot has recently joined the band.
summary The winery that justifies the hype about Waiheke Island. Consistently great wines have been produced, albeit in minuscule quantities; small wonder it has established the highest ex-winery price of $50 en primeur, and $85 upon commercial release, with a limit of one bottle per customer! For many, patronising the winery restaurant will be the only means of tasting these exalted wines. Minuscule exports to the UK, the US, Australia, Japan and Taipei.

stratford wines of martinborough NR

115 New York Street, Martinborough **region** Wairarapa
phone (06) 306 9257 **fax** (06) 306 8257 **open** By appointment
winemaker Stratford Canning **production** 2000 **est.** 1993
product range ($16–28 CD) Riesling, Chardonnay, Pinot Noir.
summary Strat Canning has worked as a winemaker in the Martinborough region for a number of years and is now also producing his own wines from 1 hectare each of pinot noir, chardonnay and riesling.

Stratford Wines of Martinborough Riesling

Produced from the 1 hectare of estate plantings of the variety; both the inaugural 1998 and 1999 vintages have been well received, and the style is quite distinct.

▼▼▼▽ **1999** Light green-yellow; a powerful bouquet with a mix of apple and more floral aromas edged with a touch of old-style kerosene. The palate is no less powerful, again showing a toasty kerosene character which normally comes with far greater age. A wine which dramatically split the judges at the Royal Easter Wine Show 2000. **rating:** 84

best drinking 2000–2003 **best vintages** NA **drink with** Strong fish dishes • $17

tai-ara-rau wines NR

Upper Stout Street, Gisborne **region** Gisborne
phone (06) 867 2010 **fax** (06) 867 2024 **open** 7 days 10–5
winemaker Jeff Sinnott **production** 1000 **est.** 1989
product range Estate Chardonnay and Merlot; Waimata Vineyard Chardonnay, Pinot Noir and Merlot.

summary Tairawhiti Polytechnic has followed in the footsteps of Australia's Charles Sturt University in making commercial quantities of wine as part of the wine industry certificate course which the institute offers. It is the only New Zealand institution to do so, drawing upon 3 hectares of chardonnay and 1.25 hectares each of pinot noir and merlot.

te awa farm winery   NR

2375 Roys Hill Road, SH 50 RD5, Hastings **region** Hawke's Bay
phone (06) 879 7602 **fax** (06) 879 7756 **open** Mon–Fri 9–5 weekends 10–6
winemaker Jenny Dobson **production** 20 000 **est.** 1992
product range ($14.95–39.95 R) Under the Longlands brand Sauvignon Blanc, Chardonnay, Pinotage, Merlot, Cabernet Merlot; Under the Reserve range Frontier Sauvignon Blanc, Frontier Chardonnay and Boundary (the latter a Bordeaux-blend).
summary The Lawson family is yet another to venture into winemaking after being contract grape growers for over 15 years. Unusually, however, when Gus and Ian Lawson decided to venture into winemaking on their own account, they decided to start again, purchasing a 173-hectare sheep property on Roys Hill Road in 1992, establishing 32 hectares of sauvignon blanc, chardonnay, merlot, cabernet franc, cabernet sauvignon and syrah. The first vintage from Te Awa Farm was in 1994 and an on-site production facility (incorporating a cellar-door sales area) was constructed over 1997, with the peripatetic Jenny Dobson now in charge of winemaking. Exports to the UK, Denmark, Singapore, Japan and the US.

Te Awa Farm Frontier Sauvignon Blanc
The estate-grown grapes are whole-bunch pressed and are then fermented and aged for nine months in French oak barriques, 40 per cent of which are new. The malolactic fermentation is suppressed.
TTTY 1998 Medium yellow-green; the bouquet is dominated by oak, which completely subjugates the fruit, and the palate does not alter the balance. **rating:** 80
best drinking 2000–2002 **best vintages** NA **drink with** Deep-fried fish • $25.95

Te Awa Farm Boundary
An estate-grown blend of 76 per cent Merlot, 15 per cent Cabernet Sauvignon and 9 per cent Cabernet Franc, each separately fermented and matured. The wine spends 18 months in French oak barrels before a light fining and bottling.
TTTT 1998 Medium to full red-purple; the aromas are slightly subdued in a savoury/gamey spectrum, but there is rather more on the palate where black fruit flavours join the more savoury earthy characters feeding through from the bouquet. The tannins are firm but suitable for the style. **rating:** 87
best drinking 2002–2008 **best vintages** NA **drink with** Ox tongue • $30

te horo vineyards   NR

State Highway 1, Te Horo **region** Wellington Region
phone (06) 364 3392 **fax** (06) 364 3392 **open** 7 days 11–late
winemaker Alastair Pain **production** 1200 **est.** 1985
product range ($9.95–19.95 CD) Chardonnay, Sauvignon Blanc, Riesling, Pinot Gris, Gewurztraminer, Merlot, Cabernet Sauvignon Cremant Méthode Traditionale; a selection of fruit wines.
summary Formerly called Grape Republic, a marketing and promotion tour-de-force using direct mail and wine club techniques, and producing a vast array of flavoured wines and smaller quantities of more expensive table wines which are distinctly austere. An underground cellar and sales area was opened in 1995. Most of the wine is sold direct ex winery.

te kairanga wines   ★★★★

Martins Road, Martinborough **region** Wairarapa
phone (06) 306 9122 **fax** (06) 306 9322 **open** 7 days 10–5
winemaker Peter Caldwell **production** 16 000 **est.** 1984
product range ($13–40 CD) At the top end is the Reserve range of Chardonnay and Pinot Noir; then the Premium range of Sauvignon Blanc, Chardonnay, Pinot Noir, Cabernet Sauvignon and Cabernet Merlot; at the bottom end the Castlepoint range of Müller Thurgau, Dry White, Dry Red and Cabernet Sauvignon.
summary Te Kairanga is an enigma. For a long time its wines were disappointing but then took a distinct turn for the better, suggesting that all of its problems were behind it. More recent tastings are less conclusive, so close and yet so far from the best of what is undoubtedly a great region. The appointment of Peter Caldwell, and the fact that it has over 30 hectares of mature vineyards will help Te Kairanga realise its full potential. Winning the trophy for Best Wine of Show at the Royal Easter Wine Show 2000 with its Cabernet Sauvignon will also help, however much it may complicate plans to phase out the production of that variety. Exports to Australia and the US.

Te Kairanga Reserve Chardonnay

First made in 1994 from the lowest-yielding and best parcels of fruit available to Te Kairanga, and the Reserve range of Chardonnay and Pinot Noir is only produced in better vintages, when exceptional levels of fruit ripeness and flavour are achieved in the winery and which then justify the use of a higher percentage of new oak. The wine spends 11 months in a mix of new and one-year-old French oak barriques and 15 per cent is taken through malolactic fermentation.

▼▼▼♀ **1998** Medium yellow-green; conventional melon and cashew aromas are mixed in with some less conventional and seemingly volatile characteristics on the bouquet. The palate has light melon and mlf cashew flavours, but at the end of the day doesn't reassure. **rating: 82**

best drinking 2000–2002 **best vintages** '94, '95, '96 **drink with** Sweetbreads • $28

Te Kairanga Reserve Pinot Noir

Based on vineyard block selections, with new clones among them, the grapes being fermented in open vats with hand plunging. The wine then spends 18 months in French oak barriques.

▼▼▼▼♀ **1998** Dense red-purple; the bouquet is complex, with ripe plum, spice, forest floor and oak aromas. The palate is opulently rich and ripe, flooded with dark plum fruit; there is also considerable extract and tannin. Needs time to resolve itself; an extremely interesting wine to watch as it matures. **rating: 90**

best drinking 2001–2006 **best vintages** '98 **drink with** Smoked quail • $40

Te Kairanga Cabernet Sauvignon

The 1998 vintage well and truly put the cat among the pigeons when it won the trophy for Best Wine at the Royal Easter Wine Show 2000, disposing of some exceptional Sauvignon Blancs and Pinot Noirs in so doing.

▼▼▼▼▼ **1998** Dense red-purple; very rich, dense prune, plum and chocolate fruit on the bouquet introduces an utterly spectacular palate which has all the foregoing and then some. No hint of green, and in many ways reminiscent of Esk Valley The Terraces from a good vintage. **rating: 96**

best drinking 2003–2013 **best vintages** '98 **drink with** Leave it in the cellar • $22

te mania estate ★★★☆

c/o The Grape Escape, McShanes Road, Richmond, Nelson **region** Nelson
phone (03) 544 4541 **fax** (03) 544 4541 **open** Mon–Fri 10–5 summer and 11–4 winter
winemaker Jane Cooper **production** 4000 **est.** 1990
product range ($16–20 CD) Riesling, Late Harvest Riesling, Sauvignon Blanc, Chardonnay, Merlot.
summary Jon and Cheryl Harrey commenced development of their vineyard in 1990, planting 4.5 hectares in that year (which came into production in 1992), and expanded the plantings in 1994 and 1995 with an additional 4 hectares. They previously sold most of their grapes to other Nelson winemakers, but since 1995 have had Jane Cooper as winemaker. Together with another vineyard owner, the Harreys have purchased a property on which they have erected a cellar-door sales facility, café and arts and crafts centre. Has a rapidly growing reputation, particularly for Sauvignon Blanc. The wines are exported to Australia, the UK, Japan and The Netherlands.

Te Mania Estate Nelson Chardonnay

Estate-grown (on the Home Block Vineyard) and only 50 per cent barrel-aged (for ten months).

▼▼▼▼♀ **1998** Medium yellow-green; elegant cashew and melon fruit aromas are supported by subtle barrel-ferment oak. The palate is unforced and elegant, with melon, citrus and cashew, which do not have to fight against the oak for expression. **rating: 92**

best drinking 2000–2001 **best vintages** '98 **drink with** Crab cakes • $18

te mata estate ★★★★★

Te Mata Road, Havelock North **region** Hawke's Bay
phone (06) 877 4399 **fax** (06) 877 4397 **open** Mon–Fri 9–5, Sat 10–5, Sun 11–4
winemaker Peter Cowley **production** 30 000 **est.** 1896
product range ($10.30–60 CD) Elston (Chardonnay), Castle Hill Sauvignon Blanc, Cape Crest Sauvignon Blanc, Rosé, Bullnose (Syrah), Coleraine (Cabernet Franc Merlot), Cabernet Merlot, Awatea (Cabernet Merlot — premium), Woodthorpe Terraces Viognier.
summary In the eyes of many, New Zealand's foremost producer of Cabernet Merlot, notwithstanding the consistency of the show success of the Vidal/Villa Maria group. The wines of Te Mata are made in a different style, restrained and elegant but always packed with fine fruit. Nor should the consistently stylish and varietally correct white wines be ignored; these too are of the highest quality. I have not tasted the '98 Coleraine or Awatea, but am reliably assured they are the greatest wines made to date by Te Mata. Initially only available via cellar door and mailing list, the wines are now conventionally distributed throughout New Zealand, and are exported to Australia, Belgium, France, Germany, The Netherlands, the UK and the US.

Te Mata Estate Cape Crest Sauvignon Blanc

Generally accepted as one of New Zealand's classic Sauvignon Blancs, even if it doesn't have the same status in export markets as does Cloudy Bay. It is a single-vineyard wine which is barrel-fermented in previously used barriques. The oak handling is very clever, providing textural richness without overt oak flavour.

▼▼▼▼ 1998 Medium yellow-green; the bouquet is very ripe, with passionfruit and peach aromas, the oak barely evident. The palate is much more restrained than the bouquet, with an attractive mineral cut to the clean finish.

rating: 89

best drinking 1999–2001 **best vintages** '91, '94, '95, '96 **drink with** Quiche Lorraine • $30

Te Mata Estate Elston Chardonnay

The grapes come from the estate-owned Elston Vineyard and from a nearby vineyard at Havelock North. The grapes are whole-bunch pressed, and are fermented in a mix of new and used barriques, undergoing a full malolactic fermentation and lees stirring. The wine spends approximately seven months in oak.

▼▼▼▼ 1998 Medium yellow-green; the bouquet is clean but complex, with obvious creamy/nutty mlf aromas. The palate is similarly complex, with the mlf influence very pronounced, and which, while adding to complexity, does strip the fruit a little. Another Te Mata wine regarded as a New Zealand classic. **rating: 88**

best drinking 1999–2003 **best vintages** '93, '94, '95, '96, '97 **drink with** Turkey • $42

Te Mata Estate Coleraine Cabernet Franc Merlot

A similar blend to that of Awatea (55 per cent Cabernet Sauvignon, 30 per cent Merlot and 15 per cent Cabernet Franc) but made from the highest quality grapes available to Te Mata, a change introduced in 1989, prior to which the wine was sourced solely from the Coleraine Vineyard. Almost invariably one of New Zealand's finest red wines, and universally acknowledged as a classic.

▼▼▼▼▼ 1997 Medium red-purple; the moderately intense bouquet is sophisticated and elegant, with a seamless marriage of fruit and oak. The similarly fine and elegant palate has great length, supported by fine tannins and a hint of toasty oak. Iron fist in a velvet glove it may be, but all you see is the velvet. **rating: 94**

best drinking 2002–2012 **best vintages** '89, '91, '94, '95, '96, '97 **drink with** New Zealand lamb • $60

Te Mata Estate Awatea Cabernet Merlot

Typically a blend of around 55 per cent Cabernet Sauvignon, 30 per cent Merlot and 15 per cent Cabernet Franc. The wine is plunged during fermentation and has a period of maceration on skins after the end of fermentation. It spends 18 months in a mix of new and used barriques during which time it is racked, and eggwhite-fined prior to bottling.

▼▼▼▼ 1997 Medium red-purple; the bouquet is of medium intensity, with slightly tarry notes to the fruit. The palate is elegant and fine, but for Australian tastes, lacking sweet fruit on the mid-palate. **rating: 86**

best drinking 2000–2007 **best vintages** '89, '91, '94, '95 **drink with** New Zealand lamb • $42

te whare ra ★★★☆

Anglesea Street, Renwick, Marlborough **region** Marlborough
phone (03) 572 8581 **fax** (03) 572 8518 **open** 7 days 10.30–4.30 (reduced hours in winter)
winemaker Warwick Foley **production** 3500 **est.** 1979
product range ($14–21 CD) An ever-changing and at times confusing range; the two constants are Starfish Cove at the bottom end and Duke of Marlborough at the top end. In between these are releases sometimes varietally identified and sometimes by informative names such as Henrietta and Sara Jennings.
summary Te Whare Ra was purchased from the founding Hogan family by Roger and Christine Smith in October 1997. By all accounts the Smiths and winemaker Warwick Foley have done much to improve the quality of the wines; the 1999 Duke of Marlborough Gewurztraminer was the gold medal winner and Champion Gewurztraminer at the 1999 Air New Zealand Wine Awards.

te whau vineyard NR

218 Te Whau Drive, Waiheke Island **region** Waiheke Island
phone (09) 377 3119 **fax** (09) 307 2322 **open** As from November 2000: 11–5 through summer months
winemaker Tony Forsyth, Herb Freidli **production** 550 **est.** 1993
product range ($38–48 CD) Te Whau Bay Chardonnay, The Point (Bordeaux-blend).
summary Tony Forsyth has established a little over 2 hectares of close-planted vines on a sheltered and steep (20°) north-facing slope. A second sheltered vineyard site has been planted with three clones of chardonnay, which produced 50 cases of Chardonnay in 1999. The first wines were made in 1999 at the on-site gravity-feed winery, complete with fully underground barrel hall. Te Whau Bay Chardonnay and The Point (a four-variety Bordeaux-blend with 54 per cent Cabernet Sauvignon, 31 per cent Merlot, 10 per cent Cabernet Franc and 5 per cent Malbec) are due to be released in November 2000.

thainstone wines   NR

Giffords Road, RD3, Blenheim **region** Marlborough
phone (03) 572 8823 **fax** (03) 572 8623 **open** Not
winemaker Graeme Paul **production** 3000 **est.** 1990
product range ($12–22 R) Sauvignon Blanc, Chardonnay.
summary Jim and Viv Murray acquired their 7-hectare vineyard in 1990; already planted to sauvignon blanc, the decision was later taken to graft part over to chardonnay, which came into production in 1997. Until 1995 all the grapes were sold, but since that time the amounts of wine made have gradually increased. There are limited exports to Canada and the UK.

the antipodean   NR

PO Box 5, Matakana **region** Northland and Matakana
phone (09) 422 7957 **fax** (09) 422 7656 **open** Not
winemaker Michelle Chignell-Vuletic **production** 300 **est.** 1977
product range ($92–100 CD) The Antipodean (a blend of Cabernet Sauvignon, Merlot and Malbec), 'A' (Sauvignon Blanc, Semillon blend), The Iconoclast (Shiraz), Obiter (Cabernet Sauvignon).
summary More words have been written about this tiny winery than almost any other in New Zealand, and almost certainly more words than bottles produced. As the product range and prices testify, not your run of the mill winery.

the denton winery   NR

Awa Awa Road, Ruby Bay, Nelson **region** Nelson
phone (03) 540 3555 **fax** (03) 540 3555 **open** 7 days 11–6 Oct–Apr
winemaker Richard Denton **production** 2000 **est.** 1997
product range ($15.50–35 CD) Riesling, Sauvignon Blanc, Chardonnay, Reserve Chardonnay, Pinot Noir, Reserve Pinot Noir, Merlot, Folly (a super-premium Merlot Cabernet).
summary Richard, and wife Alexandra, Denton discovered Nelson while on a world tour and some years later moved from their native England to Nelson to purchase the property in 1995. The first 2 hectares of vines were planted, and a winery — and the seemingly obligatory café and art gallery — appeared in time for the 1997 vintage. Richard Denton was an amateur brewer for many years and graduated to amateur winemaking before taking the final plunge into commercial winemaking. A further 3 hectares of vineyard are to be planted, and increased production will follow.

the village winery   NR

417 Mount Eden Road, Mount Eden, Auckland **region** Auckland Area
phone (09) 638 8780 **fax** (09) 638 9782 **open** Sun–Wed 10–9, Thurs–Sat 10–10
winemaker Ken Sanderson **production** 4500 **est.** 1994
product range ($7.50–28.95 R) Windmill Road range of Hawke's Bay Sauvignon Blanc, Hawke's Bay Chardonnay, Hawke's Bay Merlot, Cabernet Sauvignon Merlot Franc, Jean Method Traditional Vintage (Sparkling).
summary Enterprises such as this are not uncommon in California but it is the only one I know of in either Australia or New Zealand, with the winery established in the main street of suburban Mount Eden, which was — until owner Peter Schinckel found a loophole in the law — a 'dry' area. (New Zealand, like Australia, still has areas in which alcohol may not be sold.) The wines are made under the Windmill Road label, the winery-cum-shop stocking a broad range of wines from other producers as well as Windmill Road. Exports to Japan, Germany and Switzerland.

thornbury wines   NR

29a Ocean Beach Road, Mt Maunganui **region** Hawke's Bay
phone (07) 572 2281 **fax** (07) 575 8729 **open** Not
winemaker Steve Bird **production** NA **est.** 1998
product range ($17–25 R) Marlborough Sauvignon Blanc, Hawke's Bay Chardonnay, Hawke's Bay Merlot.
summary A most impressive newcomer, marking a partnership between Steve Bird, former Morton Estate winemaker, and Bruce and Sharon McCutcheon. The 1998 vintage relied on contract-grown grapes, with winemaking in rented space. In 1999 Thornbury acquired a vineyard of its own in Hawke's Bay, but will continue to source sauvignon blanc from Marlborough.

torlesse ★★★☆

Waipara Village, Waipara, Canterbury **region** Canterbury
phone (03) 314 6929 **fax** (03) 314 6867 **open** Fri–Sun 11–4 or by appointment
winemaker Kym Rayner **production** 5000 **est.** 1990
product range ($12.50–29.50 R) Riesling (Dry and Medium), Gewurztraminer, Marlborough Sauvignon Blanc, Chardonnay Lightly Oaked, Chardonnay Waipara Reserve, Pinot Noir, Pinot Noir Selection, Cabernet Sauvignon, Cabernet Merlot Selection, Reserve Port.
summary Torlesse was effectively reborn in 1990 when its existing shareholders purchased the business from a receiver. They include Dr David Jackson, author of several books on viticulture, and winemaker Kym Rayner; all have vineyards in the Canterbury region which supply Torlesse with grapes, supplemented by grapes purchased from the Stonier Vineyard in Marlborough. The plans are for production to increase to about 13 000 cases. Exports to Australia, Canada and the UK.

totara vineyards ★★★

Main Road, Thames **region** Waikato and Bay of Plenty
phone (07) 868 6798 **fax** (07) 868 8729 **open** 7 days 10–6 summer, 7 days 10–5.30 winter
winemaker Gilbert Chan **production** 10 000 **est.** 1950
product range ($7.95–19.95 R) Müller Thurgau, Chardonnay, Reserve Chardonnay, Sauvignon Blanc, Chenin Blanc, Cabernet Sauvignon.
summary A substantial operation which, however, has had its share of problems, leading to a decision to remove all its vineyards in 1986 under the Vine Pull Scheme; it now relies on local growers to provide the grapes for its wines. Had its moment of glory in the 1992 Air New Zealand Wine Awards when the '90 Reserve Chardonnay won the Chardonnay Trophy.

trinity hill ★★★★

2396 State Highway 50, RD5, Hastings **region** Hawke's Bay
phone (06) 879 7778 **fax** (06) 879 7770 **open** 7 days 10–5
winemaker John Hancock, Warren Gibson **production** 35 000 **est.** 1996
product range ($13.45–45.35 CD) Under the cheaper Shepherds Croft brand Sauvignon Blanc, Chardonnay, Merlot Cabernet Franc Syrah; Wairarapa Riesling; and under the premium Gimblett Road label Chardonnay, Syrah, Merlot, Cabernet Sauvignon Merlot, Cabernet Sauvignon.
summary A fast-rising star in the New Zealand firmament. A joint venture between former Morton Estate winemaker John Hancock, an Auckland businessman and a pair (a couple actually) of London restaurateurs. The venture began with the establishment of a 20-hectare vineyard on a prime Gimblett Road site, followed by the erection of a state-of-the-art winery in 1996, completed just prior to the first vintage. All of the wines so far released have achieved great critical acclaim. The vineyards now comprise 60 hectares, and the wines are exported to Australia, Brazil, France, Hong Kong, Israel, Japan, The Netherlands, the Philippines, Singapore, the UK and the US.

Trinity Hill Wairarapa Riesling

Produced from grapes grown on the famous vineyard of Neil Petrie, who supplies grapes to some of New Zealand's best winemakers.
▼▼▼▼♀ **1999** Light to medium yellow-green; interesting high-toned floral aromas with a mineral substrate to the bouquet are followed by a palate with an exceptionally long finish and aftertaste when both citrus and mineral flavours coalesce; mercifully dry. **rating:** 90
best drinking 2000–2005 **best vintages** '97, '99 **drink with** Vegetable terrine • $16

Trinity Hill Gimblett Road Chardonnay

A super-premium wine coming from the Gimblett Estate and Stockbridge Vineyard, situated adjacent to each other in the Gimblett Road area. The grapes are whole-bunch pressed, and the wine was fermented and aged in French oak barriques, 80 per cent new and 20 per cent one-year-old. The malolactic fermentation is suppressed to enhance fruit character, and the wine is blended and bottled after 11 months in oak.
▼▼▼▼ **1998** Medium yellow-green; very strong, toasty/charry barrel-ferment oak dominates the bouquet, and although the powerful palate has fresh citrus/melon fruit, the oak is just that little bit too obvious for comfort. It is a fine line to have given the '97 the benefit of the doubt and not the '98, but such is life. **rating:** 86
best drinking 2000–2002 **best vintages** '97 **drink with** Roast chicken • $34

Trinity Hill Shepherds Croft Chardonnay

While Trinity Hill has three distinct areas within Hawke's Bay — Gimblett Road, Ngatarawa and Te Awanga — the majority of the initial releases came from the Shepherds Croft Vineyard at Ngatarawa. Between 50 per cent and 75 per cent of the wine is barrel-fermented depending on the vintage (50 per cent in 1997), and given the usual lees contact, although it is not easy to tell how much (if any) was taken through malolactic fermentation.

TTTT 1999 Medium yellow-green; a stylish and sophisticated bouquet with citrus, melon and cashew aromas matched with well-balanced and integrated oak. This interplay is repeated on the palate; a strongly worked wine, but successfully so, with gentle mouthfeel and real finesse.   **rating: 89**

best drinking 2000–2002 **best vintages** '97, '98 **drink with** Tuna • $20

Trinity Hill Shepherds Croft Merlot Cabernet Franc Syrah

A blend of 47 per cent Merlot, 38 per cent Cabernet Franc and 15 per cent Syrah which has already begun the transition into an elegant mature Bordeaux style.

TTTTY 1998 Medium red-purple; an elegant cedary/savoury bouquet already shows secondary Bordeaux-like aromas. The palate has sweet, ripe red berry/cassis/plum fruit flavours supported by soft, fine tannins and nicely judged oak.   **rating: 93**

best drinking 2002–2008 **best vintages** '98 **drink with** Rack of lamb • $22

Trinity Hill Gimblett Road Cabernet Sauvignon

So far as I am aware, made its debut in 1998 alongside the Gimblett Road Cabernet Merlot.

TTTT 1998 Medium red, with just a touch of purple; the aromas are in the savoury/leafy/earthy/spicy spectrum, leading into a palate which opens with powerful blackberry/blackcurrant fruit before moving into persistent tannins running through to the finish. Right on the edge, but will likely come into balance in time.   **rating: 87**

best drinking 2003–2012 **best vintages** '98 **drink with** Charcoal-grilled beef • $35

two paddocks   NR

PO Box 369, Queenstown **region** Otago
phone (03) 442 5988 **fax** (03) 441 1123 **open** Not
winemaker Dean Shaw (Contract) **production** 650 **est.** 1997
product range ($31 R) Pinot Noir.
summary Two Paddocks (only one is presently in production) is the venture of film star Sam Neill. By 2002 both the Gibbston Valley and Earnscleugh vineyards will be in production, producing two single-vineyard Pinots.

unison vineyard   ★★★★

2163 Highway 50, RD5, Hastings **region** Hawke's Bay
phone (06) 879 7913 **fax** (06) 879 7915 **open** By appointment
winemaker Anna-Barbara and Bruce Helliwell **production** 2500 **est.** 1993
product range ($23.50–33.50 CD) Two wines only are produced: Unison and Unison Selection, both being blends of Merlot, Cabernet Sauvignon and Syrah.
summary Bruce Helliwell, a New Zealand winemaker with MSc Honours degree, met his German-born and trained viticulturist and winemaker wife Anna-Barbara while she was managing a small estate in Chianti Classico hill country. Between them, they have winemaking and viticultural experience in New Zealand, Germany, California, Italy, Switzerland and France. The vines on the 6-hectare estate are close-planted at a density of 5000 vines per hectare, with the yield reduced to only 1 kilo per vine. These are seriously good wines. Exports to Australia, the UK, the US, Germany, Belgium, Sweden and Taiwan.

Unison Selection

A premium blend of Merlot, Cabernet Sauvignon and Syrah, estate-grown on high-density, low-yielding plantings.

TTTTT 1998 Medium to full red-purple; a rich and complex array of dark chocolate, sweet berry and gently savoury aromas lead into an excellent palate with lusciously sweet and ripe cassis/dark berry fruit. You know the oak is there, but it doesn't compete, and the tannins are similarly well balanced.   **rating: 94**

best drinking 2003–2013 **best vintages** '98 **drink with** Braised oxtail • $33.50

Unison

This is the junior blend of the same three estate-grown varieties of Merlot, Cabernet Sauvignon and Syrah as the Unison Selection, and for my money there was some fairly astute selection.

TTTT 1998 Medium red-purple; the bouquet is distinctly lighter than the Selection, with rather more leafy/gamey fruit aromas; sweeter, more juicy fruit is apparent on the palate, but it lacks the depth and intensity of its big brother.   **rating: 86**

best drinking 2003–2008 **best vintages** NA **drink with** Lamb chops • $23.50

vavasour wines ★★★★★

Redwood Pass Road, Awatere Valley, Marlborough **region** Marlborough
phone (03) 575 7481 **fax** (03) 575 7240 **open** Mon–Sat 10–5 April–Sept, 7 days 10–5 Oct–Mar
winemaker Glenn Thomas **production** 25 000 **est.** 1986
product range ($14.95–27.95 R) At the top end come Vavasour Single Vineyard Sauvignon Blanc, Chardonnay; then Awatere Valley Sauvignon Blanc, Chardonnay, Pinot Noir and Cabernet Sauvignon; then Dashwood Chardonnay, Sauvignon Blanc and Pinot Noir; and Stafford Brook Chardonnay and Cabernet.
summary Vavasour has established itself as one of the most reliable and best producers in the Marlborough region. The drier, slightly warmer climate of the Awatere Valley and the unique river-terrace stony soils on which the 12.5-hectare vineyard is established are producing grapes of great intensity of flavour, which are in turn being skilfully handled in the winery by Glenn Thomas. Exports to Australia, the UK, France, Ireland and Switzerland.

vidal estate ★★★★☆

913 St Aubyns Street East, Hastings **region** Hawke's Bay
phone (06) 876 8105 **fax** (06) 876 5312 **open** Mon–Sat 11–6, Sun 10.30–5
winemaker Rod McDonald **production** 60 000 **est.** 1905
product range ($9.50–40 CD) Constant revamping of the product range (new brand managers?) keeps everyone on their toes. The Private Bin range has been replaced by the Estate Range; the Bays range introduced for restaurants; only the East Coast (at the bottom) and the Reserve range (at the top) continue (for the time being). The usual spread of varietals are covered by each range.
summary Together with Te Mata, Villa Maria and Esk Valley, consistently produces some of New Zealand's finest red wines; they have ripeness, richness and balance, a far cry from the reds of bygone years. Surprisingly, notwithstanding the success of Vidal year after year at the Sydney International Wine Competition, and notwithstanding that its wines are distributed in the UK, Canada, much of Asia and the Pacific, it has still not sought distribution in Australia. Surely it will be only a question of time, for production continues to increase.

Vidal Estate Hawke's Bay Sauvignon Blanc

The 'Estate Range' replaces the old 'Private Bin' range. From the 1997 vintage the words 'lightly oaked' were added to the label. This refers to the fact that 5 per cent of the wine is barrique-fermented and matured for three months with lees stirring.
▼▼▼▽ **1999** Light green-yellow; crisp, predominantly mineral and not particularly aromatic characters on the bouquet lead into a pleasant wine on the palate which won't frighten the horses. **rating:** 82
best drinking 2000–2001 **best vintages** '94, '96 **drink with** Poached scallops • $15

Vidal Reserve Hawke's Bay Chardonnay

One of the most highly regarded of the Hawke's Bay Chardonnays, even if overshadowed in the eyes of some by its sister wine from Villa Maria. The style is moving along with the mainstream of New Zealand Chardonnay, away from overblown, over-extractive making to a more restrained mode, but without sacrificing drinkability and accessibility. Barrel-fermented in French oak (two-thirds new), part of the ferment in a coolroom, and part ambient, remaining on its gross yeast lees (stirred weekly) before being bottled after 11 months maturation.
▼▼▼▼▼ **1998** Medium green-yellow; attractive dusty/spicy oak is woven through melon fruit on the bouquet. The palate has good flavour and length, with citrus and nectarine fruit following through the mid-palate to finish. **rating:** 94
best drinking 2000–2003 **best vintages** '90, '91, '94, '96, '97, '98 **drink with** Veal fricassee • $28

Vidal Estate Reserve Hawke's Hay Noble Semillon 375 ml

Barrel-fermented in French oak and held in oak for 12 months, but the wine has easily swallowed up that oak.
▼▼▼▼▽ **1998** Medium yellow-green; powerful honey/honeycomb/quince fruit aromas backed by subtle oak. The wine is very rich on the palate but exceptionally well balanced, the honey and quince fruit neatly offset by gentle acidity and subtle oak. **rating:** 91
best drinking 2000–2004 **best vintages** '98 **drink with** Caramelised apple tart • $40

Vidal Estate Pinot Noir

I remain to be convinced that anyone should be planting pinot noir in Hawke's Bay, particularly if they have the option of anywhere from Martinborough through to Central Otago. The maximum effort has been invested in the winery with all of the tricks of the trade being used on various parcels in an effort to invest the wine with the character missing from the grapes.

507

🍷🍷🍷🍷 1998 Medium red-purple; the bouquet is clean but, notwithstanding all of the cleverness in the making, the basic fruit is plain. The same dynamics are at work on the palate, although there are some stem tannins on the finish which give the wine interest while it is young, but will do nothing for it as it ages. **rating:** 81

best drinking 2000–2002 **best vintages** NA **drink with** Quail • $19

vilagrad wines NR

Rukuhia Road, RD2, Ohaupo **region** Waikato and Bay of Plenty
phone (07) 825 2893 **open** Tues–Sat 10–6
winemaker Peter Nooyen **production** 2000 **est.** 1922
product range Recently introduced Nooyen Reserve range of Riesling, Gewurztraminer, Chardonnay, Pinot Noir and Cabernet Merlot Malbec head the range.
summary A low-profile operation making wines of modest but consistently acceptable quality that age surprisingly well, but aspiring to greater things with the Nooyen Reserve wines. A winery restaurant is open on Sundays (and for functions at other times by arrangement).

villa maria ★★★★★

5 Kirkbride Road, Mangere, Auckland **region** Auckland Area
phone (09) 255 0660 **fax** (09) 255 0661 **open** 7 days 9–6
winemaker Michelle Richardson **production** 500 000 **est.** 1961
product range ($7.50–39.95 CD) A large range of wines under the Private Bin label, basically varietally identified, stands at the bottom end of the portfolio; next comes the Cellar Selection range of Chardonnay, Sauvignon Blanc, Cabernet Merlot; then Wairau Valley Reserve Sauvignon Blanc; at the top end the Reserve Bin range of Barrique Fermented Chardonnay, Marlborough Chardonnay, Sauvignon Blanc, Gewurztraminer, Noble Riesling, Cabernet Merlot and Cabernet Sauvignon.
summary Whether viewed on the basis of its performances at Sydney International Winemakers Competition or on any other show result over the last few years, Villa Maria has to be rated one of New Zealand's best large wineries. The quality of the wines, both white and red, is exemplary, the flavours magically full without going over the top. Not surprisingly, the wines are exported to Europe, North America and Asia, but — as is the case with Vidal — so far, not to Australia.

Villa Maria Reserve Gewurztraminer

The first Reserve Gewurztraminer since 1994, grown on the Simcox Vineyard in Hawke's Bay. While my fellow judges were far less impressed, I accorded it gold medal points at the Royal Easter Wine Show 2000.

🍷🍷🍷🍷 1998 Bright yellow-green; the wine has a delicate yet intense bouquet with seductive rose petal and spice aromas. The palate, too, neatly balances intensity with delicacy; fruit-fresh, clean and dry. **rating:** 92

best drinking 2000–2004 **best vintages** '99 **drink with** Steamed Chinese fish with ginger • $20

Villa Maria Cellar Selection Sauvignon Blanc

Drawn from the Wairau and Awatere Valley regions.

🍷🍷🍷🍷 1999 Light to medium yellow-green; clean; some light, somewhat amorphous tropical fruit aromas are followed by a clean, light- to medium-bodied palate which is well balanced, if a little plain. **rating:** 84

best drinking 2000–2001 **best vintages** NA **drink with** Fish soup • $18

Villa Maria Private Bin Sauvignon Blanc

Formerly a blend of Marlborough, Te Kauwhata and Hawke's Bay grapes but now entirely sourced from Marlborough and made at Villa Maria's Marlborough winery.

🍷🍷🍷🍷 1999 Light green-yellow; a clean fresh but rather neutral bouquet lacks varietal character; there is slightly more to be found on the palate, with some herb and faint gooseberry flavours; the balance is good enough. **rating:** 84

best drinking 2000–2001 **best vintages** NA **drink with** Gazpacho • $15

Villa Maria Reserve Clifford Bay Sauvignon Blanc

A wine which made its first appearance in 1996 from grapes grown in the Awatere Valley. Right from the outset the wine has established itself as by far the best Villa Maria Sauvignon Blanc, a status reflected in continuing show success, the '99 keeping the pace with a gold medal at the Air New Zealand Wine Awards 1999.

🍷🍷🍷🍷 1999 Light yellow-green; the bouquet is clean and of moderate to full intensity, with a mix of herb and tropical fruit, yet is not fragrant. The palate has considerable power and intensity, with quite luscious tropical fruit. The finish is powerful yet not aggressive; all in all, a very good wine in the grand style. **rating:** 93

best drinking 2000–2002 **best vintages** '97, '99 **drink with** Prawn and avocado salad • $25.50

Villa Maria Reserve Barrique Fermented Chardonnay

One can legitimately argue about the level of oak in this wine; whether one really likes it or not is a question of personal style preference, but there is no doubting the complexity and power of the wine. A Bob Campbell Classic, and five stars from Michael Cooper.

TTTY 1998 Medium yellow-green; extremely spicy/dusty oak utterly overwhelms the fruit on the bouquet, and achieves much the same on the palate, where some fruit can be perceived. The points may seem extreme, particularly given the 94 points I accorded the '97 vintage, but there really is no halfway point with a wine such as this. You will either love it or hate it. **rating:** 81

best drinking 2000–2003 **best vintages** '90, '91, '94, '96, '97 **drink with** Moroccan chicken stuffed with raisins and pine nuts • $35

Villa Maria Reserve Hawke's Bay Chardonnay

Surprisingly, this is the first vintage of this wine. It is sourced from three different vineyards, the lots being kept separate until final blending. Fully barrel-fermented, with 60 per cent undergoing malolactic fermentation and 25 per cent lees stirred. Kept in barrel for 11 months. A prolific show medal winner throughout 1999, culminating in the trophy for Best Chardonnay at the 1999 Air New Zealand Wine Awards, and a runner-up for Champion Wine of Show.

TTTTT 1998 Excellent bright green-yellow. The bouquet shows very clever winemaking, with a sophisticated mix of nutty cashew, fig and melon aromas. The palate, too, shows sensitive handling, with nectarine and citrus fruit dominant among the many flavours, and leading through to a long, lingering finish. Unquestionably at the top end of New Zealand Chardonnay. **rating:** 95

best drinking 2000–2004 **best vintages** '98 **drink with** Braised pork hock • $29.95

Villa Maria Reserve Marlborough Chardonnay

As the label suggests, made entirely from Marlborough region grapes drawn from Villa Maria's two best vineyards in the region, predominantly hand-picked. The wine is 100 per cent barrel-fermented in a mix of new (60 per cent) and one-year-old (40 per cent) oak. Given eight months lees contact, with partial barrel stirring, and 25 per cent malolactic fermentation. Sophisticated winemaking, to say the least.

TTTY 1998 Medium to full yellow-green; a wine which is loaded to the gills and beyond with oak on both the bouquet and palate. Quite obviously, the wine has appeal to both public and critics alike, but the older I get, the more I want wine to taste of wine, not oak. **rating:** 80

best drinking 2000–2002 **best vintages** '94, '96, '97 **drink with** Coquilles St Jacques • $30

Villa Maria Reserve Hawke's Bay Merlot

A blend of 94 per cent Merlot and 6 per cent Malbec selected from individual blocks on the Ngakirikiri vineyard. open fermentation with hand plunging, and 10 per cent being run off for barrel-fermentation is followed by maturation in new and one-year-old barriques for 18 months.

TTTTY 1998 Medium to full purple-red; shows the sweet, lush dark plum fruit of the vintage, coupled with the sweet French oak on both the bouquet and palate, again with sumptuous sweet plum and berry fruit. A show style which duly won a gold medal at the 1999 Air New Zealand Wine Awards, and scored gold medal points on my score sheet at the Royal Easter Wine Show 2000. **rating:** 91

best drinking 2003–2008 **best vintages** '96, '98 **drink with** Venison medallions • $35

Villa Maria Reserve Merlot Cabernet

A blend of Cabernet Sauvignon and Merlot grown on the Villa Maria Ngakirikiri vineyard blended with Merlot from Bridge Pa. The percentage of Merlot and Cabernet respectively is not stated but is necessarily Merlot-dominant. The wine spends 18 months in a mix of predominantly French, and a little American, oak, part new, part used.

TTTTY 1998 Medium red-purple; for once the oak is not dominant on a bouquet which is nonetheless quite complex, with gentle savoury and dark chocolate overtones to the fruit. The palate opens up with attractive red fruit flavours before fairly solid tannins — part, from the fruit and partly from oak — appear on a slightly grippy finish. Gold medal Air New Zealand Wine Awards 1999. **rating:** 92

best drinking 2003–2010 **best vintages** '85, '87, '90, '91, '92, '94, '95, '98 **drink with** Rich, soft ripened cheese • $35

voss estate ★★★★

Puruatanga Road, Martinborough **region** Wairarapa
phone (06) 306 9668 **fax** (06) 306 9668 **open** 7 days 11–6 summer
winemaker Gary Voss **production** 2000 **est.** 1988
product range ($16–28 CD) Reserve Chardonnay, Sauvignon Blanc, Pinot Noir, Waihenga Cabernet Merlot Franc.

summary Voss Estate has been established by Annette Atkins, Gary Voss and Murray Voss, with 9.5 hectares of vineyards (5.5 hectares of pinot noir, 2 hectares chardonnay, 1 hectare of riesling and half a hectare each of cabernet sauvignon, merlot and sauvignon blanc). Production is largely estate-based, with some grapes purchased from other Martinborough growers. Exports to Australia and Canada.

waiheke vineyards ★★★★

76 Onetangi Road, Onetangi, Waiheke Island **region** Waiheke Island
phone (09) 486 3859 **fax** (09) 486 2341 **open** Not
winemaker Paul Dunleavy, John Dunleavy **production** 1300 **est.** 1990
product range ($35–49 R) Te Motu (Cabernet Merlot), Dunleavy Merlot Franc.
summary The venture of the Dunleavy family headed by long-term, but now-retired, Wine Institute of New Zealand chief executive Terry Dunleavy. Produced outstanding wines in 1993 and 1994, providing yet further evidence (if any was needed) of the suitability of Waiheke Island for the production of ripe, full bodied, Cabernets. Exports to the UK, Ireland, France and the US.

wai-iti river vineyard NR

Livingstone Road, Waimea West, Nelson **region** Nelson
phone (03) 542 3205 **fax** (03) 542 3205 **open** By appointment
winemaker Dave Glover (Contract) **production** 1000 **est.** 1993
product range ($17–30 CD) Riesling, Chardonnay, Pinot Noir, Cabernet Sauvignon.
summary Chan and Philip Woollaston planted their small (6-hectare) vineyard on the Waimea Plains near Nelson in the winter of 1993 on old riverbed gravels. The cellar-door sales and tastings opened on schedule in 1999.

waimea estates ★★★☆

148 Main Road, Hope, Nelson **region** Nelson
phone (03) 544 6385 **fax** (03) 544 6385 **open** Oct–Mar 7 days 10–6, Apr–Sept Fri–Sun 10–5
winemaker Michael Brown, Bruce Collie **production** 5500 **est.** 1997
product range ($15–29 R) Riesling, Sauvignon Blanc, Chardonnay, Pinot Noir, Cabernet Merlot released under the Waimea Plains label.
summary Former orchardists Trevor and Robyn Bolitho diversified into viticulture in 1993 and by 1999 had 37 hectares of vineyard established, with a further 18 hectares to be planted in the spring of 2000. Part of the production is sold to other producers, but since 1997 Waimea Estates has produced wine under its own label. In 1998 a winery was built on site with an ultimate production capacity of 50 000 cases. The quality of the wines so far released has been consistently good. Exports to Australia.

Waimea Plains Nelson Riesling

Fresh, lively and well balanced; can be drunk immediately or cellared for up to five years. One of the features of the Riesling is that the acid and residual sugar balance is achieved without the obvious use of residual sugar.
▼▼▼▽ **1999** Light green-yellow; the bouquet is clean, solid, with ripe, sweet lime aromas. The palate loses the plot to a degree, with plenty of tropical flavour, but lacks continuity and, despite all that flavour, is slightly hollow.
rating: 80
best drinking 2000–2005 **best vintages** NA **drink with** Stuffed capsicum • $22

Waimea Plains Nelson Sauvignon Blanc

Right from the outset the quality of the Sauvignon Blanc has been excellent, usually in a rich, aromatic, user-friendly style. The grapes are typically taken from six different sites on two different vineyards, resulting in six separate pickings.
▼▼▼▼▽ **1999** Light green-yellow; voluminous passionfruit and gooseberry aromas swirl from the glass, followed by a rich, full-flavoured palate featuring the same fruit characters but avoiding going over the top. **rating:** 91
best drinking 2000–2001 **best vintages** '97, '99 **drink with** Calamari • $15

waipara downs NR

State Highway 7, Bains Road, RD3, Amberley **region** Waipara
phone (03) 314 6873 **fax** (03) 314 6873 **open** By appointment
winemaker François Crochet **production** 800 **est.** 1989
product range ($12–16 CD) Chardonnay, Pinot Noir, Cabernet Sauvignon, Port.
summary Six hectares of vines on a 320-hectare farm puts Waipara Downs into perspective, but does not diminish the enjoyment Ruth and Keith Berry derive from producing their wines from the limestone soils of the Waipara Valley. The wines have been consistent bronze and silver medal winners in New Zealand wine shows. The wines are distributed in Australia through Negociants.

waipara springs wines ★★★★

State Highway 1 North, Waipara, North Canterbury **region** Waipara
phone (03) 314 6777 **fax** (03) 314 6777 **open** 7 days 11–5
winemaker Kym Rayner, Stephanie Henderson-Grant **production** 10 000 **est.** 1990
product range ($12–28 CD) Sauvignon Blanc, Chardonnay, Riesling, Pinot Noir, Ram Paddock Red, Two Terrace Red.
summary Owned by Bruce and Jill Moore and the Grant family, represented by Andrew Grant and Stephanie Henderson-Grant. The initial plantings of 4 hectares in 1982 have now risen to 20 hectares, providing all of the grapes for the significantly increased production. The wines have deservedly gained an excellent reputation; exports to Australia, the UK, the US and Canada.

Waipara Springs Dry Riesling

A wine which provides one answer to the question why so many New Zealand Rieslings are appreciably sweet: it's very easy for the acid to present a formidable barrier when the wines are dry.
♥♥♥♥ 1999 Medium green-yellow; the bouquet is quite aromatic, with Germanic lime juice aromas. The palate opens with lots of limey fruit then penetrating, biting acidity takes over. Technically, the acid won't soften, but the overall palate-feel will, and the wine will richly repay cellaring. **rating: 85**
best drinking 2004–2009 **best vintages** NA **drink with** Spicy Thai soup • $15

Waipara Springs Botrytised Riesling 375 ml

Not produced every year, but only when there is a significant amount of truly noble rot (or botrytis). The grapes must have been picked when exceedingly ripe, for, notwithstanding its sweetness, the wine retains 12.5 degrees alcohol.
♥♥♥♥♥ 1999 Glowing yellow-green; there are intense apricot, peach, honey and honeycomb aromas followed by an intensely rich and sweet palate with the same flavour spectrum, and very good acidity to provide balance. **rating: 95**
best drinking 2000–2005 **best vintages** '99 **drink with** Sweet cake • $28

waipara west NR

376 Ram Paddock Road, Amberley, RD2, North Canterbury **region** Waipara
phone (03) 314 8699 **fax** (03) 314 8692 **open** By appointment 10–4 most weekdays
winemaker Petter Evans **production** 6000 **est.** 1989
product range ($12–35 CD) Riesling, Sauvignon Blanc, Chardonnay, Pinot Noir are the premium varietals; Ram Paddock Red and Two Terrace Red are second-label blends.
summary Waipara West is situated at the gorge of the Waipara River. The vineyard is surrounded by steep banks and planted on naturally sloping terraces which vary in height and aspect. Seventeen hectares of chardonnay, sauvignon blanc, riesling, merlot, cabernet sauvignon, cabernet franc and pinot noir have been planted, with the very experienced Petter Evans (ex-St Helena) in charge of winemaking. Almost all of the wine is exported, chiefly to the UK.

wairau river wines ★★★★

Corner Rapaura Road and SH 6, Blenheim **region** Marlborough
phone (03) 572 9800 **fax** (03) 572 9885 **open** 7 days 9–5
winemaker John Belsham **production** 20 000 **est.** 1978
product range ($17–40 CD) Riesling, Botrytised Riesling Reserve, Sauvignon Blanc, Sauvignon Blanc Reserve, Chardonnay, Chardonnay Reserve; Philip Rosé Estate is the second label introduced in 1995.
summary Phil and Chris Rose have been long-term grape growers in the Marlborough region, having established 110 hectares of vineyard progressively since 1978. The first wines were made under the Wairau River label in 1991 by contract-winemaker John Belsham, and all of the vintages to date have been of exemplary quality, particularly the tropical-accented Sauvignon Blanc. Exports to Australia (all States), Canada, the US, the UK, Germany, Hong Kong, Singapore and Sweden.

Wairau River Sauvignon Blanc

The Sauvignon Blanc accounts for 8000 cases of the total Wairau River production, and is exported to both the UK and Australia with great success. The consistency of the wine over the '91 to '99 vintages shows why, if you except the very difficult '95 vintage.
♥♥♥♥ 1999 Light to medium yellow-green; the bouquet is in typically restrained mode, crisp and minerally with moderate intensity. The palate has good mouthfeel on entry, and good balance and length, but doesn't have quite the amount of weight or fruit intensity one would like to see on the mid-palate. **rating: 87**
best drinking 2001–2002 **best vintages** '91, '92, '93, '94, '96, '97, '98 **drink with** Deep-fried calamari • $18.50

Wairau River Botrytised Riesling Reserve

An extraordinary wine of great intensity and style, irresistible at any price.

▼▼▼▼▽ **1998** Glowing yellow-green; a very intense bouquet with strong botrytis influence, the aromas primarily of cumquat, apricot and lime. The palate is much tighter than the bouquet — a thoroughly good thing — with more lime juice coming through on a long, lingering, intense finish. **rating:** 92

best drinking 2001–2011 **best vintages** '97, '98 **drink with** Fruit tart •$40

waitiri creek wines   NR

State Highway 6, Gibbston Valley RD, Queenstown **region** Otago
phone (09) 520 0572 **fax** (09) 520 0965 **open** due December 2000
winemaker Rudi Bauer (1998), Dean Shaw (1999) Contract **production** NA **est.** NA
product range ($18–30 R) Gewurztraminer, Chardonnay, Pinot Noir.
summary In a move reminiscent of the 1840 stone gaol which was relocated in 1965 to house the then Hordern's Wybong Estate Winery in the Upper Hunter of New South Wales, Waitiri Creek's cellar door is housed in a 110-year-old Rimu church which has been moved to the site, and which is due to open in December 2000.

walker estate   NR

Puruatanga Road, Martinborough, Wairarapa **region** Wairarapa
phone (06) 306 9615 **fax** (06) 306 9615 **open** Not
winemaker James Walker, Chris Lintz (Contract) **production** NA **est.** 1988
product range ($14.50–22 CD) Riesling, Rosé, Notre Vigne.
summary The Walker family (Liz, Brendan and son James) established what they believed to be a two-variety vineyard, riesling and shiraz, in 1988. Until 1993 the grapes were sold to other Martinborough winemakers, but since that time have been vinified under the Walker Estate label. The intriguingly named Notre Vigne (our vine) stems from the fact that the vines thought to be shiraz are in fact of an as-yet unidentified variety, with DNA testing failing to reveal the answer. The wines made from the mystery grape are extremely powerful, densely coloured and most unusual.

walnut ridge   ★★★☆

159 Regent Street, Martinborough **region** Wairarapa
phone (06) 306 9323 **fax** (06) 306 9323 **open** 7 days 11–5 Dec–Jan, weekends 11–5 Feb–Nov
winemaker Bill Brink **production** 650 **est.** 1986
product range ($17–36 CD) Sauvignon Blanc, Botrytised Sauvignon Blanc, Pinot Noir, Cabernet Sauvignon.
summary While Bill Brink produces both Pinot Noir and Cabernet Sauvignon, he falls on the Pinot Noir side of the argument so far as Martinborough is concerned. That view, mind you, is not so surprising when you find that the first release from Walnut Ridge was the 1994 Pinot Noir, which was awarded a silver medal at the 1995 Air New Zealand Wine Awards. As to the rest, I should quote Bill Brink, who says that he 'came to New Zealand via the somewhat circuitous route of Samoa and the Peace Corps in 1973. After a number of years in public service and doing the Dominion crossword, and a change-of-pace year at Victoria University deliberating the obfuscatory logic of "existential deterrence", I came to Martinborough and began the development of what has become Walnut Ridge'. Exports to Australia and the UK.

west brook winery   ★★★☆

215 Ararimu Valley Road, Waimauku, Auckland **region** Auckland Area
phone (09) 411 9924 **fax** (09) 411 9925 **open** Mon–Sat 9–5, Sun 11–5
winemaker Anthony Ivicevich **production** 8000 **est.** 1937
product range ($10.95–21.95 CD) Marlborough Riesling, Sauvignon Blanc, Barrique Fermented Chardonnay, Hawke's Bay Chenin Blanc, Merlot, Henderson Cabernet Merlot; also under the Blue Ridge label are Sauvignon Blanc, Marlborough Chardonnay and Cabernet Merlot.
summary West Brook made its last vintage at the old Henderson winery in 1999 and has now moved to a new winery in the Ararimu Valley. It is reasonable to expect that the already impressive range of wines will improve further in the years ahead.

whitehaven wine company   ★★★★

1 Dodson Street, Blenheim, Marlborough **region** Marlborough
phone (03) 577 8861 **fax** (03) 577 8868 **open** 7 days 9–5
winemaker Simon Waghorn **production** 18 000 **est.** 1993
product range ($13.50–21 CD) Riesling, Festival Riesling, Sauvignon Blanc, Barrel Fermented Sauvignon Blanc, Chardonnay, Pinot Noir; also Single Vineyard Reserve Riesling, Gewurztraminer, Pinot Gris, Noble Riesling.

summary Whitehaven is a joint venture between Greg and Sue White and winemaker Simon Waghorn. Waghorn qualified as a winemaker at Roseworthy in Australia, first becoming assistant winemaker at Cooks Wines and thereafter spending five years as senior winemaker at Corbans' Gisborne winery, where he is responsible for production of a string of gold medal winning wines. A 200-tonne state-of-the-art winery has been built which includes a restaurant and wine shop as part of the complex. As one would expect, the initial releases under the Whitehaven label have had great show success. The business has grown dramatically, and the wines are now exported to England, Japan and The Netherlands.

Whitehaven Sauvignon Blanc
The skills of Simon Waghorn are showcased with this wine, which won gold medals at both the 1999 Liquorland Top 100 Competition and the Royal Easter Wine Show 2000, awards with which I profoundly agree.
▼▼▼▼▼ **1999** Light green-yellow; a wonderfully clean and crisp bouquet with intense herb and lemon rind aromas; the palate lives up to the promise of the bouquet, long and lively, with intense lemony fruit and a clean, lingering finish. **rating: 94**
best drinking 2000–2001 **best vintages** '99 **drink with** Deep sea crab • $14.75

Whitehaven Chardonnay
A very cleverly made wine with the judicious rather than enthusiastic use of the Chardonnay tricks of the trade. Half of the wine is stainless steel-fermented, the other half fermented in French and American oak; lees stirring and partial malolactic fermentation followed for the barrel portion. It is an approach which pays good dividends.
▼▼▼▼ **1998** Medium yellow-green; attractive nectarine and peach fruit on both the bouquet and palate is gently supported by nutty, oaky nuances; very good balance and length. **rating: 88**
best drinking 2000–2002 **best vintages** NA **drink with** Grilled salmon • $15.50

william hill winery   NR
Dunstan Road, RD1, Alexandra **region** Otago
phone (03) 448 8436 **fax** (03) 448 8434 **open** Mon–Sun 10–4.30
winemaker Gerry Rowland, David Grant **production** 2000 **est.** 1982
product range ($16–25 CD) Riesling, Gewurztraminer, Chardonnay, Pinot Noir.
summary Notwithstanding that the William Hill vineyards extend to 9 hectares, production grew painfully slowly in the early years. A new winery was commissioned for 1995 (happily an exceptional vintage for Central Otago) which offers contract-winemaking services for other wineries in the region. Exports to the US.

winslow wines   NR
Princess Street, Martinborough **region** Wairarapa
phone (06) 306 9648 **fax** (06) 306 9271 **open** 7 days 10–5.30 Aug–April, winter by appointment
winemaker Elise Montgomery, Steve Tarring **production** 625 **est.** 1985
product range ($19–36 CD) St Vincent Riesling, St Vincent Reserve Riesling, Rosetta Cabernet Rosé, Petra Cabernet Sauvignon and, at the pinnacle, Turakirae Reserve Cabernet Sauvignon Franc.
summary The Bio-Gro™ managed estate plantings of 2.2 hectares are planted to cabernet sauvignon (2 hectares) and cabernet franc (0.2 hectares). Owners Jennifer and Steve Tarring buy the remainder of the grapes for the small production from contract growers.

wither hills vineyards   ★★★★☆
16 Salisbury Street, Herne Bay, Auckland **region** Marlborough
phone (09) 378 0857 **fax** (09) 378 0857 **open** Not
winemaker Brent Marris **production** 20 000 **est.** 1992
product range ($19.95–35 R) Sauvignon Blanc, Chardonnay, Pinot Noir.
summary The Marris family have been grape growers in Marlborough for 12 years and now have 83 hectares under vine, with a further 32 hectares available for planting. Since Brent Marris left his position as chief winemaker for Delegat's, production of Wither Hills has increased rapidly, though part of the estate grapes are still sold. Having initially secured a reputation with the Sauvignon Blanc and Chardonnay, Brent Marris leapt to prominence with his 1998 Pinot Noir. Exports to Australia, the US, Singapore and Brazil.

Wither Hills Sauvignon Blanc

First made in 1994; and has established itself as an extremely reliable, stylish example of Marlborough Sauvignon Blanc, made in a no-frills, no-nonsense fashion.

TTTT 1999 Light to medium yellow-green; the bouquet is clean, with moderately ripe fruit running from lemon/mineral through to tropical, spicy aromas. The palate is well balanced, with plenty of flavour running throughout; crisp finish. **rating: 89**

best drinking 2000–2001 **best vintages** '94, '97 **drink with** Fresh scallops • $19.95

Wither Hills Chardonnay

First made in 1992 from the estate-owned vineyards in the Wairau Valley; the second vintage (1994) established the reputation of the wine by winning a gold medal at the Air New Zealand Wine Awards. The wine is 100 per cent barrel-fermented and lees stirred, remaining in oak for 12 months.

TTTT 1998 Medium yellow-green; in the mainstream of New Zealand Chardonnay style, with fairly potent barrel-ferment aromas on the bouquet. The palate is rich and round, with figgy melon fruit, but I would still prefer a little less oak and a little more fruit focus. That said, a smart wine. **rating: 89**

best drinking 2000–2002 **best vintages** '92, '94, '96, '98 **drink with** Prawns with walnuts • $29

Wither Hills Vineyards Pinot Noir

First made in 1997, matured for 14 months in a mix of predominantly new (80 per cent) French oak. The wine represented a solid start, but few could have been prepared for the impact of the 1998, which won just about every accolade and trophy possible, including the trophy for Champion Wine at the 1999 Air New Zealand Wine Awards (the first time that award has been won by a Pinot Noir) and almost routinely winning the trophy at the Sydney International Wine Competition 2000 for Best New Zealand Pinot Noir.

TTTTT 1998 Medium to full red-purple; an exceedingly complex bouquet with excellent fruit and oak balance and integration; savoury more than primary fruit; an element of volatile lift is evident but does not mar the wine. The palate has great structure and intensity, with plum and spice flavours supported by perfectly judged tannins. **rating: 97**

best drinking 2000–2005 **best vintages** '98 **drink with** Breast of squab • $35

woodfield estate   NR

57 Duncan Road, Hamilton **region** Waikato and Bay of Plenty
phone (07) 827 7170 **fax** (07) 827 7140 **open** Tues–Sun 10–5
winemaker Brian Mahoney **production** 500 **est.** 1994
product range ($14–25 CD) Chardonnay, Cabernet Merlot.
summary June and Brian Mahoney have established a small winery and cellar-door facility in an architect-designed farmhouse style, and use natural winemaking methods (minimal additives, minimal filtration, no stabilisation) in handling the Waikato-grown grapes they use to make their wines.

index

more titles by james halliday
from harpercollins*publishers*

James Halliday's Australian and New Zealand Interactive Wine Companion

the new edition of the interactive CD-ROM for PC and Mac features James Halliday's detailed assessments of more than 3400 wines and 1300 wineries; an itinerary to help plan winery tours; vertical tasting notes of over 90 classic wines, many going back 40 or 50 years; the 'Wine Organiser', a cellar holdings and tasting notes program (compatible with previous versions); and interactive wine region maps. With search and print facilities throughout, the *Interactive Wine Companion* is the perfect addition to every wine lover's collection.

ISBN: 0 7322 6835 4

Wine Atlas of Australia and New Zealand

New revised edition

this new edition offers all the detail and research of the previous edition, and more. Including maps of Australia's new wine regions, profiles on Australia and New Zealand's top winemakers and wineries and stunning photographs, the *Wine Atlas of Australia and New Zealand* is an indispensable reference tool.

ISBN: 0 7322 6448 0

Classic Wines of Australia

this unique book provides a comprehensive insight into the greatest wines made in Australia over the past 50 or more years. James Halliday's notes on vertical tastings of these wines cover all the most famous names; equally absorbing are the notes for the classics of tomorrow, wines known only to a chosen few. A brief introductory background is given to each of the wines chosen, and tastings range far and wide across sparkling wines, white table wines — both dry and sweet — dry reds and fortified wines.

Some readers will already have cellars that include a number of these wines. Hopefully others will be inspired to start collecting wines and experiencing first-hand the magical transformation of a vibrant young wine into a seriously graceful old wine.

ISBN: 0 7322 5851 0

Collecting Wine:
You and Your Cellar

a necessity for every wine enthusiast, this book contains valuable information on how to start and maintain a cellar, how to choose white and red wines for cellaring, the most efficient cellar racking systems and the problems a bottle may encounter during its life. It also provides Australian and imported wine vintage charts and recommends wine merchants, auction houses, societies and literature.

ISBN: 0 7322 6528 2